GOETHE

Goethe

A LIFE IN IDEAS

MATTHEW BELL

PRINCETON UNIVERSITY PRESS
PRINCETON & OXFORD

Copyright © 2025 by Princeton University Press

Princeton University Press is committed to the protection of copyright and the intellectual property our authors entrust to us. Copyright promotes the progress and integrity of knowledge created by humans. By engaging with an authorized copy of this work, you are supporting creators and the global exchange of ideas. As it is protected by copyright, any intentions to reproduce, distribute any part of the work in any form for any purpose require permission; permission requests should be sent to permissions@press.princeton.edu. Ingestion of any IP for any AI purposes is strictly prohibited.

Published by Princeton University Press
41 William Street, Princeton, New Jersey 08540
99 Banbury Road, Oxford OX2 6JX

press.princeton.edu

GPSR Authorized Representative: Easy Access System Europe - Mustamäe tee 50, 10621 Tallinn, Estonia, gpsr.requests@easproject.com

All Rights Reserved

Library of Congress Cataloging-in-Publication Data

Names: Bell, Matthew, 1964– author.
Title: Goethe : a life in ideas / Matthew Bell.
Description: Princeton : Princeton University Press, 2025. | Includes bibliographical references and index.
Identifiers: LCCN 2024047807 (print) | LCCN 2024047808 (ebook) | ISBN 9780691153957 (hardback) | ISBN 9780691275161 (ebook)
Subjects: LCSH: Goethe, Johann Wolfgang von, 1749-1832. | Authors, German—18th century—Biography. | Authors, German—19th century—Biography. | BISAC: BIOGRAPHY & AUTOBIOGRAPHY / Philosophers | HISTORY / Modern / 18th Century | LCGFT: Biographies.
Classification: LCC PT2049 .B45 2025 (print) | LCC PT2049 (ebook) | DDC 831/.6—dc23/eng/20241217
LC record available at https://lccn.loc.gov/2024047807
LC ebook record available at https://lccn.loc.gov/2024047808

British Library Cataloging-in-Publication Data is available

Editorial: Ben Tate, Josh Drake
Production Editorial: Elizabeth Byrd
Jacket: Karl Spurzem
Production: Danielle Amatucci
Publicity: Alyssa Sanford (US), Carmen Jimenez (UK)
Copyeditor: Reese M. Heitner

Jacket Credit: Sueddeutsche Zeitung Photo / Alamy Stock Photo

Printed in the United States of America

10 9 8 7 6 5 4 3 2 1

LEVERHULME
TRUST

Lou   Flo   Cec

> Es ist doch nichts besser, als wenn man sich liebt und zusammen ist.

CONTENTS

Acknowledgements ix
Permissions xi

Introduction: The Compromise — 1

1 Hometown: Frankfurt, 1749–1765 — 15

2 'I'm Not a Christian': Leipzig, Frankfurt, Strasbourg, 1765–1771 — 33

3 'Moses! Prophet! Evangelist! Apostle, Spinoza or Machiavelli': Frankfurt and Wetzlar, 1771–1775 — 63

4 The Intellectual Love of God: Weimar, 1775–1786 — 126

5 'In Conversation with Things': Italy, 1786–1788 — 207

6 Transformations: Weimar, 1788–1794 — 236

7 Church Militant: Weimar, 1794–1805 — 305

8 'My Emperor': Weimar, 1805–1814 — 414

9 'What More Could Grandpa Want?': Weimar, 1814–1825 — 505

10 'These Very Serious Jokes': Weimar, 1825–1832 — 580

Note on Translations, Editions, and Referencing 659
List of Abbreviations 661
Notes 665
References 725
General Index 741
Index of Goethe's Works 751

ACKNOWLEDGEMENTS

AS WITH ANY project of this size, a considerable burden is borne by those close to the author, in this case this book's three dedicatees, who have lived with and supported me and my writing about Goethe for many years. Their contribution to the contents of the book is, as Goethe might have said, 'inkommensurabel'. And they have made me laugh so much. My sister Sarah Delaney has been a tremendous support, especially during the last weeks of our mother and stepfather's lives in spring 2024. The memory of Ann and Pete and their famous generosity lives on in the blessedly large blended family they left behind.

Academic friends, colleagues and students have left their mark on my work in all sorts of ways, though of course they take no responsibility for its flaws. In the beginning was Ray Ockenden, who first introduced me to Goethe. I was subsequently supervised by Jim Reed, the most admirable *Doktorvater*. Colleagues and students in the German and Comparative Literature programmes at King's College London have provided a sounding board for over thirty years. In ways that might not immediately be apparent to them, decisive contributions were made by David Ricks, Michael Silk, Sebastian Matzner, Rosa Mucignat, and Daniele Vecchiato. I have also benefitted from the learning and generosity of Barry Nisbet, Ritchie Robertson, Jeremy Adler, John Williams, Clark Muenzer, Dan Wilson, Charlotte Lee, Horst Lange, and the organizers of and participants in the colloquia of the Goethe-Lexicon of Philosophical Concepts. Members of the English Goethe Society have heard me speak about Goethe more often than is healthy. Soon after I started writing, Doriane Zerka provided invaluable assistance with the typescript and Harry Ritchie offered sensitive guidance on how to communicate. Simon Glendinning and Jane Darcy have been wonderful conversation partners throughout. Once most of the book was drafted, Catriona MacLeod and Claudia Nitschke were kind enough to read it and make judicious suggestions. Lisa Barnard gave me a much-needed shove when I was struggling to write the conclusion.

I would like to thank the Leverhulme Trust for the award of Research Fellowship RF-2019-640, which funded an invaluable period of study leave in 2020.

The project was originally proposed to me by Ben Tate of Princeton University Press more years ago than either of us would care to remember. The fact that Ben has accompanied the project throughout its lifespan, offering wise and astute advice, has made all the difference. Working with other colleagues at PUP has been a pleasure from beginning to end; my thanks go to Elizabeth Byrd and Josh Drake. The team at Westchester Publishing Services have been a marvel, turning my erratic typescript into a much more polished object: I am immensely grateful to Angela Piliouras and Reese Heitner.

PERMISSIONS

Chapter 4

'Myth and "Metaphysical Reach" in Goethe's Iphigenie auf Tauris', in: *Poetry and Poetics, Greek and Beyond: Essays in Honour of M. S. Silk*, ed. Fiona MacIntosh and David Ricks, Routledge / Centre for Hellenic Studies, forthcoming 2025.

'This Was a Man!' Goethe's *Egmont* and Shakespeare's *Julius Caesar*', *Modern Language Review* 111 (2016), 141–61.

Chapter 6

'The Poetic Coherence of Goethe's Venetian Epigrams', *Publications of the English Goethe Society* 78 (2009), 117–30.

Chapter 7

'Society and the Sources of Legality in Goethe's *Die natürliche Tochter*', *Colloquia Germanica* 55 (2022), 9–20.

'Charakter (Character)', GLPC 1/2 (2021), https://doi.org/10.5195/glpc.2021.41.

'Embracing the Enemy: The Problem of Religion in Goethe's "Confessions of a Beautiful Soul"', in: Juliana de Albuquerque and Gert Hofmann (eds.), *Anti/Idealism: Re-interpreting a German Discourse*. Berlin and Boston: De Gruyter, 13–26.

'Goethe's Two Types of Classicism'. *Publications of the English Goethe Society* 64–65 (1996), 97–115.

Chapter 10

'Sorge, Epicurean Psychology, and the Classical *Faust*', *Oxford German Studies* 28 (1999), 82–130.

GOETHE

Introduction

THE COMPROMISE

ON 12 NOVEMBER 1723 Professor Christian Wolff left the Prussian university town of Halle accompanied by a group of students. On crossing the River Saale and leaving Prussian territory, he paused to refund the students their fees for the lectures he would not be able to give. Hours earlier he had received a cabinet order issued by King Friedrich Wilhelm I. The order removed Wolff from his university post and decreed that 'within forty-eight hours of receipt of this order he is to leave the town of Halle and all other royal lands on pain of the noose'.[1] The news of Wolff's banishment came as a shock. Professor Joachim Lange of the theology faculty at Halle was unable to sleep or eat for three days, or so he later claimed.[2] Lange's distress, assuming it was genuine, was presumably aggravated by guilt. For several years Lange and his colleagues in Halle's staunchly Pietist theology faculty had been trying to undermine Wolff. The cause was a dispute about the overlapping claims of theology and philosophy. Its roots lay in the claim of Spinoza and his allies that all truths in theology must conform to philosophy.[3] Theology must either submit itself to philosophical judgement or retreat to a space that did not impinge on the real world. The feud between Wolff and Lange may also have been personal. There were suggestions that Lange was jealous, for there were more empty benches in his lectures than in Wolff's.[4] In a university system that required students to pay lecture fees directly to their professors, the competition to recruit students could be deeply divisive. The antagonism had broken into open warfare on 12 July 1721, on the occasion of Wolff ending his term as university pro-rector and handing over to none other than Lange. Wolff's oration at the end of his term was designed to aggravate the Pietists. He praised Confucius as a forerunner of his own philosophy and argued that Chinese moral philosophy proved that it was possible to be good without being Christian. The speech was both a provocation to Lange and an unwise admission by Wolff that his own philosophy had no need of Christianity. It was obvious that Lange would use his position as pro-rector to undermine Wolff. Getting their revenge in first, Wolff's students took to the streets. There were shouts of 'Long live the old pro-rector, death to the new one Lange!' The students sang obscene songs outside Lange's home.

The whole episode was tragic, comical, depressing, and bizarre. The official reason for Wolff's banishment was alleged atheism.[5] The unofficial reason was stranger. Wolff had not helped his cause by involving the government in his dispute with the theologians. In March 1723 one of Lange's supporters, Daniel Strähler, published the first instalment of a multipart critique of Wolff's philosophy. Without even reading Strähler's argument, Wolff complained to the government that Strähler was bringing the university into disrepute by criticising him personally. Strähler was forbidden to continue his critique. With his proxy out of action, Lange published his own critique of Wolff, which began a public duel of essays lasting from July to November. There were three further attacks by Lange and three parries by Wolff.[6] Lange also demanded that a royal commission be established to investigate Wolff's dangerous teaching. Wolff had sympathizers at the Prussian court, and at first it seemed that no action would be taken against him. However, Wolff's bothersome appeals to the authorities about Strähler had evidently caused annoyance in more traditionalist factions at court. A military crony and member of the King's 'tobacco cabinet' explained to the King that Wolff believed in Leibniz's doctrine of preestablished harmony. (In fact Wolff did not assert that preestablished harmony was true; he merely treated it as the most plausible of all available conjectures.) According to this doctrine souls and bodies do not interact causally, they only appear to do so. In reality they have been set in harmony by God, in the same way as two clocks can be set to tell the same time. One implication of Leibniz's doctrine is that all human actions are preordained by God and therefore divinely sanctioned. Hence, so the King's smoking crony averred, the King's soldiers could desert and argue that God had willed them to do so. For the Soldier King this was too much, and he immediately banished Wolff on pain of execution by hanging.

German intellectual life in the early to mid-eighteenth century involved significant compromises and dangers. Censorship was an ever-present threat, even if an incoherent one. Censorship was hard to enforce because of the patchwork of legal jurisdictions that made up the Holy Roman Empire of the German Nation. Wolff fled from Prussian Brandenburg into nearby Hessen-Kassel, where he safely took up a chair at the University of Marburg.

FIG. 1. Professor Christian Wolff, during his time at the University of Marburg, etching by Johann Georg Wille

Censorship was also often counterproductive. In the fifteen years following his banishment, around two hundred essays and pamphlets were published on Wolff's philosophy.[7] He became German philosophy's leading figure, the 'dominant progressive philosopher' in the Empire,[8] and a hero of the Enlightenment. In Paris, the *Encyclopédie* devoted an article to him. Nonetheless censorship was existentially threatening because the penalties could be so severe and so unpredictable. Wolff was banished and threatened with hanging by personal order of the King and for reasons that he could not have foreseen and were arguably beyond his control—an obscure metaphysical theory he did not even subscribe to. He was accustomed to feuding with the theologians in Halle. They had been trying to silence him for some time. Lange's colleague August Hermann Francke had been warning his students against attending

Wolff's lectures since 1712.⁹ Lange starting planting informants in Wolff's lectures in 1717. For years the structures of university governance protected Wolff against these intrigues. What they could not protect him against was the King's personal intervention.

Eighteenth-century Germans understood the flaws of monarchical government. They knew it was prone to the arbitrary abuse of power Wolff had experienced. However, monarchy was the system almost all of them lived under, and they believed in the security and stability it afforded. There was relatively little systematic criticism of monarchy as a form of government.¹⁰ The answer to abuses of power was not to exchange monarchy for a republic. Instead, Germans tended to place their hope in sensible government. It was an attitude that had become widespread in the aftermath of the Thirty Years' War. After the peace of 1648, political discourse focused on reviving the German lands from three decades of bloodshed, destruction, famine, and disease. Governments were urged to provide sound administration, good public order, and physical and moral welfare—what was known as 'Polizei'.¹¹ The ideal state was a highly regulated commonwealth that could increase the welfare of its subjects.¹² There was a preference for policies that produced results, less so for deliberation on the constitutional structures that underpinned them or might guarantee the rights of their subjects. Wolff gave rational form to this view in his *German Politics*, published during his pro-rectorship at Halle in 1721. His argument follows the Aristotelian theory that there are three basic forms of government, distinguished by the number of persons making up the ruling authority in each: monarchy (rule by a single person), aristocracy (rule by a group), and 'polity' (rule by the whole community). Each form is capable of providing blameless and effective government. Wolff's solution to arbitrariness and abuse of power is not to analyse the merits and flaws of the forms of government and reach a view on which is best. He treats them as equally valid. He does show glimpses of republicanism: he writes approvingly of the freedoms provided by a 'polity', which one can also term a 'free republic', he says.¹³ However, he soon restores parity between the three forms of government by observing that the 'ignorance and obstinacy' that can arise in a 'polity' causes as much damage as the abuses of power under aristocracy and monarchy.¹⁴ On the question of democracy his view is clear, and was shared by almost all of his contemporaries: popular suffrage cannot produce good government.¹⁵ 'Democracy' is in fact his name for the corrupted form that a 'polity' will descend into if the common people impose their selfish interests on the state. In general, however, constitutionality and representation have only very limited impact on the quality of government. Wolff's language is dominated instead by moral psychology. What distinguishes effective from corrupt government is whether rulers promote the interests of the state or their own selfish interests, and whether they do so is decided chiefly by their moral character.

Wolff's compromise with political reality involved shifting the focus of criticism away from political systems and towards the safer ground of personal morality. In doing so, he insisted on a political role for the scholar-cum-official class to which he belonged. He repeatedly affirmed the need for monarchs to take advice from philosophers. Ideally the modern monarch should be a philosopher himself, but since this was rarely the case, the monarch should employ a caste of educated officials to draw up the state's laws,[16] just as Chinese governments had done.[17] The idea of philosophers advising on legislation was wishful thinking, of course. The vast majority of German territories were ruled by autocrats and enjoyed no representative democracy. There were many consultative bodies, such as the noble diets or city councils, but these played only a minor role in legislation and administration. Their main role was to allow the estates (nobility, town burghers) to bring complaints to the notice of their prince. Moreover, the estates were medieval institutions that did not reflect the interests of the modern university-educated class of officials, let alone the professoriate. If the professoriate had any influence, it was felt indirectly through the universities' role in educating government officials. The German lands were unusual in Europe for having a very large number of universities and for educating government administrators to a high level. The science of government (*Kameralwissenschaft*) was taught extensively, alongside economics, law, and other relevant disciplines. A lively public sphere had emerged, including a growing circulation of newspapers and journals. The largest and most diverse publishing industry in Europe gave Wolff and his class many opportunities to present their ideas on government. This was one of the contradictions of eighteenth-century German society. The professoriate enjoyed high status and profile, but this was not matched by their political influence. When philosophers published unsolicited advice to monarchs—for instance in the venerable literary tradition of the 'mirror of princes', which reached back to the Middle Ages and beyond—the advice was usually more moral or educational than directly political. That accorded with Wolff's political theory, which held that the welfare of the state depended on the monarch's moral qualities. It has long been argued that the German intelligentsia's self-image and its claims to a leading role in state and society were out of step with political reality, and it is hard to disagree.

1740 brought hopeful signs for the progressive wing of the Enlightenment. Friedrich Wilhelm I was succeeded by Friedrich II (Frederick the Great). The new Prussian king was reputed to be cultured and enlightened. Wolff had refused the old Soldier King's invitations to return to Halle, but he accepted Frederick's invitation, at the second time of asking. His return in December 1740 was a triumph. The same year he published the first volume of his *Law of Nature Treated in the Scientific Manner*, which presented a more liberal version of Rationalism than the *German Politics*.[18] Whereas Aquinas, the first theorist of natural law, had originally determined the source of law to be God's will, Wolff sought to distance law from theology. Natural law was a product of human reason. It was the same move as he had made in his Chinese oration of 1721. One benefit of distancing philosophy from theology in this way would be to reduce sectarianism. If theology was cut off from philosophy, then sectarian divisions would lose their philosophical footing and instead become mere matters of social practice or private conviction. Natural law would thus give philosophical sanction to the settlement of 1648 and the religious peace it had brought to places like Wolff's hometown of Breslau (Wrocław). (Wolff's philosophy proved popular across Germany's confessional divide and was taught at Catholic universities as much as Protestant ones.) At the same time, Wolff faced the familiar danger of being seen to come too close to Spinozan naturalism.[19] For Spinoza there was only one natural law, and that was the 'impersonal, morally neutral' law of nature itself.[20] Wolff kept to a middle way. His natural law occupies the realm of reason, an autonomous place insulated from both the accusation of Spinozan atheism and interference by the theologians.[21] Reason has authority over all human beings by virtue of its very nature, and it can be known by all humans, again by virtue of its nature. The natural character of human rights flows from reason's universality. In contrast to his great predecessors in natural law, Samuel von Pufendorf and Christian Thomasius,[22] Wolff argues that there are human rights that we are born with (*iura connata*). These are so absolute and fundamental that human action or reflection cannot alter them. They include both 'negative' freedoms, such as freedom from persecution, albeit on a limited scale,[23] and 'positive' rights to such goods as sustenance, habitation, and work.[24] To be sure, existence in the state requires that we sacrifice some rights, and the sacrifices might need to be extensive. Nonetheless, the *iura connata* are so fundamental that they continue to exist even if surrendered: the modern state is a compromise between the absolute validity of our rights on the one hand and limitations to our rights on the other.[25] In international law, Wolff argues for parity of esteem for states.²⁶ Relations between states are not a function of power; we do not respect a state because it forms part of an international balance of power. On the contrary, we owe all states a duty of esteem because they all promote the perfection of their subjects.²⁷ In this sense, Wolff's conception of natural law draws on Aristotelian and Leibnizian notions of perfectibility. The law is the unfolding of reason towards a perfection that imitates the perfection of God.

Any hopes that princes might abide by natural law or that Frederick II might prove a more enlightened ruler than his father were immediately challenged. On 16 December 1740, only ten days after Wolff's triumphant return to Halle, Frederick launched an attack on Austrian Silesia. His military successes were greeted enthusiastically in the mainly Protestant northern and central heartlands of the Enlightenment. The wave of support for Frederick made the Wolffians' intellectual balancing act even more difficult. Frederick's aggression and the accompanying tightening of political restrictions in Prussia made Wolff's theory of natural law seem overly optimistic. It might still be argued that Frederick was a positive embodiment of the power of the rational state and was maintaining the Enlightenment principle of religious freedom. Germany's leading playwright and critic, Gotthold Ephraim Lessing, was not convinced. In an angry outburst to his friend Friedrich Nicolai, he claimed that Frederick's version of the Enlightenment amounted to little more than scorn for all religion.²⁸

Criticism of Wolffianism grew through the 1750s and '60s. As with Wolffianism itself, it is hard to class its critics as either liberal or conservative. Justus Möser, a legal official in the prince-bishopric of Osnabrück, made his reputation by defending the rights of the traditional estates against the arbitrariness of the territory's secular authority. Möser's essays present a wider critique of modern rationalizing tendencies in politics and culture. He has been claimed as a protoconservative by Klaus Epstein and Karl Mannheim,²⁹ and as an inheritor of traditional estates-based conservatism by Panajotis Kondylis.³⁰ The conservative tendency in Möser's thought is grounded in a sceptical attitude to rationality. All attempts to reason about ultimate truths lead to more doubt, and so reason is a poor guide to organizing society. We would be better advised to accept things as they are and use tradition and history as our guides. However, as Beiser has shown, Möser was concerned to revise natural law, not abandon it. Möser rejects the basis of Wolffian moral psychology. Whereas Wolff argues that our sense of good and evil is a form of knowledge, Möser proposes the reverse: our knowledge derives from affects and inclinations.[31] For Möser, Wolffian natural law is not really natural; it is in fact rational. Möser replaces reason with nature as source of natural law.[32] In political terms, the universal laws of Wolffianism divert the state from the true plan of nature in all its variety and pave the way for despotic uniformity.[33]

Critics could argue that 'nature' in Wolff's philosophy was not nature, and 'human nature' was not human nature.[34] For Wolff, the natural world was organized rationally. Each organism or other natural entity had its own function within nature as a whole, and the purpose of the whole was to satisfy the claims of reason. The beauty of nature could only be understood on the assumption that it was created by a beneficent divine architect. To be sure, much of Wolff's theory of nature was more empirical and commonsense than its critics gave it credit for, but its critics did have an easy time ridiculing the notion that, say, rats existed in order to provide food for cats. Wolffian nature was a rationalist construction. Demands for a more authentic conception of nature that offered greater existential intensity became more urgent in the late 1750s, following Rousseau's *Discourse on the Arts and Sciences* (1750) and *Discourse on the Origin and Basis of Inequality among Men* (1754). German intellectuals, including Möser, tended to view Rousseau's denunciations of modernity as extreme. However, Möser agreed with Rousseau's rejection of rationalist culture, especially the culture of the Rococo.[35] Rousseau was an ally against attempts by Frederick II and Johann Christoph Gottsched to rationalize German literature—or to Frenchify it, which amounted to the same thing. Gottsched, the most prominent Wolffian after Wolff, was also attacked for his attempts to standardize the German language on the model of the Saxon dialect. A prolonged dispute broke out in 1740 between Gottsched and the two Swiss philologists Johann Jakob Bodmer und Johann Jakob Breitinger. It is noteworthy that for the critics of Rationalism—Möser, Bodmer, Breitinger, Johann Georg Hamann, and his protégé Johann Gottfried Herder—language and literature were a key focus. Of all of them, Herder was the closest to Rousseau. He worked out a new version of Rousseau's conjectural history of civilization that centred innate human creativity at the source of human history.[36] More generally, Herder presented a progressive anti-Rationalist alternative to Wolff. His first important intervention was his 1765 essay 'Problem: How philosophy can become general and useful for the benefit of the people'. Even though Wolff had done much to make the style of philosophical exposition more accessible and had written in plain and lucid German,[37] the content of his philosophy remained abstract and his view of human nature overly rational. Herder's counterproposal is that philosophy should be 'taken back to anthropology', which has the further consequence that philosophy must be 'modified according to the varieties of the population'.[38] If philosophy has to conform to human variety, then Wolff's *iura connata* would cease to exist. Wolff's and Herder's versions of a progressive Enlightenment could hardly have been more different.

The critiques of Wolffian rationalism were persistent and well made, but the critical voices were scattered and at the margins of the German-speaking world: Möser in Osnabrück in the northwest, Bodmer and Breitinger in Zurich, and Hamann and Herder in far-flung East Prussia. While their ideas were well received, they did not change opinion significantly in the central Lutheran heartlands of the Enlightenment. They did not find anything like the wide approval or institutional acceptance that Wolff's philosophy enjoyed. They did little to change the terms of the Wolffian compromise with monarchic power.

———

Wolffianism was still the dominant philosophical tradition in the German lands in the 1760s, as Goethe's writing career was beginning. His arrival on the literary scene in the latter years of Wolffianism shaped certain key features of his intellectual development. Above all he reacted against the unnatural conceptions of nature in Wolffianism. He found several allies, including Rousseau, Spinoza, Möser, and Herder. Much has rightly been made of Herder's influence on the young Goethe. Herder channelled Goethe's literary talent away from an uninteresting Rococo style and towards new and more natural modes of expression, for instance, the popular songs sung in rural German communities (*Volkslieder*). Herder also influenced Goethe's intellectual development by giving him resources in the battle against Wolffianism. However, Goethe had already found key allies in this battle, notably Rousseau and possibly Spinoza. (The date of Goethe's first meaningful engagement with Spinoza is contested,[39] but it is certain that Goethe knew about Spinoza before he met Herder in 1770.) Goethe's literary career went on to span sixty-five years, during which Europe's cultural and intellectual landscape changed profoundly. Although he insisted he was not a philosopher, he read widely in philosophy. He was friendly or acquainted with several of the most prominent figures in the golden age of German philosophy: Herder, Jacobi, Schiller, Reinhold, Fichte, Schelling, Hegel, and Schopenhauer. Perhaps because he was not a philosopher by vocation, and so was less interested in creating a self-consistent philosophical system, an extremely wide variety of intellectual influences left traces in his writings. He was the kind of writer who responded to the good, the bad, and the simply interesting in what he read, whether or not he agreed with it. He wrote in a dizzying range of genres and disciplines. His literary works include arguably the single richest corpus of lyric poetry in modern Europe. There are also epics and artfully wrought cycles of poems. His dramatic works range from small comic pieces and libretti for musical theatre, through bourgeois social plays and large-scale historical dramas, to the huge and barely stageable phantasmagoria of *Faust*. In addition to four extremely diverse novels, he composed numerous shorter prose narratives. He wrote a very large body of critical and historical writings on literature and the visual arts. In science, which from 1780 onwards occupied as much of his time as literature, he wrote essays on geology, meteorology, optics and colour, botany, entomology, and mammal zoology. Many of his critical and scientific writings are shot through with a philosophical desire to question and understand what we know, how we know it, and what it means. This is particularly true of the mass of aphorisms he produced from the 1790s onwards. His poems, plays, and prose narratives are also philosophical, in the sense that they create fictional worlds in which philosophical ideas are put to the test. If not a philosopher by vocation, Goethe was a decidedly philosophical writer. This is why it makes sense to think of his writing career in terms of both his literary and his intellectual development. This book focuses on the latter, and of course in doing so it presents only part of the picture. It does include analyses of some of his literary works because they are philosophical in the sense described above. However, its main focus is on his career as a thinker, on a life lived in constant close contact with philosophical, religious, aesthetic, scientific, and political ideas.

Goethe's cultural legacy is well known. His intellectual legacy has been no less important, but is less familiar. One indication of the power of his influence is that some of the major figures of the nineteenth and twentieth centuries built their intellectual careers around the reception of his ideas. Four examples are Matthew Arnold, Friedrich Nietzsche, Max Weber, and Oswald Spengler. It was not just that these four found ideas in Goethe's writing that they could make their own. It was that they had a deep and broad allegiance to a Goethean way of thinking and sustained that allegiance for the duration of their intellectual careers. Arnold ranked Goethe among the four most powerful influences on his life.⁴⁰ Arnold's vision of Victorian high culture as 'the best which has been thought and said in the world'⁴¹—a notably Goethean formulation⁴²—was based on the classics and the Bible. The latter, Arnold wrote, 'will forever remain, as Goethe called it, not only a national book, but the Book of the Nations'.⁴³ Arnold regretted the decline of religious belief, and yet he agreed with Goethe—and with Goethe's favourite philosopher Spinoza, to whom Arnold came via Goethe—that religion must do without the supernatural.⁴⁴ Unlike Goethe, Arnold was politically liberal, though in a limited sense, and the limits on his liberalism were again Goethean. Freedom was a philistine concept, and liberalism must be tempered by 'renouncement' and experience.⁴⁵ 'Renouncement' was one of Goethe's signature ideas, and it was from Goethe that Arnold learned that the reasons for 'renouncement' came from our personal experience. This is the meaning of Arnold's best known statement on Goethe: 'Goethe's profound, imperturbable naturalism was absolutely fatal to all routine thinking; he puts the standard, once for all, inside every man instead of outside him.'⁴⁶ For Nietzsche, Goethe represented a different kind of naturalism, 'healthily restrained celebration of the sensuous'.⁴⁷ The image of Goethe in Nietzsche's writing is unusual (for Nietzsche, that is) because it is consistently positive and without the ambivalence or reversals that characterize Nietzsche's attitude to his other 'heroes'. Consequently Nietzsche associates Goethe with all of his 'familiar, eternally recurring preoccupations and obsessions'.⁴⁸ Everything Nietzschean also seems to be Goethean. Weber became dedicated to Goethe in his teens when, according to his wife Marianne, he read all forty volumes of the Cotta edition of Goethe's works.⁴⁹ Weber's writings on sociology and politics are scattered with quotations from Goethe, but his reception of Goethe was not shallow. Of special importance to him were the two *Wilhelm Meister* novels and *Faust*, which helped to form his notions of the specialized vocation and active asceticism.⁵⁰ He shared with Goethe an ambivalence about modernity: a belief that modernity consisted in and must be met with practical engagement, alongside a sense that modernity had lost contact with beauty and spiritual richness. Scepticism about modernity was Spengler's dominant mode, most famously in his *Decline of the West* (1918–1922). In the preface to a 1922 edition of *Decline* Spengler wrote that 'Goethe gave me the method, Nietzsche the questions.'⁵¹ The work's subtitle, *Outlines of a Morphology of World History*, indicates what Spengler had in mind, for *morphology* was one of Goethe's signature concepts. According to Spengler's morphological method, cultures undergo evolutionary processes that dictate the forms they take. Again there is a vein of naturalism in Goethe's influence, which for Spengler expresses itself as a scepticism about civilization. Spengler dismisses the progressive model of historical development and replaces it with a cyclical one. For the epigraph of *Decline* Spengler used some verses by Goethe that advertised that cyclical model: 'in the infinite the same thing / Flows on eternally repeating itself' ('im Unendlichen dasselbe / Sich wiederholend ewig fließt').[52]

Goethe's theory of morphology was a biological, not a historical theory, and it enjoyed its most fruitful reception in nineteenth-century evolutionary science. Again, his scientific legacy is not as well known as it might be. As Robert Richards has shown, Goethe's 'conceptions in morphology, the science virtually of his own creation, had a solid empirical footing and provided purchase for the emergence of evolutionary theory in Germany and England'.[53] A line of influence leads from Goethe's work on mammal anatomy through Carl Gustav Carus and Richard Owen to Darwin. In the first edition of *The Origin of Species*, Darwin cited Goethe's theory of the 'compensation of growth'.[54] In the third edition, he added a historical preface in which he acknowledged Goethe's work on mammal morphology in the mid-1790s.[55] Other evolutionary biologists promoted Goethe's work, notably Étienne Geoffroy Saint-Hilaire, Ernst Haeckel, and Thomas Henry Huxley. Goethe's holistic vision of nature inspired Alexander von Humboldt to develop his conception of ecology.[56] Huxley, on being invited to write an editorial for the first edition of the new science journal *Nature* in 1869, offered his own translation of a rhapsodic prose poem 'Nature' that was at the time generally attributed to Goethe.[57] Darwin admired Huxley's translation.[58] Other aspects of Goethe's work in biology have been less influential, but have still found resonance. The botanist Agnes Arber published a translation of Goethe's essay on plant metamorphosis.[59] Her own theory of plant form grew out of her reception of Goethe.[60]

The wider reception of Goethe's science is a more mixed picture. The theory of light, optics, and colour on which he worked for nearly twenty years has been largely (and rightly) rejected, and it prompted some nineteenth-century scientists to deny Goethe's scientific work any credibility whatsoever. The physicist and physiologist Hermann von Helmholtz argued in a lecture of 1853 that Goethe was really an intuitive artist, not a scientist. (In 1875 he added a postscript to the lecture in which he acknowledged that Darwin's theory of evolution was 'unmistakably' based on the same ideas as Goethe's.)[61] Helmholtz's friend the physiologist Emil du Bois-Reymond made a similar argument in 1882. He set Goethe up as example of the damage done to German science by philosophical speculation.[62] In the developing split between the two cultures of science and the humanities, Goethe's science was forced onto the humanities side. This had an unfortunate consequence. His expulsion from science allowed him to emerge as a mediating figure between the two cultures or as a throwback to a golden (or just different) age before the split occurred. Heinrich Henel claimed that 'the real importance of Goethe as a student of nature lies in the fact that he was the last great figure in the Western world to offer an alternative to what is now known as science.'[63] The idea of Goethe as an alternative to modern materialist science was one of his main attractions to Rudolf Steiner and the anthroposophists. Steiner promoted Goethe's scientific writings as an alternative to the dominant materialist trend in modern science. Anthroposophy has applied its own version of Goetheanism to a wide range of disciplines, including agriculture, medicine, and education.

Goethe's political legacy is less well known than his scientific legacy but just as contested. It is only in recent years that his political thought has begun to be analysed systematically. Much of the earlier political reception of Goethe was based on either partial and tendentious interpretations or somewhat fuzzy notions of his symbolic value for the German people. The earliest trends in political Goethe reception tended to pick out supposedly socialist or liberal elements in his work, especially in the two *Wilhelm Meister* novels.[64] With the advent of German unification in 1871, Goethe for the first time became a political figure and a symbol of Germanness, even being equated with Bismarck.[65] 'Germany', wrote Herman Grimm, 'was chosen by fate to have produced men like Luther, Goethe, and Bismarck.'[66] Grimm claimed that Goethe's German would become the language of the German Empire. Grimm's intentions were liberal. The Nazis reenvisioned Goethe in their own image: Faust was a symbol of the German *Volk* and its mission to assert itself in the world.[67] With the defeat of Nazism and the foundation of the German Federal Republic, Goethe resumed his role as a spiritual forerunner of liberalism. It was a fortunate coincidence that the new Republic's constitution was promulgated in 1949, the two hundredth anniversary of Goethe's birth. Goethe became the exemplary 'good German' and he prefigured the clauses in the Federal constitution that protected the free unfolding of the human personality.[68] In the German Democratic Republic the image of Goethe took its lead from the Hungarian Marxist György Lukács's *Goethe and his Age* (1947), which presented Goethe as having the unusual ability to rise above his class-consciousness and analyse the 'German misery' of the late eighteenth and early nineteenth centuries. Lukács's view spread to the German left in the West in the 1960s. Goethe's novel *Werther* became a symbol of political alienation. At the same time, for the student movement of the 1960s and '70s, the postwar

Goethe cult seemed part of the Federal Republic's failure to fully recognise the crimes of the Nazis.[69]

In an article published in 1998, Ekkehart Krippendorff notes that scholars have neglected the subject of Goethe's politics.[70] In fact it has long been recognised that his politics contained an authoritarian strain.[71] His opposition to free speech, democracy, and civil rights for Jews—indeed civil rights for anyone—is well known. In the 1990s the work of W. Daniel Wilson brought to light Goethe's authoritarian activity as a minister: his role in suppressing popular demands for rights and in the surveillance of freemasons, students, and professors at the University of Jena.[72] Wilson's conclusions are contested, but their tenor fits with Goethe's well-documented opposition to democracy and civil rights. This raises in a particularly stark form the question of how we can make sense of the contrast between the authoritarian politician and the seemingly liberal writer and thinker. Krippendorff lists the many ways in which Goethe engaged with politics as a minister of state, writer, and observer of a politically tumultuous era. He concludes that Goethe does not fit into the familiar political spectrums of conservative-progressive or right-left: 'However, he was by no means unpolitical, to which status he has been overwhelmingly reduced for the sake of convenience'.[73] The fallacy of the 'unpolitical Goethe' has not only been a matter of convenience, a way of avoiding using the ill-fitting and anachronistic right-left spectrum. It goes back to Thomas Mann's decidedly political defence of Goethe during World War I. For Mann, the 'unpolitical Goethe' was a true representative of the German bourgeoisie, whose proper role was indeed to be unpolitical.[74] Krippendorff's answer to the problem of Goethe's contradictoriness is that Goethe was primarily interested in political results, not ideas: he was a doer, not a thinker.[75] Of course, the idea of being a deliverer of results flatters every politician's self-image, and Goethe was no less guilty than any politician of presenting himself as a selfless and unideological servant of the people. And while there is some truth in that image, we should set against it the fact that he thought and wrote about political practice and ideas continually from his student days onwards. We certainly cannot explain the gap between his authoritarian politics and liberal attitudes to culture and science by pretending that he did not think about it. A more historically accurate answer to the problem will be evident from the story of Christian Wolff and the uneasy compromise of the eighteenth-century German intelligentsia between intellectual freedom and political unfreedom. For Goethe, however, the compromise with power took a less liberal and progressive form.

1

Hometown

FRANKFURT, 1749–1765

GOETHE'S HOMETOWN was a peculiar mixture of new and old, liberty and prejudice, power and irrelevance. Its position at the junction of arterial trade routes made Frankfurt a commercial hub—on the River Main near its confluence with the Rhine and on the north-south land highway. It was said of Frankfurt in Goethe's day that commerce was 'the soul of the city'.[1] Commerce gave the city its traditions, its political institutions, its wealth, its calendar. At the two trade fairs at Easter and Michaelmas the tents of the merchants formed a city within a city, all under the protection of a grant of Imperial privilege of 1240. Well before the eighteenth century Frankfurt was also one of Europe's great financial centres, especially after the arrival of wealthy Jews expelled from the surrounding Catholic cities in the sixteenth century. The oppression of Calvinists in the Low Countries and France and immigration from Italy added to this influx of wealthy and well-connected financiers. Its location also made Frankfurt a meeting place of the German territorial princes and their representatives. It was a place of parleys and treaties. Its commercial and political significance had been recognised in 1372 when it won the status of a Free Imperial City, which made the Frankfurters uncommonly proud. In 1562 it acquired the honour of becoming the site of the Emperor's coronation. The ceremonial importance was not matched by real political power. Frankfurt was a tiny territory with no military resources of its own. By the mid-eighteenth century the real power lay in Vienna and Berlin.

Frankfurt's medieval traditions were still visible. According to Heinrich Sebastian Hüsgen's guidebook of 1802, the city contained sixteen churches, three chapels, and six convents.[2] These formed the city's medieval cityscape, along with the so-called Old Bridge (in fact rebuilt in the 1740s) and the two

FIG. 2. View of Frankfurt from the west, by J. C. Zehender (1770)

ancient wooden cranes on the Main wharf.[3] In many ways Frankfurt was more like a very large and traditional village.[4] The streets were dirty because of the many pigs that ran free despite repeated ordinances of the city council to control them. Further problems were caused by the homeless. The city council repeatedly tried either to drive out beggars or put them to work cleaning the city's streets—another way of solving the pig problem.[5] However, there was no mass of labourers because the city council feared unrest and blocked attempts at establishing manufacturing industry.[6] The only physical evidence of urban modernity lay outside the city walls, where the wealthy patricians and burghers built their summerhouses.[7]

The city's social structure was also traditional, and religion was its most important marker. According to a popular Frankfurt saying, the Catholics had the churches, the Calvinists had the money, and the Lutherans had the power. It is possible that Goethe's lifelong distance from organized religion grew out of distaste for Frankfurt's institutionalized discrimination. The city officially converted to Lutheranism in 1530, and shortly thereafter Catholic worship was banned. Only Lutherans could be members of the city's ruling council, practise the law, and take up other esteemed professions and trades. The right to public worship, and with it the city's oldest churches, was restored to the Catholics following the Imperial Diet of 1548, which established an uneasy settlement. The city was governed by its Lutheran majority but owed fealty to its Catholic overlord, the Emperor in Vienna. The Calvinists had to wait until the Peace of Westphalia in 1648 for legal recognition, after which Frankfurt was bound to permit Calvinist worship within its territory, though it was still forbidden within the city walls. This was despite the Calvinists' considerable commercial influence, for they managed the Frankfurt Stock Exchange for most of the eighteenth century. Astute observers, including Goethe's great uncle Johann Michael von Loën, saw that the restrictions imposed on the Calvinists expressed the Lutherans' fear of growing Calvinist power.[8]

Fear was also at the root of the persecution of Frankfurt's Jews. The city council defended the Jews' economic rights, but only because Jewish moneylenders brought wealth to the city, and all the better since, like many European governments, the city would periodically expropriate Jewish property.[9] At the beginning of the century three thousand souls inhabited the Jewish ghetto at Jews' Lane (*Judengasse*).[10] The ghetto's population was tightly regulated. Immigration and marriage were restricted: only twelve Jewish marriages were permitted per year. Jews were confined to the ghetto between sunset and dawn and on Sundays and holy days. They were allowed to walk in the streets in groups of no more than two and then only if they wore a yellow ring sewn on to their clothing. Jews were permitted to promenade on the Sabbath in a dilapidated suburb on the banks of the Main known as the Fishers' Field, where fishermen used to dry their nets.[11] Out of fear of 'contamination', Jews were not allowed to employ Christian servants or wet nurses or to touch fruit and vegetables in the market.[12]

Within the Lutheran citizenry more subtle discriminations of status were made. Status was regulated by a clothing code that went back to the middle of the fourteenth century.[13] Often flouted, these ordinances were periodically renewed until the middle of the eighteenth century. They dictated the outward appearance of each rank of burghers, down to the most trivial detail. According to an ordinance of the 1750s, all burghers had to carry a lantern after dark, the nobility being permitted three candles in theirs, the wealthier burghers two, and the rest only one.[14] To belong to a status group was to win privileges and accept limitations. Above all it was to submit oneself to social control. On moving to university in Leipzig Goethe would find a more modern and stylish city. Leipzig did make him nostalgic for Frankfurt's medieval charms, but on returning home after graduation he described Frankfurt as a 'wretched hole'.[15] In later life he felt pride in the city's political self-rule and its patrician oligarchs' self-confidence. Yet after leaving the city aged twenty-six he returned for only a few brief visits in his long lifetime. Throughout his life his attitude

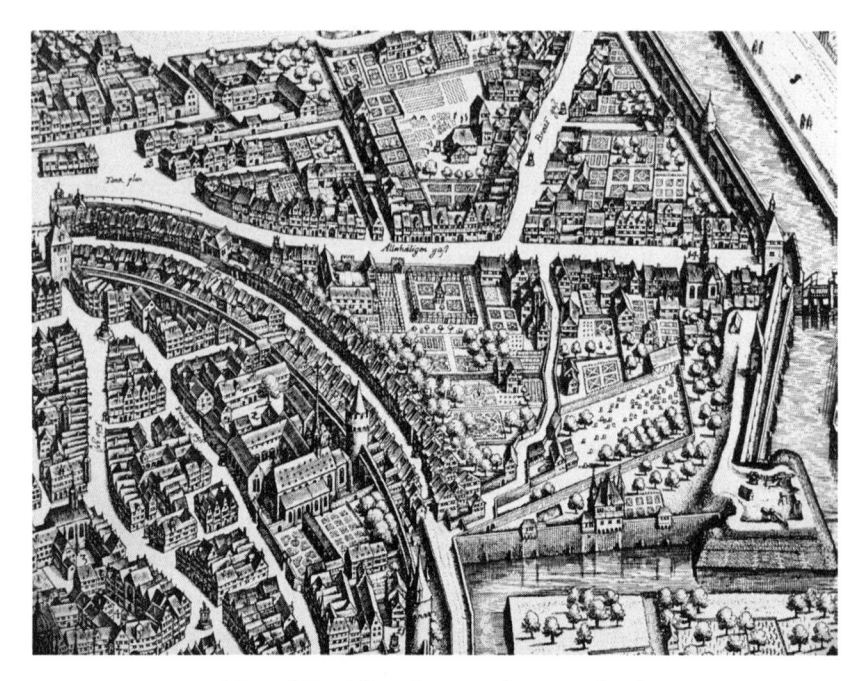

FIG. 3. Map of Frankfurt showing the curved Judengasse
and its tightly packed dwellings (1628)

to Frankfurt alternated between nostalgia for its charms and a dislike of its restrictions and parochialism.

The city's ordinances divided the burghers into five ranks. Only the top two ranks qualified for election to the council. The second rank included the highest practitioners of the crafts and trades and the wealthier burghers. The first rank comprised the councillors of the top two benches, the nobility, advocates, and the College of Graduates in medicine and law. Within the first rank there were further discriminations. The nobility consisted of two societies, the Alten-Limburgs and Frauensteins, of which the former deemed themselves the true patricians.[16] In 1782 in distant Weimar, Goethe was raised into the Imperial nobility. Much later it was reported by Eckermann, perhaps unreliably, that Goethe thought little of his elevation, for he had always counted himself a Frankfurt patrician.[17] By the traditional Frankfurt criteria he was not a patrician at all. The error was understandable insofar as he qualified for the

College of Graduates, which did belong to the same clothing rank as the Alten-Limburgs. It was also true that latterly members of the College of Graduates, including Goethe's maternal grandfather, had occupied the highest offices in the city government. Some commentators, among them von Loën, even argued that commercial activity did not detract from nobility. But these were unusual modernizing arguments, and even on von Loën's definition, Goethe's bloodline was not distinguished enough for patrician status. His family, though comparatively well off and able to live a *rentier* lifestyle, had a worryingly lowly recent past that would take two or three generations to wash clean.[18] It is possible that Goethe had in mind a further and more tendentious theory of von Loën's, that true nobility was not a social condition, but a moral one, 'an elevated condition of virtue'.[19] It was true that the traditional social order was beginning to show signs of flexibility. The notion that a man might be elevated to the aristocracy by virtue of his personal qualities or achievements was no longer unconscionable. More likely though it was Goethe's later conservatism—his commitment to the idea of the aristocracy in the wake of the French Revolution—that made him want to present himself as a patrician by birth and not merely a member of the lower aristocracy by elevation.

In comparison with other great German commercial cities, Hamburg and Bremen for instance, Frankfurt was politically backward. Its merchant class had little say in the city's government.[20] Such reform as did happen was imposed from above by the Emperor in Vienna. During the late seventeenth and early eighteenth centuries the Frankfurt burghers repeatedly complained to the Emperor about mismanagement, corruption, and nepotism.[21] In 1712 an Imperial commission was imposed on the city that settled matters, mostly in favour of the burghers. It was thanks to these reforms that Goethe's maternal grandfather, Dr Johann Wolfgang Textor, rose to the post of *Schultheiß*, the city's chief magistrate and highest official. Goethe was descended from lawyers on both his mother's and father's side. His maternal grandfather Textor had studied law at the University of Altdorf, and as was traditional he completed his training at the Imperial law courts in Wetzlar. On his return to Frankfurt, his ability was quickly recognised, and in 1727 he was appointed to the council. The previous year he had married Anna Margaretha Lindheimer, whose family was connected by marriage to the Frauensteins. The couple moved into the rear portion of his father's substantial property in the new town, which included a fine garden, but they were never wealthy. Textor was a natural diplomat, and he rose rapidly through the ranks of the city government despite or perhaps because of which he remained a controversial character. Whether

Textor was indeed corrupt, vane, and intemperate, as the doctor and scientist Johann Christian Senckenberg claimed, is not known.[22] Goethe gives a much warmer portrayal of his grandfather in his autobiography. Weekly visits to the Textor home for Sunday lunch were a highlight of the week for young Wolfgang. Among his earliest poems were New Year's greetings to his maternal grandparents.

Goethe's humble ancestry was on his father's side. His paternal grandfather, Friedrich Georg Göthe, was the son of a cobbler and was apprenticed as a tailor in a small village in Thuringia. From these beginnings he rose to earn a comfortable fortune though his status as a tradesman excluded him from the top levels of Frankfurt society. His journeyman years had taken him to Lyon, a centre of the silk trade, where he acquired the skills that would bring him success on his return to Germany—as well as an accent on the *e* at the end of his surname. Göthé left Lyon in 1685, after Louis XIV abolished the religious freedoms French Calvinists had enjoyed under the Edict of Nantes. He settled in Frankfurt, where his business grew rapidly. In 1687 he married his first wife Anna Elisabeth Lutz, the daughter of a master tailor. She died in 1700, having given birth to five children, including two sons, Hermann Jakob and Johann Michael, the latter of whom appears to have had a learning disability. In 1705 Goethe (as he now styled himself) married the childless widow Cornelia Schellhorn, owner of the Weidenhof, one of the city's most reputable inns. The marriage was a union of two well-off members of Frankfurt society[23] though not in the same league as the Calvinist banking families.[24] Friedrich Georg now left tailoring and developed his new wife's wine merchant business, a commercially astute decision as it turned out. The family could now aspire to the social ascent for their children that was not possible for themselves. Their son Johann Caspar, born in 1710, was sent away to finish his schooling at the Casimirianum in Coburg, the preferred choice of wealthy Frankfurt burghers. From there he proceeded to a legal training at the universities of Gießen and Leipzig.[25] By graduating as a doctor of civil and church law, Caspar completed his family's social ascent from the level of minor tradesmen to the College of Graduates. However, his education had progressed at a leisurely pace and was further delayed by a lengthy grand tour through Italy, as far south as Naples, where he was one of the first Germans to witness the excavations at Herculaneum. On the return route he stayed for five weeks in Milan where he apparently had an affair, before registering briefly at the University of Strasbourg and returning to Frankfurt.[26] If Caspar was to build a successful career, he now needed to show a greater sense of purpose, but there was little sign of it. In order to practise as an advocate, he needed to complete the formality of registering as a citizen. Why he decided not to is unclear. Perhaps he was waiting for political events to untangle themselves. Following the death of the Habsburg Emperor Karl VI in October 1740, Karl Albrecht of Bavaria enjoyed a short tenure as Holy Roman Emperor, with his court at Frankfurt. During the city's brief spell in the sun of Imperial politics, Caspar applied for the position of Imperial Councillor, which he was granted on payment of an administrative fee. If Caspar was hoping this would lead to a political career, his hopes were disappointed when Karl Albrecht died in January 1745. After this unlikely episode of failed opportunism, Caspar did not take up politics or the law. He may have made an error in throwing in his lot with Karl Albrecht. Once the Habsburgs reclaimed the Imperial throne, his disloyalty in siding with the Bavarian usurper may have made him unpopular in Frankfurt, which was after all an Imperial city. But this does not explain his continuing reluctance to embark on a public career. After a year or two the stain of disloyalty would have washed off. In any case, he could still have enjoyed a career as an advocate, and after showing proper diligence and loyalty to the city, made his way in the administration. A quite different account of Caspar's career is presented in Goethe's autobiography, *Poetry and Truth*, written ten years into the next century. According to this version, Caspar intended to work his way up through the Frankfurt administration, beginning by applying for a junior unpaid position, but his application was inexplicably rejected, and in a fit of pique he decided never to work for the city again. This account also seems implausible. If he seriously intended to work his way up through the administration, he would have registered as a citizen, which he chose not to do.

More probably Caspar was a victim of Frankfurt's obsession with status. He would have been barred from the top of the Frankfurt administration by the fact of his lowly ancestry. His social standing was quite different from that of his future father-in-law, Johann Wolfgang Textor, who became *Schultheiß* as a relatively impoverished burgher, but who was a third-generation member of the College of Graduates. Textor had little money but a solid pedigree; Caspar had money but no pedigree. A further obstacle was that in 1741 his half brother Hermann Jakob, a tinsmith by trade, had been nominated for a position on the third bench of the council. As it happened, Hermann Jakob failed at the final stage—a drawing of lots instituted as part of the Imperial commission's attempts to combat nepotism and to weaken the hold of the nobility on the council. Had his half brother been successful, Caspar would have been barred from the council by the anti-nepotism provisions. After 1741 he may have felt that if he put himself forward, he would be treading on his half brother's toes. Indeed in 1747 Hermann Jakob Goethe was nominated again and this time was successful in the lottery. A seat on the council benches was now blocked to Goethe's father. So it seems most unlikely that he seriously intended to make his career in the city administration. An alternative would have been to practise as an advocate and then become a diplomatic representative of a foreign prince. It is possible that he considered leaving Frankfurt to go into foreign service, and this was why he did not become a citizen.[27] Frankfurt citizenship was not to be taken on lightly, for anyone renouncing it had to forfeit one tenth of their wealth to the city.[28]

Following his half brother's election, a new prospect emerged: starting a family. A son would suffer from less social stigma, as he would be one generation further removed from the taint of Friedrich Georg Goethe's humble birth. He would also benefit from being the son of an Imperial Councillor, no matter the circumstances under which the title was granted. And by declining to make a career in the Frankfurt administration for himself, Caspar ensured that his son would not fall foul of the anti-nepotism provisions. In 1748 he made a calculated and successful attempt to marry well. Johann Wolfgang Textor had been appointed *Schultheiß* in the summer of 1747. He had four young daughters, the eldest of whom was of marriageable age. It was a good match for both sides. On 20 August 1748 Catharina Elisabeth Textor and Johann Caspar Goethe were married in the Church of St Katharine by the family pastor Dr Johann Philipp Fresenius. From this point Caspar's focus would be his family, his dynasty. Having foregone a career for himself, he would ensure a career for his male progeny. Every provision would be made, and so, when his new wife was seven months pregnant, on 25 June 1749 he finally registered as a citizen of Frankfurt. The timing ensured that a first son would naturally inherit citizenship and thus be eligible for election to the city council.

Caspar brought his bride to live in his mother's house. The house was formed from two adjoining dwellings originally built around 1590 by Dutch émigrés in the traditional timbered style, with the first and second floors overhanging the road. It stood on a street named the Great Deer Ditch (*Großer Hirschgraben*). As the house was built over an infilled ditch, it had roomy cellarage for the valuable stock of wine that Caspar's mother Cornelia retained after she was widowed and sold the Weidenhof.[29] By the early eighteenth century it was one of Frankfurt's better addresses. It ran from southern end of the Horse Market (*Rossmarkt*), the city's largest central square, down to the French Church and the Weißfrauenkloster against the walls in the city's southwestern corner. The Weißfrauenkloster was a convent founded in the thirteenth century, originally dedicated to taking in penitent prostitutes from the streets. (The idea of the penitent 'fallen woman' would be an abiding theme in Goethe's writing.) The houses on the Hirschgraben were also of late medieval construction. The interior of the Goethe house was a warren, the result of two dwellings of unequal size and shape being knocked together. There was no garden, just a small backyard, but the upper floors at the rear of the house had views over the extensive gardens to the west behind the grander houses of the Gallows Lane (*Galgengasse*).

Here Goethe was born around midday on 28 August 1749. It was a very long labour and a difficult birth. According to family legend, the baby seemed to be stillborn and was only revived with great effort. The next day the child, named Johann Wolfgang after his mother's father, was baptized into the Lutheran confession by Dr Fresenius.[30] Grandfather Textor was his godfather. He commemorated the birth of his first grandson by planting a plum tree in his garden. The child seems to have been an anxious infant, prone to temper tantrums. It was a blessing when on 7 December 1750 his mother gave birth to a daughter, Cornelia Friederike.[31] The children formed a strong and lasting bond. By the age of three or four the two of them looked so similar they were sometimes taken for twins.[32] Of a further five children born after Cornelia, all but one died before the age of three. A son, Hermann Jakob, was born in November 1752 but suffered from poor health and died in 1759. Allegedly Wolfgang was more annoyed than saddened by his young brother's death. He had prepared a body of teaching materials that he would have tried out on the young boy, but now he had lost that opportunity.[33]

In 1752, Caspar began the project of educating his dynasty. From 1752 to 1755 Wolfgang attended the kindergarten of Madame Hoff, where he began to learn to read and may have picked up some French, for Madame Hoff was a descendant of Huguenot immigrants. Cornelia joined Wolfgang at the kindergarten in May 1753. This initiated a pattern of the two children being educated together. During the week, the children would spend all day at the kindergarten. On Sundays after church, lunch would be taken at the Textor grandparents' house. Wolfgang also spent long hours in the company of his father's mother, Cornelia, whose favourite he was. Until her death in 1754 at the age of eighty-six, she occupied a large room giving onto the backyard of the house on the Hirschgraben. For Christmas 1753 she presented the children with a puppet theatre, or so Goethe records in his autobiography *Poetry and Truth*. What the autobiography fails to mention is that it was paid for by Caspar.[34] It may be that Goethe simply did not know that his father had paid for the puppet theatre. Or it may be that in recollecting the gift while he was writing *Poetry and Truth*, he was recycling his own fictional account in his semi-autobiographical novel *Wilhelm Meister's Apprenticeship*. Here, Wilhelm's paternal grandmother gives Wilhelm the theatre. His father, a lonely figure, cannot empathize with his son and has only scorn for his bumbling attempts to stage puppet plays. In any case, we should be sceptical about the traditional view of Caspar as a stern, unbending, and irritable educationalist, a force against which the young Wolfgang rebelled, as psychologically plausible as it sounds. This view was based on naïve readings of the *Wilhelm Meister* novel and *Poetry and Truth*, neither of which are reliable sources.

On grandmother Cornelia's death in 1754, her son Caspar began a major refurbishment of the house. The main aim was to integrate the two original buildings and so create gracious living and reception areas linked by elegant staircases and halls. In the process the façade would be modernized. The rebuilding displayed Goethe's father's desire to combine the practical and the elegant, while avoiding excessive luxury or ostentation. The house was richly but not extravagantly decorated in the modern style. Caspar knew his place within Frankfurt's social hierarchy. He wanted to enjoy his wealth without drawing too much attention to it.[35] He designed the new house himself, assisted by his engineer friend Johann Friedrich von Uffenbach.[36] The one self-conscious addition to the exterior was a new coat of arms above the front door, comprising elements of the Textor arms in the upper field with an ascending line of three lyres in the lower, which represented Caspar's devotion to the arts. The house would henceforth be known as the Three Lyres. Grandeur was reserved for the interior. The main staircase was remodelled after the staircase in the town hall built for the coronation of Karl VII. Caspar's and Catharina's initials were worked into the wrought-iron railings on its first landing, displaying the strength of the marital bond to visitors.

During the renovation of the house, home schooling was impossible, so for nine months Wolfgang was sent out to Johann Tobias Schellhaffer for arithmetic and handwriting. It was a difficult period because of Schellhaffer's use of corporal punishment and fights between the boys in his charge. For the next stage in his education, Caspar mistrusted Frankfurt's only grammar school, the Gymnasium Moeno-Francofurtanum, and so Wolfgang was educated at home, in the company of Cornelia from 1757. Caspar employed an interesting and colourful team of tutors. By appointing a different tutor for each subject, Goethe's father was also able to retain control of the overall shape of the curriculum for himself, which was no doubt part of his plan. There were three objectives: to prepare Wolfgang for training as a lawyer, to provide a broad humanistic education, and to equip him with accomplishments befitting his social rank. Despite Caspar's reputation for rigid and overbearing didacticism, Wolfgang thrived on his father's programme, to the extent that he became as didactic as his father. More than anything, Caspar created an environment in which his children could teach themselves. He had collected a varied library. Two thousand volumes were put up for auction when the library was dispersed after his death,[37] but at its peak the library was larger. The classics were covered in the way one would expect of the period: a good representation of the Latin authors, almost all in the original, a less strong showing of the Greek authors, mainly in translation or bilingual editions. These were the most important resources for Wolfgang. His father's library was Wolfgang's springboard for exploration of ancient and modern literature. In addition to the Greco-Roman classics, there were the canonical Italian authors from Dante to Goldoni, French authors principally of the seventeenth century, Germans (mainly contemporary prose), and even some English. Shakespeare was present in a complete edition by Nicholas Rowe of 1709. Much of the English literature was in translation, but Goldsmith, Richardson, Sterne, and Thomson were in English. Naturally there was also a generous selection of religious works, ranging rather wider than Caspar's own Lutheranism. His wife's interest in Pietism was represented by a number of devotional works. One surprising absence was philosophy, apart from a few works by Aristotle, Albertus Magnus, and Leibniz. There were a handful of scientific works, including Linnaeus's *Systema naturae* of 1748. Caspar also collected widely in the arts and 'naturalia'. He favoured contemporary artists from Frankfurt and the surrounding area, who tended to paint in the Dutch realist style. He also owned a few minor seventeenth-century Dutch paintings. Often local artists would visit and set up their easels in the Goethe house. There were also some old firearms, valuable pieces of pottery, worked gemstones, and statuettes, in particular Venetian pieces collected on his travels, and a good number of mineral specimens. Of the approximately eighty private art collections in

Frankfurt at the time, Caspar's was one of the smaller ones,[38] but it appears to have been well known in the city.

From 1756 Wolfgang learned Latin under Johann Jacob Gottlieb Scherbius, a Lutheran theology candidate of Turkish descent. Latin was, of course, a necessity for a legal career. As a Protestant theologian Scherbius could also teach Ancient Greek, which, while of no practical use for the law, was of great interest to Wolfgang. His father was happy for Wolfgang to diverge from what was strictly necessary for his career. He believed firmly in a rounded education, including the arts. 'Everyone must learn to draw', Goethe records him saying.[39] The drawing tutor was Johann Michael Eben, a copperplate etcher. The lessons consisted mainly in copying facial expressions from the standard books by Le Brun and Piazetta.[40] Thanks to Caspar's patronage of local artists, the painter Johann Ludwig Ernst Morgenstern was employed to correct Wolfgang's productions.[41] Further lessons in architectural draughtsmanship and mathematics were given by Johann Friedrich Moritz, the Danish legate and advocate. Modern languages played an important role in Caspar's scheme, and as with the ancient languages, formal instruction could be reinforced by reading literature in the original language from Caspar's library, whether Dante or Corneille or Goldsmith. First came French, taught by another Huguenot, Mademoiselle Gachet. Italian lessons were provided for Cornelia, with Wolfgang listening in. The tutor was a colourful former Dominican monk, Domenico Antonio Giovinazzi. He first entered the Goethe household in order to help Caspar write (in Italian) the journal of his grand tour, 'Journey through Italy 1740'. Last in the roster of languages, the whole family began to learn English with a theology student, Johann Peter Christoph Schade, who had spent eight months in England.[42] Wolfgang was a talented linguist. The comprehensive linguistic curriculum taught in the Goethe house was extended even further when the twelve-year-old Wolfgang asked to learn Yiddish, an extraordinary request in the light of Christian attitudes towards Jews. His father acceded, and lessons were given by a converted Jew, Carl Christian Christfreund.[43]

In matters of religion Wolfgang increasingly went his own way. He inherited neither his father's orthodox Lutheranism nor, except briefly, the more passionate Pietism of his mother. He learned the standard forms of Lutheran catechism and worship, but the only part of his religious studies that had any appeal were the stories of the ancient Jews in the Old Testament. As a linguist and budding scholar of the ancient world, he wanted to read it in the original Hebrew, and for that his obliging father provided yet another tutor, Johann Georg Albrecht, Rector of the Gymnasium Moeno-Francofurtanum. Even at this early stage,

Wolfgang's interest in scripture seems to have been more literary than religious. The Old Testament was one of the earliest and purest examples of human storytelling and poetry. What little we know of his early religious attitudes suggests he tended towards a typical mid-eighteenth-century rational Lutheran optimism. There was no deeply rooted faith, and seeds of doubt were sown early. The elder Hüsgen, who became a mentor to Wolfgang, pointed him towards scepticism. In *Poetry and Truth* Goethe presents Hüsgen as otherworldly and ascetic: he 'stood in opposition to God and the world'. An amusing and lapidary statement of Hüsgen's sums up his beliefs and character: 'Even in God I find errors'.[44] He recommended that Wolfgang read Agrippa von Nettesheim's 'Invective on the Uncertainty and Vanity of the Sciences' (1527).[45] According to Agrippa, the lauded philosophy of the ancients was of little value. It was just a rationalized form of myth and poetry. Moreover, the ancient philosophers seldom agreed with one another, and the debates that raged between their schools had more to do with polemic than truth. Anyone looking to philosophy for a single coherent truth was bound to be disappointed.[46]

In describing his departure from Christianity in *Poetry and Truth*, Goethe makes much of the impact of the huge earthquake that struck Lisbon on 1 November 1755, destroying the city's medieval centre and killing as many as sixty thousand citizens. In the autobiography Goethe claims that his faith in a benevolent God was deeply shaken by the earthquake and the philosophical debates that followed it. It is likely that the six-year-old Goethe was aware of the earthquake. It is less likely that he had any understanding of its theological significance. More likely is that while he was planning *Poetry and Truth* around 1810,[47] he came across Voltaire's and Rousseau's responses to the earthquake. In other words, his sense of the earthquake as a theological problem was formed long after the event. His religious education was probably more deeply affected by the feeling, shared by many of Frankfurt's Lutherans, that church services were dry and uninspiring. The Goethes' and Textors' pastor Dr Fresenius was a particular target of these complaints. Within the Goethe household matters were not improved by Caspar's insistence on reading to the family the early volumes of Archibald Bower's *History of the Popes* (1748–1766), a Protestant assault on the doctrine of papal supremacy. It was dull material, but Caspar would never give up reading a book part way through, so the family had to endure to the bitter end.[48] Fresenius and Bower, however different, were symptoms of one malaise. Both institutionally and intellectually, the Lutheran Reformation had ossified. In the region of Frankfurt there had long been alternatives to Lutheran orthodoxy, notably the Pietism that had put down roots in the court of Darmstadt and the University of Gießen, and promised Lutherans a more passionate and individualized experience of Christianity. Through the first half of the century there had been constant quarrels between orthodox Lutherans and Pietists. Fresenius was an outspoken critic of Pietism.[49] But Pietism continued to offer many Lutherans what they felt was a more vivid relationship to God. Had this not also been the original motivation of Luther and the other reformers—to bring Christians closer to their God? And had not the reformers themselves been branded heretics? One result of the long historical process of reformation was that the charge of heresy was increasingly a compliment. The Pietist Gottfried Arnold's *Impartial History of the Church and of Heretics*, published in Frankfurt at the beginning of the century, offered many examples of this. Arnold adopted the Protestant narrative according to which the church had been in decline since the days of the apostles, but he took the narrative further than the Reformers, by including Protestantism within the general story of degeneration. If the Reformation had renewed the church somewhat, it was a brief interval in a general process of decline. Since the decline was continuing, there was need for a new reformation, such as the Pietism espoused by Arnold. For Goethe the attraction of Arnold's argument lay in what it implied about heresy. The continuing story of the church's decline created space for heterodox figures on the margins of Christianity. Eccentric and troubled though these figures might be, they had reason to dissent, and the church, by branding them as heretics, was merely displaying the reflex response of an institution interested chiefly in sustaining its authority. Arnold taught Goethe to feel sympathy for rebels and antipathy towards institutions.[50]

From the middle of the century Frankfurt was riven by political divisions. As a Free Imperial City it owed fealty to the Emperor under whose direct control it was. During the reform crisis of the early eighteenth century, Vienna's intervention had caused disquiet among Frankfurt's Lutheran patriciate, whose grip on the city council and pride in self-rule the Viennese reforms had undermined. Loyalty to the Habsburgs was also weakened by the Lutheranism of Frankfurt's constitution. Confessionally and culturally, Frankfurt had more in common with predominantly Lutheran Prussia. Not that Prussia treated Frankfurt any more gently than Austria did. In 1753 Frederick II had abused Frankfurt's territorial sovereignty by having Voltaire arrested by Prussian agents at the Golden Lion inn, as he was passing through on his way home from Potsdam.

When war broke out again between Prussia and Austria in 1756, a substantial part of the Frankfurt citizenry sided with Prussia, as in 1740, and they were buoyed by Frederick II's early victories.[51] In the autumn of 1758, with the war turning against Prussia, Austria's ally France moved an army east over the Rhine, pressing back the Prussian-allied Hanoverians under Prince Ferdinand of Brunswick. The French commander requested entry into Frankfurt as a friendly force, which the city council refused, but in January 1759, thanks to the suspicious negligence or incompetence of the city militia, the French marched into Frankfurt without bloodshed. Frankfurt was now in the Imperial camp. Of more immediate consequence, the city had to provide lodging for the French officers, and the smart and roomy Three Lyres was chosen as quarters for the King's Lieutenant and civil governor of the city, François Théas de Thoranc, an urbane and melancholic nobleman from Grasse in the Midi. Thoranc's residence in the Goethe house was profoundly humiliating for the anti-Imperial and pro-Frederick head of the family. The pain was all the greater because the family's loyalties were split. Caspar could count on young Wolfgang's support, but his wife remained quietly loyal to the Empire like her father Schultheiß Textor. No doubt the feeling of being undermined by his wife and in-laws grated on Caspar. His feelings of humiliation were deepened by the continuous disruption at the Three Lyres. Thoranc was responsible for adjudicating conflicts between the French military and the local population, which created a constant traffic of arrestees and complainants. The tension boiled over after a pitched battle between the French and Hanoverian armies a few miles northeast of Frankfurt in April. In *Poetry and Truth* Goethe describes listening to the guns and cannons through a top-floor window. The French eventually prevailed. According to Goethe's account, when Thoranc and Caspar met on the staircase of the Three Lyres after the battle, the Frenchman cheerfully commented on the outcome, to which Caspar retorted, 'I wish the devil had taken the lot of you—even if he'd had to take me too!'[52] Thoranc was outraged and threatened to have Caspar thrown in gaol. Only the tactful intervention of Goethe's mother spared him. There was another flare-up that Goethe did not report in *Poetry and Truth*. In early 1760 at a party to celebrate the christening of the latest Goethe son Georg Adolph, Caspar accused his father-in-law of accepting a bribe to let the French army into the city. The two

FIG. 4. The Goethe family in shepherds' costumes in an imagined landscape, sketch by J. C. Seekatz (1762)

men drew swords and were only just prevented from doing one another serious harm. These eruptions of bottled-up humiliation were nonetheless more comic than tragic. Thoranc treated his hosts with consideration and kindness, and he did much to enliven and modernize the city. A French theatre was established, and Wolfgang was allowed to attend and sit in the seat reserved for grandfather Textor. It was here that he had one of his earliest encounters with the work of Jean-Jacques Rousseau, whose opera *The Village Soothsayer* (1752) was performed in 1759. The French occupation introduced house numbering, street lighting, and regular refuse collections.

At the end of May 1761, the Goethes were finally relieved of their French lodgers, in exchange for more congenial guests: the family of Heinrich Philipp

Moritz, legate of the Danish crown and various German princes.⁵³ Moritz was an acquaintance and was typical of the society that Caspar kept. In *Poetry and Truth* Goethe gives the misleading impression that as a non-patrician his father was isolated from Frankfurt society. In fact he had a wide social circle and hosted fortnightly evening parties at the Three Lyres, where music, food, wine, and learned discussions were enjoyed. Most of Caspar's friends were educated men of his own class: lawyers, scholars, and physicians.⁵⁴ Some masonic songs found in his library indicate that he may have been a freemason.⁵⁵ Parties were also laid on for the children, who were evidently very sociable. The Englishman Harry Lupton organized a regular fashionable soirée at which English was spoken.⁵⁶ Beyond this, we know little about Goethe's friendships. *Poetry and Truth* tells a story of his friendship with a group of youths of lower social status and a girl named Gretchen, slightly older and wiser than him. Some members of the group took advantage of Goethe's connection to the council in order to spin a fraud. Wolfgang was accused of being party to the conspiracy, and under interrogation he revealed Gretchen's identity, only to be consumed with guilt afterwards. The story is so close to his *Faust* that it must be fiction—a lively, verbally gifted lover; a wise but quiet and demure beloved named Gretchen; his dangerous friends and associates; the girl suffering greater punishment than the boy; his deep guilt.

The plan was for Wolfgang to start university in autumn 1765, aged sixteen. His father appointed a private tutor to prepare him. One of the subjects to be studied in advance of his matriculation was ancient philosophy. His earlier reading of Agrippa's 'Invective' had provided him with an argument against the philosophers. Formal philosophy was unnecessary, since its contents already existed in religion and poetry.⁵⁷ However, he was beginning to discover that philosophy had its merits. With his tutor, he read the single-volume abridgement of Johann Jakob Brucker's *History of Philosophy*.⁵⁸ Brucker reinforced something that Goethe had picked up from Gottfried Arnold and that would be of immense consequence for his philosophical education. It concerned the Rationalist philosopher Spinoza, decried near universally in the eighteenth century as a dangerous atheist. Contrary to Spinoza's reputation, Brucker and Arnold both give accounts of him that are in several points sympathetic. Arnold insisted that Spinoza was not in fact an atheist, but a deist. Nowhere in Spinoza's writings is the existence of God denied. On the contrary, Spinoza writes effusively of the divinity of nature.[59] There was also much to be admired about Spinoza as a person. In the face of persecution he remained honest and virtuous. Brucker states that Spinoza 'lived soberly and quietly, unacquainted with ambition, desire for wealth or envy, disagreeable to no one, courteous in his manners'.[60] Brucker and Arnold both quote from Spinoza's personal correspondence. In later life, Goethe would be as interested in Spinoza's letters as in his major philosophical works, the *Ethics Demonstrated in the Geometric Manner* and the *Theological-Political Treatise*. Although the focus on Spinoza's character might suggest Goethe's amateurishness as a philosopher, he could argue—and later would repeatedly do so, most eloquently in the case of the art historian Winckelmann—that the man and his thought were cut from the same cloth, and that the letters had the virtue of being lived philosophy. There is no documentary evidence that Goethe read Spinoza before 1773 despite Martin Bollacher's claims.[61] However, there is good reason to believe that he formed an impression of Spinoza from Arnold and Brucker, and that his fondness for heretics would have made Spinoza interesting to him.

In the year before his departure, the strands of Goethe's education were leading in diverse directions, no doubt as Caspar planned, though with fraught consequences. His father's plan was for Wolfgang to study law at Caspar's alma mater, Leipzig. Wolfgang's interest was in languages and literature, especially the works of Hebrew, Greek, and Roman antiquity. The new University of Göttingen, founded in 1734 by George II, King of Great Britain and Elector of Hanover, offered the most exciting opportunities. Two of Germany's most energetic and innovative scholars taught there, the classicist Christian Gottlob Heyne and the Hebraist Johann David Michaelis. Heyne was one of the founders of modern classical philology, noted for his interdisciplinary work on classical mythology. Michaelis analysed the social origins of the Mosaic law, and in particular its roots in early pastoralist society, an approach that would have appealed to the sceptical but myth-loving Goethe. Wolfgang imagined himself following in the footsteps of Heyne and Michaelis and becoming a professor of ancient languages.[62] However, the struggle over his career was brief and conclusive. Reluctantly he followed his father.

2

'I'm Not a Christian'

LEIPZIG, FRANKFURT,
STRASBOURG, 1765–1771

ON 3 OCTOBER 1765, after a journey of four days, Goethe arrived in Leipzig. On 19 October he matriculated at the university.[1] Leipzig was, in some senses, a more modern version of Frankfurt: a predominantly Lutheran commercial city with a political importance that was more symbolic than real. In its layout and architecture, Leipzig was more impressive, and in cultural terms there was no comparison. Much of the medieval city had been demolished and replaced with larger and more uniform modern buildings in wide tree-lined avenues. In 1660 street cleaning was instituted and in 1701 street lighting, fifty years before the French introduced it to Frankfurt. From 1650 Leipzig hosted the world's first daily newspaper, published by Timotheus Ritzsch. Leipzig was an example of neoclassical and Enlightened urban and cultural renewal. Not for nothing was it nicknamed 'the Little Paris'. Indeed, if any city deserved the title of Germany's cultural capital, Leipzig did. It was by far the most important centre of the Protestant German publishing trade. All of the arts were cultivated. With hindsight, its musical culture seems especially strong. At the beginning of the century Telemann had founded a conservatoire, the *Collegium Musicum*. From 1723 to his death in 1750, J. S. Bach was cantor of St Thomas's and director of the city's church music. The city was home to the oldest public opera house and concert hall in Germany. Although he occasionally attended concerts, Goethe had relatively little interest in music and was even less interested in entering churches to hear it. But there were numerous fine art collections, and an art academy was founded in 1764 under the direction of the painter and sculptor Adam Friedrich Oeser. Opportunities to discuss the arts with a like-minded Enlightened elite existed in the city's clubs, salons, and coffee houses.

By Goethe's time the university, founded at the beginning of the fifteenth century, was one of the leading universities of Protestant Germany and in the vanguard of the Enlightenment. In 1682 Otto Mencke, professor of politics and ethics at Leipzig, published Germany's first academic journal, the *Acta Eruditorum*. In 1687 Leipzig broke the hegemony of the Latin language by hosting the first university lecture in German, by the philosopher Christian Thomasius. Gottsched, the Wolffian, taught in Leipzig for forty years until his death in 1766. It was from Leipzig that the call went out for the modernization of German literature, for a new poetics based on a reworking of Aristotle, and a classicizing dramaturgy purified of the crude and improvised horseplay that passed for comedy on the German stage.

———

Having matriculated, Goethe had to decide on his course of study. If he still nurtured hopes of defying his father and studying the Greek and Roman classics, he was disappointed by the professor whom his father had recruited as his director of studies, Johann Gottlob Böhme, a historian who also taught international law. Goethe may have assumed Böhme would support his literary and classical aspirations: Böhme wrote poetry in Latin.[2] However, Böhme believed that poetry was not a fit object of study for a serious young man, nor would he be discharging his duties properly if he allowed Wolfgang to violate his father's wishes. After a series of uncomfortable arguments, Goethe backed down with some minor concessions. His course of study was to be broad based, as was normal for students in their first year, but its trajectory would be towards graduation in law. To that end Böhme recommended philosophy, law, and the history of institutions for Goethe's first semester. There were other foundational courses to be taken, including basic algebra and geometry which, in addition to philosophy, were taught by the Wolffian Johann Heinrich Winckler.[3] In recognition of his other interests, Goethe was permitted to attend a class on literary history and a practical writing class with Professor Gellert. He would also visit a class on Cicero by the classicist Johann August Ernesti.

He attended lectures assiduously at first, but soon became disenchanted. Philosophy made no more sense to him than it had in Frankfurt. Logic told him nothing that his common sense could not have said. The elegant mathematical method of Wolffianism only offered an unexciting commitment to moderation in all things, on which basis everyone might qualify as a philosopher.[4] As for law and the history of institutions, they were just as dull at university as they had been at home. Even the writing class with Gellert was a disappointment. He submitted some of his poems and Gellert returned them covered in red ink, but with no insights as to their merits or faults, perhaps because Gellert simply disliked poetry or because he was more concerned about the neatness of his students' handwriting than their poetic talent.[5] A course on literary history, based on the Lutheran theologian Johann Christoph Stockhausen's *Critical Outline of a Select Library for the Lovers of Philosophy and the Beaux Arts* (1752), proved no more enlightening and left no mark on him. Ernesti's course on Cicero's *Orator*—unpromising material in any case for a budding poet—was equally disappointing. As a philologist, Ernesti was an innovator. He discovered some hitherto unknown features of the sequence of tenses in Latin, mainly through an analysis of Cicero's prose style. He also made ground in the study of the manuscript traditions of classical authors. This kind of microscopic philology was, however, quite different from the broader historically and socially informed study of antiquity that Heyne and Michaelis were developing at Göttingen.

Amid these disappointments Goethe developed a strong scepticism about the university as an institution. Tellingly, even the great Gottsched, the renewer of the German theatre and arbiter of taste in poetry, the embodiment of Leipzig's aspirations to cultural modernity, became a figure of fun for Goethe. The whole of Leipzig despised the man, Goethe wrote to his friend Riese.[6] His disillusionment culminated in an unfortunate episode in, of all places, Böhme's lectures on the institutions of the Holy Roman Empire. Instead of diligently taking notes, Goethe occupied the time by filling the margins of his exercise book with cartoons of the various characters described in Böhme's lectures. This greatly amused his neighbours in the lectures, but it also came to Böhme's notice, with predictable consequences. The episode confirmed Böhme in a view of Goethe that was becoming widespread in Leipzig. The young man was flighty and unserious.

There were two sides to Goethe's behaviour in Leipzig. He enjoyed his new social life and behaved according to the fashionable conventions of dress, language, and conduct. One of Goethe's contemporaries as a student, the Lutheran theologian's son Carl Wilhelm Jerusalem, dismissed Goethe as a fop.[7] Writing to Cornelia in December 1765, Goethe complained about how busy he was with his studies and social life.[8] If he soon began to devote less time to his studies, the time he freed was easily filled by socializing in the smart circles to which his wealth and good connections gave him access. He did engage fully with Leipzig society. Indeed, he could be socially brilliant, a performer and entertainer of exceptional magnetism, though needless to say his ability to monopolize people's attention did not always go down well. 'He would get uncommonly puffed up', said another contemporary.[9] Inside, however, there was still a quirky, turbulent, often naïve Frankfurt boy. He had to be told how to dress properly. The clothes he had brought with him from Frankfurt were not in the latest style.[10] He spoke strangely too, an effect in part of his Frankfurt dialect and in part of his strangely earthy and antiquated vocabulary. Within a year of matriculation his disaffection with his studies was affecting his life more generally. As he wrote to Cornelia in October 1766, 'I've fallen out of favour with those to whom I was once permitted to pay my respects [...]. I'm therefore considered to be socially surplus to requirements and incorrigible'.[11] The narrowing of his social circle brought benefits.[12] He developed fewer, more intense friendships. In March 1766 a Frankfurt acquaintance arrived in Leipzig, Johann Georg Schlosser, a lawyer ten years Goethe's senior. The occasion of Schlosser's stay in Leipzig prompted a visit to the great Gottsched. It began comically. By mistake Schlosser and Goethe were admitted to the room where Gottsched was dressing, and they found him without his usual seventeenth-century-style waist-length periwig. His state of baldness did not perturb the great man, who took the wig from his servant, boxed his ears, and proceeded to launch into a long disquisition.

Increasingly Goethe distanced himself from the university. With Schlosser he began to lunch at an inn belonging to the tinsmith and wine merchant Christian Gottlieb Schönkopf. The relationship between Goethe and the Schönkopf family became close, so much so that he seemed part of the family, or so he later claimed.[13] A friendship developed between Goethe and Schönkopf's daughter Anna Katharina or Käthchen (Goethe also called her Annette), who was three years older than him. A match between the two was out of the question though there was probably some allure in the idea of escaping from the social life that his rank dictated. Later that year, at the same time as his resigned letter to Cornelia, he became close friends with a student eleven years his senior, Ernst Wolfgang Behrisch, a fellow visitor to the Schönkopfs. Until Behrisch departed under a cloud in autumn 1767—he had written some satirical verses against Professor Christian August Clodius—Goethe and the magnetic, witty, and quirky Behrisch were fast friends.

As Goethe retreated from university life and the Leipzig *beau monde* into smaller social groups and strong personal bonds maintained by correspondence, he remained connected to the wider literary world, above all through the theatre. The theatre became the outer expression of his literary persona. It was the end product for which his feverish, experimental letter-writing was a preparation. He had arrived in Leipzig with a batch of dramatic drafts based on stories from the Old Testament. These half-written plays and plans expressed his image of himself as a student of the ancient world in the manner of Heyne and Michaelis. The truths of the ancient world, which underpinned and prefigured all our modern wisdom, were to be unlocked by means of the study of ancient history and society, and then portrayed on the tragic stage. The most complete of the plays, nearly finished by the time Goethe arrived in Leipzig, was a tragedy about Belshazzar.[14] In May 1767 Goethe told Cornelia he was working on a play titled 'The Heir of Pharaoh'.[15] Nothing remains of it, and what little remains of *Belshazzar* suggests that he was uncertain about his direction. He began to write it in rhymed alexandrines, the traditional metre of French and German tragedy, and used by English playwrights before Marlowe and Shakespeare. Alexandrines are capable of flexibility, but can sound plodding and statuesque, as if every rhyming couplet were an attempt at a weighty epigram. That is how the surviving passages from the first act of Goethe's *Belshazzar* read. However, at some point he appears to have switched to blank verse,[16] the more supple metre of Marlowe and Shakespeare.[17] The surviving fragments document a young playwright's uncertain response to literary fashions.

Goethe's understanding of drama underwent a change in 1767. The stimulus was Aristotle's *Poetics*, which he may have been prompted to read by Lessing's theatre reviews in his *Hamburg Dramaturgy* (1767–1768). Lessing's neo-Aristotelianism was more in tune with the Enlightenment's modernizing spirit. The rules governing drama, notably the strict adherence to the unities of place, time, and action, were to be relaxed and brought into conformity with reason and nature. Dramatic form must flow from the nature of the play's subject matter, but not in the hidebound manner of Gottsched. It is likely that Goethe felt his plays on Old Testament subjects did not conform to the new models of tragic drama, or that their cumbersome alexandrines made them feel obsolete in comparison to Lessing's prose plays. In October 1767 the Old Testament plays were consigned to the flames in one of Goethe's periodic *autos-da-fé*, as he wrote to Cornelia: 'Belshazzar, Isabel, Ruth, Selima, etc. etc. have made amends for their sins of youth in the flames no less'.[18] In the same letter he acknowledged the interest Cornelia had shown in a play he had begun in Frankfurt, a pastoral drama titled *Amine*.[19] In Leipzig, between February 1767 and April 1768, he set about rewriting it under the new title *The Lover's Temper*. It is the only complete dramatic work surviving from Goethe's Leipzig years. It was first published in 1806. The genre of the pastoral comedy had become a Leipzig speciality, 'reformed' by Gottsched in his *Critical Poetics*, and supposedly perfected by Gellert. The characters of pastoral comedy are types more than real characters, generally one dimensional, with suitably inauthentic classicizing names and inhabiting an artificial world, lacking any social or historical hinterland. The early scenes of *The Lover's Temper* make clear what social norms the characters are expected to adhere to: the sociable pleasures of dance and music, chastely erotic love affairs (which generally climax with kissing), and a balance of sensibility and equanimity. The play's moral is simple: a true lover cannot also be a hater; a person that *truly* loves one other person can hate no one.[20] The morality is as idealized as the setting. The plotting is also weak. The lovers are persuaded to overcome their flaws by being shown, in each other's behaviour, an image of their own. The flaw in the plot is that the resolution comes not from their own passions but the intervention of a third party, Egle, for whom there is nothing at stake. Egle represents a disembodied didactic principle, rather like the tutor in Rousseau's great educational novel *Émile*. In the same way as the pastoral scenario is irrelevant to the play's themes and action, the role of Egle is extrinsic to the psychological story the play tells.

The Lover's Temper was an exercise in playwriting to a fashionable Leipzig formula, with little thought as to how the formula could be bettered or made relevant to Goethe's own experience. The same is true of most of the poems Goethe wrote while in Leipzig. They were part of a tradition of lightweight and playful poetry, and as in *The Lover's Temper*, Goethe was influenced by local Leipzig models. Christian Felix Weiße's *Playful Songs* (1758) were the main influence on the three series of poems Goethe produced in Leipzig: *Annette*, dedicated to Käthchen Schönkopf; *Songs with Melodies*; and *New Songs, Set to Melodies by Bernhard Breitkopf*. The poems were attempts to force his verbal talent, with its tendency to ramble erratically, into tidy, conventional forms. If he was beginning to feel his way towards an authentic poetic voice, it would be a long and tortuous process. In February 1766 he composed a poem for the wedding of his uncle Johann Jost Textor, which won high praise in Frankfurt. Goethe subsequently submitted it to Professor Clodius for critical appraisal who returned it covered in red ink. Clodius disapproved of the way Goethe's poem applied the paraphernalia of Greco-Roman gods and goddesses to human subject matter—an irony given that Clodius was known for his academicist alexandrines sprinkled with Greco-Latin vocabulary. By way of revenge Goethe parodied Clodius's style in a jokey encomium to the local Leipzig patissier Hendel. As was the way in the gossipy city, the poem became news and caused some upset:

> O Händel, dessen Ruhm von Süd zum Norden reicht,
> Vernimm den Pään, der zu deinen Ohren steigt!
> Du bäckst, was Gallier und Britten emsig suchen,
> Mit schöpfrischem Genie: originelle Kuchen.[21]

> O Händel, whose repute extends from south to north, / Hear the paean that ascends to your ears! / You bake what Gauls and Britons eagerly seek, / With creative genius: original cakes.

The verses contained a squib on the fashionable theory of 'original genius' that had been popularized by one of Goethe's favourite British poets, Edward Young, and it attests to his increasing interest in English literature. In March 1766 he read William Dodds's anthology *The Beauties of Shakespeare* (1752).[22] The impact of English poetry is felt most strongly in his letters. Writing to his Frankfurt friend Riese in April 1766, he complains of suffering from melancholia and compares himself to a worm in the dust who aspires to be an eagle,[23] an image probably drawn from Young's *Night Thoughts*.[24] The letter to Riese alternates between addressing Riese directly in prose and taking stock of Goethe's poetic predicament in Young-style blank verse. The letters from Leipzig are very diverse, even erratic, and often self-consciously so. Some are entirely in French, others in rather poor English, and others switch between French, English, and German. The inserted fragments of verse are similarly polyglot. Some are quotations; others are his own, like the lines to Riese, though clearly imitative. They draw on contemporary German, English, and French poetry as well as also older models. These were the poets Goethe recommended to his sister: Gessner, Klopstock, Tasso, Ariosto, Milton, and Young. He was also reading the standard work on poetics, Boileau's *L'Art poétique* (1674), which he found correct and pleasant but lacking in heart and feeling.[25] The hegemony of neo-Aristotelian classicism was beginning to wane. The poetic legislators were on their way out. Young stressed the importance of inspiration, not rules. In December 1766 Gottsched died, the great bulwark of Wolffianism and neo-Aristotelianism. After Clodius's stinging criticism of his Textor wedding poem in 1766, Goethe briefly stopped writing poetry. He resumed in the spring of 1767, but was forced to acknowledge that the results were not good.[26] The Clodius experience deterred him from seeking professorial advice. Independence suited him better: 'If I have genius, then I'll become a poet, even if no one can improve me; if I have none, then all their critical judgements won't help'.[27] Genius is unteachable. Creativity does not respond to commands. Still Goethe felt that he was no longer the ten-year-old writing poetry for his grandparents. He was at least confident enough to be able to consign his earlier work to the fire and preserve the newer, better work.

Poetry gave Goethe less pleasure than drawing and painting. Two months after arriving in Leipzig he began private drawing lessons with the Director of the newly established Art Academy, Adam Friedrich Oeser.[28] A bond soon developed with Oeser and his family, which lasted beyond Goethe's departure from Leipzig in 1768. Indeed, Oeser's influence was arguably the most enduring and significant of all Goethe's experiences in Leipzig. Oeser was an enemy of the ornate baroque manner in art, and preferred a clean and natural neoclassical style. As Goethe put it shortly after his return to Frankfurt in autumn 1768, Oeser had shown him 'the path to truth and beauty'.[29] Oeser's taste was influenced in turn by his friend Johann Joachim Winckelmann. Oeser had taught Winckelmann drawing ten years earlier in Dresden, and the two had shared lodgings. Now working as Prefect of Antiquities at the Vatican, despite his barely concealed homosexuality, Winckelmann had become a celebrity and perhaps the best known German writer in Europe. Oeser received news that Winckelmann was planning a trip to Germany in the spring of 1768 and would visit Leipzig, which created great excitement among Oeser's pupils. The excitement was far exceeded by the devastation that struck them in June. Winckelmann reached Vienna, but got cold feet and turned back to Italy. In Trieste he was murdered by the cook and petty thief Francesco Arcangeli, for the sake of some medals he had received from Maria Theresa in Vienna. His murder preserved Winckelmann's reputation at its zenith and ensured that he would be known not only as a great art historian, indeed the founder of art history, but also as a tragic and much-loved personality. If some of the great literary celebrities of the eighteenth century suffered from egregious and widely decried personal flaws—avarice in the case of Voltaire, neglect of his children and paranoia in the case of Rousseau—Winckelmann's character made him a hero. Moreover, as a homosexual man, he was an outsider and a victim of Christian morality.

At the time, Winckelmann's impact on Goethe was probably less strong than that of the French aesthetician Charles Batteux. In his second semester, from Easter 1766, he attended Gellert's lectures on Batteux's *The Fine Arts Reduced to a Single Principle* (1746). The importance of Batteux's theory for Goethe has gone practically unnoticed, perhaps because Herder, his mentor in aesthetic matters from 1770, disliked Batteux. *The Fine Arts* divided the arts into three categories. 'Mechanical' arts such as agriculture and politics are to be valued solely for their utility.[30] The fine arts of poetry, painting, and music have no utility. They only serve to give us pleasure. A third, mixed type, both useful and beautiful, includes architecture, eloquence, and history. Thus far Batteux was broadly in accord with Aristotle, who had distinguished between fine and useful arts on the grounds that the fine arts employed ideals and the useful arts were grounded in facts. However, Batteux's 'single principle' has nothing to do with the fine arts' lack of utility. The principle is the beautiful imitation of nature. Taken literally, the principle of imitation is uninteresting, and it had been exhaustively worked out in Jean-Baptiste Dubos's *Critical Reflections on Poetry and Painting* (1719). Batteaux's theory was more sophisticated and subtle. He did not mean imitation in the strict sense. Instead, artists create an ideal type of nature in their imagination by selecting aspects of nature and forging them into a new entity. This entity Batteux called 'beautiful nature' (*la belle nature*), and despite its name it was both natural and unnatural. The artist's task is 'to select the most beautiful parts of nature and form them into an exquisite whole, more perfect than nature, without, however, ceasing to be natural'.[31] Hence the term 'beautiful nature' is misleading. For one thing, by 'nature' Batteux does not mean the natural world. He means things as they are, including human nature and therefore the whole social world. Second, art is not an imitation of this broadly conceived 'nature', but the creation of a simulacrum of it in the artist's imagination. Thus whereas older theorists like Dubos had located the source of inspiration in nature proper, Batteux shifts the source of creativity away from objects and into the subjectivity of the artist. *La belle nature* is the product of an artist's 'enthusiasm'. In this sense Batteux's theory of art is 'expressivist', like Young's 'original genius'. This was why Batteux struck his Anglophile German readers as much more modern than Dubos.

Batteux's theory appealed to Goethe in several ways. It was more modern than the neo-Aristotelian theories of Dubos, Boileau, and Gottsched. It was largely in accord with the aesthetic preferences that Goethe assimilated in Leipzig, notably Oeser's and Winckelmann's preference for the art of antiquity and Athenian sculpture in particular. Batteux also suited the less rule-abiding mood of the 1760s. He reacted against the idea of aesthetic laws. His *Fine Arts* had nothing of the hidebound and rationalistic character of Dubos and Gottsched. He recognised that the artist's imagination was the engine of creativity, which he defined in terms of enthusiasm, much as Young did. As Goethe put it in a letter to Langer from Frankfurt in October 1769, to write in the spirit of Batteux was to write 'without a touch of imitation, everything [is] nature'.[32] Furthermore Batteux shared Rousseau's conviction that education was more about learning than being taught. Taste can only be taught if the student is allowed to develop his faculties freely. The foundations of Goethe's mature understanding of art were laid in Leipzig. In later life he would repeatedly return to Batteux's *la belle nature*.[33]

There is very little evidence of Goethe engaging with Christianity during his time in Leipzig, whether at church or in private. Towards the end of his studies, after Behrisch had left, he came under the sway of another elder mentor, Ernst Theodor Langer. A committed Lutheran, Langer saw Goethe as a challenge. Langer's employer had warned him against becoming acquainted with 'such a dangerous individual' as Goethe.[34] Langer tried to interest Goethe in Christianity, but failed, even when Goethe fell seriously ill in the summer of 1768 and, by his own admission, was open to religious sentiment. Writing to Langer several months after his return to Frankfurt, Goethe summed up the failure of Langer's efforts:

> To be sure I recognise the effect your sermon has had on me. Love and courtesy towards religion, friendship towards the Gospels, a holy reverence for the Word. In sum, everything you could have done. Of course even with all that I'm not a Christian, but is it the business of any human to make me one?[35]

In *Poetry and Truth* Goethe tries to sum up the religious tendencies of the age and his attitude towards them as a student. He identifies two emergent trends in Christianity: a deistic natural religion and a fascination with oracular obscurity. He claims that he tended towards the former.[36] Deism certainly comports with other views he held in the late 1760s, in particular his interest in the historicity of ancient Hebrew and Greek literature and Rousseau. In the summer and autumn of 1767 he read *Émile*.[37] By the end of the book he had decided that he was a committed Rousseauian. Writing to Cornelia in October 1767 he stated his Rousseauian creed:

> Don't laugh at this foolish-seeming philosophy, the propositions that seem so paradoxical are the most wonderful truths, and the corruption of the modern world resides only in the fact that people ignore them. They are grounded in the most honourable truth: *plus que les moeurs se raffinent, plus les hommes se depravent* [the more our morals are refined, the more depraved men become].[38]

These views coalesced into an attitude towards religion typical of the radical Enlightenment. The original archaic, natural religions, such as we find in the Old Testament, have declined into modern, civilized, debased religions. Civilization has deposited layers of cultural sediment on top of natural religion, and this sediment has hardened into a firm doctrinal and institutional crust. We are now imprisoned in the cage of religious doctrines and institutions we have unwittingly built for ourselves.

The exchanges with Langer happened after Goethe went down with a serious lung infection in the summer of 1768. There had been a pattern of lung problems and depression since 1765.[39] By the spring of 1768 he was heartily sick of his studies in Leipzig, as he wrote to Behrisch: '3 months Behrisch, and after that it's over'.[40] His mood had worsened: he later admitted to Johann Christian Limprecht that he had been an 'unbearable person' during these months.[41] One night in June he awoke with a massive pulmonary haemorrhage. After several weeks confined to his bed and still seriously ill, he was driven home from Leipzig, setting off on his nineteenth birthday. Even before the collapse of his health, he had begun to bid farewell to the whole Leipzig episode. His own literary productions were now foreign to him, he would later claim in *Poetry and Truth*.[42] So was the modern German literature he had imitated in Leipzig. In a book swap with Langer, Goethe gave away 'whole basket-loads of German poets and critics' in exchange for 'a number of Greek authors', who would cheer him up during his recovery, he thought.[43] In turning away from modern literature and towards the ancients, he was reverting to the comforting solidity of true beauty and nature, not its refined, civilized form. No doubt the frustration of his plans to study the classics at Göttingen was still a source of resentment. Leipzig, the city of fashionable modern poetry and theatre, had been a disappointing failure—a shipwreck, as he put it in *Poetry and Truth*.[44]

For the next few months he was more or less bedbound. Once he began to convalesce, he occupied himself with drawing, reading, and writing. As he put it to Langer, 'I'm writing an appalling amount, partly due to my mood, partly to deal with the boredom'.[45] Compared to his letters from Leipzig, those written in his bedroom in the Three Lyres were less idiosyncratic, less performative, more communicative. There were painful personal matters to reflect on. Rereading the letters and poems written in Leipzig he was struck by their superficiality.[46] On the other hand, he realized that in leaving Leipzig he had distanced himself from German culture. In Frankfurt, aside from the occasional concerts he attended with Cornelia, there was no cultural or intellectual life of note. 'I know nothing, for I'm completely disconnected from all the *beaux esprits*', he wrote to Friederike Oeser.[47] Nonetheless, the eighteen months Goethe spent in Frankfurt were an important phase of his intellectual development. 'During my illness I've learned a lot that I couldn't have learned at any other point in my life', he wrote to Käthchen Schönkopf on 30 December;[48] and again two months later, 'As of the 3rd of March I've been here for half a year, and I've also been sick for half a year; in that half year I've learned a lot'.[49]

―――――

What did he think he had learned? Reviewing his time in Leipzig he recognised his own complicity in the awkward relationship with Käthchen Schönkopf. He knew that he was at least half to blame even if he had not done anything obviously blameworthy. He worked through these feelings of semi-guilt in a new play, *Partners in Guilt*. While writing, he read Shakespeare's *As You Like it* and *A Winter's Tale* and Heinrich Wilhelm von Gerstenberg's grim Shakespearean tragedy *Ugolino*. There is little evidence of Shakespeare in *Partners in Guilt*. Like *The Lover's Temper*, it was written in the French style, in imitation of Molière and using alexandrines. The setting, however, was closer to home: an inn in contemporary Germany. There is a reference to political events in Poland, which would culminate in the first partition of Poland in 1772. The plot spans one night, in which a group of persons, bound together by ties of blood, desire, and obligation, become complicit in guilt. The play opens on a solitary male figure in a carnival costume and mask, the low-rent criminal Söller. (His name is a pun on the German word for 'debt'.) The scene is the inn belonging to Söller's father-in-law. Söller has crept into a rich guest's room to steal some money. As he pockets the money, Söller hears his inquisitive father-in-law approaching the room to nose for political gossip among the rich man's letters. Söller hides in an alcove and hears the innkeeper being disturbed in turn by his daughter Sophie, Söller's wife. The innkeeper leaves in a hurry, thinking himself undiscovered, but drops his candle on the way out, which Sophie finds. She has come for an assignation with the rich man Alcest, an old beau of hers. Overheard by Söller in his alcove, Sophie delivers a soliloquy criticising him and praising Alcest. (During his concealment, Söller maintains a commentary on what he has overheard, and his interspersed comments contain some snappy situational comedy.) The assignation does not go well. Sophie declares her love for Alcest, but when he tries to embrace her, she breaks away, claiming that it would ruin their friendship. All four characters have something to hide. All are pursuing illicit aims. As these aims bring them to the same place at the same time, they become half aware of the secret actions of the others and prone to false suspicions. All four have thus made themselves appear culpable and half aware of one another's guilt, even if only Söller has actually committed a crime.[50] The play now follows Söller's, Sophie's, and her father's increasingly desperate attempts to conceal or explain away their guilt until Alcest, to whom circumstances have given the role of investigator, begins to suspect Söller of the theft. Alcest correctly infers that Söller had overheard him and Sophie, and at knifepoint he forces Söller to admit that 'I stole your Lordship's money, and you—you stole my wife'.[51] In the final scene Alcest and Söller are joined by Sophie and her father, who are still trying to conceal their own guilt by accusing one another of the theft. Alcest informs them that Söller is the thief, but that they are all in fact guilty in different ways. Alcest therefore suggests that Sophie, Söller, and the innkeeper split the money, reflecting their shared complicity. Finally he threatens Söller with a suspended sentence of hanging if he should steal again.

Although *Partners in Guilt* displays considerable technical proficiency,[52] its effect is weakened by the imbalance between its characters and the mystery of Alcest's superior status. The social status of the innkeeper, Sophie, and Söller is fully explained by their circumstances, but Alcest's status is not. He is wealthy enough to force the others into dependency on him and socially elevated enough to be suspected by the innkeeper of carrying confidential diplomatic letters. Compared to the denizens of the inn, he possesses superior insight, intuition, and force of character. This and his social superiority explain why at the end of play he can dispense seemingly unofficial justice that the others mutely accept. The ending is patently a sticking-plaster solution though arguably all the better for it. Guilt and complicity are neither erased nor atoned for by Alcest's disbursement of his money. On the contrary, the gift of the money confirms that debt is a condition of human social life. Alcest's money is shared, and by accepting it the others reaffirm that they are beholden to him. The stress is thus on complicity, not on guilt alone. It is not that the characters inherit some atavistic condition of guilt. They are not irredeemably fallen. Rather they create for themselves a messy human state of complicity, a collaborative effort driven by their interlinked but incompatible desires. Here is the first glimpse of a distinctively Goethean idea—that humans are in a seemingly permanent state of semi-guilt that comes about through human urges and the accidents of social relations, from which there is no escape. As Goethe commented on the play in *Poetry and Truth*, 'let him who is without sin cast the first stone'.[53]

Through the autumn of 1768 Goethe's health seemed to be improving. He was treated by Dr Johann Friedrich Metz, a Pietist and alchemist. Metz was known to prepare secret remedies based on alchemical recipes. His father had been acquainted with the famous Swabian Pietist, theologian, and alchemist Friedrich Christoph Oetinger.[54] Thanks to this connection Metz junior enjoyed high standing among the Frankfurt Pietists. He was less well regarded by the medical establishment, which imposed strict regulations on the production and dispensing of medicines, so that Metz was not allowed to prescribe his panacea and instead advised his patients to read the original alchemical writings. Goethe's health deteriorated sharply and on 7 December reached a crisis. He was suffering from crippling stomach pains. The family feared for his life. Johann Christian Mellin, a Pietist friend of Langer's, led a watch by his bedside. Finally his mother persuaded Dr Metz to administer some of his illegal panacea. After two days of continued pain, Cornelia recorded in her diary that Goethe was showing signs of recovery.[55] After a further week or two the danger passed.[56]

The relief felt at Goethe's recovery, especially that of his father, gave rise to a quiet revolution at the Three Lyres. Goethe's mother had inclined towards Pietism for some years. More recently she had become close to a leading light of the Frankfurt Pietists, Susanne von Klettenberg, a relative by marriage, member of the Frauenstein college, and canoness of the Weißfrauenkloster at the south end of the Großer Hirschgraben. Now Metz's panacea and the attentiveness shown by Mellin and his Pietist friends persuaded Goethe's father that Pietism should be fully welcomed into the house.[57] Caspar approved the purchase of new Pietist literature from Halle.[58] Regular Pietist meetings were held. The impact on Goethe was twofold. He felt drawn to his mother's Pietist friend Fräulein von Klettenberg, who was also physically infirm.[59] Indeed, symbolically Pietism seemed to offer some spiritual compensation for physical weakness. In the middle of January 1769, shortly after his recovery, Goethe wrote to Langer that Metz's treatment had been good for his 'soul', and that 'the Saviour has finally caught up with me, I fled him too long and too fast, then he grabbed me by the hair of my head'.[60] Was this a genuine religious awakening? The language of the letter to Langer recalls the playful self-dramatization of Goethe's letters from Leipzig, and the allusion to the strange prophet Habakkuk in an apocryphal later addition to the Book of Daniel—'And the angel of the Lord took him by the top of his head, and carried him by the hair of his head'—is typically idiosyncratic.[61] The choice of Habakkuk was probably suggested by the prophet's doubts. He is the only Old Testament prophet to question the workings of God explicitly. Earlier in the letter to Langer Goethe writes of 'Worries! Worries! Always weakness of faith'. His brief brush with Christianity was dogged by uncertainty: 'I'm sometimes exceedingly peaceful concerning it, sometimes when I'm quiet really quiet, and I feel all the goodness that has poured over me out of the eternal spring'.[62] The spring might be God, but it might equally be nature. A more compelling attraction of Pietism was its primitivism. The Pietists wanted to revive the practices of the earliest Christians. In tight, nonhierarchical communities of true believers, they would be freed from the structures of institutional religion, and instead devote themselves to personal confession, documented in a spiritual autobiography. This was a version of the original revolutionary Christianity of the apostles, not yet tainted by centuries of corruption and inertia, just as Gottfried Arnold had described it in his *Impartial History*, which Goethe read intensively in 1769. 'It is so pleasant', Goethe wrote in *Poetry and Truth*, 'to think oneself back into the times of the apostles, where everything appeared so fresh and unmediatedly spiritual, and in this respect the communities of the [Pietist] brethren possessed something magical, insofar as they seemed to continue, nay to immortalize that very first condition'.[63] In September 1769 he visited the Pietist circle in Marienborn.[64] However, contact with the Pietists and their primitive faith did not result in the desired spiritual awakening, not least because they rejected him: 'I was, however, forced to recognise that neither the Brethren nor Fräulein von Klettenberg were willing to count me as a Christian, which disturbed me'.[65] It was disturbing indeed that there was no place for him in this revival of the earliest and truest faith. If not in this most original and natural form of religion, where would he find his spiritual home?

More fruitful, at least in the short term, was the interest in alchemy prompted by Metz and the Pietists. Opinion may have been divided on the efficacy of Metz's panacea, but personal experience is a strong incentive to believe, especially when that experience has involved being restored to good health from death's very door. Goethe would often rank the evidence of his own experience above any theoretical grounds, sometimes stubbornly and irrationally so. Metz's panacea gave him a reason to believe in alchemy. There were other, less tangible but more significant reasons. The practice of alchemy was common among Pietists. Both Pietism and alchemy were on the margins of eighteenth-century thought. There was something anti-bourgeois and anti-modern in Pietism and alchemy that appealed to the young contrarian Goethe. One lesson he had learned from Gottfried Arnold was that 'the spirit of contradiction and love of paradox resides in all of us'.[66] As it happened, Fräulein von Klettenberg, whose uncle Johann Hektor von Klettenberg had toured the German courts promising to turn base metals to gold, was studying Georg von Welling's *Magical-Cabbalistical and Theological Opus* (*Opus mago-cabbalisticum et theologicum*, 1719). Goethe was able to assist her in understanding its alchemical prescriptions. He bought his own copy of Welling and made copious notes in its margins.[67] He started to experiment with alchemical equipment.[68]

Goethe's interest in occultism broadened from Welling to take in a number of writers from the fifteenth through seventeenth centuries: Basilius Valentinus, Paracelsus (Philippus Theophrastus Aureolus Bombastus von Hohenheim), Franciscus Mercurius van Helmont, Eirenaeus Philalethes (George Starkey), and Anton Josef Kirchweger. Writing to Friederike Oeser in February 1769, Goethe talks of devoting himself to 'philosophy', by which he means a strange cocktail of alchemy, occultism, and Neoplatonism. Out of this he devised a personal philosophy-cum-religion, sitting in his bedroom at the Three Lyres. *Poetry and Truth* contains a long account of this odd construct,[69] which seems to derive partly from Welling and partly, probably by contamination with Goethe's much later natural philosophy, from Romantic notions of cosmic polarity and conflict.[70] As for what he actually thought during his convalescence in Frankfurt, a better indication is contained in the journal he kept from January 1770. These 'Ephemerides' list a wide range of reading—significant quotations are copied down and differences of philosophical opinion duly recorded. The material on alchemical, occult, and Neoplatonic topics makes up only a very small part of the whole.⁷¹ His interest in alchemy and other occult 'sciences' was one among many.

———

His alienation from the contemporary cultural scene did not last long. As soon as he had recovered, he began to catch up with the latest literature and criticism. He read Lessing's essay on the Laocöon group, in which Germany's foremost critic argued, in direct opposition to Goethe's hero Winckelmann, that poetry and the visual arts were incommensurable systems, for whereas the former expressed itself in and through the temporal successiveness of words, the latter could only indicate the passing of time metaphorically. Goethe saw a plaster cast of the Laocöon group in October 1769 on a trip to Mannheim.⁷² He expressed his disagreement with the formidable Lessing in an essay that has not survived. In his notebooks the following year he engaged with Lessing's essay at length, taking issue with Lessing's claim that for the Greeks 'beauty was always the highest law of the visual arts'.⁷³ Goethe preferred to say that truth was the highest law, a view more in tune with Batteux and Winckelmann. Goethe also read the latest work of a new star in German criticism, Johann Gottfried Herder. Whereas Lessing continued the broadly rationalist tradition, Herder connected with newer currents in German thought, in particular Johann Georg Hamann's anti-Rationalist exploration of language—'reason is language'—and the Göttingen school of classical and biblical studies. One of the principle arguments of Herder's *Critical Forests* (1769) confirmed Goethe's sceptical view of philosophy. For Hamann, 'poetry is the mother tongue of the human race' and therefore has priority over philosophy and religion.⁷⁴ In this spirit, Herder argued that each nation has its own incommensurable 'genius', formed from its historical and climatic circumstances and the nature of its language. The Old Testament was not the word of God. It was the poetry and law of the ancient Israelites. It expressed the native genius of the ancient Jewish people. Might there also be a native genius of the German people? New investigations of the deep European past offered promising intimations. In a long letter to Friederike Oeser of February 1769 Goethe refers to the poems of 'Ossian', the ancient Scottish bard recreated by James Macpherson in the 1760s, and he sets Ossian squarely in the historical framework outlined by Herder. Ossian's poems were composed 'in the spirit of his times', Goethe argues—'im Geiste seiner Zeit'.⁷⁵ In the *Critical Forests* Herder had introduced the term *Zeitgeist* into the German language.⁷⁶

As for modern literature, alongside Gerstenberg's *Ugolino*—a grim tragedy of imprisonment, starvation, madness, and necrophagia—Goethe was most impressed by Wieland. In February he read Wieland's satire about the cynic Diogenes, *The Mad Socrates*, and was strongly affected by it.[77] Wieland's Diogenes is a satirical foil to modern thought, and the narrative frame of the work pokes fun at the Catholic church.[78] Wieland further confirmed Goethe's dislike of modern philosophy and institutionalized religion.[79] Goethe knew what Wieland's targets were and was not misled by critics who, with quaint literal-mindedness, claimed Wieland was satirizing the philosophy of Ancient Greece.[80] But Wieland's greatness also reminded him of the 'famine conditions of good taste in Frankfurt', as he wrote to Wieland's publisher Philipp Erasmus Reich.[81] Wieland was a figure of real substance, a true teacher: 'After [Oeser] and Shakespeare, Wieland is the only one I can recognise as my true teacher, others showed me that I was at fault, these men showed me how I could do it better'.[82] He was still smarting from the unproductive and pedantic criticisms he had received from Gellert and Clodius in Leipzig. But they were dwarves, whose criticisms had no purchase on the great writers, among whom Rousseau also belonged. To Oeser he wrote: 'Voltaire could not lay a glove on Shakespeare, no small *esprit* can negate a greater one. *Émile* remains *Émile*, even if the Berlin pastor blows his top [. . .]'.[83] In his growing excitement about the prospects for contemporary German literature, he was all the more conscious of his own failings as a poet. As winter turned to spring he conducted another *auto-da-fé*. His Leipzig poems now seemed cold and superficial to him. He also destroyed several plays, some of which were quite substantial fragments of three or four acts, according to *Poetry and Truth*.[84]

———

It was during a bout of melancholic inactivity in winter 1769/70[85] that he started to keep the 'Ephemerides'. Although these jottings mainly listed his reading material, they were a sign of his growing intellectual determination. His future career was also becoming clearer. He would be leaving for Strasbourg in a few months, where he would complete his doctoral dissertation and so assuage his father's disappointment that his son had returned from Leipzig without graduating. Caspar had tried unsuccessfully to hide it during Wolfgang's illness, but the household sensed his anger and had to tiptoe round him for fear of causing a scene.[86] In some ways the 'Ephemerides' preempted the continuation of his legal studies. They are not simply a commonplace book, an accumulation of interesting literary and philosophical titbits. Like a conscientious law student, Goethe feels bound to argue with the texts he cites. Some material is promptly dismissed: the theory that spiders are the product of women's menstruation[87] or, more controversially, the traditional and well-attested theory of the four humours, on which Goethe agreed with Paracelsus that 'their grounds are nothing but a fleeting speculation'.[88] He also criticises the overly rationalistic ancient medics for being obsessed with the number seven. Goethe was becoming something of an empirico-sceptic, like Hume and Hamann.

In matters of religion, he had two concerns. One was the sociopolitical ambivalence of religion. On the one hand, religious dissent threatened to overturn the social contract that guaranteed peace and security. As Voltaire put it in his 'Epistle to the Author of the Book *The Three Impostors*' of 1769, Luther and Calvin had 'troubled the earth'.[89] (In fact the text to which Voltaire was responding was a biography of Spinoza compiled from the work of Gabriel Naudé and Pierre Charron, and not a version of the early eighteenth-century *Treatise of the Three Impostors*; the *Treatise* and the biography had originally been published together, which probably created the confusion.)[90] Goethe evidently agreed: this is the spirit in which, in the 'Ephemerides', he defends Giordano Bruno against the damaging accusation of atheism.[91] However, complete freedom of religious belief was intolerable, and there could be no room for atheism. Only with a clear awareness of the immortality of the soul and the possibility of punishment after death could people be persuaded to behave morally. As Voltaire's 'Epistle' inimitably put it, 'If God did not exist, it would be necessary to invent him'.[92] The empirico-sceptical standpoint, allied to the Voltairean belief in the moral necessity of religion, lies behind Goethe's reaction to Spinozism, as recorded in the 'Ephemerides'. Goethe had been reading the *Bibliographia Antiquaria* of Johann Albert Fabricius (1668–1736), in which Spinoza was attacked for equating God with nature. Goethe's reaction is that 'it is difficult and dangerous to discuss God separately from nature [. . .], we can only know God by means of insight into nature, hence it seems absurd to me to accuse of absurdity those who by means of a most philosophical form of reasoning join God with the world'. Joining God with the world was of course precisely what Spinoza had done. Philosophically then, Goethe cleaves close to Spinoza. However, in the final sentence of his commentary on Fabricius, Goethe joins orthodox opinion in regretting the ill effects of 'Spinozism', though without blaming Spinoza himself: 'I should if at all possible withhold my signature from any sect, and I deeply regret that Spinozism, because the worst errors have flowed from precisely this source, was born a twin to this purest of doctrines, albeit an utterly dissimilar one.'[93] Quite how Spinozism is 'dissimilar' to the doctrine of the unity of God and nature is not explained, which is hardly surprising given that the doctrine is entirely consistent with Spinoza's, as Goethe might have recalled from his reading of Pierre Bayle. Indeed, the 'regret' concerning Spinozism seems even odder when we consider that Goethe had been at pains to defend Bruno, whom Bayle viewed as an ally of Spinoza, as Goethe well knew.[94] We should surely not read much into Goethe's inconsistency. It is probably best read as an uncritical acceptance of orthodox anti-Spinozism.[95] In any case, at this stage Goethe may not have actually read Spinoza, but only read about him.

The inconsistency concerning Spinoza was an aberration. Goethe persisted in reading, defending, and advocating unorthodox thinkers. As well as defending Bruno, the notebooks contain several quotations from Rousseau's typically aggressive letter to M. de Beaumont, Archbishop of Paris, in which Rousseau defends *Émile* against criticisms grounded in orthodox theology. For instance, Goethe quotes Rousseau's attack on the Catholic doctrine of original sin: 'Original sin explains everything except its own origin, and it's this origin which is in need of explanation'.[96] While one might, at a push, be able to construct an argument for the inheritance of sin by one generation from another, the claim that humans were from their very origins in a state of sinfulness was irrational and unnatural. It made God appear arbitrary. No rational or natural religion could subscribe to this view.

Goethe arrived in Strasbourg at the beginning of April 1770, and on 18 April he matriculated at the university. The city had much in common with Frankfurt. It was largely medieval, its skyline dominated by the single spire of its unfinished medieval minster. In the days after his arrival Goethe wrote to Limprecht that Strasbourg was 'very mediocre'.[97] Over the summer months he acquired a wide circle of friends, including some who would have a powerful influence on him during the next few years. Despite the allergy to all things Gothic that Goethe had inherited from his father,[98] the medieval minster came to fascinate him. He would regularly climb the tower to admire its construction and the views it afforded of the city and environs. His interest in the minster was just one sign of a mind beginning to open itself up to the past. During his stay in Strasbourg he discovered a passion for the remnants of the region's medieval and ancient history, thanks to Johann Daniel Schöpflin's *Alsatia Illustrated* (1751–1761), a massively rich and learned account of the region's antiquities.[99] In Strasbourg, on the borders of the German-speaking world, Goethe's understanding of Germany was to change fundamentally: 'Germanness emerging', he wrote later in his notes for *Poetry and Truth*.[100]

At first his attention was drawn to France. On 7 May the Austrian Archduchess Maria Antonia, fourteen-year-old daughter of Empress Maria Theresa, passed through Strasbourg en route from Vienna to Versailles, where she was to marry the French Dauphin Louis-Auguste. There was a ceremony on her entry into French territory at Strasbourg, at which point she renounced her Austrian territories and titles and took on her French ones, including the ill-starred French version of her name, Marie-Antoinette. To accommodate this rite of passage, a suite of reception rooms had been built on a neutral island in the Rhine and decorated with a set of ornate Gobelin tapestries based on cartoons by Raphael. Goethe bribed the attendants to see the tapestries, and the impression Raphael's compositions made on him reminded him that it was his destiny to travel to Italy on the grand tour. 'To Italy Langer! To Italy!', he wrote to his Leipzig mentor. He was, he admitted, jumping the gun: first he must travel to 'school' in Paris, after which Rome would be his 'university'.[101]

The study of law continued to be a millstone. Reporting back to Susanne von Klettenberg in Frankfurt, he claimed to be enjoying his legal studies,[102] but in a more private letter to Langer he joked: 'What I'm studying? In the first place, the distinctions and subtleties by means of which people make right and wrong nearly identical'.[103] As in Leipzig he was advised on his studies by a mentor, though this time a far more congenial one—the spirited and avuncular Johann Daniel Salzmann, who had earned a reputation for probity and effectiveness in administering the charitable funds disbursed to the city's orphans. In fact Goethe needed to do very little to pass the examinations and was left with plenty of spare time, which he devoted not only to general reading and brushing up his Greek, but also to the study of the twin sciences of medicine and chemistry. In the autumn he began to attend Professor Jacob Reinhold Spielmann's chemistry lectures and the anatomical demonstrations of Professor Johann Friedrich Lobstein.[104] Although he was only a dilettante medic, he took the subject seriously enough to follow Dr Johann Friedrich Ehrmann on his hospital rounds,[105] where theory gave way to a pleasingly empirical Hippocratic method.[106] Finally he attended Ehrmann's son's classes on obstetrics. Medical students were prominent in Goethe's social circle. The main event was lunch at the table of the Lauth sisters, presided over by the popular Salzmann. The lunch parties were evidently entertaining and certainly more interesting than the local Pietists, whom Goethe found 'boring', he told Susanne.[107] Ironically it was a Pietist student who would engage Goethe's attention in the late summer, Johann Heinrich Jung, son of a tailor from a village west of Cologne. Goethe was fascinated by Jung's life story—his struggle to gain an education, the twists and turns of his spiritual journey towards Pietism, and not least his stormy relationship with his father. He and Jung became fast friends. Jung seemed unconcerned by Goethe's 'free-thinking' attitudes towards religion. What mattered was that despite his heterodoxy and sometimes excitable behaviour, Goethe did not mock religion.[108]

Several weeks after Jung arrived in Strasbourg to begin his medical studies, a more notable visitor settled in the city, Johann Gottfried Herder, whose essays on contemporary culture Goethe had read in 1769. Herder was emerging as one of Germany's leading cultural commentators. In the first place he was a powerful advocate of a popular, bottom-up Enlightenment. Philosophy should leave the lecture theatre and become an active force in ordinary life. Of course, the idea of a popular Enlightenment was also central to Wolffianism and the tradition of popular philosophy that had grown out of it, but Herder was scathing in his rejection of the Rationalist metaphysical tradition, in particular its arrogant presumption that human reason could comprehend and transform the world. The chief purpose of Herder's writing, at least during this first, most creative phase of his career, was to reorientate us away from abstract and arrogant reason and towards the more concrete and contingent human faculties of sensation and language. By nature an awkward, sometimes irascible character, Herder was already out of sorts on arriving in Strasbourg, having taken up the ill-fitting role of tutor and companion to the sixteen-year-old son of the Prince-Bishop of Lübeck. He resolved to end the appointment and remain in Strasbourg in order to be treated for the unsightly and uncomfortable effects of a blocked tear duct. He hoped that the cosmetic improvement to his eye would make him a more pleasing husband for Caroline Flachsland, the sister-in-law of a minister at the Hessian court in Darmstadt. However, the surgical procedure, conducted by Lobstein, further soured his mood. Confined to his darkened room, in great discomfort and disappointed by the failure of the surgery, he could at least enjoy the company of his new young friend Goethe. Herder gave him the nicknames 'Sparrow' and 'Woodpecker', and the two spent days together in conversation.[109] Herder was an enabler and a stimulus. He had a far wider knowledge of literature than Goethe, ancient and modern, German and foreign, including the comparatively obscure literatures of Scandinavia and the Baltic.[110] His presence was enriching, challenging, and enlivening. He brought Goethe up to date with the latest German and, more importantly, English literature, including two novels that were to become firm favourites of Goethe's: Goldsmith's *Vicar of Wakefield* (1766) and Sterne's *Tristram Shandy* (1759–1767).[111] Herder's views were not always complimentary; he sharpened Goethe's sense of the shortcomings of much contemporary literature. Even the classics were subjected to his critical scrutiny. Ovid's *Metamorphoses* contained no real truth; it was overcultivated, mannered, and derivative.[112] He was especially critical of French culture. In 1769 he had travelled by boat from Riga to Nantes, then on to Paris, with high hopes of encountering French culture in its home. However, the journal of his travels, the gist of which he no doubt communicated to Goethe in Strasbourg, turned into a Rousseauian critique of the French Enlightenment.[113] By early April 1771 Goethe had abandoned his own plans to travel to Paris, probably on Herder's advice.[114]

Herder also pointed Goethe to Robert Lowth's essay *On the Sacred Poetry of the Hebrews* (1753). Lowth was the first writer to take seriously the poetic structure of the psalms and prophecies of the Old Testament. Through Lowth Goethe came to see the psalms and prophecies as documents of a primal poetry, a poetry of the people in its most natural form. The ideas Goethe encountered in Herder's darkened room would set Goethe on the path to becoming Germany's national poet. Herder deserves much credit for this transformation, but they were not Herder's ideas. As Goethe put it, 'the author from whom he had learned the most' was the 'magus of the north' Johann Georg Hamann.[115] Hamann enjoyed a polymathic education though he was hampered by a stutter and a hypochondriacal temperament. In the employ of a Riga trading house he had travelled to London, where he fell in with bad company and spiralled down into a dissolute life. He was rescued by intensive reading of the Bible and became convinced of the sacred nature of the text. Also during his stay in London he encountered David Hume's sceptical version of empiricism, which turned him decisively away from Enlightenment rationalism. Reason was powerless to guide us; it was the imagination and not reason that created our image of the self and world. Hume's arguments could also be applied to religious faith. Faith could not be justified by reason, only by faith itself. All other attempts to justify faith led not to faith but to its refutation, in other words to Spinozism. Up to a point Hamann's ideas confirmed what Goethe had already learned from other sources, but Hamann went much further in stressing the priority of language over reason.[116] Language, Hamann argued, is not created by reason, but by our emotions and our sensory experience. Humans are at heart sensuous and emotional creatures. We respond most powerfully to a language that is tangible, a language of metaphors and stories. Accordingly God chose to give us his revelation using the vivid language of the psalms, parables, and prophecies, a pictorially rich language. And we should follow the model of scripture; we should reject attempts to force language into conformity with reason, for instance, by standardizing language as has happened with French, for any such procrustean system will rob language of its vigour. Linguistic 'correctness' is a false idol. By the same token, the abstract language of most philosophy is unnatural, as is the modern trend for presenting philosophy in the form of geometry. (Goethe would ignore this feature of Hamann's thought; if he was aware of any conflict between Hamann's emphasis on natural language and Spinoza's geometrical method, he makes no mention of it.) Philosophy should rather organize itself according to the patterns of natural language. For as a matter of historical fact, philosophy has always been preceded by and is therefore subordinate to natural language. God is 'the poet at the beginning of days', not the first philosopher.[117] Not least among the virtues of Hamann's work was that by celebrating the poetic qualities of natural language, he enhanced the status of poetry itself. Of all forms of discourse, poetry was closest to the origins and essence of language. In his characteristic rhapsodic style Hamann proclaimed that the original and most natural form of language is poetry:

> Poetry is the mother tongue of the human race; even as the garden is older than the ploughed field, painting than script; as song is more ancient than declamation; parables older than reasoning; barter than trade. A deep sleep was the repose of our farthest ancestors; and their movement a frenzied dance. Seven days they would sit in the silence of deep thought or wonder;— and would open their mouths to utter winged sentences.[118]

Poetry was not only the primal act of human creativity; it was rooted in the natural lives of ordinary people, especially those who lived beyond the reach of modern urban civilization. In addition to travelling the Alsatian countryside to see the ruins described in Schöpflin's *Alsatia Illustrated*, Goethe followed Herder's lead in collecting examples of popular rural song. Herder made Hamann's theory of language real; he provided the impulse to collect poetry and the revelation that this poetry belonged to a population and hence a nation. Here was the first inkling that the poet might best speak to his nation through the medium of such natural, primal poetry.

Germany had no national poet, no national canon, nor any established repertoire of national myths, legends, or history that might furnish a national poet with material. There was nothing in German to compare with Shakespeare.

Among Goethe's new circle of friends Shakespeare was a passion. Two new friends were among the enthusiastic admirers: Franz Lerse, an Alsatian theology student, and Jakob Michael Reinhold Lenz, an erstwhile theology student from Seßwegen in modern Latvia. Goethe gave Lerse a copy of *Othello* inscribed 'To his and Shakespeare's worthy friend Lerse, in everlasting memory. Goethe'.[119] In Strasbourg Goethe made his first attempt at a play in the style of Shakespeare, a drama on the life and assassination of Julius Caesar. He abandoned the Caesar project in its infancy, and only a page or so survives, although enough to give insight into the development of this new Shakespearean style of German drama. It was a style that Goethe invented and would soon perfect, perhaps only tenuously Shakespearean, but a response to Shakespeare that would move modern literature in an entirely new direction. It was to be a new kind of historical drama. Instead of compressing the events of a year or two into five acts, as Shakespeare's *Julius Caesar* did, or abstracting the philosophical truth of history from the brute historical facts, as Aristotle ordained, Goethe's Caesar play covered the whole of Caesar's political career, a span of around forty years. The action would have consisted of a series of snapshots from this career, not so much the moments of high historical drama in the public arena, but private conversations that shed more light on Caesar's character. Its politics appear to have been pro-Caesar. Bodmer reports Goethe saying that Caesar's assassins, Brutus and Cassius, were 'villainous because they killed Caesar by ambush and from behind'.[120] Forty years later he would state in the historical part of his *Theory of Colour* that the assassination of Caesar was 'the most tasteless deed ever done'.[121] The portrayal of Caesar in private would presumably have been more positive than Shakespeare's Caesar, with his mixture of arrogance, imperiousness, vanity, and insight. The Caesar play came to nothing, but a full-length play in the same format on a quite different subject would follow in winter 1771 and its publication in 1773 would make Goethe a figure of national importance.

———

The first works that give a clear indication of Goethe's ability and his future as Germany's national poet were not drama but poetry. In October 1770, on one of his tours through Alsace, Goethe passed through the village of Sessenheim, where he became acquainted with the family of the Lutheran Pastor Johann Jakob Brion. At the Brions' Goethe played his usual role of jester, entertaining the family, and especially Pastor Brion's daughters, with comical stories and

FIG. 5. The vicarage at Sessenheim, drawn by Goethe (1770)

performances. A rapport developed with the middle of the five Brion children, Friederike, aged eighteen. Over the next eight months Goethe visited Sessenheim on four further occasions. Very little documentary evidence has survived of his relationship with Friederike. The story is recounted at length in *Poetry and Truth*. Aside from this unreliable evidence there is one surviving letter from Goethe to Friederike.[122] The other thirty or so letters to her were apparently destroyed by her younger sister Sophie. There are also three poems in which she is mentioned by name, plus several others of which she is evidently the subject.

Some important details of the account in *Poetry and Truth* are inaccurate, but more importantly the whole story is coloured by the passage of time and Goethe's later agenda. Writing forty years later it made sense to Goethe to represent the Sessenheim episode as a rural idyll in the manner of Rousseau or Goldsmith. On Friederike's sense of her own appearance, Goethe writes in *Poetry and Truth* that 'she did not compare herself [with other people]'.[123] She was not afflicted by *amour-propre*, the obsession with competitively projecting an image of oneself, which according to Rousseau undermines the moral fabric of modern civilization. The Sessenheim vicarage is example of natural human life unaffected by the ills of civilization. *Poetry and Truth* presents Goethe as a glamorous intruder into this idyll. His superior social status and education was attractive to the Brion daughters, as was his ability to entertain and bewitch with his hilarious stories.[124] However, all this magnetism pulling Friederike towards Goethe was a deceit, for there was never any realistic hope of marriage, given their wholly different social status and life experience. By entertaining a relationship that was doomed to fail, he destroyed the rural idyll in the very process of enjoying it, which only served to prove Rousseau right. In May and June 1771 Goethe paid his final visit to Sessenheim: 'It was a distressing time, the memory of which is no longer present to me', he writes in *Poetry and Truth*, misleadingly, for the implication, no doubt designed to fit his later image of himself as both destroyer of simplicity and survivor of emotional shipwrecks, was that by wiping his memory clean he was able to avoid the worst effects of guilt.[125] This was not how it appeared at the time. In the months and years immediately after the events of May and June 1771, he rewrote the narrative several times. The repeated motif is of male desire destroying female innocence, resulting in a deep sense of guilt. Only later would the guilt be expunged and the whole episode reframed as a conflict between nature and civilization.

One version of the narrative appears in the poem 'Little Rose on the Heath' ('Heidenröslein'). It is a strikingly laconic poem in the manner of popular song, but what Herder described as its 'children's tone'[126] contrasts shockingly with its dark content. The language is idiomatic. In order for the rhyme scheme to work, it requires pronunciation in Goethe's own Frankfurt dialect, so that it feels rooted in a sense of place. The story is of an impetuous boy finding and plucking a rose. By way of defence, the rose's prickle stabs the boy—a fruitless act of resistance, for the boy plucks it anyway:

Heidenröslein

Sah ein Knab' ein Röslein stehn,
Röslein auf der Heiden,
War so jung und morgenschön,
Lief er schnell es nah zu sehn,
Sah's mit vielen Freuden.
    Röslein, Röslein, Röslein roth,
    Röslein auf der Heiden.

Knabe sprach: ich breche dich,
Röslein auf der Heiden!
Röslein sprach: ich steche dich,
Daß du ewig denkst an mich,

Und ich will's nicht leiden.
    Röslein, Röslein, Röslein roth,
    Röslein auf der Heiden.

Und der wilde Knabe brach
's Röslein auf der Heiden;
Röslein wehrte sich und stach,
Half ihm doch kein Weh und Ach,
Mußt' es eben leiden.
    Röslein, Röslein, Röslein roth,
    Röslein auf der Heiden.

Little Rose on the Heath

A lad he saw a little rose growing, / Little rose on the heath, / 'Twas so young and morning-fair, / Run he did to see it close, / Saw it with great joy. / Little rose, little rose, little rose red, / Little rose on the heath.
The lad he said: I'll break you, / Little rose on the heath! / Little rose said: I'll prick you, / So you'll think of me forever, / And I'll not put up with it. / Little rose, little rose, little rose red, / Little rose on the heath.
And the wild lad broke / The little rose on the heath; / Little rose guarded itself and pricked, / But its woe and pain was vain, / Had to just put up with it. / Little rose, little rose, little rose red, / Little rose on the heath.

A speaking rose is within the conventions of popular song, but its words also take us to a darker place, where the rose represents a young girl, whom the boy deflowers. Now the double meanings are accentuated, and we realize how much complexity is concealed within the poem's apparent naivety. 'Morning-fair' ('morgenschön') takes on the meaning of virginal purity. The 'red' ('roth') at the end of the first line of the refrain—the only line in the poem that does not rhyme—stands for blood. The 'wild' boy's 'joy' is violent sexual desire that disregards the girl's refusal to give consent. The consequences for the girl are physically real and painful. The rhyme of 'you' ('dich') and 'me' ('mich') shows that her fate is bound to his actions. The rose/girl also acquires a stoical dignity. The repeated second line of each verse—'Little rose on the heath'—does not change from verse to verse, suggesting her steadfastness, while the first line describing the boy does change, indicating his wildness. The sense of her steady resolve is reinforced by her claim that he will 'forever' ('ewig') think of her. The rose's prickle symbolizes the prick of conscience. The idea of a permanent state of guilt is reinforced by the repeated refrain. Hence the repeated refrain, which looks at first sight like a conventional feature of popular song, becomes intrinsic to the darker psychological meaning of the story: a pattern of male sexual violence leading to recurrent guilt. And all of this psychological depth is achieved without breaking the naïve conventions of popular song.

———

The relationship with Friederike and the composition of his first groundbreaking lyric poems coincided exactly with his preparations for graduation. To obtain his doctorate in law, Goethe was required to submit a thesis, have it published, and defend it in a viva. The thesis has not survived. According to *Poetry and Truth*, its title was 'De Legislatoribus' ('On the Lawmakers') and its subject was the relation between secular and church law. It was submitted to the faculty in June 1771. Excellent though parts of it were judged to be, the dean of the law faculty Professor Johann Friedrich Ehrlen politely indicated to Goethe that it could not be accepted, as publication would inevitably be blocked by the religious censors. Goethe's argument was that secular law must have precedence over church law, which he justified with jurisprudential and historical arguments. The reaction of the Strasbourg professoriate suggests that it was the historical arguments that caused most upset. A member of the faculty of theology, Professor Elias Stöber, described Goethe in a letter as 'a crazed mocker of religion'.[127] Goethe claimed that religions had been created not by saintly prophets acting as mouthpieces for the word of God, but by political leaders. As he put it in *Poetry and Truth*: 'I demonstrated that all public religions had been introduced by military leaders, kings, and men of power, indeed this was even the case with the Christian religion.'[128] In effect Goethe was denying the divine origins of Christianity. He extended the argument to the Old Testament. The laws of Moses were not divine teachings. They were mere ceremonial laws of the Israelite nation. Religions were imposed by the state as a means of ensuring social welfare and the state's political control. The argument was not new. It had been worked out in detail one hundred years earlier in Spinoza's *Theological-Political Treatise*, which concluded that 'religion was adapted to the advantage of the republic'.[129] Whether Goethe took this argument directly from Spinoza is not clear. He could have found it in other sources. Spinoza's ideas on the relation of church and state had fed into the radical Enlightenment and been adopted by more moderate anticlerical thinkers such as Voltaire, who may have been Goethe's source.[130] Either way, it was explosive, especially in Strasbourg, with its fine balance between Catholic and Protestant confessions. In *Poetry and Truth* Goethe advanced the rather strange argument that he had always intended that the thesis be censored, for he did not wish to become a published author.[131] Implausible though this seems, Goethe must have known that by building his doctoral thesis upon a notorious Spinozist argument he was risking censorship. Perhaps he was taking revenge on his father for continuing to push him into a legal career he had little interest in.

The thesis was duly withdrawn, and instead of graduating with a doctorate, Goethe submitted himself for the licentiate—a qualification one level below the doctorate, but still sufficient to allow him to practise law in Frankfurt. Students sitting for the licentiate were required to assemble a collection of controversial legal propositions, which were then to be defended in a public viva. Goethe duly collected fifty-six propositions and had them published by the university press in advance of the public defence on 6 August 1771, at which his friend Lerse took the role of Goethe's adversary. The subject matter of the propositions was far broader than the thesis, covering numerous areas of law, including the penal code and regulations governing legal qualifications. The controversial argument of 'De Legislatoribus' makes an appearance in proposition 42: 'On all public matters the [secular] judge adjudicates; on hidden matters the church adjudicates'.[132] The proposition grants practically no authority to church law, which cannot even rule concerning the priesthood if the matter has any bearing on the common good of society. Another position he defended for the licentiate made a strong claim for vesting absolute secular authority in the person of the monarch: 'All legislative power rests with the prince. And the power to interpret the law'.[133] The position implied a defence of autocracy against Wolffian natural law. Goethe believed in autocracy from an early age and continued to do so, as is suggested by the unfinished Caesar play and his later comments on it. Whether he knew it or not, his position echoed a conservative line of argument in Spinoza's *Theological-Political Treatise*. Spinoza held that the legal authority vested in a prince was legitimate.[134] It was senseless to remove a monarch. States should retain their existing constitutional arrangements. (Goethe was certainly no supporter of Spinoza's theory of the democratic state in which 'because not all men can equally think the same things, they agreed that the measure which had the most votes would have the force of a decree, but that meanwhile they'd retain the authority to repeal these decrees when they saw better ones'.)[135] Despite these Spinozist elements, the university records report that the viva was passed 'with applause'.[136] He was now qualified to embark on a career as an advocate at home in Frankfurt, without the doctorate.

3

'Moses! Prophet! Evangelist! Apostle, Spinoza or Machiavelli'

FRANKFURT AND WETZLAR, 1771–1775

GOETHE RETURNED to Frankfurt in August 1771, two weeks before his twenty-second birthday, with his licentiate in law, but not the doctorate his father had expected. The licentiate did at least allow him to practise and use the title of Doctor in Frankfurt. The literary fragments he brought home from Strasbourg amounted to scattered, unfinished projects and a few extraordinary short poems. During the next four years, most of which he spent at the Three Lyres, his confidence in his writing grew in fits and starts. By the end of 1774 he was the most fêted author in Germany. The path to celebrity was rocky, and he remained uneasy with his fame. Until autumn 1774 his publications were either anonymous or as a member of a coterie of coauthors. He actively sought anonymity, so as to avoid the awkwardness of having to explain views that were out of step with the intellectual mainstream and liable to be misunderstood. In December 1774, at the height of his celebrity, he wrote to a friend and fellow author about an anecdote in Rousseau's *Émile* that he had 'always found remarkable'.[1] In this anecdote a lady warned Rousseau against expressing one of his heterodox opinions: 'Keep quiet, Jean-Jacques, they won't understand you'. Goethe's interest in Rousseau was the crux of the matter. By this point he had read *Émile*, the epistolary novel *Julie, or the New Heloïse*, some minor works, and possibly the *Discourse on the Origin of Inequality*. There are hints in the play *Clavigo*, which he wrote in spring 1774, that he was aware of Rousseau's *Constitutional Project for Corsica*, which envisaged a patriotic republic that would resist all the damaging tendencies of modernity, such as urbanization, commerce, and finance. Rousseau's theory that the progress of civilization had enfeebled human nature was anathema to most educated Germans; it ran counter to Wolffianism's progressive tendency. There was also the risk of trouble with the authorities. The Strasbourg theology faculty, in preventing publication of Goethe's doctoral dissertation, had given a reminder of the ever-present threat of censorship. Deist writings occasioned some of the century's most egregious cases. The impieties contained in the 'Profession of Faith of a Savoyard Vicar' in Book IV of *Émile* had led to an order for Rousseau's arrest. The author fared better than his book, which the Paris parliament ordered to be 'lacerated and burned by the executioner of high justice'.[2] There was also the case of the saintly Spinoza, expelled from his synagogue and placed under a general ban at the age of only twenty-four. Goethe continued to follow the Spinozan view that human institutions cannot embody the divine will. In our world, religion cannot escape being shaped by political power.[3] The reputation he acquired once his identity was no longer anonymous confirmed the point of the anecdote. From 1774 onwards his contemporaries became intensely interested in the outlandish Dr Goethe, son of a wealthy Frankfurt family, a bizarre genius with unconventional opinions.

On his birthday, 28 August 1771, he applied for admission to the magistracy, which was granted three days later, and on 3 September he was formally inducted as an advocate and citizen. His first case began in the middle of October. During the next four years he took on only twenty-eight cases. At first it did not matter that he was only practising the law in his 'leisure hours', as he wrote to Salzmann.[4] His father was happy to help him with his briefs and took pride in his literary productions. Goethe later claimed that his father had wished him to have a literary career, alongside law and politics, and had kept copies of his unpublished writings.[5] A mixed career of this kind was the norm for eighteenth-century men of letters, and so Goethe was following a well-trodden path. The problem was his utter disdain for the law, which made the balancing act unstable. Johann Georg Christian Kestner believed, probably because Goethe told him, that he 'hated the study of law'.[6]

Goethe wrote his first substantial work in 1771 and published it in 1773: a play titled *Götz von Berlichingen with the Iron Hand*. The path to publication was tortuous and illustrates the mixture of uncertainty and confidence about his literary career. The impulse for the play came from two sources: his experience of medieval history and art in Strasbourg, and Götz's autobiography, which he found in the Frankfurt city library in September 1771, though his father may also have owned a copy. He drafted a version of the play in just six weeks, under the title *History of Gottfried von Berlichingen with the Iron Hand*, *dramatized*.⁷ In February 1772 he wrote to Salzmann that his success in completing the play had given him new confidence as a writer: 'prospects expand daily and obstacles remove themselves'.⁸ A copy was sent to Herder in January 1772. After a long wait, a broadly positive verdict arrived around the beginning of July.⁹ The play sat in a drawer for another six months, while Goethe was at the Imperial Court in Wetzlar. He began revisions in the winter of 1772/73, toning down the sexual impropriety of some of the later scenes, which might have proved embarrassing, and adjusting the language. The first version drew heavily on the rough, archaic German of Luther's bible and the southern German dialects of Goethe's day, but the experiment in historical and regional style was patchily executed. In the revised version published in 1773 he made more thorough use of archaic and regional dialects to differentiate the characters.¹⁰ Above all he sought to create a richer portrayal of the sixteenth century which, as he had learned from Herder, was the crucible of modernity.¹¹ With the revisions completed in March 1773, the play was ready for publication. Encouraged by his Darmstadt friend Johann Heinrich Merck, and perhaps still smarting from his failure to interest a publisher in *Partners in Guilt*, he decided to publish the play himself—a not uncommon tactic in an age when authors generally saw publishers as rapacious and dishonest. The plan was for Goethe to source the paper and Merck to arrange the printing. Given the exorbitant price of paper, this left Goethe footing the lion's share of the cost. Copies were ready in June. Unfortunately, Merck had departed for Russia, leaving Goethe to distribute the copies, a task for which he was unprepared and unsuited.¹² As he sent the copies out slowly and erratically, the pirate publishers were able to saturate the market with reprints,¹³ and the venture was a financial failure. At least the response to the play from his growing circle of acquaintances was overwhelmingly positive.¹⁴ The author of *Götz von Berlichingen* was greeted as the messiah that the new generation of German cultural nationalists had so eagerly awaited. The poet Gottfried August Bürger even called Goethe 'the German Shakespeare'.¹⁵

For the next generation of writers in Germany, Britain, and France—the first Romantic generation—*Götz von Berlichingen* was an inspiration, and through their responses to it *Götz* changed the history of modern literature. While the play is set in the early sixteenth century and documents the end of the Middle Ages, it is also an affectionate recreation of the medieval world. 'The Middle Ages are in actual fact the hero of this remarkable drama, one sees them living and acting, and that is what one is interested in', wrote the French critic Jean-Jacques Ampère in 1826—a review that Goethe translated into German, so highly did he rate it.¹⁶ Goethe's medievalism was an inspiration for the hugely popular Waverley novels of Walter Scott, who translated *Götz* in 1799, and it also inspired the later generation of French Romantics, and indirectly the medieval fantasy worlds of J. R. R. Tolkien and George R. R. Martin. The play's second great contribution to literary history was the innovative manner in which Goethe represented late medieval Germany. The play is a coherent attempt at worldmaking, with detailed attention to linguistic, ethical, social, and political features of the early sixteenth century. In this respect Goethe created something utterly unlike his hero Shakespeare's history plays, which made no effort to create a world different from Shakespeare's own. Even in the eighteenth century the 'presentist' attitude to the past was still the norm: historical drama clothed its characters in the apparel, language, and manners of the eighteenth-century French court. It aimed at grandeur, not historical authenticity. *Götz von Berlichingen* changed all this. After *Götz* it became the norm for literature set in the past to recreate a sense of that past, even if the fictional past was always inflected by modern concerns.

The play revolves around the relationship between Götz and his old friend Weislingen, now in the service of Götz's archenemy the Prince-Bishop of Bamberg. In Act I Götz succeeds in kidnapping Weislingen and persuading him to change sides. To confirm the renewal of their alliance, Weislingen is betrothed to Götz's sister Maria. In Act II the chronically weak and indecisive Weislingen is tempted back to Bamberg by the bishop's courtier Liebetraut. There Weislingen falls in love with the femme fatale Adelheid von Walldorf, who persuades him to return to the bishop's service as his ambassador to the Emperor. Götz meanwhile has begun another feud with the city of Nuremberg and ambushed some of the city's rich merchants. In Act III Weislingen, representing the bishop's interests, persuades the Emperor to send a force of soldiers to besiege Götz's castle. After resisting valiantly, Götz hands himself over to the Emperor's forces on the assurance that he will be treated as a free man, but instead in Act IV the Swabian court at Heilbronn sentences him to imprisonment. Götz's ally Franz von Sickingen, now married to Maria, surrounds Heilbronn and rescues Götz by threat of arms and fire. Act V is overshadowed by the violence of the Peasants' War. The rebels try to recruit Götz as their leader. With misgivings he accepts, on condition that the peasants refrain from violence, but his trust in the peasants is betrayed when they burn down the town of Miltenberg. Götz is captured again by Weislingen's soldiers, and the plot spirals into utter chaos. Adelheid, now bored of Weislingen, betrays him by seducing Götz's page Franz and persuading him to poison Weislingen. The guilt-racked Franz commits suicide. Adelheid is sentenced to death by a secret court and assassinated. In the 1771 version she seduces her assassin and stabs him to death, though not before he is able to fulfil his commission by throttling her—they die together in her bed. (This scene was the main casualty of Goethe's 1773 revisions.) Under house arrest in his castle at Jaxthausen, Götz falls into a deep melancholy and dies whilst proclaiming his freedom.

Götz owed much of its popularity to its being so utterly different, in style and atmosphere, from the common run of German historical and political dramas. The play's language has striking historical, regional, and social colour. The voices of the lower classes, such as foot soldiers and even gypsies, are heard in new and sympathetic ways. Their roles go well beyond mere serving and spear-carrying. The action of the play has movement and vigour. It ranges over a large swathe of southwestern Germany. All this novelty might seem to have political implications. The more traditional forms of historical and political theatre reinforced an image of the existing social order. *Götz* not only broke with the conventions of traditional theatre; it also identified its hero with the politics of freedom. However, despite signalling a revolution in the theatre, the play's politics are far from revolutionary. At its heart is an argument about historical change. In the fourth of his *Critical Forests* (1769), Herder proposed that the era of the Emperors Maximilian I (reigned 1508–1519) and Charles V (reigned 1519–1556) was the crucible in which the medieval world dissolved and modern Europe was formed.[17] *Götz von Berlichingen* is set during this period and traces the emergence of modernity out of the Middle Ages. Götz himself represents the values of the medieval world. He embodies what Herder called the 'chivalric mind': 'the *mixture* of concepts *of honor* and *love* and *faithfulness* and *worship* and *bravery* and *chastity*'.[18] His death enacts that part of Herder's vision concerned with the passing of the Middle Ages. The play is haunted by a sense of regret, guilt even, at the loss of the great age of 'German freedom'. Götz embodies this freedom in its literal, political sense: as an Imperial Knight, he represents a class of minor territorial rulers who enjoyed the right of direct appeal to the Emperor and made up a not insignificant part of the Empire's military forces. In the sixteenth century the military role of the Imperial Knights was under threat from advances in the technology of warfare: the advent of firearms and artillery and an increasing dependence on infantry instead of cavalry, which would make the Knights redundant.[19] The Knights were also known for disrupting the Empire's peace and welfare with their endless feuding and preying on innocent tradesmen—a practice that Goethe's Götz unashamedly continues. However, the play makes it clear that the view of the Knights as unruly and recalcitrant disturbers of the peace is a misrepresentation from the biased perspective of modernity.[20] As Herder would argue in his essay *This too a Philosophy of History for the Formation of Humanity* (1774), the spirit of one age—its *Zeitgeist*, to use Herder's word[21]— always includes a negative and distorted view of the age that preceded it. We see the cultures of the past through the lens of their decline, and so the mere passage of time inevitably leads us to disparage the past. This is how our sense of historical progress is formed, not by one civilization giving way to a better one, but by the inevitable decline of every civilization and our tendency to treat that period of decline as if it represented the civilization as a whole. Herder also pointed Goethe to a quite different assessment of the Imperial Knights in Justus Möser's historical essays. Möser understood the Knights' feuding not as chaotic violence, but as a form of political self-regulation.[22] His work formed a further ingredient in Goethe's understanding of German history and the condition of modern Germany—alongside the ideas of Rousseau, Hamann, and Herder.

For most of Act II, the setting switches between Götz's castle at Jaxthausen and the bishop's palace in Bamberg—a Rousseauian contrast between nature and civilization. Aside from the suitably sardonic courtier Liebetraut (Lovetroth—the name is ironic), the bishop's palace is populated by ignorant prelates and an oleaginous lawyer, who goes by the professional Latin name of Olearius, a vain attempt to conceal his German name Öhlmann (Oilman). Olearius is tasked with educating the ignorant clerics in a new legal system. The Codex of Justinian is steadily replacing Germany's traditional, precedent-based legal system, which at least had the virtues of familiarity and proximity.[23] He is an unappealing figure who is clearly intended as a satirical comment on the emerging modern bureaucratic state. The nature of this new bureaucracy was defined by Max Weber in the early twentieth century. Weber viewed modernity as an increasing rationalization and instrumentalization of human life, the triumph of technology and rationality over the human spirit. Under the old system, political power was vested in a prince who embodied, interpreted, and articulated the polity's traditions directly to his subjects. The prince was the immediate source of law and its interpretation and application. In the modern rationalized state, a class of officials like Olearius will stand between the prince and his subjects. The old common law dispensed by the prince in person will give way to a new system of law administered by a caste of bureaucrats. What was direct, natural, and familiar will become mediated, artificial, and alien.

It is from this false modernizing tendency that Götz seeks to rescue Weislingen. Like Götz, Weislingen is an Imperial Knight, but he has abandoned the chivalric life. He has left his ancestral lands in the hands of a manager, so that he can live off the income as an absentee landlord and courtier in Bamberg. In doing this, Weislingen is following the direction of travel of the modern economy. The economic elite distance themselves from labour on the land in favour of a cash economy. Again, a sense of proximity is being lost. Yet the new cash economy creates a prison for us, for we are now slaves to the very financial instruments we created in order to give us control over our lives. Weber famously described modern economic rationality as a garment that felt like a 'casing hard as steel'. (The standard but less accurate translation is 'iron cage'.)[24] Rousseau described the modern cash economy with the metaphor of chains: 'Give money, and soon you will have chains. The word *finance* is a slave's word [...]. In a truly free state the citizens do everything with their hands and nothing with money'.[25] Götz knows that he can only rescue Weislingen by encouraging him to return to his ancestral lands. In order to do so, Götz supports the betrothal of Weislingen to his sister Maria, in all sincerity and without any suggestion that she is being exploited. The paradox of liberating Weislingen by binding him to Maria is lost on Götz, but Maria is aware of it, for she tells Weislingen that 'loving embraces are like chains'.[26] It seems that imprisonment awaits at every turn.

A further complexity is that the contrast between Jaxthausen and Bamberg is not as clear as it first appears. Jaxthausen is also afflicted by the debilitating effects of civilization. Götz's son Carl is learning from books, not by roving the countryside as Götz had done. Books, Rousseau argued in *Émile*, should be excluded from a child's education. They have a doubly debilitating effect. They interpose themselves between the child and the world. A child learning through books learns others' opinions instead of forming opinions of its own that would be more reliable and would fully develop the child's faculties. Books also excite the imagination and so increase our desires beyond what is attainable.[27] Like Weislingen, then, Carl is destined for the modern condition of weakness in which our desires always exceed our capabilities. A third case, that of Götz's page Georg, seems to offer some hope for Jaxthausen, but ends in tragedy. Götz indulges Georg's dressing up in armour that is too big for him. Georg's playacting seems harmless and no doubt expresses his deep commitment to Götz and the medieval way of life, which is no doubt why Götz indulges him. By indulging Georg, Götz encourages him to play a role he is too young for. Georg's precocious ambition will eventually kill him, and Götz must take some responsibility for his death.

Despite Götz's efforts, Weislingen is beyond rescue. His imagination has been stimulated by life at the Bamberg court, where the cash he draws from his estates enables him to cut a fine figure in the competition for social and sexual prestige. In a civilized place such as Bamberg, the competitive desires of our *amour-propre* are liable to expand without limit and far outrun our capacity to satisfy them. It is in this mismatch between our imagined desires and our power to attain them that modern man's fundamental weakness lies, and this weakness is the greatest source of wickedness in modern civilization. 'All wickedness comes from weakness', was Rousseau's grim conclusion in *Émile*.[28] Weislingen is the epitome of modern weakness. He has the name to match his condition: the German for 'weakling' is *Weichling*.[29] (The similarity is clearer in the 1771 version where his name is spelt Weisling.) In his weakness, Weislingen is divided against himself, torn between the factitious self of *amour-propre* and the authentic self of *amour de soi* and *pitié*. Weislingen acknowledges that his self has split in two when he succumbs to Götz's attempt to win him back: 'I'm no longer myself, and yet I'm myself again'.[30] At Jaxthausen he is forced to admit that the sense of freedom he felt at Bamberg was a lie, and that he depends on the very people he would place himself above. Götz is proof of this painful point for Weislingen, for Götz is at ease with his people at Jaxthausen, neither ruled by nor ruling them, and therefore truly free:

> Oh why am I not as free as you! Gottfr[ied] Gottfr[ied]! In your presence I feel my worthlessness completely. Dependence! An accursed word, and yet it seems as if I were destined for it. I left Gottfried in order to be free; and only now do I feel how much I depend on the little people I seemed to rule. I don't want to see Bamberg again. I'll break with all of them, and be free. Gottfr[ied] Gottfr[ied] you alone are free whose great spirit is self-sufficient and needs neither to obey nor to rule in order to be something.[31]

Weislingen's predicament is that of a civilized, modern person. At the very point of becoming free from the bonds that tied him to the land, he is imprisoned by a new set of bonds created by his desire and imagination. Liebetraut, following his success in persuading Weislingen to return to Bamberg, understands Weislingen's problem: 'He wanted to without wanting'.[32] A further moment of vivid symbolism adds to the picture of his divided self. Riding up to Bamberg's gates, Weislingen feels his horse shy and refuse to enter—a symbol of the conflict between Weislingen's natural, animal desire for self-preservation (the horse) and his conscious mind governed by inauthentic *amour-propre* (the rider). It is the *amour-propre* that wins out and fatefully drives Weislingen into Bamberg and to his death.

Like Weislingen, Götz suffers the gradual erosion of his freedom. His fate follows a model Goethe would set out in a rhapsodic speech in honour of Shakespeare's name day in October 1771. Shakespeare's plays 'all turn on this secret point (which no philosopher has yet seen or located) at which the particularity of our self, the pretended freedom of our will, collides with the inevitable course of the universe'.[33] Until the end Götz remains loyal to the Emperor, in his own rough-hewn and idiosyncratic fashion. His attitude to the Emperor is expressed in the famous words he shouts down to the imperial troops besieging his castle at Jaxthausen: 'Tell your captain that the Emperor has, as ever, the respect I owe him; your captain, on the other hand, tell him he can kiss my arse.'[34] From Götz's loyalty to the Emperor it has been inferred that Goethe himself was a supporter of the Empire. However, Götz's position is not quite so straightforward. His loyalty is to the person of the Emperor, not to the Empire as a political entity. The captain is an agent of the Emperor, but not the Emperor himself, and therefore he cannot command Götz's loyalty. Götz refuses to acknowledge the new political world in which the Emperor's power is no longer expressed in person, but is instead mediated through the technologies of administration and war, in this case the new army of foot soldiers. By contrast, Götz has practically nothing to say about the politics of the Empire. For him, the Empire is only a collection of territories that need to be defended against external enemies, notably the Turks. What binds Götz to the Empire is personal loyalty to the Emperor born of the shared experience of warfare—another relic of the medieval world that is being eroded by the technology of modern warfare and the modern bureaucratic state.

Even when Götz comes closest to open rebellion against the Empire, he remains loyal to the Emperor and his own aristocratic class. In Act V the already broad panorama of the play widens further to encompass the Peasant's War of 1524–1526. At first Götz declines the peasants' request that he lead them. It is only when the violence of the revolt becomes intolerable that he joins them, hoping that he might be able to rein them in. Between the play's 1771 and 1773 versions, Goethe's attitude towards the episode seems to have changed in ways that shed light on his politics. In the 1771 version a justification is given for the peasants' violence. They have captured and plan to murder a local nobleman, Count Otto von Helfenstein. In response to Helfenstein's wife's entreaties, the peasant leader Metzler explains that Helfenstein had imprisoned a peasant for poaching a deer; the peasant's wife had begged for mercy, but Helfenstein had given none; nor will the peasants spare him now.[35]

The peasants' cause is therefore a rough-and-ready form of justice. They demand retribution for the injustices they have suffered: their exclusion from good hunting grounds and Helfenstein's lack of compassion. However, in the equivalent 1773 scenes, Metzler's dialogue with Helfenstein's wife is omitted and with it goes the justification of the peasants' cause.[36] Metzler merely crows that Helfenstein and twelve other aristocrats, along with around seventy other victims, have been herded together and slaughtered.[37] The peasants' violence is indefensibly bloodthirsty. As for Götz's involvement in the revolt, the changes Goethe made in 1773 are ambivalent. By removing the peasants' justification for killing Helfenstein, he might seem to have made Götz more culpable, in the sense that Götz is joining an indefensibly violent revolt. On the other hand, Götz is a member of the ruling aristocracy and is chiefly concerned to end the violence. By removing whatever cause there had been for the violence, Goethe makes Götz's intervention to end it all the more praiseworthy. If we follow this latter argument, the 1773 version gives support to the role of the ruling class as guardians of the social order—a position with which Goethe, never a friend of revolution, seems to have sympathized. The omission of the peasants' justification for killing Helfenstein also changes our perception of Weislingen. In the 1771 version, the story of Helfenstein's cruelty might have served as a counterexample to Weislingen and Bamberg. Helfenstein was an aristocrat ruling his lands in his own person in the traditional manner and doing so cruelly—perhaps, one might infer, the aristocrats' lands would be run better by commercial managers, such as Weislingen employs, or bureaucrats like Olearius. In the 1773 version, with the Helfenstein story omitted, there is no such example of cruel, personal aristocratic management. By omitting the Helfenstein story, Goethe removed an argument against the traditional aristocracy. In the 1773 text the only remaining example of traditional aristocratic rule—as opposed to the absent landlord Weislingen and the modernizing Bishop of Bamberg—is Götz, who is an exemplary shepherd of his people and 'needs neither to obey nor to rule in order to be something', in Weislingen's words.[38] The 1773 version presents a more consistent picture of a cohesive and humane medieval social order threatened by the advance of modernity.

Against this picture of medieval cohesiveness, the Peasants' War represents the growing distance between aristocracy and peasants and the fracturing of society. It is one more aspect of modernity that Götz struggles nobly but vainly to resist. In the last few scenes the general fragmentation of society affects him directly, and he falls into a dissociated sensibility—a deranged melancholy that makes him a ghostly shadow of his former robust self, in a land broken by envy and no longer tended by human hands:

> ELISABETH: What a despondent darkness! I cannot find you any longer.
> GOTTFRIED: Whom were you seeking. Surely not Gottfried von Berlichingen. He is long gone. The fire of envy has burned his roofs they have fallen in, and have also broken down the walls, it was overgrown with ivy, the peasants took away the stones to build the foundations of their houses. Wolves were dwelling in the undergrowth, and the owl sits in the wall, you will only find the ruined dome of a once proud castle here, where the ghost of its old owner flits about moaning.[39]

The tone of pessimism that dominates the final scenes of the play is moderated only slightly in its very last exchange, as Götz dies:

> GOTTFRIED: [...] Freedom. Freedom! [*dies*]
> ELISABETH: Only up there, up there where you are. The world is a prison.
> MARIA: Noble noble man. Woe to the century that spurned you.
> LERSEE: Woe to posterity if it disregards you.[40]

The gesture towards posterity is a reminder that, despite the pervading sense of decline, we may still have some control over our fate. By appreciating Götz, posterity may be able to reverse the decline enacted in the play. The only hope the play offers is that we might somehow preserve the natural, close, and familiar bonds between us.

Goethe's main activity on his return to Frankfurt was as an essayist and book reviewer. From autumn 1771 to the end of 1772 he produced a body of essays and reviews, which represented his first entry into the public literary world. These writings set forth the new tastes in art and literature he had learned while in Strasbourg. Some of his artistic tastes were unconventional, for instance, his love for medieval Gothic architecture. The theory he developed to support his tastes was a distinctive amalgam of the new and the traditional, based partly on his enthusiasm for Rousseau's, Herder's, and Hamann's theories of culture—preferring the natural and primitive to the artificial and civilized—and partly on more mainstream thinkers such as Batteux. Contrary to what is commonly believed, Goethe did not merely follow Herder's views on the arts. Herder disliked every aspect of Batteux's aesthetic theory[41] whereas Goethe remained committed to Batteux, writing a very positive review of a new edition of Johann Adolf Schlegel's translation of Batteux's *Fine Arts* in 1772.[42] Also contrary to a clichéd view of what was to become the *Sturm und Drang* movement, Goethe was consistently opposed to the idea that the arts should imitate nature. Genius does not follow nature; it creates in a manner *analogous* to nature. 'This is what we think', so proclaimed a review Goethe coauthored with Merck, 'that genius does not imitate nature, rather it creates as nature does'.[43] It was a fine but important distinction. Genius has its own autonomous wellsprings and energy. It gives expression to the deep human drives of self-preservation that Rousseau defined as *amour de soi*. Indeed, in a sense art *is* self-preservation, as Goethe put it in a damning review of Johann Georg Sulzer's *General Theory of the Fine Arts*. ('Very easy to translate into French, could actually even be a translation from French', he mocked.)[44] For Goethe, art is an expression of the energy of a human protecting himself against the amoral, destructive-creative forces of nature:

> What we perceive of nature is force consuming force; nothing stable; everything passing; a thousand seeds trampled, every instant a thousand more born, grand and significant, infinitely various; beautiful and ugly, good and evil, everything coexisting with equal right. And art is precisely the contrary, it arises from the efforts of the individual to preserve itself in the face of the destructive force of the universe.[45]

In creating beautiful and enduring forms, artists assert themselves against the formless and ephemeral chaos of life. This is not to say that artistic creativity is altogether spontaneous. Genius does not exist in isolation. It can be inspired by examples, which stimulate artists to their own creative acts, as much by competition as by imitation. What cannot inspire genius, however, is abstract rules or prescriptions. The reaction against rules and principles might be taken—again a clichéd view—to entail that great art disregards form, but that would be quite wrong. Great art does contain structure, above all harmony, proportion, and a sense of scale. Indeed great art is precisely the creation of such patterns in the face of the chaos of nature. This is consistent with Goethe's understanding of the appreciation of the arts, which is a matter of sensation, not of judgement: the harmony of great artworks appeals to our sensibility, not our reason.

In autumn 1771, alongside his work on *Götz*, Goethe planned two events, in Strasbourg and Frankfurt, to celebrate Shakespeare's name day, possibly on the model of celebrations held in Stratford-on-Avon in September 1769, at which the actor David Garrick gave a festive oration. Aside from organizing the events, with food, drinks, and music at the Frankfurt event funded by Goethe's father, Goethe wrote a short triumphal speech in Shakespeare's honour. The focus of the speech was the genius of Shakespeare. It contains some general statements about the distinctive features of Shakespeare's theatre, but gives no examples from the plays. Also inspired by his experience in Strasbourg, and focusing principally on the creative artist, was an essay 'On German Architecture', in praise of the architect of the Strasbourg cathedral, Erwin von Steinbach. Merck arranged for the anonymous publication of the essay in Frankfurt. Subsequently it was republished by Herder in his miscellany 'On the German Character and Art' in 1773. In his review of the volume, Matthias Claudius praised the 'enthusiasm and patriotic warmth' of Goethe's essay.[46] Goethe's greatest effort went into a journal, the *Frankfurt Scholarly Notices*. The journal was the latest in a series of attempts to revive an academic review journal that would promote the University of Giessen, Frankfurt's closest academy. The project was initiated by the Hessian government in Darmstadt, and it found willing participants in the so-called 'circle of the holy ones' in Darmstadt, with Merck and Schlosser taking on the editing and with Herder as the most prominent reviewer. Goethe, still an unknown author, was recruited by Merck and probably wrote around eighty reviews, as well as helping Merck and Schlosser with the editing.[47] Later in the year the relationship between the team and the publisher Deinet became strained, partly because the reviews were perceived as overly critical and not sufficiently academic in style. The team made no attempt at the kind of encyclopaedic coverage expected of an academic review journal. From the outset the plan was to cover only such examples of the literature in science, law, and theology as were of general interest. The main focus was to be culture, history, and politics, with a special emphasis on English literature. For Goethe the *Frankfurt Scholarly Notices* provided a platform for his Rousseauian critique of modern culture; it gave him an opportunity to attack what he saw as the unhealthy dominance of philosophical and aesthetic theory over practice, the feebleness of modern sensibility, and the sterile uniformity of modern nations, in comparison to the vigour and individuality of older, non-European, and 'primitive' cultures.

As Goethe later put it in *Poetry and Truth*, describing his and Herder's turn towards Germanness in Strasbourg: 'so it was that on the border of France all at once we were freed and unbound from all things French'.[48] All of the essays and reviews Goethe wrote during 1771 and 1772 criticise either commonplace Enlightenment assumptions or French writers. The longer pieces serve as a springboard for Goethe to develop his own ideas, which, ironically, owed much to Rousseau and hence to the French Enlightenment. That is how his claim to have been 'freed and unbound from all things French' is best understood. In the essay 'On German Architecture' he attacked Marc-Antoine Laugier's argument that the fundamental unit of architecture is the column; classical temples are the models for modern palaces. Goethe's seemingly literal-minded response is that walls are a more basic unit. But the real reason for this sally into architectural history is to defend the Strasbourg cathedral against the Enlightenment's low opinion of Gothic architecture. Alongside *Götz von Berlichingen*, 'On German Architecture' is one of the earliest attempts to rehabilitate the Middle Ages. The eighteenth century's chief objection to Gothic architecture was its excess of ornamentation.[49] Goethe argues that the ornamentation of the cathedral is not excessive since it is in harmony with the scale and structure of building.[50] The 'colossal' cathedral wears its ornamentation lightly.[51] The core argument, therefore, is not that some new aesthetic criterion has to be devised to justify the cathedral, but that classical and neoclassical architecture do not have a monopoly on formal harmony. The cathedral can be justified with the very criteria used to attack it.[52]

Within Goethe's defence of the Strasbourg minster is contained a more general argument. Any culture, and not just Greco-Roman antiquity or neoclassical modernity, can produce beautiful forms. True art springs not from rules or principles, of which some nations or historical periods might have a greater command, but from the natural and universal human need for self-preservation—Rousseau's *amour de soi*. True genius is not concerned with anything outside itself; it is not afflicted by the unhealthy tendency to compare ourselves with those around us (*amour-propre*):

> For in man there is a creative force which becomes active as soon as his existence is secure. When he is free from worry and fear, this demigod, restless in tranquillity, begins to cast about for matter to inspire with his spirit. And thus savages decorate their coconut-fibre mats, their feathers, their bodies, with bizarre patterns, ghastly forms and gaudy colours. And even if this creative activity produces the most arbitrary shapes and designs, they will be harmonious despite the apparent lack of proportion. For a single feeling created them as a characteristic whole.
>
> This characteristic art is in fact the only true art. If it springs from a sincere, unified, original, autonomous feeling, unconcerned, indeed unaware of anything extraneous, then it will be a living whole, whether born of coarse savagery or cultured sensitivity. You see endless variations of this in different

nations and individuals. The more the soul develops a feeling for proportion, which alone is beautiful and eternal, whose fundamental harmony we can prove but whose mysteries we can only feel, in which alone the life of the god-like genius dances to blissful melodies, and the more deeply this beauty penetrates the mind so that both seem to have originated as one and the mind can be satisfied with nothing but beauty and produces nothing but beauty—then the more fortunate is the artist, the more glorious is he, and the deeper we bow before him and worship God's anointed one.[53]

Harmony is the product of a single self-consistent act of creation by artists who are 'unaware of anything extraneous', that is to say anything outside the circle of their immediate experience. This is why the traditional aesthetic principle of decorum or appropriateness is damaging, as Goethe claimed in a 1775 essay on the French sculptor Étienne Maurice Falconet. Decorum requires that the external trappings of an artistic representation, such as the style of clothing worn by a figure in a painting, must be appropriate to the subject matter. In many cases this is obviously nonsense: it would be ridiculous and unnatural to demand that representations of the Virgin Mary always dressed her in clothes appropriate to a Jewish woman of the first century B.C.E. Instead—and this is how Goethe's opposition to decorum connects to the argument about the self-consistency of characteristic art—artists should begin with what they know and love:[54] 'start from what's at home, and then extend yourself, as well as you can, across the whole world'.[55] In the spirit of Rousseau, Goethe believes that self-consistency is most likely to be found in ancient or 'primitive' cultures, where the connection to 'what's at home' is likely to be stronger. In 'civilized' nations this connection is lost. The vigour of the senses is dimmed and mediated by the artificial systems of religion, class, the law, and above all the social relations that give rise to *amour-propre*:

> As soon as a nation is civilized, its ways of thinking, acting, feeling become conventional, and it ceases to have character. [...] The arrangements of religion, the relations of class that are so closely associated with them, the oppressive power of the law, the still greater oppressive power of social relations and a thousand other things mean that a civilized person and a civilized nation can never be truly their own creature.[56]

Truly great, characteristic art is produced only by artists and nations who have retained their character, who have not fallen into 'the vile and deceiving uniformity that prevails in our morals', as Rousseau put it in the *First Discourse*.[57]

One purpose of engaging in this prolonged assault on French culture and conventional Enlightenment ideas was to show that Germany, if it were to create its own culture, must draw on its own historical resources. The greatest model for Germans to emulate was Shakespeare. In the Shakespeare oration Goethe again targeted French culture. French appropriations of Greek tragedy are embarrassing, he argues, as French courtly culture is petty and trivial compared to the authentic, vigorous popular culture of ancient Athens. A mark of its inferiority is that the French tragic theatre of Corneille and Racine needed the aid of rules, the infamous three unities of place, time, and action. In fact these are 'oppressive bonds on our imagination'.[58] Shakespeare had no regard for rules at all. He was a free spirit or, using one of Goethe's favourite words in the early 1770s, a wanderer. Shakespeare's theatre has a very simple recipe. It sets the struggles of the mighty individual within a complex play of historical forces. (In the same way, Goethe set Götz in opposition to the changes Germany was undergoing in the early sixteenth century.) As Goethe put it in a review of an adaptation of *Cymbeline*, Shakespeare's abiding subject is 'the life of history'.[59] Against the grandeur of the historical pageant, Shakespeare sets 'colossal' characters. (Goethe does not mention any characters or plays by name though it is likely he had in mind Cassius's description of Julius Caesar: 'he doth bestride the narrow world / Like a Colossus'.) As well as measuring up to the historical moment they inhabit, Shakespeare's characters are products of 'nature'. The belief that what Shakespeare created was in some sense nature or that Shakespeare was a conduit through which natural creativity flowed—these were commonplaces of eighteenth-century criticism, for instance in Pope's preface to his edition of Shakespeare, which Goethe knew.[60] Goethe's version of the 'nature' trope is that Shakespeare's characters comprise equal quantities of good and evil, are capable of equally egregious virtues and vices, as if they were a microcosm of the balance of good and evil that makes up the cosmos. Evil and moral ugliness are just part of the complexion of Shakespeare's people, and any worthwhile aesthetic theory must be able to accommodate this fact. Goethe claims that Sulzer's *General Theory of the Fine Arts* cannot, because it holds that the purpose of art is to beautify nature.[61] Batteux's theory can, because Batteux believes that 'la belle nature' need not actually be beautiful, despite its name.[62] By the same token, the charge that Shakespeare's plays are formless and his characters crude has no merit. We in the eighteenth century, Goethe explains in the Shakespeare oration, can barely comprehend Shakespeare's colossal characters with their mixture of good and evil because we have grown up in a world in which everything is 'corseted and prettified'.[63]

Shakespeare was therefore the model for a renascent German literature. Goethe was keen to find other writers who might play the same role. They fell into two broad types. Some were primitive (or supposedly primitive) European models. In autumn 1771, encouraged by Herder, he read James Macpherson's recreations of a supposedly ancient Scottish bard Ossian.[64] Around the same time he sent Herder a collection of twelve songs he had found in villages in the Alsace.[65] Herder had coined a new word for this kind of poetry: the *Volkslied* ('popular song'). In the spring of 1773 Goethe read the poet and *Meistersinger* Hans Sachs, another example of the creative ferment of the sixteenth century. His other main interest was Ancient Greek literature. In July 1772 he wrote Herder a long account of his reading of the lyric poet Pindar—'I'm living in Pindar now [...] the Greeks [are] my only study'.[66] He felt that Pindar had opened his eyes to a new vision of poetic 'mastery': it was all about 'getting stuck in', he wrote to Herder.[67] He also read Homer, Plato, Xenophon, Theocritus, and the Anacreontic poets. As for modern German literature, in 1772 he read Lessing's new play *Emilia Galotti* and Wieland's political novel *The Golden Mirror*. However, the effect of all this reading—of which the examples listed above are a small sample—was not to encourage him to enter the public arena as a poet. He did not want to be known as a poet, according to Friedrich Wilhelm Gotter.[68] With *Götz von Berlichingen* still lying in a drawer, Goethe's semipublic literary face was that of an anonymous, provocative reviewer, and essayist, not a poet, novelist, or playwright.

From May to September 1772 he took a break from his life of part-time advocacy, part-time writing, and part-time wandering through the Hessian countryside. On 25 May he enrolled as an intern at the Imperial Chancery Court in Wetzlar, a town of five thousand, of whom around nine hundred were directly attached to the court.[69] The large numbers of ambassadorial representatives of the German principalities, plus their families, gave Wetzlar a cosmopolitan atmosphere that was at odds with its small size and largely medieval profile. The chancery court had originally been responsible for maintaining peace among the German principalities. It was also a court of appeal for lower regional courts in matters of civil law, and a court of first instance in cases of family and inheritance law brought against the imperial princes and free Imperial Cities, such as Frankfurt. During Goethe's presence in the summer of 1772, in addition to its usual business, the court was preoccupied with a decade-long visitation tasked with examining and reforming its practices, which were a byword for corruption, legal chicanery, and general foot-dragging.

Goethe shared lodgings with Jakob Heinrich von Born, a longtime acquaintance and son of Leipzig's mayor. They lodged in the house of the procurator Georg Wilhelm Ludolf. Goethe appears to have made virtually no use of the opportunities to witness the court's proceedings that were the purpose of his internship. He soon joined the daily lunch party at the Crown Prince Inn, an assembly of twenty-five young men, including some old acquaintances from his legal studies in Leipzig. The lunch party had formed itself into a 'Knights' Table'—a parody, complete with pointless and arcane rituals, of the masonic lodges of strict observance that were springing up across Germany. 'There was not a trace of purpose to be found beneath these crusts', he wrote dismissively in *Poetry and Truth*.[70] Among his fellows at the Knights' Table was Carl Wilhelm Jerusalem, a member of the Duchy of Braunschweig-Wolfenbüttel's legation. Jerusalem was a committed Britophile: he read English literature, imitated the English style of dress, and was a devotee of David Hume's philosophy, a rare thing in Britain, let alone Wolffian Germany. Possibly inspired by Jerusalem, Goethe renewed his interest in the recent English literature that appealed so much to the melancholic sensibility he and Jerusalem had in common: Goldsmith, Young, Gray, Macpherson's *Ossian*.[71] Despite a later claim by the Hamburg lawyer Johann Arnold Günther that 'Goethe and Jerusalem lived [in Wetzlar] in heartfelt amity and with precisely the same convictions',[72] Goethe's relationship with Jerusalem was not close. The philosophically inclined Jerusalem referred to Goethe as 'a fop'.[73]

In early June, in the nearby village of Garbenheim, Goethe was introduced to Kestner, a member of the Electoral Hannoverian legation, and on 9 June he met Kestner's betrothed Lotte Buff at a ball in the village of Volpertshausen. Goethe was 'boisterously jolly' at the ball, Kestner said: 'he's like that sometimes, and yet at other times melancholic'.[74] He became closely attached to Lotte and was a frequent guest at her family's home. According to Kestner, Goethe 'passed for a philosopher here, a title which however he did not wish for himself'.[75] Kestner evidently thought Goethe was a noteworthy personality, for he wrote the most detailed account we have of Goethe at this time:

> He possesses what they call genius and a quite extraordinarily lively imagination. In his feelings he is violent. [...] He does whatever crosses his mind, without bothering whether it pleases others, whether it's fashionable, whether decorum permits it. Any sense of constraint is

anathema to him. [...] He has a high opinion of Rousseau, is however not a blind devotee of him.[76]

Although Kestner and Goethe maintained a friendly and respectful manner to one another, Kestner grew uncomfortable with the hours Goethe was spending with Lotte.[77] The awkwardness, though largely Goethe's fault, was not helped by the fact that Lotte and Kestner's betrothal had not been made public, and 'she was far too bashful to admit to it to anyone'.[78] After two months she delivered a sermon to Goethe: he could hope for no more than friendship from her. He seemed depressed at the news.[79] He indicated to Lotte and Kestner that he would be leaving in September. At his last meeting with the couple there was a strange conversation about life after death. Goethe again seemed 'full of discontent and had all manner of fantasies'.[80] The next day he left Wetzlar, without saying farewell in person; he left a letter for the couple. He walked down the Lahn valley for several days to the Rhine, then to Coblenz, where he stayed with Sophie von La Roche, author of the celebrated sentimental novel *History of Fräulein von Sternheim* (1771). Also present at the La Roche home at Ehrenbreitstein were Merck and Franz Michael Leuchsenring, the latter with a folder full of various treasured pieces of correspondence including letters by Rousseau's friend Julie Bondeli.[81]

Kestner was one of several acquaintances who recorded unease at Goethe's religious unorthodoxy. 'He has respect for the Christian religion, but not in the form in which our theologians imagine it', Kestner wrote.[82] In the winter of 1772/73 Goethe returned to the religious themes of his doctoral dissertation. By New Year he had drafted two short pieces, both in the form of missives from fictitious Lutheran pastors: 'Letter from the pastor of *** to the new pastor of ***' and 'Two important hitherto unanswered Biblical questions'. Both texts were published anonymously and with fictitious imprints, the former claiming on its title page to be a translation from the French, in a nod to Rousseau's Savoyard Vicar in *Émile*, and the latter claiming to be by 'a country priest in Swabia', in imitation of Hamann's 'Supplement to the Socratic Memorabilia'. However, the content of the pieces owes more to Spinoza than either Rousseau or Hamann.[83] Both pieces are primarily concerned with church politics. At the core of both is the argument of Goethe's doctoral dissertation: religious doctrines and institutions are by their nature political, for whatever religious feelings a person may have privately will always be compromised by social and political power as soon as they come into contact with the public world. In the 'Letter' an experienced pastor writes to his new young colleague in the neighbouring parish to advise him against following his predecessor's practice of anathematizing unbelievers. Goethe knew how it felt to be on the receiving end of exclusion when the Frankfurt Pietists had refused to accept him as a Christian. His fictional pastor writes that 'the doctrine of the damnation of the heathens' is obnoxious, and he goes on to confess that 'in secret' he believes in Origen's heretical doctrine of the *apokatastasis pantōn*, the resurrection and reconciliation of all humans, believers and nonbelievers alike, which Goethe probably learned of through Gottfried Arnold. Clearly one cannot preach such doctrines, the pastor admits. Indeed, Christianity is riven by such deep divisions that there are numerous doctrines on which it would be unwise to preach. For instance, by preaching on the reality or otherwise of the sacrament—a key bone of contention within the reformed churches since the time of Luther—one would inevitably upset the sensibilities of some believers. Such doctrinal matters should be left to the individual conscience: 'To force opinions on someone is cruel enough, but to demand of someone that they must feel what they cannot feel—that is tyrannical nonsense'.[84] For a pastor to seek to impose orthodoxy on his flock is illiberal. Spinoza had made the same argument in the *Theological-Political Treatise*:

> [. . .] since [the nature of Religion] consists not so much in external actions as in simplicity and honesty of heart, it is not the domain of any public legislation or public authority. For simplicity and honesty of heart are not instilled in men by the command of laws or by public authority, and absolutely no one can be compelled by force or by laws to become blessed. For this, what is required is pious and brotherly advice, good education, and above all, one's own free judgment.[85]

Because there is no general standard of piety nor any natural law that dictates what we should believe, faith can only be a private and not a political matter. Yet at the same time, it is right and proper for the state to impose a church on its subjects for reasons of social order. The degree to which doctrinal unity is enforced or conversely doctrinal liberality is permitted—such matters are, the pastor insists, 'political considerations'.[86] Similarly, the creation of the reformed churches by Luther and Calvin were political acts.[87] The essay thus presents an ambivalent picture: the state enforces public worship, while good pastors protect their flocks by refusing to enforce doctrinal orthodoxy.

The political nature of religious institutions is reaffirmed in the second piece, 'Two important hitherto unanswered Biblical questions'. Goethe again uses the innocuous mask of a Lutheran country pastor, whose son, to his dismay, has just returned from university full of systematic modern theology. In contrast to these cold and subtle doctrines, the fictional pastor insists that 'the only usable religion must be simple and warm', which seems harmless enough until he continues: 'of the only true religion, it is not ours to judge who will determine the genuine relationship of the soul to God but God himself'.[88] Again, individual conscience is the final arbiter of faith, and it is illiberal to intrude into this private space. Having made the argument for freedom of conscience, the fictional pastor proceeds to ask a seemingly unrelated question: 'what was written on the tablets of the covenant?' His answer is 'not the Ten Commandments'.[89] Before Moses received the commandments, he had already written the words of the Lord in a book. These prior commandments were the terms of the alliance God made with the Jews;[90] they were the means of achieving and maintaining unity among Moses's people. The origins of the Mosaic law were therefore political, not moral or divine. It is the argument of Goethe's doctoral dissertation, and it is also one of the key arguments of Spinoza's *Theological-Political Treatise*: 'the whole law of Moses, was concerned with nothing but the Hebrew state'.[91] The creation of public religion is a political act, not a divine one.

The winter of 1772/73, when he wrote the two essays, was the high point of Goethe's engagement with the question of the origins of religious institutions. At the same time he planned a drama on the prophet Mohammed, of which two short fragments remain, written in a mixture of prose and 'Pindaric' free verse. The subject had probably been in his mind since autumn 1771 when, inspired by discussions with Herder, Goethe began to read a new German translation of the Qur'an by David Friedrich Megerlin, also consulting Jean Gagnier's *Life of Mohammed* (1732). Goethe's account of the Mohammed fragment in *Poetry and Truth*, aside from erroneously dating its composition to 1774, correctly connects the project with his Spinozist theory of the political origins of religion. For Spinoza the originators of religions were indeed great teachers of humanity. However, as Goethe put it in *Poetry and Truth*, these exceptional individuals, in translating their inner feeling of the divinity into outer forms, 'encounter the crude world' and so must 'surrender those high qualities and finally renounce them altogether. The heavenly, eternal is submerged within the body of earthly intentions and carried off to mortal destiny'.⁹² In other words, the religious instinct, here expressed by Mohammed's pantheistic nature-worship,⁹³ must engage with and be shaped by politics. Mohammed begins as an enthusiastic preacher of the divine, formulates his feelings as a monotheistic faith, and enforces this by means of political and military power.

By summer 1773 his religious heterodoxy was becoming a problem. It did not take long for informed readers to connect the two anonymous essays to *Götz von Berlichingen*, and then to link all three to the name of Dr Goethe in Frankfurt. His views on religion thus became part of his persona from his very first entry into the public literary world. While some liberal or modernizing Protestants might welcome the toleration espoused in the two essays, the seeming uncertainty of Goethe's own position led to a spate of questions. Did he in fact espouse the *apokatastasis pantōn*? Was he a Christian at all? In May 1773 he read Spinoza, possibly seeking confirmation that his arguments were robust. To his new friend Johann Caspar Lavater, a Zwinglian pastor and writer from Zurich, Goethe admitted in November that 'I am not a Christian'.⁹⁴ This was not to say he did not believe—it was just that the objects of our belief are more or less interchangeable, as he put it in a letter to Betty Jacobi: 'whether you believe in *Crist* [sic], or *Götz* or *Hamlet*, that is all the same, just so long as you believe in something. Believe in nothing, and you'll lose faith in yourself'.⁹⁵ While faith is a psychological necessity, there is no need for its object to be religious. What matters is the human engagement, the empathy or sympathy that faith expresses, as he wrote to Lavater's friend Johann Conrad Pfenninger:

> And so the word of man is to me the word of God, whether it was priests or whores who collected it and rolled it up into a canon or scattered it as fragments on the ground. And with fervour in my soul I embrace my brother Moses! Prophet! Evangelist! Apostle, Spinoza or Machiavelli. To everyone however I can say, dear friend you sense the individual things powerfully and wondrously, the whole is as much of a mystery to you as it is to me.⁹⁶

Faith is thus an expression of compassion. What matters is that our compassion engages with the world. The reference to Spinoza and Machiavelli is not an empty provocation. The point is that where faith and human sympathy are concerned, the moral categories of good and evil are irrelevant. We simply do not have a sense for them. This was the argument of the Shakespeare oration. Shakespeare's characters engage us because they are indissoluble amalgams of good and evil. To Sophie von La Roche, who had briefly been betrothed to Wieland, Goethe wrote of his love-hate relationship with his favourite German author: 'Good and evil roars past ears that cannot hear them. And is evil not good and good not evil? Do I hate Wieland or love him?—in truth it's all the same—I feel compassion for him—'.[97] The natural human capacity to feel concern or compassion, rooted deep in our nature, dwarfs any reasoning about good and evil or indeed the truth or otherwise of religious doctrine. Compassion generates all other human feelings and dispositions, as Rousseau had argued.

In autumn 1773 Goethe began work on an ambitious drama on the subject of Prometheus, in which he sought to express his new synthesis of Spinoza and Rousseau. He did not finish the play, but extensive fragments have survived. His main sources for the myth were Benjamin Hederich's *Comprehensive Mythological Lexicon* (1724) and the fifth-century B.C.E. Athenian tragedy *Prometheus Bound*, traditionally ascribed to Aeschylus. He was also reading Wieland's *Essays on the Secret History of the Human Understanding* (1770),[98] which was critical of Rousseau on some points, though there is no sign in Goethe's unfinished drama of a response to Wieland's arguments. The action of Act I concerns the politics of Prometheus's relations to the Olympian gods, who have offered Prometheus a place on Olympus and lordship of the earth. Prometheus rejects their offer, for it would mean sharing with the Olympians what he alone has created. When Minerva hears Prometheus criticise the gods for their lack of wisdom, she promises to lead him to the 'source of all life' ('Quell des Lebens all'),[99] over which Jupiter has no control—in other words, fate or nature. (Goethe used the phrase 'the source of life' several times in the 1770s; it is similar to Spinoza's *natura naturans*, the primal and inaccessible generator of all natural phenomena.) In Act II Mercury reports to the gods that Minerva has betrayed them and Prometheus's creatures now have life. Mercury offers to descend to the earth and proclaim Jupiter's lordship to men, but Jupiter is reluctant to provoke conflict, as he believes humans are already too strong and think themselves godlike. Meanwhile Prometheus is teaching men how to build shelters out of trees. The crude shelters are an allusion to Rousseau's *Discourse on the Origin and Foundations of Inequality*, in which the construction of shelters out of tree branches was the first revolution in human history and led to the development of the family and of private property, and hence the first mischiefs and divisions in society.[100] Goethe thus acknowledges Rousseau's model of the decline of civilization, yet his Prometheus teaches men that there is a natural balance in human iniquity. If a man steals another man's goat, so be it; society will rectify things:

PROMETHEUS: Laß ihn.
    Ist seine Hand wider jedermann
    Wird jedermanns Hand sein wider ihn. [...]
    Ihr seid nicht ausgeartet meine Kinder!
    Seid arbeitsam und faul
    Und grausam mild
    Freigebig geizig!
    Gleichet all euern Schicksals Brüdern
    Gleichet den Tieren und den Göttern.[101]

Leave him! / If he raises his hand against people, / People will raise theirs against him. [...] / You are not debased, my children, / Be industrious and lazy, / And cruelly gentle, / Generously greedy, / Be like all your brothers-in-fate, / Be like animals and like gods.

Human sensibility has not yet been debased by the advent of private property and the family. Humans are still what they were created to be: part animal and part divine. (Goethe may have been prompted by Wieland's reckoning with Rousseau's claims about the state of nature in his 'Dream Dialogue with Prometheus', in which Prometheus declares that he will create a race between gods and animals.)[102] Yet Goethe's Prometheus makes mankind, both in his divine and animal aspects, subject to fate, not the gods: there is to be no divine intervention from outside the natural world. The fragment ends with a dialogue between Prometheus and Pandora, in which Prometheus contends that the fear of death which separates mankind from animals—'one of man's first acquisitions on moving away from the animal condition', according to Rousseau's *Discourse*—is merely the counterpart to joy.[103]

The fragments of 'Prometheus' are a fascinating fusion of Goethe's thinking in 1773, as his responses to his main influences—Rousseau, Spinoza, and perhaps also Shakespeare—began to mature. The plot, insofar as we can piece it together, is a piece of eighteenth-century conjectural history that imagines how the early history of humankind may have unfolded. Humans are caught in a struggle between two forces: the powerful but selfish Olympian gods and the benevolent but flawed Prometheus, for whom autonomy is to be preserved at the cost of self-destruction. Or to return to the conjectural mode, the fragments imagine two forces driving civilization: greedy and fearmongering institutions and a culture of ingenuity and self-reliance. This conjectural history seems to offer an alternative to the Rousseauian model of decadence and decline. Instead Goethe's humans wear a more Spinozan aspect: human nature retains its uncorrupted essence, part animal and part divine. Of course the divine element in humans amounts to nothing more than intelligence and consciousness: the ability to create culture and the ability to experience the keenest joys and fears. Thus while humans are spared the worst of Rousseauian corruption, Goethe is more sceptical than Rousseau about our original nature. (The cliché of the noble savage was a common target for criticisms of Rousseau.) Goethe's humans are by nature prone to extreme emotional states, like Shakespeare's characters with their extremes of good and evil. Human nature is something of a monstrosity, albeit one for which we must show the utmost compassion.

There is one further Prometheus fragment which may have been written at the same time or possibly later, and which took on a life of its own. It was published separately by Fritz Jacobi in 1785 and then included by Goethe in his collected works in 1790. In 1819 Franz Schubert composed a powerful setting of the text. This fragment of a monologue expresses central doctrines of Goethe's Spinozism. In it Prometheus challenges Jupiter's claim to divine omnipotence. In doing so he also challenges traditional Christianity, for this is the monologue's real subject, of course, not the religion of the Ancient Greeks. Goethe's jumping off point was Lucian's dialogue *Jupiter Catechized*, which he probably read in Wieland's translation. Lucian has the cynic Cyniscus ask whether Jupiter can overturn the decisions of fate, to which Jupiter replies that he cannot. God is ruled by fate or, as Spinoza and Goethe would have it, by the laws of nature. Nature is self-consistent; its laws are universal; no god can interrupt them. Jupiter's anger—his use of the thunderbolt to punish and intimidate humans—is in fact the work of fate, governed by no divine rationality. Therefore humans should assign no special meaning to god's supposed punishments. Our prayers and offerings to Jupiter are pointless since in fact Jupiter is not in command:

> Bedecke deinen Himmel Zeus
> Mit Wolkendunst!
> Und übe Knabengleich
> Der Disteln köpft,
> An Eichen dich und Bergeshöhn!
> Mußt mir meine Erde
> Doch lassen stehn.

Und meine Hütte
Die du nicht gebaut,
Und meinen Herd
Um dessen Glut
Du mich beneidest.

Ich kenne nichts ärmers
Unter der Sonn als euch Götter.
Ihr nähret kümmerlich
Von Opfersteuern und Gebetshauch
Eure Majestät und darbtet wären
Nicht Kinder und Bettler
Hoffnungsvolle Toren.[104]

Cover up your heaven Zeus / With cloudy haze! / And practise, like a boy / Who's beheading thistles, / On oaks and mountain peaks! / This my earth you must / However leave standing.
And my hut / Which you did not build, / And this my hearth / Whose glow / You envy me.
I know nothing more impoverished / Under the sun than you Gods. / You nourish meagrely / With sacrificial levies and the breath of prayer / Your majesty and would waste away / Were not children and beggars / Hopeful fools.

Here we come to the nub of Spinoza's argument about the psychology of belief and disbelief, as Goethe understood it. Prometheus knows that Lucian's Cyniscus was right: Jupiter cannot overrule fate. By the same token he must think that God has no existence outside the natural laws that shape our world. What Prometheus is unable to do, however, is attain the spiritual calm that should flow from this knowledge. He cannot convert his knowledge that fate or nature is supreme into the kind of calming doctrine that Goethe found in Spinoza. This is because the Prometheus who rails against an impotent Zeus is still a slave to the passions kindled by the faith of his childhood, as he tells us in a passage of spiritual autobiography:

Als ich ein Kind war
Nicht wußte wo aus wo ein
Kehrt mein verirrtes Auge
Zur Sonne als wenn drüber wär
Ein Ohr zu hören meine Klage

Ein Herz wie meins
Sich des bedrängten zu erbarmen.

Wer half mir
Wider der Titanen Übermuth
Wer rettete vom Tode mich
Von Sklaverei?
Hast du's nicht alles selbst vollendet
Heilig glühend Herz?
Und glühtest jung und gut,
Betrogen, Rettungsdank
Dem Schlafenden dadroben.

Ich dich ehren? Wofür?
Hast du die Schmerzen gelindert
Je des Beladenen
Hast du die Tränen gestillt
Je des Geängsteten.
Hat nicht mich zum Manne geschmiedet
Die allmächtige Zeit
Und das ewige Schicksal,
Meine Herrn und deine.[105]

When I was a child / Didn't know which way was up or down / My eye went astray and turned / To the sun as if beyond it there were / An ear to ear my lament / A heart like mine / To have mercy on the afflicted. Who helped me / Against the Titans' insolence? / Who rescued me from death / From slavery? / Did you not achieve all this yourself / Sacredly glowing heart? / And glowed on young and good, / Deceived, with thanks for salvation / To the one who sleeps up above.
Me honour you? What for? / Have you ever eased the pains / Of one who's troubled / Have you ever stopped the tears / Of one who's anguished. / Was I not forged into manhood / By almighty time / And eternal fate, / My rulers and yours.

Prometheus's recollection of his youth sheds a troubled light on his atheism. We can now see it as the disappointed bitterness of one who had expected too much, one who had been 'afflicted', 'troubled', 'anguished' and who wept but whose 'sacredly glowing heart' nonetheless gave thanks to the sleeping God in heaven. (The language of Prometheus's religious experience has a Pietist flavour.) The appeal to a deaf God only leads to disappointment. Prometheus the young Pietist has therefore flipped over into Prometheus the grown-up militant atheist. The fragment of spiritual autobiography explains Prometheus's very un-Spinozan anger, for Prometheus has ignored precisely the advice that Spinoza gives us about worshipping God: 'He who loves God cannot strive that God should love him in return.'[106] In *Poetry and Truth* Goethe claimed that this advice gave him peace and consolation.[107]

When Goethe began writing *Faust*, probably in 1771, he could have had no idea that it would be a project that would accompany him for the rest of his life or that later ages would see it as one of the defining works of modern Europe. There is arguably no work that better encapsulates our modern ambition to know and control our world and the unease that comes with that ambition. No other work better embodies the historic changes that occurred in the last quarter of the eighteenth and first quarter of the nineteenth century and created the world we now live in. The history of the composition and publication of *Faust* is tortuous. In its final form, *Faust* has two parts. *Part One* was published in 1808. This is the version of *Faust* that embodies the relentless yet uneasy movement of modernity, the spirit that has come to be known as 'the Faustian'. Most of the passages that express this idea were composed after Goethe resumed work on *Faust* in 1797, after a long hiatus. The earliest drafts of *Faust*, begun in Frankfurt sometime between 1771 and 1773 and left unfinished in 1775, present a different picture of modernity, one that expresses Goethe's peculiar reception of Rousseau and Spinoza. He probably wrote the core scenes of this early *Faust* in concerted bouts during 1772 and 1773. After that he worked on the play sporadically, dashing off some lines when the inspiration took him and adding them to his 'Faust bag'. When the Swiss medic Johann Georg Zimmermann visited Goethe in September 1775, Goethe showed him a bag of scraps of paper and pronounced: 'Voilà mon Faust!'[108] Despite the chaotic form of the manuscript, Zimmermann wrote that 'his *Faust* is a work for all Germans. He read me a few fragments of it in Frankfurt which thrilled me one moment and made me laugh my head off the next'.[109] This early version of *Faust*, the so-called 'Original Faust' (*Urfaust*), has come down to us in a copy made by a Weimar court lady, Luise von Göchhausen. She probably made her copy directly from Goethe's manuscript in 1777 or 1778. When the copy came to light in the late nineteenth century, it was presumed to contain all the material Goethe had written up to 1775—the complete contents of the bag he showed to Zimmermann. However, reports by other contemporaries suggest that the bag contained more material than the Göchhausen copy.[110] Visiting Goethe in 1774, the poet Heinrich Christian Boie was able to report that 'Dr Faust is almost finished',[111] which cannot be said of the *Urfaust*. The most obvious sign of the *Urfaust*'s incompleteness is the absence of some core ingredients of the Faust legend, in particular the scenes in which Faust summons the devil, questions him about the nature of hell, and makes the infamous pact. None of these scenes are in the Göchhausen copy. Nor does the copy include the ending of the pact and Faust's death. One can argue that some of these gaps have artistic merit. Certainly some of them, in particular the gaps between the Gretchen scenes in the second half of the *Urfaust*, conform to Herder's understanding of the structure of folk poetry, which proceeds, he says, in 'leaps and bounds', and with no regard for linear plotting.[112] These scenes are the opposite of Lessing's play *Emilia Galotti*, about which Goethe wrote to Herder in July 1772 lamenting its pedestrian and overly logical plotting: '*Emilia Galotti* is [...] only reasoned [...]. With half a brain you can find out the reason for every scene, every word even'.[113] The gaps in the Gretchen story contribute to its startling effects. Moments of high drama and public action are passed over—Faust's night with Gretchen, the death of Gretchen's mother and brother, Gretchen's murder of her baby, and her trial and execution. Instead Goethe dramatizes the episodes between them: moments of social comedy alternating with a close focus on Faust's and Gretchen's reflections and, increasingly, their desperation. The decision to avoid the expected events and to focus instead on social comedy and interiority, with their occasionally painful contrasts in tone, was inspired. On the other hand, to argue that the omission of the pact scene has artistic merit is surely to make a virtue of necessity. As for the *Urfaust*'s ending, the impact of the scene in the prison cell before Gretchen's execution is devastating, and there are few tragic climaxes to match it in the Western canon—and yet we know that Goethe did not view this as the conclusion of the play. So the reader of the *Urfaust* is left with a conundrum. It remains unknowable exactly which of the gaps and loose ends are artful creations, and which Goethe had simply not got around to filling.

By Goethe's day there existed a wide variety of Faust plays, ranging from serious tragedies in the manner of Marlowe's *Doctor Faustus* to the popular puppet plays that Goethe saw in Frankfurt in his childhood. Goethe had not read Marlowe, but he probably saw a tragedy based on Marlowe's play performed by the Lepper-Ilgner company in Strasbourg.[114] There was also a continuing tradition of chapbooks, including a version by Nikolaus Pfitzer in 1675 and one in 1725 by an anonymous self-styled 'Christian-minded' author. Goethe probably knew several versions from this tradition, and it is difficult and probably fruitless to try to identify which of these he drew on. The most striking feature of his *Faust* is its sheer variety. It was, as Zimmermann reported, a mixture of strongly contrasting forms and moods, from the broad comedy of the puppet theatre to the high pathos of Marlowe. In its variety of modes and styles it is again unprecedented among the works of the Western canon. Homer, Virgil, Dante, and Shakespeare—or later Flaubert and Tolstoy—created exemplars of the genres they wrote in. *Faust* was not an exemplar of anything but itself: it grew out of no single genre nor did it become the archetype of one. Among the high canonical works of Western literature it is unique in its variety of modes, allusions, and sources of inspiration. The reason for this variety lies in the challenges that the material posed to a writer of the late eighteenth century. Faust's rejection of conventional university scholarship and flight into demonic magic made little sense in an age that was concerned with purifying and setting sober limits on human knowledge. The devil paranoia that motivated the earliest Lutheran versions of the story was foreign to the Enlightenment—the conviction that the devil was omnipresent and that radical human sinfulness was unavoidable. So too was its Augustinian animosity towards nature and reason. Lessing had contemplated writing a version in which Faust's alliance with the devil turned out to be an illusion, but this was clearly to avoid the problem, not solve it. Goethe's unique solution to the problem of modernizing the story begins by taking seriously its historical setting in the German Reformation, in much the same way as *Götz*. The language of the *Urfaust* is strongly flavoured by the German of Luther's bible. The versification comes in part from the poetry of Hans Sachs, whom Goethe began to study in the spring of 1773. Yet while in some parts the outer form of the play draws on sixteenth-century models, its themes belong to the eighteenth century. Instead of necromancy, Faust's mental world is furnished with the 'pansophical' mysticism that had kept Goethe entertained during his long illness in 1768 and 1769, and by Pietism and its ally alchemy. A further problem was Faust's comical exploits. It is likely that Marlowe had farmed these out to a team of collaborators. The resulting scenes, including one in which Faust plays tricks on the Pope, a surefire hit in anti-Catholic England, were unworthy of the serious scenes at the beginning and end of Marlowe's tragedy. Goethe's answer was to ignore virtually all of the traditional Faustian exploits and to replace them with something thoroughly modern: a 'bourgeois tragedy', which has Faust fall in love with and abandon Gretchen, a young girl of the distressed lower burgher estate. This also helped to solve the problem of the devil. Because Goethe had dispensed with most of Faust's traditional exploits and the associated magical trickery, his Mephistopheles could be divested of most of his demonic attributes. Goethe's devil has none of the menace of Marlowe's Mephistophilis, terrifying Faustus into remaining true to his pact. When Goethe's devil intervenes in the action, he does so in ways that reinforce the social and psychological realities of Faust's and Gretchen's world. He is a devil who prods and nudges humans to do what they might have done anyway, a devil who augments and revels in our naturally destructive and stupid inclinations.

The *Urfaust* begins in a similar way to Marlowe's *Doctor Faustus*, with Faust alone in his study lamenting the unsatisfactory nature of the knowledge he has acquired as a scholar. Like Marlowe's Faustus he runs through the traditional disciplines: philosophy, medicine, law, and theology. But the emphasis is quite new. Faust spends no time picking away at the deficiencies of each particular discipline, as Marlowe's Faustus does. (Goethe will reassign this picking of holes to Mephistopheles.) Instead Faust offers a much broader and deeper critique of academic study, a critique that represents the Enlightenment's turn in on itself with the scepticism of Hume and Rousseau. First, Faust argues that the analytical attitude required of him by secular Enlightenment philosophy robs him of his ability to make a positive mark on the world:

> Mich blagen keine Skrupel noch Zweifel
> Fürcht mich weder vor Höll noch Teufel.
> Dafür ist mir auch all Freud entrissen
> Bild mir nicht ein was rechts zu wissen
> Bild mir nicht ein ich könnt was lehren
> Die Menschen zu bessern und zu bekehren.[115]

> No scruples or doubts bother me, / I fear neither hell nor devil. / But all joy has also been torn away from me, / I don't presume to know anything valid, / I don't presume I could teach anything / To improve or convert anyone.

By disenchanting the world, the Enlightenment has lost its power to move people to live better. By the same logic, such positive claims as Enlightenment philosophy makes are so abstract as to lack any relation to the real world. Our everyday experience cannot verify them. So we find that we do not really know what we claim to know. Faust turns to occult knowledge in order not to have to deal in mere empty signs:

Daß ich nicht mehr mit saurem Schweiß
Rede von dem, was ich nicht weiß.
Daß ich erkenne was die Welt
Im innersten zusammenhält,
Schau alle Würkungskraft und Samen
Und tu nicht mehr in Worten kramen.

So that I no longer with bitter sweat / Will talk about what I don't know. / So that I come to know what / Holds the world together in its innermost, / See all the effective power and seeds / And no longer go rummaging around in mere words.

Goethe may have written parts of Faust's monologue in response to sceptical arguments in Herder's *Travel Journal*.[116] Faust's predicament is also similar to Hume's in *A Treatise of Human Nature* (1739–1740). Goethe had probably not read Hume, but was certainly aware of the critique of Hume's scepticism in Hamann's *Socratic Memorabilia*.[117] He was also aware that sceptics were prone to melancholia; he had witnessed this in the case of a Wetzlar acquaintance, Carl Wilhelm Jerusalem. Faust's sceptical project also leads to melancholia—anxiety, a loss of energy and vitality, an obsessive concern with death:

Und fragst du noch, warum dein Herz
Sich inn in deinem Busen klemmt?
Warum ein unerklärter Schmerz
Dir alle Lebensregung hemmt?
Statt all der lebenden Natur,
Da Gott die Menschen schuf hinein,
Umgibt in Rauch und Moder nur
Dich Tiergeripp und Totenbein.[118]

And you still ask why your heart / Feels clamped inside your breast? / Why an unexplained pain / Arrests any vital stirrings? / Instead of living nature, / Where God created humans to be, / In smoke and must you're surrounded / By animal skeletons and bones of the dead.

The first route out of imprisonment should lead into nature, but for Faust nature is a theoretical and not a physical object. He is still a scholar, the product of an alienated civilization. The prison he is trapped in is really a mental one. Hence his escape into nature leads only into representations of it in the pansophical literature. One such is the mysterious sign of the macrocosm, and yet having momentarily admired its beauty, Faust has to acknowledge that it is just another symbol empty of life-giving reality. Eventually Faust's quest finds its destination, when he lights upon a spell to summon the Spirit of the Earth. The Spirit duly appears, its horrific visage wreathed in flame. The epiphany becomes a paradox. The Spirit does really seem to be the motive force behind natural processes, the inscape of the universe, so to speak. But for that very reason it eludes Faust's attempts to grasp and hold it. It is beyond human comprehension. It is dynamic, amoral, as destructive as it is creative, impossible to fix in a stable image:

> GEIST: In Lebensfluten, im Tatensturm
> Wall ich auf und ab,
> Webe hin und her!
> Geburt und Grab,
> Ein ewges Meer,
> Ein wechselnd Leben!
> So schaff ich am sausenden Webstuhl der Zeit
> Und würke der Gottheit lebendiges Kleid.[119]

> SPIRIT: In the tides of life, in the storm of deeds / I seethe up and down, / Weave back and forth! / An eternal sea, / A transforming life! / So I work at the roaring loom of time / And fashion the divinity's living garment.

Numerous sources have been proposed for the Spirit and its imagery.[120] Most likely it is a composite that Goethe drew from several pansophical and other sources, not that it matters overly. The meaning of the Spirit is clear. It is evidently not what Faust expected: its vision of the world is not somewhere Faust could find restorative healing or liberation from mental imprisonment. Nor is it anything he can fully know, for it has none of the fixed essences or qualities that his mind could comprehend. This is the paradox that the Spirit of the Earth represents. One source Goethe probably did draw on was Spinoza's distinction between *natura naturata* ('natured nature')—the created and knowable natural world we see around us and can comprehend in qualities and essences—and *natura naturans* ('naturing nature')—the inherent productivity of nature that is prior to our knowledge of it. The Spirit represents nature's unknowable productivity.[121]

It befits the paradoxical nature of the Spirit that its manifestation ends mysteriously. In response to Faust's claim that he resembles the Spirit—for does not Genesis tell us that we are made in God's likeness?—the Spirit answers cryptically: 'Du gleichst dem Geist den du begreifst, / Nicht mir!'[122] ('You are the likeness of that spirit which you comprehend, / Not of me!') Towards the end of the *Urfaust* Faust will imply that the Spirit did indeed put Faust in contact with another spirit, one more comprehensible to Faust, Mephistopheles. There is nothing else in the *Urfaust* to support his claim or to explain the relationship between the Spirit of the Earth and Mephistopheles. But the Spirit's words have another, altogether different meaning. What Faust is in fact a likeness of is the image of the world that he himself comprehends, the world as he imagines it. The Spirit's parting words are thus a restatement of the view first recorded in the fragments of Xenophanes of Colophon that our gods are the way they are because we created them:

> If cattle and horses and lions had hands
> or could paint with their hands and create works such as men do,
> horses like horses and cattle like cattle
> also would depict the gods' shapes and make their bodies
> of such a sort as the form they themselves have.[123]

Faust can comprehend only that divinity which he resembles, and he resembles it because he has made it in his own image. Faust's world is anthropomorphic. How could it be otherwise?

Goethe's version of Faust's opening monologue is utterly different from Marlowe's. The tragedy of Goethe's Faust is to be trapped in a human-made world—the world of civilization, as diagnosed by Rousseau. In Faust's world, as in Rousseau's, nature brings freedom, and civilization brings confinement. What Faust discovers from the Spirit is that there is no way back from civilization to nature. Nature as it is in itself is inaccessible, and the encounter with the Spirit leaves Faust with nothing to hold onto but his own mental world—the spirit that he comprehends. Thus the arc of the long opening scene begins with an urge to escape into nature from artificial and overweening reason, and ends with Faust being nudged away from nature as it is in itself and towards a pact with the devil. However, the *Urfaust*, in the fragmentary condition in which it is preserved in the Göchhausen copy, does not show us the transition from the Spirit of the Earth to the devil; it only shows Faust's despondency after the Spirit departs. As if to increase Faust's anguish, from the summoning of the Spirit he descends into the bathos of a sardonic dialogue with his assistant Wagner, who mouths the platitudes of early modern humanism—though Goethe's actual target is the shallow rationalist optimism of the eighteenth century. The dialogue with Wagner thus confirms the strange words of the Spirit of the Earth: Faust is condemned to a prison made of empty ideas. There is only one direction for Faust, towards an ever bleaker and more self-defeating scepticism, which he articulates angrily in response to Wagner's facile nostrums. Finally, in answer to Wagner's optimistic belief that humans can surely know both the world and themselves, Faust's bleakness reaches its peak. When society is told the truth, its response has been to shoot the messenger:

> Wer darf das Kind beim rechten Namen nennen?
> Die wenigen die was davon erkannt
> Die töricht gnug ihr volles Herz nicht wahrten.
> Dem Pöbel ihr Gefühl ihr Schauen offenbarten,
> Hat man von je gekreuzigt und verbrannt.[124]

> Who can call a spade a spade? / The few who've known something, / Who were foolish enough not to keep their full heart guarded, / Who revealed to the plebs what they felt and saw, / These have since long ago been crucified or burned.

The implication seems to be that in this despondent condition he is ripe for taking by the devil. If this is indeed the dramatic argument that Goethe intended, it will not be Faust's ambition to *know* that will make him susceptible to the devil, but his despondency at discovering there is nothing worthwhile that he *can know*. Quite how Goethe might have created such a deal with the devil is hard to see.

In the absence of the scenes of summoning and pact, the action jumps to two scenes that take place after the pact. The first has Mephistopheles, dressed like Professor Gottsched, preparing a naïve freshman for his first semester, by mocking the byzantine scholasticism of logic, metaphysics, and medicine and delivering an outrageous satire on the conditions of student life. The next scene takes place in Auerbach's Cellar, where the drinkers indulge in bawdy banter and self-mockery, which Mephistopheles echoes and exaggerates, while adding an element of social and political criticism that the drinkers dislike, before he bamboozles them with magic wine. Neither scene clarifies what contractual arrangements govern the relationship between Faust and Mephistopheles. What occurs after these scenes is again quite different from the chapbooks and Marlowe. Goethe's Faust does not regret his deal with the devil.[125] (He will come to despise the devil, but will not accept any responsibility for the devil's or his own actions.) There is no Christian religion in Faust's life that could serve as an obstacle to his relationship with Mephistopheles or cause him eventually to repent of it. Faust seems to inhabit a world without transcendent religious truths, a world in which supernatural beings are either incomprehensible (the Spirit of the Earth) or merely the 'brothers' of humans (Mephistopheles). Writing to Herder in 1775, Goethe opined that 'the whole doctrine' of a perfect, immortal Christ was 'a load of shit', and was designed only to infuriate an 'imperfect, needy being' like Goethe. But once we recognise God or the devil as a worldly creature, not separated from us by the barriers of immortality or perfection, then he can become 'dear to me, for he is my brother'.[126] Goethe's devil has a distinctly human relationship to Faust. In the first place, he is Faust's servant, albeit a servant on whom Faust is dangerously reliant for his access to and engagement with the world. Mephistopheles facilitates Faust's desires and thus leads him ever deeper into immorality and criminality. At the same time the worldly devil takes on the theatrical role of Faust's mocker, sardonically puncturing his high-minded pretensions and pointing out the contradictions and hypocrisy of his pursuit of Gretchen.

Whilst Mephistopheles's behaviour is clear, Faust's can seem inconsistent. The scholar seeking the essence of nature and the wooer of Gretchen are not obviously motivated by the same desire. The problem has been addressed in two ways. Beginning in the late nineteenth century, there was a tendency, led by Wilhelm Scherer and Gustav Roethe, to argue that the *Urfaust* was made of two incompatible and poorly joined halves, written at different times and in different modes.[127] Current criticism tends towards a more 'unitarian' view. At the heart of Faust's quest is the modern search for authenticity. In order to live an authentic life, the modern individual must be able to distinguish between those motivations that are intrinsic, rooted deep in our interiority, and those that are extrinsic and artificial, the products of *amour-propre*. The modern competitive public sphere demands that we construct false self-images in order to attain and secure social prestige. In the early scenes Faust's quest for authenticity involves rejecting the outer forms of knowledge in favour of an unknown inner essence of nature. In the university scenes nature holds the promise of liberation from the prison of social convention, but nature in this sense is either an imaginary goal (the sign of the Macrocosm) or utterly unknowable. This function is then taken over by Gretchen, not in the trivial sense that she is nature, but in the more interesting sense that Faust treats her as if she were nature. Here too Faust claims to prefer authentic feeling to the outer forms or 'husks' of social convention—the rituals of courtship, the institution of marriage, the church. He variously characterizes Gretchen as divine, domestic, naïve, or natural. Indeed one cause of Gretchen's tragedy (and a source of misreadings of the play)[128] is Faust's tendency to treat Gretchen not as a complex human being with her own desires and beliefs, but as an abstract idea. The true character of Gretchen, which Faust never fully grasps, is as much knowing as naïve, equally desirous to live within her social world and to escape its confines. Hence the play also has symbolic unity. It begins in the 'prison' of Faust's study. Unbeknown to Gretchen, Faust secretly visits her bedroom which he calls a 'prison'.[129] The play ends in the prison cell where Gretchen awaits execution for infanticide.[130] So Faust's adventure has freed him from the prison of his old life, but ends in a prison, with Gretchen the prisoner, the victim of Faust's quest for authenticity.

Faust imagines Gretchen as a Rousseauian child of nature, just as in *Poetry and Truth* Goethe would reinterpret his relationship with Friederike Brion. However, in the precisely drawn social reality of the drama, Gretchen is very much a part of the modern world, where status is marked by outward signs and where young burgher women have to be on their guard against sexual predation by men of higher class. The first few scenes of the tragedy of Gretchen show that she is aware of the dangers of *amour-propre* and male predatoriness, but also vulnerable to them. On their first encounter, Faust addresses her as a 'Fräulein', the form of address used for aristocratic ladies. She sees through his flattery and at the same time cannot help but be in awe of the aristocratic status she thinks he has, for surely only an aristocrat could be so arrogant. The casket of jewellery that she finds on her return to her bedroom has the intended effect on her. The scene delicately prefigures the stages of her tragic fall. Instantly she realizes something is wrong in the close and stuffy room. Perhaps a whiff of Mephistophelian sulphur lingers in the air which, being a devout Catholic, she can detect, but then the modern rationalist in her chides herself for her own timidity. As she undresses, she sings an old song:

Es war ein König in Thule
Einen goldnen Becher er hätt
Empfangen von seiner Buhle
Auf ihrem Todesbett.

Der Becher war ihm lieber
Trank draus bei jedem Schmaus.
Die Augen gingen ihm über
So oft er trank daraus.

Und als es kam zu sterben,
Zählt' er seine Städt und Reich
Gönnt alles seinen Erben,
Den Becher nicht zugleich.

Er saß beim Königs Mahle
Die Ritter um ihn her
Auf hohem Vätersaale
Dort auf dem Schloß am Meer.

Dort stand der alte Zecher
Trank letzte Lebensglut
Und warf den heilgen Becher
Hinunter in die Flut.

Er sah ihn stürzen, trinken
Und sinken tief ins Meer
Die Augen täten ihm sinken
Trank nie einen Tropfen mehr.[131]

There was a king in Thule, / A golden goblet he had / Received from his mistress / On her deathbed.
He preferred this goblet, / Drank from it at every feast. / His eyes welled up / Whenever he drank from it.
And when his death came, / He counted his towns and realm, / Bequeathed everything to his heirs, / But not the goblet.
He sat at the royal dinner, / His knights around him, / In the high hall of his fathers / There in the castle by the sea.
There he stood, the old toper, / Drank his life's last glow / And threw the holy goblet / Down into the deep.
He saw it falling, drinking / And sinking deep into the sea. / His eyes closed, / Never drank another drop.

Gretchen no doubt means to comfort herself by singing the song, but its words contain a destabilizing unconscious wish fulfilment. In imagining the king remaining true to his beloved (not his wife!) until the grave, she expresses the impossible desire of a young woman in a burgher tragedy. It is the desire to enjoy an enduring partnership with a man of higher status than her, without the security of marriage. As she finishes singing, she notices the casket of jewellery, opens it, and tries on the jewels in front of the mirror. In four quick stages, the short scene has taken Gretchen from the world of her Catholic upbringing with its preconscious protection against evil, to a modern, rational self-awareness that lacks such safety, then to an unconscious expression of her desire for social advancement, and finally to full complicity in modern *amour-propre*.

When the courtship begins in earnest, the stages by which Gretchen falls for Faust are set out with great tact. Goethe's portrayal of Gretchen, torn by conflicting motivations, is one of his greatest dramatic achievements. The detail is precise and telling—for instance her embarrassment at her lack of education and the rough skin of her hands that tells of her daily work. She is clearly aware of her own desire and what she is doing to satisfy it, but like all of us she is able to park that awareness in a place where it can be made to seem harmless, even childish:

> FAUST: Süß Liebgen!
> MARGARETE: Laßt ein mal.
>   *[Sie pflückt eine Stern Blume und zupft die Blätter ab eins nach dem andern.]*
> FAUST: Was soll das? Keinen Strauß?
> MARGARETE: Nein es soll nur ein Spiel.
> FAUST: Wie?
> MARGARETE: Geht Ihr lacht mich aus.
>   *[Sie rupft und murmelt.]*
> FAUST: Was murmelst du?
> MARGARETE: *[halb laut]*. Er liebt mich—Liebt mich nicht.
> FAUST: Du holdes Himmels Angesicht!
> MARGARETE: *[fährt fort]*. Liebt mich—Nicht—Liebt mich—Nicht—
>   *[Das letzte Blatt ausrupfend mit holder Freude.]*
>   Er liebt mich!
> FAUST: Ja mein Kind! Laß dieses Blumenwort
>   Dir Götter Ausspruch sein: Er liebt dich!
>   Verstehst du, was das heißt: Er liebt dich!
>   *[Er faßt ihr beide Hände.]*
> MARGARETE: Mich überläuft's![132]

> FAUST: Sweet darling!
> MARGARETA: Wait a moment!
>   *[she picks a daisy and plucks off the petals one by one]*
> FAUST: What is it? Not a bouquet?
> MARGARETA: No, it's just supposed to be a game.
> FAUST: How so?

MARGARETA: Leave off, you'll laugh at me.
   [*she plucks and murmurs*]
FAUST: What are you murmuring?
MARGARETA: [*half aside*] He loves me—loves me not—
FAUST: You sweet vision of heaven!
MARGARETA: [*continues*] Loves me—not—loves me—not—
   [*plucking the last petal with sheer joy*]
   He loves me!
FAUST: Yes, my child! Let this flower's word / Be the verdict of the gods: He loves you! / You understand what that means? / He loves you!
   [*he takes both her hands*]
MARGARETA: I'm shivering!

The courtship mixes confession with evasion. Gretchen knows exactly what she wants, only she would rather not admit it. Her words spoken '*half aside*' are a clear invitation to Faust, which of course she cannot utter directly. Instead she retreats into a game, so as to cloak her desire in a harmless form, but also to conceal from herself how seriously she means it. Faust is also evasive. He is bold enough to take her hands, but not to say 'I love you'. Indeed her game, which speaks of Faust in the third person ('he loves you—not'), invites him to copy her and so to avoid speaking in the first person and so taking full responsibility. The pattern is repeated by the famous scene in which Gretchen asks Faust: 'do you believe in God?' She asks the question in order to reassure herself that Faust will remain true to her, but it is another evasion: she cannot ask him directly whether he will be faithful to her. Instead she makes the calculation that if Faust is a good Christian, he will be a loyal lover. Of course, this is naïve, as if professing Christian faith really were a guarantee of good behaviour. In another sense, it is cynical, for Gretchen is abjuring her own moral responsibility and instead assigning responsibility to her faith: she is asking the church to tacitly sanction an affair outside wedlock. At the same time the question does almost achieve what she wants, for it puts pressure on Faust. He is unwilling to renounce his claim to sincerity and to lie outright, and so he is forced to give an answer that remains just within the bounds of honesty, but is couched in such enthusiastic rhetoric as to convey a strong sense of religiosity:

Wer darf ihn nennen?
Und wer bekennen?
Ich glaub ihn!
Wer empfinden?

Und sich unterwinden
Zu sagen ich glaub ihn nicht!
Der Allumfasser
Der Allerhalter
Faßt und erhält er nicht
Dich, mich, sich selbst!
Wölbt sich der Himmel nicht da droben
Liegt die Erde nicht hierunten fest
Und steigen hüben und drüben
Ewige Sterne nicht herauf!
Schau ich nicht Aug' in Auge dir!
Und drängt nicht alles
Nach Haupt und Herzen dir
Und webt in ewigem Geheimnis
Unsichtbar sichtbar neben dir,
Erfüll davon dein Herz so groß es ist
Und wenn du ganz in dem Gefühle selig bist,
Nenn das dann wie du willst,
Nenn's Glück! Herz! Liebe! Gott!
Ich habe keinen Namen
Dafür. Gefühl ist alles
Name Schall und Rauch
Umnebelnd Himmelsglut.[133]

Who can name him? / And who confess: / I believe in him? / Who can sense / And presume / To say: I don't believe in him? / He who embraces everything, / He who preserves everything, / Does he not embrace and preserve / You, me, himself? / Is not the vault of heaven above us? / Does not the earth lie firm beneath us? / And do not here and there / The eternal stars rise? / Do my eyes not look into yours, / And does not all this weigh / On your head and heart / And weave in eternal secrecy / Invisibly-visibly around you? / Fill you heart with it, no matter how big it is, / Then call it what you will, / Call it happiness! Heart! Love! God! / I have no name / For it. Feeling is everything, / Name is mere noise and smoke / Veiling the glory of heaven.

To take Faust's words at face value for a moment—and to overlook the obvious contradictoriness of expending so many words on saying that we should not be interested in mere words—the claim that the divinity is in fact unnameable smacks of deism. Faust's profession of faith is that he does not believe in the doctrines of any positive and revealed religion, but nor is he an atheist, and he will 'never rob anyone of their feelings or their creed' ('Will niemand sein Gefühl und seine Kirche rauben').[134] Nor should anyone be obliged to believe. Faust manages to express both a plausible confession of faith and sheer evasiveness. At the same time, Gretchen is a willing accomplice. She wants the relationship to last, and seeks Faust's reassurance that it will, but by asking him obliquely, she has invited him to answer obliquely. If the purpose of her question was to force him to commit to her, it has failed; if its purpose was to salve her conscience while allowing her to follow her desire, it has succeeded admirably.

After Faust gives Gretchen the sleeping potion, we do not see Faust and Gretchen together again until the final scene of the Göchhausen copy. When we next see Gretchen, she has slept with Faust and may be pregnant. The focus suddenly shifts to her private anguish and public disgrace. The next scenes have the important dramatic function of explaining why Gretchen murders her child. In a scene by a city well, a friend of Gretchen's reports gossip about another girl who is currently 'eating for two', having had a very public affair with a young man—one of those girls who had to have the best and be the first, a clear case of *amour-propre*.[135] Gretchen is convinced that her own motives were nothing of the sort: 'But everything that moved me to do it, / God! it was so good! ah, was so dear to me!' ('Doch—alles, was mich dazu trieb / Gott! war so gut! ach war so lieb!')[136] In the next scene Gretchen prays privately to the Mother of Sorrows at a shrine in the city walls. However, private convictions of purity and contrition are no defence against the social and psychological power of the church. The following scene represents the funeral service for Gretchen's mother in the city's cathedral. The focus is on the psychological effects of institutional religion. A choir sings the requiem mass, or at least those passages in it that express the terror of Christian moral teaching: God's wrath, the dissolution of the world in ashes, and a judgement from which nothing can be concealed and which will leave no sin unavenged. In addition to the choir, we hear Gretchen's terrified responses and the voice of an 'Evil Spirit', which amplifies and adds extra terror to the words of the mass. Is this the devil, or is it another manifestation of the church? For Gretchen there is no difference.

Faust is now a fugitive, and his feelings turn to fatalism, anger, and disgust, with only faint glimmerings of remorse. The closest he comes to acknowledging his responsibility is an eloquent postcoital reverie that turns into an extended image of Gretchen's destruction. He imagines her dwelling in an alpine cottage, whilst likening himself to a spring waterfall that washes away her dwelling and her life. The image hints at a historical change: a static, traditional, pre-urban (Rousseauian) way of life is destroyed by the violent, unstoppable forces of modernity. Faust seems to recognise the damage his quest for authenticity is causing. The image of the waterfall also shows the imbalance of power and status between Gretchen and himself and the impossible position his power has forced her into. That impossibility is graphically realized in the final scene, a bleak and compelling study in tragic madness, which takes place in the city gaol at midnight before Gretchen's execution. Gretchen's mind has been completely deranged by the murder of the baby and the trial. As Faust arrives to rescue her, she sings a version of the grim traditional tale of the juniper tree, in which a boy laments his murder by his stepmother. Again Goethe uses song to convey the fractured state of Gretchen's mind. Her conscious mind has lost contact with reality. When Faust enters, she fails to recognise him, at first taking him for her executioner—a grimly apt mistake, since Faust is in large part responsible for her death. When she does recognise him, she cannot engage: her consciousness is preoccupied with thoughts of her dead mother and her family's graves, which she asks Faust to tend. (There will be no space in the plot for Faust.)[137] Faust says very little in the gaol scene. He has already used up what little conscience he had. He tries to persuade her to escape with him, but his moral inadequacy makes that impossible. The presence of Mephistopheles does not help, for Gretchen has retained her visceral revulsion for the devil. It is this that irrevocably turns Gretchen away from Faust and back towards her God. At the end her faith and pity forces a decision on her. She accepts God's judgement for her crimes. And yet she cannot abandon her love for Faust either.

After returning from Wetzlar to Frankfurt in 1772, Goethe had found himself increasingly alone.[138] There was no university and only one grammar school in Frankfurt.[139] The first reading society was founded in 1787, the first permanent theatre in 1782, and the first standing theatre company in 1792.[140] In June 1773 he attended his first meeting of the Frankfurt College of Graduates, which promised the company of men of similar social standing and intellectual aspirations. He did not attend again. On 1 November 1773 Cornelia married Schlosser and moved to Emmendingen in Swabia. Friends were concerned that the combination of Goethe's unhappiness and talent would prove self-destructive.[141] Kestner proposed to Goethe that he could find employment elsewhere, perhaps at a princely court or in a council of justice. His reply to Kestner shows he considered the prospect seriously.[142] A letter from a new friend Johann Caspar Lavater to Dr Zimmermann in October 1774 suggests that he continued to do so: 'Goethe would be a wonderful active presence at a prince's court. *That's* where he belongs. He could be a king. He not only has wisdom and bonhomie, but also force of character'.[143]

Goethe's family and friends seem to have had no inkling that in February 1774, eighteen months after his abrupt departure from Wetzlar, he would suddenly begin to write a novel based on his Wetzlar experiences and friends. The two main elements of his Wetzlar life that went into the novel were his relationship with Lotte and Kestner and the suicide of his acquaintance the Humean philosopher Jerusalem in October 1772. The short novel was finished in around four weeks. Its story is simple. The hero Werther has been sent away by his mother to pursue an inheritance that she believes the family is owed. Werther has no interest in the errand. For him it is a chance to escape. The first sentence of the novel reads: 'How glad I am to be away!'[144] He has several reasons to welcome his escape. He lost his father in childhood, and his relationship with his mother is cold. He has perhaps knowingly encouraged the affections of a woman whose sister he was fond of. Earlier a woman he loved had died young. Against this background, Werther's errand turns into a quest for authenticity in the small towns and villages of rural Germany. On his way to a country ball, he meets Lotte, but fails to register the vital information that she is already betrothed. They enjoy dancing together. When the ball is interrupted by a storm, they share a moment standing at the window; Lotte mentions Klopstock's poem 'The Rite of Spring' and puts her hand on his. It is a symbolic moment: he mistakes her gesture of friendship for a sign of love and of hope for a relationship that can however only happen in the poetic and sentimental world of Klopstock's poem, not in reality. Werther now visits Lotte frequently, though eventually he must recognise that she is firmly promised to her betrothed Albert. After a strange conversation about life after death, Werther leaves Lotte and Albert, and the first part of the novel ends. As a cure for his melancholia, Werther takes a job as a secretary to a small principality's embassy. His return to the world of work and urban society goes badly. He falls out with a punctilious legate, becomes involved in another impossible relationship, this time with an aristocratic woman, and then makes a social faux pas. Unable to stand the fact he has lost face to the legate, he resigns from his post, drifts for a while, and then returns to Lotte and Albert, who are now married. The crisis comes quickly. Albert bans Werther from visiting Lotte, but Werther visits her anyway, and after reading to her from his translations of Ossian, they touch and he kisses her. The grisly ending is closely modelled on Kestner's report of Jerusalem's death in his letter to Goethe of 2 November 1772. Werther asks to borrow Albert's pistols for a journey, and then shoots himself messily, with a copy of Lessing's *Emilia Galotti* open on his desk. The novel's final sentence, reporting that a priest did not accompany Werther's coffin to the grave, is copied verbatim from Kestner's letter.

Goethe seems to have written no preparatory plans or notes, and only one short passage of the original manuscript material has survived, probably dating from the four weeks it took him to write the novel. In light of this lack of preparation and the rapid composition of the novel, the account Goethe gave later in *Poetry and Truth*—that he wrote the novel 'more or less unconsciously, like a sleepwalker'[145]—seems plausible, even if the notion of unconscious creativity served his ideological purposes in the autobiography. With hindsight there are signs that the novel was gestating as early as autumn 1772, in particular Goethe's request to Kestner for a detailed account of Jerusalem's last days. Around the same time he heard from Jerusalem's friend Christian Albrecht von Kielmannsegg that Jerusalem's health had been undermined by his 'anxious striving for truth and moral goodness'. Goethe reported Kielmansegg's view in a letter to Sophie von la Roche: Jerusalem had 'a noble heart and a penetrating mind', and a character of this kind might easily succumb to suicide.[146] Most importantly, the philosophical themes which, combined with the novel's explosive style, provide much of its tension and richness were not sudden inventions. Two sets of ideas are prominent in the novel. One is our necessary but destructive quest for authenticity, the urge to break out of the prison of convention we have built for ourselves. In modern urban societies humans are locked into a poisonous competition for social and sexual prestige. What we call culture, and especially our tendency to learn from books rather than our own experience, has imprisoned, not liberated us. The novel's hero Werther seeks to undo an education that has gone wrong and has overstimulated his imagination. It is a version of the process described in *Émile*, where the purpose of education was to prevent the child's imagination becoming dangerously prevalent. Much of Werther's argument is with himself. The product of a bookish world, he professes to dislike almost all books. In *Émile* Rousseau bans all books except one, Defoe's *Robinson Crusoe*, a story set in a world without modern books, telling of a versatile, self-reliant, practical, much-travelled hero. In the first half of Goethe's novel Werther claims that there is only one book that his sensibility can tolerate and that can pacify his overactive imagination—Homer's *Odyssey*. The *Odyssey* is set in the patriarchal, preliterate world. Odysseus is versatile, self-reliant, practical, much travelled. Like much else in the novel, Werther's choice of the *Odyssey* as his only reading recalls a Rousseauian idea.

The novel's second main theme concerns religion. For Werther, as for Faust, one route to authenticity leads via God-nature, more specifically our feeling that we are part of the natural world. However, it is a route fraught with psychological peril. We can expect too much of God-nature; we are liable to expect something in return for worshipping its divinity. However, we need to heed Spinoza's warning: 'He who loves God cannot strive that God should love him in return'.[147] A passionate love of God-nature is liable to lead to disappointment when God-nature fails to return our love. In Spinoza's world and Goethe's, God-nature works only according to natural laws and therefore cannot return the love of an individual human. The iron laws of nature admit of no exceptions for individuals. In Werther's case the resulting disappointment leads to a martyr complex. The novel's title advertises this theme, as would have been apparent to Goethe's German readers. *Die Leiden des jungen Werthers* is usually translated as *The Sorrows of Young Werther*, but *Leiden* is also the word used for the passion of Christ ('die Leiden Christi'). The title's allusion to the New Testament passion becomes a reality at the end of the novel when Werther, descending into madness, applies the words of Christ's passion to himself: 'My God, my God why hast thou forsaken me?' (Matthew 27:46),[148] 'I go ahead to my father' (John 14:28),[149] 'I take up the cold and fearful cup' (Matthew 26:42, John 18:11).[150] Allusions to Christ's passion become frequent in the final pages of the novel. They convey Werther's sense that he has become a martyr to the world. Not only has the world ignored his love, it has spurned and humiliated him. His rejection by Lotte and his social mortifications, whether they were other people's fault or his own, only compound his sense of martyrdom. His suicide is a twisted, insane parody of Christ's death on the cross.

The novel appeared in time for the 1774 Michaelmas book fair. It was published by the fashionable Leipzig publisher Johann Friedrich Weygand, who had a reputation for encouraging up-and-coming authors, though in fact he was as ruthless and cynical as the worst of the Leipzig publishing cartel.[151] Its impact was explosive and controversial. Goethe's portrayal of Werther and his world draws on fashionable models: Goldsmith's *Vicar of Wakefield* and Rousseau's *Julie, Or the New Héloïse*. However, the sensibility Werther shares with those novels is taken to a monstrous extreme. He is a 'colossal' mixture of the positive and negative, as Goethe advocated in his Shakespeare oration. Many contemporary readers failed to recognise the ambivalence, which led to somewhat partisan readings—either for or against the novel's hero. A further difficulty was how to understand the novel's social meaning. Werther abandons the standard path to self-realization of the German educated classes, which led from university to employment in a branch of the state (administration, university, church) or a profession (law, medicine), and the cultural life of the towns and cities. Indeed, contrary to a widespread view of the novel since World War II,[152] Werther does not represent the burgher culture of his time, and certainly not 'the bourgeoisie', a concept that is alien to German social reality of the 1770s.[153] Soon after moving away, he encounters a young graduate, whom he describes in a gently patronizing way:

> When he heard that I do a lot of sketching and know Greek (two great wonders hereabouts), he addressed himself to me and raked up a whole load of learning, from Batteux to Wood, from de Piles to Winckelmann, and informed me that he had read Sulzer's *Theory* (the first part) and that he owned a manuscript by Heyne on the subject of Antiquity. I let him be.[154]

The list is a sample of what a German student in the 1770s might read, including Goethe's favourites Batteux and Winckelmann. Heyne had been the main reason Goethe wanted to study at Göttingen. Werther's alternative is to seek a more authentic self-realization in the rural small towns and villages, and away from the urban culture of the universities. Parts of his quest for authenticity read like a recreation of Rousseau's world. As the destination of his country walks, Werther chooses a hamlet, Wahlheim, nestled in the foothills of the mountains, as was the village where Rousseau's Julie and St Preux lived. In Wahlheim Werther builds himself a primitive wooden shelter, which is a nod towards the hut society described in Rousseau's *Discourse on Inequality*[155] and in Goethe's Prometheus fragment. Like Rousseau, Werther believes that unspoilt human goodness can still be found in children and the common folk. Lotte is another example of innocence and authenticity, just as Gretchen was for Faust. Werther portrays her as capable of escaping all the worry and rumination that accompanies modern social life and of living entirely in the moment, in a way that Werther himself finds impossible:

> Oh you should see her dancing! She is in it heart and soul, utterly, her whole body in harmony, so without care or inhibition, as though dancing was all there is and as though she had no other thought or feeling—and it is certain that in those moments all else vanishes from her view.[156]

FIG. 6. Werther, Lotte, and her siblings, by D. Chodowiecki (1776)

The quest for authenticity is also evident in the form and linguistic texture of the novel. The first edition uses elements of regional dialect, a nonstandard, archaic orthography, and spoken idioms—inversions, ellipses, unfinished clauses, repetitions, and exclamations. Werther's German is an act of resistance against the modernizing trend towards stylistic clarity and linguistic standardization. The novel's epistolary form is another nod towards Rousseau's *Julie*, but also to the wider tradition of eighteenth-century novels of Sensibility beginning with Samuel Richardson's *Pamela* (1740). The novel in letters enacts authenticity and emotional directness. As Richardson put it, the letters in an epistolary novel are to be imagined as being 'written while the hearts of the writers must be supposed to be wholly engaged in their subjects'.[157]

Like Jerusalem, Werther is a philosopher, though one imagines him rejecting the label, as Goethe did. His philosophy is an extreme form of Sensibility, combining elements from Rousseau, Hume, and what Goethe knew of Jerusalem's own writings. Kielmannsegg had told Kestner that Jerusalem's philosophy was controversial and 'divergent' from standard views.[158] Goethe probably already knew this when he asked Kestner for detailed information about Jerusalem's philosophy in autumn 1772. According to Kestner, a manuscript draft of an essay 'On Freedom' was on Jerusalem's desk when he committed suicide. The tenor of Jerusalem's philosophy became clearer two years after Goethe's novel appeared when Lessing published a collection of Jerusalem's philosophical essays. This revealed for the first time the full extent of Jerusalem's unorthodoxy and the similarity of his ideas to Werther's. For instance, the collection published by Lessing included an essay 'On the Nature and Origin of General and Abstract Concepts', which concludes with the Humean thought that abstractions are meaningless.[159] In the same vein, Werther says that abstractions are 'miserable'.[160] Entities are distinguished from one another not by differences in kind, Werther argues, but by differences in degree. Since this is so, then our moral judgements cannot provide categorical certainty: there can be no clear line between good and evil. A much more reliable yardstick than reason is our innate moral sense, which possesses real immediacy and force. Indeed, our feelings outweigh our reason, so that one might even agree with Hume that 'reason is, and ought only to be the slave of the passions, and can never pretend to any other office than to serve and obey them'.[161] Goethe had made the same point in some drafts of an unfinished epistolary novel he worked on around the spring of 1770: 'better bad through feeling than good through reason'.[162]

At no point in the novel is any explicit mention made of philosophers, but then that is also the point because Werther's arguments do away with the need for philosophy as it was commonly understood by Goethe's contemporaries: the philosophy of the immortal soul, moral reasoning, the good life—all the safe and wholesome doctrines of Wolffianism. In Werther's view, all a person really needs is selfless compassion and practical common sense. However, proper selflessness means renouncing the idea that God-nature should return our love. And in order to understand fully why that renunciation is necessary, we would need to follow Spinoza's argument against final causes in nature, set out in the appendix to Part I of the *Ethics*. It would become a core belief of Goethe's to which he returned repeatedly in later life, especially once he began to study science. Spinoza explains why we so often fail to understand the true character of God-nature. Humans make the mistake of thinking that the causes of things are akin to human purposes, as if God-nature were a superhuman intelligence who planned the universe for our sake:

> Men commonly suppose that all natural things act, as men do, on account of an end; indeed, they maintain as certain that God directs all things to some certain end, for they say that God has made all things for man, and man that he might worship God.[163]

This is not an occasional or minor mistake. It is almost universal, and its effects are profound. Virtually all human thought is vitiated by it. The structure of our understanding of the universe depends on it. Knowing this, we can now understand why the desire that God-nature should return our love comes so naturally to us, despite seeming strange when considered in the light of reason. Our imagination presents us with a false picture of a world that operates according to human purposes, and so it is entirely natural for us to expect the world to behave as we would or as we would want it to. For Werther this poses a special danger. He wants to find an authentic way of living, and this requires him to construct an ideal of authenticity which he can then pursue *in the world*. But the ideal of authenticity is his ideal, which he has imposed on the world. The result is solipsism. The further he goes in his quest for authenticity, the more his world comes to resemble himself, and the less he is able to escape his own imagination, until of course a crisis occurs.

One of the difficulties readers have with the novel is that it constantly reminds them, with indications that are sometimes obvious and sometimes very subtle, of the gap between how the world is and how Werther imagines it. Just as the epistolary structure and the linguistic texture of the novel are designed in accordance with Werther's quest for authenticity, so too they show signs of his solipsism. The novel is quite different from any earlier epistolary novel. The correspondence is entirely one sided. Until the last few pages, when the editor narrates Werther's final days, the reader sees nothing but Werther's letters and the occasional footnote added by the editor. We see none of his correspondent Wilhelm's letters. Werther's sensibility becomes an echo chamber. There is no other voice that can correct his errors. For many readers this represented a liberation of the self from the chains of convention, but the novel's one-sidedness soon creates doubts. Werther feels that Lotte loves him, but does she really? And if she does not, does it matter, so long as the feeling of being loved makes Werther happy? As he puts it to Wilhelm, 'Are they phantoms, if they make us happy?'[164] Werther's immoderate and uncontrolled sensibility— 'better bad through feeling than good through reason'—becomes a problem.

A more subtle sign of these problems is the village of Wahlheim. The name is in fact a pseudonym invented by the narrator. (The novel is full of these reality effects, which tease the reader by pretending that real people, places and events are hidden under a cloak of fiction.) Wahlheim means 'home of choice', as if the village were the place Werther had chosen to settle. In fact, and contrary to a stubborn myth about the novel, he does not live there at all. There is good reason to suppose he does not spend even one night there.[165] In fact,

Wahlheim is the destination for his walks from the town and a stopping off point en route to Lotte's family in their hunting lodge. His recreation of Rousseauian hut society in Wahlheim is a performance. He actually lives in a nearby town. He is an urbanite who uses the countryside for his own pleasure and to project a self-image. Worse still, and in an ominous irony, Wahlheim prefigures his grisly suicide. As he sits at the inn at Wahlheim cooking peas and reading Homer, he imagines himself as one of the suitors of Homer's Penelope, feasting on Odysseus's oxen while the hero labours to return from Troy.[166] Werther fails to mention—and the reader should assume he has failed to notice—the rather obvious parallel between the situation in the *Odyssey* and his own triangular relationship with Lotte and Albert. If Werther is the suitors, then Lotte is Penelope and Albert is Odysseus. Any reader would know that the suitors are arrogant and selfish. An attentive reader will also notice that Werther's daydream points to the climax of the *Odyssey*, when Odysseus returns to Ithaca and brutally slaughters the suitors—a grim prefiguration of Werther's fate.

Werther's first crisis is reported in his letter of 18 August, just a week after a long conversation with Albert about suicide. The letter describes in direct and powerful terms Werther's plunging from ecstasy into terror. It begins with a despairing question: 'Does it have to be the case that what made a person's felicity will become the source of his wretchedness?'[167] The 'what' is his relationship to God-nature: 'The full and warm feeling of my heart for living Nature', which has now become 'my unbearable tormentor, a spirit of torture pursuing me wherever I go'. A long paragraph now repeats the hymnic praise of nature in winding, cascading sentences which are such a feature of the early part of the novel. It is obvious though that a gap has begun to open between Werther's imagination and God-nature. A brief paragraph in the middle of the letter signals the distance: that was then, and this is now. There follows another long rhapsodic paragraph, but this time the mood is one of horror:

> It is as though a curtain has been drawn back from before my soul and the scene of unending life transforms itself in front of me into the abyss of the ever open grave. How can anyone say: this *is*—since everything passes, everything rolls by with the speed of lightning, so rarely does a life run the whole course its energies are for but is rapt away with the torrent, sunk and smashed to pieces on the rocks? Every moment eats at you and at those around you whom you love, every moment you are a destroyer and are bound to be. Your most innocent stroll costs a thousand tiny creatures their lives, one footstep shatters the laborious buildings of the ants and stamps

a little world into a vile grave. Oh, it is not the great and rare disasters of the world that touch me, not the floods that wash away your villages nor the earthquakes that swallow up your cities. What undermines my heart is the devouring force which lies hidden in the universe of nature and which creates nothing that does not destroy its neighbour and itself. And so I reel in fear, the energies of heaven and earth weaving around me. And all I see is an eternally devouring, eternally regurgitating monster.[168]

The sheer terror of this passage has virtually no precedent in eighteenth-century literature, not even in the darker moments of the Gothic. The philosophical structure of Werther's experience derives from Spinoza's warnings about loving God-nature too passionately. By filling God-nature with human purposes, we have become unable to see that God-nature works only according to its own iron laws. Therefore we should not expect God-nature to repay our love; our worship should be a selfless 'intellectual love of God' ('amor dei intellectualis'). The psychology is similar to Prometheus's switch from boyhood piety to adult rage. Enthusiasm is liable to flip over into disappointment, worship into terror, and the higher the former, the deeper the latter. Just as the symmetry of the two states is close, so the shift from one to the other is shockingly sudden. An illusion is destroyed by the rapid drawing of a curtain, just as when it suddenly dawns on a person that their relationship with God is not just bothered by nagging doubts—faith has been altogether and irrevocably lost.

The novel was (and remains) a challenge for readers because Werther's quest for authenticity is so closely bound up with his melancholia. Werther's philosophy is designed to cure his melancholia, but may also be a product of it. Goethe intended that these dilemmas would exercise and challenge the reader's capacity for sympathy. Werther has great allure, but his treatment of Lotte and her marriage is negligent at best and cruel at worst. The novel pulls us in different directions. It reads like an authentic document whilst pushing the limits of what counts as appropriate in the eighteenth-century novel—appropriate in morality, religion, literary form, linguistic expression. Its position on suicide is ambivalent. In their debate reported in the letter of 12 August, Albert argues that suicide is a form of moral weakness, whereas Werther defends the view that suicide is the symptom of an illness and therefore beyond moral censure. A review in the Hamburg paper the *Reichspostreuter* on 11 November 1774 listed a number of features of the novel that would become commonplaces of its contemporary reception. It was based on a true story. It is full of powerful emotions that speak to young readers in particular. It excuses Werther's suicide 'in every way', but the arguments are specious in ways that its young readers may not grasp. 'We wish therefore that it had never been written [...]. We tremble to think of the consequences that could ensue from it for many, and it would be reasonable that this kind of book should be banned by every state that is concerned above all with the preservation of its citizens'.[169] The next year reports began of copycat suicides, or what has become known as the 'Werther effect'. The reports and their connection to Goethe's novel are anecdotal but not implausible. A pattern of imitative behaviour emerges. For instance, during Goethe's lifetime there were eleven reports of suicides where a copy of Goethe's novel was found in the pocket of the victim or on their desk or under their pillow.[170]

The reception of *Werther* had a profound effect on Goethe's literary and intellectual career. In the year and a half after the novel's composition—from the spring of 1774 to the autumn of 1775—his writing was subject to two contradictory impulses. He knew he could speak to an audience hungry for Sensibility, and yet he felt uneasy about the new literary market that he was helping to create, for at some level he believed his readers did not understand him—nor even *want* to understand him. In his best works of the period—*Werther* and the sentimental drama *Stella*—he concealed a more sceptical meaning under layers of irony. Some of his other work was simply lightweight—full of sentiment but either contrived or lacking depth and complexity, seemingly written only in order to leverage his success.

Werther ends with a verbatim quotation from Kestner's report on Jerusalem's death in November 1772: as Werther's body was carried to the grave, 'no priest attended'.[171] Goethe's distaste for Christianity's moral purism remained strong. In his reply to Kestner, he went so far as to blame Jerusalem's father, a moderate Lutheran pastor and theologian:

> Unhappy Jerusalem [...] Unhappy man. But the devils, those shameful people who enjoy nothing but the chaff of vanity and have idolatrous lust in their hearts and preach idol-worship and inhibit nature in its goodness and overstretch and ruin our powers, they are to blame for this misfortune, for our misfortune. May the devil their brother take them all. If the accursed priest his father is not to blame, then God have mercy on me for wishing he should break his neck like Eli.[172]

The charge was grossly unfair but contained a small grain of truth. Part of what creates the suffering of people like Jerusalem is a twisted system of morality that puts more emphasis on sinfulness than on sympathy and understanding. The same argument appears in a review Goethe coauthored for the *Frankfurt Scholarly Notices*, which concluded that 'excessively strict religious morality pursued beyond the bounds' was to blame for turning people into enemies of religion:

> Thousands have become such privately and publicly for this very reason, thousands who would have loved Christ as their friend, if he had been portrayed as a friend and not as a splenetic tyrant ready to let fly with thunderbolts wherever there is not the highest perfection. We must say it outright for it has long troubled our hearts: Voltaire, Hume, la Mettrie, Helvetius, Rousseau, and their whole school have not done morality and religion nearly so much damage as the strict, sickly Pascal and his school.[173]

In May 1775 Goethe wrote to Herder in even blunter terms about the appalling moral rigorism of Christianity and his own preference for a Rousseauian morality of sympathy:

> If only the whole doctrine of Christ were not such a load of shit which makes me, as a human being, as a limited, needy thing, makes me furious, then [Christ] would be dear to me. Even as God or the Devil portrayed in this way is dear to me, for he is my brother.[174]

Bodmer reported Lavater's conclusion that Goethe was 'the warmest friend and most dangerous foe of religion and virtue'.[175]

The guardians of morality in the Lutheran and Catholic faculties of theology and censorship offices reacted to *Werther* predictably, if a little slowly. The novel was banned in Electoral Saxony in 1775 and in Denmark and Austria in 1776. The verdict drawn up by the Leipzig theologians for the Saxon commission of books was written by Goethe's old teacher Professor Ernesti.[176] Lotte and Kestner were dismayed by the novel. It was not just that Goethe had borrowed so freely from Kestner's report on Jerusalem's circumstances, including the detail of the loan of the pistols. Jerusalem had shot himself with a pistol borrowed from Kestner—by having Werther kill himself with Albert's pistol, Goethe clearly identified Albert with Kestner and cruelly reminded Kestner of his own small part in Jerusalem's suicide. Worse was that friends might identify the fictional Lotte with Lotte Kestner and infer that Lotte and Kestner's marriage was unhappy. Exactly what Goethe thought about these sensitive matters is not known.

For a while he defended the novel. Lavater reported a conversation in which Goethe argued that, far from condoning suicide, the novel explained what causes it and what follows from it in much more vivid ways than any moral teaching can.[177] In March 1775 he wrote to Auguste von Stolberg that he was 'fed up with the digging up and dissecting' of his 'poor Werther'.[178] Soon he gave up talking about the novel. In December 1774 he wrote to Sophie von La Roche, who as a fellow novelist might be expected to understand his predicament:

> Today I got back a copy of *Werther* that I had leant out and had been passed around from hand to hand, and see, at the front on the blank page is written: Tais Toi Jean Jaques [*sic*] ils ne te comprendront point! [Keep quiet, Jean-Jacques, they won't understand you at all]—That had the strangest effect on me because this passage in *Émile* was always remarkable to me.[179]

Goethe did not turn his back on his new readership, but he became still more nuanced, more ambivalent in his portrayal of Sensibility and the quest for authenticity. The *Sturm und Drang* movement, which he had initiated with *Götz* in 1773, was over almost as soon as it began—for Goethe at least, if not for the 'Goetheans' around him.

In June 1774 Lavater visited Frankfurt, followed in July by the educator and Rationalist theologian Johann Bernhard Basedow. It was agreed that Goethe would accompany Lavater on a river trip down the Rhine. In the middle of July they sailed to Bad Ems on the Lahn, and then further down the Rhine to Neuwied, parting company at Cologne. Goethe proceeded to Düsseldorf, where he made another new friend, the philosopher Fritz Jacobi, son of a wealthy sugar merchant and younger brother of the poet Johann Georg Jacobi. During these early days of their friendship Fritz Jacobi and Goethe debated Spinoza's philosophy. In *Poetry and Truth* Goethe devotes a long passage to explaining the two great merits he found in Spinoza: the 'peaceful effect' of Spinoza's dispassionate method on his excitable mind,[180] and the metaphysical naturalism which held that 'nature works by eternal, necessary laws that are so divine that the divinity itself could not change anything in them'.[181] On the same journey Goethe told Lavater that this man whom Christians had showered with obloquy was in fact a saint. Lavater recorded a fragment of the conversation:

> [Goethe] maintains nobody has expressed himself concerning the divinity as closely to the Saviour as [Spinoza]. Moreover, all of the recent deists have simply plundered him. He was an extremely just, honest, poor man. *Homo temperatissimus* [the most moderate of men]. [...] He denied the prophecies

and was a prophet himself. [...] His correspondence is the most interesting book one can read concerning honesty [and] philanthropy.[182]

Goethe reached home in the middle of August after a month of travels. He now began to receive visits at the Three Lyres from literary notables, including the poets Klopstock and Heinrich Christian Boie. In the middle of December a party of nobles passed through Frankfurt on their way to Paris. They were from the small Duchy of Sachsen-Weimar-Eisenach in Thuringia—the Duke Carl August himself, not yet eighteen, with his governor Count von Görtz, his younger brother's tutor Major von Knebel, the chief equerry Freiherr von Stein, and the ducal physician. Goethe was invited to breakfast with the party, and the meeting was such a success that he accompanied them on the next leg of their journey as far as Mainz. The subjects of discussion included Möser's *Patriotic Fantasies* and, somewhat awkwardly for Goethe, a savage skit he had written, *Gods, Heroes and Wieland*, against Wieland's reworking of Euripides's *Alcestis*. Wieland had been working as Carl August's tutor since 1772. Evidently Goethe was able to make good some of the damage, for he entered into a friendly correspondence with Knebel.

He reacted to finishing *Werther* by immediately throwing himself into another project, *Clavigo*, a conventional five-act prose tragedy. He wrote it in the space of a week in May 1774, soon after sending the fair copy of *Werther* to Weygand. *Clavigo. A Tragedy by Göthe* was published by Weygand in autumn 1774, the first work to carry his name. The play is based on an autobiographical anecdote by Beaumarchais. The Spanish royal archivist Clavico, a writer and social climber, had twice annulled his engagement to Beaumarchais's sister. Beaumarchais travelled to Spain to confront Clavico and force him to make a written confession of his actions. In dramatizing this confrontation Goethe translated some passages directly from Beaumarchais, which no doubt expedited the writing of the play. In Act V, however, Goethe departed from his model, first by having Beaumarchais's sister Marie die of a broken heart when she finds Clavigo has abandoned her for a second time, and then in a final coup de grace having Beaumarchais kill Clavigo in a scuffle on the street. The play was relatively successful, on the page and stage. Numerous productions were put on across Germany in the next few years. The play went through several official editions and was reprinted by the pirate publisher Himburg.

However, it was utterly different from *Götz* and *Werther*. In September 1773 Goethe had written to Kestner that he was working on 'a drama for performance' which would show people that he could 'follow rules and represent morality

[and] sensibility'.[183] The play in question was probably not *Clavigo*, but *Clavigo* does conform exactly to this plan. In the conventional five-act format, with the action spanning no more than a few days, and the setting in (mainly) domestic spaces in the city of Madrid, it is self-contained, with a small cast of characters of similar social status, and little in the way of a backstory to be expounded in Act I. Clavigo has abandoned Beaumarchais's sister Marie, not without remorse, in favour of continuing his social ascent at court, with the support of his crudely drawn, Machiavellian sidekick Carlos. Summoned from France to avenge Marie's lost honour, Beaumarchais confronts Clavigo at his home and demands that Clavigo issue a public declaration of his betrayal of Marie and her good character. The meeting ends in a compromise: Clavigo will write the declaration, but Beaumarchais will not publish it until Clavigo has had a chance to woo Marie again, which he does successfully. Carlos, however, persuades the weak and pliable Clavigo that marriage to Marie would be a poor match compared to his elevated prospects if he were to continue his social climbing without her. This argument appealing to *amour-propre* persuades Clavigo rather too easily. Carlos now engineers Clavigo's escape, by claiming that the declaration was forced on him at gunpoint. When the news reaches Marie, she faints and dies. (Some contemporaries, Wieland among them, found this implausible.)[184] As Clavigo happens to be passing Marie's home one night, he encounters her coffin and becomes involved in a scuffle with Beaumarchais, who stabs him. The play ends with a reconciliation between Beaumarchais and the mortally wounded Clavigo.

Clavigo was Goethe's only attempt at a 'bourgeois tragedy' in the tradition of Lillo, Diderot, and Lessing—or at least the only one that remains strictly within that world. The purely domestic plot, without any tyrannical nobles or scheming politicians, means that the play has little political interest. Its social interest is also modest, for we do not actually see Clavigo in action as a social climber. In *Poetry and Truth* Goethe claimed that Clavigo's betrayal of Marie was one of the forms, along with Weislingen in *Götz*, through which he processed his guilt concerning Friederike Brion.[185] The affinity to Weislingen also appears in a letter to Schönborn of June 1774: 'My hero [is] an uncertain, half great half little person, a pendant to Weislingen in *Götz*, or rather Weislingen himself in the full roundness of a protagonist'.[186] The play lacks the psychological depth of *Götz*, chiefly because Clavigo's social ascent is motivated extraneously by the villainous sidekick Carlos, which detracts from the 'full roundness' of Clavigo. Carlos also makes the plot disappointingly thin. He is the major force behind Clavigo's reverting to type, and yet for all his big talk of decisiveness, Carlos is only a cheerleader, not an agent of deeds, nor is his motivation for influencing Clavigo at all clear—he has no skin in the game. The betrayal of Marie thus becomes oddly mechanical. *Clavigo* belongs to a series of projects through which Goethe hoped to repeat the success of *Werther* in the theatre—projects that largely failed. Merck reacted to Clavigo by scolding Goethe for reverting to convention and betraying his mission as Germany's meteoric new genius: 'As far as I'm concerned you should never write such rubbish again; the others can do that'.[187]

When Goethe returned to longer literary projects in the winter of 1774/75, he worked on a series of plays that touch on the Rousseauian themes of *Götz* and *Werther*, but without the intensity and conviction of his two great successes. *Hanswurst's Wedding, or The Way of the World* was planned as a carnivalesque farce in the manner of Hans Sachs, only more obscene. All that survives of it is a fragment of around two hundred and fifty lines of monologue and dialogue and a list of two hundred mostly sexual or scatological names for characters. In an opening monologue Hanswurst's guardian reports that he has been charged with educating Hanswurst in social decorum, but has only succeeded in overlaying his animalistic urges with a veneer of learning. Under the veneer of respectability humans are unfit for society. In November 1773 he had begun *Erwin and Elmire*, a slight prose play containing songs—a genre Wieland had christened the 'singing play' (*Singspiel*). He picked up the threads again in February 1775, perhaps thinking it might provide an easy hit with his new audience. Two young lovers Erwin and Elmire, driven apart by the gap between nature and civilization, are reconciled by Elmire's old Spanish tutor Bernardo. He has Erwin act the role of a hermit in a long white beard and under a vow of silence. Elmire confesses her true feelings to the hermit (Erwin), while he stands mutely listening to her in the knowledge that she must be telling the truth. For love to flourish, the ill effects of civilization must be neutralized. *Claudine of Villa Bella*, another *Singspiel*, was probably written between summer 1774 and spring 1775. The play is in the Spanish cloak-and-dagger style and portrays a sentimental young woman who, like Elmire, has fallen from nature into artifice. The two main male characters are competing brothers, the loyal Pedro, who loves Claudine, and Crugantino, who had fallen into a life of libertinage and vagabondage, but is now disaffected with his freedom and has returned home in secrecy. Claudine's envious cousins hatch a plan to upset her and Pedro. The plan involves the dangerous Crugantino wooing Claudine, possibly leading her into libertinage and destroying Pedro's hopes. During some trivial cloak-and-dagger action Pedro is wounded by Crugantino, but then the brothers are reunited in defence of Claudine. Nobility of spirit wins out over the complications of social class, pride, and so on. There is some talk about nature and freedom, but it is inconsequential. Even if Crugantino's vagabondage was intended as an authentic alternative to the ills of civilization,[188] the play treats it as a phase that Crugantino has put behind him.

Stella is an altogether more substantial and controversial work. It was probably written in a few weeks in February and March 1775. Goethe managed to sell the play, sight unseen, to the publisher Mylius, who grudgingly accepted what he knew would be a financial loss as the price for having 'this rare genius and productive writer' in his stable.[189] Inevitably the play was soon pirated. It was performed in Hamburg and Berlin, but there was little prospect of success on the stage, because the play's denouement was so outrageous. The plot is relatively simple, though it has a lengthy backstory. Some fifteen years before the action, Cezilie and Fernando married and had a daughter, Luzie. Soon Fernando abandoned them and embarked on years of vagabondage, including service in France's suppression of the Corsican rebellion in 1768–1769. Fernando now regrets having intervened on the French side against what he terms the 'freedom' of the 'noble' Corsican rebels.[190] Returning to Germany, Fernando fell in love with the wealthy orphan Stella, without admitting he was already married. Stella renounced her money, land, family, and friends[191] to elope with him, and they set up home together, with the wealth he gained on his adventures. A child was born but died, and then Fernando suddenly left Stella. This was three years prior to the action of the play. The vacuum of his departure was filled by largely accurate local gossip: he was an atheist; he had seduced and eloped with Stella; they were not married.

The play begins with the impoverished Cezilie and Luzie arriving at an inn next to Stella's estate, where Luzie has been appointed as Stella's companion. The three women bond amid effusive sentimental talk, which is thrown into disarray as Fernando has coincidentally arrived at the inn, evidently hoping to resume his relationship with Stella.[192] Luzie has bumped into him at the inn and now points out to Stella the man's resemblance to a portrait of Fernando that Stella keeps in a shrine.[193] Cezilie also recognises the picture and makes plans for Luzie and herself to leave immediately.[194] Fernando and Stella are reunited, which he describes as a religious experience: 'these moments of ecstasy in your arms, they make me good again, pious again—I can pray, Stella; because I'm happy'.[195] He seems to be one of those sentimental souls like Werther who have no formal religion but have retained religious language as a way of talking about love. Stella learns that the two women are leaving and sends Fernando to persuade them to stay.[196] In a second recognition scene, Cezilie tells Fernando with obvious irony that men are to be pitied for having to live in a woman's world and should therefore not be blamed for inconstancy.[197] Fernando now pledges himself to Cezilie, but his claim that he had in fact been looking for Cezilie and Luzie is a patent lie, as Cezilie realizes. In reply to his 'Nothing, nothing in the world will separate me from you! I've found you again', she retorts: 'Found what you weren't looking for'.[198] Fernando makes a plan for the three of them to escape, about which Cezilie is sceptical. Once he is alone Fernando realizes his situation is utterly impossible and considers suicide.[199] Fernando lies to Stella: Cezilie and Luzie want to leave but will not give a reason, he says.[200] The serving girl from the inn now appears and asks Fernando why he has not come, having ordered a carriage for three, but Fernando tries to dismiss her as 'a child'.[201] The social politics of the play are indeed subtly revealed in the way the upper class and burgher characters, including the manageress of the inn, consistently and with no good reason treat the serving classes as contemptible, stupid, and lazy.[202] Finally Fernando plucks up the courage to tell Stella he is leaving her and that Cezilie is his wife. In the ensuing distress and confusion, Stella decides to leave home and travel.[203] Cezilie and Fernando argue about the proper course of action. Fernando's answer is that Stella should be abandoned and sent to a convent. To break the impasse, Cezilie tells him a strange old story of a certain Count von Gleichen, which ends happily in a ménage à trois involving the Count, his wife and a young woman who had once rescued him from his captors. The arrangement is even approved by the Pope, it seems.[204] The play ends with Stella and Fernando seemingly accepting the logic of Cezilie's story. The trio embrace; both women pledge their love for Fernando and he asserts his possession of both of them.[205]

To some readers the ending has seemed so implausible as to represent something other than an actual domestic arrangement—perhaps a sentimental platonic union such as Werther claims he wants with Lotte, where 'all desire falls silent in her presence'.[206] This is hard to credit, since Cezilie's and Stella's prior relationships with Fernando were sexual; both produced offspring. It is hard to see why these relationships would suddenly lose their sexual character. Equally it is hard to see how the ending of the play can be read as unreal in literary terms. Exotic as the Count von Gleichen story is, with its medieval setting and its references to adventure, slavery, and treasure, still nothing in the action of the play suggests a similar departure from eighteenth-century reality. Nor is there any indication that the new ménage would follow the Gleichen story in taking the form of an official marriage—which would be a patently unrealistic idea in late eighteenth-century Germany. The ménage simply reflects what many women in the eighteenth century had to contend with. What Goethe asks us to imagine was by no means fantastical in his day. Many of his readers would have been aware of such relationships, if only by repute. The keeping of mistresses was commonplace among the higher aristocracy and not unknown among the higher burgher ranks. More intriguing than the question of realism is the strange moral psychology of the ménage. It would be easy to write it off as a male author's sexual fantasy. In fact, the play ruthlessly dismantles Fernando's character, and the ménage reaffirms this depiction of him as morally suspect. He is no Count von Gleichen.[207] Indeed, Cezilie's use of the Count von Gleichen story to interest Fernando in the ménage involves flattering Fernando by comparing him with the noble Count, and Fernando's lack of self-knowledge makes him fall for the flattery. The thought of suicide only occurs to him when he sees no way out for himself. It is not prompted by any of his very real misdeeds—his abandonment of Cezilie and Luzie, his participation in the suppression of the noble Corsican revolt, or his deceit of Stella and abandonment of her after the death of their child. His suggestion that Stella should be parked in a convent is particularly obnoxious. He is obviously without merit. With the ménage à trois, Cezilie and Stella offer him a redemption he does not deserve. How then does the arrangement reflect on Cezilie? She dreams up the plan for the ménage à trois, she deploys the story of Count von Gleichen to convince Fernando, and she persuades Stella join them. Her sardonic exculpation of Fernando—she pretends to feel sorry for men, confined as they are in a woman's world—shows she has a clear understanding of how unbalanced the relation between the sexes is. She knows that Fernando thinks Stella can be lightly cast aside and confined to a convent. As for herself, she could of course continue to live without her husband, but she would be condemned not to remarry, and would be depriving her daughter of a father. In other words, Cezilie has all the knowledge and motivation needed to make this extraordinary proposal. In the circumstances, committing herself and Stella to someone as morally fallible as Fernando may simply be the least worst of the available options. The ménage thus demonstrates the moral superiority of women. Cezilie in particular offers Fernando a redemption that he does not merit. Indeed both kinds of female virtue—the active virtue of Cezilie, who makes the best of a bad job at the end, and the passive devotion of Stella, who does little in the play but remain constant to Fernando—surpass whatever virtue Fernando possesses.

FIG. 7. View down into Italy from the Gotthard Pass, by Goethe (1775)

Stella reflects Goethe's growing scepticism about the culture of Sensibility, which is after all what lies behind the play's ending. Sensibility valued love more highly than social conventions such as marriage or monogamy. The play represents a world that has detached itself from normal social relations. Stella is an aristocrat; Fernando is independently wealthy; Cezilie and Luzie are distressed gentlefolk who stay afloat thanks to Stella. None of them practise trades or professions. The action of the play begins in an ordinary inn, which is a typical location for comedy, but it ends in the private and isolated space of Stella's estate. The movement away from civic life enables the lovers to find one another again and to form a new bond that disregards ordinary values. In turn, the ménage à trois will only push Cezilie, Luzie, Stella and Fernando further into social isolation. Although the play avoids directly addressing the social consequences of the ménage, it does subtly indicate what they might be. The high-ups will continue to be a world apart, isolated from the serving classes they despise. However, even with their separation from the world, reality will bite. People have gossiped about Stella and Fernando and will no doubt continue to do so.

This may not matter to Stella, Cezilie, and Fernando, who have no real need of society, but it is likely to matter to Luzie, whose adult life still lies before her.

1775 was a strange and chaotic year. In January Goethe met Anna Elisabeth (Lili) Schönemann, daughter of a rich Frankfurt Calvinist banking family. In April they were betrothed. In the middle of May Goethe decided to accompany the Stolberg brothers on a trip to Switzerland, where he came close to descending from the Gotthard into Italy. He returned to Frankfurt at the end of July. Within the next month or two it became clear to Goethe that he was not going to marry Lili. The obstacle was probably religion: her family's Calvinism and his family's Lutheranism, or his own heterodoxy. In early October Lili's mother publicly and embarrassingly announced that the betrothal was being broken off because of confessional incompatibility. It was at this point that Goethe decided to take up the invitation from the young Duke Carl August of Weimar.[208] Carl August had passed through Frankfurt again on 22 September en route to his wedding to Princess Luise von Hessen-Darmstadt in Karlsruhe, and his party returned through Frankfurt on 12 October. Arrangements were made for Goethe's travel to Weimar, but delays and confusion ensued, and in a panic Goethe briefly toyed with the idea of travelling to Italy instead. In the end Weimar came good.

4

The Intellectual Love of God

WEIMAR, 1775–1786

THE DUCHY of Sachsen-Weimar-Eisenach consisted of several noncontiguous territories that had only recently been unified when Eisenach was joined with Sachsen-Weimar in 1741. The home territory was centred on Weimar and the university town of Jena. Eisenach lay to the west, separated from Weimar by the lands of Erfurt and Gotha, and a smaller region surrounded Neustadt to the southeast. In addition, several tiny satellite territories included the lands around the town of Ilmenau in the upper Ilm valley. The scattered territories had never been wealthy. Their sandy soil was not fertile. Bad turned to worse under Duke Ernst August I. He unified Weimar and Eisenach, but his extravagant soldiering, hunting, and building ruined the Duchy's finances. Rescue came in unexpected circumstances. On Ernst August's death, his son Ernst August II Konstantin was a minor. Out of concern at his ill health, a rapid marriage was arranged to the fifteen-year-old Anna Amalia of Brunswick-Wolfenbüttel, who produced two sons. When Ernst August II died after only three years of rule, Anna Amalia, aged eighteen, began a sixteen-year regency on behalf of their infant son Carl August. It was the strikingly capable Anna Amalia who rescued the Duchy from impoverishment and laid the foundations for its unexpected flourishing as a centre of German culture. Among her successes was to engage Wieland as Carl August's tutor at the age of fourteen.

The town of Weimar was dominated by its *Schloss*—part palace, part fortified castle. There were few other substantial buildings, and certainly no large stock of bourgeois houses like the Three Lyres. The Duchy's population numbered around 120,000; the town's only six thousand. In 1742 the tally of houses in Weimar was reckoned at 729, of which a hundred were courtiers' dwellings. A large proportion of the residents worked directly or indirectly for the Duchy

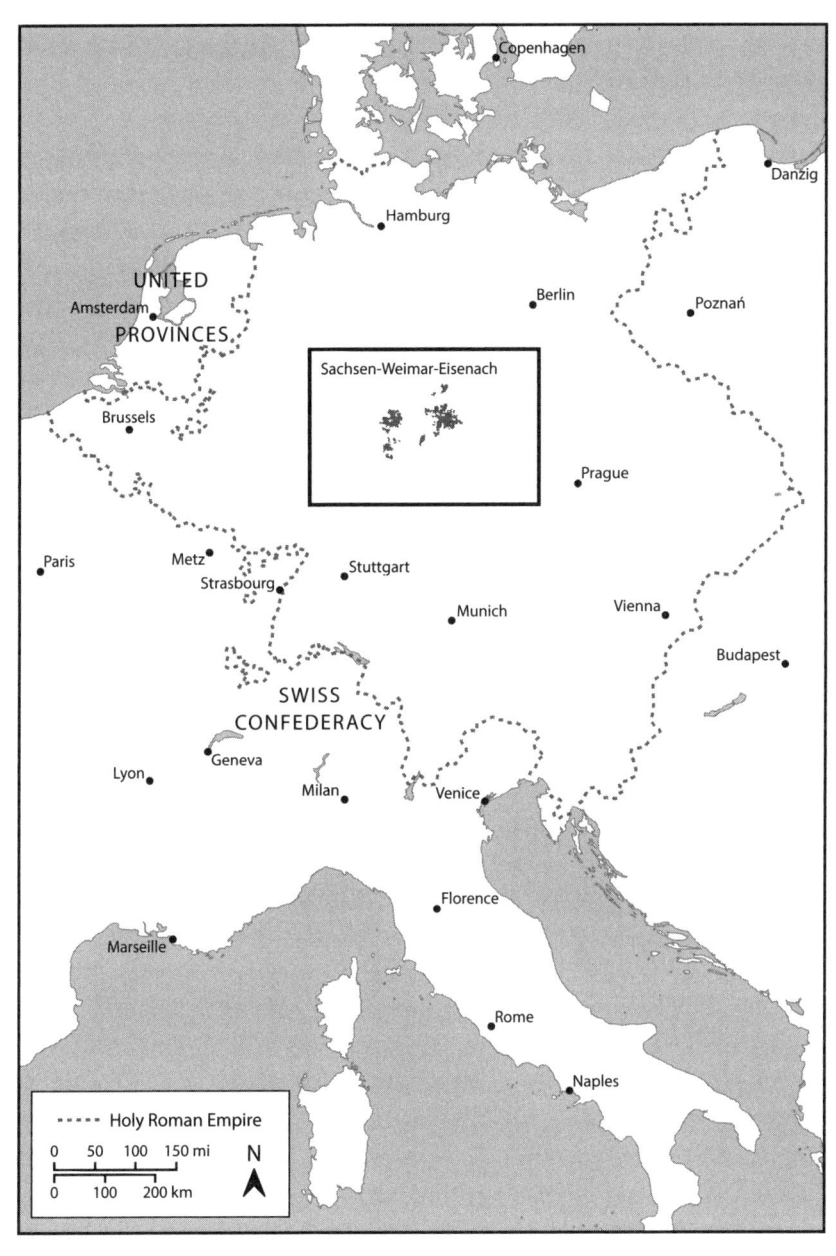

FIG. 8. The Holy Roman Empire of the German Nation
in the eighteenth century

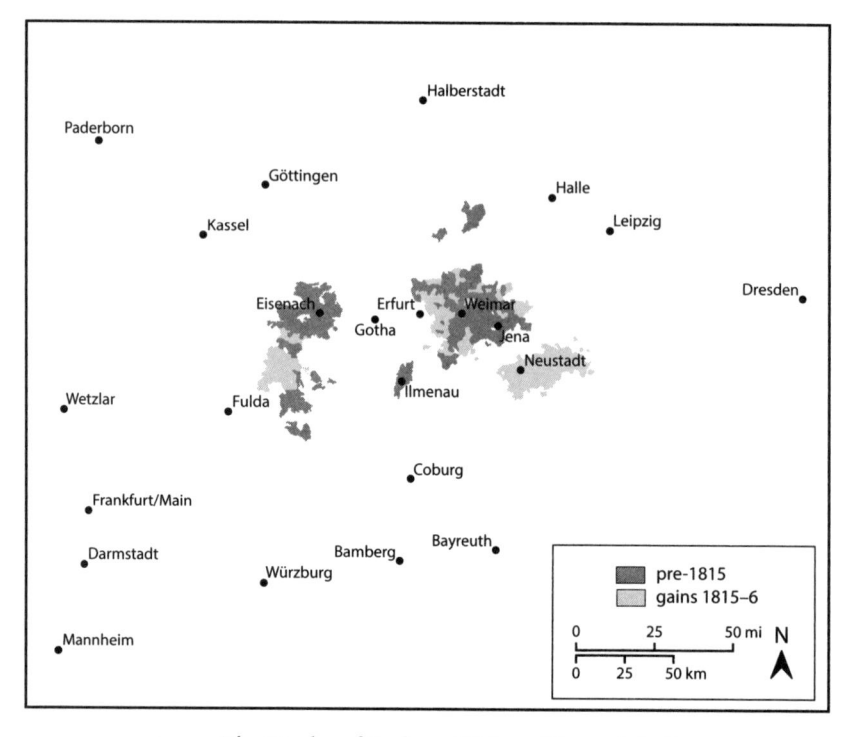

FIG. 9. The Duchy of Sachsen-Weimar-Eisenach before
and after its enlargement and elevation to Grand Duchy in 1816

and the ducal family. There was little other commercial activity and practically no manufacturing, except for a small cottage industry of stocking weavers around the town of Apolda, run by entrepreneurs who supplied the workers with raw materials and paid them on a piecework basis. The economy was almost entirely agrarian. Two thirds of the population were peasants. They were the largely unheard though not altogether silent majority. They made occasional appeals to the authorities to respect their traditional rights, and there were periodic outbreaks of unrest among the stocking weavers over reductions in their pay.[1] The authorities were concerned that these challenges would lead to public disorder, which was every eighteenth-century government's greatest concern. However, the protests generally went nowhere. There was certainly no representative forum to hear the peasants' complaints. The territory was ruled directly by the Duke through his Privy Council and lesser administrators. Even the Privy Council could only advise. It had no power to make decisions unless ordered to do so by the Duke in his absence. There was nothing resembling the oligarchic municipal government of Frankfurt.

Much has been written about Goethe's move to Weimar, and much calculating has been done of its costs and benefits for him, politically, socially, culturally, and intellectually. There has been a tendency to overstate the suddenness of the move and to imply that it was unconsidered and misguided. In fact the idea of entering the service of a prince had been floated in his circle two years before the move. He had his first contact with the Weimar court in October 1774. The charge has been made that in moving from Frankfurt to Weimar Goethe was turning his back on some aspects of modernity: urban culture, representative government, commerce. Yet Frankfurt did not feel very modern to Goethe. For its size, it was not a particularly cultured or educated city. Its social, commercial, and governmental structures were grounded in religious discrimination. And in any case, why should modernity be so important for a student of Rousseau? For all the poverty and scatteredness of its lands, Weimar offered Goethe something that Frankfurt could not. Frankfurt was hobbled by its ancient institutions, its arcane social distinctions, the jockeying for social and political power of its noble or pseudo-noble families, and its religious divisions. These had become deeply entrenched over hundreds of years, showed little sign of changing, and held no attraction for a young man in a hurry. Weimar was a newer creation. Power was more centralized. The population, the vast majority Lutherans, was more cohesive. Although Weimar society was split between the nobility and the rest, it had fewer social stratifications than Frankfurt. It was organized more vertically, with everyone's social and economic existence dependent on the Duke. There was even the promise of a ducal budget for the kind of large-scale cultural projects that were unknown in Frankfurt. Weimar gave him the prospect of getting things done.

It is not clear how long Goethe expected his stay in Weimar to be, but Carl August had a permanent arrangement in mind. In the first place, he needed a companion and mentor. On the Duke's accession, Wieland had retired from his role as tutor. A guiding hand and moderating influence was needed for the still wayward eighteen-year-old Duke. He also had to set the tone for his new court and provide entertainment, especially for his young Duchess and her ladies, a role for which Goethe's creativity and ease in the company of women made him ideally suited. Finally, the Duke needed to make his mark on the administration of the Duchy. Too young for his voice to carry much weight, he needed an older ally who would support him in any conflicts with the established Weimar families. A doctor of law from a wealthy family closely connected to Frankfurt's administration was a plausible, if not a perfect choice. Goethe was young too, and as a bourgeois he could not fully participate in courtly events.

From the outset Goethe was confident in his ability to rise to the demands that would be made of him, as he wrote to Merck in January 1776:

> My situation is promising enough, and the Duchies of Weimar and Eisenach will be a stage on which one can try out whether a role in worldly affairs suits one or not. So I'm in no rush, and freedom and sufficiency will be the chief conditions of my new establishment, even if I'm better positioned than ever to recognise the thorough shittiness of this our secular majesty.[2]

In March he wrote to Lavater: 'I have now fully set sail on the waves of the world, completely resolved: to discover, win, fight, fail, or blow myself and my whole cargo sky high.'[3] His work in Weimar was a challenge that would prove and shape his character. It was also a test of whether a person committed to authenticity could flourish in such a world and could in turn influence it. He immediately set about establishing himself. If Carl August needed Goethe as a mentor and ally, then Goethe secured his own mentor by persuading the Duke to offer Herder the position of General Superintendant of the Duchy's Lutheran church. In March 1776 Goethe's annual salary was agreed, at 1200 thalers, the second highest in the Duke's service. He moved out of his temporary lodgings in the von Kalbs' house and into his own rooms opposite the Yellow Palace. He also acquired a garden and adjoining cottage in a pleasant spot on the edge of town by the Ilm meadows—an indispensable appurtenance for a Rousseauian child of nature. The Duke paid for it.[4] For the next six years Goethe would divide his time between the garden house and town. The purchase of the garden also qualified him for citizenship, which he took up on 26 April and so confirmed his commitment to Weimar. In these early months he also made his mark by becoming close to the Dowager Duchess Anna Amalia, the Duchess Luise and other court women, notably Charlotte von Stein, the wife of the Duke's chief equerry. The relationship got off to a bad start,[5] but soon Goethe was visiting and writing to her frequently. Over 1,700 letters and brief notes from Goethe to Charlotte have survived. Often he would dine with her in the evening. In some respects their relationship was like a marriage. There was gossip and has been much speculation. In fact, having given birth to seven children in the first nine years of marriage, Charlotte felt so physically damaged that she could no longer have sex with her husband,[6] so it would seem unlikely that she did so with Goethe. More important is what Charlotte and the other women of the court meant to Goethe as a writer and thinker. Friendships with women provided an alternative to the overwhelmingly male politics and administration of the Duchy. The company of the court women was culturally richer than that of the Duke, who preferred hunting, soldiering, eating, drinking, and gambling. Goethe's writing after 1775 shows a deep gulf between the male world of power and physicality and the female world of morality and the mind. For Goethe the Weimar women were uncorrupted by 'the thorough shittiness of this our secular majesty'.[7] In this sense, the circumstances Goethe found in Weimar fitted into the model he brought with him—the idea that a pure 'source of life' flowed into and sustained humanity, but was corrupted by political power and civilization.

His earliest literary efforts in Weimar show the importance to him of women as cultural and moral models. One was the poem 'To the Moon', in six ballad-style stanzas.[8] It starts as a conventional moon poem—a lover alone at night in a foggy moonlit river valley. There is a strong sense of dreamlike haunting, of wanting to move but being stuck. The marvellous cadences of the final two stanzas imagine two lovers secluded from the world and enjoying the monstrous yet confined nature of desire, as if it were the minotaur in its labyrinth:

Selig wer sich vor der Welt
Ohne Haß verschließt
Einen Mann am Busen hält
Und mit dem geniest,

Was den Menschen unbewußt
Oder wohl veracht
Durch das Labyrinth der Brust
Wandelt in der Nacht.[9]

Blessed [is] whoever from the world / Closes herself off without hatred, / Holds a man to her bosom / And with him enjoys
That which—unknown to people / Or perhaps despised—/ Through the labyrinth of the breast / Roams at night.

The implication is that we have become or made ourselves into beings of labyrinthine emotional complexity, and now the feelings that lie beneath our consciousness seem too monstrous to indulge, except in moments of complete seclusion.

Another work inspired by Charlotte von Stein is the one-act domestic drama *The Siblings*, which Goethe wrote in a couple of days in autumn 1776. It enacts the tension between the private world of pure feelings and the public world of transactions. The setting is the bourgeois home of the merchant Wilhelm and his sister Marianne. Only Wilhelm knows that in fact Marianne is not his sister, but the daughter of the widow Charlotte who, while she lived, was Wilhelm's great love. Charlotte had rescued him from a profligate life during which he wasted his inheritance. However, just as he was beginning to turn his fortunes around under her wholesome influence, and so have some prospect of marrying her, Charlotte died. She left her daughter Marianne to Wilhelm as his ward, under the proviso that he pretend the daughter has died and that Marianne is his sister. The situation is fraught with repressed sexual tension, for Marianne loves Wilhelm and he loves her—but it is also implied that perhaps what he loves is Charlotte in the 'rejuvenated' form of her daughter, or to put it in the language used elsewhere in the play, Wilhelm's love has been 'transferred' from Charlotte to Marianne. The sense of suppressed sexual desire is heightened by the fact that Marianne sometimes looks after the neighbour's young son and is permitted by Wilhelm to share the young boy's bed, in a maternal way of course. It is certainly not overinterpreting matters to suppose that Wilhelm has a sexual fantasy in which he is in the young boy's place, enjoying lying with a woman who acts like his mother but is in fact not—like Charlotte. The play's potentially tragic complication is that Wilhelm's business associate Fabrice is also in love with Marianne, and the first half of the play is concerned with him proposing marriage to Marianne in an awkwardly roundabout manner. Not at first understanding that Fabrice might take what she is saying for an acceptance, she tells him to ask Wilhelm's permission. Again in a roundabout fashion, Fabrice broaches the subject with Wilhelm, but Wilhelm is preoccupied by his own complex feelings for Marianne and rebuffs Fabrice rudely. Under pressure and after an inner struggle, Wilhelm eventually tells Fabrice the truth about Marianne. Thus the dam is unblocked, so that Wilhelm can finally tell Marianne the truth too. The play ends with Wilhelm and Marianne embracing, though the words with which Marianne ends the play—'Wilhelm, it's not possible!'—show that she is still at a loss and much remains to be done. The feelings are such that no simple closure is possible. More abstractly, love cannot simply be transferred like money. This is Marianne's settled view, and she is undoubtedly the moral centre of the play. By contrast, the male characters live and think as merchants. Their behaviour is pragmatic and flexible. The gender difference is therefore not a matter of women's nature being different from men's. Marianne acts on principle in order to protect herself from the easy and unwelcome pragmatism of men. She has learned to adopt a principled position because her weak social position requires it of her. Morality is a shield against male power. At the same time Wilhelm is in deep perplexity: he wants to honour his devotion to Charlotte but he also loves her daughter, and yet he must accept the bourgeois social norms that require him to live with Marianne as his sister. The ending, instead of resolving the conflicts, raises them to an acute pitch. Wilhelm is no nearer to reaching equilibrium: to the very end he is represented as unsteady and troubled, almost on the verge of disintegration. It seems astonishing that on 21 November 1776 *The Siblings* was performed by the Weimar Amateurs' Theatre, with Goethe playing Wilhelm. Still, performance was an ephemeral event—publication was another matter altogether and quite impossible. When Goethe lent the manuscript out, both in Frankfurt and Weimar, he insisted that it go no further than close friends and family and that no copies be made.[10]

What did Goethe hope to achieve in Weimar? After his arrival in November 1775 he stopped writing critical essays or reviews on the subjects that interested him—religion, the arts, literature, antiquity. There were no more essays advocating a Rousseau-style reinvigoration of modern culture. The burst of public literary activity that had begun with his essay on the Strasbourg minster ended abruptly. One explanation for his retreat is that he was simply too busy, as he put it to 'the German Sappho' Anna Louisa Karsch.[11] Another explanation is that he was now living the Rousseauian theory that he had preached. He had not ceased to believe in the message of *Émile*; he now had a chance to put it into practice.[12] Much of his time was spent in the company of the Duke, to the consternation of many of the established Weimar courtiers, some of whom hated Goethe.[13] Wieland blamed these 'cabals against Goethe' on jealousy,[14] but there was also concern that Goethe was mentoring the Duke in an unsuitable manner and encouraging his wild behaviour. According to one version of the gossip, on their excursions into the countryside '[the Duke] in a brotherly way enjoys one and the same girl with [Goethe]'.[15] Johannes Daniel Falk, who much later compiled anecdotes from these years, came somewhat closer to the truth, though still not without prurience. Falk recorded that Goethe wanted to educate the Duke to behave like a Rousseauian 'natural man':

> The Duke was to become a natural man [*Naturmensch*] and to be extracted from the torturesome courtly and philistine life. They dug potatoes from the earth, cooked them with kindling in the forest, slept with girls in the forest, carved inscriptions on the trees, the traces of which can still be found twenty-five years later.[16]

Herder reported the same notion, with disapproval; he was unhappy with Goethe's attempts to induct the Duke into a 'life of nature'.[17] As Falk and

Herder implied, there was a plan for the Duke's education behind the wild and chaotic behaviour—hunting deer and boars and shooting birds; swimming in the Ilm naked after dark even in mid-winter; eating, drinking, and sleeping outdoors; growing asparagus and strawberries in the garden; ice-skating with music and fireworks. These activities seemed uncouth and indecorous for a German ducal court, and that was indeed part of the plan. During this period, Goethe's view of the Weimar court was unremittingly negative. Repeatedly he complained about the shallowness and 'poverty' of court life and indeed of society in general.[18] At least he could try to protect the Duke from its effects. His plan was to strengthen the Duke's mind and body so that he could resist corruption by society. To this extent, Falk and Herder were right. Goethe was trying to turn Carl August into a *Naturmensch*. The Duke was being immersed in nature, so that his natural vigour would prevail and he would become robust and resilient. His mind and body would be hardened in intemperate conditions—hence the swimming and skating and sleeping outdoors, especially in winter. Carl August was Émile and Goethe his Rousseau.

The craze for skating was one of Goethe's more popular innovations. There were plenty of opportunities. The 1770s were the tail end of the Little Ice Age, and the ponds and rivers around Weimar froze regularly. Goethe commemorated the skating craze in a striking poem of just seven lines, 'Ice-life Song', which he published in Wieland's *German Mercury* in 1776. The first four lines convey the grace and excitement of skating:

Eislebens Lied

Sorglos über die Fläche weg,
Wo vom kühnsten Wager die Bahn
Dir nicht vorgegraben du siehst,
Mache dir selber Bahn![19]

Carefree off over the surface, / Where the bravest risker no track / Has carved before you, / Make a track for yourself!

The structure of the long sinuous sentence conveys the patterns of the skater's tracks, and the unexpected word order creates a sense of skating into the unknown. As is usual in Goethe's poems that capture the immediacy of experience, there is a latent symbolic meaning, and the experience of the moment is also a condensed image of life more generally. The poem encourages us to skate our own new path away from what we are accustomed to. For Goethe himself, it might mean branching out from his life in Frankfurt along his new path in Weimar, as administrator of the Duchy and Rousseauian tutor to the Duke. It might be the poet of the Age of Geniuses, who creates strikingly original works that follow no established rules. The poem's second strophe of three lines turns from the outer experience towards the skater's anxiety about the ice breaking. He gives himself a repeated reassurance that if the ice does crack, it will not break with him on it, as he will already have sailed past the cracks. In the final line—'If it breaks now, it won't break with you!' ('Bricht's gleich, bricht's nicht mit dir!')—anxiety gives way to confidence. By being fully committed, by moving forward, we will not get stuck on breaking ice. Speed and confidence guarantee safety; danger comes from hesitancy. The poem conveys the victory of Goethe's confidence in his mission over his apprehensions about it.

Although he criticised the court in private, he participated fully in its daily life. His seemingly endless energy and inventiveness made him an ideal *maître de plaisir*. He would go out walking with the 'mademoiselles', dance at the frequent balls, take part in the endless cardgames and long, bibulous dinners, and organize Easter egg hunts and dancing for the children.[20] His political duties were relatively light at first. In June 1776 he took his oath as a state employee and was appointed to the Duke's Privy Council, in the face of resistance from the established Weimar families. He attended the Privy Council's weekly, sometimes twice-weekly meetings. Most of the advice to the Duke was formulated by the two established Privy Councillors, Jakob Friedrich von Fritsch and Christian Friedrich Schnauß. Goethe's contribution was limited. Once he had proved his competence, in 1779 he was appointed to the committees that reported to the Privy Council, and these demanded considerable effort: administering the roads, mining, military, and tax collection in Ilmenau.[21] One particularly delicate matter was overseeing Major von Wolfsburg, the unpopular Prussian army recruiter. Wolfsburg was permitted to enlist the Duchy's subjects to fight for the Prussians in the War of the Bavarian Succession. In some cases Wolfsburg used force, and Goethe did succeed in sparing some unwilling recruits, but there was no concerted challenge to Wolfsburg. The financial benefits of selling the Duchy's subjects outweighed any consideration of the subjects' rights. It was better to continue with the recruitment and hope that it could be hushed up. Overall Goethe's work was unappetizing and unglamorous, but it rewarded the determination and attention to detail of which he now showed himself surprisingly capable. His appointment in Weimar had been a risk for Goethe and for the Duchy's ruling family. To the seasoned councillors Goethe was the young prince's favourite and not a serious politician. While Goethe did lack experience, he worked hard and soon showed a natural talent for administration.[22] Fritsch, who had worked in the Duchy's government since 1756 and led the Privy Council since 1767, never warmed to Goethe, but grew to respect his honesty, selflessness, and energy.[23] The bourgeois Schnauß, though twenty-seven years Goethe's senior, became a firm friend.[24]

There were three aspects of the work he found particularly exhausting. The economic misery of the peasants was markedly worse than in neighbouring territories.[25] Much could have been done. The peasant smallholders and tenant farmers were burdened by a massively inequitable tax system and the detested *corvée*—the obligation to perform a number of days' work on the estates of the nobility, which forced peasants to leave their own lands untended, particularly during the critical harvest period. Repeatedly the peasants appealed to the authorities to have the *corvée* commuted into cash payments, which though burdensome would at least have given them more control over their fate, but the landowning aristocracy was set against reform.[26] This was not simply a struggle between Enlightened reformers in government and a selfish, outmoded aristocracy, as some commentators have suggested. The Duchy's largest landowner and therefore the greatest beneficiary of the *corvée* was Carl August himself.[27] Goethe occasionally complained in private about the miserable state of affairs, for instance in a letter to Charlotte von Stein in April 1782:

> One is ashamed at how much advantage one has in comparison to so many thousands. One constantly hears talk of how poor a land is, and how it is getting poorer, at times one thinks this isn't right, at times one puts it out of one's mind, when at last one sees the thing with open eyes, and sees the incurable state of it, and how we merely tinker!![28]

Though he was fully aware of the reasons for the economic misery of the peasants, he was not a reformer, at least not by conviction. The extent of his ambition was to make the existing system work as well as possible while maintaining the social order. Nor was he alone in sustaining the status quo. Herder, who was instinctively more liberal than Goethe, was involved in enforcing a new *corvée* to fund maintenance of the Duchy's church buildings, and in instituting repressive measures to enforce it.[29] There were protests and social unrest,[30] but relatively little evidence of them appears in Goethe's writings or the Duchy's records—no doubt because the Duchy, like the other German states, was eager to present itself as a beacon of peace and harmony.

Much of Goethe's energy was spent dealing with sporadic disasters. A particular menace were the blazes that tore through the tightly packed, wooden houses of the Duchy's towns. There was no systematic provision for firefighting. If he was nearby, Goethe would join in the efforts to rescue people and put out the fires, as his natural sympathy demanded, though there were times when he felt even his normally generous reserves of pity were close to depletion, as he confided to his diary following a blaze in Apolda in July 1779:

> In the night there was an almighty fire in Apolda, early in the morning as soon as I heard I went, and was roasted and soaked the whole day. The Duke was out of the Duchy in Bendeleben and Erfurt. Also burned in part were my plans, thoughts, scheduling of my time. So life goes on to the end, so too will others live after us. I can only thank God that in all the fire and water I still have a head on my shoulders, and yet I demurely await more fierce tests, perhaps within four weeks. My ideas about firefighting [were] confirmed again. [...] The Duke will believe eventually. My eyes are burning from the heat and the smoke and the soles of my feet are sore.
>
> By and by the misery is becoming as prosaic to me as a fireplace. But I will not let go of my thoughts [...]. Not one person knows what I am doing and with how many enemies I have to battle to achieve the little I do. In all my striving and struggling I beg you, you gods that watch over us, not to laugh. At most have a smile and stand by me.[31]

In all of this Goethe rightly retained his conviction that many problems were man-made and therefore soluble, at least in principle. It was a question of getting people to recognise the problem and to prioritize it above their own interests. This was the heart of Goethe's attitude to politics, as he grew into his role during his first years in Weimar. He was never a liberal. He was not interested in gaining the people's consent for the actions he deemed necessary or in protecting people's rights. As he would write ruefully to Charlotte von Stein in 1786, reflecting on ten years in the administration, executive power was really all that mattered, and without it, politics was a fool's errand: 'For I always said, whoever has to do with administration, without being ruling lord, must be either a philistine or a knave or a fool'.[32] Aside from his efforts to educate the Duke, he did not have a programme for Weimar's political renewal. He was interested in the maintenance of public order and in workable solutions to immediate problems. The main obstacle he encountered was people's intransigent individuality, as he wrote home to Frankfurt in November 1776: 'I am not exactly weighed down by business affairs, but am all the more plagued by what forms the basis of all affairs: the crazy whims, passions and idiocies and weaknesses and strengths of humans'.[33] Thus Goethe was torn in two very different directions—between sympathy for the suffering of people and an authoritarian frustration with their refusal to accept the effective remedies and sound administration he felt he could offer.

In Goethe's mind, people's 'crazy whims, passions, and idiocies and weaknesses' were to a great extent caused by religion. Two tragic deaths in 1777 and 1778 shook him and led to some sombre reflections on humans and their gods. In the middle of June 1777 he received the news that his beloved sister Cornelia had died three weeks after giving birth to her second daughter. In his diary he noted: 'Dark broken day'.[34] His grief was compounded by a sense of guilt at Cornelia's increasingly unhappy marriage to Schlosser since their move to Emmendingen in 1774. He marked her birthday in his diary in December 1777.[35] 1778 began with the tragic death of the seventeen-year-old Christel von Laßberg. Troubled by an unhappy passion, and possibly influenced by *Werther*, she drowned herself in the Ilm on the night of 16 January. She had been carrying a copy of Goethe's novel. The news was brought to Goethe while he and the Duke were out skating. The body was taken to Charlotte's house. Goethe consoled the parents. Several days later he noted in his diary: 'In silent grief busy for several days with the scene of the death, then forced back to theatrical frivolity'.[36] There was some thought of setting up a monument. Goethe spent an evening moving a large stone to the place on the bank where Christel's body had been found. Writing to Charlotte two days later, he counselled her not to be consumed by grief: 'this beguiling grief has something dangerously alluring about it, like water itself, and the reflections of the stars of heaven that shine from both tempt us in'.[37] The allure of water and its reflections are the theme of a poem he wrote in 1778, 'The Angler'. It is one of his finest *Volkslieder*, though much less well known than 'Little Rose on the Heath' and 'Alder King' ('Erlkönig'). The poem combines a ballad-like simplicity with some typically Goethean linguistic innovations that are quite foreign to the *Volkslied* tradition and belong, if anywhere, in Pindar—for instance the newly coined compound adverb 'wave-breathingly' ('wellenatmend') and the phrase 'damp transfigured' ('feucht verklärt'). Part of the effect also derives from the poem's insistent repetitions and its balancing of opposed forces—the world above the water and the world below, nature and humanity, free will and compulsion:

Der Fischer

Das Wasser rauscht, das Wasser schwoll,
Ein Fischer saß daran,
Sah nach dem Angel ruhevoll,
Kühl bis ans Herz hinan:
Und wie er sitzt und wie er lauscht
Teilt sich die Flut empor,
Aus dem bewegten Wasser rauscht
Ein feuchtes Weib hervor.

Sie sang zu ihm, sie sprach zu ihm:
Was lockst du meine Brut
Mit Menschenwitz und Menschenlist
Hinauf in Todes Glut?
Ach wüßtest du wie's Fischlein ist
So wohlig auf dem Grund,
Du stiegst herunter wie du bist,
Und würdest erst gesund.

Labt sich die liebe Sonne nicht
Der Mond sich nicht im Meer?
Kehrt wellenatmend ihr Gesicht
Nicht doppelt schöner her?
Lockt dich der tiefe Himmel nicht,
Das feucht verklärte Blau?
Lockt dich dein eigen Angesicht
Nicht her in ewgen Tau?

Das Wasser rauscht, das Wasser schwoll
Netzt ihm den nackten Fuß,
Sein Herz wuchs ihm so sehnsuchtsvoll
Wie bei der Liebsten Gruß.
Sie sprach zu ihm, sie sang zu ihm,
Da wars um ihn geschehn,
Halb zog sie ihn halb sank er hin
Und ward nicht mehr gesehn.[38]

The Angler

The water roared, the water swelled, / An angler sat by it, / Looked at his rod peacefully, / Calm to his very heart: / And as he sits, and as he listens / The rising flood parts, / Out of the turbulent water there rushes / Up a damp woman.
She sang to him, she spoke to him: / Why do you tempt my brood / With human cunning and human guile / Up into the heat of death? / Ah, if you only knew how the fishies are / So cosy at the bottom, / You'd climb down just as you are / And would only then become healthy.
Does not the beloved sun wash itself / Does not the moon [wash] itself in the sea? / Does not their face return wave-breathingly / With double the beauty? / Does not the deep heaven tempt you, / The damp-transfigured blue? / Does not your own face tempt you / Down here into eternal dew?
The water roared, the water swelled, / Wetted his bare foot, / His heart swelled so longingly / As if at a greeting from his beloved. / She spoke to him, she sang to him, / Then he was done for, / Half she pulled him half he sank in / And was never seen again.

Whereas at first sight the poem seems to be a simple ballad-like fairy tale of an angler bewitched and drowned by a water nymph, the various doublings add extra layers of meaning. The water nymph represents the natural world, which she portrays as beautiful and healthy. The beauty of the nymph's vision in stanza three, and her suggestion that the angler, like Narcissus, might be drawn into the water by his own reflection, add further layers of meaning. For is our attraction to nature not also narcissistic? Have we not anthropomorphized nature, in the same way as we create anthropomorphic gods? The fatal glamour of nature is a glamour we project onto it. Is it not narcissistic to love something that we have made in our own image? The nymph's picture of the little fish cosily at home on the riverbed, and of the sun and moon washing their faces clean in the sea, indeed the very nymph herself—these appeal to our anthropomorphic-narcissistic urge. This is the sense in which the angler both jumps and is pulled into the water—he is lured by the picture his own mind has created of a perfect but fatal world.

Much of the consternation surrounding Goethe's behaviour in Weimar concerned his heterodox religious views. A story circulated that in May 1776 Goethe had nailed a bible to a tree, and he and the Duke had taken potshots at it.[39] Goethe's friends rebutted the allegations. Despite his new responsibilities, there was no sign of him becoming orthodox. Visiting Weimar in December 1775, Fritz Stolberg noted that Goethe was worryingly irreligious. It was not the business of great minds, Goethe believed, to bow down to revealed religion.[40] The whole system of positive and revealed religion was a psychological prison built by our own infirmity of purpose and character. A short prayer-like lyric from 1776 puts the argument succinctly:

Menschengefühl

Ach, ihr Götter, große Götter
In dem weiten Himmel droben,
Gäbet ihr uns auf der Erde
Festen Sinn und guten Mut
O wir ließen euch, ihr Guten,
Euren weiten Himmel droben.[41]

Human Feeling

Ah, ye Gods, great Gods / In the wide heaven above, / If you gave us on the earth / Firm purpose and good courage / Oh we would leave for you, you good [Gods], / Your wide heaven above.

By creating positive and revealed religion, humans interfere with heaven. They do so because they lack courage and firmness of purpose, and so they contravene Spinoza's rule that a true love of the gods is psychologically resilient and unselfish: 'he who loves God cannot strive that God should love him in return.'[42] During the early years in Weimar Goethe became more assertive in his deism—or atheism, as some would have it. He was becoming particularly annoyed by Lavater's insistent harping on about Christ, as he wrote in January 1777: 'Your thirst for Christ makes me feel sorry for you. You're in a worse case than us heathens, our gods do actually appear to us in our need.'[43]

It is sometimes stated that Goethe was not an atheist or an opponent of religion.[44] Certainly even during his most militantly anti-Christian years from around 1770 to around 1800, his view of religion was nuanced. It is helpful to remember that religion is not a single, monolithic entity. Different religions—the polytheistic religion of Ancient Greece and Rome, say, or Christianity—held quite different values for Goethe. And even if he thought the outward forms of Christianity and the doctrine of Christ were damaging illusions, some elements of Christianity could be beneficial. In that sense, when Goethe wrote to Lavater that 'our gods do actually appear to us in our need', he was being provocative, but not gratuitously so. He really did think religion could be beneficial. For Goethe in the late 1770s positive and revealed religions are indeed illusions and often damaging ones, but they can also contain positive messages of human flourishing—beneficial illusions, though illusions still. The idea of the beneficial illusion forms the core of a play Goethe worked on in the winter of 1776/77. Its first draft was titled 'Sterntal' after the melancholy Baron whose cure forms the play's main action. It was performed by the court's amateur players on the Duchess Luise's birthday in January 1777. It was the first in a series of Goethe's productions in honour of the melancholy young Duchess. This first version has not survived. There was a second performance in March, this time under the title *Lila*. In this version it is the Baron's wife Lila who is melancholic. She has fallen ill after hearing the false news of her husband the Baron's death.[45] When he returns, she 'flees him as if he were a ghost',[46] for she has succumbed to the *idée fixe* that he has been captured by evil spirits who are also pursuing her, so that she now haunts the garden in a state of morbid paranoia.[47] In the first performance Goethe played the role of the therapist Dr Verazio, who instructs the patient's family and friends in a charade that will lead Lila back to health. As he puts it himself, it will be the 'masterpiece' of 'curing imagination with imagination'—using a beneficial illusion to drive out a harmful one. Under his instruction Lila's sister Marianne, posing as Almaide the leader of the fairies, reveals to Lila that her husband is alive but has been captured and put to sleep by a 'jealous demon'.[48] Marianne's story is in fact exactly what the delusional Lila already imagined to be the case. In this way Marianne enters into Lila's imaginary world and begins to take control of it. According to Marianne, the evil demon has also captured Lila's family.[49] This embellishment, which is news to Lila, appeals strongly to her melancholic pessimism. The final element of the therapy makes the link with religion clearer. Still in the guise of Almaide, Marianne explains to Lila how she must undergo a symbolic ritual in order to free herself and defeat the demon. First she must cleanse herself by washing her face and hands, so that her chains will drop away. Then she must put on a new white dress and a veil, which symbolizes the end of her black melancholia. Finally Lila's sisters inform her that she has defeated the demon, and she returns to reality. The charade has enacted the Baron's liberation from the clutches of the demon, and Lila has been persuaded that, having first believed herself guilty of failing to free him, she has now freed him by her own actions. Both were, of course, illusions, but there is an important difference between them. In the first, harmful illusion Lila was the passive victim of a process that was leading towards doom. In the second, beneficial illusion she is an active agent in a process of purification and liberation. The beneficial illusion contains a positive image of humans as masters of their fate, and not as victims, such as we find in the doctrine of original sin or the story of Christ's passion. The healing of Lila also presents a surprisingly positive view of ritual—surprising because Christian rituals such as the eucharist were often deprecated by eighteenth-century deists. The ritual that Lila performs involves purification and cleansing. It symbolizes human health. *Lila* contains the seeds of a humanistic doctrine that allows a role for religion and ritual, so long as they embody a positive vision of human nature.

After *Lila*, his next composition for the stage was strikingly different. 'Proserpina', only a few pages long, was originally composed as a freestanding dramatic monologue, in which the goddess Proserpina, recently arrived in Hades after her father Jupiter bound her in marriage to his brother Pluto, tries at first to find a way back up to the world of the living, but must then acknowledge that her search is fruitless and she is destined to live in Hades forever.[50] Goethe must have completed it by the end of 1777, for at that point he decided to include it in a new satirical comedy he wrote that autumn and winter, *The Triumph of Sensibility*. The monologue was obviously experimental. Although it has a distant affinity to the 'Prometheus' monologue—like Prometheus, Proserpina rails against the injustice of Jupiter—it has no other precedents or successors in Goethe's oeuvre. Proserpina's condition, trapped in joyless gloom among the hopeless, pitiable dead, is in the first place an embodiment of melancholia. Her insistent repeating of words is suggestive of a mind circling unhappily and unable to free itself.[51] There may have been a trigger for its composition, perhaps the composer Gluck's request to Wieland that he write a poem commemorating the death of Gluck's young niece, or it may have been inspired by the unhappiness of the young Duchess Luise, but the most important impulse was literary—Rousseau's monodrama *Pygmalion* (1770). The influence of Rousseau's concept of *pitié* is also detectable in the compassion Proserpina feels for the hopelessness of the dead in the underworld. Despite being their queen, she can do nothing to help them. She is a compassionate queen ruling over a hopeless domain. She takes pity on Tantalus and her mother Ceres, who will be anxiously searching for her. Momentarily she wonders whether Jupiter might allow her back up into the daylight. Then she bites into the pomegranate and realizes her fate is sealed. And yet the fate that ties her to Hades, triggered by the eating of the pomegranate, gives rise to a last bout of anger at Jupiter. As in the Prometheus monologue, Jupiter also stands for the God of Christianity: the German word for pomegranate, *Granatapfel*, alludes to the apple of Eden, and we are clearly expected to see a connection between Proserpina and Eve. Why has God made the world such that sensual pleasure (the apple) condemns us to eternal misery? Why make pleasure so sweet if it is destined to damn us? Why equip humans with the ability to feel pleasure if pleasure is sinful? Finally she despairs, but not without retaining some of her natural compassion, calling out: 'Give me the fate of your damned!'[52]

Goethe's decision to include 'Proserpina' in *The Triumph of Sensibility* might appear strange, for its new context completely changes the monologue's tone. The play is a satire on fashionable Sensibility and the craze for nature. In this context Proserpina's monologue reads like parody. It is possible that by filleting Proserpina's monologue into the comedy, Goethe wanted to show how easily the pursuit of authenticity could become inauthentic. The play was first performed on Duchess Luise's birthday in January 1778, and its plot and characters reflect the concerns in Weimar about the Duke's troubled relationship with his melancholy Duchess. The plot concerns the marital problems of the king and queen of the kind of fanciful realm Goethe knew from Shakespeare's comedies. King Andrason is wilful and 'humoristic'. He is relaxed about social protocol, though as one of his sister-in-law Feria's ladies points out, his informality seems like a ploy to allow him to get intimate with her attractive young ladies-in-waiting. His melancholic wife Queen Mandandane has followed her husband's example and become interested in another man, but obsessively so.[53] In search of a remedy for his wife's obsession, Andrason has visited an oracle in the mountains and received a cryptic response:

> Wenn wird ein greiflich Gespenst von schönen Händen entgeistert
> Und der leinene Sack seine Geweide verleiht [...]
> Wird die geflickte Braut mit dem Verliebten vereinet:
> Dann kommt Ruhe und Glück, Fragender, über dein Haus.[54]

> When a tangible phantom has its life taken by beautiful hands, / And the linen bag lends out its inwards, [...] / If the patched up bride is united with the beloved: / Then peace and joy will return, Questioner, to your house.

The object of Mandandane's affections is Prince Oronaro. We learn from his pompous majordomo, Merkulo, that Oronaro adores nature, but cannot bear to be outdoors, because of the unhealthy breezes, biting midges, and sundry other nuisances. Therefore he has employed a 'directeur de la nature' to create an indoor imitation of nature for him, complete with an artificial babbling brook, artificial birdsong, and artificial moonlight. 'We call it artificial nature', Merkulo says, 'for the word nature, as you will observe, has to be everywhere'[55]—no doubt a joke at Goethe's own expense, as the Weimar court's creator of natural experiences. Inside his arbour Oronaro worships a dummy of Mandandane, and he speaks to it in the language of Sensibility: 'Thou made for me alone / Found and chosen only by sympathy'.[56] Just as the artificial arbour parodies the cult of nature, Oronaro's love for his artificial Mandandane parodies the cult of Sensibility. However, Andrason's domain is little better. Mandandane has created a replica of the underworld, complete with a pomegranate tree, where she acts out her unhappy marriage to Andrason by performing the Proserpina monologue.

The play's action is instigated by Feria's ladies, who infiltrate the Prince's arbour and discover the dummy of Mandandane stuffed with straw and sentimental novels, including Rousseau's *The New Heloïse* and Goethe's *Werther*. Andrason now realizes that the first two lines of the oracle—'When a tangible phantom / Has its life taken by beautiful hands'—have been fulfilled and that 'taking the life' of the dummy refers to the removal of the novels, which gave life to the dummy and indeed to the whole artificial arbour. The animating force of 'nature' is in fact not nature at all, but a sentimental replica of it animated by authors like Rousseau and Goethe. In order to fulfil the oracle's words, the novels must be stuffed back into the dummy ('the patched up bride'). All that now remains is for Andrason to persuade Mandandane that Oronaro in fact loves the dummy, not her. This is achieved by a staged contrivance: Mandandane is made to take the dummy's place in the arbour. Oronaro, unaware that he is now faced by the real Mandandane, can no longer feel any effect. But once the dummy is switched back in, complete with its animating sentimental novels, the effect returns. Mandandane realizes that Oronaro loves the dummy and sentimental fiction more than he loves her. She is reconciled with Andrason. But for Oronaro there is no cure; he is still in love with his artificial Mandandane. Despite the satirical unveiling of Oronaro's world, some people will continue to prefer replicas of love and nature to the real thing.

———

In February 1779 Goethe began work on a new play that was far more ambitious than anything he had attempted for the Weimar stage so far: *Iphigeneia at Tauris*. Its remarkable poetic, symbolic, and philosophical coherence make it one of the most beautiful pieces of dramatic art produced in eighteenth-century Europe, even if it is more of a closet drama than a stageworthy spectacle. Its heroine Iphigeneia is one of the most sensitively drawn female characters in any play by a male playwright since Shakespeare. The play is also remarkable for its philosophical power and coherence. It presents the fullest and most subtle exploration of the conflict between political reality and personal authenticity that Goethe had yet achieved. It takes seriously the religious elements in the myth that most modern adaptations of it do not—there have been many[57]—and turns them into a cogent argument. Nor is the play's philosophy obtrusive: the ideas are made to spring naturally out of the myth and the realism of the play's (often underrated) characterization.[58]

The circumstances in which Goethe wrote *Iphigeneia at Tauris* could hardly have been less conducive to writing a neoclassical drama. For two weeks from the end of February he travelled through Jena, Dornburg, Apolda, and the other small towns and villages, inspecting the roads and checking on Wolfsburg's recruitment of soldiers for the Prussian army. Writing to Charlotte, he complained that 'the drama won't move forward here, it's cursed, the King of Tauris is supposed to speak as if not a single stocking worker in Apolda were starving'.[59] Despite his worries, work on the play progressed rapidly, whether because he had the model of Euripides's *Iphigeneia among the Taurians* to help him or because he was so energized by his plans for the material.[60] Certainly the play was not a piece of escapism—a beautiful neoclassical distraction from the ugly realities of life in the Duchy. The play addresses the political reality that Goethe was becoming more deeply enmeshed in since his appointment to the committees that reported to the Privy Council. The fundamental problem that beset the Duchy, on Goethe's view, was inconsistency. Government was not consistently focused on improving the conditions of life in the Duchy. It was too pragmatic, too easily moved by the needs of the moment. As a foil to this (male) pragmatism and flexibility, Goethe creates in Iphigeneia a woman whose circumstances force her to speak with a consistent moral voice, like Marianne in *The Siblings*. Obviously the point is not that states should be governed by women; it is that men fail to govern well because they do not attain the moral consistency that women like Iphigeneia, because of their circumstances, have to learn.

A first draft of the play was ready by the end of March, after only six weeks. Another week later the play received its first performance at the Hauptmann House on the Weimar esplanade, with Goethe playing Orestes, Prince

Constantin as Pylades, Knebel as Thoas, Seidler as the King's advisor Arkas, and Corona Schröter, the only professional actor, as Iphigeneia. Goethe designed the production, with the flats painted to resemble grand marble columns representing the temple of Artemis, and the soffits painted blue to represent a Winckelmannian clear Greek sky. He also made innovative use of a carpet to muffle footfall on stage and had the actors swathed in white 'Grecian' robes.[61] The court physician Hufeland judged the production to be 'a genuine picture of classical Greece at its most beautiful'.[62] The playwright too was pleased, not only with the play, which according to Knebel Goethe thought was his best work so far,[63] but also with the production: 'very good effect, especially on pure people', he noted in his diary.[64] If 'pure people' in the audience understood the play, Goethe could be happy, for purity is one of its key ideas. His pleasure was tempered by the knowledge that the play lacked polish. It was a 'sketch', he told Charlotte von Stein.[65] The first draft was in prose, albeit with persistent iambic rhythms. He was reluctant to lend out the text in its unfinished form, he told Lavater.[66] In search of inspiration, between March and September 1780 he studied Euripides's Greek text intensively. Another model for the polishing of *Iphigeneia* was Lessing's new play in iambic pentameters *Nathan the Wise*, which he first read in April 1780. *Nathan* too was concerned with a deist reinterpretation of religion. In August the playwright Leisewitz reported that Goethe spoke of Lessing 'with the greatest respect, especially because of his *Nathan* and his theological controversies'.[67] According to Knebel, Goethe thought *Nathan* 'the highest masterpiece of human art'.[68] *Iphigeneia* was performed again for the Duchess's birthday in January 1781 while Goethe continued to tinker with the text, but there was no breakthrough. It took the intervention of Wieland and Herder to encourage Goethe to rewrite the play in verse and so give it the polish it deserved. The resulting version, reshaped through the autumn and winter of 1786 and published in June 1787, was a hard-won triumph, not only metrically and stylistically, but also in enhancing the power of the original drama. (This is the version used in the following discussion, and not the 1779 prose version.) It was also utterly different from the dramas with which Goethe had made his name in the 1770s. The Germans in Rome to whom Goethe read the newly finished version in 1787 expected 'something Berlichingian' and were bemused.[69] His publisher Göschen wrote disappointedly to Bertuch that 'people don't understand *Iphigeneia*'.[70]

Although he modelled his version closely on Euripides's play, he was also building on the long tradition of the Iphigeneia myth, in which successive authors had rewritten, repurposed, and modernized the story. In the earliest

Ancient Greek sources, including Aeschylus's *Oresteia* trilogy, the process of modernization is already underway. When Agamemnon sacrifices Iphigeneia at Aulis in order to secure favourable winds for the Greek fleet to sail to Troy, he perpetuates a family history of blood guilt. The consequences are Clytaemnestra's murder of Agamemnon and Orestes's murder of his mother. The blood guilt is bequeathed to the next generation. In the final play of Aeschylus's trilogy, Orestes is pursued by the Furies (also euphemistically known as the Kindly Ones) to Athens where he begs Athena to intercede. She sets up a new court to try Orestes's case, which she presides. When the jury of twelve Athenians is tied, she arbitrarily casts her deciding vote in Orestes's favour. The Furies are persuaded to relent. Instead of meting out retaliatory justice, they will henceforth oversee the Athenian system of trial by jury. The trilogy thus ends by completing the transition from a primitive system of blood guilt to a modern system of trial according to the law. It shows the emergence of a modern enlightened polity. Euripides's version some forty years later explores an episode en route to the trial in Athens. Pursued by the Furies, Orestes has consulted the oracle of Apollo at Delphi. The oracle has hinted that Orestes would be freed of the blood guilt if he could rescue the cult statue of Apollo's sister Artemis from the Taurians. On their arrival, Orestes and Pylades have been captured by the Taurians, who have a tradition of sacrificing any foreigners that land on their shores. Here the action of Euripides's play begins. Orestes meets his sister Iphigeneia, for according to Euripides's version she was not in fact sacrificed at Aulis, but was spirited away by Artemis and installed as the goddess's Taurian priestess. The Greeks duly plan their escape. After a confrontation between the Greeks and Taurians, Athena intervenes to impose the victory of the Greeks over the barbarians and the removal of the statue of Artemis to Greece. Euripides's play is a piece of Greek cultural imperialism. It ends with a quite different kind of Enlightenment from Aeschylus's *Oresteia*: the assertion of the values of Greek culture over barbarism by means of divine *fiat*.

Goethe's version follows the plot of Euripides's *Iphigeneia among the Taurians* with some fidelity, except for one brilliant innovation. Euripides has the oracle of Apollo direct Orestes to steal the Taurians' cult statue of Apollo's sister Artemis. In Goethe's play, Orestes comes to realize that the oracle's vague injunction to rescue 'the sister' can be interpreted as referring not to the cult statue of Apollo's sister, but to his own sister Iphigeneia. This innovation allows Goethe to modernize Euripides's play in several ways. Now the Greeks are directed by Apollo's oracle not to steal Taurian property; rather they are charged with taking Iphigeneia, who is authentically Greek. The removal of the statue was theft; the removal of Iphigeneia is restitution. The shift from theft to restitution means that the violent standoff between the Greeks and Taurians can be resolved without divine intervention. The resolution is achieved by humans, not a *deus ex machina*. This shift from a religious to a purely human resolution is confirmed by the symbolism of Orestes's interpretation of the oracle. The oracle's reference to a 'sister' is not to a religious icon, but to a human being. The solution to the Greeks' problem is no longer a cult statue, it is Iphigeneia. In this way Goethe's play effects a transition that is far more enlightened than the victory of the Greek values at the end of Euripides's play, or even the shift in Aeschylus's *The Kindly Ones* from retaliatory to law-based justice. In Goethe's play the movement is from traditional revealed religion to a modern secular humanism. Indeed, reinterpreted in this manner, the oracle itself becomes redundant, for instead of enacting a divine ordinance, the play now effects a human desire: Iphigeneia's longing to return home to Greece, which she expresses in the play's opening monologue as she stands outside the temple of Artemis 'seeking the land of the Greeks with my soul' ('das Land der Griechen mit der Seele suchend').[71] The play is sometimes described as a meditation on the relation of the human and the divine;[72] in reality the divine turns out simply not to exist or—as Goethe's rethinking of Spinoza and Rousseau would have it—to be identical with nature and the human heart.

Goethe's innovation brought further benefits, for the shift from revealed religion to secular humanism made sense of an idea that was implicit in Euripides's version, but was not developed by Euripides, namely the significance of Artemis's rescue of Iphigeneia at Aulis. Traditionally, and as understood by Aeschylus, Iphigeneia was not spirited away, but sacrificed, and her death led to the murders of Agamemnon and Clytaemnestra, according to the logic of retaliatory justice. In Euripides's version, with Iphigeneia spirited away to safety, the transmission of the blood guilt—Clytaemnestra's murder of Agamemnon—rests not on the fact that Agamemnon has killed Iphigeneia but on the erroneous belief that he has. The continuing bloodshed thus has less to do with revenge for an actual wrong, and more to do with the Tantalid dynasty being locked psychologically in a cycle of violence.[73] In Goethe's play this psychological problem is central to the action. Humans are locked in a logic of violence and deceit from which they seem unable to free themselves. This logic is sanctioned by a belief in the old religion and its concept of blood guilt—which for Goethe is the classical equivalent of the Christian notion of original sin. Religious beliefs provide us with the means of justifying our violence to one another. It is sometimes claimed that the peaceful humanistic outcome of Goethe's play is alien to the thought-world of Attic tragedy, and that the ethics of the play are those of eighteenth-century Sensibility.[74] This misses a crucial point about Goethe's adaptation of Euripides. The innovation of having Orestes reinterpret the oracle is Goethe's way of unpacking and improving something that was already implicit in Euripides's play: the idea that violence is the product of erroneous human beliefs.[75]

A second consequence of Goethe's innovation is to make Euripides's Athenian cultural imperialism redundant. The cult statue of Artemis will remain where it originally fell to earth in the Taurian lands. Taurian culture is left intact and is not vandalized by Greek imperialism. Again this arguably makes more sense of the Greek myth than Euripides's version did, for it is obvious to an impartial spectator that Greek culture is not superior to Taurian culture. Of course, Goethe's Greeks start from a Euripidean position of Greek prejudice towards the barbarian Taurians. As Pylades puts it, 'Diana longs to be / Away from this rude shore of the barbarians / And their bloody human sacrifices' ('Diana sehnet sich / Von diesem rauhen Ufer der Barbaren / Und ihren blut'gen Menschenopfern weg').[76] But the Taurian practice of human sacrifice is really no worse than Agamemnon's sacrifice of Iphigeneia or the murderous history of the Tantalids. Greece, the land of Iphigeneia's murderous Tantalid forebears, is hardly more humane than Tauris.[77] The Taurian King Thoas makes this point when in Act V he mockingly asks Iphigeneia why he should feel obliged to be any more humane than Atreus:

> Du glaubst, es höre
> Der rohe Skythe, der Barbar, die Stimme
> Der Wahrheit und der Menschlichkeit, die Atreus,
> Der Grieche, nicht vernahm?[78]

Do you believe / The rude Scythian, the barbarian, hears the voice / Of truth and humanity that Atreus / The Greek did not hear?

In fact, Taurian culture looks well ordered enough. Unsheathed swords are not allowed in the presence of the king.[79] Thoas is supported by a clever and smooth-mannered minister Arkas, who seems rather more humane than the typical villainous princes' ministers of eighteenth-century German theatre. Thoas himself is an autocrat who claims complete obedience from his subjects. Whilst professing to be worried that the lack of a male heir undermines the security of his throne, he exploits the supposed insecurity as justification of his demands for total obedience. In this he is little different from many eighteenth-century European dynastic rulers, who identified their own interests with those of the state in the spirit of Louis XIV's dictum 'l'état c'est moi'. Arkas even suggests that Iphigeneia has introduced a modicum of liberalization to the Taurian state.[80] If so, this serves to illustrate both the Greek Iphigeneia's humanity and the receptivity of the Taurians to it. The fact that Thoas later retracts his benevolence and claims to regret it simply shows that the path from autocracy to Enlightenment is a rocky one, as any eighteenth-century European would understand.[81]

Arkas's smooth manners are, however, for political show. He mixes his praise for Iphigeneia's humanizing influence with vague threats. If she resists, Thoas will take her as his wife by force. When she reacts angrily to the threat of violence, Arkas executes a preplanned retreat to a milder but still obnoxious threat: she is to resume the tradition of human sacrifice. His tactics might seem clever but are a serious misjudgement. By provoking such a strong reaction in Iphigeneia, Arkas has not cowed her, but primed her to explode. When Thoas repeats his marriage offer, Iphigeneia's first response is to hide behind her incognito. How could Thoas marry a woman whose identity he does not know? It is a weak gambit because it invites an obvious challenge from Thoas: if she wishes to return to Greece, she must demonstrate that she has a family to return to.[82] Iphigeneia now launches into a long account of her family history, hoping that by detailing the crimes of the Tantalids she will scare Thoas off. Her words give rise to an unintended twofold dramatic irony. First, the need to deter Thoas encourages her to put the worst possible construction on her family's history and to admit that the Tantalids live under a divine curse. The gods have malign intentions towards humans. This is precisely the argument—the divinely ordained persistence of blood guilt or original sin—that Iphigeneia will later question and the play will refute. Now however she relies on imputing malignity to the gods in order to deter Thoas. She has constructed an interpretation of divine intentions that simply reflects her own needs of the moment.[83] Iphigeneia is by no means alone in making religion conform to her purposes. The play raises questions concerning the will of the gods, and all sorts of claims are made that depend on our supposed ability to read the divine will. In this sense Goethe's play is in fact quite Euripidean.[84] It exposes the knots people tie themselves in when they try to make religion serve their own ends. There are moments when characters catch themselves in the act of interpreting divine intentions arbitrarily. In the same scene, Iphigeneia is happy to criticise her own practice of imputing intentions to the gods, when it suits her to do so:

> Der mißversteht die Himmlischen, der sie
> Blutgierig wähnt; er dichtet ihnen nur
> Die eignen grausamen Begierden an.[85]

> One misunderstands the Heavenly Ones, if one / Imagines them bloodthirsty; one is merely projecting / One's own cruel desires onto them.

This is shortly after Thoas has made the same criticism of Iphigeneia: 'This is not a god speaking; it's your own heart' ('Es spricht kein Gott; es spricht dein eignes Herz'.)[86] Orestes makes a similar observation concerning Pylades's overly optimistic scheming: 'With what rare art you weave the counsels of the gods / Cleverly together with your own wishes' ('Mit seltner Kunst flichst du der Götter Rat / Und deine Wünsche klug in eins zusammen'.)[87] The characters can argue about the meaning of divine intentions, but the play, because Goethe has abandoned Euripides's *deus ex machina*, offers no evidence of any divine intentions whatsoever. The gods give no answers to any of the questions the play raises.

The second irony in Iphigeneia's narrative of the Tantalid blood guilt is that the history of the Tantalids is even worse than she presents it to be. It is only in Act II, in dialogues with Pylades and Orestes, that she learns that Clytaemnestra has murdered Agamemnon and in turn been murdered by Orestes. Of particular concern to her is the murder of Agamemnon because if it was indeed driven by Clytaemnestra's passion, it would support Thoas's claim in Act I that women are lustful and untrustworthy.[88] The story of Clytaemnestra might support Thoas's misogyny, but the play does not.[89] In fact it avoids saying anything about the *nature* of women and instead only comments on their *situation*. In her opening monologue Iphigeneia complains that 'the condition of women is pitiable' ('der Frauen Zustand ist beklagenswert').[90] The subordination of women to men is a social fact. Thoas, on the other hand, attacks women for their vicious *nature*. The play does nothing to support his view. For all that the play celebrates the unheard-of deed of a remarkable woman, and was performed as a celebration for the Duchess, it does not follow the eighteenth-century fashion for ascribing a higher degree of sensitivity or sympathy to women. Indeed, it would have been perverse of Goethe to use the Tantalid story to argue for the natural superiority of women, with Clytaemnestra having murdered her husband and

Electra having egged Orestes on to murder their mother. Iphigeneia is evidently better able to feel sympathy than the male characters, but this is because of her experience, not her natural complexion. She sympathizes with the Greek prisoners, because like them she was due to be sacrificed. The shared experience as a sacrificial victim has made her compassionate:

> Löst die Erinnerung des gleichen Schicksals
> Nicht ein verschloßnes Herz zum Mitleid auf?
> Wie mehr denn meins! In ihnen seh ich mich.
> Ich habe vorm Altare selbst gezittert,
> Und feierlich umgab der frühe Tod
> Die Knieende; das Messer zuckte schon,
> Den lebenvollen Busen zu durchbohren.[91]

> Does the memory of the same fate not dissolve / In compassion a closed-up heart? / How much more so mine! I see myself in them. / I have trembled before the altar myself, / And solemnly an early death enveloped / Me as I knelt; the knife was already quivering / Ready to pierce my breast so full of life.

Orestes thinks the priestess's help will be of no avail, but only because of the greater power of the king, though as Pylades astutely responds, male power makes men more enigmatic partners than women:

> Wohl uns, daß es ein Weib ist! denn ein Mann,
> Der beste selbst, gewöhnet seinen Geist
> An Grausamkeit und macht sich auch zuletzt
> Aus dem, was er verabscheut, ein Gesetz,
> Wird aus Gewohnheit hart und fast unkenntlich.
> Allein ein Weib bleibt stet auf einem Sinn,
> Den sie gefaßt. Du rechnest sicherer
> Auf sie im Guten wie im Bösen.[92]

> Lucky for us it's a woman! For a man, / Even the best, accustoms his mind / To cruelty and in the end makes / A law out of what he abhors, / He becomes hard and practically unrecognisable out of habit. / But a woman remains constantly set on one purpose / That she has conceived. You can count more reliably / On her, both for good and ill.

Again, the gender differences are consequences of habit and social roles. Men are less likely to show pity because they cover their true selves in a carapace of violent power. Women, having no access to power, are more likely to resort to consistent moral arguments than inconsistent political ones. The difficulty for Pylades, which he does not fully understand, is that while he might be able to rely on Iphigeneia's pity at first, an inflexible quality such as this could make her unsuitable for his flexible schemes. Iphigeneia's pity may be so inflexible as to make her reluctant to deceive Thoas.

In a society divided strictly according to gender roles, it is hard for Iphigeneia to understand her own moral capacity in anything other than gendered terms. The most obvious characteristic of women is their lack of physical power compared to men. What then can women offer in opposition to male physical (and political) power? Against the hard power of swords women have only the soft power of words. This is the case Iphigeneia makes to Thoas when confrontation between the Greeks and Taurians threatens to erupt into violence in Act V. It is the moment when she fully realizes her own moral strength:

> Beschönige nicht die Gewalt,
> Die sich der Schwachheit eines Weibes freut.
> Ich bin so frei geboren als ein Mann.
> Stünd' Agamemnons Sohn dir gegenüber
> Und du verlangtest, was sich nicht gebührt,
> So hat auch er ein Schwert und einen Arm,
> Die Rechte seines Busens zu verteid'gen.
> Ich habe nichts als Worte, und es ziemt
> Dem edlen Mann, der Frauen Wort zu achten.[93]

> Do not sugar-coat the force / That glories in the weakness of a woman. / I was born as free as a man. / If Agamemnon's son were standing opposite you / And you were demanding something improper, / He has a sword and an arm / To defend the rights of his bosom. / I have nothing but words, and it is fitting / For a noble man to heed a woman's words.

Words are, of course, only the outer form of Iphigeneia's vision of woman, just as swords are the outer form of Thoas's political power. What Iphigeneia really has in mind is the power of reasoned argument. Her experience has shown her that men are not amenable to principled arguments. Repeatedly the men put up obstacles to them, usually by appealing to 'necessity', which is as much as to say that they seek to enforce their will by appeal to political power. Pylades is particularly guilty of this move:

Das ist nicht Undank, was die Not gebeut. [...]
Braucht's Überredung, wo die Wahl versagt ist? [...]
Du weigerst dich umsonst; die ehrne Hand
Der Not gebietet, und ihr ernster Wink
Ist oberstes Gesetz, dem Götter selbst
Sich unterwerfen müssen.[94]

It's not ingratitude when necessity demands it. / [...] Is there any need for persuasion when choice is forbidden? / [...] You refuse in vain; the brazen hand / Of necessity commands it, and its grave sign / Is the highest law, to which the gods themselves / Must surrender.

Faced by male appeals to political necessity, women have no alternative but to appeal to moral principles, such as the ancient and, in Greek culture, universal law of hospitality towards strangers. This law forbids the sacrifice of the Greeks, as Iphigeneia insists to Thoas:

Wir fassen ein Gesetz begierig an,
Das unsrer Leidenschaft zur Waffe dient.
Ein andres spricht zu mir, ein älteres,
Mich dir zu widersetzen: das Gebot,
Dem jeder Fremde heilig ist.[95]

We hungrily latch onto a law / That serves our passions as a weapon. / A different [law], an older one, tells me / To oppose you: the commandment / According to which every foreigner is sacred.

As Iphigeneia's words make clear, the obscurity of divine intentions makes it difficult to know what the moral law is. How can we know that we have not just weaponized the moral law to serve our desires? One approach would be to strip away any laws that might be motivated and polluted by self-interest. This is the force of the word 'pure' that occurs repeatedly in the play, especially towards the end. Here again Goethe makes the myth do the work of motivating his characters' words and actions. Iphigeneia's quest for purity is rooted in her role as a priestess, and one of her prime duties is to keep the goddess's temple pure. She has already achieved this by ending the Taurian practice of human sacrifice. The priestly duty of purity has also spread to other areas of her life. She first expresses her desire to return to Mycenae as a vague idea—'seeking the land of the Greeks with my soul' ('das Land der Griechen mit der Seele suchend')[96]—but she soon connects her desire to return to Greece with the idea of purity. She begins to see her role as bringing about a renewal of Mycenae through her own purity, 'with a pure hand and a pure heart' ('mit reiner Hand und reinem Herzen').[97] She repeats the idea in her plea to Thoas in Act V: 'Let me, with pure heart, pure hand, / Go there and expiate our house' ('Laß mich mit reinem Herzen, reiner Hand / Hinübergehn und unser Haus entsühnen').[98] But what is purity? In the first place, it means freedom from the negative passions: sadness, anger, desire.[99] (There is an obvious similarity to Spinoza's notion of human fulfilment as a process of liberation from desires.) Another feature of purity is the absence of deceit or cunning:

THOAS: Die Vorsicht stellt der List sich klug entgegen.
IPHIGENEIA: Und eine reine Seele braucht sie nicht.[100]

THOAS: Prudence wisely takes precaution against cunning.
IPHIGENEIA: And a pure soul makes no use of it.

The ideal human condition would be to have a heart unpolluted by anger, desire and deceit, a heart through which 'the source of life / Flows pure and unimpeded' ('des Lebens Quelle [...] rein / Und ungehindert fließt'), as Iphigeneia puts it.[101] Her talk of 'the source of life' is not an empty formula or a mere poetic ornament. It employs the language of Luther's Bible (Psalms 36:9) to refer to a metaphysical entity: the divine source and origin of all things. It is the same idea as in the *Prometheus* fragment, when Minerva promised to lead Prometheus to 'the source of all life' ('Quell des Lebens all'), and Mercury voiced alarm at Minerva's revealing the Olympians' secrets: 'High treason! / Minerva [...] has opened the source of life to him' ('Hochverrat! / Minerva [...] / Hat ihm den Lebensquell eröffnet').[102] So too Faust aspired to grasp the 'sources of all life' ('Quellen alles Lebens'),[103] a project that led him to summon the Earth Spirit, which did indeed seem to be the source of all life. For all its biblical associations, the language of purity and the 'sources of life' is best understood as articulating Goethe's interpretation of Spinoza and Rousseau. The ideal state of the human mind is one freed from deception and negative passions. Once we have succeeded in so liberating ourselves, we will find that the sources of life do indeed flow pure through us, and we will have a full and disinterested appreciation of God-nature—in other words Spinoza's 'intellectual love of god' (*amor dei intellectualis*). Or in a Rousseauian sense, the sources of life will express themselves morally, in the form of pity or compassion for our fellow humans.

Act III is concerned with the recovery of Orestes. In keeping with the play's secular humanism, the pursuit of Orestes by the Furies is reimagined as a psychological problem, not a supernatural or religious one. In his dialogues with Pylades and Iphigeneia in Act II, it emerges that Orestes suffers from episodes of hallucinatory mania and a deep, settled melancholia, with its typical features of anxiety, confusion, and morbid thoughts. At first Iphigeneia tries to heal him by means of a traditional religious intercession in her role as priestess, but her imprecations have no effect, or at least not the effect she hopes for. Her presence does remind Orestes, in his confusion, of his imminent death, for she is the priestess of Diana responsible for sacrificing him. Having thus brought the prospect of death nearer, her revelation that she is in fact his sister only makes the situation worse, for by sacrificing him she would perpetuate the Tantalid blood guilt, in his imagination at least, and this vision causes him to fall into a hysterical fit and then faint. Iphigeneia has unintentionally triggered a crisis in his illness, which, in accordance with traditional medical wisdom, will begin his recovery. Left alone, Orestes wakes and imagines he has left the world of the living and is in Hades, where he is reunited with the grim figures of his dead family. When Iphigeneia and Pylades return, they are able to wake him to full mental clarity. The crisis has passed. Triggered by his sister's presence, though not at all in the manner she intended, and certainly not by virtue of her humanity or purity, Orestes has healed himself.

Iphigeneia will make a similar journey, albeit without the mania and hallucinations. It is a journey through despair, alone and without aid, for the Greek men are now preoccupied with Pylades's plan to escape with the statue of Artemis. Iphigeneia's part in the plan is to feed Thoas the lie that human sacrifices cannot be resumed, as one of the Greeks has defiled the temple with blood guilt, and so the statue must be taken down to the sea to be purified. The plan adds a further irony to the play's treatment of religion: by deceitfully invoking the religious procedure of purifying the statue, Iphigeneia would be bringing religion into disrepute. Faced with the painful prospect of lying to Thoas, she prays to the gods not only to save her, but to prove to her that they are deserving of worship: 'save me, and save your image in my soul!' ('Rettet mich, / Und rettet euer Bild in meiner Seele!')[104] The double challenge—both to save her and by doing so to justify her religious belief—expresses an emerging scepticism. Her faith is on the verge of evaporating. In this anxious mood she is reminded of a song that the Fates supposedly sang when Tantalus was cast down from Olympus. The main sense of the song—the gods may favour some humans but also turn their backs on whole generations—is followed by a melancholy coda imagining Tantalus in the underworld gloomily contemplating the fate awaiting his successors. The song seems to confirm her fear that the gods are oblivious to human aspirations and that her salvation, if there is to be one, will not come from the heavens.

Pylades's escape plan is a continuation of the cycle of crime into which people seem locked by their belief that violence and deceit are the only way forward. This is the psychological innovation that Goethe inherited from Euripides: even if Iphigeneia was not in fact sacrificed by Agamemnon, the cycle of violence seems destined to continue by virtue of our erroneous belief in it. Iphigeneia is now challenged to break the cycle. She knows the gods will give no succour, if they are even capable of listening, and so in reality her challenge to the gods is a challenge to humans. She knows that men's addiction to violence and deceit makes them unable to break the cycle. She fears that women have no weapons potent enough to counter male power. She thus persuades herself that her only option is to perform the 'unprecedented act' ('unerhörte Tat')[105] of revealing the plan to Thoas. The trigger for her decision is that Thoas seems close to suspecting the truth. Her 'unprecedented act' will be to preempt his discovering the truth by being open with him, in the hope that he will then keep his word and set her free. Her hope is that a virtuous circle will replace the vicious one:

> Auf und ab
> Steigt in der Brust ein kühnes Unternehmen:
> Ich werde großem Vorwurf nicht entgehn
> Noch schwerem Übel, wenn es mir mißlingt;
> Allein euch leg ich's auf die Kniee! Wenn
> Ihr wahrhaft seid, wie ihr gepriesen werdet,
> So zeigt's durch euern Beistand und verherrlicht
> Durch mich die Wahrheit![106]

Up and down / There rises in my breast a daring plan: / I will not escape great censure / Nor grievous ill, if I fail; / Still, I lay it on your knees! If / [You gods] are truthful, as you are extolled as being, / Then show it through your support and glorify / Through me the truth!

The gods have changed. They are no longer helpful gods who intervene to rescue humans. Instead their role is to support us when we tell the truth. Their role is thus both diminished—they do not actually intervene—and purified. Indeed it is purified because it is diminished. For we can no longer sully the gods' reputation by invoking them to sanction or make good our crimes. The old revealed religions no longer make sense, for they were invented by humans merely in order to establish political power—so Goethe's Spinozan conviction. Iphigeneia's 'unprecedented act' not only establishes honesty between her and Thoas; it also ushers in a new age of Spinozan deism.

It remains to persuade Thoas that Orestes is who he claims to be. The proof is a scar on his head resulting from an accident in childhood. The semiotics of divine intentions is replaced by a semiotics of human identity. Thoas duly accepts the sign and indicates that the Greeks are free to leave: 'Go then!' ('So geht!'). This is still the voice of a ruler granting permission; it is an exercise of power. Iphigeneia insists on more. She insists on hearing the voice of sympathy from Thoas, not power, and so she makes a generous offer of guest friendship to any Taurian who happens to reach Mycenae, and in doing so she repeats the universal law of sympathy towards strangers that she appealed to earlier in Act V:

> Bringt der Geringste deines Volkes je
> Den Ton der Stimme mir ins Ohr zurück,
> Den ich an euch gewohnt zu hören bin,
> Und seh ich an dem Ärmsten eure Tracht:
> Empfangen will ich ihn wie einen Gott,
> Ich will ihm selbst ein Lager zubereiten,
> Auf einen Stuhl ihn an das Feuer laden
> Und nur nach dir und deinem Schicksal fragen.[107]

> Should even the humblest of your people ever / Bring back to my ears the sound of the voice / I've grown accustomed to hearing from you, / And should I see your costume worn by even the poorest, / I will welcome him like a god, / I will myself prepare a bed for him, / Invite him to a seat by the fire / And ask only after you and your fate.

Shared human experience recognises no difference between great and small, Greek and Taurian, man and woman. Sympathy is universal. Thoas understands this, haltingly and grudgingly perhaps, and finally supplements his 'go!' with a more sympathetic 'fare well!' ('Lebt wohl!').[108] We finally hear sympathy emerging from the mouth of the autocratic ruler. Along with Spinozan deism, a Rousseauian vision of universal sympathy has triumphed.

By the beginning of August 1779 Goethe and the Duke had decided that they would take a month or two away from Weimar and make a journey westwards. There were blunt conversations with Anna Amalia and Carl August, probably concerning the Duke's development. Goethe had a sense that a phase of his work with the Duke was coming to an end. Eventually it was decided that they would travel to Switzerland. The Duke's formation into a *Naturmensch* would be completed. He would be finally and fully tested by the physical and mental demands of alpine travel in the autumn and winter: bathing in ice-cold alpine lakes, slogging on foot up precipitous mountain paths, acquiescing to the sublime landscape, simply seeing the world without desires or pretensions. Another turning point and culmination was Goethe's elevation to the rank of Privy Councillor. The title was not merely honorific; it carried expectations of behaviour and marked a shift to a more formal relationship. Two days after the decision was finalized, Goethe wrote to Charlotte: 'it is amazing to me that, as if in a dream, with my thirtieth year I set foot on the highest rung of honour that a burgher in Germany can climb to'. And he added in French the famous words of Christopher Columbus: 'one never goes as far as when one does not know where one is going'.[109]

On 12 September 1779 the party set out on their four-month journey. In Kassel they visited the antiquities and met Georg Forster, who had accompanied Captain Cook on his second expedition. Within a week they were in Frankfurt, staying at the Three Lyres. Goethe's mother was well, but his father's memory was failing, a prelude to his descent into dementia.[110] The next week they were in Sessenheim, an opportunity for Goethe to assuage some of his 'guiltless guilt' towards Friederike,[111] and a similar opportunity arose in Strasbourg with a visit to Lili Schönemann, now married. In Emmendingen they visited Schlosser, and from there travelled via Freiburg, crossing into Switzerland at Basle, before heading southwest down the Aare valley to Biel. Here they took a boat on the lake to pay homage to the great Rousseau, who had died in July of the previous year. From Biel they headed southeast to Berne, where they took a circular route through the Oberland. After another pause in Berne, they struck out southwest to Lake Geneva, arriving in Lausanne on 22 October. The obligatory pilgrimage was made along the northern shore of the lake to Vevey, the setting for much of Rousseau's *New Heloïse*. The leisurely ride from Lausanne to Geneva was interrupted by an invigorating excursion up to the Vallée de Joux. From Geneva the party made another pilgrimage, to Voltaire's estate at Ferney. He had also died the previous year. There were introductions to the scholarly community in and around Geneva: the naturalist Charles Bonnet, the pastor and bibliophile Anton Josua Diodati, and the mountaineer and geologist Professor Horace-Bénédict de Saussure. Goethe was less interested in learning from Saussure about the geology of the Alps than in questioning him on the next and most challenging leg of their journey, which was not to be undertaken lightly in November.[112] The tour took them in a wide curve south and east through the Valais to the Furka Pass, where they crossed into the canton of Uri and then briefly into the Ticino at the Gotthard Pass. Here Goethe could look down towards Italy and ruefully write to Charlotte that it was still not time for his grand tour.[113] From the Gotthard they passed north through Andermatt and Schwyz to Lucern, and thence to Zurich, where Lavater waited.

Goethe's estimation of Lavater as a person remained very high[114] even if he felt little but scorn for his latest writings. In Geneva the young theologian and classicist Georg Christoph Tobler, recommended to Goethe by Lavater, had shown Goethe a manuscript of Lavater's new hexameter paraphrase of the Book of Revelation. The only thing in it that spoke to him, Goethe wrote bluntly to Lavater, was Lavater's handwriting.[115] Still, he hoped that the young Duke would benefit from meeting Lavater and was not disappointed.[116] It was the last time Goethe would enjoy spending any length of time in his company. Their correspondence continued for several years, but Goethe's letters showed an increasing irritation. He found Lavater's constant harping on the subject of Christ tedious. As he put it to Charlotte in 1782, Lavater was like a person who has a detailed command of all the latest astronomy and yet ruins it all by insisting that the earth is balanced on the shell of a giant tortoise.[117]

During the trip Goethe wrote detailed descriptive letters to Charlotte. Usually at the end of the day he would slip away into another room and write even if this meant not warming himself by the fire in the main room of their guesthouse. In these letters he tried something new: expressing his relation to nature in a manner that satisfied Spinoza's principle of the intellectual love of God. The aim was to purify his observations by minimizing his own desires and pretensions, to apprehend and treat things as they truly were. At the beginning of October, as the party first entered Switzerland, they passed through the narrow gorge made by the River Birs between Basle and Moutier. That evening in Moutier he wrote up his observations to Charlotte. After describing the gorge's rock formations in detail, he added: 'My eye and my soul were able to apprehend the objects, and since I was pure and the feeling encountered nothing false, so [the objects] were able to have the effect they should.'[118] It was a matter of letting the object speak for itself. Evidently satisfied with the letters he wrote in Switzerland, in the spring he shaped them into a coherent travelogue. The two paragraphs of description of the Birs gorge, which directly precede the passage quoted above, were taken up into the revised version with only very minor changes. They are a good example of his new mode of descriptive writing:

> At one point rock walls rise vertically one above the other, at the next huge strata run diagonally down to the river and the road; broad masses are lain one on top of the other, and close by stands a line of sharp-pointed crags. Wide clefts gape upwards and blocks the size of walls have detached themselves from the remaining body of rock. Some pieces of rock have rolled down; others are still hanging up above and seem, by their position, worryingly liable at any moment to come tumbling down.
>
> Some round, some pointed, some overgrown, some bare—so are the tops of the rocks, among and high above which boldly towers some single bald summit, and on the rockface and deep in the hollows are winding weathered clefts.[119]

The *Letters from Switzerland* maintain this mode throughout. The description conveys perceptual forms: size, structure, surface, relation, orientation. It also allows the perceiving subject into the picture, both as an observing point of view and as an emotional subject who experiences anxiety ('worryingly') about the falling rocks, but is only the subtlest presence. The objects are what really matter. Wieland wrote enthusiastically to Merck in April:

> [It is] one of his most masterful productions [. . .]. It is a genuine poem, hidden though the art may be. The extraordinary thing though and what differentiates him in nearly all of his works from Homer and Shakespeare, is that the I, the *ille ego*, glimmers through, but without any boastfulness and with infinite delicacy.[120]

In retrospect the *Letters from Switzerland* look like a preparation for Goethe's career as a geologist. However, in Switzerland he had no inkling of the sudden transformation that would happen in 1780 when geology and the other branches of natural history began to be a major preoccupation. In the spring of 1776 the Duke had directed Goethe to supervise the reopening of the silver mines in Ilmenau, which had been put out of action by flooding in 1739, when the dam burst in one of the dykes used to store water to power the mine's pumps.[121] In June the Duke met with advisers, among them the director of mining in Saxony, Friedrich Wilhelm Heinrich von Trebra. In July a permanent mining commission was established under Goethe and Kalb, and shortly afterwards Goethe visited Ilmenau with the Duke and Trebra. He entered into the spirit of the endeavour by reading widely in the literature on mining and resuming the study of chemistry, which was necessary for assaying the mine's silver ore.[122] Progress was slow. The commission was snarled up in legal negotiations over the ownership of the mines. In late November 1777 Goethe set off on his first research trip to the Harz Mountains, northern Germany's most important mining region. He visited all of the operational mines in the upper Harz region, descending deep into the shafts of several of the mines around Clausthal.[123] At some point on the journey he parted with his companions and set off on his own for the highest peak in the Harz, the Brocken, infamous for its associations with witchcraft and devil-worship. Despite local warnings about the dangerous conditions, he climbed the Brocken on 10 December. He commemorated the ascent in a Pindaric ode, 'Winter Journey in the Harz'. It is his most successful emulation of Pindar, perhaps because it is his strangest—its stark and luminous imagery, rugged syntax, and abrupt shifts of focus lead to the surprising but also prosaic conclusion that the Ilmenau mining project might be the goal of his existence at the Weimar court. The poem's final strophe celebrates the Brocken and its surrounding peaks for spreading the wealth of precious metals through their veins to the surrounding principalities:

> Du stehst mit unerforschtem Busen
> Geheimnisvoll offenbar
> Über der erstaunten Welt,
> Und schaust aus Wolken
> Auf ihre Reiche und Herrlichkeit
> Die du aus den Adern deiner Brüder
> Neben dir wässerst.[124]

> You stand with unexplored bosom, / Secretly manifest, / Above the amazed world, / And look out of clouds / Onto their realms and majesty, / Which out of the veins of your brothers / Beside you you water.

If 'Winter Journey in the Harz' was a prayer for success at Ilmenau, it was not answered. The legal position was resolved only in 1783, so that at last share certificates for the project could be issued. In February 1784 the momentous formal opening of the mine was marked by a ceremony in Ilmenau. Goethe

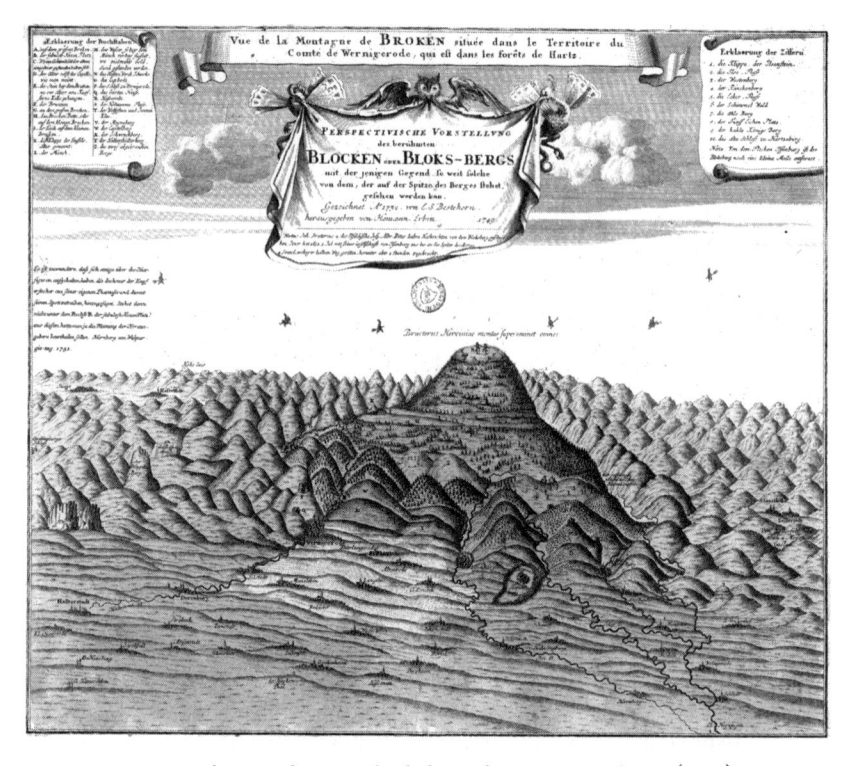

FIG. 10. The Brocken or Blocksberg, by L. S. Bestehorn (1732).
The etching includes witches circling the summit on broomsticks;
the location of the 'Witches' Altar' is marked on the summit.

delivered an ill-fated speech from memory, during which he had to pause embarrassingly for several minutes while he tried to remember the thread of his argument.[125] With the mine now open again, he had to devote time to managing the workforce.[126] With Knebel he spent two weeks in Ilmenau in June 1785 overseeing the halting progress. June 1786 saw problems with flooding.[127] By this point there was still nothing to show for all the effort and expense. It had been a costly failure.

By that point Ilmenau seemed less important than it had on his journey in the Harz in 1777. Forty years later Goethe told Friedrich von Müller that Ilmenau had made him a scientist,[128] but that was not strictly true. There is a difference between science as a technology for extracting silver ore from the earth and science proper: science as a means of understanding how the universe works. It was only in the summer of 1780 that Goethe became interested in science proper. Only now did he begin to understand how the hard-won knowledge of mining techniques fitted into a larger picture of the evolution of the earth. This new focus had one decisive trigger. In April 1780 he read *The Epochs of Nature* (1778), the fifth supplementary volume of Buffon's massive *Natural History* (1749–1788). He wrote enthusiastically to Merck:

> The Epochs of Nature by Buffon are absolutely excellent. I acquiesce entirely to it and will not allow anyone to say that it is a hypothesis or a story. [. . .] Nobody shall say anything to me against him in detail unless they can create a larger and more coherent whole. At any rate, the book seems to me less hypothetical than the first chapter of Genesis.[129]

Goethe saw two virtues in Buffon's account of the origins of the earth. First, it was synoptic and systematic: 'large' and 'coherent'. Second, it was more plausible than Genesis. That last sentence might look like damning with faint praise, but was meant more as a provocation: the story of the creation of the earth in Genesis cannot be taken seriously, and we all know that. The charge that Buffon's account is a hypothesis or story is more complex. It was a response partly to Buffon's own acknowledgement that his theory was hypothetical, and partly to his critics, who included Georg Forster. According to Buffon's account, the earth originated as a fragment of molten mineral that had been dislodged from the sun by the impact of a comet. In place of the traditional biblical chronology, Buffon proposed, on the basis of some complex calculations, that the earth was around 75,000 years old. However, he admitted that this account was hypothetical in two ways. The first was a tactical retreat in response to Christian outrage: his 75,000-year chronology was just a philosophical hypothesis, he claimed.[130] The second was a recognition that the comet theory and the calculations of the earth's cooling were conjectures. Either way, in his letter to Merck Goethe objected to Buffon's halfway retraction of his challenge to the biblical chronology. He believed in Buffon's heretical chronology and continued to advocate it. Writing to Merck in 1782, he stated that even the most recent period in the earth's history was, 'contrary to our conventional chronology, exceedingly ancient'.[131] Buffon's systematic approach and indifference to scripture commended him to Goethe. It showed convincingly that the earth was formed by the laws of nature, not divine action. Buffon's geology was further proof that revealed religion consisted largely of attractive falsehoods. Buffon's literary project—Goethe soon conceded that it was in fact a 'story', but a compelling one[132]—made a deep impression on him. By December 1781 he was planning his own 'Story of the Universe'.[133]

In 1776, at the inception of the Ilmenau project, Johann Carl Wilhelm Voigt, the younger brother of Goethe's ministerial colleague Christian Gottlob von Voigt, had been sent to complete his education at the mining academy in Freiberg under Germany's most eminent mineralogist Abraham Gottlob Werner. On his return to Weimar in 1780, Voigt was employed by the administration to advise on the geology of Ilmenau. He recommended that Goethe read Werner's *On the External Characteristics of Minerals* (1774), a rather arid exercise in what Werner termed 'geognosy'—the identification of minerals from their external appearance. In September Goethe wrote to Sophie von La Roche of his new passion: 'I am devoted [...] to mineralogy with all my soul'.[134] As the work on the mine was still in abeyance, he instructed Voigt to begin a geognostic survey of the Duchy and drafted a set of directions for him.[135] Goethe reported on Voigt's findings in a long letter to Merck in October 1780. It now seemed to Goethe that the practical value of Voigt's work for mining was the least of its merits: what mattered far more was the geognostic project of understanding the different layers that made up the earth's crust, in the manner of Buffon's *Epochs*.[136] In addition to the survey, which was published in 1781, Voigt would start a collection of minerals. Possessing physical samples was of particular value to Goethe, since he could 'not learn anything from books', he confessed to Merck in October 1780.[137] In December, in a long letter to the learned Duke Ernst of Saxe-Gotha-Altenburg, he said he would make better progress in natural history by means of what he called 'intuitive concepts', rather than by 'scholarly concepts'.[138] In fact he did learn from books: the Genevan professor Saussure's *Journeys in the Alps* (1779), a German translation of the Swede Axel Cronstedt's *Essay on Mineralogy* (1758), Barthélemy Faujas de Saint-Fond's *Studies on the Extinct Volcanoes of Vivarais and Velay* (1778) and Pierre Bernard Palassou's *Essay on the Mineralogy of the Pyrennees* (1781)—the latter two of which were essential reading, he wrote to Merck in 1781.[139] This reading persuaded Goethe that there was great progress to be made, as he wrote to Merck:

> This field has, as I'm just beginning to see, been cultivated with great diligence, and I'm convinced that, given all the existing experiments and reference books, a single great individual, who is able to traverse the world by foot or by mind, might once and for all understand and describe for us this strange composite globe, which is what Buffon has perhaps already done in the highest sense.[140]

Whereas on the trip to Switzerland in the winter of 1779/80 he had insufficient knowledge of the geology of the Alps to understand what he saw,[141] from the summer of 1780 his travels would involve making detailed observations in a 'geognostical diary'.[142] Some of these breaks from administrative work yielded poems that reflected his new interests. On 6 September 1780 he found himself in Ilmenau on official business. By way of relief from the day's stresses, he spent the evening on the Kickelhahn, a hill one and a half miles southwest of the town, from which he could enjoy the magnificent sunset, as he wrote to Charlotte: 'The sky is completely clear and I'm going up to enjoy the sunset. The view is huge but simple'. Later the same evening, he continued the letter from the hunting cabin on the Kickelhahn. He reminded Charlotte of a drawing he had done for her of the same view in 1776: 'The sun is down. It is exactly the spot from which I drew the rising mists for you, now it is so pure and peaceful [. . .]'.[143] It was probably on this evening, in the interval between writing the two passages above, that Goethe wrote the most famous poem in the German language. He scratched its mere eight lines on the hunting cabin's wall in pencil:

Über allen Gipfeln
Ist Ruh,
In allen Wipfeln
Spürest du
Kaum einen Hauch;
Die Vögelein schweigen im Walde.
Warte nur, balde
Ruhest du auch.[144]

Over all the hilltops / There's peace, / In all the treetops / You detect / Hardly a breath; / The little birds are silent in the forest. / Just wait, soon / You too will rest.

While Goethe's tendency to mythologize his own creativity has led the poem to be read as an expression of intense subjectivity, it is better understood as an exploration of how our subjectivity interacts with the world. Starting from a landscape of pine-covered hills, the poem shifts its focus to the observing self at the end of line 2 ('you detect', 'spürest du'), then moves out again to the birds in the forest (line 4), and finally back to the self again (lines 5 and 6). This alternation reflects the interaction between self and world, in which the subject is not a mere passive receiver of impressions, but is actively attentive—the verb 'spüren' (line 2) can mean *to perceive* but also *to track*. The interaction of self and world is also reflected in the way the world is presented. The focus of the subject's perceptions shifts from the mountains, to the trees, and finally to the birds. It is a movement from more distant objects to closer ones; the focus of the senses draws in towards the subject. This movement in turn corresponds to another important structural feature of the poem. The three kingdoms of the natural world are present: mineral (the mountains), vegetable (the trees), and animal (the birds). They appear in the sequence in which they emerged in the history of the earth as expounded by Buffon in *The Epochs of Nature*. Thus the movement through the three kingdoms corresponds to the movement of the subject's perceptions; objective reality and subjective perception are in harmony.

From late 1780 Goethe accompanied Voigt on his geognostical surveys. He also travelled on his own or with other companions—sometimes natural historians, sometimes local experts,[145] sometimes friends: Knebel and even the Duke. The artist Kraus sketched rock formations for him. In September 1783 he travelled to the Harz again. From Clausthal he wrote to Charlotte: 'I'm absolutely in my element here and am pleased that I find that I'm on the right track with my speculations on the ancient crust of the new world'.[146] One speculation concerned the regularity of the masses of granite. These were divided into horizontal strata intersected by fissures running north-south and further fissures running roughly east-west at uniform nonperpendicular angles to the north-south fissures. In combination, the north-south and east-west fissures created rhomboidal shapes. The second speculation was that granite seemed to form the base layer of many rock formations, and might therefore be the oldest stratum of the crust, as Saussure proposed in his *Journeys in the Alps*.[147] Through 1783 and into 1784 he became increasingly convinced that these two theories captured something fundamental about the ancient formation of the earth's crust. During a trip to Eisenach and the Thuringian Forest in the summer of 1784 he examined sandstone layers known as *rotliegend*, which also conformed to the model: 'it is a stratified formation, which is divided by large vertical fissures', he wrote in his notes.[148] In another note from the same trip he observed: 'the horizontal fissures of the strata are often invisible. / The vertical fissures visible. / Also divided by these rhomboidally. / Kind of division around a mid-point'.[149] As he wrote in 1820, when reflecting on his early geological research, 'we believed we had found that during solidification an orientation of fissures northwards occurred; the crosswise fissures crossing eastwards but not perpendicular, causing the rhomboidal peelings. We had a model in mind'.[150] The discovery in June 1784 was enough to prompt a confident letter to Herder: 'I've been diligently clambering about on the rocks, and have found much that's of use to me. Also I believe I've found or rather applied a very simple principle so as to explain the evolution of larger rock formations'.[151] The rhomboidal forms that Goethe found in granite and *rotliegend* were visible evidence of a process described in the geological literature he was reading by Saussure, Richard Kirwan, and Jean-Baptiste Louis Romé de l'Isle. The rhomboidal forms, which are shaped like massive crystals, indicated that granite was formed by a process of crystallization or, as he would put it in 1820, solidification. As for now, 'the whole structure of our earth is to be explained by crystallization', he wrote in a set of notes on the history of the formation of the earth:[152] 'When our earth formed into a body its mass was in a more or less fluid state. [. . .] / The liquefaction occurred through a fire in the core [. . .]. / The core of the earth crystallized and is probably the heaviest mass. / The external crust of the earth is granite'.[153] All of which suggests a more general claim: 'its external regular constant form [is] the perfection [*Vollendung*] of a thing',[154] or in Aristotelian terminology its *telos*. If the rhomboidal form is the form taken naturally by crystallizing granite—the form it takes when it is not subjected to external pressures—then we can say that the rhomboidal form is the perfection or *telos* of granite. The rhomboidal form may thus be said to inhere in the substance of granite; it is the direction naturally taken by the process of crystallization in granite. By this route he came to the Aristotelian doctrine of hylomorphism: the idea that form inheres in substance, and that therefore form and substance are inseparable. If there is one idea that perhaps typifies Goethe's mature thought, it is the inextricable unity of form and substance.

Goethe's interest in natural history was motivated by a number of factors, but the most important was that our relation to nature needed to be rescued from the influence of positive and revealed religion. The essays and notes he wrote in 1784 and 1785, chiefly on geological formations, were probably intended as contributions to the 'Story of the Universe' he had conceived in 1780 after reading Buffon's *Epochs of Nature*. The 'Story of the Universe' was an alternative to scripture. As Goethe understood it, natural history was in direct opposition to biblical and doctrinally sanctioned views of the history of the earth and to the account of them in Wolffian philosophy, which held that the *telos* of nature was to be useful for humans, and that natural phenomena belonged to fixed and divinely ordained kinds. This is why Goethe was especially interested in natural phenomena that seemed to confute theistic views of the world. He wanted to see nature as an independent, self-contained system that had its own *telos*, not ours. He was aware of the most heinous recent heresy of all—the idea that animal and plant species were not fixed. How else could one explain the evidence that in the more recent rock strata the fossils of extinct animals became more similar to current species? Goethe discussed these fossils in detailed letters to Merck in October and November 1782.[155] That year he read the first volume of Jean-Louis Giraud-Soulavie's *Natural History of Southern France* (1780–1784). The first edition, later censored, contained a theory of the 'metamorphosis of several species of animals' based on the fossil record: it was an early theory of evolution.[156]

A pleasant surprise came in August 1783 when the frostiness between Goethe and Herder suddenly thawed. There followed a period of vigorous intellectual exchange. Herder was working on a new universal history: *Ideas on the Philosophy of the History of Mankind*. In December Goethe wrote to Knebel about the chapters of the *Ideas* dealing with the origins of the earth: 'the day before yesterday we read the first chapters together, they are delectable. [. . .] We are in a fever of world and natural history now'.[157] As Goethe described it much later, 'our daily conversation was concerned with the primal origins of the water-covered earth and the living creatures that have evolved on it from time immemorial'.[158] Goethe would later claim that he had provided much of the descriptive material on natural history for the early parts of Herder's *Ideas*.[159] A letter from Charlotte von Stein to Knebel sheds more light on the ideas Herder and Goethe were discussing: 'Herder's new work makes it probable that we were once plants and animals'.[160] It is possible that this refers to a notion of species transformation, which Goethe may have picked up from Soulavie and passed on to Herder.

Before the rapprochement with Herder, Goethe had already begun to study anatomy. In 1778 the University of Jena appointed a young professor of anatomy, Justus Christian Loder. In the summer of 1780, while Goethe was undergoing his baptism in geology, Loder performed anatomical presentations for the Weimar court. Goethe was impressed by Loder's skill and knowledge, and in 1781 he began to attend his lectures and dissections in Jena. Anatomy combined nicely with another pastime: he could practise his draughtsmanship by drawing the human body. By November he felt that his knowledge was far enough advanced to give his own lectures on anatomy at Weimar's Free Academy of Drawing. He had devised his own method of presenting the material to the students, he told Lavater: he aimed to show them what was distinctive in the 'singular' anatomy of humans and at the same time to show how the functions of human life depended on the structure of the body.[161] Through 1782 and 1783 he continued to labour over skeletons with Loder. In May 1782 Goethe read the volume of Buffon's *Natural History* concerned with quadrupeds.[162] In April 1783 the poet Friedrich von Matthisson visited Weimar in the company of the Göttingen anatomy professor Johann Friedrich Blumenbach, who wrote to the great Heyne full of praise for Goethe's anatomical knowledge.[163] Through the winter of 1783/84 Goethe and Loder examined mammal skulls. Goethe's attention was drawn to a bone formation in the mammalian palate that carries the incisor teeth, the intermaxillary bone (*os intermaxillare*). Whereas in most mammals the sutures between the intermaxillary formation and the main maxillary bone remain visible throughout an animal's development, in adult humans the sutures seemed to disappear, due to the extreme foreshortening of the human face relative to the other apes. This led some authorities, including Blumenbach, Samuel Thomas Sömmerring (also a correspondent of Goethe's), and the eminent Dutch anatomist Pieter Camper, to claim that the intermaxillary bone was not a feature of human anatomy. (Vicq d'Azyr in France had shown that Camper was wrong, but his work was not well known in Germany.)[164] Indeed its absence from humans could be interpreted as a sign of humans' anatomical uniqueness. And since the form of the palate could be linked, speculatively of course, to the faculty of speech, the uniqueness of humans as speaking and rational beings could be related to their unique anatomy. Humans were a unique creation, godlike in form and function. Contrary to this traditionalist view, Goethe believed that his observations provided evidence of the existence of the intermaxillary sutures in humans and hence demolished the doctrine of human uniqueness. In March 1784, with a typical mixture of excitement and caution, as well as an ironic nod towards the failure of Ilmenau to yield up the hoped-for silver, he wrote to Herder, his ally in transformationist thought:

> According to the instruction of the Evangelist, I must in all haste acquaint you with a blessing that has befallen me. I have discovered—neither gold nor silver, but something that gives me inexpressible joy—
> the os intermaxillare in humans!
> Together with Loder I was comparing human and animal skulls, lit upon the traces and lo! there it is. But I beg you, don't say a word, for it must be kept secret. It will delight you too, for it is the keystone to human beings, is not absent, is here too! And how! I've also been thinking about it in connection with the whole, what a fine thing it'll be there.[165]

The vague term 'the whole' conveys an idea Goethe had learned from Buffon's *Époques*: science proper had to think universally; natural laws must be universal in their operation. It was also one of the key principles of Herder's *Ideas*: hence

Goethe's urge to tell him about the *os intermaxillare*. The particular empirical finding acquired meaning through its place in a broader argument with heretical theological implications, which were constantly in his mind and explain both his excitement and his caution.

On a purely empirical level, it is doubtful whether Goethe's discovery merits the excitement. The human *os intermaxillare* had been identified by anatomists before Goethe, as he well knew. From March to May 1784 he worked on a short essay outlining his findings and setting them in their historical context, with Loder's help. In the essay he made clear that he was only standing on the shoulders of giants: the *os intermaxillare* had been described by the greatest authorities in anatomy, Galen and Andreas Vesalius. Goethe drafted several versions of the essay. Drawings were commissioned from Johann Christian Wilhelm Waitz, a student at the Academy of Drawing. Further mammal skulls were examined: in June 1784 he received an elephant skull on loan from Sömmerring. He wrote to Charlotte: 'I have started to study the great skull and am finding more than I like, more and more new things, and yet that's why we study nature'.[166] Initially he correctly inferred that the elephant's tusks were modified incisors, but eventually concluded wrongly that they were canines.[167]

In November he sent the essay to Knebel with a full confession of the creed:

> Herewith finally the treatise from the realm of bones; I'd be glad for your thoughts on it. I have avoided mentioning the result, which Herder has already alluded to in his Ideas—namely that one cannot find the difference between humans and animals in anything specific. On the contrary, humans are related in the closest way to animals. The unity of the whole makes each particular creature what it is, and humans are humans just as much by virtue of the form and nature of their upper jaw as by the form and nature of each joint of their little toe. And thus each creature is but one tone, one shade of a great harmony, which one must also study in its entirety, for otherwise each individual is a dead letter. It is from that perspective that this little essay is written, and that is in fact the interest that lies concealed within it. [...] Just as in ancient times, when humans lay sore oppressed on the earth, it was a benison to point them towards heaven, so now it is an even greater benison to bring them back down to earth and reduce somewhat the elasticity of their attached balloons.[168]

The essay, with its Spinozan dynamite hidden safely out of sight, was finished in December. A version in Latin was produced for Camper. Goethe sent the two versions to Merck with a request that he forward the Latin one via

Sömmerring to Camper, assuming that Merck thought Camper would 'respond well to the rectification of his opinion by a layman'.[169] For whatever reasons, Merck hesitated, which annoyed Goethe and led to a permanent cooling of their friendship. He continued to remind Merck through the winter. In April he expressed scepticism to Merck about the experts' likely reaction to his findings:

> I'm genuinely curious to hear what Sömmerring said when you showed him the bones. I don't yet think he'll surrender. I wouldn't put it past a professional scholar to deny the evidence of his five senses. They're rarely concerned with grasping the living essence of the matter, and instead with what people have said about it.[170]

However, Goethe's opinion of professional scholars was not suddenly soured by his frustration over Merck's foot-dragging. He had believed for some time that his own ideas—'intuitive concepts' he called them in 1780—were simply different from the 'scholarly concepts' used by the professionals.[171] Goethe's concerns were borne out. His empirical observations did have an effect: Camper acknowledged Goethe's observation of the intermaxillary bone in the walrus; both Blumenbach and Sömmerring later altered their position on the human intermaxillary bone from denial to acceptance.[172] However, their initial refusal to recommend publication killed the essay stone dead. It was left unpublished until 1820, by which time it was only of historical interest.

In January 1785 Goethe bought a microscope in order to study the tiny, simple freshwater animals of the genus *hydra*.[173] His interest in the *hydra* was motivated by the thought, widespread at the time, that at the microscopic level there seemed to be virtually no difference between plant and animal life.[174] Hence the *hydra* and other microorganisms were of special interest to transformationists, for they indicated how simple animal life might evolve out of plants. Goethe was keen to observe any phenomena of this kind. In summer he went to see a large mushroom, to judge by his description probably a cauliflower mushroom of the genus *sparassis*.[175] In September, after rain, a large patch of yellow-green jelly fungus (*tremella*) attracted his attention.[176] Goethe thought he found some microscopic forms within the body of the *tremella*, which he believed were examples of the kind of single-celled microscopic life forms or *infusoria* found in freshwater ponds. These *infusoria* seemed to hover ambiguously between the plant and animal kingdoms. In the autumn he began to read Wilhelm Friedrich von Gleichen-Rußwurm's writings on the *infusoria*. In the spring he began to copy Gleichen-Rußwurm's experiments, which involved infusing water with various vegetable substances—potato, beer, dried mushrooms, lentils, and so on—and observing the infusions every few days as they stood in glass jars on a sunny windowsill.[177] The experiments showed that the microorganisms behaved differently in sunlight and darkness. At the time he drew no wider conclusions from the observations, but the motivation for the experiments is clear from some reflections he wrote thirty years later when reflecting on his notes from 1786. Here he commented, in the typically guarded manner of his older years, on the possibility of transformation between the plant and animal kingdoms:

> Plants and animals in their least developed state are scarcely to be differentiated. Hardly perceptible to our senses, they are a pinpoint of life, mutable or semimutable. Are these beginnings—determinable in either direction—destined to be transformed by light into plant, or by darkness into animal? This is a question we do not trust ourselves to answer, even though there is no shortage of observations and analogies on the matter.[178]

Were one less cautious, one might indeed conclude that the forms of microscopic animal and vegetable life we observe today evolved from the same ancestral microorganisms, and this is of course exactly what Goethe's comment hints at.

Having ventured into geology, anatomy, and microorganisms, it was inevitable that Goethe would become interested in botany. His ambition was to construct a unified picture of nature that was independent of divine action and wholly self-consistent in its laws and processes. Botany was the missing piece. In early March 1785 he went to Jena with Knebel to study with the botanists. In April he set up a seed tray so that he could study the development of plants from their beginnings. It gave him, as he wrote to Charlotte, 'really lovely revelations about this race'.[179] Herder wrote to Knebel that 'Goethe is diligently looking through the microscope and at plants'.[180] But it was books that would prove the most useful stepping stones. In November for the first time he looked closely at Linnaeus's *Philosophia Botanica*, having only dipped into it in the past.[181] He wrote to Knebel that he had 'made considerable progress in botany'.[182] Towards the end of the year he began to make notes on the classification of plants according to their method of embryonic development from the seed (cotyledon). The first question was whether the embryonic development of the cotyledons happened above ground (epigeal) or below ground (hypogeal). He seems to have come to the erroneous view that some plants could have both epigeal and hypogeal cotyledons. This in turn made him want to develop his own terminology for the cotyledons: the terms 'upper' and 'lower' did not seem to express the way plants developed, for the so-called 'upper (epigeal) cotyledons' seemed to have the form of leaves. Whether he knew it or not, he was becoming involved in the kind of semantic argument that he had criticised the scholars for. It would also lead him to one of his most fruitful and important insights in all of his researches into natural history. Botany was becoming an obsession. In April 1786 he wrote to Fritz Jacobi: 'Botany and the microscope are now the mortal enemies against whom I have to fight. On the other hand, I'm now living in a solitude and seclusion from the world that makes me as mute as a fish'.[183]

Befitting his new status as Privy Councillor, he began to adopt a more formal personal demeanour. Already in January 1780, on his return from the Swiss journey, his friends in Weimar, including Wieland, noted the change in his behaviour.[184] Eighteen months later, the visiting Danish theology student Friedrich Münter reported that Goethe was 'too minister-like and cold. Yet he was entirely polite'.[185] He was striving harder to maintain a high standard in his administrative work. He wrote to Kestner in May 1780 that 'order, precision, speed are qualities I hope daily to acquire some measure of'.[186] The previous day he wrote in his diary that governing a state required the ability to govern oneself by renouncing one's desires: 'the only person worthy to govern and able to govern is the person who is capable of complete self-denial'.[187] The qualities he thought necessary for an administrator were akin to the objectivity he strove for in natural history. Accordingly he began to read up on administrative finances, starting inauspiciously with the *Report to the King* (*Comte rendu au roi*, 1781) of the Director-General of Finance to the French crown Jacques Necker—inauspiciously because, despite Necker's claims for the accuracy of his statement of the monarchy's finances, his numbers massively understated the monarchy's indebtedness. Goethe was not to know this: 'it is a massive bequest to the present world and the future', he wrote to Charlotte in April 1781, 'its spirit is life-giving and its flesh is also useful'.[188] The next year Goethe wrote to Knebel that he intended to study economics.[189] He was convinced of his own dogged perseverance and capacity for order. Unfortunately he could not say the same of Carl August. Ten days before the letter to Knebel he wrote to Charlotte with one of his very rare complaints about the Duke: 'Fundamentally the Duke has a narrow perspective on things and whatever courageous projects he undertakes are done in the heat of the moment; he lacks the proper sequence of ideas and true constancy to pursue a long plan that in its full breadth and width would be audacious'.[190]

It was not that the 'order, precision, speed' and 'self-denial' necessary for politics were particularly congenial to Goethe. On the contrary, he knew that human authenticity could not long survive contact with politics. This tension was one of the themes of the drama *Egmont*, which he was struggling to complete in the years 1780–1782. The play's material came from the early years of the Dutch provinces' struggle for independence from Spanish dominion. By early 1782 it may have been substantially finished, but there were still problems with Act IV concerning the delicate matter of how to represent the despotic politics of the Spanish Grand Duke of Alba without lapsing into cliché. The language of the play also irked him: the 'overly unbuttoned and student-like nature of its style [...] contradicts the dignity of the subject matter', he wrote to Charlotte in March 1782.[191] In January 1785, hoping to finish the play, he realized that he had lost the manuscript.[192] The final impulse to finish what had been started over a decade earlier came in July and August 1787. The completed manuscript was edited by Herder, gone over once more by Goethe, and published in 1788.

Goethe had in fact begun work on the play in 1774, the year after the publication of *Götz von Berlichingen*. It was to be another prose drama in five acts set in the revolutionary sixteenth century, with a large cast ranging from the high nobility to the working classes, and a protagonist whose aspiration to live freely is out of step with the emergence of modernity. The protagonist was Lamoral, Count of Egmont, Prince of Gavre (1522–1568), a member of the Flemish high nobility and a loyal and respected statesman and general of the Empire. The historical Egmont objected to the introduction of the Inquisition into the Low Countries, was apprehended by the Spanish and tried at a special tribunal set up by Alba. Along with Philip de Montmorency, Count of Hoorn, and numerous lesser nobility, he was beheaded on the Grand Place in Brussels in 1568. In this sense the action of the play, ending in the hours before Egmont's execution, showed how even 'well-established' political institutions struggled to withstand 'firm and well-calculated despotism', as Goethe later put it in *Poetry and Truth*.[193] However, that pessimistic conclusion contrasts with the longer historical perspective. Egmont's execution was the prelude to the Eighty Years' War between Spain and the Netherlands, which resulted in the birth of a new independent, economically, and culturally rich nation, the Dutch United Provinces. Indeed, the Dutch States General chose the date of

5 June 1648, the eightieth anniversary of Egmont's execution, to promulgate the Treaty of Münster which formally recognised its independence, and so Egmont's death became part of the official narrative of Dutch greatness.

In order to tie Egmont's fate more closely to Dutch independence, Goethe compressed the events of the years 1566–1568 into a much shorter time frame. The first three acts, prior to Alba's arrival in Brussels with his army, show the city in a state of concerned anticipation verging on outright violence. Egmont meets his fellow nobleman William of Orange, who fails to persuade the peaceable and tradition-minded Egmont to join him in going into exile and leading a rebellion against the Spanish. On Alba's arrival in Act IV, a new repressive order is imposed that initially cows the citizens. Egmont is arrested after a long and tense debate with Alba. This scene was entirely Goethe's invention; it enabled him to move the action on briskly and omit the trial at which Egmont and the other nobles were convicted on trumped-up charges. The curtain falls in the hours before Egmont's execution. The most drastic changes Goethe made to the historical record were designed to shine a spotlight on Egmont. The Count of Hoorn and other nobles tried alongside Egmont are omitted entirely. Egmont becomes the sole Dutch martyr, and the play's final scene conveys his growing faith that his execution will incite the Dutch to rebellion. Egmont becomes a dashing and charismatic figure, certainly more so than the historical Egmont, who was a devout Catholic in his forties with a wife and eleven children. Unsurprisingly Goethe's Egmont has no obvious religious faith, aside from advising the citizens to 'stand firm against the foreign doctrine' of Calvinism—advice that seems designed more to maintain public order than to ensure the citizens' spiritual welfare.[194] Goethe's Egmont seems to be a younger man with no family and instead a petit-bourgeois beloved Clara, whose mother would rather she married the stolid and sensible bourgeois Brackenburg. This romantic plot, culminating in Egmont's visit to Clara in Act III, displays both his desire for authentic love and his moral irresponsibility. Marriage between Egmont and Clara is obviously impossible, and yet Egmont fails to consider what the consequences of their relationship will be for her. As in *Faust*, the bourgeois tragedy of Egmont and Clara shows that the charisma of a man of high social status creates the potential for 'guiltless guilt'—guiltless because the guilt arises out of authentic love. Egmont's political behaviour shows the same blend of authenticity and irresponsibility. His charisma and authenticity make him a suitable flag for the Dutch rebellion to rally around. Yet he is an inept politician who finds politics cold and disingenuous. Indeed, part of the play's political meaning is that the success of the

Dutch bid for nationhood depends in part on Egmont's cavalier disregard of politics. Political success depends on being unpolitical.

Egmont is not a reformer, let alone a revolutionary.[195] His understanding of the politics of the Low Countries is rooted in established rights and privileges, such as the entitlements of the local nobility or his own right to be tried by the Emperor, as a member of the Order of the Golden Fleece. When in Act IV Alba points out that the local nobility seems reluctant to share its power with the common people, Egmont replies as a good conservative should: 'this occurred centuries ago and is now accepted without envy'.[196] The Low Countries' traditional arrangements express a shared experience. By retaining them, the people place their trust in those with whom they have lived together, as Egmont puts it to Alba:

> That is why the citizens wish to retain their old constitution, to be ruled by their compatriots, for they know how they will be led and can expect these leaders to be both unselfish and to share a concern with the people's fate.[197]

Egmont's view of politics is grounded in shared experience. In Act II he encounters citizens on the street agitating for the restitution of their traditional rights. He remembers one of them, a tailor who once made livery for his men. The memory seems to moderate Egmont's initial anger towards the people on the streets, and instead of chiding them, he encourages them to restore order and confirms that they 'can rely on every kind of help' from the authorities.[198] The scene is a reworking of the opening of Shakespeare's *Julius Caesar*, which Goethe read during the early phase of work on *Egmont*.[199] In Shakespeare's scene two pompous tribunes question a crowd of tradesmen, and a cobbler makes fun of one of the tribunes, the haughty and dim-witted Marullus. Comparing the two scenes one is struck by how close Egmont is to the people: his concern for his people may be paternalistic, but he understands them and commands their respect, in contrast to Shakespeare's Marullus.

Egmont's problem is not his paternalism: it is that his trust in the past blinds him to the possibility that the future could be different. This leads him to make a series of incorrect judgements about where events are leading. He incorrectly assumes that the sensible and moderate regent Margareta of Parma will remain in post, as she has made empty threats to resign in the past. When William of Orange insists that Egmont consider what might happen if the regent did resign, Egmont incorrectly predicts that her replacement will behave broadly as she has done. Again, when Orange maintains that the King could well turn his aggression from the people to the nobility, Egmont disagrees, again wrongly, on the grounds that the Empire's constitution prevents the King from doing so. Part of Egmont's problem is a misplaced confidence in the traditional many-layered structures of the Holy Roman Empire, as understood by Möser and as experienced by Goethe in Frankfurt, and in the ability of these structures to withstand attack from 'firm and well calculated despotism'. A positive construal of Egmont's politics is that he has understood that modernity is hollowing out human individuality. It is the kind of argument Möser made in his 1775 essay 'The Current Tendency towards General Laws and Ordinances is a Danger to General Freedom'.[200] In his debate with Alba in Act IV, Egmont claims that King Philip and his advisors are making the mistake of treating people as philosophical abstractions in the hope of making them easier to control:

> He has decided what no prince has the right to decide. His will is to weaken, oppress, destroy the strength of his people—their self-confidence, their own conception of themselves—so as to be able to rule them without effort. His will is to corrupt the very core of their individuality; doubtless with the intention to make them happier. His will is to annihilate them so that they will become something, a different something. Oh, if his intention is good, it is being misguided. It is not the King whom this people resists; what it opposes is only the King who is taking the first unfortunate steps in a direction utterly wrong.[201]

The play invites us to set the flawed but authentic Egmont against the calculating and characterless Orange. Goethe modelled Orange on the description in the pro-Spanish Roman Jesuit Famiano Strada's *On the Belgian War* (1632)—'prudent and cautious, always pursuing the future in his mind'.[202] Goethe has the Regent describe Orange in these terms: 'To be frank, I fear Orange [. . .]. Orange is up to no good, his thoughts reach out to the distant future, he is secretive'.[203] Goethe also drew on the constellation of characters in *Julius Caesar*. The Regent's fear of Orange echoes Caesar's fear of Cassius because 'he thinks too much', and 'he looks / Quite through the deeds of men'.[204] For Orange, this kind of prudence is a duty. In his debate with Egmont he describes himself as a chess player:

> I do not regard any move on the other side as insignificant. And just as idle persons enquire with the greatest care into the secrets of nature, so I consider it the duty, the vocation, of a prince to know the views and strategy of all parties.

Goethe's treatment of Dutch independence is therefore not entirely optimistic. In order for the charismatic Egmont's legacy to be preserved, the tactical prudence of Orange is required, but there will be a Rousseauian price to be paid for political success. Orange is an unattractive character. His tactics are purely reactive.[205] He has no identity outside the world of politics. Egmont draws attention to this on his visit to Clara in Act III, when he describes himself as consisting of two Egmonts:

> That Egmont is an ill-tempered, stiff, cold Egmont, who has to keep up appearances, now make this face, now that [...]. But this one, Clara, this one is calm, candid, happy, beloved and understood by the best of hearts, which he too understands wholly and presses to him with complete love and trust. [*He embraces her.*] That is your Egmont.[206]

Egmont has two selves, but Oranien has no private self; he has only a 'stiff, cold' public-facing self. This is the nature of modern politics: the hollowing out of the self, the erasure of identity. As Goethe put it in a review in the *Frankfurt Scholarly Notices* in 1773, in a civilized nation one cannot be 'one's own creature'.[207] The play repeatedly raises this objection to the Spaniards' politics. In Act IV one of the citizens, Jetter, describes Alba's Spanish soldiers marching through the streets of Brussels:

> It freezes your marrow to see a body of them march down the street. Straight as posts, their eyes glued on the next man's back, not a single man out of step. And when they're on guard duty and you pass by, you feel as though they could see right into your head, and they look so stiff and grumpy that you seem to see a taskmaster at every corner. They made me feel ill. Our militia, at least, was a gay lot. They took liberties, stood about with legs straddled, wore their hats over one eye, lived, and let live; but those fellows are like machines with a devil inside.[208]

Goethe drew this image of the Spanish military, spiritually mechanized and ruled by a single will, from a passage in Herder's *This too a Philosophy of History for the Education of Humanity* which describes how the modern technological and bureaucratic state has created mechanized armies controlled by a single will: 'The army became a hired, thoughtless, forceless, will-less machine which *one man* directs in *his head*, and which he only pays as a *puppet* of movement, a living wall, to throw bullets and catch bullets'.[209] Egmont expresses a similar thought at the close of the play: the Spanish soldiers guarding him are commanded by 'the ruler's hollow words [...], not their true feelings'.[210] In the technological-bureaucratic state people have no true feelings; the state has hollowed them out. Orange may be less oppressive than the Spanish, but the play shows us how he has turned himself into a machine for politics.

Against this sombre background of Spanish oppression and the loss of authentic selfhood, the final Act presents Egmont's transformation into a martyr and symbol for Dutch independence. Alba's threats of repression have changed Egmont's attitude.[211] He now sees that the freedom of the Low Countries is at stake and war is necessary. He has ceased to be the trusting royalist and paternalist whose overriding political priority was to maintain civic order and has become a martyr for Dutch freedom. Critics have questioned whether the play properly justifies Egmont's transformation. In his 1788 review, Schiller argued that Goethe had failed to ground Egmont's martyrdom in the play's action. Although an audience might feel fear and pity for Egmont, the play shows no heroism that an audience might admire or that would justify Egmont's status as a martyr.[212] Schiller was certainly right in the sense that Egmont is not a preformed hero. He has to become one, and to do so he must undergo a psychological transformation, moving from anxiety to confidence. The transformation culminates in a dream vision of Clara arrayed as freedom. In a combination of costume, dumb show, and incidental music, the vision of Clara indicates that Egmont will win victory. Schiller complained that the dream vision was 'a leap of faith into an operatic world'.[213] Certainly, the play does move into a symbolic mode, but in Goethe's defence this transformation flows out of the play's political logic. Egmont becomes a symbol because Alba decides to make him one in Act IV. When Egmont proposes that the King should offer a general pardon, Alba argues that this would set a bad example: 'And let everyone who has profaned the King's majesty, the sanctity of religion, go about scot-free where he pleases? To serve as a shining example to others that atrocious crimes go unpunished?'[214] Alba's plan is instead to staunch the rebellion by executing Egmont as an example to the people of the Low Countries of what happens when Spanish power is threatened. Egmont acknowledges Alba's plan in his final words, urging the people of the Low Countries to ready themselves for sacrifice by following his 'example': 'Protect your property! And to preserve your dearest ones, willingly, gladly fall as my example shows you'.[215] In other words, Alba's political strategy creates the conditions for Egmont to become a symbol; Egmont's transformation is the unintended consequence of Alba's plan. It is also a consequence of Egmont's character. In order to become an ideal, Egmont must be unable to do politics well. This is because the goal of politics cannot be within the process of politics itself; it must lie outside of the political process, outside of politics in the hollow and mechanical sense represented by Orange and Alba. Egmont's authenticity and his antipathy to this form of politics is what qualifies him as a political symbol. His fullness of character motivates the rebellion. More than that, it embodies the purpose of rebellion: to enable us to be authentically ourselves. The people of the Low Countries rebel in Egmont's cause, in the cause of a life worth living.

———

In the early 1780s Goethe ceased to be a successful dramatist. He did finish *Egmont* and recast *Iphigeneia* in iambics, but these were projects begun in the 1770s. His new plans all led to failure or to inconsequential short plays, either because he could not finish what he had begun or because he could not find a theme that spoke to his real interests. In summer 1781 he began work on a Hellenizing drama, *Elpenor*. One and a half acts have survived in a manuscript of 1784. Despite some powerful rhetoric, it is not especially dramatic and has none of the thematic richness of *Iphigeneia*. A promising drama on the life of the sixteenth-century Italian poet Torquato Tasso was sketched in prose. The drafts have not survived. Goethe would take the manuscript to Italy with him in 1786 and bring it back to Weimar in 1788 still unfinished. During and after the Swiss journey he wrote a short lyric drama *Jery and Bätely*, which he described as a 'little operetta, in which the actors dress in Swiss clothes and talk about cheese and milk'.[216] The wealthy Jery is frustrated by his failure to win the hand of Bätely and conspires to win her with his old friend Thomas. In trying to prove to Bätely that she needs a strong man around the house, Thomas takes things too far and smashes her windows, which angers Jery. In the ensuing fight, Jery is beaten up by Thomas, and Bätely tells him she loves him, motivated partly by gratitude, but mainly by pity. In this Rousseauian Swiss idyll, pity, the deepest of our emotions, is what brings and binds people together. At the same time Goethe was working on a comedy, *The Birds*, based very loosely on Aristophanes's comedy of the same title, but with much less bite to its satire.[217] Writers are criticised for wanting an easy life; critics are criticised for being misanthropic and pessimistic; readers are criticised for being slavishly dependent on critics; and the population as a whole is too easily swayed by flattery and appeals to sentiment. Between summer 1781 and summer 1782 he wrote the lyric drama *The Fisherwoman* for performance at the outdoor theatre on the banks of the Ilm by Anna Amalia's summer residence at Tiefurth. Sending the text to Merck, Goethe dismissed it as a 'wood and water play'—'performed at Tiefurth it has a good effect but apologies if it is written like minutes [of a meeting]'.[218] Its main interest is that the play is built around a number of *Volkslieder* published by Herder in 1778 and 1779 and adapted for the play by Goethe, the most celebrated being 'Alder King' ('Erlkönig'). A more substantial project was *Jest, Deceit and Revenge*, an Italian-style *opera buffa* and the culmination of over ten years of work on lyric dramas and operettas. With numerous arias and fully versified recitative, it was Goethe's most ambitious attempt yet at a libretto for musical theatre. For all the effort he expended on the versification, the characters are formulaic and the plot, pivoting around the attempt by a husband and wife team of harlequins from Italian *commedia dell'arte* to trick a miserly doctor out of an inheritance he had swindled them out of, is trivial. He recruited his young Frankfurt friend Philipp Christoph Kayser to compose the music, but Kayser worked very slowly and required constant gentle coaxing by Goethe. The project was abandoned in spring 1786.

On 10 April 1782 Emperor Joseph II confirmed Carl August's application to have Goethe raised to the Imperial nobility. Aside from the personal honour, his ennoblement had the practical benefit that Goethe could represent the Duke at the other territorial courts with full diplomatic honours, which was a significant advantage for the Duke's diplomatic ambitions. In Weimar eyebrows were raised and worse. Herder wrote scathingly to Hamann about his erstwhile protégé's elevation.[219] A sad coincidence six weeks later was the death of Goethe's father, the Imperial Councillor Johann Caspar Goethe. His health had declined rapidly after Goethe's last visit to the Three Lyres on his way back from Switzerland.[220] A week after his father's death Goethe moved into new premises in the centre of Weimar: a compact but elegant house on the Frauenplan, which conveniently backed onto Charlotte's home. It was also coincidental that 1782 brought further political problems in the Empire and within the Duchy. As a result, Goethe's elevation came at the cost of even more fraught and time-consuming official activity. In 1780 Joseph II had ascended to the imperial throne and revived an old Habsburg plan for exchanging the Austrian Netherlands, a distant territory that was proving resistant to Austrian attempts to govern it, for Bavaria. The exchange would have allowed Austria to exert more influence over the Empire's internal politics. In October 1782 Wilhelm von Edelsheim, minister of the Duchy of Baden, wrote to Carl August to encourage him to join in resisting the 'slavery' that threatened the small German territories.[221] The aim was to revive a plan for an alliance of smaller German principalities that had been shelved in 1778. The League of Princes would form a third power, between Prussia and an enlarged Austria. Goethe was opposed to the plan, but Carl August was enthusiastic, envisaging a role for himself in imperial politics. Consequently Goethe spent an increasing amount of time on diplomatic business and missions, which he disliked. It was not just that the stiff formality of diplomacy was uncongenial to someone of such a practical bent. Goethe believed that his and the Duke's political energies would be better spent on making the government more effective than on diplomatic manoeuvers that were in any case likely to fail. The Duchy's domestic administration demanded their full and constant attention. In June 1782 the Duke dismissed Johann August von Kalb, the chancellor of his exchequer, with whom Goethe had lodged after his arrival in Weimar in 1775. Kalb had treated the Duchy's treasury as his private bank, and there was talk of his having leveraged his position at court to purchase some land.[222] After Kalb's dismissal Goethe delivered a harsh verdict in a letter to Knebel: 'Every day as I dig deeper into affairs, I see how necessary this step was. As a businessman he performed moderately, as a politician poorly, and as a human appallingly'.[223] Goethe cleaned up the mess by passing on the debt to the Duchy's estates in return for reducing their tax burden, which he achieved by significant cuts in the military budget. He disbanded the Duke's artillery and reduced his infantry by two thirds. It was not the end of the Duchy's financial problems. In a longstanding legal battle with the Duchy, the councillors of Ilmenau complained about the corrupt behaviour of the tax collector Gruner. Goethe investigated the case and produced evidence of Gruner's guilt, which resulted in his imprisonment, though he was pardoned a year later in the amnesty that followed the birth of the crown prince.[224] Oversight of the Ilmenau tax commission needed to be improved, and this was yet another responsibility that was laid on Goethe's broad shoulders.

The need to stabilize the Duchy's finances was confirmed by troubling instability at home and abroad. February and March 1784 brought bad flooding of the Saale at Jena, and wild boars continued to ravage the farmlands around the Ettersberg.[225] There was growing anxiety about grain prices.[226] For eight months in 1783 and 1784 the Laki volcano in Iceland spewed sulphuric plumes into the atmosphere, which blighted harvests across Europe for two years. The eruption may also have exacerbated the flooding in Jena.[227] In the 1770s and '80s rural panics because of crop failure, real or imagined, became increasingly common across Europe. For an administrator like Goethe the panics were especially worrisome as they undermined trust in government. If the undermining of government from the bottom were not bad enough, the reputation of the French monarchy was damaged in 1785 by the Diamond Necklace Affair—a conspiracy to defraud the Cardinal de Rohan by playing on his desire to win the favour of the queen. Goethe later claimed he had been deeply worried by the affair's impact on confidence in the French crown.[228] Whilst this might look like being wise after the event—it suggested that Goethe had in some sense foreseen the French Revolution—in fact he was sufficiently interested in the affair to consider writing a comic operetta on the subject in 1787.[229] It was a sign of the times, if nothing else.

A concern to ensure the effectiveness of government may have been behind Goethe's and the Duke's decision to join the Weimar freemasons. On 23 June 1780 Goethe was admitted to the masonic lodge 'Anna Amalia at the Three Roses'. Nine months later he applied for promotion to the rank of Master, the society's third level, but was only granted admittance to the second level, on the anniversary of his first joining. In February 1782 Carl August followed Goethe, and only one month later Goethe and the Duke were together elevated to the third grade. However, the lodge was shut down as a result of the Congress of Strict Observance at Wilhelmsbad in summer 1782, which reformed German freemasonry into two orders: the Chevaliers Bienfaisants de la Cité Sainte, which followed the so-called reformed Scottish rite, and the Order of Illuminati, founded by Adam Weishaupt, professor of church law and philosophy at Ingolstadt. In February 1783, Goethe and Carl August transferred their allegiance to the Illuminati.[230] Why Goethe and the Duke joined the masons is unclear, and the question is made harder to answer by the lack of clarity in the motives of the freemasons themselves. The main stated objective of freemasonry was ethical renewal. There were also political goals that troubled German rulers. The Illuminati envisaged a future Europe without princes though they had no practical or even theoretical plan to achieve it. Did Goethe and the Duke see themselves as part of this moral elite, or did their alarm at the political goals make them want to observe the Illuminati from within? Shortly after their return from Switzerland, Goethe wrote to Fritsch that he wished to become a mason in order 'to be in closer contact with people I have learned to value, and it is this sociable desire alone that makes me seek admittance'[231]—which sounds more cagey than anything.[232] He did read up on freemasonry during the years of his membership, but there is little evidence of genuine interest. Writing to Lavater, Carl August claimed that Goethe was 'no more interested in this discipline than in medicine or mathematics'.[233] In 1783 Goethe wrote to Kayser expressing his scepticism about freemasonry's secret rituals: 'if one wishes no more than to do good, then everyone can do that in plain daylight and in one's house clothes'.[234] Perhaps the clearest evidence of his attitude to freemasonry is a letter to Lavater of June 1781, written on the same day as he replied to Fritsch's letter informing him he would not be admitted to the third grade:[235]

> I have indications, even reports of a great mass of lies walking in darkness, of which you seem as yet to have no idea. Believe me, our whole moral and political world is undermined by subterranean passages, vaults, sewers, just as a great city tends to be, and of which—their interconnections and the circumstances of their inhabitants—hardly anyone thinks or imagines; only a person who has some intelligence of these will understand when all of a sudden the ground gives way there, smoke issues from a vent over there, and wondrous voices are heard here.[236]

There is circumstantial evidence that Goethe and the Duke wanted to conduct political surveillance of the masonic lodges. Certainly in later years, after the French Revolution, Goethe would undertake such surveillance, especially at the University of Jena. It is less clear that he was involved in spying in the early 1780s. Among the many negative things Herder said about Goethe's work at the Weimar court, he insisted that Goethe was averse to all 'intrigue' and would never knowingly 'persecute' anyone.[237] Fritsch does appear to have kept an eye on the Weimar lodge on behalf of the Duchy from the early 1760s. But it is unclear why Goethe would have needed to become involved, let alone the Duke. Spying was certainly beneath his royal majesty. It seems most likely that Goethe and Carl August had reason to suspect that the freemasons might have some secret influence on Germany's politics in general, including Weimar's. Perhaps they felt that, if such influence were being exerted, they would be better placed to steer it from within, and this desire to control the direction of events, as distinct from mere spying, would explain why Carl August felt the need to become involved in person. If this is the case, there is no obvious discrepancy between Goethe's infiltration of Weimar freemasonry and his wider cultural and intellectual attitudes.

Goethe's role in an execution for infanticide poses a more challenging question about how to reconcile his political and literary activities. On 11 April 1783 Johanna Catharina Höhn, a twenty-three-year-old unmarried servant from Tannroda in the Ilm district, murdered her newborn child. The judicial board reported that the case seemed clear and there were no extenuating circumstances. Things might have appeared otherwise to an Enlightened reader of Goethe's *Urfaust* or the wealth of other fictional and legal literature on the subject. It was widely acknowledged that economic deprivation, the social stigma surrounding childbirth out of wedlock, and the harsh penalties imposed on women found guilty of such 'fornication' were prima facie grounds for clemency.[238] (Public humiliation, including enforced penance at church, was still the standard punishment in Weimar, and though already abolished in Prussia, it would only be abolished in Weimar in 1786, with Goethe voting in favour of abolition.) A similar case of infanticide had been tried in 1781, and the mother, Dorothea Altwein, sentenced to death. Carl August had exercised clemency and commuted the death sentence to life imprisonment. In the case of Höhn, the Duke—who had indeed read some of the relevant legal literature and, of course, heard Goethe read the *Urfaust*—again recommended commutation of the death penalty when he sent the case back to the judicial board. How the board reacted to his recommendation of clemency is not recorded. The trial proceeded: Höhn confessed her guilt and was sentenced to death. In November the Duke sought the advice of his three Privy Councillors, possibly because the judicial board had been split on the question of the sentence,[239] or because it had voted against clemency and he wanted a third opinion. Either way, the Privy Councillors were asked to advise on two matters: the general question whether to retain the death penalty for cases of infanticide and the specific decision on clemency in the case of Höhn. Schnauß voted in favour of the death penalty in both matters. Fritsch refrained from offering an opinion on the Höhn case; on the more general matter he argued ambivalently, though privately he agreed with Schnauß. Goethe also refrained from advising on the Höhn case, but gave a clear opinion in favour of retaining the death penalty in general. In other words, it seems that the Privy Council supported the sentence originally proposed by the judicial board. On 28 November, following the public performance of a show trial, Höhn was executed. Carl August demonstrated his displeasure by absenting himself from Weimar for the execution. What responsibility should Goethe bear for the execution? Ultimate responsibility lay with the Duke, not with the Privy Council, which could only offer advice, not decide matters. The Duke had the power to overrule the court and the Privy Council and to commute the sentence. Indeed in his written advice Fritsch opined that in future all such instances should be decided by the Duke on a case-by-case basis.[240] Despite the Duke's evident distaste, he chose not to impose clemency. By seeking the Privy Council's opinion, he had followed precedent, but he must also have known that their opinion would serve him as a fig leaf. This does not exempt the Privy Council from blame. Goethe could, of course, have argued for clemency himself, and his opinion would have carried weight. He would not have been isolated in doing so, since he knew that the Duke favoured clemency and that Fritsch had expressed himself ambivalently. He must also have known that opinion in Weimar society was divided. As he knew, abolition of the death penalty was the drift of much recent Enlightened legal opinion, though some major Enlightenment voices—Montesquieu, Rousseau, Kant—argued that the death penalty was rational. But most of all, Goethe's own ethics of sympathy and his portrayal of Gretchen might have been expected to incline him towards clemency. His vote for retaining the death penalty would seem to create an egregious discrepancy between political and literary activity that is troubling and hard to comprehend. It becomes more comprehensible, if no less troubling, when one considers that the discrepancy was at least consistent. In 1771, during his legal studies in Strasbourg, he had argued for the retention of the death penalty. Only a few months later Susanna Margaretha Brandt killed her newborn child and was put on trial for infanticide in Frankfurt, inspiring the Gretchen story in the *Urfaust*. Although he created a vivid portrayal of extenuating circumstances in the *Urfaust*, and although he probed the parlous social condition of women in *Iphigeneia*, his political instinct was to support the state's power. His views on these matters were formed early and did not change significantly. He had always believed that the state was the sole source of legal authority. He certainly did not believe in rights. He followed Spinoza in asserting the state's authority to enforce religious practice, if not belief, on its subjects. He also believed that the state was responsible for enforcing public morality by means of the law. Three years later, when he voted to abolish enforced penance at church for sex out of wedlock, it was not in an uncharacteristic fit of liberalism. He was again acting in accordance with his belief in state authority, this time in a conflict between church and state. His vote granted the state the sole authority to punish its subjects, and removed any such authority from the church.[241] The distinction between state power and church power might seem artificial to us, if both are repressive. It would have seemed less so to Goethe. That is not to say that Goethe's vote to retain the death penalty for infanticide should not trouble us.

After struggling to guide the Duke and administer the Duchy since 1775, and amid the political worries of the early 1780s, it was understandable that the ideas of German cultural nationhood of the early 1770s seemed less achievable. Goethe had always been sceptical, and his scepticism had only grown. His experience did nothing to suggest that grand narratives of cultural nationhood or the renewal of the Empire were realistic. His domestic political activity revealed a social world that was driven by personal desires and lacked the consistency of purpose and action needed for grand projects. This was the subject of the writing project that occupied most of his time from 1782 onwards and was his most substantial achievement of the first decade in Weimar, alongside *Iphigeneia*: a full-length novel with the working title *Wilhelm Meister's Theatrical Mission*. His first mention of the novel dates from soon after his arrival in Weimar in November 1775, but the writing proceeded very slowly. It took him a whole year to write the twenty-three short chapters of Book One—about half the length of *Werther*, which had taken him just two months. Book Two took three years. It was only in the spring of 1782 that he began to give the novel the time it needed. By November 1785 six books were completed, a substantial draft nearly three times the length of *Werther*, though still unfinished. The novel is a delightfully detailed account of the theatre's place in German society, not so much as a force for social and cultural renewal, but as a microcosm of Germany's social problems. Book One draws on his childhood experiences in Frankfurt, in particular his privileged glimpses behind the curtains of the French theatre established by the Comte de Thoranc during the occupation of Frankfurt in the Seven Years' War. An unpublished note written for *Poetry and Truth* records for the year 1760: 'extraordinary impression of the private lives of French theatre folk'.[242] The novel is concerned more with what happens backstage than with the theatre as a public art form. Behind the theatrical illusion is something utterly ordinary. In order to create the illusion, actors must project false selves. This is why the lives of theatre folk are a microcosm of modern society. Because acting requires the creation of a false persona, it is an extreme case of the *amour-propre* that bedevils all modern civilization.

Book One follows Wilhelm as he grows up during the War of the Austrian Succession in a busy commercial town reminiscent of Frankfurt. The later books seem to be set during the Seven Years' War. Wilhelm's father Benedikt has been a partner in a successful business but is now a somewhat desolate figure. His wife is having an affair, and the introspective son feels alienated from both parents. The novel begins with a visit from Benedikt to his mother, who is making her grandchildren some puppets for Christmas. The puppet show sparks Wilhelm's imagination: it is his first experience of the theatre and the beginning of a lasting infatuation. Soon the young Wilhelm becomes an amateur theatre impresario, adapting and writing scripts, making costumes and sets, putting on puppet shows, and directing his friends in ad hoc performances. Of course he lacks the expertise needed to achieve sound results; in the 'heat of invention' things become chaotic.[243] Goethe chose the theatre as a vocation for his hero for this very reason. The theatre requires a wider range of skills than landscape painting, Werther's passion. It needs organizational and social skills and is therefore a good measure of maturity, and not only the maturity of a child moving towards adulthood. It is also a measure of a nation's political, social, and cultural maturity. This explains the change in tone that the novel undergoes. Wilhelm's bumbling childhood experiments in the theatre, which signal his immaturity, are narrated with gentle humour. However, as his theatrical mission continues into adulthood and the scene moves to the national stage, the issues become more serious and the gap between ambition and achievement in the theatre is narrated with growing scepticism.

The *Theatrical Mission* is also a novel of education. Book One traces Wilhelm's development from childhood into adulthood in the manner of Rousseau's *Émile*. Like Émile, Wilhelm is part of an educational experiment conducted by the invisible hand of fate, and as in *Émile* the experiment is designed to allow the child to express his unconscious urges freely and to experience the inevitable and all-important failures that follow. Wilhelm's theatrical desires and the challenges he faces are typical of male adolescence. His favourite teenage reading is Tasso's romantic epic *Jerusalem Delivered*, a choice that reflects his developing sexuality. Oddly, but not untypically as later events will show, Wilhelm is most fascinated by the androgyny, the as-yet-undecided sexuality of Tasso's heroine Chlorinda. At this important stage of development sex and sexuality are the powerful but confusing drivers behind Wilhelm's theatrical mission. When he organizes his friends into a theatrical company, the boys perform in order to impress the girls. The problem with love, as Goethe had learned from *Émile*, is that the lover needs to make himself lovable; he must project an image of himself to his beloved, a false and vain second self that he uses to compete with his male rivals for the girls' favour. Acting creates the perfect environment for this game of self-presentation, for acting involves the same creation of a false self-image as love does. And so in their seemingly innocent amateur dramatics, Wilhelm and his friends enter the adult world of *amour-propre*. Wilhelm struggles to keep a lid on his friends' desires and intrigues. Like them he is motivated by what the narrator describes, in terms obviously borrowed from Rousseau, as a 'most pleasurable love of oneself [*Eigenliebe*]'.[244] By 'Eigenliebe', Goethe means to evoke Rousseau's *amour-propre*.

(This was the usage in contemporary German translations of Rousseau. In Carl Friedrich Cramer's translation of *Émile*, first published in 1789–1791, *Eigenliebe* is used for *amour-propre* and *Selbstliebe* for *amour de soi*.)[245]

Book One ends with Wilhelm's entry into adulthood and his first love affair, with Mariane, an actress in a touring theatre company. Despite the shocking contrast between her chaotic domestic circumstances and Wilhelm's orderly home life, he creates an idealized image of her and of the acting profession. With his imagination and passions fully stimulated, he begins to see a future for himself away from the stolid commercial world of his family. He plans to make his name as the founder of a German national theatre.[246] The two sides of his life cannot, however, be kept separate for long. His friend Werner warns Wilhelm that Mariane is having another affair, and eventually Wilhelm learns the truth at first hand. On the night when he intended to give Mariane a romantic letter outlining his plans to leave home and seek out a friend who is a theatre director, he discovers that she is being visited by another man.

Book Two charts Wilhelm's collapse into a Werther-like sickness that nearly kills him. The pace of the narrative slows markedly, as Wilhelm ruminates on his passion for Mariane and on his now moribund literary ambitions. The narrator diagnoses melancholia: 'he was assailed by false moods, his ideas were confused and exaggerated, he was unrecognisable from his former self'.[247] After a period of sickly self-indulgence, recovery comes, and the inner core of his character reasserts itself and expels 'all the false and foreign' impulses.[248] It is a sure sign that he is cured when his instinct of self-preservation is restored and he rejects Werner's attempts to engage with him: 'he was not predisposed towards dialogue, it was not easy for him to put himself into the thoughts of another'.[249] The theatre with its unhealthy *amour-propre* continues to beckon, however. Shortly after his recovery Wilhelm meets and takes pity on a young couple, Melina and his beloved, who want to marry and escape from their petit-bourgeois lives into the theatre. Melina has even taken on a stage name: his original family name was Pfefferkuchen ('Peppercake', a type of spicy biscuit), which someone had confused with Honigkuchen ('Honeycake'), and this inspired him to change his name to the classier Latinized form Melina ('mel' is Latin for honey). As with Olearius/Öhlmann in *Götz*, the authentic identity is sacrificed for the sake of presenting a more distinguished image to the world.[250]

Book Three signals another change in the novel's atmosphere, when Wilhelm is sent out into the world to collect debts owed to the family firm. From the relatively confined space of the Meisters' hometown, the story shifts to an expansive landscape of small towns, villages, and noble estates dotted about rural Germany. The novel is no longer driven by the internal dynamic of Wilhelm's growing maturity. Now external stimuli move him from one experience to another, and the remainder of the novel has an episodic structure, in common with most eighteenth-century popular novels. Leaving home Wilhelm embarks, at first unintentionally, on a series of adventures connected with the theatre, and with each episode his involvement in the theatre deepens. At first he merely observes. He witnesses a performance put on by some miners celebrating their trade outside an inn, then a play in a theatre belonging to a philanthropic factory owner, and then a highly professional acrobatic show in a town square. These and subsequent episodes form a narrative strand in their own right, an oblique history of the theatre, from its origins in the working lives of ordinary people, through the process of becoming institutionalized, and up to the present day. The miners put on a naïve yet authentic performance reflecting and emerging out of their working lives. With the acrobats we reach an altogether different level of performance, impressively drilled yet morally troubling in its effects because the acrobats knowingly captivate their audience with their physical prowess. The difference between the miners and acrobats is felt in the social effects of each performance. The miners create a moment of joy and civic unity. The acrobats impress their audience but encourage sexual immorality among it: the female tumblers are ogled by the men in the audience, and the leading male performer supplements his earnings by serving the local ladies as a gigolo.

The conjectural history of the theatre in Book Three shows an upwards trajectory of aesthetic ambition but a descent from social cohesion into competitiveness, vanity, and immorality. In May 1782, five months before he began work on Book Three, Goethe received a gift from his mother: 'the new fine Geneva edition of Rousseau'. At first he was most excited by the prospect of reading the first part of the *Confessions*.[251] Volume VI of the edition contained Rousseau's critique of the modern theatre in his *Letter to Monsieur d'Alembert on Spectacles* (1758), which was written in opposition to a proposal by D'Alembert in the *Encyclopédie* that a standing theatre should be established in Geneva. It seems likely that Goethe read the *Letter* for the first time before he started Book Three, and that Rousseau's critique of the theatre influenced his descriptions of the miners and acrobats and the tone of his depiction of the theatre in general. Rousseau argued that some public spectacles could promote social cohesion. The public civic traditions of Geneva were examples of this, and Goethe's description of the miners' performance has a similar effect. By contrast, Rousseau believed that most modern theatre was damaging to civic morality, as the acrobats' performance in Goethe's novel is. For Rousseau, the modern theatre possesses only empty glamour. The emotional catharsis afforded by tragic drama, which modern neo-Aristotelians laud as the theatre's supreme act of grace, is in reality no such thing. On the contrary, the rationale of the theatre is entertainment. Actors aim to enflame our passions, not to purify them, which will be no surprise to anyone who knows how poorly actors behave offstage. The bad reputation of actors may not be entirely justified, Rousseau says, but it is based on a ubiquitous reality:

> I see in general that the estate of actors is one of license and bad morals; that the men are given to disorder; that the women lead a scandalous life; that both, avaricious and spendthrift at the same time, always overwhelmed by debts and always spending in torrents, are as little controlled in their dissipations as they are scrupulous about the means of providing for them.[252]

This dissipated behaviour behind the scenes is licensed by the fact that acting is the art of creating false appearances for the pleasure of others, and therefore it is an acute form of *amour-propre*. Actors invest all their efforts in creating an illusion to please an audience. As such acting represents the very worst of modern civilization, the creation of a false self in order to make a public impression:

> What is the talent of the actor? It is the art of counterfeiting himself, or putting on another character than his own, of appearing different than he is, [...] of saying what he does not think as naturally as if he really did think it, and, finally, of forgetting his own place by dint of taking another's. What is the profession of the actor? It is a trade in which he performs for money, submits himself to the disgrace and the affronts that others buy the right to give him, and puts his person publicly on sale.[253]

Central to the ill repute of actors is their need to be something they are not: rich, virtuous, heroic, noble. The effort of *seeming* consumes and destroys their ability to *be* themselves: 'an actor on the stage, displaying other sentiments than his own, saying only what he is made to say, often representing a chimerical being, annihilates himself, as it were, and is lost in his hero'.[254] Solid, virtuous *amour de soi*, the core of human character and the source of virtue, is hollowed out and replaced by vain, malignant *amour-propre*.

The *Theatrical Mission* is sceptical about the theatre, and becomes increasingly so in Book Three. Goethe's imaginative recreation of the lives of theatre folk is more generous and his scepticism less harsh than Rousseau's, but the reasons for it are similar. Wilhelm has fallen for the superficial glamour of Mariane's life and fails to see the penury that makes her dependent on her lovers' gifts. From Book Three the impact of Rousseau's vision of the theatre becomes apparent. The novel repeatedly highlights the difference between (artificial) seeming and (authentic) being. Forced by Werner to confront the truth about Mariane, Wilhelm continues to idealize the acting profession, now in the shape of the Melinas, even though Madame Melina has only modest acting talent and her husband none whatsoever. Wilhelm mistakenly idealizes the role of the playwright and the educative role of the theatre as a whole, despite the lack of any evidence that playwrights and their work educate the people. He continues on his mission despite the kind of setbacks that would defeat a less idealistic person. Even where he seems closest to realizing his theatrical ideals, the novel shows that his ideals are in conflict with human realities. Although Wilhelm's development towards maturity represents a progression, it is dogged by continual reminders that the theatre is far from realizing its civilizing mission. Indeed, in one respect the novel's trajectory is retrograde, for whereas Wilhelm is idealistic about the theatre in Books One and Two, and the narrator seems to support his ambition, in the later books he becomes disenchanted, his ambition is undercut by irony, and the narrator grows more distant. At each stage of his theatrical journey, Wilhelm seems more out of place. His upbringing, even if it failed to excite his imagination, had a certain bourgeois moral solidity. The narrator refers to the 'good conscience' that tells Wilhelm he ought to return home.[255] There is some prospect of his making a good commercial career in the theatre, for in the theatre, as in commerce, money is king. Yet the income of theatrical companies is erratic, their financial management is chaotic or even criminal, and whatever comes in is instantly frittered away. There is no discipline or prudence and consequently no financial stability. The other factor that makes Wilhelm unsuited to the theatre is his half-formed genius as a playwright. Actors are interested only in dramatic effect, not in artistic excellence. Theatre managers are concerned only with filling seats. The nature of the theatre means that Wilhelm's potential cannot be realized and his talent and 'good conscience' are out of place.

His next encounter is with a touring theatre company under the management of the rather masculine Madame de Retti. What had been an oblique history of the theatre now becomes explicit: Madame de Retti recounts her attempts to regularize and professionalize the theatre by insisting on proper rehearsal time and by banning improvisation. Here Goethe fictionalizes one of the prominent figures of eighteenth-century German theatre, Friederike

Neuber, the actor and collaborator of Gottsched. Despite Madame de Retti's well-intentioned rationalizing and modernizing efforts, her company remains chaotic. The Wolffian theory does not convert into practice. A reading of Wilhelm's *Belshazzar* play generates heated enthusiasm but ends in drunkenness and smashed glassware, which sickens Wilhelm.[256] Nevertheless he is persuaded to allow the company to perform the play. Now a worse problem emerges. Bendel, the company's leading male and Madame de Retti's lover, is an alcoholic who gets too drunk to perform on the first night. Wilhelm reluctantly takes the role himself. Preparing to go on stage, 'he looked at himself in the mirror, and the old spirit of the theatre came over him'.[257] The mirror represents the vanity of the theatre, and it has an effect on Wilhelm akin to a haunting, both familiar and disquieting. His performance is a success, but once the initial thrill has subsided, he resolves not to repeat it.

The temporary success of *Belshazzar* is overshadowed by the familiar problem of money. Madame de Retti and Bendel try to abscond with the takings. Even though Melina stops them (for less than altruistic reasons, as it turns out), the theatre's survival still depends on a substantial subsidy from Wilhelm—or rather from his father's company, on whose behalf Wilhelm is supposed to be collecting debts, so that he has a supply of ready cash. A solution to the financial problem appears in the form of an invitation to perform at the estate of a local aristocrat. The company, now led by Melina, decamps to the Count's chateau, where it is shabbily treated at first. Once settled, the familiar chaos of theatre life resumes, and the difference between seeming and being becomes acute. The actresses fool around with the resident soldiers. The money the actors earn is wasted on high living. Once the company's task is completed—they perform a play for a visiting Prince, complete with an awkward allegorical prelude in praise of the Prince written by Wilhelm—they are dismissed and feel aggrieved. The aristocrats are only interested in the theatre as a means to project their own status. They have no interest in genuine patronage, in supporting the theatre for the sake of art. Aristocratic patronage is clearly not a solution to the theatre's financial problems.

During his collaboration with the company, first under Madame de Retti's management, then under the utterly incompetent Melina, Wilhelm continues to be torn between his idealized theatrical mission and revulsion at the actual state of the theatre. He spends much of this time away from the actors in the company of Philine, a pretty young woman of easy manners and generous sexuality, and two mysterious misfits: a young androgynous girl Mignon, who was abused by the manager of the acrobats and now feels indebted to Wilhelm for rescuing her, and the 'Harpist', a melancholic wandering minstrel. Mignon in particular provides Wilhelm with sanctuary from the chaos of the theatre. Her childlike dependence on him—she calls him her 'father'—'gave his being a certain consistency, greater strength, and substance'.[258] Becoming a surrogate father to Mignon seems to do Wilhelm good. All aspects of the relationship—her arrested sexuality, the purity of her inwardness, her dependence on Wilhelm's paternal sympathy—stand in marked contrast to the licentious, impure, adult world of the theatre.

During Wilhelm's stay at the chateau a further source of spiritual nourishment is provided by Jarno, an otherwise cold and cynical officer, who recommends to Wilhelm that he read the plays of his namesake William Shakespeare. The sudden appearance of Shakespeare on Wilhelm's cultural horizon signals that the novel's oblique history of German drama has arrived at the present day, that is to say the rediscovery of Shakespeare by the 'geniuses' of the *Sturm und Drang*. However, Wilhelm immerses himself in Shakespeare without any prospect of performance. His life has split into two halves, one his engagement with the theatre, the other his private existence with Philine, Mignon, and the Harpist, and Shakespeare is decidedly part of his private existence. His first attempt to make Shakespeare live is a disaster. With his small entourage Wilhelm acts out the role of Prince Hal among his friends at the Boar's Head tavern, and he even dresses in pseudo-Shakespearean style. The company, still smarting from its bad experience at the chateau, decides to reconstitute itself as a republic, with Wilhelm as its leader. Wilhelm proposes that they take a dangerous route to the next town, through an area where volunteer militia units are rumoured to be active. The company supports him, carried away by the romance of the idea. While lunching in a forest clearing, they are ambushed by bandits. Badly injured in a skirmish, Wilhelm is helped by a mysterious woman in white, the 'Amazon' as he terms her—another case of ambiguous gender.

The novel's final episode takes place in the city of H*** where Wilhelm finally reaches the destination he had intended for himself and Mariane in Book One. There he meets his friend the theatre director Serlo and Serlo's troubled actor sister Aurelie, and he hopes to find Mariane.[259] Serlo is the closest the novel comes to showing us a successful theatre director at work. He is obviously more canny and able than Madame de Retti, though he shares her financial incompetence and shows typical theatrical vanity. Still, he is open-minded about what might appeal to German audiences and listens sympathetically to Wilhelm's advocacy of Shakespeare. With Serlo the novel brings us to the cusp of a truly German theatre of the kind that cultural nationalists since Lessing had envisioned. Even so, the novel continues to highlight the theatre's ambivalence. Ever manipulative, Serlo takes advantage of the news that Wilhelm's father has died and his mother is to remarry—a strong hint that Wilhelm's destiny is to play Hamlet!—to convince Wilhelm that his future is with the theatre. Even so Wilhelm's feelings are mixed, not least because, now standing near his mission's end, he recalls the absent Mariane, who was there at the beginning:

> 'So here I stand', he said to himself, 'not at the forking of the path, but at my goal, and yet I dare not take the last step, dare not grasp it. Yes, if a profession, a mission was ever clear and explicit, then this is it. At the same time everything happens by mere chance and without my doing, and yet everything is just as I had devised and planned it. Very strange! A person might be familiar with nothing more than with his hopes and wishes, long nourished in his heart, and yet when they confront him, when they force themselves upon him, he does not recognise them and recoils from them. Everything that I allowed myself to dream before the unhappy night that separated me from Mariane now stands before me and offers itself to me. I wanted to flee here, and I have been gently led here; I wanted to seek shelter with Serlo, now he seeks me and offers me conditions that as a beginner I had no right to expect. Was it then merely love for Mariane that fettered me to the theatre? Or was it a love of art that bound me tighter to her?'[260]

What is absolutely clear is that Wilhelm's decision, whichever way it falls, will result from a tangle of motives, not all fully conscious or understood. In the final chapter Serlo, Aurelie, and Philine implore Wilhelm to join Serlo's company as its lead male, and he accedes, though he is numb to their excitement, and moments later a vision of the mysterious Amazon floats unbidden through his mind.

At this point the novel fragment breaks off, at what appears to be the end of Book Six. The moment seems both decisive and fateful, more so than the endings of Books One through Five. Wilhelm's mission is on the verge of completion. He has joined a theatre company that seems capable of performing plays that would speak to the nation. *Hamlet* would be an obvious choice, especially given the unconscious motivation provided by Wilhelm's father's death and his mother's impending remarriage. Perhaps Serlo's company would even become a standing theatre though how it would be funded is unclear. Werner's commercial success might provide funds; the aristocracy certainly cannot be relied on. It is possible that Wilhelm would go on to establish a national theatre and find and marry Mariane, so fulfilling the promise Wilhelm made in his letter to Mariane in Book One—a tidy if idealistic ending which was hardly in keeping with the German cultural and political scene in the mid-1780s. Even if such an ending is plausible, it seems likely that Wilhelm would continue to face the amateurism, chaos, and selfishness that had already dismayed him in the theatre. The picture at the end of Book Six is further complicated by loose ends that seem to point in other directions. The mystery of Mignon surely requires resolution, and her relationship with Wilhelm warrants further development. So too does the figure of the elusive and attractive Amazon, whom Wilhelm tried unsuccessfully to find in Book Five. There is no evidence in the existing fragment that the Amazon has any connection with the theatre. Despite this she may point towards a role for the aristocracy in Wilhelm's life, perhaps as a patron. One further possibility then is that, after a brief period of success with the manipulative and vain Serlo, Wilhelm would move in an altogether different direction, away from the theatre. Perhaps Jarno would be proved right when he said that Wilhelm was 'neither born to the theatre nor can be educated for it'.[261] At any rate, the novel evidently had some way to go before its conclusion, as Goethe ruefully observed in a letter to Charlotte on the day he completed Book Six: 'If it carries on like this, we'll be old before we see this work of art completed'.[262] On 8 December he wrote again to Charlotte that he had drafted a plan for the completion of the novel in six further books, but the plan has not survived.[263] He may also have come up with a new title for it.[264] In the spring of 1786 he began work on Book Seven, but little was written.[265] The novel was one of the works Goethe took with him to Italy, Mignon's home. In Vicenza with its Palladian villas, he felt he had found her birthplace.[266] More ideas for the novel continued to come,[267] including a plan to conclude it in Wilhelm's and his own fortieth year,[268] but the only progress he made was to accumulate more material.[269] Gradually the novel slipped out of his mind.

It may be that speculating on its conclusion is the wrong way to think of the novel's unfinished state. It feels more like a novel that exists for the sake of the process Wilhelm goes through, than a narrative heading towards resolution. The issues are too intractable and too real to be resolved. There had been a time when German intellectuals hoped that a national theatre might be a cure for the nation's ills, but in the 'Theatrical Mission' the institution of the theatre suffers from those very ills to an acute degree: the theatre is the patient, not the doctor. In particular there is a painful gap between being and seeming. Indeed the theatre is constituted by this gap, and so it is utterly unsuited to cure society's ills. The latter parts of the novel, especially those involving Mignon, suggest that a cure might come from personal authenticity. But that seems to be a long way off since the very characters who hint at such authenticity—Mignon, the Harpist, even Aurelie—have been deeply damaged by the violent passions of others.

———

In September 1784 Goethe received a welcome visit from Fritz Jacobi. In Weimar Jacobi also met Herder in person for the first time, which he judged a great success.[270] One of the main subjects of discussion was Spinoza. In Jacobi's view, which would develop fully during 1784 and 1785, Spinoza was a prime example of the failing of all rationalistic philosophy. In its passion to explain, Jacobi believed, rationalistic philosophy confused the conditions of existence, such as could legitimately be explained in terms of natural causes, with the conditions under which humans justify ideas, which could not. By replacing justification with causation, philosophers had eliminated human freedom and rationality. Spinoza's philosophy, with its almost complete denial of free will, was merely the most logical version of this fallacy. Herder rejected Jacobi's interpretation of Spinoza and was pleased to inform Jacobi that, after the latter's departure, Goethe had reread Spinoza and reached the same view as Herder.[271] However, this was not the reason for Goethe's renewed interest in Spinoza. For Goethe the attraction of Spinoza had less to do with Jacobi and Herder's debate about the principles of rational justification than with the metaphysics of science. In this latter regard, Goethe was happy to concede Jacobi's view of Spinoza as the most coherent exponent of what in the next three years would come to be known by a novel name: scientific realism. Spinoza's position—on this Goethe and Jacobi agreed—was that all natural phenomena were subject to causal laws. The world was fully explicable in terms of natural causation, and there was no room for supernatural causes. Spinoza was a thoroughgoing realist, as Goethe wrote to Jacobi in June 1785:

> On this we are in agreement and were so from the very first, that the idea you present of Spinoza's doctrine is much closer to ours than we could have expected from what you said in person [. . .].
>
> You acknowledge the utmost realism which is the foundation of the whole of Spinozism, on which everything else rests, from which everything else flows. He does not prove the existence of God, existence is God. And if others therefore berate him as an atheist, so I should like to name and praise him as *theissimus*, even *christianissimus*.[272]

The idea that Spinoza's philosophy was close to or expressed the essence of Christianity was not new: it went back to Spinoza's friend Jarig Jelles, who made the claim in his preface to Spinoza's *Opera Posthuma* (1677).[273] Goethe concluded by making explicit the connection between his own efforts in natural history and Spinoza's theory that all phenomena are modifications of the single entity we call God or nature:

> Forgive me if I much prefer to fall silent when the subject of discussion is a divine being, which I only know in and through *res singulares* [individual entities], the closer and deeper contemplation of which nobody can encourage more than Spinoza, even if to his view all individual things seem to disappear.[274]

Goethe's claim that Spinoza 'encouraged' his work on natural history should be taken at face value. He did not claim to be interpreting Spinoza's philosophy, and he made it clear that he did not accept Spinoza's view that there were no *res singulares*.[275] There exists a short essay in Charlotte von Stein's hand that, since its discovery at the end of the nineteenth century, has been taken to represent Goethe's understanding of Spinoza and accordingly appears in most editions of Goethe's writings under the title given to it by a nineteenth-century editor: 'A Study after Spinoza'.[276] If the attribution to Goethe were correct, and if indeed the essay did express his understanding of Spinoza (despite the fact that Spinoza is not named in the essay), then it would represent at best an idiosyncratic interpretation of Spinoza, and at worst an elementary misunderstanding.[277] However, there are good reasons to suppose Goethe was not its author and that he did not in fact attempt to reinterpret Spinoza in this fashion.[278] In any case, he was not especially interested in the details of Spinoza's ontology, the question of whether the world consisted of discrete individuals or a single set of modifications of God-nature's essence. Nor was he interested in following step by step the rationalistic path of knowledge that Spinoza had laid out, leading from 'an adequate idea of the absolute essence of certain attributes of God to the adequate knowledge of the essence of things', even if he did quote precisely these words against Jacobi in 1785.[279] What appealed most to Goethe about Spinoza was the demonstration that nature works only according to natural laws. These universal laws are always and everywhere the same, allowing of no interruption by extraneous powers such as divine intervention. The chief benefit of Spinoza's metaphysics was therefore a negative one: Spinoza totally excluded religion from the study of natural history. This was different from Leibniz, who, as had become clear after the publication of a new edition of Leibniz's *Complete Works* by Louis Dutens in 1768, had forfeited his own claims to rationalism by defending aspects of revealed religion, such as the miracle of transubstantiation. There were also moral or psychological benefits to Spinozism. Spinoza recommended that we should love Godnature but have no expectation that our love would be reciprocated. Indeed, to suggest that because Goethe's own practice as a natural historian did not follow Spinoza's doctrines in detail, Goethe must therefore have misunderstood Spinoza, is to miss the point grossly. Goethe did study Spinoza and seek to familiarize himself with the technicalities of Spinoza's system, but not with the aim of developing his own Spinozan ontology or epistemology. His interest was in the implications of Spinoza's thought for him as a natural historian and a human being.

The debate with Jacobi might have ended there, but Jacobi's tenacity and fondness for polemics caused matters to take an unexpected turn. Towards the end of 1783 Goethe had given Anna Amalia a poem for her handwritten 'Tiefurt Journal'. Though the journal circulated privately, the contents were always prone to leak out into the wider world. At some point in the next two years the poem reached Jacobi in Pempelfort, and he published it, with his own emphases added in order to make the sense clearer, and with Goethe's name appended to it. The book in which Jacobi published the poem—*On the Doctrine of Spinoza, in Letters to Herr Moses Mendelssohn* (1785)—made the sensational claim that Lessing had been a crypto-Spinozist. Goethe's poem occupies pages 2 to 5, after a quotation from Descartes and before Jacobi's foreword.[280] His intention in printing the poem in such a prominent position was clear: the poem was to be read as evidence for Jacobi's polemical thesis that Spinozan ideas had a pervasive influence in Germany. The fact that Jacobi's foreword to the book is dated 28 August 1785, Goethe's birthday, may have been a coincidence, though a mischievous joke on Jacobi's part cannot be ruled out.

> Edel sei der Mensch,
> Hülfreich und gut!
> Denn das allein
> Unterscheidet ihn
> Von allen Wesen
> Die wir kennen.
>
> Heil den unbekannten
> Höhern Wesen,
> Die wir ahnden!

Ihnen gleiche der Mensch;
Sein Beispiel lehr uns
Jene glauben.

Denn unfühlend
Ist die Natur;
Es leuchtet die Sonne
Über Bös' und Gute,
Und dem Verbrecher
Glänzen wie dem Besten
Der Mond und die Sterne.

Wind und Ströme
Donner und Hagel
Rauschen ihren Weg,
Und ergreifen
Vorüber eilend
Einen um den andern.

Auch so das Glück
Tappt unter die Menge,
Faßt bald des Knaben
Lockige Unschuld
Bald auch den kahlen
Schuldigen Scheitel.

Nach ewigen ehrnen
Großen Gesetzen
Müssen wir alle
Unseres Daseins
Kreise vollenden.

Nur allein der Mensch
Vermag das Unmögliche,
Er unterscheidet
Wählet und richtet,
Er kann dem Augenblick
Dauer verleihen.

Er allein darf
Den Guten lohnen,
Den Bösen strafen;

Heilen und retten
Alles Irrende, Schweifende
Nützlich verbinden.

Und wir verehren
Die Unsterblichen,
Als wären sie Menschen,
Täten im Großen
Was der Beste im Kleinen
Tut oder möchte.

Der edle Mensch
Sei hülfreich und gut!
Unermüdet schaff er
Das Nützliche, Rechte
Sei uns ein Vorbild
Jener geahndeten Wesen.[281]

Noble may man be, / Helpful and good! / For that alone / Differentiates him / From all beings / That we know.
Hail to the unknown / Higher beings / That we imagine! / Let man be like them; / Let his example teach us / To believe in them.
For unfeeling / Is nature; / The sun shines / Upon the bad and the good, / And on the criminal / As on the best shine / The moon and the stars.
Wind and rivers / Thunder and hail / Rush on their way, / And grab hold of—/ Racing headlong—/ One [person] after another.
So too fortune / Gropes among the crowd, / Now grabs the boy's / Curly-haired innocence, / And next also the bald / Guilty pate.
Following eternal, brazen, / Mighty laws / All of us must / Fulfil our existence's / circles.
Yet humans alone / Are capable of the impossible, / They distinguish, / Select and judge, / They can give the moment / Permanence.
Only they are allowed / To reward the good, / Punish the wicked; / Heal and rescue / All erring, wandering things / Usefully gather.
And we honour / The immortals, / As if they were human, / Achieving on the grand scale / What the best [human] on the small scale / Achieves or would like to.
May the noble man / Be helpful and good. / May he unwearied create / What's useful, what's just, / Be to us a model / Of those imagined beings.

The verses are an argument rather than a poem, but it is a subtle and intricate argument that works as much by poetic implication as it does by direct statement. Its meaning is intended to be semi-obscure. Indeed, for its publication in the Göschen edition of his *Writings* in 1789, Goethe added a title that further cloaked his true intentions, 'The Divine'. In reality the poem is only about 'the divine' in a very limited sense. It might seem at first sight as if the poem says we should derive our morality from the gods. Certainly nature cannot be the source of our morality, for it only obeys its own iron laws and pays no mind to human cares. This view Goethe shares with Spinoza, though he also illustrates his point with a very obvious allusion to Matthew 5:45: '[God] causes his sun to rise on the bad as well as the good'.[282] But whereas the evangelist's argument is that God's universe is just, Goethe means no such thing: his universe is morally neutral. The allusion to Matthew is another decoy.[283] So what is the source of our morality? We might appear to be in a world resembling Kant's,[284] where nature works according to its own laws, whereas morality is the preserve of rational beings. However, in Kant's world the source of morality is reason. Goethe's poem points to a quite different source: our ability to *intuit* or *imagine* things. The verb Goethe uses is 'ahnen' (also spelt 'ahnden'), which has a range of meanings, from 'foretell' through 'intuit' to 'imagine'. This raises a question: is the thing that is foretold or intuited or imagined a real entity or a fiction? Here the context provides the reader with a clear steer, for Goethe contrasts *ahnen* (line 9) with the verb *kennen* (line 6), which unambiguously means 'to know', and the position of the two verbs in their respective lines makes it clear that they are antithetical: knowledge is opposed to imagination. (Jacobi understood this: in the version of the poem that he published he printed the verbs *ahnen* and *kennen* with emphasis and thus made the antithesis even clearer.) Hence in lines 5 and 6 the things that make up the natural world are described as the 'beings that we know'. The gods, on the other hand, are 'unknown' beings that have to be foretold or intuited or imagined. So the antithesis of *ahnen* and *kennen* leads us to a narrower sense of *ahnen*. The things that we *ahnen* are indeed imaginary entities. Thus one thing the poem definitely does *not* say about morality is that it comes from the gods. We have moved beyond positive and revealed religion. It becomes clear on careful reflection, as it became clear to Iphigeneia, that the gods, despite all our talk about them, do not exist. We merely imagine them as part of the process by which we invent morality. The gods are a psychological trick we play on ourselves. This is what lurks behind Jacobi's use of Goethe's poem in *On the Doctrine of Spinoza*. Jacobi correctly saw that the argument of Goethe's poem was Spinozist, and it was Spinozist in the strong sense in which

Jacobi understood Spinozism. As he put it in On the Doctrine of Spinoza, 'Spinozism is atheism'.[285]

Goethe was at first amused by Jacobi's unauthorized publication of the poem: it was 'a great prank', he told Charlotte.[286] He wrote more sternly to Jacobi, but was soon mollified. Still, he advised Jacobi that it would have been preferable to print the poem anonymously.[287] As the debate continued, Goethe began to let his irritation show at what he thought was bad faith on Jacobi's part. As with Lavater, with whom Goethe finally broke in the summer of 1786, he had limited patience for friends who insisted on letting their religion interfere with science. Jacobi's fideist philosophy—his belief that only faith in a personal God could adequately justify our knowledge of the world—was an egregious error, which in fact only served to reveal its own inadequacy as an argument, he told Jacobi:

> I can't let you get away with this manner, it is only appropriate for faith-sophists for whom it must be a matter of some importance to obfuscate all certainty of knowledge, to cast over it the pall of their own vague cloudy realm, since they are unable to shake the foundations of truth.[288]

Eventually in a long letter of May 1786 Goethe brought down the shutters on what he now considered to be mere polemical mischief-making by Jacobi. He ended by reaffirming his commitment, as far as the justification of knowledge was concerned, to Spinoza's theory of the highest form of knowledge, *scientia intuitiva*, quoting the definition of it in Part II, Proposition XL of the *Ethics*: 'This kind of knowledge proceeds from an adequate idea of the formal essence of certain attributes of God to the adequate knowledge of the essence of things'.[289] God may have blessed Jacobi with great wealth and a family, neither of which Goethe had, but he had also punished Jacobi with the curse of metaphysics, whereas God had blessed Goethe with a love for the physical world 'so that I might have good cheer in contemplating his works'.[290]

By the middle of the 1780s Goethe's friends were beginning to worry that his political duties were affecting his health. Knebel noted repeatedly in his diary that Goethe was gloomy.[291] The Herders both wrote to their friends of his 'suffering'.[292] In February 1785 he began to withdraw from his duties, no longer attending all of the once- or twice-weekly meetings of the Privy Council. In the spring the Duke became concerned that Goethe was taking too long to recover from an illness, and Knebel noted his repeated relapses.[293] A more traditional kind of cure was called for. So in the summer of 1785 he travelled to the Bohemian spa Carlsbad (Karlovy Vary) to take the waters. He enjoyed it so much that it became a fixture in his calendar. The spa visit was probably what finally decided him that he needed a much longer break to recover from the stresses of his work and stave off the recurrence of his melancholia. This meant Italy, but a trip to Italy had to be financed, and his spendthrift habits had left his coffers bare. For this reason, in spring 1786 he enlisted Bertuch to enter into negotiations with the publisher Göschen for a complete edition of his works.[294] Aside from money, the attraction for Goethe was to have a clean and authoritative edition of all his works, free from the misprints, cheap paper, and general shoddiness of the pirate editions. For Göschen, aside from adding Goethe to his stable, the appeal was the as yet unpublished material, notably the soon to be versified *Iphigeneia*. There were also the incomplete works—*Faust, Egmont, Tasso*—which could be published as unfinished fragments, painful though that was for Goethe. The deal was agreed at the beginning of July 1786. On 23 July he made arrangements with Seidel for his departure. He instructed his banker Paulsen that during his travels payments were to be made to him under the pseudonym Johann Phillipp Möller.[295] The next day he wrote a brief farewell to the Duke and set off for Carlsbad: 'I'm going in order to mend various deficiencies and fill up various gaps; may the healthy spirit of the world stand by me!'[296]

5

'In Conversation with Things'

ITALY, 1786–1788

'3RD SEPT. At 3 A.M. I stole out of Carlsbad, otherwise they wouldn't have let me go.'[1] So begins Goethe's 'Diary of my Italian Journey for Frau von Stein'. The secretiveness was part necessity, part superstition.[2] Before he departed, he told no one the full extent of his plans, not even the Duke, who first learned of his plan for a longer break after Goethe had left.[3] He told Charlotte von Stein and Knebel that he was extending his summer cure a little,[4] 'to strengthen myself morally and physically', he wrote to Knebel.[5] His friends might well have assumed that he was going on another geognostic tour in Thuringia or the Harz or Bohemia. There had been no mention of Italy. The risk that he might once more have to abort the Italian trip in the Alps was too great.

As he travelled south through Bavaria, he grew more convinced that he had been wise to travel incognito, styling himself as Johann Phillipp Möller, an artist. In Regensburg he was recognised by a clerk in a bookshop.[6] His itinerary took him through Munich, across the Alps at Mittenwald and down into Austria, through Innsbruck, and up to the Brenner Pass. He was already aware that in his desperation to reach Italy he was rushing past sights that merited a proper visit.[7] From the Brenner he descended along the River Adige to Bolzano, where he enjoyed his first taste of Italy proper. He continued to Lake Garda and Verona, where he paused for four days and wrote his first letters. He now revealed to Charlotte and the Herders that he had escaped to Italy[8] though he wrote to Seidel that he would not show his hand fully until he reached Rome.[9] From Verona he travelled east, stopping for a week in Vicenza to admire the architecture of Palladio and for two days in Padua before he sailed down the River Brenta and into the Venetian lagoon. He celebrated the occasion with suitable pomp in his diary:

And so it was written on my page in the book of Fate that on the evening of 28th September, at five by our clock, sailing from the Brenta into the lagoons, I should see Venice for the first time and shortly thereafter disembark on and visit this wonderful island city, this republic of beavers. Thus, thank God, Venice is no longer a mere word for me, a name that has so often caused me anxiety, who have forever been a mortal enemy of empty words.[10]

He stayed in Venice until the middle of October, spending the early mornings working on *Iphigeneia* and the remainder of the day visiting sights or simply wandering through the labyrinth of narrow streets. In an alley by the Rialto several days after his arrival he had his first fleeting sight of one of the infamous Venetian prostitutes.[11]

The journey from Venice to Rome was even more of a headlong dash than his escape from Germany. Through Bologna, into the Apennines and south to Perugia, he reached Rome in just two weeks, barely leaving his carriage to see the wonders of Florence.[12] At the beginning of November he could finally write to his friends from Rome to apologise for his secretiveness and reveal the full extent of his plans. Rome was his destination, for now at least, and he gave the impression to the Duke, whether honestly or not, that he would not stay for more than a few months: 'My desire to see this country was overripe; now that it is satisfied, my friends and fatherland will once more become truly and profoundly dear to me, and my return will be welcome'.[13]

In Rome he devoted himself to methodically visiting the architectural sites, palazzi, and churches. He particularly enjoyed clambering about on the precarious ancient ruins.[14] He could no longer remain incognito. For one thing, he needed company, and the large number of Germans in Rome, especially artists, provided it. He was particularly pleased with the company of Angelika Kauffmann and Johann Heinrich Wilhelm Tischbein. The latter had been in Italy since 1783, funded by Duke Ernst of Gotha on Goethe's recommendation. There were also outings to the hill-town Frascati, where a group of artists studied under the genial guidance of the landscapist Philipp Hackert, recently appointed court painter to King Ferdinand of Naples and Sicily. An unexpected new friend was the writer Carl Philipp Moritz, who had suffered a miserable upbringing in a poor Pietist family and become renowned for his *Magazine for Empirical Psychology*, an innovative compendium of case histories. 'He is like a younger brother of mine', Goethe wrote to Charlotte, 'of the same nature, only neglected and damaged by Fate at exactly those points where I was blessed and favoured. It gave rise to a strange reflection on myself'.[15] Ten days after they first

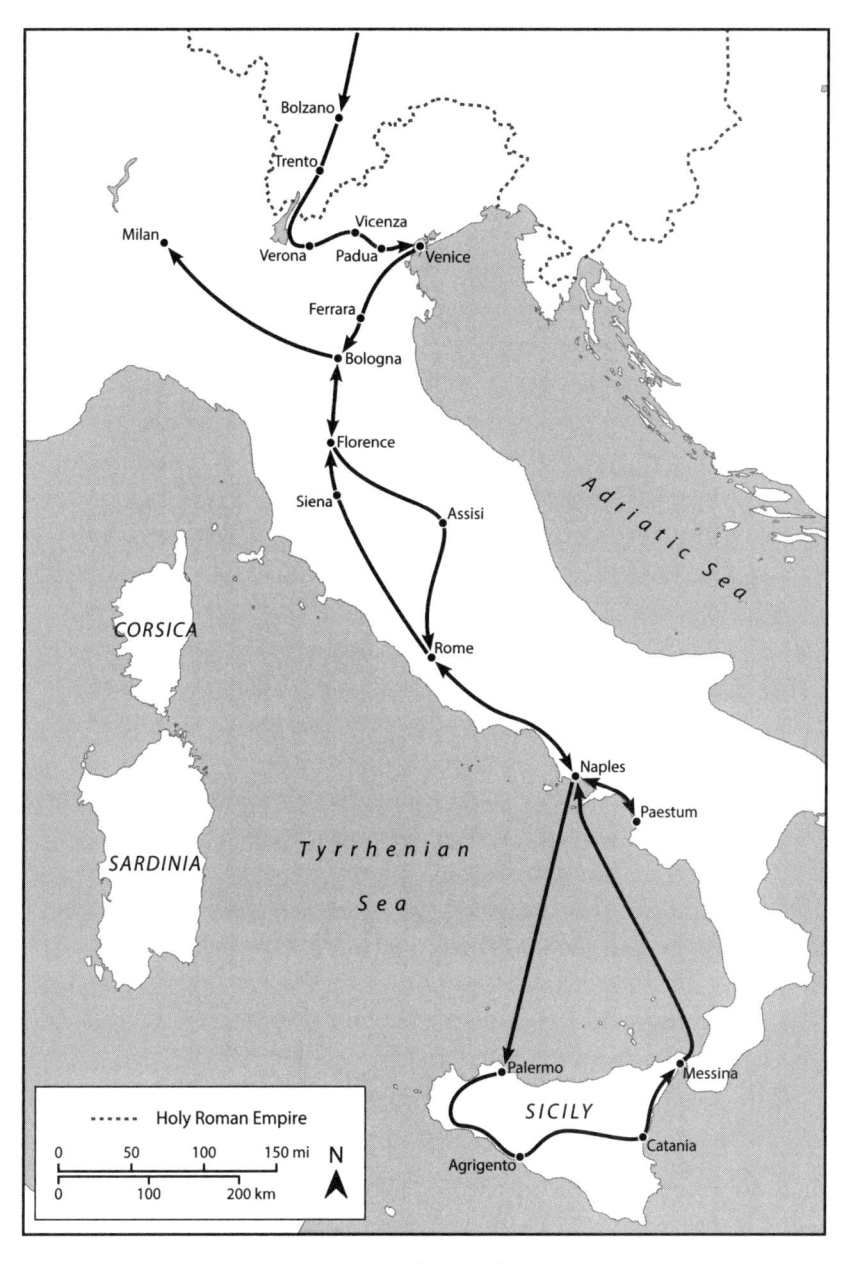

FIG. 11. Goethe's route through Italy in 1786–1788

FIG. 12. Goethe at the window of his lodgings on the Corso in Rome, by J. H. W. Tischbein (1787)

met, Moritz broke his arm in a fall from a horse during one of the group's outings. Goethe tended Moritz with great compassion and diligence, often sitting up with him through the night while his arm mended.¹⁶

In December he was thinking that in the new year he might head south to Naples in early 1787 before returning via Rome to Germany in April or May. By the first week of January the plan had changed. He would extend his stay by a year; from Naples he would visit Sicily, a relatively simple matter given his connection with the court of Naples and Sicily through Hackert. In late February 1787 he packed up his belongings and set off for the south with Tischbein. By the end of the month he was visiting Hackert in his rooms in the royal palace in Naples. Two days later he made his first ascent of Vesuvius, which was spitting stones and belching smoke. During his stay in Naples, Vesuvius became an old friend: he made the dangerous ascent to the crater three times. There was also a visit to another famous Neapolitan attraction, Emma, the young wife of Sir William Hamilton, Britain's honorary consul to the court of King Ferdinand. Hamilton was a knowledgeable collector of ancient art, notably the so-called Etruscan vases that were being excavated in large numbers at Pompeii and Herculaneum. In fact they were not Etruscan at all, but either Greek imports or made locally by Greek settlers in the colonies around the Bay of Naples. Goethe saw Emma perform her 'attitudes', in which she portrayed scenes from mythology and ancient works of art by posing in alluring postures and making quick changes of drapery, designed as much to reveal as to conceal.

Confronted by the sea, he had doubts about Sicily.[17] He was buoyed by meeting the painter Christoph Heinrich Kniep, who would accompany him. They visited the Doric temple precinct at Paestum, his first and somewhat disconcerting sight of a Greek temple. The transport to Sicily was arranged, and during an anxious wait for the seas to calm, there were conversations about other possible adventures, maybe to the Dalmatian coast and even Greece.[18] His reservations about sea travel—so far he had only made one brief excursion beyond the Lido at Venice—were confirmed by the stormy crossing to Palermo. He lay below deck thinking about *Tasso*.

The circuit of Sicily lasted six weeks—from Palermo with its luxuriant public gardens, down to the Greek temples of Agrigento on the south coast, then inland via Caltanisetta to Catania and Taormina on the east coast, where the strong winds forced him to abort an ascent of Etna, and finally north to Messina. In Palermo he investigated the occultist mountebank Giuseppe Balsamo, 'Count Cagliostro', who had begun his criminal career forging signatures on legal documents and in 1785 was accused of involvement in the Diamond Necklace Affair and briefly imprisoned in the Bastille.[19] Posing as an Englishman, Mr Wilton, and claiming to have news of Balsamo's release from the Bastille and flight to England, Goethe was able to get access to the family though he learned little beyond the exceptional piety of Balsamo's mother.[20] In Agrigento he reconsidered and rejected a plan to travel to Malta. An ascent of Etna had to be aborted because of bad weather. On the return journey to Naples the passengers mutinied as the becalmed ship threatened to drift onto the rocky coast, but

FIG. 13. View from Mt Etna by Goethe (1787)

Goethe calmed them, encouraging them to pray to the Virgin Mary and not to distract the crew from their work. The account of the episode in Goethe's *Italian Journey* reads like an allegory of his political work in Weimar.

He left Naples reluctantly at the beginning of June 1787. He regretted foregoing a closer look at the most recent lava flows. He would remain in Rome until April 1788, practising his drawing of landscapes and studies of architecture and the human body, and mixing with the community of German artists. In the spring he may have had an affair with a young Roman widow. Attempts to identify her have been unconvincing.[21] In April he was forced to say farewell to her and his close friends Angelika Kauffmann, Moritz, and the artist Friedrich Bury. According to a later report by Caroline Herder, during the fortnight leading up to his departure from Rome 'every day he cried like a child'.[22]

———

Giuliano Baioni has argued that Goethe's time in Italy was a complete withdrawal from the social and political realities of his life in Weimar.[23] In an obvious sense this is true: Italy was a holiday and was not Weimar. However, his past and presumed future in Weimar was often on his mind. Throughout his time in Italy he was under constant pressure to justify his absence from Weimar. His justifications took several forms. Obviously the trip was a cure for the anxiety and exhaustion he had felt after ten years of political work in Weimar. It was 'morally therapeutic', he said.[24] However, the letters to Weimar make surprisingly little of his need for recuperation, and somewhat more of his anguish at postponing the Italian trip for so long. It was as if he were reluctant to blame the Duke for his exhaustion and preferred to emphasize the psychodrama of his failure to see Venice and Rome before his late thirties. 'I feel as if I had been born and brought up [in Italy], and were now returning from a journey to Greenland, a whale-fishing trip';[25] 'I now see in real life all the dreams of my youth; the first etchings I can remember (my father had hung the views of Rome in an anteroom) I now see in reality';[26] 'I can hardly express to you how good it feels that so many dreams and wishes of my youth are now dissolving, that I now see in real life the objects that from my youth onwards I saw in etchings and of which I heard my father speak so often'.[27] He needed to convince his friends that his absence would have a tangible benefit, and so his letters repeatedly rehearse the idea that Italy has been his 'rebirth', that he will return to Germany 'reborn'.[28] The phantoms of distant Italy he had grown up with were being replaced by solid impressions. He felt as if his mind were gaining a new 'inner solidity'[29] or 'elasticity'.[30] 'All day I'm in conversation with things'.[31] There were moments when this turn from the imagined to the tangible took on an extreme realism, for instance one week after his triumphant arrival in Venice:

> On this journey I hope and intend to achieve a settled view of the fine arts, really impress their sacred image on my mind, and keep them as a source of private pleasure. But then to turn my attention to craftsmen and when I come back study chemistry and mechanics. For the time of beauty is over, our day demands only what is an urgent and strict necessity.[32]

Of all the ingredients of his Italian therapy the most beneficial was *seeing* Italy: its climate, its geology, its flora, its people, its art and architecture. Repeatedly his letters and diary return to the experience of seeing. 'It's hard to express how happy my manner of observing the world makes me and what I'm learning every day!';[33] 'You know my old method of treating nature; I'm treating Rome in the same way and it's coming to meet me, I'm continuing to see and to study things from the bottom up'.[34] Seeing things with a clear eye had to be worked at, he told Charlotte.[35] In doing so he would rid himself of the damaging 'pretensions' that had haunted him: 'my training in seeing and reading all things as they are, my fidelity in allowing my eye to be clear, completely divesting myself of all pretension—these make me deeply, quietly happy. Every day a remarkable new object, every day new, great, strange images and an overall experience that one has long thought and dreamt but can never arrive at with the imagination.'[36]

But to what purpose was he being reborn? He knew that he was more than ever committed to the Duke, who had generously allowed him this furlough of twenty-one months. On his return he would remain in the Duke's service and dependent on the Duke's wishes and favour. Still, he hoped it would be a new relationship.[37] He made it clear to the Duke that he would need more time to write, not least in order to memorialize his Italian experiences. Writing from Rome in March 1788, he sought approval for his plans for the return journey and added a further request:

> As I could, according to these indications, arrive home no earlier than the first half of June, so I would like to add a further request: that after my arrival you would grant the same leisure to me when I am present as you already have to me during my absence. My desire is [...] to add up the sum of my journey and to include in the last three volumes of my writings the mass of the many recollections on my life and the many thoughts about art.
>
> I can permit myself to say that after this year and a half of solitude I have rediscovered myself; but as what? As an artist![38]

By art Goethe did not mean the visual arts, even though he devoted more time in Italy to drawing than to writing, producing more than 450 landscapes and 350 studies of architecture, perspective, anatomy, and sculpture.[39] More than a quarter of his surviving 2,500 drawings and watercolours were made in Italy. He needed to relaunch his literary career, and the mass of drafts and notes on Italian subjects would be the springboard. The diary he had written for Charlotte, covering the journey from Carlsbad to Rome, was already a substantial and well-finished piece of work. After his arrival in Rome his notes became more functional and fragmentary, but he did recommence his correspondence with his Weimar friends, who received infrequent but lengthy letters from him. Just as much as the diary for Charlotte, these were intended as preparatory drafts for a more finished travelogue. In fact the travelogue remained unwritten until much later; he only began work on his *Italian Journey* in 1813. In the meantime, and to make good in some measure the debt to his friends, in 1788 he published a series of short essays in Wieland's *German Mercury*, under the heading *Extracts from a Travel Journal*. It was the kind of writing Goethe had produced in large quantities before 1775 and virtually nothing of since then. Aside from these pieces, he wrote little new work in Italy. If he was to be reborn as a writer, it would evidently not be as a poet, for he wrote virtually no new poetry in Italy. There was a new but soon abandoned tragedy on the Phaeacian princess Nausicaa from Book VI of Homer's *Odyssey*. In this tragic version the relationship between Odysseus and Nausicaa would be deeper than in the *Odyssey*. Odysseus would be 'half guilty, half guiltless', according to the recollections in the *Italian Journey*.[40] Nausicaa would not recover from the affair. Only a few pages of drafts have survived.

Aside from the journals and letters, his main literary activity in Italy was providing finished copy for the Göschen edition of his *Writings*. In a letter to the Duke from Rome in December 1786, he returned again to the theme of Italy as a rebirth: 'When I undertook to have my fragments published, I considered myself dead; how happy I'll be when, by completing what I had begun, I can once more confirm myself as living'.[41] *Iphigeneia* was versified after an arduous struggle. *Egmont* was completed and revised. Some work was done on *Torquato Tasso*. Two new scenes were drafted for *Faust*. The lyric dramas *Erwin and Claudine* were revised and some of their flaws removed. The *Meister* novel was left untouched. Some of the burden of the unfinished works had been lifted.

Scientific observations were part of the therapeutic regime. The lush and sometimes unfamiliar flora he saw as he went further south drew him towards botany. But in this as in other fields of natural history, he followed his nose. Crossing the Alps he became preoccupied by the weather, notably the forms of clouds and the regional and local patterns of rainfall either side of the Alps. At this time cloud types had not yet been systematically classified. The first classification to make compelling sense of the forms of clouds—and the basis of the standard modern nephology—was published by Luke Howard in 1803. Goethe's first intuition was that the shapes of clouds depended upon air pressure, though he preferred the term 'elasticity'. (Measuring air pressure would become a lifelong habit.) He was conscious of his lack of schooling in matters of terminology, as he wrote to Charlotte in his diary: 'altogether my terminology is not the best; when I return, then we shall compare my notes and experiences with the principles of the experts in physics, their theories and experiences. Sadly I'm not educated, as you know'.[42] His observations do have merit. In conditions of high elasticity, the large, compressed, discrete masses of cloud will tend to disperse into thinner blankets of cloud at higher altitude. (In Goethe's German these are termed 'lamb clouds'.) Indeed, what Goethe describes here conforms exactly to the transition between cumulus and cirrocumulus clouds observed by Howard. In alpine regions, the skeins of high lamb clouds are caught by the mountains and form towering white clouds, with greyer striated clouds beneath them. If the high pressure continues, these clouds will also be dispersed and blown away by the wind. It may also happen that the sun causes meltwater on the high mountains to evaporate, and when the air is sufficiently saturated, the water vapour forms clouds that can build up to such an extent that a storm happens.[43] In this way, weather patterns are affected not just by changes in latitude, but also by high mountain ranges and in particular by the alpine range that spreads east to west across this region of Europe. Indeed, the effects caused by the Alps can dwarf the effects of latitude, so that the differences in weather conditions to the north and south of the Alps are much greater than would be found between two similar latitudes that are not separated by high mountains.[44] This at any rate was the experience of a traveller exchanging the cold and wet of Germany for dry, balmy Italy. It was also a serious attempt at a holistic model of the weather that accounted for air pressure, humidity, and geography, all on the basis of observations.

The changes in climate allowed Goethe to confirm Linnaeus's observations on the environmental variations in plant forms, due to changes in warmth, sunlight, air pressure, humidity,[45] and even the effects of salty marine air. On the Lido at Venice he found the plants as rich in sap as river plants and as tough skinned as mountain plants.[46] In the university botanical gardens at Padua his attention was drawn to a two-hundred-year-old fan palm. Its leaves, entire at the base, veined halfway up, and frayed at the top, were of special interest, as was its flower, which seemed, in terms of its outer form at least, to bear absolutely no relation to the rest of the plant.[47] Among the few books he took with him on the journey was an old edition of Linnaeus's *Genera Plantarum* (1737).[48] Indeed, he did not imagine finding anything other than confirmation of the Linnaean system of plant classification.[49] He would only realize later that in some part—the part of his theory focusing on leaves—his own way of conceiving of plant classification was incompatible with the Linnaean method, which was based strictly on the ordering and form of the sex organs and took no account of other relationships between plants. In the meantime, he continued to adhere broadly to Linnaean principles.

In late March 1787 in Naples he made his first mention of an 'original' or 'archetypal plant' (*Urpflanze*).[50] Several weeks later in the botanical gardens at Palermo he found the most luxuriant and diverse range of flora he had yet seen,[51] perhaps including evidence of the *Urpflanze*:

> In the face of so many new and renewed forms, the old whim occurred to me again as to whether among this multitude I might find the *Urpflanze*. For such a thing must exist! How else would I be able to recognise that this or the other form is a plant, if they are not all formed according to one pattern?[52]

It is surprising that he refers to the *Urpflanze* as an 'old whim'. Neither here nor in any of his subsequent references to the *Urpflanze* in Italy is there evidence of a fully worked out model of what the *Urpflanze* actually is. What is clear is its purpose. The idea is to show in a visual model that all existing forms of plants are related to one another. In this sense, the *Urpflanze* is the vegetable equivalent of his search for a relationship between mammalian skulls. Furthermore, the logic of the *Urpflanze* dictates not only that all existing plants are related, but also that there is an almost infinite number of other possible plant forms. That is to say, the plant species that currently exist or have ever existed are only a small fraction of the complete range of possible plants. By extrapolation from the *Urpflanze* one can envisage the full mutability of the vegetable realm. The *Urpflanze* also entails that the transformation of plants is governed by regularity, or as Goethe puts it 'an inner truth and necessity'.[53] This regularity must be visible in the relation between successive stages in the development of a plant. It must also apply to the animal kingdom and therefore be indicative of a deeper developmental law.[54] Responding from Rome to Herder's new Spinoza dialogue *God: Some Conversations*, Goethe drew a parallel between his *Urpflanze* and Spinoza's view of God-nature: 'in botany I have come across a ἓν καὶ πᾶν [one and all] that amazes me'. According to Jacobi's *On the Doctrine of Spinoza*, Lessing had used the Greek phrase (originally from Heraclitus or Xenophanes) in the context of his admiration for the Spinozism of Goethe's 'Prometheus'.[55] In the letter to Herder, Goethe uses the phrase as a nod towards the Spinozan notion that nature in all its ramifications is characterized by a law-like unity. For all these reasons, then, it seems clear that even in 1787 Goethe knew that the *Urpflanze* was at heart both a metamorphic theory—it involved claims about how organisms develop—and a morphological one—it was a way of envisioning the unity of nature. The morphological dimension was not in itself new; it can be read across from his work on mammalian skulls. The metamorphic dimension was a new departure. In August 1787 he wrote to Knebel of finding a proliferous carnation, where out of the corolla of the parent plant grew four fully formed carnations.[56] He took this to indicate that the plant, from stem to flower and sex organs, is one complete and repeatable developmental unit.

One of the additions Goethe made to his 'Faust sack' while in Italy is closely connected with his morphological studies. It is a monologue of some thirty lines that Faust utters in a stormy forest. He begins by invoking the Earth Spirit, whom he credits with inducting him into the study of natural history:

> Erhabner Geist, du gabst mir, gabst mir alles,
> Warum ich bat. Du hast mir nicht umsonst
> Dein Angesicht im Feuer zugewendet.
> Gabst mir die herrliche Natur zum Königreich,
> Kraft, sie zu fühlen, zu genießen. Nicht
> Kalt staunenden Besuch erlaubst du nur,
> Vergönnest mir in ihre tiefe Brust,
> Wie in den Busen eines Freund's, zu schauen.
> Du führst die Reihe der Lebendigen
> Vor mir vorbei, und lehrst mich meine Brüder
> Im stillen Busch, in Luft und Wasser kennen.[57]

Sublime spirit, you gave me, gave me everything / I asked for. It was not in vain that you / turned your face towards me in the fire. / [You] gave me wonderful nature for a kingdom, / the power to feel it, to enjoy it. It is not / only a coldly marvelling visit that you permit me, / you grant me to look into the depths of its breast, / as if into the bosom of a friend. / You lead the series of living beings / before my eyes, and teach me to recognise my brothers / in the silent bush, in air and water.

The Earth Spirit has given Faust insights into nature. The 'series of living things' is evidently orderly and intelligible, for it passes before his eyes in sequence. 'Bush and sky and sea' indicate the classificatory sequence of mammals, birds, and fish. The whole sequence must also include human beings, because the living things are Faust's 'brothers'. There is more than just a hint of the transformationist arguments Goethe had discussed with Herder in 1784, as they worked on the early chapters of Herder's *Ideas*. As Herder put it, 'The animals are humans' elder brothers'.[58]

———

Reaching Italy and in particular Rome was, Goethe told his Weimar friends, a blessed release from long anguish and frustration. What he had missed, and what he now experienced in abundance, was immediate contact with ancient objects: architecture, sculpture, pottery, but also the land itself, the sky and mountains, the seascapes, and cliff-hugging settlements. They were places that might, without being too fanciful, be imagined as the islands of Homer's *Odyssey*, or the streets through which Propertius, Ovid, and Martial had walked. In Rome and Sicily the descriptions in the ancient poets turned into 'sensuous concept[s]'.[59] Goethe was amazed to see his first Roman amphitheatre in Verona, which gave him an insight into the relation between popular behaviour and classical architecture, and his first Roman temple in Assisi, where he appreciated how the location of a temple was crucial to its place in city life—'so natural, and so great in its naturalness', he wrote.[60] Several weeks after arriving in Rome, however, he began to realize that the rebirth would also involve 'more effort and worry than pleasure'.[61] He was returning to school, or more precisely returning to the university education in the classics that his father had forbidden him:

> I thought I'd learn something proper here; but the idea that I'd have to go back so far into my schooling, that there was so much I'd have to unlearn, indeed relearn—that didn't occur to me. [. . .] I'm like an architect who wanted to build a tower and had laid poor foundations.[62]

He was studying Winckelmann again,[63] with a view to identifying 'the styles of the various peoples of antiquity and the periods of these styles, for which Winckelmann is a reliable guide'.[64] He also read Vitruvius and Palladio on ancient architecture: 'with architecture things are getting better daily. When you get into the water, you learn to swim. I've now made rational sense for myself of the orders of the columns and can generally answer the question "why?" Now I retain in my mind the dimensions and proportions, which as a mere task of memory were always incomprehensible and impossible to remember'.[65] The theory did not always prepare him for the experience. At Paestum he was shocked by the 'stubby, wedge-shaped, closed-packed massive columns' of the Doric temples. He concluded that we moderns are so habituated to the later, slender style that we find the earlier style hard to appreciate.[66] The slimmer columns of the so-called Temple of Concordia at Agrigento, a masterpiece of the high classical style and the best-preserved Greek temple outside Athens, were more to modern taste. Sometimes Winckelmann was not a reliable guide. Also at Agrigento, Goethe admired the Phaedra sarcophagus and took it to be an example of the mature, beautiful style of Greek art, following Winckelmann, whereas in fact it was a Roman imitation. Still, the true meaning of the sarcophagus was clear to him, as it had been to Winckelmann: 'here the main intention was to represent beautiful young men'.[67] Greek art was all about beautiful typicity.

Experiencing the reality of ancient art and life helped him to form a clearer view of the distance between modernity and antiquity. The distance was best understood in terms of the modern prevalence of the imagination. The ancients represented things, he wrote to Herder on returning from Sicily to Naples, whereas we moderns represent our consciousness of things:

> [The ancients] represented existence, we normally represent the effect; they portrayed what's fearful, we portray fearfully; they what's pleasant, we pleasantly etc.
>
> From here derives all exaggeratedness, all manneredness, all false elegance. If what I'm saying isn't new, then at least my vivid feeling of it was occasioned anew.[68]

In Sicily he thought he had experienced something of the Homeric world. In a short essay written probably in June 1787, he tried to explicate an obscure passage in Book X of the *Odyssey*, which the translators Bodmer and Voss had construed differently.[69] Goethe's interpretation of the passage is almost certainly wrong. Homer names a Laistrygonian hill-town as *Tēlepylos*, 'far-gated'. Goethe wrongly reads the word as an adjective though to be fair it was a reading supported by other authorities at the time. More important was the general inference he drew from the passage. For Homer the town was not unique but a typical Mediterranean fortified hill-town. Homer was the poet of the typical and the symbolic, not of arcane detail.

Before Italy Goethe's knowledge of the visual arts was based on two foundations. His father had brought him up on the Dutch style of domestic and landscape painting. In Leipzig Oeser taught him a Winckelmannian neoclassicism. Both traditions were largely secular. Italy presented him with a wholly new experience. He was immersed in the art of the Italian Renaissance, and he found three new heroes to worship: Raphael, Michelangelo, and Palladio. By July 1787 he was confident that his eye was better educated: 'In time I could become a connoisseur'.[70] His aim was to be able to make his own autonomous, self-reliant judgements: 'In art I have to reach the point where everything becomes intuitive knowledge and nothing remains tradition and name only'.[71] It was, he stressed repeatedly, the same process as he had employed in educating himself as a natural historian, even if nature was a more dependable subject of study than art.[72] One of his earliest reactions to art in Italy, in the church of San Giorgio in Verona, was horror at the paintings' appalling subject matter.[73] The artists seemed to be fixated on showing the degradation or demeaning of human nature. Several weeks later in Bologna he formulated his horror:

> What can you say but that you'll be driven mad by the nonsensical subjects. [...] One is always in the anatomy theatre, on the gallows, at the knacker's yard, always the suffering of the hero, never his deeds. Never an immediate interest, always something phantastical and extraneous that has to be waited for. Either evil-doers or ecstatics, criminals, or fools. [...] There is nothing there that provides any notion of humanity.[74]

This view is entirely consistent with the humanism of *Iphigeneia*: humans thrive when they are not subject to morbid and fearful religious beliefs. By contrast, the serene, neoclassical architecture of Palladio beautified human dwellings and places of worship and thereby exalted human nature. Goethe admired Palladio's villas and palaces in and around Vicenza. In Padua he acquired a copy of Palladio's *Four Books on Architecture* (1570), which he studied in depth:

> Aside from some diligence on *Iphigeneia*, I've spent most of my time on Palladio, and cannot tear myself away. [...] In Verona and Vicenza I saw what my eyes could see, it was only in Padua that I found the book, now I'm studying it and the scales are falling from my eyes, the fog is parting and I can understand the objects.[75]

It was not only that Palladio's buildings embodied an admirable neoclassical humanism. Goethe saw in Palladio, as in Raphael, an example of an artist who by dint of diligent application to the fundamentals of his craft was eventually able to create art with a supreme lightness of touch. Palladio and Raphael exemplified the ultimate development of an artist, the *telos* of the creative spirit, who gradually, and without hindrance from inimical external influences, followed the rules of art to their perfection:

> I have got to know better two people to whom I give the epithet 'great' without reservation—Palladio and Raphael. There was not a hair's breadth of arbitrariness about them, what made them so great was that they simply knew the boundaries and laws of their art in the highest degree and moved with lightness within them, practised them.[76]

What are the laws of art? In part they are determined by the medium the artist works in. Oils are different from watercolours. Rough porous limestone—as used at Paestum, which is distant from any sources of good marble—is different from the fine Pentelic marble of Athens. The fact that the temples at Paestum had to be built from relatively poor stone imposed constraints on the architects. The columns had to be relatively short and fat. These constraints forced the architects of Paestum, so Goethe decided, to adopt the Doric style.[77] The history of art was bound up with the material conditions of its production. It was gratifying to apply his knowledge of geology and mineralogy to art.[78] Shortly after his return to Weimar, while he was meditating what to publish from his stash of Italian notes, he wrote to Heyne in Göttingen:

> If I were inclined to put pen to paper, then at first it would be very simple things. E.g., to what extent the material used for building requires the wise artist to build thus and not otherwise. So the different types of stone shed an agreeable light on architecture, each change of the material and mechanical craft imposes on the work of art a different determination and constraint. The ancients, from all I have been able to observe, were especially clever in this regard and I have often engrossed myself in these thoughts with great interest.
>
> You will see that I do very much begin from the earth and that it may seem to many as if I were handling this most spiritual matter in too earthly a manner; but if I am permitted to make this observation: the Greek gods were enthroned not in the seventh or tenth heaven, but on Olympus, and trod their enormous steps not from sun to sun but at most from mountain to mountain.[79]

In contrast to the Christian art of the Renaissance, the more humane art of the Greeks recognised its proper place on the earth we inhabit, not in some fantastical space above us. Thus reading the history of art in terms of materials was consistent with his Spinozan humanism. As he put it to Wieland, in connection with the essays he was publishing in the *German Mercury*: 'natural history, art, manners, etc., with me everything is amalgamated'.[80] The different branches of knowledge belonged to one tree. That much was implied by Spinoza's theory of knowledge: there was only one *scientia intuitiva*, only one fundamental way of grasping the universe, only one truth.

On the face of it, consistency is one thing Goethe's theory of art appears to lack. The problem went back to Winckelmann. If all art is situated in history, defined and described by the new discipline of art history that Winckelmann had founded, it must follow that the criteria by which art is to be judged must themselves be historical. Ancient Greek art obeys different rules from Renaissance art. And yet Winckelmann insisted that there were absolute (Neoplatonic) norms of beauty. For Winckelmann, ancient art is both an unrepeatable historical phenomenon and, paradoxically, an ideal we should emulate.[81] Goethe's route round this paradox involved making art contingent upon nature. Writing in Rome in January 1787 he stated the problem and where he hoped to find the solution:

> First one is required [...] with every work of art to inquire as to the era that gave rise to it. We are urged by Winckelmann to separate the periods, to recognise the specific style used by the nations and gradually developed by them in the sequence of time and then finally depraved. [...] The second thought is exclusively concerned with the art of the Greeks and seeks to investigate how those incomparable artists proceeded in developing from the human figure the sphere of divine form that is completely perfect. [...] My supposition is that they proceeded according to exactly those laws according to which nature proceeds and on whose trail I am.[82]

Later in 1787, responding to Herder's Spinoza dialogues *God: Some Conversations*—and it is no accident that Goethe was brought to these conclusions after being reminded of Spinoza—he expressed the effect made on him by the few perfect works he had seen (or thought he had seen) by the Greeks in their best period:

> So much is certain, the ancient artists had just as great an understanding of nature and just as secure a conception of what can be represented and how it must be represented, as Homer. Sadly the number of artworks of the first rank is very small. But if one only sees these, then one can wish for nothing more than to understand them correctly and then depart in peace. These high works of art were at the same time produced as the highest works of nature by human beings according to true and natural laws. Everything arbitrary, everything imagined falls away, here is necessity, here is God.[83]

The language is unmistakably Spinozan.[84] It is also connected to the theory of natural forms Goethe developed during his geological studies in the early 1780s. The crystalline rhomboid forms of granite were the *telos* of the rock's formation; they were the forms granite took if no extraneous factors interrupted its development. Artistic creation has its own analogous natural logic, its own way of naturally unfolding from within. If this unfolding takes its natural course and is not interrupted by arbitrary or merely imagined notions, such as the fantastical ideas in much Renaissance art, it can generate works of perfect beauty in the same way that nature does.

The idea is spelt out in more detail in a short essay published in the *German Mercury* in February 1789, titled 'Simple Imitation of Nature, Manner, Style'. Ostensibly the essay has the modest aim of clarifying terminology. Once understood correctly, the terminology has its own internal structure and sequence, ascending from *simple imitation* through *manner* to *style*. *Imitation* is a matter of conscientiously reproducing the forms and colours of the objects. By means of *imitation*, a 'competent but limited' artist can portray 'pleasant but limited' objects. Still, the results can be 'sure, powerful and rich'.[85] An anxious feeling that *simple imitation* is not enough may impel an artist to turn to *manner*. What then happens is that artists select which features of the object to represent and by doing so create their own 'language' of representation. So what is being portrayed is now not the object, but the mind of the artist.[86] In this respect, *manner* is what we moderns do, as compared to the *style* of the ancients: they 'represented existence, we normally represent the effect' of existence, as Goethe wrote to Herder in May 1787. *Style* adds a third process, the 'exact and deep study of the object itself', which involves a comparative study of 'the series of forms'. (Again Goethe connects his theory of art with his work in natural history.) *Style* thus rests 'on the deepest foundations of knowledge, on the essence of things insofar as it is permitted to us to know this in visible and tangible forms'.[87]

Writing thirty years later, Goethe made a striking claim about the knowledge he had brought back from Italy to Weimar in 1788. In addition to studying nature and the arts, he had observed 'the manners of nations' and learned 'how from the meeting of necessity and chance, drives and will, motion and resistance a third product emerges, which is neither nature nor art but both simultaneously—necessary and random, intentional and blind. I understand human society'.[88] The lapidary last sentence seems surprising, until we recall that in the mid-1780s Goethe had worked closely with Herder on the latter's *Ideas on the Philosophy of the History of Mankind*, assisted also by Knebel. One impulse in the *Ideas* is to explain human history and culture in terms of natural causes, whether the reactions of humans to their material environment, especially geography and climate, or the expression of innate drives and physiology in human behaviour. The same impulse is strong in Goethe's writings in Italy. Perhaps the first impression any German traveller would form of Italian society would be that the climate's relative warmth allowed Italians to live and work outdoors more than northerners did.[89] Moreover, a nation that lives outdoors enjoys a less isolated, more cohesive form of social existence. It is more of a nation.[90] In Vicenza he noted that 'the Vicentines [...] have a free kind of humanity that derives from their constantly public life'.[91] His Italian writings are full of comments of this kind, as well as more analytical passages. There are several accounts of the peculiarities of Italian culture such as the idiosyncratic method of timekeeping or the chaotic and initially repellent Shrovetide festivities in Rome. There are attempts to explain the character of the larger Italian cities by speculatively reconstructing their origins. Descriptions of the Greek and Roman antiquities attempt to explain them in terms of anthropology. In each case, Goethe believes that Italians lived as a group of people in constant close contact with one another by virtue of living and working outdoors. The oddness of Italian timekeeping makes sense when we think that Italians value their evening promenades, which bring to a close the public daylight hours and signal the beginning of nighttime privacy. This explains why the Italian clock begins and ends around nightfall.[92] Equally Verona's Roman amphitheatre is a product of natural human behaviour in a public space. People would have crowded round any outdoor spectacle and set up seats on wooden planks and barrels; the rows behind would have drawn up wagons to sit on. In this way a natural amphitheatre was formed out of materials lying to hand. The architect of the Roman amphitheatre simply gave this popular behaviour the permanence of stone. Understanding how the amphitheatre at Verona was built depends on our thinking of the people behaving en masse. Goethe put the same idea to work in his speculations on the origins of Venice, Rome, and Naples. His speculative history of the 'beaver republic' Venice is similar to Herder's in *This too a Philosophy of History*. Venice was originally a place of refuge. Successive waves of refugees fled to the safety of the islands in the Venetian lagoon. 'The main idea that forces itself upon me here is once more the people [*Volk*]. A great mass! And an existence that is necessary, not arbitrary'.[93] Once in the lagoon, the limited amount of dry land forced the Venetians to build upwards—hence Venice's many towers—and to use water as their main means of transport. So it was that in Venice the canals replaced roads.[94] Rome was a different case. The origins of Rome were also driven by the needs of the people, but the environment forced quite different decisions on its first inhabitants. The location of Rome is swampy and prone to flooding. Clearly no prince in his right mind would lead his people to such an unfavourable place. Goethe's theory was that Rome's seven hills must first have been occupied by herdsmen and 'riffraff'. The hills were not a defensive refuge from the surrounding countryside. Rather they were the only place to build securely in a region whose low-lying land was swampy. So the people gradually built up and fortified the hills and then proceeded to drain the surrounding marshy valleys.[95] It was a gradual process of occupation and fortification. The origins of Venice and Rome contrasted again with those of Naples, which is surrounded by fertile agricultural land and enjoys a balmy climate. The land around Naples provided all the sustenance the people needed, and this happy situation is reflected in modern Neapolitans' behaviour. Their efforts are dedicated to living a carefree life. Unlike the Venetians, they have no interest in becoming rich: why should they, when their immediate needs are so well provided for? In one of the *German Mercury* essays Goethe addressed a charge levelled against Naples: that its population comprises thousands of *lazzaroni*, homeless folk who live on the street and are completely idle. Writing to Charlotte from Naples, Goethe insisted that this was a myth created by northern preconceptions: 'When one looks at this city on its own terms and really in detail, and doesn't look at it from a northern political standard, then it is a grand, wonderful sight, and you know that this is exactly my manner'.[96] Closer examination shows that the *lazzaroni* do not exist.[97] To be sure, there are many raggedly dressed people who resemble beggars, but these people are in fact gainfully occupied.[98] They only appear to be idlers because they live and work outdoors all year round in a land that provides for their needs. Naples simply demands less economic effort and ingenuity of its inhabitants.[99]

The most substantial and well crafted of Goethe's writings on the anthropology of Italy, and the strongest justification for his claim to have 'understood human society', is his essay on the Roman Shrovetide carnival, which he witnessed in 1787 and 1788. He probably made detailed notes during his second stay in Rome and wrote them up in the winter of 1788/89. The small volume was published by the Berlin firm of Unger at Easter 1789. Goethe lavished considerable care on the design of the volume. A pleasantly rounded Roman typeface was used instead of the traditional German *Fraktur*. His Frankfurt compatriot Johann Georg Schütz provided engravings of the carnival costumes. Goethe's description of the carnival emphasizes the role of the people in creating their own culture: 'The Roman carnival is a celebration that is actually not *given to the people, but that the people gives to itself*.[100] The streets of Rome, in particular the narrow, ruler-straight Corso running for one mile from

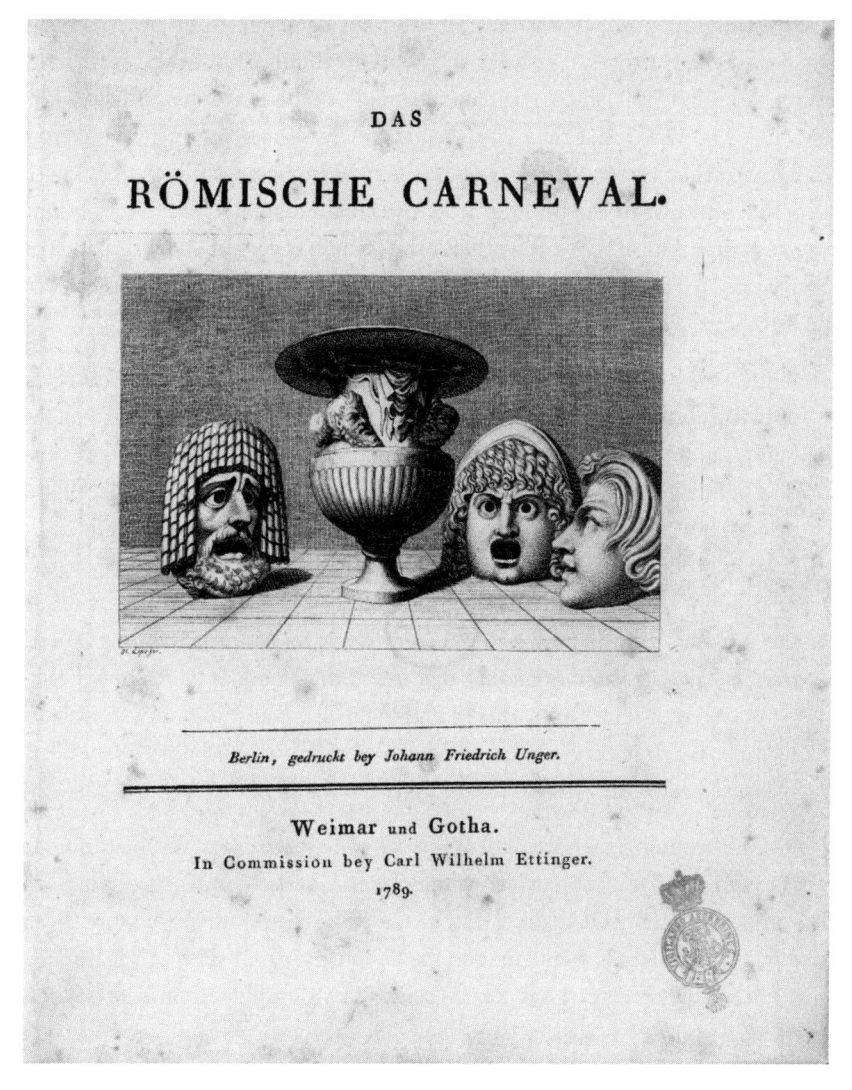

FIG. 14. Title page of Goethe's 'The Roman Carnival',
with vignette etched by J. H. Lips (1789)

the Porta del Popolo down to the Piazza Venezia, determines the form of the festival. The shape of the Corso means that the carnival is all about movement along it and spectating from the buildings and piazzas either side of it. Masses of people are brought into a space too small for them, which creates an intense, half-organized competition for space that is at once playful and menacing. He was fascinated by the danger and tension of the carnival, which seemed to hold a symbolic meaning. It was an embodiment of primal human drives, an organized chaos expressing the crisis moments of human life: sex, birth, and death. As individuals, the participants seemed to experience the carnival without fully knowing what they were doing or why. There was a long, fevered buildup to the climax of the carnival: the mad horseraces down the Corso, which in contrast to the buildup were over in an instant.[101] Evidently there were unconscious motives at work, for the festivities passed 'like a dream, like a fairy tale'.[102] He concluded the description with a reflection on the carnival's unconscious symbolic meaning:

> If during the course of these follies the crude *pulcinella* indecently reminds us of the pleasures of love to which we owe our existence, if a *baubo* divulges in the public square the secrets of a woman in childbirth, if the many candles lit at night remind us of our final solemnities, then in the midst of the nonsense we are made aware of the most important scenes in our life. [. . .] If we may continue to speak more earnestly than the subject seems to permit, then we will observe that the most vivid and highest pleasures, such as the horses as they fly past, only come into view for a moment, move us, and hardly leave a trace in our souls, that freedom and equality can only be savoured in the frenzy of madness, and that the greatest joy only stimulates us most when it verges the most closely on danger and desirously takes pleasure in sweetly anxious emotions close at hand.[103]

The anthropological notes and essays are of no less interest for the thoughts about method that unobtrusively guide them. Goethe was aware of the need for objectivity. As well as divesting himself of the prejudices of a northern mentality, he sought to blend in with the people he was observing. He noticed that the people of Verona had a keen sensitivity to foreigners, and so he took to dressing and behaving like a middle-class Veronese, partly for the pleasure it gave him, but also because it allowed him to get close to the people without attracting their attention.[104] Again in Naples he used stealth: 'today I stole through the city observing, as is my manner'.[105] It is no exaggeration to claim that Goethe was, however briefly and informally, a pioneer of ethnographical fieldwork. By studying people as a mass he believed he could understand better the law-like regularities of human behaviour. Humans as a mass are truer to type because a mass of people is less liable to be affected by an individual's arbitrary whims. Repeatedly he stressed that the behaviour he was studying was the natural behaviour of ordinary folk, not the behaviour dictated to them by a ruler. So in *The Roman Carnival*, when he asks whether the carnival can in fact be understood at all, he answers the question by pointing to the almost complete absence of state organization or policing of the festivities: 'The state makes few arrangements and little expense. The circle of pleasures moves of its own accord, and the police regulates it with a very gentle hand'.[106] This is why he feels able to claim that the carnival is a natural expression of the Roman way of life.[107] It is the same argument as he made for rhomboidal form being the natural perfection or *telos* of granite, assuming it was allowed to crystallize without external impediments.

Above all Goethe's Italian anthropology is concerned with beginnings. His speculative histories of the great Italian cities have a genetic form. They seek the traces of ancient origins that persist in modern life. Italy was fertile ground for such work because so much of Italy's ancient history is still visible today. He believed that modern Italian society also preserved remnants of ancient behaviour, for instance the convention by which male actors played female roles in the theatre. Even so, the modern Italian *Volk* was less cohesive than it had been in antiquity: to fully appreciate the natural form of the amphitheatre in Verona one would have to have seen it full of ancient Veronese, when 'the *Volk* was still more of a *Volk* than it is now'.[108] In antiquity the drive for self-preservation was undimmed, and the colours and flavours of human behaviour were stronger.

It was fortunate that the two acts in prose of a play about Torquato Tasso were among the fragments Goethe packed in his trunk for Italy because the material would come to life again south of the Alps. In October 1786 he visited Ferrara, where the play is set, and in Rome in February 1787 he paid homage at Tasso's grave in the church of San Onofrio across the Tiber. He also saw the wax bust of Tasso in the monastery library. He finished the play in summer 1789 in Weimar. It was published in Volume VI of the Göschen *Writings* at the end of the year. Finishing the play at some distance from his pre-Italian life perhaps allowed him to make public the criticisms of courtly life that he had only expressed privately to Charlotte von Stein and Knebel. The action takes place at the Ferrara court's summer palace at Belriguardo, where the Duke, his sister Princess Leonore, and her Florentine friend Leonore Sanvitale are spending the spring, and their court poet Tasso is completing his epic poem *Jerusalem Delivered* (*La Gerusalemme Liberata*). Although they have only recently arrived to enjoy the spring in the countryside, their relationships are already testy: the opening dialogue between the Princess and Leonore Sanvitale is full of veiled competitiveness. Indeed, in the first two acts much of what is said appears inconsequential, but behind the courtly politeness matters of great significance are being mooted. This sense of hidden agendas and desires, played out over the course of a single day and between only five speaking characters, gives the play an atmosphere of claustrophobia that is essential to its meaning.

The main conflict arises out of a seemingly trivial event, and its triviality will matter. The Princess and her friend Leonore Sanvitale want to crown Tasso with a garland, so elevating him to the same status as Virgil and Ariosto, whose busts the ladies have just crowned. At first Tasso demurs, then reluctantly accepts. The timing is fateful because at this moment Antonio Montecatino, the Duke's minister, returns from conducting a successful diplomatic mission at the Papal See. As will become clear, seeing Tasso crowned and praised arouses jealousy in Antonio. In the same way as the two ladies compete to be the subject of Tasso's poetry, Tasso and Antonio are in competition for the Duke's favour. It is a competition Tasso is destined to lose, not so much because of his personal failings—the others accuse him of immaturity, solipsism, and paranoia—as because he has nothing to offer the Duke but cultural prestige. Antonio offers something more tangible and valuable: hard political power. Precisely in order to stress this contrast between politics and poetry, Antonio makes pointedly dismissive comments about the limited value of the arts and about Tasso's standing as a poet. In a clear sign of how power works here, Antonio's dismissiveness incurs no censure from the Duke. Indeed, at the end of Act I Antonio withdraws with the Duke, and Tasso with the ladies, which shows how politics trumps culture.

The play is a remarkable study of the fraught and twisted psychology that comes with relationships of competition and dependence. At the beginning of Act II, Tasso makes it clear to the Princess that he adores her. She evidently needs him to prop up her fragile self-esteem, for she suffers from constitutional weaknesses of mind and body.[109] Although (or perhaps because) he recognises the unbridgeable social gap between them, he proposes to her a Rousseauian idyll, albeit in words adapted from the real Tasso's pastoral play *Aminta*:[110] a world in which 'whatever pleases is permitted' ('erlaubt ist was gefällt'),[111] in which no social divisions exist to inhibit true feelings. This is one of the virtues of his poetry: it expands our sense of what human nature is capable of. Fantastical as his vision is, Tasso articulates it in easy, flowing cadences and precise imagery.[112] The Princess's defensive reply, quoting Guarini's *The Faithful Shepherd* (*Il pastor fido*), makes for a stark contrast: 'what's proper is permitted' ('erlaubt ist was sich ziemt').[113] She struggles to express herself, speaking in halting, flat-footed sentences.[114] More damaging than her evident lack of conviction is her need for his attention, which makes her unable to dampen his enthusiasm. When he anxiously confesses that he has heard rumours about her being courted by various princes, she unwisely reassures him that 'I know of no relationship yet that would tempt me' ('Noch weiß ich kein Verhältniß, das mich lockte').[115] Tasso can reasonably understand this as encouragement.

Buoyed by the hope of success with the Princess, Tasso tries to repeat his success with Antonio, but their long dialogue becomes increasingly antagonistic. Tasso grows more agitated and Antonio more caustic. Antonio even stoops to implying that Tasso has enjoyed the Princess's sexual favours. He picks up Tasso's incautious use of the words 'delight' ('Wollust'), which can denote both sexual and nonsexual pleasure, and 'without reserve' ('ohne Rückhalt'). He replies with a chain of sexual innuendos—conquest, broad roads, unlocked gates—that culminate in the low implication that Tasso's conquest of the Princess is akin to picking up a prostitute on the street:

> Scheint es doch,
> Du bist gewohnt zu siegen, überall
> Die Wege breit, die Pforten weit zu finden. [...]
> Wer angelangt am Ziel ist, wird gekrönt,
> Und oft entbehrt ein Würd'ger eine Krone.
> Doch gibt es leichte Kränze, Kränze gibt es
> Von sehr verschiedner Art, sie lassen sich
> Oft im Spazierengehn bequem erreichen.[116]

Yet it seems / You're used to conquering / To finding the roads broad everywhere, the gates wide open. [...] Whoever reaches their goal gets crowned, / And often a worthy man misses out on a crown. / Yet there are easy garlands, there are garlands / Of very different kinds, they can / Often be had easily enough just by going for a walk.

The antagonism escalates until Tasso finally challenges Antonio and draws his sword, at which point, and unluckily for Tasso, the Duke appears. His appearance at this instant might be chance, but it also gives some credence to Tasso's feeling that he is being watched. He may be overreacting. He may also be right. After hearing both men tell their side of the story, the Duke confines Tasso to his quarters. Act II ends with the Duke instructing Antonio to restore peace, after Leonore has visited Tasso to calm him down.

Act III returns to the ladies' competition to be Tasso's muse. Leonore has a secret plan to take Tasso to Florence, chiefly to satisfy her own pride and vanity, but also as a weapon in the political conflict between the city-states. When she proposes to Tasso that leaving Ferrara would be good for him, he sees through her plan. As he had said of her in Act II:

> So liebenswürdig sie erscheinen kann,
> Ich weiß nicht wie es ist, konnt' ich nur selten
> Mit ihr ganz offen seyn, und wenn sie auch
> Die Absicht hat, den Freunden wohlzuthun,
> So fühlt man Absicht und man ist verstimmt.[117]

As likeable as she can appear, / I don't know why it is, I could seldom / Be completely open with her, and even if she / Has good intentions towards her friends, / One senses intention and one is put off.

His scepticism is justified. Because he recognises *amour-propre*, Tasso is neither calmed by Leonore's visit, as the Duke hoped, nor won over by her secret strategy. Next Antonio visits to give Tasso his freedom. Tasso's response is to negotiate with the Duke. In return for his service, Tasso should be free to travel to Rome where learned men can advise him on how to finish his poem. Antonio now finds himself in an invidious position, for if he antagonizes Tasso, the Duke could hold him responsible for the loss of Tasso's services. We do not see how Antonio presents Tasso's proposal to the Duke—unenthusiastically, one suspects. Instead Act V begins with Antonio reporting to the Duke that he has gone to Tasso a second time—from which we can infer that the Duke was not happy with the Rome plan—and has failed to persuade Tasso to relent. Tasso now comes negotiate with the Duke in person and adds a further request, that the Duke return to him the manuscript of *Jerusalem Delivered* that Tasso had solemnly presented in Act I. The Duke rejects the request and instead proposes that a copy be made which Tasso can take with him. The purpose of the Duke's counterproposal is to prevent Tasso from selling his poem to another prince, for a copy of the manuscript would have minimal value, if it were known that the original were still in the Duke's possession. The Duke continues to treat Tasso like a possession or a child. At least this is how Tasso sees it, not unreasonably.

The play reaches its climax in a second dialogue between Tasso and the Princess. He reveals to her that his plan is in fact to visit his sister in Sorrento, which would signal his complete withdrawal from the public competition for prestige and the politics of the Italian city-states. However, it seems that Tasso has only floated this idea in order to alarm the Princess and force her to acknowledge how much she needs him, which she duly does: 'I have to leave you, and leave you / Is what my heart cannot do' ('Ich muß dich lassen, und verlassen kann / Mein Herz dich nicht').[118] When she realizes her error in leading Tasso on, it is already too late and Tasso tries to embrace her, in a flagrant breach of court etiquette. As it happens, the Duke, who as the stage directions state was slowly approaching, has been watching them, which again suggests that the court practises surveillance, intentionally or otherwise. The Duke orders Antonio to restrain Tasso and departs with the Princess. In a highly ambiguous final scene, Antonio tries—genuinely and despite Tasso's accusation that Antonio is a 'tyrant's tool'—to get Tasso standing on his own two feet again. Tasso begins to come round, but is haunted by his victimhood. In a tragic relapse into bare, pitiable animality, he clings on to the one thing he knows he still possesses:

> Nein, Alles ist dahin!—Nur Eines bleibt:
> Die Träne hat uns die Natur verliehen,
> Den Schrei des Schmerzens, wenn der Mann zuletzt
> Es nicht mehr trägt—Und mir noch über alles—
> Sie ließ im Schmerz mir Melodie und Rede,
> Die tiefste Fülle meiner Noth zu klagen:
> Und wenn der Mensch in seiner Qual verstummt,
> Gab mir ein Gott, zu sagen wie ich leide.[119]

> No, it's all over!—One thing alone remains: / Nature has bestowed tears upon us, / The cry of pain, when finally a man / Can't bear it any more—And me above all others—/ In my pain she left me melody and words, / To lament the deepest fullness of my need: / And if in their torment people fall silent, / A god gave me to tell how much I hurt.

Antonio takes Tasso's hand. Tasso speaks the last words of the play: a long metaphor reminiscent of the extended metaphors of Homer. He acknowledges the ambivalence of his relationship with Antonio. He first compares Antonio to a rock and himself to the storm-tossed waves; then he imagines a ship breaking up and its pilot (Tasso) cast onto the rock (Antonio) that both breaks and saves him.

In March 1789 Caroline Herder recorded that Goethe had told her 'in confidence the actual meaning of this play: it is *the disproportion of talent with life*',[120] as if Tasso's character were incompatible with success in other walks of life or indeed with life itself, which is more or less what the Duke thinks. But it is not what the play says.[121] Tasso does have flaws, but so do the play's other characters. The Princess is painfully naïve and dreamy though not averse to coquetry. Leonore is a vain and cynical schemer. Antonio is a social climber with a streak of cruelty and a dirty mind. The Duke has fewer and less grievous personal flaws, as one would expect from an advocate of autocracy like Goethe. Still, he is thoroughly patronizing. He calls the women children and pretends to be Tasso's doctor.[122] He presides over a court that is at best deadly dull and at worst a surveillance state. The aristocrats are all infected by *amour-propre*. In their world Tasso becomes an instrument by means of which they seek to project their own self-image. Antonio belittles Tasso because he wants to reserve that role for himself. Nor is the problem of this problem play that real life cannot accommodate poetry. Tasso's poetry is manifestly a superior alternative to courtly *amour-propre*. Only Tasso is capable of an expansive and generous vision of life. He expresses love and sympathy in ways that no other characters do. His words have energy and conviction. Rightly understood, and not treated as a tool of social prestige, his poetry is alien to self-interest. This social fact is what defines the contrast between Tasso, the contemplative poet, and Antonio, the political man of action—and not some tired Platonic antithesis of ideal and reality. The Duke follows this latter clichéd path of pigeonholing the poet as an ineffectual idealist or a patient in need of treatment. The ending of the play, when Tasso and Antonio are reconciled, awkwardly and ambivalently to be sure, shows that there needs to be a route out of the tired, old antitheses, but it does not show what the route might be.[123] Antonio extends the hand of sympathy and Tasso acknowledges it. In the long metaphor with which Tasso ends the play we see that the old relationship between poetry and power is over. Tasso imagines himself as a wave of the sea; in quieter times the surface of the water (poetry) had reflected and beautified the sun and stars (the Duke and his court), but no longer:

> In dieser Woge spiegelte so schön
> Die Sonne sich, es ruhten die Gestirne
> An dieser Brust, die zärtlich sich bewegte.
> Verschwunden ist der Glanz, entflohn die Ruhe.[124]

> In this wave so beautifully was mirrored / the sun, the stars rested / On this breast, that moved so tenderly. / The sparkle has vanished, the peace has fled.

If Tasso's poetry is the unstable sea, then Antonio is a rock which a shipwrecked sailor can cling to. Now that traditional courtly poetry, a reflection of untouchable celestial bodies, is a thing of the past, there is some hope in an alliance of the bourgeois poet and politician. However, the hope is not defined. Tasso understands that it is time to move on, though how and where is unclear. The relationship of poetry to power remains an 'open-ended dialectic'.[125]

In this sense, *Tasso* is an inversion of Goethe's experience of liberation in Italy, his escape from the world of power into the world of beauty, albeit in the knowledge, as he wrote in Venice, that 'the time of beauty is over, our day demands only what is an urgent and strict necessity'.[126] But *Tasso* is not simply about Goethe. It tackles wider issues concerning the place of art in the modern world. If art is to aspire to formal ideals—to represent a divine or natural necessity, not a political one—it cannot at the same time serve the needs of political power or social prestige. Tasso faces the same challenge as Iphigeneia: to develop a voice that is authentic and free from political necessity. Like her, he feels compelled to say what political necessity would prefer not to be said. The question is whether such artistic authenticity is possible in the modern world,[127] in which everything is subject to economic, political, and military necessity. 'The time of beauty is over', and art has become part of the economy and politics, or as Hans Reiss aptly put it, 'poetry produces fame',[128] like a machine. The Duke employs Tasso in order to promote himself and his territory in the struggle for dominance among the Italian city-states. For the women of court, Tasso's poetry serves either as a substitute for sexual fulfilment (the Princess) or to burnish a self-image (Leonore). At the root of all this instrumentalization of art is modern *amour-propre*. Civilization drives us to create false self-images in order to succeed in the competition for social attention. The tragedy of Tasso is not that he goes mad or that his poetic métier makes him incapable of living in the real world. His tragedy is that his belief that he is being persecuted, while perhaps not warranted in all its details, is certainly warranted in the more general sense that culture, like religion, is subject to political exploitation.

6

Transformations

WEIMAR, 1788–1794

ON HIS return to Weimar Goethe immediately plunged back into the round of lunches and suppers at court, where he enthusiastically recounted his experiences in the beautiful south. Not everyone shared his excitement. 'Goethe has returned [...] and we've heard nothing but Italy, Italy, Italy', wrote Frau von Wedel.[1] Though eager to talk, he was reluctant to lend out the manuscript of his travel journal. 'My intention was to throw it in the fire', he wrote to Herder who was about to set off for Italy: 'I know how it works. One person sees the thing and then another, it gets copied and finally I have the displeasure of seeing these private bits [*pudenda*] printed somewhere'.[2] Instead he extracted a few short essays from his drafts and published them in Wieland's *German Mercury*. The complete journal, with its story of personal renewal and its infectious excitement at the experience of Italy, would have to wait thirty years for publication.

The question of his official duties also had to be settled. He could not return to the workload that had run him into the ground before Italy, yet he expected to continue living in the style to which he was accustomed, and only Weimar could guarantee the desired balance of financial security and leisure to write. As in his dealings with publishers, he struck a deal with Carl August that reflected his high estimation of his worth. He would be relieved of most of his duties. Continuing as the Duke's senior advisor in all matters, he would still have a vote on the Privy Council, though attending only sporadically. His advice and company would have to justify the high price of his services. For the Duke, as for the publishers, he was an expensive luxury. Unlike the publishers, however, Carl August did not try to cheat him out of his dues and could therefore count on his unwavering loyalty. Four years later, on the death of his uncle Hermann, there was talk of offering Goethe a position on the Frankfurt city council. Out of gratitude to Carl August he declined.[3]

In addition to his advisory role, he would continue to administer the Duchy's roads and waterways and the ill-fated Ilmenau mines with their associated finances. From the spring of 1789 there was also the hugely expensive remodelling of the ducal *Schloss* to oversee. Another new role, befitting his national standing as a writer and his interest in natural history, was to take charge of the University of Jena. It was important and delicate work. The university was a major source of income for the Duchy and a showcase of its intellectual and cultural liberality. One of Goethe's first acts was to approve the appointment of a new nonstipendiary professor of history, the once radical playwright Friedrich Schiller.[4] For the impecunious Schiller, who had led a nomadic existence since his escape from the employ of Duke Carl Eugen of Württemberg, Jena seemed a safe harbour and a beacon of freedom from princely interference.[5] The reality was more complex. While most of the Jena professoriate shared Schiller's view of Jena's liberality, the Weimar government was tightening its political control of the university. A particular concern, as in the early 1780s, was the academics' interest in freemasonry.[6] The government decided not to permit secret societies in Jena, whether because the political ideals of the freemasons were dangerously radical or because the existence of these 'subterranean paths, vaults and sewers', as Goethe had written to Lavater in 1781,[7] might undermine trust in the state. In spring 1789, when a new masonic lodge was mooted, Goethe was obliged to read the riot act, as he reported to Carl August:

> Jena, as you know, was threatened with a lodge, Bertuch immediately gave up on the idea and has also put Hufeland right, [but] Bode clings to this plaything so firmly that it would not be easy to talk him out of it, in the meantime I have in all frankness explained the situation to him and shown him why you would neither give your consent to such an establishment nor turn a blind eye.[8]

In addition to putting pressure on individuals, Goethe and the Duke decided on a public information campaign. Goethe proposed publishing a piece in Bertuch's *General Literary News* that would 'deal a heavy blow to all secret societies'.[9] Of special concern was the progressive theologian Carl Friedrich Bahrdt in Halle, who was recruiting for his German Union, a more radical successor to the Illuminati. Bahrdt was arrested by the Prussian authorities in the same month as Goethe and the Duke blocked the new masonic lodge in Jena.[10] As well as preventing the spread of secret societies in the Duchy, Goethe and the Duke were keen to distance themselves in public from the taint of association with Bahrdt and the Illuminati, not least in order to reassure the Duchy's more powerful neighbours that Weimar's intellectuals and the students and professors at Jena were not the source of radical ideas.[11] However, the problem did not go away; in the summer of 1789 a visitor recorded rumours that students were still planning to resurrect the order of Illuminati.[12]

The winter of 1788/89 was brightened by a visit from Moritz. Goethe helped to build Moritz's reputation by publishing extracts from his essay 'On the Creative Imitation of Beauty' in Wieland's *German Mercury*. Carl August also put in a good word for Moritz which led to his appointment to the Berlin Academy of Sciences and then to a chair in antiquities at Berlin's Royal Academy of Fine Arts. It was the culmination of a stellar career for the son of a poor hatter. Another younger man who enjoyed Goethe's support was a local author, Christian August Vulpius. It was the family's history and not the quality of Vulpius's writing that engaged Goethe's sympathy. 'Empty, shallow, tasteless, and repugnant' was his verdict on a volume in which Vulpius's poems appeared.[13] Vulpius's father had struggled to make a living as a scribe and archivist in the miserably paid service of the Weimar dukes.[14] In 1782 he was accused of malpractice, possibly for forging claims for long-overdue expenses.[15] Goethe was party to the decision to sack the aging Vulpius. After his death in 1786, the Vulpius household consisted of Christian August, his aunt, his half sister, and his sister Christiane. They were only saved from destitution by Christiane's work in an artificial flower factory set up by the Bertuch family to support Weimar's petit-bourgeois women. Shortly before Goethe's return from Italy, Christiane's brother set off on a tour of southern Germany, so in early July 1788 it was Christiane who had the task of pleading with Goethe to renew the financial support for her brother that had lapsed during Goethe's absence.[16]

On 11 July or a day or two earlier Christiane probably called at the Frauenplan and spoke to Goethe's servant Seidel.[17] It seems that on 12 July, either at the Frauenplan or his garden house, Goethe and Christiane met. This was the date they would celebrate as the anniversary of their 'marriage'. It was a turning point in his life, he wrote in 1796: 'my marriage is now eight and the French Revolution seven years old.'[18] The relationship continued in secret through the summer, autumn, and winter. It helped that Christiane was a free agent.[19]

FIG. 15. Christiane Vulpius, by Goethe (c. 1789)

She had no father whose consent had to be sought. Her brother, technically the head of the family, was on his travels, now supported by subsidies and bearing introductions to Goethe's friends and acquaintances, including Jacobi who was looking for a secretary and a tutor for his children.[20] Perhaps Goethe hoped to keep Christiane's brother safely remote from Weimar and in ignorance of the relationship for a few months longer.[21]

News of the affair broke in February 1789.[22] Charlotte von Stein had special reason to feel aggrieved. The coldness between her and Goethe was, she believed, entirely of his making. He had left her for Italy and failed to make amends on his return.[23] It galled her that news of his latest recklessness was brought to her by her son Fritz, who chanced upon Christiane alone at Goethe's garden house. The court ladies quickly formed a view of Christiane. Caroline Herder opined that before this improbable liaison with Goethe, Christiane had been 'a common wh[ore]'.[24] Nor was the philandering Duke much amused, later claiming that 'the Vulpius woman spoiled everything'.[25] Social life had to continue. Goethe was the Duke's ever-present lunch guest. If the talk at court touched on Christiane at all, she was referred to as 'the von Goethe housekeeper', which covered the truth of the relationship in a veil of semi-decency.[26] Goethe managed to compartmentalize the two halves of his life, his professional and courtly role, and his personal and poetic existence. In some sense the compartmentalization merely continued the practice he had developed in his first decade in Weimar.[27]

Towards the end of October 1788, some ten weeks after he first met Christiane, Goethe began to write a series of poems he described as 'erotica'. Not *'erotica'* in the modern sense of the word, these were simply poems about *eros* or sexual love. He wrote the first 'eroticon' after Knebel gave him a new edition of the Roman love poets Catullus, Propertius, and Tibullus.[28] Contrary to their vague and functional title, the 'erotica' grew into a coherent cycle of poems, probably inspired by Book I of Propertius's elegies. Goethe realized that beneath the casual surface of Propertius's first book was an artfully constructed narrative.[29] But the 'erotica' were not narrow imitations. Though he wrote them 'in the manner of Propertius', as he later put it, he did not imitate or rework whole poems by Propertius.[30] Rather he treated the corpus of Latin poetry—not only the 'triumvirate' of Catullus, Propertius, and Tibullus, but also Virgil, Horace, Ovid, and others—as a quarry from which he could mine motifs and scenarios. The process of mining Latin poetry and setting the elements in a quite new context helped him to create a consistent voice and a coherent world: the poems are (almost) all written in the voice of a German tourist and poet visiting Rome, studying its culture, and enjoying an affair with a Roman woman. While there is some looseness in the cycle's narrative sequence, and the position of some poems seems interchangeable, there is a clear story. The poet arrives in Rome anticipating his sexual liberation, for he evidently believes that such liberation is to be expected, as Goethe had read in Winckelmann's letters. The affair begins suddenly, and the suddenness needs to be justified. Yet erotic and intellectual fulfilment overcomes all doubts, even if social disapproval causes some short-lived awkwardness and misunderstandings between the lovers. Finally the affair is made public by the poet releasing his poems to the world.

Beyond the coherence of voice, situation, and story, the 'erotica' also embody the view of human nature and the arts that Goethe formulated in Italy.

In this sense the 'erotica' are Goethe's fullest and subtlest reckoning yet with his Italian experience. As he wrote to Jacobi eighteen months later, he was 'studying the ancients and following their example, as far as one can in Thuringia'.[31] The tourist who speaks the poems represents more than just Goethe: he is a typical German traveller following in the footsteps of Winckelmann. Or he is any northern European who has become aware of the traces of a fuller humanity in our distant past and to whom Rome promises a sexual and cultural awakening, replacing the ice and gloom of the north, both climatic and moral, with a southern existence of erotic freedom and creativity. Further, by situating the poems in Rome, Goethe allows his German tourist to encounter Greco-Roman art in its proper milieu and to address the same questions as Winckelmann struggled with. Confronted by the best that has survived of ancient art, especially its sculpture, what is an adequate response? The answer lies in a further Winckelmannian characteristic of Goethe's fictional tourist: because he is a poet, he responds to ancient sculpture by creating a written analogue of it, in the same way as Winckelmann developed a new form of writing about art in his lyrical descriptions of the Belvedere Apollo and the Belvedere Torso. The best examples of ancient sculpture challenge us to reimagine our own lives. Faced with this challenge, the creative writer must forge a personal response, both an intellectual and a sensuous reawakening. To his Weimar friends it seemed that Goethe had 'become sensuous', as Charlotte complained to Caroline Herder.[32] The poet of the heart had become a poet of the body. But this was an unjust verdict on the poems, for in fact the poet of the heart had become a poet of the mind as well as the body. Certainly Goethe did think of art in what might seem 'too earthly a manner', as he wrote to Heyne in July 1788.[33] And in the 'erotica' sex is rendered as physically and graphically as public poetry could dare in eighteenth-century Germany. One poem ends by imagining the creaking of the poet's bed as he and his beloved make love; in another the poet taps out the rhythm of a hexameter on his sleeping beloved's naked back; and another constructs an analogy between the fire in his hearth and the arousal he experiences when his beloved visits, both morning and evening. Yet all of this sensuality is also saturated in classical learning, for it makes rich and clever use of tropes and motifs from the Roman elegists. In this way, the poems raise philosophical questions about the physical-cum-mental nature of humanity and the importance of art as a phenomenon that speaks to both mind and body. The sensuousness of the 'erotica' is that of a natural historian, philosopher and classical scholar, as well as a lover.

The argument of the 'erotica' centres on the idea that substance contains its own form, as Goethe had concluded from his geological studies in the early 1780s. The analogy between geology and art was by no means far-fetched. At Paestum Goethe had seen how the materials determined the temples' forms. By the same token, there was an affinity between a particular poetic mood—for instance, the elegiac mood of Propertius and his confrères—and the forms of the elegiac couplet they used. This affinity between form and substance is evident everywhere in the 'erotica'. The poems are supremely well-crafted and intricate structures of remarkable balance and parallelism. The balance is evident in the poems' form. The idea of a fusion of two elements or of the suspension of opposites is an intrinsic feature of the elegiac couplet, with its pair of lines, hexameter and pentameter, each divided into two parts by a midline caesura. Goethe's handling of the form shows how well he understood it. Balance is also evident in the poems' argument, which hinges on the fusion of two forces, the mental and the physical, the formal and the substantial. Because they argue for the union of the mental and the physical, it is necessary that the poems achieve a balance of intellectual complexity and physical directness, and this is why, at the same time as they are highly intricate structures, the 'erotica' also convey an air of Rousseauian naturalness. They reimagine classical antiquity as a state of nature which we can now, even if only briefly, recapture through *eros*. The natural Rousseauian character of *eros* appears in several of the poems, most clearly in a poem that contrasts grandeur and simplicity: Rome's architecture and the fine clothing of its polite society on the one hand, and on the other the plain private spaces inhabited by lovers and the simple woollen dress and light linen shift worn by the poet's beloved. The second half of the poem proposes that her simple clothes are not only unpretentious and natural; they are also quick and easy to remove, so as to reveal love in its true and authentic nakedness:

> Schon fällt dein wollenes Kleidchen
>   So wie der Freund es gelöst faltig zum Boden hinab.
> Eilig trägt er das Kind, in leichter linnener Hülle
>   Wie es der Amme geziemt, scherzend aufs Lager hinan.
> Ohne das seidne Gehäng und ohne gestickte Matratzen,
>   Stehet es, zweien bequem, frei in dem weiten Gemach. [. . .]
> Uns ergötzen die Freuden des ächten nacketen Amors
>   Und des geschaukelten Betts lieblicher knarrender Ton.[34]

Already your little woollen dress falls, / As soon as your friend has loosened it, in folds to the floor. / Hurriedly he carries the child, in her light linen covering, / As befits a nurse, playfully to the bed. / Without the silken hangings and embroidered mattresses, / It stands, comfortable for two, open in the broad room. / [. . .] We're delighted by the pleasures of genuine naked Amor / And the shaken bed's charming creaking sound.

The poems have their own simplicity of style to match their representation of unadorned sensuality. They use a direct mode of expression and a standard conversational language, with little of the redundant adjectival ornament normally found eighteenth-century neoclassical verse. In this respect, the 'erotica' preempt the argument of the 1802 version of Wordsworth's preface to the *Lyrical Ballads*. When Wordsworth asks, 'what is a Poet? to whom does he address himself? and what language is to be expected from him?', his answer is: 'He is a man speaking to men'.[35] Poetic language should be simple and direct. What distinguishes a poet from other people, however, is the 'more lively sensibility' that means the poet 'rejoices more than other men in the spirit of life that is in him; delighting to contemplate similar volitions and passions as manifested in the goings-on of the Universe, and habitually impelled to create them where he does not find them'. The poet's business is to give voice to the energy and life force that flows through all things, and to find analogies between the private passions of people and the universal forces of nature. To discover these connections is to possess 'a disposition to be affected more than other men by absent things as if they were present'. This is how Goethe understands elegiac poetry, not as lament or sadness, but a way of being 'affected more than other men by absent things as if they were present', as Wordsworth put it. Absent things are recreated in their emotional and physical fullness. Elegy conjures up the past and makes it present once more, so that the sadness of remembrance of things past is outweighed by the joy of rediscovering and reexperiencing a history of moments of fulfilment— not only one's own history, but the long artistic tradition of sexual, emotional, and intellectual fulfilment.

In his study in Weimar in the chilly winter of 1788/89 Goethe recreated the warm sensuality and aesthetic excitement of Rome, as 'a man speaking to men' and as a student of the Roman elegists. The argument of the 'erotica' is encapsulated in the fifth elegy, one of Goethe's very finest poems. The poem celebrates the fulfilment of the poet's erotic and intellectual desires in Rome:

Froh empfind' ich mich nun auf klassischem Boden begeistert,
  Lauter und reizender spricht Vorwelt und Mitwelt zu mir.

Ich befolge den Rat, durchblättre die Werke der Alten
  Mit geschäftiger Hand täglich mit neuem Genuß.
Aber die Nächte hindurch hält Amor mich anders beschäftigt,
  Werd' ich auch halb nur gelehrt, bin ich doch doppelt vergnügt.
Und belehr ich mich nicht? wenn ich des lieblichen Busens
  Formen spähe, die Hand leite die Hüften hinab.
Dann versteh ich erst recht den Marmor, ich denk' und vergleiche,
  Sehe mit fühlendem Aug', fühle mit sehender Hand.
Raubt die Liebste denn gleich mir einige Stunden des Tages;
  Gibt sie Stunden der Nacht mir zur Entschädigung hin.
Wird doch nicht immer geküßt, es wird vernünftig gesprochen,
  Überfällt sie der Schlaf, lieg' ich und denke mir viel.
Oftmals hab' ich auch schon in ihren Armen gedichtet
  Und des Hexameters Maß, leise, mit fingernder Hand
Ihr auf dem Rücken gezählt, sie atmet in lieblichem Schlummer
  Und es durchglühet ihr Hauch mir bis in's Tiefste die Brust.
Amor schüret indes die Lampe und denket der Zeiten,
  Da er den nämlichen Dienst seinen Triumvirn gethan.[36]

Happily now I feel myself inspired on classical soil; / Past and present both speak louder and more enticingly to me. / I follow the advice and leaf through the works of the ancients / With a busy hand, daily with new pleasure. / But through the nights Amor keeps me otherwise engaged; / If I only become half learned, yet I am doubly contented. / And am I not educating myself, when the graceful bosom's / Forms I trace, drawing my hand down her hips? / Only then do I understand marble correctly; I think and compare, / See with a feeling eye, feel with a seeing hand. / If my beloved then steals from me several hours of the day, / She gives me hours of the night in recompense. / It's not always kissing, there's sensible talk; / If sleep overcomes her, I lie and think a lot. / Often I've composed poems in her arms, / And counted the hexameter's measure softly with fingering hand / On her back. She breathes in graceful slumber, / And her breath warms me through to the depths of my breast. / Amor meanwhile trims the lamp and thinks of the times, / When he did the same service for his triumvirate.

Love has many dimensions, encompassing physical sex, companionship ('sensible talk'), and above all mutual enrichment. In the first half of the poem, love aids the comprehension of classical art; and in the second, it inspires his poetry, for his beloved is also his muse. The scene is set by the directness of the opening: the word 'happily'. The rest of the first line expresses Goethe's approach to ancient art. Inspiration comes from being on the very ground from which the great works of ancient art physically emerged. On classical soil the poet can feel and understand the materials of ancient sculpture. This is how the first half of the poem concludes, with an awareness of how marble of different types can be worked. Before that conclusion, we are taken through an argument about learning and sensing. The second couplet presents reading as the physical action of leafing through a book's pages. Goethe drew the advice to study the ancient texts, along with the image of the hand turning a book's pages, from Horace's epistle 'On the Art of Poetry', but he moves beyond Horace to Winckelmann and a more active form of learning. In his descriptions of the Belvedere statues Winckelmann alternated between describing the statues and telling the heroic stories of the mythical figures represented by them, so that his reader could imagine the sculpted body in action and thus appreciate its moral as well as its physical beauty. Scholarship enriches sensuous experience. Or as Eckermann claimed Goethe to have said about Winckelmann, reading him was not so much about learning things as about becoming something.[37] So Goethe's tourist in Rome has his physical pleasure enhanced daily by reading. The lines that follow acknowledge the unnatural separation of mind and body that bedevils modern thought and has caused modern culture to denigrate sensuousness and sexuality—only to firmly reject that separation. Lying in bed with his beloved, he traces the outlines of her body with his fingers, and the understanding he gains of the human form reinforces his understanding of the statues. Sight—the sense most closely associated with the mind and rationality—is enriched by and enriches touch—the sense that occupies the lowest position in the traditional hierarchy, the earthiest sense. By levelling the hierarchy of the senses and placing earthy, sensuous touch alongside rational vision, the tourist finds a richer and deeper knowledge, even of the technicalities of the different types of marble used in ancient art and architecture. This is the meaning of the claim that he now appreciates marble by 'comparing'. Behind this image we can infer the art-historical arguments about the grain of marble: the finer-grained marbles, with their softer texture and milkier tone, were better suited for rendering human bodies. Such is also the gist of Goethe's image of his tourist tracing the outline of his lover's 'graceful' ('lieblich') breasts and her hips, whose smooth contours could be rendered in milky Parian marble. (Winckelmann used the same term, *lieblich*, to describe the soft, charming style of later forms of ancient art, after the end of the more austere 'high' style of the Parthenon friezes.)[38] So, following Winckelmann, and in particular Winckelmann's letters, Goethe finds sexuality and connoisseurship mutually enriching.

The second half of poem repeats motifs from the first half and applies them to poetry. Again the poet is a would-be connoisseur learning to appreciate sculpture by tracing the form of his beloved's breasts and hips, but now he is using her back to softly tap the rhythm of a hexameter line. What was the mutual enrichment of touch and vision in the first half of the poem is now the interaction of the two lovers. He uses her body to mark time; she meanwhile exhales her warm breath into his mouth. In doing so she inspires him, for the Latin verb 'breathe into' (*inspiro*) is the source of the word 'inspiration'. By breathing into his chest she literally and physically enacts the idea of poetic inspiration. She is his muse in both a traditional poetic sense and in a tangible, physical sense. The idea of inspiration is made earthly. So that he can continue writing his poems at night, his lamp is trimmed by the god of love *Amor*, who thus connects the modern poet to his classical forbears. Some things are permanent, such as love and its praise in poetry. The poet has recreated antiquity in the modern world, recreated a natural and authentic form of life within inauthentic civilization, albeit within the privacy of his bedroom and in the imagined yet concrete world of his poems.

All of which was to remain relatively private for the time being. Goethe circulated the 'erotica' among his friends, but he took no steps to publish the cycle. In January 1791, sometime after the mood that inspired the 'erotica' had left him, he wrote to Knebel that he had considered publication but had been deterred by Herder.[39] That was not the end of the road for the 'erotica'. As Goethe remarked to Göschen in July 1791, the poems were 'waiting for the point at which they would be published'.[40] That month one 'eroticon' appeared in the *German Monthly* under Moritz's coeditorship. The poem was simply titled 'Elegy. Rome 1789'—no doubt Goethe thought it appropriate to blend the location in Rome that had inspired the poems and was their subject with the date when he had written them in Weimar. Publication of the rest of the 'erotica' would have to wait.

———

The revolutionary waves that broke over France in the summer of 1789 had begun to swell while Goethe was in Italy. If he was aware of the growing crisis, he could afford to ignore it as he lingered in the Arcadian south. In 1786, with some heavy debt redemptions due, the financial problems of the French monarchy became so dire that the controller of the crown's finances, Charles Alexandre de Calonne, was able to persuade Louis XVI to convoke an assembly of notables to authorize new taxes. The convocation of the assembly would present a veneer of national representation, but its membership would be nominated by the crown, in order to ensure compliance. The plan was an admission that the crown's finances were far worse than had been apparent from Necker's optimistic *Comte rendu* of 1781, which Goethe had greeted so enthusiastically. The plan was also a disastrous failure: the assembly refused to grant new revenues, and its proceedings sparked a public debate about the politics of popular representation which the crown proved unable to quell. In summer 1788, with awful weather causing falls in tax revenue, the fateful decision was made to set the date of 1 May 1789 for the convocation of the Estates-General. The elections for the Estates in the spring of 1789 created unprecedented popular engagement; they were the largest exercise in popular democracy ever witnessed in Europe up to this point.[41] Once the Estates met, the crown's problems only deepened, for the debates about representation now had an active and theatrical focus, with the players on stage cheered or booed by an increasingly turbulent Paris audience. On 12 July 1789 the revolution proper began, when groups of Parisians, reinforced by mutinous guardsmen, broke down sections of the Paris customs wall and set light to its gatehouses. What happened two days later simply added more powerful symbolism. On 14 July the Bastille Saint-Antoine, a medieval fortress-turned-prison, was surrounded by a crowd containing mutinous guardsmen armed with two cannons. Its governor surrendered, thus giving rise to the myth of the 'storming' of the Bastille. The King's ministers advised him that he could no longer rely on the army's support.

Across Europe observers looked on with amazement. The events of 14 July 1789 resonated so strongly because the Bastille was a state prison: its fall represented the humbling of Europe's most powerful autocratic state. What had seemed settled and inevitable—the absolute power of the French monarchy at home and the diplomatic and military supremacy of France in Europe—was marvellously altered. The very shape of history was changing, and in sudden and unpredictable ways. Among the most profound changes wrought by the revolution was a quickening of consciousness—political but also social, intellectual, and cultural. News from Paris spread through educated Europe in the increasingly popular and avidly read newspapers. An international audience impatiently awaited the next day's news. The revolution turned the consumption of news into a form of entertainment.

Fascinated and enthused though many Germans were, revolution did not break out in Germany. In some territories peasants rebelled by refusing the *corvée*, deliberately breaking hunting and forestry laws or protesting against supposed grain hoarding. The political fragmentation of Germany meant that these protests were confined to their localities. Any local unrest was contained by territorial armies, which were rarely overstretched. Because peasant unrest seldom spread across territorial borders, there were none of the great rural panics that raged across France. Germany also lacked social unity. The coming together of the three estates in the French national assembly had no equivalent east of the Rhine. The German aristocracy and clergy lined up foursquare behind the old regime. Many German intellectuals supported the revolution, but in the absence of meaningful representative bodies or a German Paris, there was no theatre of politics where debates about representation could take to the stage. In any case, German intellectuals largely followed the Wolffian tendency to view politics in terms of its moral or rational aspirations, not its constitutional methods. Their goal was Enlightenment, and whether it was achieved via an absolutist or a constitutional route made little difference for most of them.[42] When the French Revolution became factional or 'political', as Wieland lamented in 1791, German intellectuals could revert to the comfort and security of enlightened absolutism.[43]

The threat of revolutionary contagion was felt right across Germany even if actual rebellions were rare. The Revolution loosened people's tongues and made the atmosphere more febrile.[44] Sachsen-Weimar soon felt the effects. In the summer of 1790 a cluster of villages in neighbouring Saxony went into open revolt. Following the abolition of the nobility in France in June 1790, there were similar demands in Saxony.[45] The authorities were right to fear the spirit of revolution, for in Germany the abolition of the nobility was a strikingly new demand that threatened to import the politics of Paris. The government in Weimar responded to the unrest on its doorstep by suppressing free speech and introducing modest reforms to mitigate some of the hardship experienced by the peasants. This dual approach, combining a threateningly large stick and a meagre carrot, was designed to deal with the symptoms rather than the underlying condition.[46] The authorities believed that their main task was to quell 'a frenzy of imitation' and 'a spirit of revolt'.[47] In March 1790 the Privy Council urgently dispatched Goethe to Jena to subdue a spat between the students and the military. 'For the moment I hope to cover it up', he wrote to Herder.[48] In a small university town it was normal for violence to break out now and again between the students, townspeople, and military. But the alarm about foreign radical contagion made the Weimar government more sensitive than usual. Its reaction was to erode the university's autonomy, while it projected to the world its reputation for intellectual liberality.[49] Any disorder had to be quietly suppressed before it was infected with revolutionary 'reasoning' about politics.[50] Goethe approved of the measures and led their execution.

The Revolution also had longer-term effects on Germany. For all the political differences between France and Germany, the underlying similarities gave cause for hope or anxiety, depending on one's point of view. The Revolution brought into question the long-accepted facts of autocratic government and aristocratic social dominance. In theory if not in practice, it reshaped the politics of the *ancien regime* into new conflicts and made the old tensions more antagonistic—monarchists against republicans, conservatives against progressives, traditionalist Christians against advocates of religious liberty. The new ideological order took shape slowly. It would take time before the idea of progress was fully aligned with that of democracy. Equally, the ideology of conservatism crystallized gradually, only emerging fully in the 1830s. A consistent enemy of the Revolution, Goethe was part of this piecemeal reshaping of modern politics. Like his compatriots, he slowly developed a coherent post-revolutionary politics—in his case, a thoroughgoing if idiosyncratic protoconservatism. Some elements of his conservatism predated the revolution: his trust in princes as the source of law and the state as the guarantor of public order, his belief in the importance of a ruler's good character, his Rousseauian scepticism about modernity, his resistance to the universalizing claims of philosophical reason. In his administrative labours up to 1786, Goethe was not a reformer. Although he expressed dismay privately about the Duchy's politics and economics—'everything with us is inconsistent and not followed through', he wrote to Charlotte six weeks before the outbreak of the Revolution—he had no difficulty writing in the same letter that the burghers should acquiesce to aristocrats running the government.[51] The events of the Revolution did not cause him to change that view.

In early May 1789 Christiane was pregnant. A decision loomed. Goethe could have paid Christiane off or he could have found her a place to live and continued to visit her. Either would have been standard behaviour for a man of his class. He decided instead to go his own way, whether out of love for Christiane or a sense of responsibility or most likely both.[52] They would set up home together though not in the house on the Frauenplan, as Carl August made clear to him. The court ladies would not tolerate their cohabiting within the city walls. It was indecent and illegal. Pregnancy out of wedlock was punishable by payment of a penitential fine to the church authorities, a portion of which, ironically, would normally find its way into the pocket of the superintendant of the Lutheran church, Herder.[53] So a plan was hatched for Goethe to set up home just outside the city walls, in the Hunstmen's Houses. At the beginning of December, with the birth expected in the coming weeks, Christiane's condition suddenly deteriorated.[54] Fearing for her life, Goethe refused to leave the house. After three weeks of anxiety, he could stand it no longer and fled to Jena.[55] On Christmas day an urgent summons brought him rushing back to Weimar. Christiane gave birth to a healthy son. Two days later he was christened Julius August Walther in the sacristy of the Church of St James.

The latter stages of Christiane's pregnancy and August's birth on Christmas day 1789 brought the 'erotica' to a natural conclusion. The god of love had done his work by producing a child. In the winter of 1789/90, as baby August was nursed, Goethe's mind turned from love to reproduction. In the first two months of 1790 he read the collection of Roman poems known as the *Carmina Priapeia*. These earthy and jocular elegies celebrated the god Priapus, an odd amalgam of a Greek deity from Lampsacus in Asia Minor and a local Roman fertility god, whose statue, sporting a massive phallus, had stood in many Roman gardens and vineyards. Goethe wrote two Priapic poems of his own and a set of scholarly notes on the original Latin text. The two poems served as a framing device for the 'erotica'—in the first Priapic poem the elegies are referred to as flowerbeds in a garden over which the god Priapus stands guard, his huge erect member poised threateningly to 'punish from behind' any 'enervated, ashamed' hypocrites who trespass in the garden of love.[56] Priapus is thus added to the pantheon of tutelary deities of natural, sexual love—along with Amor the god of love, the Goddess Opportunity, who provides lovers with spontaneous sex, and the Goddess Discretion, who guards their secrets. Goethe's Priapus also has a cultural role as the guarantor of poetic liberality, defending the free realm of poetry against the hypocritical attentions of the Christian moralists. The Priapic poems, like the '*erotica*', give sensuality a broader cultural, even intellectual dimension. In 1781 William Hamilton had discovered at Isernia in Abruzzo what he thought was a modern survival of the ancient Priapic cult. The worship of Priapus briefly became a favourite topic of northern European libertines. The wealthy gentleman scholar Richard Payne Knight published an account of it in his *Discourse on the Worship of Priapus* (1786–1787). Goethe shared the view that these southern

Italian remnants of the worship of Pripaus represented a wholesome pre-Christian attitude to the body. He had witnessed this easy sensuality in Hamilton's Naples. He read the Priapic poems in a 1664 edition of the *Priapea* edited by Friedrich Lindenbrog and containing exegetical and textual notes by Caspar Schoppe and Joseph Justus Scaliger, and he built on their work by writing his own commentary on the poems. His commentaries on the *Priapeia* were serious scholarship; they included several proposals for emendation of the Latin text of the *Priapeia*, two of which have found favour with modern scholars.[57]

Also around the time of August's birth, he began to read the Roman epigrammatist Martial's fourteen books of caustic, anarchic epigrams that treat sex as a series of tawdry transactions. Switching to the cynical mode of Martial at this moment, just as his relationship with Christiane was blessed by their first child, was not as surprising as it might seem. A year earlier Knebel had regretfully reported to Herder that Goethe had returned from Italy with 'a load of restricted ideas'.[58] Goethe shared with Knebel an attachment to the Epicurean philosophy of Lucretius, which was solidly focused on the material world: 'for my own part I more or less support the philosophy of Lucretius and confine all my pretensions to the sphere of life', he wrote to Fritz Stolberg in February 1789.[59] But unlike Knebel he drew the further conclusion that humans should confine their knowledge of nature to particular things—'that our being is too limited to form any conception of the existence and essence of things, that everything must *absolutissime* be restricted to individual existences'.[60] His friends had already seen signs of Goethe's new realism in his letters from Italy. If in the latter books of his *Ideas* Herder was expounding humanity's future perfectibility, Goethe could only concur, he wrote to Charlotte from Rome, subject to the proviso that the world would become 'one great hospital and each person another's humane nurse'.[61] Human nature was simply too fragile to sustain humanity. The revolutionary talk of freedom made him aware of other constraints on human ambitions. It was these realities that made the caustic voice of Martial seem apt. He quickly wrote one hundred or so epigrams in the style of Martial. At their head he pinned an epigraph from Martial that confirmed the realism of his new poetic mode: 'our pages have a human flavour'.[62] They presented humans as they really were and not as we might hope them to be. In Italy he had decided that the honour and glory of art consisted in representing human beauty. Now he felt that human sensuousness was in fact all that art could represent, as he wrote to Meyer in April 1789: 'my conviction is that the highest aim of art is to represent human forms, with the greatest sensuousness and beauty possible. As for moral objects, art should only select those that are intimately related to the sensuous'.[63] In giving the arts the ambition of representing human sensuousness, he was also setting their limits.

Shortly after beginning the epigrams, in March 1790 he set off again for Venice. Carl August had asked him to meet Anna Amalia there, at the end of her tour of Italy.[64] At the Duke's expense, he was to show her the sights of the Most Serene Republic and accompany her back to Weimar. The timing of the trip was poor. The enforced separation from the most vital part of his new existence, Christiane and August, soured his mood. Worse was to greet him on arriving in Venice on the last day of March. Anna Amalia's party had been delayed by several weeks, and Goethe was left kicking his heels in a cold and flooded Venice, where it was unpleasant to sightsee or amble through the streets as he had in the autumn of 1786. The second stay in Venice had dealt his love for Italy 'a fatal blow', he wrote to Carl August four days after his arrival.[65] And after the passionate and subtle praise of love expressed in the '*erotica*', the epigrams he was now writing seemed, he wrote to the Herders, to reflect the frustrating time he spent waiting for Anna Amalia in Venice.[66] However, Italy was still Italy, and the '*erotica*' and epigrams were similar enough in Goethe's mind for him to bind the manuscripts of the two cycles together in a single collation and give them similar titles: 'Elegies. Rome 1788' and 'Epigrams. Venice 1790'.[67] Just as the elegies drew widely on Latin poetry and blended the motifs of the Roman elegists into a whole that expressed his own philosophy, so too the epigrams were not only written 'after the manner of Martial', as he put it later to a French supporter.[68] Soon after arriving in Venice, he bought a pocket-sized edition of the Roman satirist Juvenal, which he proceeded to annotate, so that the epigrams also contain elements of Juvenalian satire—the roving perspective of the Roman flaneur,[69] and a moralizing tone that ironically undermines itself.[70] By blending Martial's cynicism with Juvenal's satire, Goethe created another distinctive voice for himself.

The most significant difference between the Roman '*erotica*' and the Venetian epigrams was that the former were written before the French Revolution, and the latter were written during it. The epigrams still argue for sexual liberation, but to a less optimistic conclusion. The subject matter and attitudes of the epigrams are largely the same as those of the '*erotica*'. Social life is tedious and stultifying. Sex should be celebrated, not hidden. Indeed sex is essential to human fulfilment, but our Christian civilization denigrates and devalues sex, to our personal and cultural detriment. Conventional morality is hypocritical, guilt ridden, and unnatural. Christianity is a sham and a deceit. It is not a suitable belief system for any rational man.[71] It morbidly sucks the life out of us. By contrast, sex is life giving: there is more vitality in the phallus of Priapus than the dead bones of saints honoured by Christian worshippers.[72] In Venice the sexual message is exemplified by the ubiquitous prostitutes, though Goethe's presentation of these wary and fast-moving 'lizards', as he terms them,[73] is ambivalent, because of his anxiety concerning the syphilis that was rampant in the city. Yet even this anxious note of caution occasions an ironic joke. The miracles with which Christ removed the sins of humanity would now be better employed in freeing people from the curse of syphilis. We need a new redeemer to make sex healthy again, as it was for the ancients.[74] Of course, such miracles are impossible, and so the risk of syphilis must be avoided, and thankfully the prostitutes can be employed safely to give hand jobs in the backstreet coffee houses.[75]

The Venetian epigrams make clear the full extent of the deception that afflicts modern civilization, and more trenchantly than the 'erotica'. The deception affects not only our sexual morality, but also, in the wake of the Revolution, politics and religion. Whereas the Roman *erotica* create a semi-serious form of deism—a polytheistic religion that reflects the sexual needs of humanity, with Amor trimming the wick of the poet's candle, Priapus guarding the lovers' garden, and the Goddess Opportunity presiding over the lovers' spontaneous lovemaking—the Venetian epigrams dismantle Christianity with a vigour and openness that Goethe had not dared since *Faust* in the early 1770s. One thing that could be said in favour of the Revolution, at least early in 1790, was that it brought an end to the *ancien regime* that had kept the truth hidden—a concealment in which Goethe had colluded in his years as a courtier and administrator in Weimar, but from which he had liberated himself in Italy and with Christiane in Weimar. An epigram addressed to 'the plebs' takes pleasure in the paradox that the plebs worship the authorities that have prevented them from knowing the truth:

> Dich betrügt der Regente, der Pfaffe, der Lehrer der Sitten
>   Und dies Kleeblatt wie tief betest du Pöbel es an
> Leider läßt sich noch kaum was rechtes denken und sagen
>   Das nicht grimmig den Staat, Götter und Sitten verletzt.[76]

> You're deceived by the ruler, the priest, the teacher of morals, / And this cloverleaf how deeply you worship it, plebs. / Sadly hardly anything sensible can be thought or said / Which does not fiercely damage the state, gods and morals.

Aside from reprising the trenchant and pessimistic view expressed by Faust in the *Urfaust*—that we cannot aspire 'to know anything correct', and that those who *do* manage to call a spade a spade are liable to end up 'crucified or burned'— the epigram is a pointed reference to the situation in France. The 'cloverleaf' represents the threefold function of censorship in the French state before the Revolution—censorship that protects the state, the Catholic church, and sexual morality, by suppressing sedition, heresy, and pornography.[77] This suppression of the truth had ended, symbolically if not actually, on 14 July 1789 with the storming of the Bastille, the majority of whose inmates had in fact been publishers and printers of illicit writings, not common criminals. In this sense, the storming of the Bastille liberated the truth. Other epigrams confirm this surprisingly liberal view. The poet of the epigrams, if not a political revolutionary, is at least a revolutionary in a more general, moral sense:

> Tolle Zeiten hab ich erlebt und hab nicht ermangelt
> Selbst auch thöricht zu sein wie es die Zeit mir gebot.[78]

Crazy times I've experienced, and have not refrained from / Being foolish myself, just as the times demanded of me.

There is a virtue in the revolutionary speakers heard now on Paris street corners—speakers who in fact played an important role in radicalizing a largely illiterate Parisian working class[79]—even if Goethe believed the content of their revolutionary talk was mad:

> Jene Menschen sind toll, so sagt ihr von heftigen Sprechern
> Die wir in Frankreich so laut hören auf Straßen und Markt.
> Auch mir scheinen sie toll doch redet ein Toller in Freiheit
> Weise Sprüche wenn, ach! Weisheit im Sklaven verstummt.[80]

Those people are mad, you say of the vehement speakers, / Whom we hear in France speaking so loudly in streets and markets. / They seem mad to me too; yet a madman when free utters / Wise sayings, whereas, alas! wisdom in slaves goes unheard.

If he showed some sympathy for the Parisian sansculottes, it was ironic, and he certainly did not support their radical ideas. Matters of political constitutionality and representation had no purchase on him. What mattered was that states were governed well, for social and political unrest was caused by poor government, whether it was the financial incompetence under Louis XVI or— though his loyalty to the Duke would not allow him to say so publicly—the lack of consistency of Weimar's government under Carl August:

Diesen Amboß vergleich ich dem Lande den Hammer dem Fürsten
    Und dem Volke das Blech das in der Mitte sich krümmt.
Wehe dem armen Bleche wenn nur willkürliche Schläge
    Ungewiß treffen und nie fertig der Kessel erscheint.

This anvil I compare to the nation, the hammer to the prince, / And to the people the tin that bends in between them. / Woe to the poor tin, when only arbitrary blows / Strike randomly, and the pot is never finished.

He continued to believe that government should be in the hands of men like himself, who were willing to make sacrifices for the sake of the people. Had he not sacrificed his literary career and his physical and mental health during the first Weimar decade? Exciting though the talk of liberty might be, in the end it was only talk and could not be the foundation of good government:

Alle Freiheits Apostel sie waren mir immer zuwider
    Denn es suchte doch nur jeder die Willkür für sich.
Willst du Viele befrei'n so wag es vielen zu dienen.
    Wie gefährlich das sei willst du es wissen? Versuchs.[81]

All the apostles of freedom, I could never abide them, / For each sought only license for himself. / If you wish to free many, then dare to serve many. / You want to know how dangerous that is? Try it.

The antidemocratic animus of the first two lines might initially seem to be qualified by lines 3 and 4, which invite the 'apostles of freedom' to share the responsibility for government. Is there perhaps some virtue in revolutionary popular sovereignty? However, the emphatic final invitation to 'try it' indicates that Goethe believes popular sovereignty will always fail. The idea of liberty always comes a distant third behind an ethic of service and a direct experience of government, and this in turn implies that experience of ruling must first be sought within the existing structures of government. Experience comes before constitutional change. The invitation to the apostles of freedom to rule the state is only a rhetorical gesture.

The Revolution had already spilt over into Germany, as an idea if not as political reality. It is this idea of a German revolution that Goethe resists in the epigrams. Talk of liberty and fraternity on the level of national politics is pointless; at best it is the talk of wise fools, at worst that of selfish conmen. That said, the epigrams are not altogether caustic. There is a recognition of hunger and poverty. The empty and self-serving politics of liberty should be resisted and replaced with more limited ambitions:

> Warum schreit das Volk und rennt so? Es will sich ernähren
>   Kinder zeugen und die nähren so gut es vermag.
> Merke dir Reisender das und tue zu Hause desgleichen
>   Weiter bringt es kein Mensch, stell er sich wie er auch will.[82]

> Why are the people shouting and running around so? They want to feed themselves, / Have children, and feed them as well as they can. / Take note of that, traveller, and do likewise at home. / That's the most a person can do, try as he might.

The epigrams are true to Goethe's new 'restricted' ideas. They limit our moral aspirations to common sense, procreation, and sustenance for ourselves and our families. Sympathy and pity are confined to the small sphere of the household; they have no force in the larger domain of territorial or national politics.

If Germany did not have a political revolution, it later became a cliché that it experienced a philosophical one, a 'revolution of the spirit'.[83] Its source was unexpected. Immanuel Kant, born a generation before Goethe in 1724, held the chair of logic and metaphysics at the university in his hometown of Königsberg. For the first half of his academic career Kant was just one among many German philosophy professors who held loosely to Wolffianism and picked eclectically from the latest French and British ideas. Prior to the 1780s he was best known for his *General Natural History and Theory of the Heavens* (1755), an attempt to explain the origins of the solar system on Newtonian principles. It was not clear to anyone except his closest friends and associates that Kant was brewing a philosophical revolution. Since the late 1760s he had been working on a radically new conception of metaphysics that aimed to resolve the conflict between empiricism and rationalism. The first hint came in his inaugural dissertation *On the Form and Principles of the Sensible and Intelligible World* (1770), in which he drew a distinction between the sensuous world of external phenomena and the intellectual principles of time and space that structure our experiences.[84] During the next decade he fell silent as he worked out his new 'transcendental' philosophy. The first aim of the transcendental philosophy, set out in the *Critique of Pure Reason* (1780), was to validate and justify the knowledge of the world that we can reliably acquire, for instance Newtonian physics. Kant was not a sceptic about science or everyday experience. He was convinced that the stance of empirical realism—that scientific and everyday knowledge could contain truth—must be valid, as far as it went. The proviso is crucial, for he also believed that empirical realism was insufficient *on its own*, because it could not explain how our knowledge came to conform to the objective world. As a matter of convenience—Kant's argument is famously hard to summarize—the problem can be illustrated by the principle of causation. Physics requires that we think of not just some but *all* phenomena as conforming to laws of cause and effect. If it is to be valid at all, the principle of causation must apply universally. However, once we place our own thinking selves within the empirical realm, as we must if we are to interact with the world, we have no choice but to admit that our own capacity to think is also subject to the laws of cause and effect. If this were the end of the matter, reason itself would become a product of cause and effect. In Kant's terminology, reason would be 'conditioned' or 'determined'. But if our reason were indeed so conditioned by particular causes—by causes pertaining at one place and time but not at others—reason could not possess the universality that would allow us to apply it to an understanding of *all* causes, as is required by the universality of causation. Reasoning about universal laws would become impossible, for reason that is merely local cannot justify a principle that is universal. Hence, because we must be able to use reason universally, reason must be exempted from the causal, empirical realm—it must be 'unconditioned'. So instead of holding that objects in the world condition our reasoning about them, we must hold that our reasoning conditions the objects. This was Kant's revolution: a shift from a world in which objects condition a subject's thoughts to one in which thoughts in the subject condition objects. In order to illustrate the magnitude and necessity of the revolution, he called it a 'Copernican revolution'. After this revolution, while we can still hold a realism about the empirical realm, we must think of the structuring principles that cover or 'transcend' all empirical knowledge as inhering not in the objects, but in the intellect of the subject. Only in this way did Kant believe that we could make sense of the split between sensuous phenomena and the intellectual principles of space and time. In addition to space and time, he identified twelve further 'pure concepts of the understanding' or, following Aristotle, 'categories', such as causation. These transcendental concepts, like the forms of time and space, were not properties of an external reality, but ideal properties of the human intellect, indeed properties of any conceivable intellect. This is the essence of Kant's doctrine of 'transcendental idealism'.

At first the public response was muted. Many readers were baffled by Kant's new-fangled terminology and dreadfully tangled sentences, or they found the new system too revolutionary. Cogent criticisms began to emerge in the mid-1780s. There were two related problems, both stemming from Kant's attempt to make a categorical distinction between thinking subjects on the one hand and objects of thought on the other. In 1787, in the midst of the furore over his revelations concerning Lessing, Fritz Jacobi made the first telling criticism of Kant's project. Jacobi saw the *Critique of Pure Reason* as a failed attempt to address the problem of determinism that flowed out of the philosophy of Spinoza. Once we think of the physical world as governed by cause and effect, logic forces us down a path towards complete determinism and the denial of free will. Kant promised an escape from this inexorable slide, but one that defied logic, as Jacobi saw it. Kant seemed willing to grant that objects caused our sensations, and to this extent our thinking was conditioned by cause and effect. Yet at some point in the process of knowledge forming in the mind, Kant mysteriously turned the tables so that our knowledge became conditioned by a freely operating intellect. Where in the process of acquiring knowledge did this pivot take place? Where did causation suddenly cease to operate and the free intellect take over? What guarantee could Kant give that the location of the pivot was not arbitrary? Jacobi claimed he could find no coherent answer within the *Critique*:

> I must confess that this circumstance caused me not a little delay in my study of Kantian philosophy, with the consequence that for several years in succession I had to begin the *Critique of Pure Reason* over again, because I was continually confused by the fact that I could not enter the system without [the premise of causation], and could not remain in the system with the same premise.[85]

There was a second, related problem that offended both common sense and the very empirical realism that Kant had claimed to justify. It would become a particular concern for Goethe in his work on natural history. A primary objective of natural history is to divide objects into classes—stuff such as giraffes and mountains. If we accept a distinction between subject and object, we must take a view on which side of the subject-object gap the division into classes occurs. Kant is clear about this: the division of phenomena into giraffes and mountains lies in the subject and not in the objects themselves. Nature itself does not distinguish between giraffes and mountains—it is we who do so, a view that to many seemed irredeemably bizarre.[86]

Before his return from Italy Goethe was quite unaware of Kant's revolution. During the autumn and winter of 1790/91 he read the *Critique of Pure Reason* and the third in Kant's series of transcendental writings, the *Critique of Judgement*. The copies of both works in his library contain extensive markings, for the most part pencil lines indicating passages that he thought noteworthy. There is also evidence of an encounter with Kant's work two years earlier. In February 1789 Wieland wrote to his son-in-law Carl Leonhard Reinhold, who was lecturing on the new Kantian philosophy in Jena, that Goethe had been reading the *Critique of Pure Reason* 'with great application'.[87] Wieland also mentioned that Goethe was keen to meet Reinhold for a 'lengthy conference' on Kant. Reinhold gave Goethe private tutorials on Kant's philosophy in 1789.[88] However, Goethe later wrote to Jacobi that 'there was no chance of holding a conversation with [Reinhold], I have never been able to learn anything through him or from him'.[89] It may have been the failure of the tutorials with Reinhold that encouraged Goethe to return to Kant in the autumn of 1790. A more urgent motive was the publication of the *Critique of Judgement* at that year's Leipzig Easter book fair, for its second half was concerned with a matter of vital interest to Goethe: the nature and competence of our judgements about causality in the natural world and above all about the apparent purposiveness of organisms. The first half of the *Critique of Judgement*, concerning aesthetic judgements, was of much less interest to him;[90] he was scathing about Kant's discussion of the arts and Kant's failure to recognise the centrality of imagination in our mental lives.[91]

During these early encounters with Kant's philosophy, Goethe was trying to complete a short essay on his theory of plant metamorphosis and to develop his ideas about comparative anatomy. In an unpublished sequel to his first attempt to set out the theory of plant metamorphosis, written between the summer and winter of 1790, Goethe acknowledged Kant's 'new philosophy', and in the manuscript added a marginal note citing the title of Kant's *Critique of Judgement*, which he began to study no later than the first week of October. On 6 October, following several conversations with Goethe in Dresden,[92] Christian Gottfried Körner wrote to Schiller that 'Goethe has found nourishment for his philosophy in [Kant's] critique of teleological judgement'.[93] In the second metamorphosis essay Goethe addresses the question of teleology directly: are natural historians helped or hindered by assuming that organisms are designed for purposes extraneous to them? His answer is that they are hindered. The *Critique of Judgement* supported his belief. However, it is unlikely that he learned anything new from Kant on this point. He was already confirmed in his opposition to the idea of teleology in nature by two favourite thinkers: Spinoza and Buffon. Much later in life, he claimed that his opposition to final causes first came from Spinoza.[94] When he resumed work on mammal osteology late in 1790, after reading the *Critique of Judgement*, he jotted a note by way of reminder to himself: 'Buffon against *causae finales*'.[95] Spinoza and Buffon, not Kant, were the sources of Goethe's opposition to teleology.

Goethe was much less receptive to Kant's construal of the subject-object divide. As a natural historian he found it hard to comprehend how the division of nature into classes could be a property of subjects and not of the objects themselves. At the end of October 1790, a few weeks after his conversations with Körner in Dresden, Goethe met Schiller in Jena and the conversation inevitably turned to Kant. Schiller, quickly becoming a convinced Kantian, was less impressed than Körner by Goethe's grasp of the new philosophy. He wrote to Körner that Goethe found philosophy too 'subjective'. 'Overall his way of thinking is too sensuous', Schiller continued.[96] Goethe would later make his opposition to Kant more explicit: 'It strikes me as dangerous that Kant defines as knowledge that which our soul brings to cognitions'.[97] In Goethe's view, the way nature is divided into classes is a property of nature itself, not of the mental apparatus we use to grasp the world. Kant's 'pure concepts of the understanding' are not knowledge. The content of knowledge is in objects, not subjects. As Goethe wrote some thirty years later, reflecting on the early 1790s, '[I] tended in such matters wholly towards a strict realism'.[98] The problem with Kant's philosophy was that 'it never gets to the object', he wrote in 1831.[99]

Things came to a head when Goethe began to work on the theory of optics, for his work on optics forced him think about experimental method. Writing in 1793 about the ways in which different scholarly and scientific disciplines could contribute to the study of optics, he acknowledged a role for 'the critic'— by which he meant a practitioner of Kantian philosophy, whose task would be to analyse the method and significance of experiments and the argumentation connecting observation with theory.[100] For Goethe, the primary role of the new philosophy is to be a handmaiden to science. Kant's philosophy can help us to avoid methodological missteps, but makes no positive contribution to the content of scientific knowledge. (Kant said as much himself.) It has nothing to say about the concepts with which we grasp nature. This is because Goethe locates the subject-object divide in a different position. In what might seem to be a nod to Kant, he draws a distinction between subjective and objective optical experiments. However, this has nothing to do with Kantian philosophy; it has nothing to do with the ways in which subjects construct propositions about objects. For Goethe, objective optical experiments were those in which the experimental apparatus was part of the phenomenon, such as when Newton used prisms to refract a beam of white light and produce spectral colours. In a subjective experiment, on the other hand, the prism is used by the observer to witness the phenomenon; it is part of the observation, not part of what is observed.[101] But in both cases the totality of the subject-object divide inhabits the phenomenal world; it does not, as it did for Kant, mark the border between the phenomenal world and the noumenal world of the free intellect.

This explains another difference between Goethe and Kant: their use of the term 'mode of representation' (*Vorstellungsart*). In German philosophy before Kant's transcendental turn, a *Vorstellungsart* denoted a perspective on something, formed of whatever experiences or preconceptions or purposes one brought to the matter. For instance, when considering a duck, the hunter and the natural historian have different *Vorstellungsarten* of the duck, for they approach it with different experiences, preconceptions, and purposes. So we might say the natural historian and the hunter have different theories of what a duck is. Kant adopted the term in the *Critique of Pure Reason*, but in a new and peculiar way. It denotes the set of framing concepts with which our understanding apprehends and gives structure to experience. So for instance, time is not a property of objects, but of the subject's own cognitive faculties: '[time] is to be viewed in reality not as an object but as the mode of representation [*Vorstellungsart*] of myself as an object'.[102] Goethe, both before and after his reading of Kant, used the term in its ordinary pre-Kantian sense. In a draft written in summer 1788, 'Laws of the Development of Plants', he used the term *Vorstellungsart* to describe the botanical theories of epigenesis and preformation. These two *Vorstellungsarten* are, he thinks, competing theories that account equally well for the same phenomena, albeit in different ways. But he is far from suggesting that the division of reality into structures is a *Vorstellungsart*, as Kant did. Indeed, Goethe insists that the theories of epigenesis and preformation are 'fundamentally compatible'[103] and therefore amenable to being reconciled by a third theory—his own, of course. By contrast, Kant believed we are inescapably confined to our *Vorstellungsart*, because it is built into our cognitive faculties. For Goethe, it is possible to move between different *Vorstellungsarten*, because it is possible to change the experiences or preconceptions or purposes with which we view the world.

He applied the same understanding of *Vorstellungsarten* to a troubling disagreement between the mineralogists Voigt and Werner. The disagreement was worrying because Goethe admired both men's expertise, and because it cast doubt on his own understanding of the formation of the earth. Two competing theories claimed to explain the origins of rock formations: Vulcanism and Neptunism. The former held that rock formations were produced by volcanic action, the latter that they were laid down by sedimentation out of the earth's primordial seas. Goethe had at first been undecided between the two, though Werner's support for Neptunism carried weight with him. Voigt, in his first venture into print in 1786, argued that the so-called horn-slate was a form of lava, contrary to his teacher Werner's theory. Since Goethe was then nearing the volcanic hotspots of southern Italy, Voigt asked him to look out for samples of horn-slate.[104] Troubled by Voigt's apostasy, Goethe wrote to him recommending moderation in his criticisms of Werner; Goethe would try to resolve the dispute once he was back in Weimar.[105] In September 1789 Werner visited Weimar, and Goethe heard the Neptunist arguments expounded by the master. He was now convinced that Werner was right, he wrote to Voigt's elder brother Christian Gottlob; the younger Voigt must be allowed an honorable retreat from his Vulcanist heresy.[106] The message clearly got through to the younger Voigt, who wrote an emollient letter to Werner in early October.[107] At this point, prior to a meeting Goethe had planned with Voigt for November, Goethe wrote a brief essay, 'Proposals for a compromise to unify the Vulcanists and Neptunists concerning the origins of basalt'. Surprisingly given Goethe's sympathy for Werner's Neptunism, he argued that both perspectives, having good arguments on their side, might be subsumed under a higher perspective.[108] The compromise involved imagining a superheated volcanic sea. The deposition of basalts in this sea resulted from repeated cooling and melting, and 'thus the volcanic islands and promontaries rose upwards, thus huge bays developed, thus did whole costal volcanic regions originate'.[109] It was an ingenious solution, which made room for Voigt's theory of horn-slate while preserving the essence of Werner's Neptunism. It was also a precipitate attempt to find answers where none were available, since Goethe and his contemporaries had very little understanding of subterranean geological processes or geological chemistry.

———

The botanical observations Goethe brought back from Italy posed a new problem. Italy had shown him a wealth of alien and exotic flora. This raised with new urgency the question of how plants were to be classified. The method of classification used by Linnaeus in the *Systema Naturae* of 1735, to which Goethe still adhered in Italy, was based on the morphology of the reproductive organs. In simple terms, Linnaeus's 'sexual classification' involved organizing plants into species according to the number of their pistils and stamens. Linnaeus's method seemed unnatural. It took no account of the overall form or structure of the plant. Goethe's first attempt to bring order to his Italian observations, and to solve the problem of classification, was a short essay written in the summer of 1788, during the early weeks of his relationship with Christiane. Here for the first time Goethe explored the idea of a general 'type' ('Typus') of plant anatomy. (The notion of an 'archetypal form', *Urbild*, was one of the substantive theories espoused by Kant that Goethe found appealing.)[110] By 'type' he meant a set of features that all members of a class of plants shared. However, describing these features proved difficult because they could vary so much in even closely related species. Thus he was already forced to acknowledge that there would be 'great difficulty' in defining 'such a Proteus': 'it escapes even the sharpest comparative perception and can barely be got hold of incompletely and even then only in contradictions'.[111]

Frustrated by the challenge of defining the 'type', he tried a different approach: analysing and describing the stages of a plant's growth. The basic structural element of plant growth is defined by a stem node. Plants grow by repeating the development from one node to the next. From each node grows either a new section of stem or a set of leaves or axial buds. The stem, leaves, and buds are thus variations on a single basic developmental unit. One might term this unit a leaf, as Goethe had first guessed intuitively in the botanical gardens in Palermo in April 1787.[112] To be sure, the label 'leaf' was a flag of convenience. One might just as well say that a stamen is a contracted petal as that a petal is an expanded stamen.[113] Still, there were good reasons for maintaining that the leaf was fundamental. Leaf forms do persist in some transitional phases of plant growth. For instance, tulips have transitional forms that are half green leaf and half coloured petal.[114] A venerable fan palm he saw in the botanical gardens at Padua,[115] already over two hundred years old in 1786, showed different forms of leaf: entire at the base of the plant and increasingly frayed towards the top. The leaf was not simply a leaf: it was an element that metamorphosed into a variety of different forms.

The key to understanding plant development was therefore the notion of metamorphosis, and this was Goethe's focus as he organized and wrote up his observations. In the winter of 1789/90 he completed an *Essay in Explanation of the Metamorphosis of Plants*. First he tried and failed to interest Göschen in the essay, then offered it to Carl Wilhelm Ettinger in Gotha, on the same worthless assurance he had offered to Göschen: that the publisher could have first refusal on all his future works.[116] Ettinger published it at Easter 1790, printed in well-spaced roman type and with generous margins—an expression of Goethe's new Italian sensibility. The essay, in 123 numbered paragraphs, is primarily concerned with describing the development of a generic flowering plant and thus explaining how its component parts metamorphose into one another. The description in all its careful detail is the vehicle for Goethe's true purpose, which is to show that metamorphosis is governed by certain 'laws of transformation'.[117] The main drivers of metamorphosis are the twin forces of expansion and contraction. In Kant's *Metaphysical Foundations of Natural Science*, Goethe found the notion that the phenomena of dynamic physics can be expressed in terms of two pairs of forces, expansion-repulsion and contraction-attraction. (Of the ideas in Kant's work that appealed to Goethe, this was the only one that was new to him.) In the metamorphosis essay Goethe applies Kant's physical forces to plant growth. For instance, the corolla is formed by expansion of the calyx, whereas the stamen is formed through contraction of the corolla. Thus the forces of expansion and contraction operate in alternating sequence.[118] Implicit in this model of alternating expansion and contraction, though he was not confident enough to state the thesis openly, is that nature has a fixed amount of material. An organism cannot expand endlessly; expansion must alternate with contraction. This theory of the economy of nature would play an important role when Goethe returned to the study of mammal osteology in 1790.

The essay further implies that the plant has a 'goal', something akin to Aristotle's notion of an entelechy. The plant's goal is production of a seed. It is therefore not a goal in the teleological sense criticised by Buffon. Rather it is a goal intrinsic to the life of the plant, namely the production of new plants. In this sense, it would appear that Goethe shares Kant's view that organisms possess their own intrinsic purposiveness. In the *Critique of Judgement* Kant argued that organisms are distinguished from mechanisms insofar as the latter have only power of movement whereas organisms have power of development and reproduction, and these constitute their intrinsic purposes.[119] However, the metamorphosis essay was published six months before Goethe read the *Critique of Judgement*, so Goethe's notion of natural purposiveness cannot have been influenced by Kant's. In any case, Goethe's essay is less interested in the purposiveness of nature than in the laws that govern it. These laws impose

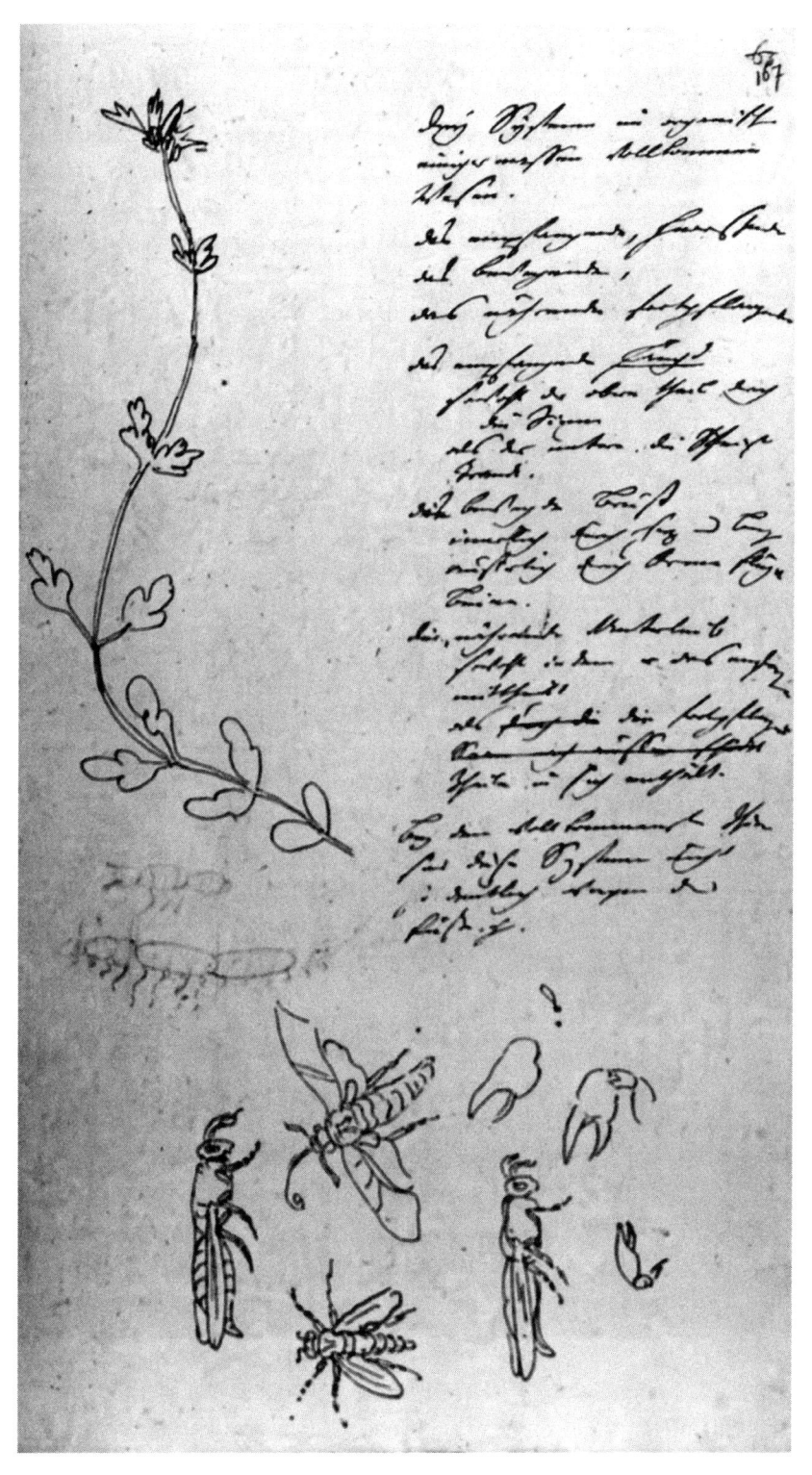

FIG. 16. The metamorphosis of a typical flowering plant
and various insects, by Goethe (c. 1788)

upon plant growth two tendencies of divergence and reintegration. The parts of a plant extend out from the stem in divergent directions; we see this in the pairs of opposed leaves that grow out from the stem nodes of flowering plants. These opposed parts then grow closer together and in the flower organize themselves around a central focus, before finally fusing into the corolla. In a simpler form, this process of *anastomosis* can be seen in the veins of a leaf.[120] The veins grow out of a single stem vein, and as they diverge and increase in number, they decrease in diameter, so exemplifying the law of expansion and contraction. At the point of their greatest refinement the veins of separate structures meet and fuse so as to form a circulatory system. *Anastomosis* can also be observed, Goethe argues, as a plant's development reaches its goal of reproduction, for the pistils and stamens, having grown out of the calyx into separate structures, enjoy what Goethe terms 'a spiritual *anastomosis*':[121] the stamens release pollen that is taken up by the pistils, and in this way the reproductive material circulates from one to the other.

In the first place the metamorphosis essay is a theory of the mechanisms that drive plant growth. The individual elements of the theory are not in themselves novel, and yet the theory as a whole is, and it is supported by fresh, detailed, meticulous observations. It was well received in particular by younger and more adventurous botanists. Positive reviews soon appeared in the journals,[122] and Goethe's name began to be cited as an authority on botany, though he only became aware of his new reputation somewhat later.[123] From late 1794, he found an attentive audience in the young naturalist Alexander von Humboldt. Goethe's botany was formative influence on Humboldt's geographical botany of Central and South America. Humboldt was excited by Goethe's holistic approach to nature.[124] Joachim Dietrich Brandis, a student of Lichtenberg and Blumenbach, based his own theory of a single, unifying and nonmaterial life force on Goethe's essay (*Essay on the Life Force*, 1795).[125] Goethe's work reentered the mainstream of botanical research in the twentieth century. One of the most eminent botanical morphologists of the twentieth century, Agnes Arber, published an English translation of Goethe's essay in 1946.[126] Acknowledging and building on Goethe's argument that plant development consisted in the metamorphosis of leaves, Arber went on to develop her own Goethean theory that leaves were partial shoots.[127]

With the metamorphosis essay published, Goethe returned to the study of mammal skeletons. The work was interrupted by the trip to Venice in the spring of 1790 though a fortuitous incident promised to unlock one of the mysteries of the mammal skeletal type. On 22 April Goethe and his amanuensis Götze were walking in the Jewish cemetery on the Lido. Götze picked up a fragment of a sheep's skull and presented it to Goethe 'as if it were a Jew's head'.[128] By chance, Götze's crass anti-Semitic comment helped Goethe with his model of mammal osteology,[129] as he wrote to Caroline Herder in May.[130] The insight is usually supposed to have been that the sheep's skull had a strong resemblance to a vertebra. Might a mammal's skull not actually be a metamorphosed vertebra, in the same way as the calyx of a flowering plant was a metamorphosed leaf? Goethe's letter to Caroline Herder does not state this, and Robert Richards has questioned whether Goethe's writings in this period show any evidence of the skull-vertebra theory.[131] As a theory of the development (ontogeny) of the individual mammal it is in any case incorrect: the development of embryos shows that the skull does not develop out of the vertebrae.[132] But this would be to miss the point, for Goethe was in fact interested in the development of species, not individuals: phylogeny, not ontogeny. The skull form of each mammal species must result from a set of transformations of the mammal type, and these transformations could be understood in terms of the same forces that shaped plant metamorphosis, such as the Kantian forces of expansion and contraction. It was these transformations that interested Goethe.

Inevitably the question arises how close Goethe came to a modern theory of evolution. Buffon's view was that transformation had occurred between species but not between genera. This made sense of some of the fossil evidence available at the time, for instance megafauna such as the aurochs, which can be considered to be ancestors of domestic cattle. It obviously falls far short of being a fully worked out theory of evolution. In recent years a consensus has emerged that Goethe held a transformationist theory of this kind. Within this consensus there is a spectrum of views as to how well developed Goethe's theory was. At one end of the spectrum, Margrit Wyder has argued that Goethe's theory represented a step towards a properly historicized theory of transformation,[133] but that his moves in this direction were reluctant and unintentional.[134] At the other end, Robert Richards considers that Goethe was a genuine forerunner of Darwin's theory of evolution.[135] The evidence of Goethe's unpublished drafts on mammal osteology of the early 1790s suggests that even Richards has understated how close Goethe came to a fully worked out theory of evolution. In these drafts Goethe made a number of conceptual moves that Darwin would also make. Indeed Goethe came close to making the most important move of all: to a theory of natural selection. The central question in his osteological notebooks is how the forces of transformation act on a species. His answer, like Darwin's, is to imagine the ecological niche that a species inhabits. While the modern concept of an ecological niche was not known to Goethe, he grasped the underlying idea. There are features of an animal's environment that force it to develop certain 'aids to life', in other words the features of its anatomy that enable the animal to thrive in its environment. He concentrated on two of these: the forms of the jaw and of the limbs.[136] Much of the empirical detail of the osteological drafts of the early 1790s concerns mammal teeth, and teeth were the reason for his interest in skulls. The way in which an animal feeds determines the form of its teeth and, because each mammal jaw is equipped to carry certain types of teeth, the teeth determine the form of the jaw and hence of the skull. Indirectly then, the shape of a mammal's skull is determined by its diet. The argument concerning mammal limbs is more obvious and at first sight somewhat banal. Comparison of the bodies of fish and seals shows a similarity of function; both body forms are, in modern parlance, adaptations to life in water. The point of comparing such different organisms as fish and seals is that they belong to entirely different classes (*pisces* and *mammalia*), and are therefore so remotely related that the body form of a fish cannot be a transformation of that of a seal or vice versa. To put it another way, the fish-like bodies of seals have descended from ancestors that were not fish-like at all. The adaptations of fish and seals to life in water must therefore have evolved independently, in both cases in response to the aquatic environment. As Darwin puts it in the 'Morphology' chapter of *On the Origin of Species*, 'the shape of the body and fin-like limbs are only analogical when whales are compared with fishes, being adaptations in both classes for swimming through the water.'[137] To what extent did Goethe think in these evolutionary terms? The answer is to be found in the distinction he makes between the development of the individual organism (ontogeny) and the development of the species (phylogeny). The argument about the convergent evolution of the body forms of fish and seals is phylogenetic, and Goethe stresses precisely this point: 'the existence of a creature we call "fish" is only possible under the conditions of an element we call "water," so that the creature not only exists in that element, but also evolves [*werden*] there.'[138] There is only one way to construe this statement: a species evolves in response to environmental pressures.

At the same time, the argument concerning fish and seals eliminates the need for final causes. (In his 'Morphology' chapter Darwin also comments that it is 'hopeless' to explain these relationships 'by the doctrine of final causes.')[139] It can now be shown that the purpose of an organism is to thrive and reproduce in the niche it evolved in. This section of Goethe's argument ends with a vision worthy of Darwin and comparable with the famous 'entangled bank' passage in *On the Origin of Species*. After repeating the distinction between phylogeny and ontogeny, Goethe widens his view to consider what an evolutionary niche really looks like:

> How admirable that nature must use the same means to produce a creature as it does to sustain it! We progress on our path as follows: first we viewed the unstructured, unlimited element as a vehicle for the unstructured being, and now we will raise our observation to a higher level to consider the structured world itself as an interrelationship of many elements. We will see the entire plant world, for example, as a vast sea which is as necessary to the existence of individual insects as the oceans and rivers are to the existence of individual fish, and we will observe that an enormous number of living creatures are born and nourished in this ocean of plants. Ultimately we will see the whole world of animals as a great element in which one species is created, or at least sustained, by and through another. We will no longer think of connections and relationships in terms of purpose and intention. This is the only road to progress in understanding how nature expresses itself from all quarters and in all directions as it goes about its work of creation.[140]

The idea that species evolve in a niche and that the niche comprises other species—the niche inhabited by pollinating insects comprises flowering plants—is another similarity between Goethe's conception of evolution and Darwin's.

A further similarity is the principle of the economy of nature that Goethe had first employed in the essay on plant metamorphosis. It is a 'general law of development' that nature alternates between 'giving and taking away':[141] 'nature cannot give without on the other hand taking away, and she can take nothing without on the other hand giving'.[142] This is because nature has a fixed 'budget' which it must disburse according to a law of compensation, which determines that expansion of one element of an organism must be compensated for by contraction of another. For instance, those ungulates that have no horns have, by compensation as it were, a full complement of upper incisors and canines (e.g., horses), whereas the ungulates with horns lack a full complement of those teeth (e.g., rhinoceroses).[143] The economy of nature has evidently driven evolution down either of these two paths. The budget is either spent on horns or on upper incisors and canines, but does not suffice for both. The law of compensation was by no means new. Among eighteenth-century natural historians it was advocated by Charles Bonnet,[144] and it can be found as early as Aristotle, who proposed that among members of the same genus of animals 'the parts are identical save only for a difference in the way of excess or defect.'[145] In the first edition of *On the Origin of Species* Darwin cited Goethe and Etienne Geoffroy Saint-Hilaire as the authors of this 'law of compensation or balancement of growth.'[146] Darwin thought the application of the law was confined to a small number of cases. However, he did find the metaphor of the economy of nature useful in a different, more general sense that he made frequent use of: 'namely, that natural selection is continually trying to economise in every part of the organisation.'[147]

The economy of nature is just one instance of a more general feature of Goethe's theory of mammal osteology and of his work on natural history as a whole. Throughout his writings are scattered references to the creativity of nature. In the osteological writings of the early 1790s he refers to nature's 'formative power' and to the 'primal power of nature'. While easily dismissed as poetic formulae, these notions do important work. Goethe's osteological writings of the early 1790s are explorations of the ways in which the 'primal power of nature' creates animal bodies, just as Spinoza's *natura naturans* creates *natura naturata*. We cannot of course perceive the 'primal power of nature', at least not directly. We can however infer the constraints under which it creates animal bodies, for everything we see in the natural world is marked by those constraints. For instance, we cannot perceive the forces behind the Kantian phenomena of expansion and contraction directly, but only as they act through the limitations imposed by the economy of nature, for instance in the form of ungulate horns and teeth. The 'primal power of nature' creates under the constraint of a fixed budget or law of compensation. The key point here, and one of Goethe's most important insights, relates to causation. In his geological work in the 1780s he took up Aristotle's idea that substance contains a form that is intrinsic to it and will be expressed so long as the substance can emerge in freedom. This idea does more interesting work in his osteological writings in the 1790s. We do not see directly the forces that create the body forms of fish and seals; what we see is the effects of natural constraints on those forces. We see the 'primal power of nature' working indirectly via the aquatic environment in which fish and seals evolved. In other words, Goethe's theory of nature relies on an underlying principle of indirect or negative causation. The created world comes about through nature's creative force being filtered by a set of constraints. Fish and seals have their streamlined bodies and fins or flippers because these are the body forms that are not filtered out by the aquatic environment. Put simply, what evolves is what is not prevented from evolving. Goethe evidently felt that the notion of indirect or negative causation needed justification. He was alert to the sensitivities of those who were committed to a God or nature that creates directly, that makes the imprint of its creating hand visible in the very forms of its creatures. Goethe's theory deprives God or nature of that direct creative power. Nature acts indirectly and in ways that involve the complex interaction of forces, some creative, some restrictive, such as the aquatic niche in which fish and seals evolved. He spells this aspect of his theory out immediately before and as a defence of his vision of 'the entire plant world [...] as a vast sea':

> We show disrespect neither for the primal force of nature nor for the wisdom and power of a creator if we assume that the former acts indirectly, and that the latter acted indirectly at the beginning of all things. Is it not fitting that this great force should bring forth simple things in a simple way and complex things in a complex way? Do we disparage its power if we say it could not have brought forth fish without water, birds without air, other animals without earth, that this is just as inconceivable as the continued existence of these creatures without the conditions provided by each element? Will we not attain a more satisfactory insight into the mysterious architecture of the formative process, now widely recognised to be built on a single pattern, by examining and comprehending this single pattern more fully and then looking into the following question: how does a surrounding element, with its various specific characteristics, affect the general form we have been studying? How does the form, both determined and a determinant, assert itself against these elements? What manner of hard parts, soft parts, interior parts, and exterior parts are created in the form by this effect? And, as indicated before, what is wrought by the elements through all their diversity of height and depth, region and climate?[148]

This is the point at which Goethe comes closest to Darwinian evolution by natural selection. Darwin's natural selection operates by way of negative or indirect causation.[149] His great breakthrough was to realize that natural selection was a constraint on nature's productivity. Animals can only reproduce insofar as they are allowed to by their fitness for the environment they inhabit. Thus, organisms acquire form not because some natural force causes them to do so, but because the pressures of the competition to survive and breed do not *prevent* them from doing so. The limiting factor of the evolutionary niche is responsible for the wondrous diversity of natural forms. Goethe's view is strikingly similar. What creates living forms is not just the primal force; it is the primal force being allowed to do certain things by the environment it is in.

The question therefore arises: if Goethe's osteological writings contain some modern evolutionary ideas, why do they contain no fully worked out theory of evolution? Having discovered some of the key elements of a full evolutionary theory—the complex, multicausal niche, the economy of nature, evolution as negative causation—why did Goethe not go into print as an advocate of transformationism? The answer to this question has several parts. In some respects Goethe's ideas harked back to ancient and outmoded traditions. His theory of the type can be criticised for its ambiguity. It can be interpreted to mean that animal genera were fixed: the type of each genus is a kind of neo-Platonic blueprint drawn up by nature that allows for some degree of transformation between species within a genus, but not between the different genera.[150] At other times Goethe views the type as more fluid.[151] It has also been argued that Goethe's thinking about animal species was not properly historical,[152] but he can hardly be blamed for this, since he and his contemporaries had no conception of the immensity of evolutionary time. Despite James Hutton's 1788 *Theory of the Earth*, the idea that geological time was immensely long was only popularized in the early 1830s by Charles Lyell's *Principles of Geology*. To conceive of the immensely long course of evolutionary time would have taken an extraordinary leap of the imagination in the 1790s. Having said that, Goethe's osteological drafts of the early 1790s do contain clear evidence of a properly historical notion of evolution. The formation of species happens not in some Neoplatonic realm of ideas, where blueprints are drawn up before being mysteriously manifested on earth. On the contrary, Goethe states unambiguously that the evolution of fish and seals happened in the sea and the evolution of pollinating insects happened on earth among flowering plants.

The main problem with Goethe's writings on mammal osteology is not that they are insufficiently evolutionary. It is that he did not complete them. They consist of three fragmentary and unfinished drafts. An 'Essay on the Forms of Animals' was written in late 1790.[153] He planned to publish the essay in the spring of 1791, a year on from the plant metamorphosis essay. However, other more urgent matters distracted him: in the winter of 1790 he began to work on the theory of optics and colour. The two other drafts date from 1794: an 'Attempt at a General Theory of Osteology' and an 'Attempt at a General Comparative Theory'. Again, other business got in the way of the completion of these drafts. In the summer of 1794 Goethe accepted an invitation from Schiller to contribute to a new literary journal. It was the beginning of the closest and most intense working relationship of his life. So the three osteological drafts remained unfinished and known only to his close friends and collaborators until he eventually published the material in 1820, by which time his ideas were no longer new.

———

After his return from Venice in 1790, his osteological researches gave way to a new fascination with coloured light and optics that would occupy him for the next twenty years. It is fair to say that his studies in colour present a problem. Much of his effort was expended on a quixotic attempt to disprove Newton's theory of the diverse refrangibility of light. Some parts of the campaign against Newton have merit, in particular his ideas about the physiology of colour vision and the use of colour in art. These have led Boyle to argue that the real focus and value of these efforts was the human experience of colour and not the physics of light and optics: his work is best understood as a phenomenology of colour.[154] His campaign against Newton also led Goethe to interesting reflections on the philosophy of science and the ways in which the Newtonian orthodoxy became institutionalized. These are an early example of 'science studies'. However, the considerable effort he expended over more than twenty years only really makes sense in the context of his wrongheaded campaign against Newton. The ideas about physiology, art, and the philosophy and history of science were products of the campaign against Newton, and not the other way round. All of which begs the question, why did Goethe devote so much time to such a flawed project? He was certainly not driven by the passion to defend the unity of nature against religion, as he had in his work in natural history in the 1780s. His work on optics had none of the radicalism of his geology, botany, and (especially) mammal anatomy. However, his campaign against Newton was a battle against an orthodoxy, and that certainly made it attractive to him. But above all, it was a matter of what he was fighting for. Newton's experiments involved holding human perception at arm's length. The experimental apparatus and setup were elaborate and arguably unnatural; they created a gap between the experimenter and the phenomenon. The results were expressed in complex mathematical form and as quantities rather than perceivable qualities, which seemed perverse to Goethe given that the subject, colour, was that most perceivable quality of all. In these two senses Newton's experiments were the antithesis of Goethe's humanism, his belief in the fundamental soundness of human thought and sensation. Needless to say, the motivation for his work on colour was more complex than this, but if we want to identify one leading motive for his campaign against Newton, it was the defence of a vision of nature in which *human* nature was primary.

The campaign against Newton revealed the limitations of Goethe's humanism, and the incident that first triggered his interest in colour illustrates these limitations. In the winter of 1789/90 he borrowed a set of prisms and other apparatus from Christian Wilhelm Büttner, formerly professor of natural history and chemistry at Göttingen. Goethe kept the prisms for some time without using them while he put the finishing touches to the essay on plant metamorphosis. By January Büttner was asking for their return. Goethe had already packed the apparatus when on a whim he decided to recreate Newton's experiment. Instead of following Newton's method—blacking out the windows and having a beam of light enter the darkened room through a pinhole[155]—he trusted his own ordinary experience. He simply put the prism to his eye and looked through it in broad daylight. At first he was disappointed not to see the spectral colours, but as his gaze alighted on the boundaries between the dark window frames and the pale sky outside, the colours emerged faintly where the dark frames met the light sky. According to his later account, he said to himself, 'as if by instinct', that 'the Newtonian doctrine was false'.[156] He did acknowledge later that the spectral colours could be produced by refraction through a prism, but he insisted that this was a subordinate phenomenon and Newton's results were artefacts of a contrived experiment. He thought he had stumbled upon a more fundamental phenomenon that any human could readily experience: what are known as boundary colours. There followed a sudden revelation. The boundary colours were produced not by the splitting of white light but by the interaction of light with dark. The colours were intermediate states between pure white light and complete darkness.

Goethe's accounts of his experience with Büttner's prisms date from nearly twenty years after the event. His letters and diaries from early 1790 are silent on the matter. No doubt the accounts he wrote later dramatize the moment of discovery. He set great store by its suddenness, for he believed that this was how some scientific discoveries came about—from a sudden insight or aperçu. Whether or not the insight actually was a sudden revelation, the experience in January 1790 seems to have been the foundation for the work on light and colour that would occupy him on and off for twenty years. He quickly designed a set of experiments to show that colours were produced at the boundaries of light and dark surfaces.[157] He made two cardboard surfaces, one consisting of a white strip on a black background and the other a black strip on a white background. With the cards arranged so that the strips are horizontal, and the prism held on one card and orientated so that the strip can be seen through its refractive angle, the prism can now be moved slowly away from the card. As the prism reaches about halfway between the card and the observer, coloured bands begin to emerge along the top and bottom margins of the two strips. These bands display the chromatic aberrations that Newton had seen, but not in a spectral array of six colours matching the colours of the rainbow. Instead there was a pair of coloured bands. The white strip on the black background was fringed on its top edge by a cyan band shading into purple and on its bottom edge by yellow shading into orange. The black strip on a white background produced the opposite arrangement, with orange shading into yellow on the top edge, and purple shading into cyan on the bottom. The observation demonstrates that in each pair of coloured bands the paler colour (yellow or cyan) adjoins the white area and the darker colour (orange or purple) adjoins the black. This configuration of colours and their relation to black and white proved that colours were produced by the interaction of light and dark.

The observations with Büttner's prisms might not have had such a profound effect had Goethe not already been fascinated by the phenomena of colour. Indeed, his work on colour was never purely scientific.[158] His interest in meteorology led him to observe the colour of the sky as it changed with weather and climate. His Italian notebooks are full of references to the deep blue of the southern sky, in contrast to the less intense colours north of the alps. He saw connections between the quality of the Italian light and the colours used in Italian Renaissance art. Indeed, his interest in the artistic use of colour was unusual for its time since art historians and theorists tended to be more interested in shape than colour. A first tentative essay on colour was drafted in May 1791, under the title 'On Blue'.[159] He planned to send it in to the *Magazine for the Latest News from Natural History* published by the Jena mathematician Johann Heinrich Voigt. As is clear from a letter to Voigt, the essay was inspired by attempts to refine the colorimetry of blue, by Professor Saussure among others.[160] Although Goethe rarely makes explicit mention of colorimetry, much of his concern with colour is best understood in this context. One of the main contributions of Goethe's work on optics would be to argue for alternative view of the shape of colorimetric space—not an open, linear segment, like the Newtonian spectrum, but rather a closed, continuous arrangement that can be visualized as a circle. In the essay 'On Blue' Goethe makes several observations concerning blue that at first seem disconnected. A pure Berlin blue, viewed away from direct light, seems much darker than other colours. Even in the absence of blue in the sky and in a curtained room, shadows appear blue. The first inference is that 'a pure deprivation of light is in and of itself blue'.[161] Presumably the further inferences are that blue is one of the primary spectral colours and the colour space occupied by blue neighbours that of black.

By spring 1791 he had a more ambitious plan, and by the end of August, after months of observations and drafting, he was able to publish an advertisement for his forthcoming *Essays on Optics*, which would appear in two parts in October 1791 and May 1792. The intense personal significance of his first venture into print on the theory of colour is suggested by the date given in the advertisement: 28 August, his forty-second birthday. It was a relaunching of his scientific career. He recognised the failure, as he now saw it, of his *Essay in Attempt at Explaining the Metamorphosis of Plants*. He had made the mistake of writing the *Metamorphosis* essay for the scholarly community.[162] In the *Essays on Optics* he would write for a lay audience—hence the efforts he devoted to describing his observations in terms that laypeople would be able to follow, and hence also the inclusion of a set of images, printed on loose-leaf cards, that would help his readers to replicate his observations.

The *Essays* are not a fully worked out theory of colour. At several points in the step-by-step description of his observations, Goethe insists that he is proceeding with caution, as if he is reluctant to make substantive theoretical claims. Nor do the *Essays* conform to the traditional model of eighteenth-century disquisitions on colour, which normally begin with a summary of Newton's work.[163] Instead Goethe begins with some remarks on how we experience colour in nature and the importance of colour for painting. Any scientific theory of colour must take these human experiences and practices into account.[164] With this emphasis on ordinary human experience, an assault on Newton is being prepared covertly, for by making ordinary human experience central to his account of colour, Goethe is preparing the ground for his argument that Newton's theory of the refrangibility of white light is unnatural. Humans experience white light as a single and simple phenomenon. This matters for the scientific understanding of colours because humans are reliable measuring instruments. Humans are equipped to apprehend nature. From this humanistic doctrine it will follow that white light must be unitary and fundamental, for that is how we experience it: white light is 'the simplest, most fundamental and homogeneous thing we know'.[165] The humanistic argument is not spelt out in the *Essays on Optics*, but it is implied, and the implication is anti-Newtonian. That is confirmed when Goethe turns to address Newton's reputation. At first he shows restraint. Newton is not named and is instead referred to as a 'profound thinker'.[166] Perhaps Goethe thought that an explicit polemic might deter his lay readers. Yet the polemical intention soon becomes clear. The Newtonian doctrine is like a 'castle' built in the middle of the field of knowledge. Its followers form a 'party' which one must join or be forever excluded.[167] The language implies that the Newtonian orthodoxy did not establish itself by virtue of being true.

Having implied his opposition to Newton, Goethe proceeds to the heart of the matter. Newton's *experimentum crucis* does not yield the kind of 'pure experiences' that should be the foundation of science,[168] where 'pure' means: accessible to the human senses in their unaugmented state. The experiment suffers from three defects. First, it requires a complex and contrived experimental environment that is hard to reproduce because it is so far removed from ordinary human experience.[169] Second, it depends on the theory that white light is composite, which contradicts common sense. Third, the experiment's conclusion that the refractive angles of the spectral colours are quantitatively constant implies that colours are mathematical quantities, whereas we experience them as qualities.

After this provocative beginning, the main body of the *Essays* makes only very modest claims. Explicit discussion of theories of light is avoided in favour of teasing references to a 'law' which is 'constant'.[170] The phenomena of boundary colours are presented through a range of observations, each under subtly different conditions. The prism is moved back and forth between the eye and the object. Prisms of different shapes are used. The relation of the black and white fields on the object cards is alternated, and different shapes are tried. In the second volume of the *Essays* grey and coloured shapes are introduced, and a massive water prism is described. Under these varied conditions the observer witnesses the boundary colours entering and withdrawing from our experience.[171] The 'law' of colours is thus a law of the *appearance* of spectral colours to the human eye. It is a law that emerges out of an array of phenomena. In this way Goethe's readers are invited to adopt a different method from Newton's, indeed the reverse of the Newtonian relationship between experimentation and hypothesis. Newton's complex and demanding *experimentum crucis*, which involved precise control of several parameters, was designed to decide between two hypotheses. The hypothesis of Descartes, Hooke, and others was that refraction produced colours by changing the patterns of the pulses that made up light and that refraction was therefore a *modification* of white light. Newton's hypothesis was that refraction produces colour by splitting light into its components, and thus 'Light itself is a *Heterogeneous mixture*

FIG. 17. Goethe, etching by Ramberg,
probably after the 1791 portrait
by J. H. Lips (1792)

of differently refrangible Rays'.[172] The experiment was designed to test the hypotheses; the hypotheses preceded and mandated the experiment. In Goethe's *Essays* the relationship between experiment and hypothesis is reversed, or so the reader is to believe. The process begins with an observation, which is then multiplied under varied conditions, so providing an exhaustive resource of observations of similar phenomena. If repeated carefully and in a logical sequence, the observations would, Goethe believed, lead any observer to the same inductive conclusions. In Goethe's mind, this was the correct scientific method, as established by Francis Bacon.

In principle, the debate whether hypotheses or experience should have precedence can be decided either way. In practice, Goethe's model of experience-led science was of much less use in physics than in natural history. Indeed, it can be argued that one of Goethe's mistakes was to import a methodology from natural history into physics. Sensing that his method needed further amplification, in the spring of 1792 he drafted a short essay now known by the misleadingly Kantian title 'The Experiment as Mediator between Subject and Object'. The title was invented thirty years later. Preparing to publish the essay in 1822, Goethe admitted to Riemer that he could not remember its original title, and Riemer was left to devise one. The title chosen, whether by Riemer or Goethe, reflects Goethe's feeling that Schiller wanted to 'harmonize such utterances with Kantian philosophy'.[173] In fact the terms *subject* and *object* are not used in the essay. In a letter to Schiller of 1798 Goethe referred to the essay under the title 'Precautions of the Observer',[174] which suits its contents better. The precautions to be taken by the observer have nothing to do with Kant's theory of the subjective constitution of our knowledge. They are closer to Spinoza than Kant.[175] The precautions Goethe recommends are both negative and positive: errors to be avoided and good practices to be cultivated. On the negative side, observers are warned against the mistaken assumption that phenomena have human purposes, as Spinoza had argued in the appendix to Book I of the *Ethics*.[176] Their limited experience should not lead people to overlook relevant data. They should resist the temptation to enviously exclude others from their own discoveries, or to overlook relevant theories due to their unfamiliarity with the history of the subject. By avoiding these errors, observers can guard against settling on 'an idea conceived in undue haste'.[177] The greatest risk lies in making overly hasty inferences from one or more experiments, such as the *experimentum crucis*, for we are all prone to excessive haste in connecting our experiences with one another and in seeing individual experiments as representative of general truths. Experience is wide and multifarious: the observer must not narrow his field of view unduly, and certainly not down to a single experiment. The observer who does so may be guilty of unwittingly claiming dominion over the phenomena, which is more easily done when their number is limited. The few phenomena collected in this way look more like a despotic court than a free republic, and history can quickly turn such closed systems into a sacred shrines or sects. With these 'precautions', Goethe laid the ground for his later polemics against Newton.

Goethe must have known his criticisms of Newton could be turned against himself, for his own understanding of colour did in fact originate from a small set of observations that he rashly solidified into a theory: 'an idea conceived in undue haste'. The positive recommendations spelt out in the second part of 'Precautions of the Observer' are designed both to avert this criticism and to justify the experimental method used in the *Essays*. The essence of the argument is that an individual experiment has to be one member of a larger series. The phenomena themselves are manifold, and they change in subtle ways as the conditions under which they are viewed are altered. Not only that, the phenomena present themselves to the viewer in multidimensional ways. For instance, colours present themselves to the human eye in (at least) two ways.

They can stand in contrast to one another, as we can plainly see when we juxtapose colours and find that the degree of contrast between two colours depends on which colours are juxtaposed; to produce the highest contrast with blue, we must juxtapose it with yellow. Equally, colours sit next to neighbouring colours. For instance, red will always be found neighbouring yellow in the spectrum. To fully explore these phenomena, we must conduct a series of observations that are themselves manifold and multidimensional, and which faithfully reproduce the natural affinities and relationships between the phenomena.[178] Only with this variety of experiments can we begin to see patterns unfolding— not dissimilar to the patterns we see when comparing mammal skeletons or the parts of flowering plants. Having varied the experiments in this way, we should eventually be able to see the patterns as a single phenomenon, and the series of observations that disclose them as one observation. This holistic observation is a 'higher' kind of experience, and it is the proper destination of all empirical observation:

> In the first two parts of my *Essays on Optics* I sought to set up a series of contiguous experiments derived from one another in this way. Studied thoroughly and understood as a whole, these experiments could even be thought of as representing a single experiment, a single piece of empirical evidence explored in its most manifold variations.
>
> Such a piece of empirical evidence, composed of many others, is clearly of a higher sort. It shows the general formula, so to speak, that overarches an array of individual arithmetic sums. [...] those who wish to be honest with themselves and others will try by careful development of individual experiments to evolve empirical evidence of the higher sort. These pieces of evidence may be expressed in concise axioms and set side by side, and as more of them emerge they may be ordered and related. Like mathematical axioms they will remain unshakable either singly or as a whole. Anyone may examine and test the elements, the many individual experiments, which constitute this higher sort of evidence; it will be easy to judge whether we can express these many components in a general axiom, for there is no arbitrariness here.[179]

The underlying doctrine is clear: observation is preferable to abstraction; the scientific process should begin with observations, not hypotheses, and it should culminate in super-phenomena, not theories. In reacting to Newton, Goethe returned to the methods he had used in the 1780s in geology, botany, and anatomy.

When the process of reconstituting the French state began in earnest in summer 1790, the German territories were also forced to confront the challenge of reform. Reluctantly at first, during the 1790s Goethe came to play a role in rejuvenating the *ancien regime* model. His first task was to revitalize the Weimar theatre. For five years the court had been fed a diet of comedies, *Singspiele*, and comic operas by the travelling troupe of Giuseppe Bellomo, and its cost was fully subsidized by Carl August. He now hoped to establish a more modern court theatre, partly subsidized and partly commercial. In January 1791 his patience with Bellomo's whinging actors finally snapped,[180] and it was decided that a remnant of the Bellomo troupe would be retained[181] under a new director. In some ways Goethe was a perfect fit for the role. He was a decisive and experienced administrator, a charismatic leader, a competent amateur actor, and had once been a successful theatrical writer. Of equal importance was his clear sense of a new aesthetic direction, which he had trialled successfully in the 1779 production of *Iphigeneia*. Within a few weeks of Bellomo's final performance in April, he was planning wholesale changes to the repertoire and reforming the company's overly casual and naturalistic acting style.[182] The aim was to train a company that could perform an expanded and enriched repertoire, including more foreign plays. Carl August would subsidize one third of the costs. The remainder would be funded by ticket sales, including a season ticket at reduced rates, which was carefully budgeted by Goethe's experienced deputy Franz Kirms. In this way, the theatre would find a balance between being attuned to the tastes of a paying audience and representing the aesthetics of a conservative but cosmopolitan court. The hybrid nature of the project suited Goethe's interests, even if he sometimes felt shackled by the 'torture' of three weekly performances, as well as a summer season at Bad Lauchstädt.[183] He showed considerable perseverance and would remain in charge for twenty-six years. The changes he brought about had a lasting effect on the aesthetics and practices of the German theatre.[184]

The first of his own plays to be staged, in December 1791, was a comedy he had begun in Rome: a satirical dramatization of the Diamond Necklace Affair.[185] It was his first in a series of attempts to use the theatre to move public opinion against the Revolution or at least against the idea of a revolution in Germany. Initially conceived as an operetta, *The Mystified Ones* centred on an unproven allegation that the conspiracy had been led by the swindler, forger, occultist, and freemason Balsamo ('Count Cagliostro'). It is not clear whether

Goethe actually believed the allegation, and the play is vague on this point. Its two plot strands, the conspiracy of the necklace and the antics of the mountebank Count Rostro, barely come into contact with one another. More important for Goethe was the social phenomenon of Cagliostro and the threat it posed to the sociopolitical order. As he had written to Lavater in 1781, 'our whole moral and political world is undermined by subterranean passages, vaults, sewers',[186] by which he meant secret societies. By the time he reworked the operetta as a play in prose, in spring 1791, the Illuminati had become an ingredient in conservative explanations for the French Revolution.[187] The Illuminati and other secret societies claimed to recognise no distinctions of class or estate. The abolition of the nobility in France in June 1790 seemed to conservative conspiracy theorists to be the fulfilment of this masonic aspiration. Goethe's Count Rostro is said to believe that 'all estates are equal',[188] which makes him not only a politically subversive mason, but also a forerunner of the Revolution. By early September 1791 the play was finished and had a fantastical new title,[189] *The Great-Copt*, an allusion to Cagliostro's claim that he was an emissary of a mysterious figure of that name. The claim was no mere eccentricity on Cagliostro's part: some masons believed that their organizations were led by shadowy 'unknown superiors'.[190] In the play, Count Rostro's occult antics were to culminate in a dramatic revelation of the Great-Copt in person, which would be the Count's ultimate gift to his adoring followers, but of course the Copt turns out to be none other than Rostro himself.

In the main plot a Marquise and her husband conspire to defraud a cathedral Canon. The Marquise tricks the Canon into purchasing a necklace that will win the Princess's favours for him. In fact the Marquise has forged a letter from the Princess to the Canon and is pretending to be the Princess's confidante. The main motivation for the conspirators is simply greed. In a parallel plot Count Rostro seeks to burnish his reputation as an occultist, but is dogged by a sceptical Baronet. (The fact that the Baronet is of the lowest rank of the nobility and has the good sense to disbelieve the Count identifies him with Goethe.) The two plots are linked somewhat loosely by the Marquise's niece, who is being trained by the conspirators to pose as the Princess but instead reveals the plot to the Baronet. Dutifully he informs the authorities, and in the final act the royal guardsmen intervene to arrest the conspirators, picking up Count Rostro along the way. The Captain of the guard is under instruction to hush things up so as not to undermine public confidence—a key principle of Goethe's own political practice. The Marquis, Marquise, and Count are sent to prison, and the Canon into exile. The niece begs to be sent to a convent, and the Baronet is left to regret that he was unable to do more to protect her.

The play suffers from two main weaknesses, both indicative of Goethe's political uncertainty during 1790 and 1791. The masonic plot of Count Rostro and the affair of the necklace are connected by a slender thread, and the connection between them only makes sense if we accept the conservative conspiracy theories that blamed the freemasons for the revolution. Absent this belief, there is little to persuade an audience that the atmosphere of mysticism and credulity created by Count Rostro is anything other than scenery, or at most evidence that society is riddled with self-destructive and venal criminality. The second problem concerns Goethe's treatment of the Revolution. The play seems to argue that the primary cause of the Revolution was the French nobility's lack of moral backbone. The play was published in 1792, but readers found it 'flat' and 'empty' and lacking the passion and feeling they expected of Goethe.[191] Writing much later, Goethe blamed the negative response on his satirical rejection of the high ethical ideals of freemasonry.[192] More likely is that he sacrificed dramatic interest to his propagandistic aims. The play affirms the paternalistic politics practised by the Weimar regime both before and after the Revolution. In order to preserve the social and political status quo, embarrassing mishaps are to be resolved and subversive activities suppressed quickly and quietly.

In 1792 the Revolution descended into chaos, with war between France and the great European monarchies and an increasingly paranoid and bloodthirsty mood in Paris. The mood in Germany was also becoming febrile. Writing to Voigt from Coblenz in July, Carl August insisted that 'it was by no means a fantasy if [the coalition powers] feared the transplanting of new French ideas to German soil. I have obtained proofs here, and no secret is being made of the fact that if Austria, Prussia, and Russia were not pushing against the tide with such force, the unrest would already now be breaking out in several parts of Germany'.[193] The government in Weimar settled on a policy that combined suppression of dissent and punishment of agitators, albeit with a degree of leniency. In the autumn, with Carl August now away on campaigns, revolutionary leaflets were found circulating in Eisenach, and some primitive revolutionary clubs were formed.[194] The Duke demanded a thorough investigation and exemplary punishments. Once a handful of agitators had been denounced and imprisoned, the Privy Council reverted to a more lenient approach, which Voigt tried to package suitably to the absent Duke. With Goethe's support, Voigt argued that the troublemakers could be ignored as they had not in fact meant to threaten the Duke directly: 'Goethe is also of the opinion that what has happened (particularly since it was not directed against your august self but rather in Eisenach against the somewhat rigid aristocracy there) should on this occasion be forgotten'.[195] The unrest continued through the winter and into the summer of 1793, when the stocking workers of Apolda rioted after their pay was reduced.[196] The government suppressed the riots and introduced some modest defensive reforms.[197] Then some of the wealthier peasants in Eisenach appealed for their *corvées* to be commuted into cash. The Privy Council was initially sympathetic but eventually decided to resist the appeals.[198] Leniency was one thing, genuine reform another.

The University of Jena was a greater source of worry and was Goethe's responsibility. Autonomous student societies were a traditional part of university life and not ordinarily known for political subversiveness. In January 1792, in a statement to the Privy Council concerning the abolition of student societies and the archaic practice of duelling, Goethe put his view bluntly: 'One should destroy all secret societies come what may'.[199] The university senate promulgated the ban at the beginning of February, and for a time order was maintained. Voigt kept a number of students and professors as paid informers, an arrangement Goethe was aware of.[200] In June the fragile peace was broken by violent rioting, probably triggered by the government's surveillance activities. In the middle of July the unrest culminated in the students marching out of Jena in a column and so hitting the government where it hurt most: its purse. The authorities had overreacted. Their mistake was to believe the conspiracy theories that cast students as revolutionaries, and Goethe was as guilty of this error as his colleagues in the Privy Council. The behaviour of a handful of professors and other intellectuals may have contributed to the error. By 1792 Carl August had become deeply suspicious of the 'race' of professors and in the summer ordered Voigt to have his spies report on them.[201] In Weimar itself, the notables were causing problems. Carl August was annoyed by Wieland's overly liberal opinions on the Revolution.[202] In October 1792 Kirms wrote to him that two more notables were causing friction at court with their support for the Revolution. One was Herder, as the Duke already suspected, and the other was almost certainly Knebel.[203] Carl August instructed Kirms to tell Knebel to hold his tongue.[204] Goethe and Voigt put financial pressure on Herder.[205] More troubling was Bode, whose independent wealth made him less easy to cow.[206] When he died in December 1793, Charlotte von Stein, a bitter opponent of all things revolutionary, expressed her relief: 'So, one bel esprit and friend of the Revolution fewer in the world'.[207]

Goethe reacted to the crisis of 1792 by starting work on a play about the politics of Germany in the wake of the Revolution. Although he left it half finished, he evidently felt it was important, as he returned to the play several times in later life. The finished scenes are an uneasy mixture of personal confession and propaganda. The early manuscripts have no title. In 1814 he added the title *Breme von Bremenfeld*—the name of the agitator who plans an uprising in the petty German principality where the play is set. In 1815, when revising the still unfinished text and adding a synopsis of the missing scenes, he changed the title to *Signs of the Times*, before settling on *Agitated* in 1816 (literally 'The Agitated Ones', *Die Aufgeregten*). Although he later dated the writing of the play to 1793–1794,[208] the spring and summer of 1792 seems a more likely date, before the Revolution entered its bloodiest phase and the war of the first coalition began in earnest. The play makes no mention of the war and reflects a less negative view of the Revolution than Goethe would reach at the end of the year.[209]

The setting is a German principality ruled by a countess in the name of her young son. She has just returned from Paris where she witnessed 'extraordinary events, but little to cheer the soul', she tells her son's tutor. The tutor, who holds a master's degree, represents the worrisome elements of the German intelligentsia who sympathized with the ideals of the Revolution: people like Herder, Knebel, and Wieland, the former tutor to Carl August. Envying the countess her trip to Paris, the tutor is intoxicated by 'the greatest deeds the world has ever seen, [...] the rapture that took hold of a nation at the moment when it first felt itself free and unbound from the chains it had borne for so long that this heavy alien burden had, as it were, become a part of its miserable, sick body'. The Countess deflates his rhapsodic enthusiasm, but he still maintains that the revolutionary violence was admirable: 'to err with the best and highest intentions is always more praiseworthy than to act fittingly with mean intentions. One can stumble on the right path and walk straight on the wrong one—'.[210] The scene is unfinished; the tutor's speech breaks off, and the debate is not resolved. Later, in conversation with her adviser—a loyal, thoughtful, staunchly pro-aristocratic bourgeois based no doubt on Goethe himself—the Countess, while seeming to confirm part of the tutor's defence of the revolution, makes a more general point about oppression:

> Having observed how unfairness so easily mounts up from generation to generation, how noble deeds are for the most part particular to the person, and how only selfishness is, as it were, heritable; having seen with my own eyes that human nature can be oppressed and debased to a miserable degree, yet not be altogether subjugated and destroyed: I have made it a firm principle to strictly avoid every single action that seems to me unfair and to speak my mind out loud about such actions among my family, in company, at court, and in the city. I will no longer be silent at any injustice, no longer tolerate any pettiness under a guise of greatness, even if I should be denounced with the hated name of 'democrat'.[211]

Eckermann reports a conversation of 1824 in which Goethe supposedly claimed that the Countess's 'sentiments were thoroughly respectable. They were my sentiments at the time and still are today'. The Countess was a model of 'how the aristocracy should in fact think. The Countess has just arrived back from Paris, she has witnessed the revolutionary events there, and the lesson she has learned from them is by no means bad'. For himself, he could 'never be a friend of the Revolution', Goethe added, 'for its horrors touched me too closely and enraged me by the day and the hour, while back then its beneficial effects were not apparent. Also I could not be unconcerned about people seeking to bring about similar scenes in Germany in a *contrived* manner, which in France had been the result of a deep necessity'.[212] Eckermann's reports of Goethe's words should always be treated with a large pinch of salt, and the view of the play conveyed in this report is slightly misleading. By claiming that the Countess had learned a lesson from events in Paris, Goethe's reported words impose a definitive meaning on words that are open to interpretation. The Countess does not connect her talk of unfairness and oppression with the Revolution. Her words are more general: unfairness accumulating over generations, a seemingly endless legacy of selfishness. To suggest that she has been humanized by her experience of the Revolution, which she says offered little to cheer her soul, is to read into her words something that is not there. Nor does she state that she concluded from the suffering of the French peasants that her own subjects should be treated better. If there is a lesson to be learned from the oppression of the peasants, the Countess—so her words clearly imply—already knew it before her trip to Paris. The Revolution, one might easily conclude, happened because the French monarchy failed to follow the wiser and more moderate course of reform pursued by German princes and their advisers, as Carl August and Goethe persuaded themselves.

The Countess is part of the myth of German princely benevolence cultivated by the Weimar regime. Aside from the Tutor's enthusiasm, the play says nothing about the French revolutionaries as people, and only negative things are said about their German fellow-travellers. A revolution in Germany is neither necessary nor justified—a conclusion that conforms closely to the opinion of the Weimar regime at the time. The abuses suffered by German peasants and the exclusion of the burghers from power are not sufficient grounds for political reform.

The spread of revolutionary ideas in Germany is represented by the barber Breme, a faux intellectual and braggart. His chief contribution to the progress of humanity will be the revolutionary book he is writing on the theory of barbering. His spurious claims to be a friend of humanity are further undermined by his greed. By way of a reward for leading the revolutionary uprising, he demands kickbacks from his corevolutionaries: the remission of his debt of two hundred thalers to the church, the gift of a parcel of land, and the marriage of his daughter to one of his fellow revolutionaries' sons.[213] Breme's ridiculous shallowness and hypocrisy represents Goethe's view that revolutionary agitation is merely a vehicle for self-interest. It shows how unable Goethe still was to take the Revolution seriously. However, he is careful to acknowledge that the peasants have real grievances. The Countess's wild and archconservative daughter Friedericke wants to hunt in the peasants' fields even before the crops have been brought in.[214] When she is told the peasants have just complaints about their oppression, she suggests shooting them.[215] However, it is not a straightforward matter of the aristocrats oppressing the peasants. The peasants' main grievance is the local aristocrats' illegal extension of the *corvée*. The grievance hangs on the existence of an ancient document setting out the peasants' rights and duties. The peasants are withholding their labour until the document is produced, and thus obstructing the Countess's laudable aim of improving the territory's roads. It turns out that during the war the Countess's corrupt administrator—not her advisor, but a man of altogether lower status and morals—stole the document and now hopes to exploit it for his own advantage, which further confirms the Countess's view that self-interest is endemic in human affairs. The corrupt administrator is Breme's equal in greed and selfishness and his counterpart on the side of the authorities. The main dramatic function of the administrator's crime, however, is to shift blame away from the ruling nobility. The peasants' main grievance is the fault of a corrupt bourgeois official, not of the aristocratic rulers or indeed of the system over which they preside.

The Countess and her adviser concoct a clever plan to regain the document, but as the Countess's daughter Friedericke rightly sees the plan will reward the administrator for his crime. Before the plan can be put into action, therefore, she threatens the administrator at gunpoint and forces a confession from him. Thus it is the archconservative, hunting-mad Friedericke who solves the play's main political problem and removes the peasants' grievance. She does so in an act of spontaneous, only half-conscious violence. So the play suggests that despite the arbitrary nature of aristocratic rule and the well-known moral variability of rulers from one generation to another, the aristocracy is capable of ruling the territory in the interests of all. Even with the capricious Friedericke in charge, there could be no reason for a revolution in Germany. Indeed it is precisely because the aristocratic system throws up such characters—noble individuals with an instinctive, barely enunciated sense of fairness, in whom, in other words, character is a more powerful force than ideas—that the aristocratic system of government is right for Germany.

In June 1792 Goethe returned to the house on the Frauenplan, and in return for Carl August purchasing the house for him, he agreed to accompany the Duke on the coalition campaign against France.[216] It was, Knebel drily noted, typical of Goethe's 'peculiar system of compliance' towards the Duke.[217] On 8 August Goethe set off disconsolately to join Carl August at the coalition base in eastern France. In Frankfurt he found his mother healthy and in good spirits.[218] In Mainz he was entertained by Professor Sömmerring. The political divisions among Sömmerring's guests made for awkward conversation, particularly with the republican Georg Forster.[219] On 27 August he reached the Prussian camp near Longwy, where he was greeted by heavy rain, a sea of mud churned up by the horses and wagons, and an army riddled with dysentery.[220] The Duke at least seemed to be enjoying himself. Perhaps, Goethe wrote with forced optimism to Voigt, Carl August would be able to reflect with pleasure for the rest of his life on his military exploits in France.[221]

The allies' optimism seemed justified. The French army had crumbled in the Austrian Netherlands in the spring, General Lafayette had defected and been replaced by the untried Dumouriez,[222] and Longwy and Verdun had fallen swiftly in August. News of the September massacres in Paris added to the impression that the Revolution was about to collapse.[223] By 19 September the armies had converged around Valmy: the French under Dumouriez and

Kellermann and the Prussians under the Duke of Brunswick. The sides were evenly matched numerically, but the French occupied easily defensible ground. Because of the tortuous route of their approach, the coalition forces were facing east with their backs to Paris, so that the French armies stood between the coalition forces and their main supply lines, though at the time this seemed unimportant, as a quick victory was expected. However, the battle proved totally inconclusive. The French lines held firm in their superior position against the repeated advances of the Prussian infantry, which failed to get close enough to make the allies' superior discipline count. Brunswick finally called off the assault around four o'clock in the afternoon.

Writing nearly thirty years later, Goethe claimed he had recognised the importance of Valmy at the time. On the evening after the battle, with Prussian officers gathered glumly round a campfire, Goethe (so he later wrote) had answered their requests for some consoling wisdom with these famous words: 'From here and now begins a new era of world history, and you can say that you were there'.[224] In all likelihood it was only during the week-long standoff following the battle that the truth dawned on the coalition forces. The cannonades of the French artillery had been highly effective, and the conscript army of the Revolution had shown far better discipline than expected. On 27 September Goethe wrote to Knebel of the growing realization that the French army was made of sterner stuff than they had first thought: 'I'm very glad that I've seen this all with my own eyes and that, whenever people speak of this important period, I'll be able to say: *et quorum pars minima fui* [and in these things I played some small part]'.[225] The comment to Knebel may have been a first draft of the later, more famous apophthegm about 'a new era of world history'. Or perhaps the story he told twenty years later was accurate. Either way, he did realize on the day or very soon after that he had witnessed history being made at Valmy.

With no prospect of a decisive victory and cut off from its main supply chains, the coalition army withdrew. Slogging through mud and rain, it reached Verdun by 10 October and Luxembourg five days later. In Verdun Goethe tried to minister to some of the sick troops.[226] From Luxembourg he wrote to his mother that 'no pen or tongue can describe the misery of the coalition army'.[227] Their slow progress meant that the Prussians found their retreat blocked by the French army of the Rhine under Custine, which had moved north from Worms to surround Mainz on 18 October and captured the city three days later. Being forced north to evade the French forces did, however, compensate Goethe with a visit to Jacobi—a great relief after the misery and humiliation of the campaign. During the retreat he worked on an allegorical fiction, titled *The Journey of the Sons of Megaprazon*, which portrayed the social and intellectual forces of the Revolution and counterrevolution in the form of a fantastical Rabelaisian travelogue. Quizzed by the Jacobis, he read some unfinished drafts to them. The surviving fragments outline several episodes in the sea journey of Megaprazon's seven bickering sons, who represent the fractured state of the German intelligentsia, politicised by the constant flow of sensational news from France. As with *The Great-Copt*, there is a tension between a desire for objectivity—in this case by using the distancing effect of allegory—and a compulsion to put across his own opinion with some clumsy satire. The reading did not go down at all well.[228] The project seems not to have survived this first encounter with an audience.

The aftermath of Valmy was a triumph for the French armies and a disaster for the coalition. Dumouriez allowed the Prussians to retreat into Germany, and then took his army north to overrun the Austrian Netherlands. The French army of the south invaded Savoy and captured Nice. The central army under Custine took the Rhine and Main cities of Speyer, Worms, Mainz, and Frankfurt in rapid succession. Thankfully for Goethe's mother, Frankfurt remained in French hands for only six weeks.[229] It was the first failure of the French attempts to 'liberate' the Germans. On 19 November the National Convention, which had been convoked in the summer to produce a new republican constitution, declared that it would support all foreign peoples that wished to 'recover their liberty'. However, the Frankfurt guilds informed Custine that they were happy with their traditional political and social order and wished to retain it. Three days later, when the Prussians arrived, the Frankfurt city guard vigorously attacked their French occupiers from the rear and opened the gates for their liberators. The French occupation of Mainz was altogether more tragic. Two weeks after the Prussians recaptured Frankfurt, the convention ordered its generals in occupied territories to introduce the full gamut of revolutionary policies by abolishing serfdom, seigneurial dues, tithes, and the nobility. When the news of Custine's northward march reached Mainz, most of its nobles, higher clergy, and grander burghers packed up and fled. On 22 October Custine entered the city to take up residence in the Elector's palace. So began the Mainz 'revolution' that rumbled on through the winter, spring, and summer. One of Custine's first acts on taking the city was to inform the guilds that citizens would have a free vote on their future.²³⁰ The promise of democracy was a sham. No meaningful opposition was tolerated.²³¹ Since the New Year Custine had set up seven new gallows, no doubt in order to give encouragement to the citizens.²³² The vote was limited to adult males who had shown their fitness by signing a formal oath of loyalty 'to the people and the principles of liberty and equality'. On election day, 24 February, most citizens stayed at home.²³³ To the people of Mainz the French were alien invaders, not liberators. The Revolution's anti-Catholicism was obnoxious to a solidly Catholic population for whom religious traditions were also a source of civic pride. The people of Mainz can hardly have been encouraged to welcome the Revolution by the execution of Louis XVI on 21 January, one month before the Mainz vote. In any case, the fate of the 'revolution' was sealed by the Prussian forces, which by the end of March had cut off any traffic between Mainz and France. The Mainz Jacobins and others suspected of revolutionary sympathies were now exposed to violence at the hands of the local population. A group of clubbist leaders caught escaping from the city were taken to Frankfurt. As they were led through the centre of the city, they were pelted with eggs and fruit, spat at, and insulted. Witnesses were appalled by the violence of the counter-revolutionary reprisals.²³⁴ A new question thus arose: how should the authorities deal with Germans who had not only agitated for revolutionary change, but actively collaborated with the French occupiers?²³⁵ Once Mainz was completely encircled on 14 April, the question became urgent.

At end of January 1793, immediately after the execution of Louis XVI, Goethe began work on another attempt to process the Revolution: a version of the part comical, part didactic medieval epic poem on the mischievous Reynard the Fox. It was his first successful attempt to make poetry of the Revolution. In his childhood Goethe had read Gottsched's prose retelling of the celebrated Low German *Reynke de Vos* of 1498, illustrated with prints by the Golden Age Dutch painter and printmaker Allaert van Everdingen. Traditionally the tale of the fox was accompanied by prose glosses drawing out the moral lessons of each episode. Goethe decided to do without the glosses and to replace Gottsched's moralizing Enlightenment manner with the objective narrative style of Homer, possibly inspired by a 1793 essay of Herder's which called the Low German *Reynke* 'the Ulysses of all Ulysseses'.²³⁶ To create the proper dignity of the Homeric style he composed his version in dactylic hexameters. In

February 1793 he bought Johann Heinrich Voß's translation of Virgil's *Georgics*, in which Voß expounded his purist views on the use of the hexameter in German. Goethe found Voß's prescriptions 'sibylline'.[237] Instead he aimed, as he wrote to Jacobi, for ease and naturalness.[238] Indeed, far from Homer's epic dignity, Goethe's hexameters have the lightness and irony of mock epic, which he reinforced by sprinkling the narrative with the kind of erotic innuendos he had enjoyed using in the 'erotica' and Venetian epigrams.[239] The mock-epic mode suits the utterly amoral antihero Reineke. The chaos he creates with his murdering, raping, thieving, and deceit expressed Goethe's growing despair about politics.[240] Reineke's bloodthirsty deeds are narrated with gruesome precision but also a lightness of touch that ironically conveys the commonplaceness of such bloody violence. At the opening of the first canto, when King Nobel the lion summons all his vassals to court, the narrator stresses that Reineke, the only absentee, has made enemies of all the others: 'everyone had accusations, he had abused all of them' ('Alle hatten zu klagen, er hatte sie alle beleidigt').[241] Reineke's deeds drive the narrative and his speeches form a large part of the poem, but he stands apart from the other animals—he is both an agent and an unveiler of corruption.[242] He succeeds in his trickery by exploiting and thus revealing the greed of the other animals, especially King Nobel's love of money, which Reineke excites by falsely claiming to have accumulated enormous treasure. Reineke is twice arraigned and sentenced for his crimes. Finally he survives by winning the right of single combat with Isegrim the wolf, a much stronger opponent, whom he defeats by first distracting him and then mauling his genitals: he 'grabbed his sensitive parts and pulled them, / Ripped him horribly, I'll say no more', says the narrator ('Bei den empfindlichsten Teilen ergriff er denselben und ruckte, / Zerrt' ihn grausam, ich sage nicht mehr').[243] Following his sly and vicious victory, Reineke is acclaimed by the other animals and appointed treasurer of the realm by King Nobel. The thief is put in charge of the realm's money, which seems fitting.

The eighth canto contains the poem's most overt comments on the Revolution. Reineke complains that King Nobel is unfairly persecuting him, for the King treats all property as his own, and anything else is stolen by the stronger animals, the bear and the wolf.[244] The distribution of wealth is inequitable; the strong get rich while the less strong are plundered. Goethe no doubt had in mind the unfair burden of taxation borne by the commoners under the *ancien regime*. Two passages invented by Goethe and not in Gottsched's version further illustrate the disorder of the realm.[245] Reineke claims that the animals—he means the head of each animal family—are driven by their desire to assert their power over other families. The result is chaos. In a well-ordered polity, each head animal would look after and keep in order his family, but people lack any kind of discipline:

> Es läßt sich ein jeder
> Alles zu und will mit Gewalt die andern bezwingen.
> Und so sinken wir tiefer und immer tiefer ins Arge.[246]

Everyone allows themselves / Everything and wants to dominate others by force. / And so we sink ever deeper and deeper into wrong-doing.

There is no prospect of social or political progress while the world is gripped by universal selfishness. The situation is not helped by the realm's spiritual leaders, who instead of exercising a moral and moderating influence over their flock, merely pursue their own greedy desires in public and so normalize hypocrisy.[247] Needless to say, Goethe did not mean his cynical analysis of society to give ammunition to the revolutionaries. The cynicism of *Reineke the Fox* is the same as that of the *Venetian Epigrams*, where he excoriated the triad of statesmen, clerics, and teachers of ethics under the French *ancien regime*. His intention was in no way to advocate revolution. What he meant was that there could be no return to the thievery, corruption, and hypocrisy of the *ancien regime* and to what the decidedly anti-revolutionary Edmund Burke termed 'that system of Court Intrigue miscalled a Government'.[248]

The sustained and painstaking work on *Reineke*, extending over three months, was a sign of the pleasure he took in it and the relief its distanced objectivity gave him from the constant talk of politics. By contrast the next piece he wrote, a short comedy *The Citizen General*, was a direct intervention in German politics and was written in the course of just three days in April.[249] The rapid composition was possible because the play's mode, setting, and characters were based on models Goethe knew well: two comedies by Christian Leberecht Heyne, the first of them a translation of a French original. Goethe had staged Heyne's plays several times during the previous two years. As for his new play's anti-revolutionary purpose, he would be pleased, he wrote to Bertuch from Marienborn, if *The Citizen General* 'served as a shibboleth to unmask foolish or malicious non-patriots in Germany'.[250] Writing in the *Campaign in France* nearly thirty years later, he claimed that he knew several 'noble spirits' who were infected by the revolutionary fervour. He probably meant Herder and Knebel.[251] And in a chronicle of the year 1794, also written later, he recalled that French revolutionary songs had been circulating and had reached him 'via persons one would not have suspected'.[252] The play addressed the question of what was to be done with Germans who sympathized with the Jacobin puppet government of Mainz, and how the situation should be managed in the best interests of the Duchy.[253]

The play is set in the rural idyll of the wealthy peasant Märten's farm. His daughter Röse has just married her sweetheart Görge. Tensions persist however. Märten is jealous of his son-in-law, and Märten's friend the local barber-cum-bonefixer Schnaps teasingly treats Röse as if she were still unmarried. Understandably Görge will not allow Schnaps in the house, an annoyance to Märten who depends on Schnaps for the latest political news. Schnaps will turn out to be an empty-headed fantasist, like Breme in *Agitated*. But he is not solely to blame. He and Märten are mutually dependent victims of revolutionary intoxication. Märten desires more information than he needs; Schnaps claims to have more information than he actually has. The tensions reach down into the heart of the household, for Märten overrides Görge's banning of Schnaps from the farm. It is thus unclear who is the head of the household, Görge or Märten. The Revolution has made the peasants unable to regulate their own households. This instability contrasts with the highly idealized rural setting of the play. The peasants live under the jurisdiction of their seigneur, a nameless nobleman, and it is he who provides the ultimate guarantee of social stability. The peasants are looking forward to seeing the seigneur married soon. His marriage is the final piece in the jigsaw of the social order. It will ensure continuity for the future, for this is a traditional dynastic territory in which the noble family provides both the actual grounds for political stability and a symbolic model for it: the seigneur is the symbolic 'father' of the peasants, and they are his 'children'. The stable foundation afforded by seigneurial society contrasts with the unstable and ephemeral world of politics that Märten and Schnaps would be part of, though in reality they cannot. In this way, the play embodies a central tenet of Goethe's emerging philosophy. Society is underpinned by the family, a timeless anthropological foundation deeper and more stable than whatever happen to be the politics of the day.[254] Beneath the superficial destabilization emanating from France, peasant life is shown to be contented and successful. Röse and Görge are happily married, and Märten, unusually for a German peasant, is rich.[255] There are no grounds for political change.

Schnaps claims the Jacobins in Paris are aware of his qualities and want to recruit him, and he shows Märten his liberty cap and 'uniform of freedom', which however is too tight for him—a symbolic indication that foreign ideas do not 'fit' the Germans.[256] At this point, the return of Görge from work in the fields sets off a chaotic chain of events in the farmhouse that ends with Röse's milkjug being broken and Schnaps being locked in the back room. Märten finally comes to his senses, though only out of panic at the thought of his family being tainted by association with Schnaps's Jacobinism. The village Judge arrives just as peace is about to be restored. He sees through the family's pretence that nothing has happened and finds the damning evidence of the liberty cap, but he overreacts, and it takes the arrival of the nobleman to finally restore order. Even in legal matters the seigneur has authority, and for good reason. When Schnaps is brought in wearing his ill-fitting uniform, the Judge overzealously speaks of torture and inquisition. Harsh punishment of Jacobins was of course one of the options open to the German authorities. However, patient questioning by the nobleman reveals that Schnaps acquired the uniform from a prisoner of war. If this is true, the nobleman reasons, Schnaps should be treated leniently and with a minimum of fuss: 'I know what I have to do. If this all turns out to be true, then a trivial matter of this kind must not be admonished; it will only arouse fear and mistrust in a peaceful land. We have nothing to fear. Children, love one another, cultivate your land, and keep house well.'[257] Like the guard captain in *The Great-Copt*, the nobleman follows a pragmatic policy of hushing up the revolutionary intoxication. His pragmatism is one of a broader set of policies. The time-honoured ways of life, grounded in family and the soil and governed by a paternalistic local nobility—and not, it should be noted, by the legally qualified Judge—are to continue unchanged. There are no real grievances behind Schnaps's revolutionary talk and therefore no grounds for reform. The revolutionary intoxication is a foreign import, and only faux intellectuals and fantasists take it seriously. The whole political situation is more farce than tragedy.

The humour of *The Citizen General* 'involves constructing a community of laughter to fend off the blandishments of change'.[258] The play also contains a rebuke. After seeing its second performance in Weimar, Caroline Herder wrote compliantly to Goethe: 'even if one *has* received a gentle slap on the wrist or two, the [play as a] whole was so beneficent and satisfying that one was pleased to receive them.'[259] The message understood by Caroline and presumably by her less emollient husband was that the regime would overlook their revolutionary sympathies, so long as they renounced them. Weimar would present a united front of peace, stability, and continuity. This was also the message for consumption by a wider German audience. If the Duchy presented a picture of stability and quiet, this was because any revolutionary intoxication was superficial and ephemeral, and the authorities were treating it with leniency.[260] The play is not least an exercise in conservative propaganda. It creates the pretence that the authorities in Weimar were acting just like the nobleman: gently, quietly, paternalistically. There is no evidence that Goethe wrote the play to order. Still, it is hard not to read the play in the context of the Duchy's public relations. In December 1792 Count Görtz, Weimar's and Prussia's ambassador to the Regensburg Imperial Diet, was directed to propose a ban on the sending of French newspapers by the Imperial post. His response to the Weimar Privy Council was to argue that a ban would be useless, as newspapers were easy to conceal. Instead he suggested that a writer in Weimar should produce counterrevolutionary propaganda. Schnauss reported Görtz's suggestion approvingly to Carl August. Goethe must have been aware that the idea was circulating. Even if *The Citizen General* was not prompted directly by Görtz's suggestion, it satisfied the Duchy's public relations needs perfectly,[261] and it seems likely that this was Goethe's intention. This may be why Goethe chose to have Unger publish it anonymously and as a stand-alone volume in June 1793, but not to include it in *Goethe's New Writings*.

On 12 May 1793 Goethe set off for the Prussian camp at Marienborn. It was a wrench to leave home again just eight months after Valmy. August had measles and Christiane was pregnant again. (A baby girl, Karolina, was born on 21 November but died after only two weeks.) In Frankfurt Goethe had a difficult conversation with his mother. For the first time he revealed to her the existence of Christiane and their three-year-old son. His mother cannot have reacted well, for although she sent a greeting and gifts to Weimar, Christiane's reply to her went unanswered. It took two years for Frau Goethe to reconcile herself to treating Christiane and August as part of the family.[262] On 27 May he reached the camp. At least the weather was much better than at Valmy, and the roomy tent that served as his quarters was comfortable enough. However, the relative comfort could not mitigate the madness of war: 'the chaos, confusion, inhumanity around us is too great', he wrote to Herder four days after reaching Marienborn. That night mayhem struck the Prussian camp when the French garrison launched a sortie that left around ninety Prussians killed or wounded, including two officers from Carl August's Weimar detachment. Goethe sent Herder a detailed account of the sortie.[263] Generally he kept himself to himself. Aside from invitations to the headquarters, he stayed in the tent correcting *Reineke*, making notes on optics,[264] and writing not altogether reassuring letters to Christiane and his friends. On a less serious note, he had a lucky escape on his way to Mainz, just avoiding a meeting with Lavater, who was now trying to ally himself with Kantian philosophy. In a letter to the Herders Goethe vented his scorn at Kant's latest essay, *Religion within the Bounds of Pure Reason*, which gave some succour to the peddlars of piety like Lavater: 'Kant, after spending a long lifetime cleansing his philosophical gown of numerous squalid prejudices, has sacrilegiously soiled it with the stain of radical evil, for that the Christians be enticed to kiss its hem'.[265] The uneasy standoff around Mainz ended on 18 June with the commencement of a brutal bombardment of the city. Goethe wrote to Christiane of his fear that the beautiful medieval city would be devastated: 'when I eventually tell you all about this you won't believe that such a thing could happen'.[266] It was a 'tragic spectacle', most of all for the unhappy burghers of Mainz who had fled the city and were now condemned to watch it burn. 'The situation of the Mainz emigrés is the most tragic in the world', he wrote to Voigt.[267] His own condition was comfortable. He and Carl August were promoted to superior lodgings in a house on the road to Alzey, after its previous occupant Prince Louis Ferdinand embarrassingly caught a bullet in his backside. Goethe ensured the house and the square it overlooked were kept tidy and presentable.

In the middle of July, with six thousand dead and one thousand wounded in the city, the French commanders had had enough. The terms of the capitulation were signed on 23 July, and the next day the French garrison filed out under Prussian protection. The military on both sides strove to maintain an air of orderliness. As the French General Dubayet passed through the camp at Marienborn he pronounced the words guaranteeing free passage three times: 'I count on the loyalty of the King of Prussia'. Carl August stepped forward and gave a reassurance that the column would be allowed to pass unmolested.[268] The fate of the collaborators was not so clear. The capitulation agreement contained a secret annex detailing their treatment. Any who so wished were to be given free passage to the French border under Prussian escort.[269] In addition, the main text of the agreement allowed free passage for French political operatives in their own wagons, which afforded German collaborators an opportunity to be smuggled out.[270] Those who surrendered to the Prussians were eventually treated with leniency. No collaborators were executed or given long prison sentences.[271] Initially, however, the Prussian military incarcerated many in miserable conditions and subjected them to starvation.[272] Some had already suffered reprisals during the occupation and siege, and once the French began to leave, the reprisals took on a new and horrific intensity. Goethe observed the operation of this lynch justice. 'The final days of the capitulation, the handover, the departure of the French have been among the most interesting of my life', he wrote to Jacobi on 27 July. Loyalist Mainz emigrants waited outside the city for the emerging collaborators, some of whom were torn away from the column and robbed and beaten, before being handed over to the Prussians. Other loyalists began to return secretly to the city: 'the people started to run through the city and overpower those who had remained behind'. Goethe evidently thought that the Prussians were intentionally turning a blind eye to the reprisals, and he approved: 'The policy of leaving the matter to chance and having the arrests done from below as it were seems good to me. The evil that these people have wrought is great. The fact that they have now been abandoned by the French is just the way of the world and may serve as a lesson to any rebellious people'.[273] It is noteworthy that in this private letter to Jacobi Goethe takes a quite different view from the official policy of leniency advocated in *The Citizen General*. The truth was that Goethe felt the Mainz loyalists had right on their side in punishing the revolutionaries.

The account of events Goethe wrote nearly thirty years later, *The Siege of Mainz*, acknowledges the justice of the reprisals but conceals this within a story that is closer to the official version and even creates a role for Goethe as the guarantor of the collaborators' safe passage. In a vivid passage he imagines himself at an upper window of Carl August's quarters, looking down on the departing column of French troops. At his side is Charles Gore, the father of Carl August's English mistress. A group of French infantry is passing below, accompanied by some young women of Mainz at whom a crowd of loyalist bystanders hurl abuse. Next a man on horseback draws the crowd's attention. There are shouts of 'Stop him! Kill him!' Some among the crowd identify the man as an architect who had allegedly plundered the cathedral chapter and set fire to it. The crowd is about to attack the architect when Goethe races downstairs and out into the square shouting 'Stop!' Having distracted the crowd, he tells them that 'these were the quarters of the Duke of Weimar, and the square was sacred':

> If they wanted to make a disturbance and wreak vengeance, then they should go elsewhere. The [Prussian] King had promised safe conduct to all the French, and if he had wanted to set conditions and except certain people from safe conduct, he would have stationed observers and either turned back or taken prisoner those who were guilty. [...] And they, the

people in the crowd, no matter who they were or how they got there, had no other role to play here in the midst of the German army than to remain peaceful spectators; their misfortune and their hatred [...] gave them no rights here, and once and for all I would allow no violence in this place.²⁷⁴

The lecture pacifies the crowd, and the architect is allowed to pass unharmed. On going back into the house, Goethe is upbraided for his audacity by Gore. A semi-humorous argument ensues. Goethe finally ends the debate with what he feels is a conclusive argument: 'I kept pointing out to him in jest the clean square in front of the house, and finally I said impatiently: "It is simply in my nature, I prefer to commit an injustice than to endure disorder"'.²⁷⁵

Goethe's intervention to save the architect and his half-humorous argument with Gore are in all likelihood fictions invented by Goethe when he wrote *The Siege of Mainz* almost thirty years later. There is no corroboration of the story either in Goethe's letters at the time or in the many surviving eyewitness accounts.²⁷⁶ It is hard to believe that such a visible intervention by the famous Goethe would have gone unnoticed and unrecorded, especially since he was known to be quartered in the building outside which the episode supposedly took place. But the accuracy of the narrative is one thing, its political meaning another. The anecdote articulates Goethe's political philosophy of the early 1790s—the same political philosophy that he dramatized in Friedericke's intervention at the end of *Agitated*. The anecdote in *The Siege of Mainz* acknowledges that the vengeful loyalists have some right on their side, ugly though their reprisals might be. So much is implied by Goethe's comment to Gore that in preventing the reprisals he was committing an injustice; *ergo*, to have allowed the reprisals would have been just. To that extent the anecdote echoes Goethe's private letter to Jacobi. So if the lynch justice of the mob has right on its side, why does Goethe stop it? The answer is not, as has often been claimed, that as a matter of political principle he preferred order to justice. The anecdote makes it clear that what is at stake is not orderliness in *principle*, but the orderliness of this particular space directly outside the Duke's quarters. He knows full well that disorderly reprisals are happening elsewhere; what is important is that they should not happen 'in this place'. Further, Goethe knew that the treatment of the collaborators in Mainz was a pressing political issue, and one with ramifications for the treatment of revolutionaries in Germany more generally. How is the problem of German revolutionaries solved by Goethe's answer to Gore? In his answer Goethe implies that his first duty is the maintenance of order in the public and very visible space before the Duke's quarters. Moreover, the jest about keeping the space in front of the Duke's quarters tidy is also symbolic. The space before the Duke's quarters stands for the Duke's public reputation as a gracious and gentle ruler, which Goethe is bound to burnish and protect. The anecdote thus reflects with striking honesty, once its nonliteral meaning is discerned, the reality of the Weimar government's reaction to the French Revolution. Officially, as the propaganda of *The Citizen General* has it, collaborators and fellow-travellers were being treated with leniency. Unofficially, however, repressive measures were applied or tolerated, insofar as they could be kept relatively quiet and would not threaten to spoil the Duke's reputation for humanity and Weimar's status as a beacon for intellectual liberality. The anecdote as a whole expresses this uneasy tension between public leniency and covert repression.

On a still more general level, it articulates one of Goethe's core political beliefs, as did the archconservative Friedericke's spontaneous intervention at the close of *Agitated*. Goethe's answer to Gore is that he intervened because it is in his nature to do so: '"It is simply in my nature, I prefer to commit an injustice than to endure disorder"'. This is in reply to Gore bemusedly asking 'what bug' has bitten Goethe to make him behave so rashly. Gore's question and Goethe's answer are designed to show that Goethe acted on impulse, as did Friedericke when threatening the administrator in *Agitated*. In racing down to the street and plunging into the angry crowd, he acted spontaneously and instinctively. His lecture to the bystanders was a piece of improvisatory theatre. The whole episode is a display of his spontaneous genius. In the 1790s he decided that genius, whether it be his own poetic creativity or the scientific aperçus behind his refutation of Newton or the political action of Friedericke in *Agitated*, sprang from unconscious sources. It was a psychological and naturalistic alternative to rationalistic understandings of the self—for instance, Kant's notions of the 'transcendental unity of apperception' that lay behind all of our knowledge, or the 'good will' that grounded our morality.

The comparison with Kant is pertinent because Kant's ethics were part of the philosophical landscape in which German protoconservatives formulated their opposition to the Revolution. An example is the Hanoverian philosopher and statesman August Wilhelm Rehberg (1757–1836). As a matter of pure philosophy, Rehberg agreed with Kant that morality could only be justified by pure reason. As a practical matter though, Rehberg believed that pure reason was too remote from us to provide any usable principles.[277] Kant's Categorical Imperative—'act only according to that maxim through which you can at the same time will that it should become a general law'[278]—was based on the idea that in order to have true moral worth, the maxim of an action (that is to say, the principle that justified it) must not be in contradiction with itself. For instance, one could not claim moral value for one's actions if while advocating the law one was at the same time making oneself exempt from the law. Rehberg's objection was that Kant had only demonstrated that morality consisted in noncontradictoriness: Kant had only told us what moral truth was *not*, not what it was.[279] Therefore, Kant's moral theory had no purchase on politics.[280] Faced with the failure of ethical reason to justify politics, Rehberg reverted to historical precedent and tradition, like Edmund Burke and other protoconservative thinkers. Goethe shared Rehberg's dislike of rationally based politics. Like Rehberg, he was happy to concur with Kant's view that morality was justified by pure reason.[281] But like Rehberg, he thought that Kant's rational justification of morality yielded no practical results. However, he differed from Rehberg in the sense that his opposition to Kantian morality involved a deeper scepticism about reason than Rehberg's—a scepticism that derived from his naturalism about mental states. Since his adolescence in Frankfurt he had considered reason to be a subjective matter. Reason only ever expressed the interests of humans in particular social situations. It was the view he expressed in his Strasbourg dissertation and the unfinished Mohammed drama. The divinity had no universal legislative force because it was always compromised by political reality; religions were first and foremost political movements. Goethe's conservative reaction to revolutionary politics in 1792–1793 was indeed an extension of his long-held views on religion. For Goethe, political principles were not pure, disembodied ideas of reason any more than religions were pure expressions of faith in the divinity. They could only ever manifest themselves in the compromised, conflict-ridden space of politics. Goethe's opposition to political ideals is therefore also different from the view articulated by Isaiah Berlin in his essay 'My Intellectual Path'—that the ultimate political ideals, while worthy, were liable to be in conflict with one another. Berlin's liberal view was that the ideals of 'liberty and equality, spontaneity and security, happiness and knowledge, mercy and justice' were not only empirically incompatible, but also conceptually so, and therefore 'the very idea of the perfect world in which all good things are realised is incomprehensible, is in fact conceptually incoherent'.[282] Goethe's argument is more conservative than Berlin's. He believed that political ideals only ever expressed the social and personal interests of their advocates. As he put it in one of the *Venetian Epigrams*: 'All the apostles of freedom, I could never abide them, / For each sought only license for himself'.[283] The rational discourse of freedom was rational in name only; it only ever expressed one person's desire to pursue his own interests at the cost of another's. Which moral or political principles should have priority within this conflict-ridden reality? Reason itself was incapable of providing an answer, because in practice reason was *normally* in conflict with itself, just as political actors and parties were.

The episodes in *Agitated* and *The Siege of Mainz* represent what happens when political rationality confronts reality. In *Agitated*, the Countess's and her adviser's plan to reclaim the vital documents involves rewarding the administrator for his misdeeds. Thus the peasants' rights (and with them the social and political order) can be restored, but only at the cost of unfairly rewarding the administrator for his crime. Rights are in conflict with justice. In *The Siege of Mainz*, the just desires of the loyalists are in conflict with a general sense of lawfulness. The architect can be handed over to the mob, in which case justice will be served at the expense of general lawfulness. Alternatively, the architect can be spared, in which case lawfulness will be preserved at the expense of justice. How are we to resolve these conflicts of principle? Goethe's answer is that, since political ideas are never accessible in anything like their pure, rational form, reason is powerless and only our spontaneous resources of good character can cut the Gordian knot of political conflict.

After publishing the second of the *Essays on Optics* in May 1792, Goethe must have realized that a mere phenomenology of colour would not suffice. If his work was to stand a chance of displacing Newton's, it would have to be a comprehensive theory of colour, including a full reckoning with Newton. At first, in summer 1792, he intended to add a third volume to the *Essays*. This would treat the intriguing phenomenon of coloured shadows, which had the potential to undermine Newton's theory of diverse refrangibility. When coloured lights (green, red, and blue) are placed side by side and equidistant from a white surface, the additive effect of the lights will produce a white reflection. If a thin object such as a pencil is placed between the lights and the surface, seven types of shadow appear—blue, red, green, black, cyan, magenta, and yellow. The problem for Newton's theory is that our perception of the coloured shadows cannot be explained simply in terms of the radiation emanating from each of the shadowed areas. For instance, if the blue light is blocked and only the green and red lights illuminate the surface, the surface will be perceived as yellow, not because the radiation is in the yellow spectrum, but because, as is now known, a mixture of red and green light stimulates the cones in the human retina to the same degree as yellow light, so that the eye can only perceive yellow. The best Goethe could do was to infer that the effects were explained by the different strengths of the lights. Thus, when two lights of different intensities are introduced to a darkened room and a shadow is cast, the stronger light will cause a yellowish shadow to be cast by the weaker light, and the weaker light will cause a shallower, broader blue shadow to be cast by the stronger light. In this way he sustained his underlying belief that colours arose from light being modified, not from being split—they were effects that 'happened to light' but were 'not derived from light' itself, as he wrote in the camp at Marienborn in July 1793.[284]

In 1791 Sömmerring had advised him that progress with his studies required an 'exact analysis of the power of vision',[285] and in summer 1794 he would finally follow the advice. When considering coloured shadows in 1793, he had not yet thought much about the physiology of the eye. As well as receiving valuable support from Sömmerring, in August 1793 he succeeded at last in interesting the physicist Lichtenberg in his work, though only briefly. He sent Lichtenberg the third, unpublished part of the *Essays on Optics*, which included his discussion of coloured shadows. Two months later Lichtenberg sent Goethe a long critical reply, in which he explained how difficult it was to isolate objective from subjective colours. The implication was that Goethe's theory of coloured shadows might amount to a confusion of objective with subjective phenomena. Towards the end of his letter Lichtenberg pointed to the phenomenon of contrastively coloured afterimages:

> It is, for example, certain that if one looks through a red glass for a long time and then suddenly removes it, then for an instant the objects appear greenish; if on the other hand one looks through a green glass, then they initially appear reddish. This is connected to Buffon's *couleurs accidentelles* that are observed in the eyes.[286]

If the afterimages were accidental properties of light, and not light in its essential quality, might this not also be true of the coloured shadows and even the boundary colours that were the empirical basis of Goethe's theory? In his reply to Lichtenberg, Goethe insisted that there were regularities in the accidental colours.[287] However, this still begged the question where the dividing line was to be drawn between subjective and objective optical phenomena.[288] So the theory of coloured shadows turned out to be a stumbling block, and Goethe soon abandoned the third part of the *Essays*. Unsure how to proceed, he drafted several essays during the next two years, some intended to summarize his theory, some outlining further experiments, others treating discrete aspects of optics such as its history. The drafts included his first attempt to write the history of colour theory and thereby 'to discover the moral-political causes of the dominance of this or that theory', since it was evidently not by virtue of any empirical warrant that Newton's theory had achieved its ascendancy. Indeed, that it had remained ascendant for so long was surprising, given its evident flaws.

In the most substantial draft, planned during the siege of Mainz and written later that year, he attempted for the first time a systematic analysis of the errors in Newton's theory of differential refrangibility. First there was the question whether observation or hypothesis had priority in the process of investigation. On the face of it, Newton followed Francis Bacon's principle that we should take account of all the possibilities and begin by eliminating the untenable ones, rather than rushing to a positive conclusion or, as Newton put it, constructing hypotheses. Up to this point, Goethe should have welcomed Newton's cautious method. However, the explanations Newton rejected did not in fact address the main issue, namely Newton's claim that the spectral colours must result from the splitting of white light since the spectral image appears in the form of an elongated oblong, not in the form of a sphere as was predicted by pre-Newtonian theories of refraction. A second problem, to which Goethe attributed great importance, was the manufacture of the first achromatic lenses by John Dollond in 1757. Newton had maintained that all lenses must generate spectral colours, which was consistent with his view that colours were produced by differential refraction through lenses. Dollond had shown empirically that this was not the case by manufacturing lenses that showed no chromatic aberrations. Again Goethe could justly accuse Newton of following his own desire to rush to a hypothesis—'the arbitrariness of his own mind'—instead of observing the phenomena 'on the free path of nature',[289] as Goethe put it, once more implying that his own method was more liberal than Newton's. There were strong grounds for a more robust and detailed scrutiny of Newton's method than anyone had hitherto undertaken. There were also grounds for Goethe's view that the dominance of the Newtonian orthodoxy was to be explained by factors that were not strictly scientific in nature. Yet the task of forming these insights into a fully worked out theory was beyond him.

7

Church Militant

WEIMAR, 1794–1805

IN JULY 1794 Goethe wrote to Meyer that some of his Weimar friends were 'behaving in a manner bordering on madness'.[1] In September he wrote to Caroline Herder, in what may have been a warning to her husband, that 'sadly the spirit of the age is having an ill effect on friendship'.[2] In July and August a trip to Dessau, Leipzig, and Dresden with the art historian Meyer provided relief from the 'quarrels that are now confusing the world'.[3] On his return he learned that his mother, fearing another French invasion, had packed up her things and sent them away from Frankfurt.[4] He feared that he might be forced to emigrate.[5] In April 1795 Prussia and France concluded the Peace of Basle. France withdrew its troops from the east bank of the Rhine, but in a secret annex to the treaty Prussia recognised French control of the west bank, which meant that tensions between France and the German lands were bound to continue. In any case, Britain and Austria were still at war with France. Basle was a false dawn. War continued to threaten the German lands for the next twenty years, as did revolutionary ideals. Although the new French Convention retreated to a less liberal constitution, the ideals of liberty, equality, and fraternity were still destabilizing the German states.

Even during the height of the Terror, the Weimar government had continued its finely balanced policy of tolerating known supporters of the Revolution among the Jena professoriate and binding them into near silence, if not active conformity with the Duchy's conservative politics. After the Kantian Professor Reinhold left Jena at Easter 1794, there was pressure to appoint a high-profile successor who could continue the teaching of the new philosophy. The choice, which Goethe later called reckless,[6] was Johann Gottlieb Fichte, a much-lauded young Kantian. In 1793 Fichte had published the anonymous first instalment of his *Contribution to the Rectification of Popular Opinions Concerning the French Revolution*. Alongside a deeply unpleasant strain of anti-Semitism, Fichte defended the principles of the Revolution, if not its realization in practice. His authorship of the essay became public knowledge immediately. Voigt certainly knew, which means that Goethe did too. The authorities must have assumed Fichte could be persuaded to moderate his views, like Herder, Hufeland, and Schmid. Indeed, Fichte gave Hufeland a commitment to that effect. Nonetheless caution dictated that he be monitored, and Goethe was charged with doing so.[7] His behaviour soon gave cause for concern. He was reported to have claimed in a lecture that in twenty to thirty years' time there would be no more princes or kings[8] though he denied doing so. Goethe met Fichte to impress upon him the need for discretion, and he duly fell into line for a time.

Aside from burnishing Jena's credentials as a leading school of philosophy, Goethe hoped that Fichte might provide a new stimulus to his scientific work. Fichte's new project, the *Theory of Science*, certainly promised as much. On receiving proofs of an outline of the *Theory*, Goethe replied with polite irony that Fichte would 'do humanity an invaluable service by giving a scholarly foundation to what nature has silently long agreed upon'. He hoped that Fichte might reconcile him 'with the philosophers, whom I cannot do without and with whom I can never agree'.[9] He would be disappointed. Fichte's starting point seemed promising. In the *Critique of Judgement* Kant had argued that the free moral self and our intelligence that apprehends the world cannot be reconciled, unless we 'look beyond the sensible [realm] and seek the unifying point of all our faculties *a priori* in the supersensible'.[10] Fichte agreed that the ground of the self could not be found 'in consciousness qua an empirical state [...]. The absolute subject, the I, is not given by empirical intuition'. Still, we can deduce the ground of the self: 'it is [...] posited by intellectual intuition'.[11] Fichte termed this act of positing the self a 'deed-action' ('Tathandlung') in order to distinguish it from the facts ('Tatsachen') of consciousness. For the 'deed-action' to become conscious, it needed a trigger or check to its activity.[12] From this trigger derive the objects of empirical consciousness. During the process of acquiring knowledge I abstract from it, until my reason presents to me a consciousness of my absolute freedom; I come to realize that I am not determined by anything but myself.[13]

Goethe committed himself to following Fichte's philosophy, but did so 'with difficulty and from a distance'.[14] In spring 1795, after consultations with Fichte, he resorted to asking Jacobi for help in refuting him.[15] In the meantime

Fichte's position at Jena was becoming uncomfortable. Although his lectures were popular, he had become a target for student rancour. In February and April students threw stones through his and other professors' windows. When Fichte complained to the authorities in Weimar, Goethe wrote gleefully to Voigt: 'So you have seen the absolute *I* in great dismay, and indeed it is most discourteous of the non-*Is*, whom one has posited, to fly through his windows. He is suffering the same fate as the creator and preserver of all things whose trouble with his creations, as the theologians tell us, never ends'.[16]

The summer of 1794 brought Goethe real support in his scientific studies from two young Prussian aristocrats, the brothers Wilhelm and Alexander von Humboldt. Their enthusiasm and knowledge more than made up for Goethe's disappointment with Fichte. The younger brother Alexander had trained in mineralogy with Werner at Freiberg though he was more interested in the natural history of fungi and lichens than in mining. In his mycological studies, published in 1793, he moved beyond descriptive natural history and envisaged a universal geography of plants that would show in what conditions each species grew. It was the first step in a massively ambitious project that would eventually take him on a five-year journey through South and Central America. In December Goethe made a special outing to meet the brothers in Jena. Alexander was moved by the 'boundlessly' warm welcome Goethe gave him.[17] Later Goethe would write to Carl August that Alexander was 'a veritable cornucopia of the sciences. His company is exceptionally interesting and educative. One would struggle to learn from books in a week what he puts forth in one hour'.[18] Alexander's interest in ecology complemented Goethe's theory of species transformation: his belief that the plant world was 'a vast sea which is as necessary to the existence of individual insects as the oceans and rivers are to the existence of individual fish, and [...] that an enormous number of living creatures are born and nourished in this ocean of plants'.[19] Goethe's vision of nature as an interconnected web was an inspiration for the younger Humboldt. Humboldt has been credited with originating the modern notion of ecology. In South America he became deeply troubled by human destruction of the natural environment. The vision and the conceptual tools for his understanding of the environment came in part from Goethe,[20] and it may be that they already discussed these ideas in the mid-1790s. In an epigram of 1798, Goethe formulated what is now a central principle of ecological thought. The natural environment must be understood as a whole consisting of mutually dependent parts. This is why human intervention in the environment, for instance to destroy pests, is likely to do more harm than good. Instead we should leave nature to regulate itself:

> "Sprich, wie werd' ich die Sperlinge los?" so sagte der Gärtner:
>   "Und die Raupen dazu, ferner das Käfergeschlecht
> Maulwurf, Erdfloh, Wespe, die Würmer, das Teufelsgezüchte?"—
>   Laß sie nur Alle, so frißt Einer den Anderen auf.[21]

> "Tell me, how do I get rid of the sparrows?" said the gardener, / "And the caterpillars as well, also the beetles' entire kind, / Moles, flea beetles, wasps, the worms, that work of the devil?" / Leave them all alone, then each will eat up the other.

More generally, the friendship with Humboldt marked the beginning of a school or tradition of Goethean science. In turn, Goethe recognised with remarkable prescience how much Humboldt would contribute to natural history, writing to Unger in 1797: 'What he can do in the future for the natural sciences is incalculable'.[22]

After the burst of theorizing on mammal osteology in the early 1790s, Goethe spent the middle years of the decade on empirical work. He experimented with growing plants under glass of different colours. The effects on growth rates were measured, and the resulting variations in the plants' colour noted.[23] There was a strong correlation between exposure to sunlight and green pigmentation though Goethe had no understanding of the chemistry of chlorophyll, which was first isolated in 1817. In summer 1796 a massive population of magpie moths gave him the opportunity to study the emergence of moths from their pupae. He was amazed that in just twelve minutes the newly emerged moths' wings grew by half an inch in length and the same proportionally in width: 'the most beautiful phenomenon I know in organic nature (which is saying a lot)'. Glued to his microscope he observed, measured, dissected, and subjected the pupae to various environmental conditions. The phenomenon was a challenge to the standard models of organic growth. The conclusion he reached about the rapid growth of the wings was correct:

> It is obvious that one cannot imagine this growth as if the solid parts of the wings grew so much in such a short time, rather I think of the wings, all completely composed of the finest *tela cellulosa* [cellular thread], now being expanded at such great speed by the influx of some elastic fluid or other,

whether of an airy, vaporous, or damp nature. I'm convinced one will be able to observe something similar in the development of plants.[24]

In autumn 1796 he studied the internal organs of frogs, confident he would be able to 'work right through this new field of organic nature' during the winter months.[25] From October to December he devoted his spare time to anatomical studies of fish and birds.[26]

The letter about moth wings was written to the playwright Friedrich Schiller, a new and unexpected sounding board for Goethe's thoughts about natural history. Schiller shared Goethe's liking for Rousseau, though he belonged to a more liberal tradition of Rousseau reception, and he was much less interested in science. During a visit to Weimar in 1787 he wrote to his friend and benefactor Körner:

> Goethe's spirit has shaped all the people who are numbered among his circle. A haughty philosophical disdain for all speculation and investigation, an attachment to nature and a retreat into the five senses that's taken to the point of affectation, in short a certain childish naivety of reasoning characterizes him and his whole sect here. They prefer to look for plants or do mineralogy than get lost in empty demonstrations. The idea can be very healthy and good, but one can also overdo it.[27]

In Schiller's sometimes envious imagination, admiration for Goethe's skills as a writer competed with resentment at the Privy Counsellor's Olympian hauteur.[28] For several years Schiller studied him from a distance, first from Leipzig, then from Jena following his election to a chair in history in 1789. Goethe had supported Schiller's appointment—another talented but politically radical young writer and intellectual. But Schiller's appointment was completed before the Revolution, and his earlier radicalism seems not to have been held against him. It was only during the Terror that the authorities decided Schiller should be monitored.[29] By then Schiller had grown more tolerant of the old regime in Germany, in common with many German intellectuals. In 1794 his politics were closer to Goethe's than they had been five years earlier. History had brought them together in other ways. Since publishing *Don Carlos* in 1787, Schiller had written nothing for the stage. Goethe finally published *Egmont* in 1788 and *Tasso* in 1790, both conceived many years earlier. Since then

Germany's two greatest living playwrights had stopped writing the serious large-scale dramas that promised to create a national culture. Instead, both had turned towards aesthetic theory, in part out of disenchantment with the reading and theatre-going public's seeming preference for sentimental content above literary merit. While Carl August's patronage allowed Goethe to ignore the literary scene, Schiller's finances were parlous. Since 1791 he had also lived off patronage that came to an end in 1794. That spring he concluded a contract with the Stuttgart house of Cotta to edit a new literary journal *The Horae*, named after the Greek goddesses Eunomia (good government), Dike (justice), and Irene (peace). As he wrote in an advertisement for the journal, these were the forces of 'world-sustaining order, from which all good things flow and which have their aptest symbol in the even rhythm of the course of the sun'.[30] The appeal to a well-ordered natural and political cosmos marked a turn away from the Revolution.

The story of the beginnings of their friendship is preserved in a short reminiscence Goethe wrote in 1817 titled 'Fortunate [or happy] Occurrence'. In this account Goethe highlighted a conversation between them on 20 July 1794. There are no exactly contemporary records of the conversation, but it almost certainly did occur, and letters between Goethe and Schiller one month later tend to corroborate the 1817 account. The conversation supposedly turned on the central question of Kantian philosophy: the relation between subject and object. Following a botanical lecture by Professor Batsch at Jena's Society for Research into Nature, Schiller and Goethe find themselves leaving the hall together. They agree that Batsch's 'piecemeal' manner of presenting botany robs nature of its coherence. By way of contrast to Batsch's method, Goethe explains his theory of plant metamorphosis, complete with the *Urpflanze*. Schiller's lapidary response is damning: 'that isn't an experience, it's an idea'. In this way, according to Goethe's account, Schiller has identified the crux of the subject-object dilemma 'with ultimate rigour' and shown that Goethe has failed to solve it.[31] Worse still, he has cast Goethe in the role of an idealizing subject, much to his annoyance. At this tipping point in the conversation, the most likely outcome is that the two men part as antagonists, with Schiller having made a standard antirealist critique of natural science, and Goethe being reminded of an 'old resentment' against Schiller and his like—he had apparently read Schiller's essay *On Grace and Dignity* (1793) with distaste. However, Goethe composes himself and offers a gently self-mocking riposte: 'I'm happy that I have ideas without even knowing it, and can even see them with my own eyes'.[32] The riposte solves nothing, of course; it is merely a holding position. It reaffirms Goethe's image of himself as an intuitive observer of nature and an instinctive thinker, while merely parking the question of how ideas relate to experience. But by parking the question Goethe allows the conversation to continue, in the course of which they can agree where the bone of contention lies and express the hope of conciliation: 'If [Schiller] considered to be an idea what I expressed as an experience, still between the two some mediating or connecting element must prevail!' Goethe's account now moves swiftly to the moment at which he and Schiller agree to collaborate. The subject matter has shifted from philosophy and botany to aesthetics and culture, and specifically *The Horae*, to which Schiller has invited Goethe to contribute. The whole course of the argument is summarized thus: 'in this way, by means of that greatest of all contests, between object and subject (a contest perhaps never to be decided), we put the seal on an alliance that endured uninterrupted and had many good results for us and others'.[33]

Goethe published 'Fortunate Occurrence' alongside his writings on morphology from the 1790s. This may explain why botany looms so large in the narrative. Schiller presented a quite different picture of the conversation, superficially at least, in a letter to Körner of 1 September 1794. His letter reports conversations about art and art theory that he had had with Goethe six weeks earlier, in other words around 20 July; there is no mention of philosophy or botany. Schiller does stress that they reached agreement 'by completely different routes', which confirms Goethe's account of their antagonistic premises:

> Between these ideas there appeared an unexpected agreement, which was all the more interesting, as it genuinely emerged from a complete difference of perspectives. Each was able to give the other something he lacked, and to receive something in return.[34]

Their complementarity is also the theme of a long letter from Schiller to Goethe of 23 August, ten days before his letter to Körner. The letter is a masterful combination of analysis and empathy, couched in the finely balanced rhetoric in which Schiller was a virtuoso. It was something of a risk, as Schiller undertook to hold up a mirror to Goethe's whole intellectual and poetic character, and to do so in a determinedly abstract and philosophical manner, which he must have known Goethe might dislike. The risk was justified by the letter's two momentous aims. In June Schiller had invited Goethe to contribute to *The Horae* both as a writer and editor.[35] Ten days later Goethe accepted enthusiastically.[36] No doubt the conversations on 20 July were mainly concerned with establishing the common ground on which they would build their collaboration, and the main subject matter must have been art and art theory, just as Schiller told Körner on 1 September. Any further discussion was cut short by a hastily arranged trip Goethe had to make to Dessau and Saxony. Schiller's letter of 23 August had the task of picking up the conversation where it had left off a month earlier. A more delicate task was to confirm Goethe's place in the engine room of the new journal. Schiller was aware of the need to respect Goethe's standing as Germany's preeminent writer. On the other hand, as chief editor of the journal Schiller knew he must position himself as Goethe's intellectual equal. The framework Schiller chose for this risky gambit was the idea that their 'unexpected agreement' had 'emerged from a complete difference of perspectives', as he put it to Körner. To make the gambit work, Schiller had to show how the results of Goethe's scientific intuition—the *Urpflanze*—were actually in conformity with Kantian idealism or Schiller's version of it. Indeed, Schiller wanted to show that as a Kantian (of sorts) he could make the journey to Goethe's *Urpflanze* from a starting point in theoretical reflection about the purposiveness of organisms, as Kant had outlined in the *Critique of Judgement*. In other words Schiller would demonstrate that the *Urpflanze*, and with it Goethe's whole intellectual project, could be validated not only by Goethe's empirical observations but also by the speculations of Kantians like himself. By showing how the truth could be arrived at from these two opposed directions, Schiller gave an elegant demonstration of his and Goethe's complementarity. To add to the risks of the undertaking, he needed to celebrate Goethe's intuitive empiricism while explaining why Goethe neither had nor needed any awareness of the conformity of his thought processes to Kantian idealism. Goethe was to be lauded for not knowing the claims of reason. At the same time Schiller would show that Goethe's ignorance of reason was balanced by a complementary deficit on reason's side. This is why Schiller's letter portrays the process of Kantian analysis as haunted by elegiac sadness. The philosophers' analytical method involves dissecting things, and all analysis is laborious and uncreative. Only intuitive geniuses like Goethe can truly create:

> In your correct intuition is found everything (and far more completely) that analysis laboriously seeks, and it is only because this exists as a totality within you that your own wealth is concealed from you: for, sad to say, we only know that which we take apart. Therefore minds like yours seldom know how far they have penetrated, and how little cause they have to borrow from philosophy, which can only learn from them. The latter can only dissect what is given to it, but the giving itself is not the job of the analytical thinker, but of the genius which under the obscure but secure influence of pure reason connects things according to objective laws.[37]

Goethe's *Urpflanze* is congruent with Kant's philosophy without his knowing it. Indeed, his ability to create synthetic concepts like the *Urpflanze* depends on this very ignorance of philosophy. In portraying Goethe as possessing an unconscious genius from which Schiller increasingly felt himself excluded, Schiller has been accused of wishful thinking and of overlooking Goethe's engagements with the philosophy of Kant and Fichte.[38] The accusation underestimates Schiller's intelligence and tact. For one thing, Schiller succeeded in doing exactly what Fichte had failed to do: he made Goethe believe that natural science, as Goethe practised it, might engage with the new philosophy in productive ways. (It can only have worked to Schiller's advantage that the conversation of 20 July occurred one month after a bemused Goethe received the drafts of Fichte's *Theory of Science*.) Moreover, it is unlikely Schiller would have styled Goethe as an unconscious genius, if he had not known it would appeal to Goethe. Certainly it conforms to Goethe's riposte on 20 July as reported in 'Fortunate Occurrence'—'I'm happy that I have ideas without even knowing it'.[39] It is possible that Goethe did formulate the riposte in these or similar words on 20 July, and that Schiller expanded Goethe's words in writing the letter of 23 August. It is also possible that their discussions of art and art theory on or after 20 July touched on the notion that artistic creativity was in some part an unconscious process. In October Goethe spoke to Dorothea Veit in precisely these terms:

> When I make a poem, I must reveal it only once it's finished, otherwise people will knock me off course, and such is the case in all art. [...] Genius seems to me to be like an adding machine; the wheels are turned and the result is correct; the machine doesn't know why? or how?[40]

Subsequently Schiller and Goethe would repeatedly claim that artistic creativity was at root unconscious: 'all creativity is the work of nature' and not reflection.[41] Before the alliance with Schiller, Goethe was already using the idea of unconscious creativity in a variety of ways—for instance Friedericke's spontaneous intervention at the close of *Agitated*, which succeeds where political reason cannot. In 'Fortunate Occurrence' Goethe framed his and Schiller's argument about the *Urpflanze* in terms that resemble both Schiller's letter of 23 August and the spontaneity of Friedericke: the dilemma of experience and ideas may perhaps 'never be decided' by philosophy; if some point of congruence does exist, its nature is mysterious. Schiller's picture of Goethe's naivety does the same, but within a Kantian framework.

Schiller had spent the previous three years attempting to define the mysterious point of congruence, an endeavour that eventually brought him to the complementarity theory in 1793 or 1794. During 1793 he drafted a series of letters to his benefactor Prince Friedrich Christian von Schleswig-Holstein-Augustenburg. The letters set out his views on the power and responsibilities of art in a modern polity. After the letters were destroyed in a fire, Schiller redrafted and expanded them, now with more explicit reference to Kant's theory of the rational will and to the Robespierrist argument that human nature could be purified and reformed through political terror. Schiller believed the Robespierrist argument was circular: human selfishness is to be reformed by politics, but how can it do so when politics is already vitiated by human selfishness? By contrast, Schiller believed that only once a purely rational state was constituted could human reason prevail. As things stood, however, our political arrangements were the product of necessity, in the sense that they were designed in an ad hoc way to satisfy the human need for physical and emotional security, as a bulwark against the dreaded Hobbesian *bellum omnium contra omnes* ('war of all against all'). In order to create the state of reason, we would have to dismantle the state of necessity. The French Revolution showed how precarious such a transition was, for by Schiller's Kantian definition the freedom of the rational will cannot appear in a world ruled by necessity. In order to effect the move with confidence from the existing state of necessity to the ideal state of reason, we would need to be given some kind of visible warrant of rational freedom that could guide us in the phenomenal realm. Schiller's diagnosis of the Revolution is therefore informed by what he and Fichte viewed as Kant's failure: the acknowledgement in the *Critique of Judgement* that our moral will and our intelligence that apprehends the world cannot be reconciled, unless we 'look beyond the sensible [realm] and seek the unifying point of all our faculties *a priori* in the supersensible'.[42] Schiller's and Fichte's projects were based on the same understanding of Kant and shared a common objective: to show that there is a point of congruence between moral reason and intelligible experience that we can actually know. The main body of the Augustenburg letters is concerned with finding that point of congruence. We need not follow all the stages of Schiller's somewhat convoluted argument. The point on which it turns is that human culture does in fact contain an analogue of Kant's distinction between intelligible experience and moral reason. It is an analogue that has been lying in plain view, for our whole cultural history displays it. All culture is at root a form of play, and all play comprises two elements: the materials or content we work with (Kant's content of experience) and the rules or forms within which we contain them (an analogue of Kantian moral reason). The greatest works of art display a perfect harmony of form and content, in which each element asserts itself without diminishing the other, so that each is, as it were, free. Thus art is the point of congruence for which we have been searching. It is the warrant in the sensuous world of the unity of our rationality in the supersensible world. In this way, the finished version of the letters grounds Schiller's theory of aesthetics in the complementarity theory. Form and content are complementary opposites, each representing an antagonistic drive within humans. In reconciling the antagonism, art can be the school for human nature. The title Schiller finally decided on was *On the Aesthetic Education of Man*.

Art is the answer to chaotic Robespierrism. Art can purify human nature and make us fit to build the state of reason. Since the opening letters offer aesthetic education as a solution to a political problem, one finding of Schiller's argument might have been that aesthetic education should be the work of politically minded artists, and some passages in the *Aesthetic Education* do suggest such a role for the poet, perhaps as the kind of politically and socially aware playwright that Schiller had once been and might once more become, albeit in a less radical guise. However, the ending of the *Aesthetic Education* avoids this conclusion and suggests instead that the 'aesthetic state' or 'state of aesthetic semblance', if it exists at all, is only distantly connected to political and social reality:

> But does such a state of aesthetic semblance really exist? And if so, where is it to be found? As a need, it exists in every finely attuned soul; as a realized fact, we are likely to find it, like the pure church and the pure republic, only in some few chosen circles, where conduct is governed, not by some soulless imitation of the manners and morals of others, but by the aesthetic nature we have made our own; where men make their way, with undismayed simplicity and tranquil innocence, through even the most involved and complex situations, free alike of the compulsion to infringe the freedom of others in order to assert their own, as of the necessity to shed their dignity in order to manifest grace.[43]

We should not expect art to give us clear answers to the day's political questions. Cotta had wanted Schiller to edit a journal of European politics, but Schiller felt alienated from politics, and his advertisement for *The Horae* laid a strict injunction of silence concerning 'the favourite theme of the day'. Instead *The Horae* would 'create a narrow, intimate circle for the Muses and Graces':[44] a space in which art could be discussed for its own sake and on its own terms, undisturbed by news from France and its fevered reception in Germany.

On 27 August Goethe replied to Schiller promising his full and uninhibited collaboration.[45] The next day he wrote to Fritz von Stein of the relief that *The Horae* promised 'at a time when miserable politics and disastrous, vacuous partisanship threatens to end all friendly relations and destroy all scholarly connections'.[46] On 30 August he sent Schiller an essay he had written at some point in the previous year or two, 'To What Extent Can the Idea that Beauty is Perfection with Freedom be Applied to Organic Beings'. It may have been a response to Schiller's essay *On Grace and Dignity*, and certainly it picks up the Kantian themes that had motivated Schiller's essays on aesthetics. Goethe probably sent Schiller the essay because it had emerged in their conversations that they had both travelled the same path of trying to refute Kant's claim that, with some limited exceptions, aesthetic judgements are subjective and to discover an objective criterion of beauty that involved freedom. Goethe's essay argues that the more an animal species's body parts are *coordinated with* one another (as opposed to *subordinated to* one another), the more beautiful the species will seem to us. Nothing came of the essay, but its themes—in particular the notion that humans were the most perfect species by virtue of their higher degree of freedom—would reemerge in his aesthetic and scientific thinking in 1798 and after.

His first new composition for *The Horae*, titled *Conversations of German Emigrés*, was a series of six stories set in a frame, in the manner of Boccaccio's *Decameron*. The stories were adapted from stories by others.[47] Despite this, they are knitted together effectively, both by their shared themes and tone and by the political and aesthetic discussions that make up the surrounding frame. The storytellers in the frame are sheltering from the French armies in 1793. Unlike Boccaccio's characters sheltering from a plague, Goethe's are deeply affected by the events around them.[48] As an extended family of German aristocrats, they own properties in French-occupied lands either side of the Rhine. The allies have driven the French back over the Rhine and encircled Mainz, allowing the family to return to its smaller property on the east bank. The head of the family is the widowed Baroness von C.—capable, broadly educated, intellectually acute, and usually able to maintain her volatile family's good humour.[49] Aside from the Baroness, the strongest characters are her 'lively, vehement, imperious' daughter Luise, who bears a strong resemblance to Friedericke in *Agitated*, and their revolutionary cousin Karl. They receive a visit from their still homeless west-bank relatives, the Privy Councillor von S.

and his family. He is a principled man, a lover of 'consistent behaviour', but independent-minded in some matters.[50] Having experienced at first hand the 'arbitrariness' and 'spirit of oppression' of the French and participated in the Valmy campaign, he has become gloomy and prone to passionate outbursts.[51] The Privy Councillor is a fictional other self of Goethe, one who has let the revolutionary temper of the times wear him down, in a way Goethe understood. During the Privy Councillor's visit the siege of Mainz begins, and the political arguments in the house become heated. The Privy Councillor argues that the Mainz revolutionaries should be punished and left at the mercy of the city loyalists or, as his antagonism with Karl escalates, that they should be hanged. Karl, not wanting to be outdone in bloodthirstiness, paints a picture of the guillotine cutting a swathe through Germany. Finally, Karl insults the Privy Councillor, who leaves in a rage. The Baroness tries to restore calm by proposing to the remaining members of the family that they may talk about politics in private, but in company must try to retain their 'social cultivation' and 'good tone'.[52] A companion of Karl, a wise old Catholic cleric, proposes that they tell one another stories. The stage is thus set for a process of aesthetic education. Storytelling will cure them of the ill effects of politics and restore them to polite sociability.

All six stories hinge on intimate relationships, actual or prospective. The characters resist or are frustrated in what they desire or what might seem to be in their interests. In none of them is there a direct route from an intention to a moral goal. It might appear that in the fifth and sixth stories the practice of renunciation provides a shortcut to moral and social harmony. In the fifth story, a busy merchant sets off on a journey leaving his young wife with the instruction that she should find a lover; she falls in love with a young lawyer who urges her to join him in renunciation for one month before they become lovers, and through this practice of renunciation she discovers her moral self. In the sixth, a young man, Ferdinand, steals money from his father in order to impress a young woman, until he finds out he has an aptitude for business; because he reforms just in time, he is forgiven when the theft is discovered. A discussion between the old cleric, Luise, and the Baroness interrupts the story of the young wife and the lawyer. The cleric makes the startling claim that there is only one moral story, and it is this: a story that demonstrates our power to overcome our desires. Luise objects that we might in fact be motivated by our desires to overcome our desires; we might be naturally inclined towards self-denial. If we can be inclined towards self-denial, if narratives can show how such natural inclinations lead to self-denial, then there may be an infinite number of moral tales, just as there can be an infinite number of natural inclinations. The debate has now landed in the realm of moral philosophy. In formulating the debate Goethe was responding to an argument in Kant's *Groundwork for the Metaphysics of Morals* (1785). Kant confronted a ubiquitous argument of eighteenth-century ethics: because all moral actions can be construed as being motivated by personal interests, there is no such thing as a *purely* moral act. When I give to charity, I am not only obeying a moral imperative to help the less fortunate; I am also acting in my self-interest by reinforcing an image of myself as a benevolent person. My charitable donation makes me feel or look better. Kant acknowledges that an act motivated by such self-satisfying urges would indeed not be truly moral: it might be done *in accordance with* moral duty, but not *out of* moral duty, and only the latter counts as truly moral. What empirical evidence is there that pure morality is achievable? Kant admits there is none.[53] Luise's understanding of the stories is aligned with this conclusion. The acts of renunciation by the young wife, the procurator, and Ferdinand are *in accordance with* moral duty, but not *out of* moral duty, and yet they still lead to morally good outcomes. Indeed, in any narrative that leads to self-denial or renunciation, self-interest always helps to bring the outcome about. Consensual as ever, the Baroness concludes the debate by acknowledging the equipollence of Luise's and the cleric's arguments: 'It is true, a heart that tends to the good is, when we become aware of it, bound to delight us; but there is nothing in the world more beautiful than inclination guided by reason and conscience'.[54] No doubt Goethe also had in mind Schiller's letter of 23 August with its subtle and powerful bid to establish the two of them as complementary opposites working at a common endeavour.

The Baroness's diplomacy is effective, but it does not answer the questions raised by the stories. The stories are not balanced in the way the Baroness proposes, nor is any such balance desirable in narrative fiction. The stories are in fact formed of a manifold of psychological causes and effects. The route to self-denial via the shortcut of Kant's ethics may be signalled, but it is not taken. If it were, the stories would vanish and be replaced by the cleric's ethical formula: 'man has in himself the power to act against his inclination from the power of what is right'.[55] The cleric admits as much: 'This is not the only moral tale I can tell; but they all resemble one another so closely that one always seems to be telling the same one'.[56] But the stories only 'seem' to be the same if we insist on reducing them to the formula. In fact, poets have a more complex and earthbound task. Their concern is with human psychology—'empirical psychology, where we poets are in actual fact at home', as Goethe would put it to Schiller in 1801.[57] Moreover, the narrative imagination is not confined to a binary choice between psychological causes and decisions of reason. In the first two stories, most of the narrative is concerned with the actions of seemingly supernatural poltergeists, and in the intervening discussion there is much talk of possible explanations for the seemingly supernatural effects and their very plausibility. Much of this discussion is accompanied by evasions. So at the end of the first story, Luise's elder brother Friedrich claims he has an explanation for the mysterious events, but when pressed he refuses to divulge it, and instead launches into the next story.[58] The search for the truth is postponed by more storytelling; the intellect gives way to the imagination. At the end of the fourth story, Friedrich begins to tell the company about a lucky talisman that has been passed down the male line of his family. When quizzed, he says he has already revealed too much.[59] Again rational explanation is subordinated to the rights of the imagination. Indeed, by asserting the rights of the imagination, we can *purposely* forestall the claims of the intellect, and this is indeed what happened when the old cleric proposed storytelling as a way to heal the family's political divisions.

In August 1795 Goethe decided that he would use the final sections of the *Conversations* to take this dichotomy of imagination and intellect to an extreme conclusion. He told Schiller he would end the *Conversations* with a fairy tale, 'a product of the imagination' which would 'issue out into infinity',[60] in other words the imagination would permanently forestall reason. The fairy tale is introduced in a discussion following the final story. Karl, the advocate of revolutionary liberty, declares a liking for fairy tales, the products of a liberated imagination. In reply, the cleric promises the family a fairy tale which, he tells them, 'will remind you of nothing and of everything'.[61] Indeed, nothing in the 'Fairy Tale' (so its title) is real. It takes place in a symbolic landscape populated by fantastical figures: three will-o'-the-wisps; four kings made of different metals; a beautiful princess whose name identifies her as a lily; a sad and ghostly prince who has lost the symbols of his sovereignty; a threatening giant whose shadow is however stronger than its body; an old man dressed as a farmer with a lamp that turns ordinary substances into precious ones; and a gold-eating snake that metamorphoses into a bridge in a final act of self-sacrifice. We are told the symbolic meaning of some of the figures: the gold, silver, and bronze kings are said to represent sovereign wisdom, charisma, and power respectively. They are the three elements of government. Most of the figures lack such definition, though they are still plainly symbolic. In part the symbolism derives from the actions they perform. They undertake tasks involving movement, utterance and ritual, often governed by strict rules—crossing the river, paying dues, and fetching and ferrying symbolic items. The actions are accompanied by momentous transformations of shape, size, colour, substance, and so forth. So on the other hand, 'everything is symbolic', as Schiller put it, and 'one cannot resist seeking meaning in everything'.[62] In this sense, the 'Fairy Tale' does indeed 'issue out into infinity'—an infinity of meanings that reason cannot determine.

The symbolic nature of the 'Fairy Tale' means that any interpretation will be tentative. However, the three kings indicate that the tale's interpretation must involve politics. The purpose of the symbolism of the 'Fairy Tale' is to express politics in a manner that is not overtly political. In this sense, the 'Fairy Tale' conforms to the programme of Schiller's *Aesthetic Education*. The creative imagination thrives on freedom. It cannot be tied to specific political issues of the day, and yet the 'Fairy Tale' is thoroughly political. It is Goethe's first and best developed statement of how a modern state should be constituted in the light of the Revolution. At the end of the tale, the gold, silver, and bronze kings pass on their attributes to the prince, signifying his readiness for kingship. The fourth king, though made of a bizarre alloy of metals and destroyed before the tale ends, has asked one of the tale's key questions: 'who shall rule the world?'[63] Among the tale's possible meanings then, must be an answer to the questions raised by the French Revolution.[64] It begins in a world suffering collapse and threatened by great peril, with its inhabitants scattered and incapacitated. It ends in a utopian manner, with its inhabitants reunited and their powers revived, its material substance reconstructed and beautified, and its political and social order restored. The first feature of the world we encounter is the 'great river, which was newly swollen with heavy rain and overflowing'.[65] The river represents the quickening course of historical events that threaten to overwhelm society. It gives rise to the practical problem that it can only be crossed in certain highly constrained circumstances. It is guarded by the threatening giant, whose shadow can however serve as a bridge, though only at dawn and dusk. The giant thus embodies fear and hope—the two contrasting responses to the Revolution. The combination of opposites is typical of the tale's symbolism, which continually represents the duality of the historical moment. The world's collapse contains the potential for its restoration. The river separates two domains. On one side is the princess Lily's park. Her name connects her to the French crown through its symbol the fleur-de-lis. Her touch is cursed and blessed: it kills living beings and brings the dead back to life. This is her peril, but the farmer with the lamp reassures her that she should think of 'the greatest misfortune as the greatest good fortune, for the time is at hand'.[66] The ominous statement 'the time is at hand' is both a refrain and a magical formula: once the farmer has spoken it three times, the final suite of transformations begins. The key transformation is performed by the snake, which metamorphoses into a bridge that permanently reunites the two halves of the world. This enables the prince to claim his tokens of majesty from the three kings. The princess can be united in love with the prince. The city is miraculously rebuilt, and though the giant briefly threatens it by causing chaos on the bridge, its time has passed. The prince wants to fight the giant, then shows self-restraint in pondering whether to confront him with symbolic objects (sceptre, lamp, oar) rather than his sword, but the farmer states that even this is unnecessary, and moments later the giant is transformed spontaneously into a massive column that serves the city as a sundial. Peace returns; the prince, princess, and their retinue can enter the palace. There is one further moment of chaos when the people threaten to tear one another to pieces over gold coins scattered by the departing will-o'-the-wisps, but it is a momentary aberration, and order is soon restored. The monarchy has been reestablished; the temple is now the most visited in the world. The city has a grand new plaza and bridge. The people go about their daily business in comfort and security.

The central symbol of the 'Fairy Tale' is the new bridge. In the first place, it is a means of safely crossing the river, instead of the constrained and dangerous options that existed before: a ferryman's shaky boat that could only carry passengers in one direction, the giant's ominous shadow. The new bridge thus overcomes the danger of the overflowing river (the Revolution). More generally, the bridge simply enables movement, which is perhaps the most obvious structural feature of the 'Fairy Tale' as a whole. In practical terms, the bridge brings harmony; it brings people together, brings unity to the lands. Indeed it makes the lands into nations, as the farmer points out: 'these neighboring banks have been brought to life as nations and united'.[67] Hence the new bridge is a key ingredient in modern nation-building. For the people who use it, the bridge boosts the economy and serves as a pleasant amenity, with covered colonnades for pedestrians either side of the central roadway. It is a marvel of design and construction, immense and fantastical. The central roadway has room for wagons and livestock to travel in both directions. The covered colonnades on each side accommodate many thousands of pedestrians. It forms part of the renovated city's urban planning, for the bridge connects with the similarly colonnaded plaza in front of the restored temple. The elements of the new city are strongly reminiscent of Palladian urban design. The temple is a rotunda topped with a dome: more classical temple than Christian church. The bridge is based on descriptions of a design by Palladio himself.[68] But for all its imposing materiality, the bridge is as much spiritual as physical. It is a memorial to the snake's act of self-sacrifice and its love for the other figures in the tale, especially the princess of whom the snake was particularly fond. The bridge thus embodies the highest value of the tale: love.

The sociopolitical argument of the 'Fairy Tale' is clear enough. Brown is surely right to conclude that it describes how to curb and channel the disruptive energies of the Revolution and restore the monarchy.[69] A key question posed by the narrative is who shall perform the processes of transformation, curbing, and channelling. How is an ideal polity constituted? According to Schiller, Goethe stated that the 'Fairy Tale' represents the need for '"the mutual assistance of powers and their reliance on one another"'.[70] The tale shows how a variety of agents with diverse and complementary capabilities cooperate. The farmer formulates a similar idea twice: 'no one can help on their own, but only when one joins with many others at the right time'[71] and 'we are met at a fortunate hour. Everyone perform your office, everyone do your duty, and communal good fortune will assuage individual griefs just as communal misfortune destroys individual joys'.[72] It is the first time Goethe formulated his vision of a successful state that relies on the collaboration of individuals with diverse and complementary abilities. It would become a favourite motif in his political thought. In 1796 he included it in the closing book of the *Wilhelm Meister* novel, in the somewhat less optimistic words of the Abbé: 'All men make up mankind and all forces together make up the world. These are often in conflict with each other, and while trying to destroy each other they are held together and reproduced by Nature'.[73] Although the Abbé seems less hopeful than the farmer in the 'Fairy Tale', the underlying idea is the same. Society is akin to an organism, in which a collection of diverse parts, each with different capabilities or functions, contributes to the functioning of the whole. The constituent elements of a polity will have powers of varying kind and degree. Inequality is an essential feature. The fact that the unequal parts work together, even if they are often in conflict—and it should be remembered that the world of the 'Fairy Tale' was close to disintegrating—is due to the force of circumstance: either the logic of rule-bound behaviour in the 'Fairy Tale' or 'nature' in the words of the Abbé. This rule-bound, natural force causes society to remain cohesive and reproduce itself, despite the conflicts within it. Behind this vision of conflict-ridden but cohesive society lies Goethe's idea of the natural environment as a web of mutually dependent species.

In the 'Fairy Tale', the figures all contribute to the utopian transformation, but their contributions are of unequal value. The populus is largely passive, a product of transformation, not a driver of it. The farmer with the magic lamp is exclusively active. He is the tale's supreme agent and the originator of the words 'the time is at hand'. Exactly what the old farmer represents is unclear. His age suggests the old regime or perhaps tradition. His lamp that transforms the ordinary into the precious suggests art or the imagination. As a farmer he is associated with natural processes. He acts as advisor to the prince. The relation between the monarchy and the people is strikingly traditional. In their final transformation, the prince, princess, and their entourage enjoy a kind of apotheosis, lit by a heavenly light that amazes the people. Having thus awed and dazzled, they disappear into hidden halls that lead to the palace. There is no suggestion that the people will have access to the palace; there will certainly be none of the popular storming of the royal palaces at Versailles in October 1789 or the Tuileries in August 1792. As Goethe put it in an epigram in 1795:

> Willst du frei seyn mein Sohn! So lerne was rechtes, und halte
>   Dich genügsam, und sieh niemals nach oben hinauf.
>
> Do you want to be free, my son? Then learn something proper, and exercise / Restraint, and don't ever look upwards.[74]

Nothing is said about how the monarchy will make laws or exercise power. The constitutional reforms of the Revolution's early years play no part in the 'Fairy Tale'. An insight into how the monarchy might exercise its power is given by the last of the inset stories and the discussion that follows it. The story ends with the reformed Ferdinand becoming a father and bringing up his children. In order not to lose the capacity for self-denial, occasionally he foregoes a pleasure. He imposes the same rule on his children, for instance, by arbitrarily denying one of them a favourite food, and they accept this without complaint. The Baroness approves of Ferdinand's practice and draws an analogy with the state:

> [She] confessed that on the whole friend Ferdinand was probably right, for in a kingdom too everything depended on the executive power; the legislative could be as rational as it liked, it would avail the state nothing if the executive were not powerful.[75]

Goethe's fixed political belief since his law dissertation was that a state needed a powerful executive above all else. The question of the executive's legitimacy was secondary, for legitimacy derived not from popular consent or any other form of constitutionality, but from power and its effective exercise. The 'Fairy Tale' confirms this unequal relation between executive, law, and people. The monarchy is arrayed in the symbols of wisdom, charisma, and power, while its subjects' role is confined to commerce, travel, and worship. The people are the engine of the economy. Their activity fills the bridge with wagons and livestock. Yet they are an unindividuated mass whose pursuit of commerce is motivated by base avarice and a lack of self-restraint. When the departing will-o'-the-wisps shower them with gold, the people become violent and incapable of self-control, in contrast to the prince's self-restraint in not attacking the giant:

> Greedily the people continued to run about for a while, jostling and tearing at one another, even when the gold coins stopped falling. At last they gradually dispersed, set out on their journeys, and to this day the bridge teems with travellers, and the temple is the most frequented in the entire world.[76]

They are clearly not capable of self-government.

———

Goethe set out the reasons for his opposition to democracy in a pair of Horatian epistles that appeared in the first two volumes of *The Horae*. The first is concerned with the massive growth of the literary market. Everyone is now reading and writing, resulting in a constantly shifting literary scene that lacks any objective and enduring aesthetic values. In the absence of aesthetic objectivity, people are driven by self-regard:

> Reden schwanken so leicht herüber hinüber, wenn viele
> Sprechen und jeder nur sich im eigenen Worte, sogar auch
> Nur sich selbst im Worte vernimmt, das der andere sagte.
> Mit den Büchern ist es nicht anders.

> Talk fluctuates so readily, back and forth, when many / Are speaking and everyone hears himself in his own words, and even / Only [hears] himself in the words that another spoke. / It's no different with books.[77]

The underlying problem is self-love: wanting one's own opinions to be confirmed and those of one's antagonist refuted or ignored. The argument's Rousseauian tenor is confirmed by the extreme, anti-modernizing conclusion Goethe draws. To restore stability, the literary world needs to shrink. The right to write needs to be restricted. The seemingly unfinished second epistle makes this point, using young women as the example. What begins with praise of young women for their domestic work ends as diatribe against the expansion of the literary world. The argument is obviously sexist, but it has as much to do with social class as gender. The young women stand for 'the mass' of people and how they ought to behave.[78] The population at large should work and not read or write. The patriarch of such a 'kingdom'—Goethe means the family patriarch surrounded by his busy daughters but also metaphorically the state—will be surrounded by industrious workers who will not need books.[79]

The antidemocratic politics of the two epistles make clear why Goethe responded in the way he did to an article by Daniel Jenisch, a Berlin theologian and lecturer on French language and literature. Jenisch had argued that only a mature political culture can create classic works of literature. France enjoys maturity; Germany does not. Even the Terror would not stop French writers producing classic works. It may be that Jenisch's reference to the Terror raised political suspicions in Goethe.[80] But that alone does not explain why Goethe titled his critical response 'Literary Sansculottism' or why its tenor is so much more political than Jenisch's original essay. The point of the provocative title was to imply that Jenisch had levelled down any distinctions of literary quality in the same way as the sansculottes wanted to abolish social distinctions. Jenisch had underrated the achievements of German authors. Goethe singles out Wieland as an example of an author deserving more respect than Jenisch was willing to give. The lack of literary judgement is bad enough, but behind it lies a worse error: a confusion of political partisanship with aesthetic judgement. Jenisch seems to have political reasons for preferring French literature to German. Although parts of the essay are confrontational, Goethe agrees with some of Jenisch's analysis. The problems of German literature *are* sociopolitical in nature. In the absence of a unified political nation, there can be little hope of a unified literary nation. However, in Goethe's view the sort of social and political changes that would foster a classic German literature are politically undesirable:

> And yet the German nation should not be blamed if its geographical situation binds it closely together whilst its political situation fragments it. We do not want the kind of upheavals that could prepare the way for classical works in Germany.[81]

Goethe must have known that some German Jacobins viewed German particularism as an obstacle to political revolution.[82] Goethe now agreed: one of the reasons why particularism was worth saving was that it impeded revolution.

After the first volumes of *The Horae* appeared in early 1795, Schiller and Goethe grew increasingly convinced that they were fighting a battle with the reading public on multiple fronts. At Easter 1795 Cotta reported from the Leipzig book fair on negative reactions to Schiller's *Aesthetic Education*, which appeared in the first two volumes of *The Horae* (*Die Horen*).[83] Some readers were perplexed by Goethe's *Conversations*.[84] Further problems soon emerged. There were accusations of plagiarism against articles by Schiller's protégé Woltmann and Herder—the latter, most damagingly, by the classicist Friedrich August Wolf. There was also a moral scandal. In autumn 1794, Goethe read the *Roman Elegies* to a delighted Schiller. With some of the more delicate content removed, in particular the autobiographical elements that identified Goethe as their author, the *Roman Elegies* were published in *The Horae* in the middle of 1795. Outrage inevitably ensued. According to Böttiger, Herder proposed changing the name of Schiller's journal from *The Horae* (*Die Horen*) to *The Whores* ('die Huren').[85] Moralistic reactions to the *Elegies* would become a major factor in Goethe's attitude to the reading public in the following years. The tipping point was reached in November 1795, with the publication of translations of Plato's dialogues by Fritz Stolberg, including a preface that tried to recruit Plato for Christianity, and a negative review of the *Aesthetic Education* by the Kantian philosopher Friedrich August Mackensen. In late October, on hearing of Mackensen's review, Goethe proposed holding an annual review of the responses to *The Horae*: 'when such things are tied up in bundles, they burn better'.[86] Schiller agreed: 'We're living in the age of vendetta. It is a veritable church militant [*ecclesia militans*], I mean *The Horae*'.[87] Goethe was more energized by Stolberg's distasteful recruiting of Plato for Christianity[88] than by Mackensen's narrow Kantianism. He knew that Schiller would share his distaste, because Stolberg had published a negative commentary on Schiller's poem 'The Gods of Greece' in 1788. The German literary world seemed ill disposed to their aesthetic project and the pagan humanism at its heart. Goethe repeated his proposal: they should issue a forthright statement of their opposition to the 'half measures' ('Halbheit') of the German reviewers, critics, and journal editors, to be published regularly in a foreword or afterword of *The Horae*. As he would write in a review in 1804: 'Intolerance always expresses itself through action and effect, and it can only be countered through intolerant action and effect'.[89]

In December the proposal began to take shape, albeit in an unexpected way. Instead of a review of reviews, Goethe and Schiller hit upon the idea of writing a series of polemical epigrams, in the playful manner of Martial's *Xenia*. Each distich would target one of their antagonists, not only those like Mackensen who had criticised *The Horae*, but a much wider cast of characters. Some, like Stolberg, were old enemies. Others were representatives of cultural and intellectual tendencies Goethe and Schiller disliked. It would be a broad offensive against the conditions that made a disinterested appreciation of art impossible in Germany. The plan was to write several hundred epigrams and edit these down to a collection of around one hundred. Work began in earnest in January 1796, and the final selection was made that summer. It was decided that Schiller's annual *Almanac of the Muses for the Year 1797*, published in October 1796, would be a more suitable vehicle for them than *The Horae*. The effect of the *Xenia*, foreseen by Schiller, was to antagonize large sections of the literary world—and to sell well. Going through three editions, a total of more than three thousand copies, the 1797 *Almanac of the Muses* was the most popular such almanac in the eighteenth century.[90] And by a satisfying irony, also foreseen by Goethe and Schiller, in buying the *Almanac* in such large numbers the Germans were buying poetry that attacked them for not buying poetry:

> *An die Xenien*
> 'Deutschland fragt nach Gedichten nicht viel!' ihr kleinen Gesellen
>   Lärmt bis jeglicher sich wundernd ans Fenster begibt.
>
> *To the Xenia*
> 'There's not much demand for poems in Germany!' You little companions, / Make a racket until everyone goes to the window in surprise.[91]

As a publishing phenomenon, the *Xenia* bucked the trend away from poetry and towards the 'goddess of the marketplace, clear prose.'[92] Clear prose has the advantage of conveying clear meaning, but the desire for clear meaning devalues beauty:

> *Die Bedeutung*
> Was bedeutet dein Werk? So fragt ihr den Künstler, den Dichter,
>   Freunde fragt ihr mich so, so kennt ihr das Schöne noch nicht.
>
> *Meaning*
> What does your work mean? If you ask this of the artist, the poet, / Or ask it of me, you don't yet know what beauty is.[93]

The content of art becomes its sole purpose; its form becomes irrelevant.[94] The desire for clear meanings reduces reading to a banal exercise in extracting useful or congenial messages, which generally means moral content. The state of German literature—its miserable 'half measures'—is attributable to this preoccupation with morality. Beneath this preoccupation lies a deeper sociocultural pathology: the dominance of mind over body. The point is made in an epigram titled 'The moral faculty':

> *Die moralische Kraft*
> Kannst du nicht schön empfinden, dir bleibt doch vernünftig zu wollen,
>   Und als ein Geist zu tun, was du als Mensch nicht vermagst.[95]
>
> *The moral faculty*
> If you can't sense beautifully, you can always will rationally, / And thus do as a mind, what you're incapable of doing as a human being.

Morality diminishes the body and turns us into insubstantial parodies of true humanity. It was the argument at the heart of the *Roman Elegies*. True art is always embodied. Aesthetic education is education of the mind *and* the body. The pathological condition of modern humanity consists in our lacking sensuous refinement.

The special role of the human body in art is the theme of a provocative piece of satire Goethe wrote during the *Xenia* campaign—so provocative that he waited until 1808 to publish it. In February 1796 he promised Schiller some passages from the journal of his Swiss tour with Carl August in 1779, but then changed his mind, as the journal now struck him as overly subjective. Instead he wrote a fictional narrative which would frame and explain the journal's subjectivity—a 'passionate fairy tale', as he put it to Schiller.[96] The framing narrative takes the form of a set of letters written during a Swiss tour by Werther. Goethe evidently felt that *Werther* was a symptom of the sickness afflicting German culture: the tendency to prefer sympathetic content above the rigours of form. Thus the 'Letters from Switzerland' would serve as an explanatory prequel to both the 1779 journal and *The Sorrows of Young Werther*, killing two subjective birds with one objective stone. The *Letters* represent Werther before his descent into suicidal self-absorption, and accordingly Werther's writing in the *Letters* is measured and sober in comparison to the novel. The main body of Werther's narrative is merely a prelude to the final few pages, which clinch the argument about subjectivity. Werther acknowledges that his development as an artist is hampered by his lack of appreciation for the naked human body, the sight of which in a portrait of Danaë leaves him 'in a listless state'.[97] By way of a remedy, he first has his friend Ferdinand bathe naked in a lake and then arranges for a young woman, 'a Venus', to strip naked in front of him.[98] He seems unaware that in fact he has engaged the services of a prostitute, and because of this naivety, what should be the climactic section is in fact an anticlimax. His imagination does become enflamed as the girl performs her striptease.⁹⁹ Stunned by the 'eery' effect this has on him, he is speechless:

> She stood, as Minerva might have stood before Paris, modestly she climbed onto the bed, in her naked state she tried to find sleep in various postures, finally she seemed to be asleep. She stayed a while in the most delightful pose, I could only gape in wonder. Finally a passionate dream seemed to disturb her, she sighed deeply, vigorously changed her posture, mumbled the name of a lover, and seemed to stretch her arms out towards him. 'Come', she finally called in a distinct voice, 'come into my arms, my friend, or I'll really go to sleep'.¹⁰⁰

Faced with the reality of female nudity, Werther invents a more modest version of what he is doing. Before engaging the woman, he said he wanted a Venus—the only female figure in Greek art that is routinely portrayed naked—but now he imagines her as a chaste Minerva. Incapable of sensuality, his imagination prevents him from seeing the reality: the woman is awake and is asking him to join her in bed. His sexual failure is at the same time a failure to be fully human, and it points forward to Werther's emotional problems in *The Sorrows of Young Werther*. Behind Werther's failure lies the modern tendency to denigrate the body.

By 1794, all but one of the major works begun in the 1770s and '80s were published. Only the *Meister* novel resisted his repeated attempts to complete it. He tried in 1788, 1791, and in March and December 1793. Finally in May 1794 he submitted himself to the discipline of a contract with Unger in Berlin, who would encourage and cajole him over the next two years,¹⁰¹ so that the novel's four instalments were published in time for the biannual book fairs. On agreeing the contract, Goethe recruited Herder to advise on the revision of the novel. It was an unfortunate choice. Herder had no stomach for Wilhelm's sexual relationship with Mariane, which Goethe made more prominent in the revised version of Book I. The story of Wilhelm's childhood would now be told not by the narrator but by Wilhelm himself, to Mariane as she lay in his arms. With Herder's involvement ending nearly as soon as it had begun, the new friendship with Schiller was opportune. Schiller would not let prudishness get in the way of his remarkably acute literary judgement. In autumn 1794, his role in the *Meister* revisions was formalized. Goethe asked him to read each book of the novel in manuscript and make suggestions as to how the narrative should unfold. Goethe would then make use of Schiller's 'anticipatory criticism' in writing the next book.[102] Book by book the manuscript was posted to Schiller and received a prompt and penetrating response. Further discussions took place during Goethe's frequent visits to Jena.

The effect of having Wilhelm narrate his childhood was to put some distance between his subjective experiences and desires and the now more objective narrator. Goethe wanted to steer the novel away from the autobiographical 'pseudo-confession' of the first book, as he wrote to Herder in May 1794,[103] and towards Homeric objectivity. A second change was to amplify the novel's scepticism about the theatre as the vehicle of cultural nationalism. After the Revolution, cultural nationalism was not just obsolete but dangerous. Germany did not want the kind of upheavals that could bring about a national literary culture. The increased scepticism about the theatre and cultural nationalism is evident in two comments made by Jarno in the new material written from 1794 onwards. In Book III Jarno recommends to Wilhelm that he forget the theatre and commit himself instead 'to an active life'.[104] In Book VII he is blunter: 'I think [. . .] that you should abandon your association with the theatre, for you have no talent for it'.[105] It is a striking retreat from the aspirations of the 1770s, especially considering that it was Jarno who first advised Wilhelm to read Shakespeare, and that Shakespeare was the model for a new national theatre heralded by Goethe's generation.

What then is the new 'active life' that Jarno recommends to Wilhelm? How will a bourgeois German contribute to public life after the Revolution? The answer would have to wait for Books VII and VIII. However, the revisions to the early books do invite the reader to see Wilhelm's career as an education for an active life. The impulse probably came from the new Göschen edition of Wieland's *Complete Works*, beginning in 1794 with the *History of Agathon*, the philosophical novel of education (*Bildungsroman*) originally published in 1766–1767. With its classical setting, erotic themes, and ironic treatment of Agathon's education, Wieland's novel provided Goethe with a model for reinventing *Meister*. Like Agathon, Wilhelm is idealistic about the power of education, but motivated as much by sexual desire as by a desire to learn. This is another effect of reframing the story of Wilhelm's childhood within his relationship to Mariane. Wilhelm now thinks his childhood interest in the theatre was only a juvenile enthusiasm, whose shortcomings are now clear to him at his higher plane of development, or so he tells Mariane during one of their late-night trysts:

> It is always pleasant, my dear, to remember old times and our past, but harmless, mistakes. Especially when this occurs as we feel we have achieved

a high point from which we can now look about and reflect on the path that brought us to this lofty view. It is pleasant and satisfying to remember the obstacles that we sadly thought were insurmountable, and then compare what we, as mature persons, have now developed into, with what we were then, in our immaturity. I cannot tell you how happy I am now that I can talk to you about the past—now that I gaze out towards the joyous landscape that we shall travel hand in hand.[106]

The claim to have ascended to a sovereign, objective standpoint from which he can reflect objectively on the course of his education is premature and will be ironized by events, not least by his failure to see the truth of Mariane's circumstances, as half actress and half prostitute. At the same time as ironizing Wilhelm's confidence, the novel becomes more positive about the educative value of error. When Wilhelm is preparing to leave home, he looks at his library of critical writing on the arts and rereads his own efforts in the genre; his old friend Werner questions their value, and Wilhelm replies: 'It is not the business of a pupil to finish a thing. It is enough that he tries his hand'.[107] Error is a necessary part of education, for it is through error that the student teaches himself. Teachers in the conventional sense are nowhere to be seen in the early parts of the novel. Instead Wilhelm meets mysterious strangers, who seem to have special insight into his circumstances. On the night of his planned departure from Mariane, as he is about to deliver the letter outlining his secret plan to join the theatre director Serlo, Wilhelm meets such a stranger, who turns out to have facilitated the sale of Wilhelm's grandfather's art collection. (In 1795 Goethe's mother, encouraged by Goethe, sold the Three Lyres and with it his father's paintings.) Wilhelm's favourite painting in the collection was of a story from Plutarch: the prince Antiochus sick with longing for his father Seleucus's young bride Stratonice. The stranger is somewhat dismissive of the painting, and Wilhelm is forced to acknowledge that it was the subject matter and not its execution that attracted him, a classic instance of the dilettantish preference for content over form that Goethe and Schiller were now campaigning against. Still, the stranger does not seek to put Wilhelm right: he is merely a catalyst for Wilhelm's development, not a teacher. Where the stranger does intervene decisively is to censure an offhand comment by Wilhelm about destiny. Wilhelm asks him to explain his beliefs, and receives an equivocal answer:

> It is not a matter of believing, or trying to make sense out of what is otherwise incomprehensible, but simply of deciding which way of looking at things [*Vorstellungsart*] suits us best. The texture of this world is made up

of necessity and chance. Human reason holds the balance between them, treating necessity as the basis of existence, but manipulating and directing chance, and using it. Only if our reason is unshakeable, does man deserve to be called a god of the earth. Woe to him who, from youth on, is prone to find arbitrariness in necessity and ascribes a certain reasonableness to chance and accepts this religiously. For that amounts to denying one's rational self and giving free play to one's feelings. We think we are god-fearing people if we saunter through life without much thought, we let ourselves be carried along by happy chance, and then finally declare that our wavering existence was a life governed by divine guidance.[108]

The stranger is evidently a Spinozist, for along with his protestations of the unfathomability of things, he believes that reason requires us to admit the iron necessity of nature.[109] Everything else that can be said about life is merely a *Vorstellungsart*, a partial and provisional perspective on the ultimate reality. What is to be avoided above all is the superstitious belief that contingent events have a purposeful shape. We can and should learn from our errors, but we should not believe that they were part of a preordained plan.

By June 1795 the six books of the *Theatrical Mission* were fully revised and reshaped into the first four books of the *Apprenticeship*. Book V of the *Apprenticeship* broke new ground. The *Theatrical Mission* had ended at a forked path, with Wilhelm's decision to join Serlo's company, prompted by his father's death, and his vision of the mysterious Amazon, which indicated a quite different direction for his life. In the *Apprenticeship* more is made of this episode. Between the news of his father's death and Wilhelm's decision to join the company are two new chapters that detail Wilhelm's deliberations. A letter arrives from Werner outlining how the family's commercial and domestic arrangements will change after old Meister's death. According to Werner's plan, Wilhelm will become a land agent, for Wilhelm had sent his father some notes on the agricultural economics of the regions had travelled through. In fact, the notes were not firsthand observations: Wilhelm had cobbled them together out of books with his friend Laertes's help. Werner's misplaced image of him brings home to Wilhelm how unsuited he is to a commercial career. He responds to Werner with a firm but emollient letter. His future, he is convinced, is in the theatre, and his mission will have a social purpose. He now understands that a burgher's personal development is hindered by the social privileges of the nobility. The burghers are the engine of the economy, but that is all they are. By contrast, the aristocracy's function is public self-presentation. (The same social division appears at the end of the 'Fairy Tale'.) A burgher cannot be an artist and an aristocrat cannot be useful. Wilhelm does not mean that burghers cannot create great literature: he means that they cannot project the role of artist onto the national stage. 'The differences are not due to any pretentiousness on the part of the aristocracy or the submissiveness of the burgher estate, but to the whole organization of society', he says.[110] Wilhelm aims to bridge the gap by means of the 'harmonious development of [his] personality' in the theatre. It is no longer simply a theatrical mission: it is a theatrical mission in the service of social reform. For the first time the novel gives an indication of what the 'active life' advocated by Jarno might actually be. It is to be a transformational building of bridges similar to the snake's in the 'Fairy Tale'.

The contract with Serlo is signed. One of Wilhelm's conditions is that Serlo's company will perform *Hamlet* uncut. He soon realizes this is not only impractical but also undesirable. To the British island nation the subplots involving ships and pirates made sense; to a German audience they do not, and so Wilhelm cuts them. *Hamlet* is thus made to conform to modern German neo-Aristotelian aesthetics, but in a serious-minded fashion. This is no mere sentimental bowdlerization. On the contrary, Wilhelm insists on the poetic justice of ending with a stage littered with corpses. The rehearsals proceed well. On the whole the company is run professionally, though the management has some alarming blind spots. No one is available to play the role of the ghost, and Serlo seems so relaxed about this oversight that the reader suspects he is planning a *coup de théâtre*. It is one of a number of mysterious events surrounding the production. One night Wilhelm is visited in his bedroom by an unidentified woman, who may be Philine or even Mignon. Philine certainly intimates her intention to seduce him though the priggish Wilhelm cannot see it. The first night of *Hamlet* is a huge success. The psychodrama of the play gets inside the actors' heads and creates an electric atmosphere. When the ghost appears played by a mysterious actor—two unknown men dressed like monks have been seen backstage—there is palpable fear. The ghost leaves behind a veil, embroidered in which are the words 'For the first and last time, young man, flee!'[111] After this excitement, however, subsequent performances feel flat. A few days into the run the actors' lodgings burn down. It seems that the now deranged Harpist may have caused the fire, and he makes an unsuccessful attempt to kill Aurelie's young son Felix. The company starts to disintegrate. Philine leaves accompanied by a mystery guest whose red military uniform reminds Wilhelm of Mariane. Aurelie falls ill, almost on purpose. The Harpist is entrusted to a doctor, who recommends that Aurelie read an autobiography of a saintly woman or 'Beautiful Soul'. Melina sees an opportunity to oust Wilhelm and persuades Serlo to make the repertoire less highbrow. Aurelie succumbs to her illness. Wilhelm is eased out of the company. Before she dies Aurelie asks him to deliver a conciliatory letter to the man who is generally believed to be the father of Felix. At the end of Book V, with his theatrical mission incomplete and now unravelling, Wilhelm leaves the company.

Book VI consists entirely of the 'Confessions of a Beautiful Soul', the autobiography Aurelie was prescribed by the doctor. Some of the material came from the diaries of Goethe's Pietist friend Susanne von Klettenberg. (The diaries have not survived, and so we do not know to what extent he used them.) Writing to Schiller in March 1795 he referred to Book VI as his 'religious book'.[112] The novel's sudden shift to religion is an unexpected departure, but it is not unconnected with the main narrative. Book VI is another story of education that raises questions about the relation between subjective self and objective world. The Beautiful Soul's story begins with a lung haemorrhage in her ninth year, followed by a nine-month convalescence—the first of a series of symbolic rebirths. The first two thirds of her narrative is concerned with the contrast between her spirituality and her unsuccessful relationships with men. Faced with an empty social world full of libidinous men of whom many have the pox, she clings to the idea that God is an invisible friend. This becomes a leitmotif.[113] Her isolation is brought into sharp focus with the appearance of the Uncle, her father's childless stepbrother, an aesthete and educationalist, who shares her dislike of society but for different reasons. His wealth enables him to dispense largesse to the family. He entails his estate on her youngest sister on condition of her marrying a man he approves of. The Beautiful Soul receives a position as a secular canoness, which gives her an opportunity to live in a way that suits her religious convictions. The last third of the narrative presents challenges of a different kind. Her youngest sister reluctantly marries, an event both social and aesthetic, and managed in meticulous detail by the Uncle at his estate. However, the Beautiful Soul's development halts and goes into reverse. Kept awake night after night by a second haemorrhage, she imagines her disembodied soul reflecting on her body from the outside. The final episodes of Book VI are stories of dying and growing up. The youngest sister, despite a fractious marriage, gives birth to two daughters and a son, but the mother and her husband soon die, he after a fall from his horse and she after giving birth to a second son. The orphaned children are educated under the Uncle's supervision by a mysterious French Abbé. The children will become the spiritual descendants of the Uncle and not of the Beautiful Soul.

In March 1795 Goethe wrote to Schiller that the 'Confessions' were founded upon 'the most noble deceptions and the most delicate confusion of the subjective and the objective'.[114] The Beautiful Soul projects her own subjective morality onto objective reality—that is what her private God really is, a projection of her subjectivity. To be sure, the 'deceptions' about which Goethe wrote to Schiller are 'noble' and the 'confusion' is 'delicate' because they derive from the admirable impulse to find in the world the moral goodness that is in oneself. In this sense, the Beautiful Soul is an example of the process Goethe described in 'The Divine'. The gods have no objective existence; we create them and fill them with the best of ourselves, in order that we can find them worth believing in. The fact that we believe in them only shows how successful the moral trick is that we play on ourselves, and how nobly it is motivated. By contrast the Uncle has a Spinozan humanist attitude to religion:

> 'If we can think it possible', he said to me one day, 'that the Creator of the world should take on the form of His creature and should inhabit the world for a time after the world's fashion, then this creature must seem perfect indeed if the Creator Himself could ally Himself so closely with it. In the concept of humanity there cannot be a contradiction with the idea of godhead, and if we often feel remoteness and difference from the godhead, then it is our urgent responsibility not to dwell on our weaknesses and faults like the devil's advocate but to seek out our finest qualities by which we can legitimately confirm our godlikeness'.[115]

The Uncle's philosophy reinterprets and reframes the Beautiful Soul's subjective god within a version of Spinozism that preserves the positive elements of her story. The Beautiful Soul becomes a lesson; her life becomes part of the family archive from which subsequent generations will learn.

At the beginning of Book VII Wilhelm arrives at Lothario's estate with the firm intention of upbraiding him over his neglect of Aurelie, but instead he is persuaded to connive in the deceit of another victim, the beautiful and highly strung Lydie, who is in love with Lothario. The doctor has ordered that Lydie be removed from the estate while Lothario recovers from a wound suffered in a duel with her ex-husband. The plan is for Wilhelm to take her off on a wild-goose chase in pursuit of Lydie's childhood friend Therese. Wilhelm's moral misgivings about deceiving Lydie are trumped by his desire to find the Amazon, for he has taken too literally Jarno's description of Therese as 'a real Amazon'.[116] He realizes his error when he finally meets her at her small, immaculately managed estate. She has focused her energy on the estate in response to the end of her engagement to Lothario, when it emerged that Lothario had once had an affair with Therese's mother. Lothario is also progressing towards more focused activity. He had previously travelled to America to fight on the United States' side in the War of Independence, but has since realized that his reforming zeal would do more good at home. Wilhelm reacts to Lothario's plans with respect, but also envy because of Therese's understandable love for Lothario. Amid the political excitement, it emerges that Felix is not the son of Lothario and Aurelie after all, but had only been entrusted to Aurelie's care by an elderly woman. Wilhelm does not yet know that the old woman was Mariane's maid Barbara, and that Felix is his and Mariane's son. Jarno, who presumably does know, urges Wilhelm to return to the town and collect Felix and Mignon. When Wilhelm meets Barbara, she gives him the shocking news that Mariane died after giving birth to his son Felix. Wilhelm refuses to acknowledge Felix until incontrovertible evidence emerges in the form of letters to him from Mariane that Werner had intercepted. Before he leaves, he resolves to write to Werner with the news that he plans to renounce the theatre and join the reform project of Lothario and his associates. On his return to Lothario's estate Jarno invites him to a ceremony in the mysterious ancient tower in the centre of the castle. Wilhelm is led through a symbolic darkness into an archive holding manuscripts bearing the names of Lothario, Jarno, and others. He is given a 'certificate of apprenticeship' by the Abbé, containing a series of allusive aphorisms.

Book VIII opens with the arrival of his old friend Werner. The family firm is to enter into the joint purchase of a new estate with Lothario. In addition to securing Felix's patrimony through this enterprise, Wilhelm realizes he needs to find a mother for Felix. Therese is a candidate close to hand, and he proposes to her by letter. In the meantime, the ailing Mignon is to be cared for, and Wilhelm is sent off to see Lothario's sister Natalie who is looking after the child. It transpires that Natalie is the mysterious Amazon. At this point the situation between Lothario, Therese, Natalie, and Wilhelm escalates. Therese accepts Wilhelm's offer of marriage, under Natalie's influence, but it soon emerges that Therese is not her mother's daughter, and thus the obstacle preventing her marriage to Lothario never existed. When Therese receives the news about her parentage from Natalie, she suspects that they are all being played, a feeling Wilhelm shares, even though his desire for Natalie is now in competition with that for Therese. At this moment, Mignon collapses and dies, her weak heart finally giving way at the prospect of Wilhelm marrying. The tragedy of Mignon's death suddenly gives way to comedy with the arrival of Friedrich, the brother of Natalie and Lothario. Friedrich confesses to Wilhelm that he was the young person who went off with Philine in Book V. She is carrying their child, though Friedrich admits with remarkable equanimity that the child was conceived around the time of Philine's nighttime visit to Wilhelm and may be Wilhelm's. Urgent discussions take place concerning the marriages, led by the Abbé, though it is agreed that the whole messy situation should be hushed up.

Amid the discord and confusion comes a brief moment of harmony, as Mignon's body is laid to rest in the Hall of the Past. However, the placid and classicizing ceremony occasions a dramatic revelation. On seeing Mignon's corpse, the Marchese Cipriani, an old family friend recently arrived from Italy, recognises her as his long-lost niece. He now reveals the whole grim backstory of Mignon and the Harpist. Mignon was the issue of an unknowing incestuous relationship between the Marchese's sister Sperata and his brother Augustin (the Harpist), which drove them both into profound religious melancholy. The Harpist/Augustin now appears with the doctor, strangely calm because he has stolen a flask of opium that gives him the option of committing suicide. Further tragedy ensues when Augustin rushes in with the news that Felix has unwittingly drunk the opium, which Augustin had poured into a glass. Fearing Felix's death, and now aware of his own backstory—he had found the Marchese's account of it in the Abbé's room—Augustin opens the veins in his neck and though initially saved by the doctor, later removes the bandages and dies. Yet Felix has not actually drunk the poison; he only claimed to have drunk from the glass, because he feared his father's anger at his bad habit of drinking straight from bottles. Natalie, whom Felix does not fear, elicits the truth from him. It takes the wise fool Friedrich to cut through the whole knotty episode. He hints at a possible relationship between Wilhelm and Natalie, who has proved herself a fit mother for Felix. All of this is aggravates Wilhelm, who delivers an understandably ill-tempered outburst at Lothario and is angry at Friedrich for his indiscretion, until Lothario reveals to Wilhelm that Therese had promised her hand to Lothario on the condition that Natalie should marry Wilhelm. Friedrich interrupts the tense discussion saying that he has overheard Natalie telling the Abbé she consents to marrying Wilhelm. Friedrich compares Wilhelm to Saul, son of Kish, 'who went in search of his father's asses, and found a kingdom'. Wilhelm's reply, and the final words of the novel, are a fitting mixture of acceptance and incomprehension: 'I don't know about kingdoms', says Wilhelm, 'but I do know that I have found a treasure I never deserved. And I would not exchange it for anything in the world.'[117] It is not clear whether the treasure is Felix or Natalie or the fact that the three of them seem to fit together as a family.

With the tortuous narrative of Books VII and VIII, Goethe wanted to impose a strict causal necessity on Wilhelm's fate. As he wrote to Unger, the novel was 'among all my works the most logical and, in more than one sense, the hardest, and yet it must, if it is to succeed, be composed with the utmost freedom and lightness'.[118] The novel is hard in the sense that Wilhelm's path is so tortuous as to confound rational interpretation. The stranger whom Wilhelm meets at the end of Book I is therefore right to be pessimistic about our ability to find meaning in the events of our lives: 'Woe to him who [...] ascribes a certain reasonableness to chance and accepts this religiously. For that amounts to denying one's rational self and giving free play to one's feelings'.[119] Yet as Schiller observed in July 1796, Goethe had made life difficult for himself by dropping some obvious hints as to the novel's message, such as might placate his German readership's desire for a clear moral meaning.[120] This was another tension in Books VII and VIII, in addition to the tension between the narrative's difficulty and the 'freedom and lightness' of the style. At various points we are told that Wilhelm has reached his goal or that the aims of his education have been fulfilled, but these assertions of pattern and meaning turn out to be provisional and uncertain. They are only limited and partial perspectives on Wilhelm's life; they are *Vorstellungsarten*, like the idea that nature has a purpose or exists for our benefit. (The word *Vorstellungsart* occurs seven times in the finished novel, and six of these belong to the post-1794 revisions.) However, this should not lead us to dismiss everything as meaningless chaos. In particular we cannot and should not want to forget our past—a truth that is embodied by Felix who is a living reminder of Wilhelm's infatuation with Mariane and the theatre. So the Society of the Tower is surely right to preserve an archive of human development and education, containing the biographies of its members and other significant persons, including the Beautiful Soul. At the same time, we should be sceptical when, at the end of Wilhelm's induction into the Tower, the Abbé announces to him: 'Hail to you, young man. Your apprenticeship is completed, Nature has given you your freedom'.[121] The Tower's wisdom is provisional. Its members do not even agree what purpose it serves. Natalie disdains the Abbé's liberal educational theory, even though he was her teacher and the Tower's guiding spirit. She even implies that he has now seen the error of his ways. She has developed her own educational method, less liberal than the Abbé's. The proliferation of theories is another example of the novel's multiperspectival manner.

The ending of the novel presents perhaps its biggest tension. The Tower's social reform plans, and hence its answer to the Revolution, involve mending the breach that the Revolution created between burghers and aristocrats. While in America Lothario had written to Jarno that 'I will return, and in my own house, my own orchard, in the midst of my own people, I will say: *Here, or nowhere, is America!*' Reform begins at home, at his own estates. His farm workers are to be released from the remains of their feudal obligations; tenant farmers may get some extra rights, including freedom from the *corvée*. Aristocrats will now have to pay taxes, so that this historic privilege that separated them from the peasants and burghers will end. At least some of society's ancient divisions and inequities will be eliminated. The reform plans of Books VII and VIII involve pooling the resources of aristocratic land ownership and bourgeois commerce. Werner will lead the family firm in a joint venture with Lothario. The novel ends by confirming a series of marriages between burghers and aristocrats. However, the Tower does not arrange the marriages; it has to wait for ungovernable desire and chance to arrange them. The Abbé sets himself up as matchmaker, but this goes down poorly with the others. Wilhelm offers sardonic resistance: 'I would think one should leave the pastime of arranging marriages to those who are in love with each other'. And when the Abbé gives solemn confirmation of the arrangements, Friedrich pointedly dismisses him: 'Your appearance is a formality, we don't need you gentlemen anymore'.[122] Indeed the Abbé seems to be more of an obstacle than an aid. Wilhelm is particularly dismayed to hear that he is being manipulated. In this tense and febrile atmosphere Friedrich mischievously suggests that Wilhelm should marry Lydie, which angers Wilhelm. Natalie springs to Wilhelm's defence, and this in turn prompts Friedrich to mock his sister. Natalie will not marry, Friedrich says, until a way can be found for her to offer herself 'as a supplement to someone else's existence' because 'some bride or other is missing'.[123] In any case, it turns out that the cold and sceptical Jarno has already proposed to the overwrought Lydie, a most implausible match, as both Friedrich and Natalie observe. In the chaotic comedy of the marriages there is however a pattern. The chaos is resolved by natural means that accord with the principle of complementarity. The partners complement one another. The highly strung Lydie is paired with the coldly rational Jarno. The dashing and romantic Lothario with his political plans matches the practical, homely Therese. Natalie and Wilhelm are the strangest pairing. Wilhelm's life has been driven by an urge to find fulfilment in love that borders on desperation in Books VII and VIII, and he has run through a series of passions and affairs.

Natalie, on the other hand, seems almost loveless. As Friedrich would have it, Natalie will not marry until she can selflessly offer herself to fill a gap. For her, love is just a matter of social duty, assuming she feels love at all. When Wilhelm asks her whether she has ever been in love, her paradoxical reply—'Never—or always!'—expresses a dispassionate lucidity that contrasts with Wilhelm's obscure and confused passions. In attempting to move on from the chaos of the Revolution, and in pairing the partners up according to the principle of complementarity, the last two books of the *Apprenticeship* resemble the 'Fairy Tale'. As we learn in the 'Fairy Tale', 'no one can help on their own, but only when one joins with many others at the right time'.[124] And according to the scroll Wilhelm receives in the Tower, 'All men make up mankind and all forces together make up the world. These are often in conflict with each other, and while trying to destroy each other they are held together and reproduced by Nature'.[125] Individuals can only see things through their own *Vorstellungsart*; only the totality of individuals would bring about a totality of *Vorstellungsarten* and thus a complete and rational picture of the world. A successful society requires individuals with diverse and complementary abilities to come together. As in the 'Fairy Tale', the parties come together along routes that reason cannot foresee, but in the *Apprenticeship* the result seems more provisional and less stable. The Abbé's control over his friends is limited. Their coming together is driven by the order of nature, working through the contingent and labyrinthine twists of Books VII and VIII. Their relationships do not seem altogether stable, as befits a novel set in contemporary Germany.

The Peace of Basel seemed to provide some security for Weimar and the other principalities of northern and central Germany. It removed the threat of French or Prussian domination and secured the particularism of the *ancien regime*. However, since the fading of the dream of a Protestant-led German cultural nation, it was less clear what Germany was. This suited Goethe. Italy had made him feel more European than German. A cosmopolitan Europe based on classical humanism seemed more congenial than a Protestant German nation. Secure in its particularism, Weimar could reach out into the wider world. For Goethe, particularism was not a neutral fact or a second best. It is easy to overlook the high value Goethe placed on particularism—easy because his writings on the subject in the mid-1790s, though extensive, are scattered and not in the finished form he hoped for them. In 1795 he began work on an ambitious project that would defend and celebrate particularism. It was the most ambitious project of his career thus far. Its subject was the cultural history of the city-states of Renaissance Italy, chief among them Florence. The argument was that the cosmopolitan humanism of the Renaissance had grown out of the particular circumstances and character of the city-states. This was Goethe's alternative to the failed project of German cultural nationalism, and so the Italian Renaissance was not merely of historical interest. It had lessons for modern Germany. If such a supreme artistic flowering as the Renaissance, embodying cosmopolitan and humanist values, could grow in the soil of Italian particularism, could the same happen in Germany? How could such polities be preserved? How could a polity maintain its inner unity and cohesion? How important was the competition between polities? After the French Revolution there were also lessons to be learned from the eventual decline of Florence. The independence of the German principalities was threatened by the Revolution, a Prussian-dominated north German confederation, and the continuing Austro-Prussian duopoly. The decline of Florence in the sixteenth century seemed to have been caused by similar pressures: the rise of the great nation-states France and Spain, and revolutionary elements within Florence itself. Goethe set out to answer these questions in the form of a large-scale cultural history tracing the origins and achievements of the Renaissance city-states, culminating in Florence's golden age and decline. Between 1795 and 1797 he devoted much of his time to preparatory reading and note-taking. A third trip to Italy was needed, preferably with Meyer, to collect information and see the artworks at first hand. He would also make up for neglecting Florence on his headlong race to Rome in autumn 1786. He began to make plans for the journey while finishing the 'Confessions of a Beautiful Soul' in the summer of 1795. Over the next two years, his plans were repeatedly frustrated by events at home and abroad. In October 1795 Meyer set off for Italy on his own. Goethe took out his travel diaries and notes from the first Italian journey and began to put them in order 'with great pleasure' and with a view to publishing them.[126] The only immediate result was an essay titled 'Architecture' based on the original notes and prompted in part by his work on the restoration of the ducal palace.[127] There were distractions, the first being the birth of a son Karl on 1 November 1795. Sadly the baby died at not quite three weeks old. The plans had to be put on hold again in the spring of 1796 because of Napoleon's dramatic victories in northwestern Italy.[128] Departure was rescheduled for August 1796 but again postponed.[129] The plan was still alive in December.[130] After Austria sued for peace in April 1797, Goethe hoped to set off in early or late summer.[131] Eventually the plans ran into the sand, and he made do with a trip to Switzerland in the summer and autumn of 1797, where he met the returning Meyer in Stäfa, near Zurich. The trip to Italy did not happen, and the grand cultural history remained unwritten.

During Meyer's travels the two corresponded regularly. Goethe asked Meyer for details of Italy's 'climate, customs and practices, current conditions, and whatever else, also something about prices. All such notes will have great value in the future'.[132] The aim was to create 'a picture of Italy according to the revolutions of its land and states since the earliest times'.[133] The notes he wrote—'my *collectanea* for the understanding of Italy'[134]—were detailed and extensive. They began with Italy's geology and landscape and extended to the history of the Renaissance, encompassing agriculture, industry, trade, political organization, building, everyday life, language, and the arts.[135] The guiding principle was that 'everything humans do cultivates them': all our activities, from farming and hunting, through commerce, the law, politics, and so on together make up our culture.[136] The scope and method is similar to that of Herder's *Ideas for the Philosophy of the History of Mankind*, only more concrete and detailed. An example of the concreteness of Goethe's plans are his notes on the cultivation and use of the olive. He documented its history, its various species, the methods of its processing, and its uses—for 'oil is an ingredient of life for the Italians'.[137] Observations of the same kind are scattered through the diaries of his journey through southern Germany and Switzerland in 1797, along with details of reading matter on the history and politics of German and Swiss towns. As well as the 1795 essay on architecture, he wrote a short account of the construction of the Basilica of St Peter's[138] and compiled a long bibliography of architectural writings.[139] The most substantial remnant of the project was his translation of the autobiography of the Florentine goldsmith and sculptor Benvenuto Cellini, begun early in 1796, published in part in *The Horae*, and finally appearing in its entirety in 1803. Some of the *collectanea* found their way into the seventeen appendices he added to the Cellini autobiography, including a short history of Florence under the Medicis.[140]

At first Cellini's *Vita* interested Goethe as a source of information.[141] It was the richest contemporary account of the history of Renaissance art. Goethe was fascinated by the concrete details of Cellini's circumstances and his descriptions of the techniques of sculpture and metalworking.[142] He soon came to see that Cellini's life was also typical and symbolic. In a plan for *Poetry and Truth* written fifteen years later, Goethe gave Cellini as a representative of the principle that 'a person can only live with his own kind, and not even with them, for he cannot tolerate anyone being his equal for long'.¹⁴³ Most striking of all was Cellini's character. He was energetic, lustful, assertive, self-confident, keenly aware of his own value as an artist, and willing and able to stand up to the powerful. The autobiography made no attempt to hide the negative side of his character: he was a street brawler, impulsive, proud, vengeful, painfully conscious of his status and reputation. Worst of all he was physically and mentally abusive towards his model Caterina and used sex as means of punishing her. As an artist, however, Cellini embodied qualities that Goethe came to value, most of all the idea that the worth of his work lay in the work itself and not in his reputation. So confident was Cellini in the excellence of his work that he could ask to be paid not according to the terms of a contract drawn up in advance, but on the basis of the quality of the work he delivered. At heart Cellini was supremely competitive, and thus he typified Florence. Competitions for artistic commissions were common in Florence. Cellini claimed that this was the reason for Florence's artistic preeminence: the early dukes of Florence had 'only succeeded in making this most noble of all schools so perfect by understanding how to encourage competition among all the artists; in this way, the amazing dome and doors of [the baptistery of] San Giovanni were finished as well as so many other temples and statues, and their city had become as famous for its talents as no other had been since the ancients'.¹⁴⁴ Cellini internalized the practice of competition. As was the norm, he competed against his contemporaries in Florence, and most enthusiastically of all against 'the beast' Baccio Bandinelli.¹⁴⁵ More praiseworthy though was to compete against an artist of great skill,¹⁴⁶ and the more skilled the competitor, the more honourable the competition.¹⁴⁷ Most ambitious and meritorious of all was to compete against one's greatest forebears, in Cellini's case Michelangelo and the ancients.¹⁴⁸ The idea of artistic competition became central to Goethe's understanding of the character of the artist, probably from his work on Cellini's *Vita*. Where Cellini fell down in this regard was his tendency to brag, which did not comport with the proper nature of artistic competition, as Goethe would later write in his account of his travels in Italy: 'one should not compare oneself with [the artistic forebear], but emulate him in private, hope for oneself what he has achieved'.¹⁴⁹ Still, Cellini was exemplary in having made competition the principle that governed his work. So too, more importantly, was the city of Florence: the most perfect example of a polity whose cultural influence belied its size.

Cellini was an exemplary figure of the sixteenth century, like Götz, Faust, Egmont, and Tasso. In all these exemplary lives Goethe saw the advent of modernity. Political modernity with its new technologies of government was displacing the traditional forms of life. Larger, bureaucratically organized states began to dominate the smaller, more organic ones. The traditional virtues of honour and loyalty to the ruling house were threatened by a new force of political idealism, or what Goethe termed 'enthusiasm'. (In the *Venetian Epigrams*, he had used the word 'enthusiast', *Schwärmer*, to designate the French Revolutionaries and the Christians whom he supposed to be their spiritual counterparts.)[150] This clash of forces is apparent towards the end of Goethe's account of the history of Florence in the tenth appendix to his Cellini translation. His account builds up to Florence's apogee under the Medici family, which is 'opposed ungratefully, mulishly, terribly by a hideous, fantastical monster, the monk Savonarola', an 'impure enthusiast'.[151] The Medici line fails from within, in the person of Pietro, youngest son of Cosimo I de' Medici, a man 'as incapable as he was unfortunate', who spent much of his adult life as a hanger-on at the Spanish court.[152] Medici rule is then interrupted by a chaotic sixteen-year republic. Here Goethe quotes a passage from Machiavelli's *History of Florence* on the instability all republics suffer from:

> Most cities, says Machiavelli, particularly those that are not well organized and are governed under the name of a republic, have frequently changed the manner of their administration, and usually for this reason: not because of a struggle between freedom and servitude, as many believe, but because of a struggle between servitude and lawlessness.[153]

The advocates of republicanism are not fighters for freedom. The alternative they offer to autocracy is mere chaos or 'license'. Goethe had made the same point concerning the French Revolution in his *Venetian Epigrams*: 'All the apostles of freedom, I could never abide them, / For each sought only license for himself' ('Alle Freiheits Apostel sie waren mir immer zuwider / Denn es suchte doch nur jeder die Willkür für sich').[154] However, the intrinsic instability of republic government meant there could be no return to stabler times. External and internal pressures on Florence caused the restored Medici dukes 'to think more of their safety than of adorning the city'.[155] An exception was Cosimo II de' Medici, in whom Florence enjoyed a 'change of fortune',[156] albeit a temporary one. It was only by means of marriages to Austria and France that Cosimo could keep the city secure. In effect Florence became a client state. Cosimo's reign was therefore only a temporary and partial reprieve, before Florence inevitably succumbed to the forces of political modernity.

Goethe's history of Florence reveals his interest in 'how old constitutions that are grounded only in existence and self-preservation behave in times of evolution and change'.[157] These words are from a letter written in Zurich to Schiller towards the end of Goethe's journey through southern Germany and Switzerland in autumn 1797. It was a poor substitute for the planned trip to Italy, but it did allow him to continue thinking 'about the characteristics of cities',[158] as he noted in his diary. In Frankfurt he took note of recent books on the city's constitution.[159] He discussed the city's current and past politics with the syndic Karl Friedrich Wilhelm Schmidt and Professor Sömmerring.[160] He continued to think about politics in Switzerland: 'observations on the position of the canton [Schwyz], in relation to political circumstances', he noted on 30 September.[161] Never a friend of democracy, he thought that some Swiss cantons, with their traditions of popular government, must have difficulty finding consent for highly advantageous public works. Any landowner who might be disadvantaged by the works would be able to block progress.[162] His settled view was that democratic government could not consistently pursue the common good. The system of government was only one factor among many. Travelling through southern Germany, he made notes on the location and construction of towns, with his typically painterly eye. He made a habit of surveying each town. So in Stuttgart at the end of August he records rising at 6 A.M. to make his 'usual tour' on his own to reconnoitre the city and its surroundings.[163] The traditions of urban organization, the quality of roads, municipal buildings, and public hygiene—all of these gave rise to reflections on 'the concept of religious and secular administration [*Polizey*]'.[164] In Heilbronn he found evidence of sound public administration. The government had always been well resourced. The city enjoyed fertile agricultural land which was divided relatively evenly between its citizens. A peaceful spirit of civic equality seemed to have been long established, with no powerful spiritual or secular lords to upset the balance of power.[165] Like Frankfurt, Heilbronn had an oligarchic government open only to Protestants and graduates. In other words, it was a well-educated oligarchy of relatively uniform character. A sign of the city's continuing good governance was that it was still able to expand by buying up parcels of land on its borders. Goethe thought this an admirable policy, which might have benefitted German Imperial Cities in general, by insulating them against the troublemaking of unruly neighbours or the aggression of domineering larger states seeking to exploit disputes over land ownership. He was keen to find any policies that might ensure the survival of the smaller cities and principalities.

His observations in Germany would not feed directly into the Italian project, but they were of the same kind and were motivated by the same concerns. In Switzerland, while he consulted with Meyer on how to process their Italian *collectanea*, he was taken with a new poetic plan, an epic on the story of William Tell. The story gelled with his interest in the history of the Italian city-states and the southern German cities. It would tell how the small area around Lake Lucerne succeeded in defending itself and its culture against the Holy Roman Empire, a mighty multinational state. The symbolic figure of Tell would reflect his fatherland, and so the geographical detail would be an important part of the poem, as he reported to Schiller from his lodgings with Meyer in Stäfa:

> I have once more been able to realize fully in my imagination the confined, highly symbolic location where the events play out, as well as observing the character, morals and customs of the people in these areas, insofar as one can in such a short time, and now it is a matter of luck whether anything will come of the project.[166]

Nothing did come of the project, for Goethe at least. In 1803–1804 Schiller wrote his play *Wilhelm Tell*, using the very details Goethe had observed, or so Eckermann later claimed.[167]

Goethe believed that small polities enjoyed social and cultural advantages over larger ones. In larger polities the relationships between people became more abstract or (as we might say today) virtual, and less real. He noted the effect when in 1803 the physician Hufeland visited from Berlin where in 1801 had been appointed to a post with the title of Privy Counsellor. In a small polity like Weimar a Privy Counsellor really did give counsel. In Berlin the title was merely honorific.[168] It was a small example, but it meant something to Goethe. There has been much debate about Goethe's decision to remain in Weimar. Did he regret not moving to a large city? Was his defence of small polities like Weimar merely self-justification? In part these questions stem from an unwillingness to acknowledge how deep Goethe's sympathy was for protoconservative ideas. Ever since the early 1770s it had been his settled belief, learned first from Rousseau, then consolidated by Möser and Herder, that small polities were likely to retain their character and identity better than large ones. Weimar's size was one of the reasons he had moved there: to be in a place where his ability could make a material difference. During the journey in late summer and autumn 1797 he reflected on the question of size. The fabric of culture was made up of a tight weave of beliefs and attitudes. In larger polities, the public sphere was made of the much looser fabric of the economics of consumption: culture existed to provide diversion or entertainment. In larger polities, culture was something to be consumed, not an authentic expression of selfhood. The ties that bound people together and created social cohesion tended to loosen in proportion to the economic opportunities available to them. In smaller polities, the creators of culture could still shape public sentiment. In August 1797 he wrote to Schiller from Frankfurt:

> I had a very strange realization of what the public is actually like in a large city. It exists in a constant orgy [*Taumel*] of acquisition and consumption, and what we call sentiment can neither be produced nor communicated. All entertainments, even the theatre, exist only to provide diversion. The great fondness of the reading public for journals and novels arises out of precisely this: because the former always and the latter mostly pile diversion on diversion.[169]

If public sentiment cannot be shaped, it risks becoming irrevocably partisan, like political opinion after the Revolution. Cultural debate becomes politicised. The cultural goods created by one party become the target of a second party determined to destroy the first's reputation. These are the cultural politics of the modern city. In a smaller polity or one in which the government was still capable of setting the tone, the damage might be containable, so long as 'it had not yet become policy that in one and the same state or one and the same city a party was permitted to destroy what others had just created'.[170] Such decisive action was only possible in smaller polities governed by regimes with unfettered executive power. As Böttiger noted, Goethe vigorously opposed anything he thought would undermine Weimar's cohesion and common good.[171]

Goethe planned the Tell epic shortly after finishing *Herrmann and Dorothea*, an epic poem of two thousand lines in nine cantos, closely modelled on some features of Homer's *Iliad*. The composition of *Herrmann and Dorothea* coincided with work on Books VII and VIII of *Wilhelm Meister's Apprenticeship*, and it was finished in June 1797, less than two months before his departure for southern Germany and Switzerland. *Herrmann and Dorothea* is set in contemporary small-town Germany and reflects Goethe's concerns about the survival of the smaller polities. The story concerns the romance of Herrmann,

FIG. 18. Frontispiece of *Herrmann und Dorothea* by J. W. Meil (1797)

the son of a wealthy Innkeeper in a small German town near the Rhine, and Dorothea, an emigré from the German lands on the east bank of the Rhine. Herrmann rides out to give food and clothing to a train of refugees passing close to his hometown. There he falls in love with Dorothea. His father the Innkeeper is unhappy because Dorothea is a destitute refugee, and not the wealthy hometown bride he was hoping Herrmann would marry. The father therefore sends his friends the Pastor and the Apothecary to assess Dorothea's suitability. A Judge travelling with the refugees tells them about Dorothea's heroic defence of some young women against attempts to rape them. Herrmann brings Dorothea home with him, but out of an understandable fear of rejection—she wears an engagement ring—he does not reveal his love for her and instead pretends that his family wants to employ her as a maid. The pretence breaks down during a fractious debate back at the inn. Still, the debate reveals Herrmann and Dorothea's love for one another, and they are betrothed by the Pastor with the father's at first grudging consent. The poem ends with a long monologue by Herrmann extolling the blessings of property ownership, German steadfastness in the face of the 'fearful movement' of current events, God, law and family, and above all peace, which is the poem's final word:

> Und gedächte jeder wie ich, so stände die Macht auf
> Gegen die Macht, und wir erfreuten uns Alle des Friedens.[172]
>
> And if everyone thought like me, then power would stand up / Against power, and we would all enjoy peace.

The poem is set against the background of the revolutionary wars, though it is not clear exactly when. Herrmann's longing for peace might be a response to the successes of the Revolutionary armies in late 1794 and early 1795, before Peace of Basle, or perhaps it is the summer of 1796, when the French invaded southwestern Germany again.[173] One thing is clear: the Jacobin Terror has ended, as the Judge's speech in canto VI makes clear. Herrmann's closing monologue evokes an attachment to the social status quo but also hopes for national renewal. It shows the deep attachment of Germans to their hometown.[174] It portrays a Germany that acknowledges the Revolution in neighbouring France but follows its own path to nationhood. This was how the poem was read by many at the time and in the nineteenth century, and its seemingly sentimental view of Germany made it his greatest publishing success since *Werther*. Recent readers have tended to find more complexity and irony in the poem, and in particular a more balanced view of the Revolution than Herrmann's closing monologue implies or than Goethe had managed in his earlier attempts to write about the Revolution. The liberal aims of the early Revolution are shown in a positive light by the Judge in canto VI. Equality and freedom are valid goals in response to the long history of the church's and the aristocracy's dominance ('idleness and selfishness'):

> Denn wer leugnet es wohl, daß hoch sich das Herz ihm erhoben,
> Ihm die freiere Brust mit reineren Pulsen geschlagen,
> Als sich der erste Glanz der neuen Sonne heranhob,
> Als man hörte vom Rechte der Menschen, das allen gemein sei,
> Von der begeisternden Freiheit und von der löblichen Gleichheit!

Damals hoffte jeder, sich selbst zu leben; es schien sich
Aufzulösen das Band, das viele Länder umstrickte,
Das der Müßiggang und der Eigennutz in der Hand hielt.[175]

For who will deny that his heart was lifted high, / His chest was freer and beat with purer pulses, / When the first glimmer of the new sun rose, / When we heard of the right of men that was common to all, / Of inspiring freedom and of praiseworthy equality! / Back then everyone hoped to live for himself; it seemed / The bondage would loosen which cast a net round many lands, / Which idleness and selfishness held in its grasp.

Dorothea herself has felt both the positive and negative effects of the Revolution. Her fiancé died fighting for the Revolution's ideals. She even wears the three colours of the Revolution, albeit so subtly as to seem accidental.[176] This more balanced view of the Revolution is supported by the objectivity of the Homeric style. The Homeric narrator does not express opinions, least of all political ones.[177] Moreover, the nineteenth-century nationalist reading of the poem is only weakly supported by Herrmann's closing monologue, which is more universalizing than nationalist.[178] Herrmann represents Germany as a place of tradition and (potentially) strength, but not as a nation state.[179] German statehood might in fact be dangerous if it led Germans to import the foreign idea of revolution. There is nothing in Herrmann's speech to contradict the anti-nationalist view Goethe expressed in 'Literary Sansculottism'.

Recent criticism has also asked how seriously we can take the content of the poem and the hometown values it seems to present. It may be that the poem is best understood as an example of mock-epic,[180] and that the Homeric manner both lends grandeur to the world it depicts and gently undermines it.[181] Goethe saw the issue slightly differently. He was conscious of writing to satisfy the thirst of his bourgeois readers for the subject matter they liked. 'In *Herrmann and Dorothea* I have, as regards the subject matter, done what the Germans want, and now they are extremely satisfied', he wrote to Schiller in January 1798. But in satisfying his readers he had also tricked them into accepting his own brand of high-classical art, 'like a card-sharp whose aim must be that no one understands how the trick has been produced'.[182] His point was not, or at least not in the first place, that the Homeric style allowed him to ironize the values his poem seemed to extol. It was that the poem's values and scenario were a Trojan horse for its high classical style. It was proof that the

Germans would stomach any writing, so long as its setting and sentiments appealed to them. What the objectivity and distance of the Homeric style certainly does is allow for nuance in the representation of Herrmann and Dorothea's world. This is by no means a homogeneous world, and the Homeric style sheds light on its internal divisions. In December 1796, with most of the poem finished, Goethe wrote an elegy announcing it, also titled 'Herrmann und Dorothea'. The elegy notes that the epic will represent German society according to its naturalness. It will take us into the quiet homes of the burghers where people grow up 'according to nature' ('nach der Natur'). The elegist hopes that these people, 'the healthy breed' ('das gesunde Geschlecht'), will triumph in the revolutionary wars. By contrast, in canto VI the Judge blames the end of the liberal phase of the Revolution on 'a corrupted breed, not worthy enough to bring about good' ('ein verderbtes Geschlecht, unwürdig das Gute zu schaffen'),[183] the opposite of the rural hometown folk who live close to nature. Schiller used similar language in the Augustenburg letters: the Jacobins were 'a corrupted generation.'[184] It was the language of the day.[185] Its ultimate source was Rousseau's analysis of the corrupting effects of civilization. Thus far, the imagery of naturalness seems to favour the Germans; the poem is an affectionate portrait of 'the pure humanity of the existence of a small German town', as Goethe wrote to Meyer in December 1796.[186] However, Herrmann's hometown is not as free of corruption as it might seem. There are signs that competitive *amour-propre* is beginning to take hold. His father the Innkeeper is wealthy. His social and political outlook reflects how Goethe's urban readers wanted to see themselves. They were the cultivated burghers of the medium and large German towns—orderly, rational, cosmopolitan-minded, and progressive. His father wants Herrmann to acquire the same civilized and orderly standards:

> Darum hab' ich gewünscht, es solle sich Herrmann auf Reisen
> Bald begeben, und sehn zum wenigsten Strasburg und Frankfurt
> Und das freundliche Manheim, das gleich und heiter gebaut ist.
> Denn wer die Städte gesehn, die großen und reinlichen, ruht nicht,
> Künftig die Vaterstadt selbst, so klein sie auch sei, zu verzieren.[187]

> That's why I've wished that Herrmann should go on his travels / Soon and at least see Strasbourg and Frankfurt / And friendly Mannheim, which is built evenly and serenely. / For whoever has seen the cities, the large and clean ones, will not rest / In adorning his own hometown in future, however small it might be.

The ambition to emulate the cities may be admirable, but in canto V, close to the centre of the poem and also at its moral centre,[188] the Pastor presents a very different image of hometown life and contrasts it with the competition for prestige in the cities. First he praises the slow rhythms of the peasant life, then turns to the peaceful hometown burghers, whose virtues are quite different from those of the Innkeeper's speech:

> Und Heil dem Bürger des kleinen
> Städtchens, der ländlich Gewerb mit Bürgergewerbe gepaaret!
> Auf ihm liegt nicht der Druck, der ängstlich den Landmann beschränket;
> Ihn verwirrt nicht die Sorge der vielbegehrenden Städter,
> Die dem Reicheren stets und dem Höheren, wenig vermögend,
> Nachzustreben gewohnt sind, besonders die Weiber und Mädchen.
> (V, 19–38)

And hail to the burgher of the small / Town, who combines rural trade with burgher's trade! / On him lies none of the pressure that anxiously confines the countryman; / He is not confused by the worry of the townspeople who desire much, / Who, having little wealth, are accustomed always to emulate those richer and those higher, / And especially the women and girls [do so].

The position of this speech at the heart of the poem indicates its centrality to the poem's meaning. It is also close to Goethe's post-Basle interest in the future of the small German polities. The Pastor diagnoses the discontents of urban modernity in terms of Rousseau's competitive *amour-propre*. The economy of a larger town brings with it competition for social prestige. Urban burghers of modest means cannot help but emulate their richer and higher-born compatriots. This unhealthy competition weakens the traditional fabric of society, for it causes envy. Another Rousseauian hallmark is the Pastor's comment about women's *amour-propre*. In *Émile*, Rousseau argued that women were especially susceptible to *amour-propre* because they must not only *be* virtuous and attractive, they must also *appear* so.[189] One of the tensions between Herrmann and his father is Herrmann's shyness in the company of the girls his father wants him to marry. They mock Herrmann for not following the latest fashions. The Pastor's speech makes clear that Herrmann's father has misunderstood the situation. The girls are caught up in an unpleasant competition for social prestige. Their *amour-propre* prevents them from seeing the goodness in Herrmann that lies beneath superficial appearances.

The Pastor's speech, with its distinction between the progressive burghers of the cities and the peasants and burghers of the timeless rural towns, is not only placed at the centre of the poem; it also precedes and frames the Judge's speech about the Revolution in canto VI. The Judge's political analysis accords with the Pastor's social analysis. The Judge praises the noble goals of the early stage of the Revolution which was a legitimate response to the longstanding wrongs of the *ancien regime*. This evidently reflects Goethe's opinion of the progressive German intelligentsia, for instance Herder, Knebel, and the Jena professors Hufeland and Fichte. But the Revolution then descends into violence. First, the new liberators of France are challenged by 'a corrupted breed'. Goethe's readers would detect a reference to the Jacobins here, though as we have seen the Rousseauian language also points to a broader category: the part of the urban bourgeoisie that is motivated by *amour-propre*. Worse is to come after the defeat of the French armies in western Germany. In their retreat, the French become desperate and descend into mindless violence, which triggers a reaction from the Germans, who also descend into animality. At this point in the Judge's narrative, his earlier republican language of liberty versus bondage is replaced by the conservative language of lawfulness versus license:

Sprech' er doch nie von Freiheit, als könn' er sich selber regieren!
Losgebunden erscheint, sobald die Schranken hinweg sind,
Alles Böse, das tief das Gesetz in die Winkel zurücktrieb.[190]

People should not talk of freedom, as if they could govern themselves! / Let loose, as soon as the constraints have gone, there emerges / All evil, which the law had driven into the corner.

The Judge's speech thus shifts in a way that closely resembles Machiavelli's analysis of republican governments in his *History of Florence*. Many believe that by abolishing monarchy they will replace bondage with freedom, says Machiavelli. This is the opinion of the republicans, but they are wrong. In fact, replacing a monarchy with a republic is merely to replace the necessary 'constraints' of the 'law' with license and lawlessness.

In light of the strictures on women's reading that Goethe expressed in the first epistle, one might expect the hometown society of *Herrmann and Dorothea* to display negative female stereotypes or traditional gender roles. In some ways it does, as we saw in the case of the young women's superficial love of fashion. Dorothea presents a more complex case. When in canto VII Herrmann and Dorothea meet at the well and he offers to carry one of her pitchers, she refuses, telling him that service is woman's lot. She then qualifies her statement by adding that a woman's service may be her route to mastery, which resembles the misogynist cliché that women's lack of social power is only an appearance and in reality women are in charge. However, in some ways Dorothea really is in charge. In canto VI the Judge recounts how, during the chaos after the French withdrawal, Dorothea killed one of a crowd of would-be rapists and saw off the rest of them. Again the meaning is reinforced by a Homeric archetype. The man's death is described in the manner of the *Iliad*: she 'struck him mightily down; he fell at her feet as his blood flowed' ('Hieb ihn nieder gewaltig; er stürzt' ihr blutend zu Füßen').[191] Again, in canto VIII as she and Herrmann walk up the steps to the inn before their fateful encounter with Herrmann's father, she stumbles and he supports her: Herrmann 'carried with manly feeling the woman's heroic stature' ('trug mit Mannesgefühl die Heldengröße des Weibes').[192] Although he supports her, the stereotypical gendering of feeling woman and heroic man is reversed. She becomes one of the statuesque heroines of ancient myth captured in Greek sculpture. She is a survival from a heroic age, a gift of god, *dōron theou*, as the Greek etymology of her name has it.

The idea of spontaneity is important for the resolution of *Herrmann and Dorothea*, as it was for *Agitated*. Dorothea's defence of the women shows that she is capable of acting out of a spontaneous impulse of sympathy or pity. The idea of spontaneity is first raised by the Pastor in canto V and becomes important towards the poem's close. Much is gained by acting on feeling and little by reflecting, the Pastor argues, for reflection may only serve to confuse our healthy impulses:

> Der Augenblick nur entscheidet
> Über das Leben des Menschen und über sein ganzes Geschicke;
> [...] Immer gefährlicher ists, beim Wählen dieses und jenes
> Nebenher zu bedenken und so das Gefühl zu verwirren.[193]

> Only the moment is decisive / In the life of a person and his whole fate; / [...] It's always more dangerous, when choosing, to consider this and that / At the same time and so to confuse one's instinct.

Even if deliberation were not liable to confuse us further, by the beginning of the final canto the situation has become so tangled as to be insoluble by reason. On reaching the inn with Dorothea, Hermann takes the wise Pastor to one side and begs him to resolve the 'knot'.[194] Instead of reflecting on the wisest course, the Pastor spontaneously—'his spirit commanded him' ('da befahl ihm sein Geist')[195]—manoeuvres Dorothea into a position in which she has no choice but to reveal her feelings for Herrmann. With that, the 'knot' has been cut. The Pastor feels justified in his instinctive action. Herrmann's final speech repeats the Pastor's preference for spontaneity over reasoning, but now in a more explicitly political context. Dorothea has recalled her erstwhile fiancé's departure for Paris, where he found only prison and death. She repeats his apocalyptic words on leaving her. The world was in flux, he said: 'The basic laws are dissolving of the most firmly established states' ('Grundgesetze lösen sich auf der festesten Staaten').[196] 'Grundgesetz' also means *constitution*;[197] the fiancé's words refer specifically to the reform of the French state, as well as to basic laws in general. It is against this memory of constitutional reform that Herrmann makes his final speech. Germans should not 'sway this way and that' ('wanken hierhin und dorthin'),[198] he says, echoing the Pastor's argument against deliberation. Instead, Herrmann insists that people should hold on to what they have: lawfulness must be preserved. As Machiavelli argued in his *History of Florence*, the republicans erred in their optimism. The alternatives on offer in a revolution are not servitude and liberty, but servitude and lawlessness. Now we see the significance of Dorothea's words to Herrmann at the well. To accept a life of service is also to choose lawfulness. As it happens, and to her good fortune, service is not what she gets, but events have shown she was right to accept the bargain.

———

The partnership with Schiller reawakened in Goethe a public confidence and eagerness for controversy that had been dormant since his move to Weimar in 1775. On finishing *Herrmann and Dorothea* in the summer of 1797, he returned to the Old Testament and began to study the story of the Israelites' forty-year wanderings through the wilderness in the last four books of the Pentateuch. What emerged was a set of notes and a more-or-less continuous draft of an essay. In 1812 he revised the draft. It was finally published in 1819. On one level, it resembles the kind of Bible criticism practised by Johann David Michaelis, Johann Gottfried Eichhorn, and others.[199] It tries to uncover the historical events behind the implausible Mosaic narrative. The Israelites cannot have spent forty years in the wilderness. Most likely forty was just a stock way of saying 'a large number'. A more reasonable duration would have been four years. However, alongside this scholarly mode is an argument in the spirit of Spinoza's *Tractatus Theologico-Politicus*. The Mosaic laws were added by later authors in order to cover up embarrassing historical facts, fill gaps in the narrative, and impose a false interpretation long after the event.[200] In reality, the establishment of the Mosaic law was motivated by political needs, not religious or moral beliefs. The story of Moses's leading the Children of Israel through the wilderness is a story about nation-building. The material Goethe wrote in 1797 and the revised version of 1812–1819 both reinterpret the Mosaic narrative in these political terms, albeit with different emphases. Horst Lange has argued that the essay expresses Goethe's distaste for nationalism.[201] Certainly nationalism was a cause for concern after Valmy, and the drafts do describe a murder committed by Moses in Egypt as a 'patriotic assassination'.[202] However, nationalism was much less of a concern for Goethe in 1797 than it would be when he returned to the drafts in 1812. The idea of Judaism as a national religion is not prominent in the 1797 drafts. The 1812–1819 version is more overtly anti-nationalistic: it refers to Jehovah twice as a 'national God'.

The core of the 1797 essay is a study of the pathological psychology of Moses and his people which was caused, Goethe argues, by the violent competition for military and political power between the Israelites and their neighbours. A further dimension of the 1797 draft is provided by parallels between Moses's leadership of the Israelites and 'the modern French'—in other words the Revolution. His explanation of Moses's leadership follows the same pattern as the history of the Revolution recounted by the Judge in canto VI of *Herrmann and Dorothea*. What began as a justified rebellion against years of oppression descends into cruelty and violence. For even if we absolve Moses of the stupid cruelty of leading his people through the desert for forty years, still his leadership was violent and incompetent. Even so, Moses was a product of his nation and his time. The Israelites' humiliating subjection by the Egyptians was intolerable to a proud people. In the same way it was understandable that the French rebelled against years of misrule, according to the Judge in *Herrmann and Dorothea*. Their oppression at the hands of the Egyptians primed the Israelites to follow a leader with a 'lively feeling for right and wrong' as well as a tendency for violent actions.[203] This explains the murder of the firstborn sons of the Egyptians, which Goethe blames on a crack unit of Israelite assassins. This 'cruel policy'[204] was perfectly designed to undermine the legitimacy of the Egyptian state, for it destroyed the principle of primogeniture on which Egyptian society was founded. The Israelites' successful assault on the Egyptian state then hardened into a policy. From this point on the raison d'être of the Israelite state would be conquest by force. Goethe probably intended a parallel with the French state's wars of liberation from 1793 onwards. With the Moses project, in its 1797 form, Goethe used the new reality of the Revolution to revisit and retest his long-held support for Spinoza's argument that the institutions of religion have their origins in nation-building. The Revolution had rewritten the principles on which the French state was founded, more than once. The need for rewriting was understandable: the history of misrule and oppression was real and painful. But in the end the rewriting only served to cover up or legitimize a will to power and a psychopathology of violence.

The years 1796 and 1797 were Goethe's most productive as a poet since the elegies and epigrams of 1788–1790. His productivity was stimulated by Schiller, and as in the *Xenia* it was a competitive collaboration. The most brilliant evidence of their collaboration is the series of ballads they wrote in 1797. Each of the ballads is unique in its patterns of rhyme and rhythm, each is a display of poetic virtuosity and the very opposite of the 'half measures' Goethe and Schiller decried. Poetry should not present some rose-tinted sentimental or glibly rationalized image of how we want humans to be—'staid and natural', ('bieder und natürlich'), as Goethe put it in 'Muses and Graces in the Mark', a satire on the poems of the Brandenburg pastor F. A. W. Schmidt, another culprit of poetic half measures. The true vocation of the poet was to present an unflinching vision of how humans really are, Goethe wrote to Schiller in November 1797:

> Whatever may come, we are required to forget our century, if we want to proceed according to our convictions. For such sanctimonious drivel in matters of principle, as seems to pertain currently, has never existed before in the world [...]. Poetry is in fact grounded in the empirical-pathological condition of humanity, and who among our excellent connoisseurs and so-called poets is able to admit that?[205]

It was a provocation to the moralizing tendencies of 'our century', not an escape from it. The poems of 1796 and 1797 are part of modernity but stand athwart it. They return to the paganism of the *Roman Elegies* and have a strong strain of satirical indignation at Christianity for perverting and enfeebling human nature. The story told in Goethe's ballad 'The Bride of Corinth' is a shocking brew of sex, death, and religion, set in the early years of Christianity. The language is simple, and the complex scheme of rhyme and rhythm is handled with such ease as to feel entirely natural. It tells the story of a would-be bride and groom who have been promised to one another in childhood by their respective families. The poem begins with the young man arriving in Corinth to be wed. In the meantime, his bride's family has converted to Christianity, while the groom's family has stuck to its ancient pagan beliefs. The historical setting shows once more the emergence of problematic modernity out of antiquity. This is the reason for Goethe's choice of Corinth as the poem's location: it was one of the first Greek cities in which Christianity took root. (As we shall see, the poem contains another more specific and more challenging allusion to early Christian Corinth.) The bride's mother welcomes the groom with food and wine. As he lies down to sleep, the bride appears in his room wearing a white dress and veil. He soon notices that her skin is white too—she is a vampiric ghost. (The poem is one of the earliest modern examples of vampire literature.) The bride now tells her story. Her mother, on recovering from illness, committed the daughter to a convent, by way of thanks to God, so that rather than becoming an actual bride, the young woman became a bride of Christ. Shortly after joining the convent she died, which gives a seal of morbid finality to her incarceration. When she has finished her story, the ghost bride and her bridegroom enjoy the night together, only to be interrupted by her mother who has been lurking outside the room. Appalled, the mother assumes the groom has been visited by a prostitute. The groom dies from contact with the vampire bride. The poem ends with the bride pleading with her mother to disinter her from her coffin and burn her with groom on a funeral pyre, so that she and her groom can be reunited with their old gods:

> Höre Mutter nun die letzte Bitte
> Einen Scheiterhaufen schichte du,
> Öffne meine bange kleine Hütte,
> Bring in Flammen Liebende zur Ruh.
> Wenn der Funke sprüht,
> Wenn die Asche glüht,
> Eilen wir den alten Göttern zu.[206]

> Mother, hear now my last request: / Pile up a funeral pyre; / Open my anxious little cabin, / Bring lovers to peace in the flames! / When the spark flies, / When the ash glows, / We will hurry to our old gods.

The funeral pyre signifies the fire of love, for even in death pagans enjoy the pleasures of life. The food that the mother has brought to welcome the groom was, it turns out, pagan bread and wine, 'gifts of Ceres, gifts of Bacchus', the groom tells his bride, so quickly closing off any thought that the bread and wine might have signified the Christian sacraments. More provocative still, the figure of the bride contains a strongly anti-Christian subtext. In becoming a bride of Christ, she also comes to represent the Christian church. This is why Goethe chose Corinth as the site of the poem. In 2 Corinthians 11, Paul warns the church of Corinth of a heretical doctrine that promises another, false Christ. In fact, Paul tells the Corinthians, their church is wedded only to the one true Christ: 'For I am jealous over you with godly jealousy: for I have espoused you to one husband, that I may present you as a chaste virgin to Christ'.[207] This empty theological marriage, so Goethe's poem would have it, has supplanted the authentic pagan marriage between the bride and groom. Not only is the marriage of the church to Christ empty—because a virginal marriage is not a marriage at all—it is also contrary to good health and proper human flourishing. The colourful crowd of ancient gods has been banished from her family's now silent house, the bride tells her groom. The Christian religion that has replaced them is not only colourless and lifeless; it is a crime against human nature:

> Und der alten Götter bunt Gewimmel
> Hat sogleich das stille Haus geleert,
> Unsichtbar wird einer nur im Himmel,
> Und ein Heiland wird am Kreuz verehrt,
> Opfer fallen hier,
> Weder Lamm noch Stier,
> Aber Menschenopfer unerhört.[208]

> And the colourful throng of the old gods / Straightaway vacated the silent house. / One alone and invisible [is worshipped] in heaven, / And a saviour is worshipped on the cross; / Sacrifices fall here, / Neither lamb nor bull, / But, unprecedentedly, human sacrifices.

The inflammatory reference to human sacrifice is not an empty provocation. It is an idea that links several parts of the poem's portrayal of the new religion.[209] It is the bride sacrificed by way of thanks for her mother's recovery, for her committal to a convent is a form of sacrifice, a deprivation of all sensuous and sexual joy. It is the virginal marriage of the Corinthian church to Christ. It is the sacramental blood and wine, the consumption of Christ's flesh and blood during worship. And it can equally well apply to God's sacrifice of his son Christ on the cross.

Christian apologists might defend their religion's obsession with death by pointing to the value of faith. Christians are tested, even by the church's own doctrines, but the test stimulates faith, which proves the final guarantee of salvation and the highest human good. The poem blocks off this argument. In the figure of the bride's mother, Goethe presents a damning critique of faith-fuelled zealotry. She has sent her daughter to a convent. She spies on the household, enforcing Christian morality. Worst of all, the mother is faithless. The bond between bride and groom was a solemn oath, which the mother has broken by committing her daughter to a convent. Her faith in marrying her daughter to Christ amounts precisely to faithlessness. In this way she has destroyed one of the main arguments made in the eighteenth century for Christianity and against atheism—that because atheists do not believe in punishment in the afterlife, they have no reason not to break oaths. This was John Locke's argument in his *Letter Concerning Toleration* (1689).[210] The behaviour of the mother shows that Christians can no more be held to oaths than atheists. Indeed it is the very nature of Christianity that makes the mother break the oath: its propensity to turn us into zealots with a 'with us or against us' mentality. As Goethe's narrator puts it in the poem's second stanza:

Keimt ein Glaube neu,
Wird oft Lieb und Treu
Wie ein böses Unkraut ausgerauft.[211]

When a new belief sprouts, / Often love and faith are / Ripped out like vile weeds.

Goethe wrote 'The Bride of Corinth' on 4 and 5 June 1797. In the next three days, he wrote another ballad of the same remarkable quality and complementary to it, 'The God and the Bayadère'. Where 'The Bride of Corinth' exposes Christianity's morbidity and faithlessness, 'The God and the Bayadère' reconstructs a positive vision of what a religion of salvation through death could have been. The story, set in ancient India, tells of the great god Mahadeva visiting the earth in human form to discover whether people deserve punishment or forgiveness. He comes across the Bayadère. The Western imagination has traditionally combined in the *bayadère* the roles of temple dancer and prostitute, but in Goethe's poem she is a prostitute and dancer, and no mention is made of service in temples.[212] There are two reasons for this. Her eventual salvation is all the more provocative precisely because she has no prior connection to religion. And by casting her as a prostitute first and foremost, Goethe repeats a provocation he first expressed in one of the unpublished *Venetian Epigrams*, namely that Christ liked to associate with prostitutes:

> Wundern kann es mich nicht daß unser Herr Christus mit [illegible]
> Gern und mit Sündern gelebt gehts mir doch eben auch so.²¹³

> I'm not surprised that our Lord Christ liked to live with [illegible] /
> And sinners, that's how it is with me too.

The illegible word is generally assumed to be 'whores' (*Huren*). The point of the quip is that a genuinely merciful god extends his grace to the worst of sinners. So in visiting the Bayadère, Mahadeva is similar to Christ, a god taking on human form to share our misery and happiness and to take pity on the lowliest of sinners. The Bayadère entices Mahadeva with her dance and welcomes him into her brothel, where she tends to his 'simulated hurts' ('geheuchelte Leiden'). Mahadeva now goes on to demand 'slavish service' ('Sklavendienste') of the Bayadère, in other words sex, to which she adapts naturally. In testing the Bayadère by posing as a hurt and vulnerable human, Mahadeva blatantly attempts to break her will. He hypocritically sets her a moral standard that is unachievable for humans, at the same time as he encourages her to be immoral. This is the paradox at the heart of the Christian life: the combination of pity and moral rigour. The worst of the torture is still to come. As the god's demands on her become ever harsher and her service ever more subservient, she falls in love with him. Prostitution evolves into love, and it does so naturally at first: 'If obedience is in the spirit, / Love will not be far behind' ('Ist Gehorsam im Gemüte / Wird nicht fern die Liebe sein').²¹⁴ Still, accustomed to a life of sexual service to men, she cannot cope with the true feeling of love. The transformation of service into love causes a crisis in her, and she collapses at his feet. Eventually they go to sleep, and in the morning she wakes to find him dead in her arms—the harshest test of all, now that she loves him. The god's body is carried to a funeral pyre, and she follows hoping to throw herself onto the pyre, according to the traditional practice of *suttee*. The priests refuse her wish: because she was not married to Mahadeva, there is no duty on her to die. The priests' objection contains two thoughts, both of them contrary to humanity and nature: first, that there is an important difference between a marriage in practice and one in law; second, that *suttee* must be a self-denying duty and cannot be a self-realizing desire. However, she defies the priests and flings herself onto the pyre. The god manifests in the flames and embraces her, and together they float upwards to heaven. Not only was the priests' opposition obnoxious, it was also out of step with their god. Their doctrine is based on an artificial law of self-denial whereas the god saves the Bayadère because she has naturally realized the highest virtue of all: love. The poem closes with a moral lesson that expresses the proper spirit of Christianity, not the artificial religion of the priests:

> Es freut sich die Gottheit der reuigen Sünder;
> Unsterbliche heben verlorene Kinder
> Mit feurigen Armen zum Himmel empor.[215]
>
> The godhead rejoices in penitent sinners; / Immortals raise lost children / Up to heaven in their fiery arms.

The allusion to Luke 15:7 is unmissable: 'I say unto you, that likewise joy shall be in heaven over one sinner that repenteth, more than over ninety and nine just persons, which need no repentance'. The poem's alternative story of salvation ends with the woman of loose morals becoming a paragon of faith. And if the Bayadère's good heart is justified, so too is the god Mahadeva's. His cruelty in the opening stanzas, and not least the torment of his pretended death, gives way to a generosity of spirit that should be the nature of any god worthy of the name. This then was the reality of Christ's mission, or should have been. Salvation comes from sympathy and love, by an entirely natural route, beginning in and continuing through the body, in contrast to the self-justifying ordinances of institutional religion and its philosophical outrider, the Kantian ethics of self-denying duty.

The work on optics had stuttered to a halt in autumn 1793 after Goethe failed to win Lichtenberg's approval for his theory of coloured shadows. Insult was added to injury when Lichtenberg published an updated edition of J. C. P. Erxleben's *Foundations of Natural Science* in 1794. Lichtenberg failed to mention Goethe's experiments or even to list the *Essays on Optics* in the bibliography. (In fact Lichtenberg had made a note reminding himself to do so, but for some reason it did not happen.)[216] The omission triggered an angry outburst from Goethe in a letter to Schiller in November 1795.[217] In the four years from 1793, all Goethe's attempts to make progress were unsuccessful. It was dawning on him that the project of a general theory of colour was too ambitious. The problem of distinguishing between subjective and objective phenomena required a multifaceted solution. He set out the challenges in a complaint to Jacobi in December 1794. An alarmingly wide range of phenomena needed to be captured in experiments. These had to be arranged in a logical sequence. Full account would have to be given of the competing theories of colour. 'This requires a working through of my poor *I*, the possibility of which I previously had no inkling of'.[218] The theory of colour was as much a theory of the human mind and senses as it was of colour itself, and it required philosophical solutions. 'In compiling my physical observations, I find it has already been of great benefit to me that I am looking down on the philosophical battlefield rather more than usual', he wrote to Schiller in November 1795.[219] He had hoped that Fichte's *Theory of Knowledge* would come to his rescue, but it had not. In the spring and summer of 1795 he turned his attention to the physiology of colour vision, perhaps hoping to make sense of Buffon's *couleurs accidentelles*. Meanwhile Sömmerring was working on the physiology of the eye and the optic nerve.[220] In August he sent Goethe the results of his research.[221] However, when Sömmerring published his essay *On the Organ of the Soul* in 1796, Goethe was not convinced by the links he made between the physiology of the eye and the phenomena of vision. The idea that the soul was located in a particular part of the brain was speculative and of no scientific use. Sömmerring's work was an example of the wrong way of introducing philosophy into the science of perception.

It was only in January 1798 that he began in earnest to use philosophy to bring order and system to his work on optics. The question was how to make sense of our perception of harmonious and contrasting colours. Like others before him including Newton, Goethe used a colour wheel to express the relationship between colours. The wheel had the advantage over a linear spectrum that it expressed not only the transitions between neighbouring colours, but also contrasts between colours that occupied opposed positions on the wheel, for instance blue and orange. In this sense, the colour wheel could be considered a more faithful representation of colour space than the spectrum. This was important, since Goethe's criticisms of Newton were designed to show that the linear spectral patterns produced by Newton's experiments were mere artefacts of the experimental process and not expressions of nature. However, the colour wheel is still only an abstraction; it is not a phenomenon we observe in nature. So despite its satisfyingly complete form and its ability to express both transitions and contrasts, the colour wheel does not of itself prove that the relations between positions on it express anything about the nature of light. It is possible that the colour wheel does say something about the nature of light, and Goethe evidently thought so. It seemed to correspond to the boundary colours he had seen through Büttner's prisms. Alternatively, the colour wheel might express facts of subjective visual perception, such as Buffon's *couleurs accidentelles*, as Goethe no doubt hoped when he began to study the physiology of vision in 1795. Or the colour wheel might express some other facts about the human mind, such as the pleasure we take in the colours in art or nature. Finally, the colour wheel might be a mere artefact of the scientific process, as Goethe thought the linear spectrum was. Considered as an artefact, the colour wheel raised a further set of questions about the validity of scientific representations. A Newtonian might represent light as consisting of waves, with each colour occupying the space on a quantitative scale of wavelengths that corresponded to its differential refrangibility. However, the concept 'wave' is only a symbol, and the numerical values of wavelengths are only approximations. Perhaps science is forever doomed to use representations that do not fully express natural phenomena. Or perhaps some classes of representation are more useful in some contexts than in others.

In the *Critique of Pure Reason*, Kant had tried to demonstrate that all propositions concerning experiential and scientific phenomena must fall under the twelve 'pure concepts of the understanding'. It was therefore reasonable to wonder whether the colour wheel might be organized along the lines of Kant's twelve concepts. Schiller first suggested this idea and set out his own analysis according to the categories in a letter of 19 January 1798, as Goethe was resuming work on optics after four frustrating years.[222] As their discussions continued through 1798, applying the Kantian concepts produced results that were unexpected and in some ways disappointing. In November they discussed the differing types of colour harmony.[223] The next day Goethe drew up a table of the colour relationships and some diagrams of colour wheels. The discussion continued in the evening.[224] The focus of their conversations was the psychological and aesthetic effects of different colour combinations in painting. Since August Goethe had been rereading Diderot's *Essay on Painting*,[225] and he found Diderot's comments on colour congenial.[226] The diagrams Goethe drew after his discussion with Schiller show the various types of harmony that can be derived from the colour wheel—for instance pairs of contrasting colours linked by diameters, and triads of colours linked by equilateral triangles. Beside the diagrams Goethe wrote brief notes indicating how the various combinations related to Kant's pure concepts of the understanding in the class of quantity—the three concepts of unity, plurality, and totality. So for instance, contrasts between diametrically opposed colours on the wheel represent a maximum of plurality, in other words a totality. Triads of colours connected by equilaterals represent a 'plurality that deviates little from unity'. These triadic harmonies are 'significant, daring'. There is no further annotation or discussion. The purpose of Goethe's notes and the discussions with Schiller was to provide artists with a conceptual framework for making choices about the use of colour harmonies, and not to make truth claims about the colour wheel. It is hard to imagine the diagrams and notes generating any propositions that would satisfy Kant's requirement that we use the concepts to confirm whether our propositions about nature are meaningful.

A second problem was that the geometrical relationships between colours, whether diametrical or triadic, are crude abstractions that pay no regard to the almost infinite shadings between the different hues on the wheel. This failure of schematic representations to capture the richness of phenomena became a talking point again in January 1799, when Goethe and Schiller tried a different Kantian approach to the colour wheel. In December 1798 Goethe read Kant's newly published *Anthropology in Pragmatic Perspective*. Although the work dated from Kant's lectures decades earlier, it played a part in his system of transcendental idealism. The *Anthropology* was an analysis of the psychological faults and weaknesses that humans must contend with in their efforts to follow ethical precepts. Goethe wrote to Schiller that he found the book 'valuable' but could only stomach it 'in small doses'.[227] He was less complimentary in a letter to Voigt:

> Notwithstanding all that is excellent, acute, delightful (in which our old teacher remains ever the same), it seems to me to be prejudiced in many passages and in many more ungenerous. A wise man ought not to use the word *fool* so often, especially since pride is so irksome to him. Genius and talent are ever obstacles to him, he dislikes poets, and thank God he understands little of the other arts. In various instances he is pedantic, e.g., that he will not tolerate a mixture of the sanguine and the choleric temperaments; admittedly my expression *mixture* is incorrect, but experience teaches that there is a progression from the sanguine to the choleric through many stages. And in any case the whole division into four temperaments is mere artifice and a convenience for the sake of the observer.[228]

Despite their reservations about the *Anthropology*, Goethe and Schiller devised a colour wheel of three concentric rings based on the four temperaments. In the innermost ring were the twelve hues and in the outermost ring the temperaments. A middle ring contained twelve human occupations or types, from the ruler and the philosopher (both melancholics) to the bon vivant and the poet (both sanguine). These correspondences were based in part on cues in Kant's text, though the classification of the philosopher as melancholic was contrary to Kant's view that phlegmatics were commonly philosophical.[229] Perhaps by classifying the philosopher as melancholic, Goethe and Schiller were having a dig at Kant's grim *Anthropology*. Goethe later claimed they created several versions of this 'temperament rose',[230] but it was not a serious attempt to give philosophical form to the colour wheel. Eventually, in the final version of his *Theory of Colour* of 1810, Goethe rejected any analogies between moral terminology and colours as mere *jeux d'esprit*.[231] What he did usefully and interestingly explore, in a section titled 'Sensuous-Moral Effects of Colours', was the psychological and social aspect of our reaction to and use of colours. He also expressed reservations about the application of metaphysical concepts to colours: 'Metaphysical formulae have great breadth and depth; however, in order to fill them out adequately requires rich contents, otherwise they remain empty'.[232] The Kantian experiments had not come close to resolving the problem of the colour wheel.

In his letter of 19 January 1798, Schiller told Goethe that by applying the categories to his 'predicament' he would gain 'new faith in the regulative use of philosophy in empirical things'.[233] Schiller's formulation is somewhat confused. By 'the regulative use of philosophy' Schiller must have meant the regulative use of reason. Kant distinguished between 'constitutive' and 'regulative' procedures in the creation of scientific knowledge. The former describes what we do when we create or 'constitute' scientific knowledge: we ensure that scientific theories conform to the twelve pure concepts of the understanding (or categories). This task belongs to the faculty of understanding. The faculty of reason has no role in the constitution of knowledge. The ideas created by reason, such as the idea of the universe as a totality, cannot be found in experience and must not form part of scientific theories. The pure concepts of the understanding and the ideas of reason must be kept entirely separate, Kant insisted:

> Without such a division, metaphysics is utterly impossible, or at best is a disorderly and bungling endeavor to patch together a house of cards, without knowledge of the materials with which one is preoccupied and of their suitability for one or another end.[234]

This is the point on which Schiller seems to have been confused, and it took Goethe several weeks to reach a settled view on Schiller's advice concerning the regulative use of reason. In the meantime he thought about the history of the science of optics. He felt a 'strong desire' to write something on the history and hoped he could produce something good or even pleasing, he told Schiller.[235] The reply to Schiller's advice on the regulative use of reason came on 10 February. Goethe understood Kant's distinction between the regulative and constitutive uses of reason, at least as it related to the history of optical theory. He accepted Kant's view that scientific research is a constitutive procedure: it is concerned with what we can possibly know. However, scientists easily lapse into imagining what *ought* to be the case. In other words, they take regulative ideas of reason and use them constitutively. It is only natural, indeed it is admirable of humans to do so, to impose their idea of what ought to be on what could possibly be:

> That which strikes us so much in theory, we see in practice every day. One can hardly believe one's own eyes how much humans, in order to make something of their singular, one-sided, powerless nature, are required to close their eyes to circumstances that contradict them and struggle against them with utmost energy—and yet the reason for it lies in the deeper, better part of human nature, since man must in practice always be constitutive and actually not be bothered about what could happen, but about what should happen. Now, the latter is always an idea, and man is concrete in a concrete situation; so it goes on and on in endless self-deception, in order to bestow the honour of an idea on concrete things etc.[236]

Kant's distinction between the constitutive and the regulative proved useful, but not in the way Schiller envisaged. Instead of using reason as a regulative guide to forming scientific theory, Goethe meant to use the constitutive-regulative distinction (or confusion) as a tool for understanding the psychology and sociology of scientific research. A week later he wrote to Schiller reaffirming his understanding of the usefulness of Kant for his work on optics. There was no value in testing his theory against Kant's categories. He was only interested in using Kant to explain the history of optics: 'What actually led me to that schema according to the categories, and what necessitated my insisting on its completion was the history of colour theory'.[237] From this point on, his focus was on colour theory and its history. In February 1799, he drafted a general introduction and table of contents for the whole of his colour theory.[238] The eighth of its nine sections would be devoted to 'History of Colour Theory, perhaps'.[239] On the same day, he wrote from memory[240] a first, schematic history.[241] In the spirit of the letter to Schiller of 10 February 1798, the drafts foreground social and psychological factors. They outline how scientists have responded to their historical circumstances and how their work on colour has reflected their own needs. Over the next ten years he worked these few pages of drafts into a full-scale history. The 1810 version of his *Theory of Colour* would consist of three parts: a didactic part setting out his own observations, a polemical part criticising Newton's theory, and a historical part. The historical part was as long as the other two combined. It was a pioneering work in the history, sociology, and psychology of science.

The 'working through of my poor *I*',[242] of which he wrote to Jacobi in 1794, had become a working through of the history of science. The *I* was not neglected. The historical drafts he wrote in 1799 contained a section on his own journey towards a theory of colour. In 1800 he made a further set of notes on the history of his optical researches, under the heading 'History of the Author's Work in this Field'.[243] In 1803, in a concerted effort to finish the theory of colour, he reviewed the mass of papers he had accumulated over the years. 'I stand high enough above it to view my past being and doing, historically, as the fate of a third person', he wrote to Schiller.[244] The process of bringing himself to mind historically, as he put it in the same letter, had enabled him to overcome his natural aversion to autobiography. This was the second unexpected consequence of trying to apply Kant's philosophy to colour theory. Its significance for the remainder of his working life was immense. His literary output from 1800 onwards would be dominated by autobiography.

The attempts to apply Kant's philosophy to colour theory had one further consequence. Goethe recognised that the colour wheel was a symbolic abstraction from the phenomena. This was just one case of a more general problem. His colour theory was an assemblage of related phenomena. In order to express the theory, he needed to describe the phenomena as faithfully as possible. These descriptions were the most decisive part of his work on colour. In 1798 and 1799 he had lengthy debates with Schiller about the best form of discursive representation. He addressed the problem in the introduction he drafted in February 1799:

> In the discourse itself it has not been possible to refrain entirely from hypothetical expressions. Viewed more closely, every word is in itself hypothetical; and when presenting such simple phenomena that easily vanish from our handling of them, we have to help ourselves out with analogies, metaphors, symbols, and all manner of figurative expressions.[245]

By 'hypothetical' Goethe means that the expressions convey more than the phenomena, and the surplus meaning they convey implies an explanation of the phenomena. In this sense words are hypotheses. The structure of language is not the structure of reality. Scientific language inevitably conveys all manner of extraneous meanings. One seeming exception is the language of mathematics, which is more valid, because mathematic symbols 'have intuitions at their root'. For this reason, they 'can be identical with the phenomena in the highest sense'.[246] On a superficial reading, this seems to give mathematics a special role in natural science. Goethe knew Kant's claim in the preface to the *Metaphysical Foundations of Natural Science* that 'in any special doctrine of nature there can be only as much proper science as there is mathematics therein'.[247] Kant's argument comes down to the difference between (mathematical) quantities and (experiential) qualities. Only the former can be given a priori and thereby constitute absolute proof: 'For only the concept of magnitudes can be constructed, i.e., exhibited *a priori* in intuition, while qualities cannot be exhibited in anything but empirical intuition'.[248] This is far from being Goethe's argument. The reason for Goethe's high opinion of mathematics is that it has near-absolute purity as a sign system, in contrast to the messiness of verbal language. It is not that mathematics gives an absolute standard of proof by virtue of being completely a priori and nonempirical. On the contrary, mathematical symbols come closest to human perception by virtue of not introducing extraneous meanings. So Goethe's thinking about scientific signs and symbols revolves around the question of what gets us closest to the phenomenon, what is least detrimental to conveying human sensation. Insofar as conveying human sensation is the highest goal of scientific discourse, science is defined in terms of the *homo mensura* principle. Human sensation is the touchstone for scientific truth. Humans are the measure of nature.

Goethe still hoped for a productive dialogue with the young Kantians, and his hopes were revived in 1798, albeit in fraught circumstances. In October the *Philosophical Journal*, edited by Fichte and Niethammer, published the essay 'Development of the Concept of Religion' by Friedrich Karl Forberg, a former pupil of Fichte's. Fearing that Forberg's essay might be taken as an expression of his own views, Fichte published a companion piece, 'On the Ground of our Belief in a Divine World-Governance'. The essays were not especially controversial, certainly in comparison with Goethe's views on Christianity, and their post-Kantian idiom would have limited their appeal, had it not been for the publication of a pamphlet decrying them, *A Father's Letter to his Student Son about Fichte's and Forberg's Atheism*, which was written in an accessible style and circulated widely. The Lutheran authorities in Dresden complained about Fichte's and Forberg's essays to Duke Friedrich August of Saxony, who issued a confiscation order against the journal and threatened to bar his Saxon subjects from studying at Jena. Faced with a financial loss, Carl August ordered the university to investigate and punish the culprits. Fichte responded by threatening to resign if he were formally censured for atheism. The Duke took Fichte at his word and obliged him to leave.

Goethe's role in Fichte's dismissal is hard to judge. By the end of 1798 Carl August was so frustrated by Goethe's failure to report on the content of the Jena professors' lectures that he refused to speak to Goethe on the subject.[249] However, it is unlikely that Goethe was actively shielding Fichte and the other professors. The balance of the evidence, or the telling lack of evidence, suggests that Goethe argued for Fichte's dismissal. His correspondence with Voigt is silent on the events, probably because Goethe destroyed the relevant letters. Fichte later claimed that Goethe voted for his dismissal in the Privy Council, which was otherwise evenly split.[250] A vote against Fichte would certainly have been in keeping with Goethe's anxieties about political agitation and his opposition to freedom of expression. Any reason Goethe might have had to support Fichte earlier in his tenure had now vanished. The political risk that the authorities had taken in appointing Fichte had not paid off. Fichte's undoubted qualities as a lecturer were outweighed by his self-importance. Writing to Schlosser in August 1799, Goethe expressed regret at Fichte's departure but also bemoaned his 'foolish presumptuousness'. He continued: 'And for my own person I am ready to admit that I would vote against my own son, if he allowed himself such language against a government'.[251]

According to Fichte's son, when it was put to Goethe that in voting for Fichte's dismissal he risked damaging the university's reputation, Goethe replied: 'One star sets, another rises!'[252] He could afford to be sanguine about Fichte's departure because he had already found a replacement. The new philosophical star was the twenty-three-year-old Friedrich Wilhelm Joseph Schelling, a graduate of the Tübingen seminary. Aside from his youthful brilliance, Schelling possessed the two appealing attributes that Fichte had lacked: political moderation and an active interest in science. Writing to Voigt after his first meeting with Schelling in May 1798, Goethe opined that 'he is a clear, energetic mind, organized according to the latest fashion; I haven't noticed a trace of a sansculotte turn in him, rather he seems moderate and educated in every way'.²⁵³ Four months earlier he had read Schelling's *Ideas for a Philosophy of Nature*. There were arguments in the *Ideas* that should have appealed to him. Schelling commended Kant's definition of matter in terms of attractive and repulsive forces, and he attempted a transcendental deduction of matter as an equilibrium of opposed forces. Still, Goethe felt Schelling had fallen into the Idealist trap of deriving propositions about nature from human mental faculties: 'it is not nature as we know it, rather [nature] as it is grasped by us only according to particular forms and capacities of our mind', he wrote to Schiller in January 1798.²⁵⁴ His opinion of Schelling began to change when, during the visit in May, Schelling took part in Goethe's optical experiments.²⁵⁵ There was probably also a wider discussion of Goethe's scientific theories; Schelling had long recognised the importance of Goethe's theory of plant metamorphosis. Goethe duly confirmed his support for Schelling's appointment.²⁵⁶ In June he read Schelling's essay *On the World Soul*, where Schelling made explicit and prominent reference to Goethe's metamorphosis theory. Goethe wrote to Voigt again voicing his support for Schelling.²⁵⁷

Goethe did see hope in Schelling's *World Soul* for a fruitful dialogue between science and the new philosophy. Like Goethe, Schelling was impressed by Kant's discussion of organic causation in the *Critique of Judgement*. Organisms showed evidence of both mechanical and teleological causation. Within our empirical knowledge, these two forms of explanation were incompatible because evidence alone cannot show that a body is caused both by external forces and by internal purposes. However, the two types of cause might not be incompatible in nature as it is in itself.²⁵⁸ If the supersensible substrate of being did indeed combine mechanical and teleological causes, then nature and spirit could be unified, and Kant's philosophy of nature might be reconciled with Spinoza's.²⁵⁹ The obstacle was Fichte's transcendental philosophy of the self. Fichte had argued that the domains of purpose and causation cohere in the self prior to its objectification. Schelling realized this was not enough to satisfy Kant's argument: the two domains must also cohere in nature. Schelling's task therefore was to create a transcendental philosophy of nature to complement Fichte's transcendental philosophy of the self.²⁶⁰ In his early writings, up to and including *On the World Soul* (1798), Schelling modelled his philosophy of nature on Fichte's transcendental philosophy. The duality of nature, its empirical and transcendental aspects, were the product of the duality of the mind,²⁶¹ and so nature must be explained using the methods of cognition derived from Fichte's philosophy of the self. This was why Goethe could only muster limited enthusiasm for Schelling's system: it satisfied the demands of the subject but not those of the object. As he wrote to Voigt in June 1798, Schelling's *On the World Soul* 'contains very fine prospects and arouses an all the more lively desire that the author might make himself ever more familiar with the detail of experience.'[262]

In the winter of 1798/99, during Schelling's first semester at Jena, Goethe discussed the theory of metamorphosis with him and read the as yet unpublished textbook of his lectures, *First Outline of a Philosophy of Nature*.[263] The *Outline* was published in October 1799, followed in November by the *Introduction to his System of the Philosophy of Nature*. Goethe read the *Introduction* in September 1799, and he and Schelling went through the manuscript in detail at the beginning of October. The published version of the *Introduction* shows Schelling moving decisively towards Goethe's position.[264] The first and most important change was that Schelling now saw nature as independent of mind. The *Introduction* begins by stating that a philosophy of nature cannot be grounded in Fichte's philosophy of the self. Second, Schelling now sees nature's productivity in terms of Goethean metamorphosis. To understand nature is to grasp the essential duality of nature as productivity and product, in other words Spinoza's *natura naturans* and *natura naturata*. A natural product arises from a limitation on nature's productivity. The product contains within itself nature's infinite productivity, in the form of a drive towards infinite development, and this drive is nothing other than Goethean metamorphosis.[265] Nature provides archetypes and these undergo development according to laws of transition. The third Goethean element in Schelling's new theory is the specification of the laws of transition. Metamorphosis consists in the alternation of polar opposites and their progressive 'elevation' or 'refinement' (*Steigern*). In the case of organisms, metamorphosis tends towards ever more refined forms, the highest of which is reproduction.[266] This was the process Goethe had described in his essay on plant metamorphosis of 1790: the reproductive systems of flowering plants were an extremely refined or 'spiritual' form of anastomosis.

Schelling's shift from transcendental idealism to the philosophy of nature occurred under Goethe's mentorship. It made possible an exchange of shared enthusiasms. One was Kant's definition of matter in terms of repulsion and attraction in the *Metaphysical Foundations of Natural Science*. Another was Kielmeyer's groundbreaking lecture 'On the Relationship of Organic Forces', one of the foundational texts of the new science of biology. Goethe first read Kielmeyer's lecture in 1793,[267] and they met in September 1797, as Goethe travelled to Switzerland. He noted in his diary: Kielmeyer 'explained several thoughts to me as to how he is minded to link the laws of organic nature to general physical laws, e.g., polarity'.[268] Schelling was also a devotee of Kielmeyer's work. As for the notion of the progressive refinement of organic forms (*Steigern* or *Steigerung*), Goethe had seen it in action in flowering plants and mammals, but Schelling provided him with the terminology: Goethe first used the term *Steigerung*, which would become a signature term of his science, in December 1798 as he was reading the manuscript of Schelling's *Outline*.[269] Another shared enthusiasm was the importance of chemistry as the science that could provide links between organic and inorganic nature. Goethe and Schelling remained in close contact over the next two years. Thereafter Goethe continued to follow Schelling's philosophical evolution, not always with approval. For his part, Goethe stayed true to the position they had developed in 1799. He struggled with the transcendental aspect of Schelling's Idealism; he needed Niethammer's help to fathom Schelling's transcendental deduction of natural dynamism.[270] He saw no reason to abandon his Spinozism: the productivity of nature could be grasped by means of Spinoza's *scientia intuitiva*. As he insisted to Benjamin Constant in 1804, at its root Schelling's system *was* Spinozism.[271]

Shortly after reading Schelling's *World Soul* in June 1798, Goethe wrote a didactic poem of eighty lines in elegiac couplets, 'The Metamorphosis of Plants'.[272] The impulse for the poem probably came from Schelling. In the preface to the *World Soul* Schelling proposed that the 'earliest philosophy' had known that there were general principles governing all natural phenomena and hinted at them, albeit 'only in poetic images'.[273] This may have reminded Goethe of his old project of a poem about the universe, conceived after his Buffon-inspired turn to natural science in 1780. If he was to begin a new didactic project, plant metamorphosis was a natural place to start, not least because of the prominence Schelling gave it in *On the World Soul*. The poem is framed as a monologue spoken by the poet to his beloved. The frame gives structure and vividness to the poem's scientific contents. Naturally enough, the poet is his beloved's teacher in matters of botany. He can lead her through the material by drawing analogies between plants and humans, and so the botanical argument that makes up the body of the poem can be enriched with metaphors from human life, and the human frame around the lesson can in turn be enriched with plant metaphors. It is partly because of the rich network of metaphors and the vision they create of nature as a unity that the poem feels Schellingian. The poem is more open about the natural philosophy underlying metamorphosis than Goethe's 1790 essay—in this respect too, the impulse from Schelling is clear. The main body of the poem follows the stages of a plant's development from seed to reproduction. The external cause of plant growth is sunlight. Like Schelling in his *World Soul*,[274] Goethe suggests that light has given rise to the polarities of earthly life: the antithetical or alternating forces of stillness and movement, dryness and moistness, night and day. Behind these polar phenomena is the most general polarity of all: the power of the plant's internal developmental drive (*Bildungstrieb*), and nature's restraining hand that sets limits to nature's own productivity. Through these limitations, productivity becomes product, *natura naturans* becomes *natura naturata*:

> Doch hier hält die Natur, mit mächtigen Händen, die Bildung
>   An, und lenket sie sanft in das Vollkommnere hin.[275]

> Yet here nature, with mighty hands, stops the development / And steers it gently towards more completeness.

This process of *Steigerung* into more refined organization gives rise to the plant's reproductive organs. As in the *Metamorphosis* essay, the final step in the process of reproduction, when the stamen releases pollen to the pistils, is presented as a 'spiritual anastomosis', in suitably religious language. With the cycle of plant development completed, the poem returns to its human frame. The poet asks his beloved to recall how their relationship has blossomed from physical into spiritual love, the fruit of which is a shared view of the world. The poem thus ends with the charming prospect of the lovers enjoying the culmination of their love, a higher world in which they take pleasure in their shared appreciation of botany.

Goethe sent the poem to Knebel in July 1798, adding that he planned to write a poem in the same vein on magnetism. He had just read A. C. A. Eschenmayer's *Attempt to Derive the Laws of Magnetic Phenomena from Propositions of Nature-Metaphysics a priori*.[276] In fact, the poem on magnetism came to nothing. Although buoyed by the success of 'The Metamorphosis of Plants', he doubted whether his experiments in didactic poetry would ever amount to a full-length epic in the manner of Lucretius,[277] whom Knebel was translating. The didactic project was forgotten and then picked up again when Schelling arrived in Jena. Around the time when they edited Schelling's *Introduction* together in September 1799, they must have discussed collaborating on a didactic epic. By early January 1800 Schelling had written at least thirteen eight-line stanzas setting out the scientific programme they had agreed on.[278]

Goethe contributed only one more poem to the joint project, 'Metamorphosis of Animals'. The poem is more conventionally didactic than 'The Metamorphosis of Plants'. Indeed, it reads like a fragment of translation from Lucretius. (By the time he wrote it, Goethe had made detailed comments on Knebel's translations of the first third of Lucretius's poem.) Its tone is more austere. It speaks in the voice of a stern guide on an intellectually arduous journey up to the summit of scientific truth. There are none of the earlier poem's inviting gestures—the charming framing device of the conversation with the beloved, and the imagery linking human to plant reproduction. The poem summarizes the laws governing vertebrate morphology that Goethe had worked out in the early 1790s. Every animal is driven to express its inner teleology, the purposiveness of its nature.[279] The first law of animal morphology is that inner teleology interacts with the mechanical causes of the environment. The determinant of both inner teleology and external constraints is how an animal feeds itself. Every species receives from its archetype a particular configuration of body parts it requires for nutrition while the environment it lives in imposes constraints on the availability of food. The form of an animal is therefore the result of inner and outer causes acting in concert. This duality of causes gives nature's design its manifold beauty. The emphasis on duality is again likely to have been prompted by Schelling:

> Dieser schöne Begriff von Macht und Schranken, von Willkür
> Und Gesetz, von Freiheit und Maß, von beweglicher Ordnung,
> Vorzug und Mangel, erfreue dich hoch.
>
> This beautiful concept of power and limits, of arbitrariness / And law,
> of freedom and measure, of mobile order, / Advantage and deficit—
> may it give you great joy.[280]

The reciprocity of inner purposiveness and outer constraints is further governed by the iron law of the economy of nature: this is the reason for the empirical regularities we observe in mammals' teeth. The fragment closes by heralding the perfection of the law, which no human legislation has surpassed, and by sternly reminding us to make sober observation and not imaginative enthusiasm the measure of our knowledge. Having summarized the main ideas of morphology over sixty hexameter lines, it was perhaps hard for Goethe to see where else he could take the poem. In order for didactic poetry to sustain its interest over long stretches, a strong sense of philosophical purpose must combine with an ability to convey telling physical observations. Schelling's

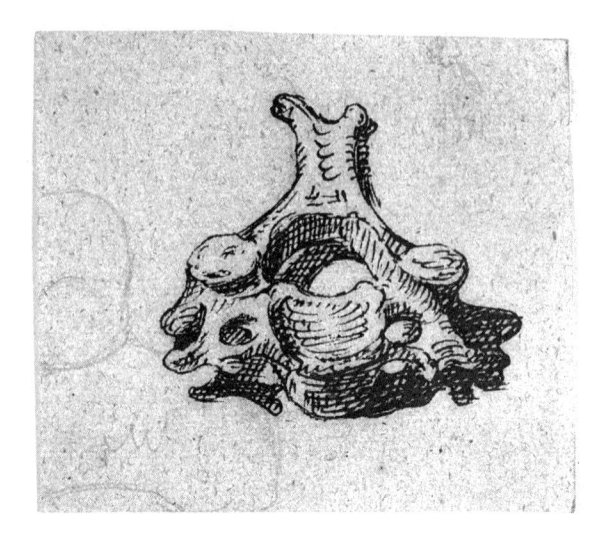

FIG. 19. Drawing of a mammal vertebra by Goethe (1790s?)

Naturphilosophie was too abstract for Goethe, both as a poet and a scientist. This was his main difference with Schelling and the other Idealists. After reading Eschenmayer's essay on magnetism, he wrote to Schiller: 'I have been able to take a good look into the workshop of the philosophers and students of nature, and I feel myself confirmed anew in my role as observer of nature'.[281] His insistence on the importance of observation at the end of 'Metamorphosis of Animals' reads like a warning to the philosophers. According to a letter from Caroline Schlegel to Schelling, in October 1800 Goethe gave up the didactic project and assigned it to Schelling instead.[282]

The end of the didactic project did not mean the end of his interest in Schelling's work or *Naturphilosophie*. For all his reservations about its distance from solid observation, the new *Naturphilosophie* encouraged him to look for principles that might unify the branches of natural science. Kant's *Metaphysical Foundations of Natural Science* had taught him that physics was the most likely source of such principles. Electricity, galvanism, and magnetism were the most promising fields of study. Through the spring and summer of 1798 he experimented with magnetism.[283] The work with Schelling on the *Introduction* in October 1799 was occasion for discussions of magnetism, electricity, and their underlying dualities.[284] In 1798 he read Johann Wilhelm Ritter's *Proof that a Constant Galvanism Accompanies the Process of Life in the Animal Kingdom*. After meeting Ritter in Jena in September 1800,[285] Goethe wrote to Schiller that Ritter was 'an amazing phenomenon, a veritable heaven of knowledge on earth'.[286] He was a proponent of what Goethe termed the 'higher physics'.[287] Still more speculative was the Schelling-influenced work of Franz von Baader. In 1800 Goethe read his essay *On the Pythagorean Square in Nature and the Four Corners of the Earth*. 'It may be that in the last few years I've become more amicable towards these modes of understanding [*Vorstellungsarten*]', he wrote to Schiller, adding however that he was still not able to understand everything Baader wrote.[288]

Schelling's theory of duality gave Goethe the best hope for building a bridge between empirical science and *Naturphilosophie*. In July 1798, after reading Schelling's *World Soul* and discussing it with Schiller, he drew up a schematic list of 'dualistic natural effects' and a 'table of physical effects',[289] comprising magnetism, electricity, galvanism, colour, sound, taste, and smell. His efforts to unify the branches of science now reached far beyond parallels he had drawn in 1790 between the polarities of plant growth and Kant's theory of attractive and repulsive matter, and the 'general dualism of nature'.[290] Schelling's *World Soul* had shown him how this dualism could be captured in its entirety. The most important advance though was to reconstruct natural processes dynamically. Any natural phenomenon must exhibit duality merely in order to be a phenomenon: 'whatever emerges into appearance must divide itself, in order to appear at all', he noted in 1805 for a series of lectures to the ladies of Weimar.[291] This is not the modest Kantian theory of the duality of empirical matter—that repulsion and attraction is all we can observe because the unity of nature is hidden from us. In Goethe's view, we observe a pulsing alternation between duality and unity in the empirical realm:

> What is divided seeks itself again and can find itself and be reunited; in the more basic sense, when it is merely blended with its opposite and merges with it, whereby the phenomenon is null or at most indifferent. The unification can however also occur in the higher sense, when what is divided elevates [*steigert*] itself and through the uniting of the elevated poles it generates a third, new, higher, unexpected thing.[292]

One polar force generates another, and their subsequent interactions generate the dualities we observe in magnetism, electricity, and the other forces in Goethe's schematic table. This very abstract model of dynamism, using Schelling's language, might serve as an analogue in the theoretical sphere to the observation of the genesis of natural forms in the empirical sphere, which Goethe still regarded as the gold standard of science and his proper domain.[293] In December 1799 he noted in his diary: 'if in the theoretical [domain] only the dynamic is fruitful, then in empirical observation only the genetic has value, for the two coincide'.[294] The field was therefore open for dialogue between Goethe as an empiricist and the 'Messrs Idealists and Dynamists', as he termed them—even if he still believed that Idealism was prone to dogmatism and pedantry.[295]

In summer 1797, Goethe resumed work on *Faust*, with understandable misgivings. 'Our study of ballads has set me on this path of mist and fog again', he wrote to Schiller in June.[296] *Faust* lacked the objectivity and clarity of form he had come to expect from poetry. The 'bizarre poem'—he did not call it a play—seemed like the unplanned and spontaneous product of poetic subjectivity.[297] Given time, he hoped that it would spring back to life: 'It would just be a matter of one peaceful month, and then the work would spring from the earth like a great colony of mushrooms, to general amazement and consternation'.[298] Its shapeless and sudden manifestation would not be the only reasons for consternation. In order to finish *Faust* he had to address the question of Faust's damnation, which he had left unanswered on publishing the work as the unfinished *Faust: A Fragment* in 1790. According to a plan written in summer 1797, the work would end with an 'epilogue in Chaos on the way to Hell'. The question was how to get there. His first task was to find some artistic and intellectual coherence in the work, with Schiller's help: 'Now I should like it if you would be so kind as to think the matter through, in a sleepless night, [and] set out for me the requirements that you would make of the whole work, and so, like a true prophet, report and interpret my own dreams for me'.[299]

Particularly challenging were the still unwritten scenes in which Faust summons the devil, makes his bargain with Mephistopheles and questions him as to the nature of the universe. Dramatic high points in any Faust play, these scenes were conspicuously missing from Goethe's pre-1775 drafts and the 1790 *Fragment*. (In nineteenth-century *Faust* scholarship this gap came to be known as the 'great lacuna'.) It may be that he had not been able to write them because he was unsure how to motivate Faust's summoning of the devil. In all versions of the story before Goethe, Faust made his bargain with the devil in order to gain knowledge. The Faust legend's special contribution to the history of our discomfort with modernity was the feeling that our quest for knowledge may have dug deeper than was safe. However, in the 1770s drafts and the 1790 *Fragment* version, Faust has already renounced all knowledge before summoning the devil and has turned instead to a more Rousseauian quest for authenticity. Somehow, at some point in hacking through the crust of the merely conventional world and digging down towards authenticity, Faust must encounter the devil, but the 1770s version does not show how the meeting comes about. It does show the logic of the relationship between Faust and the devil. The devil opens up routes to authentic experience by facilitating Faust's desires, for instance, by arranging his affair with Gretchen. Yet the devil cannot be a partner in that experience, for he turns out to be the very spirit of inauthenticity, a spirit of meaningless and superficial conventionality. Thus Goethe's portrayal of the antagonism between Faust and the devil is quite different from any previous writer's. In Marlowe's play, Faustus and Mephistophilis are antagonists concerning the fate of Faustus's soul, but they also have a common purpose: they are both concerned with amassing and exploiting power. In Goethe's version, the antagonism over Faust's soul no longer exists and is replaced by an antagonism over this world: between authenticity and triviality. But given Mephistopheles's constitutional inability to share Faust's quest for authenticity, it is hard to see why Faust would have wanted a deal with him in the first place, and this may explain why Goethe had not managed to write the scenes leading up to and including the pact. The answer Goethe found after 1797 has two components. One is Mephistopheles's and Faust's inability to understand one another, which is partly due to their very male determination to mock and challenge each other. As a result, the deal they make neither expresses their settled intentions nor satisfies their aims. The scene that produces the deal was something that Goethe, with his knowledge of the law and his fascination with the pathological condition of human psychology, could write with relish.

The other component lay close at hand in 1797. In March Goethe read the new edition of Fichte's *Theory of Science*.[300] According to Fichte, the deepest impulse in human nature was not a thirst for knowledge but a compulsion to activity, which he also termed 'striving' (*Streben*).[301] Humans were endowed with a boundless activity and striving that preceded and was not bounded by objective conditions. Instead, activity itself set those conditions in the process of its self-actualization. Moreover, in setting itself conditions, activity could not be limited by them; it must constantly move beyond them, in a kind of perpetual striving.[302] Thus Fichtean activity and striving preceded knowledge. Indeed, it was telling that Fichte's *Theory of Science* had little to say about actual knowledge, as far as Goethe could tell. The first attraction of recasting Faust as an example of Fichtean man was that his bargain with the devil would no longer be motivated by the human thirst for knowledge. Science would not be blamed for the ills of modernity. A second attraction was the connection between Fichte's absolute *I* and the Revolution. It was not just that Fichte was well known for his revolutionary sympathies. The *Theory of Science* was designed to be a philosophical justification of the Revolution, or so one of Fichte's letters proposes:

> I believe that my system belongs to [the French] nation. It is the first system of freedom. Just as that nation has torn away the external chains of man, my system tears away the chains of the thing-in-itself, or external causes, that still shackle him more or less in other systems, even the Kantian. My first principle establishes man as an independent being.[303]

Fichte's philosophy was the French Revolution's eccentric German cousin. In their very different ways, both were committed to absolute freedom. For Goethe, either kind of freedom, revolutionary or Fichtean, was anathema. The great advantage of making Fichtean activity part of Faust's mission was that Goethe could formulate the bargain with the devil as an expression not of a thirst for knowledge, but a desire for untrammelled activity and the revolutionary freedom of the absolute self.

It took Goethe several years to realize his new vision of the deal between Faust and Mephistopheles. At first he did not get far beyond planning. In autumn 1797 he composed a court masque, 'Oberon and Titania's Golden Wedding', which he later decided to include in *Faust*. In December he worked on a prologue set in heaven. It was his first confrontation with the theological controversies that he knew *Faust* would stir up, as it brought God into direct dialogue with Mephistopheles. He also began to sketch the pact scene. The next April he versified the dungeon scene, originally written in prose in the early 1770s and omitted from the 1790 *Fragment*. Scattered mentions of further work occur in his diaries through 1798 and 1799. In 1800 work began in earnest on the 'great lacuna'. Then in a new departure, in late summer 1800 he planned a suite of scenes between Faust and Helen of Troy. Helen had been a poetically powerful though fleeting presence in Marlowe's *Doctor Faustus*, though Goethe did not read Marlowe's *Faustus* until 1818. The Helen scenes required him to read up on the history of Sparta. There was also research to be done on magic and demonology. Faust was to visit the witches' gathering on Walpurgis Night, culminating in Satan holding a black mass on the Brocken. These scenes were started but never finished, and only part of the Walpurgis Night material was published. From February through April 1801 a substantial push saw the existing material, up to the dungeon scene, all arrayed in one continuous text. The philosophers in Jena were curious to know what would become of *Faust*, he wrote to Schiller in March 1801.[304] Presumably he had discussed some of his ideas with them, but he was still far from settling Faust's final fate. He had not even begun to work on the scenes surrounding Faust's death. And so *Faust* again had to be 'fragmented' as in 1790, now into two parts. The first part, extending from Faust's first monologue to the dungeon scene, was to be published under the title *Faust. The First Part of the Tragedy*. It would also include three prefatory elements: a dedicatory poem that he had written on resuming work in 1797; a prelude set in a modern German theatre; and a 'Prologue in Heaven'. Contractual details for the publication of *The First Part* were negotiated with Cotta in 1802. For various reasons—illness, dilatoriness, the Napoleonic Wars—the text was only finalized in 1806[305] and publication was delayed to 1808. Of the second part, he had drafted only the 265-line fragment titled 'Helen in the Middle Ages', in which Faust would travel back in time from the sixteenth century to an earlier age of higher beauty.

The 'Prologue in Heaven' prefigures the two parts of Goethe's solution to the problem of Faust's deal: striving and an incomprehension stemming from competitiveness. The scene begins with the three archangels Raphael, Gabriel, and Michael in turn chanting verses in praise of the physical universe. First the sun is praised, then the planet earth and its geology, and last the weather, before the three join in a reprise of Raphael's wonder at the enduring mystery of the universe:

> ZU DREI: Der Anblick gibt den Engeln Stärke
> Da keiner dich ergründen mag,
> Und alle deine hohen Werke
> Sind herrlich wie am ersten Tag.[306]
>
> ALL THREE: The sight gives strength to the angels, / Since none can comprehend you, / And all your lofty works / Are as marvellous as on the first day.

The essential nature of the universe remains a mystery. The archangels can only marvel at its awesome magnificence and the clash of opposed forces it embodies.[307] The universe is structured according to the polarities that Goethe had found in Kant's *Metaphysical Foundations of Natural Science* and developed in collaboration with Schelling, and the Archangels' vision of it resembles a Spinozan 'intellectual love of God'. Oddly though, they make no mention of organic life or human beings. That has to wait for the entrance of Mephistopheles—a troubling thought, for the allocation of natural kingdoms between the Archangels and Mephistopheles suggests that some sort of division of labour operates in heaven, with the Archangels responsible for the inorganic universe and Mephistopheles responsible for humans. He duly mimics and parodies the Archangels' words. They sang of a universe that is still as marvellous as it ever was; he mocks humans as incorrigibly bestial:

> Von Sonn' und Welten weiß ich nichts zu sagen,
> Ich sehe nur, wie sich die Menschen plagen.
> Der kleine Gott der Welt bleibt stets von gleichem Schlag,
> Und ist so wunderlich als wie am ersten Tag.
> Ein wenig besser würd' er leben,
> Hättst du ihm nicht den Schein des Himmelslichts gegeben;
> Er nennt's Vernunft und braucht's allein,
> Nur tierischer als jedes Tier zu sein.[308]

> Of the sun and planets I can say nothing, / I only see how humans toil away. / The little god of this world hasn't changed his spots / And is as bizarre as on the first day. / He'd live a bit better, / If you hadn't given him the radiance of heaven's light; / He calls it *reason* and only uses it / To be more bestial than any beast.

Mephistopheles plays the role of a grossly mocking tutelary spirit of humans, and the Lord will duly confirm him in post. First though, two opposed visions of humanity must be tested against one another. Answering Mephistopheles's sardonic mock-lament, the Lord gives the example of Faust—a counterexample to Mephistopheles's miserable image of humanity, one supposes, though the Lord does not say so explicitly. Instead he deploys his sovereign gift for remaining above the fray by retreating into safely oblique generalities, as good teachers often do. When Mephistopheles objects that Faust's questing mind is bizarre, the Lord insists that striving is never without error, but can eventually find its way:

> DER HERR: Wenn er mir jetzt auch nur verworren dient;
>   So werd' ich ihn bald in die Klarheit führen.
>   Weiß doch der Gärtner, wenn das Bäumchen grünt,
>   Daß Blüt' und Frucht die künft'gen Jahre zieren.
> MEPHISTOPHELES: Was wettet Ihr? den sollt Ihr noch verlieren!
>   Wenn Ihr mir die Erlaubnis gebt

Ihn meine Straße sacht zu führen!
DER HERR: Solang' er auf der Erde lebt,
Solange sei dir's nicht verboten.
Es irrt der Mensch, so lang er strebt.[309]

THE LORD: If he now serves me in confusion, / Soon I'll lead him into clarity. / The gardener knows, when the sapling comes into leaf, / That blossom and fruit will adorn future years.
MEPHISTOPHELES: What will you wager? You're going to lose him, / If you give me permission / To lead him gently along my path!
THE LORD: For as long as he lives on earth, / It is not forbidden to you. / Humans err for as long as they strive.

Faust is to emerge out of error and confusion and into clarity. This is the first hint at his ultimate fate, but it is vague and tantalising. For one thing, it is not clear what the Lord is referring to by 'clarity'. Is it a state attained during a person's life? So will Faust realize the error of his ways before he dies? Or does 'clarity' refer to the salvation of his soul? If the latter, what sort of thing is a soul that attains clarity? Is it a personal identity or a more generalized intellect such as the 'eternity of mind' (*mentis aeternitas*) that Spinoza argued for in Part V of the *Ethics*?[310] And who effects the emergence into clarity? Does it need the Lord's grace, or will Faust find clarity through the propensity of his own nature? On this last question, the Lord seems to sit on the fence, imagining himself as a gardener tending Faust, his plant. The plant may need tending, but its blossoming and fruiting are in its nature. Either way, the Lord seems confident in the ultimate outcome of Faust's bargain with Mephistopheles, and so it makes no sense for him to accept Mephistopheles's offer of a wager, and he does not. In his eagerness, Mephistopheles does not grasp this point: he believes they have made a bet. (His misunderstanding prefigures his confused bargain with Faust.) The Lord knows otherwise and ends their debate by reaffirming that Mephistopheles cannot corrupt humans, only spur them to greater activity. He then commands the Archangels to resume their song:

Des Menschen Tätigkeit kann allzuleicht erschlaffen,
Er liebt sich bald die unbedingte Ruh;
Drum geb' ich gern ihm den Gesellen zu,
Der reizt und wirkt und muß, als Teufel, schaffen.—
Doch ihr, die echten Göttersöhne,
Erfreut euch der lebendig reichen Schöne!
Das Werdende, das ewig wirkt und lebt,
Umfass' euch mit der Liebe holden Schranken,

Und was in schwankender Erscheinung schwebt,
Befestiget mit dauernden Gedanken.[311]

For the activity of a person can all too easily slacken, / They love absolute rest; / That's why I'm happy to give them the companion / Who goads and acts upon and must, being a devil, create.—/ But you, true sons of the gods, / Take pleasure in beauty vividly rich! / What becomes, eternally in action and living, / May it embrace you with love's delightful limits, / And that which hovers in wavering appearance, / Make it firm with enduring thoughts.

The Lord's command to the Archangels to lend the permanence of thought to fleeting appearances gives a further hint as to what Faust's fate might be. Mind will confer its eternity (*mentis aeternitas*) on matter. Aside from Spinoza, Goethe may have had in mind Schiller's post-Kantian argument in the *Aesthetic Education*. In Kant's form-substance duality, intellect gives form and intelligibility to the manifold of formless and fleeting sensations. In Schiller's elaboration of Kant, the permanence of true art comes from the forms that structure its content.

The 'Prologue in Heaven' is followed by Faust's first monologue, the summoning of the Earth Spirit, the dialogue with Wagner (all in the same form as in the 1790 *Fragment*), and the new material that fills the 'great lacuna'. When Goethe eventually filled the gap, the result was close to twelve hundred lines of verse. If the drama slows to a crawl, the poetry is magnificent. The new material comprises the conclusion of the argument of the first monologue, a walk with Wagner outside the city gates, and two scenes titled 'Study'. In the first, Faust summons the devil, and in the second the deal is struck. The argument is dense and complex. In motivating the meeting between Faust and Mephistopheles, Goethe faced the delicate task of balancing Faust's pessimism and melancholia against his striving. Faust wants to give up on life while still longing to live. He despairs at the thought that we are hemmed in not by inauthentic conventions, but by the consequences of our actions: 'Ah! our very actions as well as what we suffer, / They inhibit the course of our life' ('Ach! unsre Taten selbst, so gut als unsre Leiden, / Sie hemmen unsres Lebens Gang').[312] The error of the absolute idealist (or the political revolutionary) is to think that in remaking the world, we can avoid the consequences of such remakings. In fact, even if we were absolutely free to act (we are not), we could never be free of our actions' consequences. As the reality of humanity's Sisyphean condition dawns on Faust, he catches sight of a bottle of poison, and his pain is suddenly relieved. Suicide offers the prospect of release from the anguish of endless striving: 'I see you, the pain is eased, / I hold you, the striving abates' ('Ich sehe dich, es wird der Schmerz gelindert, / Ich fasse dich, das Streben wird gemindert').[313] But suicide is not a simple matter, and the condition of humanity is 'pathological', as Goethe wrote to Schiller in November 1797.[314] Faust's hope of release from striving is contradicted by his own words.[315] His first thought about suicide is that it will liberate his spirit from the physical world, and he will pass from this conditioned world into 'new spheres of pure activity' ('neue Sphären reiner Tätigkeit').[316] If he desires more activity, then evidently a release from striving is not what he really wants. Striving is in the nature of humans, as the Lord told Mephistopheles in the 'Prologue in Heaven'. As Faust lifts the poison to his lips, a bell rings and a choir begins to sing of Christ's resurrection. It is Easter. Even though he is an unbeliever and has no faith in the miracle of the resurrection, the singing jolts him back to life. There is no objective truth in Christianity, but there is a subjective one, in Faust's own past. The Easter chorus reminds him of his youth, when he did believe. This is the first of two short passages of spiritual autobiography, both in the language of Pietism. Faust remembers himself as a child in fervent prayer, wandering the countryside, 'amid a thousand burning tears' ('unter tausend heißen Tränen').[317] It is the first time that anything of this sort appears in a version of the Faust legend.[318] In no previous version is Faust said to have been a believing Christian. It is likely that in casting the adult Faust as a lapsed Pietist, he was thinking back to the 'Prometheus' monologue of 1773. Prometheus describes the faith of his youth in the language of Pietism, and Faust does the same here. The reason for Faust's lapse from Pietism is made clear in the second passage. On their walk outside the city walls Faust tells Wagner that he once helped his father to treat the citizens during an outbreak of plague. Back then he had wandered outside the city praying for a cure, but of course his prayers were not answered, any more than Zeus answers Prometheus's prayers. And like Prometheus, the disappointed Faust then veered from one extreme to another, from passionate Pietist faith to angry atheism. The problem is our failure to heed Spinoza's advice that 'he who loves God cannot strive that God should love him in return'.[319] The correct attitude is the intellectual love of god.

The scene 'Outside the City Gate' introduces Faust to Mephistopheles, in the form of a black poodle that approaches Faust and Wagner as they return at dusk. The meeting is triggered by two lyrical monologues that express Faust's isolation from society and its 'ocean of error'. Part of Faust wishes to live on the earth and enjoy its pleasures; his other part wishes that airborne spirits might carry him away from the here and now wrapped in a magical cloak. At this point the black dog appears, as if Faust's talk of magical spirits has invited Mephistopheles into his world. At first Faust perceives some magic in the dog whereas to the complacent rationalist Wagner it is just a dog. At the end of the scene Faust disappointedly accepts Wagner's view, for on closer acquaintance, the dog is merely trained to obey a person's commands. Ironically, Wagner has helped Faust even closer to the truth than Faust realizes. Far from being one of the airborne spirits Faust desperately longed for, and far from releasing Faust from his confinement, the dog is a mere projection of human conventionality, and a narrow and literal-minded one at that. This is indeed exactly what Mephistopheles will turn out to be.

The scene shifts back to Faust in his study, with only the dog for company. The summoning of Mephistopheles now plays itself out, but again in an unexpected and original manner. Traditionally, Faust sets out with the explicit aim of summoning the devil. In Goethe's version, the summoning proceeds not along the rails of Faust's intention, but according to the logic of the situation and his unwitting desires. The process begins with Christianity. Returning to his study after dark, he craves the security of scripture—another pendular swing in his life as a Pietist and atheist. The return to scripture seems to make the dog agitated, as if Faust's desire for religious comfort were distressing it. The result is a bizarre contrast between the high pathos of Faust's ambition and the comedy of Mephistopheles in dog form. Faust opens his Bible—he calls it 'the holy original' ('das heilige Original'),[320] by which he must mean the Greek New Testament—and begins to translate the first verse of the Gospel of John. The scene is rich in allusions, historical and modern. The historical Faust was a contemporary of Luther, the greatest modern translator of the Bible. So in having Faust translate the Bible, Goethe cheekily associates the devil-summoning Faust with the devil's self-professed greatest enemy Luther. The scene of translation is also a typical scene of Renaissance humanism: the return to the textual sources in order to separate the pristine truth from the deadwood of tradition. The choice of John is significant because John's first verse—'In the beginning was the word'—contains a semantic crux. 'Word' is the traditional translation of the New Testament Greek *logos*. Alternative renderings of *logos* include *discourse* or *speech*, or even *reason*, *logic*, or *idea*. There was a tendency during Goethe's lifetime to interpret *logos* in terms of (some form of) reason. Lessing, Kant, Herder, Fichte, Schleiermacher, Hegel, and Schelling all did so.[321] Faust joins this trend. He has his own reasons. As his first monologue has told us, words are only representations of things and not the things themselves. By this reasoning, words cannot enjoy the originary status they are given in John's first verse. Faust's first alternative translation is '*Sinn*' (*sense* or *intention*). But this too lacks the energy and concreteness necessary to make things happen, and so next he tries '*Kraft*' (*force*), a favourite word of Herder's. The trajectory away from words and towards activity leads him to write his final version 'confidently' ('getrost'),[322] as he puts it: 'in the beginning was the *deed*' ('Im Anfang war die *Tat*'). The final version expresses Faust's commitment to activity above all things and his closeness to Fichte's theory of the primal 'deed action' (*Tathandlung*). And so the German tradition that began with Luther's Reformation culminates in Fichte's philosophy of revolution. As soon as Faust utters these words, the dog begins to advertise its magical nature again by changing its shape. Mephistopheles evidently thinks that Faust's Fichtean translation of the Gospel is the ideal occasion for him to tempt Faust into a pact.[323] Faust duly performs the binding spells, and Mephistopheles appears in the form of a travelling student—in fact a parody of Faust himself.

In their first dialogue Mephistopheles's prevailing mode is mockery of Faust and of himself. He seems unable to take anything seriously. He represents human rationality satirically turned in on itself. The same behaviour persists through the next scene, in which the bargain is struck. Faust is again at a low ebb. He has realized that the sardonic Mephistopheles cannot give him anything worth having. When he tells Mephistopheles so and mockingly challenges him to show all the futile and worthless things he has to offer, Mephistopheles ignores Faust's mocking tone (or affects to do so) and promises to oblige him. The dialogue is a virtuoso portrayal of two competitive antagonists so confident in their own rightness that they do not hear or care what the other is saying. Faust is convinced of the high seriousness of a mission that comes from the inalienable core of his being, or so he claims. In fact, the terms of the deal he proposes are as much a product of his impulsive desire to prove Mephistopheles wrong. Mephistopheles is guided by two conflicting motives: the need to do a deal and the conviction that humans are already damned, as he put it in the 'Prologue in Heaven'. The contradiction in his motives makes him both too eager and too casual. Faust knows that he has to tread carefully, for the devil is a self-interested and unreliable partner, but he loses all caution under Mephistopheles's provocation. As a result, neither pays much attention to the terms of the deal. Indeed, nowhere in the remaining action of *The First Part* will either of them refer back to the terms of the wager.[324] It is a lesson in how not to make a contract, written by a lawyer who understands the dangers lying in wait for 'pathological' humans who choose to make contractual commitments:

> FAUST: Was willst du armer Teufel geben?
> Ward eines Menschen Geist, in seinem hohen Streben,
> Von deinesgleichen je gefaßt?
> Doch hast du Speise, die nicht sättigt, hast
> Du rotes Gold, das ohne Rast,
> Quecksilber gleich, dir in der Hand zerrinnt,
> Ein Spiel, bei dem man nie gewinnt,
> Ein Mädchen, das an meiner Brust
> Mit Äugeln schon dem Nachbar sich verbindet,
> Der Ehre schöne Götterlust,
> Die, wie ein Meteor, verschwindet.
> Zeig mir die Frucht, die fault, eh' man sie bricht,
> Und Bäume die sich täglich neu begrünen!
> MEPHISTOPHELES: Ein solcher Auftrag schreckt mich nicht,
> Mit solchen Schätzen kann ich dienen.
> Doch, guter Freund, die Zeit kommt auch heran
> Wo wir was Gut's in Ruhe schmausen mögen.
> FAUST: Werd' ich beruhigt je mich auf ein Faulbett legen;
> So sei es gleich um mich getan!
> Kannst du mich schmeichelnd je belügen,
> Daß ich mir selbst gefallen mag,
> Kannst du mich mit Genuß betrügen;
> Das sei für mich der letzte Tag!
> Die Wette biet' ich!
> MEPHISTOPHELES: Top!
> FAUST: Und Schlag auf Schlag!
> Werd' ich zum Augenblicke sagen:
> Verweile doch! du bist so schön!
> Dann magst du mich in Fesseln schlagen,
> Dann will ich gern zugrunde gehn![325]

> FAUST: What can you offer, poor devil? / Was a person's spirit, in their high striving, / Ever comprehended by your like? / Sure, you have food that never satisfies, have / Red gold that without pause / Like quicksilver runs through one's fingers, / A game at which one never

wins, / A girl who in my arms / Is already making eyes at my neighbour, / Honour, the beautiful pleasure of the gods, / Which disappears like a meteor. / Show me the fruit that rots before it's picked, / And trees that come into new leaf every day!

MEPHISTOPHELES: A task like that does not scare me, / I can be of service with treasures like that. / But good friend, the time's coming / When we should treat ourselves to a proper feast at our ease.

FAUST: If I should ever lay myself down on a bed of sloth, / May that be the end for me! / If you can ever flatter me into / Being pleased with myself; / If you can trick me with pleasure, / May that be my final day! / That's the wager I'm offering!

MEPHISTOPHELES: Done!

FAUST: It's a deal! / If I should say to the moment: / Stay a while! You are so fair! / Then you may bind me in chains, / Then I'll gladly perish!

The key to the deal is Mephistopheles's offhand reference to 'ease' ('Ruhe'), which so irritates Faust that he hastily overcommits himself to constant activity. With the wager agreed, Faust expatiates on his new refusal to rest. He will turn his back on all those human experiences that philosophy had traditionally held to constitute a good life: happiness, fulfilment, beauty, truth. In their stead, he will taste all the experiences humans know, though none of them will endure and they will all be subject to the remorseless onwards rush of time. From experiencing all forms of pain and pleasure, it is a small step to Faust wishing to share 'what's allocated to the whole of humanity, / [...] the highest and deepest [...], / Its pleasure and pain [...]' ('was der ganzen Menschheit zugeteilt ist, / [...] das Höchst' und Tiefste [...], / Ihr Wohl und Weh [...]').[326] Like the delicious torment Mahadeva inflicts on the Bayadère, Faust's wager is to be a test of humanity's ability to endure the full and contradictory range of its experience. When Mephistopheles objects that this all sounds a bit too much like God, Faust simply states: 'But that's my will!' ('Allein ich will!'). The absolute ego must have its freedom, even if it has no other purpose than to test itself and humanity at large. The wager has come to embody the spirit of modernity in its purest and most concentrated form: the active self bounded by no material conditions or particular purposes. Experience has no limits, activity has no goals, other than to offer itself in a wager that tests its own essence of activity.

What does the 'great lacuna' material mean for the Gretchen scenes? In the second half of the nineteenth century there emerged a view of *Faust* as an allegory of modern progress,[327] which, though sometimes too simplistic, is broadly true to Goethe's text and intentions. In the wake of the unification of Germany in 1871 and the new nation's rise to great power status by 1900, Faust's crimes were often glossed over or seen as justified by the higher cause he represented: a spirit of progress and striving.[328] Nationalistic interpretations of this kind reached their most extreme form during the Third Reich. For the Nazis, Faust was a Titanic figure and the epitome of National Socialism.[329] Goethe's poem was the foundational myth of modern 'Germanic-Nordic culture'.[330] The 'Prologue in Heaven' appeared to justify the 'Faustian' principle, as it was commonly called after the Great War. The wager scene could serve as a grand statement of modern man's self-denial for the sake of humanity or the German *Volk*. As for Gretchen, as a victim of Faustian striving she evoked the 'final and holiest sacrifice' that German women could make for the *Volk*.[331] In fact, the themes of striving and activity are almost entirely absent from the Gretchen scenes, as if they belonged to a different world—to the divine order of the 'Prologue in Heaven' and the poisonously masculine cut and thrust in Faust's study. The word *striving* appears only once during the Gretchen scenes, in the reworked and versified dungeon scene. Faust seeks desperately to persuade Gretchen to escape with him: 'FAUST. [*striving away*] Come with me! Come with me!'; ('[*fortstrebend*] Komm mit! Komm mit!').[332] Shortly afterwards Gretchen experiences the last-minute revelation that she must die to atone for her crimes. The appearance of *striving* at this point, just as the moral implications of her tragedy become clear to Gretchen, shows the gulf between Faust's striving and Gretchen's painful moral awakening. Apart from impinging on the Gretchen scenes in this one instance, the themes of striving and activity form a frame that surrounds them. It is a frame that is foreign to Gretchen's feelings and conscience, indeed to any moral feeling at all. Its effect is to heighten the beauty and tragedy of Gretchen's love for Faust and the queasy feeling readers have that Faust is using Gretchen as a piece in some greater game, much like Mahadeva uses the dancing girl in 'The God and the Bayadère'. There is no morality in boundless striving, and nowhere does Faust mention sympathy for the plight of his fellow humans. In aspiring to embrace all the highs and lows of human life, to expand his own self into some all-encompassing, quasi-divine sensorium, while neglecting to think of actual moral feelings, Faust has imprisoned himself in a logic of acquiring experience for acquisition's sake. He has created for himself the existential equivalent of Max Weber's economic iron cage, by which modern humans seek to control the world, but by which they are themselves imprisoned and controlled, so as to become, in Weber's words, 'sensualists without heart'.[333]

With Faust's overweening wager, the 'great lacuna' was filled. The one further addition was the Walpurgis Night scenes, including the masque 'Oberon and Titania's Golden Wedding'. The scenes form a retarding element in the action. By postponing the hammer blow of the dungeon scene, they increase its effect. There is therefore a dramatic logic in the virtual nullity of what occurs in the Walpurgis Night scenes. After the death of Gretchen's mother and brother and the requiem mass in the cathedral, Faust and Mephistopheles are banished from city. Mephistopheles takes Faust on an adventure up the Brocken to experience the crazed phantasmagoria of the witches' sabbath. The mindless babbling and cavorting of the witches is interwoven with passages of satire on modern politics and culture. Amid all the unreality, Faust catches the briefest glimpse of the tragedy of Gretchen. While he dances with a sexy young witch, he sees a vision of Gretchen with manacled feet, dead eyes, and a knife-thin red line around her neck. The shock is quickly removed if not forgotten. The scene switches immediately to 'Oberon and Titania's Golden Wedding'. The masque consists of a parade of characters representing tendencies in modern German culture whose words are gently self-satirizing. It is the war of the *Xenia* by other means. In addition to retarding and heightening the denouement, the masque reminds us of the tragic vision of Gretchen in amongst the dross of modernity. A further section of the Walpurgis Night material was not published. Goethe began to draft a black mass which would form the climax of the whole bizarre intermezzo. Around one hundred lines of the manuscript have survived. The outlines of the scene are clear. It was to have been a parody of church ritual presided over by Satan himself, complete with his obscene sermon to the flock in praise of avarice and sexual desire. The coarse humour and brutal honesty of the drafts are reminiscent of the *Venetian Epigrams*. The whole scene would have served as a companion piece to the requiem mass in the cathedral. Needless to say, the drafts were not published during Goethe's lifetime.

Schiller's *Horae* was wound down at the end of 1797. In the months before the final issue appeared, Goethe and Meyer discussed plans for a successor. Provisionally titled 'The Artist',[334] the new journal's focus would be different. In the first place, it would be a vehicle for Goethe's and Meyer's studies for their grand project on the history of Italian art. In spring 1798 Schiller and Goethe pitched the proposal to Cotta.[335] By the end of June a decision had been made on the title: *The Propylaea* (*Die Propyläen*), referring to the monumental gateways that stood on the approach to Ancient Greek temple precincts, for instance, on the Athenian acropolis. The title captured the provisional and introductory nature of the project. The journal was to be a gateway to something larger and grander, the new art made by German artists: 'Our intention thereby is to stimulate and to provoke, not to establish or build, even if we have derived our title from a building', Goethe wrote two years later.[336] It was also provisional in the sense that its contents consisted in large part of the fragments of their unwritten history of the Italian Renaissance. When Goethe pitched the project to Cotta in May 1798, he admitted that the contents would be 'fragmentary' though an attempt would be made to bring coherence by beginning each volume with a theoretical introduction.[337] Indeed, there is reason to suppose that the gateways of the journal's title refer to these introductions—a set of imposing entrances to the historical and theoretical world beyond. *The Propylaea* was not a commercial success. Starting in October 1798, six volumes appeared in all. The print run of the first three volumes was 1,350. Only 850 subscribers were recruited. By the third year of publication, the print run had to be reduced to 750 and payments to writers were paused in order to save money.[338] In July 1800 the journal was put on ice.[339] For a time Goethe and Meyer discussed resuming publication, but nothing happened.

It would be easy to explain the journal's failure as a consequence of the narrow classicism it seemed to espouse and the local interests it represented, but that would be unfair. *The Propylaea* had the sincere aim of stimulating, provoking, and thereby creating a national discussion about the arts. As Goethe put it to Cotta in November 1800:

> The greatest difficulty will be to draw the creative artist out the narrow solipsism into which he must fall insofar as he mainly has a small audience that usually consists only of patrons and friends. So if one can give them and their works publicity, so that the fatherland gets to know its artists and the artist his fellow artists, then a more public awareness must spread across the whole field.[340]

The main vehicle for this national awareness was an annual prize, funded by Duke Carl August, for the best work of art on a set topic. The prize competition arose out of the need to decorate the refurbished ducal palace.[341] Goethe could have bought the art on the secondhand market, and it is to his credit that he chose instead to use the rebuilding of the palace as an opportunity to encourage up-and-coming German artists. And even if one of the goals was to promote Weimar as a leader in the German art scene, he could argue that fostering cultural competition between the German principalities was in the spirit of the Italian Renaissance. He was also conscious of the requisitions of Italian art by Napoleon, which made him think wistfully how the spirit of the Renaissance had formed Italy into 'one great body of art'.[342] The requisitions made him feel more strongly than ever the need to 'intervene in the practical side of art'.[343] He outlined his arguments in the long introduction that made up one quarter of the first volume. Its composition and multiple revisions lasted through the spring and summer of 1798. The first volume also included a dialogue 'On Truth and Likeness in Art', inspired by Giorgio Fuentes's decorations at a production of Salieri's opera *Palmira, Queen of Persia* that Goethe saw in Frankfurt in August 1797. Later volumes contained further theoretical pieces on the arts: an exchange of letters on the various approaches to art titled 'The Collector and his Family'; two short pieces on the correct choice of subjects for painting and sculpture; an essay on the Laocoon group; and a translation of Diderot's *Essay on Painting*, interleaved with Goethe's comments. Piecemeal though the presentation was, *The Propylaea* and annual prizes were Goethe's most concerted bout of writing on aesthetic theory since the early 1770s.

Aside from the ambition to foster public debate about art, *The Propylaea* and annual prizes had an ambitious theoretical aim: to establish the proper competency of aesthetic judgement. Kant's critiques had established the competency of theoretical and practical reason but failed, in Schiller's and Goethe's view, to do the same for aesthetic judgement. The first target of Goethe's critique was the fallacy that art should be judged in terms of its fidelity to nature: 'the eternal lie of the connection of nature and art', as he had put it to Meyer in 1796.[344] The second target was the tendency to judge art in terms of its supposed morality. The proper object of aesthetic judgement lay between these two improper objects, neither fidelity to nature nor to our moral feelings. Rectifying the naturalistic fallacy involved reworking Batteux's notion of 'la belle nature'. Batteux is now presented as the 'apostle of the half-true gospel of the imitation of nature, which is so welcome to those who merely trust what their senses tell them and are not aware of what lies behind it'.[345] However, Goethe seems to have misremembered Batteux's actual argument that 'la belle nature' was not about simple imitation of nature at all. In fact Batteux's view was similar to Goethe's. Art involved the creative construction of a new nature. What distinguishes Goethe from Batteux is the question of whether the products of the artistic imagination possess any objectivity. For Batteux the question does not arise. Goethe had decided in Italy that great art possessed objectivity: 'These high works of

[Ancient Greek] art were at the same time produced as the highest works of nature by human beings according to true and natural laws. Everything arbitrary, everything imagined falls away, here is necessity, here is God'.[346] But in the 'Simple Imitation' essay of 1789 he could only give a vague indication of what the 'necessity' was to which great art conformed. It rested 'on the deepest foundations of knowledge, on the essence of things insofar as it is given to us to know them in visible and tangible forms'.[347] By 1798 it was clearer to him what these 'deepest foundations' were, thanks to Kant's *Metaphysical Foundations of Natural Science* and Kielmeyer's lecture on organic forces. In the introduction to *The Propylaea* Goethe maintains that artists can benefit from understanding the science of the 'reciprocity' and 'polarity' of colours.[348] The objectivity of art consists not in its fidelity to particular natural objects, but in following the lawlike patterns of nature in general, such as the polarities that exist in colour.

Thus far the theory would arguably just be a new kind of naturalism, a naturalism of laws rather than empirical appearances. It would not explain what distinguishes art from our scientific understanding of nature. Goethe's answer to that question is to return to Moritz's notion of perfection (*Vollkommenheit*). In the *Critique of Judgement*, Kant denied that perfection could be a meaningful criterion of beauty, because aesthetic judgements were judgements about subjective states, whereas judgements concerning perfection were objective.[349] Goethe was strongly committed to the thought that beauty consisted in objective perfection. Artistic perfection consists in the harmony and coherence with which the object is represented.[350] A perfection of this kind will strike the viewer as having its own objective necessity or rightness. Of course, any art will (subjectively) speak to the senses and the imagination, but truly beautiful art will do more than this. It will transcend the viewer's arbitrary individuality and force upon the viewer an impression of absolute lawlikeness. In this sense it will appeal to something higher in the human mind, a sense of wholeness:

> The worst picture can speak to the sensibility and imagination, by setting it in motion, freeing it and making it independent; the best work of art also speaks to the sensibility, but in a higher language, which one must of course understand; it captivates the feelings and the imagination; it deprives us of our liberty, we cannot do as we please with perfection, as we wish; we are forced to surrender ourselves in order to get ourselves back from [the work of art] exalted and improved.[351]

Without labouring the fact of Goethe's antipathy towards liberalism, we can note that the liberating effect of art—which was still present in Schiller's *Aesthetic Education* despite his opposition to the Jacobins—is subordinated to a higher state of being in which liberty or autonomy has been transcended. The proper effect of art is not to make us free individuals. It is to make us conform to an objective necessity that overrides our individuality. It is a Spinozan condition in which individuality is sacrificed for the sake of a higher knowledge of the nature of things. The same idea of necessary objectivity should guide our judgements of artists. The more perfect the work of art, the less it displays the individuality of the artist:

> The result of a true method is called style, as opposed to manner. Style elevates the individual to the highest point that the species is capable of attaining, which is why all great artists resemble one another in their best works. So Raphael used colour like Titan wherever his work succeeded best. Manner on the other hand individualizes the individual, if one can put it so.[352]

The anti-individualism of Goethe's argument explains his intense and relentless criticisms in his commentary on Diderot's *Essay on Painting*.[353] Both here and elsewhere Goethe repeatedly stresses his profound respect for Diderot's intellectual brilliance.[354] Brilliant minds stimulate competition and opposition: 'the most supreme effect of the spirit is to call forth spirit'.[355] And again: 'Only in action and reaction do we find pleasure'.[356] However, Diderot was an advocate of individualism in art. His *Essay on Painting* is in fact a mixture of naturalism and sentimental moralizing.[357] And it was because Goethe respected Diderot so much that he felt he had to go through the time-consuming process of separating the wheat from the chaff in Diderot's essay.

Diderot's sentimental moralizing was an instance of the second widespread abuse of aesthetic judgement: our tendency to substitute moral criteria for aesthetic ones. To a large extent, Goethe's discussions of moralizing in aesthetics recapitulate the arguments of the *Xenia* campaign against the artistic 'half measures' of contemporary German literature. A new direction (for Goethe) was to develop Moritz's analysis of literary dilettantism of the late 1780s. Amateurish writers lapse into dilettantism because they mistakenly believe that their sensitivity amounts to creativity. In early 1799 Goethe, Schiller and Meyer held lengthy discussions on dilettantism.[358] Goethe drew up two sets of schematic notes on the subject, which he hoped would feed into *The Propylaea*, but nothing came of the plans. The aim was to construct a psychological typology.

The types of dilettantism included the naturalistic fallacy, the mixing of genres, sentimental moralizing, the aping of fashion, and an overly florid or morbid imagination.[359] Again, the project has a Kantian flavour. It resembles Kant's *Anthropology in Pragmatic Perspective*, which Goethe read several weeks before the discussions on dilettantism, with a mixture of grudging admiration and distaste. The *Anthropology* was a typology of moral flaws. Kant itemized and schematized the pathologies that cause us to fall short of the ideal of free and rational behaviour. However, just as Goethe found Kant's *Anthropology* dogmatic and illiberal, so the divide between Goethe's aesthetic ideal and dilettantism is less rigid than Kant's divide between morality and pathology. He allowed that some of the very greatest artists might be thought of as representatives of dilettantish tendencies: Michelangelo, Correggio, and Raphael might be the 'kings or high ambassadors of whole types' of dilettantism.[360]

Another new direction for Goethe is the idea that the highest and the proper object of art is to represent human beings.[361] It would become central to his understanding of art. Again, Kant was an important reference point. Kant argued that ideal beauty 'can be expected only in the human figure'.[362] As expected, Goethe differs from Kant on the nature of human beauty. For Kant human beauty was moral. For Goethe it comprises the whole of our mental and physical being. The importance of this doctrine for Goethe is evident in the fact that human subjects make up all of the topics Goethe and Meyer set for the annual art competition, and the holistic view of humans comes across strongly in their judgements on the submissions. The purpose of the competition was to encourage artists to reflect on how to approach their subject matter. If the imagination is to construct reality and not merely reproduce it, then choices have to be made. Goethe's essay on the Laocoon group provides a lesson in choice and composition. The Laocoon sculptor has succeeded in finding 'the highest moment to be represented'—that is to say, the moment that captures the widest range of human experiences and emotions in a single image. The Laocoon sculptor has chosen a moment that captures three distinct emotions: anxiety, terror, and sympathy.[363] In temporal terms, the figures represent the anticipation of the tragedy to come (anxiety), the experience of the tragedy at its height (terror), and reflection on its effects (sympathy). The sculpture thus combines three temporal moments in one image, despite Lessing's claim in his essay 'Laocoon or the Limits of Painting and Poetry' (1766) that the visual arts were nontemporal in nature. The group's posture is perfectly chosen to reveal the force of the sea serpent's attack. The whole of Laocoon's body is straining to withstand its constricting power, and yet the serpent's posture is also designed to highlight the point in Laocoon's side where the snake is biting him.[364] The group is therefore 'a model of symmetry and multiplicity'.[365] It is as perfect an example as one could hope for of how an artist should approach the challenge of selection and a lesson for artists entering the annual prize competition. The purpose of the competition was to encourage artists to attain the kind of holistic understanding of composition shown in the Laocoon group, and Goethe and Meyer chose their topics to provoke this kind of deliberation. For the 1801 competition they chose Achilles on Scyros—a famous topic portrayed in Statius's unfinished epic the *Achilleid*. The material posed a peculiar challenge because the elements in the narrative were so diverse,[366] not least Achilles disguising himself as a young woman in order to conduct an affair with the daughter of the king of Scyros. In announcing the prize topic, Goethe could not resist teasing the competitors: 'We will not preempt the artists and will say only so much: this subject has only *one* moment in which all the motifs come together'.[367]

Like *The Propylaea*, the aim of the annual prize competition was to put the high philosophy of art into practical action, but as with *The Propylaea* the effect of the prize competition fell short of Goethe's expectations. The competitions have been criticised for a doctrinaire and old-fashioned classicism. It is true that the subjects Goethe and Meyer proposed were mostly taken from Homer and the Greek tragedians, and this may have distracted potential entrants from the competition's purpose. Goethe was disappointed by the relatively small number of artists who entered their work for the first year's competition. He expected several dozen but received only nine. The next year the number of submissions rose to twenty-seven, which gave him grounds to hope that he could encourage a national debate on the arts.[368] The hope was realized in part. The most positive consequence of *The Propylaea* and the competitions was that Goethe was now in conversation with a new generation of German artists, notably Philipp Otto Runge, with whom he corresponded until Runge's early death in 1810.

―――――

The topics from Homer that Goethe set for the annual competitions arose from his rereading the *Iliad*, from December 1797 into the spring of 1798. The success of *Herrmann and Dorothea* tempted him to try a more ambitious imitation of Homer.[369] After some reading and deliberation he chose as his subject matter the episode in the Trojan War between the end of Homer's *Iliad* and the death of Achilles. The narrative would be based loosely on the fourth-century C.E. Latin prose translation of a Greek chronicle of the Trojan War attributed to Dictys of Crete. He worked on the 'Achilleid' for several weeks in the spring of 1798 and again in spring 1799, before abandoning it as a fragment of 650 lines. The problem was that the subject matter contained too much sentiment and pathos for the Homeric manner; it tended more towards tragedy than epic, he wrote to Schiller in May 1798.[370] The Homeric style of *Herrmann and Dorothea* added a distanced and ironic dimension to the poem's commentary on the spirit of the times, even if the tension between the Homeric form and the modern content was lost on his German readers. The 'Achilleid' lacks this tension. The poem's Homeric style is mere pastiche.

A second attempt at writing in the Greek style was his work on the Helen episode of *Faust* in September 1800. His plan was to incorporate a full-scale Greek tragedy into *Faust*,[371] but he only managed to write 265 lines. Unlike the 'Achilleid', however, the Helen material mattered to him, and he did not abandon its main theme. It was a first attempt to represent the exclusion of absolute beauty from the world, forced out by the lust for power of those surrounding it. Helen is the victim of the machinations and power plays of her husband and the ugly monster Phorcyas. In the brief fragment we see enough of Helen to appreciate her moral as well as her physical beauty. She is a gracious queen who defends her maidservants against Phorcyas's calumnies, and a noble spirit weighed down by the memory of her past and anxiety about her future. One reason for his lack of progress with Helen was that another play on the same theme of beleaguered beauty took his attention. One evening in November 1799 Schiller showed Goethe the first volume of the memoirs of Stéphanie-Louise, illegitimate daughter of Prince Louis-Francois de Bourbon-Conti, which had been published the previous year.[372] Goethe dove into the book and the next day asked for the second volume. Within three weeks he had drafted the full outline of a play on the subject. During the winter he wrote the first act, but the work stalled, and the play was only finished in March 1803. Moreover, *The Natural Daughter* was only the first play of a planned trilogy. It was premiered in Berlin in April 1803 and published by Cotta in July. In summer 1804 Goethe tried to write the second and third parts of the trilogy, without success.[373] The play remained an unfinished prelude, a gateway to the real action of the unwritten second and third plays. *The Natural Daughter* was a 'mere exposition', he is reported as saying much later,[374] a chain of mere motivations.[375]

The play loosely follows Stéphanie-Louise's *Memoirs*. Its heroine Eugenie is the illegitimate daughter of a high-ranking but vain and sentimental Duke in a monarchy that bears a close resemblance to prerevolutionary France, though no place names or dates are given, and Eugenie is the only character who bears a name. The Duke is to ask the King for Eugenie's legal recognition in return for the Duke's switching from the anti- to the pro-crown party at court. However, the Duke's legitimate son and Eugenie's half brother is opposed to the plan, which he thinks will diminish his patrimony. He plots to have Eugenie kidnapped by her Governess and shipped away, under the pretence of her death in a riding accident, to the disease-ridden tropical colonies ('the islands'), which is as good as a death sentence. The half brother does not appear in the play; we only see the instruments of his power—the Duke's treacherous Secretary, Eugenie's Governess, whom the Secretary manipulates, and a weak-willed Secular Cleric. All this is by way of backstory. In Act I the Duke presents Eugenie to the King and makes his request. The King appears to accede and sets a date for her appearance at court, but he is a weak character, unable to control the machinations of the high nobility. As the Duke observes, the King's 'leniency breeds temerity' among his nobles.[376] Whether the King is only weak is not clear—it is possible he has been manipulated into participating in the plot to kidnap Eugenie. Either way, the King insists that the Duke and Eugenie keep the matter secret, lest the news cause resentment. In Act II the Secretary explains the plot to kidnap Eugenie to the Governess, who rightly guesses that Eugenie is to be exiled to her death in the islands. Torn between the controlling power of the Secretary and her duty of care for Eugenie, the Governess tries to avert the worst effects of the conspiracy by persuading Eugenie to renounce her claim to recognition, but Eugenie is simply too excited by her prospects. Indeed, she breaks her word to her father and unlocks a secret cabinet containing jewels to be worn on the day of her presentation at court. (Like Friedericke in *Agitated*, Eugenie is impulsive and confident in her own aristocratic superiority.) The conspiracy comes into effect in Act III. The Duke learns of Eugenie's apparent death while out riding. The Secular Cleric plays his part by reporting that Eugenie's body was so horribly mangled in the accident as to be unrecognisable. In Act IV the scene shifts to the harbour of a coastal town, where Eugenie is to embark for the islands. Still hoping to avert her transportation, the Governess shows the order for Eugenie's arrest, a royal *lettre de cachet*, to a Magistrate, who is horrified by the abuse of power the document represents. The Governess persuades the Magistrate to save Eugenie by marrying her. The Magistrate asks Eugenie to marry him and delivers a homily on marriage, but she rejects him, as the marriage would make her beholden to him and would end her hopes for recognition by consigning her to his lower social class. In Act V Eugenie is now in chains waiting to embark. She begs the regional Governor and the Abbess of a local convent to help her, but they both baulk at the sight of the *lettre de cachet*. Undecided what to do, Eugenie entrusts her decision to a fanatical old Monk. He tells her to go to the islands, where she will do good work by giving comfort to the ill. He regrets his own return from the islands to the corrupt mainland which, he says in a premonition of the Revolution, is threatened by collapse. Eugenie accepts the Monk's vision of the kingdom, but instead of following his advice, she decides to stay and fight for the *ancien regime*. She therefore accepts the Magistrate's offer of marriage, on condition that the marriage will not be consummated until some unspecified time in the future: he is to hide her at his country estate and keep her identity secret; eventually she will summon him and their marriage might perhaps then be consummated. He accepts all her terms and she offers him her hand.

Goethe acknowledged that *The Natural Daughter* was not an easy play to stage; to make it stageworthy, he would have to rewrite it completely, he wrote to Zelter.[377] He told Germaine de Stael that it was 'an artist's experiment'.[378] On the page, it is a mysterious and occasionally beautiful poetic drama, full of symbolic action and language. Its elevated rhetoric constantly aspires to poetic beauty, but just as often it serves as an instrument of its speakers' power, and in this respect it is similar to *Torquato Tasso*. Its beautiful and impulsive heroine is surrounded by characters whose intentions are either self-serving or obscure. Reflecting on the play much later, Goethe described it as a repository for his thoughts about the causes and effects of the Revolution: 'In the plan I made myself a vessel in which I could set down, with suitable seriousness, everything I had written or thought over many a year about the French Revolution and its effects'.[379] The central argument is that the *ancien regime* was corrupted by conflict between interests, both personal and factional, which the crown was too weak to suppress. Naturally enough, this reflects Goethe's perspective as an *ancien regime* minister whose first responsibility was to maintain his Duke's executive power. However, what is most interesting about the play, as a political document, is Goethe's understanding of the *ancien regime* as a legal structure. The play contains the most detailed and complex reflection on the operations of the law of any of Goethe's works.[380] The plot concerns the treatment of illegitimate children by French inheritance law before and during the Revolution, and through this medium it reflects on the social and political nature of the law in general. While Goethe drew extensively on the memoirs of Stéphanie-Louise de

Bourbon-Conti, he moved sharply away from his source in choosing to make Eugenie's husband-to-be a well-respected legal officer. In Stéphanie's memoirs, the husband who is forced on her is a minor official of the crown, and Stéphanie portrays him as ill mannered and venal.[381] Goethe's Magistrate is an officer of one of France's thirteen provincial appeal courts and is reputed to be of good character.[382] By making this change, Goethe associated Eugenie's husband-to-be with that class of bourgeois regional lawyers and officials that played such an important role in the Legislative Assembly elected in September 1791—the second and more radical phase of the Revolution. In Goethe's notes for the second and third plays in the trilogy, the Magistrate becomes part of a revolutionary underground movement. He is the most positive representative of the Revolution in Goethe's writing. The change also means that the discussions between Eugenie and her husband-to-be concerning their marriage and the *lettre de cachet* are informed by his knowledge of the law. Much of the action of Acts IV and V is concerned with the different characters' reactions to the *lettre de cachet*, and they reveal how social class affects attitudes to the law and legality. The *lettre* is shown to three characters in turn: the Magistrate, the provincial Governor, and the Abbess. The three characters represent the three estates: the third estate, the nobility, and the clergy. The Governor and Abbess are reluctant to act against the *lettre de cachet* because they are part of the aristocratic world that such royal instruments as *lettres de cachet* support. The Governor reacts to the *lettre* with a disquisition on legal rights. What might at first sight appear to be Eugenie's rights as a natural person in fact boil down to rights over property, or so the Governor argues. Because cases in inheritance law are matters of money and not human sentiments, they typically descend into bitter and unfeeling disputes. It is a view that reflects prerevolutionary French inheritance law, which was defined largely in terms of social rules governing the ownership of property.[383] The revolutionary assertion of basic human rights changed all this, as Goethe knew. In November 1793, the Law of Brumaire Year II gave some inheritance rights to illegitimate children.[384] It was a notable advance for its time.[385] In January 1794, the Law of Nivôse Year II decreed that all persons be treated equally for the purposes of inheritance, with no precedence for men above women or for older above younger siblings.[386] As a result of these two innovations, inheritance law became less a matter of socially differentiated property rights and more a matter of the fundamental human rights of a natural person. Notwithstanding his pessimism then, the Governor's reading of the law is plausible. Things look bleak for Eugenie.

By contrast, the Magistrate draws a distinction between two spheres of legality—a distinction which is of great importance for what happens in Act V. In many cases the law serves the interests of the people. In the case of the *letter de cachet*, however, all that matters is power:

> Nicht ist von Recht, noch von Gericht die Rede;
> Hier ist Gewalt! entsetzliche Gewalt,
> Selbst wenn sie klug, selbst wenn sie weise handelt.[387]

> There is no question here of law or judgement; / This is power! horrific power, / Even if [it acts] prudently, even if it acts wisely.

The Magistrate's appalled reaction to the *lettre* reflects progressive opinion in France before and during the Revolution. The *lettres de cachet* were a prerogative of the crown, unchallengeable in law and thus an expression of the absolutist principle that kings could disregard or even contradict the law: *rex solutus est a legibus*, kings are exempt from the laws. In 1770 a remonstrance by Malesherbes, the President of the Court of Aids, pointed out that *lettres de cachet* could be issued by designated minsters of the crown without the crown's knowledge. There were therefore *lettres* in circulation about which Louis XV knew nothing and which did not express the royal will in all its majestic wisdom. Mirabeau, in his bestselling radical essay of 1782, *On Lettres de Cachet and State Prisons*, made no distinction between legitimate and illegitimate letters: all *lettres de cachet* were abuses of power. These criticisms bring into focus two aspects of the *lettre de cachet* in *The Natural Daughter*. We are not told how the *lettre* came into being—whether it was a result of the King's changing his mind about recognising Eugenie, perhaps under pressure from a faction at court, or it was a spurious letter produced without the King's knowledge by one of his ministers. The play does not exclude the possibility that this *lettre* belongs to the spurious type criticised by Malesherbes. The Magistrate's reaction, on the other hand, is much closer to Mirabeau's radical essay. The power expressed in the letter is or should be illegal, he says, regardless whether it was an expression of the King's wise and prudent will or not. This takes us to the heart of the play's representation of law and legality. Repeatedly and in a variety of ways, the play suggests that the ultimate sources and justification of legality are inaccessible to us. The language of fate is ubiquitous: the words *Schicksal* and *Geschick* together occur thirty times. Power is referred to in abstract language. Vague indications are given of remote or inaccessible sources of power. Ultimately the law is just brute power, undefined and ominous.[388] For the

Magistrate, a bourgeois revolutionary, this represents a systemic problem, as he bleakly tells Eugenie: 'You will not find the source of the evil, / And if found it will continue to flow forever' ('Des Übels Quelle findest du nicht aus, / Und aufgefunden fließt sie ewig fort').[389] Even if it were possible to identify the source of the *lettre*, the Magistrate claims, the abuse of power would not stop because it is part of the very bedrock of the *ancien regime*, namely the principle that *rex solutus est a legibus*.

By contrast to the Magistrate's radical opposition, and in a strange paradox, Eugenie maintains her strong allegiance to the crown to the very end, despite the fact that the legal instrument that threatens to destroy her is a pure expression of the crown's sovereign power. The play's aristocratic supporters of the *ancien regime*, the Governor, the Abbess, and Eugenie, are in a perplexing situation. They refuse to criticise the legality of the *lettre de cachet*, and yet they can say nothing meaningful about the sources of that legality. The Magistrate, despite his progressive politics, has come to the same conclusion: as a legal officer he can carry out the law within everyday bourgeois life, but there exists a higher domain where he and the legality he represents have no power whatsoever:

> Was droben sich in ungemess'nen Räumen,
> Gewaltig seltsam, hin und her bewegt,
> Belebt und tötet, ohne Rat und Urteil,
> Das wird nach anderm Maß, nach andrer Zahl
> Vielleicht berechnet, bleibt uns rätselhaft.[390]

> Whatever up there in uncharted spaces, / Strange beyond our ken, moves back and forth, / Gives life and takes it, without counsel or judgement—/ Is by another standard, another measure / Calculated perhaps, remains a mystery to us.

The meting out of life and death arbitrarily is a reminder of Princess Lily in the 'Fairy Tale', who symbolically represents the French crown, and who lives with the paradoxical curse and blessing that any living being she touches dies, but her touch can also bring the dead back to life. Her touch is her own magical *lettre de cachet*.

Eugenie and the Magistrate thus represent a conflict between a well-regulated bourgeois sphere and a royal sphere that is impenetrable and endowed with great but arbitrary and ambivalent powers, and this conflict is not resolved at the end of the play. When Eugenie finally accepts the Magistrate's proposal of marriage, the resulting compact by no means represents Eugenie (or even Goethe) accepting the claims of the bourgeoisie as preeminent, as is argued by Boyle.[391] Eugenie accepts the proposal entirely on her own terms. She will not consummate the marriage, thus rejecting the central pillar of the institution of marriage. She will go into hiding at the Magistrate's rural estate, so exempting herself from any of the usual duties or status of a wife in bourgeois civil society. In response he accepts all of her conditions. He acknowledges his powerlessness in this instance, despite being an officer of the law, and promises to be at her command. In securing these terms for herself, Eugenie carves out a space outside the laws that govern marriage in bourgeois civil society, a space where she can continue to be an aristocrat in a bourgeois world. The Magistrate accepts Eugenie's terms without any negotiation. He is as submissive towards the nobility as Wilhelm in Books VII and VIII of *Wilhelm Meister's Apprenticeship*. What persuades the Magistrate to accept Eugenie on such unfavourable and illegitimate terms? In part it is her beauty and aristocratic lineage which combine to make her a goddess in his eyes, his own Helen of Troy. In part it is his acknowledgement of *ancien regime* realities. Ordinary people have no power over the ultimate sources of legality; the pact we make when we enter this higher world is to accept our own powerlessness. Goethe's own prosaic view of the question of legality, a view he formed during his doctoral studies in Strasbourg and maintained throughout his life, was that the only real source of legality was secular and military power,[392] and that all legislative power was vested in a state's ruler: 'all legislation is the province of the prince'.[393] He was, of course, deeply sceptical about the law as a branch of academic study and as a practice. His experience of administering Sachsen-Weimar taught him that the power of the executive was much more important to the health of a polity than the quality of its laws. As the wise and well-read Baroness in the *Conversations of German Emigrés* puts it: 'the legislative could be as rational as it liked, it would avail the state nothing, if the executive were not powerful'.[394] While *The Natural Daughter* does give space to the Magistrate's radical critique of *lettres de cachet*, and no doubt Goethe did lament the failure of the French crown to find better ways to keep its subjects in order, the play's imagery and its conclusion lend stronger support to an aristocratic, top-down worldview, in which a mysterious royal sovereignty is the ultimate source of all legality.

Until 1798 the main impact of the Revolution on Sachsen-Weimar had been the threat of imported revolutionary ideas taking root among the local population and the threat of invasion by the French revolutionary armies. The Revolution could therefore be dismissed by conservative German regimes as an external matter, and a case could be made for ignoring its political content. This was the position of the government of Sachsen-Weimar. After the breakdown of peace in 1798 and Napoleon's coup against the Directory in 1799, the nature of the threat changed. In 1800 the Austrians were driven out of northern Italy and southern Germany. Austria made peace with France at the Treaty of Lunéville in 1801. The treaty established total French sovereignty over the German territories west of the Rhine. By way of compensation to the German principalities that lost territories to France, numerous smaller territories east of the Rhine were annexed to larger ones, and over seventy religious territories were secularized. So began the most significant reorganization of the Holy Roman Empire since the end of the Thirty Years' War. The arrangements were confirmed at the Imperial Recess (*Reichsdeputationshauptschluss*) of 1803. All told some 110 small German territories east of the Rhine disappeared for good.

The effects of the Imperial Recess on Sachsen-Weimar were indirect but no less sudden. The incorporation of the Archbishopric of Würzburg into the Electorate of Bavaria and the confirmation of freedom of the press there led to the revitalization of its university. A department of Protestant theology was established in the hitherto solidly Catholic university. Competition for Jena also came from the University of Halle, now more generously funded by the Prussian government. The result was that Würzburg and Halle offered substantially better conditions than Jena to a professoriate that had begun to have doubts about the liberality of Jena after the dismissal of Fichte. The mood in Jena was aggravated by personal disagreements between professors and a growing atmosphere of acrimony.[395] The year of 1803 saw an exodus of professors. Schelling left for a chair in Würzburg, followed by the philologist Schütz, the theologian Paulus, and the economist and jurist Hufeland. The anatomist Loder, with whom Goethe had worked closely since the 1780s, left for Halle. The *General Literary Journal* (*Allgemeine Literatur-Zeitung* or *ALZ*) under the editorship of Schütz and Hufeland left for Halle at the end of the year.

The Jena crisis of 1803, like Weimar's treasury crisis of 1782, showed Goethe at his energetic best. It was his responsibility to prevent the university dwindling into insignificance, a threat that he and other members of the Weimar elite took very seriously.[396] During the summer and autumn he worked on recruiting replacements for the departed professors. Ironically, the departure of the *ALZ* turned into a boon for Goethe. In August it was decided that the *ALZ* would continue to publish in Jena, under the new name of the *Jena*

General Literary Journal (*Jenaische Allgemeine Literatur-Zeitung, JALZ*), edited by the classicist Heinrich Carl Abraham Eichstädt. Goethe set about engaging a 'company of reliable men' who would be the backbone of the reviewing team.[397] As the first edition went to press in January 1804, he could write confidently to Schiller: 'All in all I've learned that a higher level of culture is widespread in Germany, the possessors of which will all gradually congregate to us'.[398] In the first few years of the *JALZ*, Goethe contributed most of the reviews on literature. Thanks to his and Eichstädt's efforts, the *JALZ* was able to compete with the *ALZ* and eventually overtake it. Unlike *The Horae* and *The Propylaea*, the *JALZ* made no great claims for aesthetic regeneration, nor was it dominated by the new philosophy. (The *ALZ* under Schütz continued to be the house magazine of Kantianism.) The *JALZ* fitted in with Germany's traditional periodical culture. Goethe gladly took the chance it gave him to be reconciled with the German republic of letters.

In 1799 he came into possession of a collection of letters from Winckelmann to his friend Hieronymus Dietrich Berendis, erstwhile secretary of Anna Amalia. The letters reminded Goethe of how much he owed to Winckelmann, at precisely the time when he was setting out his own philosophy of art in *The Propylaea*. They prompted him to return to Winckelmann's writings on art history and, for the first time, to make explicit his own debt to Winckelmann, as he wrote to Schiller in August 1799: 'Recently I've been diligently studying Winckelmann's life and writings. I must try to clarify for myself in detail this valiant man's achievement and influence.'[399] So began a new project, slowly at first. In his commentary on Diderot's *Essay on Painting* he made the first tentative step by setting his own Winckelmannian aesthetics in a Kantian frame. Since 1798 he had tried and failed to reconfigure his work on optics and aesthetics along Kantian lines. In the process, and in his dealings with Fichte and Schelling, he came to the view that the new philosophy was an expression of modernity's unhealthy tendency to treat objective facts as if they were states of mind. The Kantian focus on the thinking subject, far from clarifying our relation to objective fact, was getting in the way. Although he had cordial relations with the young Idealists in Jena, notably the brothers August Wilhelm and Friedrich Schlegel, he disliked their new conception of art because of its blurring of genres and its view of art as a vehicle for the new philosophy. It was surely just one small step from there to an openly religious view of art, which had to be combatted now, just as it had been in the *Xenia*. As Goethe wrote to Meyer in 1805: 'It's time to announce what we think about this tomfoolery; for nothing good will come of peace with such people: they will just run amok all the more brazenly.'[400] In his return to Winckelmann there was much more at stake than Winckelmann's life and work. It was also part of his battle to win back cultural and intellectual ground from the Romantics and Idealists.

The Winckelmann project was collaborative from its inception. In September 1799 Goethe and Meyer began to plan a history of eighteenth-century art, the germ of which went back to Meyer's travels in Italy from 1795 to 1797 and their joint project on Italian art.[401] Meyer was also helped by Karl Ludwig Fernow, who returned to Jena in 1803 from a seven-year stay in Italy. The resulting 'Outline of the Art History of the Eighteenth Century' was the largest part of the Winckelmann volume. A second essay by Meyer assessed Winckelmann's achievement as an art historian. Goethe provided an edited text of the letters to Berendis. By way of an advertisement, in February 1804 he published a set of notes on the letters in the *JALZ*.[402] The volume was topped and tailed with a preface by Goethe and a list of all Winckelmann's extant letters in chronological order, again by Goethe. In its final stages the project faltered while Goethe waited for Wolf in Halle to finish an essay on Winckelmann's education as a classicist. In December 1804 Goethe started work on the essay in which he expounded Winckelmann's cultural and philosophical significance. It appeared in the volume anonymously and untitled, gathered with Meyer's and Wolf's essays on Winckelmann under the heading 'Sketches for a Portrait of Winckelmann'. The writing of the essay proceeded slowly and was interrupted by a life-threatening illness in the early months of 1805. With the essay finished, the volume was published in May.

Writing to Schiller in 1798 on the 'Achilleid', Goethe admitted that there were features of Homer's poetic style and beliefs that it would be hard for him, as a modern, to reproduce:

> If I'm to have success with a poem that is to some extent a continuation of the *Iliad*, then I will have to follow the ancients even in those matters for which they are criticised; indeed I must make my own that which discomforts me; only then will I be more or less certain of not completely missing the sense and tone.[403]

Goethe goes on to identify two of these 'important points': the intervention of the gods in human affairs and Homer's use of extended metaphors. However, the way Goethe expresses himself in the letter—'to follow the ancients', that is to say to follow the practice of antiquity in general and not just the Homeric epics—suggests that he might have had in mind a more sensitive matter for which the ancients were criticised, namely homosexuality or 'Greek love', as it was commonly called in the eighteenth century. The 'Achilleid' fragment contains two references to Greek love. Goethe's narrator specifies that Ganymede, Zeus's young cupbearer, serves only Zeus; the other Olympians are served by the Graces and Hebe. Homer organizes the staff differently: Ganymede serves all the gods. By highlighting Zeus's special relationship with Ganymede, Goethe puts extra emphasis on the relationship's homoerotic nature.[404] There is also a brief reference to the love of Achilles for Patroclus. His mother Thetis describes Achilles remembering his dead friend 'longingly', a word that suggests mourning a lost lover.[405] For Goethe, 'following the ancients' meant being open about homosexuality. One remarkable feature of the Winckelmann essay is how open Goethe is about Winckelmann's homosexuality. The essay is organized in a loosely chronological sequence of twenty-five sections, each with a lapidary heading. The last section, 'Demise', contains Goethe's final valediction. He makes no specific mention of the well-known manner of Winckelmann's death at the hands of Francesco Arcangeli in Trieste. Instead he ends with the consoling thought that by dying in his prime Winckelmann was spared the pains and indignities of old age. These are the closing words of the essay:

> Now in the memory of posterity he enjoys the advantage of appearing forever vigorous and strong: for it is in the form in which a person leaves the earth that he walks among the shades, and it is thus that Achilles remains present to our minds as a youth forever striving. That Winckelmann departed early is also to our advantage. The breath of his strength wafting from his grave fortifies us and arouses in us the most animated urge to continue, now and forever, with enthusiasm and love what he began.[406]

As in the *Roman Elegies*, Goethe not only accepts the substance of Winckelmann's aesthetics; he also enacts it by portraying him in prose that emulates Winckelmann's own enthusiastic descriptions of Greek statuary in his *History*. The exquisitely measured phrases and ethereal grace of Goethe's writing turn Winckelmann into a work of art to stand beside the Apollo Belvedere. (The emphasis on youth and the notion that beauty is carried in a breath of air are both in Winckelmann's description of the Apollo.) Furthermore, Goethe repays the love that is evident in Winckelmann's letters to his friends by imagining himself, his collaborators and his readers being driven by enthusiasm and love to continue Winckelmann's work. The nature of Winckelmann's love is hinted at by Goethe's reference to Achilles. The final sentences of the essay delicately urge the reader to recognise the beauty of Winckelmann's homosexuality. If Goethe's aesthetics can seem narrowly neoclassical, they are also, above all in the Winckelmann essay, genuinely inclusive.

The project arose out of the Berendis letters. The notes Goethe published in the *JALZ* begin by affirming the importance of a person's letters:

> Letters left behind by important men always have great attraction for posterity; they are as it were the only evidence of the great computation of life, of which deeds and writings represent the finished sum totals.

This is especially true of Winckelmann 'who felt himself at his freest when, with a pen in his hand, he imagined himself face to face with an intimate friend'.[407] Again in the preface to *Winckelmann and his Century*, Goethe stresses that Winckelmann was more open in private correspondence than in person. During the period covered by the letters 'Winckelmann found himself in an anxious perplexity, the direct portrayal of which one cannot read without sympathy'.[408] The as-yet-unmentioned nature of this perplexity is that in Rome Winckelmann could live, at least in private, as a gay man, but in order to secure his position as a scholar he was obliged to undergo public conversion to Catholicism. In his private correspondence he was not exposed to the pressure to conform. In company, he was reserved, but in his letters he 'felt his full natural freedom and expressed himself as he felt more often and without reservation'.[409] In the volume's preface and the first few sections of Goethe's essay, then, homosexuality is a constant undercurrent. It first surfaces in the section titled 'Friendship', in a general discussion of relations between the sexes and not specifically in relation to Winckelmann. Goethe begins the section by considering the claim that the Greeks were 'in truth whole persons'. (The reader knows and Goethe does not need to state that this is how Winckelmann presented the Greeks in his *History*.) The Greeks' wholeness found full expression in friendship—'that delight springing from the connection between similar natures'.[410] However, human relationships were ordered in a fundamentally different fashion among the Greeks. Male-female relationships were almost entirely physical and less emotionally rich than in the modern world. The most emotionally rich relationships were between 'persons of the male sex' and between women, for Goethe adds that the two young women 'Chloris and Thyia were inseparable friends even in Hades'.[411] The mention of Chloris and Thyia is a remarkable exception to the near blanket silence about female homosexuality at the time.[412] Disregarding the taboo, Goethe openly presents Chloris and Thyia's relationship as sexual. The next paragraph is nothing short of a hymn to Greek love:

The passionate fulfilment of the duties of love, the delight of inseparability, the sacrifice of one for the other, the explicit lifelong commitment, the necessity of going together into death—these fill us with amazement at the relationship between two youths, and we feel ashamed when poets, historians, philosophers, orators, overwhelm us with stories, events, feelings, and confessions of such content.

That is to say, we moderns feel ashamed by the sheer emotional depth of Greek love and the comparative poverty of such relationships among us moderns. Goethe turns on its head the Judaeo-Christian view of same-sex relationships: that they are emotionally impoverished because they do not create offspring. And having established that Greek love is rich, he can now state openly that Winckelmann felt himself at his best in his same-sex relationships: 'it is here, that W., in the midst of stress and need, felt himself great, rich, generous and happy'.[413] If any readers preferred to turn a blind eye to Goethe's intention thus far, their blindness would be sorely tested in the next section of the essay, 'Beauty'. It begins by returning to aesthetics, though it turns out that this is only an overture to Goethe's most open statement of Winckelmann's homosexuality. The argument starts from the principle, formulated in the language Goethe had adapted from Schelling, that humans are 'the ultimate product of nature in its constant self-refinement' ('der sich immer steigernden Natur').[414] To be sure, nature's inner productivity encounters obstructions, so that its products are rarely perfect. Humans only achieve true beauty momentarily. If these fomulations seem somewhat abstract, a more concrete and controversial conclusion follows. We are asked to contemplate in the abstract something that might offend us, if we had to confront its reality unprepared. It is important to understand Goethe's tactic. One aim of the essay is a frank and generous tribute to Winckelmann which accepts his homosexuality and therefore accepts what it was like for him to live as a gay man in Catholic Rome. The unobjectionable proposition that human beauty is only momentary prepares the reader for Winckelmann's lived reality. His homosexuality could rarely express itself, its full expressions were only momentary: 'So we often find W. in the company of beautiful young men, and nowhere does he appear more vivacious and lovable than in such often merely fleeting moments'.[415] It is no accident that in writing of 'beautiful young men' and 'fleeting moments' Goethe appeals to signature ideas of the modern queer aesthetic. He has taken Winckelmann's experience seriously.

At the same time, Winckelmann's homosexuality supports Goethe's argument about contemporary German cultural and intellectual life. Winckelmann represents one pole of the German mind; the other is represented by the Idealists and Romantics. The mixed results of Goethe's efforts to apply Kant's philosophy to his work on optics and aesthetics had reinforced his belief in the fundamental difference between antiquity and modernity and the rightness of Winckelmann's theory of Greek wholeness. What distinguishes us from the ancients is that we suffer from a 'barely curable divide' between the mind and body.[416] The result of the divide is that we are no longer able to trust our senses and instead we overinvest in reason. It is certainly possible to grasp the world with reason, but it is difficult. One simply has no guarantee that ideas of reason conform to reality, and so one is liable to set off in pursuit of knowledge in the wrong direction. This is the predicament of modern philosophy:

> If one were intent on accusing the philosophers of not being able securely to locate the point of transition to life, of making the most errors precisely where they want to convert their convictions into deed and action, and thereby of diminishing their standing in the world, then there would be no lack of examples.[417]

The distinction between antiquity and modernity boils down to 'the certainty of the point from which one starts out'.[418] We can now reframe the argument in terms of the arts and see more clearly how it relates to Winckelmann. The Ancient Greeks, for whom human nature was indivisible, had no conception of the tainted and fallen nature of the flesh. Greek art makes no distinction between the beauty of a body and its moral goodness. Christian art, by contrast, habitually seeks to represent moral ideas as operating separately from beautiful forms. As a result, when we view Christian art, we have no choice but to apply moral reasoning to it, which leads us into a category error. Where we should apply only our judgement, instead we apply reason. It is because of this category error that we need a Kantian critique, which can set us back on the right path of sound judgement—or in technical Kantian terms, it can show us how to avoid erring into the constitutive use of reason. The ancients had no need of such a critique and nor do modern classicists, whose judgement has been schooled in Greek beauty. Kantianism is a necessary evil for all moderns who have not had the benefit of a thorough classical education:

> While the events of recent times are on our minds, it may be the right place for an observation that we can make on our journey through life—namely that no scholar has with impunity dismissed, opposed or disdained that great philosophical movement begun by Kant, excepting the genuine

experts in antiquity who by virtue of the singularity of their study seem favoured above all other people. For insofar as they are concerned with the best the world has produced and only ever consider the lesser and worse in relation to that excellence, their knowledge acquires such depth, their judgements such certainty, their taste such consistency that within their own sphere they appear surprisingly, nay amazingly well educated.[419]

The Kantian journey is necessary if only to return us to our proper starting point: the observation of phenomena and the judgement of beautiful forms.

The argument of the essay culminates in the section 'Character'. Here Goethe concludes that the modern hypertrophy of reason is accompanied by an excess of self-consciousness. By contrast, and as Goethe has argued in the section 'Antiquity', a person with Greek wholeness will be able 'to unconsciously take pleasure in his own existence'.[420] Goethe does not mean 'unconscious' in the strong sense of being unaware or oblivious. Winckelmann did in fact attend to his own mental and emotional states. What he did not do was obsess over himself. He possessed 'that ancient peculiarity of always being concerned with himself, without actually observing himself'.[421] What Goethe means by 'unconscious' is that one's attention does regularly focus on the self but is not locked onto it. It is important that the distinction is made in this way. If our attention is locked onto the self, then we cannot help but see the world as it relates to us and not as it is in itself. We will fall into modern philosophy's error of redescribing facts about the world as facts about our own mental states. The result will be an unbalanced relation between self and world, between subject and object. One instance of an unbalanced relation is the Christian notion of a personal God, which allows us to project our own subjective wants and needs onto the universe. The argument is familiar from the 'Confessions of the Beautiful Soul' in *Wilhelm Meister*, where Goethe analysed the 'most delicate confusion of the subjective and the objective'.[422] Winckelmann had no need for a personal God. His God was purely external: it was the source of natural and artistic beauty.[423] Here Goethe clearly has in mind Spinoza's 'intellectual love of God' and his principle that 'he who loves God cannot strive that God should love him in return'.[424] A tendency to indulge in self-observation will upset our relation to the world and contravene Spinoza's principle. Winckelmann's strength of character made him immune to this error. In addition, Winckelmann had no need of morality in its strong Kantian sense. He was an example of goodness motivated by instinct and emotion,[425] and with no need for moral principles.[426] All his motives can be described satisfactorily in terms of his natural character, even the motives that resulted in the very highest moral ends. These include doing his duty, for which he was notable, Goethe says.[427] The reference to duty is an obvious allusion to Kant. Goethe's point is that Winckelmann was able to achieve everything that Kant's ethics demands, but without the need for Kantian ethical theory. He did not need to be continuously aware of his motives or to redescribe them in terms of reason.

Goethe sent the Winckelmann essay to press in the second half of April, in the middle of a recurrence of his illness. He wrote to Schiller of his hope that the text bore no signs of his poor health.[428] The following week he visited Schiller, and they met again on the way into the theatre on 1 May. Then silence. In the first week of May Goethe felt he was beginning to recover. On 9 May Schiller died. He was only forty-five years old and at the height of his powers as a playwright. Christiane learned of Schiller's death and tried at first to conceal it from Goethe out of concern for his still fragile health. In the weeks that followed Goethe tried to put on a brave face. Since spring 1804 Schiller had been writing a play on the Russian false tsar Demetrius. Goethe thought about trying to complete it, but it was a plan born of despair. He summed up the depth of his loss in a letter to Zelter three weeks after Schiller's death:

> In the time since I last wrote to you I've had few good days. I thought I'd lose my life, and now I've lost a friend and in him one half of my own existence. Actually I ought to begin a new way of life; but at my age there's no longer any way. So I only see each day that's directly before me, and do what's closest to hand, without a thought for anything that might follow.[429]

8

'My Emperor'

WEIMAR, 1805–1814

THE LOSS of half of his existence on 9 May 1805 was devastating. Goethe sought the company of friends more than ever. He was delighted at the prospect of Wolf's arrival from Halle at the end of May.[1] In the last week of June Fritz Jacobi visited, but their friendship was now overshadowed by mutual incomprehension, as Goethe wrote later: 'I no longer understood the language of his philosophy. He could not be happy in the world of my poetry'.[2] Schiller, who had become his main bridge between poetry and philosophy, was gone. On 9 August the theatre at Bad Lauchstädt was full for a performance of Schiller's *Maid of Orleans*, several hundred folk having walked the twelve miles from Halle to honour Schiller.[3] The next day Zelter arrived from Berlin to see a dramatized performance of Schiller's poem 'The Bell' for which he had composed the music and Goethe had written a poetic epilogue. Goethe wrote to Carl August: 'My joy in seeing this delightful man and possessing him for a few days is great. If soundness were to vanish from the world, it could be reconstructed from him'.[4] Wolf was also 'sound'.[5] The good sense and resilience of these friends was some consolation. As for his writing, what he wrote to Zelter three weeks after Schiller's death summed things up: 'I only see each day that's directly before me, and do what's closest to hand, without thinking of anything that might follow'.[6] His friends expected a poetic commemoration of Schiller, and at first he hoped to write a large-scale cantata, but it proved too much for him, and the 'Epilogue to Schiller's Bell' was all he managed. The poem conveyed the breadth and nobility of Schiller's vision and issued a stern summons to the Germans to rise to Schiller's high calling. However, in keeping with Goethe's retreat from cultural nationalism, the 'Epilogue' presents Schiller more as a poet of Weimar and the world than of the German nation. The phrase 'for he was ours' is strikingly repeated, but the *us* to whom Schiller belongs is as much Weimar as the German public. The poem imagines Schiller sitting in his garden in Weimar looking up at the stars and thence striding out into the intellectual world of 'truth, goodness, beauty'.[7] There is no mention of the German nation, only of the 'world' that mourns him.

Schiller's death and his own illness made Goethe all the more aware of the need to secure his legacy. In September 1799, by way of compensation for the poor sales of *The Propylaea*, Goethe had offered Cotta first refusal on any new works he might write after the completion of the Unger edition.[8] Cotta published *The Natural Daughter* and *Winckelmann and his Century*, and was promised *Faust. The First Part of the Tragedy*. Otherwise the cupboard was bare, so agreement was reached for a new edition of his works. The thirteen volumes appeared between 1806 and 1810, edited with the help of the teenaged August's tutor Riemer. Alongside the new edition, Goethe began to send Cotta the copy for his *Theory of Colour*, his conclusive statement on the subject that had exercised him since the early 1790s. Progress was slow, at times excruciatingly so. In 1800 he had decided to divide the work into three parts.[9] The first, 'didactic' part would contain his observations of boundary colours, his research on the physiology of colour vision, and discussions of the role of colour in the other sciences and in culture. The second, 'polemical' part would detail his objections to Newton. The third part would recount and analyse the history of the subject from antiquity up to the present. The obstacles were formidable and the work exhausting. It was a 'Sisyphean stone', he wrote to Knebel in March 1806.[10] The observations had to be described with great care, for it was necessary to show how the boundary colours appeared and disappeared when subjected to a range of subtly varied circumstances. The polemics against Newton could hardly be anything other than a sustained act of destruction, which was not in Goethe's nature. In April 1807 he wrote to Alexander von Humboldt in Berlin: 'I'm now on the thorny polemical path. It is an unfriendly and also thankless task to show, step by step and word by word, that the world has been wrong for a hundred years'.[11] As for the historical part, the greatest challenge was the sheer quantity of material.

His grief over Schiller and the hard labour on the *Theory of Colour* and the new Cotta edition set him on a lonely path. Increasingly he parted ways with mainstream German intellectual life. The main reason was the changing political and cultural climate. Following the Imperial Recess of 1803, and as Napoleon's hold over Europe grew tighter, the conservative reaction to the Revolution spread more widely in Germany, at the same time as Catholicism was emerging as a cultural force. Although he shared the national movement's conservatism in politics, his distaste for its nationalism and its connection with Catholicism weighed more heavily with him.

In many of Goethe's comments on the emergence of cultural Catholicism there is a sense of disappointment and betrayal. In July 1805 he added a brief damning passage to a review by Meyer of the Riepenhausen brothers' work on Greek painting. Goethe had initially considered the Riepenhausens to be allies in his campaign to restore classical objectivity in the visual arts. For the prize competition of 1803 they submitted examples of their reconstructions of the paintings of Polygnotus at Delphi. Goethe thought the Polygnotus reconstructions admirable and wrote encouragingly of the Riepenhausens' efforts.[12] Things turned sour the next year. The Riepenhausens submitted a drawing of the deluge for the 1804 prize competition which clearly displayed their turn towards a Catholic conception of art.[13] In 1805 they published the first volume of their Polygnotus reconstructions, now with a commentary that Goethe found insufferably 'portentous, nebulous'. He smelt the same 'neo-Catholic sentimentality' in it as he had found in some of the earliest Romantic writings: the *Heart-Outpourings of an Art-loving Friar* (1797) by Wilhelm Heinrich Wackenroder and Ludwig Tieck's novel *Franz Sternbald's Wanderings* (1798).[14] The Riepenhausen brothers had indeed converted to Catholicism in 1804. Goethe's reaction alternated between militancy and resignation even within the same letter to Meyer. The neo-Catholic tendency had to be combatted now, he wrote: 'It's time to announce what we think about this tomfoolery; for nothing good will come of peace with such people: they will just run amok all the more brazenly'.[15] He would take more decisive action, as soon as time or his humour allowed: 'I shall write a portrayal of the whole neo-Catholic artists' thing; in the meantime we can leave it to ripen and wait to see whether anyone of an old heathen sensibility pipes up'.[16]

Goethe's wavering stemmed from an ambivalence in his attitude towards religion. It is overly crude to describe him as anti-Catholic or even anti-Christian. He was not ill disposed towards Christianity in itself. Since his doctoral studies in Strasbourg he had taken the Spinozan view that religion served a sociopolitical purpose. The state should support well-regulated churches in order to maintain the social order. It is noteworthy how much time and effort Goethe devoted to making sense of the religious situation in Germany in the years immediately after Schiller's death. His most valued conversation partner in matters of religion was Carl Friedrich Reinhard, Napoleon's ambassador to the puppet Kingdom of Westphalia, whom Goethe first met in Carlsbad in

May 1807. That summer he had long conversations with Reinhard on the relative merits of Protestantism and Catholicism,[17] and he made extensive notes on the subject in his diary in September.[18] There were also disputations on the subject with his son August and Riemer.[19] Both faiths suffered, to Goethe's mind, from a tendency to conceal God. The pathological belief in an invisible God was of course a key theme of the 'Confessions of a Beautiful Soul'. The gods of the Greeks or of Winckelmann were by contrast vivid and beautiful expressions of the human and natural worlds. There were of course important differences between Protestantism and Catholicism, which Goethe elaborated in his diary.[20] The invisible God of the Protestants was a moral force and the site of endless recriminations of conscience and self-doubt. The Catholics were more confident in their hope of redemption. Their God was the divine glory that lent its power to a pantheon of 'identical, similar, and subordinate gods': Christ, the Virgin Mary, the angels, and so on. In this sense the Catholic heaven was 'rich and full', like the Greeks' Mount Olympus. In a similar vein, Catholic practice had less interest in the moral self-improvement than Protestantism and instead assigned the role of conscience to the confessor. Thus, while the two faiths were different ways of organizing the same basic ideas, Catholicism did have greater aesthetic potential because it tended to externalize the divinity more than Protestantism did. Indeed Protestant poetry, which Goethe felt had an aristocratic air about it, only made itself look ridiculous whenever it tried, in its loftily moralizing manner, to give expression to the Catholic faith:

> Tending towards Protestantism is what all those do who want to distinguish themselves from the plebs; indeed I've noticed that if one wants to give expression to the Catholic religion and mythology in the Protestant poetic manner, one can make oneself ridiculous, even in a sense despicable. And so there arises, as on great feast days, a throng at the church door, with some wanting to enter and others wanting to leave.

The growing debate about cultural Catholicism was 'a sign of the times'.[21]

In early May 1808 Friedrich Schlegel visited Goethe in Weimar, fresh from his formal conversion to Catholicism in the cathedral of Cologne a week earlier. They discussed Schlegel's new enthusiasm for the medieval painting of Cologne and his essay *On the Language and Wisdom of the Indians*, published in the week of his conversion. Schlegel believed he had won Goethe over to his Romantic viewpoint, quite wrongly as it turned out.[22] After the visit, Goethe read Schlegel's Indian book carefully. He also reread Schlegel's review of the first four volumes of the new Cotta edition of his works. The closer reading lowered Goethe's opinion of Schlegel. For instance, Schlegel rated Goethe's classical elegies far lower than his lyric poems in modern meters, from which Goethe quite reasonably inferred that Schlegel's judgements were not based on aesthetic merit, but on moral and religious criteria. According to Schlegel, lyric poetry was an expression of profound religious mystery. It was exactly the same absurd language as the Riepenhausen brothers had used in their commentary on the Polygnotus reconstructions.[23] And as with the Riepenhausens, it felt like a betrayal of their earlier commonality of purpose. The case of Schlegel was worse, both because he had been a promising classicist and because of the deliberate manner in which he had smuggled his ulterior purpose and his Catholic values into a purportedly objective evaluation of Indian culture. Goethe expressed his distaste in a letter to Reinhard:

> The calculated intent of every line became clear to me, but my insight only became complete when on p. 97 of the little Indian book I saw the miserable devil and his grandmother with all their eternal stinking retinue smuggled back into the circle of good company in a most skilful manner.[24]

He wrote to Zelter on the same day that Schlegel's Indian essay was 'an utterly crass Christian-Catholic confession of faith' and 'a declaration of his conversion to the one redeeming church'. Put simply, it was 'hocus pocus'.[25]

The Schlegel affair was not representative of Goethe's attitude to Catholicism or to Romanticism. Better examples were the fate of his short-lived friendship with the Romantic playwright Zacharias Werner and his treatment of the plays of Heinrich von Kleist. Goethe at first reacted with indifference or distaste to Werner's plays.[26] He changed his mind after meeting Werner in Jena in December 1807. Werner subsequently held court in Weimar for several weeks, and it seemed that he might become Goethe's protégé. At the end of January 1808 Goethe staged Werner's play *Wanda, Queen of the Sarmatians*. He was able to appreciate Werner's charisma and talent at the same time as recognising the distance between them, as he wrote to Jacobi at the time: 'It's thoroughly strange for me, an old heathen, to see the cross planted in my own soil and to hear Christ's blood and wounds preached in poetry, without it revolting me'.[27] Werner left Weimar in March, a few days before Friedrich Schlegel's ill-fated visit. It may be that the breakup with Schlegel affected Goethe's view of Werner. By the time of Werner's return in December 1808, Goethe's interest in him was extinguished. Their friendship ended in a very public argument at a lunch party in late December, when Goethe accused Werner of a 'lopsided religiosity'.[28] Goethe continued to help Werner, but without much enthusiasm.[29] His reaction to the more talented Kleist took a similar course. In March 1808 Goethe staged Kleist's brilliant but difficult comedy *The Broken Jug*, which went down badly with the Weimar audience, whether because Goethe chose to introduce two misplaced intervals into the performance or because the text Goethe used included an overlong variant ending which Kleist later shortened.[30] Goethe thought the play overly static and an example of 'the invisible theatre'—a theatre of the mind rather than the stage.[31] It was another case of his promoting the work of a young author whom he thought talented but misguided. In summer 1807 he carefully read Kleist's play *Amphitryon* and was 'astonished', before rejecting it as another 'sign of the times'.[32] As for Kleist's medievalizing drama *Käthchen von Helbronn*, Goethe allegedly found it 'a bizarre mixture of sense and nonsense' and threw the copy into the fire with the words: 'I won't stage that even if half Weimar demands it!'[33] It was not that Goethe was opposed to Romanticism in principle or in practice. But as he had argued in the Winckelmann essay, modern self-consciousness takes us on a long and circuitous journey that can only lead back to where we started from. Ironically Kleist came to the same conclusion in a short anecdote 'On the Puppet Theatre' published in 1810. Our self-consciousness alienates us from our nature, and in order to find ourselves again 'we shall have to go all round the world and see whether [paradise] might be open somewhere at the back again'.[34] Goethe very much appreciated the more naïve expressions of Romanticism, such as Clemens Brentano and Achim von Arnim's collection of poems *The Boy's Magic Horn*, which he reviewed enthusiastically in the *JALZ*.[35] Nor did he dislike medieval culture. In 1806 he became aware of the early thirteenth-century *Lay of the Nibelungs*. He admired its naïve power and 'hyperpaganism'.[36] In November and December 1808 he read the whole epic to the Weimar ladies. It was only a shame, he wrote to Knebel in November, that our perception of the Middle Ages was being corrupted by 'our modern religious Medievalists'.[37] What he disliked was the Romantic tendency to subordinate poetry to philosophy or religion.

In autumn 1805 Goethe delivered lectures on physics at the Wednesday Club, which he had just founded to provide diversion and education for the Duchess Luise and the other ladies of court. Charlotte von Schiller took notes.[38] During his collaboration with Schelling, his scientific interests had shifted away from geology, botany, and biology. He continued to make observations, especially on geological tours of the land surrounding his summer haunts of Teplitz and

Carlsbad, but he had nothing new to say on the subject. The theories he had developed in the 1780s and '90s stood firm. In autumn 1806 he decided to edit his groundbreaking morphological essays from the mid-1790s, and wrote two prefatory essays, but nothing was published. His attention was now focused on electricity, magnetism, galvanism, and chemistry,[39] where he could observe the phenomena of polarity he had discussed with Schelling. Although he carried out experiments, including observations of the pile battery invented by Alessandro Volta in 1799, his thinking remained largely speculative. The aim was a unifying theory of the phenomena of polarity in physics. Goethe was one of many who had such hopes, but he did not live to see the great unifying theory of James Clerk Maxwell in the third quarter of the nineteenth century. One abiding question for Goethe was where the observed polarities sat in relation to the Kantian subject-object divide—the question that still bedevilled his work on optics. There is evidence that Goethe accepted Kant's view that polarity resided in the structures of our understanding. The first of his physics lectures in autumn 1805 contained the maxim that 'whatever emerges into appearance must divide itself in order to appear'.[40] In Kantian terms, phenomena are understood only insofar as they conform to the polarities inherent in human understanding. On the other hand, as a committed Spinozist Goethe found it hard to resist the thought that the phenomenal polarities were generated by the inner essence of nature. As he later noted in his diary in connection with the geologist Friedrich Wilhelm Heinrich von Trebra's observations on the mineral spring at Berka, the chemical-electrical polarities were precisely those by which 'nature right into its innermost core is enlivened and moved'.[41] So it was not just that electricity, magnetism, and chemical reactions happened to appear to the intelligence in polar configurations. The polarities were in fact the ontological ground of nature. If this could be demonstrated, and if the electrical, magnetic, and chemical polarities could be fitted into a scheme that also included light and colour, then his observations in optics would be securely grounded. The ultimate goal of a unified theory of nature was therefore to demonstrate that the polarities of colour had an ontological, and not merely phenomenological, ground. Even after the publication of the *Theory of Colour* in 1810, the unification theory remained a distant goal, as he wrote to Knebel in 1813:

> I won't deny that the unification of tellurian and ferro-magnetism with the other polarities of physico-chemical nature, which has so far not been achieved, would be a scientific event I'd like to experience. Most gratifying of all for me would have to be if that very magnetism could be conformed with colour.[42]

He wrote to the physicist Thomas Johann Seebeck in the same vein, adding that success in finding a unified theory of this kind would mean 'the whole of science would forever be secure'.[43] In the meantime, Kant's phenomenological view of polarities was a useful holding position.

In the absence of an ontological ground for his observations of boundary colours, he still needed to find a justification for his belief that the boundary colours were objective states of light, or more generally a reason for supposing that human visual perception captured things as they actually were. In summer 1805, during the early stages of writing the didactic part of the *Theory of Colour*, he translated a sentence from Marsilio Ficino's Latin version of Plotinus's *Enneads*: 'Nor could the eye in truth ever see the sun, unless it had been made sunlike'.[44] Soon after, he wrote the following verses:

> Wär' nicht das Auge sonnenhaft,
> Die Sonne könnt es nie erblicken;
> Läg' nicht in uns des Gottes eigne Kraft,
> Wie könnt' uns Göttliches entzücken.[45]

> If the eye were not sunlike, / It could never see the sun; / If God's power were not in us, / How could the divine delight us?

These verses abbreviate and simplify Plotinus's argument. In particular, what for Goethe is a state of sunlikeness, is in Plotinus's Greek and Ficino's Latin the result of a process. The eye has *become* kindred or similar to the sun, by virtue of its descent. This becomes clear in Plotinus's surrounding argument, which Goethe read in the original Greek, in a copy lent him by Wolf:[46]

> To any vision must be brought an eye adapted to what is to be seen, and having some likeness to it [*pros to horōmenon syngenes kai homoion poiēsamenon*]. Never did eye see the sun unless it had first become sunlike, and never can the soul have vision of the First Beauty unless [the soul] itself be beautiful.[47]

According to Plotinus's Neoplatonic argument, the eye can see because it shares in the nature of the divine from which the forms of things also emanate. Obviously, biological species transformation is alien to this argument, and yet Plotinus's talk of 'becoming' presents a temptation to anyone who might want to find authority for transformationism in this unlikely ancient source. That is to say, rather than reading the passage in its proper sense, one might instead construe it as arguing that the eye has evolved to see by virtue of inhabiting a niche in which the sun is operative. The eye is like the sun and of kindred nature (*syngenes*) because it has been caused (*poiēsamenon*) to become so. Indeed, this is precisely what Goethe does in the introduction to the *Theory of Colour*. He uses Plotinus's Neoplatonic argument to make a transformationist point:

> The eye has light to thank for its existence. Out of the indifferent subsidiary organs of animals, light calls forth an organ that becomes of its ilk [*seines Gleichen*]; and so the eye develops for light with the help of light, so that the inner light can meet the outer light.
>
> In this context we recall the ancient Ionian School which always repeated so emphatically: like is only perceived by like; and also the words of an ancient mystic, which we might express in German as follows.[48]

There follow the four lines of verse in which Goethe adapted the 'ancient mystic' Plotinus. The verses, as we have seen, ignore the causal element in Plotinus's argument and represent the eye's sunlikeness as a state. However, the passage in which Goethe introduces the verses not only picks up Plotinus's claim that the eye's sunlikeness is the result of a process, but makes it explicitly transformationist. Light turns parts of simple organisms into the more advanced animal eye. Organs that were 'indifferent' to light come to be more interested in it, as we might say, through their interaction with light, and in doing so they develop the ability to see, so that the eye becomes 'sunlike', as Plotinus had put it in his ancient mystical manner. The purpose of the argument is to show that human sense perception is designed to capture the way the world really is. It thus answers one of the questions that gave rise to Kant's *Critique of Pure Reason*: how can we be sure that empirical statements relate to actual objects and not just to our cognitive apparatus? Goethe answers Kant's question by means of a transformationist or evolutionary theory of perception. The fact that the eye evolved in a world full of light guarantees that there is a close fit between our visual perception and what light makes visible. It guarantees that what the eye perceives is what light reveals. Goethe makes the point a second time in some notes on the physiology of vision he probably wrote at the same time as the Plotinus translation in August 1805. The eye's ability to reproduce the phenomena of light results from the eye having evolved in response to light: 'The eye is the ultimate, highest effect of light on the organic body. The eye, as a creation of light, does everything that light itself does'.[49] The transformationist argument could not be clearer, but Goethe was no more able to explain the mechanism of transformation in 1805 than he had been in the early 1790s, and so the argument remained a speculative intuition.

Nonetheless, it was clearly an altogether different argument from the theistic claim of Locke that humans were designed by God to experience nature through their unaided senses.[50] Goethe's argument has no need of God, since the 'design' of human vision is accomplished by nature itself through the process of transformation.

Even if he had been able to explain the mechanism of transformation, his argument would have been open to an obvious neo-Darwinian objection. According to modern Darwinism, a creature's eye has evolved not so as to see light, but so as to enable the creature to survive and reproduce. Accurate vision is only accurate to the extent and in the manner that is required for an animal's survival in its evolutionary niche. Since each species has its own survival needs, in terms of diet, predator species, and so on, it is likely that each species has evolved different visual capacities. The capacity of each species' eye will be unique to it, in terms of colour discrimination, field of view, depth of field, sharpness, motion detection, and so on. Eagles have different visual capacities from humans. Therefore the fact that the human eye has evolved in a world of light is not in and of itself proof that the human eye faithfully captures objective reality. In order to claim that the human eye faithfully captures objective reality, one would also need to argue that human vision has evolved to an optimal state. It would be necessary to argue that there is something special about the human evolutionary niche. The argument might take the form that other animals have specialized needs. For instance, as Goethe saw in the 1790s, the jaws and teeth of ungulates have evolved specifically to cut and chew grass, whereas the jaws and teeth of carnivores have evolved to catch hold of and tear through flesh. To continue with the example of jaws and teeth, one would then argue that the jaws and teeth of humans are nonspecialized, as humans are omnivores and do not catch prey with their mouths, or use them for fighting as apes do. And this is indeed exactly what has happened: in the course of evolving from our primate ancestors with their long, sharp canines set in strong and relatively large, protruding jaws, we have evolved smaller and more uniformly sized teeth set in a jaw that protrudes much less. More generally, it could be argued that human anatomy lacks specialist adaptations, as compared to other mammals. This is indeed exactly what Goethe had argued in his essay 'To what extent the idea that beauty is perfection with freedom can be applied to organic creatures'. So for instance, while a mole is perfectly adapted to its niche, it is however 'ugly', because it lacks the freedom to perform actions that are not mandated by its particular survival needs. Or as we might also put it, the mole is constrained by the fact that it is adapted to a highly specific niche.

Humans are not so constrained; they are, in Goethe's words, 'practically liberated from the chains of animality'.[51] Returning to vision, one might reasonably speculate that the human eye is also liberated from the specialized needs of a particular evolutionary niche. It is not compromised in the way the eyes of other animals are. It is optimized for everything. For instance, humans have good general vision, including good discrimination of colour. By contrast, dogs have very poor colour vision, but exceptionally good movement detection, as they are much more dependent on hunting moving prey than humans are. Based on this argument, it would be reasonable for Goethe to think that the transformationist account of the eye is an argument for the objectivity of human vision and against Kant's transcendental idealist theory of cognition.

Goethe did not spell out the defence of his transformationist account of vision; he had given little thought to mammal osteology since the mid-1790s. The reconstruction presented here is based on arguments that Goethe made at different times but did not join up in the way I have here. He did explain human vision in terms of species transformation. He did believe that the human body was less compromised by the demands of its habitat and way of life than other animals' bodies. Most importantly, he believed that the human senses were accurate measuring devices. As he wrote to Zelter in 1808, 'the human being in itself, insofar as it makes use of its healthy senses, is the greatest and most accurate physical apparatus there can be'.[52] Or again in conversation with Riemer in 1809: 'The human being is the greatest and most general apparatus for physics'.[53] Goethe's first aim in using the *homo mensura* principle was to defend his observations of the boundary colours and to differentiate them from Newton's *experimentum crucis*, with its complex and contrived experimental setup, as Goethe saw it. Hence his letter to Zelter continues thus:

> And this is precisely the greatest bane of recent physics, that experiments have, as it were, been divorced from human beings, and that people want to know nature merely in what artificial instruments reveal of it, indeed that people thereby seek to limit and prove what nature can do. It is exactly the same with calculation. There is much that is true which cannot be calculated, as well as much that cannot be conveyed in one decisive experiment. However, the human being is so advanced that what is otherwise unrepresentable is represented in him.[54]

Goethe does not explain his claim concerning the limitations of complex experimental apparatus and mathematics. However, his views of the use of mathematics in science can easily be reconstructed from other sources. According to Goethe, mathematics has three virtues. First, mathematical proofs are necessary truths,[55] capable of providing absolute justification. They are 'pure and certain'.[56] If true, they are true always and everywhere.[57] Second, because numbers and other mathematical symbols have no intrinsic propositional or referential content—the number four does not represent a thing or attitude—they have the advantage of not importing any extraneous meanings into the description of phenomena. This is why mathematical expressions are pure, and why symbols 'that are derived from mathematics [...] can become identical with the phenomena in the highest degree'.[58] Third, mathematics is the appropriate way to understand space, movement, and the sciences concerned with it,[59] such as astronomy.[60] Indeed, space is a mathematical concept. In these respects, Goethe agrees with Kant. There are two important differences between Goethe and Kant. Kant viewed mathematical propositions as synthetic and hence capable of producing new knowledge. Goethe, admittedly in a conversation much later in life, shared Hume's view that mathematics was analytical and could not generate new knowledge.[61] Second, Goethe was happy to grant that the phenomena of astronomy could be expressed in mathematics because space is by definition quantitative. The same did not apply to colour. Goethe disagreed with Newton's finding that the angle of diffraction of the spectral colours was meaningful. For Goethe, the science of colour was qualitative, not quantitative. The point is made in a short draft probably written in the winter of 1805/6 in which he discussed the nature of the colour wheel or spectrum: 'where nature has put such subtle and important differences in related phenomena, one should talk of qualities rather than numerical relationships'.[62] And again: 'one can see very well that one should talk not of number but of an infinitely vivid play'.[63] Talking to Riemer in 1807, Goethe stressed the difference between the 'infinitely vivid play' of natural phenomena and the rigidity of mathematics: 'mathematical formulae, applied outside their sphere, i.e., space, are rigid and lifeless'.[64] In this, Goethe followed Buffon, who had argued in the introduction to his *Natural History* that mathematics simply cannot capture the quality of lived experience.[65] More specifically for Goethe, it cannot distinguish between the subtly nuanced qualities we experience when we perceive colour.

Through 1805 and 1806, with a speed that seemed unbelievable, Napoleon crushed first Austria and then Prussia. After defeating them both at Austerlitz in early December 1805, he resumed the work of reorganizing the German principalities he had begun at the Imperial Recess of 1803. The result was the

Confederation of the Rhine, an agglomeration of German states tied into alliance with France and serving as a buffer between France and the great powers of central Europe. In its first incarnation of July 1806 the Confederation comprised sixteen German territories, including the major kingdoms and principalities of Baden, Bavaria, and Württemberg plus a number of minor principalities and duchies. On 1 August, the Imperial Diet was informed by a French envoy that Napoleon no longer recognised the existence of the Holy Roman Empire, and on the same day nine of the princes who had formed the Confederation issued a proclamation justifying their actions on the grounds that the Holy Roman Empire had ceased to function since Austerlitz. Despite these avowals that the Empire was dead, the Austrian government was concerned that Napoleon, now in control of a sizeable part of Germany and its electoral votes, might crown himself Holy Roman Emperor and so claim precedence over the Austrian crown. Therefore, on 6 August Francis II of Austria took the desperate step of abdicating from the Imperial throne and releasing the German lands from their obligations to the Empire.

The news of the 1 August proclamation reached Goethe six days later as he travelled home from Carlsbad. He wrote laconically in his diary: 'Argument between my servant and the coachman on the box seat, which got us more worked up than the breakup of the Roman Empire'.[66] He was more sardonic in a letter to Wilhelm von Humboldt in Rome two weeks later. The German public were hungrily reading essays by advocates of 'the old patriotism', he said, but it was in vain; no amount of recycling of Germany's history could prevent the Empire passing away.[67] He had never felt a strong allegiance to the Empire. He rarely referred to it by its formal title, and when he did, as in his laconic diary entry, it carried a hint of Voltairean mockery. His dislike of the new-found Prussian patriotism also turned out to be well founded, for Prussia's actions created a near-fatal hazard for Weimar. Napoleon's creation of the Confederation of the Rhine prompted Prussia to join the Fourth Coalition against France. On the day it joined there was an inconclusive battle between small French and Prussian contingents near the town of Schleiz, a stopover on Goethe's route to and from Carlsbad. It was en route to Schleiz on 7 August that Goethe had learned of the Confederation's secession from the Empire. By 13 October the main French and Prussian forces were disposed either side of the Saale valley between Jena and Naumburg. The next day Napoleon's armies crushed the Prussians in two engagements near Jena and Auerstedt. That evening French troops entered Weimar. Many of Goethe's friends and acquaintances had their property burned or plundered. Goethe was spared, apparently through the bravery of Christiane and one of the Weimar residents who had sought shelter in the house on the Frauenplan. Somehow they were able to eject from Goethe's bedroom two French infantrymen who, having demanded entry to the house, had got drunk on Goethe's wine.[68] Riemer later wrote a detailed report of the events. Goethe's diary for 14 October merely notes: 'half past five entry of the chasseurs. Seven o'clock burning, plundering, dreadful night. Preservation of our house through steadfastness and good fortune'.[69] In a letter written on 20 October, Heinrich Voss recorded Goethe's words to his assembled friends two days after the battle:

> I was moved at how Goethe, on the second evening after the battle as we were gathered around him, thanked Mlle Vulpius for her loyalty in these unruly days and ended with the words: 'God willing, at noon tomorrow we will be man and wife'.[70]

Further damage to the town was averted by the steadfastness of Duchess Luise. Together with Voigt she made representations to Napoleon, who arrived in Weimar the day after the battle. Goethe was invited to participate in the negotiations, but declined, pleading illness.[71] Goethe and Christiane were married on Sunday 19 October. The wedding ring was engraved with the symbolic date of 14 October. The story has attracted some scepticism, but there is no good reason to doubt that Goethe did indeed propose marriage to Christiane out of gratitude for her steadfastness and loyalty.

No doubt there were also other motives for the hurried marriage, conscious or otherwise. The fate of other houses in Weimar made Goethe alarmed that his papers might be stolen or burned. His manuscript notes and drafts for the *Theory of Colour* were a special worry. The defeat at Jena-Auerstedt could also have made him aware of how dependent he was on Carl August, who was now in exile as a defeated Prussian general. Goethe had no security of income or property beyond the favour of the Duke. As for Christiane and their son August, the current ad hoc arrangements would be threatened if the Napoleonic legal code were introduced to Weimar. The code contained no provisions for the recognition of illegitimate children. The rushed marriage to Christiane may have been a reaction to the threat of a new legal situation in Weimar. If so, it did not mean that Goethe supported the introduction of the code or the universal bourgeois rights enshrined in it. During the Weimar Privy Council's discussions of the code in 1807, Goethe did not argue in its favour. To his mind the code was just a fact of modern life to which one must resign oneself, as a letter from J. C. Voght makes clear. Voght notes that Goethe's son was going to Heidelberg to study law, 'in other words, the Napoleonic Code. I found Goethe resigned to all of this. The old world was over. It was our duty to help to build the new world'.[72]

The title Goethe gave to the first, 'didactic' part of his work on optics, *Outline of a Theory of Colour*, reflects its provisional nature and hasty composition.[73] He finished writing its latter sections and then revised the whole text under the stress of the events of autumn 1806, 'a time which made calm composure of the spirits impossible', he wrote at the end of the *Outline*.[74] The finished text consists of 920 numbered sections plus a foreword, introduction, appendix, and conclusion. Its main body is divided into six sections dealing with: first, the physiology of colour vision; second, the physics of the incidence and diffraction of light; third, the colours produced by chemical reactions; fourth, general observations on the properties of coloured light; fifth, the relations between the science of colour and other fields; and sixth, the psychological effects of colour, above all in the arts. Some parts of the text resemble collections of notes, rather than a finished argument, and there is a great deal of repetition. The meaning is easy to summarize, in part thanks to the *Outline*'s repetitive nature, as Goethe wrote after publication in 1810 to Reinhard:

> Long though the work is, and strange though it may seem in its detail, nonetheless it is thoroughly consistent, and what it presents and intends can be summarized very briefly, indeed to an extent it repeats itself on every sheet.[75]

The challenge he had faced in the 1790s was how to justify his version of colorimetric space, namely the colour wheel. He was convinced that the colour wheel was a valid model of natural phenomena, and not just a fact of subjective visual perception, like Buffon's *couleurs accidentelles*. The truth of the colour wheel is the fact that 'repeats itself on every sheet'. The aim of the *Outline* is to show that the colour wheel is both subjectively and objectively real; it is 'complete, easily applicable, and natural'.[76] The chief advantage of the wheel, as opposed to the spectrum, is that it expresses both of the relations between colours that are found in nature. First, like the spectrum, it juxtaposes those colours that can be generated from one another. One position on the wheel can be generated from its neighbour by the means of darkening or intensification (*Steigerung*). So the derived colours, red and violet, arise from the effect of darkness on the primary colours yellow and blue respectively.[77] Alternatively a colour can be generated from its neighbour on the wheel by additive mixture: green arises from blue by mixture with yellow. However, unlike the spectrum, the colour wheel can also represent relations of opposition or contrast between the colours that sit on opposite sides of the wheel. Contrasting colours are not merely of use to artists, nor are they only subjective. The contrasts exist in objectively nature, for instance in the phenomena of boundary colours. Therefore, the core idea of the *Outline*—the idea that is repeated on every page—is that the colour wheel, with its relations of opposition and proximity, represents the ways that colours naturally appear in all of their domains: the physiology of visual perception, the physics of refraction and diffraction, the chemistry of coloured substances, the practice of artists, and so on. Indeed, in a more abstract manner of speaking one might say that in all cases where light appears, it does so subject to the laws of contrast and proximity as represented by the colour wheel. In other words, the colour wheel serves as a unifying theory of light although properly speaking it is not a theory at all. It is a symbolic representation of the primal phenomenon (*Urphänomen*) of boundary colours. This is the sense in which Goethe was content with his Kantian holding position. We cannot represent light itself; indeed we cannot even see it. We can only represent and see its phenomena. The colours are these phenomena, and like all phenomena they are present to us in the form of polarities.[78] In the case of colour, the polarities are the contrasts between opposed positions on the wheel and the relations of intensification and mixture between neighbouring positions.

The first of the *Outline*'s six main sections (and the first to be written) is the section on physiology. This might suggest that the physiological section has primacy in the *Outline*'s meaning. Accordingly one might read the *Outline* as a phenomenology of colour vision: an account of the ways in which an embodied human subject experiences the world of light and colour.[79] This is only half true. It is certainly not the case that the physiological section is better worked out and more finished than the other sections. It was only a sketch, Goethe wrote to Schultz in 1814.[80] The physiological section comes first for reasons of argumentative strategy, not because it constitutes the main argument. It is framed by the transformationist view of perception, set out in the *Outline*'s introduction. This is the argument that 'out of the indifferent subsidiary organs of animals, light calls forth an organ that becomes of its ilk; and so the eye develops for light with the help of light'.[81] The evolution of the eye to serve the purposes of light means that there is a tight fit between the capacity of the eye to see light and the objective effects of light. Thus the transformationist account of vision gives us reason to believe that the physiological colours will correspond to objective colours. There is no gap between subject and object. The same conclusion is stated in the section on physiological colours.[82] Goethe begins by maintaining that this important area of optics has been neglected and misunderstood. Hitherto the physiological colours, such as coloured afterimages, had been treated as phantoms or irregularities. The subjective experience of colour is too full of anomalies to be aligned with the objective facts of colour. Goethe cites several authorities for this view, including Boyle and Buffon.[83] In opposition to them, Goethe claims that the physiological colours exhibit the same laws of 'chromatic harmony' as all other phenomena of coloured light. The eye is subject to the law of the colour wheel. The physiological colours will show the same patterns of contrast and proximity as the boundary colours. In other words, in the section on physiological colours Goethe sets himself the task of showing how this seemingly most irregular area of optics can be brought under the same unifying theory as all other areas. Insofar as the physiological colours represent perhaps the greatest obstacle to a unifying theory based on the colour wheel, then by demonstrating that the obstacle can be overcome Goethe provides an extremely powerful argument in favour of the universality of the colour wheel. This is the main reason why the section on physiological colours comes first.

The section on physiology contains some striking empirical findings. The underlying theory is that the eye is an active organ, not merely a passive screen.[84] This comports with Goethe's argument throughout the *Outline* that colours are energies. The eye, therefore, must be its own energetic system, capable of opposing its own energies to the energies of light and colour. The physiological colours result from the eye's transitioning between states of excitation and rest, and these transitions conform to the law of polarity. States of excitation are caused by light. Put simply, the brighter the light the greater the excitation. This explains why white images appear larger than black images of the same size. They seem larger because the retina is more active when stimulated by the brighter tone of white, whereas black leaves the retina in a state of rest.[85] In its natural condition, the eye is continually restoring itself to equilibrium, but the process is not instantaneous. This explains why we see afterimages. When we look at a window frame against the dark early morning sky and then close our eyes, we briefly see the afterimage of the frame in black against a white background. This is the result of the tissue of the retina being activated in opposition to the stimulus. Coloured afterimages display the same law of polarity, insofar as the colours of the afterimages tend to be the spectral opposites of the colours of the actual images: a yellow image will produce a blue afterimage. We can infer from this that in its constant transitioning from stimulation to equilibrium, the eye obeys a law of polarity:

> The eye cannot and may not for one moment endure in a particular condition determined by an object. Rather it is forced into a kind of opposition which, in opposing one extreme to the other or a middle state to another middle state, connects the opposed states as it were, and strives towards wholeness in sequential succession as well as in simultaneity and sameness of location.[86]

The phenomenon of opposition is analogous to another physiological norm, namely the alternating systole and diastole of the lungs. Like systole and diastole, the behaviour of the eye exemplifies the underlying law of physiology that one state will call forth its opposite:

> In this way, breathing in presupposes breathing out and vice versa; so each systole presupposes its diastole. It is the eternal formula of life that is expressed here. When darkness is presented to the eye, [the eye] demands light; it demands darkness when it is presented with light, and thereby it displays its vitality, its right to grasp the object by producing something out of itself which is opposed to the object.[87]

The same explanation can be used to resolve the problem of coloured shadows, which had held Goethe up in the 1790s. The colour of the shadows is determined not by the addition or subtraction of spectral colours; that is to say, the shadows are not objective properties of coloured light. Rather they are determined by the physiology of the eye opposing one colour to its spectral opposite. In this way the argument concerning physiological colours is completed. The coloured shadows obey the law of chromatic harmony represented by the colour wheel, but they do so through the reactive physiology of the eye. And the reason why the physiology of the eye obeys the law is that it developed in such a way as to correspond to the objective properties of light. The eye exhibits a pattern of polarities because light does so.

The longest and most important part of the *Outline* is the section on the physics of refractive and diffractive colours. It describes in detail Goethe's observations of boundary colours and shows how these correspond to the colour wheel. The experiments themselves are little different from those set out in the *Essays on Optics* of the early 1790s. Their role in the *Outline* as a whole is crucial.

432   CHAPTER 8

FIG. 20. One of the tables to illustrate Goethe's
observations of boundary colours (c. 1810)

By performing the experiments themselves, readers of the *Outline* can themselves progress from simple everyday observations to the highest and most symbolic phenomena. What is new in the final version of the *Outline* is that the boundary colours are interpreted in terms of polarities, as was the case for the physiological colours. The most important polarity is that of darkness and light. Again the connection with the physiological section is important. The eye is a dynamic organ that constantly transitions between darkness and light. The darkness in the eye is not merely an absence of light: it is a force or presence of equal status to light. The same is true for the physical colours produced by means of refraction and diffraction. Darkness is not the absence of light; it is light's polar opposite and antagonist. Just as light can be darkened by turbid media such as atmospheric dust and water vapour, so too darkness can be weakened by the presence of light. It is through the conflict of these two antagonists that colour arises. The primary colours are yellow and blue; they arise first and in the most primal and immediate circumstances. Yellow arises though the darkening of white light, for instance in a turbid medium. This is why we see sunshine as yellow if there is mist or dust in the atmosphere, and an increase in the amount of mist or dust will turn the sun redder, which accounts for red sunrises and sunsets. Blue, on the other hand, arises through the lightening of complete darkness. Hence the absolute blackness of space appears blue to us when it is lightened by sunshine beginning to penetrate the atmosphere. In this sense, the colours we see in turbid media are the primal or originary phenomena (*Urphänomene*). They need no further explanation.

The theory of turbid media is Goethe's alternative to Newton's account of light passing through prisms. Goethe argues that his turbid media and Newton's prisms are two types of the same class of things: dioptric colours, the colours generated by light passing through a more or less transparent medium. The section on dioptric colours is subdivided into two. The first class of dioptric colours involve turbid media, and the second class transparent media, such as prisms. Goethe further distinguishes between subjective and objective dioptric colours of the second, transparent class. The former arise when we look through a prism at boundaries between light and dark tones. (The distinction between subjective and objective is not a Kantian one; by subjective, Goethe means that the eye is part of the experimental setup.) The subjective dioptric colours of the second type are the boundary colours. The objective dioptric colours of the second type—when light is passed through a prism to fall on a surface—comprise Newton's experiments with prisms. The purpose of the complex division of the argument into sections is to aid Goethe's case against Newton. The spectral images produced in Newton's experiments are in fact composite phenomena and the result of contrived experimental setups, and in Goethe's arrangement of the topics they occupy a subordinate position. Outside of Newton's contrived experiments, what ordinarily happens when a beam of light passes through a prism is that the image of the hole that gave the beam its shape is projected onto the surface, with a reddish-blue boundary at its bottom edge and reddish-yellow boundary at its top edge. It is only when the hole is narrowed to an extreme degree that these two coloured boundaries come together to form a single spectrum ranging continuously from blue to yellow. Thus Newton's experiments are only a very special and contrived case of the boundary colours. As Goethe would put it in the polemical part of the *Theory of Colour*, in the *experimentum crucis* 'the scientist puts nature on the rack and forces her into confessing what he had already decided in advance'.[88]

The third main section of the *Outline* concerns chemical colours. During his discussions with Schelling in 1799 and 1800 Goethe had begun to see how the latest discoveries in chemistry might form part of a unifying theory of matter. The plus and minus of galvanic phenomena could be connected to chemical processes of oxidation and reduction, and chemical reactions could be conceived as the coming together of elements with opposed qualities, as Schelling believed.[89] At this stage, however, Goethe's understanding of chemistry was limited. It was in 1810, with the appointment of Johann Wolfgang

Döbereiner to the chair in chemistry at Jena, that Goethe's interest in chemistry would peak. With Döbereiner's encouragement, he would understand chemistry as the science that underpinned the unifying theory he hoped for[90] and as the dynamic science par excellence.[91] The section on chemical colours in the *Outline* reflects the limited state of his knowledge in 1806. He wrote it hurriedly in three weeks in November.[92] In some ways it seems divorced from the systematic presentation of colour elsewhere in the *Outline*. There are some empirical correlations: for instance, the chemical polarity of acid and alkali corresponds to the opposed sides of the colour wheel. Alkalis tend to blue, and acids to yellow. The argument is mainly concerned with durable colours, not with colours in dynamic chemical processes.[93] The argument that white minerals represent the highest form of chemical colour is arbitrary, as Goethe acknowledges: the white colour is an accidental property resulting from the chaotic structures of masses of transparent crystals.[94] The whole section has more to do with pigments and dyes than with chemical processes.

In emphasizing the properties of dyes, Goethe was probably thinking of the final main section of the *Outline*, concerning the psychological effects of colour. Its chief purpose was to help painters reach a more theoretical understanding of colour, and so its focus moves decisively away from the domain of science proper. Since the very beginnings of his interest in science in 1780, he had been sceptical about science as a profession. In part, the section on the psychology of colour reflects his longstanding plain man's view that those working practically and technically—artists and dyers—have 'purer and more correct views than scholars in natural science'.[95] The final section of the *Outline* presents a systematic-looking, but in fact rather arbitrary attempt to assign human values to the colour wheel. Colours on the positive side of the colour wheel, from yellow through deep orange, have an energizing, vital quality. Colours on the negative side, from blue through indigo, have a restless quality of longing. In other words, both sides are energetic, but one is the energy of life, and the other has the paradoxical quality of stimulus at rest. Red, which is at the top of the colour circle and results from the complete intensification of colour, represents 'gravity and dignity, benevolence and grace'.[96] Green, which joins the two sides of the circle at the bottom, has the quality of satisfaction.[97] It is therefore an ideal colour for decorating rooms.[98] The colour wheel can also help us to understand colour combinations of various sorts. As Goethe had proposed in the physiological section, it is the nature of the eye to counterpose one colour with the colour diametrically opposed to it on the colour wheel. This counterposing action of the eye expresses a demand for 'totality and harmony' of colour.[99] The pairs of diametrically opposed colours represent this harmony and totality. Of course, artists are not limited to diametrically opposed contrasts. There are also 'characteristic' colour combinations that create their own peculiar effects, such as the 'poor' and 'mean' effect of blue and yellow, which also happens to be satisfying because of its relation to green.[100] Equally there are 'characterless' combinations that are to be avoided, such as green and blue, which is 'mean and repulsive'.[101]

The aim of the section on the psychology of colour is not to dictate to artists, but to encourage them to think in more theoretical terms about the effects of colours and their contrasts. For all their instinctive and learned sureness of touch, artists have hitherto suffered from a 'fear of theory'.[102] Goethe's aim is to liberate artists from the shackles of mere empiricism and to empower them to explore colour more reflectively. In the history of the reception of Goethe's *Theory of Colour*, this part has, without doubt, had the greatest and most creative influence. For instance, J. M. W. Turner applied Goethe's ideas in his pair of paintings 'Light and Colour (Goethe's Theory)—the Morning after the Deluge—Moses Writing the Book of Genesis' and 'Shade and Darkness—the Evening of the Deluge', both exhibited in 1843. Turner had read Charles Eastlake's 1840 translation of the *Outline*. The two paintings represent two polarities of the colour wheel. In the former, the light of creation shines golden through the turbid medium of the beginning of the deluge. In the latter, the darkness of the end of day is turned blue by the fading sun. One effect of Goethe's theory was to help artists to break away from the representational use of colour.[103] This explains why his theory became so influential among the abstract and nonrepresentational artists of the early twentieth century, such as Robert Delaunay, Paul Klee, Adolf Hölzel, and Wassily Kandinsky.[104] The use artists made of Goethe's theory of colour could not have been anticipated by him but was entirely in the spirit of the *Outline*.

The second of the three main parts of Goethe's work on colour, between the didactic part and the historical part, was the polemical part. He began work on it with enthusiasm,[105] but soon felt dispirited. It was a thankless task and a 'thorny path', he wrote to Alexander von Humboldt in April 1807.[106] What made it so difficult was that he felt he had to pick apart Newton's experiments in fine detail and dismantle the later reception of Newton's theory. This meant he had to move beyond the narrow analysis of Newton's experiments that he had worked out in the 1790s *Essays on Colour*. He needed a range of arguments of different kinds: logic, observation, method, written style, epistemology, and sociology.[107] And so he embarked upon a more general *Unmasking of Newton's Theory*—this was the title he gave the polemical part. Newton's work was to be unmasked as something other than it purported to be. It was both less and more than the set of scientific observations that Newton claimed it to be. Newton's observations actually fell short of proving his theory, and yet they had been inflated into a political, social, and cultural phenomenon. Therefore Newton's work needed to be judged both in terms of how well warranted it was as science and what factors had led Newton and his followers to believe it. He soon realized that a full treatment of the nonscientific factors that had led to the canonization of Newton would have to wait for the third part, which would eventually be titled *Materials for the History of Colour Theory*. In very rough terms then, the *Unmasking* and the *Materials* treat two different matters and are different kinds of argument. The former picks apart the scientific and methodological claims of Newton's work. The latter reconstructs the historical and nonscientific context of its discovery. In practice, the distinction is often blurred, and much of the *Unmasking* is also concerned with nonscientific matters. In any case, understood together and in respect of their common purpose, the *Unmasking* and the *Materials* represent one of the earliest essays in what has come to be known as science studies.

Goethe's main methodological criticism of Newton concerns the relation between theory and observation. In Goethe's view, Newton and his followers were guilty of positing hypotheses and then designing experiments to justify them: 'hypotheses had been put at the head, according to which one was able to artificially organize the phenomena and to transmit with great confidence a bizarre doctrine of meagre content'.[108] There are two arguments here, only one of which has merit. Goethe seems to think that the temporal sequence is a problem and that hypotheses should follow experiments, not precede them. However, the temporal sequence is of no consequence. All that matters is the logical or probative relation between experiment and hypothesis: does the experiment support the hypothesis or not? The criticism that does have merit is that Newton's experiments did not *prove* his hypotheses. Goethe realized that Newton's claim to have proved his theory by experimentation could be refuted if it could be shown that the same experiments could equally well support different hypotheses. If this could be shown, then it might reasonably be argued that Newton's theory was not fully proved by the evidence. The theory was 'underdetermined' by the evidence, in modern philosophical parlance.[109] Goethe illustrates the point with a lighthearted anecdote concerning his old acquaintance Basedow:

On this occasion, it occurs to us that Basedow, who was a heavy drinker and in his best years and in good company was of pleasant humour, always used to maintain: the conclusion *ergo bibamus* [therefore let us drink] followed from every premise. The weather is nice, *ergo bibamus*! It's a miserable day, *ergo bibamus*! We're among friends, *ergo bibamus*! There are some rotten beggars in the company, *ergo bibamus*! So Newton adds his *ergo* to the most varied premises. The refracted image is fully and constantly coloured; therefore light is differentially refrangible. The image has a white centre; and yet it is differentially refrangible. In one instance it is completely white; and yet it is differentially refrangible.[110]

The underdetermination argument is the strongest argument in the *Unmasking*. However, what it implicated was not necessarily what Goethe wanted to show, and Goethe was indeed aware of this difficulty. The underdetermination argument shows that Newton's hypothesis is not proved by his experiments. It does not prove that Newton's hypothesis is incorrect. It merely shows that Newton's hypothesis is one among several possible hypotheses. Goethe knew this, and so near the beginning of the *Unmasking* he states that 'we do not presume whatsoever to prove that Newton is wrong'.[111]

If the underdetermination argument does not disqualify Newton's theory, then it also gives us no grounds for preferring Goethe's theory to Newton's. What grounds can we have then for preferring Goethe's theory? Goethe has two contradictory answers to this question, and the contradiction lies at the very heart of the *Theory of Colour*. His first answer is that there is no reason to prefer any theory to Newton's. This is the implication of the underdetermination argument: no theory will ever be fully determined by the evidence. Goethe makes this argument in the paragraph leading up to his statement that he does not presume to prove Newton wrong:

> The phenomena can be observed very accurately, the experiments can be set up cleanly, one can adduce observations and experiments in a particular order, one can derive one phenomenon from another, one can present a certain sphere of knowledge, one can raise one's observations to certainty and completeness, and that, I would have thought, would be enough. Deductions, however, each person draws for himself; nothing can be proved by them, especially not -ities and -itions. Everything that is an opinion about something belongs to the individual, and we know all too well that conviction depends not on insight but on the will, that nobody understands anything other than what suits him and what he can therefore assent to.[112]

Goethe expressed an even more extreme scepticism in conversation with the historian Luden in August 1806: 'Everyone has his own truth. Mathematical truth is however the same for everyone'.[113] Understood in this light, the meaning of the *Theory of Colour* would be strictly empirical, limited to the set of observations it describes. It could make no claims to theoretical truth whatsoever. There is good reason to construe the *Outline* in just this way. Goethe had argued in the 'Precautions' essay of 1792 and in a short draft titled 'The Pure Phenomenon' of 1798 that the meaning of science resided not in theory or explanation, but in carefully structured series of observations, structured indeed in such a way that one phenomenon could be seen to stand at the head of a pyramid of all phenomena. All phenomena could be derived from other phenomena, with the exception of the one phenomenon at the apex. This 'pure phenomenon' stood, as it were, in the stead of a theory or explanation. It can be argued that the *Outline* is just such an ordering of phenomena, in which phenomena are derived progressively from others until we reach the apical pure or primal phenomenon (*Urphänomen*). The primal phenomenon of colour is the behaviour of light passing through a turbid medium. Insofar as the other phenomena can be derived from this, the primal phenomenon stands in place of a scientific explanation.

There are two reasons why this interpretation of the *Theory of Colour* will not do. First, despite his disavowal, Goethe did in fact try to show that Newton's theory was wrong. For instance, he set great store by the falsification of Newton's belief that all lenses were chromatic. Second, it is not clear how one phenomenon can be said to be derived from another without constructing some form of explanatory model. Goethe evidently believed that he could avoid this difficulty. He acknowledged that the ordering of phenomena required an element of theorizing, whilst insisting that the theorizing could be kept honest, as it were, by dint of constant self-criticism or 'irony', as he put it, in a passage that he adapted from Rousseau's *Émile*:[114]

> For merely looking at a thing cannot move us forward. Every looking shades into considering, every considering into thinking, every thinking into connecting, and so one can say that we theorize with every observant look at the world. However, to do this with consciousness, with self-knowledge, with freedom and, if one might use a daring word, with irony— such adroitness is necessary if the abstractness that we fear is not to become damaging and the experiential result we hope for is to become properly lively and useful.[115]

The first part of the argument is persuasive. Observations do not happen in a vacuum. The second part—the notion that the vitality and usefulness of experience has to be preserved—has more to do with the aesthetics of science than its merit. The value of science surely has more to do with whether it is true and whether we need it, than with how well it avoids abstraction and preserves the vitality of lived experience. Goethe evidently believed otherwise. Modern science risked losing touch with lived experience, which would be a significant loss for humanity. Indeed, this concern with the aesthetics of science explains much of the argument of the *Theory of Colour*.

Despite Goethe's anti-theoretical stance, there is in fact an explanatory model at the heart of the *Theory of Colour*, which purports to show that the boundary colours represent the true nature of coloured light and Newton's experiments do not. So why did Goethe sometimes insist that his own work on colour was merely empirical whilst also claiming that his theory was superior to Newton's? Why did he both claim that he was not seeking to disprove Newton and devote so much effort to disproving him? The answer lies in the beliefs that became increasingly important to him through the 1790s: the underlying polarity of all physical forms and the *homo mensura* principle. Goethe repeatedly expressed the hope that a unifying theory of physics might be discovered. This theory would construct relations between the polarities that structured all physical phenomena. For instance, it would show how magnetic polarities related to electrical polarities. But what form would the proof of the relation take? Clearly it could not be a mathematical proof, such as Maxwell's equations, given Goethe's allergy to the application of mathematics to physics. As he wrote in the winter of 1805/6, 'where nature has put such subtle and important differences in related phenomena, one should talk of qualities rather than numerical relationships.'[116] Goethe's science of colour was a science of qualities, not quantities. It had more in common with the premodern science of the Aristotelian tradition than with the modern, post-Cartesian science of Newton. It required no measurements and therefore no instrumentation beyond unaided human vision. Hence Goethe could put his faith in the *homo mensura* principle. Qualities and their relations can readily be perceived through the senses. A human being equipped with healthy senses is an entirely adequate scientific instrument.

―――

The letter to Zelter in which Goethe set out the *homo mensura* principle—his belief that a human being was 'the greatest and most accurate physical apparatus there can be'[117]—was also concerned with the theory of musical tone. His interest in the subject had begun on reading Ernst Chladni's *Acoustics* (1802) and with Chladni's visit to Weimar in 1803. From 1808 the theory of musical tone became a preoccupation in his correspondence with Zelter. In 1810, with the *Theory of Colour* finished and his self-image as a scientist still buoyant, he began to set out his ideas on musical tone in the form of a large table. The project soon stalled. It was probably the victim of his turn away from scientific theorizing in the years following the publication of the *Theory of Colour*, when the negative reception of his work on colour soured his relationship with the scientific community. He was also conscious of his limited knowledge of music theory.[118] Still, the 1810 table gives a clear indication of the theory's outlines.[119] On one point his thinking about music seems to differ from his approach to colour. Goethe was happy to grant Pythagoras's discovery that musical tuning had an objective basis in mathematics. Even so, he insisted on the priority of the *homo mensura* principle. A trained human ear gave a more acute sense of tone than mathematics ever could, he wrote in the same letter to Zelter: 'What is a string and all the mechanical dividing of it compared to the ear of a musician?'[120] The theory outlined in the table is structured according to the polarities found everywhere in nature. Musical polarities could be found in the contrast of major and minor keys and in the relation of unstressed and stressed beats. A requirement of Goethe's polarity theory was that there was equivalence or near-equivalence between the two poles. Thus, in contrast to the traditional notion that minor keys were derived and not natural—as argued by Rousseau and d'Alembert and following them Zelter[121]—Goethe sees the major and minor keys as having equal standing. Major keys are generated by rising scales and minor keys by falling ones. Together they express the essential duality of human nature. Major keys express our engagement with external objects, and minor keys our reflection on our self. The human body is central to an understanding of tone, just as it is for the experience of light. The ear is the supreme device for apprehending tone, even if it is a more passive organ than the eye. Likewise, the voice is the supreme instrument for the production of music. In this regard, Goethe agreed with Rousseau. In these respects, Goethe's thinking about music tended in the same direction as his work on colour: towards an idiosyncratic form of anthropocentrism and away from the mathematical or numerological tendencies found for instance in the 'pure' music of J. S. Bach or the transcendentalism of the Romantics.

On 17 May 1807, Goethe began work on his first large-scale literary project since Schiller's death two years and eight days earlier. It was a struggle to return to creative work, and the omens were not good. On 10 April the Dowager Duchess Anna Amalia died after a short illness.[122] Goethe wrote a eulogy in her honour. Her death intensified his feeling that his own literary success belonged to a half-forgotten past. Editing his works for the new Cotta edition hardly helped, as he wrote to Zelter: 'In general I've felt very strongly in editing my works how alien these things are to me, and that I have hardly any interest in them anymore'.[123] The new work was a product of the relationship with Cotta. It was a sequel to *Wilhelm Meister's Apprenticeship*, titled *Wilhelm Meister's Journeyman Years*. He had first mentioned the plan in a letter to Cotta in May 1798, during negotiations for *The Propylaea*. Seeking to sweeten the arrangement, he sent Cotta a list of writings that were in draft or planned, including 'letters of a traveller and his pupil, under romantic names, following on from *Wilhelm Meister*'.[124] Like his other large projects, the *Journeyman Years* developed slowly and haltingly, repeatedly postponed in favour of more appealing or urgent work. By April 1807 he had decided that the novel would have several short freestanding stories embedded in it, in the manner of the *Conversations of German Emigrés*, which he now reread, along with Bocaccio's *Decameron*, Marguerite de Navarre's *Heptameron*, Antoine de la Sale's *Cent nouvelles nouvelles*, and the *One Thousand and One Nights*. The first element he wrote was a story in four chapters that is conventionally referred to as 'St Joseph the Second'. There followed five further stories, not all of them finished at the first attempt: 'The Nut-brown Girl', 'The Man of Fifty Years', 'The New Melusina', 'The Dangerous Wager', and 'The Foolish Pilgrim'. A seventh story titled 'The Elective Affinities', after the Swedish chemist Torbern Bergman's *Dissertation on Elective Attractions* (1775), grew into a full-length novel, which occupied Goethe through 1808 and into the summer of 1809. With *The Elective Affinities* published, he returned to the *Journeyman Years* that November. By June 1810 he had drafted a substantial portion of its first part, only to postpone the work again as his attention switched to his own autobiography. Eventually he resumed work on the novel in 1820 and published it the following year. A second, expanded version followed in 1829. In the meantime, all but one of the component stories he wrote in 1807 appeared, in finished or unfinished form, in Cotta's annual *Pocketbook for Ladies*.

FIG. 21. Giotto, *The Flight into Egypt*, Scrovegni Chapel, Padua (1303–1305)

'St Joseph the Second' is the most substantial of the 1807 stories. ('St Joseph the Second' is in fact the title of the second of the tale's four chapters; the others are 'The Flight into Egypt', 'The Visitation', and 'The Lily Stem'.) If his diary is to be believed, Goethe wrote the four chapters in four days.[125] They were published in 1809 in the *Pocketbook for Ladies* under the title 'Wilhelm Meister's Journeyman Years. Book One' and appeared in more or less the same form in the 1821 version of the novel. The style of the story is simple, almost naïve. It is the literary equivalent of the Nazarene style of Goethe's young friend Phillip Otto Runge's painting *Rest on the Flight into Egypt* of 1806. (Runge wrote to Goethe in December 1806 that he was working on the painting.)[126] The story's richness comes from the strange and yet mundane parallels it relates between the lives of its characters and the gospels. Wilhelm and his son Felix are beginning their descent from the mountains, possibly in the

Ticino, although no placenames are given in the story. On their descent they meet a family: two young parents accompanied by two sons on foot. The mother riding on a donkey also has a babe-in-arms. Wilhelm is amazed—the language of wonderment occurs throughout the story—by the family's resemblance to medieval and Renaissance paintings of Mary and Joseph's flight into Egypt. The dark-haired father leads the donkey. The mother wears a blue cloak over a red dress, as Mary does in traditional depictions of the scene. Two older boys carry switches of brush and resemble the angels shown in some paintings carrying palms. One of the boys has golden hair, like the golden halo on the head of the angel in Giotto's *Flight into Egypt*. Wilhelm is also struck by the fact that the mother is riding a donkey, not a horse. There is something mysteriously archaic about the family, and the story repeatedly hints that the world it represents is removed from modernity, perhaps an escape into a pre-modern past. At the end of the first chapter, Wilhelm agrees that Felix will accompany the family and Wilhelm will join them the following day, after he has collected his papers from the hut at the mountaintop.

As Wilhelm climbs back up the mountain, the sun is setting, but his ascent postpones the moment when the sun disappears: 'He ascended the path and in this manner delayed the sunset',[127] as if he were briefly able to hold back time. The impression that time is being halted points to the theme of archaism and prefigures the old-fashioned world Wilhelm and Felix are entering, with its pre-industrial society and economy. The political order belongs firmly in the *ancien regime*. The land is governed by a secular duke whose dues and tithes Joseph collects.[128] There are no signs of modern culture such as books, or modern industry such as coalmining or manufactures. The economy is predominantly agricultural. The residents of the valley live in 'harmony with their surroundings'.[129] The world resembles Goethe's Rousseauian vision of Switzerland:

> The inhabitants are closer to one another and, if you will, also farther apart; their needs are simpler but more pressing. Each person must rely more upon himself, must learn to depend on his own hands, his own feet. Labourer, courier, porter—all are combined in one person; everyone is also closer to his neighbour, sees him more often, and is engaged with him in a common venture.[130]

The mountainous landscape isolates people and so makes them self-reliant, which is possible because the modern division of labour has not yet occurred. Equally, isolation makes people more dependent on their nearest neighbours. Joseph and the symbolic life he lives represent this society in its pure form. He lives by the craft of carpentry, like his biblical namesake. His family dwells in a restored part of an ancient monastery, the uninhabitable parts of which have been left to merge with nature; indeed the trees and bushes growing through the ruins seem almost to have preserved the ruins. It is another sign of human life thriving in nature's embrace.[131] The restored parts of the monastery resemble a museum. At dinner 'the dishes and goblets likewise evoked earlier times'.[132] The portrayal of this cutoff world raises a question. It is a Rousseauian idyll of naturalness and social cohesion, but whether it could be a model for modern society is highly doubtful, for history has moved on. Goethe still felt a strong attachment to the Italian project of the mid-1790s and its ideal of the small state, even if that world was being swept away by the torrential force of Napoleonic modernity. That much is clear from the second part of 'St Joseph the Second'. Wilhelm and Felix stay with the family at their home in the monastery. The story of his life that Joseph tells Wilhelm explains the mystery of his family's resemblance to the holy family, as represented in Italian Renaissance art. At first sight, it seems to be an extreme case of life imitating art. It is all the more unusual in that conscious mimicry has combined with chance. As so often in Goethe's fictions, the complex weave of accident and intent is hard to tease apart. His parents named Joseph after the monastery and abbey of St Joseph where he grew up. His name in turn made him interested in the story of the biblical Joseph, which was painted on the walls of the chapel in a suite of ten scenes taken mainly from the Gospel of Matthew. The scenes begin with Joseph's training as a carpenter and end with a badly damaged painting portraying Joseph making a throne for Herod with Jesus's miraculous help. This last damaged panel represents a story from the apocryphal Arab Gospel of the Childhood of the Saviour.[133] The second main theme of the story is therefore the relation of art to life, and in particular the tendency of dilettantes to confuse the two, for this is what Joseph the Second has done.[134] (Dilettantism in the visual arts was much on Goethe's mind; he discussed the subject over dinner chez Knebel on 19 May 1807, two days after starting work on the story.)[135] Whilst noting the closeness to Goethe's thinking about dilettantism, it would be harsh to characterize Joseph's attitude to art as amateurish bungling. After all, this is an isolated rural location, and its people have no access to high culture beyond the images painted on the chapel walls. The meaning of Joseph the Second's life lies in the ways he carves out a sound, natural, and moral existence in parallel with the gospel paintings. The parallels are at one level banal—Joseph the Second chose to become a carpenter in imitation of the biblical Joseph—and at another level oddly coincidental, and their total effect on Wilhelm, before he understands the history, is miraculous. And yet the explanation of the parallels makes them feel entirely normal. It is just what one would expect of a tiny isolated rural community.

The main part of Joseph the Second's story concerns him meeting and eventually marrying his wife Marie. The story takes place during chaos at end of the war, with marauding bands of displaced labourers and servants roaming the mountains. Marie and her first husband are attacked and separated. Joseph finds her and immediately falls in love. At this point he does not know her name is Marie and that she therefore fits neatly into his gospel-inspired life. He takes Marie, who is pregnant, to a local woman Elisabeth, who looks after young mothers. This is another extraordinary instance of life imitating art by pure chance, for Marie's visit to Elisabeth echoes the visitation of the biblical Mary to her cousin Elizabeth in the gospel of Matthew. When the modern Marie and Elisabeth meet and embrace, Joseph the Second announces 'You have a visitation',[136] as if to emphasize the echo of the Bible story, though it is not made clear whether he is aware that this is what he is doing. There may be an element of unconscious inspiration at work. Joseph now goes home to fetch his mother. He finds out from the militia that Marie's husband has died of his wounds. A week later he is summoned to see Marie and finds her holding her newborn son in brilliant white swaddling clothes, which reminds him of one of the chapel wall paintings, specifically the lily stem growing between Mary and Joseph 'as evidence of their pure relationship'.[137] He takes the resemblance as a portent of future happiness, and when Marie thanks him for his care for the orphaned baby, he answers 'unthinkingly': 'He is an orphan no longer, if you are but willing!'[138] Wisely Elisabeth ushers him out. It is too soon to be thinking of marriage. He continues to visit Marie, and eventually she pays his family a visit. He shows her the wall paintings and speaks enthusiastically of the duties of a stepfather, which brings her to tears. Duty requires that she mourn her husband for a year, though as Joseph observes, 'Life belongs to the living, and all who live must be prepared for change'.[139] After living happily betrothed for a while, they are married and begin a family. Joseph the Second ends his story with a strange reference to the donkey, which has remained part of their life.[140]

Everything that Wilhelm had at first thought miraculous about the family turns out to have entirely natural origins, as if an understanding of the true causes of things dispels our false belief in miracles. This is Goethe's 'heathen' response to the religious art of the Nazarenes. But the naturalism of the story goes deeper, for Joseph the Second's narrative not only explains his own family's seemingly miraculous appearance. It explains miracles more generally, and this is why Goethe used the story of the birth of Christ to the Virgin Mary, the greatest miracle of all, as the story's iconic model. Joseph's life story can be read as a series of conjectures as to how the miraculous gospel story might have arisen from the facts of ordinary life, and therefore how the evangelist Matthew (or whoever wrote the gospel) might have drawn the story from his lived experience. In other words, the story of life imitating art provides a model for how its opposite might have happened: art imitating life. The fact that ordinary mundane human existence can imitate the extraordinary and miraculous is simply the obverse of the fact that the miraculous originates from the ordinary. The spirit of this argument is captured in a diary entry Goethe wrote in August 1809: 'Polarity of faith and hope. Hypothesis that the detail of Christ's passion was modelled on the ordinary circumstances of an execution and was applied to a worthy man'.[141] The story of Christ's passion was invented, or so we can conjecture, by conflating two experiences: an execution and the moral worth of an outstanding individual. The experiences are factually unrelated but our mind finds it attractive to associate them, for we are caught in a constant oscillation between hoping that the world makes moral sense and wanting to find our hopes realized in the facts of experience. This is what we call faith. Nowhere in 'St Joseph the Second' is it explicitly stated that we should read the story in this manner, but there are strong hints to do so. The story begins with Felix picking up a piece of fool's gold on the mountainside. When he asks Wilhelm why it is called 'cats' gold' (*Katzengold*), Wilhelm answers with a pun: 'Because it's false, and cats are generally considered false'.[142] The two meanings of *false*—incorrect and deceitful—hint at a feature of the story to come. Joseph the Second is a false Joseph, both in the unexceptional sense that he is not the original Joseph and in the more interesting sense that his mimicking of the biblical Joseph is a conscious counterfeit.[143] This duality—the resemblance of one thing to another and the conscious counterfeiting of a resemblance—is precisely what we see in Joseph the Second's life. In some respects, he happens by chance to resemble the biblical Joseph, and in other respects he manufactures his resemblance to Joseph. In this way, the narrative tells us that Joseph the Second is not just performing his life story; he is also its author. This is confirmed by Joseph's occupation. His profession as a carpenter is secondary to the role of tax collector that he inherited from his father.[144] He chose carpentry in imitation of the biblical Joseph, but he would not have had to make the choice had not his primary occupation as tax collector for the local duke required him to have a second trade. His occupation as tax collector is a very obvious allusion to the apostle

Matthew, who was traditionally thought to be the author of the gospel on which the wall paintings are for the most part based. And while Joseph the Second creates his life on the model of the wall paintings, his primary model is the Joseph of the gospel. Wilhelm makes this clear on discovering his wife's name: 'I almost feel as if I had been transported back eighteen hundred years'[145]—not back to the creation of the wall paintings or the Italian Renaissance, but to the time of the gospel itself, to the original fiction on which all of it is based.

When read from this perspective, some otherwise trivial details of the story take on new meaning. For instance, the Elisabeth of Joseph's story cares for young unmarried mothers. This fact is not stated in Joseph's story, but it is clearly implied by the fact that the mothers she cares for give birth at her house and not in their own homes, and that the tasks Joseph carries out for her and the messages he carries between her and his mother are kept secret from him. Secrecy is required in order not to offend public morals. The implication is that the story of the Virgin Mary's visitation to Elisabeth in the gospel might have originated from the historical existence of a wise midwife who helped unmarried pregnant women. A similar argument can be made concerning the incongruous donkey. In the New Testament the donkey is a symbol of the humility of the Holy Family and later of Christ. The story of Joseph the Second conjectures an origin for the biblical symbol: donkeys are the ideal beast of burden in the mountainous terrain surrounding Nazareth.

In addition to giving a psychosocial explanation for the origins of faith—a natural history of religion—the story has a typically Goethean political dimension. In his role as tax collector and hence as a modern analogue of the evangelist Matthew, Joseph the Second serves a secular lord. As a tax collector, he is a living embodiment of Christ's reply to the Pharisees' question whether Jews should pay taxes to the Roman emperor: 'Render [...] unto Caesar the things which are Caesar's'.[146] Joseph's existence is guaranteed by his duke. Indeed, the whole story is an extension of the authority of Joseph's overlord. In this sense, 'St Joseph the Second' develops the Spinozist arguments of the essay 'Two important hitherto unanswered Biblical questions' of 1772, the fragmentary Mohammed play of 1773, and the Moses drafts of 1797. It shows how faith originates and is institutionalized in the context of political power. Herein lies the significance of the final, damaged panel of the monastery's wall paintings. Joseph the Second explains to Wilhelm that it was the final, now almost completely obliterated, panel that had inspired him to take up carpentry. The subject of the panel is the commission Joseph received from King Herod to build a throne that would fit between two columns in his palace. On delivering the throne, Joseph finds that it is too narrow and tall for the space. The young Jesus, who has accompanied Joseph, provides a miraculous solution to the problem. He takes hold of one arm of the throne and instructs Joseph to take the other. They pull, and the throne miraculously becomes exactly the right size. The panel thus represents Christ's miracle working in the service of political power. The figure of Christ the miracle worker is in fact an extension of the power of the king of the Jews. However, the panel's Spinozist story has nearly vanished, in two ways. First, the story does not occur in the canonical gospels, but only in an apocryphal Arab Gospel. It has disappeared from authorized Christianity. Second, the panel has been worn away and the image is barely visible. In these ways, the political origins of Christianity have become practically invisible to modern Christians.

———

Between October 1807 and June 1808, Goethe wrote the strikingly beautiful short drama *Pandora*, in an extreme Hellenizing style.[147] Leopold von Seckendorf and Joseph Ludwig Stoll had asked Goethe for a piece for their new literary journal *Prometheus*,[148] which they hoped would contribute to the cultural regeneration of the German-speaking lands after the disasters of the previous two years: Austerlitz, the dissolution of the Holy Roman Empire, Jena-Auerstedt. Goethe's play was to have had two parts, but he did not finish the second, which would have offered a prospect of Germany's rising from the ashes of 1806 and would have made sense of the play's title, *Pandora's Return*. For all its beauty, the mood of the first part is bleak. It dwells on the anthropological constants that drive the destructive forces of modernity. It had been a recurrent theme in Goethe's writing, since at least the mid-1780s, that beauty belonged in the past, and the present was a 'statistical' age.[149] As he had put it in Venice in October 1786: 'the time of beauty is over, our day demands only what is an urgent and strict necessity'.[150] Pandora herself is beauty, but she has disappeared from the world. The play's main characters are the brothers Prometheus and Epimetheus and their respective children Phileros and Epimeleia. The two families embody the progressive and retrograde principles in human nature. Thus the names Prometheus and Epimetheus, instead of signifying the gifts of foresight and memory, denote limitedness: Prometheus is locked into seeing only the future and Epimetheus only the past. In another divergence from the Greek mythic sources, in which the names carry a clear bias in Prometheus's favour, Goethe's Prometheus is no less deficient than

Epimetheus; indeed in some ways Epimetheus is the more sympathetic character, for he has cherished beauty and his actions are less destructive than his brother's. The deficiency of Epimetheus is not that he thinks too late, but that his emotional commitment to the past confines him to a melancholy twilight world of memory and dreams:

> Denn Epimetheus nannten mich die Zeugenden,
> Vergangnem nachzusinnen, Raschgeschehenes
> Zurückzuführen, mühsamen Gedankenspiels,
> Zum trüben Reich gestalten-mischender Möglichkeit.[151]

> For my progenitors named me Epimetheus, / To ponder on what's in the past, / To bring back what happened swiftly, through arduous play of thought, / Into the turbid realm of form-mixing possibility.

In its stark polarities, *Pandora* follows the model of an essay prize Goethe and Schiller set in 1801, which required 'a condensed luminous representation of that which is constant in humans, to which the chief phenomena of progressive, static, and retrograde culture can be attributed'.[152] The schematic nature of *Pandora* might appear off putting. So too might the studious use Goethe made of a range of classical metrical forms and massive compound words. During his work on the play, the classicist Wolf published a dedicatory essay to Goethe in the first volume of a new journal, *Museum of the Study of Antiquity*, edited by Wolf himself and Philipp Buttmann. Wolf praised Goethe's contributions to classical studies and credited him with creating Germany's reputation as the great nation of classicists.[153] In fact, the poetry of *Pandora* is hauntingly beautiful, for instance, when Epimetheus recollects his brief relationship with Pandora and struggles to overcome his inability to pursue an act of will single-mindedly:

> Wer von der Schönen zu scheiden verdammt ist,
> Fliehe mit abegewendetem Blick!
> Wie er, sie schauend, im Tiefsten entflammt ist,
> Zieht sie, ach! reißt sie ihn ewig zurück.[154]

> Whoever is doomed to part from their beautiful one, / Should flee with averted gaze! / If, seeing her, he catches fire in his deepest self, / She'll pull him, ah! she'll wrench him back for all time.

The play begins with an elaborate, painterly description of the stage setting, 'in the grand style after the manner of Poussin',[155] a manner Goethe considered apt for 'heroic' subjects.[156] In a later description of the citadel of Luxembourg, based on his experiences during the 1792 campaign in France, Goethe described how the city's fortifications and dwellings seemed to grow organically out of its dramatic landscape of rocks and rivers. The intimate unity of landscape and civilization required a Poussin to portray it.[157] The heroic manner of Poussin conveyed, Goethe thought, the temporal forms of civilization emerging out of the eternal forms of nature. The stage of *Pandora* is divided into two sides, one belonging to Epimetheus, the other to Prometheus. Prometheus's world is a hillside pockmarked with mines and interlaced with a maze of paths and stairs. There is some limited building, but it is 'all crude and coarse' and 'without any symmetry'.[158] The Promethean side represents the progressive forces of labour and technology exploiting the earth's inorganic resources. In the world of Epimetheus, organic nature is cultivated in a comfortable and orderly manner, with 'well-tended gardens'[159] and wooden houses, 'separate properties' whose wants seem to be already 'satisfied'. This is another aesthetic advantage Epimetheus seems to have over Prometheus. Epimetheus's world, though stagnant, is in harmony with nature, whereas Prometheus's people are waging war against nature. As Prometheus's blacksmiths sing:

> Erde sie steht so fest!
> Wie sie sich quälen läßt!
> Wie man sie scharrt und plackt!
> Wie man sie ritzt und hackt!
> Da soll's heraus.[160]

> The earth, it stands so firm! / How it allows itself to be tortured! / How people scrape and pick at it! / How people tear and hack it! / That's where it's heading.

Even if its underlying polar structure betokens an anthropological constant—the polarity of progressive and retrograde forces—other elements of *Pandora* allude to a historical moment, the moment at which Promethean modernism tips over into war. Prometheus's metalworkers have been making gear for farmers and fishermen, but now he now commands them to divert all their resources to the manufacture of weapons.[161] There is an allusion here to the ancient motif of ploughshares being turned into swords. Goethe knew the motif from Lucretius and Virgil.[162] As a classical motif, it hints at 'that which is constant in humans', as Goethe put it in the 1801 essay prize. That said, *Pandora* is also a product of the recent past and present in 1807. Prometheus's army of warriors suggests Napoleon. In depicting Prometheus's world as a militaristic one, in which society and the economy are shaped by the need to wage war, Goethe may have been influenced by Friedrich von Gentz's acute analysis of the Napoleonic regime in his *Fragments from the Most Recent History of the Political Balance of Power in Europe*, which Goethe read immediately upon its publication in spring 1806.[163] According to Gentz, the fact that Napoleon's ascent to power was based on military victory had tied him to a logic of continued military success. Having risen to power as a military leader, Napoleon had no choice but to continue to wage war. The idea was not entirely new to Goethe: it confirmed his view, expressed in the 'Mohammed' fragment of the early 1770s, that the state derived its legality from military power. There are also traces of Fichte in Prometheus's preference for action over rest: 'A real man truly celebrates by his deeds!' ('Des echten Mannes wahre Feier ist die Tat!').[164] In his diary for August 1806 Goethe noted having 'found Fichte's theory in Napoleon's deeds and methods'.[165] Not only was Napoleon the 'Mohammed of the World'. By crowning himself Emperor of the French he had also become a Fichtean 'positer [...] of the empirical universe'.[166] The comparison with Fichte was a *jeu d'esprit*, but no less truthful for that. The Promethean state is one that thrives on creating opposition. It exists in a perpetual condition of partisanship, Prometheus says: 'An active man's source of comfort should be partisanship' ('Des tät'gen Manns Behagen sei Parteilichkeit').[167] Prometheus embodies precisely those features of modernity that Goethe abhorred.

The children, Prometheus's son Phileros and Epimetheus's daughter Epimeleia, reflect the character of their respective fathers, so that in the younger generation the progressive and retrograde tendencies are now gendered. As in *Faust*, the modernizing male principle drives the action and is the chief cause of destruction. The main plot concerns the children's relationship. Epimeleia and Phileros are in love and have kissed. In expectation of more intimacy, Epimeleia leaves her garden gate open for Phileros, but instead she is visited by an opportunistic herdsman who tries to have his way with her. Phileros witnesses this and jumps to the false conclusion that Epimeleia is being unfaithful. He kills the herdsman and chases Epimeleia, threatening to kill her too. In her flight she finds her father Epimetheus, who cannot prevent Phileros from wounding her, though not gravely. Both Epimetheus and Prometheus are powerless to help. Indeed Prometheus makes things worse by threatening to have Phileros chained and drowned in the sea, in response to which Phileros takes matters into his own hands by throwing himself off a cliff. The action ends with his rescue from the sea by the followers of Eos, the dawn. The ending of the play suggests that the reckless forces of modernity might be moderated, but not halted. Prometheus recognises his people's blindness, but not his own. Nor does he acknowledge that his brother Epimetheus might be a helpful antidote against destructive modernity. Epimetheus does not appear at the end of the play. His absence means the brothers cannot yet be reconciled. If Prometheus has given an inch of ground, Epimetheus has given none. According to Goethe's notes, in the second part of the drama Pandora would return bringing the gifts of scientific knowledge and artistic beauty—gifts that belong to the world of Epimetheus, not Prometheus.[168] While Phileros changes sides, Prometheus and his followers remain opposed to Pandora's gifts. Phileros and Epimeleia will become priests of Pandora's cult on earth. Epimetheus will be rejuvenated and ascend to heaven with Pandora. However, on earth the place of the arts and sciences looks insecure. During Pandora's brief epiphany Prometheus's followers, 'the violent ones', are temporarily paralyzed by her.[169] Yet presumably they will wake and once more seek to possess and reify Pandora's gifts. The smiths will build fences, and in the marketplace the tradespeople will be riven by strife. Modern humanity will continue to suffer from the Promethean curse of partisanship and to abuse its potential for true aesthetic being.

Even though Napoleon's victories were already the stuff of legend, Goethe had only begun to pay close attention to him in 1804, after Napoleon's dragoons secretly crossed the Rhine into Germany and seized Louis Antoine de Bourbon, Duke of Enghien. The immediate trigger for Enghien's capture and hurried execution was the false charge that he had plotted to assassinate Napoleon. Many Germans were outraged by the execution of a prince of the blood. The Russian Tsar Alexander I considered it grounds for war against France. Goethe disagreed and accepted the false charge against Enghien for his 'reckless revolutionary behaviour', as Eckermann has him describe it.[170] In Goethe's eyes, Enghien was another Brutus, guilty of unlawfully plotting to strike down a prince. The case of Enghien goes some way towards explaining the controversial matter of Goethe's support for Napoleon. In his view, which had remained unchanged since his studies in Strasbourg, legality was grounded in the power of the prince, not in any abstract notions of right. Because revolution or rebellion undermined a prince's power, it must also undermine legality and the functioning of the state. This predisposed Goethe to side with Napoleon and against Enghien. He came to see Napoleon as a supreme embodiment of princely power and fountainhead of law. It was precisely by amassing so much power that princes like Caesar and Napoleon could work for the good of their people. It was all to the good that in winning power they had defeated dysfunctional forms of government: the chaotic Roman Republic in Caesar's case and the hopelessly divided Directory in Napoleon's. His support for Napoleon was probably also confirmed by his favourable view of Machiavelli. In the mid-1790s Goethe had accepted Machiavelli's view in his history of Florence that republics were not grounded in liberty and were not capable of stable and effective government. In spring 1806, he read Machiavelli again, this time *The Prince*.[171]

The figure of Julius Caesar also served to bind Goethe to Napoleon. In autumn 1808 Napoleon invited Tsar Alexander I and the German princes to a conference in Erfurt. Among the many meetings, performances by the Comédie Française starring Napoleon's favourite actor Talma, and other displays of Napoleonic power and glory, one event has acquired legendary status: the interview between Napoleon and Goethe on the morning of 2 October. The traditional view has been that Goethe was courted by Napoleon and won over by the personal interest Napoleon took in him. The truth is more complex, as Gustav Seibt has shown.[172] During a conversation with Carl August at Erfurt, Napoleon invited himself to Weimar to hunt with the Duke. This is probably why Carl August hurriedly summoned Goethe to attend him in Erfurt. Goethe's role was to make arrangements for Napoleon's visit.[173] The programme was to include a hunt, a gala dinner, a performance by the Comédie, a ball, and a tour of the battlefield at Jena followed by breakfast outdoors. Arriving in Erfurt late on the evening of 29 September, Goethe set about making the arrangements with Napoleon's staff. On the morning of 2 October he was invited to an audience with Napoleon, who greeted him with the dramatic words 'Vous êtes un homme' (in Goethe's version) or 'Voilà un homme' (in the more detailed account recorded by the twenty-nine-year-old Friedrich von Müller, who had represented the Duchy in the delicate negotiations with Napoleon after Jena-Auerstedt). Goethe and Napoleon discussed *Werther*, the theatre, and Goethe's domestic circumstances, and Goethe was evidently impressed by Napoleon's literary knowledge. As with most of Napoleon's actions, the conversation had an ulterior motive: to win Goethe over as a propagandist and, if possible, to persuade him to come to Paris and write a Caesar drama. Müller reports the invitation as follows:

> Tragedy ought to be school of kings and nations, that is the highest a poet can achieve. You for instance ought to write the death of Caesar in a worthy manner, more sublimely than Voltaire. That could be the finest task of your life. The world should be shown how Caesar would have made them happy, how

everything could have been different, if he had been given time to execute his high-minded plans. Come to Paris, I absolutely demand it of you.[174]

Among the events Goethe had to arrange for the visit to Weimar was a production of Voltaire's *The Death of Caesar*. It was Napoleon's choice, and his motive for choosing it was obvious. After the performance Goethe was treated to another interview with the Emperor, during which Napoleon repeated his proposal that Goethe should write a new Caesar tragedy 'in a different sense', as Goethe noted later.[175] Another note written by Goethe's secretary John suggests that Napoleon's choice of Voltaire's *Caesar* was intended to show Goethe how much better he could do: 'Occasion for invitation to write a Brutus'.[176] Not only that, the implication is that Goethe understood why Napoleon had chosen Voltaire's play: to manufacture the 'occasion' to repeat his invitation. This choreographed effort on Napoleon's part would make more sense if during the meeting in Erfurt four days earlier Goethe had told Napoleon of his own Caesarist sympathies, though there is no evidence in the surviving record that he did so.

Following the two Emperors' visit to Weimar, Goethe was awarded the Legion d'honneur by Napoleon and the Order of St Anna by the Tsar. He was deeply affected, especially by the French honour. In 1809 Wilhelm von Humboldt wrote to his wife Karoline that 'Goethe doesn't go anywhere without the Legion medal, and he always refers to the person who gave it to him as "my Emperor"!'[177] Goethe was not alone. After the performance of Voltaire's *Caesar*, Napoleon held a long conversation with Wieland and likewise awarded him the Legion d'honneur. Despite his insight and scepticism in political matters, Wieland was as affected as Goethe. The Legion d'honneur was a sign 'that the greatest man of all the centuries' thought favourably of him, and as such the decoration was 'of endless value' to him.[178] It was also of value to the Duchy. Several factors combined to make the political optics of Weimar's accommodation with the Napoleonic regime complex: Weimar's ties to Russia, Carl August's participation at Jena-Auerstedt on the Prussian side, and the nationalist and anti-Napoleonic sentiments of many Germans, not least the students at Jena. At the highest level of the Duchy's government, sympathies were divided. Goethe and Voigt were keen advocates of accommodation, whereas the Duke and Wolzogen were not.[179] However, in 1808 accommodation was a necessity, and it could only be to the Duchy's benefit that its greatest public assets, its poets Goethe and Wieland, had been honoured by Napoleon and that this exceptional distinction was widely reported in the newspapers.[180]

It no doubt suited the Duke's purposes that the Duchy found favour with Napoleon, whilst the reputational damage of sympathizing with Napoleon was borne by Goethe and Wieland and not by Carl August himself. This is not to suggest that the admiration Goethe felt for Napoleon was part of a concerted diplomatic strategy. It is simply to acknowledge that its diplomatic significance was a convenient fact.

Despite his admiration for Napoleon, Goethe published practically nothing that was unambiguously pro-Napoleonic. During the five years from the congress of Erfurt to Napoleon's defeat at the Battle of the Nations at Leipzig, his only explicit pro-Napoleonic publication was in three sets of stanzas he composed in honour of the Austrian Emperor Franz I, his second wife Empress Maria Ludovica, and his daughter (by his first wife) the French Empress Marie-Louise, who had married Napoleon in 1810. The occasion was the royals' visit to Carlsbad in July 1812, which Goethe was asked to commemorate by the town's burghers. The stanzas have little interest as poetry: the most persuasive sections recall with affection the founding of Carlsbad by Emperor Charles IV in 1370, but otherwise the laudatory tone feels rather bland and abstract. The third set of stanzas, dedicated to Empress Marie-Louise, celebrates Napoleon for bringing an end to the 'gloomy night'[181] of the French Revolution and for bringing unity to Europe 'through wise decision, through battles of power'.[182] However, Goethe puts more emphasis on the advent of peace than on Napoleon's victories. The final line of the stanzas associates Napoleon with God, but again the emphasis is on peace: '*He* who can will all, also wills peace'. The Carlsbad stanzas of 1812 do celebrate Napoleon at the height of his power, but they put more emphasis on the resulting peace than on the power itself.

Goethe's attitude to Napoleon was not simply starry-eyed admiration or the egotism and indifferentism that Gentz accused him of after the Battle of Leipzig in 1813.[183] There was some truth in both of these criticisms. Goethe was deeply affected by the meetings with Napoleon in October 1808, and he did believe that accommodation with the victors was the most sensible policy, for resistance would only be damaging, as he commented to Riemer shortly after the Battle of Jena-Auerstedt.[184] This was also why, in a review in the *JALZ*, Goethe praised the Berlin court historian Johannes von Müller's speech 'The Glory of Frederick', delivered in Berlin in January 1807. In Goethe's view Müller rightly stressed the need for accommodation with the French occupiers.[185] Subsequently the *JALZ* came out as a strong supporter of the Confederation of the Rhine.[186] Again in 1811, Goethe reviewed an essay by the historian Georg Sartorius on the Ostrogothic Kingdom in Italy. He wrote to Sartorius conveying his complete agreement with Sartorius's argument that the Romans should have accommodated with the Ostrogoth invaders. Instead the Romans were motivated by a nationalist politics of empty sentiment:

> The Romans' hatred towards even the mildest victor, their delusion of extinct virtues, the wish for a different situation without having a better one in view, groundless hopes, hit-or-miss ventures, alliances from which no salvation was to be hoped, and whatever all the miserable consequences of such times might be—all of this you have portrayed splendidly and you demonstrate that everything did in fact happen thus in those times.[187]

Goethe's praise for Sartorius's history of Rome under the Ostrogoths was an oblique way of expressing his view of Germany under Napoleon. The German nationalists were guilty of a politics of vain and foolish sentiment that paid no regard to reality or to the good that could be done with power.

However, Goethe's main reason for supporting Napoleon, as he clearly stated in the Carlsbad stanzas, was that Napoleon had brought an end to the chaos of the Revolution and returned the French state to its former strength. This was the deeper truth of Napoleon. He was another example, like Mohammed—to whom he was often compared at the time for precisely this reason—of how legality was grounded in military power and not in abstract principles of right. In this sense too, Napoleon had overcome the French Revolution, with all its empty talk of laws based on rights. Even after Napoleon's defeat at the Battle of Leipzig, when his power was clearly in decline, Goethe continued to argue for the Napoleonic system, as it kept order and made things happen. Wilhelm von Humboldt, a supporter of the national movement, commented with horror at Goethe's reluctance to accept the new nationalist movement and his enduring Bonapartism:

> He does earnestly believe in [the liberation of Germany], but imagines with many digressions, unclear expressions and gestures that he had got used to the former conditions, that everything then was in good order and that the new conditions were hard to stomach.[188]

His disagreement with Newton turned Goethe into a historian of science. Indeed, the history of colour theory Goethe finally published in 1810, under the title *Materials for the History of Colour Theory*, has a claim to be the first true history of science—that is to say, a history that does more than merely parade the great men of science past the reader in chronological order, a history that gives as much space to incorrect as to correct theories, and a history that seeks to understand how both incorrect and correct theories developed and to set them in their social and political contexts. Goethe's innovations as a historian of science stemmed from his disagreement with Newton. If Goethe was right about colour and Newton was wrong, then a special and unusual historical explanation was required to show why the Newtonian paradigm had become dominant. Clearly the reasons for the Newtonian paradigm's success were not strictly scientific. Instead they must have been social and psychological. A history of colour theory of this kind would run counter to standard Enlightenment narratives. Put simply, the standard Enlightenment view was that the science of the past was a garden rank with the weeds of error and containing only a few flowers of truth, to use Donald Sepper's metaphor. The history of science showed how scientists rooted out the weeds and cultivated the flowers.[189] When Goethe first started work on the history of colour theory, it was not clear to him that he would have to diverge from standard Enlightenment models, nor did he understand what form the history would take, beyond the very general notion that it would be 'the history of the human mind on a smaller scale', as he wrote to Wilhelm von Humboldt in February 1798.[190] Writing to Schiller ten days later, he followed the standard Enlightenment model: the history of science 'is divided into two parts, the history of experiences and the history of opinions'.[191] That is to say, there were experiences that supported correct theories, and there were mere opinions that seemed to support incorrect ones. He already understood that the latter part, the 'history of opinions' and incorrect theories, needed to be framed in a way that could show how and why the errors of the Newtonians had arisen. At first he hoped that he could use Kant's categories as a framework,[192] though he did not know exactly how. In fact, his correspondence with Schiller in 1798 and 1799 shows that Goethe was more interested in Kant's distinction between the regulative and constitutive uses of reason, the former valid and the latter invalid.[193] Newton's overly hasty theorizing was a case of the invalid constitutive use of reason: he had illegitimately used an idea of reason to form an empirical theory. However, the Kantian framework did nothing to help Goethe explain the acceptance of Newton's theory by other scientists, the intelligentsia and the general public. After drafting plans for the historical material in January and February 1798, he worked on it sporadically over the next ten years, including one concerted stint in Göttingen in summer 1801 researching the history of physics in Britain.[194] It was probably in Göttingen that he first began to understand the shape of his history of colour theory and to focus on 'what happened' in science and not on 'what ought to happen', as he put it to Meyer in July 1801. In other words, from this point onwards his history of colour theory would be concerned as much with incorrect theories as with correct ones.[195]

The final push to finish the *Materials* began in summer 1808 and continued through 1809 and into spring 1810.[196] Most of the work involved curating the corpus of material he had spent ten years gathering. Some of the material was obscure, some of it of uncertain authorship, in particular one crucial Ancient Greek text, and most was in foreign languages. The confusing state of the textual material was probably why Goethe decided that the *Materials* would include long passages of original text. The Ancient Greek and Latin texts were translated into German, including extracts from Knebel's still unpublished translation of Lucretius. Some texts were reproduced in full, others summarized or paraphrased or represented by an analytical table of contents. Some of the work was philological. Goethe enlisted Wolf to help him with the fraught question of the authorship of the Ancient Greek *On Colours*, attributed either to Aristotle or his pupil Theophrastus. *On Colours* was an especially important text for Goethe, and he was pleased that Wolf deemed it 'genuinely ancient and worthy of the Peripatetic School' and probably by Aristotle himself.[197] The importance of the text lay in the fact that this first systematic account of colour supported Goethe's own view that the spectral colours are generated from the combination of light and darkness. Aristotle's authority counted.

By reproducing long extracts of text, Goethe was also able to convey another feature of the historical record. He believed strongly in the power and character of the individual voice. He had held this view since his first emergence onto the German literary scene with *Götz* and *Werther*. It was the reason for his valuing Spinoza's and Winckelmann's letters more highly than their published philosophical and historical writings, and it was the rationale for the polyphonic elements in his own prose writings, such as the 'Confessions of a Beautiful Soul' and *Conversations of German Emigrés*. In the *Materials* he gives the following reason for reproducing texts, rather than conveying their sense through his own narrative: 'One should, we are told, stick not to the word but to the spirit. However, usually the spirit destroys the word or transforms it in such a manner that little remains of its previous manner and meaning.'[198] The structure and indeed the title of the *Materials* reflected Goethe's feeling that the history of science was a polyphonic discourse. In a similar vein, during his collaboration with Schiller he had repeatedly argued that a full understanding of the world could only be achieved by taking multiple different perspectives. As he wrote to Schiller in 1798, at the beginning of his historical studies: 'Only the totality of humanity perceives nature, only the totality of humanity lives humanity. Try as I might, in all the famous axioms I can only see the expressions of one individual'.[199] Individuals can only express their own *Vorstellungsart*; the totality of individuals would represent a totality of *Vorstellungsarten* and thus a complete picture of nature. This further explains why the *Materials*, in their final published form, look more like an artist's workshop than a finished work of art.

Interspersed between the quotations and descriptions are several reflective essays on questions of historiography and on topics such as the formation of intellectual and textual traditions and authority. The intellectual originality of the *Materials* lies in these reflective essays, in which Goethe tries to answer the historical questions that arose from his disagreement with Newton. Broadly speaking the reflective essays fall into two groups: an earlier group that fills the historical gap between antiquity and the early modern period, and a later group concerned with the period during which Newton formulated his theory and his followers established it. The earlier essays, in particular the three sections titled 'Lacuna', 'Transmission', and 'Authority', are concerned with the textual tradition that emerged out of antiquity, dominated by a small number of individuals: Plato, Aristotle, and the authors of the Bible. The argument is concerned with the qualities of these texts that made them canonical; it is not concerned with the social circumstances of either the authors or the texts' later reception. It is important to stress this point, because Goethe's argument will change when he comes to discuss the circumstances surrounding the origins and reception of Newton's theory. This latter sequence of essays, in particular the essays on the early years of the Royal Society and the essay titled 'Newton's Personality', deal with the social and political contexts of seventeenth- and eighteenth-century science and the psychology of theory formation. Between the earlier and later essays, there is a tactical shift in focus. The focus switches from an era that fosters great individuals writing works of extraordinary power, to an era in which scientists are embedded in a social order that complicates and inhibits their efforts. For an example of the latter, we can look back to Goethe's 1805 essay on Winckelmann. Winckelmann's individuality emerges most powerfully in his letters, where he writes as a private individual. By contrast, he wrote his formal essays on art history as a participant in a public culture of learning, and the essays are blighted by the need to engage in public debate, which causes them to appear 'baroque and bizarre' to any reader who is not informed about the intellectual life of Winckelmann's time.[200] Goethe makes a similar argument concerning Newton's errors and the triumph of his doctrine. Whilst the era in which Plato and Aristotle lived allowed them to project their individuality freely, the era of Newton did not. Newton's evident brilliance was constrained by his intellectual climate, which in turn fostered the reception of his false doctrine.

Goethe offers two explanations for the preeminence of Plato, Aristotle, and the Bible in the Western tradition. The first is that the three corpora have presented their readers with an interlocking and mutually supporting group of texts. For instance, the Bible has become central to the Western tradition because it combines mutually supporting narrative and doctrine in a way practically no other text does. However, this dense mixture of narrative and doctrine makes the Bible a highly interpretable text. That need for interpretation was answered by the work of Plato and Aristotle. Both were examples of high intellectual ambition in extensive and coherent form. The former was more spiritual in its orientation; the latter built its intellectual insight on a wide base of experience. Plato points towards heavenly ideals, like an obelisk; Aristotle appeals to our experience, like a broad-based pyramid. The antithetical character of the two was a key reason for their success, for they were able to divide the claims of reason between themselves and so to achieve a kind of exclusivity. One was either a Platonist or an Aristotelian. Or to put it another way, if one wanted to be an anti-Platonist one became an Aristotelian and vice versa. The second reason for the preeminence of Plato, Aristotle, and the Bible concerns reason itself. The claims of the Greek philosophers drew their force from reason. In an important sense, the Bible was similar, for it makes its claims on the grounds of moral conscience. Both of these modes of thought, reason and the moral conscience, originate in the noumenal realm. Consequently, Goethe concludes, reason and morality are powerful and unquestionable sources of authority: 'So reason and its relative conscience have immense authority, because they are unfathomable'.[201] This is not to say that Goethe believed in the truth claims made by the Greek philosophers or the Bible. For Goethe, reason is not accessible to us in the empirical realm except in the form of mathematics. His argument that the claims of reason have authority is an argument about the perceived status of reason, not its actual warrant.

The core argument of the three sections 'Lacuna', 'Transmission', and 'Authority' concerns two types of historical era. The course of history has the form of a cyclical alternation of antithetical eras. Before considering the nature of these two types of era, it is important to note that Goethe is not altogether sceptical about progress, and the alternation between antitheses is only part of the pattern of history. Goethe is not as sceptical as the Rousseau of the first *Discourse*, according to whom history is the eternal cyclical recurrence of similar patterns. On the contrary, Goethe thinks that cyclical alternation occurs in tandem with progress: his vision of history is of a pattern of rising cyclicality, an ascending spiral. (In 1808 Goethe wrote to his son August, studying the history of philosophy in Heidelberg, that 'in the earthly domain everything is after all repetitive. [...] There is no shortage of spirals and other even stranger lines'.)[202] We are bound to alternate between antithetical positions, but we can make progress as we do so. Scientific knowledge can advance even as it repeats the forms it has taken in earlier eras.

The emphasis in the *Materials* is less on progress and more on the two antithetical historical periods, or 'moments of world history', as he terms them. The two 'moments' are characterized in the first place in social terms:

> The first [moment] is the one in which individuals develop freely side-by-side; this is the epoch of becoming, of peace, of nourishment, of the arts, of the sciences, of congeniality, of reason. Here everything works inwardly and in the best periods strives for happy domestic edification; yet this condition eventually dissolves into tribalism and anarchy.[203]

The description of the first moment is couched in abstract, nonspecific terms, as it must be, because these are forms and structures that recur in different ages. Even so, it is possible to infer which ages Goethe would have had in mind. For instance, the apogee of classical Greek culture in the fifth century B.C.E. saw the free development of the individual among other free individuals, the triumph of reason and science, and the flourishing of the arts, at least according to the Winckelmannian view of Ancient Greece to which Goethe subscribed. Further, the notion that 'everything works inwardly' towards 'happy domestic edification' seems to imply societies that were small in scale, like the Greek *poleis*. It might further imply an economic model based on relatively small-scale land ownership, as was the case in classical Athens. The great age of classical Greece was followed by the descent of the city-states into the 'tribalism and anarchy' of the Peloponnesian War and the Hellenistic era. A similar argument could be made for the Italian Renaissance. These were small-scale polities that fostered the arts and sciences but eventually declined into the chaos of war and vendetta. Whilst the argument is primarily political, it also applies to the history of philosophy. The leading philosophers of antiquity, Plato and Aristotle, drew their authority from the ultimately unfathomable source of reason. The claims of reason are not subject to arbitration, both because reason originates in the unfathomable noumenal realm, and because *pure* reason has no purchase on phenomena, the domain in which we can arbitrate claims. Therefore adherence to the philosophy of either Plato or Aristotle became a matter of mere tribal allegiance, and for this reason too the first moment of world history tended to descend into 'tribalism and anarchy'.

In the sense just outlined, the decline of the first moment, whether in classical Greece or Renaissance Italy, resulted partly from internal contradictions. It 'dissolve[d] into tribalism and anarchy'. Periods of peace and liberty cannot endure, because individualism contains the seeds of partisanship and anarchy. Goethe's description of the second moment makes it clear that the newly awakening forces of the second moment are also responsible for destroying the first. The second moment instrumentalizes the scientific inventions of the first. Invention becomes exploitation, science becomes technology, and technology—as Herder argued in *This too a Philosophy of History*—was the precondition for the military-political institution of the nation-state. Goethe's account of the second moment is as follows:

> The second epoch is that of exploitation, of war, of consumption, of technology, of knowledge, of the intellect. The effects are directed outwards; in the finest and highest sense, this moment can provide stability and pleasure under certain circumstances. However, such a condition readily decays into selfishness and tyranny, whereby however it is by no means necessary to think of the tyrants as individuals; there is a tyranny of large masses which is most violent and irresistible.[204]

Such is the condition of much of modern Europe since the late Renaissance. Technology has supplanted the arts; the nation-state has superseded the city-state. By the 'tyranny of large masses' Goethe evidently has in mind the French Revolution, but possibly also the descent of the Florentine state into chaos with Savonarola, as Goethe had described in his appendix to Cellini's *Life*. The Italian Renaissance city-states (first moment) were succeeded by the powerful nation-states France, Spain, and Austria (second), which instrumentalized the inventions of the Renaissance. In the same way, first the Macedonian and then the Roman Empire (second moment) overwhelmed the classical Greek city-states (first) and instrumentalized their inventions. The Romans exploited Greek culture and science for the purpose of technology and empire-building. Admittedly, all of these great second-moment nations and empires were capable of periods of 'stability and pleasure', but they have also tended to descend into tyranny.

As in *Pandora* with its depiction of the antithetical cultures of Epimetheus and Prometheus, in the *Materials* Goethe evidently ranks the first moment of world history above the second. The most important factor in the relative standing of the two moments is the capacity of the individual to withstand the force of tradition, or more accurately to create the tradition anew. Tradition— or one might even say *the* tradition—is created and sustained by individuals: 'The weak thread which, from out of the sometimes very broad weft of knowledge and science, persists uninterruptedly through all ages, even the darkest and most confused, is borne by individuals'.[205] He made the same point more trenchantly in conversation with Riemer in September 1807: 'In all periods, it is only the individuals who have had an effect on science. Not the age. It was the age that executed Socrates by poison, the age that burned [Jan] Hus; the ages have always remained the same'.[206] The history of scientific truth, then, is a history of individuals, whereas the history of scientific error involves both individuals and social groups. The justification for this individualism is contained in Goethe's analysis of the notion of tradition. Of course, traditions do not come into being through mere passive inheritance, like family heirlooms. A tradition that passes unchanged down the generations will die. Traditions develop through an active process of recreation. They are made and remade through the conflict between two forms of authority: the authority of what has been transmitted, such as the great texts of Plato, Aristotle, and the Bible, and the authority of people's lived experience. This is what great individuals do. They set their own experience up against transmitted authority:

> We are constantly at war with transmission, and equally the requirement that we should experience the present on our own authority is the call-up to a momentous conflict. And yet any person on whom some original potency has been bestowed will feel the calling to survive this double struggle, which is not made easier, but harder, by the progress of the sciences. For in the end it is only ever the individual who is to challenge nature and transmission in all their growing breadth.[207]

An original individual can stand up against tradition and remake it. The great mass of people do not have this capacity. In itself this is not an objectionable proposition. It amounts simply to defining originality as the capacity to remake tradition on the basis of one's own experience, and to asserting that originality is a rare gift. However, Goethe draws a sharper conclusion. Because the original individual stands against tradition, whilst the mass of people do not, it follows that the individual will be in conflict with the mass:

> [Individuals] of the best kind are born in this century as in any other and always behave in the same manner towards the century in which they occur. That is to say, they stand in opposition to the masses, indeed in antagonism to them. In this regard educated eras have no advantage over barbaric ones: for at any time virtues are rare, shortcomings common. And is it not also the case that even in the individual a mass of errors stands against a single aptitude?[208]

Because the second moment of world history does not foster the individual, tradition is not reinvented and instead is merely exploited. Science is reduced to mere technology. The intellect ossifies. Such is the condition of modernity. Of course, it would be quite wrong to claim that science has not made progress. However, in most cases the progress has amounted to amassing new data, and data is not the same as knowledge. Data needs to be interpreted; data without understanding is empty. Hence Goethe can argue that the modern world has been arrogant. Modern scientists have collected large amounts of data, and yet they have arrogantly exaggerated the importance of that data.[209] Hence, we may be mistaken in thinking that we now stand on a higher plane of knowledge than our forbears did. Even the spiral model of history might exaggerate the progress we have actually made:

> The sciences have expanded admirably, but by no means in a steady progression, nor even stepwise, but instead in the form of ascent and descent, moving forwards or backwards in a straight line or in a spiral, whereby it is self-evident that in every epoch people have believed that they were far advanced above their predecessors.[210]

The stress is on the word *believed*, which can of course be read in two ways: perhaps our belief in scientific progress is warranted, and perhaps it is not.

Goethe's analysis of the second moment provides the core ideas for his account of Newtonianism. In the same way as the largely positive first moment fostered Plato's and Aristotle's valid and unjustly neglected insights into the nature of colour, the less positive second moment encouraged Newton's errors and their dissemination. During his research in Göttingen in 1801, Goethe came to see the Royal Society as the main force behind the discovery and propagation of Newton's theory. It was the Society's flawed practices and worldview that allowed Newton's erroneous doctrine and his false conception of scientific method to take root. However, Goethe did not want the blame to fall on the Society itself. Rather, in the *Materials* he takes a wider view of the

Society's work by setting it in its historical context. The story he tells highlights the advantages and disadvantages conferred on the Society by its sociopolitical circumstances. Naturally, the negative factors outweigh the positive. So for instance, Goethe argues that the Society was part of a scientific milieu that invested great quantities of time, effort, and money in gathering data, without a commensurate effort to understand the data. This milieu was formed by certain social and political changes in seventeenth-century England, including some liberal and egalitarian trends that Goethe disliked. The nucleus of the Society was formed in Oxford during the Civil War, when the royalist university was occupied by Parliamentarian forces. A group of scholars conceived the admirable project of studying nature for its own sake and apart from the politics of the day. In Goethe's account, these early meetings sound like the programme he developed with Schiller in the first years of their partnership in the wake of the Revolution:

> They held fast to blameless nature, banned from their meetings all the more earnestly any controversies concerning either political or religious subjects, and with their pure love of truth they nurtured in private that aversion to enthusiasm, religious fantasies, the prophecies emerging therefrom and other monstrosities of the day.[211]

The origins of the Society lay in a milieu that was loyal to the monarchy but turned its back on the wider world and on politics and religion in particular. On moving to London after the Restoration, the Society expanded its membership while retaining its character. Many of the new members were from the higher and lower aristocracy,[212] which conferred further benefits, in particular since the minor aristocrats had largely been excluded from court and forced to return to husbanding their rural estates, where they developed practical skills and habits of diligence.[213] This view of the aristocracy is again typically Goethean. He welcomes the idea of the higher nobility as patrons of science, as he will also do in three later sections on eighteenth-century German science.[214] At the same time, he acknowledges the role played by England's economically and socially useful minor nobility, who resemble Lothario's circle in Books VII and VIII of *Wilhelm Meister's Apprenticeship*. Having thus organized itself from the ground up, as it were, the Society was blessed by the patronage of Charles II, which conferred the further advantage of making the Society socially fashionable. With the bulk of fashionable London opinion behind it, the Society could now take advantage of England's expanding economy and colonial trade. Merchant adventurers and colonial authorities answered the Society's requests for information, and a great wave of data began to pour into London.

The profusion of data is one of modernity's distinguishing features, and the question of what to do with it is at the heart of Goethe's analysis of the Royal Society and modern science more generally. His answer involves a statement both of his views on scientific method and of his anti-republican politics. Despite his experiments with Kant and Schelling in the 1790s, Goethe still considered himself an empiricist. He believed that his work on colour amounted to an ordering of the phenomena. Accordingly, in the section of the *Materials* concerned with the Society's *Philosophical Transactions*, he maintains that empiricism can be the route to scientific truth, albeit under favourable conditions. At first, the random collecting of empirical data will tend to obstruct the progress of science. However, if scientists persist and learn how to organize their data, an organizing principle will arise spontaneously out of the material.[215] This is Goethe's understanding of his own method, as he first described it in the 'Precautions' essay in the early 1790s. The methods employed by the Royal Society are its antithesis: the Society practised empiricism but failed to learn how to organize the data, for reasons that were connected with its intellectual, social, and political climate. Although the Society was born in the seclusion of royalist Oxford, it could not avoid being contaminated by the climate of republicanism. The Society's motto *nullius in verba* ('take no one's word for it') was a product of mid-seventeenth-century English republicanism, likewise the Society's distrust of authority and order.[216] The consequences for the Society were that it failed to recognise disciplinary boundaries and therefore to give its work a coherent internal structure. The meetings and the *Transactions* comprised a piecemeal and arbitrary mixture of different scientific disciplines and subject matters.[217] Existing research programmes were dismissed, as was any sense of a systematic foundation. Each project or experiment was treated as a fresh start. The experiments carried out at the meetings were done in isolation and with no sense of how they could be analysed and reduced to their component parts, nor any sense of how their conditions might be varied so as to produce different results. Had they been able to do so, Newton's *experimentum crucis* would not have enjoyed its exaggerated and unhealthy influence.[218]

Goethe was not in fact averse to radical empiricism. In his view, nature itself consists only of phenomena and knows nothing of method or theory. In this sense, one might compare natural phenomena to equal citizens living in a free republic. However, whilst a natural republic is conceivable, a human one is not. Humans are incapable of sustaining republican government. They need the order and hierarchy provided by monarchy and aristocracy. Goethe makes this metaphorical use of his political argument in a later section of the *Materials*:

> All these phenomena, whatever their names are, have an equal right to be fundamental phenomena. The physiological, physical, chemical colours cited by us are all equally authorized to speak to the attention of observers and theorizers. Nature alone has a truly republican character, whereas humans incline towards aristocracy and monarchy, and the individual character of the latter occurs everywhere, especially in theorizing.[219]

Science requires order and hierarchy just as society does. The Royal Society's aversion to authority led it down the path of a chaotic 'republican' empiricism. Goethe draws a contrast, at once methodological and political, between the Royal Society and the French Academy. The latter's practice was 'just as methodical as that of the English; but a kind of sensible order reigns in it'.[220] (Goethe no doubt chose the word 'reigns' for its political connotation; he meant to contrast the true monarchy of France with the semi-democratic constitutional monarchy of England.) The result was that when English scientists did theorize, they had no awareness that they were doing so and consequently no capacity to see the contents of their theories, for instance mechanistic or atomistic models of matter, for what they were: incomplete theories that explained the phenomena from only one limited perspective.[221] Still worse was the Society's liking for mathematical forms of explanation. Mathematics is helpful for solving technical problems, such as a rise in the use of optical apparatus. However, in natural theory mathematics amounts to the most extreme form of idealism, insofar as it reduces phenomena to numerical idealizations. In this way, a paradox arose in the Society's practice. Out of fear of theory's idealism, its members committed themselves to the most idealistic theory of all.[222]

The sociopolitical analysis of the Royal Society's failings is followed and complemented by an essay titled 'Newton's Personality'—a companion piece, albeit an antithetical one, to the 1805 eulogy of Winckelmann.[223] In some ways, Newton deserves to stand alongside Winckelmann. Goethe is willing to grant Newton's genius, especially in mathematics. His judgement of Newton's personality is generally positive. Although he repeatedly accused Newton of deceit and dogmatism in the *Unmasking*, in 'Newton's Personality' he treads more cautiously at first, and though the conclusion is the same as in the *Unmasking*, it is reached via a more abstract argument about the structures of human thought. Indeed, the argument goes well beyond the particulars of Newton's personality and returns to the criticisms of Kant's anthropology that he had first spelt out in the Winckelmann essay. As in the Winckelmann essay, character is the key concept. Character is a force of nature. All beings possess it, even the worm that writhes when it is disturbed. To possess character, a being must merely experience itself as a unity. It must have some kind of self it wants to preserve as 'undivided and undeflected'.[224] In this sense, character is close to Rousseauian self-preservation (*amour de soi*). It is an inner force or propension, a gift of nature. By defining character as a natural force Goethe means to distance himself from Kant, in two ways. Although the resources of character lie deep in our nature and beyond our understanding, its attributes belong entirely to the phenomenal realm, unlike Kant's moral will or transcendental unity of apperception, with their source in the noumenal realm. Whereas the Kantian moral subject is motivated by a noumenal will (*Wille*), character is a matter of willing or desiring (*Wollen*).[225] The Kantian *Wille* is orientated only and always towards what is right. Its focus is on moral ideas within the self. It is grounded in freedom. *Wollen* has no regard for moral ideas. Its focus is on external objects. It is grounded in nature.[226] The second distinction from Kant concerns the moral value of *Wollen*. *Wollen* is by no means morally inferior to *Wille*. On the contrary, our natural *Wollen* is just as capable of attaining those moral ends that we judge to be good. The point is not to reject moral systems such as Kant's, at least not at this point in the argument. Goethe simply believes that there is an adequate way of describing human behaviour that makes no reference to moral judgements. That part of the argument was spelt out in the Winckelmann essay. Winckelmann's behaviour could be described without reference to morality. He was an example of goodness resulting from instinct and emotion, and with no need for moral principles.[227] All his motives could be formulated satisfactorily in terms of his natural character, even the motives that resulted in the very highest moral ends, such as Kantian duty. Character, therefore, can in some cases fully replace and be the equal of a system of morality based on reason.

In addition to arguing that Kantian ethics is unnecessary, Goethe believes that it misconstrues the relation between the self and external reality. It is at this point that the critique of Kant connects with Goethe's analysis of Newton's science. Although Newton's character was sound, his relation to external objects was unbalanced by the fact that the 'organ' with which he apprehended the world was mathematics.[228] Like Kant, Goethe equates mathematics with reason, but unlike Kant, he considers the noninductive nature of mathematical proofs to mean that mathematics has no necessary relation to and is liable to diverge from natural phenomena, so that it 'can, like any thoroughly applied maxim, lead to error and indeed make the error enormous and pave the way for future embarrassments'.²²⁹ The same is true of (Kantian) ethics and reason, which leads to the paradox that 'the more moral and rational a person is, the more deceitful he is likely to be'.²³⁰ The argument is reminiscent of Mephistopheles's claim in the 'Prologue in Heaven' that reason only encourages humans 'to be more bestial than any beast ('Nur tierischer als jedes Tier zu sein').²³¹ Mathematical physicists like Newton must therefore have a problematic relation to empirical fact. They will be in constant disagreement with their experience of the world. They may achieve some degree of awareness of this disagreement, but the awareness will be short lived, for nobody can tolerate living in constant disagreement with themselves. There is an easy way out of this bind. One can simply blame one's errors on circumstances or other people. A strong character like Newton's will be too honest to do this, and so is bound to end up in a relationship to itself that Goethe terms 'ironic':

> So finally, out of the conflict between a rationally judging consciousness and our certainly modifiable and yet unalterable nature there arises a kind of irony in and with ourselves, so that we playfully treat our flaws and errors like badly behaved children, who would perhaps be less dear to us if they were not afflicted by such bad habits.²³²

Goethe thus arrives at his settled view of Newton's character and work. Newton's commitment to mathematics puts him in the paradoxical position of feeling obliged to tolerate his own flaws precisely on account of their being flaws. The same is true of any strong character who apprehends the world through the idealizing modes of reason or mathematics.

Goethe had reached the view that the irony of Newton's science consisted in his being able to affirm two contradictory beliefs. The same kind of irony is the principle literary feature of a novel that Goethe wrote during two breaks from his work on the *Materials for the History of Colour Theory* in 1808 and 1809. When Goethe first conceived of the story, he meant it for the *Journeyman Years*.²³³ The earliest evidence of his work on the novel dates from the summer of 1807, after he had emerged from his mourning for Schiller to begin work on the *Meister* sequel. By the beginning of May 1808, he had a detailed plan for the first part of the novel and a title: *The Elective Affinities*.²³⁴ He must also have realized by this stage that it had outgrown the other stories he was writing for the *Journeyman Years* and that it deserved his full attention, for at the end of May he decided to draw a line under his work on the as yet unfinished *Pandora* and to put the *Materials* on hold, so that he could devote himself to the novel instead.[235] On 1 June he began to dictate it and on 30 July reached a conclusion. The next day he returned to work on the *Materials*. By the spring of 1809 he decided that the novel required 'filling out and completing'[236] though there is little to suggest that the main themes and narrative changed much during the period of writing that followed in spring and summer of 1809.[237] Final corrections were made in July,[238] and the novel was published by Cotta in October.

The Elective Affinities is the most extraordinary product of the creative burst that started two years after Schiller's death. In some ways it is an unexceptional novel: a tragic love story of two women and two men living on a small aristocratic estate in contemporary Germany, told by a conventional anonymous narrator in prose that shifts, somewhat disconcertingly, between warm affection and cool analysis.[239] However, the novel is also pervasively, almost excessively symbolic, and the symbolism, combined with the odd use of scientific ideas, conveys an impression of hidden significance, an impression Goethe encouraged in his comments to friends and acquaintances. The result has been a flood of interpretations that shows little sign of abating. The novel's title derives from the chemical theory expounded in Torbern Bergman's *Dissertation on Elective Attractions* (1775). Many early readers of the novel assumed that Bergman's theory, which is discussed by the characters Charlotte, Eduard, and the Captain early in the novel, provided a key to the novel's meaning. Bergman's chemical model governed how the characters' relationships evolved, as if the characters were elements subject to the laws of chemical bonding. However, the significance of the theory lies less in its content, or in whether it predicts the characters' behaviour, than in the ways in which the characters discuss and interpret it.[240] Their discussion brings to light a flaw in their reasoning, the same flaw Goethe had found to be at the root of many scientific errors, namely the constitutive use of reason. As he tried to apply Kant's philosophy to his work on colour in 1798, this was the insight that had persuaded him that he needed to write a history of the science which would form the third part of his *Theory of Colour*. The error arises when we apply an idea of reason, for instance, the idea that nature is ultimately a unity, to our understanding of phenomena. In imposing the idea of unity on nature, we become prone to drawing erroneous connections between unrelated phenomena, such as chemical reactions and human relationships. The error is seen most commonly in our use of symbols. Indeed the error is hard to avoid, given that our language is thoroughly symbolic. Thus the symbolic language of *The Elective Affinities* is as likely to deceive as to illuminate, and as the events of the novel unfold, it becomes increasingly hard to know which it is doing.[241] In this sense, the novel, with its welter of possible meanings and its analytical narrative, is closely related to the *Materials* and shares their interest in the psychological and social factors that drive the production of knowledge.[242] In August 1808, at the end of the first phase of work on the novel, he told Riemer that 'his idea in the new novel *The Elective Affinities* was to represent social relations and their conflicts conceived symbolically'.[243] Some early readers were scandalized by Goethe's portrayal of marriage and adultery, but again the meaning of the novel lies less in the content of any view of marriage or any moral position on adultery which the narrative might seem to give support to, than in the ways people create and use such models—the ways in which they try to impose an intellectual or moral unity on the social world, which is another example of the constitutive use of reason. In this sense, the themes of the history of science and the history of human relations run along parallel lines. For in the same way as the characters are unaware of the forces that govern their knowledge of things, they are also unaware of the great social and political changes going on in the wider world, in particular the end of the Holy Roman Empire and the great modernizing forces unleashed by Napoleon.[244]

The novel's action begins at the estate of an aristocratic couple, Charlotte and Eduard. Once childhood sweethearts, each was obliged to marry a wealthy older spouse against their inclinations. Now both widowed, they have been reunited and have withdrawn from public life to live on Eduard's estate. Eduard hears that his old friend the Captain is looking for employment, and decides he would like the Captain to stay with them and help to improve the estate, including the construction of a new pavilion. Charlotte is unwilling to have their privacy disturbed, but at the same time she hears from the boarding school where her daughter Luciane and orphan niece Ottilie are being educated that the niece is not making good progress. Recognising that Ottilie will have to move, probably to their estate, Charlotte reluctantly agrees to invite the Captain. One evening soon after the Captain's arrival, the three friends discuss Bergman's theory that the dissolution and recomposition of compounds is driven by the natural affinity of some elements for others, as if the elements were endowed with the human power of choice. The conversation becomes more playful, and the friends apply the chemical theory to their own relationships, in particular the foursome that will be formed once Ottilie arrives. Shortly thereafter Charlotte learns of Luciane's unkind behaviour towards Ottilie, and the decision is made to invite Ottilie. The two men work together on the estate while the women manage the household, for which

Ottilie shows great aptitude. This recombination of their relationships was foreseen by Eduard during the chemical discussion. What he did not foresee was that he should feel increasingly drawn towards Ottilie, and Charlotte towards the Captain. The dangerous shift in their relationships is highlighted by the visit of some old friends, a Count and Baroness who are conducting an adulterous affair and who entertain controversial modern views concerning marriage. One evening, after mentioning a friend's opinion that marriage vows should be limited to five years, the Count asks Eduard to lead him to the Baroness's bedroom in the ladies' wing of the house. Once there, Eduard decides to visit Charlotte, and the two make love, though Eduard has Ottilie in mind and Charlotte the Captain. (Fritz Jacobi condemned this 'double adultery of the imagination' as the 'apotheosis of sinful desire'.)[245] The next evening, after their guests depart, Eduard, Charlotte, and the Captain are to try out an expensive new boat that Eduard has ordered for the pond, but at the last minute Eduard decides he wants to see Ottilie instead. They meet at the house and embrace. Meanwhile, having run the boat aground, the Captain carries Charlotte to safety and they kiss. Life continues, with the four seemingly in denial of their situation. In a letter the Captain announces his departure to take up a position arranged for him by the Count, and the next morning he is gone. Charlotte and Eduard discuss what is to happen to Ottilie, with Eduard claiming it would be in her interest to stay with them, and Charlotte seeing through his dishonesty. Instead Eduard leaves, having given Charlotte an undertaking that he will have no contact with Ottilie so long as she remains at the estate. Eduard wishes for a divorce but Charlotte writes to him that she sees hope for their marriage. In despair Eduard decides to risk his life by entering military service. Charlotte tells Ottilie none of this.

The first half of Part II moves slowly, interrupted by extracts from Ottilie's 'diary', through which a red thread of 'love and devotion' runs, according to the narrator.[246] Above all the diary represents Ottilie's preternatural receptivity. Luciane visits the estate and a social whirlwind ensues. Charlotte gives birth to a son, Otto, the original name of both Eduard and his friend the Captain. Ottilie takes care of the baby. The arrival of an aristocratic English guest and his account of his rootless life make Ottilie vow to herself to bring Charlotte and Eduard together again. The English Lord's companion discovers what may be a rich seam of coal on the estate, its location unwittingly indicated to him by Ottilie. Despite the Lord's scepticism, the companion proceeds to test whether Ottilie has sensitivity to metals, which she does indeed seem to possess. Eduard's military campaign has ended with victory and honours. The

Captain, now a Major, tries unsuccessfully to persuade Eduard to abandon his hopes for Ottilie and to return to married life with Charlotte. In response, Eduard persuades the Major that he should consider marrying Charlotte. To present this plan to Charlotte, the two men travel to a village next to the estate. The Major goes to the estate but finds Charlotte away on a visit. Eduard is too impatient to wait and secretly enters the park, where he finds Ottilie by the lake, where they embrace and kiss. Ottilie decides to row back across the lake, but in her haste she drops baby Otto in the water and he drowns. The Major arrives and reveals his and Eduard's plan to Charlotte. Charlotte agrees to a divorce, blaming herself for causing her son's death by not agreeing sooner. When the Major asks her if he can hope for her hand, she neither consents nor refuses. Ottilie however vows never to marry Eduard and threatens to drown herself if Charlotte agrees to the divorce. Ottilie reveals to Charlotte that she would like to teach at the boarding school and Charlotte agrees, on the condition that Ottilie commit to never see Eduard again. Eduard attempts to intercept Ottilie at the inn where she is staying over, and while he waits for her he writes her a note asking her to accept a meeting with him and not to go to the boarding school. But before she can see the letter, they meet. He gets her to read the letter, but on doing so she makes a gesture that seems to decline his request. The next morning, again silently, she asks to be taken back to the estate. On arrival there with Eduard, Ottilie presses his and Charlotte's hands together. Eduard seems deranged, insisting that Charlotte marry the Major, and she agrees, on condition that Ottilie agrees to marry Eduard. Ottilie, still silent and now refusing food, writes a letter to her friends begging that they have patience with her. One evening the couples' friend and local fixer Mittler is discoursing to Charlotte and the Major on the Ten Commandments; Ottilie enters the room just as Mittler comes to the Seventh Commandment on adultery. The maid Nanny finds Ottilie near to death in her room. Having secured Eduard's commitment to live, Ottilie dies. Eduard starves himself to death, admitting that he is merely mimicking Ottilie and does not have the 'genius' to be a true martyr.[247] Charlotte suspects suicide, but is persuaded that Eduard's death surprised him. He is buried next to Ottilie.

Not for the first time, some of Goethe's readers were outraged at the novel's flagrant breach of norms concerning marriage and adultery. In conversation with Riemer, Goethe acidly retorted that morality does triumph in the novel because 'Ottilie must starve to death and Eduard likewise, after they have given free rein to their inclinations'.[248] The comment was as glib and unworthy of the novel's richness as were the accusations against it, and no doubt that was

Goethe's point. To judge a novel in moral terms was to apply a false standard. The complexity of the narrative and the characters' relations to one another bring into doubt any straightforward view of marriage. At several points the novel does seem to take a stand on the question of marriage. In doing so, it reflects trends of the day, for instance the liberal attitudes to marriage of the young Romantic circle in Jena, as idealized in Friedrich Schlegel's scandalous novel *Lucinde*—scandalous because at the time of its publication Schlegel was living openly with the recently divorced Dorothea Veit. (Goethe did not altogether disapprove of the younger generation's liaisons. In 1803 he used his influence in Weimar to expedite the divorce of Caroline and August Wilhelm Schlegel, so that she could marry Schelling, with whom she had been living adulterously since 1800.) To some extent Goethe's novel shares the view of an aphorism by Friedrich Schlegel: 'That which people term a happy marriage is to love what a correct poem is to improvised song'.[249] In the figure of Mittler—he is a staunch defender of the traditional view of marriage, but also an unsympathetic meddler and a cause of damage—the novel seems to reject the traditional view.[250] As for the four main characters, they profess to treat marriage as a solemn institution, otherwise they would not go through such contortions to ensure that their marital status reflected their affections. Nor do they commit adultery in the literal sense. (Boyle has suggested that the very terse narration of the Captain's carrying Charlotte from the stranded boat might conceal an act of sexual intercourse, but there is scant support for such a reading.)[251] However, Ottilie eventually abandons these attempts to make marriage reflect affections, not because she has been persuaded by Mittler's moralizing on adultery, but because she is appalled by Eduard's failure to keep his word to Charlotte. What value could there be in making a contract with a man who is so quick to break his word? Ottilie's decision has more to do with moral questions of good faith and constancy than with the question whether marriage is a natural state or not. The theoretical question of marriage is thus undercut by the narrative and becomes less and less relevant. It is not at all clear how we are supposed to judge the suggestion, reported by the Count, that marriages should be limited to a five-year term, whereupon they may be renewed or dissolved. On the one hand, the proposal does recognise that feelings change and marriage should change to keep pace with them. On the other hand, the fixed five-year term is artificial and only half serious. It reads like a parody of liberal Romantic thinking about marriage.

For all the novel's equivocation concerning theories of marriage, the fate of actual marriages cannot help but force the theoretical question on the reader. At first, Charlotte and Eduard's marriage seems to be grounded in affection and nature. It is a union of a man and woman who were once young lovers but were unnaturally forced into unloving marriages. However, doubts soon emerge as to whether their marriage is natural after all. On finding one another again, they were no longer the young lovers they had once been, and though Eduard was keen to marry, Charlotte was less sure, precisely because of the passage of time. Indeed, before they were reunited, Charlotte had unsuccessfully tried to interest Eduard in marrying Ottilie. In Charlotte's mind, marriage to the wealthy aristocrat Eduard would have been an 'excellent match' in social terms for the parentless and displaced Ottilie.[252] The narrator does not say explicitly what Charlotte thought Eduard would stand to gain by marrying Ottilie, but the reader can infer Charlotte's thought process from what the narrator says about her marriage to Eduard. Once reunited, Charlotte and Eduard felt no special need to marry and at first cohabited 'undisturbed' for a time[253] until Eduard insisted on marriage. Charlotte was reluctant, but she could not refuse for long what the impulsive and overbearing Eduard 'seemed to think [his] only hope of happiness'.[254] Her reluctance stemmed from an anxiety that women age faster than men. Instead of marrying Eduard, she had been ready to let nature take its course even if Eduard eventually lost interest in her and moved on to a younger woman. At first this seems a remote possibility until it actually happens and Eduard falls in love with Ottilie. Charlotte's attitude to marriage explains why she had previously thought Ottilie a good match for Eduard. He would do better marrying a young woman than one of his own more advanced years. Perhaps Charlotte's theory of marriage should be consigned to the same bizarre class of theories as the Count's. And yet it contains a prophetic truth: Charlotte and Eduard's marriage does become an impediment to the natural course of love and desire. All of this serves to remind the reader—or at least the reader who is able to connect the novel with Goethe's views on the relation between scientific theorizing and empirical observation—that theorizing is necessary, but should be allowed to evolve gently out of the phenomena.

The Elective Affinities is as much concerned with science as it is with marriage, and the two discourses run along parallel lines. One small detail illustrates this. According to the Count's friend's view, marriage vows ought to be renewed every five years, because our affections can change quickly. We should respond to our mutable world by changing our arrangements. By contrast, Eduard, in a similar formulation, expresses the opposite view. The Captain admits that he had learned Bergman's theory ten years ago and it may now be out of date. In reality, by 1809 it was. Bergman's theory had been overtaken by the more quantitative approach of Claude Louis Berthollet's *Studies in the*

Laws of Affinity (1801).²⁵⁵ In response, Eduard expresses his annoyance at the need to relearn what he thought he knew:

> 'It is a bad business', Eduard cried, 'that we cannot nowadays learn anything that will last a lifetime. Our forefathers stuck to the teaching they were given when they were young, but we have to unlearn everything every five years if we are not to go completely out of fashion'.²⁵⁶

In a novel that takes so much care over fine detail, it is surely significant that in both cases—the Count's friend's theory about marriage and Eduard's annoyance about scientific progress—a five-year period is mentioned. Eduard's resistance to change thus represents the conservative counterpart to the Count's embracing it. More generally, the significance of the discussion of Bergman's theory is what it says about our attitudes to knowledge in a complex and mutable world. The same is true of the novel's concern with science more widely. The novel is less interested in the substance of science than in how we react and adapt to the unavoidable fact that scientific truth changes. The novel reflects the full range of questions Goethe had grappled with since becoming interested in the science of colour: the proper method for conducting science, the meaning and conduct of experiments, the need for and risks of theorizing, the nature of scientific language and symbols, the existence of a variety of *Vorstellunsgarten*, the newly emergent areas of science championed by Goethe's friends the *Naturphilosophen*, and—most important of all—the fact that science has a history. This is not obvious at first sight. The novel's title and the discussion of Bergman's theory in Chapter 4 of Part I suggest that the theory of elective affinities will serve as a model for understanding human behaviour. The theory of elective affinities seems to express a paradox or irony, as Goethe would put it: we are both free to choose and compelled by our character. Much of the action of the novel can certainly be read in this way. What we think of as the characters' free choice may also be an expression of their 'certainly modifiable but ultimately unalterable nature', as he put it in the essay on Newton's personality. Kantian reason might require us to think of ourselves as free, but moral freedom is also just a *Vorstellungsart*—an alternative way of describing what would have happened anyway. However, it turns out that the chemical discussion that leads the reader down this path is something of a bluff—one of Goethe's literary card tricks which directs the reader's attention away from a deeper and even more controversial truth. Much of the reception of the novel in the nineteenth and twentieth centuries fell for the trick. It wrongly assumed that the behaviour of the four main characters followed the pattern of chemical recombination set out in Bergman's theory, and that the theory of elective affinities was therefore a key to the novel's meaning. In fact, the significance of the chemical discussion is more interesting and modern than this. For one thing, the term *elective affinity* is a metaphor drawn from human affairs, a 'moral' metaphor, as Goethe would put it. Shortly before the novel was published, Goethe issued a brief advertisement for it:

> It might seem that his continuing work in physics has led the author to this strange title. He might seem to have noticed that ethical analogies are very often used in natural science, in order to bring closer something far removed from the sphere of human existence; and so he might, in a moral case, have led a chemical analogy back to its spiritual origin, and all the more so since everywhere there is after all only One Nature, and likewise the traces of gloomy passionate necessity continuously wind through the realm of cheery rational freedom and are, perhaps not even in this life, to be erased only by a higher hand.[257]

At first sight the meaning seems clear. The purpose of using Bergman's theory is to show that humans are not free. Yet the advertisement is full of hesitancy and equivocation. For one thing, while Bergman's theory might be an apt description of chemical bonds, it originally derives from the sphere of human affections. Are we to think that chemical compounds exhibit human free will? Of course not— nor should we think that Bergman's theory means that humans are unfree, or not in any straightforward sense. Shortly before sending Cotta the advertisement, Goethe made a similar observation to Riemer: 'the moral metaphors in the sciences (e.g., that of 'elective affinity' invented and used by the great Bergman) are intellectually richer and can be connected better to poetry, indeed to society, than any others'.[258] The metaphor in Bergman's theory forms a bridge between science and society, and the bridge is poetic in nature, but for that very reason it is an unsafe bridge. A more sober view of moral analogies in science appears in the first part of the *Theory of Colour*, where Goethe states that moral analogies are 'mere metaphors and in the end just dissolve into games of wit'.[259] Charlotte makes exactly this point during the discussion of Bergman's theory:

> These comparisons are very entertaining, everyone likes playing with analogies. But a human being is after all superior by several degrees to those natural substances, and having been rather lax in our use of the fine words 'choice' and 'elective affinity' we might do well to return to our inner selves and ask in all seriousness what the validity of such expressions in this context is.[260]

Analogies between chemical reactions and human relationships are entertaining enough, but they are self-evidently misleading. On the one hand then, *elective affinity* is a handy anthropomorphism:[261] it allows us to understand nature in the only way we can, as human beings. On the other hand, it is liable to be the source of self-deception, which is indeed how things play out in the novel.

As Jeremy Adler has shown,[262] a close examination of the chemical discussion in the novel confirms the need for caution. Eduard proposes that a reaction will take place between two compounds, Charlotte–Eduard and the Captain–Ottilie, resulting in two new compounds: Charlotte–Ottilie and Eduard–the Captain. Represented graphically, the reaction involves the elements switching positions diagonally or 'crosswise',[263] as the Captain puts it.

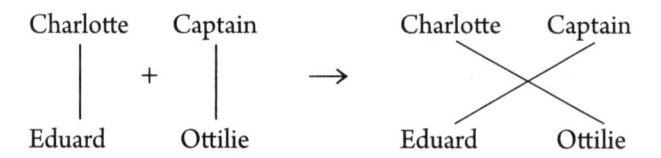

$$
\begin{array}{cc} \text{Charlotte} & \text{Captain} \\ | \quad + \quad | \\ \text{Eduard} & \text{Ottilie} \end{array} \longrightarrow \begin{array}{cc} \text{Charlotte} & \text{Captain} \\ \times \\ \text{Eduard} & \text{Ottilie} \end{array}
$$

However, the starting position posited by Eduard misrepresents the actual state of their relationships, for there is no preexisting bond between the Captain and Ottilie. A more accurate representation of the reaction would be that an initial bond between Charlotte and Eduard is dissolved by the arrival of the Captain, resulting in a new bond between Eduard and the Captain:

$$
\begin{array}{c} \text{Charlotte} \\ | \quad + \text{ Captain} \\ \text{Eduard} \end{array} \longrightarrow \begin{array}{c} \text{Captain} \\ \text{Charlotte} + \quad | \\ \text{Eduard} \end{array}
$$

The arrival of Ottilie results in Charlotte now pairing with her, so that the 'compounds' are now Charlotte–Ottilie and Eduard–the Captain. There now follows the 'crosswise' reaction between the two compounds:

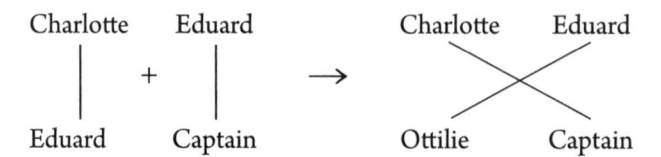

$$
\begin{array}{cc} \text{Charlotte} & \text{Eduard} \\ | \quad + \quad | \\ \text{Eduard} & \text{Captain} \end{array} \longrightarrow \begin{array}{cc} \text{Charlotte} & \text{Eduard} \\ \times \\ \text{Ottilie} & \text{Captain} \end{array}
$$

Thus, what the chemical model predicts, when applied to the relationships as they actually are and not as Eduard imagines them to be, is the new bonds of Charlotte–the Captain and Eduard–Ottilie, which is indeed what happens. If we ask why Eduard fails to apply the model correctly, one answer is that he is not really interested in the science, except insofar as he can use it to persuade Charlotte that the invitations to the Captain and Ottilie will not result in Charlotte being on her own. He uses the model to serve his interests. Two further details deserve mention. The Captain claims that he could illustrate the model better by showing his friends a range of different experiments, which he can only do once his supply of chemical compounds arrives: 'As soon as our chemistry cabinet arrives we shall show you various experiments which are very entertaining and which will give you a clearer idea than words, names, and technical terms may do'.[264] It is a typically Goethean idea. There should be a range of different experiments, not just one, and the experiments should be observed directly, and not through the veil of symbols, words, and formulae. A second easily overlooked detail is that the reaction discussed by the friends is described as 'crosswise'. A reader familiar with Goethe's work on colour might detect an allusion to Newton's *experimentum crucis*. What the friends have done, led by the impulsive Eduard, is commit the Newtonian error of drawing conclusions from a single experiment and of obscuring the phenomena behind formulae and theories.

The language of experimentation peppers the novel. This is more natural in German: the German verb *versuchen* is the equivalent of English 'try', but the noun *Versuch* means both 'attempt' and 'experiment'. During the chemical discussion, the Captain uses the noun *Versuch* in its scientific meaning; if he had his materials with him, he would show his friends the 'experiments' (*Versuche*). But even before the discussion of Bergman's theory, Charlotte and Eduard speak as if they are conducting an experiment. In breaking down Charlotte's resistance to inviting Ottilie and the Captain, Eduard exclaims: 'In God's name let us make a trial [*Versuch*] of it'.[265] When Charlotte accedes, she repeats the word *Versuch*. It is natural to conduct experiments, to try out scenarios whose consequences we cannot predict, but in doing so we risk making the errors that the friends make during their discussion of Bergman. We risk interpreting a single phenomenon as a guide to the future and so giving it a significance it should not have. We risk jumping to hasty conclusions or imagining that the consequences of our actions will be what we desire rather than what experience tells us. The problems of experimentation are spelt out again in Part II of the novel where, instead of looking back to a theory that may now be out of date, as the Captain admits Bergman's theory might be,[266] Goethe gives his readers a glimpse of what might be the science of the future. In late March 1808, as he was about to start work on the novel in earnest, Goethe read Johann Wilhelm Ritter's work on the influence of geomagnetism on natural organisms, or 'Siderism' as Ritter termed it. Ritter believed that an ability to sense geomagnetism might explain water divining and other such phenomena. On 5 April Goethe discussed Ritter's work on 'Siderism, dowsing rods, and other things' with the physicist Seebeck.[267] Either Goethe or Seebeck or both were sceptical, for in his diary the next day he recorded another conversation with Seebeck on 'Galvanism, mysticism, and the like'.[268] And again in August he recorded a 'conversation about magnetism and the derivation of miracles from known or misunderstood, half-known phenomena'.[269] The novel is equivocal on the subject of Siderism. Late in the novel an English Lord visits the estate along with a companion who practises Ritter's Siderism. The Lord's companion is described as 'a sensible, tranquil, and observant man'[270] though the Lord is sceptical about his friend's beliefs. The companion hears from Ottilie that there is one path through the grounds that she avoids, since a particular spot on the path always causes her to feel a shiver and triggers a habitual ache on her left side of her head. He claims to have seen clear evidence of a seam of coal at this spot on the path—how he has done so is not explained—and wants to test Ottilie for her divining abilities. The test consists of the subject holding a thread from which a piece of special metallic mineral hangs. Charlotte tries the test first, and the thread does not move, but in Ottilie's hand the thread describes clear circles. The companion's 'delight and avidity were such that he would not cease and begged again and again for the experiments to be repeated and varied'.[271] He offers to cure Ottilie's headaches by a mysterious method about which the reader is told only that the companion's offer is 'well intentioned',[272] but that Charlotte, quickly realizing what the method is, becomes uneasy and brings the conversation to a close. Presumably the treatment involves passing of magnetized objects over the subject's body in order to bring its forces into alignment.[273] The narrator does not state why Charlotte is apprehensive. Perhaps she is aware of well-publicized anxiety that male practitioners of this art used it to seduce young women. (Franz Anton Mesmer, its first practitioner, was forced to leave Vienna in 1777 because of such suspicions, and the French Royal Academy's 1784 report into animal magnetism confirmed these alarms.) More importantly, the debate about animal magnetism reflects a divide in the German intellectual landscape after

Prussia's defeat at Jena-Auerstedt in 1806. Before 1806 most German scientists did not take animal magnetism seriously, but after Prussia's collapse some major figures in the Berlin medical establishment, including Hufeland and Reil, championed it. The popularity of animal magnetism was part of a wider shift in German public life away from the Enlightenment and towards *Naturphilosophie*, which became a strange bedfellow of German nationalist ideology—a grasping at miraculous remedies after Germany's collapse.[274] If there is any conclusion to draw from the novel's treatment of Siderism, either from the companion's enthusiasm about phenomena that are not yet understood or from the Captain's lecture on a science that may already be obsolete, it is that scientific knowledge is in motion, driven forward both by new discoveries and by our hopes and desires, for better or worse.

At the heart of the novel's treatment of science is the insight that the errors we make arise from 'the deeper, better part of human nature', as Goethe wrote to Schiller in 1798. We cannot help but use reason constitutively:

> Man must in practice always be constitutive and actually not be bothered about what could happen, but about what should happen. Now, the latter is always an idea, and man is concrete in a concrete situation; so it goes on and on in endless self-deception, in order to bestow the honour of an idea on concrete things etc.[275]

In thinking constitutively, we imagine that nature forms a unity, that the phenomena of nature must be interconnected. Human relationships must behave like chemical compounds. Geomagnetism must be detectable by human sensibility. Phenomena become symbols for one another. Scientific knowledge is symbolic knowledge, as Goethe told Riemer in 1805:

> All our knowledge is symbolic. One thing is the symbol for another: magnetic phenomena are the symbol of electrical ones, both the same thing and the symbol of the other thing. Likewise the colours [are] by virtue of their polarity symbolic for the poles of electricity and the magnet. And in this sense science is an *artificial* life, a marvellous confluence of fact, symbol and analogy.[276]

But being a symbol of a thing is not the same as being identical with a thing. Symbolic knowledge requires us to make comparisons, and the idea that nature is ultimately a unity can lead us to find comparisons where none exist. Symbolic knowledge carries risk. It gives our will a role in the production of knowledge. It may result in our ignoring facts in favour of desires and wishes.

If we ask why *The Elective Affinities* is so densely symbolic, then Goethe's concern with the symbolic nature of our knowledge is certainly one answer. Some of the novel's symbolism conveys knowledge, some does not. Of all the characters, Eduard is most guilty of the latter, for instance when he ascribes special significance to a group of plane trees he planted in his youth and a glass with his initials engraved on it. The glass is especially meaningful because the initials, E and O, can also stand for Eduard and Ottilie, and when the glass is tossed in the air at the topping-out ceremony for the new pavilion and caught by one of the crowd, Eduard interprets it as a sign that his relationship to Ottilie is unbreakable. *The Elective Affinities* is a story about how we ascribe meaning to things. The point is made eloquently by the Captain and Eduard during the discussion of Bergman's theory:

> 'It was an analogy which misled and confused you', said Eduard. 'All we are concerned with here is earths and minerals, but human beings are very narcissistic, they like to see themselves everywhere and be the foil for the rest of creation'.
>
> 'They do indeed!', said the Captain, and he continued: 'That is man's way with everything he encounters outside himself. He credits the minerals and the plants, the elements and the gods with his own wisdom and his own folly and with his will and whims'.[277]

People tend to interpret their lives in terms of a small number of easily grasped heuristics or rules of thumb. These include the assumption that the future will resemble those aspects of the past that are most present or meaningful to us, such as Eduard's plane trees and his glass. It is in the hope of returning to 'a past happiness' that Charlotte breaks her contract with Eduard and lets Ottilie leave the estate, with the result that Ottilie and Eduard meet. It is because they imagine they have returned to their former happiness that Charlotte, Eduard, and the Captain ignore Ottilie's deteriorating health. An image of the past is repeatedly imposed upon the present, finally with tragic results. Twice the narrator describes the will to return to a former situation as an illusion.[278] In the penultimate chapter, when Ottilie begins to look over Eduard's shoulder as he reads, as she had done on her first arrival at the estate, the narrator coolly observes that 'the disagreeable and uncomfortable feelings of their middle period had been entirely extinguished'.[279] As the novel approaches its tragic close, it becomes increasingly painful to read, because of the unbearable tension between the negligence of Charlotte, Eduard, and the Captain, and gravity of the situation developing around them.

The novel's social vision is also balanced between an obsolescent present and an uncertain future. Charlotte and Eduard's estate resembles one of the petty principalities of the eighteenth century, albeit on a smaller scale. It is, as the narrator, says 'a little world'.[280] The domain is ruled by aristocrats from their *Schloß*. It has a military and an administration (the Captain), a church, a legal branch (Mittler trained as a lawyer), a cultural sector, science and medicine, agriculture, and crafts- and tradespeople—in other words, all the features of an eighteenth-century German principality. Like the Duchy of Sachsen-Weimar, it has paths that need improving, areas that are agriculturally unproductive, and traditional features that need updating (the churchyard). In reality the traditional Germany of which the estate is a fictional microcosm was under threat. Many of the old principalities and ecclesiastical lands had been amalgamated into larger territories under the Imperial Recess of 1803 and the Confederation of the Rhine. Moreover, the novel has nothing to say about the German cities. Indeed, the political, economic, and social changes that gathered pace under Napoleon are almost entirely hidden from the reader's view. The novel is a microcosm of an increasingly obsolete German society whose continued existence requires artifice. The park overlooked by the *Schloß* is to be turned into a garden in the relaxed English style that became fashionable in Germany in the third quarter of the eighteenth century. The estate's village is to be incorporated into the park and made a picturesque feature of it, to which end it must be tidied up along the lines of the 'Swiss neatness and cleanliness' that Goethe so admired.[281] The purpose of all this work is aesthetic, not social or economic. There is little thought of increasing the estate's agricultural productivity. The biggest project, the new pavilion, is to serve the purposes of pleasure. Flowers are grown for decoration. The paths are relaid to make leisure walking more pleasurable. The functions of the house are improved with beauty and the safety of its occupants and guests in mind. The old crockery with its poisonous lead glaze is replaced, the apothecary is replenished, and a surgeon is employed. The church's cemetery is levelled and turned into a garden. The whole estate is mapped and archived.[282] The word 'work' occurs frequently in the novel, but most often in the context of the embellishment of the estate. When an opportunity for economic exploitation presents itself—the seam of coal discovered by the English Lord's companion—its economic benefit is ignored. There is no thought to entering the modern industrial age of Prometheus. The estate is a model, a toy. The novel presents an image of the minor rural aristocracy adhering to its increasingly unproductive and financially unsustainable patterns of life, with no thought of modernizing itself.

The Romantic poet Achim von Arnim wrote to his future wife Bettina Brentano that Part I of the novel portrayed the 'boredom of unoccupied, inactive happiness'.[283] This is not entirely correct. The estate's inhabitants are in fact employed, even if only in embellishing the estate. Their productivity, such as it is, serves the purpose of decoration. Eduard plays the flute amateurishly, accompanied by Ottilie. Luciane acts out *tableaux vivants*. The Count is a connoisseur of music, Luciane's fiancé of architecture, and the English Lord of landscape gardening. The young architect paints the chapel ceiling. The four main characters are keen readers of all manner of material, some of which Ottilie copies into her notebooks.[284] The estate may be economically unproductive but it is culturally active, even if its productions are private entertainment by dilettantes. The novel presents a mixed picture of this dilettantism, as Goethe did in his discussions of dilettantism with Schiller in the late 1790s. There is a degree of affection as well as gentle mockery in the presentation of all this artistic and semi-artistic activity. However, in the absence of meaningful economic activity, the costs of all this aesthetic production must be met. In the novel's first sentence Eduard is described as a 'rich baron in his best years'. One can assume Charlotte is well off too, as her first husband is described as wealthy. However, they are not rich enough to fund their lifestyle and the works on the estate, for they are obliged to sell off a parcel of land. Perhaps this outlying estate that generated practically no income might have been improved to increase its productivity, but that would have required investment, and Charlotte and Eduard's wealth is devoted to providing entertainment and embellishment, not to generating wealth. Overall, the impression is given of a social milieu that is more interested in maintaining an aristocratic lifestyle than in retaining its social relevance and economic power.

The Elective Affinities does not depart from Goethe's long-held view of the role of the aristocracy in Germany. Charlotte and Eduard's isolated and economically weakened estate is just one possible form of aristocratic life—a cultured dilettantism that has precipitated the estate's decline into social and economic insignificance. In the *Apprenticeship* Goethe had presented the more optimistic prospect of a progressive and economically active alliance between the aristocracy and the bourgeoisie. And even within *The Elective Affinities* there are nuances among the foursome of main characters. Ottilie embodies an ethic of service which gives her a steadily increasing role in running the estate. The idea of service was central to Goethe's view of his first decade in Weimar. He had proved himself fit for government by serving the people, unlike the French revolutionaries who had no experience of service. Ottilie's ethic of service also comes with a habit of subservience, which has conservative political implications. Charlotte takes exception to Ottilie's overly servile habit of always bending down to pick up anything anyone has dropped. In reply Ottilie explains how she had been affected by the story of Charles I standing before his 'so-called' judges and having to humiliate himself by bending down to pick up the knob of his cane. (The word 'so-called' is a detail that hints rather obviously at promonarchist sentiment.)[285] Shortly after this passage, Eduard explains to the Captain that he prefers to avoid dealing with burghers and peasants unless he can give them direct orders. The Captain replies in the manner of an eighteenth-century absolutist government minister: 'Anything which is really for the common good will be done by the unrestricted exercise of sovereign power, or not at all'.[286] The Captain is a member of the military-administrative elite[287] that was becoming increasingly prominent under Napoleon and was able to sell its services to any administration. His comment to Eduard shows his awareness that his administrative skills will be all the more effective if he serves an administration with an all-powerful executive function.

Goethe still believed, as he had in the 1790s, that the aristocracy must validate itself anew through economic activity and service to society. By contrast, in his portrayal of Charlotte and Eduard's estate he reflected nostalgically and ironically on a world that Napoleon threatened to sweep away. As he explained to Riemer, the novel represented the 'condition of the Germans before the invasion of the French', a condition in which 'each individual could develop in its own way'.[288] It is true that political questions are marginal to the story of *The Elective Affinities*. There is a hint that the novel takes place during the Napoleonic Wars: Eduard decides to enlist 'with a commander of whom he could say: under his leadership death is likely and victory certain'—manifestly Napoleon himself.[289] It is tempting to take this as an allusion to the earth-shattering events of 1806 and after, and to read the absence of any explicit awareness of them on the part of the characters as evidence of the characters' blindness to the world around them. Indeed, Eduard himself offers a commentary on this blindness: '"What strange creatures we are," said Eduard with a smile. "As though by removing the thing that worries us out of our sight we could thereby be rid of it"'.[290] There is of course good reason to ignore politics, if one is powerless to affect it, and in this regard the novel's characters share the predicament of Weimar after 1806. Perhaps the most apt commentary on the place of politics in the novel is a letter Goethe wrote to Cotta in October 1807. He was alarmed that Cotta's journals were publishing opinions on the Duchy's membership of the Confederation of the Rhine. He begged Cotta, not for the first time, not to publish these voices, hinting that his future relationship with Cotta might depend on Cotta's compliance:

> Whereas on the aesthetic side I am happy to impart to you what we have and what we produce, and in addition some material will follow on other public matters, I must once more expressly beg you to turn away from your pages anything that relates to our political existence and does not come from me.
> We have never been politically significant.
> Our significance consisted entirely in a promotion of the arts and sciences that was out of all proportion to our powers. In other respects we are now very insignificant and more so than before. So for as long as the situation of all Germany is not settled, all the states, and especially the smaller ones, have grounds to wish that they be ignored, and that absurd reports invented and spread by the disquiet of unpaid novelists or by their idleness and ill will should not be picked up by such organs with which one is on good terms and which one is oneself minded to support. Forgive me for mentioning this point again. It is a more important matter now than ever.[291]

In times of war, a state whose cultural prominence dwarfs its political power risks attracting the unwanted attention of its more powerful neighbours. This had long been one of the fates that threatened Weimar, as Goethe well knew, and even more so now under Napoleon than in the period of Austro-Prussian dualism of the 1770s and '80s and the Revolutionary wars of the '90s. Among the many things Goethe put into the novel was an image of Weimar's political and economic weakness, as refracted through the medium of Charlotte and Eduard's estate, and a gently satirized image of its cultural importance, in the form of aristocratic dilettantism. Still, the role of politics in the novel should not be overstated. Its scope is much broader than politics, and what it has to say about science is more important. If Goethe used the novel to reflect on the powerlessness of Germany's smaller states, more salient are his (again ironic) reflections on modernity in general. And since, as Goethe concluded of Newton, irony consists in holding two contradictory views at the same time, then the novel is certainly ironic.[292] For it expresses both a resignation at the old world being overtaken by the new, and a recognition that it is our duty to act as the midwives of modernity, in whatever ways we can.

―――――

Writing in 1811 to his old Frankfurt friend Klinger, Goethe spoke of overcoming his habitual dislike of revisiting the past: 'Until now it has been my habit, or bad habit, to eradicate rather than preserve the past. Now may the time of preservation dawn, even if it is too late'.[293] With *The Elective Affinities* finished, he began to think about writing his autobiography. He had many reasons to conquer his aversion, some more and some less decisive in shaping the autobiography's final form. Among the more decisive was his attempt to make sense of his work on colour. In 1800 he had made some notes on the history of his own optical researches, under the heading 'History of the Author's Work in this Field'.[294] In 1803, in a concerted effort to finish the theory of colour, he reviewed the mass of papers he had accumulated over the years. 'I stand high enough above it to view my past being and doing, historically, as the fate of a third person', he wrote to Schiller.[295] The process of 'bringing himself to mind historically', as he put it in the same letter, whilst it enabled him to overcome his aversion to autobiography, also forced upon him an awareness of the gap between past and present. Schiller's death in 1805 increased this sense of distance. It seemed that a curtain had come down between the present and the past, or perhaps a series of curtains, for Schiller's death was preceded by Herder's passing in 1803 and followed by the Dowager Duchess Anna Amalia's in 1807. With Herder, Schiller, and Anna Amalia gone, it felt like the end of the era of Weimar's greatness. In January 1806 he briefly considered editing Schiller's literary remains.[296] Instead, he began work on the edition of his own writings that he had contracted with Cotta, another act of preservation and a reminder of the strangeness of the past.[297] He wrote to Zelter in May 1807 that 'overall while editing my works, I have felt very vividly how alien these things have become to me, and indeed that I barely have any interest in them any longer'.[298]

The aftermath of the Battle of Jena-Auerstedt in October 1806 had threatened to destroy Goethe's papers, but it was not just his papers that were threatened. As Goethe observed in a review for the *JALZ* in 1806, the extraordinary recent events were causing the memory of what had happened thirty or forty years earlier to dim. The past needed to be recovered.[299] The main trigger for his decision to write an autobiography was the death of his mother in September 1808, with which a whole world of memories threatened to slip into oblivion. The private record of his childhood in Frankfurt would vanish just like the cultural and intellectual life of Late Enlightenment Germany that was being obscured by Napoleon's remaking of Germany.[300] In the year after his mother's death, he began to make preparations. In October 1809, he wrote a first set of notes, to which he added steadily as the research and writing proceeded.[301] A schematic plan was written in Carlsbad in May 1810.[302] That July he read Voltaire's letters of 1755,[303] the year of the Lisbon earthquake, in order to remind himself of the shock the earthquake caused to the European mind. That autumn he received a set of his mother's anecdotes from Bettina Brentano in Frankfurt. From spring 1811, he wrote almost without interruption for two years. The autobiography appeared in three parts in 1811, 1812, and 1814—the last part delayed by the military campaigns of 1813 and 1814. The three parts covered the period from Goethe's birth up to the publication of *Clavigo* in summer 1774. A planned fourth part, which was to cover his move to Weimar in 1775, was postponed. If he were to proceed beyond 1774, he risked offending acquaintances who were still alive, notably Lili von Türckheim (née Schönemann). And whereas he had originally hoped that the autobiography would reach beyond 1775 and into his Weimar years, he must have realized by 1814, in his mid-sixties, that he would be unlikely to finish such a massive work. The first three parts, up to 1774, already totalled over 1,600 pages in the first edition published by Cotta. In addition, the years after 1775 involved even greater sensitivities of a personal, social, and political nature. The result was that the volumes published by 1814 ended with Goethe's literary breakthrough in 1773 and 1774, and so the story culminated and had its very purpose in his emergence as the liberator of German literature, the author of *Götz* and *Werther*. Much of Goethe's research for the autobiography was intended to explain this breakthrough. In the first place, he had to reconstruct the social world of mid-century Frankfurt and the German cultural and intellectual scene of the 1760s and '70s, against which the young poet reacted. By the standards of eighteenth-century autobiography, his research was remarkably systematic, even if it was limited to the sources he could lay his hands on: the personal letters and diaries that had escaped his earlier burnings, papers recovered from the Three Lyres, books from his father's library, and above all the Ducal library in Weimar. He paid particular attention to the writers who had influenced him in the early 1770s. He reread Goldsmith's *The Vicar of Wakefield* (1766) and 'The Deserted Village' (1770), Prévost's *Manon Lescaut*, and of course Spinoza's *Ethics*. Even with its gaps and biases, there is something encyclopaedic about the breadth of his depiction of the world he grew up in.[304]

However, among all the impulses and sources that fed into the autobiography, one stands out. It is signalled at a significant moment more or less halfway through the second of the three parts. Reflecting on his discovery that he was indeed a poet, Goethe comments that his peculiar talent derived from a compulsion to transform his responses to the world into poetry. It was a way to make sense of things outside him and in doing so to find some measure of mental equilibrium—a necessity for an unstable young man who tended to lurch from one extreme to the other. He concludes the passage by stating that the purpose of the autobiography is to supplement his poetic works:

> And so began that tendency which throughout my life I have never overcome, namely to transform whatever gladdened or tormented me, or otherwise occupied my mind, into an image, a poem, and to come to terms with myself by doing this, so that I could both refine my conceptions of external things and calm myself inwardly in regard to them. It is likely that no one needed this talent more than I, since my nature kept propelling me from one extreme to the other. Therefore all my published works are but fragments of a great confession, which this little book is a bold attempt to complete.[305]

This passage has been the subject of much sterile debate between advocates of biographical readings of Goethe's poetry and their opponents, with the result that its real meaning is often overlooked. It is a platitude that poetry occupies a space between the poet's sensibility and the external world.[306] That is not what is interesting about the passage. Goethe's experience of editing his writings for the Cotta edition of 1806–1808 was one of bafflement. He knew that his writings related to historical realities, but he could no longer recall those realities or how he had reacted to them at the time. The autobiography was an attempt to make good that deficit. In that sense, the autobiography was a supplement to his earlier writings, as presented in the new Cotta edition. It filled in the gaps around them, so to speak. But because the autobiographical supplement was written decades later, it could only be a fictional reconstruction, not a factual record. (Goethe was in any case sceptical about historians' claims to objectivity, as he had told Luden at some length in 1806.)[307] The autobiography was a precarious venture, which despite its huge bulk deserved, Goethe thought, to be called a 'little book'. This is the more interesting sense in which his poems are the fragments of a great confession. By 'a great confession' Goethe meant his autobiography, which, like the poems, was an attempt to bring out the symbolic truth of his character and its relation to history. And like the poems, the autobiography must be in large part fictional, not least because the veil that the passage of time had drawn over his past meant that there could be no easy distinction between fiction and truth. It was not a simple matter of the autobiography supplying the truth in between the fiction of his poetry. Indeed the very fictional nature of the autobiography made it an appropriate, if problematic, supplement to the twelve volumes of the new Cotta edition. Consistently in his diaries and letters Goethe referred to the autobiography as a fiction. It was the 'fairy tale of my life',[308] 'my biographical poem',[309] 'my biographical jokes',[310] 'my poetic truth',[311] 'the three volumes of my life-poem, or if you will my poet's life'.[312] The title he actually chose was 'From my Life. Truth and Poetry' ('Aus meinem Leben. Wahrheit und Dichtung'), which he soon rejected, however, because the juxtaposition of two hard *d*s sounded ugly, he told Riemer in October 1811.[313] Instead he decided on *Poetry and Truth* (*Dichtung und Wahrheit*). The title was potentially misleading, probably intentionally so. It seemed to point to an all-too-obvious distinction between poetic fiction and biographical truth, or at least it did if the 'and' was understood as connecting two contrasting entities. But *and* can also express identity, and that is how it should be understood here. The poetry is truth and the truth is poetry. The whole is a symbolic truth. The autobiography was merely the results of his life, but the truth they expressed was a general, symbolic one, which the autobiographical facts merely served to confirm. The title *Poetry and Truth*—or *Truth and Poetry* as Goethe later persisted in naming it[314]—signified this higher tendency. The facts only had value insofar as they meant something.[315] The main impulse for *Poetry and Truth* was the need to embed the writings of the new Cotta edition in a greater and symbolic whole.

The autobiography's symbolic truth consisted in a view of the poet's response to the historical circumstances into which fate had cast him, or indeed the response to history of any outstanding individual. Goethe addressed the question of his own relation to history in the first two paragraphs of *Poetry and Truth*'s first chapter, albeit with a playfulness and irony that would characterize the whole work:

> It was on the 28th of August, 1749, at the stroke of twelve noon, that I came into the world in Frankfurt on the Main. The constellation was auspicious: the Sun was in Virgo and at its culmination for the day. Jupiter and Venus looked amicably upon it, and Mercury was not hostile. Saturn and Mars maintained indifference. Only the Moon, just then becoming full, was in a position to exert adverse force, because its planetary hour had begun. It did, indeed, resist my birth, which did not take place until this hour had passed.
>
> These good aspects, which astrologers in later years taught me to value very highly, were probably responsible for my survival, for the midwife was so unskilled that I was brought into the world as good as dead, and only with great difficulty could I be made to open my eyes and see the light. It was a harrowing experience for my family, but at least the townspeople had some benefit from it, inasmuch as my grandfather, Johann Wolfgang Textor,

who was chief magistrate, was moved by this to appoint an official birth assistant and to introduce, or reintroduce, the instruction of midwives. That was probably a fortunate thing for many a child thereafter.[316]

The positive birth sign stands for Goethe's good fortune in being born with a strong character. In this sense, astrology is a handy symbol. However, the reader may feel that the neatness strains credibility. The time of Goethe's birth at exactly twelve noon is too tidy to be true (of course it was not) and the use of astrology seems incredible, coming from a careful scientific empiricist. In this second sense then, the handy symbolism emphasizes the fictional nature of the autobiography. All autobiography is (or should be) symbolic in a higher sense. The truth is that the human character is irreducible and mysterious. In this respect, *Poetry and Truth* is entirely different from its most important predecessor, Rousseau's *Confessions*. Rousseau claimed he was providing an exhaustive and meticulous analysis of how his childhood shaped his adult character, with all its neuroses and paranoia. The method was empirical. His adult character was the sum of his childhood experiences. The *Confessions* was an attempt at maximum transparency.[317] Although Goethe's autobiography does share some features with Rousseau's—Goethe did after all refer to his own as a 'confession'—the method is entirely different, in particular as regards the relation between nature and nurture. The difference can be illustrated by a false start he made during the early stages of work on *Poetry and Truth*. In an early draft, he represented his character in accordance with his theory of metamorphosis, a model of steady and predictable development. Subsequently he abandoned this approach in favour of a more mysterious model, of which the astrological symbolism is part. The change expressed his belief that character comprises a considerable element of irrationality,[318] in keeping with his definition of character in the essays on Winckelmann and Newton, where character is an irreducible and inexplicable urge of self-preservation and self-assertion. Accordingly, the relation between self and world changes. The metamorphosis model implied that the environment was on the whole a benign influence. But as is clear from the *Materials* and his attempts to understand the phenomenon of Napoleon, he no longer thought of human life in this way. For one thing, strong individuals were more likely to find themselves in opposition to their historical circumstances than in accord with them, as he had explained to Riemer in 1807 concerning the executions of Socrates and Jan Hus.[319] It was still possible for a strong individual to gain advantage from his historical circumstances, but any benefit was as likely to result from a relation of antagonism as from one of nurture. Sometimes the world might suddenly and inexplicably place an obstacle in the way of a person's development. Goethe formulated this model of sudden opposition in terms of a concept that he labelled 'the daemonic', without however explaining precisely what the concept meant.[320] The antagonistic factor in his birth sign is the moon, which 'exert[ed] adverse force'. The human counterpart to the moon is the midwife who through her ineptitude caused him to seem stillborn. However, her ineptitude is not lethal, for the innate strength of the newborn child wins through. Moreover, in response to the midwife's error, his grandfather institutes proper training for midwives, to the benefit of the city's newborns and mothers. In this way, the laconic and symbolic account of his birth establishes a pattern for the whole autobiography. Goethe is a paradigmatic strong individual who faces antagonistic historical circumstances, but instead of stifling his development, the circumstances are a stimulus, which bring about a renaissance of German culture. This is the symbolic meaning of the autobiography.

The anti-factual discourse of astrology is one of many manners and styles, some seemingly factual, others blatantly anti-factual, by means of which Goethe constructs the autobiography's symbolic and poetic meaning. The most prominent anti-factual discourse in the early books of *Poetry and Truth* is the fairy tale. In fact the word *fairy tale* (*Märchen*) occurs forty times in Parts I, II, and III. It was a term Goethe favoured when he wanted to indicate that the gap between fact and fiction was narrower than might be expected. The autobiography as a whole was the 'fairy tale of my life'[321]—a blend of fact and fiction conveying a higher symbolic meaning. Book 2 of Part I contains a fairy tale proper, under the title 'The New Paris, A Boy's Fairy Tale'. The tale relocates elements of the Greek myth of the Judgement of Paris to the Frankfurt of Goethe's youth and turns it into a parable of the young poet's quest to find his métier. Its hero is a narcissistic young man,[322] who finds himself in a magical garden, has to fulfil a number of tests, and is rewarded with the choice of three women. His immaturity prevents him from understanding what his task means, and instead he has a tantrum and breaks things. Ushered out of the garden, he sees three symbols inscribed on the outside wall. He desires to paint the figures 'as I saw them',[323] but when he returns, the images have changed. The tale illustrates that in order to find his way as a poet, he must somehow deal with and make productive the guilt arising from his selfishness and impulsiveness.

Guilt becomes a central theme, and the fictional styles of discourse become its literary vehicle. Feelings of self-recrimination are both enhanced and blunted by being transformed into fairy tales. Goethe evidently believed that the fictionalizing of guilt was both a survival mechanism and an act of poetic candour. By elevating guilt onto the poetic plane one could preserve it, whilst also drawing its poison. The most striking case of the fictionalizing of guilt is Goethe's retelling of his relationship with Friederike Brion in 1770–1771. There are practically no reliable sources of evidence for the relationship, and Goethe had little to go on besides his memory and the poems he had written and books he had read at the time. Those early lyric poems, especially the guilt-ridden 'Little Rose on the Heath', speak of his feelings of remorse for the damage he had done to Friederike. The account in *Poetry and Truth* associates his guilt with his self-fashioning as a poet. The whole episode is framed by his leaving behind his true self—a young enlightenment intellectual at university in Strasbourg and an opponent of established religion—and constructing a new fictional self that can enter into the rural idyll of Friederike's home village of Sessenheim. The key that allows him to enter her world is itself a fiction: Oliver Goldsmith's novel of rural England *The Vicar of Wakefield*. The narrative of the relationship with Friederike contains so many references to and citations from *The Vicar* as to suggest that Goethe reconstructed the autobiographical events almost entirely out of Goldsmith's novel.[324] The Sessenheim home, like Goldsmith's vicarage, becomes a moral and religious idyll, an atavistic recurrence of Old Testament patriarchy that confers religious certainty and confirms the triumph of divine good over evil. This is the idyll that the young Goethe comes close to destroying. His career as a poet and intellectual requires him to take a path of autonomy and self-assertion that will lead him to reject established religion and morality. Goldsmith's *Vicar* plays a complex dual role in this story of the poet discovering his mission. As well as providing the model for the Sessenheim idyll, *The Vicar* is the new gospel Goethe brings to the Brion household. His enthusiasm for Goldsmith's novel has recently been kindled by his new mentor Herder. At first he hesitates to share his enthusiasm with Friederike and her family. The parallels between Wakefield and Sessenheim are just too striking. His reservations are overcome when Friederike tells him she likes to read novels that contain characters like herself.[325] (Friederike's comment is modelled on a passage in *Werther* where Lotte says that she likes to read novels about people like herself. The allusion to *Werther* points towards Goethe as the author of a novel that will also prove destructive.) Goldsmith's novel is a mirror of manners, but the effect of sharing the novel with the Brions is to bring established religious, moral, and social norms into question. When he finally reads to the Brion family from *The Vicar*—in fact his hand is forced when his travelling companion Weyland unexpectedly produces the book—they see themselves reflected in it, as if 'in a mirror that was by no means disfiguring'.[326] The symbolic gift of the novel thus prefigures Goethe's role as Germany's national poet, a role into which he walks only half-consciously and which will result in his showing the Germans an image of themselves in *Götz* and *Werther*. But the effect of *The Vicar* on the Brions (and of *Götz* and *Werther* on the Germans) is by no means as simple as flattering their self-image. The poet, as both participant in and observer of the Sessenheim idyll, stands both inside and outside his audience's community. Outside of the seemingly secure idyll of rural and small-town Lutheranism, there is no moral code that can serve as a reliable guide for life. In the less stable reality of Enlightenment Germany, there is only the much weaker philosophical principle that we must do what feels appropriate to us. Goethe spells this out immediately after recounting how he read the novel to the Brions:

> As they progress in their cultural development, all people of good quality sense that they have a double role to play in the world, a real and an ideal one, and this feeling must be viewed as the basis of every noble impulse. We learn only too clearly the real part assigned us; as far as the other is concerned, we can seldom be certain of it. Let a person seek his higher purpose on earth or in heaven, in the present or the future; for all that, he will still remain exposed inwardly to eternal vacillation, and outwardly to ever-disturbing influences, until he resolves once and for all to declare that the right thing is whatever conforms to him.[327]

To construct a moral self based on ideals is to expose oneself to permanent instability, like Faust in his study alternating between optimism and scepticism. Our ideals continually run up against reality, and the only stable position is one that builds a more modest morality on the foundation of our actual character and place in the world. There may be some consolation here for the Brions in their traditional, firmly rooted idyll, but not for the modern and mobile Goethe. This is why Goldsmith's *Vicar* and 'Deserted Village' are dangerous gospels. They represent worlds like that of the Brions as belonging already to the past:

> 'The Deserted Village' by Goldsmith could not fail to have great appeal for everyone at that particular stage of cultural development and in that mental environment. Everything we liked to feast our eyes on, everything we loved, esteemed, and passionately looked for in the present, so as to participate in

it with youthful energy, was portrayed here, not as alive and active, but as a faded bygone existence.[328]

For Goethe's generation then, the Brions' world was fast becoming a lost paradise, a world left behind by modernity, and this further explains his reluctance to read Goldsmith to the Brions. The young Goethe in Sessenheim seems dimly aware that creation requires destruction. Making the new means unmaking the old. For a poet, whose task is to produce a world out of his imagination, the self-assertive process of creation involves a threat to reality. In Sessenheim, faced with a real Wakefield, he becomes culpable, like the destructive boy in 'The New Paris', 'Little Rose on the Heath', and the Gretchen episode in *Faust*. The power of the Sessenheim episode comes from Goethe revealing this as yet only dim awareness of his own destructive modernity. As the autobiography moves slowly forward to its culmination, the publication of *Götz* in 1773 and *Werther* in 1774, Goethe makes the reader increasingly aware that his emergence as Germany's national poet has resulted from a series of acts of self-assertion that both preserve his world and destroy it.

In the same way as in the *Materials*, the story Goethe tells in his autobiography of his emergence as Germany's national poet is a story of the individual's struggle with and against his historical circumstances. The main purpose of the autobiography, announced by Goethe in its foreword, was to set his development as a poet in its historical context:

> For the chief goal of biography appears to be this: to present the subject in his temporal circumstances, to show how these both hinder and help him, how he uses them to construct his view of man and the world, and how he, providing he is an artist, poet, or author, has reflected them again for others.[329]

Goethe's portrayal of his historical circumstances is unusual for its detail and breadth, and that is part of what makes the autobiography so fascinating. More interesting still is the way Goethe configures the relation between himself and his time. The more-or-less settled view of late eighteenth- and early nineteenth-century philosophical opinion, from a range of thinkers as diverse as Hume and Hegel, was that individuals soak up influences from their environment. The membrane that separates the self from society is highly permeable. That was the guiding principle of Rousseau's *Confessions*. Goethe's view is different. *Poetry and Truth* says very little about him absorbing the environment. The individuals it represents are more like discreet atoms. The external world acts on them chiefly as a brake or accelerator, which slows or speeds up the inner compulsion that drives them. That inner compulsion, however, retains its unique and irreducible character. If the individual 'creates a view of the world and humans' out of his circumstances, then that view is as likely to be formed by reacting against the culture of his day as from absorbing it. Thus the symbolic meaning of *Poetry and Truth* accords with Goethe's view that character was a largely unconscious and irreducible entity, especially in the case of a poet, in whom genius was an unconscious force. The symbolic meaning of his own career as a poet was the projection of his own individuality, at times fostered by circumstances and at times obstructed by them. A set of notes he made probably in the last year of his life captures the essence of the autobiography's argument:

> If I were to express what I have meant for the Germans in general and for young poets in particular, then I might well call myself their *liberator*; for they have learned from me that just as a human being lives from the inside outwards, so too the artist must exert influence from the inside outwards, insofar as, however he might conduct himself, he will only ever bring his own individuality to light.[330]

Or again as Riemer reported him saying in 1807, 'In all periods, it is only the individuals who have had an effect on science. Not the age'.[331] Thus the autobiography's unusually broad and detailed account of German culture in the middle of the eighteenth century was not intended to show how the young poet absorbed his environment. On the contrary, the environment either allowed him to develop unchecked or it obstructed his development and forced him to forge his own distinctive path. What helped him was as often as not having to find his way round obstacles.

As an account of the evolution of German ideas and culture and of Goethe's place in them, *Poetry and Truth* expresses a kind of dialectic. Goethe was familiar with the dialectical argument of Hegel's *Phenomenology of Spirit* (1807) and was on good terms with its author, even if he complained that Hegel was incapable of expressing himself clearly.[332] Like Hegel's *Phenomenology*, Goethe's autobiography is a story of reaction and counterreaction, of one age overcoming, denying, and preserving the last. As he put it in a letter to Buchholtz in February 1814, his autobiography showed 'how a successor period always seeks to suppress and negate its predecessor, instead of thanking it for stimulation, communication, and transmission'.[333] Like Hegel, Goethe has a dynamic and conflictual view of history. In his commentary on Diderot's *Essay on Painting* he observed that 'the most supreme effect of the spirit is to call forth spirit',[334] and that 'only in action and reaction do we find pleasure'.[335] Or again in the 1813 essay 'Shakespeare neverendingly': 'this is the quality of mind, that it constantly excites minds'.[336] The idea is expressed in Book 7 of *Poetry and Truth*:

> And that is what histories, and above all biographies, should be about, for people have enduring significance not for what they leave behind, but for the effects they have and the use they make of things and how they stimulate others to effect and make use.[337]

However, Goethe's dialectic is not Hegel's. Reaction and counterreaction are not a dialectic of ideas or thought-worlds, as in Hegel's view. Rather they are moments of the assertion of personal individuality. It is a dialectic of lived experience, not of reason. Hegel's notion that human actions embody a logical necessity was anathema to Goethe's naturalism. This is why Goethe's account of his intellectual environment in *Poetry and Truth*, rich and broad as it is, does not portray a battleground of ideas, a contest between religious, moral and aesthetic systems, or a conflict between different forms of consciousness and their objects, such as Hegel sets out in his *Phenomenology*. For Goethe, ideas are always subsidiary to individual persons and their needs. In January 1811, hoping to make sense of the history of eighteenth-century philosophy, he read the *Comparative History of Systems of Philosophy* (1804) by the French Kantian Joseph-Marie de Gérando, in which he found his individualistic view confirmed. There could never be any agreement on philosophical principles, because principles were only ever expressions of individual humans, as he wrote to Reinhard:

> In reading [de Gérando's] work I understood once more what the author clearly expressed: that the various modes of thought are grounded in the variety of humans, and for precisely this reason a consistency and uniformity of conviction is impossible.[338]

For this reason, Goethe could not agree with Hegel, even if he shared Hegel's political commitment to the state. It might be expected that Goethe would have aligned with the so-called 'Right Hegelians', who interpreted Hegel as arguing that the real can be reconciled with the ideal and that this reconciliation was to be found in the existing institutions of the modern state. The history of spirit culminated in institutions such as property, contract, law, marriage, and the church, which satisfied the demands of human self-consciousness.

However, Goethe's model of dialectic has nothing to do with politics in this sense, or at least not directly. There is a less obvious sense in which Goethe's dialectic is political. In Goethe's portrayal of German cultural history, the chief motive force behind change is intergenerational conflict, which is more psychological than rational. The course of history is not determined by a dialectic of reason. The argument of *Poetry and Truth* is of a piece with Goethe's practice since the French Revolution. It plays down the role of ideas in shaping human social and political life and instead emphasizes the role of character. For instance, where Goethe discusses philosophy in *Poetry and Truth*, he shows little interest in its intellectual content. The rise and fall of philosophies has little to do with their intrinsic qualities as philosophy, and much more to do with their ability to foster an active and productive life. He describes his generation's relief upon realizing that they could happily do without philosophy: 'Philosophy and its abstruse demands were put aside'.[339] Their loss of faith in Wolffianism is thus attributed partly to its abstruse nature and partly to the crushing, 'daemonic' effect of the Lisbon earthquake, but not to Wolffianism's flaws *qua* philosophy. Spinoza receives due credit, of course, albeit with reservations. Goethe stresses that his interpretation of Spinoza was idiosyncratic, and the effect of the *Ethics* on him was more emotional than intellectual:

> I could not possibly give an account of what I read out of this work, or into it. Let me just say, I found something in it to calm my emotions, and it seemed to open a broad, free view over the physical and moral world.[340]

He quotes his favourite Spinozan dictum—'he who loves God cannot strive that God should love him in return'[341]—but it serves as much as a warning against philosophy as an enticement to it.

The anti-rational tenor of *Poetry and Truth* was part of Goethe's broader reaction against the trends of the day: Catholicism in the arts, the blending of philosophy and poetry by the Romantics, the resurgence of the idea of Germany among nationalist opponents of Napoleon. *Poetry and Truth* was Goethe's attempt to put his own version of German cultural history into the public domain at a time when German cultural history was a subject of intense and prominent discussion, for instance, in the Romantic literary histories of the Schlegel brothers. The early stages of Goethe's work on *Poetry and Truth* coincided with the publication in 1809–1811 of August Wilhelm Schlegel's 1808 Vienna lectures *On Dramatic Art and Literature*. Schlegel's lectures were dismissive of European neoclassicism and perfunctory on eighteenth-century German drama, including Goethe's and Schiller's plays.[342] Although Schlegel praised Goethe's poems and prose, he did so while recruiting Goethe to Romanticism. For Schlegel, the period immediately preceding Goethe was something of a void.[343] Goethe shared some of Schlegel's negativity about the literature of the Enlightenment. The mid-century German literary landscape he describes in *Poetry and Truth* is on the whole rather drab.[344] The exceptions are, of course, Winckelmann, Lessing, and Wieland though even here the dynamics of cultural history are made to serve Goethe's overarching purpose of a psychological dialectic. As far as he can, Goethe represents his path out of this largely barren period of German culture as a personal odyssey.[345] He praises Lessing's *Minna von Barnhelm* as an 'unattainable model' of the art of dramatic exposition.[346] *Nathan the Wise*, the Laocoon essay, and the 'Hamburg Dramaturgy' receive honourable mentions. However, on the occasion of Lessing's visit to Leipzig for the Easter fair in 1768, the student Goethe is described as avoiding him out of youthful wilfulness, suggesting the young poet's half-conscious *agōn* with the established writer. The same pattern applies to Wieland. There is praise for Wieland's writings while Goethe's infamous skit 'Gods, Heroes, and Wieland' is characterized as a spontaneous reaction to Wieland's imagined character.

Most controversial of all, at the height of Napoleon's occupation of Germany, was the place of French culture in Goethe's early life. One element of Goethe's argument is that he and his generation liberated German culture from French tyranny and were thus implicitly a model for German nationalism under Napoleon. The trigger for his generation's reaction against France is not however the Frenchification of the German courts, which would have been the obvious way for Goethe to align himself with German nationalism in the 1810s, if he had wanted to do so. Instead he chose to situate his reaction against France in a more obscure context: the publication of Holbach's materialist *System of Nature or the Laws of the Physical and Moral World* during Goethe's studies in Strasbourg in 1770. The reaction against Holbach is presented as a liberation from French culture: 'So it was on the French border that we were suddenly rid and free of everything connected with the French.'[347] However, the reaction is as much against the dead hand of philosophy as against any specifically French form of culture. Elsewhere in *Poetry and Truth*, French culture is treated more positively. Goethe's father's unhappiness at the French occupation of Frankfurt in the Seven Years' War is seen as small-minded and resentful—a not-so-subtle dig at German nationalists under Napoleon.[348] By contrast, the head of the French occupying forces, Count Thoranc, assumes great importance in Goethe's cultural education by exciting Goethe's love of the theatre.[349]

The clear implication is that Frankfurt benefitted from the French occupation. Goethe's father's resistance is unmasked as the politics of resentment and empty sentiment, which fails to acknowledge the good that could be done with Thoranc's absolute executive power. So the effective French executive is contrasted with Frankfurt's ineffectual traditional republican government, which was only ever the expression of the commercial interests of Frankfurt's Lutheran leadership. As Goethe wrote to Zelter in 1805, 'the gentlemen of Frankfurt know the value of nothing but money'.[350] The account of the French occupation of Frankfurt conforms entirely to Goethe's attitude towards Napoleon's Confederation of the Rhine, in a manner that cannot have been intended otherwise than to aggravate German nationalists.[351]

At the end of 1812, after the publication of *Poetry and Truth*'s second part, Goethe mounted a more explicit attack on Romanticism and Catholicism in the arts. These twin trends amounted to an art of mere ideas, not an art of imaginative sensuous representation, he believed. In short, they were not art. The argument is made in two short, seemingly very different essays written in November and December 1812: 'Myron's Cow' and 'Era of Forced Talents'. At first sight, the former essay is a philological exercise: a reconstruction of Myron's now lost bronze sculpture of a heifer. The aim seems to be to reconstruct the sculpture on the evidence of a number of Roman epigrams that praise its verisimilitude. In fact, the epigrams say little about the form of the sculpture, and Goethe is surely right to argue that their fantastical descriptions of people mistaking the sculpture for a real cow are mere exercises in exaggeration.[352] What the epigrams do tell us is that the Greeks and Romans continued to admire the sculpture and that there must have been something exceptional about its composition. The obvious option for the artists would have been to compose a group consisting of a cow with a suckling calf,[353] and three of the epigrams support this conjecture. However, Goethe's discussion of the conjecture is only a preamble to the essay's main argument. The mother cow represents an activity to which humans can relate and it thus exemplifies a principle of Greek art, namely that art aims to elevate humans and make them godlike. This is an altogether higher aspiration than the modern tendency to represent God in human form:

> The Greeks' goal is to deify man, not to humanize gods. It is a theomorphism, not anthropomorphism! Furthermore, it is not the animal in man that is to be ennobled, but rather the human element in animals is to be

emphasized, so that we can delight in them in a higher artistic sense, just as we do with living animals which, following an irresistible instinct, we are fond of choosing as our companions and servants.[354]

In the version of the essay published in 1818, this passage is preceded by the unfinished sentence: 'But how weak, in comparison with such a grandiose concept, appears a Madonna and Child . . .'. In the original 1812 manuscript the comparison is fully spelt out. Modern representations of the Madonna and Child tend to 'debase' our sensuality, not ennoble it. The principles animating ancient art are altogether more noble than our modern Christian ideas of beauty, which tend to sacrifice sensuous beauty at the altar of a mere idea, an invisible God. The essay is another exploration of how the ideal can be achieved through sensuous means.

In the essay 'Era of Forced Talents', begun immediately after 'Myron's Cow' but never finished, Goethe presents an account of the consequences of taking the opposed course: seeking to represent a wholly nonsensuous entity. The specific target is contemporary German poetry in its Romantic and Christian expressions. The essay's argument is unusual, insofar as the two trends Goethe identifies as leading to this modern error were in some respects admirable and were the work of two of his most valued collaborators, Schiller and Johann Heinrich Voß. Schiller was a pioneer of a new high-concept, Kantian style that placed ideas at the heart of poetry. According to Schiller, the task of poetry was to embody 'an idea or concept', Goethe says,[355] which paved the way for the intellect to become more active in poetic creation, such that it 'could [. . .] imagine that it was making poetry'.[356] It is a dangerous approach, of course, for it invites the intellect to usurp the role of the imagination. Poetry is thereby instrumentalized as a medium for the presentation of concepts. The second trend was the improvement in understanding of poetic meter thanks to Voß, which led to the current popularity of complex and technically demanding Italian and Spanish forms such as *ottave rime* and the sonnet. The combination of these two trends, in themselves not without merit, has created the space for a new and altogether less healthy tendency: the debasing of poetry to mere rhymed philosophy. Combined with the emergence of a Christian trend in the visual arts, it threatens to ruin poetry.

At first Goethe was reluctant to accept that the tragedy of the Grande Armée in Russia at the end of 1812 and the allied victory at Leipzig in October 1813 signalled the end of the Napoleonic era. In the week following the battle he suffered the humiliation and expense of having twenty-four Austrian officers billeted with him for three days, including the Austrian commander Hieronymus Karl, Count of Colloredo-Mansfeld. On Colloredo's arrival, Goethe greeted him wearing both his Legion d'honneur and Order of St Anna. Wilhelm von Humboldt reported Colloredo's disgust on seeing Goethe wearing Napoleon's medal: 'Fie! How can a person wear something like that!' While Colloredo depleted his host's stock of food and wine, Goethe hid in the rear part of the house. The unsavoury atmosphere can hardly have failed to remind Goethe of his more considerate treatment by Napoleon's Marshals Ney, Lannes, and Augereau in the traumatic days following Jena-Auerstedt, as well as Thoranc's impeccable behaviour at the family home during the French occupation of Frankfurt. Unlike his father, however, Goethe grudgingly accommodated to the new circumstances. On the evening of Colloredo's departure Humboldt reported that Goethe was no longer wearing the Legion d'honneur.[357] At first he refused to contribute to the celebrations of victory over Napoleon. In December the historian Luden invited him to contribute to a new nationalist journal *Nemesis*, which he politely declined citing concerns over its editorial policy.[358] In private he expressed reluctance to be associated with a project that seemed unnecessarily aggressive towards the French and out of step with the official allied policy of clemency.[359] Nor did he celebrate the allies' occupation of Paris in April 1814. In his diary he noted 'news of the capture of Paris. Joyous gunfire all day'.[360] It was other people's joy. Two weeks later Charlotte von Stein could write to her son Fritz that Goethe 'does not seem to share our enthusiasm; one is not permitted to speak of political matters in his presence'.[361]

In the middle of May Goethe received an invitation from Iffland in Berlin to write a *Festspiel* in honour of the allied victory. It was to be performed on the allies' triumphal return from Paris. A week later, he sent Iffland an outline for the short play, though he admitted that the task had at first scared and only later excited him.[362] It is customary to read *The Awakening of Epimenides* as an expression of Goethe's guilt at failing to side with the national movement against Napoleon, and no doubt he did see Iffland's invitation as an opportunity to do public penance. However, the piece was more (and more ambivalent) than a simple shifting of position on the politics of the day, not least because of its use of an obscure myth and the antiquarianism of its style and meter. It was another *Pandora* though without that play's emotional power. As a celebration of Germany's liberation from Napoleon, it was a failure, and it is hard to see how Goethe could have thought it would succeed. He drew the outline of the plot from Diogenes Laërtius's *Lives of the Eminent Philosophers* together with elements from Plutarch's *Life of Solon*. According to Diogenes, the Cretan sage Epimenides was put to sleep for fifty-seven years and on awakening he found everything around him changed and another man in possession of his family's sheep. No doubt these two elements appealed to Goethe: Epimenides's reputation as a sage and his awakening to an utterly changed reality. In Goethe's version Epimenides is then put to sleep for a second spell, on the order of the gods, this time so as to shield him from the ill effects of war and tyranny. During his second sleep, three rival daemons representing war, cunning, and oppression drag his country down into chaos. Opposed to them are three female allegories representing the virtues of faith, love, and hope. The figures of faith and love are deceived and overpowered by the daemons. Only hope remains free. On waking, Epimenides laments the destruction and his having not shared his people's suffering through it, and yet at the same time his prophetic insight is confirmed by the gods. The piece ends with a celebration of the armies and their prince returning victorious from war.

The figure of Epimenides patently represents Goethe or more generally the spirit of German art as it ought to be: a visionary figure whose gaze is fixed on nature and other universals and overlooks his countrymen's immediate political concerns. In this light, *The Awakening of Epimenides* does indeed seem to be an act of self-criticism.[363] However, Epimenides's regret is a purely personal matter and it has no wider meaning for the nation. Indeed, the priests reassure him that his absence was necessary and beneficial. It has preserved his purity of feeling, and it is by virtue of that purity, untouched by war and chaos, that Epimenides will continue to think differently from the people.[364] Epimenides the prophet is blessed to be honoured in his own land, but is also at cross purposes with it. In this connection, it is important to note that according to Plutarch Epimenides was valued by the Athenian people, and his expertise in religion was of great help to Solon in his reform of the laws of Athens. Thus while Epimenides represents the apolitical nature of poetry, his wider vision also contributes to the rebirth of the state. In this sense, although the play seems at first sight to express Goethe's regret at his distance from the Germany of 1814, it also expresses his long-held political beliefs. The poet's refusal to think about the national politics of the present day is necessary in order to uphold a more universal political vision. This slippage between two ideas—poetry both as apolitical and as a deeper vision of a well-ordered society—is surely tactical, insofar as it allows Goethe to pay his dues to the national movement whilst retaining his own political vision. When Epimenides awakes to find chaos, he laments that there is 'no trace of art, of order not a trace!' ('Nicht Spur von Kunst, von Ordnung keine Spur!').[365] The spirits who bring him messages from the gods show him a representation in marble, a relic of the past that has escaped destruction and is therefore at one and the same time beyond history and historical in a universal sense. The marble sculpture represents the deeper political vision that Epimenides is to embody: a father sits in his throne-like armchair surrounded by family, servants, and domestic animals, enjoying a good meal and a rest.[366] The vision is of a patriarchal utopia, where the family clearly stands for the nation with the father-cum-prince at its head. The final chorus of *Epimenides* enacts the event for which the piece was commissioned: the triumphal entry of the victors into Berlin. It does so in a manner that confirms Goethe's adherence to the old ways. The chorus gives voice to the newly liberated German people, but again the politics they enunciate appeals to an older ideal of 'German freedom'. Credit for liberating the land is given to the prince, not the people. The new political order will be a reassertion of monarchy. The people will be 'free in their own way' ('nach eignem Sinne frei'),[367] which implies that local practices and traditions will have priority over abstract ideals of freedom. There is certainly no sign of freedom in the revolutionary or even the Napoleonic sense of universal human rights. That had only led to war and disorder. The finale thus envisages a future based on the prerevolutionary German system. Epimenides will be free to ponder the universals of science and art, while the Germans are bound into the local, paternalistic forms of government. And these two strands of German life, so the piece proposes, may be at odds with one another. Epimenides can express regret for his alienation from the people, but he is told clearly that it is in the nature of his free, stargazing intellect to be at odds with the people and their political lives. If *Epimenides* expresses Goethe's solitariness in 1814,[368] it also expresses his long-held belief in a German nation free in spirit but not in politics.

9

'What More Could Grandpa Want?'

WEIMAR, 1814–1825

GOETHE HAD mixed feelings about the defeat of Napoleon. The allied victory promised an end to the wars that had plagued Europe and caused instability in Germany since 1792. On the other hand, it was a victory for the German nationalists, whose (often liberal) politics Goethe disliked. Aside from any personal allegiance Goethe had to 'my Emperor', Napoleon had come closest to embodying his ideal of the prince: a victorious warlord as the supreme embodiment of law and untrammelled executive power. Another worry was the appearance of 'Asiatic' hordes among the Russian armies. Goethe first saw the Bashkir Cossacks in Dresden in April 1813, accompanied by a camel—'a true Asiatic hallmark', he wrote to Christiane.[1] It was less charming when on 6 November, three weeks after Napoleon's defeat at Leipzig, twelve Cossacks appeared outside the house on the Frauenplan expecting to be billeted. Goethe refused, which resulted in a standoff lasting two hours, until the Cossacks were accommodated elsewhere. Germans had become accustomed to seeing danger coming from the west, but now they would have to worry about a peril from the east, he told Luden shortly afterwards. The replacement of French officers by Bashkir Cossacks seemed a dubious exchange.[2] As it became clear that the Cossacks would not lay waste to the Duchy, anxiety turned to fascination. In January 1814 he attended Islamic prayers in the main assembly hall of Weimar's senior school. In earlier times such an event would have seemed so preposterous that 'one would not have permitted a prophet to utter' it, he wrote to Trebra; 'and yet it has happened, we were present at the Bashkir worship, saw their mullah, and welcomed their prince at the theatre'.[3] Some of

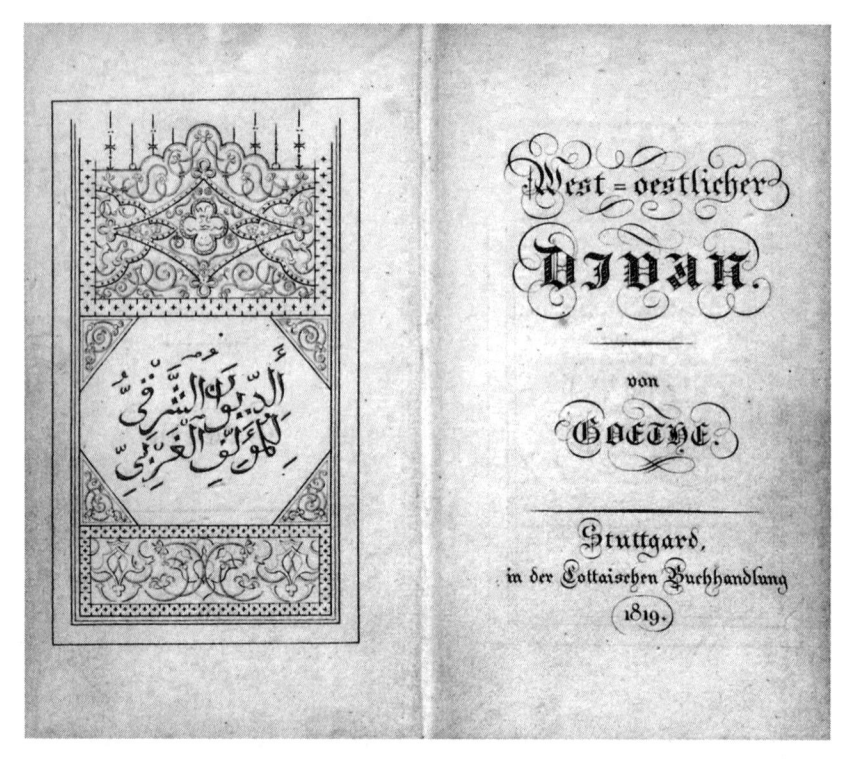

FIG. 22. Title page and frontispiece of Goethe's *West-Eastern Divan* (1819)

Weimar's 'religious ladies' even borrowed a translation of the Qur'an from the library.[4] During the next four years Goethe became an enthusiastic student of Islamic beliefs and cultures.

One benefit of the new peace was the ability to travel freely. With Napoleon now confined to the island of Elba (or so it seemed), in late July 1814 Goethe set off for a tour of the Rhine. In his luggage he carried the two volumes of Joseph von Hammer-Purgstall's translation of the fourteenth-century Persian poet Hafez. At the end of the first day's travel he noted in his diary 'Hafez. Glorious day'.[5] In the carriage he had written 'several poems to Hafez, most of them good', he wrote to Christiane.[6] The poems were written to but also in imitation of Hafez, in a double homage. By the end of July he had written enough poems in this new manner to think of them as a collection or *divân*, in Hafez's Persian.[7] In the winter he broadened his studies of Middle Eastern poetry by reading historical works by William Jones, Thomas Hyde, Thomas von Chabert, and Edward Scott Waring. By the end of 1814 there were thirty poems,[8] including one, 'Hegira', finished on Christmas Eve, which achieved the difficult task of summarizing in one coherent poetic argument across seven stanzas the themes of the whole *divân*, at least as Goethe understood it at that point.[9] The title 'Hegira'—the reference is to Mohammed's *hijrah* or flight from Mecca to Medina in 622 C.E., from which the start of the Islamic calendar is dated—stands for the poem and the whole *divân*.

Hegire

Nord und West und Süd zersplittern,
Throne bersten, Reiche zittern,
Flüchte du, im reinen Osten
Patriarchenluft zu kosten,
Unter Lieben, Trinken, Singen,
Soll dich Chisers Quell verjüngen.

Dort, im Reinen und im Rechten,
Will ich menschlichen Geschlechten
In des Ursprungs Tiefe dringen,
Wo sie noch von Gott empfingen
Himmelslehr' in Erdesprachen
Und sich nicht den Kopf zerbrachen.

Wo sie Väter hoch verehrten,
Jeden fremden Dienst verwehrten;
Will mich freun der Jugendschranke:
Glaube weit, eng der Gedanke,
Wie das Wort so wichtig dort war,
Weil es ein gesprochen Wort war.

Will mich unter Hirten mischen,
An Oasen mich erfrischen,
Wenn mit Karawanen wandle,
Schawl, Kaffee und Moschus handle.
Jeden Pfad will ich betreten
Von der Wüste zu den Städten.

Bösen Felsweg auf und nieder
Trösten Hafis deine Lieder,
Wenn der Führer mit Entzücken,

Von des Maultiers hohem Rücken,
Singt, die Sterne zu erwecken,
Und die Räuber zu erschrecken.

Will in Bädern und in Schenken
Heil'ger Hafis dein gedenken,
Wenn den Schleier Liebchen lüftet,
Schüttelnd Ambralocken düftet.
Ja des Dichters Liebeflüstern
Mache selbst die Huris lüstern.

Wolltet ihr ihm dies beneiden,
Oder etwa gar verleiden;
Wisset nur, daß Dichterworte
Um des Paradieses Pforte
Immer leise klopfend schweben,
Sich erbittend ew'ges Leben.[10]

Hegira

North and West and South splinter apart, / Thrones crack, empires tremble. / Flee now, you! in the pure East / To drink the air of patriarchs, / Amid loving, drinking, singing, / The spring of Chisr shall rejuvenate you.
There, in purity and justice, / I will delve into human races / To the very depths of their origins, / Where they still received from God / Heaven's lessons in earth's languages / And didn't torture their brains. Where they honoured fathers highly, / Warded off any foreign service; / I'll enjoy the limitations of youth: / Broad the faith, narrow the thought, / Just as the word was so weighty there, / Because it was a spoken word.
I'll mix with herdsmen, / Refresh myself at oases, / When I stroll with caravans, / Trade in shawls, coffee, musk. / Every path I'll tread, / From the desert to the cities.
Up and down frightening cliff paths, / Hafez, your songs will give comfort, / When the driver with delight, / On the mule's high back, / Sings to wake the stars / And terrify bandits.
In baths and inns I'll / Commemorate you, holy Hafez, / When my beloved waves her veil, / Makes fragrance waving her amber locks. /

Yes, the poet's whispering of love / Will make even the houris lecherous.
If you want to envy me this / Or even spoil it for me, / Just know this, that poets' words / Hover about the gates of paradise / Knocking softly, / Asking to be granted eternal life.

While superficially the *divân* poems present an image of the serenely aging poet luxuriating in Middle Eastern exoticism, they also have a political message. The first stanza of 'Hegira' focuses on Europe's political disintegration while overlooking Germany's liberation and reconstruction, and so presents a strikingly anti-nationalist perspective. Goethe wrote to Knebel in February 1815, referring to his work on the *divân* as a whole, that 'I bless my decision to make this *hegira*, which has distanced me from the times and my dear central Europe; this should be considered a great blessing from heaven which does not befall everyone'.[11] What is the poet of the *divân* escaping from, what exactly is collapsing, and whose thrones and empires we are to be alarmed about? The most obvious candidates in 1814 were Napoleon's empire and his puppet kingdoms. In other words, the poet turns his back on Europe *because* the Napoleonic order is ending. The poem's first stanza makes no mention of what most Germans were welcoming: the liberation of Germany and the prospect of a (possibly more liberal) post-Napoleonic reconstruction. By the time Goethe wrote 'Hegira', the reconstruction had been underway for some three months at the Congress of Vienna. He followed the congress closely and knew its host and organizer Metternich personally. He drew little pleasure from the proceedings, as he wrote to his fellow Napoleon-sympathizer Sartorius in February 1815,[12] nor did he place much trust in the great powers' high-minded aim of establishing a 'general, eternal peace', as he wrote on New Year's Day 1815,[13] a week after writing 'Hegira'. It was the Wolffian law of nations all over again, which had been shattered by Frederick the Great's invasion of Silesia in 1740. Another poem written in early 1815 portrays the Holy Alliance against Napoleon as angels who, having defeated the devil, 'afterwards obviously found / It's pretty good to be a devil'.[14] There was no escape from the messy reality of politics via politics itself.

The argument against contemporary politics is supported by a cultural and historical argument in favour of the authenticity of the ancient East. In the first stanza the temporal dimension of the poet's journey is only hinted at. In travelling to the East, the poet is returning to the ancient past, to breathe the same air as the patriarchs. The sequence of the compass points in the first three lines—from north through west and south to east—runs anticlockwise and thus hints that the journey to the East will also be a turning back of the clock. Likewise, the mysterious reference to the ancient Persian sage Chisr points to the age of the patriarchs, for according to Hammer-Purgstall, Chisr was believed to be contemporary with Moses.[15] The spring signals a return to the wellsprings of our culture. The German 'Quell' means both *spring* and *origin*. These hints at a return to antiquity become explicit in the second and third stanzas, which explain why the flight into the past is necessary and what the purity and justice of the ancient East consist in. The unifying idea is that at the very origins of our history, human knowledge possessed an immediacy and authenticity that we have lost. It was an age in which humans received divine lessons from God in earthly tongues, when God gave the laws of Judaism to Moses or when Allah spoke through his prophet Mohammed. As Goethe put it in a letter to Christian Heinrich Schlosser in January 1815, the ancient East was a 'land of faith, revelations, prophecies, and promises'.[16] God and the world spoke directly to humans. Words still possessed the immediacy of the feelings and things that gave rise to them. This (again) Rousseauian or Hamannian or Herderian vision of the origins of language finds its poetic expression in the extraordinary couplet 'Wie das Wort so wichtig dort war, / Weil es ein gesprochen Wort war' ('Just as the word was so weighty there, / Because it was a spoken word'). The meaning is reinforced by verbal effects that are both artless and artful. The couplet achieves an exceptional coherence, thanks to the repetition of the words 'Wort' and 'war', the unusual rhyme of 'Wort war' and 'dort war', and the sevenfold alliteration of *w*. The words 'wichtig' (weighty) and 'gesprochen' (spoken) occupy the same position in their respective lines, so emphasizing their connection at the heart of the argument. 'Wichtig' denotes both importance and weight. Ancient words did not merely refer to things, they conveyed the substance of those things. The syncope of the adjective 'gesprochen'—standard grammar requires the inflected form 'gesprochen*es*'—implies a state of language without or before the complex grammar of adjectival agreement: a language that is spoken not written. In this primal condition of language, meaning and verbal form are identical. Words embody the spirit of their users. From his limited knowledge of Arabic, Goethe felt that 'perhaps in no other language are spirit, word and writing so primally co-embodied', as he wrote in the same letter to Schlosser.[17] In contrast to this inspired ancient world stands modernity, where God has fallen silent and humans worry themselves to death in abstract thought. The symbolic escape from modern Europe is not a pessimistic act. By embarking on a *hegira* to the ancient East, the poet finds restoration from the ills of modernity. There is much value to be found at the roots of human history, in the Muslim East as in the classical West. The resemblance between this poetic *hegira* and Goethe's flight to Italy and classical antiquity in 1786 was no coincidence. Two weeks before writing 'Hegira', he reread the diary of his Italian journey.[18] The poem may have been prompted by reading a letter he had written to Carl August from Venice in October 1786, in which he described his flight to Italy as a 'hegira'.[19] The letters and diaries from Italy were shot through with the language of rebirth. More specifically, the argument of the poem 'Hegira' shows similarities to the *Roman Elegies*, which likewise begin with the poet-traveller seeking shelter from the political north and which enact the discovery of a new vein of love poetry and earthly holiness. Like the *Roman Elegies*, the *Divan* makes a broader critique of modernity that goes well beyond the politics of 1814. Sensuality trumps moral censure. Immediacy trumps intellectual abstraction. Antiquity trumps but also rejuvenates modernity. The east (or south) reenlivens the west (or north). It is at the historical and geographical wellspring of our culture that we find the resources to make our culture new.

How close did the subsequent *Divan* poems stick to the programme set out in 'Hegira'? Despite the inspired mood that Goethe found in late summer 1815, the genesis of the *Divan* was long and complex. His research during the winter of 1814/15 led to personal contacts with some of the leading orientalists of the day: Heinrich Friedrich von Diez in Berlin, Georg Wilhelm Lorsbach in Jena, and Antoine Isaac Sylvestre de Sacy in Paris. He read more widely in the Qur'an and Persian poetry. There were also travel writings by Pietro della Valle, Jean Chardin, and Jean-Baptiste Tavernier, which he had known for some time and now reread. By May 1815 he had written one hundred or so poems,[20] and by end of 1815 the collection numbered 170. In late May, during a second journey to the Rhine, Main and Neckar, he began to organize the poems into groups. In Frankfurt he stayed with the banker Johann Jakob von Willemer and his new wife and erstwhile ward Marianne née Jung. The relationship between Goethe and the thirty-year-old Marianne, awkwardly infatuated on Goethe's part, generated a series of love poems between the fictional poet Hatem and his beloved Suleika. (After Goethe's death Marianne revealed that she had written some of these poems.) During the return journey to Weimar in October Goethe organized the *divân* into books. It is likely that at this point he formed the intention of publishing the poems. However, for various reasons publication was piecemeal and protracted. One concern was that his readers would not understand the poems' manner and their Persian-Arabic frame of reference. At this point he began to plan a series of explanatory notes and essays, which would help to bring the East nearer. Another sign of his uncertainty was the plan to publish a small selection of the *Divan*'s poems in Cotta's *Pocketbook for Ladies*. Both plans were delayed by the loss of Christiane from kidney failure on 6 June 1816. Her health had been poor for a year. Goethe retreated into his grief. His diary records: 'Approaching end of my wife. Her nature's final dreadful struggle. She passed around midday. Emptiness and deathly stillness within me and without'.[21]

The twelve poems published in Cotta's *Pocketbook* in 1817 did indeed bemuse their readers, not least because it was unclear whether they were translations or original poems.[22] He returned to his plan for a set of explanatory notes 'for the better understanding' of the poems, relying on Hammer-Purgstall's new study of the *History of the Rhetorical Arts of Persia with an Anthology of Two-Hundred Persian Poets*, together with upwards of twenty other sources.[23] Preparations for printing began in spring 1818. The *West-Eastern Divan* was finally published by Cotta in 1819, accompanied by an equal weight of notes and essays under the laconic title 'For Better Understanding' ('Besserem Verständniss'). Included in the notes was a section titled 'Future Divan' which explained what was missing from the *Divan* and might be added later. Evidently the *Divan* was not definitive or complete.[24] The protracted genesis is revealing not least for what it tells us about the unity and underlying meaning of the *Divan*. Attempts to find unity in the collection have mainly been of three kinds. An older tradition of scholarship saw the *Divan* as an intellectual project concerned with Goethe's peculiar notion of faith in the physical universe, which expresses itself in the *Divan* in a strangely ethereal form.[25] More recent scholarship has tended to read the poems as a response to the events of early 1814.[26] A third approach has viewed the poems as a concerted statement on poetry itself and the proper use of the poetic imagination.[27] However, the *Divan*'s genesis casts doubt on its unity. The *Divan*'s overall structure was by no means clear during the inspired early months of writing. Goethe began to group the poems in separate named sections or 'books' only once he had already written most of them. In May 1815 he made a first attempt to group the poems into thirteen books. One of these, the 'Book of Friendship', was never written, so that the 1819 first edition of the *Divan* consisted of twelve books. The reduction to twelve had a further consequence. In 1815 he decided that a set of political poems, the 'Book of Timur', would stand in the seventh, central position of the *Divan*. This political core of the *Divan* would have involved using the fate of the Mongol warlord Tamerlane as an Oriental analogue of Napoleon and as a vehicle for reflection at length on the collapse of Europe in 1814. Goethe announced the plan, prematurely as it turned out, in an 1816 advertisement for the *Divan*: 'Timurnameh, the Book of Timur, concentrates momentous world events as if in a mirror, in which, to our consolation and disconsolation ['Untrost', a neologism], we see the reflection of our own fate'.[28] With the reduction from thirteen to twelve books and the resulting shift of the 'Book of Timur' away from the numerical centre of the *Divan*, Goethe's focus switched away from the politics of the day. In the 1819 first edition, the 'Book of Timur' contains only two poems, far fewer than Goethe planned in 1815 and 1816.

At the same time, the vision of the *Divan*'s main themes and modes, set out carefully in 'Hegira' at the end of 1814, remained intact. This was because the *Divan* drew on long-held beliefs and interests that were not products of the moment: beliefs about modernity and antiquity and in particular the contemporary relevance of the politics, religion, and poetry of the Middle East. It is in this sense that we should understand 'Hegira'. One reason why the poem makes no mention of the politics of restoration that were occupying Europe's statesmen in Vienna is that the *Divan* is concerned with a broader political, intellectual and cultural regeneration, drawing on the ancient Middle East. To be sure, the composition of individual *Divan* poems was dependent on Goethe's spontaneous 'humour', as he wrote to Riemer in August 1814.[29] Among the immediate triggers for the *Divan* poems were the collapse of the Napoleonic Empire, his travels to the Rhine in 1814 and 1815, his return to the study of optics in January 1815, and the relationship with Marianne von Willemer in summer 1815. Yet the *Divan*'s main underlying arguments and their realization in an imaginative journey to the East were by no means spontaneous. He had been familiar with Hafez's poems and the early medieval Persian collection the *Mu'allaqāt* for many years.[30] He had translated one of the *Mu'allaqāt* poems, via William Jones's English, in 1783.[31] His research on Persian and Arabic culture in the winter of 1815/16 drew on new sources such as Hammer-Purgstall, but also involved rereading 'with a purpose' material he had 'long since studied', such as the travel journals of della Valle, Tavernier, and Chardin.[32] The imaginative journey to the East, he wrote to Schlosser in January 1815, allowed him to make a return visit to the Palestine he had loved since his youth.[33] As he wrote to Rochlitz in 1812, his studies of the ancient Middle East, beginning in his youth, had provided him with a resource to draw on for his whole life.[34] At the root of this interest was his first formal piece of writing, the Strasbourg law dissertation 'On the Lawmakers', which was concerned in part with the political foundations of Judaism. He first encountered the Qur'an in David Friedrich Megerlin's translation in 1771, which was the inspiration for the unfinished political tragedy on Mohammed. His fascination with the ancient Middle East did not wane. For instance in 1797 he made plans and drafts for an essay on the great nation-builder Moses,[35] which harked back to an argument in the essay 'Two important hitherto unanswered Biblical questions' of 1772–1773.[36] This is why the Old Testament looms so large in the *Divan* and the accompanying essays 'For Better Understanding'. In the years before 1814 his interest in the Middle East was still active. He read Conrad Engelbert Oelsner's account of the early history of Islam shortly after its publication in 1810.[37] In 1812 he resumed work on the 1797 Moses drafts, adding six introductory paragraphs. Around the same time he dedicated several pages of *Poetry and Truth* to his childhood interest in the history of the Israelites in the Pentateuch. Several weeks after witnessing Islamic prayers in Weimar in January 1814, he acquired a collection of Turkish and Arabic manuscripts for the ducal library, which included a copy of the Qur'an and some commentaries on it; he was occupied with the manuscripts for months thereafter,[38] during which time he received Hammer-Purgstall's Hafez translations from Cotta. The first day's travel out of Weimar in late July 1814, when he wrote 'several poems to Hafez, most of them good' was not so much a sudden new departure. It was more the unblocking of a dam.

The *Divan* allowed him to respond more reflectively to the political and cultural needs of the time. The poems' purpose, he wrote to his daughter-in-law Ottilie in 1818, was 'to liberate us from the limiting present and momentarily to relocate us, as far as our sensibility is concerned, to a boundless freedom.'[39] Indeed, the freedom was something that he found in the Persian poets themselves: 'Overview of the world, irony, free use of talent are things we find in all the poets of the Orient', he wrote in spring or summer 1818.[40] He found that this reflective mode of poetry 'was congenial to my years', he wrote to Zelter in May 1820, a year after the *Divan*'s publication. It allowed him to observe serenely 'the changeable goings-on of the world, ever recurring in their circular and spiral forms'. His mind could hover between observation of the real world and 'unconditional acquiescence to the unfathomable will of God'. Real things could be 'purified, resolving into symbols. What more could grandpa want?'[41] (His daughter-in-law Ottilie gave birth to his first grandchild in April 1818.) Indeed, in the section of 'For Better Understanding' titled 'Future Divan', he imagined that his position in the Orient would give him daily new inspiration for poetic reflection on the duality of things: 'for everything is reflection there, which sways back and forth between the sensuous and the super-sensuous, without coming down on one side or the other'.⁴² The poetic principle of swaying back and forth is exemplified in one of the *Divan*'s most celebrated poems, 'Gingko Biloba', a meditation inspired by a leaf of the gingko tree. He wrote the poem in September 1815, during his infatuation with Marianne von Willemer, but it is by no means only or even primarily a love poem:

Gingo Biloba

Dieses Baum's Blatt, der von Osten
Meinem Garten anvertraut,
Giebt geheimen Sinn zu kosten,
Wie's den Wissenden erbaut.

Ist es Ein lebendig Wesen?
Das sich in sich selbst getrennt,
Sind es zwey? die sich erlesen,
Daß man sie als Eines kennt.

Solche Frage zu erwiedern
Fand ich wohl den rechten Sinn;
Fühlst du nicht an meinen Liedern
Daß ich Eins und doppelt bin?⁴³

This tree's leaf, which from the East / Has been entrusted to my garden, / Gives a secret meaning for us to savour, / Such as edifies a person who knows.
Is it One living being? / That has divided itself within itself, / Is it two? that have elected / To be known as One.
To answer such a question / I have surely found the right meaning; / Don't you feel from my poems / That I am One and double?

In the obvious sense that the leaf has arrived in the poet's garden from the East, like the poems of Hafez, the poem symbolizes the *Divan* as a whole. It exemplifies Goethe's comments concerning the *Divan* in his letters to Zelter, Ottilie, and others. The poem 'purifies' a physical object, the gingko leaf, by resolving it into a symbol. In doing so, the poem also hovers between two realms. It 'sways back and forth between the sensuous and the super-sensuous, without coming down on one side or the other'. At first sight the poem suggests that this relation between the phenomenon and its 'secret meaning' is straightforward, for there is a 'right meaning' that answers the question as to the leaf's

FIG. 23. Manuscript in Goethe's hand of 'Gingko Biloba', made for Marianne von Willemer (1815)

origins. The 'right meaning' is that the leaf is either one divided leaf or two fused leaves. However, this 'right meaning' is not straightforward. For one thing, it is formulated as a question, not an answer, and it thus passes the task of answering the original question back to the reader. In this sense, the poem does indeed 'sway back and forth' between two states, determinacy and indeterminacy, answerability and unanswerability. In trying to determine the nature of the leaf's super-sensuous symbolic meaning, the poem hovers between two constructions of its unity and duality, between which it is impossible to decide. Does the phenomenon of unity-cum-duality result from the splitting of a unity or the fusing of a duality? In this sense, the poem expresses a conclusion that Goethe had arrived at during the course of his scientific research in the 1790s, beginning with his reading of Kant's *Metaphysical Foundations of Natural Science* in 1790 and culminating in the collaboration with Schelling at the end of the decade. The conclusion is spelt out in the section of the *Outline of a Theory of Colour* titled 'Relation to General Physics':[44]

> Honest observers of nature, no matter how differently they think on other counts, will however agree with one another that everything that is to appear, that is to encounter us as a phenomenon, must point towards either an original dividing that is capable of uniting or an original unity that can attain division, and must present itself in such a way. To divide what is united, to unite what is divided—this is the life of nature; this is the eternal syncrisis and diacrisis, the inhaling and exhaling of the world, in which we live, move and exist.[45]

The traditional assumption that the poem's 'secret meaning' is a cryptic allusion to the relationship with Marianne von Willemer therefore falls well short of the full sense of the poem. Indeed the poem may not have been fully worked out when Goethe sent it, or according to Sulpiz Boisserée some lines from it, to Marianne in the middle of September 1815.[46] It is likely that the poem only reached its final form several days later, after a conversation between Goethe and the philologist Friedrich Creuzer in Heidelberg in late September. According to Creuzer this conversation concerned the dual nature of ancient myths and the distinction between knowing and believing. Creuzer pointed out to Goethe that the figures of Greek myth had a double meaning. They were both their literal selves and also symbolic abstractions: 'for those who believed, the strict understanding of the word was enough, but for those who knew [*den Wissenden*] the higher meaning was disclosed in secret [*geheim*] mysteries'.[47] The poem hovers on this margin between knowledge and faith, public beliefs and esoteric mysteries. Therefore what the poem says about human unity in duality needs to be understood more widely. It is the unity and duality of the culture of East and West and of Goethe's rewriting of Persian and Arabic poetry. The poet of the *Divan* is Goethe or Hafez (or the Hatem of the 'Book of Suleika') or both. Western culture does originate from the Middle East but is also different. Dialogue itself is marked by unity and duality. All deep and genuine dialogue—and the *Divan* poems are full of dialogue[48]—requires both the autonomy of two participants and their coming together in a conversation. Hence the poem is also a comment on Goethe's relation to his audience. The poet is in union with those who know but is separated from his wider readership. The poems of the *Divan* require effort to penetrate their esoteric thoughtworld. Goethe both feared and was pleased that most readers would not make this effort. In an important sense, therefore, the poet of the *Divan* is a purveyor of esoteric knowledge, like his forebear Hafez—the 'interpreter of secrets' according to Hammer-Purgstall.[49] Paradoxically it is an esoteric knowledge that can be expressed publicly, in poems that despite their esoteric content give immediate and accessible pleasure. No doubt Goethe's self-image as a scientist also played a part in the formulation of the poem. He had committed his theory of colour to print, but its reception was marked by a divide between the enthusiastic support of a few initiates, including Hegel and Schopenhauer (a new young friend in 1814),[50] and wider incomprehension or neglect.

The poems of the *Divan* present subtle variations on the themes of 'Hegira' and 'Gingko Biloba': the nature of language; love and the tension it creates between self-realization and self-sacrifice; the relation between phenomena, knowledge, and faith; the connections between the poet and his social and political world; and between past and present. The *Divan* is a collection of things and themes found and meditated on, and the meditations evolve from poem to poem. The connections between poems are sometimes direct, sometimes allusive. These juxtapositions give the *Divan* the character of a rather loose warp and weft, to use one of Goethe's favourite images. Perhaps therefore the best way to capture the *Divan*'s underlying unity is through the fiction of the traveller-merchant-poet-lover who is the poems' main voice, in the same way as the equally diverse poems of the *Venetian Epigrams* are unified by the fiction of the poet-tourist in Venice. The poet of the *Divan* is more self-consciously fictional and his identity and beliefs are harder to pin down. In 'Hegira' the poet becomes a merchant. In the 1816 advertisement for the *Divan* Goethe confirmed this identity, albeit somewhat evasively: 'The poet regards himself as a traveller. He takes pleasure in customs, habits, objects, religious convictions, and opinions, indeed he does not disconfirm the suspicion that he himself is a Muslim'.[51] The fiction of the poet as a merchant captures this evasive stance: merchants must identify with what they sell and with the people they sell to, and yet selling is a mere transaction, a relationship of non-identity. It becomes hard to summarize the *Divan* without lapsing into contradictions. And this is surely part of the point: we have fallen from the direct, unmediated world of the patriarchs, in which words shone with spirit, into the complex, shifting, polyphonic, and in many ways unreal world of modernity.

The collection of notes and essays under the laconic and rather vague title 'For Better Understanding' presents a different kind of problem. It consists of a sequence of fifty-nine notes and essays of varying lengths on a range of topics. Some of these are connected to one another in obvious ways. The first main sequence of notes covers aspects of the history of the Orient in chronological order, from the first Hebrew peoples up to the High Middle Ages. There follows a suite of accounts of the life and character of seven medieval Persian poets. A further set of notes analyses the main features of Persian and Arabic poetry, drawing heavily on Hammer-Purgstall's *History of the Rhetorical Arts of Persia*. Within this grouping is a somewhat ill-fitting essay titled 'Natural Forms of Poetry' ('Naturformen der Dichtung'), which rehearses Aristotle's analysis of the three fundamental literary modes of poetry, epic, and drama. Its purpose is to build a bridge between Persian and Arabic poetry and Goethe's own neo-classical theory of literature. The last main sequence describes and evaluates Western writing on the Orient from Marco Polo down to Hammer-Purgstall. Allowing for some brief deviations, these sequences of argument can be understood as contributions to the better understanding of the *Divan* poems and the Persian and Arabic history and culture that lies behind them.

The most conspicuous element of 'For Better Understanding', by virtue of its length and its incongruity, is a long essay titled 'Israel in the Wilderness'. Its origins lay in the essay on Moses that Goethe had drafted in spring 1797, between *Herrmann and Dorothea* and 'The Bride of Corinth'. In March 1812 he returned to the essay adding six introductory paragraphs, probably soon after writing the section of *Poetry and Truth* that dealt with his childhood interest in the fate of the first families of Israel. It is also possible that he was prompted to return to the essay in March 1812 by the promulgation, two weeks earlier, of the Prussian Edict of Emancipation, which granted Jewish Prussians equality in law and the right to military service.[52] He was opposed to all such moves towards emancipation, chiefly because they threatened to limit the legal and executive authority of the prince.[53] The 1797 draft was ostensibly intended as a rehabilitation of Moses. Goethe had analysed the text of the Pentateuch into its component parts in order to show that the forty years of the Israelites' wanderings was the result of a later recension of the text, which had had the perhaps unintended effect of making Moses seem cruel by leading his people in an irrational and bizarre zigzagging course through the wilderness. By showing that the forty years was in fact only four years, Goethe was able to claim that Moses was less incompetent and cruel than the Pentateuch makes him out to be. But within this exercise in biblical criticism were elements that also offered oblique commentary on the Terror. If Moses was a violent and indecisive leader, that was because he was the product of a nation made violent during their oppression by the Egyptians. The march through the wilderness and the various laws and customs it gave rise to were an exercise in nation-building; the creation of a national God provided justificatory cover for a nation that, in the process of escaping from Egypt, had made the right of military conquest into its first principle and had cloaked this aggression in the ideology of a divine mission. In the same way, the French had justified their wars of conquest from 1793 onwards by appealing to the ideology of liberty, fraternity, and equality. In the new version of the Moses drafts, expanded in 1812 and published in 1819 in 'For Better Understanding', Goethe retained most of 1797 text, but made a number of small but significant changes. The timespan of the wanderings is further reduced to two years. The other changes reflect Goethe's new political priorities, in particular his opposition to nationalism. (The word 'nation' does not appear in the 1797 text.) The unflattering portrayal of Moses is broadly the same as in the 1797 text: a man called to action, but prone to violence and incapable of planning. Some details are altered for the 1812–1819 version: there is more emphasis on Moses's doubt and indecision, perhaps in order to suggest a negative comparison with Napoleon.[54] Goethe contrasts Moses with his strategically astute father-in-law Jethro, the leader of the Midianites, who cleverly encouraged Moses to lead his destructive people away from the Midianites' lands. Just as Moses's violence is the product of his people's imprisonment in Egypt and expresses the birth pangs of the Israelite nation, Jethro's cleverness is a product of the Midianites' political independence. Jethro and the Midianites thus embody Goethe's continuing belief that Weimar was best served by using its independence to avoid the wars into which alliances had dragged it. The essay is also given a new framing. World history is marked by alternating periods of faith and unfaith. Periods of unfaith are distasteful, unpleasant. Such was the age of Moses, in which the Israelites lapsed from Abraham's benevolent faith in a providential God into a less appealing belief in a warlike national God who was simply a projection of Moses's own aggression—'as the man is, so too is his God', Goethe concludes. Goethe's hypothesis then is that the Pentateuch contains an original stratum that narrates Israelite nation-building. This explains Goethe's extraordinary conjecture in the 1812–1819 text that Moses did not die on the summit of Mount Nebo while contemplating the Promised Land, but was murdered by Joshua and Caleb out of frustration with his failure to fully establish Israelite nationhood. The new version of the text thus foregrounds the pathologies of nationalism—an element that was not present in the 1797 draft. The negative view of nationalism in the 1812–1819 version was probably the product of the work in spring 1812, at the zenith of Napoleon's empire and before the Grande

Armée set off to Russia that June. The implicit contrasts between Moses and Napoleon that run through the text express Goethe's belief in an independent Weimar and his dislike of the German nationalist movement. Moses is a poor military leader: he fails to channel and control the violence of his people; he introduces laws that have little rhyme or reason beyond providing cover for nationalist aggression.

Goethe had long believed that the origins of political authority lay in military power. He was firmly opposed to the view that political power was based in natural law. Even the rather limited constitution that Carl August introduced in Weimar in May 1816, which allowed a role for the traditional estates but maintained the Duke's absolute power, was too liberal for Goethe.[55] The argument is spelt out in another section of 'For Better Understanding' titled 'Government'. The origins of the ancient Persian and Arabic states lay in the power to declare and wage war. The narrative of the Pentateuch as interpreted in 'Israel in the Wilderness' is an example of this process. Moses murdered an Egyptian lord who had mistreated an Israelite. The killing gave expression to the Israelite people's resistance to their Egyptian oppressors, as described in Exodus: 'the Children of Israel sighed by reason of the bondage, and they cried, and their cry came up unto God by reason of the bondage'.[56] In Goethe's version of the narrative, the slaying of the firstborn children of the Egyptians was not a plague visited on them by the Lord, but an act of political terrorism by an elite force that embodied the popular will of the Israelites and echoed Moses's killing of the Egyptian lord. It made sense, therefore, for the Israelites to confer sovereignty on Moses, who had been the first to strike out against the Egyptians. The ensuing flight of the Israelites from Egypt and their wanderings through the wilderness were both a military adventure and a process of state-building. The process is summarized as follows in the section of 'For Better Understanding' on ancient Oriental governments:

> So we find in the very ancient Orient that all sovereignty can be derived from the right to declare war. Like all others, this right lies initially in the will, the passion of the people. A member of the tribe is injured, and straightway the mass rises up spontaneously to take revenge on the offender. However, because the mass can act and be effective, but not lead itself, instead it confers, by means of a vote or tradition or custom, the leadership in battle to a single person, whether for one campaign or for several; it bestows this dangerous role on a capable man for his lifetime, and eventually on his descendants. And so an individual, by virtue of competence in waging war, acquires the right to declare war.[57]

The *Divan*'s political tenor was not lost on Friedrich von Müller who, on hearing Goethe read from the *Divan* in February 1819, concluded that 'Goethe seems to be using [the *Divan*] as the vehicle for his political confession of faith'.[58] The essence of the *Divan*'s politics is that political power derives originally from military power, and not from natural law. Autocracy is a fact of normal political life, and we have little choice but to learn to accommodate to it. In this sense, the politics of the *Divan* have the character of a naturalistic description of political authority. Through military power a government acquires 'right'. The powerful have the right to exert power because they alone possess the ability to make and enforce laws. Right is not a normative notion, not a transcendental standard of justice. Goethe never believed in any such thing. Right is only acquired and sustained by means of power. Of course other forms of political organization than autocracy do occur. However, they are temporary and unstable, nor do they provide any more comfort and liberty for the individual than does a well-ordered autocratic regime. And even if we wanted to change our form of government, our power to do so would be limited. Political organization comes about not through action based upon reason, but according to its own natural logic: the dialectic of freedom and servitude. Freedom without a degree of servitude is impossible; indeed freedom causes servitude.

It is in this context that we should understand Goethe's defence of 'oriental despotism'. It is worth noting that the much more liberal Herder had defended oriental despotism in *This too a Philosophy of History*. For Herder, there was a close fit between the politics of the ancient Middle East and its forms of social and economic existence, and therefore Enlightenment philosophers were wrong to dismiss oriental despotism out of hand. Goethe acknowledges the Enlightenment critique of oriental despotism, before presenting his own more nuanced revision of it. Modern Western readers might well be put off by Persian and Arabic poets kowtowing to despots. However, this behaviour was merely a formalized and courtly version of the perfectly natural obeisance to the ruler that we find in the Old Testament, which is in turn only an extension of the obeisance properly owed to God. Thus, faith in secular princes derives originally from the Abrahamic faith in divine providence.[59] Goethe finds a further nuance in the historical evolution of the Persian poets' panegyrics. In their earliest expressions, the panegyrics were less overt, more subtle. In their later expressions they tended towards parody.[60] In different ways therefore and at different times, praise of despots in Persian and Arabic poetry was qualified. Indeed, the panegyrics were part of a conversation that was embedded in political and social structures. Here again Goethe projects his own political views onto his oriental models. The poet's task is to sustain and defend the autocrat's rule, to the extent that, in an admittedly highly idealized sense, the poet becomes a kind of coregent alongside the despot: 'It is striking [that the ruler] is hereby obliged to choose a coregent for himself, who can stand by him [...], and in actual fact keep him on the throne. It is the poet who works with and next to him and elevates him above all mortals'.[61] The idea is expressed, from the poet's point of view, in the first stanza of a poem from one of the *Divan*'s explicitly political poems—perhaps one of the poems Müller heard Goethe recite in February 1819. Since power is a fact of political life, the poet must converse with tyrants and can even take pleasure in doing so:

> Übermacht, Ihr könnt es spüren,
> Ist nicht aus der Welt zu bannen;
> Mir gefällt zu conversiren
> Mit Gescheiten, mit Tyrannen.[62]

Overlordship, as you can detect, / Cannot be banished from the world; / I enjoy conversing / With clever people, with tyrants.

The same argument is made in the brief account of the twelfth-century Persian poet Anvari in 'For Better Understanding'. Goethe defends Anvari and by extension all poets who consort with princes. Anvari was simply responding to political reality, and it would be a travesty of history to ignore this fact: 'We cannot therefore accept that he is blamed, after so many centuries, for the circumstances in which he lived and made use of his talent. What would become of a poet if there were not high, mighty, clever, active, and fine people whose advantages he could not use to develop himself?' To make such a charge would be akin to asking a court jeweler to work as a common paviour.[63] Goethe's political vision thus has poets becoming part of the structure of the autocratic state. Indeed the literary world in some sense mimics the structure of the political world, as he found in Hammer-Purgstall's account of the court of Mahmud of Ghazni in his *History of the Rhetorical Arts of Persia*:[64]

> Many poets assembled at Mahmud's court, they speak of four hundred who plied their trade there. And just as everything in the Orient subordinates itself, accommodates to higher commands, so the prince appointed a poet-prince to them who was to test them, judge, encourage them to works appropriate to the talent of each. This post should be considered one of the highest at the court: he was minister of all the scholarly, historical-poetic activities; it was through him that the tokens of favour were apportioned to

his subordinates, and when he accompanied the court, it occurred in such a great entourage, in such a stately procession, that one might have well have taken him for a vizier.[65]

One reason why the literary world should accommodate itself to the political world is that it is pointless and even counterproductive to criticise the organization of the state. To be sure, states can change their political organization, but only according to the natural dynamics of power, as the study of history teaches us. All states consist of conflicting factions that compete to control a fixed budget of political power. The supremacy of one faction will inevitably result in the oppression of another. Power, in whatever form, is all there is. Ideologies such as political liberty are simply the cloaks that power wears. The political rationality that liberals appeal to is largely impotent. Factions may appeal to the idea of freedom in a variety of ways. Freedom can be the covert ideology of secret conspiracies that plot to instal themselves in power. It can be the public ideology of revolutionaries when they justify overthrowing the state. Or it can be an ideology of despots who seek to sustain their power by turning the population against an external enemy and to exploit foreign war in order to quell internal dissent. In all these cases freedom is not what it claims to be. It is simply an expression or tool of power.

The arguments about political power are spelt out in the section of 'For Better Understanding' titled 'Postscript', which follows Goethe's discussion and defence of oriental despotism. Reflecting on the long history of politics helps us to clarify political universals:

> As a rule, when assessing the various forms of government people do not pay enough attention to the fact that in all of them, whatever their name, freedom and servitude exist together in a polar relation. If power resides with the individual, the masses are subservient; if power resides with the masses, then the individual is disadvantaged; this then proceeds through all the stages until perhaps somewhere, albeit only for a short time, an equilibrium is found. To the student of history this is no secret; at turbulent moments of life, however, one cannot find clarity on it. And so one never hears more talk of freedom than when one party wants to suppress the other and there is no other prospect than power, influence, and wealth changing hands. Freedom is the silent watchword of covert conspirators, the loud battlecry of public revolutionaries, indeed it is the slogan even of despotism, when the latter rouses its oppressed masses against an enemy and promises them salvation from external oppression forever.[66]

As in 'Israel in the Wilderness', Goethe understands the idea of political freedom as a cloak for the exercise or pursuit of power. In this sense, the vision of political history in the *Divan* is still shaped by the French Revolution and its aftermath;[67] nor had it changed much since the *Venetian Epigrams* in which he excoriated the 'apostles of freedom' who only sought power for themselves. There was a clear distinction in his mind between the political ideology of freedom and the actual condition of freedom, which was generally confined, he thought, to private behaviour and beliefs. Political freedom was specious, private freedom real. Even under Persian despotism, the individual was allowed 'freedom and autonomy of thought'.[68] Despotism is really no different from any form of government: it shapes a subject's behaviour in ways that are not necessarily any worse than under a republic or aristocratic oligarchy:

> No one denies a physical-environmental influence on the development of the human form and physical characteristics, but people rarely consider that the form of government also produces a psychological-environmental condition in which character develops in various ways. We are not talking about the mass of people, but about important, eminent figures.
>
> In a republic, there develop great, happy, calmly and untaintedly active characters; if the republic develops [*steigert sich*] into an aristocracy, the result is worthy, consistent, capable men, admirable in giving and obeying orders. If a state lapses into anarchy, reckless, bold people immediately emerge, despisers of morals, acting forcefully in the moment, appalling, rejecting all moderation. Despotism on the other hand creates great characters: in capable minds there develop wise, calm overview, rigorous activity, firmness, decisiveness, all characteristics that are needed in order to serve the despot and will procure for these people the first roles in the state, in which they will develop into rulers.[69]

The argument is an abbreviated and much altered version of Plato's discussion of four types of (defective) government and their 'corresponding types of men' in Book VIII of the *Republic*.[70] Where Goethe has republican, aristocratic, anarchic, and despotic governments, Plato has monarchy ('praised by a majority of people'), oligarchy (the second most favoured but 'a constitution full of bad aspects'), democracy (which eventually leads to anarchy),[71] and tyranny ('the worst disorder of a state'). Plato regards all these forms as defective in different ways and to varying degrees. By contrast, Goethe assigns high standing to the republican, aristocratic, and despotic forms, and only anarchy is notably worse. It is Goethe's equivalent of Plato's democracy. The nuances of

Goethe's argument show that, while the three superior forms of government are far superior to anarchy (or democracy), they are not of equal standing. The verb he uses to indicate that a republic can 'develop' ('steigert sich') into an aristocracy implies an improvement. Plato likewise views the timocratic form of aristocracy as superior to oligarchy, though in Goethe's version the historical sequence is the reverse of Plato's. Goethe's version, which has republicanism developing into aristocracy, is instead closer to Machiavelli's *History of Florence*, which he had used for his Cellini translation and was echoed in the Judge's account of the Revolution in *Herrmann and Dorothea*. According to this analysis, republicanism is inherently unstable. Goethe further implies that aristocracy and despotism are higher versions of republicanism. Despotism represents an advance on republicanism in the sense that the 'calmly and untaintedly active characters' of a republic are replaced by the 'wise, calm overview, rigorous activity' of men in a despotism. The qualities are broadly the same, only under a despotism they became more excellent. Furthermore, the leading men in an aristocracy and a despotism can possess a firmness of character that is absent in a republic, and likewise there is the prospect of active involvement in government in an aristocracy and a despotism which again is not mentioned in the context of republicanism. (This is the very opposite of what a modern liberal would presume.) In summary then, Goethe's reworking of Plato reflects his view that democracy-anarchy is the very worst type of state, and that aristocratic and despotic states tend to be superior to republics.

These arguments concerning the nature of political power and the relative merits of various forms of government lie behind the two political poems in the 'Book of Timur' that focus more narrowly on Napoleon. The longer of the two poems, 'Winter and Timur' is in fact a free translation of William Jones's Latin version of a fifteenth-century Arabic poem. Goethe was no doubt attracted to the poem because it placed Timur (Tamerlane) in a situation much like Napoleon's during his retreat from Moscow. Timur shelters from the freezing weather in his camp where he is visited by a hostile personification of Winter. The first third of the poem sets the scene; the remainder consists of Winter's threatening speech to Timur. The second poem, 'To Suleika', shifts to the more intimate sphere of the poet's relation to his beloved. The two poems are linked by a seemingly negative characterization of Napoleon that turns out to be more ambivalent than at first sight. In 'Winter and Timur' Winter begins its speech by addressing Timur-Napoleon as a 'tyrant of injustice' ('Tyrann des Unrechts') whose armies and flames have killed thousands of the faithful. However, the poem moves away from the moral wrong of Timur's actions to focus on the sheer natural force of his leadership, comparable in its devastation to Winter itself. Timur is thus an exemplification of Goethe's belief that political power is a natural force that exceeds moral judgement. If Timur has a weakness it is that he is less powerful than Winter; the actual natural force trumps the political one. Beyond this symbolic gesture, the poem gives no clear answer to the question how we should judge Napoleon. That task is left to the second poem, 'To Suleika', which returns to the dominant mode of the *Divan*: a poem of four stanzas in rhymed trochees that resolves a physical object into a symbol and meditates on its ambiguous meaning. It is arguably the darkest and most chilling of all Goethe's statements on politics. The speaker of the poem is presumably the poet Hatem who will sing Suleika's praises in the next section of the *Divan*, the 'Book of Suleika'. Here he observes that Suleika's beauty is enhanced by a perfume that requires the distillation of thousands of roses. These must perish in order to delight Suleika's lover:

> Dir mit Wohlgeruch zu kosen,
> Deine Freuden zu erhöhn,
> Knospend müssen tausend Rosen
> Erst in Gluten untergehn.

> To caress you with fragrance, / To enhance your pleasure, / A thousand roses budding must / First perish in heat.

In perishing, the roses achieve immortality, in the sense that their essence can be bottled and preserved and the perfume's effect can be immortalized in poetry. However, there is already an implied parallel between the heating of roses to produce their perfumed essence and the devastation wrought by the flames of Timur's armies. The final stanza brings out this symbolic connection between the destruction of the roses and the murder wrought by Timur:

> Sollte jene Qual uns quälen,
> Da sie unsre Lust vermehrt?
> Hat nicht Myriaden Seelen
> Timurs Herrschaft aufgezehrt!

> Should that torture torment us, / When it increases our pleasure? / Were not myriads of souls / Consumed in Timur's lordship!

As in 'Gingko Biloba', the question is answered evasively with a further question, nor is the evasion merely rhetorical. (Although the poem ends with an exclamation mark, the last couplet is evidently a question: Goethe no more observes standard rules of punctuation in the *Divan* than he did in his poetry of the 1770s.)[72] The question is not hard to answer. Timur's lordship caused thousands of deaths. What is disturbing is the parallel that the poem implies between the relatively trivial distillation of roses to make perfume and the thousands of human lives lost for the sake of Timur's (or Napoleon's) greatness. Does the poem really mean to imply what it seems to—that we should feel a mixture of pleasure and pain at Timur-Napoleon's murderous greatness, in the same way as our pleasure at Suleika's perfume is haunted by grief? It is hard to avoid the conclusion that it does, especially when we recall Goethe's often-stated admiration for Napoleon, even after the Russian campaign, for instance his comment reported by Sulpiz Boisserée in October 1815: 'All resolute [or decisive; *entschieden*] natures were a cause for happiness to him, so too Napoleon'.[73] Firmness of the will was the basis of character, as he had written when analysing Newton's character in the *Materials for the History of Colour Theory*: 'the main foundation of character is a resolute will, without regard for justice and injustice, for good and evil, for truth and error: it is what every party values highly in its members'.[74] The best construction that can be put on the poem is that it is not intended as a moral justification of Napoleon. It is simply a naturalistic statement about our reactions of mixed horror and pleasure, of appalled fascination at the sight of true greatness. Yet Goethe's reluctance to condemn Napoleon and his preference for a naturalistic over a moral view of political history are surely two sides of the same argument. The argument seems to be that political right is not the same as moral right. Political greatness costs lives and so it must both fascinate and appal us.

A noteworthy achievement of the *Divan*, perhaps second in importance to the exceptional beauty, richness, and vigour of many of the poems, is what Goethe called his 'appropriation of orientalism'.[75] By 'orientalism' he meant, neutrally and unproblematically, the scholarly study of the East.[76] He devoted considerable time and effort to reading and assimilating the scholarship, especially during the writing of 'For Better Understanding' in 1818. He used at least 120 sources: editions, translations, monographs, articles, and reference works.[77] The extent of his reading is explained by the fact that the literature of the medieval Middle East was much less familiar to him and his audience than were the Greek and Roman classics that he appropriated in the *Roman Elegies* and the *Venetian Epigrams*. As we have already seen, there is a similarity between the method of the poem cycles. In the *Elegies* and *Epigrams*, as in the *Divan*, appropriation meant more than merely immersing oneself in a foreign literature. It was a process of making a foreign perspective one's own, merging the self with something other, and so creating a hybrid voice. The *Divan* poems resulted from a similarly creative blending of Eastern and Western elements. In some respects the project was more challenging, and not just because of the alienness of the Orient. European attitudes to Islam were changing. Outright fear of the Ottoman Empire was giving way to an uneasy ambivalence, which was reflected in Goethe's unfinished tragedy on Mohammed of the early 1770s—Mohammed was both a power-hungry ideologue and the hero and lawgiver celebrated by Voltaire and Rousseau.[78] By 1800, however, these Enlightenment debates were overtaken once more by geopolitical concerns. The French campaigns in Egypt and Syria of 1798–1801 turned the Middle East into a battleground of the European colonial powers. Napoleon's forces included a contingent of over 150 scientists and scholars. The result, sponsored by Napoleon himself, was the monumental *Description of Egypt*, published between 1809 and 1821. In this sense, the colonial project of territorial acquisition fostered the intellectual project of Orientalism, as criticised by Edward Said. In colonizing the East, the West asserted its own supposed political, intellectual, and technological superiority.[79] This Orientalism was in considerable part an exercise in Western self-affirmation, in which the peoples of the East could be classed as primitive 'others' and defined in terms of a range of supposedly non-European characteristics: sensuous, irrational, violent, despotic, fanatical.

Said's political critique of Orientalism obviously belongs to an intellectual climate quite different from Goethe's. However, Goethe was familiar with contemporary critiques of the European colonial trading system, for instance in Herder's *This too a Philosophy of History* and Goldsmith's 'The Deserted Village'. Herder's essay establishes a link between colonialism and European intellectual arrogance. However, Europe's intellectual superiority is a myth, and Herder treats it with sarcastic disdain. In its place he proposes a new method of historical and cultural investigation. There is no single or universal standard by which we can judge cultures. All such presumptive standards, not least eighteenth-century European rationalism, are tied in an organic relation to the natural and human environment that produced them. Intellectual cultures are products of their historical and geographical positions. At different times and places humans have thought and acted in fundamentally different ways. Every culture should therefore be approached with the presumption that it is valid on its own terms. The 'appropriation of orientalism' in the *Divan* employs the Herderian argument that it is not possible to frame the East within European rationalism.

Still, it is reasonable to ask whether Goethe's habits of thought lapsed into the Orientalism described by Said, shaped as they were by his Western perspective and by his reliance on the academic literature, some of it from the colonial powers Britain and France.[80] It is not hard to find examples of this Saidian kind of Orientalism in the *Divan* and especially in the notes and essays of 'For Better Understanding'.[81] For instance, Goethe makes some notably negative comments about the religious art of medieval India, with its 'monstrous, grotesque images whose empty bodies were filled with gold and jewels', which were 'even now [...] abhorrent to any pure sensibility'.[82] These comments echo the British colonialist discourse of the time. However, they occur in the context of a discussion of Muslim antipathy towards Indian culture. That is to say, the negative view of Indian religious art is historicized and positioned within a particular non-European cultural context. The universalizing observation that 'any pure sensibility' will find Indian aesthetics abhorrent is an aside, not the main argument. Likewise, the somewhat ill-fitting discussion of Aristotle's natural forms of poetry, with its claims to universality, is contradicted elsewhere in 'For Better Understanding'. For instance, Goethe criticises William Jones for trying to force Persian poetry into a framework defined by the Greek and Roman classics. Evidently Jones could not help himself; we all make judgement easier for ourselves by drawing comparisons, and the classical heritage was just part of Jones's British cultural patrimony.[83] What we see in these examples then is an ambivalence on Goethe's part. The desire to make normative judgements is tempered by a Herderian relativism about values. The ambivalence occurs in a laconic form in the four lines of poetry the Goethe used an as the epigraph of 'For Better Understanding':

> Wer das Dichten will verstehen
> Muß in's Land der Dichtung gehen;
> Wer den Dichter will verstehen
> Muß in Dichters Lande gehen.
>
> Whoever wants to understand how to write poetry / Must enter the land of poetry; / Whoever wants to understand a poet / Must enter the poet's land.

The two couplets have usually been understood as making a single point. To understand a foreign culture, we must feel our way into it. 'For Better Understanding' will therefore immerse us in medieval Persian and Arabic culture.[84] However, it was not Goethe's way to say the same thing twice, and the couplets are better read as using similar formulations to make two different points. The subject of the first couplet is an abstraction: the principles of writing poetry, the realm of poetry. The subject of the second is a concrete particular: one poet and that poet's culture. Read in this way, the epigraph has a quite different meaning. To understand poetry, two kinds of knowledge are necessary: knowledge of the general, universal rules of poetry, as set out by Aristotle for instance and found in the 'land of poetry', and knowledge of the cultural context of any particular poet. Thus the two couplets tell us that 'For Better Understanding' will contain both types of knowledge: Aristotelian universals and Herderian cultural specifics. Normative, universalizing judgements do play a part in Goethe's writing on the East. However, as in the case of his criticism of Jones, he shows how and why these normative arguments have come into being. He makes clear their positionality. In other words, he obeys his own theory of modes of perspective (*Vorstellungsarten*). All knowledge is governed by our perspective on it, but in understanding a perspective we also become able to set it in relation to other perspectives.

Goethe valued orientalism as a form of poetic creativity. This is the second and arguably more important difference between his 'appropriation of orientalism' and the colonial Orientalism analysed by Said. The *Divan* is not an attempt to define and classify the essence of the Orient. Rather it shows us a poetic imagination moving back and forth between East and West, bringing the East to the West and the West to the East. The treatment of religion is a case in point. Goethe does not altogether avoid the Orientalist cliché of Muslim fanaticism. A series of poems in the 'Book of Hafez' play with the thought that the poet may be subject to the *fatwā*, a decree of censure issued by an Islamic religious leader. Hafez's Muslim faith is ambivalent, hovering between his reputation as the preserver of the Qur'an and a worldliness that Goethe tinges with Western traits. As the poem 'Revealed secret' puts it, Hafez is 'blessed without being pious' ('ohne fromm zu seyn, selig').[85] His poems portray the diversity of human desires. So in the poems of the 'Book of the Tavern' ('Schenkenbuch') Goethe plays with the poet's desire for the young man who serves his wine. These homoerotic elements are not altogether foreign to medieval Persian poetry, but in the *Divan* they become part of a thoroughly Goethean view of the nature and mission of poetry. The doctrine emerges at various points in 'For Better Understanding'. For instance, Goethe finds that fairy tales were ideally suited to the Persian and Arabian sensibility, with its 'oriental sensuousness, soft serenity, and easygoing idleness'.[86] He considered *1001 Nights* to be the highest expression of this type of writing, a work designed not for moral improvement but rather to lead people 'into absolute freedom'—freedom of the imagination, of course, and not political freedom.[87] Attempts by the dogmatic Islamic authorities to suppress this kind of writing could not succeed, and poetry did indeed flourish under the rule of the Barmakids.[88] Goethe thus adopts some of the clichés of Orientalism, and the conflict between poetry and Islam that he depicts is thoroughly Western. It reflects his own long-held view that poetry is incompatible with Christian morality. With his 'thoroughly sceptical flexibility',[89] Hafez is an oriental Goethe, whereas the illiberal and unpoetic elements in the Qur'an are the mirror image of the inhumane morality of Christian teaching. The Muslim East is not much different from the Christian West.

In the *Divan* Goethe's poetic imagination moves back and forth along two axes, between East and West and between the distant past and the present. In the same way as he grants a modern liberal Western sensibility to Hafez, he attributes the vitality of Western culture to the ancient Middle East. The Eastern past feeds the Western present. That is the programme set out in 'Hegira': a flight from present not only to avoid Europe's political collapse, but also to heal the pathologies of modernity by tapping into the purity and vitality of the ancient East. As we saw in 'Gingko Biloba', one pathology of the present is the alienation of the poet from his audience. The poems of the 'Book of Discontent' make this alienation their main theme, for instance, the tightly argued poem 'And whoever Frenches or Britishes' ('Und wer franzet oder brittet'), with its stern, epigrammatic ending. The poem begins with a wistful acknowledgement that the modern national literatures of Europe are driven by a vanity that is hard to escape. However, the focus on nations, the geographical axis of the *Divan* as it were, gives way to the axis of time. The poet's pathological relation to his audience can be healed by the knowledge that true poetry exists in a much longer temporal dimension—the three thousand years that separate modernity from the Old Testament and Homer:

> Und wer franzet oder brittet,
> Italiänert oder teutschet,
> Einer will nur wie der andre
> Was die Eigenliebe heischet.
>
> Denn es ist kein Anerkennen,
> Weder vieler, noch des Einen,
> Wenn es nicht am Tage fördert
> Wo man selbst was möchte scheinen.

Morgen habe denn das Rechte
Seine Freunde wohlgesinnet,
Wenn nur heute noch das Schlechte
Vollen Platz und Gunst gewinnet.

Wer nicht von dreytausend Jahren
Sich weiß Rechenschaft zu geben,
Bleib im Dunkeln unerfahren,
Mag von Tag zu Tage leben.[90]

And whoever Frenches or Britishes, / Italianizes or Germanizes, / One and all only desires / What his *amour-propre* demands.
For there is no recognition / From the many or the one, / If it brings no profit today, / When we wish to make ourselves out to be something.
Tomorrow may what's right find / Its friends well disposed, / Whereas today what's base / Wins all the honours.
Whoever is unable to give a full account / Of three thousand years, / Will remain in the dark, inexpert, / And live from day to day.

Modern European writers suffer from pathological Rousseauian *amour-propre* ('Eigenliebe'), which is the hallmark of modern civilization. (In *Émile* Rousseau argued that modern authors write for immediate praise, not for posterity, as they ought and as the ancients did.)[91] Understandable though their desire for praise might be, it is ultimately empty because genuine quality is obscured by their constant jockeying for position, and only the future can judge what has real merit. A person who understands this will take the long view, reaching back to the sources of our culture three millennia ago.

The poem has been read as a criticism of nationalism,[92] and Goethe's antinationalism is certainly evident in the *Divan*, for instance in 'Israel in the Wilderness'. However, the gesture of the first two lines is not so much directed at modern national poets as at all European poets. There are passages in 'For Better Understanding' that are more accepting of national identities, for instance the Sultan Mahmud of Ghazni's fostering of Persian nationhood. Nationhood does need to be put in its proper place, however. Nationhood can foster civic virtues, such as religion, but it derives its force from poetry, which connects us directly to our past:

> [Mahmud], himself of Persian stock, did not succumb to Arab narrowness, he knew well enough that the finest house and home for religion was to be found in nationhood; the latter was grounded in poetry, which hands down

to us ancient history in fabulous images, gradually emerges into clarity and introduces the past to the present without discontinuity.[93]

Nationhood is not bad, but nor is it the foundation of our identity, as a nationalist might wrongly suppose. Beneath nationhood lies poetry's capacity to create a national tradition. And if we dig even deeper to the roots of our sense of identity we find language. Poetry gains its power to shape our identity from its closeness to the origins of language. It is grounded in a set of primal elements ('Urelemente') that express the most important everyday experiences. For the pastoralist peoples of the Middle East these facts were animals: camels, horses, sheep. The original poetry of the Orient was based on these primal elements of language. The earliest poets thus possessed the advantage of being closest to 'the natural source of impressions' and could 'mould their language poetically',[94] forming new compound words out of the primal elements. Later poets lost this advantage; their language became artificial, derived. Goethe's orientalism aims to revitalize poetry by returning to the roots of language, to a vitality of utterance that modernity has for the most part lost.

Among the ideas given poetic form in the *Divan* is a Rousseauian, declinist model of civilization. The declinism is however by no means pessimistic. There is hope in poetry, which still has the capacity to revitalize modernity and cure its pathologies by reaching back to the vigour of the ancient Middle East, by reinvesting words with the direct power they once possessed, and by transforming things into symbols. Likewise the historical argument of 'For Better Understanding' looks back into the distant past, draws back the veil of civilization, and rediscovers the reverence for nature that constituted the ancient religions of the Orient. This, alongside a critique of nationalism, is the argument of 'Israel in the Wilderness'. The religion of Abraham and the other Old Testament patriarchs was a benign, stargazing providentialism that was only later obscured and perverted by the aggressive national religion of Moses. The ancient religion of the Persians suffered the same fate at the hands of Mohammed. The original Persian faith was grounded in nature-worship:

> The reverence for God of the ancient Persians was grounded in observation of nature. In praying to the creator they turned to face the rising sun, the conspicuously most glorious of phenomena. There they believed they saw the throne of God, sparkled about with angels. Everyone, even the lowliest of them could daily enact afresh the glory of this heart-uplifting observance. The poor man left his hut, the warrior his tent, and the most religious of all functions was performed.[95]

These primal and direct experiences are preserved in the oldest layers of sacred scripture, but also they glimpse through the more modern poems of Hafez. Modern poetry cannot fully recover the primal immediacy of things, for it inhabits a civilized world of opinions and values, a world of *amour-propre*. What it can do, however, is cultivate a sceptical and ironic awareness of its own modernity. Hafez's poems preserve some of the natural vigour that has been dimmed by the process of civilization. He can still perceive the secrets of the divinity, albeit from a distance. At the same time, he must acknowledge the newer religion of Islam, albeit at arm's length. Hafez is thus the model for the modern poet, able to tap into a still vibrant life force, his sensuousness moderated by the process of civilization, and sceptical about any values and ideas he seems to advocate:

> Out of [Hafez' poems] there streams an ever-flowing, temperate vitality. Content with little, cheerful and canny, taking his portion of the fullness of the world, peering into the secrets of the divinity from a distance, and yet rejecting religious observance and sensuality, the one as much as the other—in the very way that this kind of poetry, whatever it seems to promote and teach, must retain throughout a sceptical flexibility.[96]

In describing Hafez's poems, he was of course describing his own *Divan*. The lot of the modern poet is to hover between possibilities, to treat the world with irony, in the sense that he articulated in the *Theory of Colour*—the capacity to affirm two contradictory possibilities simultaneously, to think of the gingko leaf as both one split leaf and two fused leaves, to be both moral and sensuous, pious and worldly, modern and ancient, Western and Eastern.

Goethe continued to work on *Poetry and Truth* through the middle years of the decade until he reached the year 1775. There were two obstacles to his continuing: the fact that Lili Schönemann was still alive, and the personal and political sensitivities of his first decade in Weimar. The next section of his life story that could be published was his time in Italy. He began reviewing the material in 1813, including the journal he had written for Charlotte von Stein of his flight to Italy, his stay in Venice, and the early part of his first stay in Rome. He had written the journal, the original and extraordinarily vivid text of which has survived, with the intention of circulating it among his friends or perhaps even publishing it, as he wrote to Charlotte from Venice in

October 1786.[97] After he returned to Weimar in 1788, he changed his mind. The journal was too subjective. Instead he published a number of short essays on topics from his journal in a more objective style.[98] He continued to contemplate revising the whole journal in the 1790s, but adapting it to a more objective manner was too large and intractable a task, as he wrote to Schiller in 1796.[99] The Italian journal and letters expressed an understanding of Italy that he now considered immature. They depicted a character escaping from oppression, rather than one achieving intellectual freedom. It was only after writing *Poetry and Truth*—the story of his innate genius emerging in opposition to the world—that he appreciated the significance of the Italian material. It would be the story of a northern mind sloughing off its youthful subjectivity and maturing into objectivity in an alien and beautiful land. Much of this was already in the original journal written for Charlotte. The journal required little editing. He completed most of the work by summer 1814, when his attention switched to the *Divan* poems.[100] The sections covering his time in Rome, Naples, and Sicily required more editing and some fresh composition[101] because the source material was patchy. (It is not clear how much new writing was needed as he destroyed almost all of the notes he had written after his first arrival in Rome.) In 1816 and 1817 he published the first two volumes of the Italian journal as *From my Life: The Second Section's First and Second Parts*, carrying over the title he had used for *From my Life: Poetry and Truth*. These first and second parts of the Italian journey extended to his return from Naples to Rome in June 1787. His second stay in Rome up to April 1788 would form the third part, but this remained unwritten until 1829, when it was published together with the first two parts in Volumes XXVII to XXX of the *Complete Final Authorized Edition* under its now familiar title—*Italian Journey*.

The new plan was to turn his Italian papers from a travel journal into an autobiography. Part of the work involved stitching together individual episodes into larger units of life story. Some elements that were more appropriate to a travel journal had to be removed or shortened, for instance descriptions of artworks. There are few such descriptions in the finished Parts One and Two of the *Italian Journey*, a fact that disappointed some contemporary readers.[102] They did not find the guide to Italian art and history they might have expected. Indeed, Goethe makes a virtue of his refusal to describe artworks. Literary description is a poor substitute for direct experience. Worst of all is the Romantic habit of concentrating on the subject matter of paintings and its meaning, which tends to give too much latitude to the viewer's imagination and too little to the form of the artworks themselves, to their artistic autonomy, as

Moritz would have put it. Also disappointing for the Romantic generation was Goethe's lack of interest in medieval art, which loomed large in the German Romantic image of Italy. Instead, he gives pride of place to revivers of the classical tradition such as Palladio and Raphael.[103] The few descriptions of artworks that he retained in the *Italian Journey*, for instance his account of Palladio's Villa Capra 'La Rotonda' near Vicenza, are written in such a way as to show the gradual opening of his sensibility to art,[104] in opposition to the Romantic vision of art, which begins with the imagination 'anticipating' the meaning of art, usually in religious terms.[105] For Goethe, the virtue of art resides in disclosing through its formal perfection the Spinozan natural-cum-divine order of things.[106]

Nor did this now thirty-year-old journal from the days of the *ancien regime* speak to a contemporary audience. One might contrast Goethe's silence on Italy's political and social misery[107] with Byron's decidedly political portrayal of Italy in his 1819 poem *The Prophecy of Dante*.[108] The *Italian Journey* has plenty to say on social matters, especially in Naples, but its perspective on Italian society is a harmonizing and naturalizing one, governed by Goethe's proto-conservative assumption that since society is the product of natural forces, it is irrational to want to change it. A successful society is one in which the interests of individuals naturally converge and their aptitudes complement one another. In a note written in 1817 on the genesis of his 1790 essay on plant metamorphosis Goethe identified the three areas of knowledge in which he had made progress in Italy. The first two were the arts and nature. The third is society:

> The third thing that occupied me was the customs of nations. Learning from them how out of the clash between necessity and arbitrariness, stimulus and will, movement and resistance, there arises a third force, which is neither art nor nature but both at the same time, necessary and accidental, intentional and blind. I understand human society.[109]

Society is a natural phenomenon, albeit of a different kind from the phenomena of physics and biology. This is the meaning of the claim that society is 'neither art nor nature', but is in fact 'both at the same time'. The duality is expressed in pairs of opposed concepts that resemble Kant's and Schiller's duality of nature and freedom. However, in Goethe's pairs of concepts—'necessity and arbitrariness, stimulus and will, movement and resistance'—there is a progression towards something that we would associate more with nature than with freedom. The last pair, 'movement and resistance', might be read in terms of the conflict model of *Poetry and Truth*: the individual, with its arbitrary free will ('movement'), comes up against larger social trends ('resistance'). However, it can also be read in terms of the polarities of matter that Goethe had found in Kant's *Metaphysical Foundations of Natural Science*, and which he used in the *Metamorphosis* essay. Society is governed by a polarity and in this sense it obeys natural laws. It is nonnatural in the sense that one of the poles is arbitrary and not lawlike. The *Italian Journey* is mainly concerned with the natural side of the polarity, not with arbitrary individuals. There are some of the latter, including a tyrannical governor of the city of Messina, from whom Goethe has to escape hurriedly by taking ship back to Naples. Yet his main interest is in society as a natural phenomenon. Society is an organic product of its climate, in the broad Herderian sense of the term—climate proper, landscape, agriculture, the economy, religion, and government. The *Italian Journey* makes a virtue of Goethe's matter-of-factness. Readers might be put off by some of the unpoetic topics: agriculture, urban sanitation, the working lives of Neapolitans. But encountering these mundanities is all part of the effort a traveller must make to understand the alien land and its culture. As Herder argued in his *Ideas*, together these form an organic whole. Each part of a civilization has evolved through interaction with the other parts. In this sense, one cannot reasonably find fault with any aspect of a civilization. To do so is to deny the organic nature of a civilization and to import a standard of judgement that is foreign to the civilization in question. While Goethe often expresses annoyance with life in Italy, he is also aware of the risk of travellers imposing their own standards on a foreign land. In particular, he resists the censorious attitude of Northern outsiders who view Italians as lazy and chaotic. The argument comes to a head at the end of Part Two, before his return from Naples to Rome in June 1787. It is prompted by a claim in Volkmann's guidebook that there are 'thirty to forty thousand' unemployed people in Naples who loaf about the streets taking advantage of the city's balmy climate and the bountiful food produced from its fertile soils.[110] Goethe presents an extended analysis of the city's economy, in order to show that most Neapolitans are in fact usefully employed, and that the fabled ease of Neapolitan life is not to be equated with idleness. On one level the passage is a defence of his beloved Naples, and because Naples was originally Greek, it is also a defence of a Winckelmannian vision of Greek grace and ease, albeit in a modern incarnation. On another level, it is an essay in the social theory that Goethe had held to since the mid-1790s. All members of a well-functioning polity are parts of an organic whole. For society to function, the abilities and activities of each need to complement those of their fellow citizens. The argument is repeated at the beginning of the final passage in Part Two, as Goethe says farewell to Naples: 'each person [is] only to be considered as a supplement to all others'.[111] Individuals can only flourish if their differences complement one another. When this occurs, the claims of society and the individual are mutually supportive. Naples is therefore a model polity. It is also highly unusual. As a rule, successful polities are generally small Rousseauian ones; Naples, perhaps the third largest city in western Europe around 1800, is a glorious exception.

What sympathetic readers like Wilhelm von Humboldt did find to their liking in the *Italian Journey* was a subjective account of Italy that was experienceable by them and so paradoxically had a quality of objectivity.[112] For readers in the later nineteenth century Goethe became the exemplary traveller in Italy. Northern Europeans followed in his footsteps, thinking as they travelled that they were reliving an experience of Italy as a timeless land of ease and beauty.[113] However, this was a misinterpretation of Goethe's intentions and of the more intriguing story of personal development that the *Italian Journey* tells. Thanks to the original papers Goethe had saved, Parts One and Two have great immediacy and freshness,[114] compared to the artful composition and distanced ironies of *Poetry and Truth*. That immediacy is indeed part of the argument of the *Italian Journey*, in three important ways. First, it expresses the principle of autopsy. A thing can only truly be known if you have seen it for yourself, just as the descriptions of art in Winckelmann's *History*—the historical importance of which Goethe had stressed in his essay of 1805[115]—urge us to experience art for ourselves, and just as the nature of coloured light could only be understood, Goethe thought, by those who had repeated his observations with prisms. Second, Goethe presents sensory immediacy as an alternative to his own unhealthy Wertherian tendency to apprehend objects with the imagination, which was, much to his annoyance, being revived by the Romantics. And third, seeing Italy at first hand is part of the *Italian Journey*'s story of rebirth and healing after the ten exhausting years as a minister in Weimar. The healing power of Italy came not only from its azure skies, balmy climate, and ease of life, as a clichéd reading of the *Italian Journey* might have it. Equally important was the sheer effort involved in seeing and experiencing Italy at first hand. As Goethe notes in Rome in December 1786, the journey has involved 'more effort and worry than enjoyment'.[116] The effort consists in encountering new and alien objects, which have to be experienced, not merely imagined. To understand objects is to understand oneself. As Goethe notes in Verona: 'I am making this strange journey not to deceive myself, but to get to know myself in the objects'.[117] One would be deceiving oneself if one substituted one's own imagination for the objects themselves and one's own direct sensory experience of them. It would also be self-deception to resist being changed by the experience. The *Italian Journey* is a story of mental adjustments, some small, some large. In the background is the ghost of the irredeemable Werther with his pathological refusal to renounce his imagination. Goethe recounts meeting a Malteser in Palermo who, on learning that he is German, asks Goethe how the author of Werther is faring:

> After a short pause, as if I were deliberating, I answered: The person about whom you're kindly enquiring—it's me!—With obvious amazement he recoiled and exclaimed: A lot must have changed then! Oh yes, I added, between Weimar and Palermo I've gone through quite a change.[118]

The most important change narrated in the *Italian Journey* is his gradual discovery at first hand that the classical tradition is more discontinuous and heterogeneous, indeed stranger, than he had been taught. This historical lesson goes hand in hand with an aesthetic one. One of his main aims on the journey is to practise his aesthetic judgement on the best artworks there are, which requires him to return to the origins of the classical tradition. The *Italian Journey* is a story of a quest for the origins of beauty in Greek antiquity. The aesthetic education thus *begins* from the position of an educated person of the eighteenth century, who views Greek art through the lens of Renaissance revivals of antiquity. The two artists who receive most attention in Part One of the *Italian Journey* are Renaissance artists who are the models of the revival of antiquity—first Palladio in Vicenza, Venice, and the Veneto, and then the paintings of Raphael, starting with his 'Ecstasy of St Cecilia' in Bologna and culminating with the 'School of Athens' and his other Vatican frescoes.[119] Palladio and Raphael achieve a perfection about which nothing meaningful can be said other than that it is perfect.[120] The challenge these works present us with is not deciphering or describing them; it is being open to their salutary effect. However, this is only the first stage of the journey. During his first stay in Rome in the winter of 1786/87 Goethe begins to question neoclassicism. He becomes dissatisfied with Roman art, which consists largely of copies of Greek works.[121] The dissatisfaction provides a stimulus for his onwards journey to Naples and Sicily and the further mental adjustments that the journey requires. The journey south from Rome narrated in Part Two brings greater changes. The most acute is his first encounter with the Doric temples at Paestum. It is a challenge to a habituated mentality. The evolution of Greek architecture from a heavy and rugged to a more slender and graceful style has accustomed us to the latter:

I found myself in a totally alien world. For as the centuries progress from the earnest to the pleasing, they move humans along with them, indeed they breed them thus. Our eyes, and through them our whole inner being, are now so exclusively directed and specifically oriented to a slenderer type of architecture that these blunt, cone-shaped, dense columnar masses make us feel uncomfortable, even intimidated. But soon I pulled myself together, remembered my art history, bore in mind that the spirit of those times was in keeping with such architecture, pictured to myself the austere style of their sculpture, and in less than an hour I felt reconciled. Indeed I praised my tutelary genius for having let me see these very well-preserved remains with my own eyes, since no picture can give an adequate idea of them.[122]

In Sicily there are more Doric temples to see at Segesta and Agrigento, and hence more opportunities to become 'reconciled' to the austere style and to train the aesthetic sense. Returning to Naples, he can revisit Paestum and reach a more educated view of what had originally intimidated him.[123]

Sicily and Naples are the culmination of the *Italian Journey*. The quest for the origins of beauty ends where Greek influence was at its strongest and where the remains of Greek art and architecture are best preserved. However, while the aesthetic part of the project might be complete, the existential and psychological part is not. He hopes that he will reap existential benefits from discovering Greek beauty. Specifically it will cure him of his hypochondria by subordinating his imagination to his senses.[124] However, this succeeds only in part, and his overactive imagination is still troublesome throughout the Neapolitan and Sicilian legs of the journey. Three weeks after arriving in Naples, he reflects on his alienation from his former self:

Naples is a paradise, everyone lives in a kind of drunken oblivion of themselves. It's the same with me, I seem to be a completely different person. Yesterday I thought: 'Either you were mad before, or you are now'.[125]

Magna Graecia is a land of madness and sanity, darkness and light, danger and ease. For instance, the ease and leisure of Neapolitan life is threatened by Mount Vesuvius.[126] The extremes of life in Naples cause the imagination to run riot. There are other reasons for hypochondria, not least the sea crossing from Naples to Palermo. The two weeks before the crossing are full of uncertainty. The narrative flow of the journal breaks down into a staccato series of anxious reflections, ending with an admission of how close he still is to the hypochondria of his youth:

Sometimes I'm reminded of Rousseau and his hypochondriacal affliction, and yet I am beginning to understand how so finely organized a mind could be put into disarray. If I did not feel in such great sympathy with natural things, and if I did not see that in this apparent confusion there are a hundred observations which can be compared and put in order, just as a surveyor tests many individual measurements by drawing a line through them, I would often think that I myself was mad.[127]

The six-week tour of Sicily is also full of stark contrasts. In a revealing formulation, he describes Sicily as 'hyper-classical terrain' ('überklassische[r] Boden').[128] Unlike mainland Italy which largely fits within our preconceptions of the classical tradition, Sicily's hyper-classicism bursts the confines of the classical tradition. Adding to the uncertainty is the prospect of continuing the journey to Greece itself. On the day before embarking at Naples for Sicily, he receives an unnerving invitation:

As I was taking leave of him, the Prince of Waldeck made me uneasy by suggesting nothing less than that on my return I should arrange to accompany him to Greece and Dalmatia. Let him who goes out into the world and becomes involved with it beware lest he lose his bearings or even his mind! I am not capable of writing another syllable.[129]

The possibility of extending the trip to Greece becomes part of the psychodrama of Sicily. The second part of his tour of Sicily includes an ill-advised shortcut through the island's bleak interior from Agrigento to Catania via Caltanissetta, and a final brief stay in earthquake-ravaged, autocrat-ruled Messina. It is a foretaste of what Greece would be like for the eighteenth-century tourist: temples reduced to rubble, a society ruled by tyrants, a once rich but now empty land. The most challenging experience is that Sicily is both hyper-classical and a depressing shadow of its former glory. The painful reality is summed up by his account of a planned but unwritten tragedy on the story of Nausicaa, the princess of the Phaeacians whom Odysseus visited. Homer's Phaeacia was commonly identified with Sicily, and accordingly in the *Italian Journey* Goethe presents the Nausicaa plan as if it were a product of his time in Sicily, whereas in fact he had first had the idea well before he arrived there.[130] In the *Italian Journey*, the Nausicaa plan represents his 'final breakthrough to Greece'.[131] But by linking the Nausicaa plan so closely to Sicily, Goethe also implies that his work on the tragedy is of one place and time, limited, nontransferable, even alien to the modern and northern worlds to which he would eventually return. Nausicaa remains unfinished because it is Sicilian. It is a symbol both of Goethe's closeness to Homer's Greece and of the gulf that separates him from it. The meaning of Sicily is thus highly ambivalent. Sicily is a Homeric land, but the closer one gets to the origins of beauty in Ancient Greece, the more one is forced to realize that Ancient Greece is irretrievably lost and alien.

The journey to the Rhine and Main in summer 1814 and a shorter trip early in summer 1815 yielded a publishing project that would accompany Goethe for the rest of his life. It is known today by its eventual title *On Art and Antiquity*. A better title might have used the plural *Antiquities*, since the subject was not classical antiquity (or at least not to start with) but the medieval antiquities of the Rhine and Main region. The original title was *On Art and Antiquity in the Rhine and Main Regions*, and the three instalments of the first volume, published in 1816 and 1817, lived up to the title. The first instalment contained a travelogue of the cultural sites Goethe visited in the area in 1814, not unlike the latter stages of the *Italian Journey*. The first instalment of the second volume (1818) took a turn towards cultural polemics against Romanticism and nationalism. From 1820 onwards, the periodical became a platform for literary reviews in which Goethe promoted what we now call 'minor literatures' and his thoughts about 'world literature' (*Weltliteratur*). Goethe wrote most of the content himself, so that it was a highly subjective kind of periodical. As he would write at the end of his life in an essay titled 'A Word for Young Poets', a person can 'only ever bring his individuality to light'.[132]

The anti-Romantic tendency was in fact present from the beginning of *On Art and Antiquity*, and the project as a whole typifies Goethe's uneasy attitude to German nationalism in the post-Napoleonic years. His trip to the Rhine and Main in 1814 would not have happened without encouragement from the Catholic art collector Sulpiz Boisserée, who owned an important collection with his brother Melchior in Heidelberg. At the first meeting with Sulpiz Boisserée in Weimar in 1811, Goethe was suspicious because Boisserée was an acolyte of Friedrich Schlegel and therefore, as it seemed to Goethe, a proponent of Romanticism and the new Catholic tendency in the arts. With tact and diplomacy however, Boisserée encouraged Goethe to reconsider German medieval culture. The timing was fortunate. It was in 1811 that Goethe wrote to his old Frankfurt friend Klinger that he was overcoming his habitual dislike of revisiting his own past[133]—a past in which Goethe, along with Herder, had instigated the first German wave of medievalism. Boisserée primed Goethe to be receptive to the medieval art he would see along the Rhine and Main. There were also political imperatives. Goethe had contacts with ministers in the Prussian-governed Rhine.[134] After the liberation of the German Rhine from the French, and in response to the Prussian minister Freiherr von und zum Stein, in February 1816 Goethe composed a memorandum on the state of cultural treasures and institutions in the region. His focus on Germanic antiquities and his contacts with Prussian authorities might suggest that *On Art and Antiquity* was a contribution to the nationalist project of pan-German reconstruction after Napoleon. However, we should also bear in mind Goethe's positioning of himself in the post-Napoleonic cultural landscape. One might equally see *On Art and Antiquity* as his attempt to occupy a space in German cultural politics created by the clean start of the Restoration: to position himself once more as *praeceptor Germaniae*, and not to cede the position to others like Schlegel.

Despite returning to the Middle Ages, he did not alter the fundamentals of his understanding of art. On the contrary, he assimilated the medieval material into his settled method of viewing art.[135] From the first instalment of the second volume (1818) he adopted two tactics.[136] One was to analyse Renaissance art as if it were classical, and thus to pull the rug away from under the Romantic theorization of art. In the new Catholic writing on the arts, he found a tendency to approach artworks as if they were objects of spiritual contemplation. He preferred to focus on the concrete particulars of artworks, such as form and colour, and to consider the implications of an artist's choice of subject matter. The other tactic was to undertake reconstructions of artworks that were fragmentary or lost. His interest in the fragmentary had begun with his essay on the Strasbourg minster of the early 1770s, and he was prompted to resume it by the plans for the completion of the cathedral of Cologne which he discussed with the Boisserées in autumn 1814. His attitude to reconstructions had, however, been changed by his reading of Winckelmann, who had persuaded him that reconstruction was a branch of art history, and it must take account of the artwork's literary and intellectual context.

Towards the end of his life, Goethe was increasingly seen as a rigid and doctrinaire defender of an outmoded neoclassicism. There is some truth in this view, but it does not get to the root of Goethe's thinking about the arts. It is impossible to overlook his polemics against modern art theory in *On Art and Antiquity*. For instance, in March 1817 he wrote to Knebel:

> My second Rhine and Main instalment will be at your service very soon and will land like a bomb in the circle of the Nazarene artists. Now is the

right time to attack a twenty-year nuisance, to assail it with force, and to shake it at its roots.[137]

The attack on the Nazarenes in the second instalment came in an essay drafted by Meyer with additions by Goethe, 'Modern German religio-patriotic art'. The first instalment of the second volume of *On Art and Antiquity*, published in 1818, signalled a change in direction: it began with the essay 'Myron's Cow', in which Goethe treated classical art as normative. However, Goethe was worried by the charge of doctrinaire neoclassicism, and so alongside 'Myron's Cow', he included an essay titled 'Ancient and modern',[138] in which he rebutted the charge. The essay is Goethe's most effective statement of a position beyond the conflict between the ancients and the moderns, and between neoclassicism and Romanticism. The essay treats these dogmas as one-sided attempts to get at the essence of art, which consists in communication. All artworks communicate the mood and character of the artist: 'Every artistic product puts us in the mood that the author was in. If it was pleasant and light, then we will feel free; if it was constrained, worrisome and troubled, then it will confine us'.[139] He goes on to quote some comments by Carl Ernst Schubart which state a preference for Shakespeare over Goethe. Goethe explains this preference in terms of the favourable historical circumstances that Shakespeare enjoyed but that he, Goethe, did not. This explains Shakespeare's remarkable facility in speaking to us. By the same token, Ancient Greek artists were more favoured by history than we moderns are. Their artists benefitted from an ethos of moral goodness in combination with physical beauty (*kalokagathia*), and from a polytheistic religion that imagined the gods as physically and morally idealized human types. This is why, as an empirical matter, Greek art is excellent. However, in theory any art or artist could be favoured by history and thus emulate Greek excellence. Any art could possess the communicative immediacy of the best Greek art:

> Clarity of vision, serene receptiveness, ease of communication, that is what delights us, and when we maintain that we find all this in the genuine Greek works, and indeed accomplished in the noblest subject matter, the worthiest content, with assured and perfected execution, then one will understand us if we always proceed from this point and always tend towards it. Let everyone be a Greek in their own way! But do be it![140]

The kernel of the argument is therefore not that Greek art is normative. What is normative is directness or immediacy. If we ask what immediacy means, or what immediacy is a characteristic of, then we return to communication. Art is communication by one human to another. Immediacy in art means directness of communication, without any hindrance or inhibition or mystification. And if we ask what is communicated, Goethe's answer is: the artist's humanity, which speaks to the audience's humanity.

The essential—one might even say extreme—humanism of Goethe's writings on art is connected to the *homo mensura* principle that had become central to his scientific thinking. Just as human perception is the ultimate guarantee of scientific truth, so in the arts the direct representation of human nature is the criterion of good art. Furthermore, human nature is the best subject matter for art. So in an essay of 1817 titled 'Flower painting', Goethe begins by stating that 'the human form, and specifically in its dignity and fullness of health, [remains] the main goal of all visual art'.[141] And in an essay of the same year on Leonardo's *Last Supper*, Goethe shows that a key factor in the painting's success was Leonardo's decision to focus not on the Christian mystery of transubstantiation, which was hardly a suitable subject for visual art, but on the emotions of the disciples. These Leonardo is able to convey with physical immediacy, for instance in their hand gestures. Leonardo's subject matter is not a theological idea but a human situation.[142]

The excellence of Ancient Greek or Renaissance Italian art is thus a matter of historical fact that can be explained by theory. Ancient Greek sculpture focused almost exclusively on the human form. In doing so, it was nurtured by the Greek humanistic culture of *kalokagathia* and its polytheistic religion. A similar case can be made for the Italian Renaissance, which was only able to excel in art because it rediscovered Greek humanism. These humanistic cultures helped their artists to overcome the inhibiting factors that had constrained earlier artists. According to Winckelmann, the Ancient Greeks achieved artistic greatness when they abandoned the melancholy, funereal style of Egyptian art.[143] In the same way, Goethe argues, the artists of the Italian Renaissance could excel once they had freed themselves from the 'mummy-like' ('mumienhaft') style of Byzantine art.[144] Humanity is, of course, not the sole property of the Greeks or even Europeans. The *Divan* was an exploration of non-European humanity. Thus, although its main reference points are Ancient Greece and the Greek-inspired Renaissance, Goethe's theory of art is no more monocultural than it is dogmatically neoclassical. Of course, his judgements suffer from cultural blinkers. On several occasions he attacks Indian religious art, in sharp contrast to his very positive appraisals of classical Indian literature. The reasoning is that representations of the gods in Indian art substitute animal for human forms, and thus amount to ugly caricature.[145]

There are two further elements in Goethe's very late writing on art that make his theory more flexible. The first concerns the nature of realism in art. Since learning about Batteux from Gellert's lectures in 1766, Goethe had believed that art is created when an ideal type of nature is formed in the artist's imagination. Selected aspects of (actual) nature are forged into a new idealized entity—Batteux's *belle nature*. Batteux's doctrine can still be found in the writings of Goethe's final years. For instance, in his analysis of Mantegna's *Triumphs of Caesar*, published in *On Art and Antiquity* in 1823,[146] Goethe complains in his familiar aristocratic manner that when common folk demand art that represents the real, they merely want to drag artists down to their own level.[147] True realism consists not in slavishly imitating the real; art cannot remain on the level of mere stuff. The task of the artist is to create ideal types of the real. In this sense, the Batteux-style argument might give more flexibility to Goethe's humanism and could even have created a place in his canon of art for Indian religious images. These do represent ideal types after all, and are not slavish representations of real persons or animals. However, the doctrine of ideal types has two aspects. It makes room for something beyond mere realism, but an artistic ideal type must still be a type *of* reality, *of* humanity. Indeed, this is the grounds for Goethe's longstanding misgivings about allegorical art and literature. The problem with allegory was that it replaced human ideal types with mere abstract ideas: 'allegory transforms the phenomenon into an idea', as he put it in a maxim probably written in the 1820s.[148] Allegorical representations were no longer representations *of* actual things. This was the deeper source of his prejudice against Indian art.

He was undoubtedly aware of the limitations of his humanist version of Batteux's theory of ideal types. Even if it avoided the pitfalls of rudimentary realism, it still required the artist to prioritize the human form. He felt justified in supposing that the human form is the highest subject matter because the human form holds special interest for us. However, a theory that explains artistic excellence purely in terms of the human form is obviously deficient. Several essays and drafts from this period show Goethe wrestling with the question how we should understand nonhuman subject matter in the visual arts, for instance the essay on 'Flower painting'. The argument is developed furthest in a set of essay fragments and drafts on landscape painting written at various points between 1818 and 1829.[149] These include two schemas and one continuous draft of six manuscript pages,[150] the last of which Goethe probably dictated in May 1829.[151] This material takes the form of a history of landscape painting, which is further grounded in a history of perception and mentalities. As Trunz has commented, Goethe's method in this draft advances far beyond the standard practices of art history in his day, which were generally content to describe the contents of artworks and comment on whether their compositional elements (line, colour, perspective, and so on) were successful or not.[152] Goethe's novel approach is to interpret the forms of landscape painting as reflections of how we have understood our natural and social surroundings. Under 'forms', Goethe understands such elements as the disposition of vertical and horizontal landscape features or of buildings and human and animal figures. Early landscapes tend to present features that are 'earnest and at the same time threatening'.[153] The sense of threat is expressed through vertical elements: steep mountains and cliffs. It is a world in which humans have not mastered their surroundings. At the same time this verticality reflects a growing sense that landscape must be made interesting to the eye. Steepness causes us to be engaged by depth of field.[154] With the advent of the Florentine Renaissance, fuelled by the wealth of merchants and bankers, and later with the economic success of the Low Countries, landscape begins to shift the viewer's perspective to a higher level. We look down on landscapes from a higher point of view and see wider vistas, as Goethe notes: 'Demands of wealth. / Hence high standpoints, broad vistas'.[155] Wealth and the confidence it brings make the landscape less fearful, and instead it becomes a space for imaginative play.[156] Depictions of the land tend to ignore its economic use value, and instead present it as graceful wilderness.[157] Grace is conveyed through pleasing effects of distance, now no longer threatened by ominous verticality. Landscape painting has thus completed a Winckelmannian historical progression from the austere to the graceful.

The wider significance of the drafts on landscape painting was to allow Goethe to expand his narrow concern with the representation of the human form in art, while retaining its humanist framework. The history of landscape painting shows us that the humanist view of art can have a broader and more flexible meaning. Painted landscapes are representations of human nature, indirectly at least, in the sense that they represent the forms of human perception and mentalities. The great landscape artists thus satisfy Goethe's demand that art communicates human sensibility with immediacy. He could have applied the same argument to Indian art. However, his frame of reference, formed by his experience since childhood and latterly by his massive collection of copperplates, remained almost exclusively European, and this

Eurocentrism, typical for its time, better explains his antipathy to Indian art than any deficiency of his theory.

In 1815 Goethe's longstanding interest in meteorology took a new and more active turn. The impetus came when Carl August urged Goethe to find out about Luke Howard's classification of clouds. A new German translation had recently appeared of Howard's 1803 *Essay on the Modification of Clouds*, and Carl August had seen a summary of it by the German physicist Ludwig Wilhelm Gilbert. Howard had devised the first and, as it has turned out, remarkably enduring classification of clouds into types, based partly on their shape and colour and partly on altitude. Carl August was chiefly interested in weather forecasting and its potential benefits, not least for the Grand Duchy's struggling farmers, and he decided that Goethe should be responsible for establishing a network of weather stations around the Grand Duchy. Howard's classificatory system appealed to Goethe's interest in giving order to the natural world, and Howard soon ranked among Goethe's pantheon of great classifiers, along with Werner on geognosy and Linnaeus on plants and animals. To someone of Goethe's orderly cast of mind, clouds were especially challenging and attractive, because their airy and ephemeral quality seemed to contradict his cherished idea of natural form. As he put it himself, he was excited by 'the forming of the formless, a lawlike change of shape in the infinite'.[158] The result was a series of short notes and essays, including an encomiastic biography of Howard and a series of poems written in 1822 to honour Howard and celebrate his achievement. Behind the scenes, he continued to promote Carl August's plan for weather stations. Inspired by Howard, he made his own observations of the weather, especially during his holidays at the spas of Carlsbad and Teplitz.

What interested Goethe about the weather, at least since Italy had reconnected him with the world of things, was its nature as an interconnected system. One problem was how the meteorological phenomena we observe—rain, clouds, wind, atmospheric pressure—correlate with one another. Are changes in one phenomenon reliably correlated with changes in others? Intuitively this seems correct, and Goethe believed that his observations confirmed it: 'We find [. . .] the atmospheric phenomena always conditioned one by another; barometer reading, prevailing wind, movement, and shape of clouds directly relate to one another'.[159] The question then was how and why. Is the weather a self-contained system, or is it causally influenced by some exogenous factor, such as the influence of the sun or the moon? In Italy, he had come to think that the 'elasticity' or pressure of the atmosphere was somehow decisive. This was an attractive conclusion because it promised to adhere to a simple and regular law and because atmospheric pressure was easily measurable. (The barometer had been invented in mid-seventeenth-century Italy, probably by Evangelista Torricelli.) As Pascal had predicted, and his brother-in-law Florin Périer had verified empirically, atmospheric pressure is correlated inversely with altitude. Moreover, atmospheric pressure was invisible to the naked eye. It was a hidden quality that might provide the secret key to the other atmospheric phenomena. After first learning about Howard's classification of clouds at the end of 1815, Goethe's next task was therefore to try to correlate the types of clouds with barometer readings, and this occupied him through 1816.[160]

The most obvious empirical regularity in the barometer readings was a correlation between higher pressure and clear skies. From this Goethe inferred that air of higher pressure was capable of absorbing or dissolving or dispersing moisture.[161] Behind this inference was the model of conflict that Goethe had used in the *Theory of Colour*, in this case the conflict between air and moisture. A further complication, however, was Howard's demonstration that cloud types also varied with altitude. In order to explain this, Goethe had to posit a further conflict between the layers of the atmosphere. In a short essay titled 'Cloud Forms according to Howard', mainly consisting of observations of weather in Carlsbad in summer 1820, he proposed that cloud formation is largely dictated by conflict or struggle between upper and lower regions of the heavens.[162] However, the data was proving too complex to bring into a single explanatory model, and so in 1820 he abandoned the project of a unified meteorology with atmospheric pressure as its core phenomenon. There were just too many variables, as he wrote to Carl August in January 1821:

> The meteorological problem is to be sure just much too complicated. What must soon occur to the observer and what I've noticed for two years is that all the symptoms, whether they be barometric, thermometric, hygrometric, and just so the cloud forms, mean something different in each season, and no less in different climates or altitudes etc., for which reason then the judgement, however much mental agility one has, is made difficult.[163]

The problem of correlating meteorological data required the ability to process huge amounts of data, which only became possible with the advent of supercomputers in the second half of the twentieth century. In the absence of this technology, Goethe could only make progress by speculating on exogenous causes for the patterns of the weather and specifically changes in atmospheric pressure. In 1822 he believed he had found the answer. There appeared to be a correlation between atmospheric pressure and oscillations in earth's magnetic field. The answer harked back to his speculations on electricity, galvanism, and magnetism between 1805 and 1815. The goal of physics had to be a unifying theory of forces, which would explain the phenomena of electricity, galvanism, magnetism, and even colour with a single model. Once such a model was found, he wrote to Seebeck in January 1813, 'the whole of science would forever be secure'.[164] The idea of a correlation between atmospheric pressure and 'tellurian' magnetism was therefore a satisfying solution, albeit an incorrect one. It appealed to his intuition that the earth was a single closed system. It allowed him to avoid the problem of the multiple variables that were in play in atmospheric data. The weather was a system not because atmospheric conditions were produced by laws of mutual interaction, or indeed because the weather was affected by factors external to our planet such as the sun or moon. Rather the systematic character of the weather was caused by the earth itself: 'The causes of the changes in the barometer [...] are not cosmic, not atmospheric, but *tellurian*'.[165] Goethe believed that several pieces of data justified his tellurian model and disqualified endogenous atmospheric models. First, an endogenous explanation for changes in barometric pressure seemed incompatible with the fact that barometric pressure correlated with some atmospheric phenomena but not others. For instance there seemed to be an inverse correlation between pressure and precipitation,[166] but there was no correlation between barometric pressure and temperature.[167] Second, the regularity in barometric pressure posited by Pascal seemed to relate not to the distance of any given point above the earth's surface, but to its height above global sea level and hence also its distance from the centre of the earth. This indicated to Goethe that barometric pressure did not correlate with the weight of air pressing down on the lower atmosphere. It might however correlate with gravitational force. Furthermore, the fact that rises and falls in barometric pressure seemed to be the same across large areas was consistent with the tellurian model, or so Goethe thought.[168] However, this key piece of evidence was not as strong as Goethe believed, because the only data he had was from a relatively small corner of central Germany.[169]

In January 1825 Carl August wrote to Goethe asking for his thoughts about the relation between atmospheric pressure and weather conditions. The answer came in the form of an essay, 'Attempt at a Theory of Weather'.[170] The essay was a reckoning with ten years of meteorological observations, reading, and discussion with friends and experts. It also gave Goethe the opportunity to set out his tellurian model of climate. The essay was not published until after Goethe's death, whether because he viewed it as a private communication or because of justified hesitancy concerning the tellurian model. Indeed, Goethe's scientific achievement in meteorology was limited. His impact was more practical than theoretical. He pushed forward Carl August's plan for a network of weather stations in the Grand Duchy. He tried to link up atmospheric pressure data from Germany and Britain. He promoted a kind of citizen science project in meteorological measurements.[171] However, the kind of theoretical models that Goethe hoped for required a much wider network of weather stations than were available to him.

———

Geology was the science in which Goethe was most active after the Restoration. He continued to make observations, especially during his visits to the spa towns. He wrote numerous short notes on rock formations, theoretical pieces on crystallization, and book reviews. It was also the discipline in which he enjoyed the greatest recognition, including an honorary diploma from the mineralogical society of St Petersburg in 1818 and correspondence with several geologists eager to win his support for their theories. In February 1816 he received a request from the geologist Karl Cäsar von Leonhard, who wanted Goethe's opinion on his theory that crystalline minerals were formed in the primordial epoch. Goethe drafted a short essay and then a long letter, in which he half agreed with Leonhard. Crystallization, or 'solidescence' as he also termed it,[172] had occurred in the primordial formation of minerals and it was continuing. It was a fundamental process. Minerals have an intrinsic tendency to find regular crystalline form, if they are able to develop freely. Form inheres in matter. It was the doctrine of hylomorphism that he had adopted in the mid-1780s as a way of explaining the regular seams he had found in the Harz Mountains. He revisited this old doctrine several times between 1815 and 1825.[173] No doubt, by restating the theory he hoped to secure his geological legacy. However, there was more to it than just geological science and the question of his legacy. Goethe's theory of solidescence was a compromise between the Neptunism of Werner, whose death in 1817 prompted reassessment of his work, and the increasingly popular Vulcanist theories. It has been argued that Goethe moved away from Werner in the years after 1815,[174] and he certainly did portray Werner as dogmatic.[175] Werner's Neptunism was a monocausal explanatory model which absolutely excluded any effects of heat on rock formation. Goethe's view was more pluralistic. Instead of positing a single causal factor, he allowed for the action of heat, chemistry, water, and wind erosion.[176] Arguably this made his approach overly vague, for it was not entirely clear what sort of process solidescence was. He had first proposed this compromise back in the mid-1780s, as a way of making peace between Werner and his pupil Johann Carl Wilhelm Voigt. His position had not changed significantly since then. However, the times had changed. The Revolution had sharpened Goethe's dislike of political partisanship, and after 1815 nationalist and liberal movements were gaining ground across a wide front, from South America to Spain, Italy, Greece and the German student movement centred in Jena of all places. Dogmatism in science seemed to him an example of partisanship. So his compromise position in geology, or at any rate the manner in which he presented it after 1815, was a response to political as well as scientific partisanship. His pacific and undogmatic doctrine of solidescence was an antidote to the tumultuous, volcanic times.[177] By returning to his geological discoveries of the mid-1780s, from a time before Europe was shaken by revolution, Goethe thought he was contributing to the reestablishment of a sensible peace. However, he could not and did not maintain an impartial or undogmatic stance, in politics or in science. He disliked partisanship because it was detrimental to the harmonious and effective functioning of society. Antipathy to disruption can be conservative, and Goethe's was. He could conceal neither his dislike of revolutionary politics nor his 'aversion to violent explanations' in geology, as he wrote in 1820.[178] And so in another way, he actively sided with the minority anti-Vulcanist (and conservative anti-revolutionary) viewpoint, as he told Müller in 1812: 'posterity shall know that at least one sensible man lived in our age who saw through these absurdities. I find it ever more the case that one should stick with the minority, which is always the more sensible'.[179]

Goethe had less success in securing his legacy in optics and colour theory, at least among scientists. By 1815 the science of physical optics was drawing ever more heavily on mathematical models and techniques. He was well aware of the accusation that his own work made no use of mathematics.[180] His response to this charge in 1815, in a conversation with Boisserée, was that his theory of colour was thoroughly mathematical in the same sense as Spinoza's *Ethics*: it used a strictly logical method.[181] It was a weak defence and probably not meant seriously, but it shows he was aware how much the accusation threatened his legacy. An example of the weakness of his theory of optics was his work on birefringence. Some transparent materials such as calcite crystals have two refractive indices, so that a ray of light falling on a calcite crystal can split into two rays that form a double image. In 1817 the physicist Thomas Johann Seebeck asked Goethe to write a short history of recent research into birefringent phenomena. Goethe read some of the latest, mainly French literature on the subject. His interest was stimulated by the fact that some double images underwent colour shifts, and so he began to make his own observations of these so-called 'entoptic' colours. However, he did not join the mainstream scientific debate about the physics of birefringence. It was not only the mathematical methods that put him off. Birefringence was key evidence in debates about the nature of light, and it added new heat to the dispute between the corpuscularians, who followed Newton in holding that light consisted of minute particles, and the advocates of the wave theory. The whole debate was anathema to Goethe, since it continued the old Newtonian error of forcing light into unnatural experimental conditions in order to 'anatomize' it, and to express the results mathematically. Science of this kind no longer corresponded to what our senses told us. Jean-Baptiste Biot had proposed that light consisted of pulses with two perpendicular dimensions which could therefore be polarized when passed through a suitable medium. Goethe was unimpressed: 'Now in order to conceal a false proposition with proofs, here yet again the whole mathematical armoury was set in motion, so that nature disappeared entirely to our outer and inner sense'.[182] For Goethe, Biot's theory of polarization was just another example of the anatomization of light,[183] and he chose not to engage with Biot's work. (Whether he understood enough of the mathematics to do so is another matter.) Instead he treated birefringence in the same way as he had treated the border colours: by viewing the phenomena first under natural light and then in an array of modified conditions. His belief was that coloured birefringence appeared only 'under certain conditions', as he wrote to Reinhard in 1818,[184] and these could be identified by varying the experimental context. It was the same experimental practice as he had pursued in his *Optical Essays* in the 1790s and in the *Theory of Colour*. In this connection it is worth observing that the term 'entoptic', which Goethe used to refer to the phenomena of birefringence, is more commonly used to refer to visual phenomena that are generated by and within (*ent-*) the eye (*ops*). Indeed it can be argued that Goethe's work on birefringence shares some features with his earlier work on physiological colours. As he wrote to Reinhard, the entoptic colours were 'a phenomenon different from all others hitherto known and yet related to them in the most intimate way'.[185] It is its relatedness to physiological colours that explains Goethe's intense interest in birefringence. Increasingly he felt that the physiological colours were the most important of all the coloured phenomena, and not the boundary colours. The physiological colours were, he noted in his essay *Chromatics* of 1821, 'the beginning and end of all colour theory [...] and instead of them being considered fleeting errors of the eye, as previously, [they] are now confirmed as the norm and guiding principle of all else that is visible'.[186]

The point of similarity between birefringent and physiological colours was that both occurred in opaque media. The interest in opaque media was the most significant new development in Goethe's thinking about colour after 1815. It was not based on any new empirical discoveries. It was in fact a metaphysical construct by which Goethe tried to make sense of the visible world. The phenomena of vision appear only within opaque media. It is only within opaque media that the human eye can withstand the power of light. By contrast, both absolute light and absolute darkness are intolerable to the eye. The theory of opaque media is the central argument of the *Chromatics* essay:

> Above all one must attend to the fact that our eye is equipped neither for the most powerful light nor for the deepest darkness; the former blinds, the latter denies in excess. The organ of vision is, like the others, dependent on a middle station. Light, dark, and the colours that arise between the two are the elements from which the eye draws and creates its world. From his principle flows everything else, and whoever grasps and learns to apply it will easily warm to our presentation.[187]

Now it is immediately obvious, and certainly of little scientific interest, that the eye needs opacity in order to be able to tolerate light. It is obvious that opaque media reduce light to tolerable levels. What is less obvious in Goethe's new metaphysics of the visible is the relation between vision, opacity, and darkness. Goethe seems to want us to think that both light and darkness are reduced by opacity, but in what sense could opaque media *reduce* darkness? The idea seems to be that darkness acts as a kind of vacuum, and only when it is filled by an opaque medium such as air, can space produce light. In this sense we might think of absolute light and darkness as merely spiritual forces, that is to say forces that cannot have any effect on the world until they enter into a bodily medium. Opacity is that bodily medium. An otherwise dark vacuum (spirit) can only manifest light when it is filled with air (body). Thus in Goethe's new metaphysics of the visible, light and darkness are spiritual forces, and opacity is the bodily substance that they require in order to become manifest. The passage in which Goethe formulates this argument is rather dense and not a little obscure:

> It seems as if one can, in explaining, describing, specifying opacity, not justifiably avoid the transparent. Light and darkness have a common field, a space, a vacuum, in which they are seen appearing. This is the transparent. (Without transparency there is neither light nor darkness. This vacuum is however not the air, although it can be filled with air.) Just as the individual colours relate to light and darkness as their generative causes, so their physicality, their medium, the opaque [relates to] the transparent. (The former give the spirit, the latter the body to colour.) The first reduction in the transparent, i.e., the first slightest filling of space, equally the first approach to something bodily [or] impervious is the opaque. It is accordingly the most delicate material, the first layer of physicality. (The spirit that wishes to appear weaves itself a delicate opacity, and the imagination of all peoples has spirits appearing in a mist-like garment.)[188]

I have described this metaphysics of the visible as new, but in fact it complements Goethe's established system. It was the capstone of the metaphysics of light that he first set out in the *Theory of Colour*. One key to understanding this whole strange construction is that for Goethe darkness was not merely the absence of light. Darkness was in fact a positive antagonist of light. This was a view he arrived at early in his experiments with prisms in 1790. The fact that the boundary colours appeared at the margin of pale and dark surfaces required him to think that both light and darkness were involved in the generation of colour, and that darkness, like light, had a colour-generating effect. The world of colour was in fact the result of a struggle between the opposed forces of light and darkness. It was within this struggle, within the beautiful world of colour, that humans lived their lives. Goethe's late theory of the opaque purported to explain what it was about the physical world that made it visible. We live in a space filled with degrees of opacity. As a physical theory of light this is obviously deficient. However, it makes very good sense as a theory of coloured pigments. Opacity is one of the fundamental qualities of pigments. Paint is not merely colour; it is coloured opacity. Artists layer pigments on top of one another in order to create effects of varying density and opacity, as well as colour. Indeed the *Theory of Colour* was as much about coloured pigments, their uses and meanings, as it was about the physics of light. Repeatedly in his last years Goethe insisted on the 'practical advantages' that artists could gain from his theory.[189] In 1829, trying to explain his colour theory to the portraitist Stieler, he wrote that 'it's best to talk to the practical artist'.[190] Goethe's metaphysics of colour speak to the artist, and that is where his colour theory had its main legacy. Unsurprisingly, most scientists remained baffled by it.

By some distance, Goethe's most significant scientific legacy was his work on animal morphology. After the Battle of Jena-Auerstedt and the threat it posed to his papers, he had decided to republish the essay 'On the Metamorphosis of Plants' and other unpublished papers on plants and mammals.[191] During 1806–1807 he had drafted two introductory essays that sketched the development of his scientific thinking, 'The Undertaking is Excused' and 'The Intention Introduced'. Then he seems to have abandoned the project, perhaps because of the more urgent need to complete the *Theory of Colour*. In 1816 he took up the plan again, in the context of Cotta's new edition of his works. There followed a series of volumes between 1817 and 1824, titled *On Science in General, especially on Morphology*. They contained a heterogeneous combination of material, not all of it by Goethe himself. Of the material by him, some was new and some old, some of the old material previously published, some not. He made no significant changes to the already published material, no effort to update their findings.[192] This, together with the heterogeneity of the contents, gives the volumes the feel of an archive, rather than a coherent set of arguments. In 1817 he wrote a third introductory essay 'The Content Prefaced'.[193] This short piece ends with a statement that new 'deepening' trends in philosophy were making his old ideas relevant again. It does not state which philosophy he is referring to, but the essay's argument implies that he had in mind new developments in transformationist thinking. In the first two decades of the century transformationism was for the first time being debated openly. In 1809 Jean-Baptiste Lamarck presented a fully worked out theory of species evolution in his *Philosophie zoologique*. He was opposed by the palaeontologist Georges Cuvier, who believed that species were fixed. As far as we know, Goethe did not read Lamarck's *Philosophie zoologique*, only his annual meteorological survey for 1809,[194] but in the last two years of his life he did intervene in the French debate that developed out of Lamarck's transformationism in

1830. In 1817 that 'volcano' had not yet 'erupted', as Goethe would later joke.[195] 'The Content Prefaced' only hints broadly at the philosophical environment. It mentions some biologists by name, but these were of earlier generations: his predecessors in animal morphology Buffon and Daubenton, and his interlocutors of the 1780s Sömmerring, Camper, and Merck. The essay also highlights the collaboration with Herder in the early 1780s: 'Our daily conversation concerned the primal beginnings of the water-earth, and the organic creatures that had developed on it since ages ago'.[196] In this way he states his own (and Herder's) primacy in transformationist science. Moreover, in the first volume of *On Science in General, especially on Morphology*, 'The Content Prefaced' is placed directly after the 1807 piece 'The Intention Introduced', in which Goethe speculates on how the division between the kingdoms of plant and animal life might have been caused by the presence or absence of light. The passage is striking because it allows for transformation to have taken place at the very root of the evolution of life. Its claims are thus far broader than the narrow form of transformationism that is sometimes attributed to him.[197] According to that narrow Buffonian transformationism, transformation occurs only at the level of species. 'The Intention Introduced' speculates that transformation may lie at the root of animal life itself. It is powerful evidence for the case that Goethe believed in the stronger form of transformationism. Taken together then, 'The Intention Introduced' and 'The Content Prefaced' situate his biology at the beginnings of transformationist science and accord transformationism a much greater range and power than was normally done.

Following the publication of Parts One and Two of the *Italian Journey* in 1817, Goethe stopped working on his autobiography for two years. In accordance with his principle of not writing about his life in Weimar, the next phase of his autobiography that he could take on when he resumed work in 1819 was his participation in the allied invasion of France in 1792 and the siege of Mainz in 1793. Aside from this negative reason, there were positive reasons for writing about the two campaigns. The first was their historical significance. Goethe could assume that his readers would be interested in his experience of these momentous events 'in which I played a tiny part' ('quorum pars minima fui').[198] He had written these words a week after the Battle of Valmy. The Latin was a self-mocking travesty of Aeneas's mournful words in Virgil's *Aeneid*, as he begins to tell Dido of the fall of Troy: 'piteous things which I saw for myself,

/ and in which I played a major part'.[199] The travesty of Virgil expressed Goethe's feeling that the campaign was part of the epic story of the Revolution, and its outcome, the debacle at Valmy and the miserable retreat, was tragic, but the tragedy was also travesty. It was not a story of human heroes made playthings of the gods. It was more of a tragicomedy, a story of ordinary human misjudgements, unfounded optimism, bad weather, and not much fighting. That perspective was evidently still fresh in his mind in 1819. The epigraph Goethe chose for the *Campaign in France*—'I too [was] in Champagne'—was a travesty of the classical epigraph of the *Italian Journey*—'I too in Arcadia'. The French campaign was a modern travesty of his encounter with antiquity in Naples and Sicily. This was another reason for writing up his experiences in the wars of 1792–1793. He had returned from Italy in 1788 full of optimism and with a new intellectual purpose which the revolutionary world he returned to would not acknowledge. There is indeed a further joke in the epigraph 'I too in Champagne', for the name Champagne was the French equivalent of the Latin *campania*, that is to say the 'blessed countryside' (*campania felix*) surrounding Naples, where Goethe most fully experienced the culture of antiquity. The contrasts between the Neapolitan *campania* in spring 1787 and Champagne in autumn 1792 were plain: the balmy Italian skies versus the torrential rain of northeastern France, the fabled ease and bounty of Naples versus the stress and deprivations of an army on the move, and above all peace versus war. The French campaign and the siege of Mainz were expressions of the modern revolutionary world and a mean travesty of antiquity.

Another reason to write up the events of 1792 and 1793 was their political relevance in 1819. Goethe first mentioned his plans for the *Campaign* in his diary for 24 October 1819, one month after the promulgation of the Carlsbad Decrees on 20 September. The Decrees were a response to the murder of the playwright August von Kotzebue earlier that year. Kotzebue had been a target of the younger generation since his spat with the Schlegels in 1798. His success on the German stage was the object of snobbish envy.[200] (Despite presiding over six hundred performances of Kotzebue's plays during his tenure as director of the Weimar court theatre, Goethe shared this view and in particular mocked Kotzebue's popularity among women.)[201] Kotzebue's attacks on liberalism and nationalism worsened his reputation and led to false accusations that he was a political agent of the Russian Emperor.[202] In October 1817, on the fourth anniversary of Napoleon's defeat at Leipzig and shortly before the supposed three hundredth anniversary of the beginning of the Reformation, Lutheran student fraternity members and professors convened at the Wartburg outside Eisenach. Among the celebrations was a ritual burning of selected anti-nationalist and anti-Lutheran books, including Kotzebue's *History of the German Empire*. In March 1819 the Jena student and fraternity member Karl Ludwig Sand stabbed Kotzebue to death in Mannheim. Goethe reacted to the news with a not uncharacteristic equanimity verging on satisfaction. Kotzebue's impudence and conceit had got their deserts; his assassination was the 'necessary consequence of a higher universal order', he told Müller.[203] The Carlsbad Decrees used Kotzebue's murder as a pretext for dissolving the student fraternities, suppressing freedom of the press, and providing for the persecution of the liberal and nationalist 'demagogues'. Around this time Goethe was in contact with the Decrees' architect Metternich and must have been party to his thinking.[204] Despite his own conservatism and his long-standing opposition to freedom of the press, Goethe disapproved of the Decrees, which he believed would only fan the flames. His narrative of the failed military intervention of 1792 can be read as an oblique comment on the Decrees. Specifically, there was a parallel in Goethe's mind between the Decrees and the Brunswick Manifesto of July 1792, by which the allies meant to intimidate the French into surrender but instead fuelled the radicalism of the Revolution and inspired the French defence at Valmy. Goethe's dislike of the Decrees was not a sign of any liberalism on his part. What troubled him was the unwisely antagonistic tactics of his own side, in keeping with his long-held view that the government of Weimar should present a liberal face while covertly rooting out rebels. As he had written to Fritz Jacobi after the liberation of Mainz in July 1793, the allies were right to turn a blind eye to loyalist reprisals against the Jacobins, as long they were not seen to be doing so.[205] Liberties should be suppressed but it was unwise to be caught in the act.

In reconstructing his experiences during the campaigns, he had little to draw on from his own archive. He had preserved a series of maps of the campaign with dates and locations noted on the reverse. Beyond this he had no diaries and few letters of his own. His main source was the diary of Carl August's manservant Wagner. There were also two long letters by his own servant Goetze.[206] Goethe read a dozen or so published sources from both sides in the war, including the memoirs of the French generals Custine and Dumouriez and a collection of letters by French emigrés.[207] The project was of course politically sensitive. Valmy had been a disaster, and the reasons for the allies' failure lay not only in the astuteness of the French generals and the effectiveness of their artillery. The allied high command had been overconfident and had made a series of tactical and logistical errors. Goethe's narrative in

Campaign in France generally avoids direct comment on these errors. The only criticism, and an oblique one at that, is a reference to critical comments expressed by a retired cavalry officer in Trier and others, presumably including Goethe himself.[208] By way of explanation for the disaster, Goethe reports the excuse given by the allied commander-in-chief the Duke of Brunswick that the weather was to blame.[209] While partly true, the excuse is clearly blind to the full reality. In a piece of historical writing, such reticence on Goethe's part about the reasons for the failure would have been a significant shortcoming. However, the narrative is a work of autobiography, not history. It does not give the reader an analysis of the campaign, or at least not explicitly. Instead it presents the perspectives of Goethe and other parties whom he chances to meet. It begins not with a summary of the background of the war, but *in medias res*, with Goethe's arrival in Mainz at the end of August 1792 en route to joining Carl August's regiment at Longwy, which had been captured by the allies several days earlier after a brief siege. The advance through eastern France continues successfully, albeit in worsening weather, until it stalls in confusing circumstances in the Argonne Forest. The climax of the first part of the narrative is the stalemate at Valmy. Throughout this first part, Goethe presents himself as distant from the allied high command and its thinking, although in reality he must have been well informed about their strategy. But according to the narrative of *Campaign in France*, Goethe is more interested in his optical research than in the campaign. With the allied retreat from Valmy the narrative becomes darker. Only now does Goethe begin to write about the epidemic of dysentery among the allied troops (though he does not name the disease)[210] and the extensive loss of horses and baggage trains. His account of the retreat is suitably grim and is relieved only by excursuses on the citadel of Luxembourg's architecture and topography and the antiquities of Trier. The contrast between the optimistic advance to Valmy and the miserable retreat reflects the subjective experience of Goethe and others in the allied force. The failure of the campaign and the misery experienced by the soldiers is presented as a realization that dawns only gradually and late. Goethe 'formed the narrative in the shape of his own process of realization'.[211] To put it more bluntly, it is a study in illusion and disillusionment. Hence, Goethe's response to the allies' failure at Valmy on 20 September is a loss of faith: 'it had been my own absolute faith in such an army and in the Duke of Brunswick which had enticed me to participate in this dangerous expedition'.[212] But there are also signs early in the narrative that Goethe is sceptical. In Mainz, he hears from a young emigré woman of her plan to return to France via Trier, but he warns her that this would be premature.[213] In Grevenmacher, between Trier and Luxembourg, he reports the postmaster's worrying news about the allies' supply chains.[214] However, Goethe's worries about the campaign, presented almost apologetically and as a symptom of his isolation, are set against an overly optimistic groupthink. As social beings, people convince one another of pleasing illusions, in this case the illusion promoted by the emigrés that the revolutionary armies will surrender or defect en masse.[215] Goethe disliked the emigrés intensely, not least for only pursuing their own selfish interests, but the emigrés were not solely to blame. Even the early parts of the *Campaign*, when read carefully, contain enough signs that the whole enterprise is based on an illusion. The epigraph 'I too in Champagne' is part of this illusion, with its suggestion of a celebratory progress through France. Before the campaign Carl August had claimed that 'we will drink champagne without having to fire a shot'.[216] In the epigraph we can hear Goethe's acknowledgement that he suffered from the same illusion that the French would crumble and the allies would stroll into Paris. In this sense, the *Campaign* is a study of the obstacles that society at large places in the way of an individual's path to the truth. When society wants to believe a comforting illusion, an individual will struggle to find the truth and convince his fellows of it. The idea was by no means new: it had loomed large in his work on optics. It was especially germane to the writing of the *Campaign in France* and *The Siege of Mainz*, because the events of 1792 and 1793 came soon after Goethe's return from Italy. These were the years in which the intellectual gains from Italy should have borne fruit, but did not. They were years in which he felt intellectually and socially isolated. In the *Campaign* he exaggerates the feeling of isolation, and he gives two explanations for it, a new and an old one. Both explanations appear in the strange last quarter of the *Campaign*, which narrates his parting company with the Duke at Koblenz and his circuitous journey home via Dusseldorf, Duisburg, and Münster. First he visits the Jacobis at Pempelfort, where there is disagreement concerning his recent attempts to make poetic sense of the Revolution in his Homeric version of *Reynard the Fox* and his unfinished skit 'Journey of the Sons of Megaprazon'. The stay at Pempelfort shows how the Revolution has isolated him from German intellectual and cultural life. His isolation and, as he saw it, his objectivity are set in opposition to the hyper-factionalism surrounding the Revolution. He had long been a critic of political factions. This is the key to Goethe's analysis of what went wrong in the campaign, just as it was to the 'Megaprazon' project. The allies fail to grasp reality because they are victims of factional groupthink. They have swallowed their allies the emigrés' propaganda. In Goethe's view the Brunswick Manifesto was a product of this emigré propaganda and of the factionalism it represented. In the *Campaign* Goethe is strongly critical of the Manifesto, though he does not name it. The Manifesto grew out of revolutionary factionalism and turned it into an even worse tribalism. At the same time it gave the allies an 'invented' 'pretext' for war and a spurious unity.[217] (Goethe is careful to state that his own loyalty is not to the allies but to Duke Carl August.)[218] Like the Revolution which gave rise to it, the Manifesto divided society into two warring tribes.

The critique of factionalism can be heard from the beginning of Goethe's narrative. When he arrives at the captured town of Longwy, he finds that its residents have split into two factions, reflecting the wider political atmosphere. It is in this context that we should read the commendable antiwar stance of the *Campaign*. Goethe's politics were rooted in a conviction that the Old Regime could have prospered, had it only followed the model of Rousseau's Geneva, Justus Möser's Osnabrück, or his own Weimar: small polities in which social relations were organic and people's abilities complemented one another. Exactly what form government took was relatively unimportant. What mattered was that the state was stable and the executive function was strong. Political factions were an impediment to good government. They created instability, were socially divisive, and distorted the proper functioning of the executive, replacing pragmatism with ideology. Politics after the Revolution was marred by a pernicious and unnatural factionalism, which was the root cause of the war. Throughout the *Campaign* Goethe is at pains to highlight glimpses of an alternative. Scenes of war are contrasted with those of daily life. He enjoys seeing folk getting on with their lives regardless of the chaos around them, for instance the waitresses who serve him dinner in Verdun.[219] The political leadership of Verdun might have changed, but good character and steadfastness mean that high politics can be ignored. People prefer to live in quiet domestic simplicity, but 'we had disturbed all this, this is what we were destroying'.[220] Ordinary folk can almost always live a good, simple life, as long as politics and war do not disturb it. This is why Goethe is at pains to defend rural Champagne against charges of poverty, just as he had defended the economy of Naples in the *Italian Journey*.[221] Were it not for the war, the people of Champagne would be happy. The emphasis on peace and prosperity furnishes part of his argument against the war. Eighteenth-century invading armies conventionally fed themselves by living off the land, but legal foraging often gave way to illegal and violent looting. This is Goethe's specific charge against the conduct of the war and against war in general. As he puts it in the *Campaign*, 'hunger knows no law' and 'war [...] cancels all rights of ownership'.[222] And it is not only the inhabitants of the occupied lands who suffer. The need to loot also causes moral damage to the occupying soldiers, for they alternate between paying the inhabitants for food and unlawfully stealing from them, while hiding the violence and lawlessness behind an agreeable mask:

> Thus we continued between order and disorder, between conserving and destroying, between robbing and paying, and this is what it must actually be that makes war so corrupting for the soul. One plays first the part of the bold soldier, the destroyer, and then that of the gentle person, the giver of life [...]. In this way a type of hypocrisy is born, a type which has its own character and is quite different from priestly hypocrisy or courtly hypocrisy, or whatever the other kinds may be called.[223]

Whereas the military looks law-bound and orderly, it suffers from tensions between order and disorder that make it psychologically unstable and prone to inauthenticity or insincerity. In this more general moral sense then, war destabilizes order.

The second explanation for his isolation appears in the narrative of a meeting with Professor Plessing in Duisburg. Plessing was the real-life figure behind the melancholy loner in the 1777 ode 'Winter Journey in the Harz': a man consumed and alienated by his failure in love. The meeting with Plessing returns the narrative to the period of *Werther*, when Goethe suddenly broke onto the German literary and intellectual scene. The point of the Plessing episode is to show the difference between Goethe as a national figure in the 1770s and an isolated figure in 1792 and subsequently—a figure who is isolated despite having things of national importance to say, like the visionary sleeper Epimenides. The meeting with Plessing also explains why Goethe abandoned his role as poet of the nation. The sentimentality of 1770s Germany, its preference for ideas and feelings above facts, was blinding the cultural and intellectual nation to the reality of its politics. Ideology trumped practicality and pragmatism. The era of ideology in the 1770s and '80s paved the way for the Revolution itself and the age of hyper-factionalism that followed it.

In the spring of 1820 he returned to *Wilhelm Meister's Journeyman Years*, which had been neglected since the brief burst of work on it in 1807. In that first phase of composition, he had written 'St Joseph the Second' and five other diverse stories that have no obvious connection to Wilhelm. A seventh story turned into *The Elective Affinities*. Then in 1809 his attention was diverted elsewhere, first to *Poetry and Truth* and then the *Italian Journey* and the *Divan*. The Meister project was not altogether forgotten. He published 'St Joseph the Second' and another story, 'The Foolish Pilgrim', in Cotta's *Pocketbook for Ladies* in 1810. Three more of the 1807 stories appeared in the *Pocketbook* between 1815 and 1817. In May 1820 he drafted a new story, 'Where is the Traitor?', and finally in the autumn he returned to the novel's frame narrative. He worked intensively on the novel through the winter of 1820/21, and Part One was finished and printed in May under the title *Wilhelm Meister's Journeyman Years or The Renunciants. A Novel*. The frame was much less substantial than the narrative of the *Apprenticeship*. The six 1807 stories already nearly sufficed for the first part of the novel, he wrote to Cotta in October 1820.[224] This was a very different kind of novel from the *Apprenticeship*. It was a hybrid creation, where the inset stories were at least as important as the narrative of Wilhelm's travels that framed them. In this sense, critics have interpreted the novel as a collective or aggregate entity.[225] Its loose central coherence, its many-layeredness and profuse reference to other texts and forms of discourse all give the impression of an archive, somewhat like Goethe's *Morphological Notebooks* and *On Art and Antiquity*.[226] It is as if he wanted the reader to take responsibility for making coherent sense of the text.[227] The narrative voice seems much less interested in Wilhelm's story, which is just one among many narratives that are collected and archived.[228] In addition to its unusual form, the novel presents a jarring combination of subject matter. Some highly romantic sections contrast with others on economics, education, and migration. The romantic and decidedly non-romantic elements provide the novel's two main themes. One is the erratic nature of (mainly male) desire, which cannot be governed other than by acts of renunciation, in keeping with the novel's subtitle. The other main theme is how to respond to the accelerating and centrifugal forces of modernity. The chief response is of course education, though the educational ideas described in the *Journeyman Years* are somewhat less optimistic than those in the *Apprenticeship*. Indeed, the responses to modernity in the novel tend to be piecemeal, incomplete, and conservative. The discussions of the economy and work led nineteenth-century critics to read the novel as a protosocialist text.[229] More recently critics have acknowledged the conservative elements that make up of much of the novel's archival contents.[230]

The narrative begins with Wilhelm and Felix descending from the Alps into the Italy of Mignon and the Marchese, where they will wander in pursuit of continually changing objects and purposes. The most prominent of these is a small casket that Felix finds after they leave Joseph's family. Wilhelm has learned that Jarno is in the area and is learning the craft of mining under the pseudonym of Montan. Fitz, a young boy who will turn out to be a burglar, claims to know where to find Jarno/Montan. In the mountains a storm has left some fallen trees blocking their path, and Fitz sets off to find a way round, after warning Wilhelm and Felix against going into a nearby ravine which no one may enter or even approach without being harmed. Felix is tempted into the cleft and emerges with the splendid-looking casket made of gold and enamel and no larger than a small octavo volume.[231] Fitz's prohibition and Felix's excitement suggest that the mysterious locked casket may be a symbol of hidden desires. Perhaps it is a modern Pandora's box containing the very desires that it is our task to renounce, according to the novel's subtitle. This romantic element contrasts with the meeting with Jarno that immediately follows it. Jarno and Wilhelm discuss the theory and practice of education. Jarno recommends that Wilhelm have Felix educated at a nearby utopian institute called the Pedagogical Province. The Province is one of a number of vehicles in the *Journeyman Years* that Goethe uses to convey his thoughts about education. The novel's thoughts on education have a certain uniformity and retain the Rousseauian principle of the *Apprenticeship*. The priority of education is the formation of a robust character. Beyond this, the *Journeyman Years* tends away from the *Apprenticeship*'s goal of aesthetic humanity and towards a more practical engagement with the world.

Having sought Jarno's opinion on the casket—he says it should not be opened, which would in any case require a key of considerable complexity—Wilhelm, Felix, and Fitz proceed on their journey and soon reach an estate surrounded by a high perimeter wall. Passing through a tunnel in the wall, they are trapped by a gate closing behind them and taken to a small room, where is written on the wall: 'liberation and restitution for the innocent, pity for the misled, punitive justice for the guilty'.[232] The rationale behind these words soon becomes clear. The estate belongs to an elderly man, the unnamed 'Uncle', who has offered the saplings from his extensive nursery of fruit trees free of charge to any local growers who prove themselves careful and hardworking. Other growers, who wish to sell the saplings, must pay a small charge, and the least conscientious growers are charged a higher price. This is one of the elements that nineteenth-century critics construed as evidence of socialism. However, the Uncle's economic system is redistributive on moral grounds, not on grounds of need. The Uncle's policy is evidently justified because the less conscientious growers, whom the Uncle deemed unworthy of his generosity, have tried to steal the saplings.²³³ This is why the high wall is needed, as well as 'punitive justice for the guilty'. The Uncle's policy is itself educational: it is designed to teach society the benefits of industry and to police its greed, for the moral benefit of all.

Wilhelm stays with the Uncle and his nieces Hersilie and Juliette for several weeks, during which he reads a story titled 'The Nut-brown Girl' and learns of the nieces' anger at their errant cousin Lenardo, who has not written to them during his travels. Lenardo was in fact one of the characters in the story of the Nut-brown Girl. He abandoned her and disappeared on his grand tour, and he is now dragging his feet on the way home. Wilhelm's first task is to act as go-between and errand runner for the family. His first stop is Lenardo's former tutor, an old antique collector, to whom he gives the casket for safekeeping. The collector is the one of novel's conservative principles. He represents the preservation of the past amid the destructive forces of modernity. He lives in a part of his city that escaped a terrible fire. His house full of antiques shows 'how long something can endure [. . .] as a counterweight to everything that changes and alters so fast in the world'.²³⁴ This evidence of durability prompts Wilhelm to ask the collector about the casket. In keeping with his conservative outlook, the collector advises Wilhelm to leave the casket unopened. It was found by chance, and its opening should be left to chance, for the key may turn up where it is least expected.²³⁵ At this point Felix rejoins Wilhelm, and the collector sends them on their way to the Pedagogic Province with a letter of recommendation.

There follow two long digressions describing the Pedagogic Province's educational methods and principles, separated by the story 'The Man of Fifty Years' and a romantic interlude at Lago Maggiore, the home of Mignon. On his way to the lake Wilhelm meets a young landscape painter who has set out to paint scenes from Mignon's homeland, and the two of them meet two women from the story Wilhelm has just read: a beautiful young widow and the niece of the story's title character, who were the objects of male desire in the story and are now, as Wilhelm observes, renunciants like himself. Their renunciation is put in jeopardy during the days the four companions spend together cruising the romantic lake, but in the end temptation is resisted and the young artist joins the league of renunciants. By the time Wilhelm makes his second visit to the Pedagogic Province, a year has passed, and Felix has begun to specialize in horseriding. The Province is celebrating its triennial festival, and Wilhelm is briefly reunited with Jarno, the Abbé, and Lothario. In an unsettling dreamlike interlude he sees Natalie through a telescope from the top of a mountain, which makes him anxious and nearly causes him to fall from the summit. (The unnatural foreshortening of distance through a telescope disturbs the natural spatiotemporal order.) Finally Wilhelm arrives at a settlement around a carefully preserved castle, where he finds Lenardo and Friedrich—the latter now a father of four and a more settled man than the skittish youth of the *Apprenticeship*. At this last stop on his journey Wilhelm hears or reads the stories of 'The New Melusine', 'The Foolish Pilgrim', and 'Where is the Traitor?' Lenardo has become the leader of a League of Migrants, whose principles Friedrich describes, before Lenardo delivers a rousing speech to the assembled migrants on the eve of their departure on their great journey. At this point Part One of the novel ends, with the promise of more movement in its next instalment, though it is not clear where the movement will lead or what its purpose will be.

In keeping with its subtitle, the *Journeyman Years* reads like an exercise in the renunciation of literary perfection and closure. It mimics Goethe's view of the modern world:[236] disjointed, mobile, directionless, obsessed with the new. If any principle governs Wilhelm's journey it is the rules of renunciation that teach him mobility and receptivity to new experiences and ideas. He must not lament his separation from Natalie or think about the past. He may not stay in one place for more than three days. Each time he moves it must be by at least one mile. Within this framework, the story that looms largest is Lenardo's unresolved quest to find the Nut-brown Girl Nachodine. The resolution seems to have been permanently forestalled by Lenardo's plans for migration, which can be understood as an act of renunciation similar to Wilhelm's renunciation of Natalie. Other elements may have been awaiting resolution in the second part of the novel, such as the unfinished education of Felix. Nor does Wilhelm find a craft of the kind Jarno has taken up. Plans are made, projects are initiated, but nothing is concluded. The narrative remains enigmatic.[237]

If the novel's form seems to mimic modernity, there is something antimodern about its content. The inset stories, quests, and plans represent people's reactions to disturbing forces. Some of these forces are understood, some not. The characters' reactions to them are largely defensive: the renunciation of desire, migration in the face of overpopulation, and the retreat into traditional crafts in response to the specialized modern economy. They are also incomplete responses. The inset stories are generally inconclusive. The projects launched in the face of modernity are unsuccessful or unfinished. In this respect the first story, 'St Joseph the Second', stands in antiphonic relation to the other stories. It is the only story in which the potential for tragedy is completely averted, and it contains the only example of an untroubled nuclear family.[238] Joseph is a model of successful education. He develops into the kind of robust and capable character envisaged by the Pedagogical Province. His strength of character emerges when he has to rein in his desire for Marie until she is ready to marry him. In this way his story sets a standard for masculinity that most of the male characters in the inset stories will fail to meet, for the inset tales are riddled with sexual inconstancy and rivalry, more often than not caused by men.[239] Joseph's world is threatened by war, but otherwise it is a stable world within which Joseph is again a model, combining the craft of carpentry with his role as estate manager for the local feudal lord. In the other stories the lead male characters have no craft to fall back on, and in three of the stories the potential for tragedy is triggered by poor management—no doubt an echo of Goethe's diagnosis of the causes of the French Revolution. In 'The Nut-brown Girl' Lenardo's uncle is unduly lax in collecting rents from his tenant farmers until he suddenly needs to raise funds for Lenardo's grand tour, which prompts him to expel one of the tenant farmers. The tenant's daughter, the girl of the tale's title, appeals to Lenardo for help, but Lenardo is about to leave on his tour and fails to make the girl's case, which scars him with guilt. In 'The Man of Fifty Years' Goethe returned to the social world of *The Elective Affinities*—minor landowning aristocrats dividing their time between managing their estates, serving in the army and bureaucracy, dilettantish entertainments, and potentially tragic and incestuous romantic entanglements. The events of the story are triggered by the failure of the idle brother of a Major and Baroness to manage his estate. In an effort to keep the estate in the family, the Major and Baroness hatch a plan to have the Major's son Flavio marry the Baroness's daughter Hilarie, a liaison that sails dangerously close to incest[240] and eventually triggers a tragic competition between the Major and his son Flavio. 'The New Melusine' takes place in a more fanciful world, but again a lack of discipline serves as trigger for the events. The narrator has failed since his youth to make provision for the future: 'I was not good at economy in my youth and often found myself in many a perplexity', he admits at the beginning of his story.[241] When he finds himself in the company of a mysterious woman with seemingly endless wealth, his lack of self-restraint repeatedly threatens their relationship. However, these instances of indiscipline and bad management are not presented as structural problems in society, but as instances of weak moral character, in particular the fecklessness and *amour-propre* of high-status men. In this sense, the stories do not make a case for social reform, but for the responsible conservation and management of what exists and for education that develops strength of character. They recall Rousseau's analysis of modernity and Goethe's belief that the French Revolution might have been averted by a government that displayed staunchness, consistency, and moral fibre. Indeed there were no revolutions in Germany because the German princes were, for the most part, sound and responsible managers of their domains.

The longest of the tales by some margin, 'The Man of Fifty Years' is a subtle study of the power of *amour-propre*, our desire for victory in the competition for social and sexual prestige. The Major and the Baroness's plan to have their children Hilarie and Flavio marry and so secure their idle brother's estate is scotched by Hilarie's lack of interest in Flavio. Somewhat hurriedly and ill advisedly, another plan is hatched, which would have Hilarie marrying her uncle the Major. In this new circumstance, the Major receives a visit from his old friend the actor, who has prolonged his career playing male romantic leads by means of a secret regime of restorative makeup. Feeling his inadequacy as partner for his much younger niece, the Major asks to be initiated into the actor's secrets. It remains for the Major to announce the change of plan to Flavio, who has fallen in love with a beautiful young widow. However, the widow evidently does not love Flavio, and on experiencing her hospitality, the Major begins to court her, only half-consciously, prompted by his *amour-propre* and emboldened by his newly youthful appearance. Driven half mad, Flavio returns home, where he bonds with Hilarie while she restores him to health. The tale ends, inconclusively of course, with the Major's and Flavio's desires having so scrambled and destabilized things that no matches can be made. Hilarie and the young widow respond by asserting their agency in a joint act of renunciation. Only time can repair the damage.[242] The Major's attempt to preserve his family domains by turning back time has broken apart his family and locked them into a temporal stasis.

'The Man of Fifty Years' shows how, as circumstances change, our *amour-propre* brings forth new, adventitious, and dangerous desires—desires that we would not have had if circumstances and our *amour-propre* had not suggested them to us. Our desires are inconstant and change according to how the objects of our desire love us or how these others are loved by third parties. In turn the new desires prompt us to make ourselves more appealing to the objects of our desire by altering how we appear and behave. Through this process of the making and remaking of our desires and behaviour, we may hollow out what we like to think of as our authentic character. In this sense, 'The Man of Fifty Years' returns to a theme that Goethe had addressed in the political sphere in

Egmont and in the cultural sphere in *Wilhelm Meister's Theatrical Mission*. The similarity to the *Theatrical Mission* is especially strong. As an actor, the Major's old friend is an exemplar of Rousseauian *amour-propre*. No walk of life is more liable to hollow out our authentic character than acting, which by virtue of its hollowness poses a particular danger to the community, as Rousseau argued in his *Letter to d'Alembert on Spectacles*. In the modern world desires can become almost unfathomably complex in the ways that they split, multiply, and spread through a community, stimulated always by *amour-propre*. The exceptional richness of 'The Man of Fifty Years' lies in the way it documents this proliferation of desires far beyond the simple fixing on a loved object.[243] Of all the inset stories it presents the strongest case for renunciation as a response to the modern world.

The inset stories take place in a world that seems modern but is not noticeably affected by any of the upheavals that had destabilized Europe since 1789. For all its emotional complexity, the world of the inset stories is sociopolitically stable. It is owned and run by aristocrats, for better or worse, while the rest of the people do almost all of the work. The world of the main narrative differs from this in one important respect. It is full of reformers who actively seek to change or renew the world, educationally, socially, economically, even politically. The first reformer we meet is Jarno, who believes in the power of education to equip people for the modern economy and has accordingly retrained as a geologist-miner. For Jarno, education means self-cultivation, albeit in a much more limited sense than Wilhelm's self-cultivation in the *Apprenticeship*. When in their conversation in the mountains Wilhelm praises the idea of a rounded education, Jarno corrects him: 'Now is the age of onesidednesses. Blessings on whoever grasps this and who works for his own and other people's benefit in this sense.'[244] Like it or not, we are all specialists, and the best education provides us with a specialized craft we can practise in whatever economic circumstances we meet. The idea of specialization seems to suit Jarno particularly well; he has chosen the craft of mining in order to be alone and apart from other people, who are 'not to be helped', he says.[245] The project of a national theatre with its ambition of educating the nation in a common endeavour has been consigned to the past. Gone too is the luxury of making mistakes that characters enjoyed in the *Apprenticeship*. Jarno's prescription is more austere. When he recommends that Wilhelm should have Felix educated at the Pedagogical Province—'which I would with some justice call a pedagogical utopia', he adds[246]—it is so that Felix will find a craft suited to his character. (In *Émile* Rousseau argued that everyone should learn a trade.)[247] The Province has some of the utopian character of Plato's *Republic*. The Province presumes that the results of education exist independently of our conceiving of them, in the same way that the Platonic forms are independent of our knowledge of them. Society is already out there waiting for us, and the purpose of education is to make us ready for it. Education is a matter of fitting the square peg into the square hole. Far from allowing its pupils to grow through trial and error, the Province strictly regulates their sociability. The rationale is that, if we had been left to develop freely, our social instincts would have developed into the *amour-propre* that sees only flattery or oppression in the behaviour of our fellows. If a boy is not assigned companions, then he will seek them out and 'he will find in his companions only sycophants and tyrants'.[248] The educational practice of the Province has become less liberal and more *dirigiste*. The teacher guides the pupil with a firm hand, imparting information only when necessary. When Wilhelm complains that Jarno has failed to tell them all he knows about the geology of the mountains, Jarno replies with a lesson from Lessing's *Education of the Human Race*. Teachers should tell their students only what the students can understand.[249] There will be other knowledge students are not ready for, and it is better to keep this hidden than to risk confusing students with knowledge that is beyond them.

The Pedagogical Province also resembles Lessing's *Education* in the sense that it stands within the Christian tradition, with qualifications of course, while pointing towards a synthetic religion of the future. During his two visits to the Province, Wilhelm gradually learns its methods and precepts but is also frustrated by the feeling that secret or arcane wisdom is being withheld. It appears that the people who show him round the Province are themselves not fully initiated into its *arcana*. He is repeatedly told that the whereabouts of its leader the Superior are unknown, in what eventually begins to seem like a strategy to prevent him from asking about the Province's highest secrets.[250] The most obvious real-world parallel for this is freemasonry. One article of faith of eighteenth-century masons was that their organization was led by unknown superiors.[251] The stepwise release of secret knowledge to members as they ascend through the ranks was a principle of freemasonry. As they enter the Province, Wilhelm and Felix see the boys making strange gestures of greeting. The full meaning of these greetings, they are told by an overseer who accompanies them, is not explained to the boys. What is explained to them they are instructed to keep secret, for secrecy is key to 'a sense of shame and good manners'. When Wilhelm asks about the significance of the many different coloured clothes the boys wear, the overseer answers that only his superiors can explain it.[252] On his second day in the Province, Wilhelm is admitted to its sanctum, a cluster of buildings isolated from the rest of the Province behind a wall in a forested valley and barely visible through the trees.[253] Of the three parts of the sanctum, he is allowed access only to the first two,[254] and so the Province's new religion is both revealed and concealed.

The inculcation of its synthetic religion is central to the Province's mission. One of the lessons of the *Journeyman Years* seems to be that in the modern world individualism can no longer benefit us, and that instead we require firm religious and moral precepts. Sulpiz Boisserée recorded a conversation in 1815 in which Goethe spoke harshly of liberal pedagogues like Pestalozzi who wanted 'in their madness and rage to reduce everything to the individual and be pure gods of independence'. If the aim of education was truly to 'educate a nation and resist the savage hordes', then the teaching must include 'religious, moral, and philosophical maxims which alone can give protection'.[255] Pestalozzi's principles were alien to Goethe,[256] partly because Pestalozzi failed to recognise the value of tradition, including the Christian tradition. Much more congenial to Goethe was an experimental educational project he learned of in 1817: Philipp Emanuel von Fellenberg's Pedagogical Republic at Hofwil near Bern. A follower of Rousseau and Pestalozzi, Fellenberg aimed to educate children for social usefulness by strengthening their character and taming their passions. General education took second place to finding out what single craft or science pupils were equipped to learn. Graduates of Fellenberg's project were to be virtuosi in one thing and amateurs in all the rest.[257] The educational programme was supported by an ecumenical Christianity grounded in the love of one's neighbours.[258]

The religion of Goethe's Province is the novel's greatest difficulty. The meaning of the three different gestures of greeting or 'reverences' is straightforward enough. The greetings symbolize reverence first for a God in heaven who has earthly representatives in the boys' parents and superiors; second for the earth that nourishes us, gives us ineffable joys but also the sufferings of illness and death; and third for our peers, together with whom we confront the world.[259] The last and most important of these recalls Fellenberg's love of neighbours. In response to Wilhelm's questions, it emerges that the three reverences correspond to three types of religion or three facets of the one true religion that are represented in the Province's sanctum.[260] However, it turns out that the three reverences do not tally at all well with the three forms of religion, and it is not clear whether the mismatch is meaningful or mere confusion on Goethe's part. The three facets of religion are presented twice during

Wilhelm's visit to the Province, first in an answer to his questions about the three reverences and again on his tour of the sanctum. On both occasions Wilhelm learns that the first facet of religion is a reverence for the heavens, such as we find in the pagan religions, and which corresponds to the first reverence. The second facet is a philosophical religion that represents humans in their position between heaven and earth, which does not tally with any of the reverences. The third facet of religion connects us to what is beneath us, which seems to match the second reverence and certainly has nothing to do with the third reverence and its gesture of social solidarity. The third reverence has no equivalent among the three facets of religion. This first account of the religions is followed by a second listing of the three gestures of reverence, which conforms to the initial account of the reverences. Later in the sanctum, Wilhelm is shown the first two religions again. The first is the pagan sky religion represented in scenes from the Old Testament. Here Goethe returns to Lessing's *Education of the Human Race*. The Israelites of the Old Testament were not an exceptional nation, with few virtues and most of the faults common to all nations, though they did possess admirable resilience.[261] Their holy books display just the right mix of coherence, fragmentariness, barbarity, and tenderness to stimulate us, and the Israelites' abhorrence of graven images gives free play to the imagination.[262] In sum, the merits and faults of the Old Testament make it an excellent educational tool. The second hall of the sanctum contains the second facet of religion: the philosophical religion that situates us on the earth, where the everyday and ordinary combines with the universal and miraculous. It is illustrated by scenes from life of Christ, though not his death. Wilhelm is not admitted to the third part of the sanctum, which apparently contains a religion of pain and suffering and might be construed as relating to the second reverence. Are the reverences and religions therefore two separate systems? If so, the correspondences between them or lack thereof seem odd, as does the whole context, which implies that they form a single system. Or are the three religions altered, perhaps elevated versions of the three reverences? That solution is hardly better because the all-important third reverence seems to disappear from the system of religions. The conundrum is made more confusing by the fact that Wilhelm is told how systematic the representation of the religions in the sanctum is and how much clearer it is than the confusion that reigns out in the world. A further mystery concerns the third space in the sanctum. Wilhelm is told that the boys are not admitted to the third space and are told instead where they might find instances of the third religion out in the world. There is some doubt whether the third space exists at all. The door from the second room of the sanctum leads not to the third, but back to the entrance hall. The suspicion that the third space does not exist is confirmed when the narrator tells us that in passing through the door from the second room Wilhelm 'well observed that they had made a full circuit' of the rooms.[263] It is implied that the third room contains—or would contain if it existed—an image of Christ on the cross, which however the Province would never put on display. Here Goethe evidently intends the reader to suspect that the third religion is simply absent, which makes the supposed correspondence of the three reverences to the three religions even stranger. The confusing relationship between the reverences and religions is unlikely to have been an oversight on Goethe's part. He edited the 1821 version of the *Journeyman Years* himself, and the text is clear of errors, unlike the error-strewn 1829 version.[264] How then do we read the content of the Pedagogical Province's religion? It feels serious and systematic, but is haunted by illogicality and evasion.

One explanation was suggested by the Romantic poet Eichendorff, who claimed that the whole episode of the Pedagogical Province was a parody of modern educational theories such as Basedow's.[265] Indeed, the Pedagogical Province with its unnatural paraphernalia of gestures, costumes, and often outlandish educational practices has received considerable critical venom, even mockery.[266] However, the same playfulness and artifice extends throughout the novel, as do some of the key themes, such as economic specialization. The Pedagogic Province does not feel markedly different from the rest of the text, and it contains ideas that are demonstrably Goethean. Goethe's treatment of his source material, for instance Fellenberg's Republic, is not that of a parodist. For instance, he alters the name of Fellenberg's project by changing the word 'Republic' to 'Province', presumably because of the associations of 'Republic' with political republicanism. This is an alteration designed to make Fellenberg usable, not to parody him. Likewise the dramatic arts are excluded from the Pedagogic Province, just as they were from Plato's *Republic* and should have been from Geneva, according to Rousseau. The reasons given for excluding drama from the Province conform to Goethe's longstanding love-hate relationship with the theatre and his protoconservative politics. The theatre requires the existence of an 'idle crowd' as its audience,[267] that is to say people who are neither active nor well born. Drama represents 'feigned cheer or affected pain'[268]—a traditional objection to the theatre expressed by Plato and Rousseau. Within the family of art forms, drama is the frivolous sibling who is liable to fritter away the whole family's wealth.[269] By contrast the visual arts are earnest; artists need no festivities, for their whole year is one.[270]

Architecture is the most earnest art form of all, its creations serving as a kind of urban police insofar as they strenuously avoid the errors to which excessive liberty may lead: 'one may make errors at any time; one may build none'.[271]

The Province's social makeup also reflects Goethe's attitudes. There is no talk of any class distinctions within the Province, as there were in Fellenberg's Republic. The Province's students are distinguished from one another only by their aptitude.[272] However, the Province operates a socially selective admissions policy. The 'crowd' are excluded altogether, and Wilhelm is told that the pupils are 'well born', presumably members of the aristocracy and upper bourgeoisie like Wilhelm.[273] The wellborn pupils have a natural ability to learn the reverences whereas 'the crowd' lack respect, so Wilhelm claims.[274] Goethe's politics are also reflected in the ways the Province allows students to differentiate themselves by the colours they wear. The overseer explains to Wilhelm that the boys' choice of colour is a window on their character. By allowing the boys to choose their own colours the overseers are able to assess their character,[275] as if the overseers were using Goethe's account of colour's moral meanings in the *Theory of Colour*. The boys' tendency to imitate one another may confuse things, but even imitation and the desire to be a member of a 'party' can be revealing. (Goethe disliked political parties; they were one of the flaws of republican systems.) On the occasions when fashion takes hold and the boys all begin to make the same choice of colours, the teachers gently intervene to remove the fashionable colours from their stock and replace them with different ones. The Province disapproves of uniforms and uniformity, which are the enemy of individuality and character.[276] Of course, individuality must not be confused with the independence that Goethe so disliked in Pestalozzi's practice. Individuality consists in natural difference, not an artificial striving to be novel and reject tradition. The Province fosters an individuality of character that is compatible with tradition, a sense of community, and respect for authority—the qualities Goethe found lacking in Pestalozzi's modern, liberal pedagogy. Eichendorff's theory that the Province was a satire on educational projects seems implausible.

The 1821 version of the *Journeyman Years* ends with Lenardo's speech to his League of Migrants on the eve of their departure. The speech seems designed to steel the migrants' will by showing them that migration, or movement of some less permanent kind, is a necessity in many walks of life. The speech also articulates a social, economic, and political response to the problems of post-Napoleonic modernity. In this sense it is the most openly political section of the novel. While readers of such a polyphonic text, who have worked through the sheer oddness of the Pedagogical Province, might approach Lenardo's speech with some scepticism, there are good reasons to take it seriously. Its closing position gives it weight. It combines several of the novel's threads, including the themes of specialization, education, and travel—the main elements of Wilhelm's journeyman years. The League of Migrants is evidently a product of the Pedagogical Province, whose values Lenardo affirms at the end of the speech. It is also connected to and supported by the Society of the Tower, and the reader is led to believe that it will help to realize Lothario's reform plans. Less clear is how the League will achieve its ends or how adequate its response is to the wider challenges of modernity. One of the main themes of Lenardo's speech is conservation, which the novel has raised repeatedly in symbolic form—from the ruined and yet well preserved abbey where Joseph lives and the collector in his home that was spared from fire, to the ancient castle, well preserved and periodically restored, where the members of Lenardo's League meet. The League of Migrants is a means to adapt the old world and its traditions to the needs of modernity. The Tower's project at the end of the *Apprenticeship* was to build a bulwark against revolution by acquiring and managing property and to rebuild the trust between the bourgeoisie and aristocracy that the Revolution had destroyed. At first sight, the League's project seems different. Its answer to the acceleration of life in post-Napoleonic Europe is to become mobile. That said, the League complements rather than repudiates the Tower's project. Lenardo states that property is the first and best thing humans can have. Family, community, and patriotism are all grounded in the land, just as nature intended.[277] Yet the work people do is of even greater value than their property, and work is mobile. On the other hand, the examples of migration that Lenardo's speech marshalls are as traditional as they are modern. The examples he gives of the need to move for the sake of work include trade, pilgrimage, and diplomacy, none of which are particularly modern. He makes no reference to the most obvious feature of modern mobility: the newly mobile working class that leaves the countryside for the city and its opportunities for commerce. Towns and cities are almost entirely absent from the *Journeyman Years*[278] in contrast to the *Apprenticeship*. The *Journeyman Years* portrays a rural world resembling Goethe's and Rousseau's beloved Switzerland.

The examples Lenardo gives of nations migrating for social or political reasons are from ancient history. In May 1812 Goethe read about early 'migrations of peoples' (*Völkerwanderungen*) in Christoph Meiners's *Investigations on the Differences of Human Natures*.[279] The subject was still in his mind in June 1819, as he wrote to the Austrian army topographer Ludwig von Welden.[280] If migration is an answer to the problems of modernity, then it is an ancient answer as well as a modern one. It is part of the cyclical process of history. Migrations are often followed by returns, for migration does not always lead to permanent resettlement. This is why Lenardo prefers migration to the more permanent emigration. To think that by emigrating we might slough off our past is a false hope. A newly founded state is likely to be just as 'limited' as the state we left behind. The very rationale of his model of migration implies return: like the travels of a journeyman, its purpose is to gain new experience that can enrich the home we have left and to which we will probably return.[281]

At the heart of Lenardo's model of migration is an organicist and monoethnic model of society, which is part of a defensive response to modernity. In 1815 Goethe reportedly told Boisserée that one goal of education was to resist 'the wild hordes',[282] a view probably prompted by his encounter with the Bashkir Cossacks in April 1813. Another threat to social cohesion were modern liberal moves to emancipate Germany's Jews. Lenardo specifically excludes Jews from the League. Jews met on the road should be greeted and dealt with like any other travellers with whom trade might bring mutual advantage. They should neither be slandered nor praised despite the fact that they are conmen, he says. If not in ethnic then at least in social terms, the League is inclusive, no doubt for economic reasons. Friedrich describes it as 'a large, mobile association of doughty and active people of all classes'.[283] There is an element of democracy but only on the smallest scale. If three members meet, they will rule themselves, but as soon as a fourth arrives they choose a leader to rule them. There can be no sharing of power in these larger assemblies since coregents only ever get in one another's way.[284] As it happens, in this autocratic system Lenardo is usually chosen as the leader because he inspires the greatest trust.[285] His speech also reaffirms the need for specialization that was first voiced by Jarno and is a core principle of the Province. The main purpose of the League's travels is to learn useful skills that will meet the need for specialization in a modern economy. Behind this argument lie analyses of the modern economy such as Adam Smith's though it is unlikely Goethe had Smith specifically in mind. (He was familiar with Smith's work from around 1800; in 1806 Sartorius sent Goethe two works in which Sartorius was critical of Smith's account of value.)[286] In his portrayal of the League, Goethe recognises that the modernity of the modern economy consists in specialization and the division of labour. He does not, however, accept Smith's view that the invisible hand of free trade maximises efficiency and creates social bonds. In Goethe's account, the economy can only function for society's benefit under a centralizing, *dirigiste* leadership, which must come from the very alliance of aristocracy and mercantile bourgeoisie that was formed at the end of the *Apprenticeship*. Lothario, Werner, the Abbé, and Jarno are all backers of Lenardo's League. They have put together a large insurance fund,[287] from which Wilhelm will be able to disburse. The payments will be gifts; Wilhelm will act as a benefactor though he resists the role when Friedrich first proposes it.[288] Nothing is said about the basis on which Wilhelm will hand out the money. A model might be the Uncle with his huge nursery of fruit tree saplings, from which he donates to farmers who satisfy his standards of diligence and honesty. In addition, a large tract of land has been purchased where all the members of the League can be active, even those travelling in distant parts and gathering new and useful experience.[289] This is the ultimate purpose of the League of Migrants: to bring back useful knowledge from the periphery to the centre; to use their mobility in order to consolidate the ownership and good management of old Europe. The practice of migration, as ancient as it is modern, might defend traditional ways of life.

10

'These Very Serious Jokes'

WEIMAR, 1825–1832

GOETHE'S SOCIAL life had contracted in the years after Christiane's death. By way of compensation his engagement with the wider intellectual world expanded. His daily routine included an hour or two of dictation to his amanuensis every morning before breakfast. The resulting network of correspondence grew in size and international range. He was still open to novelty and experimentation. A sign of his openness was that in January 1826 he suddenly became an avid reader of the French liberal journal *Le Globe*.[1] In January and February he read the journal's issues dating back to its launch in September 1824.[2] Thereafter it became his staple weekly reading. He was fully aware of its politics of 'absolute liberalism or theoretical radicalism', as he put it in his diary.[3] The journal was a symptom of the now well-established faultline in politics between liberals and conservatives.[4] It was another 'troubling'[5] phenomenon of modernity. As he said of the philosophy of Victor Cousin, it was a 'theory of the *Zeitgeist*'.[6] What Goethe admired about *Le Globe* was not its liberal politics.[7] It was the 'clever', 'brave', and 'purposeful' stance of the writers.[8] Everything about the journal was open and sociable, not furtive and solitary like the writing of German radicals.[9] He seemed to have come round to the opinion of Daniel Jenisch that he had criticised in his 1795 essay 'Literary Sansculottism'. *Le Globe* impressed him partly because it was French and benefitted from France's (in some respects) higher cultural and political level.[10] And as in the case of Napoleon, he liked *Le Globe* because it liked him. He was especially impressed by a long review of a French translation of his dramatic works by Jean-Jacques Ampère in spring 1826.[11] More generally, he welcomed *Le Globe* as a bridge between French and German culture.[12] Its first issue coincided with the death of Louis XVIII and the succession of his more conservative cousin Charles X. At the end of Louis XVIII's reign an attempt had been made to pass an Anti-Sacrilege Act, which was however blocked by the Chamber of Peers. Under Charles X the act was reintroduced by the ministry of the ultraroyalist Joseph de Villèle. Among other provisions intended to restore respect for the Christian religion, the act introduced the death penalty for blasphemy. It was opposed by French liberals, and this may have been another reason why Goethe read *Le Globe* with a more open mind.[13] The liberals' opposition to bigotry also helps to explain Goethe's admiration for Guizot, one of the leaders of the moderate liberal opposition group known as the *doctrinaires*. Soret reports Goethe commenting that Guizot was 'a man after my own heart, he's solid. He possesses deep knowledge, bound up with an enlightened liberalism which, rising above the parties, goes its own way'.[14] By qualifying Guizot's liberalism as 'enlightened' Goethe points specifically towards his rejection of religious bigotry.

The same attitudes mark Goethe's stance towards liberalism more generally. It was suspect and troubling, especially its radical Benthamite wing.[15] Bentham was a particular bugbear of Goethe's. He considered himself and Bentham to be at opposite ends of the political spectrum.[16] As French liberalism grew more powerful and more radical in the late 1820s, so *Le Globe* also began to worry him more. It seemed to be a destabilizing force. The French parliamentary elections of November 1827 produced a liberal majority in the Chamber of Deputies, and Villèle was succeeded by a compromise ministry led by the *doctrinaire*-sympathizing Jean-Baptiste Gay, Viscount of Martignac. When that ministry collapsed in summer 1829, Charles X reverted to the ultraroyalist Jules de Polignac. Through the autumn of 1829 Goethe followed the French newspapers closely.[17] He still approved of the practical measures advocated by the moderate *doctrinaire* faction,[18] but during the winter he became troubled by the increasingly anti-government sentiment of *Le Globe*, which he described as 'a declaration of war that puts the existence of the Bourbons in doubt'.[19] As long as the moderate French liberals advocated practical plans to reform society, Goethe approved, albeit with reservations. However, as soon as the liberal opposition threatened the legitimacy of the executive, and as soon as their opposition began to focus on constitutional matters, Goethe turned against them. On 17 March 1830 the liberal majority in the Chamber of Deputies won a vote of no confidence against Polignac's ministry. The instability proved too much for Goethe. At the end of April he announced in a letter to Zelter that he was giving up reading the French journals. His conservatism reasserted itself:

FIG. 24. Goethe dictating to his secretary John, by J. J. Schmeller (1834)

In this connection I am obliged to announce and confide something remarkable to you: namely, that after a firm, rapid decision I have abandoned all newspaper reading and am making do with whatever a social life provides me with. This is of the greatest importance. For when you look at it closely, it is mere philistinism for private people to give too much interest to what does not concern us.[20]

The growing tensions between the liberal writers of *Le Globe* and the Bourbon monarchy were also the context for Goethe's most expansive and seemingly most favourable comments on liberalism. The comments were reported by

FIG. 25. Faust and Mephistopheles on horseback, illustration for
Goethe's *Faust* by E. Delacroix (1825–1827)

Soret in a conversation about the latter's great-uncle Étienne Dumont, who was a follower, translator, and editor of Bentham. More appealing to Goethe was Dumont's work as a moderate liberal reformer of Geneva's judicial and penal systems:

> 'For me it is an interesting problem', Goethe said, 'when I see that such a sensible, such a moderate and such a practical man as Dumont could become the pupil and loyal supporter of this fool Bentham. [...] Dumont [...] is of course a moderate liberal, as all sensible people are and ought to be, and as I am myself, and in which sense I have striven to work during the course of a long life. The true liberal', he continued, 'seeks, with the means that are available to him, to do as much good as he possibly can; but he refrains from wanting to eradicate by fire and the sword the often unavoidable faults. He strives, by means of prudent progress, gradually to eliminate public deficiencies, without at the same time spoiling just as much good by means of violent measures. He makes do with the good in this ever

imperfect world until such time as the times and circumstances enable him to achieve the better'.[21]

Goethe here redefines liberalism in such a way as to fit his own self-image as a practical, prudent politician who takes concrete measures to benefit the commonwealth, but avoids anything that will destabilize the state. As in all of Goethe's comments on liberalism, favourable or otherwise, there is no mention of the liberal principles of constitutionalism, representation, and rights. Moreover, this is specifically a moderate form of liberalism, and not a radical Benthamite one. It is the liberalism of all men of good sense, for we are all liberals really. Liberalism is thus emptied of its philosophical force and watered down to insipidity. Moreover, Goethe's emphasis on practical, achievable progress conforms to his instinctive paternalism. Any signs of Goethe's warming to liberalism need to be qualified by a recognition that his instincts were paternalistic and even authoritarian. We can compare a comment he made to Müller in March 1828 concerning Wellington's conservative ministry in Britain, which he strongly welcomed. According to Müller, Goethe ridiculed constitutionalist objections to Wellington's power:

> Complaining now about Wellington's omnipotence as Prime Minister is absurd; they ought to be happy that he's finally occupied his proper place; a man who's conquered India and Napoleon is justified in ruling over a paltry island. Whoever has the highest power is right; one should bow before him in reverence.[22]

The most desirable constitution is one in which a strong executive enjoys full legitimacy, and there can be no source of legitimacy greater than military success. This is the authoritarian Caesarism that motivated Goethe's support for Napoleon and that he expressed in the fragments of his drama on Mohammed in the early 1770s.

Goethe returned to the unfinished *Journeyman Years* in spring 1824. His first task was to conclude the story of Lenardo and the Nut-brown Girl, which was the novel's most salient unresolved thread as well as the principal link between Wilhelm and Lenardo's extended family. The work continued intermittently into 1825. The task Wilhelm is set by the family is to cure Lenardo of his guilt about the Nut-brown Girl by finding her. Once cured, Lenardo can be reunited with his family, become a useful member of society, and take up his role as leader of the League of Migrants, now in alliance with the Society of the Tower. In fact, Wilhelm's search almost has the opposite of the desired effect. When he reports that he has found the Nut-brown Girl, his letter nearly prompts Lenardo to abandon his work with the League and the Tower and seek her out, until the 'great and far-reaching' plans outweigh his guilt, or so the Abbé tells Wilhelm.[23] In this sense, by finding the Nut-brown Girl Wilhelm only provides a test of Lenardo's powers of renunciation. Eventually Lenardo is led by accident to the Nut-brown Girl, now named Susanne, in the course of his research into the state of the cottage industry of cotton weaving and its unique cultures, which are threatened by mechanization. Thus the narrative of Wilhelm's quest becomes only one minor episode within the larger context of Lenardo's and the League's efforts to preserve the unique culture of old rural Europe.

The story of Susanne and Lenardo was a priority because Goethe wanted to give the novel a fitting emotional climax that would also connect its emotional centre—its focus on the damage done to women by men's desire and *amour-propre*—to the theme of modernity. One evening at sunset Susanne tells Lenardo the story of her life since their original encounter. Forced into migration, she settled with some coreligionists in the mountains and married her host's son, who soon died in an accident, followed by his parents and sisters, leaving Susanne as the sole heir to the family cotton weaving business. She is supported in her work by an assistant of her late husband, who is also in love with her but decides not to woo her because he and Susanne disagree on how they should respond to the creeping mechanization of the industry. Her inclination is to emigrate, as her husband had intended, whereas the assistant would prefer to stay. Into this tense situation comes the glamorous Lenardo, and his evening conversation with Susanne seems to be leading to a meeting of hearts, until she ends the conversation, because her feelings for her late husband are too strong to be replaced by another man. Her ailing father, after much Bible study and with the last gasp of his life, reins in Lenardo's passion by pronouncing the two of them brother and sister. The story is thus left in a tense limbo, much like 'The Man of Fifty Years'. Susanne's subsequent fate is told as one among a series of perfunctory housekeeping acts by the novel's editor in the last few chapters. We learn that Lothario, his wife Therese (now inexplicably renamed Julie), the Abbé, and Natalie have set sail for America.[24] There is no mention of a farewell between Natalie and Wilhelm or of their future together, an omission made all the more glaring by the editor's comment that the emigrants' only misgiving was not being able to say farewell to Makarie, the old disabled astronomer aunt, whom Wilhelm first met at the

Uncle's estate. Hersilie's sister Juliette has married. The characters of 'The Man of Fifty Years' are also wed. Hilarie has married Flavio (renamed Silvio), who has become a captain and inherited the family's extensive estates, and his father the Major has married the beautiful widow.[25] The passage of time has evidently healed their wounds. Makarie cures Lydie (now Lucie) of her hysteria by laying on hands.[26] The tension between Susanne and her business assistant, which had prevented the community from defending itself against the threat of mechanization, is resolved by having Susanne come to live with Makarie, as a replacement for her companion Angela, who is to marry a mathematically gifted protégé of Wilhelm's old friend Werner. The assistant will marry the sister of a harness fitter in his local community and so diversify the family's business and provide some insurance against the decline of cotton weaving. Susanne gives him the family business, by way of compensation for the loss of his prospects of marrying her.[27]

All this tidying up of loose ends was not enough, however, and in June 1825 Goethe began to draft new plans and schemas that would completely revise the novel. The first of these schemas points to a new thread in the main narrative: the fraught three-way relationship between Hersilie, Felix, and Wilhelm, which leads to another emotionally powerful climax.[28] During the second half of 1825 he decided to round out Hersilie's character and introduce Felix's infatuation with her. Hersilie becomes the most subtly drawn character of the novel's frame narrative. Both she and Juliette are highly cultured, but Hersilie has used the leisure time that wealthy unmarried women enjoy in such abundance to hone her intellect to a keen edge of Mephistophelean contradiction, which presumably betokens an underlying discontent. The maxims that her Uncle has had inscribed throughout the estate are an obvious target for her intelligence:

> 'My sister', Hersilie said, 'can interpret them all; she and the curator vie with one another in understanding them; but I find that you can reverse them and they are then just as true, if not more so'.[29]

The vividness with which Hersilie is portrayed contrasts with Felix's lack of any interiority. During their first meeting, he becomes infatuated with her, galloping off on his horse to fetch her flowers; he 'was returning with a great bunch of blooming crowns, which he waved from afar, when he and the horse suddenly vanished. He had fallen into a ditch'.[30] His infatuation is the passion of a comically and one-dimensionally impulsive youth for an urbane, witty, but unhappy older woman, more mature than him in both years and self-awareness. More broadly, it reflects a world in which women retain some of their authentic character, while men are driven by their desire to create a self-image that consumes and threatens their whole identity. Wilhelm's inner life is not much more contoured than Felix's and his behaviour towards Hersilie is distant, as she astutely complains in a letter to him:

> My situation reminds me of a tragedy by Alfieri: since confidantes are wholly lacking, everything must be dealt with in monologues. And indeed, a correspondence with you is exactly like a monologue. Your replies merely take up my syllables, like an echo, only to let them die away. Have you even once given a reply to which a reply could be given in turn? Your letters simply parry mine, keeping them at a distance. When I rise to come towards you, you point me back to my seat.[31]

Hersilie is caught between Wilhelm and Felix and can make little impression on either. Her tragedy is to be more alive than the male-dominated world she lives in. There are traces of the Gretchen of *Faust. The First Part of the Tragedy* in her, as well as the Friederike of *Poetry and Truth*. By the end of the novel she has become the most prominent woman in Wilhelm's life, overtaking the absent Natalie. The mysterious casket ends up in her possession, as if its symbolism pertained to her. Her situation, loved by Felix but in love with Wilhelm, causes an emotional turmoil from which she thinks opening the casket might release her,[32] but at the same time she hopes that the casket might turn out to be empty. She has invested it with the hope that it contains Wilhelm's true feelings towards her and at the same time that its emptiness might release her from him. Whether it contains anything at all is not confirmed, but as far as the fate of the novel's characters is concerned it might as well be empty. The only effect the casket has on them stems from what they read into it. It represents a void that begs to be filled with meaning. In this sense it is a symbol of male identity,[33] alongside its other meanings as a Pandora's box or a symbol for deism's hidden God and nature's unknowable essence. In a final confrontation with Hersilie, Felix tries to open it but the key breaks off in the lock. He then forces himself on her, and she fights him off and warns him never to visit her again, after briefly returning his kisses. He leaves with the portentous warning that he will ride out into the world until he dies. Finally, at least as far as the casket is concerned, an old goldsmith works out how to use the key, opens the casket, and promptly shuts it again, warning Hersilie that 'such secrets were better left untouched'.[34] One thing about the casket is clear: it is not the answer to Hersilie's problems. She remains bereft and alone amid the flurry of weddings and betrothals, alienated from Wilhelm and anxious about the missing Felix. His story ends with another riding accident, which repeats as near tragedy the comedy of his first accident. From a distance Wilhelm sees Felix on horseback by a river. The river bank gives way under rider and horse, and Felix would have drowned had some passing boatmen not fished him out and Wilhelm not been able to put his surgical knowledge to use by bringing Felix back to life by opening a vein. Like the climax of the story of Lenardo and Susanne, the conclusion of the story of Hersilie, Felix, and Wilhelm links the novel's emotional centre to the theme of preserving the old within the new. By bringing Felix back to life on the riverbank, Wilhelm makes possible a new bond between father and son:

> Life returned; the loving surgeon barely had time to fasten the bandage before the young man was already bravely getting to his feet, looking keenly at Wilhelm and crying out, 'If I am to live, let it be with you!' With these words he fell upon the neck of his rescuer, recognising and recognised, and wept bitterly. Thus they stood in tight embrace, like Castor and Pollux, brothers who meet halfway along the road from Orcus to the realm of light.[35]

Wilhelm and Felix seem fated to meet repeatedly on the path between life and death. Representing the steady past and the precarious future, father and son must constantly meet and revitalize one another at moments of crisis. To Wilhelm falls the task of mending what modernity has broken, a task for which his new-found role as a surgeon is surely a metaphor.

Goethe continued to add to and revise the 1821 *Journeyman Years* up to the end of 1828. The completed novel was published in 1829 as Volumes 21, 22, and 23 of his *Complete Final Authorized Edition*. The revisions and additions resulted in some shifts of focus, but the main thrust of the novel remained the same as the 1821 text. The additions included several elements that were only loosely connected to the novel's frame. Lenardo gives a detailed description of cotton weaving, based on material that Meyer had sent Goethe from Switzerland in 1810. Wilhelm has conversations with the inventor of a wax anatomical model that can replace cadavers in the teaching of dissection and so halt the rise of grave robbing. The old aunt Makarie is described, with her intuitive understanding of astronomy. There are two long collections of aphorisms, 'Observations in the Spirit of Wanderers' and 'From Makarie's Archive'. Perhaps the most obvious change of focus is that the migration plans of the League now include emigration. In the winter of 1825/26 letters began to reach Weimar from Carl August's second son Prince Bernhard, who was travelling in North America. On his return, Bernhard compiled a report of his travels, which he published in 1828 with support from Goethe. Bernhard's reports proved opportune for the work on the *Journeyman Years*, for they allowed Goethe to pick up the theme of the relation of the New World to the Old that appeared first in Book VII of the *Apprenticeship*. There Lothario was introduced as having returned from fighting on the American side in the War of Independence, an experience that drove his desire to reform his landholdings in Germany, for 'Here, or nowhere, is America!'[36] Goethe's longstanding fascination with the United States had become more intense in the post-Napoleonic period, and he read widely in the literature on and of North America, including travel journals by Ludwig Gall (which he reviewed in 1822),[37] Geoffrey Keating and others,[38] and James Fennimore Cooper's novels, starting with *The Pioneers: or The Sources of the Susquehanna* (1823), which he read in September 1826. He was especially interested in the religious tolerance and diversity of the United States and utopian social projects such as Johann Georg Rapp's Harmony Societies and their successor, Robert Owen's socialist community at New Harmony, Indiana. In these experiments Goethe found models for the remaking of society along the lines of his own post-Napoleonic version of humanism—a society built on a more human scale and free of traditional religious institutions. Accordingly, the ending of the completed *Journeyman Years* has a new focus on emigration to the United States, albeit emigration with the prospect of return to old Europe, as was the case with the Uncle, who returned from America to the cultural riches of Europe where he established an enlightened economic and legal regime. Emigration is not an end in itself, nor is it the only answer to Europe's overpopulation. After all, emigration is just another form of migration, another way to acquire new experience and test new social and economic models that could later be applied at home, as the Uncle has succeeding in doing. In this sense, the American material that Goethe added to the 1829 *Journeyman Years* has as much to do with Europe as with America.[39] It is part of Goethe's concern with the relation of the old and the new, tempered with a scepticism about any form of innovation, for as Jarno comments when he and Wilhelm look down from the mountains at the beginning of the novel: 'Down there a new world lies before you; but I'll wager it is just like the old one behind us'.[40]

The most important shift in emphasis between the 1821 and 1829 versions is not from migration to emigration, but from movement to settlement. In the 1821 text Lenardo's speech to the League of Migrants is a call to movement and ends with the rousing poem 'Don't Stay Stuck to the Ground' ('Bleibe nicht am Boden heften'). In the 1829 version, his speech contains less argument in favour of migration and more explanation of how the League will defend the social and economic order against the centrifugal forces of modernity. His speech is followed by one by a new character, Odoard, who introduces the most sustained discussion of politics in Goethe's writing since the *Divan*. Odoard has experience of turning round a poorly administered domain. His story reminds us that the main aim of reform is to correct bad management, not to reorganize society. He has turned his back on the distractions of courtly life and plans to build a new society in old Europe. His speech to the migrants also ends with a rousing poem that corrects Lenardo's by balancing the need for movement with images of settlement under strong leadership:

Bleiben, Gehen, Gehen, Bleiben
Sei fortan dem Tücht'gen gleich.
Wo wir Nützliches betreiben,
Ist der werteste Bereich.
Dir zu folgen, wird ein Leichtes,
Wer gehorchet, der erreicht es,
Zeig' ein festes Vaterland.
Heil dem Führer! Heil dem Band![41]

Staying, moving, moving, staying / From now on let them be all the same to sound people. / Wherever what we pursue is useful / Is the most valuable domain. / It becomes easy to follow you, / Whoever obeys, achieves, / Show us a solid fatherland. / Hail the leader! Hail the bond!

The fatherland is firm and solid; it is to be settled and made productive. The Uncle has inherited large tracts of land in the United States, and the League will take over management of these. Friedrich and Lenardo intend to settle there. The Society of the Tower has bought an estate contiguous with the Uncle's domains in Italy. A canal is to be built through these domains, and unproductive land is to be made productive. Lenardo proposes emigration to empty land in the United States, the *terra nullius* claimed by many nineteenth-century colonists. (His plans show no awareness that the land was in fact not empty; there is no mention of its indigenous inhabitants, despite Goethe's reading of Cooper and the discussions of indigenous peoples in Bernhard's journals. Goethe was of course aware of the criticisms made of European colonialism at the time, as he would later show in *Faust. The Second Part of the Tragedy*.) Odoard proposes that part of the League should settle in and develop unproductive land in Europe, close to the mountainous regions where food is in short supply and where cottage industry is threatened by mechanization. What Lenardo's and Odoard's plans share and what marks them out as unusual, distinctively Goethean indeed, is the emphasis on consolidating property and training its new settlers in the handicrafts and other skills needed to make it productive and create a self-sustaining community. Property ownership and labour are to be the twin pillars of the social order.[42] That much is in accordance with the more advanced economic theories of the time, for instance Adam Smith's. Yet the economic vision is also tinged with the romantic-agrarian nostalgia for small rural communities that Goethe found in Rousseau and Möser.[43] The League is opposed to mechanization and in favour of craft. Its members are idealized craftsmen and its landowners and financial backers are mostly aristocrats.[44] Goethe was by no means blind to the forces of modernity, yet his stance tended more towards rejection than acceptance. The acceleration of industry and the economy cannot be ignored, nor can it be welcomed. Any young man facing the onslaught of modernity should not overestimate his power to withstand it, nor should he merely acquiesce:

> As little as steam engines can be throttled can anything similar be done in the moral realm. The liveliness of commerce, the continual rustle of paper money, the increase in debts to pay off other debts—all these are frightful elements that the young man of the present confronts. He is fortunate if he is endowed with a moderate, peaceable disposition that neither makes immoderate demands on the world nor allows himself to be determined by it.[45]

The change in emphasis from movement to settlement completes a shift begun in 1807 and continued in the 1821 version of the novel. The overriding goal of the *Journeyman Years*, in all its variants, is a productive and stable social order, which is to be achieved by training individuals to satisfy society's needs. A well-ordered society requires a degree of conformity. In the discussions they hold between their two addresses to the migrants, Lenardo and Odoard agree that while some individual liberty must be granted, the highest aim of government is to ensure that all parts of a polity conform to the same rules. Instead of delegating the administration to local officials, which can cause the practice of government in different areas to diverge, the central administration should constantly be visiting all parts of the domain 'to maintain uniformity [or 'equality': 'Gleichheit'] in the most important matters, and to let everyone have his own will in less crucial ones'.[46] What does uniformity or equality mean here? It is not equality before the law, such as the liberal-minded Prince

Bernhard found in his travels in America, where free male citizens were not distinguished by class.[47] Goethe's analysis of society is not concerned with class nor with eroding aristocratic privileges by enshrining universal rights in a constitution. The equality or conformity proposed by Lenardo and Odoard has more to do with policing than justice. In their view, policing is a more important responsibility of government than justice. They agree that 'the greatest need of any state is courageous authority [*Obrigkeit*]'.[48] Justice may be required to settle disputes, but a strong policing function is required if social harmony is to be maintained and centrifugal forces kept in check. Only central authority has the moral propriety that makes society gel:

> There are two powers in peacetime: justice and propriety.
>
> Justice aims at obligation, government authority [*Polizei*] aims at propriety. Justice deliberates and resolves, authority supervises and commands. Justice pertains to the individual, authority to the community [or 'entirety', *Gesamtheit*].[49]

In contrasting individual justice and social propriety, Goethe is not interested in establishing individual rights within the state, in the manner of the US constitution. Rather he is interested in asserting the rights of society over the individual. This imagined state has no representative bodies through which the individual might resist state power. The claims of justice are merely those of one individual against another, such as for the restitution of damages or enforcement of contracts. Propriety, on the other hand, has a much wider reach. It embraces the norms of behaviour that society can rightfully require of the individual. These norms are evidently not enshrined in law. They are executive orders that go further and demand more than mere laws do. They are to be determined by the government's executive function and enforced by vigilant policing. In other words, this is an authoritarian state that enforces social conformity. Lenardo and Odoard give several examples of social norms that must be policed. Lenardo proposes a ban on circulating libraries and bars serving spirits.[50] (The latter were a release for working people; the former the chief point of access to culture for the majority of the literate population.) Immoderate consumption of alcohol is of course the enemy of work and the friend of unruliness. A motto for the new settlements reads: 'moderation where there is choice, industry where there is necessity'.[51] Leisure time is to be devoted to moderate pleasures, and the necessities of life—work, education, administration—are to be pursued industriously. The ban on circulating libraries might also encourage industry by preventing the idleness of novel-reading, but it will also slow the spread of the feverish reflection and discussion of current affairs. An aphorism from the 'Reflections in the Spirit of Wanderers' expresses alarm at the rapid churning of what we now call the news cycle: 'it leaps from house to house, from town to town, from empire to empire, and finally from continent to continent, always express [*veloziferisch*, from French *velocifere*]'; it is 'the greatest evil of our time, which allows nothing to come to fruition'.[52]

One significant passage in the 1821 text that Goethe omitted in 1829 describes the League's pseudo-democratic, but in fact authoritarian constitution. It is not hard to see why Goethe omitted it. No doubt authoritarianism cloaked in democracy seemed a valid response to the repressive Carlsbad Decrees of 1819. The view presented in 1829 is that questions about political organization are unimportant, since the real business of government is keeping order. A conversation between Jarno, the Astronomer, and Makarie is summarized thus: 'So long as order is maintained, the means do not matter'.[53] An aphorism from Makarie's 'Archive' asserts the government's duty to prevent the people from feeling tempted to seize power:

> We do not ask ourselves what right we have to govern—we govern. Whether the people has the right to depose us, that is something we do not worry about—we simply guard against it feeling tempted to do so.[54]

How the government guards against the temptation is not explained. A charitable interpretation would be that good government can keep the population satisfied, but the language suggests a degree of defensiveness. Behind the League's authoritarianism lurks that profound mistrust of the people en masse that was commonly felt by governments of the time. Lenardo and Odoard gesture towards democracy, but make clear their mistrust of it, though they are unwilling to explain why they are reluctant to explain their mistrust:

> As for majority rule, we have our own special views on that; we allow it to prevail, of course, in the necessary course of things, but in the higher sense we place little trust in it. On that question, however, I may not expatiate further.[55]

An aphorism from the 'Reflections in the Spirit of Wanderers' is less reticent. It is one of several passages that express a dislike of the ignorant majority:

> Nothing is more odious than the majority, for it consists of a few strong leaders, of scoundrels who accommodate themselves, of weaklings who

assimilate, and of the masses, who trundle along behind without knowing in the least what they want.[56]

The idea that the common people do not know what they want recurs in a passage in which the Uncle repudiates the Benthamite liberalism that Goethe detested:[57]

> He did not deny that he had altered the liberal motto, 'the best for the most', according to his own ideas to 'the desirable for the many'. The 'most' cannot be found or recognised, and what the best is, can even less be determined. 'The many', however, are always around us; what they desire, we can discover, what they ought to desire, we can consider, and thus something significant can always be done and accomplished.[58]

Liberalism is unworkable because there is no way to determine who 'the most' are. Liberals like Bentham who claim that policy should reflect the needs of the majority are wrong, as are democrats who believe in majoritarian government. Instead government should be in the hands of a pragmatically minded 'we'. The 'we' are presumably those with the strength of character required to make productive use of the liberties that modern civilization affords. Indeed, and again in the spirit of Rousseau, liberty is dangerous to a mind that lacks self-control, according to one of the 'Wanderer' aphorisms: 'Everything that liberates the mind without giving us more self-mastery is harmful.'[59]

The pattern of advocating strong authority and disregarding liberty is reversed when we move from the domain of politics into that of science, and expressly so, for Goethe has his characters note approvingly the contrast between authoritarian politics and liberal science. Most of the scientific content of the novel relates to the figure of Makarie, the disabled aunt who advises friends and family on their relationships and is the object of the Astronomer's awe. She is a highly idealized creation, like something out of the novels of Goethe's Romantic contemporaries. The character with whom she has most in common is Natalie, whose strangely loveless philanthropy Makarie takes to a higher level.[60] The novel hints at but never explicitly states what underlies Makarie's two gifts: her ability to reconcile people and to intuit the motions of the solar system without calculations. Both gifts stem from an intuitive understanding of the principles of attraction and repulsion. Her remarkable capacity to mirror the heavens gives rise to three passages on science towards the end of the novel: conversations between the Astronomer and Jarno, a description of Makarie's character, and several aphorisms on science in Makarie's

'Archive'. The contrast between the domains of politics and science is spelt out in a conversation between the Astronomer and Jarno:

> Church and state may if need be find cause for declaring themselves unassailable, for they have to deal with the unruly masses, and as long as order is maintained, the means do not matter. But in the sciences the utmost freedom is required, for the scientist works not for today or tomorrow but for an inconceivable progression of ages.[61]

Science needs freedom because it has no utility, or should have none if done properly. Here science differs from politics, which is utterly practical and concerned only with what works. Lenardo's and Odoard's plans are concerned with welfare, practical utility, and good order in society. Their pragmatism is most striking in their treatment of the arts. In the new settlements the arts aim only at proficiency in handicrafts which now set the standard for the fine arts. It might seem a remarkable turnaround for Goethe, but he was connecting to an Enlightenment tradition—Diderot is one example—of ranking the crafts alongside the fine arts.[62] The crafts possess that very proficiency which modern practitioners of the fine or 'free' arts (as Odoard prefers to call them) increasingly lacked. Just as the fine arts are renamed 'free arts', the crafts will be renamed 'rigorous arts'. Their practitioners will be required to adhere strictly to the traditional stages of training of the apprentice, journeyman, and master, and no leniency will be allowed in this.[63] The rigorous arts must set an example to the free arts of how success is judged, for at present there are no criteria for success in the free arts, and failure seems to count as much as success.[64] This is far removed from Robert Owen's New Harmony with its complement of scholars, about which Goethe had read in Duke Bernhard's reports, and much more like George Rapp's practical Harmonists.[65] The 'Wanderer' aphorisms have prepared the reader for Goethe's complete retreat from the free arts: 'unrestrained activity, of whatever kind, leads at last to bankruptcy'.[66] Or: 'people go wrong, in regard to themselves and others, because they treat the means as an end, so that for sheer activity nothing happens, or perhaps something detestable'.[67] Or: 'botanists have a category of plants they name *incompletae*; one may also say that there are incomplete, unfinished human beings. They are those whose actions and achievements are not proportion to their longing and striving'.[68] The novel contains a strain of distaste for the modern, Romantic ideology of complete artistic freedom.

By contrast, Makarie's world is ethereal and theoretical. As with the Platonist Princess in *Tasso* and the Pietist Beautiful Soul, Makarie's disability betokens a disengagement from the physical world and a compensatory investment in the spirit, though in her case with no negative effects. She represents a dichotomy that appears elsewhere in Goethe's very late works: the absolute irreconcilability of the *vita contemplativa* and the *vita activa*. The former is a speculative or theoretical relation to the world, in which a person can have freedom but not affect the world. The latter is an active engagement with and impact on the world that is bound to utilitarian motives and therefore totally unfree. Makarie represents intuitive science in its pure form. Her mind contains a model of the planets which seems to be innate and untaught. She intuitively produces the results of Newtonian astronomy, which the Astronomer in his bafflement is able to check against his calculations. In intuiting the motions of the celestial bodies, she renders the whole discipline of mathematics unnecessary—or at least Goethe's understanding of mathematics, which limited its application to astronomy.[69] Makarie is thus the supreme embodiment of Goethe's scientific *homo mensura* principle, the fullest formulation of which is found among the aphorisms of her 'Archive':

> The human being in himself, to the extent that he makes use of his sound senses, is the greatest and most accurate physical apparatus there can be; and that is the greatest disaster of modern physics, that it has effectively separated experimentation from the human element and recognises Nature only in what artificial instruments can register, and indeed, wants to limit and establish thereby what Nature can achieve.[70]

Along with the *homo mensura* principle, the 'Wanderer' aphorisms express Goethe's dislike of sense-extending apparatus: 'microscopes and telescopes actually confuse man's pure senses'.[71] Goethe's scepticism about sense-extenders has a precedent in Rousseau's *Émile*, as Goethe no doubt knew. In order for Émile's senses to develop fully, he should remain ignorant of microscopes or telescopes, at least until he has enough knowledge to invent them for himself. Rousseau gives the example of how Émile is to understand the sight of a stick half immersed in water:

> I would prefer that Émile never know dioptrics if he cannot learn it around this stick. He will not have dissected insects; he will not have counted the spots on the sun. He will not know what a microscope and a telescope are. Your learned pupils will make fun of his ignorance. They will not be wrong; for before he uses these instruments, I intend him to invent them. And you may well suspect that this will not come so soon.[72]

It is hardly surprising then that Makarie's other great gift—her ability to see behind people's masks to their sound inner essence—is also the product of Goethe's reinterpretation of Rousseau:

> It was as though she penetrated the inner nature of each through the individual mask covering him. Those with whom Wilhelm was acquainted stood before him as if transfigured: the benevolent insight of this inestimable woman had detached the outer husk and ennobled and revived the healthy kernel.[73]

Makarie's gift is to detach the mask made by a person's *amour-propre* and reveal the authentic character behind it. The benefit is felt by everyone whose 'husk' Makarie removes. Far from being embarrassed at being stripped bare by her penetrating gaze, people experience it as a liberation:

> The relationship to Makarie of all these persons passing through was marked by trust and respect; all felt the presence of a higher being, yet in her presence there remained to each the freedom to appear according to his own nature. Everyone shows himself as he is, more so than he ever did towards parents and friends, and with a certain confidence, for he was lured and encouraged to manifest only what was good, was best, in himself, for which reason well-nigh general satisfaction reigned.[74]

Makarie is able to reverse the process described in Rousseau's *Social Contract*. She removes the chains in which civilization and its competition for prestige shackle us, and she restores us to our authentic state as free individuals. She creates a future that resembles the past, like Lenardo's and Odoard's settler projects that undo the ills of modern civilization. Her astronomical genius is of the same kind, insofar as her imagination artlessly becomes identical with the universe. No hypotheses or theories or mathematical calculations interpose themselves between subject and object, and so her intuition recreates the universe by means of an effortless empiricism, as described by an aphorism in the 'Wanderer' collection:

> There is a tender empiricism that enters into so intimate an identification with its object that it actually becomes a theory. But this heightening of intellectual capacity is characteristic of a highly developed age.[75]

The tender empiricism is a science of the future, which can only come about once we have learned to do without the rigid, hegemonic models of thought and behaviour that plague modern science. But it is also a science of the past that renounces the microscope and telescope and the torture chamber of modern experimentation, and reverts to a method in which humans are the measure of the universe.

The novel as a whole imagines a future that resembles a Rousseauian vision of the past. It promises to cure the ills of modernity or, where a cure is not possible, at least to contain them. Its vision is often speculative or tentative, and it readily acknowledges its own unreality. The novel's Editor states that the excursus on Makarie's character is of dubious provenance and a piece of 'ethereal poetry'.[76] Readers have struggled to know how seriously to take the novel's ideas, which seem both serious and playful. The whole novel is unstable with its mixture of diverse text types and perspectives. Its makeshift nature is accentuated by Goethe's decision to introduce the fiction of the Editor and so to give the novel something of the character of a 'found text' whose contents are thereby made both more authentic and less reliable because they are not filtered through an authoritative narrator. A seemingly inconsequential example of the improvised form of the text appears in the Editor's interpolation in the middle of Book Two. The interpolation follows Chapter 7 and precedes Chapter 9, and so it appears to replace the missing Chapter 8, and yet no explanation is given for the omission. This is just one small example of the ways in which the text disturbs its readers expectations. The 1821 version was a freestanding publication; the 1829 version appeared as Volumes 21 to 23 of *Goethe's Works. Complete Final Authorized Edition*. Whereas the 1821 version had the word 'novel' in its title, the 1829 version does not. If it is not a novel, what is it?

It is hard to know how much of this makeshift character was planned and how much was an accidental product of the publication process. The original plan was for the 1829 edition to comprise two volumes, but during the printing this had to be expanded to three. Since there was not enough material to fill three volumes, Goethe instructed Eckermann to collect some aphorisms for addition at the ends of Books One and Two. Book One would end with the aphorisms 'From Makarie's Archive' and the poem 'In the Solemn Ossuary', written on the occasion of the relocation of Schiller's remains to the ducal crypt. Book Two would close with the 'Wanderer' aphorisms and the poem 'Testament'. However, the addenda arrived with Cotta too late, so that the Makarie aphorisms and 'In the Solemn Ossuary' had to be added instead to the end of Book Three.[77] Two years after the novel's publication, Goethe agreed with Eckermann's proposal that future editions should simply omit the aphorisms, at least according to Eckermann's own report.[78] Certainly there is something arbitrary about the aphorisms.[79] Other seemingly arbitrary features of the text include the renaming of some of the characters from the *Apprenticeship* and 'The Man of Fifty Years'. It is not clear to what extent these renamings are intentional. The renaming of Jarno as Montan is fully explained by his change of career. The renaming of Nachodine as Susanne and the confusion of Valerine and Nachodine is part of the logic of the story of Lenardo's search for the Nut-brown Girl: from Lenardo's perspective, identities shift and are easily confused. There is nothing in the logic of the story to explain the renaming of Therese as Julie or Flavio as Silvio. It might be argued that these are effects of Makarie's ability to remove false masks. However, the renaming of Lydie to Lucie looks like a simple scribal or typesetting error, likewise the naming of Juliette as Julie on only one occasion. The 1829 text contains numerous scribal and printing errors, at least ten times as many as the 1821 version.[80] There were practical reasons for this. The production of the 1829 text involved more stages. Goethe was not fully involved in its editing; he delegated the revision of the proofs to Göttling and Riemer.[81] Consequently it is hard to distinguish between errors and intentional confusions. It is tempting to read much (though not all) of this as belonging to the novel's strange character, its somewhat makeshift response to the challenges of modernity. And it is important not to lose sight of fact that the novel's ideas are thoroughly Goethean, no matter how unstable and confusing their textual framing.

In completing the *Journeyman Years* Goethe was clearing his desk of a project that went back to the 1790s and beyond. During work on the novel in 1827, he returned to another plan from the 1790s, an epic poem titled 'The Hunt', which he had discussed with Schiller and Wilhelm von Humboldt in the midst of their deliberations on poetic genre in spring 1797. The version of 'The Hunt' that he completed in 1827 was however not an epic but a short, dense, and pervasively symbolic prose narrative, to which he gave the plain title 'Novella'. The reason for the plain title, if Eckermann's account of a conversation with Goethe on 29 January 1827 is to be believed, was that a novella is 'an unheard of event that actually occurred'.[82] This perfunctory definition, which may or may not correspond to something Goethe said, has since become canonical in attempts to classify the novella genre. Whether it deserves that status and whether Goethe's 'Novella' even belongs to the genre so defined has rightly been questioned.[83] The narrated happenings occur within one day, which does seem appropriate to a novella, and they culminate in an extraordinary event.

The prince of a small German domain is out hunting. His wife, accompanied by his uncle and a courtier Honorio, who is in love with her, takes the opportunity of the prince's absence to pay a visit to the nearby ruined castle that had once been the ducal family's seat. While they are away a fire breaks out in the town's marketplace, some unattended gunpowder explodes, and a lion and tiger escape from the cages where they were kept by their owners, a foreign showman and his family. The lion and tiger make their way towards the ruined castle, where Honorio shoots the latter at a second attempt. The showman and his wife appear with their son and beg that the lion be spared, since the son can pacify it with his song. The prince makes provision for trapping the beast and having Honorio shoot it, should the son fail, but the lion, having wandered into the courtyard of the ruined castle, is indeed pacified by the boy. In the manner of St Jerome, the boy removes a thorn from the lion's paw which he binds. The story ends with the boy singing his song beside the docile beast, an unheard-of situation indeed:

> Were it possible to believe that the features of so fierce a monster, the tyrant of the forest and the despot of the animal kingdom, could display an expression of friendliness, of grateful contentment, then it occurred here, and in truth the child, with his transfigured look, seemed now like a mighty victorious conqueror, and yet the lion not so much vanquished—for his strength though concealed was still in him—as tamed and surrendered to his own peaceful will.[84]

At the same time as he conceived of the story in spring 1797, Goethe was thinking about Moses and the wanderings of the Children of Israel.[85] 'The Hunt' and the completed 'Novella' of 1827 were connected to the work on Moses in two ways. The core idea of 'Novella' is that aggression might be better overcome by gentle and peaceable sympathy than by force. The contrast of force and peace was at the heart of Goethe's understanding of the religion of the Pentateuch. The religion of Abraham was peaceful, whereas the version of Judaism Moses created was the product of violence. 'Novella' represents a peaceful approach to nation-building, in contrast to the aggression of Moses.[86] The second link between 'Novella' and Moses concerned the origins of poetry in the Orient. The showman and his family are not German and most likely not from central or western Europe, as is made clear in a description of the mother speaking in ways that 'would be impossible to translate [...] into our kinds of language'.[87] Her husband follows her speech with a peaceful vision of creation that resembles Goethe's ideal of Abraham invited by God to look up at the stars. The showman speaks 'with a kind of natural enthusiasm'.[88] Both speeches are described in ways that recall Herder's characterization of the language of the Old Testament in his essay *On the Spirit of Hebrew Poetry* (1782–1783), which Goethe read in spring 1797 while working on Moses and 'The Hunt'.[89] The shift to poetry at the end of 'Novella' accompanies a wider move towards the ancient Orient that recalls the *Divan*. The family's strange language, their exotic garb, and their familiarity with lions and tigers all point to them hailing from the Orient. The boy is a reincarnation of Daniel. In the song he sings in the 'hollow' (*Graben*) of hidden castle courtyard he alludes to Daniel in the 'cave' (*Gruben*)—the pun, also reminiscent of the wordplay of the *Divan*, suggests an atavistic recurrence of the mythic origins of humanity.[90] Furthermore, the final scene of 'Novella' takes place in the ancient ruins of the ancestral castle (*Stammburg*), where trees have since taken back control so as to create 'a place both haphazard and unique, where you can see traces of the long-vanished power of man in tenacious struggle with the ever-living, ever-working power of nature'.[91] The *Stammburg* thus contains another pun, for *Stamm* can mean both *family* or *tribe* and *tree trunk*. It is an appropriate site for the return to ancient oriental poetry and wisdom and to human origins. By removing the thorn from the lion's paw the boy reenacts a prototypical experience of Rousseauian sympathy.

The atavistic ending of the story contrasts with its modern beginning in the town where the ducal family now has its residence. The town is the site of business and administration. Here we are closer to the world of the *Journeyman Years* and its concern with managing the centrifugal forces of modernity. The story's dense symbolism has given rise to numerous attempts to locate it in a particular time and place in Goethe's Germany. While one might argue that these attempts miss the point, they are not altogether without merit. The geographical location of the story is clearly in the German world of petty principalities and their ducal residences. Its landscapes and flora point towards a generic or idealized location rather than a particular one. It comprises mountains, rolling hills, forest, the headwaters of a great river, and plains with arable land, and its species of trees are those found in different parts of Germany.[92] The fire that breaks out in the town might be interpreted as the French Revolution, except for the fact that fire is not a unique occurrence—the Uncle has traumatic memories of an earlier blaze in a distant town, so that the fire points instead towards a recurrent danger, such as outbreaks of popular unrest. Indeed, before the fire breaks out, the narrator gives a brief indication of the principality's social and economic development: 'The Prince's father had lived to see the time when all members of the state were expected to pass their days in equal industry and, each according to his own fashion, produce, earn and enjoy'.[93] The town has only recently reached this high point of social and economic development. Some have read this description as again relating to the French Revolution,[94] but that seems unlikely, for there is no mention of the most prominent achievement of the Revolution, its promotion of equal legal rights. More plausible is that the town represents a German town that has adopted the policies Goethe advocated after the Revolution: that all parts of society should contribute to its well-being and prosperity, including an aristocracy that has progressed from merely extracting rents from land ownership towards full economic activity. 'Novella' presents a differentiated view of the aristocracy. The Prince is an attentive administrator and loving husband. He resents the hunt separating him from his wife and diverting him from his domain's business, and so he stands in stark contrast to the male figures of the *Journeyman Years* who are typically inconstant lovers and poor administrators. The courtier Honorio fares less well. On killing the tiger he courts the Princess in embarrassing fashion: the tiger's pelt will keep her warm on her sledge. Although apparently a good marksman, he misses the tiger with his first shot. His desire to excel in the Princess's eyes makes his aim erratic. That is how *amour-propre* affects a man, enfeebling his natural ability. And of course his plea to the Princess is itself a kind of hunt, although again a hunt that goes wrong, for she easily disarms his approach. Honorio's failure is confirmed at the end of the story. The Prince's plan for dealing with the lion assigns to Honorio the task of lighting a fire to block its way—the fire being a correlate of Honorio's destructive and passionate character—but this part of the plan comes to nothing. Honorio is not needed. His passionate and violent manner has become redundant. As the story ends, the showman's wife sees the beautiful Honorio perched on a wall and staring distractedly into the setting sun, a sign that the role of aristocratic courtier has run its day. The Uncle presents a third form of existence: humans as conscientious but passive observers, the *vita contemplativa* in contrast to the positive version of the *vita activa* represented by the Prince and the negative version embodied by Honorio. His main role is to manage the work of a draughtsman who is documenting the ancestral castle—representation and not intervention. Otherwise his influence on events amounts to anxious and repeated forebodings. He dislikes the route that he and the Princess take through the marketplace. He is traumatized by his memory of an earlier terrifying fire. His role is entirely passive. He represents the ineffectual nature of conscience, ineffectual because by choosing to observe, he renounces action.

'Novella' ends with an idyllic suspension of all such contradictions. The final scene in which 'the tyrant of the forest and the despot of the animal kingdom' succumbs meekly to the power of a mere young boy embodies a harmonious reconciliation of opposites, in the manner set out in Goethe's 1818 essay 'Myron's Cow'. In that essay, the sculptor possessed the ability to represent 'the balance to be found in imbalance, the contrast to be found in things which are similar, the harmony to be found in things which are dissimilar'.[95] On this view, the ending of 'Novella' is an example of artistic perfection. But 'Novella' is narrative and not sculpture, and it is more discontinuous than its harmonizing ending suggests. It is a story composed of two quite different and only loosely connected spheres, the town and the ancestral castle. The realism of the first part of the story and its highly idealized ending are hard to reconcile. In this sense, 'Novella' shares some of the odd inconsequentiality and antirealism of the *Journeyman Years*, with its outlandish projects for managing the effects of modernity. The nature of the town and the fire that befalls it does not generate the solution provided by the boy and his family, except in the negative sense that the fire and explosion release the beasts, and Honorio's imperfect hunting of the tiger reveals a need for more sympathetic handling of them. The showman's exotic family is not a product of the town, except in the tenuous sense that they take advantage of the commercial opportunities offered by its market. Nor is it clear how the boy's song and music could resolve the problems represented by the fires that have repeatedly broken out in the town or the haplessly aggressive behaviour of Honorio. At the end of the story Honorio is ordered to return to the town. Will he be of help there? What will his future be?[96] Will he be allowed to go on his travels through Europe or even to America, as has been suggested by one critic?[97] Or will he remain at court and continue his unwelcome attentions to the Princess? Or will he manage to overcome his desire, as Lenardo seems to have done in the *Journeyman Years*? Honorio's inflammatory passions are one unresolved problem. Another problem, symbolically related to passions, is the fire and in particular the gunpowder that was detonated by it. The gunpowder is of special importance because, according to the showman, it was the explosion and not the initial fire that caused his family to lose control of the animals. Gunpowder was a prime constituent of European modernity. As Herder pointed out in *This too a Philosophy of History*, gunpowder led to the creation of highly trained and expensive standing armies and the governmental structures needed to sustain them. And as Adam Smith observed in *The Wealth of Nations*, the firepower of these armies tilted the European balance of power in favour of the larger nation states that could afford them.⁹⁸ Gunpowder was the fuel of modern European nation-building. Closer to Goethe's own experience, on the night of the Battle of Jena-Auerstedt, Weimar had been spared catastrophe, when barrels of gunpowder left lying around the town by fleeing Prussian troops miraculously failed to detonate amid the fires.⁹⁹ The explosion that releases the wild animals in 'Novella' echoes the destructive modern threats of military power, nation-building, and nationalism. The prospect of these forces being contained by the harmonizing power of art seems remote. That very remoteness is no doubt integral to the story's meaning. Like the *Journeyman Years*, 'Novella' expresses the growing gap between Goethe's understanding of modernity and the prescriptions for managing its unruly forces that he had once believed in. Art and its ally gentle human sympathy can contain some forces, but modernity may prove too explosive.

From 1827 the term 'world literature' (*Weltliteratur*) began to appear in *On Art and Antiquity* and in Goethe's letters. He has often been credited with coining the term, which is not strictly speaking true, as it had already been used twice in the eighteenth century.¹⁰⁰ However, he was the first to use it repeatedly and with a programmatic intent. His repeated uses of the term have often been anthologized and cited as foundational documents of the discipline of Comparative Literature.¹⁰¹ The text most often quoted is from a conversation supposedly recorded by Eckermann in 1827: 'National literature doesn't mean much now; it's the era of world literature, and everyone must direct their effort to accelerating this era.'¹⁰² Whether or not Goethe said these words, they have been taken as a call for a boundary-crossing conception of literature that is entirely in his spirit. Comparative Literature grew alongside and in opposition to the historiography of national literatures that dominated the era of nation-building of the nineteenth and twentieth centuries. Instead of telling the story of a nation's literature, Comparative Literature showed how literary traditions were constituted by traffic across boundaries. More recently the discipline has tried to shift the traditional canon of the 'great books' away from the major European languages and towards the nations of the global majority. That too is a Goethean idea. In these general terms, Goethe's advocacy of *Weltliteratur* deserves credit.

However, it can be reasonably argued that the credit has been given for the wrong thing.¹⁰³ On a fairly minimalist definition (of what is admittedly a contested term), world literature widens the domain of literature from the nation to the globe. It promotes the literature that circulates beyond its nation or region of origin. It can be argued that what Goethe means by *Weltliteratur* is rather narrower, and more descriptive than normative. The core of his idea is that the period after 1815 is seeing a more intense and accelerated communication between writers and critics of the major European cultural nations. New cross-boundary dialogues are beginning, in particular in the journals that have Europe-wide circulation, such as *The Edinburgh Review*, *Le Globe* (Paris), and *l'Eco* (Milan). No doubt Goethe shared with many readers in Italy, France, and Britain a feeling of relief on seeing the barriers descend that had gone up during the Napoleonic Wars. In that sense, *Weltliteratur* was a product of a specific place and time:

> For some time there has been talk of a general world literature, and with some justice: because all of the nations, thoroughly shaken up in the most dreadful wars, then turned back in on themselves, had cause to notice that they had become aware of much that was foreign, had taken this in, had sensed hitherto unknown intellectual needs here and there. Out of this there arose the feeling of neighbourly relations, and instead of shutting themselves up as before, their spirit gradually conceived of the desire to be taken up into the more or less free intellectual commerce.[104]

This narrow sense of *Weltliteratur* emerged from personal experience. He disliked much of the response to his works in Germany in the 1820s, and he found a new reception outside Germany that was welcome and reinvigorating.[105] *Le Globe* even stepped in to defend him against his German detractors, as he wrote to Zelter at the end of 1829.[106] Writing in response to a French translation of his dramatic works in 1826, he welcomed the attention now being paid to German literature in France:

> And so it may please us from a cosmopolitan point of view that a people that has gone through so many periods of examination and testing looks around for fresh sources to revive, strengthen, and restore itself to health, and hence more than ever turns outwards, and to be sure not towards a perfected, recognised neighbouring people, but to one that is vigorous and itself in the process of striving and struggling.[107]

He enjoyed seeing his work translated and was not at all worried about what gets 'lost in translation'. On the contrary, he saw translation as a gain:[108] 'every literature ultimately gets bored with itself if it isn't refreshed by foreign attention'.[109] He insisted that German writers should not be overly concerned about being misunderstood by foreign readers, translators, and critics. Much more important was the bigger prize of international reception and recognition, even where it involved misunderstandings. Indeed, misunderstandings were a necessary part of the creative process of transnational reception:

> [...] for my part I want to make my friends aware that I am convinced that a general world literature is developing, in which an honorable role is reserved for us Germans. All the nations are paying attention to us, they're praising, criticising, absorbing and discarding, imitating and distorting, understanding or misunderstanding us, opening or closing their hearts: all of this we should receive with equanimity, because as a whole it is of great value to us.[110]

This is Goethe's most significant statement on *Weltliteratur*. It contains some elements that recur in modern conceptions of world literature and Comparative Literature. For instance, he emphasizes the vagaries of exchange and reception. The exchange of literature between nations gives rise to distortions, and yet these are much less important than the fact that a productive exchange is happening. The significance of this passage was noted immediately by writers in *Le Globe* and *l'Eco*, who translated and echoed it.[111] However, Goethe's notion of *Weltliteratur* is quite different from what we understand as world literature today. By 'literature' he means intellectual traffic in the review journals. By 'world' he means the major cultural nations of Europe: Britain, France, Italy, and Germany. This was where the journals were based that he saw as the principal vehicles of international cultural traffic.

On the other hand, *Weltliteratur* did also contain a normative element: it was how literature *ought* to be. It was cosmopolitan. It reminded us that literature does not belong to the nation. It is a universal possession of humankind, as Goethe observed in a late aphorism:

> There is no patriotic art and no patriotic science. Both of these belong, like all good things, to the whole world and can be promoted only by means of general, free reciprocity of all living contemporaries, in constant reference to what is left and known to us from the past.[112]

Goethe habitually used the term *Weltliteratur* alongside language that stressed its universal nature ('general', 'all'), as if it belonged to all nations and not just the major European cultural nations. That is the theory, and it was also his practice in his literary reviews in *On Art and Antiquity* and of course the *West-Eastern Divan*. He reviewed literature from outside Europe, notably classic and modern works from India and China.[113] There are also reviews of literature in so-called minor European languages, for instance Serbian and Modern Greek.[114] Within the major cultural nations, he was interested in literature in regional dialects.¹¹⁵ This latter interest led him to coin another term, 'world poetry' (*Weltpoesie*), which must however be distinguished from the similar-looking *Weltliteratur*.¹¹⁶ *Weltpoesie* does different work from *Weltliteratur*, even if it belongs to the same project from which *Weltliteratur* sprang—that is to say, his longstanding efforts to establish a literary domain that was both socially rooted and autonomous. *Weltpoesie* is another term for 'popular poetry' (*Volkspoesie*). It is an attempt to capture the idea of a universal poetry of humankind that springs naturally from human experience, as he argues in a review of Serbian popular poetry:

> It must be striking in this connection that a half-coarse people coincides with the most practised [people] precisely at that level of a carefree lyric poetry, which persuades us once more that a general world poetry [*Weltpoesie*] exists and excels according to circumstances; neither content nor form need to be handed down to it, everywhere where the sun shines its development is assured.¹¹⁷

Weltpoesie and *Weltliteratur* are both expressions of Goethe's universalism. *Weltliteratur* expresses his desire for dialogue and mutual understanding between different national traditions. It is a cosmopolitan and civilized form of universalism. *Weltpoesie* captures his belief in an innate capacity of humans to turn their experience into poetry. It is universalism on the level of anthropology.

In early February 1825 spring tidal flooding caused devastation along the north-sea coast. Around eight hundred lives were lost. The catastrophe may have been the prompt Goethe needed to finally resume work on *Faust*, after a break of twenty years. From 1825 he worked on it in fits and starts until 1831, when, instead of releasing the text for publication, he had its second and concluding part sealed in a box for posthumous publication in the *Final Authorized Edition*. The decision to withhold *The Second Part of the Tragedy* drew an impassioned plea from Wilhelm von Humboldt in January 1832 that Goethe should not deprive himself of the pleasure of witnessing his friends' responses to the whole work. Goethe replied in March, in a letter dated five days before his death. Nothing would give him greater pleasure than to share 'these very serious jokes' with his friends, he wrote:

> But the times are really so absurd and confused that I've persuaded myself that my honest, long-pursued endeavours on this strange edifice would be

poorly recompensed and stranded on the shore, to lie like a wreck in ruins and soon be covered by the flotsam of the hours. Confusing teaching on top of confused action prevails across the world [. . .].[118]

As he foresaw, the 'strange edifice' of *Faust. The Second Part of the Tragedy* with its 'very serious jokes' was greeted with bafflement. Its seeming lack of a straightforward plot, its strange digressions, the impression that its meaning was allegorical, and its sheer length—nearly twice as long as *The First Part of the Tragedy*—were felt to sit ill with the realities of the day.[119] All of this could be and was blamed on the poet's failing powers in old age, even if *The Second Part* contained sections of exceptional moral and poetic power. A more just criticism is that its protracted genesis caused *The Second Part* to become something of a miscellany, composed of successive new strata, each layer reflecting Goethe's responses to the events and trends of the moment when he wrote it. *The Second Part*, even more than *The First Part*, served him as a vehicle for expressing what exercised him at the time. The shifts of focus were in part the result of the piecemeal and erratic working habits of an author who was not confident he would ever finish his life's work and therefore saw no reason to work on the text systematically. Instead of writing the scenes in sequence, he jumped back and forth, working on whichever passage suited his mood.[120] He began work in 1825 by returning to the Helen fragment first drafted in 1800, which would form Act III of the completed five-act *The Second Part*. In the same year he began to think about Act V. He published Act III in 1827, after which he started work on Act I. The first half of Act I appeared in the *Final Authorized Edition* at Easter 1828. The rest of Act I had to wait until early 1830. Meanwhile in autumn 1827 he started work on Act II, which he finished in late 1830. With Acts I and II written, everything leading up to the Helen scenes was now completed. Act V was written in three stages. The central scenes were written in 1825, in the aftermath of the floods. The concluding scenes were written in the winter of 1830/31 and the opening scenes in spring 1831. In May to July 1831 he wrote Act IV and so brought *The Second Part* to a conclusion.

The most significant question concerning the work's meaning—whether Faust would be saved or damned—had been settled sometime between 1797 and 1801, when Goethe had decided to replace the traditional twenty-four-year pact with a wager, which Mephistopheles had no chance of winning outright. In the 'Prologue in Heaven' the Lord states that he will be able to lead Faust into clarity, because humans, despite their confused and errant striving,[121] are guided by a natural unconscious drive or Spinozan *nisus* (inclination) towards divine transcendence. The passages of *The First Part* written in the late 1790s thus solved the human side of Faust's salvation. Faust's actions are not germane to the question of his salvation. They might be confused, even immoral, but that does not concern the Lord. According to a note written in June 1797, 'instead of reconciling' the 'contradictions' in the *Faust* material, Goethe intended 'to make them more disparate'.[122] Presumably one such contradiction was the moral disparity between Faust's guilt over Gretchen and his salvation. However, what exactly Goethe meant by making the moral disparity 'more disparate' remained unclear until a very late stage. In December 1830 he was still intending to write a closing scene in which the heavenly powers reached a final judgement on Faust[123]—the counterpart to the 'Prologue in Heaven' that preceded *The First Part*. However, soon afterwards he suddenly and very belatedly changed tack and instead ended the work with the scene 'Mountain Gorges', in which Faust's soul is carried upwards towards Gretchen and the Virgin Mary, pushed by his love for Gretchen, and pulled by Gretchen's love for him and her intercession with the Virgin Mary on his behalf. 'Mountain Gorges' was broadly consistent with *The First Part* and Goethe's thoughts about religion in the early 1770s, but it is also fair to say that in a matter of months in winter 1830/31, with the abandonment of the judgement scene, the manner in which Faust's salvation was justified took a quite different form. The final judgement on Faust was not the only important scene that fell by the wayside in the last years of work on *Faust*. Others included a plan for Faust to descend to Hades at the end of Act II or the beginning of Act III, where he would plead with Persephone for the release of Helen. A third abandoned scene was to have occurred at the end of Act IV. Having helped the Emperor defeat a rival, Faust would be rewarded with the gift of a tract of coastal marshland. The fact of the gift was retained in the final version, but the scene representing it was never written. We can only speculate on how these unwritten scenes might have changed *The Second Part*'s meaning. However, the bare fact that he did not write them is not clear evidence of a changed vision of the work's meaning.

An overly microscopic attention to *The Second Part*'s long genesis can be misleading. In the most important respects his grasp of the work's core ideas remained firm between resumption in 1825 and completion in 1831. Much has been made, quite rightly, of the impact on Goethe of the July Revolution of 1830 in Paris and his subsequent interest in the social and economic theories of Saint-Simon. Evidence of this interest can be found in Act IV and the parts of Act V written in late 1830. However, far from being a new departure, Goethe's alarm at the July Revolution and Saint-Simonism was an extension of his response to the 1789 Revolution. He saw the July Revolution as part of the process that had begun in 1789. And the two revolutions were in turn only symptoms of the forces of modernity more generally, as were the idealism of Fichte or literary and artistic Romanticism or Benthamite liberalism—'confusing teaching on top of confused action'. By 1825 he had long since made his mind up about the 'absurd and confused' state of Europe. As he had told Müller in 1812, 'posterity shall know that at least one sensible man lived in our age who saw through these absurdities'.[124] Saint-Simonism and the July Revolution merely added extra material to the swollen bag that was *The Second Part*.

Along with microscopic attention to the genesis of *The Second Part* have come overly narrow readings of it as an allegorical work, for instance Heinz Schlaffer's reading of *The Second Part* as an allegory of the nineteenth century. The difficulty that *The Second Part* poses to such readings is the sheer breadth of its historical reference. There are allusions to the French Revolution and the July Revolution, to aspects of modern technology such as land drainage and canal-building schemes, to the (failed) financial schemes of the eighteenth century, such as John Law's and Jacques Necker's attempts to rescue the French crown's finances. In Act IV Goethe made use of late eighteenth- and early nineteenth-century writings on military tactics, as well as his knowledge of the Golden Bull of 1356, which formed the constitution of the Holy Roman Empire. His childhood mentor Johann Daniel von Olenschlager had written an essay on the subject which Goethe reread while working on *Faust*.[125] The cultural and philosophical reference points are equally diverse. The court masque staged in Act I draws on descriptions of festivities in Ancient Rome and Renaissance Florence. Acts II and III are saturated in references to classical antiquity, which are carefully differentiated into separate periods of Greek myth. The second half of Act III is set in Greece at the time of the Fourth Crusade in the early thirteenth century. There are frequent allusions to contemporary literature and thought, most obviously Romantic literature and post-Kantian Idealism. Acts II and III contain numerous references to the work of current and long-dead scientists (e.g., Paracelsus). This huge diversity of reference and allusion suggests that if *The Second Part* is an allegory, then it is an allegory of modernity more generally, and that modernity—or as we might more accurately term it, the process of becoming modern—has occurred many times. Both parts of *Faust* are concerned with history as it begins to change and accelerate, whether in the sixteenth century of the historical Faust and the Protestant Reformation, which Herder had pinpointed as the beginning of modernity, or the great range of other historical turning points. This was Goethe's purpose in having the July Revolution of 1830 rub shoulders with the Golden Bull of 1356. Modernity was not something that had occurred all at once or even within the span of Goethe's own lifetime. Signs of incipient modernity can be found even in events several hundred years apart. Modernity has been in the making for centuries, emerging or threatening to emerge in fits and starts.

The central idea of *The Second Part* was a continuation of the 1790s work on *The First Part*. Faust's idealism is a symptom of this repeatedly emerging modernity. Both Faust's idealism and emergent modernity are riven by contradictory impulses. As Goethe noted when he resumed work on *Faust* in 1797, he intended 'instead of reconciling these contradictions to make them more disparate'. The contradictions become 'more disparate' in *The Second Part* because Faust's ambitions play out on a grander scale and in a more public space. As opposed to the narrow small-town world of Gretchen in *The First Part*, the main space of *The Second Part* is the Empire. In *The Second Part* Faust becomes involved in the problems of a state transitioning into modernity: the ailing economy of the Empire in Act I and the sovereignty of the Emperor threatened by civil war in Act IV. The whole project of social-political modernity culminates in Faust's grand plan to found a new society on his strip of reclaimed coastal land in Act V, a society liberated from ancient social and political constraints and dependent only on its own resources—for which Goethe drew on the theories of Saint-Simon. In between these economic, political, and social events, Acts II and III see Faust undertaking interior journeys into a no less ambitious intellectual and aesthetic world. This is the modern ambition to understand the origins of life itself (Act II), followed by the Winckelmannian desire to create pure beauty by imitating the art of antiquity (Act III). What binds these elements together is the desire to realize an idealistic vision in the larger world—in contrast to *Part One*, in which Faust seeks to realize a more natural and authentic form of life in academe and the small world of Gretchen. Faust's ambitions in *The Second Part* are noble, but are confounded by 'real and fantastical' errors. Modernity's economic, political, and social woes can be solved only temporarily and by means of fragile illusions. Faust does this by funding the Empire's economy with dubious money (Act I), by securing sovereignty with a magical army and then seeing it partly relinquished in concessions to the grand nobility (Act IV), and by creating a new society seemingly independent of the economy and politics of the Empire, but in reality dependent on the brutal colonial trade and the church (Act V). Acts II and

III show him escaping from reality into an ideal that is also an illusion, though one that tragically seems more real than reality: the quest for the origins of life (Act II) and for perfect beauty (Act III). These ideals are not merely abstract. They are anchored in Goethe's experience of modernity: his sense that science had more to say than modern politics, in particular the politics that led to and followed from the French Revolution, and his distaste for formless and inward-looking Romanticism, which modernity seemed to prefer to his own attempts at reviving the ancients. The contradictions between Faust's ideals and reality do indeed become 'more disparate'.

In spite of *The Second Part*'s densely allusive character, its accumulation of multiple layers of historical reference and the several long digressions from Faust's quest, it is not hard to discern the plotline that connects the political Acts I, IV, and V to the scientific and aesthetic Acts II and III. In Act I Faust makes use of Mephistopheles's power to gain access to the Emperor and position himself as the solution to the Emperor's financial troubles. But Faust has ulterior and higher motives. Helping the Emperor overcome his financial difficulties is only a means to an end. Indeed the financial wizardry is not a real solution at all, but merely a quick fix that serves the higher purpose of cementing Faust's position at court and winning him the role of the Emperor's master of pleasures, which Faust parlays into the role of the Emperor's mentor and *praeceptor Germaniae*. (*The Second Part* is full of echoes of Goethe's career as boon companion, mentor, and minister to Carl August, as well as leader of the German literary renaissance.) Faust's higher goal is to solve the underlying political problem of this or indeed any state—that its welfare depends on the character of its rulers and people. This goal too will turn out to be unrealizable. The Emperor and his court prove to be immune to education by Faust. Worse still, Faust conjures an image of Helen and Paris for the court's edification and then falls in love with the projected Helen. (The summoning of and marriage to Helen was a traditional element of the Faust legend, as Goethe pointed out in an advertisement for the 1827 publication of Act III. Between the publication of *The First Part* and starting work on *Part Two* in 1825 he had read Marlowe's *Doctor Faustus* with its soaring invocation of 'the face that launched a thousand ships'.)[126] In doing so, Faust makes the mistake to which all purveyors of intoxicating pleasure are prone: he gets high on his own supply. This leads to the disaster at the end of Act I when his desire for the conjured apparition of Helen causes it to explode and plunge the court into chaos. Faust's excessive desires thus become a symbol of the Empire's problems. The lesson of Act I is that in order to educate the Empire Faust must educate himself. Act

II sets Faust's spirit on a journey to antiquity in order to find Helen's ideal beauty and so to reconcile his own spiritual idealism with a suitably ideal physical form. In this quest Faust is accompanied by a Homunculus created by his old assistant Wagner through a mixture of alchemy and modern chemistry. The Homunculus is a preternaturally gifted mind with no body and hence is a symbol for Faust's spirit and for the disembodied mind of modern Europe that is Faust's spiritual home—the world of the philosophy of Kant and Fichte, which cannot 'securely locate the point of transition to life', as Goethe put it in the Winckelmann essay.[127] The main part of Act II sets Faust on the quixotic quest to find the real Helen, in parallel with the Homunculus's quest to become embodied. Both quests involve an adventure into distant antiquity, where life was originally formed. Act II ends with a celebration of the generation of life from the sea, but it is an ambivalent ending, for in finding embodiment in the sea, the Homunculus also destroys himself, drowning in the very element that gave him body. The ambivalent ending of Act II prefigures Faust's fateful union with Helen in Act III. Now Faust appears in the guise of a Frankish crusader and is united with Helen in medieval Sparta, but the union is ephemeral, and their offspring Euphorion, again preternaturally gifted but unable to accept physical limitations, dies and is followed to Hades by his mother Helen. After this tragic failure, in Act IV Faust returns to the Empire and makes a second attempt to influence the Emperor, this time using Mephistopheles's power to win a civil war against an 'Anti-Emperor'. As in Act I, gaining the Emperor's favour is only a means to a higher end, this time to acquire a tract of marshy coastline which Faust will drain and settle with a new and freer society, a people committed to the same restless striving as Faust himself. But this project too is morally questionable and its fate is uncertain, in part because it involves brutal colonization and mass industrialization, the human costs of which Faust can neither contain nor fully acknowledge. What the classical adventure of Acts II and III and the land reclamation project of Act IV and V have in common is Faust's well-intentioned commitment to forces that he can neither fully understand nor control.

Act I appears to pick up the story shortly after the prison scene at the end of *The First Part*. An exhausted Faust lies in a pleasant meadow seeking sleep and watched over by Ariel and a chorus of fellow spirits. *The Second Part* thus begins with one of the contradictions that Goethe had decided to make 'more disparate'. A seemingly oblivious Faust being tended by kindly spirits in idyllic surroundings contrasts starkly with the madness, agony, and moral triumph of Gretchen visited in prison by her destroyers Faust and Mephistopheles.[128] It is the scandalous disparity between a person's fortune and their merit. Faust's misdeeds are not ignored. Ariel refers to him as a 'man of misfortune' ('Unglücksmann'),[129] which points to the misfortune he has both suffered and caused. If this appears to assert a false equivalence between Gretchen's suffering and Faust's, that is because Ariel is a nature spirit and nature is amoral.[130] Ariel's role is not to justify or teach Faust but to restore him to health, even if this involves erasing the trauma of the prison scene in order that he can find rest.[131] Faust learns no moral lesson from Gretchen's sacrifice. The lack of moral development will be a recurring pattern in *The Second Part*, for instance in Faust's encounter with the figure of Care in Act V. If *The Second Part* is an oblique history of civilization and if Faust represents European modernity, then it is a history without moral progress. As he wakes, it becomes clear that a memory of his wrongdoing remains lodged in his consciousness, albeit an emotional rather than a moral one:

> Des Lebens Fackel wollten wir entzünden,
> Ein Feuermeer umschlingt uns, welch ein Feuer!
> Ist's Lieb'? ist's Haß? die glühend uns umwinden,
> Mit Schmerz und Freuden wechselnd ungeheuer,
> So daß wir wieder nach der Erde blicken,
> Zu bergen uns in jugendlichstem Schleier.

> We wanted to ignite the torch of life. / A sea of fire surrounds us, what a fire! / Is it love? Is it hate? that burn all around us, / Alternating drastically in pain and pleasures, / So that we look to the earth again, / To hide ourselves in its youthful veil.

This prompts Faust to shift into the thought patterns of Goethe's science. He imagines the fire of love or hate as the sun, which is just rising and which the human eye cannot bear to look on. Even if it could, it would see nothing, for as Goethe had written in the didactic part of the *Theory of Colour*, 'light of the highest energy, such as that of the sun [...] is blinding and colourless'.[132] Instead he turns to contemplate a waterfall in which a rainbow has formed:

> Der spiegelt ab das menschliche Bestreben.
> Ihm sinne nach, und du begreifst genauer:
> Am farbigen Abglanz haben wir das Leben.

> That mirrors human endeavour. / Ponder it, and you'll grasp more precisely: / The coloured refraction is where we have our existence.

Faust arrives at the Goethean insight that coloured, refracted light is all we can ever perceive. A traditional symbol of mediation between the human and the divine,[133] the rainbow here represents the distinction between our coloured world of phenomena and the transcendent reality behind, which consists in blinding colourlessness. To commit ourselves to a world of colour, as we must, is to resign ourselves to never seeing the pure divine light, but it is a resignation that humans are incapable of sustaining, as Goethe wrote in the introduction to his *Theory of Weather*:

> Truth, [which is] identical with the divine, can never be known directly by us; we only perceive it in reflection, in examples, symbols, in single and related phenomena; we perceive it as incomprehensible life and can never renounce the wish to comprehend it anyway.[134]

In the rainbow Faust sees a symbol of the inaccessibility of the ideal. The same idea will recur at the end of *The Second Part*. Of course, Faust will not be able to renounce the desire to realize the ideal, with all the human damage that such an impossible pursuit brings.

After the symbolic first scene, Faust plunges into the messy politics of the Empire. The remainder of Act I is a colourful rendering of the Imperial court experiencing the birth pangs of modernity:[135] lawlessness and violence, selfishness and partisanship at the expense of the commonwealth, and an almost universal corruption.[136] The Emperor's legislative and executive power is threatened, as his Chancellor ominously puts it: 'When all are doing harm [and] all are suffering, / Sovereignty itself vanishes' ('Wenn alle schädigen, alle leiden, / Geht selbst die Majestät zu Raub')[137]—an echo of the opening of Emperor Charles IV's *Golden Bull*: 'any realm that is divided against itself will be laid waste: for its princes have become the accomplices of thieves.'[138] The Empire is threatened by a political revolution like those of England in the mid-seventeenth century and France in 1789, and for the same reasons. The Emperor's power is diminished by the financial strain of running an expensive court and by the ambitions of the great princes on whom he depends to maintain order. Worse still, the young Emperor is bored by his princes' complaints about the parlous state of the Empire's finances. At this moment of crisis, Mephistopheles gains the Emperor's ear by posing as his fool, while his actual fool is insensible with drink. This enables Mephistopheles to offer the Emperor a quick solution to his problems. The solution is to issue Imperial banknotes based on the surety of any buried treasure that might be found in the Empire, which belongs to the Emperor by right of an obscure law. As Grappin has noted, the buried treasure alludes to a plan devised by radicals in the French Constituent Assembly to issue *assignats* against the collateral of land seized from the church—even though the land had yet to be expropriated.[139] The point is that Mephistopheles's assurances that such treasure could be found if needed are entirely empty. The treasure may not exist. Moreover, like the issuing of *assignats* by the Constituent Assembly, it is an attempt to solve a liquidity crisis that instead will make matters worse by causing massive inflation, as the availability of currency outstrips that of goods. But people are blinded to the longer-term risks by the illusory wealth showered on them in the short term. Suddenly the Empire can pay its bills, the princes can restore order, and the courtiers can afford their pleasures. Not everyone is so naïve. The Emperor is uneasy about the means by which the new wealth was created. He appears to have signed the guarantee without knowing it, and the paper currency was manufactured suspiciously quickly and as if by magic. He demands to be shown evidence of the buried treasure that supposedly guarantees the new currency. He is understandably worried by the sudden orgy of spending at his court, and when he offers a prize to any courtier who can come up with a plan to invest soundly, the winner is his fool, who proposes to invest the cash in property and so avoid the effects of the credit-induced inflation affecting consumer goods. It is now clear why Mephistopheles needed to replace the fool in order to promote the refinancing scheme. The fool was the Emperor's wisest adviser, a prosaically literal drunk at a court that is (metaphorically) drunk on new money.

Between Mephistopheles's proposition to the Emperor and the latter's realization that the new money might not be what it seems, Mephistopheles and Faust lay on a masque for the court's entertainment. The masque occupies around one eighth of *The Second Part*, and it is hard not to feel that its length blunts the effect of Goethe's acute analysis of the modern state. However, its meaning for the drama is clear. The Emperor's qualms are outweighed by his desire to be freed of the cares of state and to have the time and money to spend on court festivities. It is the intoxication of the masque that dulls the Emperor's scruples about signing the surety. The masque removes the Emperor's cares, just as Faust had his cares removed by Ariel at the beginning of Act I. Like Faust, the Emperor lives in a world that is both real and unreal, for the masque is unreal in the sense that it is an intoxicating illusion, paid for moreover by illusory wealth, and yet it reflects the Empire's social, economic, and political reality. As Williams puts it, the masque shows 'the acquisition, distribution, and exploitation of wealth, the harnessing of the resources of the state, and the responsibility of the ruler to ensure the economic, and therefore the social and political, stability of the realm'.[140] The masque gives the Emperor the opportunity to understand his Empire, but the masque's intoxicating effect ensures that the lesson remains only half learned.

In creating the masque Goethe drew on a number of sources including Mantegna's painting 'Triumphs of Caesar', Dürer's etching 'Triumph of Kaiser Maximilian I', and Antonio Grazzini's historical account of the triumphal masques of Renaissance Florence. The Florentine detail was important, because the Florentine masques were precisely the model imported from Italy to Germany in the late Middle Ages. The masque thus also serves as an example of cultural rebirth and the advent of modernity. It falls into two halves. The first half consists of a succession of figures or groups dressed and speaking as representatives of social or cultural types, all announced by a Herald. This part is both a diversion from the reality of imminent collapse that faces the Empire[141] and a sober portrayal of the Empire's condition: the selfishness that drives an emergent modern society, the transactional forces of exchange in the economy and sexual relations,[142] and the *amour-propre* that motivates people to promote themselves at the expense of others.[143]

In the masque's second part the Emperor and his court join in the procession and turn it into a riot. Two figures preside over the chaos and express its dual essence as illusion and reality: a Boy Charioteer who symbolizes the spirit of poetry, and the figure of Plutus, the god of wealth. The Boy Charioteer represents the extravagance of the imagination. He scatters jewels to the crowd, which turn into insects as people grab them. It is a society like that described by Rousseau in his *Second Discourse*, in which people lust after imaginary goods that harm them by stimulating the unsatisfiable desires of the imagination.[144] The Boy Charioteer is followed by the god of wealth Plutus, played by Faust, and Mephistopheles in the guise of Greed, who bring the masque to its climax, for Plutus and Greed represent people's deepest urges. Plutus opens crates of money which however are an illusion, just like the paper money created by Mephistopheles. Greed then reveals the reality beneath Plutus's gold by shaping it into a phallus which he directs at the terrified women. A riot of figures follows: fauns, gnomes, giants, nymphs, all representing the Emperor's court and led by the Emperor himself in the guise of Pan.[145] As Plutus-Faust observes, people do not see what is driving them or where it will lead, blinded as they are by greed.[146] The Emperor as Pan desires only that everyone is happy,[147] but as his Herold wisely observes, his desire to please everyone shows that he has more power than wisdom.[148] The masque ends with a conflagration representing the volcanic catastrophe, perhaps even a revolution, towards which the Empire seems to be heading.

It is in the hangover after the riot that the Emperor begins to have suspicions about his new wealth, though his doubts do not last, as he is distracted by Faust and Mephistopheles's next promise of education-cum-entertainment: a portrayal of Helen and Paris, both of them representing absolute beauty combined with sexual allure. The process by which Faust and Mephistopheles conjure the images of Helen and Paris is one of the most mysterious episodes in *The Second Part*, and no doubt intentionally so. Part of the mystery stems from Goethe's Winckelmannian and Platonic view that the classical is a domain outside space and time. As he had suggested in his essay on Winckelmann, the art of Ancient Greece was a kind of Kantian *noumenon*. Beauty is objectively real but exists in a domain we cannot access. This is why, in order to summon Helen, Mephistopheles directs Faust towards a realm outside of time and space[149] where he will find the mysterious Mothers. The name for these obscure figures may have derived from one or other of two passages in Plutarch,[150] which associate the Mothers with the Platonic forms. Mephistopheles adds some Kantian language of his own, the word 'schemas' ('Schemen'), that is to say the mental, nonexperiential objects from which we derive a priori concepts. The *schemas* exist outside of time but allow us to think coherently *in* time. Mephistopheles blends these Platonic and Kantian hints with a very Goethean way of speaking about the fluidity of natural phenomena:

> Gestaltung, Umgestaltung,
> Des ewigen Sinnes ewige Unterhaltung.
> Umschwebt von Bildern aller Kreatur;
> Sie sehn dich nicht, denn Schemen sehn sie nur.[151]

> Formation, re-formation, / The eternal occupation of the eternal mind. / With images of every creature hovering around them; / They do not see you, for they only see schemas.

This may be mere Mephistophelean mischief-making, a tantalising prompt to Faust's excitable imagination. If so, the trick works, for in the final scene of Act I, when summoning the images of Helen and Paris, Faust invokes the Mothers as the eternal blueprints for classes of empirical objects, 'you who are enthroned / In boundlessness' ('die ihr thront / Im Gränzlosen').[152] Nothing determinate can be known about the Mothers, in the same way as nothing determinate can be known about Kant's *noumena* or things as they are in themselves, and because nothing determinate can be said about the Mothers, much nonsense can be said about them. What we cannot know, we must invent, and the less we know of it, the more florid our inventions are prone to be. The subsequent scenes do not help to solve the mystery. It is not at all clear what the images of Helen and Paris are. Perhaps they are empty images projected by Mephistopheles for the entertainment of the Emperor in something resembling a magic lantern show. In any case, Mephistopheles gives no thought to how the image of Helen will work on Faust's imagination. When Faust falls in love with what he believes he has summoned from the realm of the Mothers, Mephistopheles must hurriedly destroy the illusion and cover his tracks with some magical fireworks. Or perhaps there is some supernatural reality in the figures of Helen and Paris. Unsatisfied with merely seeing them, Faust reaches out to touch Helen, causing a violent rupture in the barrier between phenomena and *noumena* and momentarily revealing the blinding power of beauty as it is in itself, akin to the blinding power of white light. The circumstances of the conjuring are consistent with both interpretations, again perhaps intentionally. The show takes place on a Hellenizing stage before a massive temple, which an architect in the audience criticises as too bulky, just as the temples of Paestum had disturbed Goethe in 1787. The reality of Ancient Greece is alien to our Hellenizing preconceptions. The behaviour of the audience confirms that what we see is shaped by what we bring to perception. The men lust after Helen and find Paris crude; the women do the opposite. A scholar finds that the image of Helen falls short of the ancient textual evidence. For the idealist Faust, the image has become a reality that he believes he has the right to possess, and so Act I ends with a self-destructive attempt to turn an idea into reality, as will Acts II and III. As for Faust's project to reform the Empire, the closing stage direction, 'darkness, tumult',[153] whether it indicates a real explosion caused by Faust's transgression or an illusion created by Mephistopheles to extricate Faust from an embarrassing situation, shows that far from reforming the Empire, Faust has left it in chaos.

Questions of reality and illusion haunt Acts II and III. In Act II Faust will travel to the Pharsalian Fields in Thessaly for the classical equivalent of the Walpurgis Night. Whether he does so bodily or only in his subconscious or imagination is unclear. The purpose of the journey is to find Helen and return her to the upper world, so that she and Faust can meet in the Peloponnese in Act III and Faust can experience true beauty in its proper physical form. Again, it is not clear how real the meeting of Faust and Helen in Act III is. Does Faust meet the real Helen, or are Faust and Helen acting out a drama? Most of Act

II is concerned with the journey to find Helen. Faust is accompanied on the journey by Mephistopheles, who is out of place in the classical world but is nonetheless tempted by the prospect of finding a classical form analogous to his own modern demonic one, a form in which he might exist in antiquity. This form will turn out to be the essence of hatred and ugliness and the antithesis of Helen. The third companion on the journey is a bizarre Homunculus created in Faust's laboratory by his assistant Wagner. The Homunculus represents the modern experience of antiquity: a disembodied mind that seeks embodiment in the classical world. Indeed, this is one meaning of Act II as a whole. The modern European mind, having become a disembodied and hypertrophied consciousness in the philosophy of Rationalism and Idealism, now realizes that it is only half alive and seeks to reembody itself through contact with the physical landscape and inhabitants of Greece—an impossible dream that can only lead to its destruction. In addition to this historical-cultural theme, the Homunculus's quest for embodiment raises pressing scientific issues of Goethe's own day concerning the origins of life. Indeed, the Classical Walpurgis Night is populated by figures from Greek myth who speak as if they were participants in current scientific and political debates, and in this way Act II becomes a vehicle for Goethe's political and scientific polemics.

Act II begins with a resumption of the university satire of *The First Part*. Several years have passed and Faust's *famulus* Wagner has taken over Faust's study, assisted by his own *famulus* Nicodemus. The name Nicodemus was most likely suggested by an interlocutor of Jesus in the Gospel of John, who argued for a literal-minded interpretation of Christ's teaching of rebirth.[154] Nicodemus thus reprises the role of the literal-minded Wagner of *The First Part*. Wagner has embarked on the project of creating life by means of chemistry, but it is not clear how far he has moved on intellectually from the dry-as-dust pedant of *The First Part*. Wagner's project echoes Faust's quest for the essence of nature in his opening monologue in *The First Part*, but whereas Faust's was an imaginative quest, Wagner has retained some of his earlier boneheadedness. The Enlightenment pedant of *The First Part*, who thought that inspiration could be constructed from elements of the literary tradition, has developed into a modern scientist who imagines that everything, even life itself, can be reconstituted from its elements. Knowledge has moved forward only to repeat the errors of the past in new form. Against Wagner's failure to make real progress, there arrives in Faust's study a recent graduate, indeed the very student Mephistopheles had teased in *The First Part*. Then a naïve freshman seeking knowledge and pleasure, in his new incarnation the Baccalaureate is a post-Kantian idealist. As in *The First Part*, the student represents an aspect of Faust—in this case Faust's commitment to the absolute self, frustrated by traditional learning and convinced that the world can be remade from within the mind. In pseudo-Fichtean language he refuses to acknowledge any authority other than the self: 'Unless I will it, no devil can exist', he proclaims ('Wenn ich nicht will, so darf kein Teufel sein').[155] Worse still and with a decidedly political edge, the Baccalaureate expresses a Manichaean vision of history, in which the future is bright and the past benighted: 'the light ahead of me, darkness at my back' ('Das Helle vor mir, Finsternis im Rücken')[156]—no doubt an allusion to the German student movement, which conservatives held responsible for the murder of Kotzebue and which was suppressed by the Carlsbad Decrees.[157] Tradition and the past deserve to die, he opines, to which Mephistopheles acidly replies that the devil's work is thereby complete:

> BACCALAUREUS: Hat einer dreißig Jahr vorüber,
>   So ist er schon so gut wie tot.
>   Am besten wär's, euch zeitig totzuschlagen.
> MEPHISTOPHELES: Der Teufel hat hier weiter nichts zu sagen.
>
> BACCALAUREUS: If you've passed thirty years, / You're as good as dead. / It'd be best to kill you forthwith.
> MEPHISTOPHELES: The devil has nothing to add here.

The scene moves into Wagner's laboratory, still decked out with the fantastical medieval apparatus of *The First Part*. Wagner is about to complete his experiment by creating a human being. The science is both outmoded and modern, a mixture of alchemy and the contemporary chemistry of crystallization. In the former context, the Homunculus is the 'filius philosophorum' of the alchemists: a vital spirit grown in a glass vial.[158] In the modern context, he is modelled on Friedrich Wöhler's synthetic creation of urea by means of crystallization in 1828. Urea was traditionally associated with sperm, and the Homunculus is therefore not a human being but only the male component of one, which will need to be united with the female component in Act III, in order to create life.[159] The literal-minded modern approach of composing life from its elements is thus incomplete. Only a visit to the mythic sources of life in deep antiquity can complete it, and that will come at the cost of the Homunculus's destruction. Aside from Wöhler's experiments, Goethe modelled the Homunculus after Paracelsus,[160] who had described a homunculus as possessing occult knowledge. Thus Wagner's Homunculus is able to see into Faust's mind and diagnose what ails him, as he lies unconscious in his study, still stunned after his attempt to touch Helen and still fixated on her. The Homunculus also recognises that Mephistopheles is a thoroughly modern and northern devil, and therefore also incomplete. For all of this, the Homunculus can prescribe a cure, a flight into antiquity, where he, Faust and Mephistopheles will find what they need to make themselves whole.

The journey leads to the site of the Battle of Pharsalus, where in 48 B.C.E. Julius Caesar defeated Pompey and confirmed Rome's descent from Republican freedom into the tyranny of empire. With some annoyance Mephistopheles objects to the Homunculus's use of the word 'free' when introducing the site of the Battle of Pharsalus. For Mephistopheles, Pharsalus was not a struggle between freedom and tyranny, for in the end all men are slaves, whatever political system they live under.[161] Politics is a recurrent theme in the Classical Walpurgis Night, alongside questions concerning the origins of the earth and life and the forces present at the creation of our world. The three companions separate and each takes a different route through a changing landscape of flooding rivers and erupting volcanoes, populated by figures from preclassical Greek myth. In populating the scenes, Goethe was careful to avoid the well-known heroes of the classical mythic cycles of Heracles, Theseus, Troy, Thebes, and so on. The Classical Walpurgis Night instead represents a stage prior even to these myths and legends, a world of unfamiliar primordial life forms and a landscape in flux, out of which the myths we are familiar with are yet to emerge. (These pre-Olympian figures were being rediscovered by the mythographers of Goethe's day;[162] Goethe was familiar with the debates between Hermann, Creuzer, Schelling, and others.) It is a time of beginnings, just as the late-medieval setting of *Faust* as a whole represents the beginnings of modern Europe. *The Second Part* contains a number of such ages of emergence. After the nonspatial and nontemporal realm of the Mothers and their schemas of nature, the Classical Walpurgis Night represents a later stage of origins, a world of concrete if outlandish forms in a landscape that is heaving and breaking: Sphinxes, Griffons, Centaurs, Sirens, Giant Ants, and one-eyed Arimaspi. The topics that arise in the equally outlandish dialogues of the Classical Walpurgis Night are the intertwined subjects of politics, geology, and the origins of life—intertwined because organic life is a product of geology, and geology is connected metaphorically to politics, for instance in the volcanic convulsions of political revolutions. According to Eckermann's much later account of what Goethe may or may not have said, the politics of the Classical Walpurgis Night was 'republican'.[163] Like all Eckermann's reports, this must be treated with caution. Certainly some of the mythical figures appear not to recognise any kind of political organization, and in that sense they might be deemed republican and give the lie to Mephistopheles's pessimistic view that all humans are slaves whatever the political order. However, much of what the creatures say about politics conforms to Goethe's long-held and decidedly anti-republican political views. These episodes comprise two contrasting models of political organization, one presented positively, the other negatively. When Faust, in his quest to find Helen, asks the centaur Chiron which of the heroes was the greatest, Chiron gives the example of the Argonauts, each of whom had a special ability peculiar to him, so that as a team they were able to complement one another:

> Im hehren Argonautenkreise
> War jeder brav nach seiner eignen Weise,
> Und, nach der Kraft die ihn beseelte,
> Konnt' er genügen, wo's den andern fehlte.[164]

> In the noble company of the Argonauts / Each was virtuous in his own manner, / and according to the power that animated him, / He was able to supplement what the others lacked.

In this way the Argonauts functioned as a single social organism while each retained his individuality.[165] Goethe considered this structure a sociopolitical ideal. He had outlined similar forms of organization in the 'Fairy Tale' and at the end of each of the *Meister* novels. As the 'Fairy Tale' shows, only organizations of this kind possess a sufficiently diverse range of abilities to survive in a world of equally diverse challenges. A further advantage of the Argonauts' form of organization is that in such a group, whose members have different roles, there will be less of the competition for prestige that is encountered in societies in which roles are duplicated and infighting is therefore endemic. The Argonauts suffered no such internal divisions. On the contrary, their diverse abilities allowed them to praise one another, as Chiron explains to Faust: 'Only in company can danger be overcome; / When one is effective, all the others praise' ('Gesellig nur läßt sich Gefahr erproben: / Wenn einer wirkt, die andern alle loben').[166]

Quite different from the small and cohesive society of the Argonauts is the military dictatorship of the Pygmies, which the Griffons and Giant Ants describe to Mephistopheles. According to Herodotus,[167] the Giant Ants picked out gold from sand and assembled it into a great hoard, which was guarded by the Griffons, only to be stolen by the Arimaspi, a tribe of one-eyed humanoids. Subsequently, as Mephistopheles moves down the River Peneios towards the sea, another enmity erupts into being. The earthquake god Seismos causes a new mountain to arise, blocking the river, turning it into a lake and creating a habitat of caves and ravines for a race of Pygmies. The earthquake is plainly intended as an allegory for political revolution. Seismos proudly claims that he has brought the mountain into being by 'shaking and breaking' the earth ('geschüttelt und gerüttelt');[168] Goethe used the same pair of verbs to describe the July Revolution in a letter to Varnhagen von Ense of 10 September 1830.[169] The new world of the pygmies is revolutionary; it is as violent as the circumstances that created it, for violence begets violence. The Pygmies drive their subjects, the Dactyls and Ants, to excavate metal ore and make armour and weapons from it.[170] Critics have tried to read the Seismos episode as a detailed allegory of the French Revolution, for instance interpreting the Pygmies' traditional enemies, the Cranes, as the anti-revolutionary coalition of Prussia and Austria of 1792, or reading the victory of the Cranes as an image of what ought to have happened in the 1790s or ought to happen in future. Neither interpretation fits well, since the Cranes win where the coalition withdrew in failure, and their victory is miserably bloodthirsty.[171] The Seismos episode is better understood as symbolizing a class of political events. The Pygmy state represents the worst of modern polities. It is riven by social discontent; the Ants and Dactyls are waiting to revolt against their Pygmy leaders.[172] The Pygmy state is similar to Weber's 'iron cage', for the metals the Ants and Dactyls mine have become the chains that bind them in slavery. Seismos has given rise to a world of wealth and violence, acquisition and possession, war and revolution. The fate of the Pygmies reflects the view Goethe set out in the Moses essay in *For Better Understanding*: violent circumstances beget violent states.

The origins of the state are tied up with the origins of the earth's surface and the organic life on it. The Homunculus's quest to become fully embodied leads him to Anaxagoras and Thales. The two Greek philosophers have observed the origins of the Pygmy state and the battle between the Pygmies and Cranes, but from very different perspectives. Anaxagoras attributes the land's geology to volcanic origins. Thales claims that life originates from water.[173] Their antagonism can be read as Goethe revisiting the debate between Vulcanism and Neptunism, and siding with the latter, but things are in fact more nuanced than that. Anaxagoras and Thales give different answers because they are answering different questions. Anaxagoras gives the standard Vulcanist answer to the question how the earth's crust has been formed, whereas Thales is concerned with the origins of life. In this sense, Vulcanism is a plausible *Vorstellungsart*, as Goethe believed when he tried to reconcile the mineralogists Voigt and Werner in 1789. However, the mentality that generates Vulcanism is revolutionary and delusional. Appropriately for a Vulcanist, Anaxagoras has a fiery, choleric nature and an affinity with the revolutionary Pygmy state, whereas Thales phlegmatically sees the impending defeat of the Pygmy armies as a pointless tragedy. Anaxagoras begins his descent into madness by praying to the moon for the Pygmies' salvation. Aside from implying his lunacy, the prayer to the moon is the reverse of Spinoza's *amor dei intellectualis*: instead of loving nature dispassionately, Anaxagoras passionately begs the moon to intervene. The misapprehension that his prayers can affect nature leads to the delusion that he is personally responsible for what nature then does, and when his imagination supplies a vision of a meteor crashing down to earth to destroy the Pygmies' home, he blames himself.[174] As Thales rightly observes, this was all just imagined,[175] and the actual phenomenon was the fall of a meteor from the moon. The Homunculus rejects the Pygmies' request that he become their ruler, and it is Thales, not Anaxagoras who leads the Homunculus off downriver towards the completion of his quest for embodiment at the mouth of the Peneios. It will be in water that the Homunculus is embodied, giving final confirmation to Thales's intuition that water is the cradle of life. In political terms, Anaxagoras's revolutionary ideology is rejected and the gradualism of Thales confirmed, alongside the small-scale organicist political organization of the Argonauts.

The final episode of Act II takes place at the mouth of the Peneios, where the gods of the sea annually celebrate the arrival of Galatea, daughter of Nereus. The scene draws on Raphael's fresco 'The Triumph of Galatea' in the Villa Farnesina, among other representations of marine pageants. The symbolism of Raphael's fresco represents both the danger and power of true love. The backstory of Galatea's triumph is that she fell in love with Acis; after he was killed with a huge rock by the jealous Polyphemus, Galatea turned him into a river spirit. In Raphael's fresco, Galatea enjoys her apotheosis as a reward for her earthly trials. In keeping with his model, Goethe made this final scene of Act II a riot of vitality and movement, with a strong undertow of sexuality. Like Raphael, he has Galatea arriving at the end of the scene on a mussel shell chariot drawn by dolphins. Her arrival is announced by Aphrodite's doves from Paphos symbolizing love. Galatea is welcomed by her father Nereus, and then Thales greets her as proof of his theory concerning the origins of life in water: 'Everything originated from water!! / Everything is sustained by water!' ('Alles ist aus dem Wasser entsprungen!! / Alles wird durch das Wasser erhalten!').[176] Goethe has Galatea's mussel chariot represent the female sexual organs, into which the Homunculus finally crashes with flashing light and convulsions of pleasure, in other words an orgasm.[177] The Homunculus's tenuous flame is extinguished in the very same orgasmic moment as he becomes physically real. The Classical Walpurgis Night has been leading up to this singular moment. Its panoply of prelegendary characters represented the forms that would emerge into history. With the simultaneous birth and death of the Homunculus, an act of sexual love brings that history into being. The Sirens conclude the festival by praising 'Eros who began everything' ('Eros, der alles begonnen!').[178]

After Galatea's festival at the end of Act II the action switches to Helen standing outside Menelaus's palace in Sparta. By omitting the planned scene in Hades where Faust would have pleaded with Persephone for Helen to be allowed to return to daylight world, Goethe created a sudden and shocking shift from Galatea's festival to the tragedy of Helen. The shift is from immortal nature to mortal beauty. Galatea is an elemental figure, constantly generating new life, immortal and subject to time only in the sense that she reappears annually under the specific atmospheric conditions of a moon halo.[179] Otherwise she is unconstrained, unlike the Helen who appears at the beginning of Act III in the midst of a very human tragedy marked by the subjection of beauty to political power. Helen has returned from Troy accompanied by a chorus of enslaved Trojan women. While Helen arrives at her palace, Menelaus has remained by the coast, and there is some uncertainty what his plans for her are. (Goethe picked up this element from Euripides's tragedy *The Trojan Women*, in which after the sack of Troy Helen is under threat of being executed by her husband Menelaus.) Goethe's Helen is painfully aware of the fate her legendary beauty has consigned her to. Her opening lines describe her circumstances in a way that is both psychologically realistic—she has been the cause of strife, and has therefore been vilified as much as admired—and unrealistically implies that she knows of the long classical tradition and hence the varied fates that her reputation would suffer in later ages:[180]

> Bewundert viel und viel gescholten, Helena,
> Vom Strande komm' ich, wo wir erst gelandet sind,
> Noch immer trunken von des Gewoges regsamem
> Geschaukel, das vom phrygischen Blachgefild uns her
> Auf sträubig-hohem Rücken, durch Poseidons Gunst
> Und Euros' Kraft, in vaterländische Buchten trug.

Admired much and much berated, Helena, / From the beach I come, where we first landed, / Still drunk from the wave's energetic / Pitching, which carried us here from the Phrygian plains / On its bristling-high back, by Poseidon's favour / and Euros's power, to fatherland's bays.

The first half of Act III cleaves close to the language and meter of Greek tragedy and contains some exceptionally powerful poetry, as if the constraints of Hellenizing prosody and style and the sense of estrangement they create in modern German become paradoxically liberating and fresh. Faust's quest for classical beauty finds realization not just in Helen, but also in the poetic properties of her tragic milieu.

The chorus of enslaved Trojan women that accompany Helen make a well-meaning attempt to reassure Helen that her beauty remains a good, even though they are in some sense the victims of her beauty, and they have their own fate as prisoners to worry about. More sympathetic and perceptive than the general run of Greek tragic choruses, they also correctly recognise that the stand-in for the palace's steward who greets them is in fact Phorkyas, the ugly and malicious offspring of the sea-god Phorkys. The audience knows more: this Phorkyas is the ancient form of Mephistopheles. The embodiment of ugliness, Mephistopheles as Phorkyas becomes Helen's antagonist. His ugliness and malice is pitted against her beauty.[181] His attacks on Helen and the chorus centre on the idea that beauty and morality are incompatible. Of course Helen already knows this; her sense of self has already been shaken, and Phorkyas's method is to scratch at an already open wound, as if his malice were habitual. However, he is also playing a longer game; his ultimate aim is to save Helen by casting her into Faust's arms. Having robbed Helen and the chorus of any hope of escape, Phorkyas now dangles a strange prospect in front of them. Some warlike northerners, 'a brave breed' ('ein kühn Geschlecht'),[182] have settled in a mountain valley of the River Eurotas. Their leader lives in a stronghold built of 'rich fantastical buildings of the Middle Ages' ('reichen phantastischen Gebäuden des Mittelalters').[183] Within this fanciful medieval unreality a real human drama will play out, for the invader is Faust, who has come to claim Helen at the head of a multinational force of crusading knights. Goethe drew this scenario from the occupation of the Peloponnese in the early thirteenth century under the Fourth Crusade by Geoffroy de Villehardouin and his nephew Guillaume. Even by the loose standards of congruity of *The Second Part*, it was daring to juxtapose the mythical age of Helen with the thirteenth century, but the symbolic purpose of the juxtaposition is clear. Faust cannot fully enter Helen's world. Pure beauty is inaccessible to him. He is an invading overlord who plagues the indigenous people. His presence in the Peloponnese is thus a doubly apt metaphor for the classical tradition in modernity. Modern culture cannot become identical with antiquity; it can only ever appropriate it.

Their first meeting does not begin well. Instead of greeting Helen formally, Faust presents her with a choice that reminds her of the harm her beauty has done. Faust blames his keen-sighted watchman Lynkeus, named after the lookout on the Argo, for not warning him of Helen's arrival and hence for the lack of a proper welcome. Faust has had Lynkeus chained up in preparation for his execution, and he now gives Helen the decision over Lynkeus's sentence. Lynkeus claims he was blinded by Helen's beauty and so unwittingly reminds her of the charge made against her by Phorkyas. It seems that true beauty cannot live long in the world without incurring blame. Faust's treatment of Helen also casts a shadow over their prospects together. The price of winning Helen is to undermine her. In this regard, the Helen scenes echo the tragedy of Gretchen in *The First Part*, for Faust's desire for the innocent Gretchen meant corrupting her and destroying the very prize he craved. As the relationship between Helen and Faust develops and they grow closer, it becomes clear that Helen is becoming more German than Faust is becoming Greek. Faust's wooing of Helen culminates in his teaching her how to rhyme like a modern. It is one of the highpoints of *The Second Part*, formulated with exceptional power and delicacy:

> FAUST: Gefällt dir schon die Sprechart unsrer Völker,
>   O so gewiß entzückt auch der Gesang,
>   Befriedigt Ohr und Sinn im tiefsten Grunde.
>   Doch ist am sichersten, wir üben's gleich;
>   Die Wechselrede lockt es, ruft's hervor.
> HELENA: So sage denn, wie sprech' ich auch so schön?
> FAUST: Das ist gar leicht, es muß von Herzen gehn.
>   Und wenn die Brust von Sehnsucht überfließt,
>   Man sieht sich um und fragt—
> HELENA: wer mitgenießt.
> FAUST: Nun schaut der Geist nicht vorwärts, nicht zurück,
>   Die Gegenwart allein—
> HELENA: ist unser Glück.
> FAUST: Schatz ist sie, Hochgewinn, Besitz und Pfand;
>   Bestätigung, wer gibt sie?
> HELENA: Meine Hand.

FAUST: If our peoples' mode of speech pleases you, / Then our song will definitely delight you too, / Will satisfy your ear and mind to the utmost. / But the surest way is for us to practise it now; / Dialogue will charm it, will summon it forth. /
HELENA: Tell me then, how am I to speak so beautifully.
FAUST: That's easy, it must come from your heart. / And when your breast overflows with desire, / You look around and ask—
HELENA: who's enjoying it with you.
FAUST: Now the spirit looks neither forwards not backwards, / Only the present—
HELENA: is our source of joy.

The joint making of rhymes is not only a flirtatious game. It is also a demonstration of power and its limits. Faust leads and Helen follows. He chooses the word that is to be rhymed with. As in the dilemma over Lynkeus, he presents her with a choice that is constrained by his power. For the remainder of Act III Helen will speak in rhymed verse, though the Chorus will resist rhyme for longer. The chorus understands that women cannot be choosers of men's desires, they can only be 'connoisseurs'.[184] Gaier has shown that these and the surrounding lines contain allusions to a motif in Rousseau's *La nouvelle Héloïse* which claims Julie's empire is the absolute and unbounded empire of desire and the will, and to a passage in *Émile* that has women being 'the natural judges of men's merit'.[185] Yet it is clear that in *Faust* women only exercise limited and constrained choice. There is an imbalance of power between men and women. Now the full significance of Faust's giving Helen the decision on Lynkeus's sentence becomes clear. Faust forced a choice on Helen by means of a threat of violence. This is the power of men and of princes above all. It is princes who, to adapt Max Weber, enjoy a monopoly on the legitimate use of physical force. Helen's sentencing of Lynkeus and her education in rhyming afford her some limited choice while making clear to her that her fate rests in Faust's hands. However, Faust is also constrained by his own power. By persuading Helen to speak in rhymes, the crusader Faust brings her into his medieval world and so undermines her Hellenic antiquity and diminishes his prize.

In order to live together, Faust and Helen must take one more step away from reality and into Arcadia. The scene in the crusader castle ends with Faust proclaiming that 'into a grove the thrones will turn, / Our happiness will be Arcadian-free' ('Zur Laube wandeln sich die Thronen, / Arkadisch frei sei unser Glück!').[186] The symbols of political power dissolve into symbols of a pastoral world. As Goethe knew from his research into the Villehardouins, Arcadia was one of the regions of the Peloponnese that resisted their occupation and remained Greek. The final scene of Act III takes place in this idealized pocket of free Greece, isolated from modernity and power, but encircled and in the end confined by it. Phorkyas appears with astonishing news for the chorus. Helen has given birth to a marvellous child Euphorion who is bound by neither time nor space and so resembles a Kantian *noumenon*. He has sprung from Helen's womb fully grown and can fly without wings. Faust and Helen however are still bound by the temporal and spatial world. Helen has ordered Euphorion not to fly, and Faust has warned him to stay in contact with the earth from which he draws his power, like Antaeus.[187] When Euphorion appears with his parents, the victory of modern culture is complete, and the chorus at last begins to speak in rhyme. Euphorion represents Goethe's perception of the Romantic poets, and specifically Byron, who had died of a fever while leading the Greek forces at Missolonghi in April 1824. In military terms Byron's fate was a grandiose and tragic failure, but in political terms he was an inspiration to the Greeks. Euphorion embodies elements of the reality and the legend of Byron. His words contain allusions to the Greek wars of independence.[188] He recognises no barriers to his movement, nor any mental barriers to his absolute selfhood. He is driven by a desire for fame, and is attracted to war, where 'death / Is a commandment' ('der Tod / Ist Gebot').[189] However, his magical power of flight—a metaphor for Byron's poetic talent—cannot bear the weight he wants it to carry. Euphorion wishes to unfurl his wings, which are in fact just a cloak that can only bear him for a moment, and finally he falls to his death, leaving behind only the symbols of his brilliance.

With the death of Euphorion, Faust has finally failed in his mission to rescue modernity from its mind-body dualism and reembody it through contact with antiquity. On his descent to the underworld Euphorion begs his mother not to leave him, and she dutifully follows him. In her farewell to Faust she sadly confirms the old saying 'that happiness and beauty do not coexist enduringly' ('daß Glück und Schönheit dauerhaft sich nicht vereint'),[190] and so she confirms what Phorkyas had said at the beginning of Act III. Phorkyas urges Faust to keep hold of Helen's clothes—the symbol or mere outer form of beauty, after its substance and genius has departed[191]—and he does so, but they dissolve into clouds that carry him off towards his next and distant meeting with Mephistopheles. The chorus leader Panthalis states that she will remain true to her mistress Helen and follow her to Hades, where those who achieved a name for loyalty retain their identity. So the classical tradition finds its form. The nameless remainder of the chorus will be resolved back into the elements, just as the Homunculus merged with the sea at the end of Act II.

With the idyll of Arcadia shattered, Faust is condemned to return to revolutionary modernity. Act IV begins with Faust alone atop a rugged German mountain from which he sees the cloud that carried him there form itself fleetingly into likenesses of female perfection—Juno, Leda, Helen, and finally perhaps Gretchen—before vanishing into the upper heavens. The cloud vision is a farewell to Faust's pursuit of a woman's love, which he will not find on this earth again, a fact that is emphasized by the arrival of Mephistopheles on a pair of magical seven-league boots. The coolly malicious Phorkyas has given way to the crude and absurd modern devil. In response to Faust's discourse on clouds, Mephistopheles delivers his own bizarre geological lecture, a parody of Vulcanism. He postulates that the devils created the rugged mountain range in a failed revolution after their expulsion from heaven. The mountains were produced by their belching and farting so much sulphur as to buckle the earth's crust. While the return to modern northern Europe has condemned Faust to solitude, it has liberated Mephistopheles to become a parodic version of himself. In his modern mode, Mephistopheles praises the chaos and mess of big cities and describes the opulent pleasure palace he has built himself near the teeming city, where he can enjoy women 'in the plural'. Faust condemns cities as breeding grounds for revolutionaries and snortingly dismisses the devil's pleasure palace as 'bad and modern! Sardanapalus!' ('Schlecht und modern! Sardanapal!')[192]—an allusion Byron's tragedy about the fall of ancient Nineveh, which was dedicated to Goethe. This exchange, written in spring 1831, a year after the 1830 July Revolution, express Goethe's dismay at the Revolution and his belief, shared with his friend the historian Niebuhr, that it sprang from the same causes as the 1789 Revolution, notably the corruption of aristocratic morals that Mephistopheles represents. The disagreement about modern society is the cue for Faust to reveal the grandiose project that will motivate the remainder of *The Second Part*, for the remainder of Faust's career will be dedicated to preventing revolutions or undoing the damage they have caused. His plan is to build a dyke to keep out the 'unfertile'[193] sea and create new agricultural land. Goethe composed these passages shortly after reading about the social doctrines of Saint-Simon, who viewed France's present revolutionary condition as an anarchic and decadent prelude to a utopia of modern industry.[194] The political significance of Faust's project is made clear by the context in which he first explains it and which Goethe has carefully prepared. It is the contrast between the aristocratic corruption and idleness represented by Mephistopheles and the commitment to work and effort advocated by

Faust. As Faust puts it, 'the deed is everything, the fame nothing' ('Die Tat ist alles, nichts der Ruhm').[195] The work ethic of the modern labourer is to replace the representational culture of the early-modern aristocracy. At the same time, and in accordance with the terms of the wager, Faust again commits himself to constant activity, but this time as a recipe for avoiding revolution. By creating new land, Faust will abrogate to himself total 'dominion' ('Herrschaft') and 'property' ('Eigenthum').[196] The effort needed to secure the new land against the sea will stifle the spirit of rebellion which, to Faust's mind, the big cities of the plain have only nurtured with their idleness and corruption. Indeed, Faust will claim in Act V that the settlers on the newly reclaimed land behind the dyke will have to work continuously to maintain it. As Saint-Simon argued, constant labour will leave no time for rebellion, and the rigours of labour will breed a healthy mentality of self-reliance. Busy folk will be inoculated against revolution.

However, Faust's anti-revolutionary vision is impure. His philanthropy is mixed with ideology, hunger for power, and pathological anxiety. From his mountaintop he has observed with anguish the repeated and unproductive advance of the waves:

Da herrschet Well' auf Welle kraftbegeistet,
Zieht sich zurück, und es ist nichts geleistet.
Was zur Verzweiflung mich beängstigen könnte!
Zwecklose Kraft unbändiger Elemente![197]

Wave upon wave rules there, driven by power, / Withdraws, and nothing is achieved. / Which could worry me to desperation! / Pointless power of untamed elements!

Behind this passage stands a poem Goethe had long cherished. The first ode of Horace's third book of *Odes* describes the behaviour of those troubled by *cura* (care, anxiety): 'if a man desires no more than suffices him, / a raging sea cannot trouble him.'[198] Unlike Horace's untroubled man, Faust is irritated by the sea and he works this worry into his modernizing ideology. Faust's vision of the sea is an image of his frustration with his own life since the wager in *The First Part*: constantly moving but achieving nothing. It contrasts with the festival of the life-giving sea at the end of Act II.

With Faust having set out his plan to prevent revolution, the main action of Act IV takes place against the backdrop of a real revolution. Mephistopheles reports that the Emperor's love of pleasure, which Faust wanted to warn against in Act I but only ended up encouraging, has pitched the Empire into anarchy. The Emperor has failed to carry out his primary duty of keeping the peace,[199] and public sentiment has turned against him to the extent that a powerful faction, consisting mainly of priests anxious to retain their wealth, has elected an Anti-Emperor (*Gegenkaiser*). The Emperor's problems provide an opportunity for Faust, as Mephistopheles explains. If he and Faust can keep the Emperor on the throne, Faust can exploit the Emperor's gratitude to request the grant of a tract of coastal land.[200] However, subsequent events cast doubt on whether the intervention of Faust and Mephistopheles is decisive in saving the Emperor, or is in fact just more Mephistophelean smoke and mirrors. Even before he receives Faust's offer of help, the Emperor has risen to the occasion. Faced with the Anti-Emperor, the Emperor has become a proper emperor. Goethe probably had Fichte's theory of identity in mind, which Hegel had developed further in his *Phenomenology*. Goethe thought that regardless of its merits as philosophy, Fichte's and Hegel's thought captured the Zeitgeist. As Goethe had joked in 1806, even a Corsican artillery officer could call himself an emperor by 'positing' a world that forced him to become one, in the style of Fichte.[201] Hence the name of the Emperor's challenger: the Anti-Emperor.

The central scenes of Act IV take place amid the battle between the Emperor's and the Anti-Emperor's armies. The centre and two flanks of the Emperor's forces are already favourably disposed when Faust arrives accompanied by three of Mephistopheles's thugs and promising the assistance of the Necromant of Norcia, a magician whom the Emperor once saved from being burned at the stake. Faust recommends that one of the thugs be incorporated into each of the bodies of troops. Mephistopheles now appears and announces that the mysterious 'mountain folk' have secured the rear of the army's position. In fact he has magically animated old bits of armour found in local castles, and these provide more shock and awe than actual fighting capability. As the armies engage and the thugs do their work, the Emperor realizes that something unnatural is afoot.[202] Sure enough, the opposing army is terrified by an illusion of flood and fire and is routed. With the Anti-Emperor defeated, the Emperor is in a strong position to reconstitute the state and augment his executive power. At least that is what would happen if the Emperor governed in a Goethean manner. In fact the reconstitution of the state results in the Emperor losing power. He is too weak and amiable to assert his advantage over the Empire's great nobles. The final scenes of Act IV between the Emperor and his nobles take place in the vanquished Anti-Emperor's tent, as if to emphasize the great opportunity that comes with the victory. The Emperor's retinue arrives in time to interrupt Mephistopheles's henchmen ransacking the Anti-Emperor's treasury—a cruder but more honest view of the Empire's politics than what is about to be transacted between the Emperor and his nobles. The following scene is based on the Golden Bull of 1356, the imperial decree that confirmed the status of the seven great nobles as imperial electors and their ceremonial duties at court. In writing the scene, Goethe referred back to his childhood mentor Johann Daniel von Olenschlager's essay on the subject.[203] Perhaps more influential was Goethe's memory of the coronation of Joseph II in 1764 and his account of it in *Poetry and Truth*. A passage in the autobiography expresses his disappointment that the momentary flickering into life of the Empire at the coronation was extinguished by dirty political compromise:

> On the one hand, I took great pleasure in these things: because [...] such symbolic ceremonies once more and for an instant represented the German Empire, otherwise scattered across so many parchments, papers, and books, as a living thing; on the other hand, I could not conceal a private displeasure when I was noting down the inner negotiations for my father's benefit and was forced to recognise that here several powers stood in opposition to one another and in equilibrium, and they were only in agreement insofar as they thought to constrain the new regent even more than the old one; that everyone enjoyed his influence only insofar as he could hope to maintain and extend his privileges and ensure his independence.[204]

There is equilibrium among the princes, but the relationship between the princes and the Empire is unbalanced. The princes gain power and the Emperor cedes it. The Emperor makes grants of land to his nobles because he is beholden to them for their support during the revolution. The scene says nothing about this leverage that the nobles possess. Indeed, instead of lifting the curtain to reveal the realities of power in the empire, the scene is full of stilted and antiquarian language that emphasizes the very *unreality* of the actions that we witness. It is a parodic display of empty pomp.[205] At least that remains the case until the newly sworn-in Arch-Cupbearer, Arch-Steward, Arch-Marshal, and Arch-Chamberlain exit, leaving the Emperor alone with the Arch-Chancellor, who is also Archbishop. Exploiting his clerical position, he warns the Emperor that he is worried for his soul, as the Necromant of Norcia is in league with Satan. Again the language verges on parody, as if to emphasize that the Arch-Chancellor is disingenuously exploiting the Emperor's weakness for his own gain.[206] Finally the Arch-Chancellor asks that the church be granted the taxes, tithes, and other income from the land that

Faust has been given and wants to reclaim from the sea. The Emperor grudgingly agrees. Evidently the church is robbing the state of its income. The reason for our seeing Mephistopheles's henchmen bagging the Anti-Emperor's treasury at the beginning of the scene is now clear. The henchmen crudely ransacked the treasury. The Arch-Chancellor steals from the Empire under a veil of political formality. Worse still, he does so by taking advantage of Mephistopheles's black magic.[207] It is not the first time that the church has profited from the work of the devil. The first casket of jewels that Mephistopheles left for Gretchen was swallowed by the church which, as Mephistopheles put it, 'has gobbled up whole countries'.[208]

Much was hanging on the completion of Act V: the conclusion of the wager, the death of Faust, and his salvation or damnation. It does not disappoint. Act V is more compelling than anything so far in *The Second Part*, in its poetic and dramatic power and the pace and logic of its plotting. The first half of Act V is as powerful a drama as any Goethe had written. However, it does not answer the questions about Faust's fate as straightforwardly as Goethe's readers might have expected. In fact both the rapid and tense early scenes and the more leisurely later ones are masterpieces of ambiguity and irony, and in this sense too they are a fitting culmination of the 'incommensurable' *Faust*. Act V falls into two parts: the scenes leading up to Faust's death and those following it. In high old age, having worked on his plan for land reclamation for some years, Faust hurries to complete the project. Standing in his way are an old couple Philemon and Baucis, with their cottage and its neighbouring chapel. These scenes depict Faust's domain, his state of mind and the removal of Philemon and Baucis by Mephistopheles and his henchmen on Faust's orders. It is a powerful and fast-moving piece of drama. Repeatedly it echoes details of the tragedy of Gretchen. The tragedy of Philemon and Baucis asks similar moral questions and answers them in ways that are even more troubling than Faust's treatment of Gretchen. Having completed his work, or at least believing it completed, Faust savours his success and dies. There follows a battle between heaven and hell over his immortal remains, a battle both comical and serious, which is won by heaven thanks to the power of love. The scenes after Faust's death revert to the kaleidoscopic, mythopoeic, symbolic mode of other scenes in *The Second Part*. In the final scene, 'Mountain Gorges', the medieval Christian imagery recapitulates, in some respects, the finale of the Classical Walpurgis Night. Faust's immortal part ascends towards heaven in search of Gretchen or an angelic image of her. The ethereal, pacific verses of the final scene, which turn Faust's fate into cosmic symbolism, are hard to square with what has happened in the first half of Act V, and no doubt intentionally so. The contradictions of the Faust drama are here raised to their highest pitch.

Act V begins with a solitary speaker, a Wanderer who now returns to the shore where he was once saved from shipwreck by the bell of Philemon and Baucis's chapel and was restored to health by the old couple. The Wanderer is a kind of everyman who represents our perspective on the drama, but also the positive side of Faust. He is a rootless wanderer who is reliant on the kindness of those more rooted than himself. He represents the incursion of the modern world into the traditional and confined world of the old couple. However, modernity has already begun to encroach on the couple's world in the form of Faust, and it has driven a wedge between the forward-looking Philemon and the tradition-minded Baucis. She feels uncomfortable about Faust's work:

Wohl! ein Wunder ist's gewesen!
Läßt mich heut noch nicht in Ruh;
Denn es ging das ganze Wesen
Nicht mit rechten Dingen zu.[209]

To be sure! It was a miracle! / Still troubles me today. / For the whole business / Was murkily done.

Baucis uses the same phrase ('nicht mit rechten Dingen') as Gretchen used of the two caskets of jewels.[210] Philemon tries to reassure her by insisting they have faith in the Emperor who granted the land. Baucis answers by pointing to the human lives lost in Faust's work and to Faust's godlessness. She shares Gretchen's ability to sniff out evil. She knows that Faust's desire for their land is tantamount to enslaving them, whereas Philemon optimistically welcomes the new home Faust has offered them. It is not just that Baucis's scruples are justified. In fact Philemon and Baucis are an important part of Faust's trading empire. They operate the warning bell that keeps the ships safe which transport Faust's wealth. Of course Faust fails to recognise the role they play and makes no provision for replacing them. Indeed the lookout tower that he wants to build on the site of their chapel will look inland, not out to sea. It will provide surveillance of his new subjects, not save lives at sea.

From the cottage of Philemon and Baucis, the scene switches to Faust's palace. The contrast between the cottage and palace recalls the French revolutionary refrain 'peace to the cottages, war on the palaces' ('paix aux chaumières, guerre aux palais'), and so reminds us of the causes of popular antagonism towards the French government. The description of Faust's palace in a stage direction recalls Louis XIV-style gardens. As an absolute ruler, Faust aspires to complete control of his world, and so the smallest lack of control—the cottage and chapel of Philemon and Baucis—creates the greatest irritation. The chapel annoys him most. It echoes Gretchen and her Catholic faith. At this point we are reminded of the sources of Faust's wealth, for a barge arrives laden with produce from all corners of the world, piloted by Mephistopheles and his three violent henchmen. Mephistopheles's report of their journey makes it clear that they have been engaged not in peaceful and lawful trade, but piracy. They set out with two ships and returned with twenty, and as he coolly observes:

> Man fragt ums Was, und nicht ums Wie.
> Ich müßte keine Schiffahrt kennen:
> Krieg, Handel und Piraterie,
> Dreieinig sind sie, nicht zu trennen.[211]
>
> It's the 'what' that people are interested in, not the 'how'. / Or else I don't know a thing about shipping: / War, trade and piracy, / They are a trinity, and inseparable.

Mephistopheles's crimes at sea and the casual way Faust overlooks them ominously foreshadow what is about to happen to Philemon and Baucis. Faust has offered the old couple an alternative dwelling and seems prepared to wait for them to make their decision, to which Mephistopheles replies caustically and candidly: 'What are you embarrassed about here, / Haven't you been colonizing for ages' ('Was willst Du Dich denn hier geniren, / Mußt du nicht längst kolonisiren').[212] Mephistopheles knows that Faust's brutal colonial system overseas is little different from what he plans to impose on Philemon and Baucis. They are the aboriginal inhabitants of a land that Faust, the colonizer, thinks he has the right to expropriate, which he can justify by pretending that the land is empty and unprofitable. (The idea that colonized land was empty, 'nobody's land', *terra nullius*, was a common trope of European colonizers and their supporters. Goethe could hardly have come closer to styling Faust as a white colonial exploiter.) Faust now asks Mephistopheles to remove Philemon and Baucis, without specifying how. He may intend to move them to their new dwelling, but he fails to give Mephistopheles an explicit instruction. Mephistopheles sees the loophole Faust has left open and promises airily to remove them. It is a familiar eighteenth-century political problem: the crown failing to control its servants properly.

The next two scenes, 'Deep in the Night' and 'Midnight', portray Faust's moral and psychological response to the murder of Philemon and Baucis and the Wanderer. At first and before he learns of the crime, he regrets his impatience, but when Mephistopheles deceitfully reports that Philemon and Baucis at first failed to respond and then fell dead from terror, Faust tries to lay the blame on Mephistopheles and his henchmen: 'Were you deaf to my words? / It was a trade I wanted, I didn't want theft' ('Wart ihr für meine Worte taub? / Tausch wollt' ich, wollte keinen Raub').[213] However, Faust is condemned by his own words, which recall the piracy ('trade', 'theft') that he has long been engaged in and to which he has turned a blind eye. Philemon, Baucis, and the Wanderer are by no means the first victims of Faust's piratical and colonizing project. The scene ends with Faust seeing four shadowy figures emerge out of the smoke rising from the old couple's cottage. In the next scene, 'Midnight', one of these four shadowy figures delivers a judgement on Faust and his project. Goethe wrote the scene in 1825 shortly after returning to *The Second Part*, and so the scene contains the verdict on Faust as Goethe conceived it at the inception of his work on *The Second Part*. At that stage he still intended to include another scene in which Faust would be judged after his death, but that scene of divine judgement was eventually abandoned, so that the judgement on Faust in 'Midnight' carries greater weight than it would have done when he wrote it in 1825. Arguably it comes close to a final verdict on Faust's achievements and crimes. At the beginning of the scene, the spectral figures that emerged out of the ruin of Philemon and Baucis's cottage materialize as four Grey Women, who personify the evils of Want, Debt, Need, and Care. All four approach the palace but only Care can enter, for the wealthy Faust does not know Want, Debt, or Need, unlike the ordinary folk Philemon and Baucis. Up to this point, Act V has shown the gulf between Faust and the old couple: his wealth, power, and amorality contrast with their poverty, defencelessness, and philanthropy. The entry of Care into Faust's palace also stresses what they have in common. According to Horace's Odes III, 1—again the main model, as it was for Faust's rage at the sea at the beginning of Act IV—Care afflicts the rich as well as the poor. It is Care who now delivers the verdict on Faust in a long and powerful dialogue that has been the subject of much critical debate and at the end of which Care blinds Faust.[214] The 'progressivists', who see in Faust's project in Act V an advance from the narrow personal aims of *The First Part* to grander social and philanthropic ones, have read Faust's dialogue with Care as a moral awakening. Even though Faust is blinded by Care, he achieves progress by acknowledging that his project will only have worth if it can be completed without Mephistopheles's magic. Immediately before Care enters his palace Faust reflects on his 'path', in words that echo his first monologue, written in the mid-1770s:

> Noch hab' ich mich ins Freie nicht gekämpft.
> Könnt' ich Magie von meinem Pfad entfernen,
> Die Zaubersprüche ganz und gar verlernen,
> Stünd' ich, Natur, vor dir ein Mann allein,
> Da wär's der Mühe wert, ein Mensch zu sein.[215]

> I haven't yet fought my way into the clear. / If I could only remove magic from my path, / Completely unlearn the magic spells, / I'd stand before you, Nature, a man alone, / Then it'd be worth the trouble of being human.

The progressivists have argued that Faust sees the damage magic has done and aspires to move forwards without it and, hence, without harm. The sceptics can object that Faust's aspiration is admirable in theory, but empty in practice, because he is too blind to liberate himself from Mephistopheles. Indeed blindness is the dominant theme of the dialogue. The blinding of Faust by Care is a symbol of his moral blindness. Goethe stresses this by having Faust's watchman, the all-seeing Lynkeus, report the destruction of Philemon and Baucis's cottage. Lynkeus's preternaturally perfect eyesight gives him the ability to see the damage Faust has done. The contrast between the all-seeing Lynkeus and the blind Faust evokes the polarity of the active and contemplative life. The *vita contemplativa* (of Lynkeus) grants moral insight, but is passive and unable to act. The *vita activa* (of Faust) is energetic but blind. Faust represents the triumph of the active principle in modernity.

The scenes 'Depths of Night' and 'Midnight' establish a moral connection between the murder of Philemon, Baucis, and the Wanderer and the visit of the four Grey Women to Faust. When Faust learns of the murder of the three innocents, he has the opportunity to reflect on his actions, and Care gives him guidance for such reflection. She describes what a life lived under the burden of care looks like: erratic, restless, blind to real human needs, and vainly charging into the future, destructive to the self and to others. Faust fails to see that the life Care describes is in fact his own. Care is an opportunity for redemption that Faust is temperamentally bound to miss. The new 'inner light' ('inneres Licht') he claims to experience, which the progressivists take for the glimmerings of conscience, in fact only spurs him to accelerate the project that already caused the deaths of Philemon, Baucis, and the Wanderer. The scene ends with Faust deciding to lead the work in person:

Auf strenges Ordnen, raschen Fleiß
Erfolgt der allerschönste Preis;
Daß sich das größte Werk vollende,
Genügt ein Geist für tausend Hände.

Strict organizing, rapid hard work / Result in the finest prize of all; / In order that the greatest work be completed, / One mind is enough for a thousand hands.

What he does not know and will never find out is that his belief in the power of one 'mind' to direct the work is true in a sense he does not intend. The German *Geist* can also mean a supernatural spirit, and indeed at the beginning of the next scene Mephistopheles appears in the guise of a foreman. He and not Faust is the 'spirit' that governs the labourers' hands. A further irony of Faust's unintended pun on *Geist* is that despite his disavowal of magic he continues to rely on Mephistopheles to finish the work. Indeed Mephistopheles's appearance disguised as a foreman reminds us of the Lutheran belief that the devil is a master of disguise and can be lurking anywhere. As Luther taught, to be free of the devil requires constant vigilance, not just a laudable aspiration. Mephistopheles now organizes his workforce of *lemures*, the restless spirits of the unburied dead, according to Roman religion. Their task, however, is not to dig the drainage ditches but rather 'a longish rectangle' ('ein längliches Quadrat'), which will be Faust's grave. In his urgency to complete the work before he dies, Faust orders Mephistopheles, believing him to be the foreman, to recruit more labourers, whether by payment, persuasion, or force. It is another sign that he has lost any moral bearings. He demands daily updates on the progress of the ditches, to which Mephistopheles offers an aside that puns on the words for ditch ('Graben') and grave ('Grab').[216]

Oblivious to Mephistopheles's dark humour, Faust now delivers a long monologue rhapsodizing on the completion of his work and attaining a genuine sublimity, though not without exaggerations. The final task is to drain a malarial swamp, after which Faust will have created space for 'many millions' ('vielen Millionen'). They will live and work behind the protection of the dyke, ever mindful of the community's need to rush and block any holes eroded by the sea. In this image of Saint-Simonian community and industry Faust claims to see the pinnacle of wisdom:

Ja! diesem Sinne bin ich ganz ergeben,
Das ist der Weisheit letzter Schluß:
Nur der verdient sich Freiheit wie das Leben,
Der täglich sie erobern muß.[217]

Yes! This is the purpose to which I am totally devoted, / That is wisdom's final conclusion: / The only way to earn freedom, as well as life, / Is by conquering it daily.

As is usual for Faust, everything is black and white. He swings between exaggerated, pathological pessimism and utopian optimism, just as he did in the monologue that opened *The First Part*. The mental swings are self-perpetuating, so that his vision of the drained land as an agricultural paradise only occasions anxiety about the sea that batters the protective dyke and threatens to inundate the land behind it. The dyke will need constant maintenance and only thus will Faust's new colonizers be able to live 'not safely to be sure, but actively free' ('nicht sicher zwar, doch thätig-frey')[218]—a commitment to permanent activity that recalls his wager with Mephistopheles in *The First Part*.[219] To witness such a society would be the greatest happiness, or so he imagines, and the monologue culminates in an anticipation of that supreme satisfaction. But if this is a vision of a new civilization, like the socialist settler societies in North America that he had written about in the *Journeyman Years* or the socialism of Saint-Simon he read about in 1830 and 1831, then it is a vision marked above all by Faust's habit of swinging between polar extremes. The freedom of his colonizers is defined not as good in itself or as the opportunity for self-realization, but in terms of what has been salvaged from the constant threat of destruction. Our enjoyment of freedom consists not in the peaceable cultivation of the land or the pleasures of communal living. There is no pastoral idyll here, as there was in Faust's vision of Arcadia in Act III. Faust's colonizers will never know peace. Their freedom amounts only to a dogged refusal to be obliterated by nature. Faust's hatred of the sea has not diminished since the beginning of Act IV. His vision may be expressed in some lofty rhetoric, but its content is pathological.

Faust's neurosis is a modernized version of the pathology which, according to Schiller's essay *On Naïve and Sentimental Poetry*, results from our losing a direct connection to nature. We are unsettled. Modernity is constantly mobile, but unlike the mobility celebrated in song 'Don't Stay Stuck to the Ground' ('Bleibe nicht am Boden heften') in the 1821 *Journeyman Years*, it is an anxious mobility, a mobility under pressure of annihilation. Evidently this symbolizes a larger problem. Faustian modernity is a treadmill, and what keeps us moving is anxiety about falling off it. The main claim Faust makes for his new colony is that it will be free. His monologue uses the words 'free' or 'freedom' four times.[220] However, the freedom will be incomplete. At the end of Act IV the Archbishop secured from the Emperor the right to perpetual tithes on Faust's colony, and he was able to do so by exploiting the taint of Mephistophelean evil. The tithes mean that Faust's colony will in fact never free itself from the *ancien regime*. Jarno's sceptical observation at the beginning of the *Journeyman Years* comes to mind, as he and Wilhelm looked down from the mountains: 'Down there a new world lies before you; but I'll wager it is just like the old one behind us'.[221] Moreover, the freedom of Faust's colony is built on forced labour. Immediately before his final monologue, Faust commanded his foreman to recruit a mass of new workers, by force if necessary.[222] On a charitable view, the forced labour might be a temporary measure needed only during the phase of drainage and construction of the sea wall. Once the land is drained and secured, the colonists can turn their efforts to farming, and then perhaps they will enjoy freedom from hardship. In this sense, the freedom Faust talks of can be understood in the narrow and paternalistic sense in which Egmont tells the citizens of Brussels that 'an orderly burgher, who feeds himself honourably and diligently, always has as much freedom as he needs'.[223] Nothing in Faust's vision suggests that the colonists will be politically free, nor would we expect that of Goethe. Faust's politics are a blend of different elements that Goethe felt were characteristic of modernity, both for good and bad. He made several additions to Act V in spring 1831 after reading, with fascinated distaste, a summary of Saint-Simon's political and economic theory in *Le Globe*. Saint-Simon envisaged a new industrial utopia led by an unelected elite of technocrats. Faust's vision, with its 'millions' of workers and Faust as its presumptive leader, resembles Saint-Simon's vision in some respects. As Gaier has pointed out, Saint-Simon believed that the leaders of his new society must be protected from the proletariat by a metaphorical dyke, which further suggests that Faust's project of reclaiming land from the sea might be a symbol for the social classes in the new industrial age.[224] Like Saint-Simon's vision, Faust's is an illusory utopia.[225] Goethe also knew of the land reclamation projects undertaken in the eighteenth century and earlier, for instance the draining of the land on which Peter the Great of Russia built St Petersburg, at the cost of two hundred thousand lives according to Voltaire's account of the life of Charles XII of Sweden.[226] Either way, as a Saint-Simonist or an Enlightened despot, Faust is an illiberal autocrat, who uses his absolute executive power exclusively for the purpose of economic and social progress, with no regard for the freedom of the individual.

Having imagined his sublime benefaction to mankind, Faust is aware that he has enjoyed a moment of fulfilment. According to the terms of the wager then, he must now die. One question remains. Faust asserts that his legacy will last forever, another typically grandiose claim. But what precisely is the legacy? Faust seems to mean his colony, but we have already heard Mephistopheles directing his labourers to dig Faust's grave, instead of continuing the land reclamation, and so there must be some doubt whether Faust's vision will ever be realized. His legacy remains an important theme in the final scene, alongside the question of how he is to be judged. In place of the judgement in heaven that Goethe had originally planned, in 1831 he decided that the final scene would represent Faust's ascension to heaven. The scene is set in a desert landscape of mountains and caves inhabited by hermits. Angels fly upwards carrying Faust's immortal remains to within sight of the heavens, where the Virgin Mary rules in splendour surrounded by penitential female sinners. The visual realization of the scene was inspired by Renaissance art. The literary mode is mystical oratorio. Its symbolic language is partly Christian and partly drawn from the long Western philosophical tradition. The scene portrays the ascension and purification of Faust's ideal essence or what Leibniz, following Aristotle, would have called his *entelechy*: the spiritual essence of Faust's being, the permanent active element of his existence. It hardly needs saying that the Christian imagery of the scene does not require us to believe that Faust's immortal remains are an actual soul or that there are such things as angels. The language changed during the text's gestation. A stage direction in an early draft, not carried over into the published text, has the Chorus of Angels 'carrying up Faust's entelechy' ('Faustens Entelechie heranbringend'). In the final manuscript, Goethe labelled Faust's entelechy his 'immortal part' ('Unsterbliches'), a decidedly neutral concept, which avoids the Christian connotations of *soul* and leaves it open exactly what Faust's immortal part is. Is it a substantial soul, or is it perhaps only a spiritual or intellectual legacy, such as the written texts that would survive the death of their author?

What is sung and enacted in 'Mountain Gorges' is a form of mysticism, rather than any Christian doctrine, and it is a mysticism that incorporates Goethe's doctrine of transformationism and his *homo mensura* principle. Faust's 'immortal part' is described as undergoing a process of becoming symbolic or ideal. In order to do so, it must first be cleansed of its earthly impurities. A chorus of More Complete Angels presents the process in language suggestive both of the extraction of metal ores and the purification of the soul by love as described in Plato's *Symposium*:

> Uns bleibt ein Erdenrest
> Zu tragen peinlich,
> Und wär' er von Asbest,
> Er ist nicht reinlich.
> Wenn starke Geisteskraft
> Die Elemente
> An sich herangerafft,
> Kein Engel trennte
> Geeinte Zwienatur
> Der innigen beiden,
> Die ewige Liebe nur
> Vermag's zu scheiden.[227]

> To us a residue of earth remains / Painful to carry, / And even were it asbestos, / It is not pure. / Whenever strong mental power / Gathers the elements / Up into itself, / No Angel separated / The unified double nature / Of the innermost pair, / Only eternal love / Is capable of dividing it.

Faust's impure connection to the earth will melt away. As Goethe noted in a maxim in *On Art and Antiquity* in 1826, this process of dissolving one's earthly connections is the very essence of mysticism:

> All mysticism is a transcending of and a releasing from some object or other that one believes one is leaving behind. The greater and more significant the thing is that one is forsaking, the richer are the mystic's productions.[228]

What is to be dissolved and left behind is Faust's attachment to the real world, which runs deep. This is the reason for the scene's flamboyant Christian imagery. As Faust's 'immortal parts' are carried upwards through the gorge, the earthly material that has accreted round them is sloughed off to leave an ideal form. The sloughing off is represented by the various hermits he passes during his ascent, who become progressively less earthly and more ideal the higher he goes. The scene begins in the gorge's lower regions, where we hear a Chorus and Echo describing a paradisal place, including peaceful lions, as at the ending of the *Novelle*—a vision of heaven that is merely an idealization of the earth. The image of paradise stands for the scene as a whole, which likewise gives voice to a human imagination that imagines heaven in ways that are limited by and to the earth. The earthly bounds of our imagination are made explicit by the hermit named Pater Seraphicus. He invites a group of infants, who have died shortly after childbirth and therefore have not experienced the earth, to see things through his eyes, an 'organ proportioned to the world and earth' ('Welt- und erdgemäß Organ').[229] The Pater Seraphicus thus represents the *homo mensura* principle and its evolutionist underpinnings that Goethe developed during his work on optics. The human eye is the measure of all visible things on earth, but being proportioned to the earth, it sees only what its evolution on earth allows it to see and no more. Above and beyond the earth, things may be measured by other standards and perceived by other organs, of which we have no knowledge.

Much of the critical debate surrounding the scene has assumed that it contains a theory of divine salvation that in some sense justifies Faust's ascension. However, insofar as any doctrine of salvation is expressed by the Angels, it is more naturalistic than theological. Salvation is a process analogous to chemical purification. It is not a winnowing of wheat from chaff or a dividing of sheep from goats. It is a process that every soul must undergo. There are indications that a selection of souls has been made, but they are highly ambiguous. The Angels state that they can save whoever has striven, which might imply that Faust has been selected for salvation because of his striving:

Gerettet ist das edle Glied
Der Geisterwelt vom Bösen,
'Wer immer strebend sich bemüht,
Den können wir erlösen.'[230]

Rescued is the noble part / Of the spirit world from evil, / 'Whosoever always striving labours, / Him can we save'.

However categorical the Angels' words sound, they are ambiguous.[231] They are usually taken to mean that striving makes a person worthy of salvation. Faust merits grace because striving has been a hallmark of his life, from the Lord's singling him out as one who strives in the Prologue in Heaven, through the striving promised in the wager, to Care's description of the blindly striving Faust. But the Angels do not conclusively say that striving makes a person worthy of salvation. Instead they say that there are those who have striven, and the Angels can save them. We are no doubt also meant to recall the words of the Lord in the Prologue in Heaven: 'man errs for as long as he strives' ('Es irrt der Mensch, solang' er strebt').[232] In this sense the Angels' words would mean that striving makes a person needful of salvation. This reading coheres better with their talk of chemical purification, which implies that people need salvation, not that they merit it. The scene contains other hints that this is a heterodox version of salvation. There are allusions to the heterodox doctrines of Origen, which Goethe had found in Gottfried Arnold in the early 1770s. According to Arnold, Origen believed in the mystical idea of purification: after death we undergo 'a true purification', and there takes place 'a mystery [...] that purifies and cleanses us'. As in 'Mountain Gorges', so in Origen even angels need purification.[233] And in the same way as Faust's 'immortal parts' progress past several hermits' cells, Origen believed that the soul must progress through various 'mansions'.[234] Origen's doctrine is the *apokatastasis pantōn*, the restitution or restoration of all things. It is a universal process, not a selection of the worthy.

Faust's 'immortal parts' now take the form of a Marian Doctor (*Doctor Marianus*) who sees the Queen of Heaven above and begs for access to her mysteries. Gaier has compared this to the very end of Dante's *Paradiso*, where Bernard von Clairvaux prays to the Virgin Mary,[235] and has pointed to the importance of cosmic love in the *Paradiso*'s finale: 'love that moves the sun and other stars' ('l'amor che move il Sole e l'altre stelle').[236] The Doctor perceives that the cloud surrounding the Virgin Mary is made up of penitent women and 'those easy to lead astray' ('die leicht Verführbaren').[237] This Chorus of Penitent Women prays to the Virgin Mary using Gretchen's words prayer to Mary in *The First Part*: 'You incomparable, / You rich in pity' ('Du Ohnegleiche, / Du Gnadenreiche!').[238] The prayer is echoed by One of the Penitent Women Formerly Known as Gretchen (Una Poenitentium sonst Gretchen genannt), again using Gretchen's words from *The First Part*. Evidently she has gone through the process of purification, leaving her earthly identity behind.[239] At this point the Blessed Boys—those poor souls who died before experiencing much of the world and have ascended with Faust—realize that Faust, as a recipient of love, will be able to teach them. Here we see another glimpse of Faust's true legacy, not as the builder of a new colony on earth, but as a teacher in heaven. (Schöne notes a further parallel with Origen's heaven, where all souls help one another.)[240] The Penitent Woman Formerly Known as Gretchen notes that while Faust is blind and unaware, still his youthful vigour will reemerge, and she pleads with the Virgin Mary to be allowed to teach the former Faust. It is noteworthy that in the hierarchy of teachers Gretchen ranks higher than Faust. The Mater Gloriosa duly invites the former Gretchen up to the higher spheres, telling her that if the former Faust is aware of her, he will follow.

The scene, and with it the whole massive edifice of *Faust*, ends with a Mystical Chorus which veers close to the Platonic doctrine that what we perceive in the world is only imperfect versions of the perfect and transcendent forms:

Alles Vergängliche
Ist nur ein Gleichnis;
Das Unzulängliche,
Hier wird's Ereignis;
Das Unbeschreibliche,
Hier ist's getan;
Das Ewig-Weibliche
Zieht uns hinan.[241]

Everything transient / Is but a likeness; / What is inaccessible [or possibly, insufficient], / Here it's an event; / What is indescribable, / Here it is enacted; / The eternal womanly / Leads us upwards.

The first three couplets are straightforward, assuming we follow David Luke's reading of 'unzulänglich' as 'inaccessible'.[242] They articulate a form of Platonism or perhaps a Goethean version of Kant or Spinoza, whereby the transient or phenomenal world is only a likeness of an inaccessible truth. That likeness is either an image (first couplet) or an enactment (second and third couplets) of what lies beyond our knowledge. Thus far the Mystical Chorus conforms to the scene as a whole. It is a mystical representation of something unknowable. The fourth couplet has proved the most controversial, not because its meaning is obscure but because of the charge of sexism. Gretchen becomes an abstraction. The life, personality, desires, and needs of a particular woman are reduced to mere 'womanhood'. Worse still, the idea that 'the eternal feminine draws us onwards' is a reminder, both in its universalism and in the idea of enticement, of the misogynist Judaeo-Christian tradition that begins with Eve tempting Adam to eat the forbidden fruit. The former Gretchen is one of those penitent women who are 'easy to lead astray' ('die leicht Verführbaren'), like Eve seduced by the serpent. Sin is blamed on the weakness intrinsic to all womanhood. In Goethe's defence, it can be argued that Mountain Gorges reduces *all* humans to abstractions, not just Gretchen.[243] The final couplet does indeed recall Eve in the Garden of Eden, but it reverses the meaning of her relationship with Adam. Gretchen leads Faust on not by seducing but by educating him, and not into sin but into greater knowledge. The process of purification and abstraction enacted in *Mountain Gorges* dissolves our pathological bondage to the earth and elevates us to a purely intellectual love of God, in the manner of Spinoza. And the highest level of elevation is in a heaven ruled by women, not men.

Several months after Christiane's death in 1816, Goethe wrote an outline of Part Four of *Poetry and Truth*,[244] dealing with the two momentous episodes of 1775: his failed relationship with Lili Schönemann and his move to Weimar. However, Lili was still alive in 1816, and Goethe did not wish to cause her discomfort, so for the time being Part Four remained unfinished and, for a while, forgotten. In 1821 he wrote an account of Lili's seventeenth birthday.[245] After briefly resuming work in 1825, he completed Part Four in 1831. The whole of *Poetry and Truth* was then published for the first time posthumously in 1833 in the *Final Authorized Version*. Part Four differs in structure from Parts One to Three. In the Preface to Part Four Goethe writes that the narrative of a life that is entwined in complex ways with its age can be made more accessible to the reader by being separated out into discrete parcels. The structure of Part Four is episodic. Key events in the life are interspersed with essays on historical, cultural, and intellectual trends. While it would be easy to write this off as the work of an old man too tired or in too much of a hurry to integrate his material effectively, Part Four does have a continuous philosophical thread. Again this thread differs from that of Parts One to Three. The relationship with Lili is paradigmatic: it was an 'irresistible desire', which however did not take account of 'external factors'.[246] It was less a clash between self and world, such as Goethe described in Part Three, and more the self blindly disregarding the world. In a series of episodes, Part Four describes the growing gap between the poet's inner being and the outer circumstances of his life and of German culture. His relationship with Lili shows his blindness to religious differences. In pursuing the prospect of marriage to her, he neglects the difference in confession between the Lutheran Goethes and the Calvinist Schönemanns and hence the reality of a multiconfessional Germany. Following the success of *Werther* the pirate publishers take the circulation of Goethe's writings out of his hands, so that he becomes two quite disconnected authors: the 'Goethe' of the pirate publishers and the poet himself. In May to July 1775, he undertook a two-month trip to Switzerland with the Stolberg brothers and visited Lavater in Zurich. The trip ends in his alienation from both the Stolbergs and Lavater and from their very different visions of German culture. Lavater is fixated on detail and incapable of coherent or methodical thought.[247] The Stolbergs are committed to a freedom of emotional expression that disregards social responsibility.[248] Each episode is a story of inner and outer worlds breaking apart.

Part Four presents Goethe as sleepwalking through a social and cultural landscape that no longer has a place for him. The climax is the faintly comical chaos of his nearly aborted move to Weimar. The real Goethe of 1775 did understand the significance of the move: he knew that he was exchanging the ossified and hierarchical oligarchy of Frankfurt for a position close to autocratic power in Weimar. The fictional Goethe of *Poetry and Truth* has no awareness of this. There is praise for Anna Amalia's achievements, but the narrative says nothing about the politics of the move and focuses instead on the comedy of its nearly not coming about: the late arrival of the carriage that was to collect him, his father's mockery of the plan to move, Goethe's decision to travel to Italy at his father's insistence, the self-interested plan[249] of Demoiselle Delph to persuade him to settle in Mannheim. In the course of the confusion, his commitment to Weimar gets lost, and the move is rescued only at the last minute by a hurried letter that reaches him in Heidelberg on his way south. His nature, as he admits, is 'planless',[250] and accordingly he tries to persuade Miss Delph that Weimar is right for him by quoting the Spinoza-inspired words from *Egmont*:

> My child, my child, not another word! As though whipped by invisible spirits, the horses of the sun, Time's horses, run away with the light chariot of our destinies; and we have no choice but to grip the reins with resolute courage and, now to the right, now to the left, avert the wheels from a stone here, a precipice there. As for the end of the journey, who knows what it is? When we hardly remember where it began.[251]

Part Four of *Poetry and Truth* is not the first autobiography to stress the role of unconscious forces. In his *Confessions* Rousseau argued that his character was unwittingly shaped by a myriad of seemingly insignificant experiences. Goethe's conception of the unconscious is different from Rousseau's and entirely new. The unconscious is a blind force within us, and especially within the genius, that drives us towards an unknown destiny. In the *Confessions* Rousseau documented in painful detail the elements of experience that combined to form his character. In Part Four of *Poetry and Truth*, Goethe depicts a character inhabited by a mysterious and unintelligible force that drives it forward and to which the narrator can only give mythic or symbolic form.[252] Its existence can only be inferred from the fact that the genius succeeds despite adverse circumstances and not having a consciously formulated plan for his life. He calls this force the 'daemonic'.

The quotation from *Egmont* connects the end of Part Four back to its beginning and suggests that Spinoza's philosophy—or Goethe's version of it—provides the key to understanding his experience. Part Four begins with his rediscovery of Spinoza and the calmness this brings him. Spinoza is a cure for the 'Werther fever' that has afflicted him in the last few years.[253] The most important insight from Spinoza is that nature obeys its own iron laws that nothing can alter, not even the God that might have created them:

> Nature operates according to eternal, necessary laws, which are so divine that the Divinity itself cannot alter them. Unconsciously, all human beings are in perfect agreement about this. Just consider how any natural phenomenon astounds and actually horrifies us if it hints at understanding, reason, or merely free will.[254]

That is to say we are all unconsciously Spinozists. We know tacitly that we cannot hope to change or direct anything in nature (or at least anything significant) by our own will. In order to live successfully in such a world, we do best to renounce rationality and instead embrace our capacity for tenacity and above all levity:

> Thanks to this, he is capable of renouncing an individual thing at any moment, if only at the next he may reach for something else, and so, unconsciously, we are always recreating our whole life. We replace one passion with another. Occupations, inclinations, favourite pursuits, whims, we try them all out only to exclaim at last that all is vanity. No one is horrified by this false, nay, blasphemous saying; indeed it is thought to express something wise and irrefutable. There are only a few persons who have had a premonition about this intolerable feeling, and they have avoided all these partial resignations by resigning themselves totally, once and for all.[255]

The partial resignations of other philosophies, such as the old admonition that 'all is vanity', are false and blasphemous, for they fail to recognise the beautiful divine order of the universe. Only a preemptive Spinozist *total* renunciation gets to the truth of the matter and offers profound calm. We must recognise that the world 'works according to laws that are eternal, necessary, and so divine that the Deity himself could change nothing about them'. This is the only moral philosophy that satisfies the beauty of the universe and consoles us for our inconsequential place in it.

———

In the aftermath of the July Revolution of 1830 Goethe's attention was focused on France for other, equally revolutionary reasons. Soret reports a conversation with him on 2 August 1830:

> The news of the beginning of the July Revolution reached Weimar today and caused general excitement. In the course of the afternoon I went to Goethe.
> 'Well', he called out to greet me, 'what do you think of this great event? The volcano has erupted; everything is in flames, and the business is no longer conducted behind closed doors!'
> 'A terrible story!', I replied. 'But what else could be expected in the circumstances we know of and with such a ministry, than it ending with the expulsion of the current royal family'.
> 'We seem to be at cross purposes, my dearest friend', Goethe replied. 'I'm not talking about those people at all; I'm concerned with entirely different things. I'm talking about the dispute, so important for science, between Cuvier and Geoffroy de Saint-Hilaire that's just erupted publicly in the Academy!'[256]

In the spring of 1830 he had read[257] about the debates between Georges Cuvier and Geoffroy Saint-Hilaire at the Academy of Sciences in Paris. The debates took place weekly in front of large audiences from mid-February, until they fizzled out in a mixture of acrimony and boredom at the end of March. Their content was very much on Goethe's territory: animal structure and species transformation. Cuvier argued that animal structure was principally determined by function; Geoffroy that its main driver was evolutionary morphology. Cuvier was a longstanding opponent of Lamarck and Geoffroy, his most prominent supporter. Soon after the debates, Geoffroy published a summary of his arguments under the title *Principes de Philosophie zoologique*, in a clear allusion to Lamarck's transformationist essay *Philosophie zoologique* of 1809. Goethe began to write an analytical summary of the debate, which he only finished in 1832. It was one of the last pieces he wrote before his death. Its aim was to inform Germans about the debate and to explain how it was connected to German biology.[258] Goethe was not a neutral observer of the debate, and his account necessarily asserts his own prominence in the field. In his diary in May 1830 he wrote that the debate was between two perspectives that he termed 'stationary' and 'progressive': Cuvier's species fixism and Geoffroy's transformationism.[259] Goethe's summary of the debate leans strongly towards Geoffroy, towards a German way of thinking about biology, and thus towards Goethe's own transformationist theory. Indeed the piece's title simply borrows the title of Geoffroy's *Principes de Philosophie zoologique*. What Geoffroy has in common with Goethe and the Germans is a synthesizing view of nature as a system, in contrast to Cuvier's atomistic and empiricist approach. It is only by viewing nature as a system that we can conceive of species transformation: 'Geoffroy [...] harbours the idea of the whole in his inner sense and proceeds in the conviction that the individual [species] can develop gradually from it'.[260] There was an underlying morphological type. Variations on the type evolved through interaction with a species' environment. These changes were furthermore governed and limited by the principle of the economy of nature, which requires that growth in one area is compensated by atrophy in another. Hence a substantial part of Goethe's summary is concerned with restating the theories he had developed in the 1790s.[261]

Much of Goethe's essay, however, is concerned less with scientific substance than with method—or with what Goethe termed 'modes of representation' (*Vorstellungsarten*). Viewed in this way, the conflict between Cuvier and Geoffroy is a 'dispute between the two classes of natural scientist, the analyzers and the synthesizers'.[262] An essay of 1823 titled 'Problem and Response'[263] helps to explain what Goethe meant by reconfiguring the fixism-transformationism debate along the lines of analysis and synthesis. Goethe wrote the essay as part of a debate with the botanist Ernst Meyer on how to define the idea of a species. How much variety can exist within a single species? Certain species, such as the Dog rose (*rosa canina*) seemed to exhibit so much variety as to be barely classifiable as a single species. The Dog rose was, in Goethe's formulation, a 'promiscuous' species.[264] It was also the kind of species that Goethe had drawn on to support his theory of plant metamorphosis. Carnations were another example. These species show an extreme abundance in the way they repeat and vary a flowering plant's basic structural elements. They are 'characterless races, to which one can perhaps barely ascribe *species*, since they lose themselves in boundless variety'.[265] They 'elude any definition, any law'.[266] Indeed, the very idea of metamorphosis—nature's tendency to repeat with variations a fundamental structural unit—seemed to break down the idea of a species. This was the conceptual problem Goethe was wrestling with in the debate with Meyer. On the one hand, the idea of a species requires form and continuity or a 'tendency towards specification'.[267] Goethe also thought of this as a 'centripetal' tendency.[268] Without it, individual members of a species would rapidly diverge from one another and the species would not endure. On the other hand, every species possessed the 'centrifugal' tendency of metamorphosis. This tendency 'leads into formlessness, destroys knowledge, dissolves it'.[269] The problem has been central to recent debates in the philosophy of biology. Evolution tells us that organisms change through time. Hence a given species concept (Dog rose) represents only a single snapshot of evolution in the course of evolutionary time. In addition, at any given time the species comprises a degree of genetic diversity—a great deal of diversity in the case of the Dog rose. If we were to plot all the members of the species as points in a two dimensional space, according to their genetic diversity, we would see a fuzzy cluster of points within a more or less clearly bounded space. If we now make this model temporal, we see that over time the fuzzy cluster would move around in the space, due to genetic drift and the evolutionary pressures of a changing environment. Thus our concept of a species has to accommodate a degree of movement. It will need to be looser and more flexible than we might have wanted. This is why Goethe begins the essay 'Problem and Response' with the phrase 'natural system: a contradictory expression'.[270] Over evolutionary time, nature is not fixed and cannot be formed into a system.

The phrase 'natural system: a contradictory expression' points towards the fact that the problem is even greater than we might have first supposed and is not confined to biological species. Goethe asks Meyer to imagine that all natural phenomena have their origin in an unknowable single act of genesis—a point in space-time, as we might put it. The diversity of phenomena that we see today has arisen by a kind of a centrifugal dispersion away from this punctual origin or, as Goethe puts it, by means of metamorphosis. If this is so, then how is it that the phenomena of nature have dispersed from their punctual origin in such a way as to have complex and durable forms which even have formal interrelationships among them? How is it that nature has structure and is not mere chaotic entropy?

> Nature [...] is life and consequence [radiating] from an unknown centre, towards an unknowable boundary. [...] The idea of metamorphosis is a highly honorable but at the same time highly dangerous gift from above. It leads into formlessness, destroys knowledge, dissolves it. It is at once the *vis centrifuga* and would lose itself in the infinite, if some counterweight were not given to it: I mean the tendency of specification, the tough capacity to endure possessed by whatever has come into being. A *vis centripeta*, which cannot be damaged by any externality.[271]

Two aspects of this passage are striking. First, Goethe's account of metamorphosis—it 'dissolves' knowledge—has some similarities with Daniel Dennett's account of Darwinian evolution in his study *Darwin's Dangerous Idea*. For Dennett, evolution functions as a 'universal solvent'[272] that dissolves all the fundamental questions of biology and even philosophy. This is why Darwinian evolution is so powerful and, for believers in a divinely organized world, so dangerous. As Goethe puts it, metamorphosis is a 'dangerous gift'. Second, Goethe makes the same move here as he does in his account of the Cuvier-Geoffroy debate: a move from visualizing the shape of evolution in terms of radiation from a single point to conceptualizing the epistemology of our understanding of concepts such as *species*. Goethe says that metamorphosis dissolves form, by which he means that species like the Dog rose that undergo extensive metamorphosis are not easy for us to define morphologically. In the same sentence he says that metamorphosis destroys knowledge. The idea of metamorphosis contradicts the concept *species*. This is the result of the synthetic method in science, which tries to conceive of nature as a whole 'system'. It destroys analytical specification. In other words, the ontology of metamorphosis and species on the one hand and the epistemology of synthesis and analysis on the other are two ways of expressing the same dichotomy. Thus when Goethe describes the Cuvier-Geoffroy debate as a conflict between analyzers and synthesizers, he is also describing the debate between species fixism and transformationism.

In the essay on the Cuvier-Geoffroy debate Goethe wanted to establish his legacy as a scientist. The essay reformulates the central question he addressed in most of his scientific work, at least in his work on geology, botany, mammal anatomy, and meteorology. If we follow Goethe in imagining all natural phenomena as having their origin in an unknowable single act of genesis, and if we imagine that the diversity of the phenomena we see around us has arisen by a centrifugal dispersion from that point, then we are faced with the problem of understanding why there should be any structure at all in the natural world, and how that structure comes about. From his neo-Aristotelian theory of hylomorphism in geology, through his work on plant metamorphosis, to his theory of the mammalian morphological type, and his interest in Luke Howard's classification of clouds, Goethe's science is unified by a desire to understand how matter achieves and maintains form. Rocks have an intrinsic tendency to crystallize in regular forms. 'The whole of plant life', as he puts it in a restatement of the argument of his essay on the 'Metamorphosis of Plants', 'is a constant sequence of perceptible and imperceptible divergences of form'.[273] Mammal skeletons are transformations of a single type (form) of skeleton. The questions we should ask of nature are questions about form.

Goethe died on 22 March 1832, aged eighty-two. He had outlived almost all of his contemporaries. Of his old Weimar friends, Charlotte von Stein died in 1827, followed by Grand Duke Carl August in 1828 and Grand Duchess Luise in 1830. Christiane had died in 1816. August, their first child and only offspring to survive infancy, died in Rome in 1830. Only Knebel outlived Goethe; he died in 1834 at the venerable age of eighty-nine.

The intellectual and cultural world on which Goethe had made such an impact as a young writer had long since gone. The changes were many and deep. Politics was now organized around the ideological poles of liberalism and conservatism. Freedom of the press, an exception when he began to publish, was now widespread. For the second half of his life, Europe had been in a state of almost permanent revolutionary upheaval. The Holy Roman Empire had dissolved itself. German literature was now recognised internationally, and German philosophy had undergone its own revolution. The disciplines of science and history were showing how much nature, society, and culture had evolved. The modern mind that was formed during Goethe's lifetime was intensely aware of its own historicity. His essay on the Cuvier-Geoffroy dispute captures an awareness of the historicity of science and of the profound mental adjustments that he and his generation had to make. Its main focus is how we can reconcile the existence of structure in the natural world with the seemingly formless flight of phenomena, how we can make sense of natural form in a universe that seems destined for entropy. We seem to inhabit a world organized around paradoxical polarities. Solid matter shifts and changes, but its underlying forms can be grasped by the mind in ways that can prove remarkably durable. In September 1826 Schiller's remains were disinterred in order to be moved to the ducal mausoleum. The skull was cleaned and briefly left with Goethe.[274] He composed a set of *terze rime* to commemorate the event. The poem ends with a meditation on the paradoxical relation of matter and mind:

> Was kann der Mensch im Leben mehr gewinnen
> Als daß sich Gott-Natur ihm offenbare?
> Wie sie das Feste läßt zu Geist verrinnen,
> Wie sie das Geisterzeugte fest bewahre.[275]

FIG. 26. Goethe in the last year of his life, photogravure after the 1832 drawing by C. A. Schwerdgeburth.

What more can humans gain in life / Than God-nature revealing itself to them? / In the way it lets what's solid dissolve into spirit, / In the way it firmly preserves what's produced by minds.

The poem consoles us with the solidity and durability of the traces that our own minds leave in the world. It accepts the paradoxical duality of the universe that is reflected in human nature.

One of the questions that has run through this book is how we might reconcile the consistent liberality of Goethe's poetic and intellectual career with the overwhelmingly anti-liberal tenor of his ministerial activity and political thought. Part of the answer lies in the compromise that the eighteenth-century German intelligentsia made with autocracy, as expressed in Wolff's political theory. But it is only part of the answer. Goethe's was an unusual form of compromise, without any of the aspirations to political rationality that were held by most of his contemporaries. Unusually for his time, he rejected Wolffian natural law and its vision of how society ought to be, and instead he accepted the reality of political power as it was and had always been. We are unfree because that is how power naturally works. At the same time, he liberated himself fully from his family's Lutheran faith and turned instead to a Spinozan deism, in which God is replaced by 'God-nature', as in the verses inspired by Schiller's skull. There is a logic that connects these two moves. Accepting the reality of political power and refusing to accept Wolff's idealized image of the natural law—this was akin to accepting nature itself. More specifically, Spinoza's argument in the *Ethics* concerning the amorality of nature had a similar logic to his argument concerning the origins of states in the *Theological-Political Treatise*. God cannot interrupt the laws of nature. The universe comes into being not by divine action but according to natural laws. It follows that the miracles that supposedly accompanied the founding of the Abrahamic faiths were not miracles at all. They were not even religious acts. They were political acts performed in order to create sovereign authority and national unity, and they were only performed under the guise of religion or dressed up as religion by later writers. A similar argument can be made for the history of civilization. The origins of civilization lie not in religious belief or political programmes, but in military and political power. Likewise the subsequent history of civilization does not follow any divine or rational plan. The history of civilization is not the progressive realization of human perfectibility, as Wolff and his followers argued. The main driver of civilization is the primary affect of self-preservation (*amour de soi*), which has an unfortunate tendency to be corrupted into a secondary and pernicious form of vain self-love (*amour-propre*). In the most successful polities, which tend to be relatively small, healthy self-preservation remains dominant. We can sometimes see the traces of self-preservation in a polity's social history, for instance in Verona or Venice, where the people gave themselves the structure of their social life, rather than having it dictated to them by autocratic military power. This was as liberal as Goethe was able to be. However, it was a political vision grounded in nature, not in rational principles. In any case, the natural course of civilization was generally that self-preservation degenerated into vain self-love, as in the portrayal of the theatre in the *Theatrical Mission* and the *Apprenticeship*. In this sense, and being mindful of the twisting course of Goethe's career and the many and various impulses that formed it, one can agree with Matthew Arnold's claim that Goethe's work shows a 'profound, imperturbable naturalism'.[276] A commitment to a more natural vision of reality and of our place in it offers the best general explanation of an intellectual life that was, in the words of 'Gingko Biloba', 'one and double' ('Eins und doppelt').[277]

NOTE ON TRANSLATIONS, EDITIONS, AND REFERENCING

All foreign language texts are given in English translation. In translating Goethe's poems and verse dramas, there is little prospect of conveying both the semantic sense and the formal qualities of the original. My translations aim to convey something close to the semantic sense and to retain as much as possible of the word order, but they convey nothing of the prosody. Goethe's original German verse is included in order to give readers a sight of its forms. The line breaks in the original verse texts are indicated approximately by obliques in the prose translations. Other translations from Goethe's writings are also mine, except for some of the prose fiction and scientific writings, where I have used published translations. In these cases, the footnoted references give the translation first, followed by an edition of the German text. Where I have adapted a translator's version, this is noted in the footnotes. For a few other frequently quoted non-Anglophone authors, for example, Rousseau and Kant, I have used published English translations and given references to an edition in the original language.

Since there is no single complete and reliable edition of Goethe's writings, it has been necessary to use more than one edition. The two main editions used are the Münchner Ausgabe (MA) and the Weimarer Ausgabe (WA). Together, these two editions contain most of Goethe's writings and are relatively easy to find in libraries. MA is used for the literary, critical, and scientific writings and WA for the letters, diaries, and some of the conversations. Full details of these editions and all other frequently used sources are given in the list of abbreviations on pages 661–63 below. All other literature (i.e., literature not cited with an abbreviation) is cited by short titles in the notes. Full details are given in the bibliography. In the case of texts for which standard numbering of lines and sections exists (Greek and Roman classics, the Bible), these numberings are used and an edition is only cited where absolutely necessary.

In the notes, personal names appear in one of two forms. Less frequently cited names are given in the form, for example, C. G. Körner, with the full name appearing in the index. More frequently cited names are given in the form of an abbreviation, for example, CG (= Christiane von Goethe). All abbreviations are unpacked in the list of abbreviations below. References to letters and conversations unpack as follows: 'CS to JGH, 13/4/1778' unpacks as 'letter from Charlotte von Stein to Johann Gottfried Herder, 13 April 1778'. Where no originator is given for a letter or diary or conversation, the originator is Goethe, so that 'To FS, 24/9/1794' unpacks as 'letter from Goethe to Friedrich Schiller, 24 September 1794', and 'Conv. FWR, 3/4/1814' unpacks as 'Goethe in conversation with Friedrich Wilhelm Riemer, 3 April 1814'. References to Goethe's diaries appear in the form 'diary' followed by the date and WA reference.

ABBREVIATIONS

AA	Anna Amalia, Dowager Duchess of Sachsen-Weimar-Eisenach
AG	Julius August Walther von Goethe
BaG	*Briefe an Goethe*, ed. Karl Robert Mandelkow (Munich: Beck, 1988)
BGG	*Goethes Gespräche*, ed. Woldemar and Flodoard von Biedermann (Leipzig: Biedermann, 1910)
CA	Carl August, Duke of Sachsen-Weimar-Eisenach
CEG	Catharina Elisabeth Goethe
CFR	Carl Friedrich von Reinhard
CFZ	Carl Friedrich Zelter
CG	Christiane von Goethe (née Vulpius)
CG	Cornelia Goethe
CGV	Christian Gottlob von Voigt
CH	Caroline Herder
CLK	Carl Ludwig von Knebel
CMW	Christoph Martin Wieland
CS	Charlotte von Stein
DVLG	*Deutsche Vierteljahresschrift für Literaturwissenschaft und Geistesgeschichte*
EA	Goethe, *Elective Affinities. A Novel*, trans. David Constantine (Oxford: OUP, 1994)
EG	Goethe, *The Essential Goethe*, ed. Matthew Bell (Princeton: Princeton UP, 2015)
ETL	Ernst Theodor Langer
FA	Goethe, *Sämtliche Werke, Briefe, Tagebücher und Gespräche* ('Frankfurter Ausgabe'), ed. Dieter Borchmeyer et al. (Munich: Deutscher Klassiker Verlag, 1985–1999)
FHJ	Friedrich Heinrich (Fritz) Jacobi
FJB	Friedrich Justin Bertuch
FJS	Frédéric Jacob Soret

FM	Friedrich Theodor Adam Heinrich ('Kanzler') von Müller
FS	Friedrich Schiller
FWHT	Friedrich Wilhelm Heinrich von Trebra
FWR	Friedrich Wilhelm Riemer
GBuG	*Goethe: Begegnungen und Gespräche*, ed. Ernst and Renate Grumach (Berlin: De Gruyter, 1965–)
GF	Goethe, *Faust-Dichtungen*, ed. Ulrich Gaier, 3 vols. (Stuttgart: Reclam, 1999)
GH	*Goethe-Handbuch*, ed. Bernd Witte et al. (Stuttgart: Metzler, 1996)
GJ	*Goethe-Jahrbuch*
GLL	*German Life and Letters*
GLPC	*Goethe-Lexicon of Philosophical Concepts*
GLTT	*Goethes Leben von Tag zu Tag*, ed. Robert Steiger and Angelika Reimann (Zurich and Munich: Artemis, 1982–1996)
GQ	*The German Quarterly*
GR	*The Germanic Review*
GüsD	*Goethe über seine Dichtungen*, ed. Hans Gerhard Gräf (Frankfurt: Rütten & Loening, 1901–)
GY	*Goethe Yearbook*
JCK	Johann Christian Kestner
JCL	Johann Caspar Lavater
JFC	Johann Friedrich Cotta
JFR	Johann Friedrich Reichardt
JGH	Johann Gottfried Herder
JHM	Johann Heinrich Merck
JHMy	Johann Heinrich Meyer
JPE	Johann Peter Eckermann
JWG	Johann Wolfgang von Goethe
KAA	Immanuel Kant, *Gesammelte Schriften* ('Akademieausgabe') (Berlin: Reimer, 1900–).
MA	Goethe, *Sämtliche Werke nach Epochen seines Schaffens* ('Münchner Ausgabe'), ed. Karl Richter et al. (Munich: Hanser, 1985–1998)
MLR	*Modern Language Review*
NA	Friedrich Schiller, *Werke. Nationalausgabe*, ed. Julius Petersen et al. (Weimar: Böhlau, 1943–)
PCK	Philipp Christoph Kayser
PEGS	*Publications of the English Goethe Society*
PS	Goethe, *The Collected Works in Twelve Volumes*, ed. Victor Lange et al. (Princeton: Princeton UP, 1994–1995)

SB	Johann Sulpiz Melchior Dominikus Boisserée
SCW	Benedictus de Spinoza, *Collected Works*, ed. and trans. Edwin Curley (Princeton: Princeton UP, 2016)
SLR	Sophie von La Roche
WA	Goethe, *Goethes Werk im Auftrage der Großherzogin Sophie von Sachsen* ('Weimarer Ausgabe'), ed. Erich Schmidt et al. (Weimar: Böhlau, 1887–1919)
WH	Wilhelm von Humboldt
YW	Goethe, *The Sorrows of Young Werther*, trans. David Constantine (Oxford: OUP, 2012)

NOTES

Introduction

1. Wolff, *Lebensbeschreibung*, 28.
2. Wolff, *Lebensbeschreibung*, 28–29.
3. Israel, *Radical Enlightenment*, 200–202.
4. Wolff, *Lebensbeschreibung*, 16.
5. Wolff, *Briefe*, 21.
6. Details in Watkins, 'Pre-established Harmony'.
7. The material is collected in Abteilung III of Wolff, *Gesammelte Werke*.
8. Whaley, *Holy Roman Empire*, II, 338.
9. Hinrichs, *Pietismus*, 397–401.
10. Israel, *Enlightenment Contested*, 196.
11. Friedeburg, *Luther's Legacy*, 14 passim.
12. Friedeburg, *Luther's Legacy*, 62.
13. Wolff, *Deutsche Politik*, 195.
14. Wolff, *Deutsche Politik*, 196.
15. Wolff, *Deutsche Politik*, 190–91.
16. Whaley, *Holy Roman Empire*, II, 200.
17. Wolff, *Deutsche Politik*, 443.
18. Whaley, *Holy Roman Empire*, II, 198.
19. Israel, *Radical Enlightenment*, 434–35, 545–49.
20. Israel, *Enlightenment Contested*, 197.
21. Israel, *Enlightenment Contested*, 195.
22. Schneidereit, 'Angeborene Rechte', 161.
23. Schneidereit, 'Angeborene Rechte', 160.
24. Schneidereit, 'Angeborene Rechte', 160.
25. Schneidereit, 'Angeborene Rechte', 171.
26. Blank, 'Wolff'.
27. Blank, 'Wolff', 477.
28. Lessing, *Werke*, XI/1, 622.
29. Epstein, *Genesis*, 297–338; Mannheim, *Konservatismus*, 138–85.
30. Kondylis, *Konservativismus*, 348.
31. Beiser, *Historicist Tradition*, 80–81.
32. Beiser, *Historicist Tradition*, 94–96.

33. Kondylis, *Konservativismus*, 348.
34. On 'nature' in the Enlightenment, see Kondylis, *Aufklärung*, 348–53.
35. Wolff, 'Rokoko', 117.
36. Piirimäe, *Herder*, 63–96.
37. Blackall, *Emergence*, 26–48.
38. Herder, *Werke*, I, 103.
39. Bollacher, *Der junge Goethe*; Bell, *Spinoza*, 147–51.
40. Simpson, *Arnold*, 1.
41. Arnold, *Culture*, 5.
42. Cp. to CLK, 22/12/1830, WA IV, xlviii, 49; MA XVII, 801.
43. Arnold, *Culture*, 29.
44. Carnegie, *Autobiography*, 299.
45. Arnold, *Culture*, 32.
46. Arnold, *Essays*, 110.
47. Martin, 'Nietzsche's Goethe', 115.
48. Martin, 'Nietzsche's Goethe', 115.
49. Weber, *Max Weber*, 53.
50. Kent, 'Weber'; Sahni, 'Will to Act'.
51. Spengler, *Untergang*, 9.
52. Spengler, *Untergang*, 6.
53. Richards, *Conception*, 408.
54. Darwin, *Origin*, 1st ed., 147.
55. Darwin, *Origin*, 3rd ed., xiv.
56. Wulf, *Invention*, 29–38.
57. Huxley, 'Nature'.
58. Fullenwider, 'Goethean Fragment', 171.
59. Arber, 'Goethe's Botany'.
60. Arber, *Plant Form*.
61. Leiber, *Weltbild*, 453.
62. Bois-Reymond, 'Goethe und kein Ende'.
63. Henel, 'Type', 652.
64. For example, Varnhagen von Ense, *Wanderer*; Grün, *Über Goethe*; Gregorovius, *'Wilhelm Meister'*; Hettner, *Sozialismus*.
65. Adler, *Goethe*, 439.
66. Grimm, 'Goethe', 171.
67. Wilson, *Pakt*, passim.
68. Adler, *Goethe*, 449–50.
69. Estermann, 'Nachkriegszeit'.
70. Krippendorff, 'Politik', 867.
71. Most conveniently, Mommsen, *Anschauungen*; Rothe, *Goethe*.
72. Wilson, *Geheimräte*; *Gänge*; *Goethe-Tabu*.
73. Krippendorff, 'Politik', 867.
74. Mann, 'Repräsentant', 313; see also Krennbauer, *Staat*.
75. Krippendorff, *Goethe*.

Chapter 1. Hometown

1. Moritz, *Staatsverfassung*, 314.
2. Hüsgen, *Wegweiser*, 1.
3. Maisak and Dewitz, *Goethe-Haus*, 12.
4. Durchhardt, 'Frankfurt', 297.
5. Durchhardt, 'Frankfurt', 274.
6. Soliday, *Community*, 145–46.
7. Maisak and Dewitz, *Goethe-Haus*, 19.
8. Durchhardt, 'Frankfurt', 294–95.
9. Moore, *Formation*, 39–42.
10. Durchhardt, 'Frankfurt', 269.
11. Soliday, *Community*, 59.
12. Soliday, *Community*, 178.
13. Soliday, *Community*, 61.
14. Maisak and Dewitz, *Goethe-Haus*, 45.
15. To J. D. Salzmann, 28/11/1771, WA IV, ii, 8.
16. Soliday, *Community*, 72–73.
17. Conv. JPE, 27/9/1827, MA XIX, 582.
18. Soliday, *Community*, 89.
19. Hansert, *Geburtsaristokratie*, 434.
20. Soliday, *Community*, 5–6.
21. Soliday, *Community*, 106–11.
22. Eulner, 'Senckenbergs Tagebücher', 242.
23. Hopp, 'Goethe Pater', 8.
24. Maisak and Dewitz, *Goethe-Haus*, 14.
25. Hopp, 'Goethe Pater', 11–12.
26. Hopp, 'Goethe Pater', 19.
27. Hansert, 'Patriziat', 63.
28. Soliday, *Community*, 55.
29. Hopp, 'Goethe Pater', 23.
30. GLTT I, 17.
31. GLTT I, 19.
32. GLTT I, 20.
33. GBuG I, 16.
34. Maisak and Dewitz, *Goethe-Haus*, 76.
35. Maisak and Dewitz, *Goethe-Haus*, 29.
36. Maisak and Dewitz, *Goethe-Haus*, 24.
37. Perels, 'Bey Herrn Rath Göthe', 88–101.
38. Maisak, 'Sammlungen', 76.
39. MA XVI, 127.
40. Maisak, 'Sammlungen', 17.
41. Maisak and Dewitz, *Goethe-Haus*, 67.
42. Klippel, *Englischlernen*, 51.

43. GLTT I, 93.
44. MA XVI, 181.
45. Agrippa, *De incertitudine*.
46. Engelhardt, *Weltansichten*, 6–7.
47. MA XVI, 837.
48. MA XVI, 156–57.
49. MA XVI, 155.
50. Maisak and Dewitz, *Goethe-Haus*, 62.
51. Durchhardt, 'Frankfurt', 282.
52. MA XVI, 111.
53. Maisak and Dewitz, *Goethe-Haus*, 54.
54. Maisak and Dewitz, *Goethe-Haus*, 97.
55. Maisak and Dewitz, *Goethe-Haus*, 98.
56. Maisak and Dewitz, *Goethe-Haus*, 98.
57. Engelhardt, *Weltansichten*, 7.
58. Engelhardt, *Weltansichten*, 8.
59. Pätzold, *Spinoza*, 19; Arnold, *Kirchen- und Ketzerhistorie*, II, 585.
60. Brucker, *Institutiones*, 676.
61. Bollacher, *Der junge Goethe*.
62. Engelhardt, *Weltansichten*, 11.

Chapter 2. 'I'm Not a Christian'

1. GLTT I, 171.
2. Biedermann, *Goethe und Leipzig*, I, 16–17.
3. To CG, 6/12/1765, WA IV, i, 22.
4. MA XVI, 296–97.
5. MA XVI, 370.
6. To J. J. Riese, 6/11/1765, WA IV, i, 18.
7. GLTT I, 217.
8. To CG, 6/12/1765, WA IV, i, 19–20.
9. GLTT I, 172.
10. GLTT I, 205.
11. To CG, 18/10/1766, WA IV, i, 81.
12. MA XVI, 370.
13. To C. G. Schönkopf, 1/10/1768, WA IV, i, 165.
14. To CG, 6/12/1765, WA IV, i, 24.
15. To CG, 11/5/ 1767, WA IV, i, 86.
16. To J. J. Riese, 30/10/1765, WA IV, i, 16–17; to CG, 7/12/1765, WA IV, i, 24–25.
17. Biedermann, *Goethe und Leipzig*, I, 118–19.
18. To CG, 12/10/1767, WA IV, i, 115.
19. To CG, 12/10/1767, WA IV, i, 112.
20. To E. W. Behrisch, 24/10/1767, WA IV, i, 123; Powers, 'The Creation of Experience', 11.
21. MA I/2, 97.

22. To CG, 30/3/1766, WA IV, i, 47.
23. To J. J. Riese, 28/4/1766, WA IV, i, 44–46.
24. See, e.g., Young, *Night-Thoughts*, 13.
25. To CG, 11/5/1767, WA IV, i, 94.
26. To CG, 11/5/1767, WA IV, i, 88.
27. To CG, 11/5/1767, WA IV, i, 88.
28. To CG, 12/12/1765, WA IV, i, 30.
29. To A. F. Oeser, 9/11/1768, WA IV, i, 178.
30. For the following account, see Young, 'Introduction', in: Batteux, *Fine Arts*, xviii–xxiii.
31. Batteux, *Fine Arts*, 4.
32. To ETL, 10/1769, WA IV, li, 37.
33. Robertson, *Enlightenment*, 468.
34. MA XVI, 358.
35. To ETL, 24/11/1768, WA IV, i, 33–34.
36. Engelhardt, *Weltansichten*, 16–17.
37. GLTT I, 246–47.
38. To CG, 12/10/1767, WA IV, i, 110.
39. To J. J. Riese, 28/4/1766, WA IV, i, 44–46; to CG, 11/5/1766, WA IV, i, 50–52; to CG, 12/10/1767, WA IV, i, 116–17; to E. W. Behrisch, 2/11/1767, WA IV, i, 127.
40. To E. W. Behrisch, 5/1768, WA IV, i, 160.
41. To J. C. Limprecht, 13–19/4/1770, WA IV, i, 233.
42. MA XVI, 358.
43. MA XVI, 358.
44. MA XVI, 361.
45. To ETL, 24/11/1768, WA IV, li, 33.
46. MA XVI, 375–76.
47. To F. Oeser, 13/2/1769, WA IV, i, 197. See also to A. K. Schönkopf, 23/1/1770, WA IV, i, 225.
48. To A. K. Schönkopf, 30/12/1768, WA IV, i, 183.
49. To A. K. Schönkopf, 31/1/ 1769, WA IV, i, 186.
50. Müller, '*Die Mitschuldigen*', 12.
51. MA I/1, 339.
52. Müller, '*Die Mitschuldigen*', 15.
53. MA XVI, 309.
54. MA XVI, 983.
55. GLTT I, 305; MA XVI, 367.
56. To A. K. Schönkopf, 30/12/1768, WA IV, i, 183.
57. To ETL, 17/1/1769, WA IV, li, 35.
58. GLTT I, 306.
59. MA XVI, 364.
60. To ETL, 17/1/1769, WA IV, li, 36.
61. Daniel 14:36.
62. To ETL, 17/1/1769, WA IV, li, 36.
63. MA XVI, 675.
64. GLTT I, 326.

65. MA XVI, 676.
66. MA XVI, 376.
67. MA XVI, 366; Engelhardt, *Weltansichten*, 29.
68. MA XVI, 367–68.
69. MA XVI, 379–81.
70. Engelhardt, *Weltansichten*, 36–37.
71. Engelhardt, *Weltansichten*, 37.
72. To ETL, 30/11/1769, WA IV, li, 39.
73. MA I/2, 525.
74. Hamann, 'Aesthetica', 2; *Sämtliche Werke*, II, 197.
75. To F. Oeser, 13/2/1769, WA IV, i, 198.
76. Herder, *Sämmtliche Werke*, III, 424.
77. To C. G. Hermann, 6/2/1770, WA IV, i, 227–28.
78. Bell, 'Fragmentariness', 382–83.
79. GLTT I, 343–44.
80. To P. E. Reich, 20/2/1770, WA IV, i, 230.
81. To P. E. Reich, 20/2/1770, WA IV, i, 229.
82. To P. E. Reich, 20/2/1770, WA IV, i, 230.
83. To A. F. Oeser, 14/2/1769, WA IV, i, 205.
84. MA XVI, 376.
85. To A. K. Schönkopf, 12/12/1769, WA IV, I, 219.
86. MA XVI, 363.
87. MA I/2, 522.
88. MA I/2, 519.
89. MA I/2, 521; Voltaire, *Œuvres*, LXX/A, 243.
90. Voltaire, *Œuvres*, LXX/A, 229.
91. MA I/2, 519.
92. Voltaire, *Œuvres*, LXX/A, 241.
93. MA I/2, 526.
94. Bollacher, *Der junge Goethe*, 21.
95. Bollacher, *Der junge Goethe*, 20.
96. MA I/2, 530.
97. To J. C. Limprecht, 13–19/4/1770, WA IV, i, 234.
98. MA XVI, 417.
99. MA XVI, 510.
100. MA XVI, 845.
101. To ETL, 29/4/1770, WA IV, li, 42.
102. To S. von Klettenberg, 26/8/1770, WA IV, i, 247.
103. To ETL, 11/5/1770, WA IV, li, 43.
104. MA XVI, 390.
105. MA XVI, 404–5.
106. MA XVI, 485.
107. To S. von Klettenberg, 26/8/1770, WA IV, i, 245.
108. GLTT I, 433; GBuG I, 178.

109. MA XVI, 433–34; to JGH, spring/summer 1771, WA IV, i, 258; GBuG I, 171.
110. MA I/2, 537.
111. MA XVI, 437.
112. MA XVI, 444–45.
113. Engelhardt, *Weltansichten*, 53.
114. GLTT I, 431.
115. GBuG I, 258.
116. O'Flaherty, *Unity*, 12–37.
117. O'Flaherty, *Unity*, 28.
118. Hamann, 'Aesthetica', 2; *Sämtliche Werke*, II, 197.
119. MA I/1, 184.
120. GüsD II/1, 74.
121. MA X, 564.
122. To F. Brion, 15/10/1770, WA IV, i, 251–54.
123. MA XVI, 503.
124. GLTT I, 416.
125. MA XVI, 532.
126. MA I/1, 830.
127. MA I/2, 902.
128. MA XVI, 506.
129. SCW II, 338.
130. GBuG I, 182.
131. MA XVI, 505–8.
132. MA I/2, 555.
133. MA I/2, 555; see Wilson, 'Fantasies', 196.
134. SCW II, 329–30.
135. SCW II, 351.
136. GBuG I, 182.

Chapter 3. 'Moses! Prophet! Evangelist! Apostle, Spinoza or Machiavelli'

1. To SLR, 22/12/1774, WA IV, ii, 218; Rousseau, *Émile*, 111; *Oeuvres* IV, 153.
2. Rosenblatt, *Rousseau*, 271.
3. SCW II, 70–72.
4. To J. D. Salzmann, 28/11/1771, WA IV, ii, 8.
5. MA XVI, 539.
6. GBuG I, 200.
7. MA XVI, 604.
8. To J. D. Salzmann, 3/2/1772, WA IV, ii, 14.
9. Neuhaus, 'Götz', 82. According to *Poetry and Truth*, Herder's verdict was negative (MA XVI, 604–5); however, the contemporary evidence does not support this later view: to JGH, 10[?]/7/1772, WA IV, ii, 19.
10. Neuhaus, 'Götz', 85.

11. Neuhaus, 'Götz', 78.
12. To JCK, mid–7/1773, WA IV, ii, 98.
13. MA XVI, 606–7.
14. To JCK, 21/8/1773, WA IV, ii, 100.
15. MA I/1, 959.
16. MA I/1, 917.
17. Meyer-Benfey, Götz, 120.
18. Herder, Writings, 310.
19. MA I/1, 918.
20. Herder, Writings, 276–80.
21. Herder, Writings, 310.
22. Neuhaus, 'Götz', 78–79.
23. Ziolkowski, Mirror, 191.
24. Weber, Protestant Ethic, 164.
25. Rousseau, Social Contract, 113; Oeuvres I, 299.
26. MA I/1, 412 (1771), 573 (1773).
27. Bloom, 'Introduction', 7.
28. Rousseau, Émile, 67; Oeuvres IV, 65.
29. Bennett, 'Three Versions', 337.
30. MA I/1, 403 (1771).
31. MA I/1, 416 (1771); 576 (1773).
32. MA I/1, 424 (1771); 584 (1773).
33. MA I/2, 413.
34. MA I/1, 458 (1771); 615 (1773).
35. MA I/1, 486 (1771).
36. MA I/1, 919.
37. MA I/1, 634–35 (1773).
38. MA I/1, 416 (1771); 576 (1773).
39. MA I/1, 496 (1771).
40. MA I/1, 509 (1771); 653 (1773).
41. Young, 'Introduction', xxxiii.
42. MA I/2, 342.
43. MA I/2, 363.
44. MA I/2, 397.
45. MA I/2, 400.
46. MA I/2, 841.
47. The figure of approximately eighty is based on MA I/2, 309–410.
48. MA XVI, 524.
49. MA I/2, 418.
50. MA I/2, 418–19.
51. MA I/2, 419–20.
52. Robson-Scott, Younger Goethe, 41.
53. EG, 871; MA I/2, 421.
54. MA I/2, 498.

55. MA I/2, 499.
56. MA I/2, 380–81.
57. Rousseau, *Discourses*, 8.
58. MA I/2, 412.
59. MA I/2, 358.
60. MA I/2, 833.
61. MA I/2, 399.
62. Young, 'Introduction', xx–xxi.
63. MA I/2, 414.
64. To JGH, autumn 1771, WA IV, ii, 3–5.
65. To JGH, 9/1771, WA IV, ii, 1–2.
66. To JGH, 10/7/1772, WA IV, ii, 16.
67. To JGH, 10/7/1772, WA IV, ii, 17.
68. GBuG I, 220.
69. Sauder, 'Wetzlar', 1150.
70. MA XVI, 567.
71. Sauder, 'Wetzlar', 1151.
72. GBuG I, 218.
73. GBuG I, 201.
74. GBuG I, 200.
75. GBuG I, 199.
76. GBuG I, 214–15.
77. GBuG I, 201.
78. GBuG I, 216–17.
79. GBuG I, 203.
80. GBuG I, 203.
81. MA XVI, 592.
82. GBuG I, 215.
83. Lange, 'Pentateuch', 106.
84. MA I/2, 431.
85. SCW II, 191.
86. MA I/2, 427.
87. MA I/2, 428.
88. MA I/2, 435–36.
89. MA I/2, 437.
90. MA I/2, 438–39.
91. SCW II, 146.
92. MA XVI, 671.
93. MA I/1, 517.
94. To JCL, 23–26/11/1773, GB II/1, 55.
95. To B. Jacobi, 2/1774, WA IV, ii, 145.
96. To J. C. Pfenninger, 26/4/1774, WA IV, ii, 156.
97. To SLR, 6/1774, WA IV, ii, 164.
98. MA I/1, 983.

99. MA I/1, 674.
100. Rousseau, Discourses, 164; Oeuvres I, 92.
101. MA I/1, 677.
102. MA I/1, 987.
103. Rousseau, *Discourses*, 142; *Oeuvres* I, 60.
104. MA I/1, 229–30.
105. MA I/1, 230–31.
106. SCW I, 550.
107. MA XVI, 667.
108. GBuG I, 373.
109. GBuG I, 373.
110. MA I/2, 747.
111. MA I/2, 748.
112. Gaskill, 'Ossian', 105.
113. To JGH, 10[?]/7/1772, WA IV, ii, 19.
114. MA I/2, 740.
115. MA I/2, 134.
116. MA I/2, 742.
117. See Graubner, 'Empiricism'; O'Flaherty, *'Memorabilia'*, 41–42.
118. MA I/2, 135.
119. MA I/2, 138.
120. Surveys in Mason, 'Erdgeist'; Keller, *'Urfaust'*.
121. Bollacher, *Der junge Goethe*, 181.
122. MA I/2, 138.
123. Diels, *Vorsokratiker*, 54.
124. MA I/2, 140.
125. Williams, *'Faust'*, 18.
126. To JGH, 12[?]/5/1775, WA IV, ii, 262.
127. Scherer, *Aufsätze*; Roethe, 'Entstehung'.
128. Boyle, 'Ahnungsloser Engel'.
129. MA I/2, 155.
130. Graham, *Portrait*, 319.
131. MA I/2, 157.
132. MA I/2, 169–70.
133. MA I/2, 173–74.
134. MA I/2, 173.
135. MA I/2, 177.
136. MA I/2, 178.
137. Williams, *'Faust'*, 119.
138. To SLR, 12/5/1773, WA IV, ii, 88; to J. Fahlmer, 18/10/1773, WA IV, ii, 110.
139. Durchhardt, 'Frankfurt', 284.
140. Durchhardt, 'Frankfurt', 289.
141. GBuG I, 240, 256; see also MA XVI, 629.
142. To JCK, 25/12/1773, WA IV, ii, 135–36.

143. GBuG I, 291.
144. YW 5; MA I/2, 197.
145. MA XVI, 621.
146. To SLR, 20[?]/11/1772, WA IV, ii, 40.
147. SCW I, 550.
148. YW 77; MA I/2, 268.
149. YW 105; MA I/2, 293.
150. YW 110; MA I/2, 297.
151. Wittmann, *Buchhandel*, 148–49.
152. Examples include Lukács, 'Werther'; Hirsch, 'Schicksal'; Scherpe, 'Werther'; Assling, *Leiden*.
153. Bell, 'Class'.
154. YW 9–10; MA I/2, 202.
155. Rousseau, *Oeuvres*, I, 92.
156. YW 20; MA I/2, 212.
157. Richardson, *Clarissa*, I, viii.
158. MA I/2, 779.
159. Jerusalem, *Aufsätze*, 17.
160. YW 16; MA I/2, 208.
161. Hume, *Treatise*, 415.
162. MA I/2, 194.
163. SCW I, 417.
164. YW 34; MA I/2, 227.
165. Gaskill, 'Wahlheim'.
166. YW 25; MA I/2, 217.
167. YW 44; MA I/2, 238.
168. YW 45–46; MA I/2, 239–40.
169. Anon., Review of *Die Leiden des jungen Werthers*, 4.
170. Mestas, 'Werther Effect', 1280.
171. YW 112; MA I/2, 299.
172. To JCK, 11/1772, WA IV, ii, 33–34.
173. WA I, XXXVII, 255–56.
174. To JGH, 12[?]/5/1775, WA IV, ii, 262.
175. GBuG I, 353–54.
176. MA I/2, 786.
177. GBuG I, 292.
178. To A. von Stolberg, 7–10/3/1775, WA IV, II, 242.
179. To SLR, 23/12/1774, WA IV, ii, 218.
180. MA XVI, 714.
181. MA XVI, 715.
182. GBuG I, 263–64.
183. To JCK, 15/9/1773, WA IV, ii, 106.
184. FA I, iv, 927–28.
185. MA XVI, 556.

186. To G.F.E. Schönborn, 1/6–4/7/1774, WA IV, ii, 171–72.
187. MA XVI, 706.
188. Wilson, 'Fantasies', 197–203.
189. MA I/2, 712–13.
190. See MA I/1, 327; MA XVI, 750.
191. MA I/2, 67.
192. MA I/2, 43–44.
193. MA I/2, 52.
194. MA I/2, 53–54.
195. MA I/2, 55.
196. MA I/2, 57.
197. MA I/2, 60–62.
198. MA I/2, 63.
199. MA I/2, 64.
200. MA I/2, 65.
201. MA I/2, 68.
202. MA I/2, 43, 46, 48, 56.
203. MA I/2, 71.
204. MA I/2, 77.
205. MA I/2, 77.
206. MA I/2, 226.
207. See also FA I, iv, 983.
208. To JHM, 7/10/1775, WA IV, ii, 299; to SLR, 11/10/1775, WA IV, ii, 299.

Chapter 4. The Intellectual Love of God

1. Wilson, *Goethe-Tabu*, 141.
2. To JHM, 22/1/1776, WA IV, iii, 21.
3. To JCL, 6/3/1776, WA IV, iii, 37.
4. GBuG II, 35.
5. GBuG I, 410.
6. Voß, *Freundin*, 18.
7. To JHM, 22/1/1776, WA IV, iii, 21.
8. On the dating, see Arntzen, 'An den Mond', 180–81.
9. MA II/1, 34.
10. To C. E. Goethe, J. Fahlmer, and J. C. Bölling, 6/11/1776, WA IV, iii, 118; to CS, 2/12/1776, WA IV, iii, 125–26.
11. To A. L. Karsch, 11/9/1776, WA IV, iii, 104.
12. For an alternative view of Goethe's political experiment, see Krippendorff, *Die Großen* and *Goethe*.
13. GBuG I, 440.
14. GBuG I, 439.
15. GBuG I, 480.
16. GBuG I, 478.

17. GBuG III, 57.
18. For example, diary, 7/10/1777, WA III, i, 51.
19. MA II/1, 11.
20. GBuG III, 42.
21. MA II/2, 934.
22. Rothe, *Goethe*, 15–16.
23. GBuG III, 44.
24. MA II/2, 932.
25. Rothe, *Goethe*, 19.
26. Wilson, *Goethe-Tabu*, 83–4.
27. Wilson, *Goethe-Tabu*, 80.
28. To CS, 5/4/1782, WA IV, v, 296.
29. Wilson, *Goethe-Tabu*, 95–6.
30. Wilson, *Goethe-Tabu*, 78–9.
31. Diary, 25/7/1779, WA III, I, 91–92.
32. To CS, 9/7/1786, WA IV, vii, 241–42.
33. To C. E. Goethe, J. Fahlmer, and J. C. Bölling, 6/11/1776, WA IV, iii, 118.
34. Diary, 16/6/1777, WA III, I, 40.
35. Diary, 7/12/1777, WA III, i, 56.
36. Diary, 18/1/1778, WA III, i, 61.
37. To CS, 19/1/1778, WA IV, iii, 208.
38. MA II/1, 42.
39. GBuG I, 425.
40. GBuG I, 391.
41. MA II/1, 25.
42. SCW I, 550.
43. To JCL, 8/1/1777, WA IV, iii, 131.
44. For example, Schings, 'Religion/Religiosität'; Nisbet, 'Religion and Philosophy', 219–22.
45. MA II/1, 137.
46. MA II/1, 139.
47. MA II/1, 139, 142.
48. MA II/1, 147.
49. MA II/1, 148.
50. MA II/1, 161–64.
51. On the repetitions, see Goebel, 'Chewing'.
52. MA II/1, 164.
53. MA II/1, 168.
54. MA II/1, 169.
55. MA II/1, 178.
56. MA II/1, 184.
57. For examples, see Hall, *Adventures*, passim; Torrance, 'Religion', 179–80.
58. Reed, '*Iphigenie*'; for a negative view, see Hall, *Adventures*, 211–13.
59. To CS, 6/3/1779, WA IV, iv, 18.

60. Reed, 'Iphigenie', 198.
61. Busch-Salmen, 'Theaterpraxis', 17.
62. GBuG II, 115.
63. GBuG II, 116.
64. Diary, 6/4/1779, WA III, i, 84.
65. To CS, 4/3/1779, WA IV, iv, 15–16.
66. To JCL, 13/10/1780, WA IV, iv, 318.
67. GBuG II, 255.
68. GBuG II, 235.
69. MA XV, 186.
70. Unseld, *Verleger*, 127–28.
71. MA III/1, 161.
72. Boyle, *Poet and the Age*, I, 447–52.
73. Reed, 'Iphigenie', 195.
74. Trevelyan, *Greeks*, xvi; Seidlin, *Essays*, 35.
75. Torrance, 'Religion', 181.
76. MA III/1, 180.
77. Reed, 'Iphigenie', 203.
78. MA III/1, 214.
79. MA III/1, 216.
80. MA III/1, 165.
81. Reed, 'Iphigenie', 211.
82. MA III/1, 169.
83. Lange, 'Isaac'.
84. Torrance, 'Religion', 181.
85. MA III/1, 175.
86. MA III/1, 174.
87. MA III/1, 181.
88. MA III/1, 173.
89. Torrance, 'Religion', 182.
90. MA III/1, 162.
91. MA III/1, 211.
92. MA III/1, 182.
93. MA III/1, 212.
94. MA III/1, 205–6.
95. MA III/1, 211.
96. MA III/1, 161.
97. MA III/1, 207.
98. MA III/1, 215.
99. For a very different (and Christian) reading of Iphigeneia's purity, see Torrance, 'Religion', 186.
100. MA III/1, 212.
101. MA III/1, 214.
102. MA I/1, 674.

103. MA I/2, 136.
104. MA III/1, 207.
105. MA III/1, 213.
106. MA III/1, 213.
107. MA III/1, 220.
108. MA III/1, 221.
109. To CS, 7/9/1779, WA IV, iv, 58–59.
110. To CS, 20/9/1779, WA IV, iv, 61.
111. To CS, 25/9/1779, WA IV, iv, 66–67.
112. To JCL, 2/11/1779, WA IV, iv, 114–15.
113. To CS, 13/11/1779, WA IV, iv, 120.
114. To CLK, 30/11/1779, WA IV, iv, 148.
115. To JCL, 28/10/1779, WA IV, iv, 111–12. See also to JCL, 7/2/1780, WA IV, iv, 172.
116. To CS, 24/11/1779, WA IV, iv, 140.
117. To CS, 6/4/1782, WA IV, v, 300–301.
118. To CS, 3/10/1779, WA IV, iv, 70.
119. To CS, 3/10/1779, WA IV, iv, 70.
120. GBuG II, 232.
121. See the account in Wagenbreth, 'Bergbau'.
122. Diary, 10/8/1776, WA III, i, 19.
123. Engelhardt, *Gespräch*, 17–26; diary, 8/12/1777, WA III, i, 56.
124. MA II/1, 41.
125. GLTT II, 429.
126. To CLK, 24/4/1784, WA IV, vi, 269.
127. GLTT II, 515.
128. Conv. FM, 16/3/1824, WA V, v, 50–1.
129. To JHM, 7/4/1780, WA IV, iv, 202.
130. Buffon, *Époques*, 69.
131. To JHM, 27/10/1782, WA IV, vi, 76.
132. To JHM, 11/10/1780, WA IV, iv, 311.
133. To CS, 7/12/1781, WA IV, iv, 232.
134. To SLR, 1/9/1780, WA IV, iv, 278.
135. To JHM, 3/7/1780, WA IV, iv, 247; 11/10/1780, WA IV, iv, 310–12; MA II/2, 483–84.
136. To JHM, 11/10/1780, WA IV, iv, 310.
137. To JHM, 11/10/1780, WA IV, iv, 311.
138. To E. von Saxe-Gotha-Altenburg, 27/12/1780, WA IV, v, 24–25.
139. To JHM, 14/11/1781, WA IV, v, 221.
140. To JHM, 11/10/1780, WA IV, iv, 311.
141. MA XVI, 786.
142. MA II/2, 490–502, 515–24.
143. To CS, 6/9/1780, WA IV, iv, 281–82. On the dating, see MA II/2, 579.
144. MA II/1, 53.
145. To CS, 10/5/1782, WA IV, v, 324–25.
146. To CS, 20/9/1783, WA IV, vi, 199.

147. Engelhardt, *Weltansichten*, 140.
148. MA II/2, 489.
149. MA II/2, 490.
150. MA XIII/2, 238.
151. To JGH and CH, 20/6/1784, WA IV, vi, 308.
152. MA II/2, 511.
153. MA II/2, 509.
154. MA II/2, 512.
155. To JHM, 27/10/1782 11/1782, WA IV, vi, 76–77, 82–83.
156. Engelhardt, *Gespräch*, 91.
157. To CLK, 8/12/1783, WA IV, vi, 224.
158. PS XII, 69; MA XII, 20.
159. GBuG III, 55.
160. GBuG II, 453.
161. To JCL, 14/11/1781, WA IV, v, 217.
162. Diary, 3/5/1782, WA III, i, 140.
163. GBuG II, 413.
164. Zammito, *Gestation*, 196.
165. To JGH, 27/3/1784, WA IV, vi, 258.
166. To CS, 7/6/1784, WA IV, vi, 291.
167. MA II, 2, 910–11.
168. To CLK, 17/11/1784, WA IV, vi, 389–91.
169. To JHM, 19/12/1784, WA IV, vi, 410.
170. To JHM, 8/4/1785, WA IV, vii, 41.
171. To E. von Sachsen-Gotha, 27/12/1780, WA IV, v, 24.
172. Richards, *Conception*, 372–74.
173. To FHJ, 12/1/1785, WA IV, vii, 8.
174. Engelhardt, *Weltansichten*, 141–42.
175. MA II/2, 562.
176. MA II/2, 562–63.
177. MA II/2, 563–80.
178. PS XII, 65 (adapted); MA XII, 15–16.
179. To CS, 1/4/1785, WA IV, vii, 35.
180. GBuG II, 518.
181. To CS, 8/11/1785, WA IV, vii, 117.
182. To CLK, 18/11/1785, WA IV, vii, 126.
183. To FHJ, 14/4/1786, WA IV, vii, 205.
184. GBuG II, 220–22.
185. GBuG II, 318.
186. To JCK, 14/5/1780, WA IV, iv, 220–21.
187. Diary, 13/5/1780, WA III, i, 118. On Spinozist resignation in Goethe's thought, see Prandi, *Happy*, 23–28; Bell, *Spinoza*, 167–68.
188. To CS, 2/4/1781, WA IV, v, 104; also to CS, 31/3/1781, WA IV, v, 101.
189. To CLK, 21/11/1782, WA IV, vi, 98.

190. To CS, 12/11/1781, WA IV, v, 213.
191. To CS, 20/3/1782, WA IV, v, 285.
192. To CS, 23/1/1785, WA IV, vii, 162.
193. MA XVI, 815.
194. Bell, *Egmont*, 151–52.
195. Reiss, 'Möser', 163.
196. EG 89; MA III/1, 307.
197. EG 88; MA III/1, 306.
198. EG 61; MA III/1, 271.
199. Bell, *Egmont*, 141–44.
200. See MA III/1, 825.
201. EG 90; MA III/1, 307–8.
202. Reiss, 'Möser', 174.
203. EG 50; MA III/1, 257.
204. *Julius Caesar*, I, ii, in: Shakespeare, *Arden*, 200–201.
205. Ellis, 'Question', 124.
206. EG 76; MA III/1, 290–91.
207. MA I/2, 380–81.
208. EG 77–78; MA III/1, 292.
209. Herder, *Writings*, 316; *Werke*, IV, 61.
210. EG 106; MA III/1, 329.
211. Hobson, 'Oranien', 269.
212. Quoted in MA III/I, 844.
213. Quoted in MA III/1, 848.
214. EG 87; MA III/1, 303.
215. EG 106; MA III/1, 329.
216. To W. H. von Dalberg, 2/3/1780, WA IV, iv, 187.
217. MA II/1, 312–37.
218. To JHM, 16/7/1782, WA IV, vi, 8.
219. GBuG II, 375.
220. To CS, 25/10/1780, WA IV, iv, 323.
221. Umbach, *Federalism*, 163; Sengle, *Genie*, 65.
222. GBuG II, 378–79.
223. To CLK, 27/7/1782, WA IV, vi, 16.
224. BGG III, 97.
225. To CA, 26/12/1784, WA IV, vi, 415–16.
226. To CA, 26/11/1784, WA IV, vi, 396.
227. Thordarson and Self, 'Laki', 16.
228. MA XIV, 14.
229. To PCK, 14/8/1787, WA IV, viii, 244–46.
230. Wilson, *Gänge*, 14–15.
231. To J. F. von Fritsch, 13/2/1780, WA IV, iv, 175.
232. Wilson, *Gänge*, 71–96.
233. Wilson, *Gänge*, 110.

234. To PCK, 15/3/1783, WA IV, vi, 137.
235. Wilson, *Gänge*, 98–99.
236. To JCL, 22/6/1781, WA IV, v, 149.
237. GBuG III, 53.
238. Wilson, 'Infanticide', 19.
239. Wilson, 'Infanticide', 25–26.
240. Wilson, 'Infanticide', 25.
241. Scholz, 'Regierungstätigkeit'.
242. MA XVI, 839.
243. MA II/2, 25.
244. MA II/2, 28.
245. Rousseau, *Emil*, II, 235–36.
246. MA II/2, 46.
247. MA II/2, 63.
248. MA II/2, 64.
249. MA II/2, 66.
250. MA II/2, 101.
251. To CS, 9/5/1782, WA IV, v, 323.
252. Rousseau, *Politics*, 306; Rousseau, *Oeuvres*, VI, 519.
253. Rousseau, *Politics*, 309; Rousseau, *Oeuvres*, VI, 524.
254. Rousseau, *Politics*, 310; Rousseau, *Oeuvres*, VI, 526.
255. MA II/2, 145.
256. MA II/2, 150–51.
257. MA II/2, 168.
258. MA II/2, 223.
259. MA II/2, 295.
260. MA II/2, 330.
261. MA II/2, 263.
262. To CS, 11/11/1785, WA IV, vii, 120.
263. To CS, 9/12/1785, WA IV, vii, 139.
264. To CS, 12/12/1785, WA IV, vii, 139.
265. To CS, 13/3/1786, 21/5/1786, 23/5/1786, WA IV, vii, 192, 220, 221.
266. MA III/1, 77.
267. To CS, 20/1/1787, WA IV, viii, 143.
268. To CA, 10/2/1787, WA IV, viii, 179.
269. MA XV, 447.
270. GBuG II, 491.
271. GBuG II, 504–5.
272. To FHJ, 9/6/1785, WA IV, vii, 63.
273. Israel, *Enlightenment Contested*, 188–93.
274. To FHJ, 9/6/1785, WA IV, vii, 62–63.
275. To FHJ, 21/10/1785, WA IV, vii, 110.
276. Suphan, 'Spinoza-Studien', 3–12.
277. Lange, 'Spinoza', 18–20.

278. Costazza, 'Aufsatz'; Engelhardt, *Weltansichten*, 164–66.
279. Lange, 'Spinoza', 20–23.
280. Jacobi, *Lehre*, 2–5; *Werke*, I/1, 2–4.
281. MA II/1, 90–91.
282. Lange, 'Isaac', 168–69.
283. Lange, 'Isaac', 169.
284. MA II/2, 597.
285. Jacobi, *Werke*, I/1, 120.
286. To CS, 11/9/1785, WA IV, vii, 95.
287. To FHJ, 26/9/1785, WA IV, vii, 101.
288. To FHJ, 21/10/1785, WA IV, vii, 110.
289. SCW I, 445.
290. To FHJ, 5/5/1786, WA IV, vii, 214.
291. GBuG II, 271, 275, 276.
292. GBuG II, 438, 441.
293. GBuG II, 519, 525.
294. GBuG III, 18–19.
295. To P. F. Seidel, 23/7/1786, WA IV, vii, 252–53.
296. To CA, 24/7/1786, WA IV, vii, 253–54.

Chapter 5. 'In Conversation with Things'

1. Diary, 3/9/1786, WA III, i, 147.
2. Conv. JPE, 10/2/1829, MA XIX, 282.
3. To CA, 2/9/1786, WA IV, viii, 11–12.
4. To CS, 23/8/1786, WA IV, viii, 7; to CS, 1/9/1786, WA IV, viii, 11; to CLK, 13/8/1786, WA IV, viii, 1.
5. To CLK, 13/8/1786, WA IV, viii, 1.
6. Diary, 5/9/1786, WA III, i, 151–52.
7. Diary, 5/9/1786, WA III, i, 154; 8/9/1786, WA III, i, 161.
8. To CS, 18/9/1786, WA IV, viii, 23–24; to JGH and CH, 18/9/1786, WA IV, viii, 24–25.
9. To P. F. Seidel, 18/9/1786, WA IV, viii, 29.
10. Diary, 29/9/1786, WA III, i, 241.
11. Diary, 1/10/1786, WA III, i, 253.
12. Diary, 18/10/1786, WA III, i, 303.
13. To CA, 3/11/1786, WA IV, viii, 40.
14. GLTT II, 569.
15. To CS, 14/12/1786, WA IV, viii, 94.
16. GLTT II, 570.
17. MA XV, 257.
18. MA XV, 278.
19. MA XV, 314–25.
20. MA IV/2, 460.
21. Bode, *Rom*, 100; Zapperi, *Inkognito*, 201–38; survey in Jost, *Deutsche Klassik*, 19–28.

22. GLTT II, 661.
23. Baioni, 'Gesellschaftsidee', 74–75.
24. To Weimar friends, 1/11/1786, WA IV, viii, 38.
25. Diary, 11/9/1786, WA III, i, 177.
26. To Weimar friends, 1/11/1786, WA IV, viii, 37–38.
27. To C. E. Goethe, 4/11/1786, WA IV, viii, 43.
28. To JGH and CH, 2–9/12/1786, WA IV, viii, 76–77; to JGH and CH, 18/9/1786, WA IV, viii, 25; to JGH and CH, 13/12/1786, WA IV, viii, 90.
29. To JGH and CH, 10–11/11/1786, WA IV, viii, 50–51; see also to JCK, 10/11/1788, WA IV, ix, 53; MA XV, 158.
30. Diary, 11/9/1786, WA III, i, 176.
31. Diary, 21/9/1786, WA III, i, 220.
32. Goethe, *Flight*, 73; diary, 5/10/1786, WA III, i, 266.
33. Diary, 3/9/1786, WA III, i, 150.
34. To CS, 24/11/1786, WA IV, viii, 66.
35. Diary, 17/9/1786, WA III, i, 206.
36. To JGH and CH, 10[–11]/11/1786, WA IV, viii, 50–51.
37. To CA, 27[–29]/5/1787, WA IV, viii, 225.
38. To CA, 17[–18]/3/1788, WA IV, viii, 357.
39. GLTT II, 671.
40. MA XV, 368.
41. To CA, 12[–16]/12/1786, WA IV, viii, 83.
42. Diary, 9/9/1786, WA III, i, 165–66.
43. Diary, 9/9/1786, WA III, i, 162–65.
44. Diary, 9/9/1786, WA III, i, 165.
45. Diary, 9/9/1786, WA III, i, 166–68.
46. Diary, 9/9/1786, WA III, i, 272–73.
47. MA XVIII/2, 452.
48. To CLK, 3/10/1787, WA IV, viii, 268.
49. To CLK, 18/8/1787, WA IV, viii, 251.
50. MA XV, 277.
51. MA XV, 299.
52. MA XV, 327.
53. To CS, 9/6/1787, WA IV, viii, 232–33.
54. To CS, 9/6/1787, WA IV, viii, 232–33.
55. Jacobi, *Werke*, I, 16.
56. To CLK, 18/8/1787, WA IV, viii, 251.
57. MA III/1, 580–81.
58. Herder, *Werke*, VI, 67.
59. Diary, 19/10/1786, WA III, i, 310.
60. Diary, 26/10/1786, WA III, i, 323.
61. To CS, 23/12/1786, WA IV, viii, 101.
62. To CS, 29/12/1786, WA IV, viii, 105.
63. To Weimar friends, 13/1/1787, WA IV, viii, 130–31.

64. To CA, [13–20]/1/1787, WA IV, viii, 137.
65. Diary, 5/10/1786, WA III, i, 267.
66. MA XV, 271–75.
67. MA XV, 336.
68. MA XV, 393.
69. MA III/2, 157–60.
70. MA XV, 449.
71. MA XV, 471.
72. To CS, 20[–23]/12/1786, WA IV, viii, 100; to CS, 29[–30]/12/1786, WA IV, viii, 105; to L. von Sachsen-Weimar, 12[–23]/12/1786, WA IV, viii, 97.
73. Diary, WA III, i, 201.
74. Diary, WA III, i, 306–7.
75. Diary, WA III, i, 250.
76. Diary, WA III, i, 309.
77. MA III/2, 165.
78. Diary, WA III, i, 265.
79. To C. G. Heyne, 24/7/1788, WA IV, ix, 7.
80. To C. M. Wieland, early 9/1788, WA IV, ix, 15.
81. Potts, *Flesh*, 8.
82. MA XV, 200.
83. MA XV, 478.
84. Compare *Ethics*, I, proposition 29, SCW I, 412; Ehrhardt, 'Herders Spinoza-Schrift', 79.
85. MA III/2, 187.
86. MA III/2, 188.
87. MA III/2, 188.
88. MA XII, 69.
89. Diary, 16/9/1786, WA III, i, 202.
90. Diary, 16/9/1786, WA III, i, 194.
91. Diary, 25/9/1786, WA III, i, 230.
92. Diary, 17/9/1786, WA III, i, 208–12.
93. Diary, 29/9/1786, WA III, i, 243.
94. Diary, 29/9/1786, WA III, i, 243–44.
95. To Weimar friends, 25/1/1787, WA IV, viii, 146–47; MA XV, 196.
96. To CS, 25[–?]/5/1787, WA IV, viii, 216.
97. MA III/2, 177.
98. MA III/2, 179.
99. MA III/2, 179.
100. MA III/2, 218.
101. MA III/2, 240–42.
102. MA III/2, 249.
103. MA III/2, 249–50.
104. Diary, 17/9/1786, WA III, i, 204.
105. MA XV, 245.
106. MA III/2, 218.

107. MA III/2, 220.
108. Diary, 16/9/1786, WA III, i, 194.
109. Vaget, 'Tasso', 241.
110. Mucignat, 'Tasso',
111. MA III/1, 453.
112. On Goethe's portrayal of Tasso's poetic creativity, see Wilkinson, 'Tasso', 77–80.
113. MA III/1, 453.
114. For a very different view, see Wilkinson, 'Tasso', 82–83.
115. MA III/1, 455.
116. MA III/1, 461.
117. MA III/1, 452.
118. MA III/1, 513.
119. MA III/1, 519.
120. Conv. CH, 16/3/1789, WA V, viii, 250.
121. In general, see Reed, 'Tasso'.
122. MA III/1, 436, 435.
123. Ockenden, 'Statues', 103–4.
124. MA III/1, 519.
125. Mucignat, 'Tasso', 29.
126. Goethe, *Flight*, 73; diary, 5/10/1786, WA III, i, 266.
127. On the authenticity of Tasso's poetry, see Wilkinson, 'Tasso', 84.
128. Reiss, 'Tasso', 104.

Chapter 6. Transformations

1. GBuG III, 215.
2. To JGH, late 7/1788–early 8/1788, WA IV, ix, 8–9.
3. To CEG, 24/12/1792, WA IV, x, 43–44.
4. To the Privy Council, 9/12/1788, WA IV, ix, 64–65.
5. FS to C. G. Körner, 29/8/1787, NA XXIV, 143–50.
6. Wilson, *Geheimräte*, 141; *Gänge*, 23.
7. To JCL, 22/6/1781, WA IV, v, 149.
8. To CA, 6/4/1789, WA IV, ix, 101.
9. To CA, 6/4/1789, WA IV, ix, 101.
10. Wilson, *Geheimräte*, 141–42.
11. Wilson, *Geheimräte*, 144–46.
12. Wilson, *Geheimräte*, 142.
13. To CS, 26/1/1786, WA IV, vii, 170.
14. Damm, *Christiane*, 19–28.
15. Damm, *Christiane*, 64–65.
16. Damm, *Christiane*, 102–3.
17. Damm, *Christiane*, 114.
18. To FS, 13/7/1796, WA IV, xi, 125.
19. Damm, *Christiane*, 115.

20. To FHJ, 9/9/1788, WA IV, ix, 20–22.
21. Damm, *Christiane*, 116.
22. Damm, *Christiane*, 122.
23. GLTT II, 675–76.
24. Damm, *Christiane*, 120.
25. Damm, *Christiane*, 9.
26. Damm, *Christiane*, 9.
27. To CLK, 21/11/1782, WA IV, vi, 96.
28. To CLK, 25/10/1788, WA IV, ix, 43.
29. Lee, *Lyric Cycles*, 9–10.
30. Luck, *Römische Elegien*, 182.
31. To FHJ, 3/3/1790, WA IV, ix, 184.
32. CH to JGH, 15/8/1788, GLTT II, 679.
33. To C. G. Heyne, 24/7/1788, WA IV, ix, 7.
34. MA III/2, 78–79.
35. Wordsworth, 'Preface', 300.
36. MA III/2, 47.
37. Conv. JPE, 16/2/1827, WA V, vi, 62.
38. Winckelmann, *Geschichte*, 229.
39. To CLK, 1/1/1791, WA IV, ix, 239.
40. To G. J. Göschen, 4/7/1791, WA IV, ix, 277.
41. Doyle, *Revolution*, 97.
42. Blanning, *Mainz*, 306–10.
43. Blanning, *Mainz*, 311–12.
44. Wilson, *Goethe-Tabu*, 40–41, 96–97.
45. Wilson, *Goethe-Tabu*, 97.
46. Wilson, *Goethe-Tabu*, 101.
47. Wilson, *Goethe-Tabu*, 103.
48. To JGH, 10/3/1790, WA IV, ix, 184.
49. Wilson, *Goethe-Tabu*, 176.
50. Wilson, *Goethe-Tabu*, 103–5.
51. To CS, 1/6/1789, WA IV, ix, 126–27.
52. Damm, *Christiane*, 133.
53. Damm, *Christiane*, 129.
54. GLTT III, 49.
55. Damm, *Christiane*, 138.
56. MA III/2, 81.
57. MA III/2, 280, 575; see also MA III/2, 283, 580.
58. GBuG III, 266.
59. To F. L. zu Stolberg, 2/2/1789, WA IV, ix, 78–79.
60. GBuG III, 266.
61. To CS, 1–9/6/1787, WA IV, viii, 233.
62. MA III/2, 83.
63. To JHMy, 27/4/1789, WA IV, ix, 109.

64. MA III/2, 486.
65. To CA, 3/4/1790, WA IV, ix, 197.
66. To CH and JGH, 15/4/1790, WA IV, ix, 199.
67. To CLK, 1/1/1791, WA IV, ix, 239.
68. MA XIII/1, 522.
69. Rasch, 'Gauklerin', 68–92.
70. Bell, 'Coherence', 123–24.
71. MA III/2, 151.
72. MA III/2, 89.
73. MA III/2, 102–4.
74. MA III/2, 94.
75. MA III/2, 103.
76. MA III/2, 99.
77. Doyle, *Revolution*, 46.
78. MA III/2, 100.
79. Tackett, *Terror*, 160–61.
80. MA III/2, 113.
81. MA III/2, 94.
82. MA III/2, 126.
83. Gebhardt, *Revolution*.
84. KAA II, 398–405.
85. Jacobi, *Werke*, II/1, 109.
86. Boghossian, 'Social Construction', 566.
87. CMW to K. L. Reinhold, 18/2/1789, GBuG III, 275.
88. Boisserée, *Tagebücher*, I, 278.
89. To FHJ, 2/2/1795, WA IV, x, 233.
90. To JFR, 25/10/1790, WA IV, ix, 235–36.
91. MA XI/2, 229–30.
92. GLTT III, 107.
93. GBuG III, 361.
94. To CFZ, 29/1/1830, WA IV, xlvi, 223.
95. WA II, xiii, 258.
96. GBuG III, 365.
97. WA II, xi, 376.
98. MA XIV, 590.
99. To C.L.F. Schultz, 18/9/1831, WA IV, xlix, 82.
100. MA IV/2, 368.
101. MA IV/2, 389.
102. KAA III, 62 (A37/B54).
103. MA III/2, 308.
104. To CGV, 9/2/1788, WA IV, viii, 340.
105. To CGV, 9/2/1788, WA IV, viii, 340–41.
106. To CGV, 19/9/1789, WA IV, ix, 153.
107. MA III/2, 604.

108. MA III/2, 299–300.
109. MA III/2, 300.
110. KAA V, 234.
111. MA III/2, 303.
112. MA XV, 327.
113. MA III/2, 366.
114. MA III/2, 336.
115. MA XVIII/2, 452.
116. GLTT III, 52; FA I, xxiv, 940.
117. MA III/2, 319.
118. MA III/2, 340, 347.
119. KAA V, 372–77.
120. MA III/2, 327.
121. MA III/2, 344.
122. To CA, 17/5/1791, WA IV, ix, 261.
123. FA I, xxxiv, 454–55.
124. Wulf, *Invention*, 29–38.
125. Zammito, *Gestation*, 277–78; GLTT, III, 371–72.
126. Arber, 'Goethe's Botany'.
127. Arber, *Plant Form*.
128. To CH, 4/5/1790, WA IV, ix, 203; also, to C. von Kalb, 30/4/1790, WA IV, ix, 202.
129. Boyle, *Poet and the Age*, I, 657.
130. To CH, 4/5/1790, WA IV, ix, 204.
131. Richards, *Conception*, 497–502.
132. Wells, *Development*, 22.
133. Wyder, *Naturmodell*, 248.
134. Wyder, *Naturmodell*, 274.
135. Richards, 'Species Evolution'.
136. MA IV/2, 146.
137. Darwin, *Origin*, 1st ed., 427.
138. EG, 939; MA IV/2, 182.
139. Darwin, *Origin*, 1st ed., 435.
140. EG, 940; MA IV/2, 183–84.
141. MA IV/2, 146.
142. MA IV/2, 177.
143. Wells, *Development*, 20.
144. Nisbet, *Scientific Tradition*, 21.
145. Aristotle, *Hist. animal.*, 486a20–23.
146. Darwin, *Origin*, 1st ed., 147.
147. Darwin, *Origin*, 1st ed., 147.
148. EG 940; MA IV/2, 182–83.
149. Barros, 'Negative causation'.
150. Wells, *Development*, 29–30.
151. Tantillo, *Will to Create*, 104–5.

152. Wells, *Development*, 45.
153. To CLK, 1/1/1791, WA IV, ix, 239.
154. Boyle, 'Embodied Cognition'.
155. MA X, 909.
156. MA X, 910; also, MA XIV, 16.
157. MA X, 910–11.
158. MA IV/2, 1063–64.
159. To CA, 17/5/1791, WA IV, ix, 261.
160. To J. H. Voigt, 6/1791 or 7/1791, WA IV, xviii, 43.
161. MA IV/2, 261.
162. To FHJ, 1/6/1791, WA IV, ix, 269–70.
163. Zemplén, *Eye*, 57.
164. MA IV/2, 271–72.
165. MA IV/2, 361.
166. MA IV/2, 268.
167. MA IV/2, 268.
168. MA IV/2, 265.
169. MA IV/2, 268.
170. MA IV/2, 266.
171. Sepper, *Goethe contra Newton*, 45.
172. Newton, 'Letter', 3079.
173. To FWR, 10/9/1822, WA IV, xxxvi, 162.
174. To FS, 18/7/1798, WA IV, xiii, 218.
175. Richards, *Conception*, 439; for an alternative view, see Förster, *Twenty-Five Years*, 254–58.
176. Spinoza, *Ethics*, 26.
177. MA IV/2, 324.
178. Sepper, *Goethe contra Newton*, 67.
179. EG 945–46; MA IV/2, 329–30.
180. GBuG III, 372.
181. MA XIV, 502.
182. To JFR, 30/5/1791, WA IV, ix, 263–64.
183. To CLK, 12/10/1791, WA IV, ix, 288.
184. Sharpe, 'Theatre', 127–28.
185. To PCK, 14/8/1787, WA IV, viii, 243–44.
186. To JCL, 22/6/1781, WA IV, v, 149.
187. Wilson, 'Dramen', 264.
188. MA IV/1, 12.
189. To JGH, 5/9/1791, WA IV, ix, 281.
190. McKenzie-McHarg, 'Unknown Superiors'.
191. MA IV/1, 951–56.
192. MA XIV, 511.
193. Cited in Wilson, *Goethes Weimar*, 222.
194. Wilson, *Goethe-Tabu*, 128–29.

195. Cited in Wilson, *Goethes Weimar*, 162.
196. Wilson, *Goethe-Tabu*, 142.
197. Wilson, *Goethe-Tabu*, 143.
198. Wilson, *Goethe-Tabu*, 145–47.
199. Wilson, *Goethes Weimar*, 82.
200. Wilson, *Goethe-Tabu*, 188–89.
201. Wilson, *Goethe-Tabu*, 215–16.
202. Wilson, *Goethe-Tabu*, 275.
203. Wilson, *Goethe-Tabu*, 256–57.
204. Wilson, *Goethe-Tabu*, 257.
205. Wilson, *Goethe-Tabu*, 269–70.
206. Wilson, *Goethe-Tabu*, 275–81.
207. Wilson, *Goethes Weimar*, 685.
208. GüsD, II/1, 16, 26.
209. Wilson, 'Dramen', 267–68.
210. MA IV/1, 155–56.
211. MA IV/1, 160–61.
212. Conv. JPE, 4/1/1824, WA V, v, 10–11.
213. MA IV/1, 150.
214. MA IV/1, 159.
215. MA IV/1, 159.
216. Damm, *Christiane*, 159.
217. GLTT, III, 170.
218. To CG, 12/8/1792, WA IV, x, 2.
219. MA XIV, 590.
220. GLTT III, 195.
221. To CGV, 27/8/1792, WA IV, x, 11.
222. MA XIV, 454.
223. To C. F. Schnauß, 10/9/1792, WA IV, x, 19.
224. MA XIV, 385.
225. To CLK, 27/9/1792, WA IV, x, 25–26.
226. To CGV, 15/10/1792, WA IV, x, 33.
227. To CEG, 16/10/1792, WA IV, x, 35.
228. MA XIV, 465.
229. To CEG, 24/12/1792, WA IV, x, 43.
230. Blanning, *Mainz*, 276.
231. Seibt, *Wut*, 29–35.
232. Seibt, *Wut*, 42.
233. Blanning, *Mainz*, 281.
234. Seibt, *Wut*, 9–13.
235. Seibt, *Wut*, 59.
236. Herder, *Zerstreute Blätter*, 219.
237. MA IV/1, 1016.
238. To FHJ, 18/11/1793, WA IV, x, 126.

239. MA IV/1, 1017.
240. MA XIV, 513.
241. MA IV/1, 282.
242. MA IV/1, 1019.
243. MA IV/1, 428.
244. MA IV/1, 370.
245. MA IV/1, 1019.
246. MA IV/1, 371.
247. MA IV/1, 372.
248. Burke, *Correspondence*, VI, 479–80.
249. To CH and JGH, 7/6/1793, WA IV, x, 75.
250. To FJB, 6/6/1793, WA IV, xviii, 49.
251. MA XIV, 512; compare GLTT, III, 244.
252. MA XIV, 24.
253. Seibt, *Wut*, 112.
254. Wilson, 'Dramen', 277–78.
255. Wilson, 'Dramen', 278.
256. MA IV/1, 105.
257. MA IV/1, 129.
258. Griffiths, *Shepherd*, 121.
259. Wilson, 'Dramen', 276.
260. Wilson, *Goethe-Tabu*, 165–66.
261. Wilson, *Goethe-Tabu*, 161–63.
262. Damm, *Christiane*, 182–83.
263. To JGH, 31/5/1793, WA IV, x, 64–68.
264. To JGH, 15/6/1793, WA IV, x, 79.
265. To CH and JGH, 7/6/1793, WA IV, x, 75.
266. To CG, 3/7/1793, WA IV, x, 86.
267. To CGV, 3/7/1793, WA IV, x, 85.
268. Seibt, *Wut*, 98.
269. Seibt, *Wut*, 91.
270. Seibt, *Wut*, 92.
271. Blanning, *Mainz*, 301.
272. Seibt, *Wut*, 102.
273. To FHJ, 27/7/1793, WA IV, x, 100–101.
274. PS V, 768–69; MA XIV, 546.
275. PS V, 770; MA XIV, 548–49.
276. Seibt, *Wut*, 124–29.
277. Beiser, *Enlightenment*, 307.
278. KAA, IV, 421.
279. Förster, *Twenty-Five Years*, 59.
280. Beiser, *Enlightenment*, 307–8.
281. To JHMy, 20/6/1796, WA IV, xi, 101.
282. Berlin, 'Intellectual Path', 23.

283. MA III/2, 94.
284. MA IV/2, 361.
285. To S. T. von Sömmerring, 12/10/1791, WA IV, ix, 287.
286. G. C. Lichtenberg to Goethe, 7/10/1793, BaG I, 140.
287. To G. C. Lichtenberg, 20/10/1793, WA IV, x, 120.
288. Förster, *Twenty-Five Years*, 173.
289. MA IV/2, 376, 378.

Chapter 7. Church Militant

1. To JHMy, 17/7/1794, WA IV, x, 174.
2. To CH, end 9/1794, WA IV, x, 198.
3. To F. von Stein, 14/8/1794, WA IV, x, 181.
4. To F. von Stein, 14/8/1794, WA IV, x, 181.
5. To FHJ, 8/9/94, WA IV, x, 192.
6. MA XIV, 27.
7. GLTT III, 316–17; Wilson, *Goethe-Tabu*, 243–45.
8. Wilson, *Goethe-Tabu*, 244.
9. To J. G. Fichte, 24/6/1794, WA IV, x, 167.
10. KAA V, 341. For the following argument, see Förster, *Twenty-Five Years*, 179–82.
11. Quoted in Förster, *Twenty-Five Years*, 162; Fichte, *Gesamtausgabe*, I/2, 48.
12. Förster, *Twenty-Five Years*, 99.
13. Förster, *Twenty-Five Years*, 203.
14. To FHJ, 8/9/1794, WA IV, x, 192.
15. To FHJ, 11/3/1795, WA IV, x, 243.
16. To CGV, 10/4/1795, WA IV, x, 250.
17. GLTT III, 350–51.
18. To CA, 2/3/1797, WA IV, xii, 54.
19. EG, 940; MA IV/2, 183–84.
20. Wulf, *Invention*, 29–38.
21. MA VI/1, 38.
22. To J. F. Unger, 28/3/1797, WA IV, xii, 79–80.
23. MA IV/2, 204–32.
24. To FS, 6/8/1796, WA IV, xi, 154.
25. To FS, 26/8/1796, WA IV, xi, 244.
26. To FS, 18/10/1796, WA IV, xi, 236.
27. FS to C. G. Körner, 12/8/1787, NA XXIV, 130.
28. FS to C. G. Körner, 2/2/1789, NA XXV, 194–95.
29. Wilson, *Goethe-Tabu*, 226–27.
30. NA XXII, 108.
31. MA XII, 88–89.
32. MA XII, 89.
33. MA XII, 89.
34. FS to C. G. Körner, 1/9/1794, NA XXVII, 35.

35. FS to JWG, 13/6/1794, NA XXVII, 14–15.
36. To FS, 24/6/1794, WA IV, x, 165–66.
37. FS to JWG, 23/8/1794, NA XXVII, 25–26.
38. Boyle, *Poet and the Age*, II, 225.
39. MA XII, 89.
40. GBuG IV, 103.
41. MA IV/1, 768.
42. KAA V, 341.
43. Schiller, *Aesthetic Education*, 219; NA XX, 412.
44. NA XXII, 107.
45. To FS, 27/8/1794, WA IV, x, 183–85.
46. To F. von Stein, 28/8/1794, WA IV, x, 187.
47. The source of the Ferdinand story has only recently come to light. See Košenina, 'Ferdinand-Novelle'.
48. Gailus, 'Form and Chance', 746–47.
49. MA IV/1, 436.
50. MA IV/1, 440.
51. MA IV/1, 440–41.
52. MA IV/1, 448.
53. KAA IV, 407–8.
54. PS X, 55; MA IV/1, 496.
55. PS X, 54; MA IV/1, 495.
56. PS X, 54; MA IV/1, 495.
57. To FS, 7/3/1801, WA IV, xv, 188.
58. MA IV/1, 467.
59. MA IV/1, 476.
60. To FS, 17/8/95, WA IV, x, 286.
61. PS X, 70; MA IV/1, 518.
62. FS to JWG, 29/8/1795, NA XXVIII, 37.
63. PS X, 87; MA IV/1, 543.
64. Among many, see Mayer, *Goethe*, 244–70.
65. PS X, 70; MA IV/1, 519.
66. PS X, 76; MA IV/1, 527.
67. PS X, 90; MA IV/1, 547.
68. Brown, 'Bridges', 5–9.
69. Brown, 'Bridges', 1.
70. FS to JWG, 29/8/1795, NA XXVIII, 37.
71. PS X, 84, MA IV/1, 539.
72. PS X, 85; MA IV/1, 539.
73. EG 713; MA V, 553.
74. MA IV/1, 682.
75. PS X, 69; MA IV/1, 516.
76. PS X, 92; MA IV/1, 550.
77. MA IV/1, 660.

78. MA IV/1, 660.
79. MA IV/1, 665–66.
80. MA IV/2, 933.
81. MA IV/2, 17.
82. Baioni, 'Gesellschaftsidee', 76.
83. JFC to FS, 13/3/1795, NA XXXV, 170.
84. FS to JWG, 15/5/1795, NA XXVII, 184.
85. MA III/2, 450.
86. To FS, 28/10/1795, WA IV, x, 317–18.
87. FS to JWG, 1/11/1795, NA XXVIII, 94.
88. To FS, 21/11/1795, WA IV, x, 334.
89. MA VI/2, 573.
90. Mix, *Musenalmanache*, 36.
91. MA IV/1, 676.
92. MA IV/1, 703.
93. MA IV/1, 745.
94. To FS, 7/12/1796, WA IV, xi, 280.
95. MA IV/1, 758.
96. To FS, 12/2/1796, WA IV, xi, 27.
97. MA IV/1, 640.
98. MA IV/1, 640.
99. MA IV/1, 642.
100. MA IV/1, 643–44.
101. Unseld, *Verleger*, 196.
102. FS to C. G. Körner, 9/10/1794, NA XXVII, 66.
103. To JGH, 5/1794, WA IV, x, 158.
104. EG 484; MA V, 191.
105. EG 660; MA V, 470.
106. EG 376; MA V, 16–17.
107. EG, 388 (adapted); MA V, 36.
108. EG 409–10; MA V, 70.
109. See MA V, 730–31.
110. EG 547 (adapted); MA V, 290.
111. EG 571; MA V, 328.
112. To FS, 18/3/1795, WA IV, x, 244.
113. EG 590–91, 593, 597, 600–602, 609–10, 612; MA V, 361, 366, 372, 376, 378, 380, 390–92, 395, 421.
114. To FS, 18/3/1795, WA IV, x, 244.
115. EG 619; MA V, 406.
116. EG 641; MA V, 441.
117. EG 749; MA V, 610.
118. To J. F. Unger, 7/3/1796, WA IV, xi, 41.
119. EG 409–10; MA V, 70.
120. FS to JWG, 8/7/1796, NA XXVIII, 254–55.

121. EG 678; MA V, 499.
122. EG 748; MA V, 609.
123. EG 721; MA V, 566.
124. PS X, 84, MA IV/1, 539.
125. EG 713; MA V, 553.
126. To FS, 25/10/1795, WA IV, x, 317.
127. To FS, 1/11/1795, WA IV, x, 324.
128. To WH, 27/5/1796, WA IV, xi, 78.
129. To FHJ, 12/6/1796, WA IV, xi, 86.
130. GBuG IV, 265.
131. GBuG IV, 312; GBuG IV, 307; to Meyer, 8/5/1797, WA IV, xii, 119–20; FS to C. G. Körner, 3/6/1797, NA XXIX, 82.
132. To JHMy, 20/6/1796, WA IV, xi, 102–3.
133. GBuG IV, 265.
134. To FHJ, 13/6/1796, WA IV, xi, 88.
135. MA IV/2, 519–605.
136. MA IV/2, 523.
137. MA IV/2, 534.
138. MA IV/2, 61–64.
139. MA IV/2, 65–70.
140. MA VII, 477–87.
141. MA XIV, 49.
142. To FS, 4/2/1796, WA IV, xi, 19; to JHMy, 8/2/1796, WA IV, xi, 23.
143. MA XVI, 851.
144. MA VII, 431.
145. MA VII, 322; MA VII, 431.
146. MA VII, 55.
147. MA VII, 183.
148. MA VII, 434; MA VII, 374.
149. MA XV, 441.
150. MA III/2, 100, 113, 127, 137, 151.
151. MA VII, 486.
152. MA VII, 486.
153. MA VII, 478–79.
154. MA III/2, 94.
155. MA VII, 486.
156. MA VII, 487.
157. To FS, 25/10/1797, WA IV, xii, 347.
158. Diary, 31/7/1797, WA III, ii, 77.
159. Diary, 9/8/1797, WA III, ii, 80.
160. Diary, 13/8/1797, WA III, ii, 81; 14/8/1797, WA III, ii, 81.
161. Diary, 30/9/1797, WA III, ii, 166. See also to FS, 10/11/1797, WA IV, xii, 355; to CA, 11/9/1797, WA IV, xii, 285; to FS, 14/10/1797, WA IV, xii, 327–28; MA XIV, 68.
162. Diary, 28/9/1797, WA III, ii, 161–62.

163. Diary, 30/8/1797, WA III, ii, 108.
164. Diary, 5/10/1797, WA III, ii, 177.
165. Diary, 29/8/1797, WA III, ii, 102–3.
166. To FS, 14/10/1797, WA IV, xii, 327.
167. Conv. JPE, 18/1/1827, WA V, vi, 26.
168. MA XIV, 104.
169. To FS, 9/8/1797, WA IV, xii, 217.
170. MA XIV, 85.
171. GBuG IV, 477.
172. MA IV/1, 629.
173. But see also Robertson, *Mock-Epic*, 219 (note 85).
174. Boa, 'Heimatliteratur'.
175. MA IV/1, 592.
176. Kluge, 'Schlußrede', 62–64.
177. Kluge, 'Schlußrede', 61.
178. Kluge, 'Schlußrede', 67.
179. Robertson, *Mock-Epic*, 224.
180. Robertson, *Mock-Epic*, 198–236.
181. Boa, 'Heimatliteratur', 35.
182. To FS, 3/1/1798, WA IV, xiii, 5.
183. MA IV/1, 593.
184. FS to F. C. von Augustenburg, 13/7/1793, NA XXVI, 263.
185. Martin, *Untimely Aesthetics*, 65.
186. To JHMy, 4/6/1796, WA IV, xi, 273.
187. MA IV/1, 570.
188. Robertson, *Mock-Epic*, 218.
189. Rousseau, *Oeuvres*, V, 210; see also Robertson, *Enlightenment*, 300.
190. MA IV/1, 595.
191. MA IV/1, 596.
192. MA IV/1, 617.
193. MA IV/1, 585.
194. MA IV/1, 620.
195. MA IV/1, 621.
196. MA IV/1, 628.
197. Adelung, *Wörterbuch*, article 'Grundgesetz'.
198. MA IV/1, 629.
199. Lange, 'Pentateuch', 104.
200. WA I, vii, 328.
201. Lange, 'Pentateuch', 103–121.
202. WA I, vii, 322.
203. WA I, vii, 322.
204. WA I, vii, 324.
205. To FS, 25/11/1797, WA IV, xii, 361.
206. MA IV/1, 871.

207. 2 Corinthians 11:2.
208. MA IV/1, 867.
209. MA IV/1, 1223.
210. Locke, *Two Treatises*, 246.
211. MA IV/1, 866.
212. Thobani, *Indian Classical Dance*, 26–31.
213. MA III/2, 104.
214. MA IV/1, 873.
215. MA IV/1, 874.
216. Mautner, *Lichtenberg*, 360.
217. To FS, 21/11/1795, WA IV, x, 335.
218. To FHJ, 29/12/1794, WA IV, x, 219–20.
219. To FS, 25/11/1795, WA IV, x, 339.
220. To S. T. Sömmerring, 25/5/1795, WA IV, x, 264.
221. To S. T. Sömmerring, 17/8/1795, WA IV, x, 287.
222. FS to JWG, 19/1/1798, NA XXIX, 189.
223. Diary, 14/11/1798, WA III, ii, 223.
224. Diary, 15/11/1798, WA III, ii, 223.
225. Diary, 11/8/1798, 12/8/1798, 24–26/8/1798, 30/9/1798, 16–21/11/1798, WA III, ii, 217, 219–20, 223–24.
226. MA VII, 542.
227. To FS, 19/12/1798, WA IV, xiii, 346.
228. To CGV, 19/12/1798, WA IV, xiii, 347–48.
229. KAA VII, 290.
230. MA XIV, 61.
231. MA X, 227.
232. PS XII, 277; MA X, 226.
233. FS to JWG, 19/1/1798, NA XXIX, 188.
234. Kant, *Prolegomena*, 81; KAA IV, 328–29.
235. To FS, 3/2/1798, WA IV, xiii, 52.
236. To FS, 10/2/1798, WA IV, xiii, 60–61.
237. To FS, 17/2/1798, WA IV, xiii, 68.
238. MA VI/2, 787–89, 801–5.
239. MA VI/2, 804.
240. Diary, 9/2/1799, WA III, ii, 232.
241. MA VI/2, 789–98.
242. To FHJ, 29/12/1794, WA IV, x, 219–20.
243. MA VI/2, 798–801.
244. To FS, 22/5/1803, WA IV, xvi, 232.
245. MA VI/2, 787–88.
246. MA VI/2, 843.
247. Kant, *Foundations*, 5; KAA IV, 470.
248. Kant, *Pure Reason*, 631; KAA III, 470 (A714/B742).
249. GLTT III, 786.

250. GBuG IV, 497.
251. To FS, 30/8/1799, WA IV, xiv, 172.
252. GBuG IV, 497.
253. To CGV, 29/5/1798, WA IV, xiii, 168.
254. To FS, 6/1/1798, WA IV, xiii, 10.
255. Diary, 28–30/5/1798, WA III, ii, 209.
256. To CGV, 29/5/1798, WA IV, xiii, 168.
257. To CGV, 21/6/1798, WA IV, xiii, 188–89.
258. Förster, *Twenty-Five Years*, 223.
259. Förster, *Twenty-Five Years*, 225.
260. Förster, *Twenty-Five Years*, 226.
261. Nassar, 'Philosophy of Nature', 317.
262. To CGV, 21/6/1798, WA IV, xiii, 189.
263. Diary, 12/11/1798, WA III, ii, 222; 19/1/1799, WA III, ii, 230.
264. Nassar, 'Philosophy of Nature', 314–19.
265. Nassar, 'Philosophy of Nature', 316.
266. Nassar, 'Philosophy of Nature', 316.
267. To JGH, 1793 or 1794, WA IV, x, 132.
268. Diary, 10/9/1797, WA II, ii, 130.
269. To CGV, 19/12/1798, WA IV, xiii, 348.
270. To F.W.J. Schelling, 27/9/1800, WA IV, xv, 117.
271. Conv. B. Constant, 27/1/1804, GLTT IV, 449.
272. WA III, ii, 212.
273. Schelling, *Ausgabe*, I, vi, 67.
274. Schelling, *Ausgabe*, I, vi, 92–93.
275. MA VI/1, 15.
276. To FS, 28/6/1798, WA IV, xiii, 197.
277. To CLK, 16/7/1798, WA IV, xiii, 213.
278. Adler, 'Schellings Philosophie', 154.
279. MA VI/1, 17.
280. MA VI/1, 18.
281. To FS, 28/6/1798, WA IV, xiii, 197.
282. Adler, 'Schellings Philosophie', 154; GüsD III/1, 331.
283. Diary, 5/5/1798, WA III, ii, 206, and onwards.
284. Diary, 10/10/1799, WA III, ii, 264.
285. Diary, 20, 27, 30/9/1800, WA III, ii, 306–8.
286. To FS, 28/9/1800, WA IV, xv, 123.
287. To FS, 30/9/1800, WA IV, xv, 124.
288. To FS, 1/8/1800, WA IV, xv, 96.
289. Diary, 13/7/1798, WA III, ii, 214; 30/7/1798, WA III, ii, 216.
290. MA IV/2, 193.
291. MA VI/2, 835.
292. MA VI/2, 835.
293. To CFZ, 4/8/1803, WA IV, xvi, 265–66; diary, 1/4/1804, WA III, iii, 102.

294. Diary, 6/12/1799, WA III, ii, 273.
295. To FS, 16/9/1800, WA IV, xv, 110.
296. To FS, 22/6/1797, WA IV, xii, 167.
297. Conv. H. Luden, 16/8/1806, WA V, ii, 43.
298. To FS, 1/7/1797, WA IV, xii, 179.
299. To FS, 22/6/1797, WA IV, xii, 167.
300. To JHMy, 18/3/1797, WA IV, xii, 74.
301. Wood, 'Philosophical Revolution', 14.
302. Förster, *Twenty-Five Years*, 206–7.
303. Quoted in Beiser, 'Fichte', 38; Fichte, *Gesamtausgabe*, III/2, 298.
304. To FS, 18/3/1801, WA IV, xv, 200.
305. Diary, 25/4/1806, WA III, iii, 126.
306. MA VI/1, 542.
307. Durrani, *Faust*, 97.
308. MA VI/1, 542.
309. MA VI/1, 543.
310. See Nadler, *Spinoza's Heresy*, 94–131.
311. MA VI/1, 544.
312. MA VI/1, 552.
313. MA VI/1, 554.
314. To FS, 25/11/1797, WA IV, xii, 361.
315. Williams, *'Faust'*, 79.
316. MA VI/1, 554.
317. MA VI/1, 556.
318. Goethe, *Faust Part One*, 152.
319. SCW I, 550.
320. MA VI/1, 568.
321. Gillo, 'Bekehrung', 472.
322. MA VI/1, 568.
323. Williams, *'Faust'*, 83.
324. Mason, *Goethe's Faust*, 307.
325. MA VI/1, 580–81.
326. MA VI/1, 583.
327. GH II, 485–86.
328. Williams, *'Faust'*, 50–51.
329. Wichert, *Mythen*, 359.
330. Wilson, *Pakt*, 174.
331. Gottschewski, *Männerbund*, 770.
332. MA VI/1, 670.
333. Weber, *Protestant Ethic*, 165.
334. FS to JFC, 29/5/1798, NA XXIX, 240.
335. GLTT III, 723.
336. To F. Müller, 19/11/1800, WA IV, xv, 151.
337. To JFC, 27/5/1798, WA IV, xiii, 163.

338. MA VI/2, 958; also to FS, 10/7/1799, WA IV, xiv, 127–28.
339. FS to JFC, 10/7/1800, NA XXX, 170.
340. To JFC, 17/11/1800, WA IV, xv, 143–44.
341. To JHMy, 15/5/1794, WA IV, x, 159–61; 19/5/1794, WA IV, x, 161–62.
342. MA VI/2, 26.
343. MA VI/2, 1085.
344. To JHMy, 20–22/5/1796, WA IV, xi, 70.
345. MA VII, 656.
346. MA XV, 478.
347. MA III/2, 188.
348. MA VI/2, 16.
349. KAA V, 226.
350. MA IV/2, 94–95.
351. MA VI/2, 19.
352. MA VII, 558.
353. To JHMy, 5–8/8/1796, WA IV, xi, 149–50.
354. MA VII, 520; to JHMy, 5–8/8/1796, WA IV, xi, 149–50; to FS, 12/8/1797, WA IV, xii, 230; MA XIV, 123–24; to CFZ, 9/3/1831, WA IV, xxxxviii, 143.
355. MA VII, 541.
356. MA VII, 519–20.
357. To JHMy, 5–8/8/1796, WA IV, xi, 149–50.
358. For example, to FS, 22/6/1799, WA IV, xiv, 117–20.
359. Niedermeier, 'Dilettantismus', 213.
360. To FS, 22/6/1799, WA IV, xiv, 117–18.
361. MA VI/2, 13.
362. Kant, *Judgment*, 120; KAA V, 235.
363. MA IV/2, 86.
364. MA IV/2, 82.
365. MA IV/2, 77.
366. MA VI/2, 504.
367. MA VI/2, 432.
368. To JFC, 16/9/1800, WA IV, xv, 107.
369. To CLK, 15/5/1798, WA IV, xiii, 145–46.
370. To FS, 16/5/1798, WA IV, xiii, 148–49.
371. MA VI/1, 948.
372. Diary, 18/11/1799, WA III, ii, 270.
373. To CFZ, 8/8/1804, WA IV, xvii, 188–89.
374. Conv. J. D. Falk, 25/1/1813, WA V, iii, 52.
375. Conv. JPE, 18/1/1825, WA V, v, 137.
376. MA VI/1, 254.
377. To CFZ, 8/8/1804, WA IV, xvii, 188–89.
378. GüsD V, 537.
379. MA XIV, 60.
380. The following interpretation draws on Bell, 'Legality'.

381. Böschenstein, 'Bedeutung', 335.
382. MA VI/1, 291.
383. Szramkiewicz, *Droit*, 60–62.
384. Darrow, *Family*, 112.
385. Tackett, *Terror*, 313.
386. Szramkiewicz, *Droit*, 88–89.
387. MA VI/1, 292.
388. Reinhardt, *Kleine und große Welt*, 256.
389. MA VI/1, 297.
390. MA VI/1, 299.
391. Boyle, *Poet and the Age*, II, 783–84.
392. MA XVI, 506.
393. MA I/2, 555.
394. PS X, 69; MA IV/1, 516.
395. To FJB, 13/5/1803, WA IV, xvi, 225; also Wistoff, *Deutsche Romantik*, 139–41.
396. JWG and CGV to CA, 31/8/1803, WA IV, xvi, 278.
397. To F. L. von Hendrich, 31/8/1803, WA IV, xvi, 280.
398. To FS, 17/1/1804, WA IV, xvii, 18.
399. To FS, 21/8/1799, WA IV, xiv, 160.
400. To JHMy, 22/7/1805, WA IV, xix, 26.
401. To CLK, 17/9/1799, WA IV, xiv, 185.
402. MA VI/2, 188–94.
403. To FS, 12/5/1798, WA IV, xiii, 141.
404. Wilson, *Goethe, Männer, Knaben*, 62.
405. MA VI/1, 798.
406. MA VI/2, 380–81.
407. MA VI/2, 188.
408. MA VI/2, 195.
409. MA VI/2, 198.
410. MA VI/2, 353.
411. MA VI/2, 354.
412. Wilson, *Goethe, Männer, Knaben*, 199.
413. MA VI/2, 354.
414. MA VI/2, 355.
415. MA VI/2, 356.
416. MA VI/2, 351.
417. MA VI/2, 371.
418. MA VI/2, 376.
419. MA VI/2, 371–72.
420. MA VI/2, 351.
421. MA VI/2, 375.
422. To FS, 18/3/1795, WA IV, x, 244.
423. MA VI/2, 375–76.
424. SCW I, 550.

425. MA VI/2, 376.
426. MA VI/2, 375.
427. MA VI/2, 376.
428. To FS, 20/4/1805, WA IV, xvii, 273.
429. To CFZ, 1/6/1805, WA IV, xix, 8.

Chapter 8. 'My Emperor'

1. To H.C.A. Eichstädt, 25/5/1805, WA IV, xix, 5.
2. MA XIV, 328.
3. To CA, 10/8/1805, WA IV, xix, 35.
4. To CA, 10/8/1805, WA IV, xix, 36.
5. To CS, 4/6/1805, WA IV, xix, 10; to CFZ, 19/6/1805, WA IV, xix, 20.
6. To CFZ, 1/6/1805, WA IV, xix, 8.
7. MA VI/1, 91.
8. To JFC, 22/9/1799, WA IV, xiv, 188–90.
9. MA XIV, 63.
10. To CLK, 14/3/1806, WA IV, xix, 115.
11. To A. von Humboldt, 3/4/1807, WA IV, xix, 298.
12. To C. A. Böttiger, 15/10/1803, WA IV, xvi, 331–32; see also conv. JPE, 27/9/1827, WA V, vi, 225.
13. MA VI/2, 1122.
14. MA VI/2, 537.
15. To JHM, 22/7/1805, WA IV, xix, 26.
16. To JHM, 22/7/1805, WA IV, xix, 27.
17. Diary, 22, 29/6/1807, WA III, iii, 227, 232.
18. Diary, 7/9/1807, WA III, iii, 271–72.
19. Diary, 9/9/1807, WA III, iii, 273.
20. Diary, 7/9/1807, WA III, iii, 271–72.
21. To CFR, 22/6/1808, WA IV, xx, 93.
22. Fröschle, *Verhältnis*, 210.
23. MA VI/2, 537.
24. To CFR, 22/6/1808, WA IV, xx, 92.
25. To CFZ, 22/6/1808, WA IV, xx, 86.
26. To CFZ, 14/7/1806, WA IV, xix, 160.
27. To FHJ, 11/1/1808, WA IV, xx, 5.
28. Conv. [unknown], 31/12/1808, WA V, ii, 237.
29. Dahnke, 'Werner', 1150.
30. Reeve, *Kleist*, 23.
31. To A. Müller, 28/8/1807, WA IV, xix, 402–3.
32. Diary, 13/7/1807, WA III, iii, 239–40.
33. GLTT VI, 458–59.
34. Kleist, *Writings*, 413–14; *Werke*, II, 342.
35. MA VI/2, 602–16.
36. Diary, 14/11/1808, WA III, iii, 399.

37. To CLK, 25/11/1808, WA IV, xx, 221–22.
38. GLTT IV, 643; see also GLTT IV, 649.
39. Electricity: diary, 5/1/1806, WA III, iii, 113. Magnetism: diary, 3/8/1808, WA III, iii, 367. Galvanism: diary, 15, 19, 20, 21, 22, 27, 31/1/1806, WA III, iii, 115–16; 21/3/1808, WA III, iii, 323; 6, 8/4/1808, WA III, iii, 327. Chemistry: MA IX, 892–93.
40. MA VI/2, 835; see also to J.S.C. Schweigger, 25/4/1814, WA IV, xxiv, 227.
41. To F.W.H. von Trebra, 6/1/1813, WA IV, xxiii, 235.
42. To CLK, 20/1/1813, WA IV, xxiii, 257–58.
43. To T. J. Seebeck, 15/1/1813, WA IV, xxiii, 247.
44. To CFZ, 1/9/1805, WA IV, xix, 54.
45. MA X, 20.
46. To F. A. Wolf, 30/8/1805, WA IV, xix, 53.
47. Plotinus, *Enneads*, 64.
48. MA X, 20.
49. MA VI/2, 815; on the dating, see MA VI/2, 1262.
50. Robertson, *Enlightenment*, 428.
51. MA IV/2, 186.
52. To CFZ, 22/6/1808, WA IV, xx, 90.
53. Conv. FWR, 28/6/1809, WA V, ii, 267.
54. To CFZ, 22/6/1808, WA IV, xx, 90.
55. GLTT V, 460.
56. MA X, 786.
57. GLTT IV, 732.
58. MA VI/2, 843.
59. Conv. FWR, 14/1/1807, WA V, ii, 158–59.
60. To CA, 14/11/1812, WA IV, xxiii, 145.
61. Conv. FM, 18/6/1826, WA V, v, 294.
62. MA VI/2, 816.
63. MA VI/2, 817.
64. Conv. FWR, 14/1/1807, WA V, ii, 159. See also conv. FWR, 14/11/1810, WA V, ii, 344; to CFZ, 12/12/1812, WA IV, xxiii, 197; MA X, 226–27.
65. Nisbet, *Scientific Tradition*, 49–50.
66. Diary, 7/8/1806, WA III, iii, 155.
67. To WH, 22/8/1806, WA IV, li, 201.
68. GBuG VI, 150–54.
69. Diary, 14/10/1806, WA III, iii, 174.
70. Quoted in Gräf, *Skizzen*, 259.
71. To CGV, 16/10/1805, WA IV, xix, 197.
72. BGG II, 258.
73. Boyle, 'Embodied Cognition', 485–86.
74. MA X, 271.
75. To CFR, 22/7/1810, WA IV, xxi, 362.
76. MA VI/2, 816.
77. MA X, 22–23.

78. MA X, 9–10.
79. Boyle, 'Embodied Cognition'.
80. To C.L.F. Schultz, 30/8/1814, WA IV, xxv, 30.
81. MA X, 20.
82. MA X, 27.
83. MA X, 27.
84. Boyle, 'Embodied Cognition', 490.
85. MA X, 30–31.
86. MA X, 35.
87. MA X, 36.
88. MA X, 350.
89. Kuhn, 'Chemie', 270.
90. Diary, 22/4/1812, WA III, iv, 271.
91. To C.J.H. Windischmann, 28/12/1812, WA IV, xxiii, 215; see also diary, 22/4/1812, WA III, iv, 271.
92. Boyle, 'Embodied Cognition', 486.
93. MA X, 159.
94. MA X, 160–61.
95. To H. Steffens, 9/10/1809, WA IV, xxi, 113.
96. MA X, 236.
97. MA X, 238.
98. MA X, 238.
99. MA X, 238.
100. MA X, 241.
101. MA X, 244.
102. MA X, 258.
103. Schöne, *Licht*.
104. Gage, *Colour*, 193–95.
105. To CLK, 13/12/1806, WA IV, xix, 245–46.
106. To A. von Humboldt, 3/4/1807, WA IV, xix, 298.
107. Sepper, *Goethe contra Newton*, 103.
108. MA X, 277.
109. Mueller, 'Equivalence'.
110. MA X, 401.
111. MA X, 288.
112. MA X, 287–88.
113. GLTT IV, 732.
114. Rousseau, *Oeuvres*, III, 352–53.
115. MA X, 11.
116. MA VI/2, 816.
117. To CFZ, 22/6/1808, WA IV, xx, 90.
118. To J. C. Planitzer, 29/12/1831, WA IV, xlix, 181.
119. MA IX, 923–26.
120. To CFZ, 22/6/1808, WA IV, xx, 90–91.

121. MA XX/1, 178.
122. Diary, 10/4/1807, WA III, iii, 204.
123. To CFZ, 7/5/1807, WA IV, xix, 323.
124. To JFC, 28/5/1798, WA IV, xiii, 166.
125. Diary, 17–20/5/1807, WA III, iii, 210–11.
126. Bersier, 'Parody', 267.
127. PS X, 100; MA XVII, 20.
128. Armstrong, 'Idyl', 421–22.
129. PS X, 104; MA XVII, 25.
130. PS X, 105 (adapted); MA XVII, 26–27.
131. MA XVII, 22–23.
132. PS X, 104; MA XVII, 25.
133. The 'Evangelium Infantiae Salvatoris Arabicum' in: Tischendorf (ed.), *Evangelia*.
134. Klingenberg, *'Wanderjahre'*, 31–43.
135. Diary, 19/5/1807, WA III, iii, 211.
136. MA XVII, 33.
137. MA XVII, 35.
138. PS X, 110; MA XVII, 35.
139. PS X, 111 (adapted); MA XVII, 36.
140. MA XVII, 36.
141. Diary, 2/8/1809, WA III, iv, 49.
142. Brown, *Cyclical Narratives*, 39.
143. Salmen, *Verlassenschaft*, 101.
144. Armstrong, 'Idyl', 421.
145. PS X, 103; MA XVII, 25.
146. Matthew 22:21.
147. For a more detailed account, see Bell, *Anthropology*, 277–87.
148. MA XIV, 197.
149. Diary, 11/9/1786, WA III, i, 175.
150. Goethe, *Flight*, 73; diary, 5/10/1786, WA III, i, 266.
151. MA IX, 152.
152. To FS, 1/5/1801, WA IV, xv, 227.
153. Wolf, [Dedication].
154. MA IX, 176.
155. MA IX, 151.
156. MA XVIII/2, 283. Seckendorf and Stoll visited Goethe to discuss Prometheus, and on the same evening Goethe was looking at engravings of paintings by the Poussins: diary, 25/10/1807, WA III, iii, 288.
157. MA XIV, 429–30.
158. MA IX, 151.
159. MA IX, 152.
160. MA IX, 157–58.
161. MA IX, 161.
162. Lucretius, *De rerum natura*, V, 1281–307; Virgil, *Georgics*, I. 121–46.

163. MA XIV, 176.
164. MA IX, 184, 1044.
165. Diary, 8/8/1806, WA III, iii, 156.
166. GBuG VI, 88.
167. MA IX, 158.
168. MA IX, 1146–48.
169. MA IX, 1147.
170. Conv. JPE, 5/7/1827, WA V, vi, 147.
171. Diary, 6, 7, 25, 26/3/1806, WA III, iii, 121–22.
172. Seibt, *Napoleon*.
173. Seibt, *Napoleon*, 115.
174. Conv. N. Bonaparte, 2/10/1808, WA V, ii, 223.
175. WA I, liii, 389.
176. WA I, xxxvi, 445.
177. GLTT V, 279–80.
178. Cited in Seibt, *Napoleon*, 150.
179. Seibt, *Napoleon*, 74.
180. Seibt, *Napoleon*, 150.
181. MA IX, 65.
182. MA IX, 65.
183. Seibt, *Napoleon*, 57.
184. Conv. FWR, 11/1806, WA V, ii, 106.
185. Seibt, *Napoleon*, 65.
186. Seibt, *Napoleon*, 67.
187. To G. Sartorius, 4/2/1811, WA IV, xxii, 28.
188. Quoted in BaG II, 565.
189. Sepper, *Goethe contra Newton*, 169.
190. To WH, 7/2/1798, WA IV, xiii, 57.
191. To FS, 17/2/1798, WA IV, xiii, 68.
192. To FS, 17/2/1798, WA IV, xiii, 68.
193. To FS, 10/2/1798, WA IV, xiii, 60–61.
194. Hennig, 'British Physics', 64.
195. To JHM, 31/7/1801, WA IV, xv, 251.
196. Diary, passim between 30/7/1808, WA III, iii, 365 and 18/3/1810, WA III, iv, 102.
197. To FS, 5/7/1802, WA IV, xvi, 100.
198. MA X, 569.
199. To FS, 5/5/1798, WA IV, xiii, 137.
200. MA VI/2, 359.
201. MA X, 575.
202. To AG, 3/6/1808, WA IV, xx, 74.
203. MA X, 568.
204. MA X, 568.
205. MA X, 568.
206. GLTT V, 121. See also GLTT V, 124.

207. MA X, 570.
208. MA X, 568.
209. MA X, 569.
210. MA X, 577.
211. MA X, 729.
212. MA X, 729.
213. MA X, 729.
214. MA X, 832.
215. MA X, 728.
216. MA X, 733.
217. MA X, 727.
218. MA X, 738.
219. MA X, 884.
220. MA X, 795.
221. MA X, 733–34.
222. MA X, 734.
223. For a more detailed treatment, see Bell, 'Charakter'.
224. MA X, 786.
225. MA X, 787.
226. Contrast Koopmann, 'Ethik', 280–82.
227. MA VI/2, 375–76.
228. MA X, 785.
229. MA X, 786.
230. MA X, 788.
231. MA VI/1, 542.
232. MA X, 789.
233. Diary, 11/4/1808, WA III, iii, 327.
234. Diary, 1/5/1808, WA III, iii, 331.
235. Boyle, 'Composition', 97.
236. Diary, 15/4/1809, WA III, iv, 22.
237. Boyle, 'Composition'.
238. Diary, 24/7/1809, WA III, iv, 46.
239. Stöcklein, *Wege*, 9.
240. Adler, 'Anziehungskraft', 145–55.
241. Blessin, *Erzählstruktur*, 50.
242. Bell, *Anthropology*, 287–325.
243. Conv. FWR, 28/8/1808, WA V, ii, 216.
244. See Boyle, 'What Really Happens'; Schwartz, *After Jena*.
245. Härtl, *Dokumentation*, 113.
246. EA 124; MA IX, 410.
247. EA 240; MA IX, 529.
248. Conv. FWR, 6, 10/12/1809, WA V, ii, 286.
249. Strack and Eicheldinger, *Fragmente*, I, 52.
250. Diederichsen, 'Wahlverwandtschaften', 142–43.

251. Boyle, 'What Really Happens', 310.
252. EA 13; MA IX, 297.
253. EA 6; MA IX, 290.
254. EA 7; MA IX, 290.
255. Berthollet, *Recherches*.
256. EA 30; MA IX, 314.
257. MA IX, 285.
258. Conv. FWR, 24/7/1809, WA V, ii, 270–71.
259. MA X, 227.
260. EA 33–34; MA IX, 318.
261. GLTT V, 97.
262. Adler, '*Anziehungskraft*', 145–55.
263. EA 34; MA IX, 318.
264. EA 32; MA IX, 316.
265. EA 13; MA IX, 296.
266. EA 30; MA IX, 314.
267. Diary, 5/4/1808, WA III, iii, 327.
268. Diary, 6/4/1808, WA III, iii, 327.
269. Diary, 3/8/1808, WA III, iii, 367.
270. EA 185; MA IX, 473.
271. EA 196; MA IX, 484.
272. EA 196; MA IX, 485.
273. For the following discussion of Mesmerism, see Bell, *Psychology*, 172–80.
274. Bell, *Psychology*, 176.
275. To FS, 10/2/1798, WA IV, xiii, 60–61.
276. GLTT IV, 638–39.
277. EA 29–30; MA IX, 313–14.
278. EA 87, 229; MA IX, 371, 518.
279. EA 230; MA IX, 518.
280. EA 51; MA IX, 336.
281. EA 43; MA IX, 328.
282. Egger, 'Diätetik', 254–55.
283. MA IX, 1220.
284. Strowick, 'Poetik', 429.
285. EA 43; MA IX, 327–28.
286. EA 44; MA IX, 329.
287. Boyle, 'What Really Happens', 311.
288. Conv. FWR, 21/11/1809, WA V, ii, 283–84.
289. Boyle, 'What Really Happens', 305; see also Schwartz, *After Jena*, 20 passim.
290. EA 12; MA IX, 296.
291. To JFC, 7/10/1807, WA IV, xix, 428–29.
292. Schmidt, 'Ironie', 166.
293. To F. M. Klinger, 8/12/1811, WA IV, xxii, 206.
294. MA VI/2, 798–801.

295. To FS, 22/5/1803, WA IV, xvi, 232.
296. Diary, 27/1/1806, WA III, iii, 116.
297. Diary, 14/6/1805, WA III, iii, 112.
298. To CFZ, 7/5/1807, WA IV, xix, 323.
299. MA XVI, 882.
300. MA XVI, 881.
301. MA XVI, 835–59.
302. Diary, 18/5/1810, WA III, iv, 120–21.
303. Diary, 21, 23, 27/7/1810, WA III, iv, 141–42.
304. Jeßing, 'Dichtung und Wahrheit', 280.
305. PS IV, 214; MA XVI, 306.
306. See also to Ludwig I von Bayern, 14/4/1829, WA IV, xlv, 241.
307. GLTT IV, 732.
308. To CS, early 10/1811, WA IV, xxii, 175.
309. To SB, 17/12/1811, WA IV, xxii, 220.
310. To CLK, 23/10/1812, WA IV, xxiii, 116.
311. To FWHT, 27/10/1812, WA IV, xxiii, 121.
312. To G. Sartorius, 24/1/1814, WA IV, xxiv, 124.
313. GLTT V, 541.
314. Conv. JPE, 27/1/1824, WA V, v, 17.
315. Conv. JPE, 30 /3/1831, WA V, viii, 71.
316. PS IV, 21; MA XVI, 13.
317. Bell, *Psychology*, 86–89.
318. MA XVI, 890.
319. GLTT V, 121; see also GLTT V, 124.
320. MA XVI, 889–90.
321. To CS, early 10/1811, WA IV, xxii, 175.
322. Ammerlahn, 'Key', 9.
323. PS IV, 58 (adapted); MA XVI, 70.
324. Grappin, 'Dichtung und Wahrheit', 107–8.
325. PS IV, 340; MA XVI, 491.
326. PS IV, 344; MA XVI, 496.
327. PS IV, 344–45 (adapted); MA XVI, 496–97.
328. PS IV, 402; MA XVI, 579.
329. PS IV, 17; MA XVI, 11.
330. MA XVIII/1, 219.
331. GLTT V, 121.
332. To CLK, 14/3/1807, WA IV, xix, 283.
333. To F. B. von Bucholtz, 14/2/1814, WA IV, xxiv, 153.
334. MA VII, 541.
335. MA VII, 519–20.
336. MA XI/2, 173.
337. PS IV, 210 (adapted); MA XVI, 300.
338. To CFR, 22/1/1811, WA IV, xxii, 21.

339. PS IV, 264; MA XVI, 383.
340. PS IV, 459; MA XVI, 667.
341. SCW I, 550.
342. Paulin, *Schlegel*, 309–10.
343. Paulin, *Schlegel*, 235–36.
344. Barner, 'Bild', 296.
345. Jeßing, '*Dichtung und Wahrheit*', 295.
346. PS IV, 261 (adapted); MA XVI, 376.
347. PS IV, 364; MA XVI, 524.
348. MA XVI, 882.
349. Jeßing, '*Dichtung und Wahrheit*', 287.
350. To CFZ, 19/6/1805, WA IV, xix, 20.
351. Seibt, *Napoleon*, 173–74.
352. MA IX, 633.
353. MA IX, 634.
354. PS III, 28 (adapted); MA IX, 638.
355. MA IX, 639.
356. MA IX, 639.
357. GLTT V, 752.
358. To H. Luden, 12/12/1813, WA IV, xxiv, 65.
359. To CLK, 22/1/1814, WA IV, xxiv, 119.
360. Diary, 9/4/1814, WA III, v, 102.
361. GLTT VI, 54.
362. To A. W. Iffland, 24/5/1814, WA IV, xxiv, 287.
363. Buck, '*Epimenides*', 347.
364. MA IX, 228.
365. MA IX, 223.
366. MA IX, 223.
367. MA IX, 231.
368. Staiger, *Goethe*, II, 528.

Chapter 9. 'What More Could Grandpa Want?'

1. To CS, 17–25/4/1813, WA IV, xxiii, 330.
2. Conv. H. Luden, 11/1813, WA V, iii, 106.
3. To FWHT, 5/1/1814, WA IV, xxiv, 91.
4. To AG, 14/1/1814, WA IV, xxiv, 110.
5. Diary, 25/7/1814, WA III, v, 119.
6. To CG, 28/7/1814, WA IV, xxv, 1.
7. Diary, 31/7/1814, WA III, v, 121.
8. To FWR, 29/8/1814, WA IV, xxv, 27–28.
9. MA XI/2, 208.
10. MA XI/1.2, 9–10.
11. To CLK, 8/2/1815, WA IV, xxv, 190.

12. To G. Sartorius, 16/2/1815, WA IV, xxv, 193.
13. See the poem 'Dem Zweyten Januar 1815', MA XI/1.1, 442.
14. See the poem 'Die Engel stritten', MA XI/1.1, 68; also MA XI/1.1, 64 and Solms, *Vorarbeiten*, 95–96.
15. MA XI/1.2, 435.
16. To C. H. Schlosser, 23/1/1815, WA IV, xxv, 164–65.
17. To C. H. Schlosser, 23/1/1815, WA IV, xxv, 165.
18. Diary, 11/12/1814, WA III, v, 142.
19. To CA, 14/10/1786, WA IV, viii, 33.
20. To CFZ, 17/5/1815, WA IV, xxv, 333.
21. Diary, 6/6/1816, WA III, v, 239.
22. MA XIV, 267.
23. Bosse, '*Noten*', 323.
24. MA XI/1.2, 201.
25. See, e.g., Korff, *Goethezeit*, IV, 496.
26. See, e.g., Lemmel, *Poetologie*, 13.
27. See, e.g., Hillmann, *Dichtung*.
28. MA XI/2, 209.
29. To FWR, 29/8/1814, WA IV, xxv, 27–28.
30. MA XI/1.2, 260–61.
31. Birus, 'Begegnungsformen', 120.
32. MA XIV, 240.
33. To C. H. Schlosser, 23/1/1815, WA IV, xxv, 164–65.
34. To J. F. Rochlitz, 30/1/1812, WA IV, xxii, 252.
35. To FS, 3, 6, 17, 27/5/1797, 21/6/1797, WA IV, xii, 115, 118, 125, 130, 163.
36. Solms, *Vorarbeiten*, 223–24.
37. MA XIV, 239.
38. Mommsen, *Arabische Welt*, 42–43.
39. To O. von Goethe, 21/6/1818, WA IV, xxix, 204–5.
40. To CFZ, 17/5/1815, WA IV, xxv, 330–33.
41. MA XI/1.2, 170.
42. MA XI/1.2, 205.
43. MA XI/1.2, 71.
44. MA XI/1.2, 608.
45. MA X, 222.
46. SB quoted in MA XI/1.2, 607.
47. Quoted in MA XI/1.2, 609.
48. MA XI/1.2, 318.
49. Hammer-Purgstall, *Diwan*, I, xii.
50. GLTT VI, 15.
51. MA XI/1.2, 316–17.
52. Schutjer, 'German Epic/Jewish Epic', 174.
53. Wilson, 'Humanitätssalbader', 147.
54. MA XI/1.2, 219, 223.

55. Mommsen, *Politische Anschauungen*, 197–98.
56. Exodus 2:23.
57. MA XI/1.2, 143–44.
58. Conv. FM, 24/2/1819, WA V, iv, 1–2.
59. MA XI/1.2, 175.
60. MA XI/1.2, 174–77.
61. MA XI/1.2, 206–7.
62. MA XI/1.2, 49.
63. MA XI/1.2, 159.
64. MA XI/1.2, 766.
65. MA XI/1.2, 156.
66. MA XI/1.2, 181.
67. FA III/2, 1484.
68. MA XI/1.2, 181.
69. MA XI/1.2, 152.
70. MA XI/1.2, 764–65; see Plato, *Republic*, VIII, 544c–d.
71. Plato, *Republic*, VIII, 562e.
72. On punctuation in the *Divan*, see Maier, 'Textgestaltung'.
73. Conv. SB, 5/10/1815, WA V, iii, 253.
74. MA X, 787.
75. Conv. SB, 3/8/1815, WA V, iii, 189.
76. Bell, 'Orientalism', 200.
77. Listed at MA XI/1.2, 842–52.
78. Elmarsafy, *Enlightenment Qur'an*, 99–165.
79. Said, *Orientalism*, 103.
80. Excellent discussion in Polaschegg, *Orientalismus*, 291–397.
81. Bell, 'Orientalism', 203; see also Nicholls, 'Natural and Human Science'.
82. MA XI/1.2, 153.
83. MA XI/1.2, 188–89.
84. Bell, 'Goethe's Orientalism', 199.
85. MA XI/1.2, 27.
86. MA XI/1.2, 150.
87. MA XI/1.2, 150.
88. MA XI/1.2, 151.
89. MA XI/1.2, 164.
90. MA XI/1.2, 54.
91. Robertson, *Enlightenment*, 438.
92. MA XI/1.2, 560.
93. MA XI/1.2, 154.
94. MA XI/1.2, 185.
95. MA XI/1.2, 139.
96. MA XI/1.2, 164.
97. To CS, 14/10/1786, WA IV, viii, 30–31.
98. MA XIV, 15.

99. To FS, 26/10/1796, WA IV, xi, 243.
100. MA XV, 680; see also to CFZ, 27/12/1814, WA IV, xxv, 117–18.
101. Wild, 'Italienische Reise', 350.
102. Wild, 'Italienische Reise', 358.
103. Wild, 'Italienische Reise', 359.
104. Osterkamp, *Im Buchstabenbilde*, 319.
105. MA XV, 663.
106. Osterkamp, *Im Buchstabenbilde*, 321.
107. Wild, 'Italienische Reise', 364–65.
108. Mucignat, 'History'.
109. MA XII, 69.
110. MA XV, 404.
111. MA XV, 422.
112. Barner, 'Klassizität', 68.
113. Wild, 'Italienische Reise', 368.
114. Wild, 'Italienische Reise', 349.
115. Barner, 'Klassizität', 80.
116. MA XV, 177.
117. MA XV, 49.
118. MA XV, 301.
119. Wild, 'Italienische Reise', 359.
120. Diary, 19/10/1786, WA III, i, 305.
121. Wild, 'Italienische Reise', 261.
122. PS VI, 179 (adapted); MA XV, 272–75.
123. MA XV, 393.
124. MA XV, 310.
125. MA XV, 254.
126. MA XV, 204.
127. PS VI, 173 (adapted); MA XV, 262.
128. MA XV, 369.
129. PS VI, 182 (adapted); MA XV, 278.
130. Wild, 'Italienische Reise', 339, 350.
131. Barner, 'Klassizität', 74.
132. MA XVIII/2, 219.
133. To F. M. Klinger, 8/12/1811, WA IV, xxii, 206.
134. Tauber, '*Kunst und Altertum*', 414.
135. Tauber, '*Kunst und Altertum*', 414.
136. Birus, '*Kunst und Alterthum*', 59.
137. To CLK, 17/3/1817, WA IV, xxviii, 23–24.
138. MA XI/2, 496–507.
139. MA XI/2, 498.
140. MA XI/2, 501.
141. MA XI/2, 437.
142. Tauber, '*Kunst und Altertum*', 424.

143. Winckelmann, *History*, 129.
144. MA XIII/2, 114; to CFZ, 31/3/1822, WA IV, xxxv, 300.
145. See the poems 'Auch diese will ich nicht verschonen' and 'Auf ewig hab ich sie vertrieben' (MA XIII, 65).
146. MA XIII/2, 119–47.
147. MA XIII/2, 121.
148. MA XVII, 904.
149. MA XI/2, 494–95; MA XVIII/2, 281–87.
150. Trunz, 'Entwurf', 167.
151. Trunz, 'Entwurf', 178.
152. Trunz, 'Entwurf', 156.
153. MA XVIII/2, 283.
154. MA XVIII/2, 283.
155. MA XVIII/2, 283.
156. MA XVIII/2, 287.
157. MA XVIII/2, 283.
158. MA XII, 262.
159. MA XI/2, 569.
160. MA XIV, 251–52.
161. MA XI/2, 568–69.
162. MA XII, 458–60.
163. To CA, 24/1/1821, WA IV, xxxiv, 113.
164. To T. J. Seebeck, 15/1/1813, WA IV, xxiii, 247.
165. MA XII, 700.
166. MA XII, 703.
167. MA XII, 704–5.
168. MA XII, 709–10.
169. Nisbet, *'Witterungslehre'*, 781.
170. MA XIII/2, 275–302.
171. MA XIII/2, 272–73.
172. MA XII, 798–805.
173. MA XIII/2, 236–39; MA XII, 774–79; MA XII, 798–805.
174. MA XVIII/2, 1227; to C. C. von Leonhard, 27/2/1815, WA IV, xxv, 214; to CLK, 17/9/1817, WA IV, xxviii, 252.
175. MA XVIII/2, 364.
176. To C. C. von Leonhard, 8/1/1819, WA IV, xxxi, 52.
177. Conv. FM, 6/3/1828, WA V, vi, 269.
178. MA XIV, 280.
179. Conv. FM, 6/3/1828, WA V, vi, 269.
180. MA XII, 582.
181. Conv. SB, 3/8/1815, WA V, iii, 191.
182. MA XIV, 258–59.
183. To CFZ, 17/5/1829, WA IV, xlv, 273–74; to C.L.F. Schultz, 19–29/6/1829, WA IV, xlv, 314; to SB, 24/11/1831, WA IV, xlix, 152.

184. To CFR, 16/11/1818, WA IV, xxx, 12.
185. To CFR, 16/11/1818, WA IV, xxx, 12.
186. MA XII, 565.
187. MA XII, 565.
188. MA XII, 603–4.
189. To SB, 26/9/1827, WA IV, xliii, 78.
190. To J. C. Stieler, 26/1/1829, WA IV, xlv, 135–36; see also to CFZ, 17/5/1829, WA IV, xlv, 273.
191. MA XIV, 172.
192. MA XII, 921.
193. MA XII, 17–20.
194. Diary, 20–22/2/1809, 7/5/1809, WA III, iv, 11, 12, 27.
195. Conv. JPE, 2/8/1830, WA V, vii, 321–22.
196. MA XII, 20.
197. For example, by Wells, *Development*, 29–30.
198. To CLK, 27/9/1792, WA IV, x, 26.
199. Virgil, *Aeneid*, II, 5–6.
200. Williamson, 'Kotzebue', 906.
201. Williamson, 'Kotzebue', 910.
202. Williamson, 'Kotzebue', 915.
203. Conv. FM, 28//3/1819, WA V, iv, 6.
204. Diary, 30/8/1819, WA III, vii, 87.
205. To FHJ, 27/7/1793, WA IV, x, 100–101.
206. MA XIV, 761.
207. Documented at MA XIV, 761–62.
208. PS V, 692; MA XIV, 440–41.
209. PS V, 674; MA XIV, 413–14. See also Saine, 'Introduction', 615.
210. Saine, 'Introduction', 616.
211. Saine, 'Introduction', 616.
212. PS V, 652; MA XIV, 384–85.
213. PS V, 619; MA XIV, 338–39.
214. PS V, 622; MA XIV, 343.
215. For example, PS V, 622, 625; MA XIV, 342, 346.
216. Quoted in Damm, *Christiane*, 163.
217. PS V, 627; MA XIV, 349.
218. PS V, 624–25; MA XIV, 345.
219. PS V, 635; MA XIV, 360.
220. PS V, 639; MA XIV, 368.
221. MA XV, 404–10.
222. PS V, 640; MA XIV, 368.
223. PS V, 637; MA XIV, 364.
224. To JFC, 23/10/1820, WA IV, xxxiii, 314.
225. See Sina, 'Kollektiv'.
226. Blackall, *Novel*, 269.
227. Vaget, 'Wilhelm-Meister-Literatur', 507.

228. Spranger, 'Perspektivismus', 228.
229. Varnhagen von Ense, *Wanderer*; Grün, *Über Goethe*; Gregorovius, 'Wilhelm Meister'; Hettner, *Sozialismus*.
230. Nemoianu, 'Conservative Contexts'; Redfield, 'Dissection'.
231. MA XVII, 40. As no translation of the 1821 version exists, all translations are my own.
232. MA XVII, 51–52.
233. MA XVII, 53.
234. MA XVII, 73.
235. MA XVII, 75.
236. Øhrgaard, 'Feldforschung', 61–62.
237. Bahr, '*Wanderjahre*', 67.
238. Henkel, 'Kritik', 84.
239. MA XVII, 961–63.
240. Koschorke, 'Textur', 594–98.
241. MA XVII, 160.
242. WA I, xxv/2, 232, 239, 243.
243. Koschorke, 'Textur', 602.
244. MA XVII, 47.
245. MA XVII, 43.
246. MA XVII, 46.
247. Robertson, *Enlightenment*, 440.
248. MA XVII, 48.
249. MA XVII, 42–43.
250. MA XVII, 77, 81.
251. McKenzie-McHarg, 'Unknown Superiors'.
252. MA XVII, 79.
253. MA XVII, 82.
254. MA XVII, 91–92.
255. Conv. SB, 5/8/1815, WA V, iii, 199–200.
256. Brown, *Cyclical Narratives*, 91.
257. MA XVII, 975.
258. MA XVII, 975.
259. MA XVII, 83.
260. MA XVII, 85.
261. MA XVII, 87–88.
262. MA XVII, 88.
263. MA XVII, 91.
264. MA XVII, 1050.
265. Brown, *Cyclical Narratives*, 89.
266. Schütz, *Pustkuchen*.
267. MA XVII, 144.
268. MA XVII, 145.
269. MA XVII, 145.
270. MA XVII, 139.

271. MA XVII, 482.
272. MA XVII, 976.
273. MA XVII, 82.
274. MA XVII, 83–84.
275. MA XVII, 93.
276. MA XVII, 94.
277. MA XVII, 230.
278. Øhrgaard, 'Feldforschung', 53.
279. Diary, 21–28/5/1812, WA III, iv, 287–89.
280. To C. L. von Welden, 17[?]/6/ 1819, WA IV, xxxi, 235.
281. MA XVII, 183.
282. Conv. SB, 5/8/1815, WA V, iii, 199–200.
283. MA XVII, 183.
284. MA XVII, 183.
285. MA XVII, 197–98.
286. Carter, 'Striving and Demand', 127–28.
287. MA XVII, 201.
288. MA XVII, 201.
289. MA XVII, 197.

Chapter 10. 'These Very Serious Jokes'

1. Diary, 1/1/1826, WA III, x, 143.
2. To CFR, 7/2/1826, WA IV, xl, 294.
3. Diary, 14/2/1826, WA III, x, 161.
4. MA XIII/1, 423.
5. Diary, 17/2/1826, WA III, x, 162.
6. Diary, 15/4/1826, WA III, x, 183.
7. To CFR, 20/9/1826, WA IV, xli, 159; C. von Sternberg, 26/9/1826, WA IV, xli, 167.
8. To CFR, 12/5/1826, WA IV, xli, 29–30.
9. To CFR, 12/5/1826, WA IV, xli, 29–30; conv. JPE, 3/10/1828, MA XIX, 256.
10. To CFR, 12/5/1826, WA IV, xli, 30; conv. JPE, 1/6/1826, MA XIX, 161; to CFR, 18/6/1829, WA IV, xlv, 293–94.
11. To CFR, 12/5/1826, WA IV, xli, 29.
12. Conv. FJS, 17/10/1828, MA XIX, 624.
13. Conv. SB, 20/5/1826, WA V, v, 286–87.
14. Conv. FJS, 3/2/1830, MA XIX, 641.
15. Conv. FJS, 3/2/1830, MA XIX, 642–43.
16. Conv. JPE, 17/3/1830, MA XIX, 664.
17. To CFZ, 9/11/1829, WA IV, xlvi, 140–41.
18. To CFZ, 9/11/1829, WA IV, xlvi, 141.
19. To FM, 26/2/1830, WA IV, xlvi, 251.
20. To CFZ, 29/4/1830, WA IV, xlvii, 43–44.
21. Conv. FJS, 3/2/1830, MA XIX, 642–43.

22. Conv. FM, 6 /3/1828, WA V, vi, 268.
23. MA XVII, 471–72.
24. MA XVII, 664.
25. MA XVII, 666.
26. MA XVII, 669.
27. On the theme of compensation in the novel, see Zumbusch, 'Kompensationslogik'.
28. MA XVII, 1057.
29. PS X, 140; MA XVII, 301.
30. PS X, 143; MA XVII, 304.
31. PS X, 319; MA XVII, 550.
32. MA XVII, 552.
33. Derré, 'Beziehungen', 44–45.
34. PS X, 416; MA XVII, 685.
35. PS X, 417; MA XVII, 687.
36. EG 636; MA V, 433.
37. Diary, 19/5/1822, WA III, viii, 198.
38. Listed in Arndt, 'Harmony', 196.
39. Noyes, 'Cosmopolitanism', 444.
40. PS X, 115; MA XVII, 267.
41. MA XVII, 641.
42. PS X, 364; MA XVII, 613.
43. Redfield, 'Dissection', 18. See Nemoianu, 'Conservative Contexts', 46–47, on how the detailed understanding and appreciation of cottage industries and home production tallies with Goethe's Möserian sympathies.
44. Redfield, 'Dissection', 18–19.
45. PS X, 298; MA XVII, 519.
46. PS X, 380; MA XVII, 635.
47. Maierhofer, 'Perspektivenwechsel', 509.
48. PS X, 379; MA XVII, 634.
49. PS X, 305 (adapted); MA XVII, 528.
50. PS X, 380; MA XVII, 636.
51. PS X, 378; MA XVII, 633.
52. PS X, 298 (adapted); MA XVII, 518–19.
53. PS X, 405–6; MA XVII, 671.
54. PS X, 425; MA XVII, 698.
55. PS X, 380; MA XVII, 634–35.
56. PS X, 311; MA XVII, 537.
57. Conv. FJS, 3/2/1830, MA XIX, 642–43.
58. PS X, 139; MA XVII, 299.
59. PS X, 301; MA XVII, 523; compare Rousseau, *Émile*, 472; *Oeuvres*, V, 431.
60. Reiss, 'Wanderjahre', 50.
61. PS X, 405–6; MA XVII, 671.
62. Robertson, *Enlightenment*, 416.
63. PS X, 383; MA XVII, 639.

64. PS X, 383; MA XVIII, 640.
65. Arndt, 'Harmony', 202.
66. PS X, 296; MA XVII, 516.
67. PS X, 296; MA XVII, 516.
68. PS X, 297; MA XVII, 517–18.
69. PS X, 182–83; MA XVII, 357–58. See also the aphorisms on mathematics at PS X, 308, 311–12; MA XVII, 533, 537–38.
70. PS X, 427; MA XVII, 701.
71. PS X, 301; MA XVII, 522.
72. Rousseau, *Émile*, 206; *Oeuvres*, IV, 353.
73. PS X, 175; MA XVII, 348.
74. PS X, 409; MA XVII, 675.
75. PS X, 307; MA XVII, 532.
76. PS X, 412; MA XVII, 679.
77. Reiss, '*Wanderjahre*', 52.
78. Conv. JPE, 15/5/1831, WA V, viii, 87.
79. Redfield, 'Dissection', 17.
80. MA XVII, 1054–56.
81. MA XVII, 1050.
82. Conv. JPE, 29/1/1827, WA V, vi, 40.
83. Boyle, 'Novelle', 11–14.
84. PS XI, 280; MA XVIII/1, 376.
85. On the Moses work, see to FS, 3, 6, 17, 27/5/1797, 21/6/1797, WA IV, xii, 115, 118, 125, 130, 163. On 'The Hunt', see, e.g., to Schiller 26/4/1797, WA IV, xii, 104–5.
86. See Steer, '"Novelle"'.
87. PS XI, 274 (adapted); MA XVIII/1, 368.
88. PS XI, 277; MA XVIII/1, 372.
89. Otto, '"Novelle"', 257.
90. Wells, 'Organic Structure', 428.
91. PS XI, 267; MA XVIII/1, 357.
92. Steer, '"Novelle"', 418–21.
93. PS XI, 265 (adapted); MA XVIII/1, 355.
94. Träger cited in Rowland, 'Chaos', 114.
95. PS III, 27; MA IX, 636. See Staroste, 'Darstellung', 326.
96. On the unresolved problem of Honorio, see Auer, 'Hearing', 64–65.
97. Otto, '"Novelle"', 255.
98. Andrade, *Gunpowder*, 115.
99. Seibt, *Napoleon*, 11.
100. FA I, xxii, 937–38.
101. For example, Said, *Orientalism*, 19–20.
102. Conv. JPE, 31/1/1827, WA V, vi, 46.
103. Bohnenkamp, FA I, xxii, 937–40.
104. MA XVIII/2, 180–81.
105. Weber, 'Weltliteratur', 1134.

106. To CFZ, 31/12/1829, WA IV, xlvi, 198–99.
107. MA XIII/1, 540.
108. Bohnenkamp, 'Orientreise', 151–52.
109. MA XVIII/2, 99.
110. MA XVIII/2, 12.
111. FA I, xxii, 954.
112. MA XVII, 844.
113. MA XI/2, 246–48; XVIII/2, 107–21.
114. MA XIII/1, 380–81, 408–18.
115. MA XI/2, 267–80.
116. Bohnenkamp, 'Orientreise', 153–54.
117. MA XVIII/2, 62.
118. To WH, 17/3/1832, WA IV, lxix, 283.
119. Schlaffer, *Allegorie*, 3.
120. Bohnenkamp, 'Arbeit', 201.
121. MA VI/1, 543.
122. MA VI/1, 1052.
123. Bohnenkamp, 'Arbeit', 210–11.
124. Conv. FM, 6/3/1828, WA V, vi, 269.
125. Olenschlager, *Erläuterungen*.
126. MA XVIII/1, 934.
127. MA VI/2, 371.
128. FA I, vii/2, 400.
129. MA XVIII/1, 105.
130. GF II, 559–60.
131. MA XVIII/1, 105.
132. MA X, 67.
133. Williams, *'Faust'*, 124.
134. MA XIII/2, 275.
135. MA XVIII/1, 653.
136. FA I, vii/2, 413.
137. MA XVIII/1, 111.
138. Fritz, *Dokumente*, 562.
139. Grappin, 'Gestalt', 112.
140. Williams, *'Faust'*, 130.
141. FA I, vii/2, 432.
142. GF II, 594–95.
143. GF II, 597.
144. GF II, 619.
145. MA XVIII/1, 141.
146. MA XVIII/1, 141.
147. MA XVIII/1, 143.
148. MA XVIII/1, 145.
149. MA XVIII/1, 155.

150. Conv. JPE, 10/1/1830, WA V, vii, 179.
151. MA XVIII/1, 157.
152. MA XVIII/1, 163.
153. MA XVIII/1, 168.
154. Williams, 'Faust', 141.
155. MA XVIII/1, 176.
156. MA XVIII/1, 176.
157. Williams, 'Faust', 142.
158. Williams, 'Faust', 143.
159. FA I, vii/2, 505–8.
160. FA I, vii/2, 514.
161. MA XVIII/1, 181.
162. Williams, 'Faust', 146.
163. Conv. JPE, 21/2/1831, WA V, viii, 31.
164. MA XVIII/1, 196.
165. GF II, 767.
166. MA XVIII/1, 196.
167. Herodotus, *Histories*, III, 102–5.
168. MA XVIII/1, 202.
169. FA I, vii/2, 658.
170. MA XVIII/1, 204.
171. Williams, 'Faust', 156–57.
172. MA XVIII/1, 205.
173. MA XVIII/1, 211.
174. MA XVIII/1, 213.
175. MA XVIII/1, 214.
176. MA XVIII/1, 230.
177. MA XVIII/1, 231; see FA I, vii/2, 575.
178. MA XVIII/1, 232.
179. Williams, 'Faust', 160–62.
180. Williams, 'Faust', 164.
181. Williams, 'Faust', 164.
182. MA XVIII/1, 249.
183. MA XVIII/1, 253.
184. MA XVIII/1, 261.
185. GF II, 893–94.
186. MA XVIII/1, 267.
187. MA XVIII/1, 268–69.
188. Listed in GF II, 842.
189. MA XVIII/1, 277.
190. MA XVIII/1, 279.
191. MA XVIII/1, 1021.
192. MA XVIII/1, 288.
193. MA XVIII/1, 289.

194. Boyle, 'Politics', 31–32.
195. MA XVIII/1, 288.
196. MA XVIII/1, 288.
197. MA XVIII/1, 289.
198. Horace, *Odes*, III, i, 25–26.
199. MA XVIII/1, 291.
200. MA XVIII/1, 292.
201. Diary, 8/8/1806, WA III, iii, 156.
202. MA XVIII/1, 301.
203. Olenschlager, *Erläuterungen*.
204. MA XVI, 201; see GF II, 944.
205. FA I, vii/2, 690–91.
206. MA XVIII/1, 1090.
207. GF II, 1008.
208. MA VI/1, 616.
209. MA XVIII/1, 319.
210. MA XVIII/1, 319, VI/1, 618.
211. MA XVIII/1, 321.
212. MA XVIII/1, 323.
213. MA XVIII/1, 327.
214. More detailed analysis in Bell, 'Sorge'.
215. MA XVIII/1, 329.
216. MA XVIII/1, 334.
217. MA XVIII/1, 335.
218. MA XVIII/1, 334.
219. Boyle, 'Politics', 42.
220. FA I, vii/2, 749–50.
221. PS X, 115; MA XVII, 267.
222. FA I, vii/2, 749–50.
223. MA III/1, 270; Robertson, 'Redemption', 53.
224. GF II, 1096–97.
225. Boyle, 'Politics', 40–41.
226. Robertson, 'Redemption', 53.
227. MA XVIII/1, 347.
228. MA XVII, 778.
229. MA XVIII/1, 345.
230. MA XVIII/1, 346.
231. FA I, vii/2, 801, GF II, 1143.
232. MA XVIII/1, 543.
233. FA I, vii/2, 790.
234. FA I, vii/2, 792.
235. MA XXXIII, 1–39.
236. MA XXXIII, 145.
237. MA XVIII/1, 349.

238. MA XVIII/1, 349.
239. GF II, 1156.
240. FA I, vii/2, 791.
241. MA XVIII/1, 351.
242. Goethe, *Faust Part One*, 149.
243. MA XVIII/1, 1165.
244. Diary, 18/12/1816, WA III, v, 295.
245. GLTT VII, 95.
246. PS V, 535; MA XVI, 731.
247. MA XVI, 801.
248. MA XVI, 763.
249. MA XVI, 829.
250. MA XVI, 827, 829.
251. PS VII, 108; MA XVI, 831–32.
252. Nicholls, *Daemonic*, 230–31.
253. MA XVI, 712–17.
254. PS V, 524; MA XVI, 715.
255. PS V, 523; MA XVI, 714.
256. Conv. FJS, 2/8/1830, WA V, vii, 320–21.
257. Diary, 7/5/1830, WA III, xii, 238.
258. To CLK, 12/9/1830, WA IV, xlvii, 217.
259. Diary, 7/5/1830, WA III, xii, 238.
260. MA XVIII/2, 509.
261. MA XVIII/2, 532–33.
262. Diary, 22/7/1830, WA III, xii, 277.
263. MA XII, 294–305.
264. MA XII, 296.
265. MA XII, 295.
266. MA XII, 296.
267. MA XII, 295.
268. MA XII, 295.
269. MA XII, 295.
270. MA XII, 294.
271. MA XII, 294–95.
272. Dennett, *Dangerous Idea*, 521.
273. MA XVIII/2, 423.
274. Diary, 24/9/1826, WA III, x, 248.
275. MA XVII, 714.
276. Arnold, *Essays*, 110.
277. MA XI/1.2, 71.

REFERENCES

Adelung, Johann Christoph, *Grammatisch-kritisches Wörterbuch der hochdeutschen Mundart* (Vienna: Bauer, 1811), https://lexika.digitale-sammlungen.de/adelung/online/angebot

Adler, Jeremy, *'Eine fast magische Anziehungskraft': Goethes 'Wahlverwandtschaften' und die Chemie seiner Zeit* (Munich: Beck, 1987)

Adler, Jeremy, *Goethe: Die Erfindung der Moderne* (Munich: Beck, 2022)

Adler, Jeremy, 'Schellings Philosophie und Goethes weltanschauliche Lyrik', GJ 112 (1995), 149–65

Agrippa (Heinrich Cornelius Agrippa von Nettesheim), *De incertitudine et vanitate scientiarum et artium atque de excellentia verbi Dei declamatio invectiva* (Antwerp: Graphaeus, 1530)

Ammerlahn, Hellmut, '"Key" and "Treasure Chest" Configurations in Goethe's Works: A Comparative Overview in Poetological Perspective', *Monatshefte* 101 (2009), 1–18

Andrade, Tonio, *The Gunpowder Age: China, Military Innovation, and the Rise of the West in World History* (Princeton: Princeton UP, 2016)

Anon., Review of *Die Leiden des jungen Werthers*, *Reichspostreuter*, 11 November 1774, 3–4Arber, Agnes, 'Goethe's Botany', *Chronica Botanica* 10 (1946), 63–126

Arber, Agnes, *The Natural Philosophy of Plant Form* (Cambridge: CUP, 1950)

Armstrong, Bruce, 'An Idyl Sad and Strange: The St. Joseph the Second Section and the Presentation of Craft-Work in Goethe's *Wilhelm Meisters Wanderjahre*', *Monatshefte* 77 (1985), 415–32

Arndt, Karl J. R., 'The Harmony Society and *Wilhelm Meisters Wanderjahre*', *Comparative Literature* 10 (1958), 193–202

Arnold, Gottfried, *Unparteiyische Kirchen- und Ketzerhistorie*, 4 vols. (Frankfurt: no publ., 1699–1700)

Arnold, Matthew, *Culture and Anarchy*, ed. Jane Garnett (Oxford: OUP, 2006)

Arnold, Matthew, *Lectures and Essays on Criticism*, ed. R. H. Super (Ann Arbor: University of Michigan Press, 1962)

Arntzen, Helmut, 'An den Mond', in: GH I, 180–87

Assling, Reinhard, *Werthers Leiden: Die ästhetische Rebellion der Innerlichkeit* (Frankfurt: Lang, 1981)

Auer, Michael E., 'Of Hearing and Hearing of "Das Unerhörte" in Goethe's "Novella"', GR 86 (2011), 58–72

Bahr, Ehrhard, 'Goethe's "Wanderjahre" as an Experimental Novel', *Mosaic* 5 (1972), 61–71

Baioni, Giuliano, 'Märchen, Wilhelm Meisters Lehrjahre, Hermann und Dorothea. Zur Gesellschaftsidee der deutschen Klassik', GJ 92 (1975), 73–127

Barner, Wilfried, 'Altertum, Überlieferung, Natur. Über Klassizität und autobiographische Konstruktion in Goethes *Italienischer Reise*', GJ 105 (1988), 64–92

Barner, Wilfried, 'Goethes Bild von der deutschen Literatur der Aufklärung: zum siebten Buch von *Dichtung und Wahrheit*', in: Wolfgang Frühwald (ed.), *Zwischen Aufklärung und Restauration: sozialer Wandel in der deutschen Literatur (1700–1848). Festschrift für Wolfgang Martens zum 65. Geburtstag* (Tübingen: Niemeyer, 1989), 283–305

Barros, D. Benjamin, 'Negative Causation in Causal and Mechanistic Explanation', *Synthese* 190 (2013), 449–69

Batteux, Charles, *The Fine Arts Reduced to a Single Principle*, trans. James O. Young (Oxford: OUP, 2015)

Beiser, Frederick C., *Enlightenment, Revolution and Romanticism: The Genesis of Modern German Political Thought, 1790–1800* (Cambridge, MA: Harvard UP, 1992)

Beiser, Frederick C., 'Fichte and the French Revolution', in: David James and Günter Zöller (eds.), *The Cambridge Companion to Fichte* (Cambridge: CUP, 2016), 38–64

Beiser, Frederick C., *The German Historicist Tradition* (Oxford: OUP, 2011)

Bell, David, 'Goethe's Orientalism', in: Nicholas Boyle and John Guthrie (eds.), *Goethe and the English-Speaking World: Essays from Cambridge Symposium for His 250th Anniversary* (Rochester, NY: Camden House, 2002), 199–212

Bell, David, *Spinoza in Germany from 1670 to the Age of Goethe* (London: Institute of Germanic Studies, 1985)

Bell, Matthew, 'Charakter (Character)', GLPC 1/2 (2021), https://doi.org/10.5195/glpc.2021.41

Bell, Matthew, 'Class', in: Charlotte Lee (ed.), *Goethe in Context* (Cambridge: CUP, 2024), 48–56

Bell, Matthew, 'Embracing the Enemy: The Problem of Religion in Goethe's "Confessions of a Beautiful Soul"', in: Juliana de Albuquerque and Gert Hofmann (eds.), *Anti/Idealism: Reinterpreting a German Discourse* (Berlin and Boston: De Gruyter. 2019), 13–26

Bell, Matthew, *The German Tradition of Psychology in Literature and Thought, 1700–1840* (Cambridge: CUP, 2005)

Bell, Matthew, *Goethe's Naturalistic Anthropology: Man and Other Plants* (Oxford: OUP, 1994)

Bell, Matthew, 'Goethe's Two Types of Classicism'. *Publications of the English Goethe Society* 64–65 (1996), 97–115.

Bell, Matthew, 'The Idea of Fragmentariness in German Literature and Philosophy, 1760–1800', MLR 89 (1994), 372–92

Bell, Matthew, 'Myth and "Metaphysical Reach" in Goethe's Iphigenie auf Tauris', in: *Poetry and Poetics, Greek and Beyond: essays in honour of M. S. Silk*, ed. Fiona MacIntosh and David Ricks, Routledge / Centre for Hellenic Studies, forthcoming 2025.

Bell, Matthew, 'The Poetic Coherence of Goethe's Venetian Epigrams', PEGS 78 (2009), 117–30

Bell, Matthew, 'Society and the Sources of Legality in Goethe's *Die natürliche Tochter*', *Colloquia Germanica* 55 (2022), 9–20

Bell, Matthew, 'Sorge, Epicurean Psychology, and the Classical *Faust*', *Oxford German Studies* 28 (1999), 82–130

Bell, Matthew, 'This Was a Man!' Goethe's *Egmont* and Shakespeare's *Julius Caesar*', MLR 111 (2016), 141–61

Bennett, Benjamin, 'Prometheus and Saturn: The Three Versions of *Götz von Berlichingen*', *American Association of Teachers of German* 58 (1985), 335–47

Berlin, Isaiah, 'My Intellectual Path', in: I. B., *The Power of Ideas*, ed. Henry Hardy (Princeton: Princeton UP, 2013), 1–23

Bersier, Gabrielle, 'Goethe's Parody of "Nazarene" Iconography: The Joseph Story in *Wilhelm Meisters Wanderjahre*', GY 9 (1999), 264–77

Berthollet, Claude-Louis, *Recherches sur les lois de l'affinité* (Paris: Baudouin, 1801)

Biedermann, Woldemar von, *Goethe und Leipzig: zur hundertjährigen Wiederkehr des Tages von Goethe's Aufnahme auf Leipzigs Hochschule* (Leipzig: Brockhaus, 1865)

Birus, Hendrik, 'Begegnungsformen des Westlichen und Östlichen in Goethes *West-östlichem Divan*', GJ 114 (1997), 113–31

Birus, Hendrik, '*Über Kunst und Alterthum* im Lauf der Jahre', in: Hendrik Birus, Anne Bohnenkamp, and Wolfgang Bunzel (eds.), *Goethes Zeitschrift 'Ueber Kunst und Alterthum'. Von den 'Rhein- und Mayn-Gegenden' zur Weltliteratur* (Göttingen: Göttinger Verlag der Kunst, 2016), 46–83

Blackall, Eric A., *The Emergence of German as a Literary Language* (Cambridge: CUP, 1959)

Blackall, Eric A., *Goethe and the Novel* (Ithaca, NY: Cornell UP, 1976)

Blank, Andreas, 'Wolff on Duties of Esteem in the Law of Peoples', *European Journal of Philosophy* 29 (2021), 475–86

Blanning, T. C. W., *Reform and Revolution in Mainz, 1743–1803* (Cambridge: CUP, 1974)

Blessin, Stefan, *Erzählstruktur und Leserhandlung. Zur Theorie der literarischen Kommunikation am Beispiel von Goethes 'Wahlverwandtschaften'* (Heidelberg: Winter, 1974)

Bloom, Allan, 'Introduction', in: Rousseau, *Emile, or On Education*, 3–28.

Boa, Elizabeth, '*Hermann und Dorothea*: An Early Example of Heimatliteratur?', PEGS 69 (1999), 21–36

Bode, Wilhelm, *Goethes Leben: Rom und Weimar, 1787–1790* (Berlin: Mittler, 1923)

Boghossian, Paul A., 'What is Social Construction?', in: Daphne Patai and Will H. Corral (eds.), *Theory's Empire: An Anthology of Dissent* (New York: Columbia UP, 2004), 562–72

Bohnenkamp, Anne, 'Goethes Arbeit am *Faust*', GJ 114 (1997), 199–217

Bohnenkamp, Anne, 'Goethes poetische Orientreise', GJ 120 (2003), 144–56

Bois-Reymond, Emil du, 'Goethe und kein Ende', in: E. B.-R., *Reden*, 2 vols. (Leipzig: Veit, 1912), II, 157–83

Boisserée, Sulpiz, *Tagebücher*, ed. Hans-J. Weitz, 5 vols. (Darmstadt: Roether, 1978–1995)

Bollacher, Martin, *Der junge Goethe und Spinoza: Studien zur Geschichte der Spinozismus in der Epoche des Sturms und Drangs* (Tübingen: Niemeyer, 1969)

Böschenstein, Bernhard, 'Die Bedeutung der Quelle für Goethes *Natürliche Tochter*', in: B. B. (ed.), *Goethe: 'Die natürliche Tochter'. Mit den Memoiren der Stéphanie Louise de Bourbon-Conti und drei Studien von Bernhard Böschenstein* (Frankfurt: Insel, 1990), 317–45

Bosse, Anke, 'Noten und Abhandlungen zum besseren Verständnis des West-östlichen Divans', in: GH I, 323–34

Boyle, Nicholas, 'The Composition of *Die Wahlverwandtschaften*', PEGS 84 (2015), 93–137

Boyle, Nicholas, 'Du ahnungsloser Engel Du!': Some Current Views of Goethe's *Faust*', GLL 36 (1983), 116–47

Boyle, Nicholas, 'Embodied Cognition: Goethe's Farbenlehre as Phenomenology', GLL 70 (2017), 478–90

Boyle, Nicholas, 'Goethe, *Novelle*', in: Peter Hutchinson (ed.), *Landmarks in German Short Prose* (Oxford: Lang, 2003), 11–27

Boyle, Nicholas, *Goethe: The Poet and the Age: Volume I: The Poetry of Desire, 1749–1790* (Oxford: OUP, 1991)

Boyle, Nicholas, *Goethe: The Poet and the Age: Volume II: Revolution and Renunciation, 1790–1803* (Oxford: OUP, 2000)

Boyle, Nicholas, 'The Politics of *Faust II*: Another Look at the Stratum of 1831', PEGS 52 (1982), 4–43

Boyle, Nicholas, 'What Really Happens in *Die Wahlverwandtschaften*', GQ 89 (2016), 298–312

Brown, Jane K., 'Building Bridges: Goethe's Fairy-Tale Aesthetics', GY 23 (2016), 1–17

Brown, Jane K., *Cyclical Narratives: 'Die Unterhaltungen deutscher Ausgewanderten' and 'Wilhelm Meisters Wanderjahre'* (Chapel Hill: University of North Carolina Press, 2020)

Brucker, Jakob, *Institutiones Historiae Philosophicae Usui Academicae Iuventutis* (Leipzig: Breitkopf, 1747)

Buck, Theo, '*Des Epimenides Erwachen*', in: GH II, 341–51

Buffon, Georges-Louis Leclerc, Comte de, *Les Époques de la Nature*, vol. 1 (Paris: Imprimerie Royale, 1780)

Burke, Edmund, *The Correspondence of Edmund Burke. Volume 6. July 1789 to December 1791*, ed. Alfred Cobban and Robert A. Smith (Cambridge: CUP, 1967)

Busch-Salmen, Gabriele, 'Theaterpraxis in Weimar', in: GH 'Supplemente' I, 1–53

Carnegie, Andrew, *Autobiography of Andrew Carnegie* (London: Constable, 1920)

Carter, William Howard, 'The Law of Striving and Demand: Goethe's *Faust* and the Economic Theories of Steuart, Möser, and Schlosser', unpublished PhD thesis (UC Santa Barbara, 2005)

Costazza, Alessandro, 'Ein Aufsatz aus der Zeit von Moritz' Weimarer Aufenthalt: Eine Revision der Datierung und Zuschreibung von Goethes Spinoza-Studie', GJ 112 (1995), 259–74

Dahnke, Hans-Dietrich, 'Zacharias Werner', in: GH IV/2

Damm, Sigrid, *Christiane und Goethe: Eine Recherche* (Frankfurt: Suhrkamp, 2001)

Darrow, Margaret H., *Revolution in the House: Family, Class and Inheritance in Southern France, 1775–1825* (Princeton: Princeton UP, 1989)

Darwin, Charles, *On the Origin of Species by Means of Natural Selection, or the Preservation of Favoured Races in the Struggle for Life*, 1st ed. (London: Murray, 1859)

Darwin, Charles, *On the Origin of Species by Means of Natural Selection, or the Preservation of Favoured Races in the Struggle for Life*, 3rd ed. (London: Murray, 1861)

Dennett, Daniel C., *Darwin's Dangerous Idea: Evolution and the Meanings of Life* (New York: Simon and Schuster, 1995)

Derré, Françoise, 'Die Beziehungen zwischen Felix, Hersilie und Wilhelm in Wilhelm Meisters Wanderjahren. Eine Textinterpretation', GJ 94 (1977), 38–48

Diederichsen, Uwe, 'Goethes *Wahlverwandtschaften*—auch ein juristischer Roman?', GJ 118 (2001), 142–57

Diels, Hermann, *Die Fragmente der Vorsokratiker* (Berlin: Weidmann, 1903)
Doyle, William, *The Oxford History of the French Revolution* (Oxford: OUP, 2003)
Durchhardt, Heinz, 'Frankfurt am Main im 18. Jahrhundert', in: Lothar Gall (ed.), *Frankfurt am Main: Die Geschichte der Stadt in neun Beiträgen* (Sigmaringen: Thorbecke, 1991), 261–302
Durrani, Osman, *Faust: Icon of Modern Culture* (Robertsbridge: Helm, 2004)
Egger, Irmgard, '"[...] ihre große Mäßigkeit": Diätetik und Askese in Goethes Roman *Die Wahlverwandtschaften*', GJ 114 (1997), 253–63
Ehrhardt, Gundula, 'Wahl-Anziehung: Herders Spinoza-Schrift und Goethes *Wahlverwandtschaften*', GJ 115 (1998), 77–95
Ellis, John M., 'The Vexed Question of Egmont's Political Judgement', in: C. P. Magill, Brian A. Rowley, and Christopher A. Smith (eds.), *Tradition and Creation: Essays in Honour of Elizabeth Mary Wilkinson* (Leeds: Maney, 1978), 116–30
Elmarsafy, Ziad, *The Enlightenment Qur'an: The Politics of Translation and the Construction of Islam* (London: Oneworld, 2009)
Engelhardt, Wolf von, *Goethe im Gespräch mit der Erde: Landschaft, Gesteine, Mineralien und Erdgeschichte in seinem Leben und Werk* (Weimar: Böhlau, 2003)
Engelhardt, Wolf von, *Goethes Weltansichten. Auch eine Biographie* (Weimar: Böhlau, 2007)
Epstein, Klaus, *The Genesis of German Conservatism* (Princeton: Princeton UP, 1966)
Estermann, Monika, 'Goethe in der Nachkriegszeit. Über das Spektrum seiner Funktionen', *IABLIS Jahrbuch für europäische Prozesse* 19 (2020), www.iablis.de/iablis/themen/2020-schach-dem-wissen/thema-2020/616-goethe-in-der-nachkriegszeit-ueber-das-spektrum-seiner-funktionen
Eulner, Hans-Heinz, 'Johann Christian Senckenbergs Tagebücher als historische Quelle', *Medizinhistorisches Journal* 7 (1972), 233–43
Fichte, Johann Gottlieb, *Gesamtausgabe der Bayerischen Akademie der Wissenschaften*, ed. Erich Fuchs et al. (Stuttgart: Frommann-Holzboog, 1962–2012)
Förster, Eckart, *The Twenty-Five Years of Philosophy* (Cambridge, MA: Harvard UP, 2012)
Friedeburg, Robert von, *Luther's Legacy: The Thirty Years War and the Modern Notion of 'State' in the Empire, 1530s to 1790s* (Cambridge: CUP, 2016)
Fritz, Wolfgang D., *Dokumente zur Geschichte des Deutschen Reiches und seiner Verfassung: 1354–1356* (Wiesbaden: Harrassowitz, 1992)
Fröschle, Hartmut, *Goethes Verhältnis zur Romantik* (Würzburg: Königshausen & Neumann, 2002)
Fullenwider, Henry F., 'The Goethean Fragment "Die Natur" in English Translation', *Comparative Literature Studies* 23 (1986), 170–77
Gage, John, *Colour and Meaning: Art, Science, and Symbolism* (London: Thames & Hudson, 2000)
Gailus, Andreas, 'Form and Chance. The German Novella', in: Franco Moretti (ed.), *The Novel*, vol. 2 (Princeton: Princeton UP, 2006), 739–76
Gaskill, Howard, 'Ossian, Herder and the Idea of Folk Song', in: David Hill (ed.), *Literature of the Sturm und Drang* (Rochester, NY: Camden House, 2003), 95–116
Gaskill, Howard, 'Room at the Inn? Werther in Wahlheim', GLL 76 (2023), 191–97
Gebhardt, Jürgen (ed.), *Die Revolution des Geistes. Politisches Denken in Deutschland 1770–1830: Goethe, Kant, Fichte, Hegel, Humboldt* (Munich: List, 1968)

Gillo, Idan, 'Die verkehrte Bekehrung in Goethes *Faust*', GQ 86 (2013), 464–82
Goebel, Eckart, 'Chewing: Goethe's *Proserpina*', PEGS 86 (2017), 139–49
Goethe, Johann Wolfgang von, *Faust, Part One*, trans. David Luke (Oxford: OUP, 1987)
Goethe, Johann Wolfgang von, *The Flight to Italy: Diary and Selected Letters*, trans. T. J. Reed (Oxford: OUP, 1999)
Gottschewski, Lydia, *Männerbund und Frauenfrage. Die Frau im neuen Staat* (München: Lehmann, 1934)
Gräf, Hans Gerhard, *Skizzen zu des Dichters Leben und Werken* (Leipzig: Haessel, 1924)
Graham, Ilse, *Goethe: Portrait of the Artist* (Berlin: De Gruyter, 1977)
Grappin, Pierre, 'Dichtung und Wahrheit, 10. und 11. Buch. Verfahren und Ziele autobiographischer Stilisierung', GJ 97 (1980), 103–13
Grappin, Pierre, 'Zur Gestalt des Kaisers in *Faust II*', GJ 91 (1974), 107–16
Graubner, Hans, 'Theological Empiricism: Aspects of Johann Georg Hamann's Reception of Hume', *Hume Studies* 15 (1989), 377–86
Gregorovius, Ferdinand, *Goethes 'Wilhelm Meister' in seinen sozialistischen Elementen entwickelt* (Königsberg: Bornträger, 1849)
Griffiths, Elystan, *The Shepherd, the Volk, and the Middle Class: Transformations of Pastoral in German-Language Writing, 1750–1850* (Rochester, NY: Camden House, 2020)
Grimm, Herman, 'Goethe in freier Luft. Zu seinem hundertfünfzigsten Geburtstag', *Deutsche Rundschau* 100 (1899), 165–71
Grün, Karl, *Über Goethe vom menschlichen Standpunkte* (Darmstadt: Leske, 1846)
Hall, Edith, *Adventures with Iphigenia in Tauris: A Cultural History of Euripides' Black Sea Tragedy* (Oxford: OUP, 2013)
Hamann, Johann Gottfried, 'Aesthetica in nuce: A Rhapsody in Cabbalistic Prose', in: J. M. Bernstein (ed.), *Classic and Romantic German Aesthetics* (Cambridge: CUP, 2003), 1–24
Hamann, Johann Gottfried, *Sämtliche Werke*, ed. Josef Nadler (Herder: Vienna, 1950)
Hammer-Purgstall, Joseph von, *Der Diwan, von Mohammed Schemsed-din Hafis. Aus dem Persischen zum erstenmal ganz übersetzt* (Stuttgart: Cotta, 1812)
Hansert, Andreas, 'Auf dem Weg ins Patriziat, Johann Caspar Goethes Stellung in Frankfurt', in: Doris Hopp (ed.), *'Goethe Pater': Johann Caspar Goethe (1710–1782)* (Frankfurt: Freies Deutsches Hochstift, 2010), 62–75
Hansert, Andreas, *Geburtsaristokratie in Frankfurt am Main: Geschichte des reichsstädtischen Patriziats* (Vienna: Böhlau, 2014)
Härtl, Heinz, (ed.), *'Die Wahlverwandtschaften': Eine Dokumentation der Wirkung von Goethes Roman 1808–1832* (Berlin: Akademie-Verlag, 1983)
Henel, Heinrich, 'Type and Proto-Phenomenon in Goethe's Science', *Publications of the Modern Language Association* 4 (1956), 651–68
Henkel, Arthur, *'Wilhelm Meisters Wanderjahre—Kritik und Prognose der modernen Gesellschaft*', GJ 97 (1980), 82–89
Hennig, John, 'Goethe's Interest in the History of British Physics', *Osiris* 10 (1952), 43–66
Herder, Johann Gottfried, *Philosophical Writings*, ed. Michael N. Forster (Cambridge: CUP, 2008)
Herder, Johann Gottfried, *Sämmtliche Werke*, ed. Bernhard Suphan, 33 vols. (Berlin: Weidmann, 1877–1913)

Herder, Johann Gottfried, *Werke*, ed. Günter Arnold et al., 10 vols. (Frankfurt: Deutscher Klassiker Verlag, 1985–2000)
Herder, Johann Gottfried, *Zerstreute Blätter. Fünfte Sammlung* (Gotha: Ettinger, 1793)
Hettner, Hermann, 'Goethe und der Sozialismus', *Deutsches Museum* 2 (1852), 121–32
Hillmann, Ingeborg, *Dichtung als Gegenstand der Dichtung. Zum Problem der Einheit des 'West-östlichen Divan'* (Bonn: Bouvier, 1965)
Hinrichs, Carl, *Preussentum und Pietismus. Der Pietismus in Brandenburg-Preussen als religiös-soziale Reformbewegung* (Göttingen: Vandenhoeck & Ruprecht, 1971)
Hirsch, Arnold, '*Die Leiden des jungen Werthers*: Ein bürgerliches Schicksal im absolutistischen Staat', *Études Germaniques* 13 (1958), 229–50
Hobson, Irmgard, 'Oranien and Alba: The Two Political Dialogues in *Egmont*', GR 50 (1975), 260–74
Hopp, Doris, (ed.), *'Goethe Pater': Johann Caspar Goethe (1710–1782)* (Frankfurt: Freies Deutsches Hochstift, 2010)
Hume, David, *A Treatise of Human Nature*, ed. L. A. Selby-Bigge and P. H. Nidditch (Oxford: OUP, 1978)
Hüsgen, Heinrich Sebastian, *Getreuer Wegweiser von Frankfurt am Main und dessen Gebiete für Einheimische und Fremde* (Frankfurt: Behrensche Buchhandlung, 1802)
Huxley, T. H., 'Nature: Aphorisms by Goethe', *Nature*, 4 November 1869, 9–11
Israel, Jonathan, *Enlightenment Contested: Philosophy, Modernity, and the Emancipation of Man 1670–1752* (Oxford: OUP, 2006)
Israel, Jonathan, *Radical Enlightenment: Philosophy and the Making of Modernity 1650–1750* (Oxford: OUP, 2002)
Jacobi, Friedrich Heinrich, *Über die Lehre des Spinoza in Briefen an Herrn Moses Mendelssohn* (Breslau: Löwe, 1785)
Jacobi, Friedrich Heinrich, *Werke*, ed. Klaus Hammacher and Walter Jaeschke, 7 vols. (Hamburg: Meiner; Stuttgart: Frommann-Holzboog, 1998–2016)
Jerusalem, Carl Wilhelm, *Philosophische Aufsätze*, ed. Gotthold Ephraim Lessing (Braunschweig: Fürstliches Waisenhaus, 1776)
Jeßing, Benedikt, '*Dichtung und Wahrheit*', in: GH III, 278–330
Jost, Dominik, *Deutsche Klassik: Goethes 'Römische Elegien'. Einführung, Text, Kommentar* (Munich: UTB, 1978)
Kant, Immanuel, *Critique of Pure Reason*, trans. Paul Guyer and Allen W. Wood (Cambridge: CUP, 1998)
Kant, Immanuel, *Critique of the Power of Judgement*, trans. Paul Guyer and Eric Matthews (Cambridge: CUP, 2004)
Kant, Immanuel, *Metaphysical Foundations of Natural Science*, ed. Michael Friedman (Cambridge: CUP, 2004)
Kant, Immanuel, *Prolegomena to Any Future Metaphysics. With Selections from the 'Critique of Pure Reason'*, ed. Gary Hatfield (Cambridge: CUP, 2004)
Keller, Werner, 'Goethes "Urfaust", historisch betrachtet', *Schriften der Goethe-Gesellschaft* 69 (2009), 311–38
Kent, Stephen A., 'Weber, Goethe, and the Nietzschean Allusion: Capturing the Source of the "Iron Cage" Metaphor', *Sociological Analysis* 44 (1983), 297–319

Kleist, Heinrich von, *Sämtliche Werke und Briefe*, ed. Helmut Sembdner (Munich: dtv, 1987)

Kleist, Heinrich von, *Selected Writings*, trans. David Constantine (Indianapolis: Hackett, 2004)

Klingenberg, Anneliese, *Goethe's Roman 'Wilhelm Meisters Wanderjahre'* (Berlin: Aufbau, 1972)

Klippel, Friederike, *Englischlernen im 18. und 19. Jahrhundert: Die Geschichte der Lehrbücher und Unterrichtsmethoden* (Münster: Nodus, 1994)

Kluge, Gerhard, '*Hermann und Dorothea*: Die Revolution und Hermanns Schlußrede—zwei "schmerzliche Zeichen"?', GJ 109 (1992), 61–68

Kondylis, Panajotis, *Die Aufklärung im Rahmen des neuzeitlichen Rationalismus* (Munich: dtv, 1986)

Kondylis, Panajotis, *Konservativismus: Geschichtlicher Gehalt und Untergang* (Berlin: Matthes & Seitz, 2023)

Koopmann, Helmut, 'Ethik', in: GH IV/1, 280–82

Korff, Hermann August, *Geist der Goethezeit. Versuch einer ideellen Entwicklung der klassisch-romantischen Literaturgeschichte* (Leipzig: Weber, 1923–1953)

Koschorke, Albrecht, 'Die Textur der Neigungen: Attraktion, Verwandtschaftscode und novellistische Kombinatorik in Goethes "Mann von funfzig Jahren"', DVLG 73 (1999), 592–610

Košenina, Alexander, 'Ein "Familiengemälde" Ifflands dient Goethe als Vorlage für seine Ferdinand-Novelle in den *Unterhaltungen deutscher Ausgewanderten*', *Zeitschrift für Germanistik* 30 (2020), 1–3

Krennbauer, Franz, *Goethe und der Staat: Die Staatsidee des Unpolitischen* (Vienna: Springer, 1949)

Krippendorff, Ekkehart, *Goethe. Politik gegen den Zeitgeist* (Frankfurt: Insel, 1999)

Krippendorff, Ekkehart, 'Politik', in: GH IV/2, 865–68

Krippendorff, Ekkehart, '*Wie die Großen mit den Menschen spielen.' Versuch über Goethes Politik* (Frankfurt: Suhrkamp, 1988)

Kuhn, Dorothea, 'Goethe und die Chemie', *Medizinhistorisches Journal* 7 (1972), 264–78

Lange, Horst, 'Goethe and Spinoza: A Reconsideration', GY 18 (2011), 11–33

Lange, Horst, 'Isaac, Iphigeneia, Christ: Human Sacrifice and the Semiotics of Divine Intentions in Goethe', PEGS 78 (2009), 166–88

Lange, Horst, 'Reconstructing a Nation's Birth: Monotheism, Nationalism, and Violence in Goethe's Reading of the Pentateuch', *Colloquia Germanica* 33 (2000), 103–21

Lee, Meredith, *Studies in Goethe's Lyric Cycles* (Chapel Hill: University of North Carolina Press, 1978)

Leiber, Theodor, *Vom mechanistischen Weltbild zur Selbstorganisation des Lebens. Helmholtz' und Boltzmanns Forschungsprogramme und ihre Bedeutung für Physik, Chemie, Biologie und Philosophie* (Freiburg: Alber, 2000)

Lemmel, Monica, *Poetologie in Goethes 'West-östlichem Divan'* (Heidelberg: Winter, 1987)

Lessing, Gotthold Ephraim, *Werke und Briefe*, ed. Wilfried Barner et al. (Frankfurt am Main: Deutscher Klassiker Verlag, 1985–2014)

Locke, John, *Two Treatises of Government and A Letter Concerning Toleration*, ed. Ian Shapiro, John Dunn, and Ruth W. Grant (New Haven: Yale UP, 2003)

Luck, Georg, 'Goethes *Römische Elegien* und die augusteische Liebeselegie', *Arcadia* 2 (1967), 173–95

Lukács, Georg, 'Die Leiden des jungen Werther', in: Hans Peter Herrmann (ed.), Goethes 'Werther': Kritik und Forschung (Darmstadt: Wissenschaftliche Buchgesellschaft, 1994), 39–57

Maier, Hans Albert, 'Zur Textgestaltung des West-östlichen Divans II: Orthographie und Interpunktion', Journal of English and Germanic Philology 58 (1959), 185–221

Maierhofer, Waltraud, 'Perspektivenwechsel. Zu Wilhelm Meisters Wanderjahren und dem amerikanischen Reisetagebuch Bernhards von Sachsen-Weimar-Eisenach', Zeitschrift für Germanistik 5 (1995), 508–22

Maisak, Petra, 'Die Sammlungen Johann Caspar Goethes im "Haus zu den drei Leyern", Goethes frühe Frankfurter Erfahrungen', in: Markus Bertsch and Johannes Grave (eds.), Räume der Kunst: Blicke auf Goethes Sammlungen (Göttingen: Vandenhoeck & Ruprecht, 2005), 23–46

Maisak, Petra, and Hans-Georg Dewitz, Das Goethe-Haus in Frankfurt am Main (Frankfurt: Insel, 1999)

Mann, Thomas, 'Goethe als Repräsentant des bürgerlichen Zeitalters', in: T. M., Gesammelte Werke (Frankfurt: Fischer, 1960), IX, 297–332

Mannheim, Karl, Konservatismus: Ein Beitrag zur Soziologie des Wissens (Frankfurt: Suhrkamp, 1984)

Martin, Nicholas, 'Nietzsche's Goethe: In Sickness and in Health', PEGS 77 (2008), 113–24

Martin, Nicholas, Schiller and Nietzsche: Untimely Aesthetics (Oxford: OUP, 1996)

Mason, Eudo C., 'The "Erdgeist" Controversy Reconsidered', MLR 55 (1960), 66–78

Mason, Eudo C., Goethe's Faust: Its Genesis and Purport (Berkeley: University of California Press, 1967)

Mautner, Franz H., Lichtenberg. Geschichte seines Geistes (Berlin: De Gruyter, 1968)

Mayer, Hans, Goethe (Frankfurt: Suhrkamp, 1999)

McKenzie-McHarg, Andrew, 'The Role of Georg Friedrich von Johnssen in the Emergence of the Unknown Superiors, 1763–64', PEGS 87 (2018), 35–50

Mestas, Manina, 'The "Werther Effect" of Goethe's Werther: Anecdotal Evidence in Historical News Reports', Health Communication 39 (2024), 1279–84

Meyer-Benfey, Heinrich, Goethes 'Götz von Berlichingen' (Weimar: Böhlau, 1929)

Mix, York-Gothart, Die deutschen Musenalmanache des 18. Jahrhunderts (Munich: Beck, 1987)

Mommsen, Katharina, Goethe und die arabische Welt (Frankfurt: Insel, 1988)

Mommsen, Wilhelm, Die politischen Anschauungen Goethes (Stuttgart: Deutsche Verlags-Anstalt, 1948)

Moore, R. I., The Formation of a Persecuting Society (Oxford: Basil Blackwell, 1987)

Moritz, Johann Anton, Versuch einer Einleitung in die Staatsverfassung der Reichsstadt Frankfurt (Frankfurt: Andreäische Buchhandlung, 1786)

Mucignat, Rosa, 'History, Prophecy, Revolution: Italian politics in Byron and Foscolo', in: Roderick Beaton and Christine Kenyon-Jones (eds.), Byron: The Poetry of Politics and the Politics of Poetry (London: Routledge, 2016), 200–212

Mucignat, Rosa, 'Tasso and the Quest for Modern Epic: Goethe's Torquato Tasso and Leopardi's Operette morali', PEGS 85 (2016), 28–39

Mueller, Olaf L., 'Prismatic Equivalence—A New Case of Underdetermination: Goethe vs. Newton on the Prism Experiments', British Journal for the History of Philosophy 24 (2016), 323–47

Müller, Klaus-Detlef, 'Goethes *Die Mitschuldigen*: Zur Aneignung der literarischen Formensprache', in: Mortiz Baßler, Christoph Brecht, and Dirk Niefanger (eds.), *Von der Natur zur Kunst zurück: Neue Beiträge zur Goethe-Forschung: Gotthart Wunberg zum 65. Geburtstag* (Tübingen: Niemeyer, 1997), 5–19

Nadler, Steven M., *Spinoza's Heresy: Immortality and the Jewish Mind* (Oxford: OUP, 2001)

Nassar, Dalia, 'From a Philosophy of Self to a Philosophy of Nature: Goethe and the Development of Schelling's *Naturphilosophie*', *Archiv für Geschichte der Philosophie* 92 (2010), 304–21

Nemoianu, Virgil, 'From Goethe to Guizot: The Conservative Contexts of *Wilhelm Meisters Wanderjahre*', *Modern Language Studies* 31 (2001), 45–58

Neuhaus, Volker, '*Götz von Berlichingen*', in: GH II, 78–99

Newton, Isaac, 'A Letter of Mr. Isaac Newton [...] Concerning his New Theory about Light and Colours', *Philosophical Transactions of the Royal Society* 6 (1671/2), 3075–87

Nicholls, Angus, 'Between Natural and Human Science: Scientific Method in Goethe's *Noten und Abhandlungen zum West-östlichen Divan*', PEGS 80 (2011), 1–18

Nicholls, Angus, *Concept of the Daemonic: After the Ancients* (Rochester, NY: Camden House, 2006)

Niedermeier, Michael, 'Dilettantismus', in: GH IV/1, 212–14

Nisbet, Hugh Barr, *Goethe and the Scientific Tradition* (London: Institute of Germanic Studies, 1972)

Nisbet, Hugh Barr, 'Religion and Philosophy', in: Lesley Sharpe (ed.), *The Cambridge Companion to Goethe* (Cambridge: CUP, 2002), 219–31

Nisbet, Hugh Barr, 'Versuch einer Witterungslehre', in: GH III, 778–85

Noyes, John K., 'Goethe on Cosmopolitanism and Colonialism: *Bildung* and the Dialectic of Critical Mobility', *Eighteenth-Century Studies* 39 (2006), 443–62

Ockenden, R. C., 'On Bringing Statues to Life: Reading Goethe's *Iphigenie auf Tauris* and *Torquato Tasso*', PEGS 55 (1984–85), 69–106

O'Flaherty, James C., *Hamann's 'Socratic Memorabilia': A Translation and Commentary* (Baltimore: Johns Hopkins, 1967)

O'Flaherty, James C., *Unity and Language: A Study in the Philosophy of Johann Georg Hamann* (Chapel Hill: University of North Carolina Press, 1952)

Øhrgaard, Peter, 'Analogische Feldforschung: Überlegungen zu *Wilhelm Meisters Wanderjahren*', GJ 114 (1997), 49–62

Olenschlager, Johann Daniel von, *Neue Erläuterungen der Güldenen Bulle Kaysers Carls des IV* (Frankfurt: Fleischer, 1766)

Osterkamp, Ernst, *Im Buchstabenbilde: Studien zum Verfahren Goethescher Bildbeschreibungen* (Stuttgart: Metzler, 1991)

Otto, Regine, '"Novelle"', in: GH III, 252–65

Pätzold, Detlev, *Spinoza—Aufklärung—Idealismus: Die Substanz der Moderne* (Frankfurt: Peter Lang, 1995)

Paulin, Roger, *The Life of August Wilhelm Schlegel: Cosmopolitan of Art and Poetry* (Cambridge: Open Book, 2016)

Perels, Christoph, 'Bey Herrn Rath Göthe auf dem Grosen Hirschgraben: Eine zahlreiche auserlesene Bibliotheck, Die Büchersammlung Johann Caspar Goethes', in: Doris Hopp (ed.),

'Goethe Pater': Johann Caspar Goethe (1710–1782) (Frankfurt: Freies Deutsches Hochstift, 2010), 88–101

Piirimäe, Eva, *Herder and Enlightenment Politics* (Cambridge: CUP, 2023)

Plotinus, *The Enneads*, trans. Stephen MacKenna, rev. B. S. Page (London: Faber, 1956)

Polaschegg, Andrea, *Der andere Orientalismus: Regeln deutsch-morgenländischer Imagination im 19. Jahrhundert* (Berlin, New York: De Gruyter, 2005)

Potts, Alex, *Flesh and the Ideal: Winckelmann and the Origins of Art History* (New Haven: Yale UP, 1994)

Powers, Elizabeth, 'From "Empfindungsleben" to "Erfahrungsbereich": The Creation of Experience in Goethe's *Die Laune des Verliebten*', GY 8 (1996), 1–27

Prandi, Julie, *Dare to be Happy: A Study of Goethe's Ethics* (Lanham, MD: University Press of America, 1993)

Rasch, Wolfdietrich, 'Die Gauklerin Bettine. Zu Goethes *Venetianischen Epigrammen*', in: Stanley A. Corngold, Michael Curschmann, and Theodor J. Ziolkowski (eds.), *Aspekte der Goethezeit* (Göttingen: Vandenhoeck und Ruprecht, 1977), 115–36

Redfield, Marc, 'The Dissection of the State: *Wilhelm Meisters Wanderjahre* and the Politics of Aesthetics', GQ 69 (1996), 15–31

Reed, T. J., '*Iphigenie auf Tauris*', in: GH II/1, 195–228

Reed, T. J., 'Tasso und die Besserwisser', in: John Hibberd et al. (eds.), *Texte, Motive und Gestalten der Goethezeit: Festschrift für Hans Reiss* (Tübingen: Niemeyer, 1983), 95–112

Reeve, William C., *Kleist on Stage, 1804–1987* (Montreal: McGill-Queen's University Press, 1993)

Reinhardt, Hartmut, *Die kleine und die große Welt. Vom Schäferspiel zur kritischen Analyse der Moderne: Goethes dramatisches Werk* (Würzburg: Königshausen und Neumann, 2008)

Reiss, Hans, 'Goethe, Möser und die Aufklärung', in: H. R., *Formgestaltung und Politik: Goethe-Studien* (Würzburg: Königshausen & Neumann, 1993), 143–87

Reiss, Hans, 'Goethe's *Torquato Tasso*: Poetry and Political Power', MLR 87 (1992), 102–11

Reiss, Hans, '*Wilhelm Meisters Wanderjahre*. Der Weg von der ersten zur zweiten Fassung', DVLG 39 (1965), 34–57

Richards, Robert J., 'Did Goethe and Schelling Endorse Species Evolution?', in: Joel Faflak (ed.), *Marking Time: Romanticism and Evolution* (Toronto: University of Toronto Press, 2016), 219–38

Richards, Robert J., *The Romantic Conception of Life: Science and Philosophy in the Age of Goethe* (Chicago: University of Chicago Press, 2002)

Richardson, Samuel, *Clarissa. Or, the History of a Young Lady: Comprehending the Most Important Concerns of Private Life* (London: Richardson, 1751)

Robertson, Ritchie, *The Enlightenment: The Pursuit of Happiness 1680–1790* (London: Allen Lane, 2020)

Robertson, Ritchie, 'Goethe's *Faust II*: The Redemption of an Enlightened Despot', PEGS 91 (2022), 43–57

Robertson, Ritchie, *Mock-Epic Poetry from Pope to Heine* (Oxford: OUP, 2009)

Robson-Scott, W. D., *The Younger Goethe and the Visual Arts* (Cambridge: CUP, 1981)

Roethe, Gustav, 'Die Entstehung des *Urfaust*', *Sitzungsberichte der Preußischen Akademie der Wissenschaften* 32 (1920), 642–79

Rosenblatt, Helena, *Rousseau and Geneva: From the 'First Discourse' to the 'Social Contract'*, *1749–1762* (Cambridge: CUP, 1997)
Rothe, Wolfgang, *Der politische Goethe: Dichter und Staatsdiener im deutschen Spätabsolutismus* (Göttingen: Vandenhoeck & Ruprecht, 1998)
Rousseau, Jean-Jacques, *Collection complète des oeuvres* (Geneva: no publ.), 1780–88
Rousseau, Jean-Jacques, *The Discourses and other Early Political Writings*, trans. Victor Gourevitch (Cambridge: CUP, 1997)
Rousseau, Jean-Jacques, *Emil oder über die Erziehung*, trans. Carl Friedrich Cramer (Braunschweig: Campe, 1792)
Rousseau, Jean-Jacques, *Emile, or On Education*, trans. Allan Bloom (New York: Basic Books, 1979)
Rousseau, Jean-Jacques, *Politics and the Arts: Letter to M. D'Alembert on the Theatre*, trans. Allan Bloom (Ithaca, NY: Cornell UP, 1968)
Rousseau, Jean-Jacques, *The Social Contract and Other Later Political Writings*, trans. Victor Gourevitch (Cambridge: CUP, 1997)
Rowland, Herbert, 'Chaos and Art in Goethe's Novelle', GY 8 (1996), 93–119
Sahni, Isher-Paul, '"The Will to Act": An Analysis of Max Weber's Conceptualisation of Social Action and Political Ethics in the Light of Goethe's Fiction', *Sociology* 35 (2001), 421–39
Said, Edward W., *Orientalism* (New York: Vintage, 2014)
Saine, Thomas P., 'Introduction' in: PS V, 609–17
Salmen, Christine, *Die ganze merkwürdige Verlassenschaft: Goethes Entsagungspoetik in 'Wilhelm Meisters Wanderjahren'* (Würzburg: Königshausen & Neumann, 2003)
Sauder, Gerhard, 'Wetzlar', in: GH IV/2, 1150–52
Schelling, Friedrich Wilhelm Joseph, *Historisch-kritische Ausgabe*, ed. Hans Michael Baumgartner et al. (Stuttgart: Frommann-Holzboog, 1976–)
Scherer, Wilhelm, *Aufsätze über Goethe* (Berlin: Weidmann, 1886)
Scherpe, Klaus, *'Werther' und Wertherwirkung: Zum Syndrom bürgerlichen Gesellschaftsordnung im 18. Jahrhundert* (Bad Homburg: Gehlen, 1970)
Schiller, Friedrich, *On the Aesthetic Education of Man in a Series of Letters*, trans. Elizabeth M. Wilkinson and L. A. Willoughby (Oxford: OUP, 1967)
Schings, Hans-Jürgen, 'Religion/Religiosität', in: GH IV/2, 892–98
Schlaffer, Heinz, *Faust zweiter Teil: Die Allegorie des 19. Jahrhunderts* (Stuttgart, Weimar: Metzler, 1998)
Schmidt, Jochen, 'Ironie und Skepsis in Goethes Alterswerk, besonders in den *Wahlverwandschaften*', GJ 121 (2004), 165–75
Schneidereit, Nele, 'Angeborene Rechte, Bürgerrechte, soziale Rechte: Christian Wolffs Lehre von den *iura connata*', *Jahrbuch für Recht und Ethik / Annual Review of Law and Ethics* 22 (2014), 159–78
Scholz, Rüdiger, 'Zum Stand der Forschung über Sachsen-Weimar und Goethes Regierungstätigkeit', *IASLonline* (February 2013), www.iaslonline.de/index.php?vorgang_id=3688
Schöne, Wolfgang, *Über das Licht in der Malerei* (Berlin: Mann, 1954)
Schutjer, Karin, 'German Epic/Jewish Epic: Goethe's Exodus Narrative in *Hermann und Dorothea* and "Israel in der Wüste"', GQ 80 (2007), 165–84

Schütz, Friedrich Karl Julius, *Goethe und Pustkuchen, oder: Über die beiden Wanderjahre Wilhelm Meister's und ihre Verfasser. Ein Beitrag zur Geschichte der deutschen Poesie und Poetik* (Halle: Anton, 1823)

Schwartz, Peter J., *After Jena: Goethe's 'Elective Affinities' and the End of the Old Regime* (Lewisburg, PA: Bucknell UP, 2010)

Seibt, Gustav, *Goethe und Napoleon* (Munich: Beck, 2008)

Seibt, Gustav, *Mit einer Art von Wut: Goethe in der Revolution* (Munich: Beck, 2014)

Seidlin, Oskar, *Essays in German and Comparative Literature* (Chapel Hill: University of North Carolina Press, 1961)

Sengle, Friedrich, *Das Genie und sein Fürst: Die Geschichte der Lebensgemeinschaft Goethes mit dem Herzog Carl August von Sachsen-Weimar-Eisenach. Ein Beitrag zum Spätfeudalismus und zu einem vernachlässigten Thema der Goetheforschung* (Stuttgart: Metzler, 1993)

Sepper, Dennis L., *Goethe contra Newton: Polemics and the Project for a New Science of Colour* (Cambridge: CUP, 1988)

Shakespeare, William, *The Arden Shakespeare Complete Works*, ed. by Richard Proudfoot et al. (London: Bloomsbury, 2014)

Sharpe, Lesley, 'Goethe and the Weimar Theatre', in: Lesley Sharpe (ed.), *The Cambridge Companion to Goethe* (Cambridge: CUP, 2002), 116–28

Simpson, James, *Matthew Arnold and Goethe* (London: MHRA, 1979)

Sina, Kai, 'Kollektiv (Collective)', GLPC 2 (2021), https://doi.org/10.5195/glpc.2021.47

Soliday, Gerald Lyman, *A Community in Conflict: Frankfurt Society in the Seventeenth and Early Eighteenth Centuries* (Hanover, NH: University Press of New England, 1974)

Solms, Wilhelm, *Goethes Vorarbeiten zum 'Divan'* (Munich: Fink, 1976)

Spengler, Oswald, *Der Untergang des Abendlandes: Umrisse einer Morphologie der Weltgeschichte* (Munich: Anaconda, 2017)

Spranger, Eduard, 'Der psychologische Perspektivismus im Roman', in: E. S., *Goethe: seine geistige Welt* (Tübingen: Wunderlich, 1967), 207–32

Staiger, Emil, *Goethe* (Zürich: Atlantis, 1952)

Staroste, Wolfgang, 'Die Darstellung der Realität in Goethes *Novelle*', *Neophilologus* 44 (1960), 322–33

Steer, A. G., 'Goethe's *Novelle* as a Document of its Time', DVLG 50 (1976), 414–33

Stöcklein, Paul, *Wege zum späten Goethe: Dichtung, Gedanke, Zeichnung* (Darmstadt: Wissenschaftliche Buchgesellschaft, 1973)

Strack, Friedrich, and Martina Eicheldinger (eds.), *Fragmente der Frühromantik: Edition und Kommentar* (Berlin: De Gruyter, 2011)

Strowick, Elisabeth, 'Poetik des Dilettantismus in Goethes *Die Wahlverwandtschaften*', *Poetica* 39 (2007), 423–42

Szramkiewicz, Romuald, *Histoire du droit français de la famille* (Paris: Dalloz, 1995)

Suphan, Bernhard, 'Aus der Zeit der Spinoza-Studien Goethes', GJ 12 (1891), 3–12

Tackett, Timothy, *The Coming of the Terror in the French Revolution* (Cambridge, MA: Harvard UP, 2015)

Tantillo, Astrida Orle, *The Will to Create: Goethe's Philosophy of Nature* (Pittsburgh: University of Pittsburgh Press, 2002)

Tauber, Christine, '*Über Kunst und Altertum*', in: GH 'Supplemente', III, 414–29

Thobani, Sitara, *Indian Classical Dance and the Making of Postcolonial National Identities: Dancing on Empire's Stage* (Abindgon: Routledge, 2017)

Thordarson, Thorvaldur, and Stephen Self, 'Atmospheric and Environmental Effects of the 1783–1784 Laki Eruption: A Review and Reassessment', *Journal of Geophysical Research: Atmospheres* 108 (2003), 1–29

Tischendorf, Constantin von (ed.), *Evangelia Apocrypha* (Leipzig: Avenarius & Mendelssohn, 1853)

Torrance, I., 'Religion and Gender in Goethe's *Iphigenie auf Tauris*', *Helios* 34 (2007), 177–206

Trevelyan, Humphry, *Goethe and the Greeks* (Cambridge: CUP, 1981)

Trunz, Erich, 'Goethes Entwurf "Landschaftliche Malerei"', in: E. T., *Weimarer Goethe-Studien* (Weimar: Böhlau, 1980), 156–202

Umbach, Maiken, *Federalism and Enlightenment in Germany, 1740–1806* (London: Bloomsbury, 2003)

Unseld, Siegfried, *Goethe und seine Verleger* (Frankfurt: Insel, 1991)

Vaget, Hans Rudolf, 'Neue Wilhelm-Meister-Literatur', GQ 56 (1983), 502–9

Vaget, Hans Rudolf, 'Um einen Tasso von außen bittend. Kunst und Dilettantismus am Musenhof von Ferrara', DVLG 54 (1980), 232–58

Varnhagen von Ense, Karl August, 'Im Sinne der Wanderer', in: K. A. V. v. E., *Denkwürdigkeiten und vermischte Schriften*, vol. 1 (Mannheim: Hoff, 1837), 413–25

Voltaire [François-Marie Arouet], *Les Œuvres complètes de Voltaire*, ed. Theodore Besterman et al. (Oxford: Voltaire Foundation, 1968–2022)

Voß, Lena, *Goethes unsterbliche Freundin Charlotte von Stein* (Leipzig: Klinkhardt und Biermann, 1921)

Wagenbreth, Otfried, 'Bergbau', in: GH IV/1, 104–7

Watkins, Eric, 'From Pre-established Harmony to Physical Influx: Leibniz's Reception in Eighteenth-Century Germany', *Perspectives on Science* 6 (1998), 136–203

Weber, Marianne, *Max Weber: Ein Lebensbild* (Heidelberg: Schneider, 1950)

Weber, Max, *The Protestant Ethic and the Spirit of Capitalism*, trans. Talcott Parsons (London: Routledge, 1992)

Weber, Peter, 'Weltliteratur', in: GH IV/2, 1134–37

Wells, George A., *Goethe and the Development of Science, 1750–1900* (Alphen aan den Rijn: Sijthoff & Noordhoff, 1978)

Wells, Larry D., 'Organic Structure in Goethe's *Novelle*', GQ 53 (1980), 418–31

Whaley, Joachim, *Germany and the Holy Roman Empire*, 2 vols. (Oxford: OUP, 2011)

Wichert, Lasse, *Personale Mythen des Nationalsozialismus Die Gestaltung des Einzelnen in literarischen Entwürfen* (Paderborn: Fink, 2018)

Wild, Reiner, 'Italienische Reise', in: GH III, 331–69

Wilkinson, Elizabeth M., '*Torquato Tasso*: The Tragedy of the Poet', in: E. M. W., *Goethe: Poet and Thinker*, ed. Elizabeth M. Wilkinson and L. A. Willoughby (London: Edward Arnold, 1962), 75–94

Williams, John R., *Goethe's 'Faust'* (London: Allen & Unwin, 1987)

Williamson, George S., 'What Killed August von Kotzebue? The Temptations of Virtue and the Political Theology of German Nationalism, 1789–1819', *Journal of Modern History* 72 (2000), 890–943

Wilson, W. Daniel, *Das Goethe-Tabu: Protest und Menschenrechte im klassischen Weimar* (Munich: dtv, 1999)

Wilson, W. Daniel, *Der Faustische Pakt: Goethe und die Goethe-Gesellschaft im Dritten Reich* (Munich: dtv, 2018)

Wilson, W. Daniel, 'Dramen zum Thema der Französischen Revolution', in: GH II, 258–87

Wilson, W. Daniel, *Geheimräte gegen Geheimbünde: Ein unbekanntes Kapitel der klassisch-romantischen Geschichte Weimars* (Stuttgart: Metzler, 1991)

Wilson, W. Daniel, 'Goethe, his Duke and Infanticide: New Documents and Reflections on a Controversial Execution', GLL 61 (2008), 7–32

Wilson, W. Daniel, *Goethe, Männer, Knaben: Ansichten zur 'Homosexualität'* (Berlin: Insel, 2012)

Wilson, W. Daniel, *Goethes Weimar und die Französische Revolution: Dokumente der Krisenjahre* (Cologne: Böhlau, 2004)

Wilson, W. Daniel, '"Humanitätssalbader": Goethe's Distaste for Jewish Emancipation, and Jewish Responses', in: Klaus L. Berghahn and Jost Hermand (eds.), *Goethe in German-Jewish Culture* (Rochester, NY: Camden House, 2001), 146–64

Wilson, W. Daniel, *Unterirdische Gänge: Goethe, Freimaurerei und Politik* (Göttingen: Wallstein, 1999)

Wilson, W. Daniel, 'Young Goethe's Political Fantasies', in: David Hill (ed.), *Literature of the Sturm und Drang* (Rochester, NY: Camden House, 2003), 187–216

Winckelmann, Johann Joachim, *Geschichte der Kunst des Alterthums* (Dresden: Walther, 1764)

Winckelmann, Johann Joachim, *History of the Art of Antiquity*, trans. Harry Francis Mallgrave (Los Angeles: Getty Research Institute, 2006)

Wistoff, Andreas, *Die deutsche Romantik in der öffentlichen Literaturkritik* (Bonn: Bouvier, 1992)

Wittmann, Reinhard, *Geschichte des deutschen Buchhandels* (Munich: Beck, 1999)

Wolf, Friedrich August, [Dedication], *Museum der Altertumswissenschaft* 1 (1807), iii–ix

Wolff, Christian, *Briefe von Christian Wolff aus den Jahren 1719–1753* (St Petersburg: Eggers, 1860)

Wolff, Christian, *Christian Wolffs eigene Lebensbeschreibung*, ed. Heinrich Wuttke (Leipzig: Weidmann, 1841)

Wolff, Christian, *Deutsche Politik: Vernünftige Gedanken von dem gesellschaftlichen Leben der Menschen und insonderheit dem gemeinen Wesen*, ed. Hasso Hofmann (Munich: Beck, 2004)

Wolff, Christian, *Gesammelte Werke*, ed. Jean École et al. (Hildesheim: Olms, 1962–)

Wolff, Hans M., 'Rousseau, Möser und der Kampf gegen das Rokoko', *Monatshefte* 34 (1942), 113–25

Wood, Allen W., 'Fichte's Philosophical Revolution', *Philosophical Topics*, 19 (1991), 1–28

Wordsworth, William, 'Preface', in: William Wordsworth and Samuel Taylor Coleridge, *Lyrical Ballads*, ed. R. L. Brett and A. R. Jones (Abingdon: Routledge, 2005), 286–314

Wulf, Andrea, *The Invention of Nature: The Adventures of Alexander von Humboldt, the Lost Hero of Science* (London: Murray, 2016)

Wyder, Margrit, *Goethes Naturmodell: Die 'Scala naturae' und ihre Transformationen* (Cologne: Böhlau, 1998)

Young, Edward, *The Complaint: Or, Night-Thoughts on Life, Death, & Immortality. Night the First*, 5th ed. (London: Dodsley, 1743)

Young, James O., 'Translator's Introduction', in: Batteux, *The Fine Arts Reduced to a Single Principle*, v–lxxiii.

Zammito, John H., *The Gestation of German Biology: Philosophy and Physiology from Stahl to Schelling* (Chicago: University of Chicago Press, 2017)
Zapperi, Roberto, *Das Inkognito: Goethes ganz andere Existenz im Rom* (Munich: Beck, 1999)
Zemplén, Gábor Áron, 'An Eye for Optical Theory: Newton's Rejection of the Modificationist Tradition and Goethe's Modificationist Critique of Newton', unpublished PhD thesis (Budapest: Budapest University of Technology and Economics, 2001)
Ziolkowski, Theodore, *The Mirror of Justice. Literary Reflections of Legal Crises* (Princeton: Princeton UP, 1997)
Zumbusch, Cornelia, '"beschädigt und wiederhergestellt": Kompensationslogik und Romanform in *Wilhelm Meisters Wanderjahren*', DVLG 88 (2014), 3–21

GENERAL INDEX

Adler, Jeremy, 478
Aeschylus: *Prometheus Bound*, 85; *Oresteia*, 148–49
Agrippa von Nettesheim, 27, 31
Albertus Magnus, 25
Ampère, Jean-Jacques, 65, 580
Anna Amalia von Sachsen-Weimar-Eisenach, 126, 441
Aquinas, Thomas, 6
Arber, Agnes, 12, 266
Arcangeli, Francesco, 40
Ariosto, Ludovico, 39
Aristotle, 7, 25, 34, 41, 169, 270, 458, 460; *Poetics*, 37; politics, 4
Arnim, Achim von, 419
Arnold, Gottfried, 28, 31–32, 47–48, 82
Arnold, Matthew, 10–11

Baader, Franz von, 377
Bacon, Francis, 278, 304
Bahrdt, Carl Friedrich, 237–38
Balsamo, Giuseppe ('Count Cagliostro'), 211, 281–82
Basedow, Johann Bernhard, 117
Basilius Valentinus, 48
Batteux, Charles, 41–42, 49, 73–74, 78, 109, 547
Bayle, Pierre, 52
Beaumarchais, Pierre, 118
Behrisch, Ernst Wolfgang, 36
Bellomo, Giuseppe, 281
Bentham, Jeremy, 581, 583–84, 594
Berendis, Hieronymus Dietrich, 406
Bergman, Torbern, 441, 470, 477

Berlin, Isaiah, 301
Bernhard von Sachsen-Weimar-Eisenach, 588–89
Berthollet, Claude Louis, 476–77
Biot, Jean-Baptiste, 554
Blumenbach, Johann Friedrich, 171, 173
Bode, Johann Joachim Christoph, 285
Bodmer, Johann Jakob, 8–9
Böhme, Johann Gottlob, 34–35
Boie, Heinrich Christian, 91
Boileau, Nicolas, 39, 41
Boisserée, Sulpiz, 543
Bollacher, Martin, 32
Bonnet, Charles, 270
Bourbon-Conti, Stéphanie-Louise de, 398, 400–401
Bower, Archibald, 27–28
Brandis, Joachim Dietrich, 266
Breitinger, Johann Jakob, 8–9
Breitkopf, Bernhard Theodor, 38
Brentano, Clemens, 419
Brion, Friederike, 57–61, 99, 119, 493–95
Brucker, Johann Jakob, 31–32
Bruno, Giordano, 51–52
Buffon, Georges-Louis Leclerc, Comte de, 165, 166, 168, 169, 170–71, 260, 363, 425
Bürger, Gottfried August, 65
Burke, Edmund, 293
Büttner, Christian Wilhelm, 274
Byron, Lord, 630

Calvin, Jean, 51, 82
Camper, Pieter, 171, 172–73

Carl August von Sachsen-Weimar-Eisenach, 118, 125, 136, 214, 239–40, 283–84, 288, 297–300, 370; education as a *Naturmensch*, 133–35, 175–76, 185, 187–88
Carlsbad (Karlovy Vary), 206
Carmina Priapeia, 250–51
Carus, Carl Gustav, 12
Catullus, 240
censorship, 1–4, 63–64, 116, 253–54
Charron, Pierre, 51
Chladni, Ernst, 440
Christfreund, Carl Christian, 26
Cicero, Marcus Tullius, 35
Claudius, Matthias, 75
Clodius, Christian August, 36, 38–40, 50
Colloredo-Mansfeld, Hieronymus Karl, Count of, 502
Confucius, 1
Corneille, Pierre, 26, 78
Cousin, Victor, 580
Creuzer, Friedrich, 517
Cronstedt, Axel, 166
Cuvier, Georges, 557, 651–52

Dante Alighieri, 26
Darwin, Charles, 12, 267–72
Defoe, Daniel, 107
deism, 64
Diderot, Denis, 364
Döbereiner, Johann Wolfgang, 433–34
Dodds, William, 39
Dollond, John, 304
du Bois-Reymond, Emil, 12
Dubos, Jean-Baptiste, 41
Dumont, Étienne, 583–84

Eben, Johann Michael, 26
Eckermann, Johann Peter, 18
Eichendorff, Joseph von, 575–76
Eichstädt, Heinrich Carl Abraham, 406
Eirenaeus Philalethes (George Starkey), 48
Empfindsamkeit. *See* Sensibility
Enghien, Louis Antoine de Bourbon, Duke of, 452

Ernesti, Johann August, 34–35, 116
Eschenmayer, Carl August, 374–5
Euripides, *Iphigeneia among the Taurians*, 146–49

Fabricius, Johann Albert, 51
Falconet, Étienne Maurice, 77
Falk, Johannes Daniel, 133
Fellenberg, Philipp Emanuel von, 573, 575
Fernow, Karl Ludwig, 407
Fichte, Johann Gottlieb, 9, 305–7, 313, 369–70, 379–80, 451
Forberg, Friedrich Karl, 369–70
Forster, Georg, 288
Frankfurt am Main, 15–22, 16, 18, 33, 105
French Revolution, 246–47, 314; reception in Germany, 247–49; 'Mainz Republic', 290–91
Fresenius, Johann Philipp, 22–23, 27–28
Friedrich II (Frederick the Great), King of Prussia, 6–7, 29
Friedrich Wilhem I, King of Prussia, 1–2, 6
Fritsch, Jakob Friedrich von, 135–36

Gellert, Christian Fürchtegott, 34–35, 38, 41, 50
Gentz, Friedrich von, 451, 455
Gérando, Joseph-Marie de, 497
Gerstenberg, Heinrich Wilhelm von, 44, 50
Giraud-Soulavie, Jean-Louis, 170
Gleichen-Rußwurm, Wilhelm Friedrich von, 173–74
Globe, Le, 580–84
Goethe, August von (Goethe's son), 250
Goethe, Catharina Elisabeth (née Textor) (Goethe's mother), 22, 24, 46–47, 296, 487
Goethe, Christiane (née Vulpius) (Goethe's wife), 238–40, 239, 249–50, 296, 413, 427, 512
Goethe, Cornelia (née Walther) (Goethe's paternal grandmother), 20, 22–24
Goethe, Cornelia Friederike (Goethe's sister), 23, 25, 26, 37, 46, 105, 138

Goethe, Friedrich Georg (Goethe's paternal grandfather), 20, 22
Goethe, Hermann Jakob (Goethe's father's half-brother), 21–22
Goethe, Johann Caspar (Goethe's father), 20–27, 29, 30, 31–32, 34, 46–47, 50, 63–64, 183
Goethe, Johann Wolfgang von
—administrative work in Weimar, 135–38, 175–76, 184–85, 205, 236–37; diplomacy, 183–84; execution of Johanna Catharina Höhn, 186–88; German revolutionaries, treatment of, 284, 293–302; Prussian recruitment in Weimar, 135; title of Privy Councillor, 160; University of Jena, 237–38, 248–49, 284, 305–7, 405–6
—alchemy, 48–49, 92
—anthropology, 224–29, 448–50
—architecture, 219–20
—arts and aesthetics, 220–4, 244–46, 275, 391–97, 543–49; allegory, 547; colour in painting, 364, 435; dilettantism, 395–96, 444; history of the Italian Renaissance, 340–45, 546; immediacy, 545–46; morality and art, 328, 395–96, 410–12; nature and art, 393–94; perfection in art, 394–5; religion in art, 221, 416–19, 445, 500–501, 543–49; subject matter of visual art, 221, 251–52, 396–97, 546–47; 'world literature' (*Weltliteratur*), 543
—biology: anastomosis, 266; botany, 174–75, 216–17, 261–66, 308, 651–55; ecology, 307–8; economy of nature, 264, 269–70, 375; entomology, 308–9; evolutionary theory (transformationism), 170, 173–4, 218, 267–72, 421–24, 557–58, 651–55; fossilized animals, 169–70; intermaxillary bone (*os intermaxillare*), 171–3; mammal anatomy and morphology, 12, 170–73, 266–73, 375, 420; metamorphosis, 217, 263–66, 265, 373–76, 651–55; microorganisms, 173–74; negative causation, 270–71; 'type' theory, 263; *Urpflanze*, 216–17, 310–13
—birth, 23
—character, theory of, 288, 467–69, 491–92, 528
—colour and optics, 273–81, 302–4, 362–69, 428–39, 456–69, 553–57; birefringence, 554–55; boundary colours as the 'primal phenomenon', 274, 277, 415, 421, 424, 429–33, 432; chemical colours, 433–34; colour wheel, 275, 363–68, 428–29, 434; coloured shadows, 302–3, 431; evolution of the eye, 421–24, 429–30; history of, 366–68, 436, 456–69, 469–71, 477; Kantian approach to, 364–69; Newton's experiments, 277–79, 424, 433, 435–39, 466; physiology of vision, 303–4, 363, 429–31; psychological effects of colours, 434–35; 'temperament rose', 365–66; turbid or opaque media, 432–33, 555–57
—cultural nationalism, 188–89, 191, 196–99, 330, 340–41, 414–15
—education, pre-university, 24–32; at university in Leipzig, 34–43; at university in Strasbourg, 52–62
—education, theory and practice, 566–67, 571–76; education of Duke Carl August as a *Naturmensch*, 133–35; Pedagogical Province, 566, 572–76
—ennoblement, 18–19, 183
—fame, attitude to, 63–64

Goethe, Johann Wolfgang von (*continued*)
—freemasonry, 185–86, 237–38, 282–83, 572
—genius, theory of, 313
—geology, 162–69, 419–20, 552–53; Neptunism and Vulcanism, 262, 552–53, 624–25; and revolution, 553; solidescence (crystallization) in rock formation, 169, 552–53
—guilt, 44–46, 58–61, 119, 177, 215, 492–93, 495
—Harz Mountains, travels in (1777), 163
—home in Frankfurt (Three Lyres), 22–24, 29, 44
—humanism and *homo mensura* principle, 273–74, 276–77, 369, 424–25, 546, 596; sense-extending apparatus, 567–68, 596
—hylomorphism, 169, 223, 229, 242
—Ilmenau silver mines, 162–64
—individualism, 463–64
—Italy, travels in, 207–29, *209*, 535–43; Agrigento, 219–20; Assisi, 219; Bologna, 221; justifications for, 212–15; Naples, 210–11, 216, 226, 228, 538–39, 541–42, 559; Padua, 216, 263; Paestum, 219, 222, 540–41; Palermo, 263, 540; Rome, 208–10, *210*, 212, 218–19, 225–29; Sicily, 211–12, 216, 542–43; Venice, 208–10, 216, 225, 266–67; Verona, 221, 225, 228, 229, 252; Vicenza, 221, 225
—legal practice, 64
—literature. (*see* Goethe, Johann Wolfgang von: arts and aesthetics)
—marriage, 427
—mathematics, 369, 424–25, 438, 439, 440, 467–69, 596
—men, pragmatism and inconstancy of, 59–61, 69–70, 119, 121–25, 132–3, 146, 565

—meteorology, 215–16, 275, 549–52; clouds, 216–6, 549–50; elasticity (pressure), 215, 550–52; tellurian theory of, 551–52
—Middle Ages and medievalism, 52–53, 64–72, 76, 419, 537, 543–44
—modernity, 67–73, 105, 129, 180, 343–44, 357–58, 378–80, 389–90, 409–13, 448–52, 568–70, 576–79, 591, 604, 609–12
—music and acoustics, 440
—orientalism, 528–32
—physics, 419–21; magnetism, 376; unifying theory of, 420–21, 434
—politics, 13–14, 19, 67, 71–72, 320–24; Carlsbad Decrees, 559–60; in the Classical Walpurgis Night, 622–25; Congress of Vienna, 506; conservatism, 249, 565, 567, 580–84; democracy, 324, 345, 462, 578, 593–94; emancipation of Jews, 519, 578; executive authority, 137, 188, 323, 347, 400, 403–4, 452–53, 485, 500, 505, 519, 563, 581, 584, 592, 615, 633, 642; French Revolution, 248–49, 253–56, 281–83, 285–88, 291–96, 320–24, 349–55, 400–404, 569–70, 602; Holy Roman Empire, 35, 67–68, 71, 179, 183–84, 189, 426, 471; July Revolution (1830), 609–10, 631; League of Princes, 184; legality, 401–4, 451, 522, 584; liberalism, 580–84, 594; liberty, 255, 524–26, 560, 591–93; Napoleonic Code, 427–28; nationalism, 325, 350, 415–16, 455–56, 499–500, 502–4, 520–21, 543–44; particularism, 325, 340–55; partisanship, 553, 562–63, 576; reforms in Weimar, 136–38, 184; republicanism, 344–46, 353, 355, 453, 466–67, 525–26, 575; Saint-Simonism,

609–10, 631–32, 642–43; spontaneity as a theory of political action, 288, 298–302, 354–55; state, ideal size of, 346–47, 461, 539, 563; state, organic theory of, 322, 339–40, 537–38, 563, 623
—publishers, 65, 75, 121, 206, 236, 264, 329, 415, 441, 485–86
—religion, 26–28, 42–43, 46–48, 51–52, 54, 61–62, 64, 81–85, 87–90, 94, 115–18, 140–43, 149–52, 158–59, 161, 204–5, 297, 412; Catholicism and culture, 415–19, 500–501; Christ, 98, 108, 116, 141–42, 253; Christianity and philosophy, 297; Christianity and sex, 250–53, 357–62; Christians, intolerance of, 360; 'Confessions of a Beautiful Soul', 334–35; religion of the Pedagogical Province, 573–75; religion and science, 165, 169, 172, 205; religion and state-building, 61–62, 81–83, 355–57, 444–48
—Romanticism, 416–19, 474, 500–501, 536–37, 539, 543–49
—science in general and philosophy of science: aesthetics of science, 438; beginnings of scientific studies, 12–13, 164–75; language of science, 368–69; polarity, 373, 377–78, 420–21, 429, 432, 439, 440, 517; *Steigerung* (progressive refinement or intensification), 373, 409; underdetermination of theory by evidence, 436–37; *Urphänomen* (primal phenomenon), 438. (*see also* Goethe, Johann Wolfgang von: humanism and *homo mensura* principle; mathematics)
—self-love, theory of, 58, 70, 74, 76–77, 98–101, 104, 119, 189, 232,

234–35, 351–52, 569–71, 587, 597; and the theatre, 189, 190–94, 468, 532–35, 570–71
—sex, 240–46, 252
—sexuality, 190, 195–96, 407–10
—Spinozism, 31–32, 51–52, 156, 161, 172, 199–205, 223–24, 335, 373
—subject-object divide, 260–61
—Switzerland, travels in (1779/80), 160–62, 166
—theatre in Weimar, management of, 281
—*Vorstellungsart* ('mode of representation'), 261–62, 331–32, 338, 377, 459
—War of the First Coalition: campaign of 1792, 288–90, 558–64; siege of Mainz, 296–302
—Weimar, move to, 125, 129–31
—women, constancy and moral strength of, 59–61, 123, 131–33, 146, 153–56

Goldsmith, Oliver, 25, 26, 80; *The Vicar of Wakefield*, 55, 108, 493–95
Gore, Charles, 298–300
Göttingen, university of, 32, 35
Gottsched, Johann Christoph, 8, 34–39, 41, 97, 291
Grimm, Herman, 13
Guizot, François, 581

Haeckel, Ernst, 12
Hafez, 506, 518, 531, 532, 535
Hamann, Johann Georg, 8–9, 49, 51, 55–56, 68, 73, 81, 94
Hammer-Purgstall, Joseph von, 506, 512, 519
Hegel, Georg Wilhelm Friedrich, 9, 496–97
Helmholtz, Hermann von, 12
Henel, Heinrich, 13
Herder, Caroline (née Flachsland), 54, 239, 295

Herder, Johann Gottfried, 8–9, 41, 54–55, 65, 73, 79, 83, 91, 94, 130, 136, 199, 284, 291, 329, 558, 601; *Critical Forests*, 49, 67; *God: Some Conversations*, 223; *Ideas*, 170, 171, 218, 224, 251, 342; 'On the German Character and Art', 75; *This too a Philosophy of History for the Formation of Humanity*, 68, 180, 225, 462, 603

Heyne, Christian Gottlob, 32, 35, 37, 109

Höhn, Johanna Catharina, 186–88

Holbach, Paul-Henri Thiry, Baron d', 499

Homer, 79; *Iliad*, 347, 354, 397–98, 407; *Odyssey*, 107–8, 113, 219–20

Horace, 240, 245, 632, 638

Howard, Luke, 215, 549–50

Humboldt, Alexander von, 266, 307–8

Humboldt, Wilhelm von, 307, 502

Hume, David, 51, 55, 80, 93–94, 110

Huxley, Thomas Henry, 12

Jacobi, Friedrich Heinrich (Fritz), 9, 87, 117, 199–201, 204–5, 217, 258, 414, 472

Jerusalem, Carl Wilhelm, 35, 80, 94, 106–7, 110–11, 115–16

Jones, William, 530

Julius Caesar, 57, 453–54

Jung, Johann Heinrich (Jung-Stilling), 54

Juvenal, 252

Kalb, Johann August von, 184

Kant, Immanuel, 204, 256–61, 279, 300–301, 366, 425, 468–69; *Anthropology in Pragmatic Perspective*, 365–66, 396; *Critique of Judgement*, 259–60, 264, 306, 312, 314, 316, 371, 393, 394, 396; *Critique of Pure Reason*, 257–59, 364, 422; *Groundwork for the Metaphysics of Morals*, 318; *Metaphysical Foundations of Natural Science*, 263, 369; *Religion within the Bounds of Pure Reason*, 297

Karlovy Vary. *See* Carlsbad

Kayser, Philipp Christoph, 183

Kestner, Charlotte (née Buff), 80–81, 106

Kestner, Johann Georg Christian, 64, 80–81, 105–7, 110–11, 116

Kielmeyer, Carl Friedrich, 372–73

Kirchweger, Anton Josef, 48

Kirms, Franz, 281

Kirwan, Richard, 169

Kleist, Heinrich von, 419

Klettenberg, Johann Hektor von, 48

Klettenberg, Susanne von, 46–48, 334

Klopstock, Friedrich Gottlieb, 39, 106

Knebel, Carl Ludwig von, 118, 224, 284, 458

Kniep, Christoph Heinrich, 211

Knight, Richard Payne, 250

Körner, Christian Gottfried, 259–60

Kotzebue, August von, 559–60

Krippendorff, Ekkehart, 14

Lamarck, Jean-Baptiste, 557–58

Lange, Joachim, 1–4

Langer, Ernst Theodor, 42–43, 46–47

La Roche, Sophie von, 81

Laßberg, Christel von, 138

Laugier, Marc-Antoine, 76

Lavater, Johann Caspar, 84, 106, 117, 141, 161, 205, 297

Leibniz, Gottfried Wilhelm, 2, 7, 25, 200–1

Leipzig, 17, 33–34

Leonhard, Karl Cäsar von, 552

Lessing, Gotthold Ephraim, 7, 111, 201, 217, 499; *Education of the Human Race*, 572–74; *Emilia Galotti*, 79, 91, 107; *Hamburg Dramaturgy*, 37; *Laocöon*, 49; *Nathan the Wise*, 147

Lichtenberg, Georg Christoph, 303–4, 362

Linnaeus, Carl, 25, 174, 216, 263

Locke, John, 360

Loder, Justus Christian, 170

Loën, Johann Michael von, 17, 19

Louis XVI, King, 53

Lowth, Robert, 55

Lucian, 87

Lucretius, 251, 450, 458

Luise von Sachsen-Weimar-Eisenach, 125, 142, 144, 427

Lukács, György, 13

Luther, Martin, 51, 82, 92

Lutheranism, 27–28, 92

Lyell, Charles, 272

Machiavelli, Niccolò, 84; *History of Florence*, 344, 355; *The Prince*, 453
Macpherson, James, 49, 79, 80
Malesherbes, Guillaume-Chrétien de Lamoignon de, 402
Mann, Thomas, 14
Marlowe, Christopher, 37; *Doctor Faustus*, 91–93, 96–97, 379, 380
Martial, 251–52
Maxwell, James Clerk, 420
Meiners, Christoph, 577
Merck, Johann Heinrich, 65, 74–75, 81, 172–73
Metz, Johann Friedrich, 46–48
Meyer, Johann Heinrich, 341–42, 407, 545
Michaelis, Johann David, 32, 35, 37
Milton, John, 39
Mirabeau, Honoré Gabriel Riqueti, Comte de, 402
Mohammed, 83–84
Moritz, Carl Philipp, 208–10, 394
Möser, Justus, 7–9, 68, 118, 179
Moses, 61, 83, 355–57, 519–21, 600
Müller, Friedrich von, 453
Müller, Johannes von, 455

Napoleon (Bonaparte), 405, 425–28, 450–51, 452–56, 526–28
Napoleonic Wars, 425–26, 501–2; Battle of Jena-Auerstedt, 426–27
Necker, Jacques, 175, 247
Neuber, Friederike, 194–5
Newton, Isaac, 273–80, 304, 435–39, 459–60, 467–69
Nietzsche, Friedrich, 10–11

Oeser, Adam Friedrich, 33, 40, 50, 220
Oetinger, Friedrich Christoph, 46
Origen, 82, 646
Ossian, 49, 107
Ovid, 55, 240
Owen, Richard, 12

Palassou, Pierre Bernard, 166
Palladio, Andrea, 220–21, 321, 537, 540

Paracelsus, 48, 51
Pascal, Blaise, 550
Paul, Saint, 359
Pestalozzi, Johann Heinrich, 573, 576
Pfitzer, Nikolaus, 92
Pietism, 1, 28, 46–48, 54, 82, 89–90, 92, 385
Pindar, 79
Plato, 79, 460
Plessing, Friedrich Victor Leberecht, 564
Plotinus, 421–22
Poland, first partition of, 44
Pope, Alexander, 78
Poussin, Nicolas, 449–50
Propertius, 240
Pufendorf, Samuel von, 6

Qur'an, 83

Racine, Jean, 78
Raphael (Raffaello Sanzio da Urbino), 53, 220–21, 540
Rehberg, August Wilhelm, 300–301
Reinhard, Carl Friedrich, 416–17
Reinhold, Carl Leonhard, 9, 259
Reiss, Hans, 235
Richards, Robert, 12, 267
Richardson, Samuel, 25, 110
Riepenhausen brothers, Franz and Johannes, 416
Ritter, Johann Wilhelm, 376–77, 480
Ritzsch, Timotheus, 33
Roethe, Gustav, 98
Romé de l'Isle, Jean-Baptiste Louis, 169
Rousseau, Jean-Jacques, 8–9, 27, 30, 40, 58–59, 63, 68–69, 73–74, 76–77, 85, 90, 93, 96, 597; *Confessions*, 491, 649; *Discourse on the Arts and Sciences*, 77; *Discourse on the Origin and Foundations of Inequality*, 63, 85–87, 109, 113; *Émile*, 38, 42–43, 50, 52, 63–64, 69–70, 81, 107, 117, 134, 190–91, 352, 438, 533, 571, 596; *Julie, or the New Heloïse*, 63, 108, 109–10, 145, 160; *Letter to Monsieur d'Alembert on Spectacles*, 192–94, 571; *Pygmalion*, 143

Royal Society, 464–67
Runge, Philipp Otto, 397, 442

Sachs, Hans, 79, 92
Sachsen-Weimar-Eisenach, Duchy of. *See* Weimar
Said, Edward, 529–31
Saint-Fond, Barthélemy Faujas de, 166
Saint-Hilaire, Étienne Geoffroy, 12, 270, 651–52
Saint-Simon, Henri de, 609–10
Salzmann, Johann Daniel, 53–54, 64
Sartorius, Georg, 455–56
Saussure, Horace-Bénédict de, 160–61, 166, 168, 169
Schade, Johann Peter Christoph, 26
Schelling, Friedrich Wilhelm Joseph, 9, 370–78, 420
Scherer, Wilhelm, 98
Schiller, Friedrich, 9, 181, 237, 259–60, 279, 309–413 passim, 414–15, 487, 501; *Almanac of the Muses for the Year 1797*, 328; *On the Aesthetic Education of Man*, 314–15; *On Grace and Dignity*, 310, 316; *The Horae*, 310–12, 314–16, 325–27; *Wilhelm Tell*, 346; *Xenia*, 326–28
Schlegel, August Wilhelm, 406, 498–99
Schlegel, Friedrich, 406, 417–18, 474
Schlegel, Johann Adolf, 74
Schlosser, Cornelia Friederike. *See* Goethe, Cornelia Friederike
Schlosser, Johann Georg, 36, 75, 105
Schnauß, Christian Friedrich, 135–36
Schönemann, Anna Elisabeth (Lili), 125
Schönkopf, Anna Katharina, 36, 44
Schopenhauer, Arthur, 9
Schöpflin, Johann Daniel, 53, 56
Scott, Walter, 66
Seebeck, Thomas Johann, 480, 554
Sensibility (Empfindsamkeit), 108–12, 115, 117, 119, 124, 143–45
Shakespeare, William, 25, 37, 44, 50, 56–57, 66, 71, 74, 78, 84–87, 196; *Hamlet*, 197, 333; *Julius Caesar*, 57, 78, 178–79

Smith, Adam, 578, 603
Sömmerring, Samuel Thomas, 171, 173, 363
Spengler, Oswald, 10–12
Spinoza, Benedictus de, 1, 6, 9, 31–32, 51–52, 64, 84, 85–90, 95, 117–18, 141, 199–201, 204–5, 256, 260, 270; *Ethics*, 111–12, 114, 205, 279, 383, 498; *Theological-Political Treatise*, 61–62, 81–83, 355–57
Statius, 397
Stein, Charlotte von, 130–33, 239
Steinbach, Erwin von, 75
Steiner, Rudolf, 13
Sterne, Laurence, 25; *Tristram Shandy*, 55
Stolberg-Stolberg, Christian zu, 125
Stolberg-Stolberg, Friedrich Leopold zu, 125, 326
Strähler, Daniel, 2
Strasbourg, 52–53
Sturm und Drang movement, 117, 196
Sulzer, Johann Georg, 74, 78

Tasso, Torquato, 39
Textor, Anna Margaretha (née Lindheimer) (Goethe's maternal grandmother), 19
Textor, Johann Jost (Goethe's uncle), 38
Textor, Johann Wolfgang (Goethe's maternal grandfather), 19–23, 29–30
Theocritus, 79
Theophrastus, 458
Thoranc, François Théas de, 29, 499–500
Three Impostors, Treatise of the (*De tribus impostoribus*), 51
Tibullus, 240
Tieck, Ludwig, 416
Tischbein, Johann Heinrich Wilhelm, 208, 211
Trebra, Friedrich Wilhelm Heinrich von, 162–3, 420
Turner, J. M. W., 435

Valmy, Battle of, 288–89
Vicq d'Azyr, Félix, 171
Virgil, 240, 450, 558–59

Voigt, Johann Carl Wilhelm, 166, 262
Volta, Alessandro, 420
Voltaire (François-Marie Arouet), 27, 29, 40, 50, 454; 'Epistle to the Author of the Book *The Three Impostors*', 51
Voß, Johann Heinrich, 292, 501
Vulpius, Christian August, 238
Vulpius, Christiane. *See* Goethe, Christiane

Wackenroder, Wilhelm Heinrich, 416
Weber, Max, 10–11, 68–69
Weimar (Duchy of Sachsen-Weimar-Eisenach), 126–28, *127, 128*
Weiße, Christian Felix, 38
Welling, Georg von, 48
Wellington, Arthur Wellesley, 1st Duke of, 584
Werner, Abraham Gottlob, 166, 262, 552–53
Werner, Zacharias, 418–19
Wetzlar, 79–80
Weygand, Johann Friedrich, 108

Wieland, Christoph Martin, 50, 85–86, 118, 120, 126, 133, 248, 284, 454, 499; *Agathon*, 330; *Essays on the Secret History of the Human Understanding*, 85; *The Golden Mirror*, 79
Willemer, Marianne von (née Jung), 511, 517
Wilson, W. Daniel, 14
Winckelmann, Johann Joachim, 32, 40–41, 49, 109, 219–20, 222–23, 240–41, 245–46, 406–13, 459–60
Winckler, Johann Heinrich, 34
Wolf, Friedrich August, 407, 414, 449, 458
Wolff, Christian, 1–9, *3*, 14; criticism of, 7–9
Wyder, Margrit, 267

Xenophanes of Colophon, 96
Xenophon, 79

Young, Edward, 39, 41–42, 80

Zelter, Carl Friedrich, 414
Zimmermann, Johann Georg, 90

INDEX OF GOETHE'S WORKS

'Die Absicht eingeleitet'. *See* 'The Intention Introduced'
'Achilleid' ('Achilleis'), 397–98, 408
'After Falconet and about Falconet' ('Nach Falconet und über Falconet'), 77
Agitated (*Die Aufgeregten*), 285–88, 294, 299–300, 302, 313, 316, 354, 399
Amine, 37
'Ancient and modern' ('Antik und modern'), 545–46
'And whoever Frenches or Britishes' ('Und wer franzet oder brittet'), 532–33
'The Angler' ('Der Fischer'), 138–40
'Attempt at a Theory of Weather' ('Versuch einer Witterungslehre'), 551–52
Die Aufgeregten. *See Agitated*
The Awakening of Epimenides (*Des Epimenides Erwachen*), 502–4, 615

Beiträge zur Optik. *See Essays on Optics*
Belagerung von Maynz. *See The Siege of Mainz*
Belshazzar, 37
'Besserem Verständniss'. *See* 'For Better Understanding'
The Birds (*Die Vögel*), 182
'Blumen-Malerei'. *See* 'Flower Painting'
'The Bride of Corinth' ('Die Braut von Corinth'), 357–60
'Brief des Pastors zu *** an den neuen Pastor zu ***'. *See* 'Letter from the pastor of *** to the new pastor of ***'

Briefe aus der Schweiz. *See Letters from Switzerland*
Der Bürgergeneral. *See The Citizen General*

Campaign in France (*Campagne in Frankreich*), 558–64
Chromatics (*Chromatik*), 555–57
The Citizen General (*Der Bürgergeneral*), 293–96, 300
Claudine of Villa Bella (*Claudine von Villa Bella*), 120–21
Clavigo, 63, 118–20
'Cloud Forms according to Howard' ('Wolkengestalt nach Howard'), 550
'The Content Prefaced' ('Der Inhalt bevorwortet'), 193, 557–58
Conversations of German Emigrés (*Unterhaltungen deutscher Ausgewanderten*), 316–24, 326, 404

'De Legislatoribus'. *See* 'On the Lawmakers'
'Diary of my Italian Journey for Frau von Stein' ('Tagebuch der italienischen Reise für Frau von Stein'), 207–8, 214, 236, 535–36
Dichtung und Wahrheit. *See Poetry and Truth*

Egmont, 176–82, 206, 215
'Einfache Nachahmung der Natur, Manier, Stil'. *See* 'Simple Imitation of Nature, Manner, Style'
'Eislebens Lied'. *See* 'Ice-life Song'

The Elective Affinities (*Die Wahlverwandschaften*), 441, 469–86
Elpenor, 182
'Ephemerides', 48–52
'Epilogue to Schiller's Bell' ('Epilog zu Schillers Glocke'), 414–15
Des Epimenides Erwachen. See *The Awakening of Epimenides*
'Era of Forced Talents' ('Epoche der forcierten Talente'), 500–501
Erwin and Elmire (*Erwin und Elmire*), 120, 215
Essay in Explanation of the Metamorphosis of Plants (*Versuch die Metamorphose der Pflanzen zu erklären*), 259, 263–66, 276, 557
Essays on Optics (*Beiträge zur Optik*), 276–80, 302
'The Experiment as Mediator between Subject and Object' ('Der Versuch als Vermittler zwischen Subjekt und Objekt'), 278–79

'Fairy Tale' ('Das Märchen'), 319–24
Faust, 10, 11, 13, 31, 90–105, 108–9
   'Urfaust', 90–105, 187–88
   Faust. The First Part of the Tragedy (*Faust. Der Tragödie erster Teil*), 218, 378–91, 415; genesis of, 90–93, 206, 215, 378–81
   Faust. The Second Part of the Tragedy (*Faust. Der Tragödie zweiter Teil*), 607–48; genesis of, 380–81, 398, 607–10
'Der Fischer'. See 'The Angler'
The Fisherwoman (*Die Fischerin*), 182–83
'Flower Painting' ('Blumen-Malerei'), 546
'For Better Understanding' ('Besserem Verständniss'), 512, 514–15, 518–26, 531–35
'Fortunate Occurrence' ('Glückliches Ereignis'), 310–11
Frankfurt Scholarly Notices (*Frankfurter Gelehrte Anzeigen*), 75–79, 116, 180

Die Geschwister. See *The Siblings*
'Gingko Biloba' ('Gingo Biloba'), 515–18, 516
'Glückliches Ereignis'. See 'Fortunate Occurrence'
'The God and the Bayadère' ('Der Gott und die Bajadere'), 360–62
Götz von Berlichingen, 64–73, 76, 78, 79, 84, 119, 176
The Great-Copt (*Der Groß-Cophta*), 281–83, 295

Hanswurst's Wedding (*Hanswursts Hochzeit*), 120
'Harzreise im Winter'. See 'Winter Journey in the Harz'
'Hegira' ('Hegire'), 507–11
'Heidenröslein'. See 'Little Rose on the Heath'
Herrmann and Dorothea (*Herrmann und Dorothea*) (epic), 347–55, 348, 356
'Herrmann und Dorothea' ('Herrmann und Dorothea') (elegy), 351

'Ice-life Song' ('Eislebens Lied'), 134–35
'Im ernsten Beinhaus war's'. See 'In the Solemn Ossuary'
'Der Inhalt bevorwortet'. See 'The Content Prefaced'
'The Intention Introduced' ('Die Absicht eingeleitet'), 420, 557–58
'In the Solemn Ossuary' ('Im ernsten Beinhaus war's'), 598, 655–57
'Inwiefern die Idee: Schönheit sei Vollkommenheit mit Freiheit, auf organische Naturen angewendet werden könne'. See 'To What Extent Can the Idea that Beauty is Perfection with Freedom be Applied to Organic Beings'
Iphigeneia at Tauris (*Iphigenie auf Tauris*), 145–59, 206, 215
'Israel in the Wilderness' ('Israel in der Wüste'), 355–57, 519–21, 600
Italian Journey (*Italienische Reise*), 536–43

Jena General Literary Journal (*Jenaische Allgemeine Literatur-Zeitung*), 405–6
Jery and Bätely (*Jery und Bätely*), 182
Jest, Deceit and Revenge (*Scherz, List und Rache*), 183
'The Journey of the Sons of Megaprazon' ('Reise der Söhne Megaprazons'), 289–90, 562–63
'Julius Caesar', 57
'Julius Caesar's Triumph, Painted by Mantegna' ('Julius Cäsars Triumphzug, gemalt von Mantegna'), 547

'Landscape Painting' ('Landschaftliche Malerei'), 547–49
Die Laune des Verliebten. See *The Lover's Temper*
Leben des Benvenuto Cellini. See *Life of Benvenuto Cellini*
Die Leiden des jungen Werthers. See *The Sorrows of Young Werther*
'Letter from the pastor of *** to the new pastor of ***' ('Brief des Pastors zu *** an den neuen Pastor zu ***'), 81–84
Letters from Switzerland (*Briefe aus der Schweiz*) (1779–80), 161–62
Letters from Switzerland (*Briefe aus der Schweiz*) (1796), 328–29
Life of Benvenuto Cellini (*Leben des Benvenuto Cellini*), 342–44
Lila, 142–43
'Literary Sansculottism' ('Literarischer Sansculottismus'), 325
'Little Rose on the Heath' ('Heidenröslein'), 59–61
The Lover's Temper (*Die Laune des Verliebten*), 37–38

'The Man of Fifty Years' ('Der Mann von fünfzig Jahren'), 569–71
'Das Märchen'. See 'Fairy Tale'
'Metamorphosis of Animals' ('Metamorphose der Tiere') (poem), 375–76
'The Metamorphosis of Plants' ('Die Metamorphose der Pflanzen') (poem), 373–74
Die Mitschuldigen. See *Partners in Guilt*
'Mohammed', 83–84
'To the Moon' ('An den Mond'), 131
'Myron's Cow' ('Myrons Kuh'), 500–501, 603

'Nach Falconet und über Falconet'. See 'After Falconet and about Falconet'
The Natural Daughter (*Die natürliche Tochter*), 398–404, 415
'Nausicaa' ('Nausikaa'), 215, 542–43
'Novella' ('Novelle'), 599–604

On Art and Antiquity (*Über Kunst und Altertum*), 543–49
'On Blue' ('Über das Blau'), 275–76
'On German Architecture' ('Von deutscher Baukunst'), 76–77
On Science in General, especially on Morphology (*Zur Naturwissenschaft überhaupt, besonders zur Morphologie*), 557–58
'On the Lawmakers' ('De Legislatoribus'), 61–62, 64, 83
On the Theory of Colour (*Zur Farbenlehre*), 57, 366, 368, 415, 422, 427, 428–39, 432, 456–69
  'Outline of a Theory of Colour' ('Didactic Part'), 428–35, 469–71, 477
  'Unmasking of Newton's Theory' ('Polemical Part'), 435–39
  'Materials for the History of Colour Theory' ('Historical Part'), 456–69
'Over all the hilltops' ('Wandrers Nachtlied. Ein Gleiches'/'Über allen Gipfeln'), 167–68

Pandora, 448–52
Partners in Guilt (*Die Mitschuldigen*), 44–46, 65

Poetry and Truth (*Dichtung und Wahrheit*), 21, 24, 27, 48, 58–59, 107, 486–500, 535, 648–51
'Priapeia', 250–51
'Principes de Philosophie zoologique', 651–55
'Problem and Response' ('Problem und Erwiderung'), 652–54
'Prometheus', 85–90, 217, 385
The Propylaea (*Die Propyläen*), 391–97, 415
'Proserpina' ('Proserpine'), 143–44
'The Pure Phenomenon' ('Das reine Phänomen'), 438

Reineke the Fox (*Reineke Fuchs*), 291–93, 562–63
'Reise der Söhne Megaprazons'. *See* 'The Journey of the Sons of Megaprazon'
The Roman Carnival (*Das Römische Carneval*), 226–29, 227
Roman Elegies (*Römische Elegien*), 240–46, 326, 511, 528–29
'Roman über das Weltall'. *See* 'Story of the Universe'

Scherz, List und Rache. See *Jest, Deceit and Revenge*
Shakespeare oration, 71, 74–75, 78
The Siblings (*Die Geschwister*), 131–33, 146
The Siege of Mainz (*Belagerung von Maynz*), 298–302
'Simple Imitation of Nature, Manner, Style' ('Einfache Nachahmung der Natur, Manier, Stil'), 224, 394
The Sorrows of Young Werther (*Die Leiden des jungen Werthers*), 13, 106–16, 138, 145
Stella, 115, 121–25
'Story of the Universe' ('Roman über das Weltall'), 165, 169

'Tagebuch der italienischen Reise für Frau von Stein'. *See* 'Diary of my Italian Journey for Frau von Stein'
Torquato Tasso, 182, 206, 229–35

The Triumph of Sensibility (*Der Triumph der Empfindsamkeit*), 143–45
'Two important hitherto unanswered Biblical questions' ('Zwo wichtige bisher unerörterte biblische Fragen'), 81–84

'Über das Blau'. *See* 'On Blue'
Über Kunst und Altertum. See *On Art and Antiquity*
'The Undertaking is Excused' ('Das Unternehmen wird entschuldigt'), 420, 557
'Und wer franzet oder brittet'. *See* 'And whoever Frenches or Britishes'
Unterhaltungen deutscher Ausgewanderten. See *Conversations of German Emigrés*

Venetian Epigrams (*Venezianische Epigramme*), 251–56, 301, 344, 361, 528–29
'Der Versuch als Vermittler zwischen Subjekt und Objekt'. *See* 'The Experiment as Mediator between Subject and Object'
'Versuch einer Witterungslehre'. *See* 'Attempt at a Theory of Weather'
Die Vögel. See *The Birds*
'Von deutscher Baukunst'. *See* 'On German Architecture'

Die Wahlverwandschaften. See *The Elective Affinities*
'Wandrers Nachtlied. Ein Gleiches' ('Über allen Gipfeln'). *See* 'Over all the hilltops'
West-Eastern Divan (*West-östlicher Divan*), 506–35, 506
'To What Extent Can the Idea that Beauty is Perfection with Freedom be Applied to Organic Beings' ('Inwiefern die Idee: Schönheit sei Vollkommenheit mit. Freiheit, auf organische Naturen angewendet werden könne'), 316

Wilhelm Meister's Apprenticeship (*Wilhelm Meisters Lehrjahre*), 11, 13, 24, 329–40
Wilhelm Meister's Journeyman Years (*Wilhelm Meisters Wanderjahre*), 11, 13, 441–48, 469, 603
    1821 version, 564–79, 598–99
    1829 version, 575, 584–99
Wilhelm Meister's Theatrical Mission (*Wilhelm Meisters theatralische Sendung*), 189–99, 215
Winckelmann and his Century (*Winckelmann und sein Jahrhundert*), 407–13, 415
'Winter Journey in the Harz' ('Harzreise im Winter'), 163

'Wolkengestalt nach Howard'. *See* 'Cloud Forms according to Howard'

Xenia (*Xenien*), 326–28

Zur Farbenlehre. *See* On the Theory of Colour
Zur Naturwissenschaft überhaupt, besonders zur Morphologie. *See* On Science in General, especially on Morphology
'Zwo wichtige bisher unerörterte biblische Fragen'. *See* 'Two important hitherto unanswered Biblical questions'

A NOTE ON THE TYPE

This book has been composed in Arno, an Old-style serif typeface in the classic Venetian tradition, designed by Robert Slimbach at Adobe.